LOCOMOTIVE DICTIONARY

AN ILLUSTRATED VOCABULARY OF TERMS WHICH DESIGNATE AMERICAN RAILROAD LOCOMOTIVES THEIR PARTS ATTACHMENTS AND DETAILS OF CONSTRUCTION WITH DEFINITIONS AND ILLUSTRATIONS OF TYPICAL BRITISH LOCOMOTIVE PRACTICE

FIVE THOUSAND ONE HUNDRED AND FORTY-EIGHT ILLUSTRATIONS

FIRST EDITION

COMPILED FOR

THE AMERICAN RAILWAY MASTER MECHANICS' ASSOCIATION

By GEORGE L. FOWLER

Associate Member, American Railway Master Mechanics' Association

UNDER THE SUPERVISION OF THE FOLLOWING COMMITTEE

J. F. DEEMS, *General Superintendent of Motive Power, New York Central Lines*
A. W. GIBBS, *General Superintendent of Motive Power, Pennsylvania Railroad*
A. E. MITCHELL, *Late Superintendent of Motive Power, Lehigh Valley Railroad*

1906

THE RAILROAD GAZETTE
NEW YORK: 83 Fulton Street   CHICAGO: Old Colony Building

THE RAILWAY GAZETTE
LONDON: Queen Anne's Chambers, Westminster, S.W.

©2010 Periscope Film LLC
All Rights Reserved
ISBN #978-1-935327-96-7   1-935327-96-8
www.PeriscopeFilm.com

ACTION OF THE AMERICAN RAILWAY MASTER MECHANICS' ASSOCIATION.

At the Thirty-eighth Annual Convention, held at Manhattan Beach, N. Y., in 1905, it was

"Resolved, That the Railroad Gazette be and hereby is empowered to publish, under the supervision of a committee of this Association, an illustrated dictionary which shall give the proper names of each and every part used in the building of locomotives."

The President of the Association appointed as members of the supervising committee, Mr. J. F. Deems, General Superintendent of Motive Power, Rolling Stock and Machinery, New York Central Lines; Mr. A. W. Gibbs, General Superintendent of Motive Power, Pennsylvania Railroad; Mr. A. E. Mitchell, Superintendent of Motive Power, Lehigh Valley.

PREFACE

The American locomotive has been developed under so many different auspices and under such widely different conditions that it is inevitable that there should be a variation of practice in both the general and detailed arrangements of the machine. That these variations are not greater than they are is undoubtedly due to the American Railway Master Mechanics' Association, which has kept the members in close touch with each other personally and with each other's practices since its organization in 1868. The good work which the several editions of the Car Builders' Dictionary has done, and the important part it has had in the technical literature of the car department, naturally suggested this publication for those having to do with the locomotive. Invaluable assistance has been rendered in the compilation, not only by the members of the supervising committee appointed by the American Railway Master Mechanics' Association and by the railroad officers of this country and of Great Britain, but also by the locomotive builders, who have been repeatedly asked for drawings and information, and who have complied with all of these requests promptly and thoroughly. They have made it possible to publish this work within a little more than a year after its authorization.

The nomenclature adopted is that which is believed to be in most common approved use, with cross-references for the more unusual terms. The engravings are placed in groups in which the parts to which they refer naturally arrange themselves. A line has been rigidly drawn separating current practice from those devices which may be considered to be still experimental. Those that have not been adopted as recognized standards have been excluded from the work, as well as those parts that have become obsolete. Examples of this will be found in the omission of those types of valve motion that have not yet established themselves, and others, such as the hook motion, that have passed out of use. Readers who miss finding here things with which they are familiar should know that the book is not prophetic and not historical; it is an undertaking for present use only.

So much courteous help has been given by the Pennsylvania Railroad, the Baldwin Locomotive Works, the American Locomotive Company and the Lancashire & Yorkshire Railway, that a special acknowledgment is due to them for drawings and other information furnished, which have served as the basis for a great part of the illustrations here presented.

New York, October, 1906.   G. L. F.

DIRECTIONS

For Using the Locomotive Dictionary

To find the meaning of a given word or term, refer to it in the alphabetical list which constitutes the first half of the book, where a definition similar to those contained in ordinary dictionaries and a reference to some engraving in the second half of the book illustrating the object—if it is capable of illustration—will usually be found. The references to the engravings are by figure numbers if the part is shown as a separate engraving or by a reference number or letter to be found on a number of similar general drawings of which the part sought is but a minor detail. Inclusive figure numbers are given at the top of each of the illustrated pages.

To find the name of any part of a locomotive or tender, examine the detailed index to engravings on the pages immediately preceding the illustrated pages until the class is found to which the object looked for belongs, bearing in mind the general divisions of the classification of engravings which are as follows:

LOCOMOTIVES, ELEVATIONS, BOILERS, CYLINDERS, RUNNING GEAR, VALVES, PILOTS, BRAKE GEAR, CABS AND FITTINGS, ENGINE FITTINGS, ENGINE TRUCKS, TENDERS, TENDER TRUCKS, STANDARDS, MACHINE TOOLS, BRITISH LOCOMOTIVES.

By referring to the engravings included in that class, a representation of the part or object sought will be found with either its name underneath or a reference number or letter by which number or letter the name may be learned from the list of names of parts accompanying the illustration and usually to be found in the immediate vicinity.

CLASSIFIED INDEX TO ADVERTISEMENTS.

(For Alphabetical Index see page following last page of illustrations)

AIR BRAKES:
Westinghouse Air Brake Co., Pittsburg, Pa.

AIR BRAKE FITTINGS:
Westinghouse Air Brake Co., Pittsburg, Pa.

ASBESTOS:
Franklin Mfg. Co., Franklin, Pa.

AXLES:
Gould Coupler Co., New York, N. Y.
Lima Locomotive & Machine Co., Lima, Ohio.
McConway & Torley Co., Pittsburg, Pa.
Prosser & Son, Thos., New York, N. Y.

BALANCE MAIN VALVES:
American Balance Valve Co., Jersey Shore, Pa.

BALL BEARINGS:
Baltimore Ry. Specialty Co., Baltimore, Md.

BELL RINGERS:
United States Metallic Packing Co., Philadelphia, Pa.

BOILER COVERINGS:
Franklin Mfg. Co., Franklin, Pa.

BOILER PLATES:
Worth Bros. Co., Coatesville, Pa.

BOILERS:
American Locomotive Co., New York, N. Y.
Ateliers Metallurgiques (Ltd. Co.), Brussels, Belgium.
Baldwin Locomotive Wks., Philadelphia, Pa.
Hannoversche Maschinenbau - Actien - Gesellschaft, Linden vor Hannover, Germany.
Locomotive & Machine Co. of Montreal, Montreal, Canada.

BOILER TUBES:
National Tube Co., Pittsburg, Pa.
Prosser & Son, Thos., New York, N. Y.
Shelby Steel Tube Co., Pittsburg, Pa.
Worth Bros. Co., Coatesville, Pa.

BOLSTERS, TRUCK:
American Steel Foundries, Chicago, Ill.
Gould Coupler Co., New York, N. Y.
Pressed Steel Car Co., Pittsburg, Pa.

BOLT AND NUT MACHINERY:
National Machinery Co., Tiffin, Ohio.

BOLT THREADING MACHINERY:
National Machinery Co., Tiffin, Ohio.

BOLTS AND NUTS:
Ateliers Metallurgiques (Ltd. Co.), Brussels, Belgium.
Columbia Nut & Bolt Co., Bridgeport, Conn.

BORING AND TURNING MILLS:
Betts Machine Co., Wilmington, Del.
Niles-Bement-Pond Co., New York, N. Y.

BORING BARS:
Quincy, Manchester, Sargent Co., Chicago, Ill.

BRAKE BEAMS:
American Steel Foundries, Chicago, Ill.
Buffalo Brake Beam Co., Buffalo, N. Y.
Davis Pressed Steel Co., Wilmington, Del.
Pressed Steel Car Co., Pittsburg, Pa.

BRAKE SHOES:
American Brake Shoe & Fdy. Co., Mahwah, N. J.

BRAKE SLACK ADJUSTERS:
American Brake Co., St. Louis, Mo.

BUFFERS:
Gould Coupler Co., New York, N. Y.
McConway & Torley Co., Pittsburg, Pa.

BULLDOZERS:
National Machinery Co., Tiffin, Ohio.

BUMPING POST:
Quincy, Manchester, Sargent Co., Chicago, Ill.

CARS:
Ateliers Metallurgiques (Ltd. Co.) Brussels, Belgium.
Pressed Steel Car Co., Pittsburg, Pa.

CAR HEATING (ELECTRIC):
Consolidated Car Heating Co., Albany, N. Y.
Gold Car Heating & Lighting Co., New York, N. Y.
Safety Car Heating & Lighting Co., New York, N. Y.

CAR HEATING (STEAM):
Consolidated Car Heating Co., Albany, N. Y.
Gold Car Heating & Lighting Co., New York, N. Y.
Safety Car Heating & Lighting Co., New York, N. Y.

CAR LIGHTING:
Consolidated Car Heating Co., Albany, N. Y.
Gould Coupler Co., New York, N. Y.
Safety Car Heating & Lighting Co., New York, N. Y.

CAR AND LOCOMOTIVE REPLACERS:
Quincy, Manchester, Sargent Co., Chicago, Ill.

CAR WHEEL BORING MACHINES:
Betts Machine Co., Wilmington, Del.
Niles-Bement-Pond Co., New York, N. Y.

CASTINGS, IRON AND STEEL:
American Brake Shoe & Fdy. Co., Mahwah, N. J.
Gould Coupler Co., New York, N. Y.
Lima Locomotive & Machine Co., Lima, Ohio.
McConway & Torley Co., Pittsburg, Pa.
National Malleable Castings Co., Cleveland, Ohio.
Pratt & Letchworth Co., Buffalo, N. Y.
Prosser & Son, Thos., New York, N. Y.
Standard Steel Works, Philadelphia, Pa.
Union Steel Castings Co., Pittsburg, Pa.

CENTER PLATES:
Baltimore Railway Specialty Co., Baltimore, Md.

COPING MACHINES:
Pels & Co., Henry, New York, N. Y.

COUPLERS, LOCOMOTIVE AND CAR:
American Steel Foundries, Chicago, Ill.
Gould Coupler Co., New York, N. Y.
McConway & Torley Co., Pittsburg, Pa.
National Malleable Castings Co., Cleveland, Ohio.
Washburn Co., Minneapolis, Minn.

CRANES:
Niles-Bement-Pond Co., New York, N. Y.
Quincy, Manchester, Sargent Co., Chicago, Ill.
Sellers & Co., Wm., Philadelphia, Pa.
Shaw Electric Crane Co., New York, N. Y.

CRANK PINS:
Prosser & Son, Thos., New York, N. Y.

CUTTING MACHINES:
Pels & Co., Henry, New York, N. Y.

DRAFT RIGGING:
Gould Coupler Co., New York, N. Y.
McConway & Torley Co., Pittsburg, Pa.

DRILLING MACHINERY:
Niles-Bement-Pond Co., New York, N. Y.

DRIVING WHEEL CENTERS:
American Steel Foundries, Chicago, Ill.

DRIVING WHEEL ROTATING MACHINE:
Sherburne & Co., Boston, Mass.

DUST GUARDS:
Symington Co., T. H., Baltimore, Md.

DYNAMOS:
Crocker-Wheeler Co., Ampere, N. J.
General Electric Co., Schenectady, N. Y.
Westinghouse Electric & Mfg. Co., Pittsburg, Pa.

ELECTRIC EQUIPMENT:
Crocker-Wheeler Co., Ampere, N. J.
General Electric Co., Schenectady, N. Y.
Westinghouse Electric & Mfg. Co., Pittsburg, Pa.

ELECTRIC RAILROADS:
General Electric Co., Schenectady, N. Y.
Westinghouse Electric & Mfg. Co., Pittsburg, Pa.

ELECTRIC TRUCKS:
American Locomotive Co., New York, N. Y.
Baldwin Locomotive Wks., Philadelphia, Pa.
General Electric Co., Schenectady, N. Y.
Locomotive & Machine Co. of Montreal, Montreal, Canada.
Westinghouse Electric & Mfg. Co., Pittsburg, Pa.

EMERGENCY COUPLER KNUCKLES:
Quincy, Manchester, Sargent Co., Chicago, Ill.

ENGINEERS:
Crocker-Wheeler Co., Ampere, N. J.

FLANGERS (SNOW):
Quincy, Manchester, Sargent Co., Chicago, Ill.

FORGING MACHINES:
National Machinery Co., Tiffin, Ohio.
Niles-Bement-Pond Co., New York, N. Y.

FORGINGS AND CASTINGS:
American Brake Shoe & Fdy. Co., Mahwah, N. J.
Gould Coupler Co., New York, N. Y.
Lima Locomotive & Machine Co., Lima, Ohio.
McConway & Torley Co., Pittsburg, Pa.
Pratt & Letchworth Co., Buffalo, N. Y.
Prosser & Son, Thos., New York, N. Y.
Railway Steel-Spring Co., New York, N. Y.
Standard Steel Works, Philadelphia, Pa.
Union Steel Casting Co., Pittsburg, Pa.

FURNACES (FORGING AND TEMPERING):
Witteman & Co., A. P., Philadelphia, Pa.

GAGES, AIR, STEAM AND WATER:
American Steam Gage & Valve Mfg. Co., Boston, Mass.
Ashcroft Mfg. Co., New York, N. Y.
Ashton Valve Co., Boston, Mass.
Star Brass Mfg. Co., Boston, Mass.

GRINDING MACHINES:
Norton Grinding Co., Worcester, Mass.

GRINDING WHEELS:
Norton Co., Worcester, Mass.

HOISTS (ELECTRIC):
Niles-Bement-Pond Co., New York, N. Y.
Quincy, Manchester, Sargent Co., Chicago, Ill.

HOISTING AND CONVEYING MACHINERY:
Quincy, Manchester, Sargent Co., Chicago, Ill.

HORIZONTAL BORING AND DRILLING MACHINES:
Betts Machine Co., Wilmington, Del.
Niles-Bement-Pond Co., New York, N. Y.

HOSE, AIR, STEAM, ETC.:
Quincy, Manchester, Sargent Co., Chicago, Ill.

HOSE COUPLERS (AIR AND STEAM):
Consolidated Car Heating Co., Albany, N. Y.
Gold Car Heating & Lighting Co., New York, N. Y.
Safety Car Heating & Lighting Co., New York, N. Y.

HYDRAULIC MACHINERY:
Dudgeon, Richard, New York, N. Y.
Watson-Stillman Co., New York, N. Y.

INJECTORS:
Hayden & Derby Mfg. Co., New York, N. Y.
Hancock Inspirator Co., New York, N. Y.
Nathan Mfg. Co., New York, N. Y.
Sellers & Co., Incorp., Wm., Philadelphia, Pa.

IRON AND STEEL:
(See Steel and Iron.)

JACKS:
Dudgeon, Richard, New York, N. Y.
Watson-Stillman Co., New York, N. Y.

CLASSIFIED INDEX TO ADVERTISEMENTS.

JOURNAL BEARINGS:
National Malleable Castings Co., Cleveland, Ohio.

JOURNAL BOX PACKING:
Franklin Mfg. Co., Franklin, Pa.

JOURNAL BOXES AND LIDS:
Davis Pressed Steel Co., Wilmington, Del.
Gould Coupler Co., New York, N. Y.
Symington Co., T. H., Baltimore, Md.

LAGGING, LOCOMOTIVE BOILER:
Franklin Mfg. Co., Franklin, Pa.

LAMPS, INCANDESCENT:
General Electric Co., Schenectady, N. Y.
Westinghouse Electric & Mfg. Co., Pittsburg, Pa.

LIGHTS, CONTRACTORS':
Wells Light Mfg. Co., New York, N. Y.

LOCK NUTS:
Columbia Nut & Bolt Co., Bridgeport, Conn.

LOCOMOTIVES, COMPRESSED AIR:
American Locomotive Co., New York, N. Y.
Baldwin Locomotive Wks., Philadelphia, Pa.
Locomotive & Machine Co. of Montreal, Montreal, Canada.

LOCOMOTIVES, ELECTRIC:
American Locomotive Co., New York, N. Y.
Baldwin Locomotive Wks., Philadelphia, Pa.
General Electric Co., Schenectady, N. Y.
Locomotive & Machine Co. of Montreal, Montreal, Canada.
Westinghouse Electric & Mfg. Co., Pittsburg, Pa.

LOCOMOTIVES, MINE:
American Locomotive Co., New York, N. Y.
Baldwin Locomotive Wks., Philadelphia, Pa.
General Electric Co., Schenectady, N. Y.
Locomotive & Machine Co. of Montreal, Montreal, Canada.
Westinghouse Electric & Mfg. Co., Pittsburg, Pa.

LOCOMOTIVES, STEAM:
American Locomotive Co., New York, N. Y.
Ateliers Metallurgiques (Ltd. Co.), Brussels, Belgium.
Baldwin Locomotive Wks., Philadelphia, Pa.
Hannoversche Maschinenbau - Actien - Gesellschaft, Linden vor Hannover, Germany.
Lima Locomotive & Machine Co., Lima, Ohio.
Locomotive & Machine Co. of Montreal, Montreal, Canada.

LUBRICATORS:
Detroit Lubricator Co., Detroit, Mich.
Nathan Mfg. Co., New York, N. Y.

MACHINE TOOLS:
Betts Machine Co., Wilmington, Del.
Cincinnati Shaper Co., Cincinnati, Ohio.
Manning, Maxwell & Moore, New York, N. Y.
National Machinery Co., Tiffin, Ohio.
Niles-Bement-Pond Co., New York, N. Y.
Quincy, Manchester, Sargent Co., Chicago, Ill.
Sellers & Co., Incorp., Wm., Philadelphia, Pa.
Steptoe Shaper Co., John, Cincinnati, Ohio.
Stockbridge Machine Co., Worcester, Mass.
Underwood & Co., H. B., Philadelphia, Pa.
Woodward & Powell Planer Co., Worcester, Mass.

MOTORS:
Crocker-Wheeler Co., Ampere, N. J.
General Electric Co., Schenectady, N. Y.
Westinghouse Electric & Mfg. Co., Pittsburg, Pa.

NUTS AND BOLTS:
Ateliers Metallurgiques (Ltd. Co.), Brussels, Belgium.
Columbia Nut & Bolt Co., Bridgeport, Conn.

OIL CUPS:
Nathan Mfg. Co., New York, N. Y.

PACKING:
American Balance Valve Co., Jersey Shore, Pa.
Franklin Mfg. Co., Franklin, Pa.
Quincy, Manchester, Sargent Co., Chicago, Ill.
United States Metallic Packing Co., Philadelphia, Pa.

PILOT COUPLERS (See Couplers, Locomotive and Car).

PLANING MACHINES:
Betts Machine Co., Wilmington, Del.
Niles-Bement-Pond Co., New York, N. Y.
Quincy, Manchester, Sargent Co., Chicago, Ill.
Woodward & Powell Planer Co., Worcester, Mass.

PLATES, BOILER AND FIRE-BOX:
Worth Bros. Co., Coatesville, Pa.

PIPE THREADING MACHINERY:
Niles-Bement-Pond Co., New York, N. Y.

PISTON RODS:
Prosser & Son, Thos., New York, N. Y.

PNEUMATIC TOOLS:
Quincy, Manchester, Sargent Co., Chicago, Ill.

POP SAFETY VALVES:
American Steam Gauge & Valve Mfg. Co., Boston, Mass.
Ashton Valve Co., Boston, Mass.
Consolidated Safety Valve Co., New York, N. Y.
Star Brass Mfg. Co., Boston, Mass.

PORTABLE TOOLS:
Niles-Bement-Pond Co., New York, N. Y.
Quincy, Manchester, Sargent Co., Chicago, Ill.
Underwood & Co., H. B., Philadelphia, Pa.

PRESSED STEEL SHAPES:
Pressed Steel Car Co., Pittsburg, Pa.

PUMPS AND PUMPING MACHINERY:
Hannoversche Maschinenbau - Actien - Gesellschaft, Linden vor Hannover, Germany.

PUNCHING MACHINERY:
Dudgeon, Richard, New York, N. Y.
Pels & Co., Henry, New York, N. Y.

RAILROAD SUPPLIES:
Manning, Maxwell & Moore, New York, N. Y.
Quincy, Manchester, Sargent Co., Chicago, Ill.
Sherburne & Co., Boston, Mass.

REDUCING VALVES:
Mason Regulator Co., Boston, Mass.

RIVETING MACHINERY:
National Machinery Co., Tiffin, Ohio.
Quincy, Manchester, Sargent Co., Chicago, Ill.

SANDING APPARATUS:
American Locomotive Sander Co., Philadelphia, Pa.

SHAFTING:
Sellers & Co., Incorp., Wm., Philadelphia, Pa.

SHAPERS:
Cincinnati Shaper Co., Cincinnati, Ohio.
Steptoe Shaper Co., John, Cincinnati, Ohio.
Stockbridge Machine Co., Worcester, Mass.

SIDE BEARINGS:
American Steel Foundries, Chicago, Ill.
Baltimore Railway Specialty Co., Baltimore, Md.

SLOTTING MACHINES:
Betts Machine Co., Wilmington, Del.
Niles-Bement-Pond Co., New York, N. Y.

SPRINGS:
American Steel Foundries, Chicago, Ill.
Ateliers Metallurgiques (Ltd. Co.), Brussels, Belgium.
Railway Steel-Spring Co., New York, N. Y.
Standard Steel Wks., Philadelphia, Pa.

STAYBOLTS:
Flannery Bolt Co., Pittsburg, Pa.

STAYBOLT SLEEVES:
American Balance Valve Co., Jersey Shore, Pa.

STAYBOLT THREADING MACHINES:
National Machinery Co., Tiffin, Ohio.

STEEL CASTINGS (See Castings, Iron and Steel).

STEEL TIRES (See Tires, Steel).

STEEL AND IRON:
Prosser & Son, Thos., New York, N. Y.
Railway Steel-Spring Co., New York, N. Y.
Standard Steel Wks., Philadelphia, Pa.
Witteman & Co., A. P., Philadelphia, Pa.
Worth Bros. Co., Coatesville, Pa.

STEEL, TOOL.
Witteman & Co., A. P., Philadelphia, Pa.

TENDER COUPLERS (See Couplers, Locomotive and Car).

TENDERS, LOCOMOTIVE (See also Locomotives, Steam).
Pressed Steel Car Co., Pittsburg, Pa.

TIRES, STEEL:
Prosser & Son, Thos., New York, N. Y.
Standard Steel Wks., Philadelphia, Pa.

TIRE TURNING & BORING MILLS:
Betts Machine Co., Wilmington, Del.
Niles-Bement-Pond Co., New York, N. Y.

TRACK SANDERS, LOCOMOTIVE:
American Locomotive Sander Co., Philadelphia, Pa.

TRUCKS, LOCOMOTIVE:
American Locomotive Co., New York, N. Y.
Ateliers Metallurgiques (Ltd. Co.), Brussels, Belgium.
Baldwin Locomotive Wks., Philadelphia, Pa.
General Electric Co., Schenectady, N. Y.
Hannoversche Maschinenbau - Actien - Gesellschaft, Linden vor Hannover, Germany.
Lima Locomotive & Machine Co., Lima, Ohio.
Locomotive & Machine Co. of Montreal, Montreal, Canada.
Pressed Steel Car Co., Pittsburg, Pa.
Westinghouse Electric & Mfg. Co., Pittsburg, Pa.

TRUCK BOLSTERS (See Bolsters, Truck).

TUBES (See Boiler Tubes).

TUBE EXPANDERS:
Dudgeon, Richard, New York, N. Y.

TURNTABLES:
Sellers & Co., Incorp., Wm., Philadelphia, Pa.

VALVE SETTING MACHINES:
Sherburne & Co., Boston, Mass.

VALVES (STEAM):
American Steam Gauge & Valve Mfg. Co., Boston, Mass.
Ashton Valve Co., Boston, Mass.
Consolidated Safety Valve Co., New York, N. Y.
Hancock Inspirator Co., New York, N. Y.
Star Brass Mfg. Co., Boston, Mass.

VALVES, BALANCE, MAIN:
American Balance Valve Co., Jersey Shore, Pa.

VESTIBULES:
Gould Coupler Co., New York, N. Y.
McConway & Torley Co., Pittsburg, Pa.

WASHER MACHINE:
National Machinery Co., Tiffin, Ohio.

WHEELS:
Ateliers Metallurgiques (Ltd. Co.), Brussels, Belgium.
Prosser & Son, Thos., New York, N. Y.
Railway Steel-Spring Co., New York, N. Y.
Standard Steel Wks., Philadelphia, Pa.

WHISTLES:
Ashton Valve Co., Boston, Mass.
Manning, Maxwell & Moore, New York, N. Y.
Nathan Mfg. Co., New York, N. Y.
Star Brass Mfg. Co., Boston, Mass.

WRENCHES:
Coes Wrench Co., Worcester, Mass.

A DICTIONARY OF THE
LOCOMOTIVE

A

A. B. C. Journal Bearing and Wedge. Fig. 4496.

Acorn. A general term for the ornaments or tips resembling the acorn, used to finish the ends of rods of various forms.

Adjusting Spring (Trailing Truck). 20, Figs. 3393-3468. A heavy spiral spring or nest of springs used for controlling the side motion of a two-wheel radial trailing truck. Also called centering spring.

Adjusting Spring Case. 21, Figs. 3393-3468. A cylindrical cast iron holder in which an adjusting spring is placed. Also called centering spring cylinder.

Adjusting Spring Seat. 22, Figs. 3393-3468. A casting, or a part of the bolster of a two-wheel trailing truck, forming a bearing for the end of the adjusting spring.

Admission. The opening of a steam port to admit steam to one end of a cylinder. If the valve has no lead, admission takes place at the moment the piston reaches the end of its stroke and just as it is to begin the return stroke.

Air Brake. Any brake operated by air pressure, but usually restricted to systems of continuous brakes operated by compressed air, in distinction from **Vacuum Brakes,** which see, which are operated by creating a vacuum. The air is compressed by some form of steam pump on the locomotive, or a motor-compressor on electric locomotives, and is conveyed by pipes and flexible hose between the engine, tender and cars to cylinders and pistons under the tender and each car, by which the pressure is transmitted to the brake levers, and thence to the brake shoes. This system is what is now termed the straight-air brake. This brake is now obsolete in steam road practice, having been replaced by the **Automatic Air Brake,** which see, and also see **Westinghouse Air Brake, Quick-Action Air Brake, Vacuum Brake, New York Air Brake.**

Air Brakes (Standards). The following standards have been generally adopted:

1. Maximum brake-pipe pressure 70 lbs. for ordinary service, 90 lbs. for double pressure control freight service, and 110 lbs. for high-speed brake service.

2. Maximum braking power for locomotives should be as follows: 75 per cent. of weight on drivers, engine in working order, for driver brakes; 60 per cent. of weight on truck and trailer wheel brakes, and 100 per cent. of the light weight of the tender for tender brakes.

3. For electric locomotives, the maximum braking power should be 100 per cent. of the weight on axles driven by motors, and 90 per cent. on free axles.

For tenders the M. C. B. Standards relating to brake levers, jaws or clevises, rods and brake beam levers, location of angle cock, etc., are commonly adopted.

AIR

Air Brake Hose. Fig. 2538. Flexible tubes made of alternate layers of rubber and canvas by which the brake pipes under engines, tenders, and cars are connected together, and compressed air, which operates the brakes, conducted through the train. The hose is made with a coupling at each end of the engine and tender, so that it can readily be connected or disconnected. Also called air hose and brake hose.

Air Cylinder. (Air Pump). 63, Figs. 2429-2435. A cylinder forming part of the air brake pump, and having its piston fastened to the same rod to which the piston of the steam cylinder is fastened. It is furnished with air inlet and discharge valves at each end, communicating respectively with the air inlet and the discharge pipe.

Air Cylinder Bracket. A projecting piece of metal bolted to the frame of a locomotive or tender, to which the brake cylinder is attached. See **Truck Brake, Tender Brake.**

Air Cylinder Gasket. See **Gasket.**

Air Cylinder Oil Cup (Air Pump). 98, Figs. 2429-2435; Fig. 2451. A small brass receptacle with a stop cock or faucet, screwed to the air cylinder of an air pump, to hold a supply of lubricant for the air cylinder. See **Automatic Air Cylinder Oil Cup.**

Air Drum. Fig. 2463; 156, Figs. 76-124. Also called **Main Reservoir** and **Reservoir,** which see. A cylindrical reservoir, made of sheet steel, into which air is pumped and stored for use in the air brake system and train air signal line. Sometimes placed under the cab deck or between the frames in front of the guide yoke; but now two are commonly used, placed under the running board near the cab, one on each side of the engine.

Air Drum Hanger. 180, Figs. 76-124. An iron strap riveted to the lower side of the running board, or to the boiler, to support the air drum.

Air Drum Head. The end of the air drum, to which the cylindrical body is riveted or welded.

Air Drum Saddle. A strip of iron fastened to the locomotive frame for supporting the air drum or drums when the drums are placed between the cylinder saddles and the guide yoke.

Air Gage (Air Brake). Figs. 2483-2486. A gage to register the pressure of air in the reservoirs, brake pipe or brake cylinders, similar to an ordinary steam pressure gage. They are made either with a single pointer, Fig. 2484, or with two pointers, Figs. 2483, 2485-2486, to indicate on one dial both the reservoir pressure and the brake pipe pressure. The latter type is called a duplex gage.

Air Gage Fitting. A pipe connection by means of which an air gage is connected to an engineer's brake valve in a locomotive cab.

Air Gage Stand. Figs. 3014-3015. A bracket or support to hold an air gage.

Air Hose. See **Air Brake Hose.**

Air Inlet. An opening for the admission of air to an air compressor. The term includes both the air strainer and air pipe.

Air Pipe (Air Brake). More properly **Brake Pipe**, which see. Often called train pipe.

Air Pipe Strainer (Air Brake). Fig. 2541. More properly **Brake Pipe Air Strainer**, which see.

Air Piston (Air Brake). 66, Figs. 2429-2435; 5, Figs. 2512-2515. The piston fitted to the air cylinder of a pump or compressor, and whose motion back and forth in the air cylinder draws in and compresses atmospheric air and forces it through suitable valves, to the main reservoir.

Air Piston Packing Rings (Air Pump). 67, Figs. 2423-2428; 6, Figs. 2512-2515. The metal rings fitted to the air piston to make it air tight in the cylinder.

Air Pump. Figs. 2423-2450, 2563. A machine attached to a locomotive for compressing air. It consists of a steam and air cylinder, the pistons in which are connected to the same piston rod, so that the air piston is worked directly by the steam piston. Suitable valves are provided for admitting and exhausting the steam and air to and from the cylinders. The steam cylinder is supplied with steam through a pipe from the boiler, and in this pipe is a pump governor, which is connected to the main reservoir in such a way that when a certain pressure of air is attained in the reservoir the governor closes the steam valve of the pump. When the air pressure falls, the governor opens the steam valve and starts the pump. The motion of the steam piston is reversed by a reversing valve on the cylinder top head, moved by a rod having a tappet on it which is raised by the reversing valve plate on the piston striking it. The reversing valve controls the admission of steam to the main valve which moves the main slide valve, which in turn, admits steam to or exhausts it from either end of the cylinder. The steam cylinder exhaust goes through a pipe to the smokebox and stack. The air cylinder takes in air through a perforated metal inlet and through disk or poppet valves at each end, and discharges it through similar valves to the main reservoir. The air cylinder is cast with corrugations or ribs to give as large a radiating surface as possible because the rapid compression of air develops a large amount of heat in it which would be destructive to packing leathers and gaskets, and cause the deposit of moisture in parts of the brake system where it would give trouble by freezing. See below and **Motor-Compressor.**

Air Pump and Motor. Figs. 2512-2515, 4628, 4666. A machine for compressing air, mounted on an electric locomotive and consisting of air cylinders, the pistons of which are gear driven by an electric motor. Also called **Motor-Compressor**, which see.

Air Pump Bracket. Figs. 2641-2643. An iron or steel casting secured to the boiler shell for holding the air pump.

Air Signal. See **Train Air Signal.**

Air Signal Reducing Valve. See **Reducing Valve.**

Air Strainer. Fig. 2541. A **Brake Pipe Air Strainer**, which see.

Air Valve (Air Pump). See **Discharge Valve.**

Air Whistle. 1. Fig. 2556. A small whistle placed in the locomotive cab for giving signals to the engineman from any part of a train. Operated by an independent line of pipe supplied with air from the main reservoir of the air brake system. See **Train Air Signal.**

2. A pneumatic signal whistle for electric locomotives.

Alexander Car Replacer. Fig. 4581.

Allen Paper Wheel. Figs. 4538-4539. A car wheel with a steel tire, a cast iron hub or center, and the space between the tire and center filled with compressed paper and held in place by wrought iron plates on either side extending from the center to the tire and bolted thereto. See **Steel Tired Wheel.**

Allen Valve. A slide valve made with a curved passage through it extending from near one edge of the face to the other. This passage conveys steam from either end of the steam chest to the steam port at the other end when the port is only slightly open, and thereby gives a higher initial pressure in the cylinder. The Allen-Richardson valve, Figs. 2126-2129, is a modification of the original Allen valve.

Alligator Crosshead. Figs. 1059-1073, 1103-1111. See **Crosshead.**

Alligator Wrench. See **Wrench.**

Alternating Current. An electric current whose manifestations cause it to appear to reverse its direction continuously and periodically. The induction produced by the variation of electric current permits a change of the electric pressure to a lower or higher voltage by means of a device called a **Transformer**, which see. See also **Direct Current.**

Alternating Current-Direct Current Motor (Electric Locomotive). Figs. 4650, 4659-4660. A motor wound with compensating field coils and supplied with a transformer, capable of operating with either alternating or direct current.

American Balanced Slide Valve. Figs. 2108-2118.

American Controller Spring. Fig. 4532.

American Railway Master Mechanics' Association Standards. See **Master Mechanics' Standards.**

American Steam Gage & Valve Mfg. Co. Vacuum valve, Figs. 1009-1011; cylinder relief valve, Figs. 1012-1014; steam gage, Fig. 3154; whistle, Fig. 3213; safety valve, Figs. 3214-3215.

American Type Locomotive. Figs. 49-50, 106-109. The prevailing type of locomotive several years ago. One having a four-wheel front truck and four-coupled driving wheels, but no trailing truck. See **Whyte's Nomenclature.**

Ammeter (Electric Locomotive). An instrument used to indicate the amount of current, or number of amperes flowing in a circuit.

Ampere. The unit of electric current.

Amperage. The amount of electric current flowing in a circuit, expressed in amperes.

Andrews Cast Steel Tender Truck. Figs. 4346-4348.

Angle Cock (Air Brakes). Figs. 2530, 2535. A cock placed in the brake pipe under the rear of the tender and at each end of each car just in front of the hose connection. This cock must always be open except at the rear end of the last car, where it must always be closed to prevent escape of air from the brake pipe and applying the brakes.

Angle Cock Body. 1, Fig. 2535. See above. Usually made of cast iron, and bored out to receive the stem or key.

Angle Cock Handle. 5, Fig. 2535. A flat or half-round piece of iron, bent to conform to the shape of the angle cock and fastened to the end of the stem or key to open and close the cock.

Angle Cock Locking Arm. Fig. 2530. A device attached to the handle of an angle cock to prevent the accidental closing of the valve by jarring or otherwise. It consists of a hinged handle fitting down over a lug cast on the body of the cock to hold the handle in place when in the wide open position. The handle can then be moved to the closed position only by lifting it off the lug and turning it.

Angle Cock Stem. 2, Fig. 2535. A slightly conical plug, ground to fit the interior of the angle cock body, and having a rectangular opening through it so as to open communication between the two ends of the angle cock body. Also called a cock key.

Angle Cock Stem Nut. 3, Fig. 2535. A nut screwed on the lower end of the angle cock stem for the purpose of holding it in place by a washer which is thereby bound against the angle cock body with any desired degree of tightness. Called also a cap.

Angle Cock Stem Washer. A flat metal ring sometimes put in between the cap and stem or key of an angle cock. See above.

Angle Fitting (Air Brake). A special pipe elbow for use with brake and signal pipe hose couplings.

Angle Globe Valve. Figs. 3016-3017. A **Globe Valve**, which see, having the inlet and outlet connections at an angle with each other, commonly 90 degrees.

Angle Iron or **Angle.** A general term applied by makers to iron or steel rolled in the form of an L, but with the corner rounded off somewhat. When the angle is rolled with a sharp interior corner and not rounded off, it is termed a square-root angle.

Angle Valve. An **Angle Cock**, which see.

Anti-Friction Metal. A term applied to bearing metals having a low coefficient of friction, such as **Babbitt Metal**, which see, and other alloys of special composition which are used for bearings.

Anti-Friction Side Bearings. Figs. 4511-4521. Devices, a few of which are shown, to eliminate the friction between body and truck in curving. The two general forms are roller side bearings and ball-bearing side bearings.

Application Chamber Pipe (Air Brake). The pipe which connects the application chamber of the distributing valve with the automatic brake valve through the independent brake valve. See **Distributing Valve**.

Apron. See **Cab Apron**.

Arbor. "A spindle or axle for a wheel or pinion; a mandrel on which a ring or wheel is turned in a lathe."—Knight.

Arc. The brilliant flash of light that occurs when a circuit carrying an electric current is opened or broken. It is sometimes very destructive in its effects unless destroyed by a powerful magnetic field.

Arc Lamp. Figs. 3267-3270. A device for producing illumination, wherein an electric arc is maintained between the ends of two rods or pencils of carbon held by suitable mechanism at a distance of 1/8 to 3/8 inch apart. With an electric current of from 7 to 9 amperes at 45 volts maintained between the carbon points, an amount of energy equal to about 1/2-horsepower, a brilliant light is produced. The arc lamp is enclosed in the case of the headlight on the smokebox. See **Electric Headlight**.

Arch. A term sometimes applied to the **Smokebox**, which see. See also **Brick Arch**.

Arch (Elliptic Spring.) The height from the center of the scrolls at the ends of the elliptics to the under side of the main leaf of the spring. Twice the arch of an elliptic spring, less the thickness of the spring bands, is the set, and is the maximum amount which an elliptic spring can be compressed. In a half-elliptic spring the arch and set differ only in the thickness of the spring band.

Arch Bar. 1, Figs. 4294-4382. A bent wrought iron or steel bar, which forms the top member of a diamond truck side frame. In the diamond truck the next lower member is the inverted arch bar, and the next lower (occasionally used) is the auxiliary arch bar. The tie bar comes under all, and sometimes becomes an arch bar.

Arched Roof. A cab roof, the surface of which is curved.

Arm. A lever or handle. See **Sand Box Arm, Reverse Shaft Arm, Rocker Arm**.

Arm Rest. Figs. 2874-2876. A wooden or metal bar or ledge attached to the side of a cab, usually upholstered, for the engineer or fireman to rest the arm upon.

Arm Rest Bracket. A shelf or bracket supporting the arm rest.

Armature (Electric Locomotive). 2, Fig. 4589; Fig. 4654. The rotating part of an electric motor, consisting of a laminated iron cylinder or core keyed to a shaft, and in the slots of which are wound the armature coils of insulated copper wire or ribbon. At one end of the core on the shaft is mounted the commutator, a copper cylinder composed of insulated segments, which are connected to corresponding armature coils.

Armature Key. A long, slender piece of steel, driven in a longitudinal slot cut on a driving axle or on an armature shaft, to hold the armature firmly on the axle or shaft.

Armature Keyway. 3, Fig. 4588. A longitudinal slot cut on a driving axle or an armature shaft for the insertion of a key used to hold the armature fast.

Armature Quill. Fig. 4654. A sleeve or tube, surrounding a driving axle but not touching it, and having an armature attached to, or built around it. A circular enlargement on the outer end of the quill carries a number of short, stout pins that fit in cylindrical pockets in the inside hub of the driving wheel.

Armature Shaft. The shaft on which the armature of an electric motor is fastened. In the case of gearless motors, the driving wheels of the locomotive are keyed to this shaft; but if the motor transmits power to the driving axle through gears, a pinion is fastened on the armature shaft which engages a gear wheel on the main driving axle.

Armored Brake Hose. Brake hose, covered with a woven wire fabric, to protect it from injury or abrasion. Another form of armored brake hose is formed by winding a continuous wire spirally around it by a machine which makes the spiral slightly smaller than the tube, so that it grips tightly. Vacuum brake hose, for vacuum brakes, is usually lined with coiled wires on the inside to prevent collapsing, but such is not properly termed armored brake hose.

Articulated Locomotive. Figs. 22, 83-87. A locomotive having two sets of cylinders driving independent groups of wheels. See **Mallet Articulated Compound Locomotive**.

Asbestos Dust Guard. Fig. 4510.

Asbestos Felt. A preparation of asbestos in loose sheets, for use as a non-conductor of heat in the covering of steam pipes. It must be handled with care to prevent tearing.

Ash Dump (Stayless Boiler). 72, Figs. 151-152. A cylindrical chute or pipe, usually 18 or 20 in. in diameter, leading from an aperture in the bottom of a corrugated firebox to the outside shell below. It is to allow the ashes to be discharged into the ash pan. See **Stayless Boiler, Vanderbilt Boiler**.

Ash Ejector. 29, Figs. 520-522. A device for removing ashes from an ash pan, operated by compressed air, and consisting of a cylinder having its piston rod connected to the ash pan dump shaft or slide rod. Air is admitted to and exhausted from the cylinder usually by a three-way cock.

Ash Ejector Valve. A three-way cock or other form of valve for operating an ash ejector.

Ash Pan. Figs. 508-549. Details, Figs. 638-720. A receptacle underneath the grate for holding the ashes that drop through the grate bars. In order to control the admission of air under the grate, it is provided with hinged or sliding openings or dampers at either end operated by rods and levers from the cab. The ashes are dumped from the bottom through one or more hoppers closed by hinged or sliding doors.

Ash Pan Angle. An angle iron hanger or support bolted to the lower rail of the frame or to the bottom of the firebox ring, to support the ash pan.

Ash Pan Axle Guard. A piece of sheet steel made fast underneath the ash pan and over or partly surrounding a driving axle for the purpose of protecting the axle from the excessive heat of the ash pan. Used on locomotives having one or more axles under the firebox.

Ash Pan Damper. 2, Figs. 508-549; Figs. 677-679. A flap or door, hinged at the top, to regulate the amount of air admitted under the grate bars. Also hung from hinge pivots and made to slide vertically in guides or ways.

Ash Pan Damper Crank. 3, Figs. 546-549; Figs. 674-676, 698-700. A bell crank transmitting the motion of an ash pan damper handle to a damper rod. In some designs, where dampers are arranged to slide vertically in ways or guides, two bell-cranks are used, one connecting the lower end of the damper handle to the damper rod, the other connecting the damper rod with the damper by an intermediate lever. The bell crank nearest the damper is provided with a counterweight to balance the weight of the damper.

Ash Pan Damper Crank Support. A casting secured to an ash pan or firebox to support the damper crank by a pin or short shaft.

Ash Pan Damper Handle. 2b, Figs. 546-549; Figs. 711-712. An operating handle attached to the ash pan damper crank and with its upper end passing up through the deck.

Ash Pan Damper Hinge. Figs. 685-686. The pivot or support on which the ash pan damper turns in opening or closing.

Ash Pan Damper Hinge Bearing. A lug on the ash pan to hold the hinge on which the damper is hung.

Ash Pan Damper Latch. Figs. 718-720. A fastening device for holding an ash pan damper in any position. A catch consisting of a small lever is secured in the casting through which the ash pan damper handle passes, and drops a pin or detent into a notch in the edge of the ash pan damper handle.

Ash Pan Damper Lever. 2i, Figs. 546-549; Figs. 703-704. A lever making connection between the damper rod and the damper.

Ash Pan Damper Lug. A projection cast on a damper for attaching the damper lever by pins.

Ash Pan Damper Rod. Figs. 705-710; 2c, Figs. 546-549. A slender bar connecting the damper with the ash pan damper crank for opening and closing the damper.

Ash Pan Damper Rod Pin. A bolt to secure the damper rod at either end.

Ash Pan Damper Shaft. 2d, Figs. 546-549; Figs. 689-692. A transverse shaft with a bell crank attached, resting in bearings on a support or bracket, for operating an ash pan damper.

Ash Pan Damper Shaft Bearing. 2e, Figs. 546-549; Figs. 693-697. A bracket attached to the frame of the locomotive for holding the end of the ash pan damper shaft.

Ash Pan Drop Cross Brace. Figs. 652-657; 5, Figs. 546-549. A transverse angle connecting the two sides of an ash pan hopper to strengthen it at the opening of the drop door or dump.

Ash Pan Drum. A hopper underneath an ash pan, used on some locomotives where the firebox is over one or more driving axles.

Ash Pan Dump. 4, Figs. 546-549; Figs. 665-667. A door or flap that closes the bottom of an ash pan hopper.

Ash Pan Dump Connection. 4a-4d, Figs. 508-549. The rods and levers comprising the mechanism for operating a dumping ash pan.

Ash Pan Dump Connection Pins. Bolts used in the ends of the rods and levers of the ash pan dump connection.

Ash Pan Dump Crank. 4e, Figs. 508-549. A crank connecting the ash pan dump with an operating rod and handle.

Ash Pan Dump Crank Support. A bracket on which an ash pan dump crank is pivoted.

Ash Pan Dump Cylinder. 29, Figs. 520-522. A cylinder in which a piston and piston rod, operated by air from the main reservoir, pushes or pulls a rod connected to the ash pan dump crank.

Ash Pan Dump Lever. 4a, Figs. 508-549. Connected to the ash pan dump and operated by a rod.

Ash Pan Dump Plate. 4, Figs. 508-549; Figs. 665-667. A steel plate or casting covering the opening in the bottom of an ash pan or ash pan hopper. Also called slide.

Ash Pan Dump Shaft. Part of an ash pan dump rigging, and attached to the handle used to move the dump plates.

Ash Pan Dump Shaft Arm. 4e, Figs. 508-549. Attached to an ash pan dump shaft for connection to the rod that operates the dump.

Ash Pan Dump Shaft Bearing. The support of the dump shaft in a bracket attached to the locomotive frame.

Ash Pan Dump Shaft Connection. The rods or bars by which an ash pan dump shaft is operated.

Ash Pan Dump Shaft Connection Rod. 4b, Figs. 508-549. A slender bar connecting the lever on the dump shaft with a lever that moves the dump.

Ash Pan Dump Shaft Handle. 4d, Figs. 508-549. A handle for operating a dumping ash pan. Usually but not always arranged to be worked from the foot plate.

Ash Pan Dump Shaft Handle Catch. A fastener for securing the dump shaft handle in place.

Ash Pan Dump Shaft Handle Lock Pin. A detent for fastening the dump shaft handle catch in place.

Ash Pan Dump Valve. A valve controlling the admission of air to the ash pan dump cylinder.

Ash Pan Heater Valve. A globe valve attached to the boiler to supply steam to a set of pipes placed in an ash pan to prevent the accumulation of snow and ice, which would interfere with the operation of the dampers and dumps or hopper slides.

Ash Pan Hopper. A receptacle fastened underneath a grate to receive and retain the ashes that fall through. More commonly, simply ash pan.

Ash Pan Slide. 4, Figs. 508-549; Figs. 665-667. A casting or plate sliding in guides to close the bottom of an ash pan hopper.

Ash Pan Slide Guide. 4c, Figs. 508-549. Ways formed on the bottom of an ash pan hopper for holding a plate or slide.

Ash Pan Support. 6, 7, 20, 20a, Figs. 508-549. Braces

or hangers to hold the ash pan and secure it to the firebox or frame. See **Ash Pan Angle.** In Figs. 638-641 the injector overflow discharge pipe is combined with the ash pan support.

Ash Pan Wheel Pocket. That portion of an ash pan that is arched or bent up to pass over an axle.

Ashton Pressure Gages. Figs. 3159-3160.

Ashton Safety Valves. Figs. 3224-3225.

Atlantic Type Locomotive. Figs. 54-59, 110-118. A locomotive having a four-wheel front truck, four coupled driving wheels and a two-wheel trailing truck. Used for fast passenger service. See **Whyte's Nomenclature.**

Atmospheric Brake. See **Air Brake, Vacuum Brake.** This term, but little used, includes both the air brake and the vacuum brake.

Aurora Metallic Rod Packing. Fig. 1021.

Automatic Air Brake. Figs. 2410-2614. One which is automatically applied by a rupture in the hose couplings or brake pipe, or by train separation. The term is indefinite, but usually refers to the Westinghouse Air Brake, Figs. 2410-2556, or the New York Air Brake, Figs. 2557-2614, which see, which are the ones in most general use throughout the world.

Automatic Air Cylinder Oil Cup. 98, Figs. 2429-2435; Fig. 2451. An oil cup for automatically supplying a proper amount of lubrication to the air cylinder of an air pump.

Automatic Coupling (Steam and Air Pipes). A device by means of which the steam, air brake and signal pipes are automatically coupled by impact. It is usually supported by a hanger from the coupler, and springs back of the head keep the parts tight together. Allowance is made for vertical and lateral movement, and provision made for interchange with cars not equipped with the device.

Automatic Lubricator. Figs. 3195-3205. A device for feeding at regular intervals a certain quantity of oil or lubricant to a cylinder or other mechanism. See **Sight-Feed Lubricator.**

Automatic Reducing Valve (High-Speed Brake). Figs. 2503-2507. A valve attached to the brake cylinder to automatically bleed the pressure down to 60 lbs. after an emergency application, when the pressure in the cylinder rises to 85 lbs. or more. The triangular port gives a graduated reduction. It also prevents the brake cylinder pressure from exceeding 60 lbs. in a service application. The triangular port then gives a wide opening.

Automatic Slack Adjuster. A device inserted in the foundation brake gear for automatically taking up the slack resulting from wear of the brake shoes and other parts.

Auxiliary Arch Bar. A wrought-iron bar sometimes used, which forms the lower member of a diamond truck side frame. See **Arch Bar.**

Auxiliary Reservoir (Air Brake). Figs. 2410-2421. A cylindrical reservoir made of steel tubing, attached to some part of a locomotive and to the under side of the tender by hangers or bands. The reservoir serves to hold a supply of compressed air to operate the brakes of the driving or truck wheels, and of the tender, and is supplied from the main reservoir on the engine through the brake pipe and triple valve.

Auxiliary Reservoir Bleed Cock (Air Brake). A faucet or cock for emptying the reservoir of any water condensed from the compressed air. More commonly **Reservoir Drain Cock,** which see.

Auxiliary Reservoir Nipple (Air Brake). See **Triple Valve Nipple.**

Axe. A steel chopping tool with a wooden handle, carried on the engine or tender for use in emergencies.

Axle. 23 and 72, Figs. 77-124, Figs. 1363-1385, 3545-3548. A shaft made of wrought iron or steel to which a pair of wheels is attached by pressing on in a hydraulic wheel press. This method suffices for tender and engine truck wheels. Locomotive driving wheels are keyed on in addition. Axles are distinguished according to their use as driving, front truck, trailing truck and tender axles, and according to the method of manufacture, as hammered, fagotted, muck bar axles, etc. The A. R. M. M. Standard truck axles are shown in Figs. 4878-4881.

Axles. (A. R. M. M. Standards.) Figs. 4878-4881.

At the convention of 1879 the Master Car Builders' Standard Axle with 3¾ by 7-inch journals was adopted as standard. Changed to Recommendations 1891. Modified to conform to M. C. B. standard 1903.

At the convention of 1890 the Master Car Builders' Standard Axle with journals 4¼ by 8 in. was adopted as standard. Changed to Recommendations in 1891. Modified to conform to M. C. B. standard in 1903.

At the convention of 1903 the Master Car Builders' Standard Axle with 5 by 9-inch journals was adopted as standard.

At the convention of 1903 the Master Car Builders' Standard Axle with journals 5½ by 10-inch was made a standard.

Axles. A. R. M. M. A. Standard. Specifications for Locomotive Driving and Engine Truck Axles.

1. *Material.*—Open-hearth steel.

2. *Chemical Requirements.*—Phosphorus, not to exceed .05 per cent.; sulphur, not to exceed .05 per cent.; manganese, not to exceed .60 per cent.

3. *Physical Requirements.*—Tensile strength—not less than 80,000 lbs. per square inch; elongation in two inches—not less than 20 per cent.; reduction in area—not less than 25 per cent.

4. *Tests.*—One test per melt will be required, the test specimen to be taken from either end of any axle with a hollow drill, half-way between the center and the outside, the hole made by the drill to be not more than 2 inches in diameter nor more than 4½ inches deep. The standard turned test specimen, ½ inch in diameter and 2 inches gage length, shall be used to determine the physical properties. (See Fig. 1.)

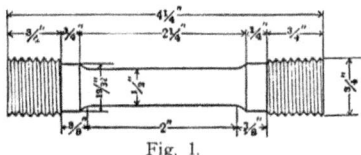

Fig. 1.

Drillings or turnings from the tensile specimen shall be used to determine the chemical properties.

5. *Stamping and Marking.*—Each axle must have heat number and manufacturer's name plainly stamped on one end, with stamps not less than ⅜ inch high, and have order number plainly marked with white lead.

6. *Inspection.*—All axles must be free from seams, pipes and other defects, and must conform to drawings accompanying these specifications.

7. Axles must be rough-turned all over, with a flat-nosed tool, cut to exact length, have ends smoothly finished and centered with 60° centers.

8. Axles failing to meet any of the above requirements, or which prove defective on machining, will be rejected.

Axle Box (British), 46, Figs. 5077-5078. A **Journal Box**, which see. See also **Grease Axle Box, Oil Axle Box**.

Axle Box Bearing (British). See **Journal Bearing**.

Axle Box Cover (British). A hinged movable cover on the tender axle box through which the lubricant is introduced. On British oil axle boxes the cover is generally bolted to the box with a strip of leather interposed to make an oil-tight joint. The oil is replenished through a small orifice closed by a screw plug or spring hinge.

Axle Box Keep (British). The lower part of a tender axle box, which in an oil box, contains the lubricant, and in a grease box simply protects the under side of the journal from dust.

Axle Box Sponge Box (British). See **Driving Box Cellar**.

Axle Box Lid (British). See **Journal Box Lid**.

Axle Collar 10, Fig. 3545. A rim or enlargement on the end of an axle which takes the end thrust of the journal bearing.

Axle Guard (British). American equivalent, pedestal. The ordinary or W pattern consists of a wrought iron plate attached to the sole bar, which permits vertical motion of the tender axle box, but restrains movement in any other direction.

Axle Guard Crown (British). The main part of the **Axle Guard**, which see.

Axle Guard Crown Washer (British). A piece of wrought iron plate, used as a washer for three or more bolts, which secure the main part of the axle guard to the tender sole bar.

Axle Guard Keep or **Horn Stay** (British). A piece of iron which secures the lower end of the jaws of the tender axle guards together.

Axle Guard Stay Rod or **Axle Guard Stretcher** (British). American equivalent, pedestal tie bar. A longitudinal bar connecting the lower ends of the tender axle guards, and keeping them the right distance apart.

Axle Guard Wing (British). The inclined part of an axle guard, strengthening it fore and aft.

Axle Guard Wing Washer (British). A piece of iron plate used as a washer for two or more bolts securing the wing of the axle guard to the sole bar. See **Axle Guard Wing**.

Axle Packing. A **Dust Guard**, which see. The journal packing is often called axle packing.

Axle Seat. 4, Figs. 3526-3540. The inside surface of the hole in a wheel which comes in contact with the axle, and not the hole itself. The corresponding part of an axle is called the wheel seat or wheel fit.

B

Babbitt Metal. "An alloy, consisting of 9 parts of tin and 1 of copper used for journal boxes; so called from its inventor, Isaac Babbitt, of Boston. Some variations have been made, and among the published compositions are:

Copper	1	1
Antimony	1	5
Tin	10	50

Another formula substitutes zinc for antimony. The term is commonly applied to any white alloy for bearings, as distinguished from the box metals or brasses in which copper predominates."—Knight.

Babbitt Metal Bearings. A style of bearing of which a great variety of forms exist, which in effect substitutes Babbitt metal in some of its many forms for brass as a bearing surface. **Lead-Lined Bearings**, which see, are different in that they merely use a thin sheet of lead over the brass, to correct slight irregularities and give an even bearing surface. The bearing or brass should be bored out to remove scale.

Back Bumper. 122, Figs. 76-124; Figs. 1531-1537. A cast iron or steel beam fastened across the frames under the deck at the back end of an engine. Also called tail piece, foot plate and deck plate.

Back Course (Stayless Boiler). 71, Figs. 151-152. The plate on a **Lentz** or **Vanderbilt Boiler**, which see, that corresponds to the outside firebox sheet of an ordinary locomotive boiler.

Back Cylinder Head. 1. (Air Brakes.) See **Non-Pressure Head**.

2. (Engine Cylinder.) Figs. 918-919, 922-925, 928-933. The **Cylinder Head**, which see, through which the piston rod passes; the head nearest the crosshead.

Back Face Plate (Steel Tired Wheels). The inner one of the two plates connecting the tire with the hub.

Back Head (Boiler). 129, Figs. 77-124; 4, Figs. 151-204. The plate forming the back end of a boiler. It is separated from the back firebox sheet by the back water space. See **Boiler**.

Back Head Braces. 9, Figs. 151-204; Figs. 265-269. Supports for the back head extending from the firebox side sheets. They are attached with pins to angle or channel brackets riveted to the inside face of the back head.

Back Head Brace Angle. 5, Figs. 151-204. A steel plate bent to a right angle and riveted inside the boiler back head to hold one end of a brace binding the back head to the firebox side sheet.

Back Head Brace Jaw. A bifurcation on the end of a back head brace for attaching the brace to a lug on the back head or boiler shell.

Back Head Brace Lug. A projection riveted to the shell or back head sheet for securing one end of a back head brace. See **Back Head Brace Angle**.

Back Head Brace Pin. 11, Figs. 151-204. A bolt passing through the jaw of a brace and through a corresponding hole in a lug, for holding the brace.

Back Head Crow Foot. 10, Figs. 151-204. A bifurcated lug riveted to the inside of the back head for the attachment of a brace.

Back Head Tee Iron. A T-shaped piece of iron riveted to the inside of the back head for the attachment of a brace. See **Back Head Brace Angle**.

Back Stop Timbers. Short sub-sills bolted and keyed by packing blocks to the center sills of a tender in line with the draft timbers, to assist the draft or center sills in transmitting the buffing shocks and strains. Usually called a buffing sub-sill.

Back Water Space. 3, Figs. 151-204. See **Water Space**.

Badge Plate (For Boiler Pressure). Figs. 237-238, 243-244. A cast or stamped metal plate fastened to the back head of a boiler or in some other prominent place in the cab to indicate the pressure allowed to be carried.

Baffle Plate. 14, Figs. 343-442. An apron for regulating the draft through the tubes, placed in the smokebox and attached to the tube sheet at an angle of 20 to 30 deg. It is intended to prevent sparks being drawn up the stack. Called also deflecting plate and diaphragm.

Bail. A curved handle of a more or less semi-circular form for a pail, bucket, lantern or other utensil. As applied to lanterns, 15, Figs. 3317-3322.

Balanced Compound Locomotive. See **Compound Locomotive.**

Balanced Valve. Figs. 2097-2192. A valve in which the steam pressure on all sides is evenly balanced. All **Piston Valves,** which see, are balanced valves, and most **Slide Valves,** which see, are balanced. Balancing is accomplished by admitting steam behind or underneath the valve over the same area as the parts normally under pressure.

Balanced Valve Regulator. Fig. 3164. A valve for automatically regulating the pressure in the steam pipe in a car heating system.

Baldwin Tandem Compound Locomotive. Figs. 47, 2207. See **Compound Locomotive.**

Baldwin Balanced Compound Locomotive. Figs. 54, 56, 63, 2193-2206. See **Compound Locomotive.**

Ball Bearing Side Bearing. Figs. 4511-4512.

Baltimore Ball Bearing Side Bearing. Figs. 4511-4512.

Band. 1. A metal strip or hoop surrounding the outside of a boiler to hold the jacket in place.

2. A piece of iron shrunk around the middle of a spring to hold its leaves or plates in their relative positions.

Barber Tender Truck. Figs. 4311-4314.

Barrel (Boilers). Also called shell. That portion of a locomotive boiler extending from the smokebox to the firebox and enclosing the tubes.

Bearing. That which supports or rests on something, and is in contact with it. Thus a block or stone on which the end of a timber rests is called a bearing. The metal block or bushing in contact with a journal is called a bearing. For M. M. Standard journal bearings see Figs. 4797-4877. See

Brake Hanger Bearing	Lead Lined Journal Bearing
Brake Shaft Bearing	Lifting Shaft Bearing
Center Bearing	Rocker Side Bearing
Dust Guard Bearing	Rocker Bearing
Journal Bearing	Side Bearing
Stop Key Journal Bearing	Truck Side Bearing
	Driving Axle Bearing
Main Rod Bearing	Side Rod Bearing

Bearing Metal. An alloy of copper and tin or copper and zinc, to which antimony and lead are sometimes added, for use in engine and tender axle bearings. See **Anti-Friction Metal, Babbitt Metal.**

Bearing Spring (British). American equivalent, bolster spring, or journal box spring. The spring which carries the weight of the vehicle and rests on the axle box. In British practice usually a half-elliptic spring.

Bearing Spring Buckle (British). American equivalent, spring band. A solid wrought iron strap which confines the plates of the bearing spring, and is generally provided with lugs on the lower side so that it cannot be moved transversely or longitudinally on the axle box. The plates are secured to the buckle by a vertical rivet.

Bearing Spring Shoe (British). A cast iron lipped rubbing piece, secured to the under side of the sole bar, on which the ends of a bearing spring bear.

Bell. 57, Figs. 77-124; Fig. 3255. A device for making a sound, consisting of a hollow, cup-shaped brass casting with a swinging rod or clapper inside, mounted on the boiler of a locomotive to give warning of its approach. Operated either by hand with a bell rope leading into the cab, or by a small air engine, or **Bell Ringer,** which see.

Bell Clapper. 8, Fig. 3255. A rod having a knob or enlargement on the end hanging from the top of a bell on the inside for the purpose of striking the bell and making a sound. Also called a bell tongue.

Bell Clapper Hanger. 4, Fig. 3255. A lug cast on the upper inside surface of a bell for the purpose of hanging the clapper. Also called bell clapper jaw.

Bell Cord or **Bell Rope.** A cord extending from the cab to the lever of the bell by which the bell is rung.

Bell Cord Bushing. Figs. 3256-3257. A thimble lining a hole through a partition for a bell cord to pass through. Usually placed in the front or rear wall of the cab, according to the location of the bell.

Bell Crank. 1. An arm or rod attached to a bell to move it and cause it to sound.

2. A pivoted crank having two arms usually at right angles to each other and in the same plane for changing the direction of motion 90 deg., more or less.

Bell Ornament. An ornament or device on top of a bell, formerly much used, but now almost obsolete.

Bell Ringer. Figs. 3261-3266. A small motor consisting of a cylinder, piston, piston rod and suitable valve for admitting compressed air to the cylinder, the piston rod of which moves, by means of a connecting rod, the crank attached to the bell and thus rings the bell.

Bell Ringer Support. A stand or bracket, bolted to the boiler to form a base to which the bell ringer is bolted.

Bell Rope. See **Bell Cord.**

Bell Rope Eye. A circular hole in the end of the bell crank arm for the attachment of a rope by which the bell is rung.

Bell Stand. 58, Figs. 77-124; 9, Fig. 3255. A stand with two arms on which the studs or trunnions of the bell yoke rest.

Bell Stand Seat. The base or support bolted to the top of the boiler, and on which the bell stand is secured.

Bell Yoke. 3, Fig. 3255. A curved piece of metal passing across the top of the bell, usually of one piece with the bell itself, and having a stud or trunnion at each end resting in and turning upon bearings on the bell stand.

Belpaire Firebox Boiler. Figs. 184-196. A boiler having a firebox with a flat crown sheet joining the side sheets by a curve of short radius and having the outside crown sheet and the upper part of the outer side sheets flat and parallel to those of the inner firebox. These flat parallel plates are then stayed by straight direct vertical and transverse horizontal stays, obviating the necessity of crown bars to support and strengthen the crown sheet.

Bend (Iron Pipes). See **Return Bend.** They are distinguished as close and open return bends.

Bending Rolls. Fig. 4888. A machine for bending metal plates to a circular form, such as boiler plates. Three rolls are arranged in pyramidal form. The two lower rolls are generally geared together and the upper roll runs free, but is provided with means for vertical adjustment and is also arranged so that it can be swung out of the way to allow the removal of the piece which has been formed. By changing the distance between the upper roll and the lower rolls, plates can be bent to varying radii of curvature.

Best, W. N., American Calorific Co. Oil Burner. Figs. 734-736, 756-757.

Bettendorf Cast Steel Tender Truck. Figs. 4342-4345.

Beveled Washer. A washer used to give an even bearing for rods which stand at an acute angle to the surface on which the nut or bolt head bears. Sometimes two such washers which come near together are cast in one piece, and are then called double beveled washers.

Bibb. A curved nozzle for conveying liquids and changing the direction of flow, usually from a horizontal to a vertical current. Hence—

Bibb Cock. Literally, a cock with a curved nozzle or spout, but commonly restricted to a cock with a plain valve without springs, moved by the hand only.

Binding Post. 28, Figs. 3267-3270. A short brass stud with a hole through it for a conductor or wire which is held fast in the top or side of the post by a thumb screw.

Blast Pipe (British). 21, Figs. 5077-5078. See **Exhaust Pipe.**

Blast Pipe Nozzle (British). 22, Figs. 5077-5078. See **Exhaust Nozzle.**

Bleeding Cock or **Bleeding Valve.** Another name for **Release Valve**, which see. The operation of releasing the brakes when applied upon a car detached from the locomotive is sometimes called bleeding. The bleeding valve is located in the auxiliary reservoir, and the brakes may be released by holding it open and allowing the air in the brake cylinder to escape.

Block. 1. "A heavy piece of timber or wood, usually with one plane surface; or it is rectangular and rather thick than long."—Webster.

2. "A pulley or system of pulleys, mounted on its frame or shell, with its bands or strap. A block consists of one or more pulleys or sheaves, in a groove of which the rope runs, fastened in a shell or frame by pins, on which they revolve; of a shell or frame enclosing the pulley or pulleys; and of a strap or band, consisting of a rope, encompassing the shell, and attached by an eye of rope or a hook to some object."—Ed. Ency.

The interior wheels are termed sheaves, which latter term is often made to designate the whole block or pulley, but incorrectly. A snatch block is a block with only one sheave, and with an opening at the side for the ready insertion and removal of the rope. Blocks without this opening, however, are sometimes loosely termed snatch blocks.

Block and Tackle. A general term applied to a pair or more of pulleys and accompanying rope. Also termed fall and tackle, or simply tackle.

Blooms and Billets (A. R. M. M. A. Standard Specifications for Steel Blooms and Billets for Locomotive Forgings).

Material.—1. Open-hearth steel.

Physical Requirements.—2. Grade "A":
Tensile strength, 70,000 lbs. per square inch.
Elongation in two inches, 20 per cent.

3. Grade "B":
Tensile strength, 80,000 lbs. per square inch.
Elongation in two inches, 17 per cent.

Chemical Analysis.—4. Grade "A":
Carbon .... .25 to .40 per cent.
Phosphorus, not to exceed...... .06 per cent.
Sulphur, not to exceed........ .06 per cent.
Manganese, not to exceed...... .60 per cent.

5. Grade "B":
Carbon .... .35 to .50 per cent.
Phosphorus, not to exceed...... .05 per cent.
Sulphur, not to exceed........ .05 per cent.
Manganese, not to exceed...... .60 per cent.

Tests.—6. One test per melt will be required, the test specimen to be cut cold from the bloom, parallel to its axis and half-way between the center and the outside. The standard turned test specimen, ½ inch in diameter and 2 inches gage length, shall be used to determine the physical properties. (See Fig. 1. **Axles, Specifications.**) Drillings or turnings from the tensile specimen shall be used to determine the chemical properties.

Stamping and Marking.—7. Each bloom or billet must have heat number and manufacturer's name plainly stamped on one end, with stamps not less than ¾ inch, and have order number plainly marked with white lead.

Inspection.—8. Blooms and billets must be free from checks, pipes and surface defects. Any blooms or billets chipped to a depth greater than ½ inch will be rejected.

9. Any billet or bloom failing to meet the above requirements will be rejected and held subject to disposal by manufacturers.

10. Inspector to have the privilege of taking drillings from the center of the top bloom billet of the ingot in order to determine the amount of segregation.

Grade "A" is intended for rod straps and miscellaneous forgings.

Grade "B" is intended for driving and truck axles, connecting rods, crank pins and guides.

Blower Pipe. 250, Figs. 77-124. A pipe to convey steam from a valve on the boiler head to the exhaust nozzle tip or base of the stack in order to create a draft and thus stimulate the fire when the engine is standing. Also used to diminish black smoke when steam is shut off, as when approaching a station.

Blower Pipe Connection. Figs. 390-393. A threaded nipple in the side of the smokebox for attaching a steam pipe while the locomotive is standing in the engine house to create a draft and start the fire.

Blower Pipe Coupling Nut. 49, Figs. 390-393. A union for joining the two parts of the blower pipe, i. e.: the one leading from the valve on the boiler head and the one leading to the stack or exhaust tip.

Blower Pipe Fittings. The couplings, unions, elbows, nipples, etc., used in connecting the blower pipe from the valve on the boiler head to the point where it enters the stack or exhaust pipe.

Blower Valve. Figs. 3027-3031. A valve attached to the boiler head, or more usually to the **Turret**, which see, to admit steam through the blower pipe to the stack, in order to increase the draft.

Blow-off Cock. Figs. 277, 3334-3339; 224, Figs. 77-124. A plug valve having a large opening, usually screwed into the front water leg of the firebox, but sometimes into the back head above the crown sheet, used for emptying the boiler and carrying off accumulated mud and loose scale. See **Pneumatic Blow-off Cock.**

Blow-off Cock Arm. The handle or lever by means of which the blow-off cock is opened and closed.

Blow-off Cock Extension. A pipe, usually having an elbow or right angle bend, screwed on a blow-off cock to conduct the water from the boiler into a pit or other opening between the rails.

Blow-off Cock Rod. A slender bar connected to a blow-off cock for operating it and extending out to the side of the engine, where it is connected to a shaft and handle.

Blow-off Cock Valve. Fig. 3339. A valve, controlling by means of air pressure, the operation of a blow-off cock. See **Pneumatic Blow-off Cock.**

Board. "A piece of timber sawed thin, and of considerable length and breadth, compared with the thickness, used for building and other purposes."—Webster. See **Letter Board, Runboard.**

Body Bolster. 5, Figs. 3614-3656; Figs. 4113-4416. The

transverse members of the underframe over the trucks which transmit the loads carried by the longitudinal sills to the truck through the center plates. Metal body bolsters are becoming standard for use on tenders regardless of whether the sills are of wood or steel. The term body transom is sometimes applied to the bolster, but incorrectly, as this term applies more properly to the cross tie timbers. See **Bolster**.

Body Center Plate. 8, Figs. 3614-3656. The center plate attached to the under side of the body bolster. See **Center Plate**.

Body Check Chain Eye. 31, Figs. 3614-3656. An eye bolt or clevis for fastening a truck chain or safety chain to the tender frame. See **Truck Check Chain Eye**.

Body Check Chain Hook. An iron hook on the **Check Chain**, which see, which enters into the body check chain eye. See Figs. 3768-3770.

Body Side Bearings. 32, Figs. 3614-3656; Figs. 4511-4521. The upper one of the two **Side Bearings**, which see, attached to the body bolster.

Body Spring. A **Bolster Spring**, which see.

Bogie (British). Figs. 5137-5140. A swiveling four-wheel truck used under engines and tenders. See **Truck**.

Bogie Frame (British). See **Truck Frame**.

Bogie Frame Cross Stay (British). See **Truck Frame Cross Tie**.

Bogie Horn Plate (British). 48, Figs. 5077-5078. See **Pedestal**.

Bogie Horn Plate Stay (British). 49, Figs. 5077-5088. See **Pedestal Cap**.

Bogie Pin (British). 52, Figs. 5077-5078. See **Center Pin**.

Boiler. Figs. 144-206; Details 207-330. A steel shell containing water which is converted into steam by the heat of the fire in the firebox to furnish energy to move the locomotive. Locomotive boilers are of the internal firebox, straight fire tube type, having a cylindrical shell containing the fire tubes or flues, an enlarged back end for the firebox and an extension front end, or smokebox, leading out from which is the stack. Boilers are classified by their shape as **Straight Top**, which see, having the cylindrical shell of uniform diameter from the firebox to the smokebox; as **Wagon Top**, which see, having a conical or sloping course of plates next to the firebox and tapering down to the cylindrical courses; as **Extended Wagon Top**, which see, having one or more cylindrical courses between the firebox and the sloping course which tapers to the diameter of the main shell. They are further classified as **Wide Firebox, Narrow Firebox, Belpaire Firebox, and Wootten Firebox**, which see. See also: **Firebox, Heating Surface, Radial Stay Boiler, Riveting, Staybolt, Tubes, Vanderbilt Boiler, Water Tube Boiler**.

Boiler Angle. A plate or strip of right angle or L section, used as a brace or strut in any part of a locomotive boiler.

Boiler Bracing. The system of stays and braces used in a boiler to enable its plates to resist the pressure imposed upon them by the steam. See **Crown Bar, Stay Bolt** and **Sling Stay**.

Boiler Check. See **Injector Check**.

Boiler Clothing Band (British). 93, Figs. 5077-5078. See **Jacket Band**.

Boiler Clothing Plate (British). 92, Figs. 5077-5078. See **Jacket**.

Boiler Filler. A metal plug screwed in a hole in the upper part of a boiler for convenience in filling with water.

Boiler Jacket. See **Jacket**.

Boiler Plate. Sheets of iron or mild steel from ¼ to ⅞-in. thick, of which the shell of a boiler is made.

Boiler Shell. The cylindrical part of a boiler in front of the firebox.

Boiler Staying (British). See **Boiler Bracing**.

Boiler Steel (Specifications for). See **Steel**.

Boiler Tee. A T-shaped piece of iron riveted to one of the boiler plates for holding a boiler brace.

Boiler Tube. See **Tube** and **Flue**.

Bolster. 5, Figs. 3614-3656; Figs. 4399-4328. A trussed wooden beam or a rolled or pressed steel shape placed across the frame of a tender truck to receive, through the center plate, the weight of the tender, and transfer it to the truck frame and wheels through the springs on which it is carried. A similar bolster is placed transversely on the under side of the tender sills, over the center of each truck, and called a **Body Bolster**, which see. It transfers the weight through the center plates to the truck bolster. Two-wheel engine trailing trucks also have bolsters, which are often combined with the journal boxes as in Figs. 3432-3435.

Bolster Arch Bar. The name sometimes applied to the upper bar in the side frame of a diamond arch bar tender truck. See **Arch Bar**.

Bolster Center Casting. Figs. 3676-3678. A hollow rectangular casting placed between the draft timbers or center sills and the body bolster plates. The king bolt passes through it.

Bolster End Cap. A metal plate over the end of the truck bolster, replacing the bolster truss rod washers used on trussed wooden bolsters.

Bolster Flitch Plates. 28, Figs. 4328-4330. The iron or steel plates of a built-up bolster, sandwiched between wood pieces. They are rarely met with now, having been almost entirely superseded by metal bolsters. They are also called bolster sandwich plates.

Bolster Guide. 5, Figs. 4294-4382; Figs. 4385-4387. Vertical posts between the top and bottom arch bars of a tender truck, primarily to stiffen the truck frame, but which serve as guides for the ends of the bolster. More commonly **Column**, which see.

Bolster Sandwich Plate. See **Bolster Flitch Plate**.

Bolster Springs. 4a, Figs. 4294-4382; Figs. 4522-4537. The main springs of a tender, carried on the spring plank and supporting the truck bolster, on which the weight of the tender body rests.

Bolster Spring Cap. See **Spring Plate**.

Bolster Spring Seat. See **Spring Plate**.

Bolster Truss Rod. 24, Figs. 4319-4323. A bent rod secured at the ends of a tender truck bolster and bearing upon a saddle or king post. Two truss rods are commonly used.

Bolt. A pin, rod or bar of metal used to hold or fasten anything in its place. Ordinarily a bolt has a head on one end and a screw and nut on the other, while a rod has a nut on both ends. Various forms of bolts, which see for further definitions, are as follows: **Carriage Bolt, Eye Bolt, Jaw Bolt, Joint Bolt, Key Bolt, Lug Bolt, Machine Bolt, Strap Bolt** or **U-Shaped Bolt**. For bolts whose names are derived from the purpose for which they serve, see **Box Bolt, Column Bolt, Hub Bolt, Journal Box Bolt, Journal Box Cover Bolt, King Bolt** or **Center Pin, Tire Bolt, Saddle Bolt, Stay Bolt, Frame Bolt, Cylinder Head Bolt, Patch Bolt**.

Bolt Cutter. Figs. 4889-4894. A machine for cutting threads on bolts by means of a die. Bolt cutters are made in various designs, as single and multiple head bolt cutters, special bolt cutters for cutting the threads on stay bolts, etc.

Bolt Head. The enlarged portion of a bolt at one end that comes in contact with the material through which the bolt is passed, and which prevents the whole bolt from going through the hole. The American Railway Master Mechanics' Association in 1899 adopted the following dimensions for square bolt heads as standard: The side of the head shall be one and one-half times the diameter of the bolt, and the thickness of the head shall be one-half the side of the head.

Bolt Header. Figs. 4933-4934. A machine for forging the heads on bolts. See also **Forging Machine**.

Booth Fuel Oil Burner. Figs. 768-771.

Boring and Turning Mill. Figs. 4895-4903. A tool for machining circular holes and turning metal. It is provided with a horizontal circular table to which the work to be machined is secured. The table is revolved on substantial bearings and the cutting tools are carried in saddles attached to a cross rail, which is secured to and has a vertical movement on the face of two uprights similar to the housings of a planer. This type of machine has supplanted the lathe for much work formerly done on the face plate. Work can be set up with greater rapidity and ease on the horizontal table of the boring mill than can be done on the vertical face plate of the lathe. In the horizontal boring and turning mill, Figs. 4895-4898, the adjustment is made by moving the table or bed carrying the work, instead of by moving the tool, as in the vertical type.

Boss or Hub (of a Steel-Tired Wheel). 3, Figs. 1353-1367. The central portion, through which the axle passes. Boss is the usual British term, but little used in the United States.

Bottom. "The lowest part of anything, as the bottom of a well, vat or ship."—Webster. See **Ash Pan Bottom**, **Lamp Bottom**.

Bottom Arch Bar. 2, Figs. 4294-4382. An inverted arch bar. The pedestal tie bar is sometimes called bottom arch bar. See **Arch Bar**.

Bottom Bolster. A **Truck Bolster**, which see, is sometimes spoken of as the bottom bolster, while the body bolster is called the top bolster.

Bottom Brace (Engine Truck). 3, Figs. 4294-4382. A flat bar bolted on the bottom of the engine truck box jaws, and frequently called a **Pedestal Binder** or **Pedestal Tie**, which see.

Bottom Truck Connection. The common name for a **Brake Lever Coupling Bar**, which see.

Box. See **Journal Box**.

Box Bearing. A **Journal Bearing**, which see.

Box Bolt. (Diamond Trucks.) The bolts holding the journal box in place. More properly, **Journal Box Bolts**, which see.

Box Cover. See **Journal Box Cover** or **Lid**.

Box Guide. See **Journal Box Guide and Pedestal**.

Box Lid. See **Journal Box Cover** or **Lid**.

Box Packing. Journal Packing, which see.

Box Steps. Tender or locomotive steps made with closed sides and backs, as distinguished from open steps which have an opening through the parts named.

Brace. An inclined beam, rod, or bar of a frame, truss, girder, etc., which unites two or more of the points where other members of the structure are connected together, and which prevents them from turning about their joints. A brace thus makes the structure incapable of altering its form from this cause, and it also distributes or transmits part of the strain at one or more of the joints toward the point or points of support, or resistance to that strain. A brace may be subjected to either a strain of compression or tension. See **Boiler Brace**, **Back Head Brace**, **Tube Sheet Brace**, **Back Brace**, **Pilot Brace**, **Frame Brace**.

Bracket. 1. An angular brace or stay to hold one piece at right angles to another. See

Bumper Bracket	Headlight Bracket
Cab Bracket	Running Board Bracket
Air Pump Bracket	Cylinder Lever Bracket

2. On cast iron tender or truck wheels, the curved stiffening ribs cast on the inside of the plate are called brackets. See **Wheel**.

Bracket Nut. A small nut, turned by a **Spanner**, which see.

Bradford Draft Gear. Figs. 3923-3926.

Brake. The whole combination of parts by which the motion of the locomotive or train is retarded or arrested. The **Foundation Brake Gear**, which see, includes all of the parts by which the pressure of the air in the brake cylinder is transmitted to the wheels.

Air Brake	High-Speed Brake Gear
Automatic Air Brake	New York Air Brake
Brake Beam	Quick Action Brake
Brake Lever	Straight Air Brake
Driver Brake	Vacuum Brake
Foundation Brake Gear	Westinghouse Automatic Air Brake.

Brake Beam. 16, Figs. 4294-4382; Figs. 4429-4458. A transverse beam of iron, steel or wood, often strengthened by a truss and carrying a brake head and shoe at each end, by means of which the pressure in the brake cylinder transmitted through the brake levers is conveyed to and equally distributed on the treads of both wheels on an axle. The brake beams are sometimes hung from the underframe or the truck frame outside of the wheels, outside hung, but more commonly between the wheels, inside hung.

Brake Beam Adjusting Hanger. 17, Figs. 4294-4382. A link sometimes attached to a brake beam to cause the latter and the brake head and shoe to maintain the same relative positions when the brakes are released, so as to prevent the ends of the brake shoes from coming in contact with the wheel when the brakes are released. It is attached to the truck transoms or truck bolster in tender trucks, by a projecting brake beam adjusting hanger carrier, and to the brake beam by an eye or clip. Sometimes called a parallel brake hanger.

Brake Beam Adjusting Hanger Carrier. See above.

Brake Beam Eye Bolt. Properly an eye bolt for fastening a lower brake rod to a wooden brake beam. They have threads cut nearly their entire length, and usually a nut is placed on each side of the brake beam, which can be screwed up so as to take up the wear of the brake shoes.

Brake Beam Fulcrum. See **Brake Lever Fulcrum**. A brake beam king post or strut is frequently called a brake beam fulcrum.

Brake Beam Hanger. 11, Figs. 4294-4382. A rod or bar by which a brake beam is hung or suspended from a tender truck. More commonly, **Brake Hanger**, which see. See also **Brake Beam Adjusting Hanger**.

Brake Beam King Post. A strut or distance piece which forms a bearing for the truss rod of a brake beam. In metal brake beams the brake lever is attached to it, and it then becomes a brake lever fulcrum.

Brake Beam Safety Chain. A **Brake Safety Chain**, which see.

Brake Beam Safety Chain Hanger. See **Brake Safety Chain Eye Bolt.**

Brake Beam Strut. A **Brake Beam King Post**, which see.

Brake Beam Support. See **Brake Hanger.**

Brake Beam Truss Rod. A rod used to strengthen a brake beam.

Brake Block. Another name for a **Brake Head**, which see. Brake block is the usual British term for the combined brake head and shoe. The two are often combined in one piece in British practice, no removable shoe being used.

Brake Carrier. See **Brake Hanger Carrier.**

Brake Chain. See **Brake Shaft Chain.**

Brake Chain Connecting Rod. An iron rod connecting the brake chain to one of the brake levers, usually the floating lever.

Brake Clevis. A **Brake Lever Fulcrum**, which see.

Brake Connecting Rod. More properly, **Brake Chain Connecting Rod**, which see.

Brake Connection. 8, Figs. 2653-2696. A **Brake Rod**, which see. A round iron rod, usually made with jaws on the ends to fit over the brake levers. They transmit the pressure of the brake cylinder piston from one brake lever to another and finally to the brake shoes. The rods take their names from the brake lever to which they are attached, which is farthest from the cylinder.

Brake Cut-out Cock. See **Cut-out Cock.**

Brake Cylinder. (Air Brake.) 60, Figs. 77-124; Figs. 2497-2499. A cast iron cylinder attached to the frame of the tender or locomotive, or to the locomotive forward truck. It contains a piston which is forced outwardly by compressed air to apply the brakes, and when the air pressure is released the piston is returned to its normal position by a release spring coiled about the piston rod inside the cylinder. On locomotives, tenders and passenger cars the brake cylinder is fitted with two heads, the pressure head and the non-pressure head, while in the freight brake the end of the auxiliary reservoir forms one head of the brake cylinder. The piston rod of the tender brake cylinder, Fig. 2499, has a crosshead at its outer end, to which is attached the cylinder lever. The piston rod of the freight brake cylinder, as well as that of the tender brake, 3, Figs. 2498-2499, is hollow and loosely encloses a push rod which is attached to the cylinder lever. The driver brake cylinder is attached either to the frame back of the driving wheels, or to one of the crossties or to the guide yoke.

Brake Cylinder Bracket. 9, Figs. 2653-2696. A plate or bar of steel riveted to the under side of a tender frame and having holes for bolts to secure the brake cylinder. See **Brake Cylinder Plate.**

Brake Cylinder Lever. (Tender Brake.) 5 and 6, Figs. 2653-2696. One of two levers which are connected together by a tie rod attached near their centers. One end of one lever is attached to the crosshead of the brake cylinder, and the corresponding end of the other is attached to a bracket on the brake cylinder head at the opposite end of the cylinder. The other ends of the levers are connected with the floating lever by rods.

Brake Cylinder Pipe (Air Brake). 1. The pipe that connects the brake cylinder with the triple valve.
2. The pipe that connects the distributing valve with all the brake cylinders in the Westinghouse E T locomotive brake equipment.

Brake Cylinder Piston Rod. 3, Figs. 2497-2499. A piston rod attached to a piston in a brake cylinder for locomotive driving, trailing, truck or tender wheels. See **Push Rod.**

Brake Cylinder Plate (Air Brake). The steel plate to which the brake cylinder is bolted and by which it is attached to the tender sills.

Brake Cylinder Push Rod. See **Brake Cylinder Piston Rod** and **Push Rod.**

Brake Cylinder Support. See **Brake Cylinder Plate.**

Brake Dog. A **Brake Pawl**, which see.

Brake Equalizer. A **Floating Lever**, which see.

Brake Eye Bolt. A **Brake Beam Eye Bolt**, which see.

Brake Finger. A **Brake Pawl**, which see.

Brake Gear. See **Air Brake Standards, Driver Brake, Foundation Brake Gear, Tender Brake, Truck Brake.**

Brake Hand Wheel. A wheel secured to a shaft around which a brake chain is wound to apply the tender brakes by hand.

Brake Hanger. 1. 11, Figs. 1294-1382. A link or bar by which brake beams and attachments are suspended from a truck or tender frame. It is attached to the truck or to the frame of the locomotive or tender by a brake hanger carrier. Brake hangers are distinguished as hooked, linked and U-shaped. Best practice locates this hanger so as to have the brake shoes a predetermined height above the rail, thus insuring the same piston travel, regardless of whether the tender is empty or loaded.
2. (British.) A wrought iron bar by which the brake block is suspended. No brake beam is commonly used.

Brake Hanger Bolt. A bolt which fastens the brake hanger to the brake hanger carrier.

Brake Hanger Carrier. An eye or U-bolt, a casting or other fastening by which a brake hanger is attached to the truck.

Brake Hanger Pin. A pin passing through the brake hanger carrier and the brake hanger.

Brake Head. Figs. 2758-62, 2778, 2784, 1459-1460; 10, Figs. 1294-1382. A metal casting secured to the end of a brake beam or hanger to hold a brake shoe. The most common form is the Christie brake head and shoe. The shoe is cast with lugs which fit into corresponding recesses in the head and a thin tapered key holds the two securely together. By withdrawing the key the worn-out shoe can be quickly removed and a new shoe substituted. In Great Britain the brake head and shoe are commonly made in one piece, and called a brake block.

Brake Hose. See **Air Brake Hose.**

Brake Hose Coupling. See **Hose Coupling.**

Brake Hose Coupling Case. See **Hose Coupling Case.**

Brake Hose Nipple. See **Hose Nipple.**

Brake Lever (Air Brake). A general term including all the levers in the **Foundation Brake Gear**, which see. See also **Dead Lever, Live Lever, Cylinder Lever, Truck Brake Lever.**

Brake Lever Bracket. A wrought iron knee on the under side of a tender, to which the fulcrum of a brake lever is sometimes attached.

Brake Lever Bracket Brace. A diagonal wrought iron brace to stiffen the brake lever bracket.

Brake Lever Connecting Rod. 8, Figs. 2653-2696. An iron rod connecting the floating levers operated from the tender brake cylinder. See **Brake Cylinder Lever.**

Brake Lever Coupling Bar (Inner Hung Brakes). 11, Figs. 1294-1382. A compression bar connecting the two brake levers (dead lever and live lever), to which it is fastened by the coupling bar pin. When the brakes are outer hung, this member becomes in tension instead of compression, and is known as the lower brake rod. It is usually called bottom truck connection.

Brake Lever Fulcrum. Figs. 4461-4463. A forked iron attached to the brake beam, by means of which a brake lever is connected to the beam. In the trussed metal brake beams the king post of the brake beam becomes the brake lever fulcrum. See **Brake Beam King Post.**

Brake Lever Guide. 15, Figs. 4294-4382. An iron bar which guides the upper end of a brake lever. Further distinguished as live lever and dead lever guides, the latter provided with pins for adjustment as the brake shoes wear, and also called a brake lever stop.

Brake Lever Jaw. A **Brake Lever Fulcrum**, which see.

Brake Lever Pin, or **Brake Pin.** A small metal pin used in the brake lever connections.

Brake Lever Spring. A **Release Spring**, which see.

Brake Lever Stop. 15, Figs. 4294-4382. An iron bar or loop attached to a truck or tender frame, and which holds the upper end of a fixed or dead brake lever. It usually has holes in it in which a fulcrum pin is inserted. By moving the pin from one hole to another the lever is adjusted so as to take up the wear of the brake shoes. More commonly called **Dead Lever Guide**, which see.

Brake Lever Strut. A brake lever coupling bar or **Bottom Truck Connection**, which see.

Brake Lever Tie Rod. 4, Figs. 2653-2696. A rod connecting the two brake cylinder levers at a point between the ends of each. Also called cylinder lever connection.

Brake Pawl. A small pivoted iron bar for engaging in the teeth of a **Brake Rachet Wheel**, which see. It is placed in such a position as to be worked in and out of engagement with the ratchet wheel teeth by the foot.

Brake Pipe (Air Brake). Figs. 2410-2421. An iron pipe connecting the engineer's brake valve on the locomotive with the brake apparatus on all the vehicles in the train, and connected between adjoining cars by flexible hose couplings. The air from the air pump or motor compressor is conveyed from the main reservoir through the engineer's brake valve to the triple valve and auxiliary reservoir under each car. The brake pipe and auxiliary reservoirs contain air at normally the same pressure, which is 70 pounds for ordinary service, 90 pounds for high pressure freight service and 110 pounds for high speed passenger service. A reduction of the pressure in the brake pipe of from 5 to 20 pounds, made by opening a small port in the engineer's brake valve to the atmosphere, causes the triple valves to close communication between the brake pipe and the auxiliary reservoir and to open communication from the auxiliary reservoirs to the brake cylinder. The compressed air stored in the auxiliary reservoir acts on the cylinder piston and applies the brakes. This is called a service application. In an emergency when it is desired to stop quickly, the engineer's brake valve is thrown to the emergency position and quickly returned to lap position. This gives a sudden reduction in the brake pipe pressure, which throws the triple valve slide valve to its extreme or emergency position. Air is admitted to the brake cylinder from the auxiliary reservoir, and also from the brake pipe through the emergency port, giving additional volume of air and therefore higher brake cylinder pressure. An emergency application travels throughout the length of the train with great rapidity. In case a hose bursts the pressure is suddenly released in the brake pipe, and the brakes are applied in the same manner, but with less force, since there is no air in the brake pipe to help out the auxiliary reservoirs. An emergency check valve is provided in the triple valves to prevent air from flowing back from the brake cylinders to the brake pipe when the emergency port is opened due to a broken hose. To release the brakes after either an emergency or service application, the brake pipe pressure is raised, and the triple valves thereby forced to the release position, connecting the brake pipe to the auxiliary reservoir and the brake cylinder with the atmosphere. The auxiliary reservoirs are then recharged with air at the brake pipe pressure, and the cylinder pressure is released. This pipe is sometimes called train pipe, train line, or train brake pipe, but its proper name is brake pipe, to distinguish it from the signal and steam heating pipes. See **Triple Valve.**

Brake Pipe Air Strainer. Fig. 2511. A wire strainer inserted in the brake pipe to prevent foreign matter from entering the brake apparatus on a locomotive or tender.

Brake Pull Rod Safety Hanger. A metal loop or eye attached to a truck and through which the lower brake rod passes. It is intended to prevent the brake rod from falling on the track in case it or its connections should break. Not commonly used.

Brake Ratchet Wheel. A wheel attached to a brake shaft, having teeth shaped like saw teeth, into which a pawl engages, thus preventing the wheel and shaft from running backward.

Brake Rod. Any rod serving to connect brake levers.

Brake Rod Guide. Any form of special support for a brake rod.

Brake Rubber. A **Brake Shoe**, which see.

Brake Safety Chain or **Link.** 18a, Figs. 4294-4382. A chain attached by brake safety chain eye bolts to a brake beam and to the truck. It is intended for the same purpose as a **Brake Safety Strap**, which see, to hold the brake beams in case a brake hanger should break. Sometimes made of a single link or bars. A brake beam safety guard is not bolted or fastened to the brake beam, but is usually a T-shaped forging, the stem being bolted to the truck frame, the cross bar hanging under the brake beam to prevent it from falling upon the track if the hanger breaks.

Brake Safety Chain Eye Bolt. An eye bolt attached to a tender truck or tender frame, and which holds a brake safety chain.

Brake Safety Strap. A strap of iron fastened to the end piece or transom of a tender truck and bent into such a shape as to embrace the brake beam. In case any of the hangers should give way, the safety strap is intended to catch and hold the beam and prevent it from falling on the track. Sometimes it is made of steel, and used as a release spring for throwing off the brake. A **Brake Safety Chain**, which see, is another device for the same purpose.

Brake Shaft. 14, Figs. 2653-2696. A vertical iron shaft on which a chain is wound and by which the power of a hand brake is applied to the wheels of a tender.

Brake Shaft Arm. A lever fastened horizontally on top of the brake shaft for turning it and applying the brake. Sometimes used instead of a brake hand wheel.

Brake Shaft Bearing. A metal eye by which a brake shaft is held in its place, and in which it turns.

Brake Shaft Casing. A tube or slot in which a tender brake shaft is enclosed.

Brake Shaft Chain. 13, Figs. 2653-2696. A chain connecting the brake shaft with the brake levers through the brake chain connecting rods, to the end of which it is attached. The force exerted on the shaft is transmitted by this chain.

Brake Shaft Chain Sheave. A roller or pulley over which a brake shaft chain passes.

Brake Shaft Connecting Rod. 8, Figs. 2653-2696. A rod which is attached at one end to a brake shaft chain and at the other to one of the levers in the foundation brake gear.

Brake Shaft Pawl. See **Brake Pawl.**

Brake Shaft Step. 11, Figs. 2653-2696. A bearing which holds the lower end of the brake shaft. It usually consists of a U-shaped bar of iron, the upper ends of which are fastened to the tender end sill, with a hole in the curved part of the bar which receives the end of the shaft.

Brake Shaft Step Brace. A wrought iron brace attached to the brake shaft step to resist the pull of the brake chain.

Brake Shoe. Figs. 2744-54, 2765-2786. A piece of metal shaped to fit the tread of a wheel and attached by a key or otherwise to a brake block or brake head. The brake shoe rubs against the tread of the wheel when the brakes are applied. Such shoes are made of cast, wrought or malleable iron or steel, usually cast iron. Also called a brake rubber. Shoes for driving and engine truck wheels are usually flanged and wear on both the tread and flange of the wheels. Shoes for tender truck wheels wear on the tread of the wheel only.

Brake Shoe Key. Figs. 2763-2764. A flat wedge-shaped piece of iron or steel inserted in a brake head to hold the shoe in place.

Brake Slack Adjuster. A device to automatically take up any slack in the brake gear between the air brake cylinder and the brake shoes, so that the piston travel shall not be too great.

Brake Staff. A **Brake Shaft**, which see.

Brake Strut. 14, Figs. 4294-4382. A compression bar or strut between the live and dead levers of a truck with inside hung brakes. Probably the term brake strut is more common than brake lever coupling bar. Brake strut should not be confused with brake beam strut. A **Brake Lever Coupling Bar**, which see.

Brake Valve (Air Brake). The valve by which the engineer operates the brakes. The proper name is **Engineer's Brake Valve,** which see.

Brake Wheel. An iron wheel attached to the upper end of the brake shaft, and by which the latter is turned to apply the brakes by hand. A brake hand wheel.

Branch Pipe. A common name for a **Tee Head,** which see.

Brass. "An alloy of copper and zinc. The term is commonly applied to the yellow alloy of copper with about half its weight of zinc, in which case it is called by engineers yellow brass; but copper alloyed with about one-ninth its weight of tin is the metal of brass ordinance or gun metal. Similar alloys used for brass for bearings of machinery are called hard brass, and when employed for statues and metals they are called bronze."—Tomlinson's Cycl. Useful Arts.

Brewer Pneumatic Fire Door. Fig. 339.

Brick Arch, 2 and 96, Figs. 721-749. A rather flat arch of fire brick, supported on water tubes or side brackets and placed across the front end of the firebox at an angle of from 30 deg. to 45 deg., with the tube sheet. Its purpose is to promote combustion and thereby diminish black smoke.

Brick Arch Stud. 1. A bolt or fastener for holding a brick arch in position.

2. A nipple or short threaded pipe, screwed into the crown sheet or tube sheet for connection to a brick arch tube.

Brick Arch Tube. Iron tubes bedded in a brick arch and having connection with the front water leg and the space above the crown sheet. Used to support the brick arch and to promote circulation. They give additional heating surface as well. See **Water Tube.**

Brick Arch Tube Nut. A nut screwed on an inclined tube making connection between the water above the crown sheet and the front water leg, to secure it in place and make a tight joint.

Bridge. 1. (Valve.) 56, Figs. 2097-2118. In a locomotive valve chamber or valvet seat, the spaces or portions of the valve seat between any two ports are called bridges.

2. (Firebox.) 1 and 92, Figs. 721-749. A firebrick wall built across a firebox in front of the tubesheet and frequently used to support the front end of the brick arch. It forms a combustion chamber in front of the tubesheet and protects the ends of the tubes from the direct heat of the fire. Also called bridge wall.

Bridge Pipe. 100, Figs. 77-124. A pipe conveying steam from the dome to the turret in the cab. Sometimes called **Turret Dry Pipe,** which see. See **Cab Turret.**

Briggs Standard Wrought-Iron Pipe Threads. At the convention of 1899, what is known as the Briggs Standard, as determined by the Pratt & Whitney gages, of threads for wrought-iron pipe and couplings, was adopted as a standard of the American Railway Master Mechanics' Association.

The gages used by the Pratt & Whitney Company were made by them from an autograph copy of a table made by Mr. Robert Briggs personally, who originally established and published these standard threads. A copy of it is as follows:

STANDARD DIMENSIONS OF WROUGHT-IRON WELDED TUBES. BRIGGS STANDARD.

Diameter of tube.			Thickness of metal.	Screwed ends.	
Nominal inside. Inches.	Actual inside. Inches.	Actual outside. Inches.	Inch.	Number of threads per inch. No.	Length of perfect screw. Inch.
1/8	0.270	0.405	0.068	27	0.19
1/4	0.364	0.540	0.088	18	0.29
3/8	0.494	0.675	0.091	18	0.30
1/2	0.623	0.840	0.109	14	0.39
3/4	0.824	1.050	0.113	14	0.40
1	1.048	1.315	0.134	11½	0.51
1¼	1.380	1.660	0.140	11½	0.54
1½	1.610	1.900	0.145	11½	0.55
2	2.067	2.375	0.154	11½	0.58
2½	2.468	2.875	0.204	8	0.89
3	3.067	3.500	0.217	8	0.95
3½	3.548	4.000	0.226	8	1.00
4	4.026	4.500	0.237	8	1.05
4½	4.508	5.000	0.246	8	1.10
5	5.045	5.563	0.259	8	1.16
6	6.065	6.625	0.280	8	1.26
7	7.023	7.625	0.301	8	1.36
8	7.982	8.625	0.322	8	1.46
9	9.000	9.688	0.344	8	1.57
10	10.019	10.750	0.366	8	1.68

Tapers of conical tube ends, 1 in 32 to axis of tube. (¾-inch per foot.)

By the late action of the manufacturers of wrought-iron pipe, 9-inch outside diameter has been excepted from the original list, as above noted, the diameter now adopted being 9.625 instead of 9.688 inches given in the Briggs table.

Broad Gage. A term applied to a gage when the distance between the head of the rails is greater than 4 ft. 9 in. The principal broad gage was 5 ft.; other gages were 5 ft. 3 in., 5 ft. 6 in., 6 ft., etc. These gages have been abandoned and the 4-ft. 8½-in. or 4-ft. 9-in. gage adopted throughout this country on all lines. The broad gages, if any exist, are confined to short branches of no importance. Tracks of 4-ft. 8½-in. and 4-ft. 9-in. gage allow cars and locomotives which are gaged by standard methods to pass over them. See **Narrow Gage, Standard Gage.**

Bronze. An alloy composed of copper and tin, sometimes with a little zinc and lead. Bronzes also often contain various other metals and chemical substances as phosphor bronze. Brass is an alloy of copper and zinc. Most journal bearings are bronzes. The variety of proportions of the various metals is very great.

Broom. A brush made of straw or twigs for sweeping the deck or foot plate on which the enginemen and firemen stand.

Broom Holder. A bracket usually placed under the cab roof or back of the cab to hold a broom.

Brush. A piece or plate of carbon or copper held in contact with the commutator of a motor or dynamo for conveying electricity to or from the armature.

Brush Holder. 3, Fig. 4589. A metal bracket or support attached to the frame of an electric motor or dynamo, but insulated from it, for holding one or more brushes in contact with the commutator. Brushes are usually secured in the holder by clamps and nuts, and their contact with the commutator is insured by springs which press the brushes against it.

Buckeye "Little Giant" Tender Coupler. Figs. 4005-4018.

Buckle Plate. See **Expansion Knee.**

Buffalo Brake Beam. Figs. 4429-4434.

Buffer. Figs. 3820-3825. An elastic apparatus or cushion attached to the rear end of a tender to receive the concussions of the cars against it. The term is generally applied to those attachments in which springs are used to give the apparatus elasticity. The term is often applied to a **Drawbar,** which see.

Buffer Bolt. 86, Figs. 3820-3825; Figs. 3867-3868. The stem or shank attached to the head of a buffer. More commonly buffer stem.

Buffer Flange. Figs. 3808-3810. A cast iron or cast steel pocket, shaped like a cylinder or like the frustum of a cone, with a flat base secured to a tender end sill and containing the spring and the stem or bolt of a buffer. Two are used, one on either side of the coupler. Also called buffing spring chamber.

Buffer Head. Figs. 3811-3813. A circular steel cup enclosing a buffer spring forming the outer surface of a buffer. Also called buffer cap.

Buffer Spring. 8c, Figs. 3820-3825. The spring that resists the compression of a train when it comes against the tender in coupling. This thrust is frequently not taken by the drawbar alone, but by the buffers which transmit it to the buffer springs, which absorb or transmit it to the tender frame.

Buffer Spring Bolt. 86, Figs. 3820-3825. A heavy rod or pin passing through a buffer spring and holding it in place. See **Buffer Bolt.**

Built-up Crank Axle. Figs. 1371-1380. See **Crank.**

Bulldozer. A machine with a reciprocating power-driven ram or head in which forgings are made. Largely used instead of a drop hammer for making duplicate pieces.

Bull Ring (Piston). See **Piston T-Ring.**

Bull's Eye. 9, Figs. 3317-3323. A convex lens, which is placed in front of a lamp to concentrate the light so as to make it more conspicuous for a signal. They are used to close the opening in fixed signal lamps on trains, and also in signal lanterns.

Bull's-Eye Lamp. See **Train Signal Lamp.**

"Bull's Eye" Lubricator. Figs. 3203-3204.

Bumper or **Bumper Beam.** 15, Figs. 77-124; 4, Figs. 2316-2318, Figs. 2319-2321. A piece of timber or a steel beam, secured across the frames of a locomotive or tender, to absorb shocks due to coupling or other collisions, and to provide a support for the coupler or draft gear. A **Pilot Beam,** which see, is the term applied to the same part when the locomotive is fitted with a pilot. See **Back Bumper** and **End Sill.**

Bumper Angle. 2, Figs. 2316-2327. A right angled iron bracket for securing a bumper beam to the side frames or sills. Usually made of cast iron.

Bumper Bar. 17, Figs. 2316-2327. A metal rod or a piece of pipe secured by brackets or posts to an engine or tender bumper for use as a hand hold for a person standing on the bumper step.

Bumper Brace. 203, Figs. 77-124. An iron brace bolted to the pilot or bumper beam at one end and the smokebox at the other.

Bumper Bracket. See **Pilot Bracket.**

Bumper Clamp. The extension of the front frame to two pieces at right angles and bolted to the bumper.

Bumper Crosstie. A transverse frame brace directly back of the bumper or pilot beam and bolted to it.

Bumper Filling Piece. See **Bumper Plate.**

Bumper Frame Bracket. 2, Figs. 2316-2327. A bracket or right angle casting for securing the bumper beam to the frames. See **Bumper Angle.**

Bumper Knee. A Pilot Bracket, which see.

Bumper Plate. An iron plate extending across the frames and covering the space between the bumper beam and the cylinder saddle.

Bumper Plate Bracket. A bracket bolted to the frames or bumper beam to serve as a support for the bumper plate. Sometimes called bumper plate support.

Bumper Plate Scroll End. A curved iron plate secured by screws to the ends of a wooden bumper beam.

Bumper Step. 197, Fig. 78. A wooden plank hung by iron brackets from the bumper beam of locomotives not provided with pilots. Also used on the back bumper of the tenders of yard or switch engines. In both cases it is intended to assist yardmen and switchmen in getting on and off the engine while making up trains, etc.

Bumper Step Hanger. A flat strip of iron bolted to the engine or tender bumper-beam to hold a bumper step.

Bumper Step Hanger Brace. A piece of iron riveted to a step hanger at the lower end and bolted through the bumper beam at the upper end to stiffen the hanger.

Burner. "That part of a lighting apparatus at which combustion takes place."—Knight. See **Headlight Burner, Lamp Burner.**

Bus, or **Bus Bar.** A metal rod or bar, for conveying electric energy. A conductor. The term is commonly applied to conductors leading from generators, motors, storage batteries, switchboards or rheostats.

Bushing. 1. "A lining for a hole."—Knight.

2. Usually a metal cylindrical ring which forms a bearing for some other object, as a shaft valve, etc., which is inserted into the hole. Often contracted into bush.

3. (Pipe Fittings). A short tube with a screw cut inside and outside, used to screw into a pipe to reduce its diameter. Generally, a bushing has a hexagonal head by which it is turned, and is sometimes called reducer. See **Lifting Shaft Arm Bushing, Bell Cord Bushing, Rocker Bushing, Cylinder Bushing, Steam Chest Bushing.**

Bushing Press. Fig. 1904. A press for forcing the bushings in driving boxes, connecting rods, etc.

Butler Friction Draft Gear. Figs. 3947-3948.

Butt Hinge. A hinge for hanging doors, etc., which is fastened with screws to the edge of a door, so that, when the latter is closed, the hinge is folded up between the door and its frame. A hinge, the two parts of which are fastened together, that they cannot readily be detached, is called a fast joint butt hinge.

Butt Joint (Riveting). Figs. 321-330. A form of connection for fastening together the ends of a boiler plate or of two plates. The edges of the plate are brought together, but not overlapped, and a strip or welt is then riveted to both plates on the inside and outside, covering the joint and holding the ends of the plate or plates firmly together. The longitudinal seams in locomotive boilers are made with butt joints.

By-Pass Valve. See **Cylinder By-Pass Valve.**

C

Cab. Figs. 2787-2817; Details, Figs. 2818-2957. A shelter built of wood or sheet steel, enclosing the back end of the boiler for the protection of the enginemen. On locomotives having broad (Wootten) fireboxes, two cabs are built; one on the waist of the boiler like a saddle; the other, much smaller, to shelter the fireman at the back end. With the latter type, a roof on the forward end of the tender is frequently used, the tender cab roof being slightly lower than that on the engine.

Cab Apron. Figs. 3782-3788; 211, Figs. 77-124. A flat iron plate hinged to the back end of the foot plate or deck to cover the space between engine and tender, and thus make a safe standing place.

Cab Apron Hinge. 212, Figs. 77-124. A rod hinge from which the apron is hung so that the latter may adjust itself to the varying heights of the engine and tender.

Cab Apron Hinge Link. A bar or link supporting the cab apron hinge.

Cab Apron Strap. A strip of iron pivoted on the hinge and fastened to the cab apron.

Cab Brace. A support, made of cast iron or steel, to hold a cab. A **Cab Bracket**, which see.

Cab Bracket. Figs. 2833-2850. A support bolted to the back end of the main frame and foot plate, and transversely thereto, to support the cab.

Cab Corner Brace. A metal post or column fastened to the rear corner of a cab, and to the back bumper on each side of a locomotive.

Cab Corner Iron. A steel angle forming the corners of a cab frame, distinguished as front or back cab corner iron, according to its location.

Cab Door. Figs. 2893-2896, 2917-2918. The movable partition which closes the opening in the front of a cab leading out to the running board or the opening over the apron. It is usually hinged to swing outward and has glass in the upper panel.

Cab Door Bracket. A projection on the front or back of a locomotive cab, to hold a hinge or pivot for a door.

Cab Door Clamp. See below.

Cab Door Fixture. Figs. 2917-2927. A device for holding a cab door in any desired position; consisting of a sliding piece fastened to the door, which piece runs on a rod passing through it and is pivoted at one end to the door frame. A clamp holds the sliding piece on the rod in any desired position and prevents the door from opening or closing.

Cab Door Fixture Slide. See above.

Cab Door Fixture Thumb Screw. 27, Figs. 2919-2920. A screw having a milled or knurled head binding the jaw and slide so that neither can move. See above.

Cab Door Handle. Figs. 2911-2912. A knob or bent piece of metal grasped by the hand to open and shut a cab door.

Cab Door Slide. 6, Figs. 2893-2896. A strip of metal on either the floor or on the under side of the upper frame or plate of a cab to form a runway or rail on which the cab door slides.

Cab Door Slide Rod. See **Cab Door Fixture.**

Cab Fittings. Figs. 2958-3207. The special devices on and near the boiler head under the direct control of the engineman. These include the steam gage, sight-feed lubricator, air pump throttle valve, blower valve, steam heat valve, air gage, cylinder cock handle, sander handle, bell ringer, injector valves, gage cocks, water gage, throttle, reverse lever, air signal whistle, cab lamp, etc.

Cab Floor Beam (Electric Locomotive). One of several transverse steel I-beams or channels forming part of the floor frame of the cab of an electric locomotive.

Cab Gangway Chain. 200, Fig. 124. A chain hung across the space between the cab and tender, as a protection to the fireman on engines with the boiler extending through to the back end of the cab.

Cab Gong. A stationary bell fastened to the ceiling of the cab and rung by a rope stretching back through the train for the purpose of signaling the engineman. Now almost entirely superseded by the air signal whistle.

Cab Gong Connection. The mechanism by which the clapper or striker of the cab gong is operated.

Cab Gong Cord Bushing. A sleeve or lining fitting a hole in the back of the cab, near the roof, to enable the cab gong cord to pass through.

Cab Gong Frame. A support secured to the roof of the cab, inside, to hold a gong.

Cab Handle. 159, Figs. 77-124. A rod or hand hold on the back of the cab to assist the men in mounting or getting off an engine.

Cab Handle Post. A rod or hand hold secured to the cab at one end and to the end of the back bumper, or tail piece, at the other. See above.

Cab Knee. See **Cab Bracket.**

Cab Lamp. Figs. 3151, 3323. Often called gage lamp. An oil lamp mounted on the top of the back head to illuminate the face of the steam and air gages. See **Gage Lamp.**

Cab Panel. See **Cab Sheet.**

Cab Saddle Plate. A steel plate fitted at right angles to the outer firebox sheet of the boiler and extending across from one running board to the other to serve as a support for the front of the cab.

Cab Seat. Figs. 2870-2882. A box or shelf, usually covered with a cushion, built on each side of the cab for the engineman and fireman to sit on.

Cab Seat Frame. A metal frame, fastened inside the cab of a locomotive, to hold a hinged or folding seat for the engineman or fireman.

Cab Sheet. Any plate forming part of a steel cab.

Cab Sides. 19, Figs. 2787-2791. The metal plates or wooden panels and posts forming the sides of a locomotive cab.

Cab Step. 229, Figs. 77-124. A step secured on each side of an engine, to each end of the bumper, to enable the enginemen to mount and dismount.

Cab Strap. A piece of iron or steel bent at right angles and riveted to the side of a cab and to the foot plate, to secure the cab to the foot plate or frame.

Cab Support (Electric Locomotive). 8, Figs. 4596-4600. One of several vertical projections cast on the top bar of the frame of an electric locomotive to support the structure of the cab.

Cab Turret. 137, Figs. 77-124; 5, Figs. 2958-2959. A distributing chamber or steam head secured on top of the boiler inside the cab, having one main valve for opening or closing communication with the steam in the boiler and a number of outlets, tapped for pipe connections, by means of which a steam supply can be taken off for the injectors, air pump, blower, steam heat, etc.

Cab Turret Dry Pipe. 100, Figs. 77-124. A pipe from the cab turret connection running longitudinally through the boiler and taking steam from the dome. Also called bridge pipe.

Cab Turret Flange. A flanged casting on the turret base for securing it to a fitting screwed into the boiler.

Cab Turret Valve. 6, Figs. 2958-2959; Figs. 3018-3022. A valve forming an integral part of the turret, seated by means of a stem turned by a handle or hand wheel, and which, when closed, shuts off all steam supply from the auxiliary devices mounted on the back head of the boiler. Also called bridge pipe valve.

Cab Ventilator. Figs. 2928-2957; 136, Figs. 77-124. A hinged door in the roof of the cab to allow a circulation of air.

Cab Window. 161, Figs. 77-124. An opening in the side or back of the cab, closed with a pane of glass mounted in a frame or sash.

Cab Window Slide. A strip of wood or metal placed lengthwise on the side of a cab to form a groove or channel in which the cab windows slide back and forth.

Cam Driver Brake. Figs. 2562-2648-2649. A form of brake for locomotive driving wheels, now rapidly going out of use. A vertical brake cylinder is mounted on the frame between two driving wheels and the piston rod is connected at its bottom end by links to two cam levers, carrying the driver brake shoes which are suspended by hangers from the engine frame. The cam levers form a powerful toggle and when the piston rod is forced down, the levers are forced out and apply the brake shoes to the wheels.

Cam Nut Wrench. (Air Brake). A special double nut spanner wrench used for adjusting the cams and taking up the slack of the cam driver brake.

Camber. The upward deflection or bend of a beam, girder, or truss.

Cap. The top or covering of anything. See **Dome Cap, Sand Box Cap.**

Cardwell Friction Draft Gear. Figs. 3927-3930.

Carline or **Carling.** 33, Figs. 2787-2791. A transverse bar of wood or iron which extends across the top of a cab roof from one side to the other, and which supports the roof boards.

Carriage Bolt. A bolt made square under the head so as to prevent it from turning when in its place. They usually have button-shaped heads and are used for fastening wooden pieces together.

Carry Iron. See **Drawbar Carry Iron, Drawbar Stirrup.**

Case. "A covering, box, or sheath; that which incloses or contains: as a case for knives; a case for books; a watch case; a pillow case."—Webster. See **Hose Coupling Case, Spring Case.**

Casey Water Gage. Fig. 3147.

Casing. 92, Figs. 77-124. A thin sheet-metal covering for the boiler, dome, sand box, cylinders and steam chest, to hold the lagging or insulation in place and protect it from mechanical injury. In Great Britain, called clothing. See **Jacket.**

Casting. Any piece of metal which has been cast in a mold.

Cast Iron Wheel. See **Wheel.**

Catch. A device to prevent a door or window from opening, usually by means of a bolt held in place by some form of spring which engages with a keeper when closed.

Cellar. A box or receptacle under a box to hold waste and oil for lubrication. See **Driving Box Cellar, Engine Truck Box Cellar.**

Center Bearing. The place in the center of a truck where the weight of the body rests. A body center plate attached to the car body here rests on a truck center plate attached to the truck. The general term center bearing is used to designate the whole arrangement and the functions which it performs, in distinction from **Side Bearing,** which see. See also **Center Plate.**

Center Pin. 5, Figs. 3344-3351. A large bolt or pivot passing through the center casting of an engine truck or the center plates of the body and truck bolsters of a tender. It usually has a washer underneath where the head bears on the center plate. For engine trucks, a key is commonly put through the lower end to prevent the engine jumping off the truck when on a bad piece of track, or in case of derailment. In locomotives having two-wheel leading trucks, such as the mogul and consolidation types, the term center pin is applied to the cylindrical casting interposed between the center casting of the truck and the coil spring directly over it. This center pin is held in place by a long, heavy bolt called a king bolt, which passes through the top of the spring cap at its upper end, and holds the outer end of the truck equalizer at its lower end. The center pin fits loosely in a shallow cylindrical casting, called a center pin guide, bolted to transverse braces. With four-wheel trucks, the casting bolted to the bottom of the cylinder saddles and fitting in the center plate or casting is called a center pin.

Center Pin Guide. 7, Figs. 3344-3351. A cylindrical casting forming part of a center plate and through which a truck center pin passes. See above.

Center Pin Washer or **Cap** (Engine Truck). 6, Figs. 3344-3351. A washer through which the center pin or king bolt passes and on which the head of the king bolt rests.

Center Plate. 8, Figs. 3614-3656; 19, Figs. 4294-4382. One of a pair of plates made of cast or malleable iron or pressed or cast steel, and having circular grooves which fit one into the other and which support the tender frame or front frame of the locomotive on the trucks, allowing them to turn freely. The center pin or king bolt passes through both, but does not really serve as a pivot. The body center plate or male center plate is attached to the under side of the body bolster or in cast steel bolsters is made an integral part of the casting. The female or truck center plate is attached to the top side of the truck bolster. When the tender is tilted, as on a curve, part of the weight is carried on the **Side Bearings,** which see.

Center Sills. 3, Figs. 3614-3656. The two main longitudinal members of the underframe of a tender which are usually close together in the center of the tender. They form as it were the back-bone of the underframe and transmit most of the buffing shocks from end to end. In steel underframe tenders the center sills are usually heavy I-beams, channels, or built-up girders.

Centering Machine. Fig. 4905. A machine for drilling the centers in work which is to be machined in a lathe, as in axles or round bars.

Centering Spring. 20, Figs. 3393-3468. See **Adjusting Spring**.

Centering Spring Cylinder. 21, Figs. 3393-3468. See **Adjusting Spring Case**.

Central Filling Piece (Steel Tired Wheels). The part surrounding the hub and connecting it with the tire. Also termed the skeleton. A wheel center is a hub and central filling piece combined in one.

Centipede Locomotive. A locomotive having a two-wheel front truck and 12 coupled driving wheels. Not in general use.

Chafing Iron or **Chafing Plate**. A metal plate to resist wear, used on brake beams, truck transoms, swinging spring planks, on the back bumper of locomotives and the front end sill of the tender.

Chafing Iron Pocket. A casting forming a flange or recess, in which a chafing plate moves.

Chain. "A series of links or rings connected, or fitted into one another, usually made of some kind of metal."—Webster. See **Check Chain, Safety Chain, Cab Gangway Chain, Uncoupling Chain**.

Chain Riveting. Figs. 319-322. A name applied to one method of setting rivets in boiler seams. Two parallel rows of rivets are put in with each rivet of one row exactly opposite a rivet in the other row. See **Staggered Riveting**.

Chamber Band. 1. A ring in the dash pot cylinder of an intercepting valve to make a close fit for the plunger.

2. (Separate Exhaust Valve.) A metal packing ring used to make a steam-tight fit between the separate exhaust valve chamber and the valve plunger, forming part of the intercepting valve of a two-cylinder compound locomotive.

Chambers Compensating Throttle Valve. Figs. 3064-3065.

Channel. A rolled steel shape of [section, sometimes used for tender sills and truck bolsters.

Check Chain. Figs. 3769-3770. A chain attached to a truck and the tender frame to prevent the truck from swinging crosswise on the track in case of derailment. Such chains are usually attached either to two or to each of the four corners of a truck and to the sills of the tender.

Check Chain Eye. See **Body Check Chain Eye, Truck Check Chain Eye**.

Check Chain Hook. See **Body Check Chain Hook, Truck Check Chain Hook**.

Check Valve. 1. (Air Brake.) Figs. 2508-2510. A pipe fitting which allows air to flow in one direction only. It is used in the main reservoir pipe of locomotive brake equipments when electric pump governors are used and arranged for operation in multiple with other governors in the train. The check valve allows air to flow from the main reservoir to the reservoir pipe, but prevents its flow in the opposite direction; so that if a compressor on another locomotive in the train starts to operate alone, and the reservoir pipe pressure is thereby increased, the check valve prevents a corresponding rise in the main reservoir pressure and the resulting difference in the pressure between main reservoir and reservoir pipe, causes the electric pump governor to cut in the compressor on that locomotive also.

2. (Triple Valve.) 15, Figs. 2490-2493. The valve under the emergency valve which prevents the escape of brake cylinder pressure back into the train line when a hose bursts or the train parts. In an emergency application, the emergency valve opens and allows the brake pipe pressure to enter the brake cylinder through the check valve, which is raised off its seat.

3. Figs. 3108, 3110. A self-closing valve so arranged that it will permit the free flow of air, gas or a liquid in one direction while preventing a similar flow in the opposite. Common uses on the locomotives are the **Injector Check** and **Water Glass Check**, which see.

Check Valve Case (Triple Valve). 13, Figs. 2490-2493. See above.

Check Valve Case Gasket (Triple Valve). 14, Figs. 2490-2493. See above.

Check Valve Spring (Triple Valve). 12, Figs. 2490-2493.

Chill. A kind of crystallization produced when melted cast iron is cooled suddenly. It is usually accomplished by bringing the molten iron in contact with a cold metal (usually iron) mold. The hardened part of a car wheel is called the chill. The mold in which a chill is produced is sometimes called a chill, but the name chill mold has been given to this.

Chill Crack. An irregular crack developed in casting upon the chilled surface of the tread of car wheels. Chill cracks not over 1/8 in. wide, and not extending to the flange, are not considered as injuring the wheel or as indicating weakness or inferior quality. Iron which makes the most durable car wheels is most liable to chill cracks.

Chilled Cast Iron Wheel. Figs. 4547-4550. A wheel cast in a chill mold. See **Chill**.

Chime Whistle. Figs. 3210, 3212. See **Whistle**.

Chimney (British). 25, Figs. 5077-5078. See **Smoke Stack**.

Chimney Cap (British). 27, Figs. 5077-5078. See **Smoke Stack Top**.

Chimney Liner (British). 26, Figs. 5077-5078. See **Smoke Stack Liner**.

Chisel. A steel cutting tool flattened at one end and ground to an edge.

Choke Fitting (Air Brake). Fig. 2547. A special pipe fitting with a restricted air passage for connection to cut-out cocks in the brake cylinder pipe of the Westinghouse ET locomotive brake equipment, Fig. 2420, to prevent loss of braking power on the entire locomotive in the event of a hose connection to the truck or tender brake bursting.

Cinder Cleaning Hole. 7, Figs. 77-124; 26, Figs. 343-442. A circular opening in one side of a smokebox. It is for the insertion of a rod or poker by means of which the cinders are pushed down in the cinder pipe at the bottom of the smokebox. The hole is closed by a cast iron lid, secured in place by a cam and handle.

Cinder Hole. 25, Figs. 343-442. A circular opening in the bottom of a smokebox to which the cinder pipe or hopper is attached. Also called spark hole.

Cinder Pipe. 3, Figs. 343-442; Fig. 407. A cast iron tube bolted to the under side of the smokebox and passing down between the frames to discharge cinders or sparks into a pit or other receptacle. Also called spark hopper pipe.

Cinder Pipe Bracket. A support for the cinder pipe.

Cinder Pocket. 1, Figs. 343-442. A **Hopper**, which see, beneath a smokebox. Also called spark pocket.

Cinder Pocket Ring. A heavy iron ring, riveted around the cinder pipe opening at the bottom of a smokebox to furnish a means of attachment for the cinder pipe.

Cinder Pocket Slide. Figs. 408-410. Also called spark pocket slide or **Hopper Slide**, which see.

Cinder Valve. Figs. 408-410. Another name for the sliding piece used to open and close a cinder pipe under a smokebox. See **Hopper Slide, Cinder Pocket Slide.**

Cinder Valve Cap. A cover fitted on the lower end of a cinder pipe.

Cinder Valve Chain. A chain attached at one end to the smokebox and at the other to the cap or cover on the lower end of a cinder pipe, to prevent the cap from being lost.

Circuit Breaker. A device for automatically opening a circuit from a trolley or third-rail shoe to the controller when the current exceeds a predetermined amount. It operates when the current for which it is adjusted pulls an iron plunger into a coil through which the current passes. The end of the plunger actuates a trip that releases the jaw or blade of the breaker, which is then rapidly opened by the tension of a spring. A magnetic blow-out device is commonly used to suppress the arc formed by the opening of the breaker.

Circumferential Riveting. 34, Figs. 151-206. The row or rows of rivets that fasten one section of the shell of a boiler to the adjoining piece on the circumference of the plate; hence the name.

Clamp. 1. "In general, something that fastens or binds a piece of timber or of iron used to fasten work together."—Webster.
  2. (Joinery.) "A frame with two tightening screws, by which two portions of an article are tightly compressed together, either while being formed or while their glue joint is drying."—Knight. See **Pipe Clamp.**

Classification Lamp. Figs. 3317-3322. See **Lamp.**

Cleaning Hole. 25, Figs. 343-442. An opening in the side of an extended smokebox for cleaning out sparks and cinders.

Cleaning Hole Plate. 25b, Figs. 343-442. A cover or lid secured by a handle and a cam on the inside for closing a cleaning hole in the side of the smokebox.

Cleaning Hole Rod (Smokebox). A metal rod, used to push cinders down to the cinder pipe by putting it through the cinder cleaning hole in the side of the smokebox.

Cleat. "1. A narrow strip of wood nailed on in joinery.
  2. A term applied to small wooden projections in tackle to fasten ropes by."—Webster.

Climax Pocket Pilot Coupler. Figs. 2377-2386.

Climax Tender Coupler. Figs. 3974-3983.

Close Return Bend. A short cast iron tube made of a U-shape, for uniting the ends of two wrought iron pipes. It differs from an open return bend in having the two branches in contact with each other.

Clothing Belts (British). See **Jacket Bands.**

Clothing Clamps (British). See **Jacket Clamps.**

Clothing Moulding (British). See **Jacket Edging.**

Clothing Plate (British). See **Jacket.**

Coach Bolt (British). American equivalent. **Carriage Bolt**, which see.

Coach Screw (British). American equivalent, lag screw, but coach screw is also used. A square-headed screw with a pointed end used to screw into wood.

Coal Pick. A curved tool or implement pointed at both ends and fitted with a handle. Carried on the tender and used to break up lumps of coal to a size suitable for firing.

Coal Sprinkler. See **Sprinkler.**

Coale Safety Valve. Fig. 3217.

Cock. "A faucet or rotary valve, usually taking its name from its peculiar use or construction."—Knight. See **Bibb Cock, Drain Cock, Cylinder Cock, Stop Cock, Angle Cock, Blow-off Cock, Cut-out Cock, Three-way Cock.**

Cock Rigging. The arrangement of rods, levers and handles for opening and closing a cock or cocks. Thus: cylinder cock rigging, blow-off cock rigging.

Cock Shaft. See **Cylinder Cock Shaft.**

Coes' Monkey Wrench. Fig. 4574.

Cold Saw. Figs. 4906-4907. A machine provided with a circular saw for cutting metal while cold. Some saws are provided with inserted cutters or teeth made of high-speed tool steel.

Cold Shot. Small globules of iron resembling ordinary gun shot, which are found in the chilled portion of cast iron wheels.

Cole Four-Cylinder Balanced Compound Locomotive. Figs. 57, 59, 116-117; Details, Figs. 2208-2215. See **Compound Locomotive.**

Cole Superheater. Figs. 486-495. Also called Schenectady superheater. A design of locomotive **Superheater**, which see, having superheating tubes nested inside of a number of enlarged fire tubes.

Collar. 1. "A ring or round flange upon or against an object."—Knight. Ordinarily an axle collar, below, is meant.
  2. (Of Journal.) 10, Fig. 3545. A rim or enlargement on the end of a tender axle which takes the end thrust of the journal bearing.

Color Coat (Painting). The coat or coats which follows the rough stuff or scraping filling coat in painting tender tanks and cabs. It is applied before the lettering and striping. The colors are mixed with turpentine and dryers, as little oil as possible being used, only sufficient to prevent the color from rubbing off. Twenty-four hours are allowed to each coat to dry, and the processes of lettering, striping and varnishing then follow, which vary greatly in the time and care given to them.

Columbia Lock Nut. Figs. 3340-3341.

Columbia Type Locomotive. Figs. 24-27, 88. A locomotive having a two-wheel front truck, four coupled driving wheels and a two-wheel trailing truck. This type is going out of use. See **Whyte's Nomenclature.**

Column (Trucks). 5, Figs. 4294-4382. The casting which separates the top and bottom arch bars of a diamond truck side frame at the center and serves as a guide for the vertical movement of the bolster. A bolster guide bar.

Column Bolt. 6, Figs. 4294-4382. A bolt passing through the arch bars and holding the column in place and the truck frame together.

Combination Lever. (Walschaerts and Joy Valve Gear). 4, Fig. 5126. Also called combining lever, or lap and lead lever. A steel arm attached to the valve stem and radius rod at its upper end, and having its lower end moved by the union link attached to the crosshead arm. Its function is to give lap and lead to the valve. See **Valve Gear.**

Combination Wrench. See **Wrench.**

Combined Air Strainer and Check Valve. (Train Air Signal System.) Fig. 2544. A device which is essentially a combination of an **O. B. Air Strainer**, which see, and a **Check Valve**, which see, for use only on locomotives equipped with the Westinghouse ET locomotive brake equipment. The strainer cleans the air supply to the train air signal system and the check valve prevents air flowing back from the signal pipe. The check valve end is connected by a pipe nipple with a special brass pipe union having a restricted passage for the air, which prevents the flow of air to the signal system from being sufficiently rapid to interfere with its proper operation.

Combined Automatic and Straight Air Locomotive Brake (Air Brake). Figs. 2417, 2421. This equipment is composed of a standard automatic locomotive brake equipment with the addition of a straight-air brake valve and a few simple parts which permit the use of straight-air on the engine and tender brakes without interfering with the automatic action when the automatic brake valve is used, both brake valves being at all times cut in. Thus an independent locomotive brake is obtained while preserving every function of the automatic system on both train and locomotive. It may be used on any class of service, freight, passenger or switching. See **Straight-Air Brake, Double Check Valve, Westinghouse SWA-SWB Locomotive Brake Equipment.**

Combustion Chamber. 31, Figs. 154-206. A compartment or space in a locomotive boiler between the firebox and smokebox. Its purpose is to promote combustion and secure additional heat from the gases before they enter the tubes. Not commonly used. The space between the firebox and the back tube sheet is sometimes called a combustion chamber. The back tube sheet is in this case set from 8 to 20 inches ahead of the throat of the firebox, because with wide, shallow fireboxes, the tubes give trouble by leaking unless kept away from the direct heat of the burning coal, where they are subjected to sudden and decided changes of temperature.

Commonwealth Cast Steel Truck Bolster. Fig. 4425.

Commutator. 1, Fig. 4589. See **Armature.**

Compound Air Pump (Air Brake). Figs. 2436-2450. An air pump having compound air or steam cylinders, or both, for supplying compressed air to the brake system with greater economy of steam consumption and greater efficiency in air delivery than can be obtained with a simple pump. See **Air Pump** and **Duplex Air Pump.**

Compound Bolster. A bolster composed of one or more sticks of timber stiffened with vertical sandwich or flitch plates of iron. The use of all-metal body bolsters is now almost universal.

Compound Locomotive. Details, Figs. 2193-2230. A steam locomotive having one or more cylinders so arranged that the exhaust steam passes from one cylinder into another cylinder or cylinders, where it performs additional work before being discharged from the exhaust nozzle and stack. Two general groups may be set off in classifying compound locomotives; two-cylinder compounds and four-cylinder compounds. The Midland Railway, England, has in service some three-cylinder locomotives in which one high pressure cylinder exhausts into two low pressure cylinders, but this method is exceptional. Two-cylinder compounds are built with the h. p. cylinder on one side and the l. p. on the other, connection between them being made through a receiver in the smokebox. An intercepting valve is provided in order to work the engine simple when that is necessary.

Four-cylinder compound locomotives are built with several different arrangements as indicated below:

(A) High pressure and low pressure cylinder on each side placed one above the other. Both piston rods drive one crosshead. (Vauclain.) Figs. 99-100.

(B) H. p. and l. p. cylinders placed one in front of the other on each side, both pistons being on one rod. (Player Tandem.) Figs. 101-105.

(C) Two h. p. cylinders between frames and two outside l. p. cylinders drive one axle. (Baldwin balanced type.) Figs. 63, 2193-2206.

(D) Two h. p. cylinders between frames drive the forward crank axle, and two outside l. p. cylinders drive the second axle. (Baldwin balanced type and Cole balanced type.) In the Cole compound the h. p. cylinders are set slightly ahead of the l. p. cylinders and of the smokebox. Figs. 116-117.

(E) Two h. p. cylinders outside drive the second axle, two l. p. cylinders inside drive the forward crank axle, the h. p. cylinders being set back of the smokebox, and each cylinder having its own valve, with independent cut-off arrangement for high and for low pressure cylinders.

(F) Two outside h. p. cylinders driving axles on a swivelling truck or bogie, and two outside l. p. cylinders driving axles on a similar fixed frame. (Mallet articulated type.) Figs. 83-87.

Theoretically the advantage of a compound locomotive over a simple engine lies in its ability to utilize a greater degree of expansion of the steam, a greater range of temperature between the live and the exhaust steam, and therefore for the same work performed, its smaller consumption of steam. With two-cylinder compounds the limit of power available is attained when the diameter of the low pressure cylinder is so great as to reach the clearance limits allowed on any particular road, in practice, about 35 inches; and in addition, they possess the defect of all two-cylinder engines, lack of balance, which is destructive to track and roadbed. With four-cylinder compounds employing a crank axle, however, the inside h. p. and outside l. p. cranks on one side are set 180 deg. apart, or at opposite dead centers, while the corresponding pair on the other side of the engine are similarly set with reference to each other, but one-quarter revolution ahead of the first pair. This produces a balanced engine, and it is found that on a locomotive of the 4—4—2 type, the four-cylinder balanced compound can safely carry 15 per cent. more weight on the driving axles than a simple engine of the same type on the same kind of track. Compared with simple locomotives doing the same kind of work, compounds show a saving in coal and water of from 20 to 30 per cent. Stated in another way, the compound develops from 20 to 30 per cent. more power than the simple engine of the same type consuming an equal amount of fuel and water. Liability to breakdowns and cost of repairs are items that usually show a balance in favor of the simple engine; but where intelligently handled and maintained, the advantages of the compound outweigh these defects.

Compression. The increase of pressure of steam confined in one end of a cylinder by the action of the valve in closing the exhaust port while the piston is moving towards that end of the cylinder and thereby diminishing the volume for the steam to occupy. To a certain extent, compression is an advantage, because the steam shut up in one end of a cylinder and compressed by the advancing piston acts as an elastic cushion to absorb the shock of the reversal of motion of the reciprocating parts of an engine.

Compressor Cradle (Air Brake). Figs. 2526-2527. A steel frame for supporting a motor-driven air compressor under an electrically propelled vehicle. The cradle is secured to the floor beams by means of brackets having pockets in which are rubber cushions so arranged as to prevent any vibrations of the compressor from being communicated to the body, and to allow its removal quickly and easily.

Conductance (Electricity). A term often used as a synonym of **Conductivity,** which see.

Conductivity (Electricity). The relative facility with which a conductor transmits electric energy. The term **Resistance,** which see, is applied to the inverse or reciprocal of this property.

Conductor (Electric Locomotive). A wire, rod, strip or rail, of metal or carbon; or an acid or a solution of a metallic salt, possessing the property of transmitting or conveying an electric current. See **Third-Rail.**

Conductor Terminal (Electric Locomotive). Figs. 4629-4630. The end of a conductor; the point where it enters the coupler socket.

Conductor's Valve. A valve for applying the train brakes, occasionally placed at some convenient point on the tender.

Conical Connection or **Course** (Boilers). 36, Figs. 151-206. That plate or course of a boiler having a tapering shape, or of larger diameter at one end than at the other. In a wagon top boiler it comes next to the firebox and in an extended wagon top boiler one or more straight courses are put in between it and the firebox.

Connecting Rod. See **Main Rod.**

Consolidated Safety Valve. Fig. 3216.

Consolidated Steam Heating Apparatus. Figs. 3168-3179.

Consolidation Locomotive. Figs. 39-44, 95-98. A locomotive having a two-wheel front truck and eight coupled driving wheels, but no trailing truck. Used for heavy freight service. See **Whyte's Nomenclature.**

Continuous Brake. A system of brakes so arranged that by connecting together the brake apparatus on the different vehicles forming a train it can be operated on all of them from one or more points on the train, as from the engine or from any of the cars. See **Air Brake, Vacuum Brake.**

Continuous Truck Frame. An iron bar which is welded together in a rectangular shape so as to form the sides and ends of a truck frame.

Control System (Type M, General Electric Co.) A system of control where one or more controllers are operated from a distance. This system has been developed with special reference to the operation of a train consisting of several motor cars or electric locomotives coupled together, all motors being controlled simultaneously by a single operator. Each motor or locomotive is equipped with a motor controller, one or two master controllers, and control couplers, together with such other apparatus as switches, fuses, rheostats, etc., as constitutes a complete operative motor car or locomotive equipment.

The motor controller consists of a number of electrically operated switches, called contactors, which close the various power and motor circuits, and which carry only the current for the operating coils of the contactors. These latter are designed to open the motor circuit contacts by gravity, and are provided with an efficient magnetic blow-out for quickly and positively disrupting the arc thus formed.

The motor controller also includes an electrically-operated reversing switch, called reverser, the function of which is to connect the motor armatures and fields in the proper relations for giving forward or backward movement of the locomotive. The reverser consists of a drum having two positions and carrying the necessary contacts for engaging fixed contact fingers, together with two operating coils, one for throwing the reverser to each position. The operation of this reverser is also effected by the master controller.

The master controller is similar in construction to the ordinary hand controller, but very small and easily operated. It is provided with separate operating and reversing interlocked handles, and has a magnetic blow-out for disrupting the arcs formed on opening the control circuit connections.

The combination of motors, rheostats, etc., effected by the motor controllers, is the same as that accomplished by ordinary hand controllers, giving series and parallel operation of motors and two economical running speeds. (See **Controller.**) Where several motor cars or locomotives are coupled together the control circuits of the various vehicles are joined together by means of couplers located at the end of each vehicle, so that all motor controller operating circuits and all master controllers are connected together, making all of the motor controllers operative from any master controller.

The couplings for connecting the control circuits between cars consist of a coupler socket fixed to the end of the car, or locomotive, and a jumper consisting of two coupler plugs connected by a multiple cable. The coupler sockets and plugs contain corresponding metal contacts for the connection of the electrical circuits.

A cut-out switch is provided on each car or locomotive, by means of which damaged motors or motor controllers may be disconnected from the energizing circuits.

Control System, Multiple Unit. See **Westinghouse Unit Switch System of Control.**

Controller. Fig. 4665. An electric switching mechanism for controlling the speed and direction of rotation of electric motors. It includes the necessary movable and fixed contacts for connecting the motors to the power circuit and to a variable resistance in the combinations necessary for starting, accelerating and reversing the car or locomotive. Nearly all railway controllers are of the series-parallel type, arranged to connect the motors first in series with each other and then in parallel across the power circuit, giving two economical running speeds. While accelerating to these speeds, variable resistances introduced into the circuit prevent undue rise of current.

The controller consists of a main cylinder, carrying the necessary contacts insulated from the shaft and from each other for engaging with fixed contacts or fingers, thus effecting the required electrical connections for reversing the direction of rotation of the motors. The arcs formed on opening the circuits are disrupted by a magnetic blow-out. The controller is enclosed in an iron casing, which protects all parts and serves to attach it to the car or locomotive.

Controller Handle (Electric Locomotive). See **Controller Lever.**

Controller Lever (Electric Locomotive). Fig. 4665. A brass arm secured to the shaft of a motorman's controller to operate it. The lever has a latch actuated by a spring, to lock it in any desired notch on the quadrant, thus giving different combinations of series or series-parallel arrangements of the motors.

Controller Notch (Electric Locomotive). See **Controller Lever**.

Contactor. See **Control System**.

Cooler Cock. 12, Figs. 4083-4085. A faucet screwed into the side of a tender tank over a truck, for connecting a small hose so as to convey water to the journal bearings in case any of them should run hot. Also called flood cock.

Cooler Cock Nipple. A nipple tapped into the side of the tank for attaching a cooler cock.

Cooler Cock Nut. A coupling nut for attaching the cooler cock hose to a truck box.

Cooler Cock Valve. A globe valve sometimes used instead of a plug cock on a tender tank.

Cooling Coil (Air Brake). Figs. 2627-2630. A coil or length of pipe placed in the air discharge pipe of the pump, having sufficient radiating surface to cool the compressed air from the temperature of discharge to that of the atmosphere, thus causing the moisture necessarily entrapped in compression to condense and collect in the main reservoir.

Cord. "A string or small rope composed of several strands twisted together."—Webster. See **Bell Cord**.

Corner Handle. More commonly a **Hand Hold** or a **Grab Iron**, which see.

Corrugated Firebox. Figs. 151-156, 5116-5117. See **Vanderbilt Boiler, Lentz Boiler**.

Cotter (British). See **Key**.

Counterbalance. 8, Figs. 1353-1367. The weight or mass of metal placed in one part of a driving wheel to balance the revolving weights of the crank pin, main or side rod, and the reciprocating weights of the crosshead, piston and piston rod.

Counter Boring. An enlargement or other alteration of form, for a certain portion of its length, of a hole bored in any substance.

Coupler. 1, Figs. 2328-2407, 3964-4062. An appliance for connecting or coupling tenders to cars and coupling cars together. By Act of Congress, Feb. 27, 1893, all engines, passenger and freight cars engaged in interstate commerce must be equipped with couplers, that couple automatically by impact and that may be uncoupled without going between the cars, on or before Jan. 1, 1898. A penalty of $100 is imposed for each violation of this act, unless the time shall have been extended for each road by the Interstate Commerce Commission after a hearing and for good cause. Of automatic couplers there are a great many; the tender couplers all conform to the contour lines adopted by the M. C. B. Association; they differ chiefly in the lock and the device for uncoupling.

2. Sometimes applied to the devices for connecting steam and air hose between the tender and cars.

Coupler Brace. 30, Figs. 2316-2327. A brace placed on each side of the pilot coupler and bolted to the bumper to assist in resisting shocks in coupling.

Coupler Horn. The projecting lug cast on the head of the coupler which bears on the face of the end sill or dead block when the draft gear is closed solid in compression.

Coupler Side Spring. A spring bearing on the bumper beam and lugs cast on the side of the coupler head as in Fig. 2368-2369 to limit the side movement of the coupler head.

Coupler Side Spring Bracket. A cast or malleable iron holder fastened to the outside of the draft timbers or sills of a tender on each side to hold a stem passing through the coupler side springs.

Coupler Socket (Electric Locomotive). Figs. 4629-4630. A receptacle made of metal and hard insulating material, having inside of it plugs connected to a circuit, leading to the controller of an electric locomotive. The socket is placed at the end of the locomotive, under the bumper, and when two locomotives are coupled for multiple unit operation, or double heading, the end or terminal of a flexible conductor or jumper connected to one, is inserted in the socket on the other, thus enabling the motorman of either locomotive to control the operation of the other.

Coupler Socket Lid. (Electric Locomotive.) 10, Figs. 4629-4630. A metal flap hinged at the top, to cover the outer end of a coupler socket.

Coupler Support. 2a, Figs. 3826-3829. A piece of cast or wrought iron fastened to a bumper and surrounding the shank or drawbar of a coupler to support and hold it in place. A **Drawbar Carry Iron**, which see.

Coupler Yoke. 3, Figs. 3826-3829. A pocket strap, U-shaped, which contains the spring and follower plates of a drawbar. It is the means of attaching the drawbar to the spring and follower plates, which are carried in the draft gear check plates riveted to the tender sills.

Coupling. "That which couples or connects, as a hook, chain or bar."—Webster. A coupling link was called simply a coupling. See **Coupler**.

Coupling Case. See **Hose Coupling Case**.

Coupling Hose. See **Air Brake Hose**.

Coupling Link. A wrought iron link or open bar by which engines and cars are coupled together by coupling pins. Chain coupling links are used with draw hooks. In consequence of the danger to trainmen attending the use of coupling links, and legislation forbidding their use after January 1, 1898, automatic couplers have almost entirely replaced them. See **Coupler**.

2. (British.) A link forming part of a coupling or draw chain. The open-ended link connected to the draw hook or drawbar is the coupling shackle. The intermediate links are sometimes termed the short links, and the end link the long link. A single long link is often used instead of three short intermediate links.

Coupling Nut. (Pipe Fittings.) A nut used to connect two pieces of pipe by what is called a union joint or **Union**, which see.

Coupling Nut Ring. A sleeve or collar forming part of a union joint. See **Union**.

Coupling Pin. A round bar of iron with which a coupling link is connected to a drawbar.

Coupling Pin Chain. A small chain attached to the car by a suitable eye to prevent the coupling pin from being lost.

Coupling Rod (British). 162, Figs. 5077-5078. See **Side Rod**.

Coupling Shackle (British). The end link of the coupling which is secured by a pin to the shank of the **Draw Hook**, which see.

Coupling Screw (British). A right and left-handed screw used in a **Screw Coupling**, which see.

Cover Plate. 1. A face plate of a steel-tired wheel connecting the tire and hub.

2. In metal underframes for tenders a plate which is riveted to the flanges of the center sills to give them additional vertical strength as a box girder. The plate riveted to the top flanges is called a top

cover plate and one riveted to the bottom flanges a bottom cover plate.

Cradle. See **Compressor Cradle.**

Crank. 1. "Literally a bend or turn; hence an iron axis with a part bent like an elbow, for producing a horizontal or perpendicular motion by means of a rotary motion or the contrary."—Webster. See **Bell Crank.**

2. An arm generally made in one piece with a driving wheel and having attached to it a pivot or pin called a crank pin or wrist pin to which a main or side rod is attached. In inside connected locomotives, including certain tyes of three-cylinder and four-cylinder compounds, the inside cranks are either forged in one piece with the axle, or preferably made separate and shrunk and keyed on. This latter form of construction is called a built-up crank axle.

Crank Axle. See above.

Crank Disk. 9, Figs. 1368-1385. One of two flat steel forgings, circular or of other shape, attached at right angles to a built-up driving axle, and having secured between them a crank pin. Also called crank web.

Crank Pin. Figs. 1130-1154. A short cylindrical shaft secured to a crank on a driving wheel, or joining the two webs or disks of a crank axle. The brass of a main rod or side rod is fitted to it, and its function is to transmit the reciprocating motion imparted to the piston, piston rod, crosshead and main rod by the expansive force of the steam, to the rotating driving wheel. Crank pins are distinguished as main crank pins if on the pair of driving wheels turned directly by the main; front crank pins if on the forward coupled or driving wheels; back crank pins if on the rear driving wheels and front intermediate or back intermediate crank pins if on front or back intermediate driving wheels between the main driving wheels and the front or back drivers, as the case may be.

Crank Pin Bolt or **Stud.** 5, Figs. 1135-1139. A stud bolt set in the end of a crank pin and on which a nut can be screwed to hold a washer in place. See **Crank Pin Nut.**

Crank Pin Bushing. 2, Figs. 1155-1229. A sleeve or collar made of brass or anti-friction metal, forced into a suitable hole in the stub end of a main or side rod and forming a bearing for the crank pin.

Crank Pin Collar. 4, Figs. 1135-1139. A circular enlargement or fillet on a crank pin, either on that portion between two rod bearings, or between a rod bearing and the face of the crank.

Crank Pin Nut. 6, Figs. 1135-1139. A nut screwed on the outer end of a crank pin to secure a cap or washer that holds the rod in place on the pin.

Crank Pin Press. (Portable.) Fig. 1909. A portable hydraulic press for forcing crank pins in and out of locomotive driving wheels.

Crank Pin Turning Machine. (Portable.) Fig. 1908. A machine for truing worn crank pins while in place on the driving wheel.

Crank Pin Washer or **Collar.** 4, Figs. 1135-1139. A circular plate with a hole in the center, held in place by a nut on the outer end of a crank pin to hold a stub end brass in place.

Crank Pin Wheel Seat. 1, Figs. 1135-1139. That portion of a crank pin that is in the body of a crank or wheel.

Crank Web. See **Crank Disk.**

"Creco" Brake Beam. Fig. 4443.

Cross Bar (Swing Link Hanger). The iron bar supporting the cross bar casting which carries the spring plank. Also called mandrel pin and lower swing hanger pivot.

Cross Compound Locomotive. Fig. 44. A two-cylinder compound locomotive, having its high-pressure cylinder on one side and its low-pressure cylinder on the other side of the engine.

Crosshead. 1. Figs. 1039-1135; 35, Figs. 77-124. A solid or built-up block of metal to which one end of the piston rod is secured, sliding in parallel ways or guides and having a pin or pivot for the attachment of the main or connecting rod. Crossheads used on locomotives are divided into four classes: (a) Four-bar guide crosshead, Figs. 1074-1077, 1084-1086; alligator crosshead for two-bar guides, Figs. 1039-1073; Laird crosshead for two-bar guides, Figs. 1078-1080; and Dean crossheads for solid guides.

2. (Air Brake.) Fig. 2546. A forked casting attached to the outer end of the piston rod, in certain classes of driver brake cylinders, to which the brake levers are connected.

Crosshead Arm (Walschaerts Valve Gear). Fig. 1812. A short bar rigidly attached to the crosshead in a vertical position, and holding one end of the **Union Link,** which see, that serves to transmit its motion to the **Combination Lever,** which see.

Crosshead Gib. 9, Figs. 1039-1086. A flat liner or rubbing piece, often made of brass, to serve as a bearing surface for the crosshead on the guides. British, crosshead shoe.

Crosshead Guide. See **Guide.**

Crosshead Key. 3, Figs. 1039-1086. A flat wedge-shaped piece of metal passing through a slot in the front end of the crosshead and through a corresponding slot in the back end of the piston rod, to fasten the rod securely into the crosshead.

Crosshead Oil Cup. 10, Figs. 1039-1086. An oil cup screwed in a crosshead to supply oil to the wrist pin.

Crosshead Plate. A flat piece of iron or steel bolted on each side of a two-bar, or alligator crosshead to hold it in place laterally.

Crosshead Shoes (British). See **Crosshead Gib.**

Crosshead Wrist Pin. 2, Figs. 1039-1086; Figs. 1126-1129. A pin or short shaft secured to the crosshead for the attachment of the front end of the main rod. It transmits the reciprocating motion of the crosshead to the main rod and forms a pivot around which the main rod turns. Also called knuckle pin.

Crosshead Wrist Pin Nut. A nut for holding the wrist pin or knuckle pin in place in the crosshead.

Crosshead Wrist Pin Washer. A ring fitted over the end of the wrist pin.

Crosstie. 13, Figs. 1446-1476; Figs. 1490-1505. A transverse brace for strengthening a locomotive or truck frame. The main frame crossties are designated according to location, as top, or bottom crosstie, back, or front, of cylinder; back of firebox; at back, main, intermediate or front pedestal, and under firebox.

Crosstie Brace (Engine Truck). 24a, Figs. 3344-3351. A transverse bar bolted at each end to the side frames of an engine truck.

Crosstie Oil Cup. A metal cup for holding oil for the purpose of lubricating a **Crosstie Shoe,** which see.

Crosstie Shoe. A metal piece attached to the foundation ring of a wide firebox, resting upon a special type of frame crosstie, to allow a slight movement of the firebox due to expansion and contraction.

Crown Bar. 7a, Figs. 151-206. A beam extending across the water space above the crown sheet of wagon top boilers to support the stay bolts holding up the crown sheet where the opening for the steam dome prevents staying the crown sheet to the outer ring sheet. They are usually supported at the ends by castings resting on the top edges of the side sheets of the firebox. Thimbles on the crown sheet stay bolts maintain the proper spacing between the crown sheet and the crown bars. Called in Great Britain a roof bar.

Crown Bar Bolt. Bolts passing through the crown bar and supporting the crown sheet. They are encased in **Crown Bar Thimbles**, which see, to preserve the proper space between the crown sheet and the crown bar.

Crown Bar Foot. That portion of the lower edge of the crown bar that rests upon the side sheets of the firebox.

Crown Bar Link. A short rod or link to connect a crown bar with a brace.

Crown Bar Separator. See **Crown Bar Thimble**.

Crown Bar Sling. A rod secured to the crown bar and supporting it from above by being bolted at its upper end to a bracket riveted to the outside sheet.

Crown Bar Sling Eye Bolt. An eye bolt screwed into a crown bar for attaching it to a crown bar sling.

Crown Bar Sling Pins. The bolts or pins holding the crown bar slings at the top and bottom.

Crown Bar Thimble. A short, hollow bolt or spacer, through which a crown bar bolt passes, placed between the crown sheet and the lower side of the crown bar.

Crown Sheet. 7, Figs. 151-206. A sheet or plate directly over the fire and forming the roof of a firebox. Being exposed to an intense heat on one side and covered with water on the other, there is a violent formation of steam on that surface. Crown sheets are sometimes made flat and sometimes curved. In any case, they must be strongly supported, and this is accomplished either by **Crown Bars** (which see), radial stays, or in the case of the Belpaire firebox, straight vertical and horizontal stays.

Cup. "A small vessel used commonly to drink out of, but the name is also given to vessels of like shape used for other purposes."—Webster. See **Oil Cup** and **Drain Cup**.

Cup Washer. A **Socket Washer**, which see.

Curled Hair. Hair from the tails or manes of cattle, horses, etc., which is first spun into ropes, then wound into coils, and either steeped or boiled in water. After this the coil is dried and the hair unwound, which leaves it in a curly and elastic state, suited for stuffing cushions, etc. Used in the Westinghouse O. B. air strainers for train air signal pipe.

Curtis Turbo-Generator (Electric Headlight). Fig. 3294.

Cut-Off. The act of closing communication between either end of a cylinder and the steam entering the steam chest, effected by the valve being moved to such a position that it closes one of the steam ports.

Cut-out Cock (Air Brake). 1. Figs. 251-2533. A valve inserted in the branch pipe from the brake pipe to the triple valve, which can be closed and the brakes on that locomotive or tender put out of action in case they are not working properly. The closing of this valve does not interfere with the operation of the brakes under any car in the train.

2. A valve which may be inserted in the pipe of the air brake equipment so as to cut off one part from the remainder of the apparatus whenever necessary.

Cylinder. 1. Figs. 788-878. A chamber or vessel whose ends are circular, and with straight parallel sides, as the cylinder of a steam engine. The cylinders used in connection with locomotives are made of cast iron, and have pistons fitted so as to work steam-tight in them. Cylinders used in brake apparatus are shown in Figs. 2497-2499.

2. (Compound Locomotives.) The high-pressure cylinder or cylinders receive steam from the boiler and exhaust it into a receiver or into the steam chest of the low-pressure cylinders. The low-pressure cylinders receive the exhaust steam from the high-pressure cylinders and expand it down further, finally exhausting it into the atmosphere through the stack.

Cylinder Attachments. The **Relief Valves, Cylinder Cocks, By-Pass Valves**, which see, attached to or used in connection with the cylinders.

Cylinder Back End (British). 39, Figs. 5077-5078. See **Back Cylinder Head** and **Cylinder Head**.

Cylinder Boring Bar. Fig. 1915. A portable machine for boring the cylinders of locomotives.

Cylinder Bushing. A cylindrical lining fitted to the inside of a cylinder for the purpose of reducing its diameter or of forming a new wearing surface for the piston when a cylinder has become unevenly or excessively worn.

Cylinder By-pass Valve. One of two small double disk valves mounted in chambers bolted to a steam chest containing a piston valve. The larger face of the by-pass valve is in communication with the interior or steam cavity of the main piston valve, while the smaller face is on the side toward the cylinder. If for any reason the pressure in the cylinder should increase to a dangerous degree, the by-pass acts as a relief valve, and opens communication between the cylinder and the steam chamber inside the main valve. When running with the throttle closed, the by-pass valves allow communication to be established between both ends of the cylinder, and the interior cavity of the piston valve equalizes the pressure.

Cylinder Casing. The outside metal sheathing or cover of a cylinder. British, cylinder clothing.

Cylinder Clothing (British). See **Cylinder Casing**.

Cylinder Cock. Figs. 973-978; 11, Figs. 982-990. A small cock screwed into the bottom of a cylinder at each end and operated by a rod from the cab to allow any accumulation of water in the cylinder to escape.

Cylinder Cock Lever. 20, Figs. 982-990. A lever pivoted to a fulcrum casting in the cab, and connected to the rod that operates the cylinder cocks.

Cylinder Cock Lever Quadrant. A curved piece of metal with notches for holding the latch of a cylinder cock lever.

Cylinder Cock Rod Guide. A slotted piece for holding a cylinder cock rod in place.

Cylinder Cock Cab Rod. 17, Figs. 982-990. A rod connecting the cylinder cock lever with another lever directly connected to the cylinder cock slide rods.

Cylinder Cock Shaft. 16, Figs. 982-990. A shaft placed transversely to the frames in bearings or hangers bolted to the frame, with an arm at each end to which the cylinder cock slides are connected.

Cylinder Cock Shaft Arm. 15, Figs. 982-990. An arm or lever connected to the rod running to the cab, or an arm connected to the cylinder cock slide rod.

Cylinder Cock Shaft Bearing. 21, Figs. 982-990. A bracket attached to the frame to hold the cylinder cock shaft.

Cylinder Cock Shank. That part of the cylinder cock that is screwed in the cylinder.

Cylinder Cock Slide Rod. 19, Figs. 982-990. A rod connecting the stems of the cylinder cocks with the cylinder cock arm.

Cylinder Cock Slide Rod Connection. The link or bar connecting a cylinder cock slide rod with its corresponding shaft arm.

Cylinder Cock Valve. A starting valve sometimes used on compound locomotives to admit live steam to the low-pressure cylinder.

Cylinder Front Cover (British). 38, Figs. 5077-5078. See **Front Cylinder Head** and **Cylinder Head.**

Cylinder Head. 1. Figs. 918-933. A metal cover for the end of a cylinder, held on by cylinder bolts or cylinder studs. The cylinder head through which the piston rod passes is commonly termed the back cylinder head, and the other the front cylinder head. In tandem compound locomotives the head common to the high-pressure and low-pressure cylinders is called an intermediate cylinder head. See **Cylinder.**

2. (Air Pump.) The cylinder heads of an air pump are known as upper and lower steam cylinder heads and upper and lower air cylinder heads.

Cylinder Head Casing. Figs. 964-968. See **Casing.**

Cylinder Head Eye-Bolt. A bolt screwed into a cylinder head with a ring on its outer end for convenience in handling in the shop.

Cylinder Head Relief Valve. Figs. 991-1014. A valve set to open at a certain predetermined pressure, to relieve the cylinder of an excess pressure caused by water or steam.

Cylinder Levers (Air Brake). 5 and 6, Figs. 2653-2696; Figs. 2703-2704. Two levers which are connected together by a tie rod attached near their centers. One end of one lever is attached to the crosshead of the brake cylinder, and the corresponding end of the other is attached to a bracket on the brake cylinder head at the opposite end of the cylinder. The other ends of the levers are connected with the floating levers by rods.

Cylinder Lever Bracket (Air Brakes). A T-shaped piece of iron bolted to the front cylinder head, to which one of the brake levers is attached.

Cylinder Lever Guide (Air Brakes). 12, Figs. 2653-2696. A guide or support for the cylinder lever. It is usually made of an iron rod bent to a U-shape and bolted to the under side of the center sills of the tender.

Cylinder Lever Support (Air Brakes). A wrought iron bar bolted to one of the center sills, on which the ends of the cylinder levers rest.

Cylinder Lubricator. See **Lubricator** and **Sight-Feed Lubricator.**

Cylinder Oil Pipe Fitting. A union on the lubricator for the attachment of the cylinder oil pipe.

Cylinder Saddle. See **Saddle.**

Cylindrical Gages. Gages made for measuring the size of cylinders and cylindrical holes, often called Whitworth gages. They consist of steel cylinders and rings hardened and ground very accurately to standard sizes. These fit into each other. The first is used for measuring the size of holes, and the last for measuring the outside of cylindrical objects, and they are called internal and external cylindrical gages. They are generally used as standards alone, from which other tools and gages are made.

D

D-Valve. Figs. 2097-2129. A steam chest valve, so-called from its shape which resembles the letter D. See **Slide Valve** and **Piston Valve.**

Dampener. 1. A device applied to a spring to cause it to act more slowly when the load is suddenly applied or removed. Fig. 4532.

2. A muffler. See **Exhaust Muffler.**

Damper. See **Ash Pan Damper.**

Davis Brake Beam Heads and Struts. Figs. 4459-4463.

Davis Counterbalance. Fig. 1326. A driving wheel counterbalance consisting of two equal weights cast in the wheel center next to the rim, 120 deg. each way from the crank pin. It is claimed that more perfect balance is thus obtained than with a single weight opposite the crank pin.

Davis Rolled Steel Wheel. Figs. 4551-4552.

Davis Pressed Steel Journal Box Lid. Figs. 4497-4501.

Davis Solid Truss Brake Beam. Figs. 4456-4458.

Dead Block. A single wooden block or stick of timber attached to the end sill of tenders to protect persons from injury, by preventing the cars and tender from coming together in case the drawbar or its attachments should give way. They are called dead blocks, from the fact that they are blocks which subserve no functions in the construction of the tender proper.

Dead Grate. 14, Figs. 546-549; Figs. 561-563. A portion of a grate surface that is made without any openings for the admission of air. Generally placed near the ends or sides of a firebox, as in those places the combustion is less active than in the center, and with open grates the fire cannot be kept hot enough. Usually cast like a shallow box and the space filled with fire clay. See **Grate.**

Dead Lever (Foundation Brake Gear). The one of a pair of truck brake levers to which the brake connecting rod is not attached. The upper end of the dead lever is confined within a dead lever guide, or brake lever stop, which latter is provided with pins to adjust the end of the brake lever as the brake shoes wear. The lever to which the power is first applied through the brake connecting rod is termed the live lever.

Dead Lever Guide or Brake Lever Stop (Brake Gear). 15, Figs. 4294-4382. See above.

Dead Wood. A Dead Block, which see.

Decapod Locomotive. Figs. 47, 101-105. A locomotive having a two-wheel front truck and ten-coupled driving wheels, but no trailing truck. Used for heavy freight service on steep grades. See **Whyte's Nomenclature.**

Decimal Gage. At the convention of 1895 the following was adopted by the American Railway Master Mechanics' Association as a standard decimal gage:

1. The micrometer caliper should be used for laboratory and tool-room work, and in the shop when specially desired.

2. The solid notch gage should be used for general shop purposes.

3. The form of this gage shall be an ellipse whose major axis is 4 in., the minor axis 2.5 in., and the thickness .1 in., with a central hole .75 in. in diameter.

4. The notches in this gage shall be as follows:

.002"	.022"	.060"	.110"
.004"	.025"	.065"	.125"
.006"	.028"	.070"	.135"
.008"	.032"	.075"	.150"
.010"	.036"	.080"	.165"
.012"	.040"	.085"	.180"
.014"	.045"	.090"	.200"
.016"	.050"	.095"	.220"
.018"	.055"	.100"	.240"
.020"	.....	.....	.250"

5. All notches to be marked as in the above list.

6. The gage must be plainly stamped with the words "Decimal Gage" in capital letters .2 in. high, and below this the words "Master Mechanics."

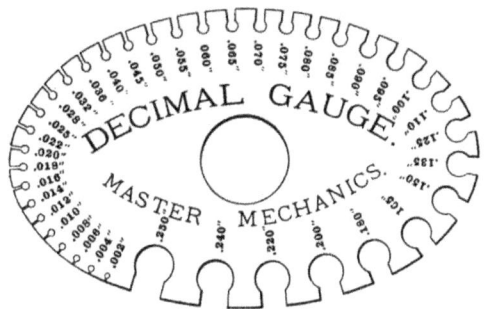

7. In ordering material, the term gage shall **not** be used, but the thickness ordered by writing the decimal as in above list. For sizes over ¼ in., the ordinary common fractions may be used.

Deck. 131, Figs. 77-124; Figs. 1519-1521, 1531-1537. The floor or platform of the cab on which the engine crew stand. Called also foot plate and foot board. It is commonly made of cast iron and serves to tie the back ends of the frames together, and to form a holder or drawhead for the tender drawbar.

Deck Beam. A beam in the form of an inverted T, with a round knob on the upper end, used in some forms of steel tender construction.

Deflector. 14, Figs. 343-442. An iron plate in the smokebox pointing downwards from just above the top rows of tubes to deflect or throw down the sparks and cinders to the bottom of the smokebox. More commonly diaphragm.

Deflector Angle. 36, Figs. 343-442. An angle secured to the inside of a smokebox to hold a deflector.

Deflector Plate. See **Deflector.**

Detroit Lubricator. Figs. 3195-3199.

Diamond Brake Beam. Fig. 4442. A trussed beam using a heavy rectangular bar for compression member and an iron rod for tension.

Diamond "S" Brake Shoe. Figs. 2773, 2783. A brake shoe with cast iron body and expanded metal inserts.

Diamond Smoke Stack. Figs. 472-478. A device for wood burning locomotives to prevent sparks from being blown out through the stack. The cap is made conical or diamond shaped and sometimes has a netting mounted across the top. A baffle plate is put in over the cylindrical body of the stack to break up the large sparks which strike it.

Diamond Truck. Figs. 4294-4330. A tender truck with iron side frames consisting of two or more **Arch Bars,** which see, and a pedestal tie bar. The spaces between the arch bars are diamond shaped, hence the name. The journal boxes are rigidly bolted to the side frames. The cross members of the truck, bolster, spring plank, etc., are either of wood or metal, or of both wood and metal combined. Metal transoms, bolsters and spring planks are in general use and increasing in favor.

Diaphragm. 1. A thin wall or partition.

2. (Valves.) Some valves are regulated by diaphragms or diaphragm plates, to which are attached springs, nuts, stems, etc., whose names explain themselves. These diaphragms all operate on the same principle. They are spring plates, which guide the rod and, assisted by spiral springs, cause the attached valves to seat or unseat at a fixed pressure.

3. (Smokeboxes.) 14, Figs. 343-442. In a locomotive smokebox, a diaphragm, called a deflector or **Baffle Plate,** which see, is placed to deflect sparks to the bottom of the smokebox and equalize the draft through the tubes.

Direct Current (Electricity). An electric current that flows in one direction continuously as distinguished from an **Alternating Current,** which see.

Discharge Pipe (Air Pump). D, Figs. 2429-2435. The pipe by which compressed air is conveyed from the air pump or compressor to the main reservoir.

Discharge Valve (Air Compressor). 2, Figs. 2512-2515. The valve through which the compressed air passes to the main reservoir. On the steam-driven air pump it is usually called an air valve.

Distance Between Backs of Flanges. At the convention of the American Railway Master Mechanics' Association in 1884, a motion prevailed that the standard distance between the backs of tires for tender, locomotive truck and driving wheels be not less than 4 feet 5¼ inches, nor more than 4 feet 5½ inches. Modified in 1903, as follows:

In the report of the Committee on Flanged Tires in 1900, they concluded it was desirable to set front and back tires on consolidation engines so that the distance between backs of flanges will be 4 feet 5⅛ inches. Therefore, the committee recommends the distance between backs of flanges be changed to read "to be not less than 4 feet 5⅛ inches, nor more than 4 feet 5½ inches."

Distance Block. A short, thick piece of wood placed between two or more objects to keep them apart, or to preserve an interval of space between them, as truck bolster distance block, etc.

Distance Piece. A metallic block to keep two objects a certain distance apart.

Distributing Valve (Air Brake). Figs. 2488-2489. The principal feature of the Westinghouse ET locomotive brake equipment. In general use, the term is often employed to include the distributing valve proper and the double chamber reservoir to which it is attached. It consists of a body in which are two sets of movable parts; the lower set, called the equalizing portion, is very similar to a plain triple valve and causes the automatic application of locomotive brakes; the upper set, called the application portion, consists of a piston and two slide valves, one of which controls the admission of air to the locomotive brake cylinders, and the other controls the exhaust. The valve has connections to the main reservoir, brake pipe, brake cylinders, automatic and independent brake valves. The two chambers of the double chamber reservoir are called the pressure chamber (larger), and application chamber (smaller). The former corresponds to the auxiliary reservoir usually installed with any triple valve; the latter is always in communication with the piston chamber in the application portion, and its pressure determines that in the brake cylinders. This valve and its reservoir perform the functions of all triple valves, auxiliary reservoirs, double check valves, high speed brake reducing valves and some other details always required in other and older locomotive brake equipments. See **Westinghouse ET Locomotive Brake Equipment, Triple Valve, Auxiliary Reservoir.**

Distribution of Steam (in Cylinders). The behavior of steam in a locomotive cylinder from the moment it enters and begins to move the piston until it leaves the cylinder on its way to the exhaust port, comprising its pressure at every point of the stroke and the rate at which changes of pressure take place. See **Indicator**.

Dividing Attachment (Vacuum Brake). Fig 5127. A device to regulate the application of the brakes to either the locomotive or train, or both. See **Ejector**.

Dome. 90, Figs. 77-124; 20, Figs. 151-206; Figs. 227-231. A cylindrical reservoir on top of a boiler and secured to it by riveting through a heavy flanged ring. Its purpose is to collect and hold dry steam. The dry steam passes through the throttle valve, dry pipe and steam pipes to the steam chest from which it is delivered to the cylinders, through the valves and steam ports.

Dome Base. 19, Figs. 151-206, 227-231. The flanged casting surrounding the joint between the dome and the boiler and fitting over the jacket.

Dome Brace. 18, Figs. 221-226. A brace secured inside the dome at one end and to the crown bars at the other, to support and strengthen the sides of the dome. Used only in wagon top boilers. British term, dome strengthening plate.

Dome Brace Foot. A lug or projection on the lower end of a dome brace for securing it to a crown bar.

Dome Cap. 23, Figs. 221-226; Figs. 232-233. The cast iron cover of a dome, bolted to the dome ring.

Dome Casing. 23a, Figs. 227-231. The outside sheathing or cover of a dome.

Dome Casing Base. The base fitted to the boiler jacket on which the dome casing rests. See **Dome Base**.

Dome Casing Ring. The cylindrical section of a dome casing, between the base and the top.

Dome Casing Top. The sheet steel, hemispherical cover on a steam or sand dome. It is usually fitted flush with the dome casing ring.

Dome Joint Ring. 19, Figs. 151-206. A flanged ring riveted to an opening in the top of a boiler and to the base of the dome to fasten the dome to the boiler shell. It is usually reinforced by another ring, inside the dome, called a **Dome Stiffening Ring**, which see.

Dome Liner. See **Dome Stiffening Ring**.

Dome Ring. 22, Figs. 151-206. A heavy cast iron ring riveted to the upper edge of a dome and having a flange to which the dome cap is bolted.

Dome Stiffening Ring. 74, Figs. 151-206. A heavy ring, made of steel boiler plate, riveted to the dome at its base and to the dome joint ring which secures it to the shell of the boiler.

Dome Strengthening Plate (British). See **Dome Brace**.

Door. That which closes an opening in a wall or partition. See **Firebox Door, Cab Door**.

Door Track. A metal bar or guide which supports a sliding door, and upon which it moves, or by which it is held in its place. They are either top door tracks or bottom door tracks. The former usually carry the weight of rear cab doors, which are hung thereon by door hangers.

Double Check Valve (Air Brake). Figs. 2508-2509. A check valve having two seats so arranged that air flowing in past either seat cannot flow out past the other, but will pass to a third connection. Such a valve is used as follows:

(1) Fig. 2509. With the combined automatic and straight-air locomotive brake equipment, a double check valve is placed between the triple valve and brake cylinder, the triple valve being connected to one seat, the straight-air pipe to the other seat, and the brake cylinder to the side connection. During an automatic application, air can flow from the triple valve to the brake cylinder, but not to the straight-air pipe. And during straight-air applications, air can flow directly into the brake cylinder, but not to the triple valve.

(2) Fig. 2508. With the Westinghouse ET locomotive brake equipment on a double end electric locomotive, a special double check valve is used in the brake cylinder pipe, so that if the flexible hose connections to either cylinder should burst, the check valve would prevent the loss of braking power on the other end. In this check valve, the valve is held midway between the two seats, when the pressures are balanced, by two springs which are not strong enough to resist an unbalanced air pressure, but will prevent the connection to either cylinder becoming closed in ordinary service.

Double Cut-out Cock or **Double Cock** (Air Brake). Fig. 2533. A special cut-out cock having connections and passages for two separate lines of pipe, so that one movement of the cock handle will affect both pipes at the same time.

Double-Ender Locomotive. Figs. 2-21, 26-30, 38, 46, 60, 75-82. A locomotive adapted to run equally well in either direction. All switching locomotives and many suburban tank locomotives are of this general class.

Double Heading Pipe (Air Brake). Fig. 2420. The pipe which connects the distributing valve exhaust to the automatic brake pipe.

Double Lip Retaining Ring (Steel Tired Wheels). Figs. 4562, 4564. One of the common methods of attaching a steel tire to the body of the wheel.

Double Plate Wheel. Figs. 4547-4550. A cast iron wheel, the rim and hub of which are united by two cast iron plates or disks. Wheels in which the double plates extend only part way between the hub and rim, the connection being made by a single plate, are often called double plate wheels. See **Wheel**.

Double Pressure Control (Air Brake). Fig. 2418. Sometimes called high-pressure control. An arrangement of the pressure governing mechanisms of the locomotive brake equipment by means of which the brake pipe and main reservoir pressures may be limited to either one of two pressures determined by the position of the handle of the **Reversing Cock**, which see. The usual pressures used with this equipment are 70 lbs. brake pipe with 90 lbs. main reservoir pressure; 90 lbs. brake pipe with 110 lbs. main reservoir pressure. It is designed primarily for use on freight engines to enable the engineer to increase the braking power on long trains, when descending grades, or to accommodate the braking power to the conditions of light and loaded cars.

Double Pressure Retaining Valve. See **Pressure Retaining Valve**.

Dovetail. "A flaring tenon adapted to fit into a mortise having receding sides so as to prevent the withdrawal of the tenon in the directions to which it will be exposed to strain."—Knight. There are many forms of dovetail joints.

Draft Connection. Figs. 3789-3819. The whole arrangement of rods, buffers and springs by which a tender is attached to a locomotive and which transmits the tractive effort to the tender and the following train.

Draft Gear. Figs. 3820-3956. A term used to designate the apparatus used under a tender or at the front of an engine to dissipate the shocks due to coupling and to provide an elastic resistance in pulling the car. Strictly speaking, the term draft gear includes only the springs or friction blocks and other parts enclosed within the coupler yoke. Draft gear and attachments include the entire apparatus by which a car is drawn, with the exception of the coupler or drawbar. Some makers furnish the complete gears, including springs, follower plates, check plates, yoke, etc. Others only the special castings or parts required, without springs, bolts or other parts which are more or less standard. See **Friction Draft Gear**.

Draft Pipe. See **Petticoat Pipe**.

Draft Pipe Bracket. 41, Figs. 343-442. A bracket or support in the smokebox for holding the draft or petticoat pipe in place. See **Petticoat Pipe**.

Draft Spring. A spring attached to a **Coupler** or **Drawbar**, which see, to give elasticity. They are usually so arranged by means of follower plates at each end as to resist either tension or compression. The usual size for draft springs is 7 or 8 in. in diameter and 8 in. in length, double coil spiral springs. They have a capacity of from 19,000 lbs. to 30,000 lbs. British, draw spring.

Drag Plate Casting (British). 141, Figs. 5077-5078. See **Drawhead**.

Drain Cock. 1. (Air Pump.) 105, Figs. 2429-2435. A small cock or faucet in the steam cylinder of an air pump to draw off water condensed from the steam.

2. (Air Brake.) See **Reservoir Drain Cock**.

Drain Cup or **Drip Cup** (Air Brake). A globular receptacle under a triple valve to collect water of condensation.

Drawbar. 1. 5, Figs. 3789-3791; Figs. 3794-3795. A rod or piece for connecting the engine and tender, secured in the draw head by a pin.

2. A heavy bar resting on the pilot and pivoted to a bracket or drawhead on the front bumper timber, with a hole or slot in the outer end for a coupling pin. Not commonly used now, being superseded by some form of pilot coupler. See **Coupler**. The term drawbar is often used synonymously with coupler.

Drawbar Bolt. An iron bolt or spindle which connects a drawbar to a draft spring and follower plates, passing through the center of the spring. A tail bolt. See **Drawbar**.

Drawbar Carry Iron. 2a, Figs. 3826-3829; 3b, Figs. 4618-4620. Often contracted to carry iron or carrier iron. A U-shaped iron strap bolted to the under side of the end sill and supporting the outer end of the drawbar or coupler. Also called **Stirrup**, which see.

Drawbar Centering Devices. Devices which take the place of a drawbar carry iron, and are designed to normally keep the coupler in the center line of draft while allowing it to move from side to side in rounding curves. Figs. 4618-4620.

Drawbar Follower Plates. 13, Figs. 3830-3854. Two iron plates which bear against each end of a draft spring and transmit the tension and compression on the drawbar to the draft springs and to the draft timbers.

Drawbar Follower Stop. 5, Figs. 3826-3829. A casting bolted or riveted to the sills or draft timbers to act as a stop to the motion of the follower. Also called check plate.

Drawbar Guide. Cast-iron lugs, or wrought plates, bearing against the sides of draft timbers over the drawbar carry iron, to resist lateral strains and protect the draft timbers from wear.

Drawbar Pocket. A **Drawbar Spring Pocket**, which see.

Drawbar Pocket Guide. A casting bolted to the draft timbers and serving as a guide or chafing plate for the **Drawbar Spring Pocket**, which see.

Drawbar Safety Lug. A horn on the upper side of a drawbar to bear against the end sill or a single dead block on the end sill, to relieve the draft spring and attachments from excessive buffing strain.

Drawbar Spindle or **Stem**. The iron drawbar bolt which passes through the center of the draw spring and follower plates. A tail bolt.

Drawbar Spring Pocket. The space at the back end of a spring pocket or strap drawbar which receives the draft springs and follower plates.

Drawbar Stem. A **Drawbar Bolt** or **Tail Bolt**, which see.

Drawbar Stirrup. A **Drawbar Carry Iron**, which see.

Drawbar Stop. A casting which limits the movement of the drawbar followers, bolted to the draft timbers. The castings for the drawbar stop are sometimes made long enough to bear against the body bolster, or a filling block is interposed between it and the drawbar, thus relieving lugs and bolts of strain.

Drawbar Yoke. 3, Figs. 3826-3854. The yoke or strap pocket that encloses the draft spring and is bolted to the end of the drawbar is called a yoke.

Draw Gear. Figs. 3789-3819. The arrangement by which the engine transmits its power to pull the tender. A rod or bar, called a drawbar, is secured in the engine drawhead casting by a pin; and its other end rests in a similar casting secured to the forward end of the tender frame. See **Draft Connection** and **Draft Gear**.

Drawhead. Figs. 3817-3819; 2377-2407. A socket or receptacle for the end of the drawbar, which is held in place by a pin. The front engine drawhead is secured to the bumper, while the back engine drawhead, holding the tender drawbar, is usually cast in one piece with the deck and foot plate. Called in Great Britain a drag plate casting.

Draw Pin. Fig. 3796. A rod or pin passing through a drawhead and a drawbar to hold them together.

Draw Pin Key. A pin or cotter passing through a slot in the bottom end of the draw pin.

Draw Spring. See **Draft Spring**.

Dressel Oil Headlight and Burner. Figs. 3295-3296.

Drilling. A term used for **Switching**, which see, or making up trains. Regulating is another term sometimes used. The British term is marshalling or shunting.

Drilling Machine. Figs. 1910-1921. A machine for drilling holes. The different types are single, double, and multiple spindle drilling machines, radial drilling machines and semi-radial drilling machines.

Drip Cup (Air Brake). A receptacle inserted in the brake pipe of each car to receive water condensing therein. A drain cup.

Drip Valve. A globe or angle valve or a plug cock used to draw off the water of condensation from a pipe, pocket, cylinder or reservoir to prevent damage by freezing.

Driver. See **Driving Wheel**.

Driver Brake. Figs. 2559-2562, 2648-2652. A brake, actuated by compressed air or vacuum apparatus, applying brake shoes to the driving wheels of a locomotive. They are either equalized brakes or **Cam Brakes**, which see. See **Air Brake**.

Driver Brake Bell Crank. A bell crank attached to a

locomotive frame for transmitting the movement of the driver brake cylinder piston rod to the driver brake rod. It is pivoted on a heavy casting bolted to the frame and called a brake bell crank bracket.

Driver Brake Bell Crank Bracket. See **Driver Brake Bell Crank.**

Driver Brake Connecting Rod. 7, Figs. 2650-2652; 6, 7, 8, 9, Figs. 4624-4627. A steel rod fastened to the driver brake cylinder lever or a brake equalizer at one end, and to the brake hanger of a driving wheel at the other end. They are distinguished as front, second, third and fourth, according to the driving wheel to which they extend.

Driver Brake Connecting Rod Equalizer. A short metal bar to which the brake rod of one of the driving wheels is attached at a point between the ends. One end of the equalizer is secured by a short link to the hanger or lever of the forward driver brake, and the other end of the equalizer is secured to the second driver brake rod. In Figs. 2650-2652, the floating lever 9 acts as an equalizer.

Driver Brake Cylinder (Air Brake). 1, Figs. 2650-2652; Fig. 2497. The brake cylinder used to operate the driving wheel brakes. See **Brake Cylinder.**

Driver Brake Cylinder Angle. An angle casting bolted to the frame of a locomotive to support a driver brake cylinder. In some designs it is located at the back end of the frames, and in others is secured to the guide yoke or other frame crosstie.

Drive Spring Pocket (Electric Locomotive). See **Driving Pins.**

Driving Axle. 72, Figs. 77-124; Figs. 1368-1370. An **Axle,** which see, on which two coupled driving wheels are mounted. They are classified as front, intermediate, main and back. In four-cylinder compound locomotives and inside-connected engines, the driving axles become crank axles. Figs. 1371-1385.

Driving Axlebox (British). 76, Figs. 5077-5078. See **Driving Box.**

Driving Axlebox Spongebox (British). See **Driving Box Cellar.**

Driving Box. 70, Figs. 77-124; Figs. 1386-1445. A box-shaped casting of iron or steel, fitted to slide vertically in the jaws or pedestals of the frame, and holding a brass or bearing resting upon the driving axle journal. British, driving axlebox. See **Journal Box.**

Driving Box Bearing. 3, Figs. 1386-1394. The brass in a driving box. It rests on the journal of the driving axle.

Driving Box Cellar. Figs. 1401-1402; 73, Figs. 77-124. A receptacle in the bottom of a driving box, to hold oil and waste, secured to the box by two bolts called cellar bolts. British, driving axlebox spongebox.

Driving Box Cellar Bolt. 6, Figs. 1386-1394. A bolt passing through the bottom of the driving box longitudinally and through the oil cellar to hold it in place. Two are used for each box. British, driving axlebox spongebox bolt.

Driving Box Saddle. 151, Figs. 77-124; Figs. 1743-1751. A ∩ shaped piece of iron resting upon the driving box and forming a base for the support of a driving spring; or hanging downward to hold the spring below the box on engines having underhung springs. Also called driving spring stirrup and driving spring seat. British, driving axle box saddle.

Driving Box Shoe. See **Driving Box Wedge.**

Driving Box Wedge. 219, Figs. 77-124; Figs. 1398-1400.

A strip of iron or steel fitted to the inside of the legs or pedestals of the frame to protect them from wear by the sliding up and down of the driving boxes. The frame legs are usually built with one slightly inclined toward the other, and the wedges are made, one with parallel sides, and the other wedge-shaped. The wedge being against the sloping leg, can be moved vertically by set screws to take up the wear of the box. The wedge with parallel sides is called a shoe. British, driving axle-box wedge or shoe.

Driving Crank. See **Crank.**

Driving Horn Block (British). 74, Figs. 5077-5078. See **Pedestal.**

Driving Pins. (Electric Locomotive.) Figs. 4654-4657. Short steel pins resembling crank pins fastened on the end of the armature quill of the Westinghouse A. C.-D. C. electric locomotive. These pins enter cylindrical pockets formed in the inside face of the driving wheel hub, and transmit the motion of the armature to the wheel through the medium of springs inserted between pin and pocket.

Driving Spring. 80, Figs. 77-124; 1, Figs. 1605-1728; Figs. 1757-1780. A half-elliptic spring built up of flat steel plates and having a saddle or stirrup resting on the driving box and one end connected to an equalizer is the common form of driving spring. In many designs, however, a helical spring bears upon the driving box indirectly by having an equalizer that rests on the box and is connected at one end to the spring. In this case, also, the spring may be helical or half-elliptic. These springs are also known as front, second, third, fourth, etc., according as they transmit their portion of the weight to the front, second, third or fourth driving wheel counting from the front.

Driving Spring Hanger. 2, Figs. 1605-1728. A piece of iron or steel secured at one end to a driving spring while the other is connected to either the end of an equalizer or to a spring set on the frame.

Driving Spring Hanger Seat. That part of the frame or of an equalizer on which a driving spring hanger is supported or suspended.

Driving Spring Staple. A **Spring Band,** which see.

Driving Spring Stirrup. See **Driving Box Saddle.**

Driving Tire. The tire of a driving wheel. See **Tire.**

Driving Wheel. 114, Figs. 77-124; Figs. 1301-1367. Any one of the wheels under a locomotive which is coupled to the main or side rods and transforms the power developed in the cylinders to tractive power at the rails. British, coupled wheel. See **Wheel.**

Driving Wheel Balance Weight (British). See **Counterbalance.**

Driving Wheel Cap. (Electric Locomotive.) Fig. 4657. A metal plate covering the opening of the outer end of a driving spring pocket.

Driving Wheel Center. 1, Figs. 1301-1367. See **Wheel Center.** The circular casting or forging having a central hub, spokes and rim on which a driving wheel tire is shrunk.

Driving Wheel Centers and Sizes or Tires. At the convention of the American Railway Master Mechanics' Association, in 1886, the report of a committee was adopted which recommended driving-wheel centers to be made 38, 44, 50, 56, 62 or 66 inches diameter. In 1887 the recommendations of a committee were adopted, making tire gages manufactured by Pratt & Whitney, Hartford, Connecticut, and here illustrated, standards of the Association. The sizes and the allowance for shrinkage are as follows:

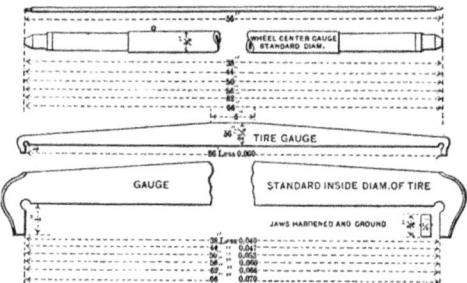

In 1893 the following sizes were adopted as standards for large driving wheels: 70, 74, 78, 82, 86, and 90 inches. Reaffirmed in 1891.

In 1896 a minimum thickness of 1 inch for the flanges of engine and truck wheels was adopted as standard practice; determination to be made by M. C. B. flange thickness gage.

Drum. 1. "A cylinder over which a belt or band passes. 2. "A chamber of a cylindrical form used in heaters, stoves and flues. It is hollow and thin, and generally forms a mere casing, but in some cases, as steam drums, is adapted to stand considerable pressure."—Knight.

Dry Pipe. 54, Figs. 77-124; 7, Figs. 343-442. A pipe conveying steam from the throttle valve and throttle box in the dome to the steam pipes in the smokebox. British, dome steam pipe.

Dry Pipe Bridle or **Hanger.** 89, Figs. 77-124. An iron band or yoke for holding the dry pipe and throttle pipe firmly in line. British, main steam pipe clip.

Dry Pipe Elbow. The right-angle bend in the dry pipe at the point where the vertical section of the throttle pipe in the dome joins the horizontal section running through the boiler to the front flue sheet in which the pipe is secured by the dry pipe sleeve.

Dry Pipe End. The end of the dry pipe attached to the tee or tee pipe from which the steam pipes lead to the steam chests.

Dry Pipe Sleeve. See **Dry Pipe Elbow.**

Duff Roller Bearing Ratchet Screw Jacks. Figs. 4578-4579.

Dummy Coupling (Air Brake). Fig. 2529. A malleable iron casting of a shape that will fit the hose coupling and attached by a chain to the end of the tender and to the front bumper of the engine, to which the coupling may be connected so as to prevent dust and dirt from getting into the brake pipe as well as to prevent damage to the coupling hose when hanging down.

Dump Grate. 15, Figs. 508-549; Figs. 564-586. A portion of a grate that is hinged so as to drop down and dump the fire into the ash pan. See **Grate.**

Duplex Air Gage (Air Brake). Figs. 2483, 2485-2486. A gage to register simultaneously on the same dial the main reservoir pressure and brake pipe pressure. For this purpose a red hand for the reservoir and black hand for brake pipe pressures are provided. An illuminated duplex air gage (Fig. 2485) is one often used in electric service, having a small incandescent lamp placed in a concealed reflector forming part of the bezel ring at the top so as to illuminate the dial without throwing light into the cab.

Duplex Air Pump (New York Air Brake). Fig. 2563. An **Air Pump,** which see, having two steam cylinders of equal diameter and two air cylinders mounted above them with pistons on the same piston rods.

The air cylinders are compounded—i. e., the large cylinder draws in air at atmospheric pressure, compresses it to about half the required pressure, and exhausts it into the small or high pressure air cylinder, where it is further compressed to the required reservoir pressure and exhausted into the main reservoir. The steam cylinders are not compounded. See **Compound Air Pump.**

Duplex Check Valve (Train Air Signal). Fig. 2510. A valve device used with an air whistle and placed between the air supply and the whistle reservoir. It allows air to flow from the supply to the reservoir only when the supply pressure is above a certain fixed amount, while it allows the air in the reservoir to flow back into the supply whenever the pressure of the supply is below that of the reservoir. By this means it is impossible for the operation of the whistle to be a serious drain on the air brake system (which is usually the source of supply), while in case of necessity, when the air brake requires an unusual amount of air, the volume and pressure of the whistle reservoir are available for braking purposes in addition to the main reservoir capacity. See **Whistle Reservoir.**

Duplex Pump Governor (Air Brake). Figs. 2460-2462. An air pump governor having two regulating portions by means of which the pressure in the main reservoir may be limited to one of two pressures, depending on which regulating portion is brought into control of the air pump. The regulation is usually made for 90 pounds low pressure and from 110 to 140 pounds high pressure.

Duplex Main Reservoir Regulation (Automatic Air Brake). An arrangement of connections between the brake valve and duplex pump governor by means of which a higher main reservoir pressure is obtained during brake applications than at other times, thereby insuring a prompt release and recharging of the brakes.

Dust Guard. Figs. 4507-4510. A thin piece of wood, leather, felt, asbestos or vulcanized fiber inserted in the dust guard chamber at the back of a journal box, and fitting closely around the dust guard bearing of the axle. It is to exclude dust and prevent the escape of oil and waste. Sometimes called axle packing or box packing. Used only on cars and tenders. British, dust shield.

Dust Guard Bearing (Axle). See above.

Dust Guard Chamber (Journal Box). See above.

Dust Shield (British). See **Dust Guard.**

Dynamo. Figs. 3289-3290, 3294. A machine for generating electricity, driven by a small engine or turbine mounted on the boiler or smoke-box to supply current to an electric headlight.

Dynamo Bracket. 3, Fig. 115. A shelf on the boiler to hold the headlight dynamo and engine or turbine for driving it.

E

Eccentric. 179, Figs. 77-124; 9, Figs. 1813-1815; Figs. 1853-1863. A disk, keyed to a shaft or axle, whose center does not coincide with the center of the axle. It rotates inside a ring called an eccentric strap which is fastened to the eccentric rod and thereby imparts motion to a link, rocker, or other device for moving a valve in the steam chest. In Great Britain, occasionally called eccentric sheave.

Eccentric Bolts. Two bolts used to hold together the halves of an eccentric strap.

Eccentric Bolt Key. A split key, or cotter, fitted through the shank of an eccentric bolt to hold the nut in place and prevent its working loose.

Eccentric Crank (Walschaerts Valve Gear). Fig. 1812. A short arm rigidly secured to the outer end of the main crank pin in such a position that the end of the eccentric crank travels in a circular path of smaller diameter than the path of the main crank pin. The eccentric crank has at its outer end a pin or bearing for the eccentric rod brass, and the eccentric rod being connected to the link, moves the valve through the medium of the radius bar or rod.

Eccentric Key. A key driven into a slot between an eccentric and a driving axle to hold the eccentric securely in its place.

Eccentric Oil Cup. A lubricant for an eccentric. Sometimes screwed into the eccentric strap, and sometimes forged or cast on it.

Eccentric Rod. 11, Figs. 1813-1815. A rod fastened at one end to an eccentric and at the other connected to either end of the **Link,** which see. It transmits the motion of the eccentric to the link.

Eccentric Rod Pin. 31, Figs. 1818-1852. A pin or pivot passing through a fork forged at the end of an eccentric rod and an eye or hole in a lug near either end of a link.

Eccentric Rod Safety Strap. A rod fastened across the engine, below the frames, to support the eccentric rods and prevent their dragging on the track in case of breakage of a rod, pin or strap.

Eccentric Sheave (British). An **Eccentric,** which see.

Eccentric Strap. 10, Figs. 1813-1815; Figs. 1864-1898. A ring fitting on an eccentric, cast in two parts, with the inner surface grooved or channeled to fit the circumference of the eccentric. The eccentric strap transforms the rotary motion of the eccentric to a reciprocating motion at the end of the eccentric rod.

Eccentric Strap Drip Plug. A plug tapped into a recess or pocket in the bottom of an eccentric strap, to serve as an oil receptacle.

Eccentric Strap Filling Piece. A thin strip of metal inserted between the edges of the eccentric straps where they are bolted together to provide adjustment for the wear of the strap and the eccentric.

Eccentric Strap Liner. A brass or composition ring inserted between the eccentric and its strap to furnish a wearing surface that can be easily and cheaply replaced.

Eight-Wheel Switcher. Figs. 19-20. A locomotive having eight driving wheels, but no front or trailing truck. Used for heavy switching service.

Ejector. Fig. 5127. An appliance for operating a vacuum brake by exhausting or "ejecting" air. It consists essentially of a pipe placed in the center of a surrounding shell or casing, with an annular opening, between the pipe and the casing. When the current of steam is admitted at the lower end and escapes at the upper end, the air in the casing is drawn out through the annular opening by the current of the escaping steam. The space is connected by a pipe with the appliances on the cars for operating the brakes. Suitable valves are also used in connection with the ejector to shut off and admit steam and air. A muffler is used to render noiseless the escaping steam. It consists simply of a box of small round balls, like shot, through which the steam must pass to escape. In the latest type a combination ejector is used having two ejector pipes, one a small one, which is kept in action continuously to maintain the vacuum in the brake pipe and a large one for use in quickly releasing the brakes after a stop.

Elbow. A short L-shaped cast iron tube for uniting the ends of two pipes, generally at right angles to each other.

Elbow Rest (British). See **Arm Rest.**

Electric Headlight. Figs. 3267-3294. See **Headlight.**

Electric Locomotive. Figs. 1585-1691. A self-propelled vehicle, running on rails and having one or more electric motors that drive the wheels and thereby propel the locomotive and cause it to haul passenger or freight cars. The motors obtain electrical energy from a rail laid near to, but insulated from the track rails, or from a wire suspended above the track, contact with the wire being made by a trolley or wheel on the end of a pole mounted on top of the locomotive. The electric rail, called a third-rail, or the trolley wire, is supplied with electricity by generators placed in a central station and driven by steam or gas engines, or water wheels. From the trolley or the third-rail shoe, electricity is conducted to a regulator or controller by means of which the motors may be started, stopped or driven at any desired speed. Electric locomotives are built either with motors mounted so as to drive the axles through the medium of gear wheels, or with the motor armature mounted directly on the axle. In this case the motor is called a gearless motor. The pressure or voltage at which electric locomotives are operated is 500 to 650 volts, direct current; and from 1,800 to 3,000 volts if alternating current is used. In this case, a transformer is placed on the locomotive which reduces the voltage from that of the trolley wire to a value suitable for the motors. Electric locomotives may be built with every axle directly driven by a motor, and thus the total weight may be made available for adhesion. In addition, two or more locomotives may be coupled and the wiring of their motors and controllers so connected that all may be operated by the controller of any one. For certain purposes, locomotives are built to be operated by a storage battery. This arrangement is only practicable for yard or switching work, where the battery can be conveniently recharged from an electric central station.

Electric Pump Governor (Air Brake). Figs. 2516-2524. An adjunct to a motor-driven air compressor, designed to open or close automatically the motor circuit when the air pressure falls below certain predetermined limits; these limits are usually 95 and 80 pounds for ordinary service, and 125 and 110 pounds for high speed service. Its function is to maintain the air pressure in the main reservoir within the limits specified.

Elliptic Spring. Figs. 4524-4531. A spring of elliptical form made of two sets of parallel steel plates of constantly decreasing length. Such springs are frequently used for bolster springs for tenders. Half-elliptic springs are used for locomotive springs. The set of elliptic springs is the total amount of bend or compression of which the spring is capable. The arch differs from half the set by the amount of the thickness of the spring band. The connection between the two halves of the elliptic spring at its extremities is termed the scroll. Elliptic springs in service are termed double or duplicate, triplets or triplicate, quadruple, quintuple, sextuple, etc., according to the number of springs used side by side and connected by a single eye bolt so as to constitute practically one spring. In tender service elliptic springs are usually duplicates. The length of the spring is the distance from center to center of scrolls when unloaded; and the height, the height over all unloaded.

Emergency Application (Air Brake). A sudden application of the brakes with maximum force caused by a quick reduction of the brake pipe pressure, due either to a broken hose, opening a conductor's valve or angle cock at some point in the train, or by turning the handle of the engineer's brake valve to the emergency portion which opens a large port to the atmosphere and reduces the brake pipe pressure. See **Brake Pipe**.

Emergency Valve (Triple Valve). 10, Figs. 2490-2493. See **Triple Valve**.

Emergency Valve Nut (Triple Valve). 28, Figs. 2490-2493.

Emergency Valve Piston (Triple Valve). 8, Figs. 2490-2493.

Emergency Valve Piston Packing Ring (Triple Valve). 30, Fig. 2490.

Emergency Valve Seat (Triple Valve). 9, Figs. 2490-2493.

End Play. 1. (Of an Axle.) The movement, or space left for movement, endwise.
2. (Of a Truck Bolster.) Usually called lateral motion.

End Sill. 4, Figs. 3611-3656. The transverse member of the underframe of a tender framed across the ends of all the longitudinal sills. In wooden underframe tenders a heavy timber approximately square in cross-section and in steel underframe tenders either a channel or a pressed plate. If the sill projects out beyond the end sheathing of the body it is known as an outside end sill. If it is framed flush with the sheathing it is usually termed an inside end sill. The British equivalent is **Head Stock**, which see. See also **Sill**.

Engine. A mechanism for converting the energy in steam, air or other gas under pressure into mechanical energy in the form of motion. Usually restricted to reciprocating engines having a cylinder, reciprocating piston and means for causing the gas under pressure to expand alternately on each side of the piston and move it back and forth in the cylinder. The term includes also the means of transforming the reciprocating motion of the piston into rotary motion, consisting usually of a crosshead, connecting rod and crank. Frequently used as meaning the entire locomotive.

Engine Bumper. See **Bumper**.

Engine Frame. See **Frame**.

Engine Frame Channel. A transverse beam of trough or channel section sometimes used to bind the frames together in front of the cylinder saddles.

Engine Frame Slab. See **Frame Slab**.

Engine Step. 210, Figs. 77-124. A shelf or bracket mounted on a locomotive to assist the enginemen in mounting or dismounting. See **Step**.

Engine Step Brace. A diagonal brace for stiffening or strengthening an engine step.

Engine Truck. Figs. 3344-3525. A metal frame carrying journal boxes and supported on one or more pairs of wheels with their axles, mounted under a locomotive and carrying part of the weight of the locomotive. Engine trucks are designated as four-wheel or bogie trucks or two-wheel or pony trucks when mounted ahead of the driving wheels, and as two-wheel or four-wheel trailing trucks when mounted back of the driving wheels. With the exception of a few designs of rigid trailing trucks, all engine trucks are made to turn about a central pivot or to allow for side displacement to enable the locomotive to round sharp curves. The term engine truck is usually restricted to the forward truck, the rear truck being called trailer or trailing truck. British, bogie. See **Truck, Trailing Truck, Tender Truck**.

Engine Truck Box. 3, Figs. 3344-3351; Figs. 3549-3610. A box-shaped casting fitted so as to slide vertically in the jaws or pedestals of an engine truck, and holding a bearing or brass resting upon the journal of the truck axle. See **Journal Box**.

Engine Truck Box Cellar. 1, Figs. 3549-3596; Figs. 3587-3589. A receptacle in the bottom of an engine truck box, to hold oil and waste.

Engine Truck Box Cellar Bolt. 6, Figs. 3549-3596. A bolt passing through a truck box cellar to hold it in place.

Engine Truck Brake (Air Brake). The arrangement of brake cylinder, levers, beams and shoes for retarding or braking the front engine truck wheels. Usually entirely separate from the driver brakes. Some locomotives have no brakes on the front truck.

Engine Truck Brake Cylinder (Air Brake). Fig. 2498; 2, Figs. 2650-2652. The brake cylinder used in connection with the air brake equipment on the forward truck of a locomotive. See **Brake Cylinder**.

Engine Truck Center Casting. 20, Figs. 3344-3351; Figs. 3352-3356. A casting bolted or riveted to the top of an engine truck and receiving directly the weight of the forward part of the engine. Also called a **Center Plate**, which see.

Engine Truck Center Pin. See **Center Pin**.

Engine Truck Center Pin Washer. 6, Figs. 3344-3351. A washer placed on the center pin to form a bearing between the head of the pin and the center plate. See **Center Pin**.

Engine Truck Equalizing Beam. British, bogie compensating beam. See **Equalizer**.

Engine Truck Frame. See **Frame**.

Engine Truck King Bolt. See **King Bolt** and **Center Pin**.

Engine Truck Oil Cup. A receptacle for holding oil and supplying it to the bearings of the engine truck boxes.

Engine Truck Pedestal. See **Pedestal** and **Truck Pedestal**.

Engine Truck Safety Chain. See **Safety Chain**.

Engine Truck Safety Chain Eye Bolt. An eye bolt in the front end of the frame on each side of the engine, for the attachment of a chain fastened to the forward corner of an engine truck to restrain its turning in case of derailment.

Engine Truck Side Bearing. 20, Figs. 3507-3525. A metal plate, block or set of rollers attached to the upper part of a four-wheel or six-wheel truck of a tank locomotive of the Forney type. It bears against a corresponding side bearing on the locomotive frame.

Engine Truck Side Bearing Pin. 21, Figs. 3507-3525. A roller forming part of an engine truck side bearing.

Engine Truck Spring. See **Truck Spring**.

Engine Truck Spring Seat. The place at which the weight of the forward end of a locomotive is transferred to the truck axles. At this place a spring band on each side of the engine truck is secured to the side frame.

Engine Truck Swing Bolster. A bolster from which the center plate of the truck is swung or suspended by means of short links hung on pivots or pins. It enables the truck to oscillate transversely to the center line of the engine, and thereby more readily adapt itself to the track when running on uneven or curved track. See Figs. 3376-3380.

Engine Truck Swing Frame. See **Engine Truck Swing Bolster.**

Engine Truck Wheel. See **Truck Wheel** and **Wheel.**

Engineer's Brake Valve (Air Brake). 235, Figs. 77-124; Figs. 2471-2482, 2567-2581. A valve in the cab for operating the air brake. It has connections to the main reservoir, brake pipe and equalizing reservoir, as well as to the air gage and the atmosphere. Commonly called brake valve.

Engineer's Brake Valve Bracket. A support in the cab to hold the engineer's brake valve.

Engineer's Brake Valve Handle. 8, Figs. 2471-2473. The lever by which the engineer's brake valve is moved to its various positions.

Engineer's Brake Valve Spindle. 12, Figs. 2471-2473. The shaft moved by the handle and carrying the engineer's brake valve.

Equalizer. Figs. 1659-1677. A beam connected at each end to a driving or truck spring, or to the end of another similar beam, for the purpose of distributing the weight of an engine or tender to two or more axles, and to prevent an excessive load being thrown upon one axle by reason of inequalities of the track or roadbed. Called also equalizing beam. Locomotives having two driving axles have these two equalized together, while those with three or more commonly have the forward driving axle equalized with the leading truck. Equalizers are always used for four-wheel engine trucks, and frequently with tender trucks. British, compensating beam. Equalizers are designated as transverse equalizers when they connect the equalizing systems on the two sides of the locomotive. They are also designated by their position as equalizer, top of box; equalizer between drivers, etc.

Equalizer Fulcrum. 1. The point at which the equalizer or equalizing beam is supported.

2. A casting bolted to an engine frame to hold an equalizer at a point between its ends. 13, Figs. 1649-1650.

Equalizer Fulcrum Gib. A small wedge or strip passed through a slot in an equalizer fulcrum to hold the beam in place.

Equalizer Fulcrum Pin. A pin or bolt for holding an equalizer. It serves the same purpose as a gib.

Equalizer Fulcrum Plate. A casting or support, bolted on or between the frames, to hold an equalizer fulcrum.

Equalizer Hanger (Engine Truck). A link or support to connect the end of a truck spring with a point on the equalizer, usually near one end.

Equalizer Nut (Engine Truck). A nut on the end of the pin or bolt that passes through the equalizer hanger and the two equalizers on each side of the truck.

Equalizer Spring. A spring which rests on an equalizing bar and carries the weight of a tender. Single or double coil spiral springs are generally used for this purpose.

Equalizer Spring Cap. A casting on top of the spring, which bears against the under side of the wheel piece and holds the spring in its place.

Equalizer Spring Seat. A casting which sets on an equalizing bar and on which the spring rests. See **Spring Plate.**

Equalizer Strap. An iron band or holder bolted to the frame, through which the equalizer passes.

Equalizer Support. The hangers or suspenders that connect the ends of a transverse equalizer to the driving springs.

Equalizer Support Bracket. A casting bolted to a frame crosstie, to hold the fulcrum of the forward transverse equalizer in ten-wheel (4-6-0) locomotives where the drivers are not equalized with the forward truck.

Equalizing Discharge Valve (Westinghouse Air Brake). A part of the engineer's brake valve which, during brake applications, equalizes the pressure in the brake pipe on long trains, and prevents the inequality in braking that would result from the sudden reduction of pressure in the brake pipe and the emergency application thereby produced.

Equalizing Lever. An **Equalizing Bar,** which see. A floating brake lever is also called an equalizing lever.

Equalizing Reservoir (Air Brake). Fig. 2487. A small cylindrical steel reservoir connected to the brake valve by a pipe. It furnishes a small volume of air for the purpose of keeping the equalizing piston of the brake valve on its seat when making service application of the brake; otherwise, an emergency application would be liable to occur even with a light pressure reduction.

Exhaust. The emission of steam from a cylinder at the end of the stroke after it has been expanded down to low pressure and has done its useful work.

Exhaust Lap. See **Inside Lap.**

Exhaust Muffler. Figs. 380-389. A device applied to the top of the exhaust pipe in the smokebox. It consists of a deep circular casting with radial apertures through which the steam discharged from the exhaust nozzle must pass. Being divided into many small discharges, the pressure of the exhaust steam is much diminished, the noise softened, and the draft on the fire reduced. A hinged flap or cover, operated by an arm and rod to the cab, enables the engineman to vary the degree of muffling or dampening as desired.

Exhaust Nozzle. 15a, Figs. 343-442; Figs. 370-379. A tip or end piece fitted on the end of the exhaust pipe or pipes, so proportioned to the size of the cylinders, front end arrangement, etc., as to cause the steam passing out of it to produce the desired draft on the fire. In Europe, a nozzle of variable size is frequently used, so as to adjust the force of the blast to the work the engine is doing.

Exhaust Passage (Cylinders). 33, Figs. 788-1029. Cored openings in a cylinder saddle casting leading from the steam chest to the base of the exhaust nozzle.

Exhaust Pipe. 15, Figs. 343-442. A vertical cast-iron pipe bolted at its base to the cylinder castings or saddles inside the smokebox, for conducting the steam exhausted from the steam chests to the upper part of the petticoat pipe and stack. British, blast pipe.

Exhaust Pipe Bolt. One of the bolts used to secure the exhaust pipe to the cylinder castings.

Exhaust Port. 36, Figs. 788-1029. An opening in a valve seat or valve chamber at the mouth of a cored passage leading to the exhaust pipe.

Exhaust Relief Valve. See **By-pass Valve.**

Expansion (of Steam). The increase in volume of steam in a cylinder after communication with the steam chest is cut off. This increase in volume is caused by the expansive force possessed by the steam and by reason of which it moves the piston.

Expansion Bracket or **Block** (British). 143, Figs. 5077-5078. See **Expansion Pad.**

Expansion Knee. 41, Figs. 77-124; Figs. 1551-1556. A thin vertical steel plate, fastened transversely to the frames at some point between the cylinder saddles and firebox to support the boiler, and possessing sufficient elasticity, by reason of its thinness, to allow the boiler to move longitudinally when expanding and contracting by reason of change of temperature. It is usual to put one knee at the guide yoke and one or two back of this, near the firebox. Also called expansion sheet and buckle plate.

Expansion Knee Plate. See **Expansion Knee.**

Expansion Link. 1. An eye bar secured to a bracket on the frame and to a thick plate or casting fastened to the outside firebox sheet. It is for the purpose of holding the back end of the boiler in such a way to the frames as to allow the boiler a little freedom to move longitudinally when expanding and contracting.

2. The term is also used to designate the link of the valve gear. See **Link.**

Expansion Link Pin. A pin or pivot holding an expansion link to the frame or firebox sheet.

Expansion Link Pin Plate. A plate or casting fastened to the outside firebox sheet to hold an expansion link pin.

Expansion Pad. 157, Figs. 77-124; Figs. 1557-1574. A plate or casting bolted to the frames, and holding a corresponding plate or pad which is riveted to the outside firebox sheet. These two pads are connected by bolts loosely fitted so as to allow the boiler to expand and contract with changes of temperature. In other forms the piece riveted to the firebox has a narrow projecting flange or lip on which rests another flange on the piece fastened to the frame. The boiler is thus perfectly free to expand longitudinally and to contract, while being held securely to the frames and allowed little movement in a vertical or lateral direction.

Expansion Pad Cap. A bent piece of metal fastened to a locomotive frame and resting on the piece secured to the firebox, these two pieces comprising an expansion pad.

Expansion Pad Liner. An iron plate interposed between an expansion pad and the outside firebox sheet.

Expansion Sheet. See **Expansion Knee.**

Extended Piston Rod. Figs. 916-917. A **Piston Rod,** which see, which extends through and in front of the piston and is carried in a stuffing box through the front cylinder head. Its purpose is to provide a front bearing for the rod and to relieve the piston rings and cylinder from wear on the bottom due to the heavy weight of the piston.

Extended Piston Rod Carrier. 3b, Figs. 916-917. A small pulley or sheave on which the extension of the piston rod is carried. It is attached to the outside of the front cylinder head.

Extended Piston Rod Casing. A pipe attached to the front cylinder head and enclosing an extended piston rod to protect it from dirt.

Extended Piston Rod Stuffing Box. 30, Figs. 916-917. The **Stuffing Box,** which see, in the front cylinder head through which the extension of the piston rod passes.

Extended Smokebox. Figs. 343-348. A **Smokebox,** which see, which extends out beyond the cylinder saddle and which has a large volume. It provides a space for the accumulation of sparks. Within certain limits extending the length of the smokebox improves the draft.

Extended Wagon Top Boiler. Figs. 144-147, 152-176. A locomotive **Boiler,** which see, having a shell made up of one or more cylindrical courses of plates next to the firebox, a conical course tapering down to smaller diameter, and one or more adjoining cylindrical courses of reduced diameter next to the smokebox. The purpose of putting in the cylindrical course next to the firebox is to provide a place for the steam dome in front of the firebox, and thus do away with crown bar staying over the crown sheet as in a **Wagon Top Boiler,** which see.

Eye Bolt. "A bolt having an eye or loop at one end for the reception of a ring, hook or rope, as may be required."—Knight. See **Bolt**; also **Brake Beam Eye Bolt, Safety Chain Eye Bolt.**

F

Face (of Rim of Car Wheel). The vertical surface of the outside of the rim.

Face Plate. 1. A metal plate by which any object is covered so as to protect it from wear or abrasion.

2. (Steel Tired Wheels.) The plates connecting the tire and hub, and bolted to each. They are distinguished as front and back face plates.

Feed Pipe. Figs. 3780-3781. A pipe for conveying water from the bottom of a tender to an injector suction pipe. Usually a piece of 3-inch rubber hose.

Feed Pipe Bracket. Figs. 3743-3744. A projection to hold an **Injector Feed Pipe,** which see.

Feed Pipe Hose Clamp. Figs. 2965-2966. A clamp or coupling for holding the feed pipe hose to the metal outlet at the bottom of the tender cistern.

Feed Valve (Air Brake). Figs. 2464-2467. Also called reducing valve, slide valve feed valve and slide valve reducing valve. A valve which automatically maintains the pressure of air supplied through the brake valve to the automatic brake system. It may be attached either to the brake valve or placed in the piping between the main reservoir and the brake valve.

Feed Valve Pipe (Air Brake). The pipe which connects the feed valve with the automatic brake valve.

Feed Valve Pipe Bracket (Air Brake). Fig. 2469. A bracket to which the pipe connections to the feed valve are made and to which the feed valve is attached, so that the latter may be removed for examination, repairs or replacement, without breaking any pipe joints.

Feed Valve Pipe Bracket Gasket (Air Brake). Fig. 2470. See **Gasket.**

Feed Water Valve Rigging. The arrangement of a cock with a shaft, rod, handle and bracket for turning on or off the supply of water in the injector supply pipe.

Female Center Plate. The body and truck center plates are sometimes called male and female plates, respectively. See **Center Plate.**

Female Gage. An **External Gage,** which see.

Ferrule. A copper sleeve fitted over the end of a tube or flue to secure a water-tight joint between the ends of the flue and the hole in the flue sheet.

Field (Electric Locomotive). 1. The magnetic flux set up by an electric current in a conductor.

2. The magnetic flux between the poles of a motor caused by the current in the field coils.

Field Coil (Electric Locomotive). 4 and 6, Figs. 4589-4590. A coil of insulated copper wire or ribbon surrounding an iron pole of a railway motor field magnet. Electric current passing through these magnet coils produces the magnetic flux in which the armature rotates, and which is called the magnetic field.

Field Magnet (Electric Locomotive). 2 and 4, Fig. 4590. The iron core and the coil surrounding it together form the field magnet of a motor.

Field Magnet Frame (Electric Locomotive). A rectangular metal frame holding the field coil or coils of a motor.

Field Strength. The density of magnetic flux between the poles of a motor.

Filling Bracket (Westinghouse Air Brake). A device which enables a "pipeless" triple valve to be used with a brake cylinder previously arranged for the attachment of the ordinary triple valve having pipe connections. The filling bracket bolts to the pressure head in place of the old triple valve, the "pipeless" triple valve then bolts to the filling bracket; the pipe connections are made to the filling bracket. See **Pipeless Triple Valve.**

Finger Grate. Figs. 528-545, 567-571. A grate made up of grate bars cast with projections or fingers on each side which interlock with the fingers on adjacent bars. When the grate bars are rocked or turned in their trunnion bearings, the fingers disengage and allow the ashes to fall through to the ash pan below. See **Rocking Grate.**

Fire Bar (British). 114, Figs. 5077-5078. See **Grate Bar.**

Firebox. 27, Figs. 151-206. The furnace, or box in which the fuel is burned. The sides and top or crown of a firebox of a locomotive boiler transmit the heat of the fire to the water, and there is an excessively active generation of steam near these parts. The front or forward sheet of the firebox has a large number of holes in which the ends of the flues or tubes are inserted. These tubes carry the products of combustion to the smokebox, and as they are surrounded by water, give up a large amount of heat to the water from the waste gases passing through them. Fireboxes are built of steel plate, except in Great Britain and parts of Europe where copper is more commonly used. Corrugated fireboxes, made in one piece, cylindrical in shape, are occasionally used. See **Vanderbilt Boiler, Lentz Boiler.**

Firebox Back Sheet. 6, Figs. 151-206. The sheet or plate at the back end of a firebox inside, in which the door or doors are located. Also called door sheet.

Firebox Back Plate (British). See **Back Head.**

Firebox Back Plate Stay (British). See **Back Head Brace.**

Firebox Back Plate Stay Jaw (British). See **Back Head Brace Jaw.**

Firebox Casing. Figs. 213-220. The covering or jacket put on outside the lagging on the firebox to hold the lagging in place.

Firebox Cross Stay. 83, Figs. 151-206. A rod or brace across the upper part of the firebox above the crown sheet, and secured to the outside sheet or shell. See **Belpaire Firebox Boiler.**

Firebox Cross Stay Pin. A bolt or pivot for holding one end of a cross stay to a bracket or lug on the inside of shell.

Firebox Crown Sheet. 7, Figs. 151-206. The plate that forms the top of a firebox. See **Crown Sheet.**

Firebox Ring. 1, Figs. 151-206; Figs. 207-212. An iron or steel bar, shaped to correspond to the ground plan of a firebox, rounded at the corners, separating the inside and outside sheets of the firebox, and to which these sheets are riveted. Also called **Foundation Ring** and **Mud Ring,** which see.

Firebox Ring Crosstie. A heavy casting secured across the frames to bind them together and at the same time support the mud ring or foundation ring at the front or back of the firebox.

Firebox Short Stay. A term sometimes used for **Staybolt,** which see.

Firebox Side Sheet. 65, Figs. 151-206. Either of the sheets forming the sides of a firebox.

Firebox Side Stays (British). See **Stay Bolt.**

Firebox Sling Stay. 14, Figs. 151-206. A rod or brace secured to a crown bar at one end and to a tee iron or lug in the top of the outside sheet at the other, by means of bolts or pins. It allows some flexibility between the crown sheet and outside sheets under changes of temperature.

Firebox Sling Stay Eye Bolt. An eye bolt sometimes used to hold the upper end of a sling stay.

Firebox Sling Stay Jaw. A forked piece for holding a sling stay.

Firebox Sling Stay Pins. 17, Figs. 151-206. Bolts or rivets to hold either end of a sling stay.

Firebox Throat Sheet. See **Throat Sheet.**

Firebox Tube Sheet. See **Tube Sheet.**

Firebox Wrapper Plate (British). 103, Figs. 5077-5078. See **Roof Sheet** and **Outside Crown Sheet.**

Firebrick. A kind of brick made especially to resist a high degree of heat, used in a firebox arch to promote uniform combustion and diminish black smoke. Also used in oil burning fireboxes to form a surface against which the burning oil may impinge. See **Brick Arch.**

Fire Door. Figs. 331-342. A door usually hinged at the side to close an opening through which coal is thrown on the fire. Some types of door are made to slide and are moved by a lever or handle. Swinging doors are made with a handle and a chain fastened to the boiler head for convenience in opening and closing. A catch or notched rod is provided, on various points of which the handle of the door may be set so as to regulate the amount of air admitted above the fire. Some doors are arranged to be operated by a rod moved by the piston of a small air cylinder, whose valve is fitted with a lever, on the end of which the fireman presses his foot, and thus opens and closes the door.

Fire Door Catch. 5c, Figs. 331-342. A catch or hook-shaped projection, on the back head on which the fire door catch strap fastens or latches.

Fire Door Catch Strap. 5a, Figs. 331-342. A strip riveted to a fire door, to hold it shut.

Fire Door Chain Hook. A hook on the fire door to which a chain attached to the back head is secured.

Fire Door Diaphragm. A term used for a fire door frame.

Fire Door Frame. 5f, Figs. 331-342. A frame to which the fire door and liner are secured.

Fire Door Handle. A handle secured to a fire door with which to open and close it. Usually made a part of the latch.

Fire Door Hinge. 6a, Figs. 331-342. The hinge or pivot secured to the back head and on which the fire door turns to open and close.

Fire Door Hinge Bracket. A bracket secured to the back head to hold the door hinge.

Fire Door Hinge Pin. 6b, Figs. 331-342. A rod or pin about which the fire door turns in opening. Part of the door hinge.

Fire Door Latch. 5a, Figs. 331-342. A strip or bar fastened to a fire door and fitting on the catch secured to the back head.

Fire Door Latch Guard. 5b, Figs. 331-342. A staple or keeper on a fire door, to limit the vertical movement of the latch.

Fire Door Liner. 5d, Figs. 331-342. A plate or shield secured to the side of a fire door next to the fire, to prevent the door itself warping from the intense heat.

Fire Door Register. 17, Figs. 331-342. A plate on the fire door with radial openings that can be partially or wholly covered by a sliding or rotating piece, to vary the quantity of air admitted over the fire.

Fire Door Shield. 18, Figs. 340-342. A curved piece fitted around the upper half of a fire door opening and projecting a few inches from the boiler back head, to protect the eyes of engineer and fireman from the intense glare and heat of the fire. Also called a hood, and frequently used as a stand for oil cans.

Fire Door Shield Bracket. A bracket secured to the back head to hold the fire door shield.

Fire Door Slide Eye. See **Fire Door Register.** An aperture in a fire door, to admit air above the fire, closed by a sliding piece.

Fire Hole Ring. 66a, Figs. 151-206. A circular or elliptical opening, closed by the fire door, formed by flanging the inner firebox sheet outward and the back head sheet inward and riveting them together.

First Course (of a Boiler Shell). 38, Figs. 151-206. That section of a boiler next to the smokebox. It is made either cylindrical in straight top and extended wagon top boilers, or shaped like the frustum of a cone in wagon top boilers.

Fixed Brake Lever. More commonly, dead lever. A brake lever, the upper end of which is fastened to a brake lever stop or dead lever guide.

Flag (for Train Signals). The standard size of flags adopted by the American Railway Association is 16 x 16 inches, and the colors indicate their purpose as follows: Red signifies danger and is a signal to stop; green signifies caution and is a signal to go slowly; white signifies safety and is a signal to go on; blue denotes that car inspectors are at work under or about the train or car, and that it cannot be moved or coupled to until the blue signal is removed by the car inspectors. In the night time lanterns with colored glass globes are used instead of flags, and the colored lights have the same meaning as the colored flags. They are used as markers or distinguishing signals on a locomotive or tender. Flags may be displayed from a staff on each end of the front bumper, on each side of the smokebox or on each of the two rear corners of the tender where suitable holders are provided.

Flag Fixture. 194, Figs. 77-124. A socket or holder for a flag staff on the front bumper of an engine. For tenders, a slotted flag holder plate is secured to each rear corner, and the flag holder, of cast or malleable iron, has a lug on it that fits the slot. The same type of fixture is also frequently used on each side of the smokebox.

Flange. 1. A projecting rim for attaching the part to any surface. The bent portion of the edge of any piece, as a boiler plate flange. See **Dome Ring.**

2. (Of a Wheel.) A projecting edge or rim on the periphery for keeping it on the rail. The inside edge of the flange which connects with the tread of the wheel is termed the throat, and the extreme outer point the toe of the flange. See **Distance Between Backs of Flanges.**

Flexible Hose Connection (Air Brake.) Fig. 2525. A short piece of rubber hose with pipe couplings on each end, placed in the discharge pipe from a motor-driven air compressor to (1) prevent any vibrations of the compressor being communicated to the piping and car body, and (2) to prevent any possible stray current from the motor from passing to the piping system. Sometimes this fitting is erroneously called the insulating hose.

Flexible Joint. Figs. 3774-3779. A joint where two steam or exhaust pipes are connected so as to provide some freedom of motion for each. A flexible joint is always placed between the tee head at the outer end of the dry pipe and the steam pipes in the smokebox. On articulated tandem compound locomotives a flexible joint is used to connect the steam and exhaust pipes of the set of cylinders on the swinging or bogie truck frame. Between engine and tender a flexible joint is used in the steam heat train pipe.

Flexible Stay Bolt. Figs. 286-305. A **Stay Bolt**, which see, having enlarged spherical ends enclosed in hollow cups screwed into the boiler plates and designed to permit of slight relative movements due to expansion and contraction of the two plates which it secures, thus preventing bending or shearing stresses in the bolt which would cause it to break.

Flitch Plates. An iron or steel plate sandwiched between pieces of wood and bolted together to give the member which they comprise greater strength. Also called sandwich plates.

Floating Lever Connecting Rod (Brake Gear). More properly a **Cylinder Lever Tie Rod,** which see.

Flood Cock. A small globe valve attached to the side of a tender tank with a tee pipe screwed on it for conveying water through rubber hose pipes to the truck boxes in case the bearings run hot. Also called a **Cooler Cock**, which see. British, jet cock.

Flue. A common name for a boiler fire tube. See **Tube.**

Flue Cleaning Machine. Fig. 4925. A device for cleaning scale and soot from locomotive boiler flues by rattling.

Flue Sheet. 30 and 42, Figs. 151-206. A plate with holes in which the flues are secured. That at the front end is called the front or smokebox flue sheet; while the other is the back or firebox flue sheet. The ends of the flues are expanded in the holes in the flue sheet, and the joints made tight by copper ferrules or thimbles slipped over the flue ends. See **Ferrule** and **Tube Sheet.**

Flue Sheet Ring. A flanged band riveted to the circumference of the front flue sheet and to the outside shell, to hold the flue sheet in place. Not commonly used, as the flue sheet is flanged to form the ring.

Flue Welding Machine. Fig. 4926. A machine for welding new ends on locomotive boiler flues.

Follower. A very common abbreviation for a **Follower Plate**, which see.

Follower Plate. See Drawbar Follower Plate, Piston Follower. The word "plate" is frequently omitted from these names.

Foot Board. See **Foot Plate.**

Foot Plate. 222, Figs. 77-124; Figs. 1531-1537. A casting secured across the frames at the back end of an engine. Called also foot board, deck, tail piece, and deck plate.

Foot Plate Key. A wedge-shaped piece of metal securing the foot plate, or deck plate, to the side frames.

Forge. Figs. 4927-4932. An apparatus containing an open fireplace or furnace, fitted with a bellows or some other appliance for producing a blast to quicken the fire, and serving to heat metal in order that it may be hammered into form. Special designs of forges are used for heating rivets, flue-welding, etc.

Forging. A piece of iron or steel, hammered or bent to shape while hot.

Forgings. (A. R. M. M. A. Standard Specifications for Locomotive Forgings.)

Material.—1. Open-hearth steel.

Chemical Requirements.—2. Phosphorus, not to exceed .05 per cent.; sulphur, not to exceed .05 per cent.; manganese, not to exceed .60 per cent.

Physical Requirements.—3. Tensile strength—not less than 80,000 pounds per square inch. Elongation—not less than 20 per cent. in two inches. Reduction in area—not less than 25 per cent.

Tests.—4. One test per melt will be required, the test specimen to be cut cold from the forging, or full-sized prolongation of same, parallel to the axis of the forging and half-way between the center and the outside.

5. The standard turned specimen, ½ inch in diameter and 2 inches gage length, shall be used to determine the physical properties. (See Fig. 1, **Axles**, Specifications.) Drillings or turnings from the tensile specimen shall be used to determine the chemical properties.

Stamping and Marking.—6. Each forging must have heat number and name of manufacturer plainly stamped on one end with figures not less than ⅜ inch high, and have order number plainly marked with white lead.

Inspection.—7. All forgings must conform to drawings which accompany these specifications, and be free from seams, pipes and other defects.

8. Any forgings failing to meet any of the above requirements, or which prove defective on machining, will be rejected.

Forging Machine. Figs. 4933-4934. A machine for forging metal into various shapes. Forging machines are generally of massive construction, and are fitted with die blocks to which dies for forming the different shaped pieces are secured. Bending and forming machines, as well as bulldozers and bolt headers are known as forging machines.

Forney Type Locomotive. Figs. 11, 12. A type of locomotive first suggested by M. N. Forney, having four or six driving wheels and a four or six-wheel swiveling rear truck, but having no front truck. A small water tank and coal bunker are carried over the rear truck.

Foundation Brake Gear. The levers, rods, brake beams, etc., by which the piston rod of the brake cylinder is connected to the brake shoes in such a manner that when air pressure forces the piston out the brake shoes are forced against the wheels. Recommended practice is that braking power should be 75 per cent. of weight on drivers, engine in working order, for driver brakes; 60 per cent. of engine weight on them for truck and trailer wheel brakes; and 100 per cent. of light weight of tender for tender brakes. Equalized pressure in brake cylinder, 60 pounds per square inch; maximum pressure in brake cylinder, 85 pounds per square inch; maximum stress in levers, 23,000 pounds per square inch; maximum stress in rods, except jaws, 15,000 pounds per square inch, no rod to be less than ⅞ inch in diameter; maximum stress in jaws, 10,000 pounds per square inch; maximum shear on pins, 10,000 pounds per square inch; diameter of pins to provide a bearing value not to exceed 23,000 pounds per square inch. The reduction of stresses in rods, levers and jaws due to friction of the foundation brake gear and the reduction of braking power due to the same cause and to the action of release springs should be neglected, because it is considered to be too difficult to determine their value even with a fair degree of accuracy. For tenders with four-wheel trucks and of various weights, the following table gives particulars as to braking:

Light Weight	Size of Brake Cylinder	Maximum Load at Middle of Brake Beam.
Over 50,000 pounds	12 inch	22,000 pounds.
Between 30,000 and 50,000 pounds	10 inch	15,200 "
Less than 30,000 pounds	8 inch	......

Foundation Ring. See **Firebox Ring, Mud Ring.**

Four-Guide Crosshead. Figs. 1074-1077. See **Crosshead.**

Four-way Cock (Air Brake). A plug or stop cock having two channels or passages in the moving portion placed in the pipe between the main brake pipe and triple valve to give the brake either automatic action or straight air, or to cut out the brake on an engine or tender entirely. Used with old forms of triple valve and now almost obsolete.

Four-Wheel Engine Trucks. Figs. 3369-3380.

Four-Wheel Switcher. Figs. 2-7, 75-77. A locomotive having four driving wheels, but no front or trailing truck. Commonly a tank locomotive, used for switching cars in small yards.

Fox Pressed Steel Tender Truck. Figs. 4349-4351. A truck, the frame of which is wrought and hydraulic forged of steel plate consisting of few pieces which are all riveted together. It is a pedestal truck with journal box springs.

Frame. 1. The outline or skeleton upon which a structure is built up. In a tender the framing is usually supposed to mean the underframe.

2. (Of a Door, Ventilator, or Window Sash.) The rectangular or curved border surrounding or enclosing it.

3. (Locomotive.) Figs. 1446-1476. A structure mounted on the wheels through the medium of springs and equalizers and carrying the engines and boiler and their attachments which together constitute a locomotive. Usually made of bars of hammered iron or rectangular section, but recently cast-steel frames have come into use with satisfactory results. British and European designers use plate frames exclusively. Engine truck frames are made of iron bars.

4. (Engine Trucks.) A rectangular structure built of wrought iron with legs or jaws for the axle boxes, welded on, and having the center plate or casting bolted on top. It supports the front end of the locomotive, and transmits its weight to the axle boxes through the springs and equalizing beams. The truck has four or two wheels, and in the latter case it is usually equalized with the forward pair of drivers. In certain designs of suburban tank locomotives, a six-wheel rear truck is used.

Frame Back Section. That portion of a locomotive frame holding the driving boxes, and back of the splice or joint on each side.

Frame Bottom Rail. 78, Figs. 76-124; 12a, Figs. 1446-1476. The bottom member of a locomotive frame between the pedestal jaws. The frame top rail is continuous over the pedestals.

Frame Brace. Figs. 1490-1518. Any member inserted between the main side frames of a locomotive to stiffen them and keep them square. See **Crosstie.**

Frame Brace to Back Head. A diagonal iron rod secured to the back head of a boiler and to the back end of the frame and foot plate on each side of the locomotive. Now becoming obsolete.

Frame Cross Plate. Figs. 1516-1518. A plate or casting secured across the frames to strengthen them; usually just in front of the cylinder saddles.

Frame Crosstie. See **Crosstie.**

Frame Filling. Figs. 1526-1530. A casting or plate bolted to the upper and lower bars of a frame for stiffening it and for the attachment of brake hangers, expansion pads, etc.

Frame Front Rail. 17, Figs. 77-124; 1, Figs. 1446-1476. The forward portion of a built-up frame, or that part between the forward driving pedestal and the front bumper. In many designs this is a single bar, but on recent large locomotives the front frame is usually made double, one bar above the other, to secure the necessary strength and stiffness.

Frame Pedestal. See **Pedestal.**

Frame Pedestal Thimble. See **Pedestal Thimble.**

Frame Splice. 6, Figs. 1446-1476; Figs. 1477-1489. The front part of a locomotive frame is sometimes called the front splice, as distinguished from the main frame, or that part that holds the driving boxes. The term is also used to designate the actual joint or connection between the two portions of a frame.

Frame Splice Keys. 7, Figs. 1446-1476. Keys driven into slots or key-ways to secure the main part of a frame to the front rail or forward portion.

Frame Top Rail. 77, Figs. 76-124; 12, Figs. 1446-1476. The top member of a locomotive frame. See **Frame Bottom Rail.**

Frame Wedge Bolt. Figs. 1463-1304. A bolt passing through a pedestal thimble or pedestal cap to adjust the position of a driving box wedge.

Franklin Fire Door. Figs. 331-332. A **Fire Door,** which see, arranged to open and shut by compressed air, worked with a foot treadle.

Franklin Institute System of Screw Threads. The **Sellers' System of Screw Threads,** which see, is often called the Franklin Institute system because it was first proposed in a report to, and was recommended by, the Franklin Institute.

Friction Draft Gear. Any form of **Draft Gear,** which see, which makes use of friction for absorbing and dissipating the energy of buffing and tension shocks transmitted through the couplers.

Front Cylinder Head. Figs. 920-921, 926-927. The cylinder head on that end of the cylinder nearest the front or pilot end of the engine. See **Cylinder Head** and **Back Cylinder Head.**

Front End. A common name for the **Smokebox,** which see, and its contained parts.

Front Frame. See **Frame Front Rail.**

Front Tube Sheet. See **Tube Sheet.**

Front Water Space. 61, Figs. 151-204. See **Water Space.**

Fulcrum. "In mechanics, that by which a lever is sustained, or the point about which it moves."—Webster. See **Brake Lever Fulcrum.**

Funnel. 1. A conical receptacle with the broad part uppermost, secured to the boiler just below the gage cocks, to receive the drip from them. Called also gage cock dripper.

2. The filling hole of the tender tank is sometimes called a funnel.

Furnace. Figs. 4935-4936. An enclosed fireplace in which a fire is maintained for the purpose of heating metal. The interior of the fireplace is usually lined with fire-brick. Various types of furnaces burn different fuels, such as oil, gas, coke and coal.

Fuse (Electric Locomotive). A short piece of metal, in the form of a wire, rod or strip, forming part of an electric circuit to protect a motor, lamp or other transformer of energy from an excessive current. For a given circuit, a fuse is used of such metal and conductivity that it will melt and thus open the circuit as soon as the limit of current carrying capacity of the circuit is reached. Fuses are generally placed in boxes, tubes, or other receptacles, to prevent the vaporized metal flying out on surrounding objects.

Fuse Box (Electric Locomotive). A fireproof receptacle, enclosing a fuse or fuses, with suitable contacts or clips for readily attaching them, and usually provided with a magnetic blow-out device. The fuse box is mounted on some part of the locomotive frame, generally near the third-rail shoe.

Fuse Terminals. The clips, clamps or binding posts used to hold a fuse in place in a circuit.

Fusible Plug. Figs. 234-236. A plug screwed into a brass thimble in a crown sheet, made of an alloy of lead, tin and bismuth, in such proportion as to give the alloy a melting point somewhat higher than the temperature of the water corresponding to the steam pressure carried. It is intended to prevent the destruction of a crown sheet by overheating when the water is low, as the melting of the plug will allow the steam to escape. In practice they are unreliable, because the melting point of the alloy often rises with long exposure to heat, and scale forming over the plug may resist a high boiler pressure after the plug itself melts.

G

Gage. 1. (Of Track.) The distance in the clear between the heads of the rails of a railroad; 4 ft. 8½ in. is the standard gage; if greater than this by more than ½ in., a broad gage; if smaller, a narrow gage. Wide gage usually means a minor and irregular or exceptional enlargement of a given fixed gage, in distinction from tight gage, a corresponding contraction.

2. A tool or instrument used as a standard of measurement of pressure or size. See **Air Gage, Cylindrical Gage, Pressure Gage, Screw Gage, Steam Gage, Water Gage.**

Gage Cock. Fig. 3127. A faucet screwed into the back head of a boiler for ascertaining the height of the water in it. Three are commonly used. For standard location see Figs. 2960-2962.

Gage Cock Dripper. Figs. 2993-2995. A receptacle or funnel placed under the gage cocks to catch the water from them and conduct it into a waste pipe.

Gasket. A thin sheet of rubber, cloth or sheet metal put in a joint between two pieces of metal to prevent leakage.

Gear. 1. In mechanics the term is used to designate a combination of appliances for effecting some result, as **Valve Gear, Brake Gear, Draw Gear,** which see.

2. Wheels are said to be in gear when they have cogs interlocking. See **Gear Wheel.**

Gear Ratio (Electric Locomotives). The relation between the number of teeth on a pinion to those on a gear wheel with which it meshes. Thus a gear wheel with 55 teeth, driven by a pinion having 11 teeth, would give a gear ratio of 5 to 1. Stated in another way, the motor armature would have to make 5 revolutions to 1 turn of the axle.

Gear Wheel. A wheel provided with a toothed periphery, for transmitting power from or to a shaft on which a similar wheel, of the same or different diameter, is secured. Electric locomotives have gear wheels fastened to the driving axle. A smaller gear wheel, called a pinion, is fastened to the armature shaft, and engages the gear wheel on the driving axle, thus transmitting the power of the electric motor to the driving wheels of the locomotive.

Geared Locomotive. See **Shay Geared Locomotive.**

Geared Motor (Electric Locomotive). An electric motor which drives an axle of a car or locomotive through the medium of gear wheels or gears.

Gearless Motor (Electric Locomotive). See **Electric Locomotive.** A motor having its armature fastened on a driving axle, thus propelling the locomotive directly, without the interposition of gears. The locomotives shown in Figs. 4585-4668 are gearless locomotives.

General Electric Headlight. Figs. 3291-3294.

Gib (for Journal Bearings). A **Journal Bearing Wedge**, which see.

Gib and Key. A fastening to connect a bar and strap together by a slot common to both, in which an [-shaped gib with a beveled back is first inserted and then driven fast by a taper key.

Glass Water Gage. Figs. 3130-3147. A gage consisting essentially of a vertical glass tube connected at the top and bottom with a boiler so as to make the height of water therein visible.

Globe Valve. A valve, the body of which is spherical or globular in shape, usually having a disk with a conical edge seating in a ring similarly ground to fit the edge. The spindle or stem that raises and lowers the disk has a thread on it working in a nut; and at the end is fitted with a handle, usually disk shaped. A number of globe valves are used on a locomotive. See **Angle Globe Valve.**

Glue. A preparation from the hoofs, horns and hides of animals, washed in lime water, boiled, skimmed, strained, evaporated, cooled in molds, cut into slices and dried upon nets. If good, it is a hard cake, of a dark but almost transparent color, free from black or cloudy spots and with little or no smell. Inferior glue made from bones will almost entirely dissolve in cold water; other kinds are contaminated with lime. Glue is better for re-melting. The strength of glue for common work is increased by adding a little common chalk.

Glue Size. One pound of glue in a gallon of water. Double size has about twice this quantity of glue. Patent size is a kind of gelatine.

Gold's Steam Heating Apparatus. Figs. 3163-3167.

Gollmar Bell Ringer. Figs. 3263-3264.

Gong. A **Cab Gong**, which see.

Gooch Valve Motion. Figs. 1809-1811. A valve motion employing two eccentrics, link, link block and rocker, very similar to the Stephenson motion but differing from it in having the link stationary and the link block movable. Not in general use. See **Valve Gear.**

Goodman Wrecking Hook. Figs. 4582-4584.

Goose Neck. 15, Figs. 4119-4120. A curved pipe, usually made of cast iron, conveying water from the valve in a tender to the suction hose that connects it to the injector feed pipe. British, swan neck.

Gould Friction Draft Gear. Figs. 3957-3961.

Gould Journal Box. Figs. 1485-1486.

Gould Pilot Coupler and Buffer. Fig. 2328.

Gould Spring Buffer. Fig. 3962.

Gould Tender Coupler. Figs. 3964-3966.

Gould Tender Vestibule. Fig. 3963.

Governor. See **Pump Governor.**

Governor Pipe Insulating Joint (Air Brake). A special pipe fitting made of brass and hard rubber, placed in the air pipe to the electric governor, to prevent any grounded current in the latter from passing into the piping system.

Governor Piston (Pump Governor). 28, Figs. 2458-2461. One of the two pistons in a pump governor. The upper piston is so placed that the **Regulating Spring**, which see, presses down on it, while main reservoir air pressure acts to force it up. The lower piston is the one which carries the spindle and disk of the steam valve to the pump.

Governor Union (Pump Governor). A brass union fitting connecting the pump governor to the pipe leading to the engineer's brake valve.

Grab Irons. Also termed corner handles and hand holds. The handles attached to tenders for the use of trainmen in boarding them. They are often more definitely specified as side or end grab iron. The term handle, though often used to designate these attachments, is not strictly appropriate to such a part, nor is it so widely in use as grab iron. The bars extending the length of the boiler and attached to the front of the smokebox are called **Hand Rails,** which see.

Graduated Spring. A form of compound spring in which only a certain number of the individual spirals come into action with a light load and the others only under a heavy load. Another method of accomplishing the same end, graduating the resistance of the spring to the load placed upon it, is the use of the keg-shaped or spool-shaped spring. Under a load the part of larger diameter closes first and that of smaller diameter is much stiffer. Graduated springs have been superseded by single and double nest coil springs of equal length.

Graduating Stem (Triple Valve). 21, Figs. 2490-2493. See **Graduating Spring.**

Graduating Stem Nut (Triple Valve). 20, Figs. 2490-2493.

Graduating Spring (Triple Valve). 22, Figs. 2490-2493. A spiral spring which acts against a collar on the graduating stem to restrain the triple valve piston from moving beyond service position when a gradual brake pipe reduction is made, but which is compressed by the piston when a sudden brake pipe reduction is made.

Graduating Valve. 1. (Old Type Triple Valves.) 7, Fig. 2490. A small plug valve that is fastened to the piston stem so that its movement is controlled by the piston. Its office is to open and close ports in the slide valve so as to control the flow of air from the auxiliary reservoir to the brake cylinder in the service application of the brakes.

2. (New Type Triple Valve.) 7, Figs. 2491-2493. A small slide valve fastened to the piston stem and sliding on the top of the main slide valve. It opens and closes ports in the slide valve which controls the flow of air from the auxiliary reservoir to the brake cylinder in service applications; from the brake cylinder to the atmosphere in release, and also controls the "quick service" and "quick recharge" features.

3. (Engineer's Brake Valve.) In the running position the air from the main reservoir has access to the brake pipe only through the feed valve attachment, which operates to limit the pressure in the brake pipe to 70 pounds when it is 90 pounds in the main reservoir. In the position for service application of the brakes the air pressure is partially released from the chamber above a piston, which is then forced upward by the brake pipe pressure below it, and opens a valve to the atmosphere, through which the brake pipe air is discharged at such a rate that the emergency action of the triple

valves on the cars cannot take place. Any degree of reduction of brake pipe pressure may be effected in this way for graduated applications of the brakes. In the position for the emergency application of the brakes, a large direct port from the brake pipe to the atmosphere is opened, which causes the instantaneous application of the brakes throughout the train.

Grate. Figs. 525-549. A set of parallel bars, commonly cast iron, at the bottom of a firebox to hold the fuel. It is usually made of a number of sections, each section comprising three or four bars resting at their ends on frames or bearers, and connected by short levers to a rod that can be moved back and forth to rock the bars and shake ashes out of the fire. For anthracite coal the grate consists of **Water Tubes** and **Pull Bars**, which see. See **Dead Grate, Dump Grate, Rocking Grate, Shaking Grate.**

Grate Bar. 7b, Figs. 525-549; Figs. 567-571. A cast iron bar or finger usually triangular in section and thinner at the bottom, cast in groups or sections, a number of which go to make up a grate. British, fire bar.

Grate Bar Thimble. A cylindrical cap or ferrule on the end of a grate bar where it rests on the side frame or bearer.

Grate Bearer. See **Grate Side Frame.**

Grate Center Frame. 24, Figs. 525-549. A casting placed lengthwise of the firebox and half way between the sides to support the grates. It has bearings on each side for the grate bars.

Grate Connecting Pins. Pins or pivots for attaching rocking grate bars to the grate connecting rod.

Grate Connecting Rod. 9, Figs. 525-549; Figs. 630-631.
  1. A rod connecting the bars of a rocking or shaking grate with a handle or lever for shaking or rocking them.
  2. A rod for tipping a dump grate.

Grate Crank. 16, Figs. 525-549. A crank attached to a locomotive dump grate and operated by the grate lever.

Grate Crank Bracket. An attachment to the frame or the side of the firebox for holding the grate crank.

Grate End Frame. 33, Figs. 525-549. A casting at either end of a firebox to hold the end portions of a grate.

Grate Frame. 31, Figs. 525-549. The rectangular ring inside a firebox in which the grate bars are carried.

Grate Frame Bearer. 32, Figs. 525-549. A bracket riveted or bolted to the bottom of the firebox for holding the frame in which the grate bars are carried.

Grate Frame Studs. Stud bolts for securing the grate frame to the sides and ends of a firebox.

Grate Frame Support. 12, Figs. 525-549. A transverse casting, of which two are commonly used, to support the frame holding the grate bars.

Grate Lever. 10, Figs. 525-549. A bar pivoted to a bracket and connected to a rod that operates the rocking grates. The upper end of the lever projects slightly above the cab deck and is generally moved by a bar having in its end a socket that fits over the upper end of the grate lever. For dump grates the lever connected to the grate crank.

Grate Lever Catch. A fastener to restrain the lever that operates the dump grate.

Grate Lever Fulcrum. 11, Figs. 525-549. The bracket on which the grate lever is pivoted.

Grate Lever Hanger. A bracket or suspender on which the grate lever of a rocking grate is pivoted.

Grate Lever Pin. A pin or pivot by which the grate lever of a rocking grate is supported and on which it turns.

Grate Rocker Keys. Keys inserted in the arms, moving the rocking grates to secure the arm to the rod by which it is moved.

Grate Rocker Trunnion. The pivot cast on either end of a rocking grate bar.

Grate Shaft. 17, Figs. 525-549. 1. The shaft or trunnion, usually cast in one piece with the dump grate, and which turns with it on the supports or bearings.
  2. The short bar to which a rocking grate lever is secured.

Grate Shaft Arm. 1. A lever fastened to the shaft that operates a dump grate.
  2. A lever fastened to a section of a rocking grate, and connected to the grate lever by a rod or pins.

Grate Shaft Bearing. 17, Figs. 525-549. A rest for either end of a dump grate shaft. Usually bolted to the under side of the grate frame. Also called grate shaft bracket.

Grate Shaft Bracket. A hanger affording a bearing for the shaft of any section of a rocking grate.

Grate Shaft Collar. A flange or enlargement formed on a rocking grate shaft to keep it in position between the bearings.

Grate Shaft Locking Pin. A key to make fast a grate shaft and prevent its moving.

Grate Side Frame. 31, Figs. 525-549. A cast-iron bar on the sides of a firebox with bearings or recesses to hold the pins or pivots of the grate bars. Also called a **Grate Bearer**, which see.

Grease Axle Box (British). An axle box which is lubricated from above by a grease composed of tallow, soda and water, which is solid at ordinary temperatures and melts should the box get warm. This form is being superseded by the **Oil Axle Box,** which see.

Grease Box. A Journal Box, which see, in which grease is used as a lubricant instead of oil.

Grease Bucket. A metal pail or bucket for holding grease for the lubrication of some parts of an engine.

Grease Chamber (British). A cavity above the journal bearing which contains the lubricating material in a **Grease Axle Box,** which see.

Griffin Cast Iron Wheel. Figs. 4547-4548.

Grinding Machine. Figs. 4937-4941. A machine for grinding, as for sharpening edge tools or for finishing accurately metal parts. Grinding machines for sharpening tools are fitted with wheels of stone, emery, carborundum, or other abrasive material. Grinding machines for finishing machine parts include plain grinding machines, universal grinding machines, etc. The grinding wheels in these special machines are generally provided with either longitudinal or cross feed, or both.

Group Spring. A helical tender spring formed of a number of separate springs, single or nested, united together by a common pair of spring plates. It is called a double, or two-group, a three-group, four-group spring, etc., according to the number of separate springs.

Guide. 119, Figs. 77-124; Figs. 1022-1029. One of two or four bars placed parallel to the axis of a cylinder and piston rod and forming ways or slides in which the crosshead moves. Single bar guides are occasionally used. Called also a slide. British, slide bar.

Guide Bar. One of the bars of a **Guide,** which see.

Guide Bearer. See **Guide Yoke.**

Guide Block. 1, Figs. 788-1029. A block or blocks bolted to the back cylinder head or to the guide yoke to form a bracket or support for a guide or guide bar. Sometimes the front guide blocks are cast on the cylinder head. British, slide bar carrier.

Guide Block Bolt. A bolt to fasten a guide block to a cylinder head or guide yoke.

Guide Oil Cup. Figs. 1030-1036. A cup or cups placed on the upper guide bar or bars to hold a supply of oil for lubricating the guides.

Guide Safety Strap (for Main Rod). Figs. 1037-1038; 214 Figs. 77-124. An open rectangular or curved piece fastened to the outer end of a guide yoke to support the main rod in case a crank pin or wrist pin breaks and the main rod drops.

Guide Step. 29a, Figs. 1022-1025. A small step fastened to a guide yoke for convenience in reaching parts of the valve gear, etc., that are located between the frames.

Guide Yoke. 14a, Figs. 1022-1025; Figs. 1596-1604. A transverse plate or casting secured to the frames by angles or knees, holding and supporting the outer ends of the guides and frequently having a brace to the waist of the boiler on each end, as well as an expansion plate for the boiler between the frames. Called also spectacle plate, motion plate, guide bearer and guide crosstie. British, slide bar bracket.

Guide Yoke Brace Angle. An angle for the attachment of a brace to the waist of the boiler and having its lower end secured to the guide yoke.

Guide Yoke Bracket. An extension on the ends of a guide yoke for holding the guides on certain types of locomotives with driving wheels spaced close together.

Guide Yoke Collar Bolt. A bolt used to secure a guide bar to a guide yoke or guide yoke collar, where the yoke is of such form that it surrounds the main rod.

Guide Yoke Knee. 1. Figs. 1602-1604. An angle casting bolted to the frame and to the guide yoke to secure them.

2. 7, Figs. 1600-1601. An expansion knee to support the boiler, and secured to the guide yoke.

Guide Yoke Sheet. 7, Figs. 1600-1601. A plate secured to the guide yoke and to an angle on the inner side of the shell of the boiler to provide a support that will allow the boiler to expand and contract. A waist sheet.

Guide Yoke Sheet Wearing Plate. A strip interposed between the shell of the boiler and the flange of the guide yoke sheet to take the wear of the sliding parts.

Gun Iron or **Gun Metal.** An alloy used for bearings, composed of copper, zinc or tin, and iron. Gun metal as commonly made consists of 90 per cent. copper with 10 per cent. tin; but zinc and iron are frequently substituted for tin, in the proportions—copper 78, zinc 20, iron 2.

Gusset Plate. A flat plate used to rivet two parts of a metal underframe together by riveting through each member and the plate or to stiffen a joint between two pieces which are riveted together by angle plates, in which case the gusset plate is riveted to the flanges of the adjoining pieces.

Gusset Stay (British). Figs. 3709-3713. A triangular plate secured to the boiler back head and to the roof sheet by angles. See **Back Head Brace**, and **Back Head Brace Angle**.

H

Hale Ash Pan. Fig. 523. A device fitted to the bottom slide of an ash pan hopper. It consists of a lever or hanger, pivoted at the upper end to a frame or bracket, and at the lower end fastened to the bottom of the hopper. When the hopper is closed the upper end of the hanger is back of the center of the hopper. Consequently, when the dump lever is operated, the hanger tends to push the bottom away from the hopper. It is intended to facilitate dumping the ash pan when the hopper is frozen.

Half Elliptic Spring. See **Spring** and **Elliptic Spring**.

Hammer (Power). Figs. 4942-4946. A machine for forging, swaging and cutting off metal. Power hammers are usually designated by their method of operation and by the shape of their frames; such as steam hammers, steam drop hammers and board drop hammers, also as single or double frame hammers. Power hammers are generally rated according to the actual weight of their falling parts.

Hand Holds. See **Grab Iron**.

Hand Hole. 60, Figs. 151-205. An opening in a water leg or in the shell of a boiler for cleaning out mud and scale. It is closed by a cast or wrought iron plate or cover held in place by studs set in a heavy ring riveted around the hole. British, mud door.

Hand Hole and Washout Plug. A plug screwed into a water leg for the purpose of washing out mud and scale.

Hand Hole Plate. 60a, Figs. 310-313. See **Hand Hole**.

Hand Hole Plate Bolt. 60b, Figs. 310-313. One of a number of bolts passing through holes in the hand hole plate cover to secure it to the ring riveted to the boiler.

Hand Hole Plate Clamp. See **Hand Hole Plate Dog**.

Hand Hole Plate Dog. 60d, Figs. 310-313. A curved piece with its ends or feet resting against the inside of a boiler near the edge of a hand hole. A bolt attached to the dog passes through a hole in the center of the hand hole plate, and a nut screwed on the end of the bolt draws the plate tight against the boiler.

Hand Saw. A hand tool with a thin flat blade having one edge serrated. Used for cutting wood.

Hand Wheel. 1. A wheel fastened to a brake shaft on the tender to apply the brakes by hand.

2. A small disk on the stem of a steam or water valve to open and close it.

Handle. "That part of anything by which it is held in the hand. A haft. As the handle of a knife or other instrument."—Worcester. They are designated by the name of the part or thing to which they are a handle, as smokebox door handle, etc.

Handle Bolt (Engineer's Brake Valve). More properly called **Handle Latch**, which see.

Handle Latch (Engineer's Brake Valve). 9, Figs. 2171-2473. An attachment to the engineer's brake valve handle which indicates to the engineer when the rotary valve is in the various positions for operating the brakes, by passing over notches in the brake valve body.

Handle Latch Spring (Engineer's Brake Valve). 10, Figs. 2171-2473. A spiral spring used with the handle latch to force it into notches in the valve body, thereby indicating when the handle is in each position required in operating the brakes.

Handrail. 6, Figs. 77-124. A piece of iron pipe secured to the boiler above the running board, on the bumper or in the cab, to serve as a hand hold.

Handrail Bracket. 52, Figs. 77-124. A post or support secured to the boiler and holding a handrail.

Handrail Flange. A flange fastened on the end of a handrail at the front of the cab.

Handrail Pillar (British). See **Handrail Bracket**.

Hanger. 1. "That by which a thing is suspended."—Webster.

2. "A means for supporting shafting of machinery."—Knight.

Harrison Dust Guard. Fig. 4509.

Harvey Friction Draft Spring. Fig. 3934.

Hayden Segmental Metallic Rod Packing. Fig. 1020.

Head. See **Brake Head, Cylinder Head, Dome Head, Draw Head.**

Headlight. 1. Figs. 77-124; Figs. 3267-3316. A lamp, with a reflector at the back, placed at the front of a locomotive to illuminate the track ahead. Oil lamps are generally used, but many headlights are fitted with an electric arc light, the current for which is supplied by a small steam turbine and dynamo unit, placed on the boiler and taking steam therefrom.

Headlight Bracket. 3, Figs. 77-124. A support secured to the side or front of the smoke-box to hold a headlight.

Headlight Bracket Column. Short posts or columns supporting a headlight on a shelf.

Headlight Bracket Stand. A support for a headlight, consisting of brackets, short posts and a shelf.

Headlight Burner. 4, Figs. 3303-3308. That part of an oil burning locomotive headlight comprising the wick and mechanism for turning it up or down.

Headlight Step. Figs. 3309-3311; 139, Figs. 77-124. A small step fastened to the side or front of a smoke-box to enable a man to reach the headlight when lighting or trimming it.

Headstock (British). American equivalent, end sill. The transverse end member of the **Underframe**, which see. It is pierced transversely in the center for the draw gear, and the buffing gear is carried near the ends.

Heater Cock. A valve attached to the boiler head, to admit steam from the boiler to the pipe running under the tender and train for heating the cars. It is a **Reducing Valve**, which see, and allows sufficient steam to pass to maintain a pressure of from 20 to 80 pounds per square inch in the train steam pipe at the valve.

Heater Cock Extension. The pipe leading from the cab turret on the boiler to the heater cock.

Helper. A term used to designate an assistant engine for trains.

Henderer's Hydraulic Claw Jack. Fig. 4580.

Hennessey Friction Draft Gear. Figs. 3949-3952.

High Pressure Control (Air Brakes). See **Double Pressure Control.**

High Speed Brake (Air Brakes). Fig. 2416. A brake equipment consisting of the ordinary quick action brake with the addition of a few attachments, the principal one being an automatic pressure reducing valve (Figs. 2503-2507), which is attached directly to the brake cylinder. The auxiliary reservoir pressure is increased from 70 to 110 pounds, and in emergency applications a pressure of about 85 pounds is obtained in the brake cylinder. This high pressure is slowly bled off through the reducing valve to 60 pounds. The operations of release and recharging take place as in the ordinary quick action brake. For vehicles operating in a high speed braked train and not equipped with the high speed reducing valve, a safety valve, Fig. 2511, is required.

Hinge. "A hook or joint on which a door, gate, etc., turns."—Webster. They are provided with a tube-like knuckle through which the **Hinge Pin**, which see, passes. The common door hinge is usually a butt or butt hinge. The strap hinge is a common form of rough hinge for heavy doors, cab aprons, tank manhole covers, etc. A T-hinge is a combination of the butt and strap hinge, one-half being of each form.

Hinge Pin. The pin passing through the knuckle of a hinge and holding the two parts together.

Hinson Friction Draft Gear. Figs. 3943-3946.

Hip Joint. The joint between the firebox and the boiler shell of a boiler with Belpaire firebox.

Hip Joint Casing. Figs. 213-215. A sheet steel cover flanged and pressed to the shape of the hip joint of a boiler with Belpaire firebox. See **Boiler Jacket.**

Hodge Brake. An arrangement invented by Nehemiah Hodge, patented in 1849, for operating the brakes on each truck of a car or tender simultaneously, and equalizing the pressure on all the wheels. The brake may have one or two levers on each truck. Underneath the body are two levers, called Hodge or floating levers, with movable fulcrums in their centers, which are connected together by a rod. One end of each of these levers is connected by a rod and chain to the brake shaft, and the other end of the floating lever is connected by a rod with the long arm of a brake lever on a truck.

Hoe. A fire tool or implement consisting of a short broad blade with a long handle at right angles to it, used for raking a fire or pulling ashes out of an ash pan.

Holder. "Something by which a thing is held."—Webster. A great variety of parts which serve this purpose are so called, as door holder, lamp holder, etc., which take their names from the thing which they hold.

Hollow Piston Rod (Tender Brakes). A brake cylinder piston rod which is hollow to receive the **Push Rod** or **Push Bar**, which see.

Hood. 1. A roof apron which is attached to the back end of the cab and extends out over the cab apron to protect the fireman.

2. A **Fire Door Shield**, which see.

Hook. A fire tool consisting of a long handle with a hook at one end used for raking or spreading fires.

Hopper. 1. (Extended Smokebox). 1, Fig. 406. A receptacle for cinders or sparks on the under side of a smokebox. It is shaped like the frustum of a cone or a pyramid, and empties into the **Cinder Pipe**, which see. Also called cinder pocket and spark pocket.

2. An **Ash Pan Hopper**, which see.

Hopper Slide. 2, Fig. 407; Figs. 408-410. 1. A piece of metal fitted in across the bottom of a cinder hopper under a smokebox for emptying it of sparks.

2. See **Ash Pan Slide.**

Hornblock (British). 18, Figs. 5077-5078. See **Pedestal.**

Hornblock Bolt (British). See **Pedestal Bolt.**

Hornblock Cap (British). See **Pedestal Cap.**

Hornblock Keep (British). See **Pedestal Thimble.**

Hornblock Tie (British). See **Pedestal Tie.**

Hose and Coupling (Air Brake). Fig. 2538. Flexible tubing with a hose nipple on one end and a hose coupling on the other for use in making the connection between adjacent vehicles of the brake pipe and train air signal pipe lines running throughout the train.

Hose. A piece of tubing made of India rubber and canvas, for conveying water, air or steam. See **Air Brake Hose.**

Hose Clamp (Air Brake). Fig. 2537. A clamp to bind the hose to the hose nipple and coupling.

Hose Collar. A collar which surrounds the hose and binds it on the nipple. Also called hose band.

Hose Coupling (Air Brake). Fig. 2539. A contrivance for coupling or connecting the ends of a pair of brake hose together, so that the air by which the brakes are operated can pass from one vehicle in a train to another. The couplings for train air signal apparatus are similar to brake hose couplings, but are arranged so that they will not couple to them.

Hose Coupling Case (Air Brake). A hollow casting which joins the main part of a coupling to which the hose is attached.

Hose Nipple (Air Brake). Fig. 2540. A short iron tube fitting into the end of the brake hose and fastened by a suitable clamp and screws. One end is threaded and screws into the angle cock.

Housing Box. A Journal Box, which see.

Hub (Wheels). 3, Figs. 1353-1367. The central portion, into which the axle is fitted. It is usually cylindrical in form and projects beyond the disks or spokes of the wheel on each side. In Great Britain termed the boss.

Hull Headlight Burner. Fig. 3297.

Hydraulic Jack. Figs. 4575-4577, 4580. A tool or machine in which the power is exerted by means of the pressure of some liquid acting against a piston or plunger, for raising heavy weights, like an engine. The head and interior tube or ram form a reservoir, from which the fluid flows to the pump, and to which it is returned in lowering. From the pump it is forced, by the downward stroke of the piston, past the lower valve into the cylinder, and, this being closed at the bottom, the ram rises. The lever, which is made with a projection on one edge, slips into a socket at the side of the head. This socket passes through an arm on the interior of the head, and to this is fastened the piston of the pump. The claw attachment is a third tube, which screws into the head, below the ram collar and outside of the cylinder, at the lower end of which is a claw projecting out at one side. They are rated so that one man can raise the weight for which they are designed. The speed of lifting is inversely proportional to the amount lifted. Ten tons can be lifted one foot in about a minute and a half.

I

I-Beam. A general term applied by makers to any form of rolled iron or steel having an I cross-section. The top and bottom parts are termed the flanges, and the middle the web. The usual dimensions are given by the total height from out to out, and vary from 3 to 24 in. When one of the flanges is simply a round bar it is termed a deck beam. I-beams are used for center and intermediate sills, also for body and truck bolsters on tenders.

Independent Brake Valve (Air Brake). Figs. 2171-2176. A rotary, straight-air brake valve used with the Westinghouse ET locomotive brake equipment for operating the locomotive brakes independently of the train brakes. See **Engineer's Brake Valve**.

India Rubber. A gum which exudes from a tropical tree growing in the East and West Indies, Mexico, South America, etc. It is prepared for use by vulcanizing with a greater or less proportion of sulphur according to the stiffness required.

Indicator. A device attached to the cylinder of a steam engine, which gives a graphical diagram of the steam distribution in the cylinder at all points in the stroke. Used chiefly for testing purposes.

Indicator Fitting. A brass fitting with a three-way cock and pipe connections for an indicator from each end of the locomotive cylinder.

Indicator Plug. Figs. 949-951. A plug screwed into a hole in the side of a cylinder near the end. When the indicator is to be used this plug is removed and the indicator pipe connection screwed in. A hole is drilled near each end of a cylinder so that an indicator diagram may be taken from either end at will.

Injector. Figs. 3088-3107. An instrument for forcing water into a steam boiler in which a jet of steam imparts its velocity to the water and thus forces it into the boiler against the boiler pressure. The injector was first reduced to practical form by Henri Giffard, an eminent French engineer, in the year 1858, and was introduced in this country by William Sellers & Co., Inc., in 1860. See **Inspirator, Metropolitan Injector, Nathan Injector, Simplex Injector, Sellers' Injector**.

Injector Bracket. Figs. 2999-3000. A projection secured to the boiler for the attachment of an injector.

Injector Check. Figs. 3108-3110. A check valve placed in an injector delivery pipe and opening against boiler pressure to admit water forced in by an injector.

Injector Check Valve. See **Injector Check**.

Injector Connecting Rods. On injectors located outside the cab, rods secured to the steam and water valves and passing through the front of the cab so that the injector may be operated from inside.

Injector Delivery Pipe. 50, Figs. 77-124. A copper or iron tube through which feed water is forced into a boiler. When the pipe is located outside the boiler, the check valve is put at the farther end of the pipe; but with injectors secured to the boiler back head, a check valve is placed close to the injector, and the delivery pipe carried inside the boiler to a point near the front end. Also called an injector check pipe.

Injector Delivery Pipe Hanger. 51, Figs. 77-124. A hanger or suspender fastened inside a boiler to support the check or delivery pipe of an injector. Used when the injectors are on the boiler backhead and deliver water through a pipe terminating near the front end.

Injector Feed Pipe. 185, Figs. 77-124. A tube secured to the water inlet of an injector and connected to the hose from the tender.

Injector Feed Pipe Coupling. A coupling or union on the injector feed pipe to connect it to the hose from the tender tank.

Injector Hole. An aperture either in the first course of a boiler, near the smokebox, or in the back head, for the injector delivery pipe to enter the boiler.

Injector Steam Valve. A valve usually arranged to take steam from the cab turret, and having a pipe through which steam is conducted to an injector.

Inlet Valves (Air Pump). 86, Figs. 2429-2435. The disk or poppet valves through which air enters the pump.

Inside Admission Valve. Figs. 2156-2157. A valve which takes live steam through a central cavity and admits it to the steam ports leading to the ends of the cylinder. The exhaust ports are at the ends of the valve. See **Valve**.

Inside Connected Locomotive. A locomotive having the main rods connected to cranks formed or built on the driving axle between the frames. Some four-cylinder compounds have two cylinders inside connected. In Great Britain many, if not most, simple engines are inside connected.

Inside Lap (Valve). With an outside admission valve,

such as an ordinary slide valve, the inside lap is the amount by which the inside edge of the valve overlaps or goes beyond the inner edge of either steam port when the valve is at the exact center of its travel on the valve face. The effect of inside lap is to delay the release of the steam from the cylinder to the exhaust pipe. Sometimes called exhaust lap. See **Outside Lap.**

Inside Stack (Smokeboxes). 5, Figs. 343-442. See **Smoke Stack Lift Pipe.**

Inside Throat Sheet. 29, Figs. 151-206. A piece or plate forming part of the front end of a firebox in boilers having the back tube sheet set forward of the front water leg, and being therefore shaped so as to correspond with the outside throat sheet. See **Throat Sheet.**

Inside Welt. 56, Figs. 151-206. A strip or narrow plate riveted on the inside of the abutting edges of two plates of a boiler to form a butt joint.

Inspection Locomotive. Figs. 31, 51-53. A locomotive having a large cab built over the front of the boiler for the use of officers in inspecting railroad track.

Inspirator. A name applied to the Hancock Inspirator, which see, a device very similar to an injector and accomplishing the same end. See **Injector.**

Insulating Hose. See **Flexible Hose Connection.**

Insulating Joint. See **Governor Pipe Insulating Joint.**

Intercepting Valve. Figs. 2216-2218, 2226. A device used on compound locomotives, consisting of a cylindrical chamber containing a valve that in one position admits live steam to the low-pressure steam chest and causes the exhaust from the high-pressure steam chest to escape to the stack. When moved to the so-called "compound" position, it closes the live steam connection to the low-pressure steam chest as well as the high-pressure exhaust to the stack, causing the high-pressure exhaust to go to the low-pressure steam chest, thus changing the engine to work as a compound. The intercepting valve is operated either by compressed air controlled by a valve in the cab, or by a rod connected to the reverse lever, which thus makes the engine "simple" in full gear, but "compound" when the lever is hooked up.

Intercepting Valve Bull Ring. A cast-iron ring forming part of an intercepting valve and holding the packing rings that make a steam-tight joint in the valve chamber.

Intercepting Valve Bushing. A cylinder of thin metal, secured inside the chamber of an intercepting valve to form a hard wearing surface for the valve.

Intercepting Valve Cylinder. A cylindrical casting set in a recess cast in the low-pressure cylinder saddle of a compound locomotive to hold the intercepting valve.

Intercepting Valve Follower. A disk or circular cast-iron piece bolted to one end of an intercepting valve to hold the bull ring.

Intercepting Valve Reducing Valve Ring. A metal ring fitted to the valve that admits live steam to the intercepting valve.

Intercepting Valve Ring. A metal ring fitted to the intercepting valve to cause it to fit steam tight in its cylinder.

Intercepting Valve Stem Nut. A nut screwed on the stem of the intercepting valve to hold the follower in place.

Intermediate Sill. 2, Figs. 3614-3656. One of the longitudinal members of the underframe of a tender placed between the center sills and the side sill. See **Sill.**

Internal Cylindrical Gage. A very accurately made, solid steel cylinder, used as a standard of measurement of cylindrical holes.

Internal Screw Gage. A solid steel cylinder with a screw thread on it, for testing the diameter of female screws.

Inverted Arch Bar (Truck Side Frames). 2, Figs. 4294-4382. A wrought iron or steel bar which rests on top of the journal boxes with the **Arch Bar,** which see, on top of it. Also sometimes called the middle or lower arch bar.

J

Jack or **Jack Screw.** Figs. 4575-4580. A machine or device for raising heavy bodies, such as a locomotive or tender to enable repairs to be made, etc. Jacks are operated either by a screw turned by a lever or by an hydraulic ram or plunger. In the screw type the head on which the weight to be raised rests has on its lower extension a threaded rod fitting in a nut or sleeve threaded to match on the interior of the base or stand. The screw is turned by a lever passing through a hole in the upper part and of sufficient length to enable one man to operate the jack to its maximum capacity. Hydraulic jacks consist of a plunger or ram under which oil or other non-freezing liquid is forced by means of a pump operated by a long handle.

Jacket. 56, Figs. 77-124. A covering of thin sheet iron over the lagging of a locomotive boiler, cylinder or other protected radiating surface. Sometimes of Russia iron, polished, but more commonly of sheet steel painted. British, clothing plate.

Jacket Bands. Strips surrounding the jacket to cover the joint between any two sections.

Jacket Clamps. Fasteners for holding the edges of the jacket in place.

Jacket Edging. A turned up moulding on the joint of the jacket sheets.

Janney Pilot Coupler. Figs. 2341-2361.

Janney Tender Coupler. Figs. 4033-4051.

Janney, R. E., Pilot Coupler and Pocket. Figs. 2373-2376.

Janney, R. E., Tender Coupler. Figs. 3967-3973.

Jaw. A Pedestal Jaw, which see.

Jerome Metallic Rod Packing. Figs. 1015-1016.

Journal. 2, Figs. 1368-1385. That part of an axle or shaft on which the journal bearing or brass rests. The part of a crank axle on which the driving box brass rests is called the main journal to distinguish it from the crank pin journal.

Journal Bearing. A block of metal usually some kind of **Brass** or **Bronze,** which see, in contact with a journal, on which the load rests. In locomotive building the term when unqualified means an engine or truck axle journal bearing. A standard form has been adopted by the American Railway Master Mechanics' Association, but its composition is not specified. See Figs. 4812-4816, etc. The Hopkins or lead-lined journal bearing is one coated on the inside with a thin sheet of lead to make it self-fitting on the journal. Babbitt metal in some of its many forms is used for car journal bearings occasionally, and almost universally for the bearings of machinery. In order that the journal bearing may be more easily removable, and to distribute the load more equally, a journal bearing key, also called a wedge, is used to hold the journal bearing in place. The term "wedge" is in very common use, perhaps more common than the name here given.

Journal Bearing Key. A metal block inserted over the top of a journal bearing. It is more commonly called a wedge. It is to distribute the load uniformly over the bearing, as well as to enable the brass to be more easily removed and replaced. The A. R. M. M. A. standard form is shown in Figs. 4803-4807, etc.

Journal Box. Figs. 4464-4495. A cast or malleable iron or cast steel box or case which encloses the journal of a truck axle, the journal bearing and key, and which holds the packing for lubricating the journal. Also called axle box, grease box, housing box, oil box and pedestal box, or simply box. British, usually axle box. The A. R. M. M. A. standard journal boxes and contained parts are shown in Figs. 4797-4877. See **Driving Box.**

Journal Box, Bearing and Pedestal. At the convention of the American Railway Master Mechanics' Association of 1881 a design of journal box, bearing and pedestal, was submitted and made standard for cars and locomotive tenders. Changed to Recommendations in 1891. Changed to standard in 1903. At the convention of 1903 the M. C. B. journal boxes and contained parts for the 3¾ by 7-inch, 4¼ by 8-inch, 5 by 9-inch and 5½ by 10-inch standard axles were made a standard of the association. They are shown in Figs. 4797-4877.

Journal Box Bolts. 8, Figs. 4294-4382. The bolts on either side of the journal box which secure it between the arch bar and the pedestal tie bar of a diamond arch bar truck.

Journal Box Cover or Lid. Figs. 4497-4506. A door or lid covering an aperture on the outside of a tender or engine truck journal box, by means of which oil and packing are supplied and journal bearings are inserted or removed. Such covers are made of cast iron, malleable iron and pressed steel. They are usually closed by a spring.

Journal Box Cover Bolt. A bolt used to fasten covers which have no hinge to the box. Two of these are usually employed to each cover. A gasket of canvas, rubber or leather is used to make a tight joint. Journal box covers are, however, now almost invariably held on by hinges and springs or some arrangement of lugs or grooved joints.

Journal Box Cover Spring. A flat spring to hold the lid in place.

Journal Box Guides. Iron bars or blocks placed one on each side of the journal boxes of some metal frame trucks in which journal springs are used. These irons, while holding the box in place longitudinally and transversely, allow it to have a vertical motion between them. When a pair of these guides is cast in one piece it is called a **Pedestal,** which see.

Journal Box Lid. Figs. 4497-4506. The iron or steel lid or cover which closes the opening in the end of a journal box through which oil and waste for the journal packing is inserted.

Journal Brass. A **Journal Bearing,** which see.

Journal Packing. Waste, wool, or other fibrous material saturated with oil or grease, with which a journal box is filled to lubricate the journal.

Journal Spring. A spring supporting part of the weight of a car which is placed directly over the journal, and which usually rests on the journal box under the truck frame. Such springs are sometimes placed above the truck frame and supported by straps, and the weight of the car is transmitted to the journal box by a vertical pin or stirrup. **Equalizer Springs,** which see, accomplish the same end as journal springs, and more effectually.

Joy Valve Gear. Fig. 5126. A form of valve gear in limited use in Great Britain which derives its motion from an arm attached to the main rod near the wrist pin. The link is pivoted at its upper end and by moving it forward or back of the central position the cut-off can be regulated for forward or backward movement of the locomotive.

Jumper (Electric Locomotive). 1, Figs. 4629-4630. A flexible cable, composed of one or more conductors, insulated from one another and covered with suitable material to resist abrasion, used to connect the controller circuits of two electric locomotives that are to be coupled for joint operation.

K

K. & M. Magnesia Boiler Lagging. Fig. 314.

Keewanee Brake Beam. Fig. 4441. A steel brake beam of rectangular cross section, and a bar for a truss rod, which is bent around the ends of the beam proper.

Kelso Pilot and Tender Coupler. Figs. 2329-2340.

Key. 1. "In a general sense, a fastener—that which fastens—as a piece of wood in a frame of a building."—Webster.

Hence, a pin inserted in a hole in a bolt and used to secure the bolt or its nut. A **Split Key,** which see, is a special form.

2. "An instrument for opening or shutting a lock by pushing the bolt one way or the other."—Webster.

3. A block over the top of a journal bearing. A **Journal Bearing Key,** which see. This part is also very commonly called a wedge.

4. A beveled bar used with a gib to form a **Gib and Key,** which see.

Key Ring Tire Fastening. A mode of securing the tire to the wheel, composed of two rings, one of U-section and the other nearly rectangular. The U-shaped ring holds the tire and wheel together, and the rectangular ring holds the former in place, filling up the grove in the tire. When both rings are in place the outer lip of the groove in the tire is slightly hammered over, thus gripping the second or key ring, and retaining it in place. See also **Tire Fastening.**

Kilowatt. See **Watt.**

King Bolt. See **Center Pin.**

Klinger Reflex Water Gage. Figs. 3130-3140.

Knee. A brace or stiffening piece, made of cast or malleable iron or steel, used to bind together two members of a structure, such as a tender frame or a cab frame, at right angles to each other.

Knuckle. 1. (M. C. B. Couplers.) The rotating coupling hook by means of which coupling is effected when the knuckle is locked by the catch or lock. It must conform to certain contour lines adopted by the M. C. B. Association in 1888.

2. (Of a Hinge.) The central tubular projections which carry the hinge pin. The term is of wide and general application in mechanics to many similar parts.

Knuckle Joint. "A joint in which a projection on each leg or leaf of a device is inserted between corresponding recesses in the other, the two being connected by a pin or pivot on which they mutually turn. The legs of dividers and the leaves of door hinges are examples of true knuckle joints. The term, however, has been somewhat commonly restricted to compound or universal joints designed to act in any direction."—Knight.

Knuckle Opener (Automatic Couplers.) The device which throws the knuckle open when the lock is lifted so that a coupling can be made. With couplers not having a knuckle opener it is necessary to go in between the cars and pull the knuckle open by hand after the lock has been lifted.

Knuckle Pin. 1. A pivot on which the knuckle of the pilot or tender coupler turns. See **Pivot Pin**.

2. A crosshead pin or wrist pin.

Krupp Steel Tired Wheels. Figs. 4553-4558.

L

Lag Screw. An iron bolt with a square or hexagonal head, and with a wood screw thread cut on it, intended to screw into woods. Lag screws are round under the head, so that they can be turned after they enter the wood. British equivalent, coach screw.

Lagging. Fig. 314; 55, Figs. 77-124. A covering laid on the outside of the boiler to prevent loss of heat by radiation. Usually composed of magnesia and asbestos and applied in sections made to fit the curvature of the boiler. It is sheathed with a sheet iron **Jacket**, which see. Formerly wood was used.

Lagging Angle. A holder or bracket secured to a boiler to hold the lagging in position.

Laird Crosshead. Figs. 1078-1083, 1112-1122. See **Crosshead**.

Lamp. Figs. 3151, 3317-3328. A device consisting of a reservoir, a wick, and a globe or chimney, in which oil or other illuminant may be burned for producing light. On a locomotive, in addition to the headlight, there are the **Gage Lamps, Signal Lamps** and **Classification Lamps**, which see.

Lamp Burner. 18, Figs. 3317-3323. That portion of a lamp by which the opening on the top of the reservoir is closed, which holds the wick, and by which the latter is adjusted. A headlight burner is a lamp burner of special form used on headlights.

Lamp Chimney. 2, Figs. 3317-3323. A glass tube which encloses the flame of a lamp, conducts away the smoke and gases and produces the necessary draft.

Lamp Fixture. A bracket secured to the boiler, in the cab, to hold a lamp that illuminates the steam gage. It is usual to place the air gage close to the steam gage so as to be seen by the same light.

Lamp Globe. 2, Figs. 3317-3323. A glass or porcelain case or vessel enclosing or surrounding the flame of a lamp or candle, and intended to protect the latter from wind. Lamp globes are approximately globular in form, but are often made of different shapes, as round, pear-shaped, egg-shaped. They frequently serve as a chimney as in the case of gage lamps.

Lamp Holder. The bracket or stand to which the gage or water glass lamp is fastened.

Lamp Reservoir. 11, Figs. 3317-3323. The portion of a lamp which holds the oil. Also called lamp fount.

Lamp Shelf. A **Headlight Shelf**, which see.

Lamp Socket. A slotted fixture or holder secured to the smokebox on each side to carry a signal or classification lamp. See **Signal Lamp Fixture**.

Lantern. A portable lamp, the flame in which is protected from wind and rain by glass, usually in the form of a globe surrounded by wires, called guards. According to the number of these wires the lantern is called single, double or triple guard. See **Signal Lamp**.

Lap (Valve). The amount by which the edges of a valve, when in the center of the valve seat or chamber, overlap the edges of either steam port. See **Inside Lap** and **Outside Lap**.

Lap Joint. Figs. 315-320. A method of fastening together the ends of a boiler plate or of two plates by laying the edge of one plate over that of the other and then riveting them. Formerly used in making the longitudinal seams in locomotive boilers.

Lateral Motion. A movement sidewise, more particularly meaning, as generally used, a side or swing motion of the bolster of a swing motion truck, in distinction from the end play of an axle under the journal. A lateral motion spring, which is slipped over a lateral motion spring pin, is sometimes used to check the lateral movement of such spring bolsters, but this end is more commonly accomplished by splaying the swing hangers outward.

Lateral Motion Spring. See above.

Lateral Motion Spring Pin. See above.

Lateral Play. Side motion of any part of a car or machinery; the space left to permit of such side motion. See **Lateral Motion** (of a Truck Bolster), **End Play** (of an Axle).

Lathe. Figs. 4947-4956. A machine for forming round pieces in which the piece to be machined is revolved in a horizontal position between two centers. The cutting tool is held in a tool post, which is secured to a carriage which travels the length of the bed and which is generally provided with power longitudinal and cross feed.

Leach Pneumatic Sander. Figs. 3253-3254.

Lead (Valves). The amount by which a valve uncovers or opens a steam port at the beginning of the stroke of the piston. This results in admitting live steam to the cylinder before the piston reaches the end of the preceding stroke.

Lead-Lined Journal Bearing. A journal bearing which has its inner surface covered with a thin layer of lead, so that it may fit itself to the journal as soon as subjected to wear. Such bearings are often called Hopkins journal bearings. A variety of other bearings are more or less similar, but a greater quantity of lead or babbitt metal is frequently used.

Leakage Groove (of Air Brake Cylinder). A small passage past the brake piston to prevent application of the brakes by trifling leakages of air.

Leather. The hide of some animal, usually cattle, which has had the hair removed and been subjected to a toughening and hardening process called tanning.

Leeds Reversible Pilot Coupler. Figs. 2370-2372.

Length (of Elliptic Springs). The distance from center to center of scrolls when the spring is unloaded.

Lens. An optical instrument for conveying rays of light upon a fixed path or fixed point. Lenses for lanterns consist of three types—bull's-eye, double convex or plano convex lens; semaphore (a mere modification of the Fresnel), and the Fresnel proper, the latter rarely used.

Lentz Stayless Boiler. A boiler having a corrugated cylindrical firebox which does not require staying. Used to some extent in Germany and Austria. See **Vanderbilt Boiler**.

Lever. "In mechanics, a bar of metal, wood or other substance, turning on a support called a fulcrum." —Webster. See **Brake Lever, Brake Equalizing Lever, Cylinder Lever, Dead Lever, Floating Lever, Live Lever, Uncoupling Lever.**

Lever Guide. 15, Figs. 4294-4382. A slotted bar to guide the upper end of a brake lever and hold it in position laterally. More properly **Brake Lever Guide**, which see.

Lever Pin. A pin or pivot passing through holes in a brake lever guide to adjust the lever in accordance with the wear of the brake shoes.

Lewis-Seley Pilot Coupler and Buffer. Figs. 2404-2407.

Lifting Link (Walschaerts Valve Gear). Fig. 1812. A short bar attached to the reverse shaft arm at one end and to the radius bar at the other to move the radius bar up or down in the link and thus move the valve in the steam chest. It performs the same function for the Walschaerts gear that the link hanger or link lifter does for the Stephenson gear.

Lifting Shaft. See **Reverse Shaft**.

Lightning Arrester (Electric Locomotive). A device for protecting electrical apparatus from damage by lightning. It usually consists of an air gap in series with a non-inductive resistance connected between the power circuit and the ground. The gap serves as an easier path to ground for high voltage discharge than that through the electrical apparatus which has a high inductance. The gap is provided with a magnetic blow-out that extinguishes the arc after discharge.

Limit Gages for Round Iron. At the convention of the American Railway Master Mechanics' Association, in 1884, the Pratt & Whitney limit gages

for round iron, shown, were adopted as standard. Reaffirmed 1891.

Nominal diameter. Of iron. Inches.	Large size, end. Inches.	Small size, end. Inches.	Total variation. Inches.
¼	.2550	.2450	.010
5/16	.3180	.3070	.011
⅜	.3810	.3690	.012
7/16	.4440	.4310	.013
½	.5070	.4930	.014
9/16	.5700	.5550	.015
⅝	.6330	.6170	.016
¾	.7585	.7415	.017
⅞	.8840	.8660	.018
1	1.0095	.9905	.019
1⅛	1.1350	1.1150	.020
1¼	1.2605	1.2395	.021

Line and Line. A term used to designate the position of a slide valve having no lap. A valve whose edge coincides with the edge of the steam port when the piston is at the end of its stroke, is said to be set line and line.

Liner. A facing interposed between two surfaces to diminish the wear. Liners are used between the driving wheel hubs and driving boxes, between the firebox and the expansion pads, etc. See **Smokebox Liner, Smokebox Door Liner**.

Link. 1. "A short connecting piece, of circular or other equivalent shape; as one of the oval rings or divisions of a chain."—Knight.

2. (Coupling Links.) A short bar with an eye at each end for connecting two things together or for supporting one from another. When used alone the term in this connection always means a **Coupling Link**, which see.

3. (Valve Gear.) 7, Figs. 1813-1815; Figs. 1911-1916. A slotted piece of metal, slightly curved, part of a valve gear. In the Stephenson gear the link has an eccentric rod attached to each end, and by means of a hanger on the reverse arm, the position of the link can be altered so as to put either eccentric rod wholly or partly in operation. In the Walschaerts gear the link is fixed or stationary in contrast to the shifting Stephenson link, being pivoted at its center to a bracket or fixed support and operated by a rod that receives its motion from a return crank on the main crank pin. To alter the position of the valve the link block is shifted, thus moving the rod attached to the valve stem. British, occasionally expansion link.

Link and Pin Coupler. An old type of drawbar by which cars were connected together by a link and a pin. There were a great variety of shapes and devices, but they have now been almost entirely replaced by the M. C. B. automatic coupler.

Link Block. 8, Figs. 1813-1815. An iron or steel block fitted on two faces to the curvature of the inside of the link and sliding in it, and having a pivot by which it transmits motion to the end of the rocker or transmission bar.

Link Block Pin. 29, Figs. 1911-1913. A pivot secured to the link block and connecting it to the rocker arm.

Link End Block. A piece forming either end of a built-up link, held to the sides of the link by a bolt passing through it. Also called a link filling piece.

Link End Block Bolt. A bolt holding a link end block in place.

Link Hanger. 1. (Valve Gear). See **Link Lifter**.
2. (Swing Motion Trucks). See **Swing Link**.

Link Hanger Eye Bolt. A bolt passing through the truck transoms, from which a short swing hanger is suspended.

Link Lifter. 14, Figs. 1813-1815. A bar by which the link is raised or lowered, having its upper end pivoted to the end of the reverse shaft arm and its lower end to a link saddle by means of the link saddle pin. On locomotives having a transmission bar, by means of which the link block moves the rocker, the lifters are often made double, one on each side of the link. Called also a link hanger. British, link suspension rod or suspension link.

Link Lifter Oil Cup. An oil cup attached to a link lifter and having an oil pipe leading from it to the bearing of the link saddle pin.

Link Motion. Figs. 1809-2096. The name given to the arrangement of links, rockers, eccentric rods, etc., for changing the relative positions of the valves and the valve seat of a locomotive and thus regulating the admission of steam to either end of the cylinders. The purpose of link motion is to enable the engineman to control the admission of steam through the slide valve ports to the cylinders, so that the locomotive may run either forward or backward, at high speed or low speed. See **Valve Gear**.

Link Oil Cup. An oil cup attached to a link to distribute oil to the inside wearing surfaces.

Link Plate (Walschaerts Valve Gear). Fig. 1812. A curved strip or covering piece, bolted to the side of the link.

Link Saddle. 28, Figs. 1813-1815. A plate or holder bolted to the link midway between the ends and carrying a pin for the attachment of the link lifter.

Link Saddle Bolt. One of the bolts that fasten a link saddle to a link.

Link Saddle Pin. 29, Figs. 1813-1815. A pivot secured to the link saddle and passing through the lower end of a link lifter.

Link Saddle Pin Washer. A washer on the end of a saddle pin under the head of the nut.

Link Suspension Rod (British). See **Link Lifter**.

Lip. See **Retaining Lip** (Steel Tired Wheels).

Little Giant Bell Ringer. Figs. 3265-3266.

Live Lever. 13, Figs. 4294-4382. The one of a pair of truck brake levers to which the brake power is first applied is sometimes given this title, the other lever being termed the dead lever.

Lobdell Cast Iron Wheel. Fig. 4550.

Lock. 1. A fastening between two pieces.

2. A device to prevent movement of one part relative to another.

3. A fastening for a door operated by a key.

4. (M. C. B. Couplers). The catch which drops in front of the tail of the knuckle and holds it in place when two couplers come together.

Lock Lifter. (Automatic Coupler). The part of the mechanism inside the coupler head in some types of M. C. B. couplers which is moved by the uncoupling rod and in moving lifts the knuckle lock so that the knuckle can open.

Lock Nut. The outer one of a pair of nuts on one bolt, which, by screwing up separately to a tight bearing, locks the inner one. A large number of special forms of lock nuts and nut locks, which serve the same purpose, are in use which are not strictly included under the above definition. Two of these are shown in Figs. 3340-3343.

Locomotive. General Views, Figs. 2-74; Elevations, Figs. 75-125. A self-propelled vehicle running on rails, for the purpose of hauling cars. It may be operated by steam, electricity, gas from volatile oils, or compressed air. Few compressed air locomotives have been built, but they resemble steam locomotives in general design and mode of utilizing the expansible fluid. See **Electric Locomotives.** Steam locomotives consist of a boiler and engine mounted on a frame supported on wheels which are turned by the engine. The boiler contains water and has a firebox forming part of it in which fuel is burned to supply heat to the water and convert it into steam. The steam passes through a valve, called a throttle valve, thence through pipes to the steam chests, from which valves, operated by a connection from the main shaft or axle, automatically admit it alternately to each end of the cylinders and exhaust it therefrom into the atmosphere through the exhaust pipes and stack. The expansive force of the steam moves the pistons, piston rods and crossheads back and forth, and, as the crosshead moves in guides, and has one end of the main rod connected to it at the wrist pin, while the other end of the main rod is connected to the crank pin on the driving wheel, the reciprocating motion of the piston is thereby changed into a rotary motion of the driving wheels. A locomotive thus transforms stored-up or potential energy of fuel into the kinetic energy or mechanical work of propelling itself and hauling cars.

During the past thirty years there has been a marked tendency toward increasing the weight of locomotives for all classes of service. In 1876 a locomotive with a cylinder 16 inches in diameter and 24 inch piston stroke was usual on American railways. Such engines had a total heating surface of between 1,100 square feet and 1,200 square feet, and weighed about 40 tons. The weights of trains were being increased and this led to the introduction of 17 inch x 24 inch cylinders until the limits of the boiler capacity to furnish steam had been reached. Up to this time the firebox was narrow and was down between the frames. The raising of the foundation ring to the top of the frames and widening it so that the outside of the firebox occupied the whole of the distance between the driving wheels, made possible an increase of grate area, and with it the heating surface and the steaming capacity of the boiler. This was an epoch in the development made by Mr. Theodore N. Ely in the Class K locomotives built for the Pennsylvania R. R. in 1881. Advantage was at once taken of this to increase the power, but it was done cautiously because of the prevailing opinion that the weight on any single wheel ought not exceed 12,000 pounds. When the track was made strong enough, weights and heating surfaces were increased until in 1890 engines with 1,800 to 1,900 square feet of heating surface were not uncommon.

The demand for increased power still continuing, the next step was to place the firebox back of the driving wheels and then widen it so as to extend over a pair of trailing wheels of small diameter that were used to carry it. This can reasonably be called another marking point in the history of the locomotive, and was first done by the Baldwin Locomotive Works in their Columbia (2-4-2) locomotive shown at the Chicago Exposition in 1893. This made it possible to obtain a firebox whose dimensions were limited only by the clearances of the right of way and the ability of the fireman to shovel coal.

With these possibilities the sizes of locomotives and boilers have been rapidly increased. The tubes have been lengthened from 12 feet or less, the common practice during the early stages of this development, to 18 or 19 feet, while tubes 20 feet and 21 feet long are in use. Heating surfaces have increased to more than 5,600 square feet, and the weights on driving wheels have risen to 28,000 pounds on each wheel. At present the limits of the fireman's endurance, the strength of materials and the weight on wheels seem to have been nearly reached.

Locomotive engineers are now looking for a practical automatic or mechanical stoker which will extend one of the limitations to higher power. When this is done the demand may come for a further increase of the tractive power of ordinary road locomotives (30,000 pounds to 40,000 pounds) to a nearer approach to certain special types that now have a tractive power of more than 70,000 pounds.

A good summary of locomotive performances is that included in the report of the tests made on the locomotive testing plant of the Pennsylvania Railroad at the St. Louis Exposition in 1904. This summary is reprinted below. Four passenger and four freight locomotives were tested at all speeds and different loads. Of the freight locomotives two were simple engines, one a two-cylinder cross compound and one a four-cylinder tandem compound. The passenger locomotives were all four-cylinder engines compounded on different systems. Two were European engines. The summary follows:

BOILER PERFORMANCE.

1. Contrary to a common assumption, the results show that when forced to maximum power, the large boilers delivered as much steam per unit area of heating surface as the small ones.

2. At maximum power, a majority of the boilers tested delivered 12 or more pounds of steam per square foot of heating surface per hour; two delivered more than 14 pounds, and one, the second in point of size, delivered 16.3 pounds. These values expressed in terms of boiler horse-power per square foot of heating surface are 0.34, 0.40 and 0.47, respectively.

3. The two boilers holding the first and second place with respect to weight of steam delivered per square foot of heating surface are those of passenger locomotives.

4. The quality of steam delivered by the boilers of locomotives under constant conditions of operation is high, varying somewhat with different locomotives and with changes in the amount of power developed, between the limits of 98.3 per cent. and 99.0 per cent.

5. The evaporative efficiency is generally maximum when the power delivered is least. Under conditions of maximum efficiency, most of the boilers tested evaporated between 10 and 12 pounds of water per pound of dry coal. The efficiency falls as the rate of evaporation increases. When the power developed is greatest, its value commonly lies between limits of 6 and 8 pounds of water per pound of dry coal.

6. The observed temperature of the firebox under low rates of combustion lies between the limits of 1,400 degrees F. and 2,000 degrees F., depending apparently upon characteristics of the locomotive. As the rate of combustion is increased, the temperature slowly increases, maximum values generally lying between the limits of 2,100 and 2,300 degrees F.

7. The smokebox temperature for all boilers, when worked at light power, is not far from 500 degrees F. As the power is increased, the temperature rises, the maximum value depending upon the extent to which the boiler is forced. For the locomotives tested, it lies in most cases between 600 and 700 degrees.

8. With reference to grate area, the results prove beyond question that the furnace losses due to excess air are not increased by increasing the area. In general, it appears that the boilers for which the ratio of grate surface to heating surface is largest are those of greatest capacity.

9. A brick arch in the firebox results in some increase in furnace temperature and improves the combustion of the gases.

10. The loss of heat through imperfect combustion is in most cases small, except as represented by the discharge from the stack of solid particles of fuel.

11. Relatively large firebox heating surface appears to give no advantage either with reference to capacity or efficiency. The fact seems to be that the tube heating surface is capable of absorbing such heat as may not be taken up by the firebox.

12. The value of the Serve tube over the plain tube of the same outside diameter, either as a means for increasing capacity or efficiency, was not definitely determined.

13. The draft in the front end for any given rate of combustion as measured in inches of water, depends upon the proportions of the locomotive and the thickness and condition of the fire. Under light power, its value may not exceed an inch, but it increases rapidly as the power is increased. Representative maximum values derived from the tests lie between the limits of 5 inches and 8.8 inches.

14. Insufficient openings in the ash pan and the mechanism of the front end, especially the diaphragm, are shown by the tests to lead to the dissipation of considerable portions of the draft force.

THE ENGINE.

15. The indicated horse-power of the modern simple freight locomotive tested may be as great as 1,000 or 1,100; that of a modern compound passenger locomotive may exceed 1,600 horse-power.

16. The maximum indicated horse-power per square foot of grate surface lies, for the freight locomotives, between the limits of 31.2 and 24.1; for the passenger locomotives, between the limits of 33.5 and 28.1.

17. The steam consumption per indicated horse-power hour necessarily depends upon the conditions of speed and cut-off. For the simple freight locomotives tested, the average minimum is 23.7. The consumption when developing maximum power is 23.8, and when under those conditions which proved to be the least efficient, 29.0.

18. The compound locomotives tested, using saturated steam, consumed from 18.6 to 27 pounds of steam per indicated horse-power hour. Aided by a superheater, the minimum consumption is reduced to 16.6 pounds of superheated steam per hour.

19. In general, the steam consumption of simple locomotives decreases with increase of speed, while that of the compound locomotives increases. From this statement it appears that the relative advantages to be derived from the use of the compound diminish as the speed is increased.

20. Tests under a partially opened throttle show that when the degree of throttling is slight, the effect is not appreciable. When the degree of throttling is more pronounced, the performance is less satisfactory than when carrying the same load with a full throttle and a shorter cut-off.

THE LOCOMOTIVE AS A WHOLE.

21. The percentage of the cylinder power which appears as a stress in the drawbar, diminishes with increase of speed. At 40 revolutions per minute, the maximum is 94 and the minimum 77; at 280 revolutions per minute, the maximum is 87 and the minimum 62.

22. The loss of power between the cylinder and drawbar is greatly affected by the character of the lubricant. It appears from the tests that the substitution of grease for oil upon axles and crank pins increases the machine friction from 75 to 100 per cent.

23. The coal consumption per dynamometer horse-power hour, for the simple freight locomotives tested, is at low speeds not less than 3.5 pounds nor more than 4.5 pounds, the value varying with running conditions. At the highest speeds covered by the tests, the coal consumption for the simple locomotives increased to more than 5 pounds.

24. The coal consumption per dynamometer horse-power hour, for the compound freight locomotives tested is, for low speeds, between 2.9 and 3.7 pounds. Results at higher speeds were obtained only from a two-cylinder compound, the efficiency of which under all conditions is shown to be very high. The coal consumption per dynamometer horse-power hour for this locomotive at the higher speeds increases from 3.2 to 3.6 pounds.

25. The coal consumption per dynamometer horse-power hour, for the four compound passenger locomotives tested, varies from 2.2 to more than 5 pounds per hour, depending upon the running conditions. In the case of all of these locomotives, the consumption increases rapidly as the speed is increased.

26. A comparison of the performance of the compound freight locomotives with that of the simple freight locomotives is very favorable to the compounds. For a given amount of power at the drawbar, the poorest compound shows a saving in coal over the best simple which will average above 10 per cent., while the best compound shows a saving over the poorest simple which is not far from 40 per cent. It should be remembered, however, that

the conditions of the tests, which provide for the continuous operation of the locomotives at constant speed and load throughout the period covered by the observations, are all favorable to the compound.

27. It is a fact of more than ordinary significance that a steam locomotive is capable of delivering a horse-power at the drawbar upon the consumption of but a trifle more than 2 pounds of coal per hour. This fact gives the locomotive high rank as a steam power plant.

28. It is worthy of mention that the coal consumption per horse-power hour developed at the drawbar by the different locomotives tested presents marked differences. Some of these are easily explained from a consideration of the characteristics of the locomotives involved. Where the data is not sufficient to permit the assignment of a definite cause, there can be no doubt but that an extension of the study already made will serve to reveal it.

Locomotive (Standard Method of Conducting Efficiency Tests). The American Railway Master Mechanics' Association, in 1894, adopted as standard a method of conducting tests of locomotives. The directions here given apply largely to both shop and road tests, but especially to the latter.

The tests are as follows:

A. Preparations for Test and Location of Instruments.

1. The locomotive should be put in good condition preparatory to the test. The boiler and tubes should be tight, and both the interior and exterior surfaces should be clean, and, if possible, free from scale. There should be no lost motion in the valve gear, and the valves should be set properly. No change in the engines should be allowed during the progress of a series of tests, unless so ordered for the purposes of the trial.

A glass water-gage should be fitted to the boiler, if not already provided, and at the side of it there should be a graduated scale to assist in correcting water quantities, caused by change of inclination of the boiler, and difference of levels when beginning and ending a test. The notches on the quadrant should be marked by large figures, so that they can be read by the cab assistant. The throttle valve lever should be provided with a scale so as to show the degree of opening of the throttle valve.

The point of cut-off of the valves should be determined for each notch in the quadrant.

2. The valves and pistons should be tested for leakage with the engine at rest. The steam valve can be tried by setting the engine so that the valve on one side will be at the center of its throw, in which position both ports are usually covered, and pulling open the throttle valve, blocking the drivers if there is a tendency for the engine to be set in motion. Leakage of the valve, if any occurs, will show itself by escaping at the open cylinder cocks. The tightness of the piston may be tested by setting the engine so that it makes steam, blocking the drivers and opening the throttle valve. This should be tried first on one cylinder and then on the other, and, if desired, it may be tried with the pistons at various points in the stroke. The leakage, if any occurs, will be shown at the open cylinder cock.

3. The following instruments should be verified or calibrated: Steam gages, draft gage, pyrometer, thermometers for calorimeter and feed-water, water meter, tank, revolution counter, indicator springs, dynamometer springs and dynamometer recording mechanism. The radiation loss on the steam calorimeter should be determined, or the normal readings ascertained, and the quantity of steam which passes through the instrument in a given time should be measured.

4. The quantities of steam used by the various auxiliaries of the locomotive can be determined by noting the change in weight of the engine standing upon scales while they are each in use under the usual conditions for known times. Similarly leakage of water and steam can be determined. The quantities can then be properly deducted from the total water used.

5. To facilitate the measurement of coal and the determination of the quantity used during any desired period of the run, it is desirable to provide a sufficient number of sacks of a size holding a weight of, say, 100 pounds, and weigh the coal into these sacks preparatory to starting on the test. If desired, the sacks may be numbered to facilitate the accuracy of record.

6. The instruments and other apparatus that should be provided and their locations are as follows:

To facilitate the work of operating the indicators and reading the instruments at the front end, the smokebox should be surrounded with a wooden

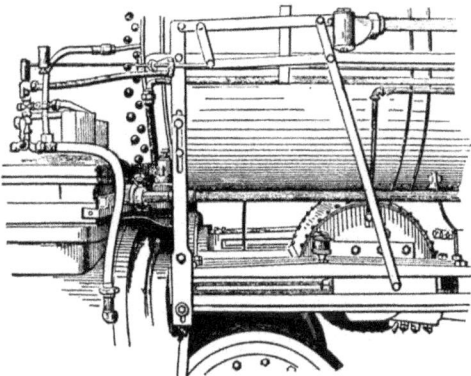

fence, or "pilot-box," as it may be called, resting on the top of the cow-catcher, and extending back far enough to inclose also the sides of the cylinders. This box is floored over above the cylinder heads, and the inclosure thus provided forms a convenient place for the accommodation of the assistants at this end of the locomotive, and it affords them some measure of protection against wind and rain, as also the joltings and vibrations due to rapid travel.

A special steam-gage with a long siphon is to be used for registering the boiler pressure. It can best be located on the left-hand side of the cab.

The indicator apparatus which is most suitable consists of a three-way cock for the attachment of the indicators, and some form of pantagraph or other correct reducing motion for the driving rig. The pipes leading from the cock to the cylinder should be ¾ inch diameter inside, and they should connect into the side of the cylinder rather than into the two heads. The indicator should also be piped so that a steam-chest diagram can be drawn by it, and from this the steam-chest pressure determined. Sharp bends in the pipe should be avoided, and they should be well covered, to intercept radiation. The three-way cock should be provided with a clamp rigidly secured to the cylinder, and thus overcome any tendency of the indicators to move longitudinally with reference to the driving rig. Absolute rigidity is highly essential in this particular. Either of two forms of pantagraph motion may be used. In both of these the reduced motion is transmitted to the indicator through a light rod, working horizontally. By this means a cord eight or ten inches in length is sufficient for connection to the indicator. Care should be taken to set the instrument in such a position that the cord pin in the end of the rod travels in a direction pointing to the groove in the paper drum. Pantagraph motions arranged as noted are preferable to the common pendulum and quadrant reducing mechanism, with its long stretch of cord.

A draft gage consisting of a U-tube containing water, properly graduated in inches, should be placed in the cab and connected to the smokebox by a ⅜-inch pipe. This long pipe steadies the water, and the readings can be taken by the cab assistant.

A pyrometer for showing the temperature of the escaping gases should be used in a position below the tip of the exhaust nozzles.

The calorimeter should be attached either to the steam dome at a point close to the throttle opening or to the steam passages in the saddle casting on one side, according as it is desired to obtain the character of the steam at one point or the other. The former location is preferred. A perforated ½-inch pipe should be used for sampling and conveying the steam to the calorimeter pipe.

The water meter should be attached to the suction pipe of the injector, and located at a point where it can be conveniently read when the locomotive is running. It should be provided with a check valve to prevent hot water from flowing back to it from the injector and a strainer to intercept foreign material.

To measure the depth of the water in the tank a metallic float should be used carrying a vertical tube which slides upon a graduated rod, the lower end of which rests upon the bottom of the tank. This should be placed at the center of gravity of the water space. If the desired location can not be used, provision should be made for ascertaining the level or inclination of the tank. The best device for this purpose is a plumb line of a certain known length, provided at the bottom with a double horizontal scale having one set of divisions parallel to the side of the tank and the other set at right angles to it. From the readings on these scales referred to, the length of the line, the level of the tank in both directions can be ascertained. A similar device should be attached to the boiler to correct for the variation of its inclination. The plumb line may be conveniently attached for this purpose at some point near the front end.

The revolution counter should be placed near the front end of the engine, in plain view of the pilot-box. It is operated through a belt from the driver axle. This recommendation applies to that form of counter which shows at a glance the exact speed in revolutions per minute.

A stroke counter should be provided for showing the number of strokes made by the air pump.

Electric connection should be made between the dynamometer car and cab, so that dynamometer records and indicator diagrams may be taken simultaneously. Another desirable provision is a speaking-tube leading from the dynamometer car to the locomotive cab, and one also to the pilox-box.

7. It is needless, except for a complete record of directions for preparatory work, to call attention to the desirability of having the test, and especially the road test, made under the supervision of a competent person, who is not only familiar with the details of the testing, but also with the proper method of firing and mechanical operation of the locomotive. This is a most important factor, for it is only the clear-headed and able experimenter who is likely to obtain satisfactory work in this most difficult department of engineering tests.

The conductor of the test is best able to determine the number of assistants required, the various duties of the men, and the manner of making records. In general, three (3) men are sufficient to conduct a locomotive test, one (1) being at each cylinder, and one (1) in the cab for taking records.

The men at the cylinders will take indicator diagrams, and one will read the revolution counter and the pyrometer. The indicator papers will be numbered in consecutive order for each cylinder before the test begins, and when the diagram is taken the papers will be deposited through a slot in a box near each assistant.

The cab assistant notes the time of leaving and arriving at stations, the position and time of opening and closing the throttle, the time of taking indicator diagrams, for which he shall determine the time and give the signal by any effective means; the time of blowing off, the time the blower is applied, the number of applications of the injector, the position of the reverse lever, the steam pressure, the draught gage, the time of passing important stations, the readings of the water glass, meter and air pump counter, the number of sacks of coal used, the reading of the tank float, the temperature of the feed-water and atmosphere, the direction and force of the wind, the condition of the rail and state of the weather. Many of these readings are as nearly as possible simultaneous with the signal for taking indicator diagrams, and one experienced man in the cab will have no difficulty in entering all of these records in a notebook properly prepared with ruled columns and headings. In case of short stops at stations, one of the men at the indicators can take the tank float observations, or any observation that is advisable at stations. The weights of coal placed upon the tender have been checked by these two persons when weighing it out to the engine. One man takes the level of the boiler at stopping places where this is required.

When the calorimeter and smoke box gas samples are used another assistant is required.

In the dynamometer car two (2) men are required, who record the time of each start and stop, the time of passing each station and mile-post, time of taking each indicator diagram as obtained from the signal given by the cab assistant, and all these events are marked on the dynamometer paper. These men, as well as one of the engine assistants, will note the direction and force of the wind, the temperature of the atmosphere and condition of the weather.

8. It is of great importance, after the preparatory work has been accomplished, that a preliminary run be made with the locomotive, in order to fairly test the apparatus and to accustom the men to their duties.

B. The Dynamometer Car.

With a suitable dynamometer car the force required to move the train, or the pull upon the drawbar, is registered upon a strip of paper traveling at a definite rate per mile. The scale upon which this diagram is drawn should be as large as is possible within reasonable limits. A scale of ¼ inch per 1,000 pounds pull is suitable, as the maximum register pull rarely exceeds 30,000 pounds.

The height of the diagram should be measured from a base line drawn upon the paper by a stationary pen, so located that when no force is exerted upon the drawbar the base line should coincide with zero pull.

The apparatus should be arranged to make a record of time marks in connection with the curve showing the pull. A chronometer should be provided having an electric circuit-breaker, by means of which a mark is made on the dynamometer paper every five (5) seconds. A better apparatus may be used in which a continuous speed curve is traced upon the paper parallel to the curve of pull. The ordinates of this curve, measured from a base line, give the speeds desired.

The location of mile-posts and other points along the route should be fixed upon the dynamometer paper by employing an additional pen, and operating it by means of electric press buttons, which are placed at convenient points in the car.

As already noted, a similar device should be provided for marking upon the dynamometer paper the time of taking indicator diagrams.

The rate of travel of the paper per mile should be such that one inch measured upon the diagrams represents 100 feet for short-distance work, and for long-distance work ½ inch to ¼ inch should be used to represent 100 feet of track. The driving mechanism for the paper should be so arranged that it can be changed to give these three proportions. It is necessary to have all the registering pens located upon the same transverse line at a right angle with the direction of the movement of the paper in order that simultaneous data may be recorded.

C. Method of Conducting the Road Test.

The locomotive having been brought to the train, the steam pressure being at or near the working point, the fire being clean and in good condition, the ash pan being also clean, observations are also taken, say, five (5) minutes before starting-time, of the thickness and condition of the fire, the height of water in the boiler, the depth in the tank, the levels, the water meter and the air pump counter, and thereafter the regular observations are carried forward, and coal is fired from the weighed sacks.

Indicator diagrams should be taken as frequently as possible, the intervals between them being not over two minutes.

Other regular observations should be taken at close intervals. Calorimeter readings, when taken, should be continued for at least five (5) minutes at one minute intervals.

At water stations careful records should be obtained of water heights and levels of boiler and tank.

As the end of the route is approached, the fire should be burned down so as to leave the same amount and the same condition as at the start. When the end is finally reached the fire should be raked and its condition carefully noted. If it differs from that which obtained at the beginning, an estimated allowance must be made for such difference.

At the close of the test the height of water in the boiler should be the same as at the beginning, or, if not, the difference, corrected for inclination of the boiler, should be allowed for.

During the process of weighing the coal into the sacks numerous samples should be obtained and placed in a covered box, and a final sample of these selected. This is to be dried and subjected to chemical analysis and calorimeter test. The sample is weighed before and after drying, and data obtained for determining the weight of dry coal used during the test. The temperature of the feedwater can be best taken at the tank cock, in order to obtain that of a mixed sample.

The duration of the road test is the length of time which the throttle valve is open.

D. The Data and Results.

The data and results of the road test may be tabulated in the form given in Table No. 1. This form corresponds in general with that recommended for shop test, namely, Table No. 2.

TABLE No. 1.

Data and Results of Road Test on ... Engine,

Made ... 19 .

General dimensions, etc. (to be accompanied by a complete description of engine with drawings and dimensions, also of train and route):
1. Kind of engine.............................
2. Size of cylinders...........................
3. Clearance of cylinders................per cent.
4. Area of heating surface...................sq. ft.
5. Area of grate surface....................sq. ft.
6. Size of exhaust nozzles..................inches
7. Average weight of locomotive and tender (including water) ....tons
8. Number of cars ....
9. Weight of cars ....
10. Length of route ....miles
11. Number of ton-miles of train load.....ton-miles
12. Number of ton-miles of total load.....ton-miles
13. Schedule time of trips......................

Total Quantities.

14. Duration of time throttle valve is open....hours
15. Weight of dry coal burned.................lbs.
16. Weight of water evaporated, corrected for moisture in the steam and loss at injector* ....lbs.
17. Weight of ashes and refuse taken from ash pan ....lbs.
18. Weight of cinders from smokebox..........lbs.
19. Percentage of ash as found by coal calorimeter test ....per cent.
20. Total heat of combustion as found by calorimeter test ....B. T. U.
21. Results of chemical analysis of coal............

Power Data.

22. Mean effective pressure, H. P. cyls..........lbs.
23. Mean effective pressure, L. P. cyls..........lbs.
24. Average revolutions per minute............rev.
25. Indicated horse-power, H. P. cyls..........H. P.
26. Indicated horse-power, L. P. cyls..........H. P.
27. Indicated horse-power, whole engine......H. P.
28. Pull on drawbar ....lbs.
29. Dynamometer horse-power ....H. P.

Averages of Observations of Instruments.

30. Average boiler pressure ....lbs.
31. **Average steam-chest pressure** ....lbs.

---
*Should be corrected for steam used by calorimeter, air-pump, blower, safety valve and whistle, to find cylinder results—line 56.

32. Average temperature of smoke-box......... °
33. Average draft suction .... "
34. Average temperature of feed-water......... °
35. Average temperature of atmosphere........ °
36. Average percentage of moisture in the steam ....per cent.
37. Maximum percentage of moisture in the steam ....per cent.
38. Weather, wind, etc. ....

Other Data.

39. Average position of throttle..................
40. Average position of reversing lever............
41. Average speed in miles per hour..............
42. Maximum speed in miles per hour............
43. Number of stops ....
44. Average number of strokes of air pumps per minute ....
45. Total estimated weight of steam used by air pump per hour ....lbs.
46. Estimated loss of steam at safety valve per hour ....lbs.
47. Estimated loss of steam at whistle per hour ....lbs.
48. Estimated weight of steam used by blower per hour ....lbs.
49. Estimated loss of steam at calorimeter per hour ....lbs.

Hourly Quantities.

50. Weight of dry coal burned per hour........lbs.
51. Weight of dry coal burned per hour per square foot of grate surface............lbs.
52. Weight of coal burned per square foot of heating surface ....lbs.
53. Weight of water evaporated per hour........lbs.
54. Equivalent weight of water evaporated per hour with feed-water at 100° and pressure 70 lbs. ....lbs.
55. Equivalent weight of water from 100° at 70 lbs. evaporated per square foot of heating surface ....lbs.
56. Weight of water consumed by engine cylinder (line 53, less sum of lines 45, 46, 47, 48 and 49).......................lbs.

Principal Results—Complete Engine and Boiler.

57. Coal consumed per I. H. P. per hour........lbs.
58. Coal consumed per dynamometer horse-power per hour ....lbs.
59. Coal consumed per ton-mile of train-load....lbs.
60. Coal consumed per ton-mile of total load....lbs.
61. Weight of standard coal consumed per I. H. P. per hour ....lbs.
62. Weight of standard coal consumed per dynamometer horse-power per hour.........lbs.
63. Weight of standard coal consumed per ton-mile of train-load ....lbs.
64. Weight of standard coal consumed per ton-mile of total load..................lbs.

Boiler Results.

65. Water evaporated per pound of coal.........lbs.
66. Equivalent evaporation per pound of coal from and at 212° ....lbs.
67. Equivalent evaporation per pound of combustible from and at 212° ....lbs.
68. Heat imparted to each pound of steam used from average temperature of feed at average steam pressure in British thermal units ....

Cylinder Data.

69. Mean initial pressure above atmosphere.....lbs.
                               H. P. Cyl. L. P. Cyl.
70. Cut-off pressure above zero ....lbs. ....
71. Release pressure above zero ....lbs. ....
72. Compression pressure above zero ....lbs. ....
73. Lowest back pressure above or below atmosphere ....lbs. ....
74. Proportion of forward stroke completed at cut-off ....
75. Proportion of forward stroke completed at release ....
76. Proportion of return stroke uncompleted at compression ....
77. Mean effective pressure (lines 22 and 23).......lbs. ....

Cylinder Results.

78. Total water consumed per indicated horsepower per hour, corrected for moisture in steam ....lbs.
79. Water consumed per I. H. P. per hour by cylinders alone (from line 56)............lbs.
                               H. P. Cyl L. P. Cyl.
80. Steam accounted for by indicators at cut-offs....lbs. ....
81. Steam accounted for by indicator at release....lbs. ....
82. Proportion of feed-water used by cylinders (line 79) accounted for at cut-off ....
83. Proportion of feed-water used by cylinders accounted for at release.
84. Total heat supplied by boiler to cylinders per hour in British thermal units ....
85. Total heat supplied by boiler to cylinder per minute per indicated horsepower in British thermal units ....
86. Total heat supplied by boiler to cylinders per minute per dynamometer horse-power in British thermal units..

The following form for the tabulation of the results of locomotive tests will be found convenient. They can, of course, be modified to suit any method of testing, whether standard or not:

LOCOMOTIVE TESTS—GENERAL RESULTS.

........................Railroad Co.
........Tests of Locomotive No. ...., between......
and..............Distance....Miles. Train No....
....Bound. ...., 19....
Kind of Coal................ Coal Analysis..........
Calorimetic Value of Coal............................
  Trip No. ....
  Date ....
  Left ....at....................

Arrived ....at.....................
Left ....at.....................
Arrived ....at.....................
1. Weather ....
2. Mean temperature of atmosphere...............
3. Direction of wind ....
4. Velocity of wind, miles per hour...............
5. Condition of rails ....
6. Weight of train in tons of 2,000 lbs., including locomotive, tender, passengers and freight ....
7. Weight of train in tons of 2,000 lbs., excluding the locomotive and tender............
8. Equivalent number of standard cars at................tons each...................
9. Size of exhaust nozzle, single or double.........
10. Maximum boiler pressure by gage.............
11. Minimum boiler pressure by gage.............
12. Average boiler pressure by gage ....
13. Prevailing position of throttle (wide open=1.00) ....
14. Prevailing position of reverse lever (notch)....
15. Prevailing points of cut-off ....
16. Schedule time in motion ....
17. Actual time in motion ....
18. Time made up in minutes.......................
19. Aggregate intermediate stops, minutes.........
20. Time during which power was developed, or throttle open ....
21. Maximum number of revolutions per minute....
22. Minimum number of seconds per mile..........
23. Maximum rate of speed, miles per hour........
24. Average speed, miles per hour..................
25. Actual weight of coal fired ....
26. Moisture in coal, percentage ....
27. Dry coal fired ....
28. Actual weight of wood used ....
29. Total weight of coal fired (wood added at .4)....
30. Weight of refuse in firebox and ash pan........
31. Weight of unconsumed coal recovered from firebox and ash pan ....
32. Total weight of coal consumed (Item 29-31)....
33. Net weight of ashes in firebox and ash pan.....
34. Weight of cinders (sparks) in smokebox........
35. Percentage of ash in coal......................
36. Percentage of cinders (sparks).................
37. Percentage of total refuse ....
38. Percentage of combustible consumed ....
39. Weight of combustible utilized ....
40. Number of miles run per ton (2,000 lbs.) of coal ....
41. Number of pounds of coal used per mile........
42. Coal used per ton of train per 100 miles........
43. Coal used per car-mile ....
44. Average weight of coal burned per square foot of grate surface per hour..................
45. Total coal per indicated horse-power developed per hour ....
46. Average temperature of feed-water ....
47. Weight of water drawn from tender ....
48. Waste of injector, leakage, etc.................
49. Weight of water apparently evaporated (Item 47-48) ....
50. Percentage of moisture in steam ....
51. Water actually evaporated, corrected for quality of steam ....
52. Actual evaporation per pound of total coal......
53. Equivalent evaporation from and at 212° per pound of coal ....
54. Equivalent evaporation from and at 212° per pound of combustible ....
55. Water used per ton of train per 100 miles......
56. Water used per car-mile ....
57. Water used per hour while developing power ....
58. Water used per indicated horse-power per hour ....
59. Water used per sq. ft. of heating surface, from and at 212° ....
60. Water used per sq. ft. of grate surface, from and at 212° ....
61. Maximum indicated horse-power developed.....
62. Average indicated horse-power developed......
63. Dry steam used per indicated horse-power, per hour, per indicated diagram..............
64. Average number of sq. ft. of heating surface per indicated horse-power................
65. Average number of indicated horse-power per sq. ft. of grate surface....................
66. Prevailing temperature in smokebox while using steam ....
67. Prevailing draft in smokebox while using steam, in inches of water ....

SHOP TEST.

A. Preparation and Location of Instruments.

In preparing for a shop test the preparations described for the road test should be followed so far as the nature of the test requires. When run as a stationary engine the locomotive is not circumscribed by the conditions of road service, and many provisions required on the road are unnecessary. It is unnecessary to determine the quantity of steam consumed by the air pump and auxiliaries, for these are not brought into use on the shop test; and no occasion exists for finding the quantity lost at the safety valve, for on the continuous shop run the steam pressure can be maintained at a uniform point, and blowing off readily prevented. It is unnecessary to use sacks for the convenient measure of coal, because the coal can be readily weighed up in lots as fast as needed for the test. It is unnecessary to provide a "pilot-box," and no fixed location of the instruments is required, as on the road test. The feed-water may be weighed before it is supplied to the tank, and the tank may be used in this case as a reservoir, the float showing its depth. The meter would thus be unnecessary as the principal instrument of measurement, but a meter is in all cases useful as a check upon this most important element in the data. The long indicator pipes required on the road test may be dispensed with and one indicator applied close to each end of the cylinder, a practice much to be preferred to the use of a three-way cock and the single indicator. The dynamometer car is not required, but its equivalent should be provided, consisting of a dynamometer which registers the pull on the drawbar in the same manner as the device used on the road.

The number of assistants required on a shop test is less than that needed for a road test. A good test can be made with four (4) assistants, distributed as follows:

One assistant for operating indicators.
One assistant for measuring water.
Two (2) assistants for general observations and coal measurement.

B. Conditions of Test.

The test should be continued for a run of at least two (2) hours from the time the normal conditions have been established.

At the close of the test the water height in the boiler and the height of water in the tank should be the same as at the beginning, or proper corrections made for any differences which may exist.

The firebox and ash pit are then cleaned, and such unburnt coal as may be contained in the refuse is separated, weighed and deducted from the total weight of coal fired. The balance of the refuse is weighed, as also the cinders removed from the smokebox.

During the progress of the test samples of the various charges of coal should be obtained, and at its close a final sample of these should be selected, dried and subjected to chemical analysis and calorimeter test. The weight of the sample is taken before and after drying to ascertain the weight of moisture contained in the fuel.

C. The Data and Results.

The data and results of the shop test can best be arranged in the manner indicated in Table No. 2. So far as these are in common with the data and results obtained on the road test, the forms used on both kinds of tests are identical.

TABLE No. 2.

Data and Results of Shop Test on....Engine, Made 19.....

General dimensions, etc. (to be accompanied by a complete description, with drawings and full dimensions).

1. Kind of engine ....
2. Size and clearance of cylinders ....
3. Area of heating surface ....
4. Area of grate surface ....
5. Diameter of exhaust nozzles ....

Total Quantities.   Whole Run.
6. Duration ....hrs. ......
7. Weight of dry coal burned, including .4 weight of wood................lbs. ......
8. Weight of water evaporated corrected for moisture in the steam......lbs. ......
9. Weight of ashes and refuse from ash pan ....lbs. ......
10. Weight of cinders from smokebox..lbs. ......
11. Percentage of ash as found by calorimeter test ....per cent. ......
12. Total heat of combustion per lb. coal as found by calorimeter test..B. T. U. ......

Power Data.
13. Mean effective pressure, high-pressure cylinders ....lbs. ......
14. Mean effective pressure, low-pressure cylinders ....lbs. ......
15. Average revolutions per minute......rev. ......
16. Indicated horse-power, high-pressure cylinders ....H. P. ......
17. Indicated horse-power, low pressure cylinders ....H. P. ......
18. Indicated horse-power, total ......H. P. ......
19. Pull on drawbar ....lbs. ......
20. Dynamometer horse-power ....H. P. ......

Averages of Observations.
21. Average boiler pressure ....lbs. ......
22. Average steam chest pressure........lbs. ......
23. Average temperature of smokebox... ° ......
24. Average draft suction .... ″ ......
25. Average temperature of feed-water.. ° ......
26. Average temperature of atmosphere. ° ......
27. Average percentage of moisture in the steam ....per cent. ......
28. Maximum percentage of moisture in the steam ....per cent. ......

Hourly Quantities.   Whole Run.
29. Weight of dry coal burned per hour.lbs. ......
30. Weight of dry coal burned per hour per sq. ft. of grate surface.........lbs. ......
31. Weight of coal burned per hour per sq. ft. of heating surface..........lbs. ......
32. Weight of water evaporated per hour lbs. ......
33. Equivalent weight of water evaporated per hour with feed-water at 100° and pressure at 70 lbs. ....lbs. ......
34. Equivalent weight of water from 100° at 70 lbs. evaporated per sq. ft. of heating surface ....lbs. ......

Principal Results, Complete Engine and Boiler.
35. Coal consumed per I. H. P. per hour..lbs. ......
36. Coal consumed per dynamometer horse-power per hour ....lbs. ......
37. Weight of "standard coal" consumed per I. H. P. per hour..............lbs. ......
38. Weight of "standard coal" consumed per dynamometer horse-power per hour ....lbs. ......

Boiler Results.
39. Water evaporated per pound of coal..lbs. ......
40. Equivalent evaporation per pound of coal from and at 212° ....lbs. ......
41. Equivalent evaporation per pound of **combustible from and at 212°** ....lbs. ......
42. Heat imparted to each pound of steam used from average temperature of feed at average steam pressure in British thermal units....... ......

Cylinder Data.
43. Mean initial pressure above atmosphere ....lbs.. ......
                                            H. P. Cyl. L. P. Cyl.
44. Cut-off pressure a b o v e zero ....lbs. ....
45. Release pressure a b o v e zero ....lbs. ....
46. Compression p r e s s u r e above zero ....lbs. ....
47. L o w e s t back pressure above or below atmosphere ....lbs. ....
48. Proportion of f o r w a r d s t r o k e completed at cut-off ....
49. Proportion of f o r w a r d stroke completed at release ....
50. Proportion of r e t u r n stroke uncompleted at compression ....

Cylinder Results.
51. Total water consumed per indicated horse-power per hour corrected for moisture in steam ....lbs. ......
52. Water consumed per I. H. P. per hour by cylinders alone (from line 51 less all measured losses) ....lbs. ......
                                            H. P. Cyl. L. P. Cyl.
53. Steam accounted for by indicators at cut-off....lbs. ....
54. Steam accounted for by indicators at release...lbs. ....

55. Proportion of feed-water used by cylinders (line 52) accounted for at cut-off ....lbs. ....
56. Proportion of feed-water used by cylinders accounted for at release..lbs. ....
57. Total heat supplied by boiler to cylinders per hour in British thermal units ....
58. Total heat supplied by boiler to cylinders per minute per indicated horse power in British thermal units ....
59. Total heat supplied by boiler to cylinders per minute per dynamometer horse-power in British thermal units.. ....

Reports should give a copy of a set of sample indicator diagrams, also combined diagram (in case of compound engines) and a chart showing graphically the principal data.

Locomotive Badge Plate. See **Name Plate.**

Locomotive Cylinder Boring Machine. Figs. 4957-4959. A special type of horizontal boring machine for boring and facing locomotive cylinders.

Locomotive Rod Boring Machine. Figs. 4960-4962. A machine for boring the ends of locomotive connecting rods. The boring spindles in this type of machine are adjustable for the different lengths of rods.

Longitudinal Brace (Engine Truck). 17, Figs. 3369-3380. Flat bars secured lengthwise of an engine truck frame between the center casting and the end pieces to strengthen it and keep it square. Usually called safety beam.

Lower Brake Rod. 14, Figs. 4294-4382. A rod which connects the two brake beams or levers of outer hung brakes. When two levers are used the rod is attached to each lever. It is sometimes supported in case of accident by a lower brake rod carrier. With inner hung brakes the substitute for the lower brake rod becomes a part in compression and is called the brake lever coupling bar.

Lubricator. 1. Any device, as an oil cup or grease cup, for holding a lubricant and supplying it to wearing surfaces. See **Oil Cup.**
2. A device for forcing oil to the valves and cylinders by means of steam pressure. **Figs. 3195-3205.**

Lubricator Steam Valve. Figs. 3206-3207. A valve, usually a globe valve, screwed into the cab turret, to control the supply of steam to the lubricator.

Lug. A projecting stud or ear to afford a bearing or point of attachment.

Lundholm Fuel Oil Burner. Figs. 772-774.

M

McCord Journal Box and Dust Guard. Figs. 4487-4489.
McLoughlin Flexible Steam Joint. Figs. 3774-3778.
McLoughlin Lock Nut. Figs. 3342-3343.
Machine Bolt. A bolt with a metal thread cut on it, and with a square or hexagonal head, especially if turned or finished. The word bolt, unqualified, usually means a machine bolt.

Magneto Speed Indicator (Electric Locomotive). Fig. 4668. A small magneto generator, driven from an axle, which shows on a dial in the cab the speed at any moment by the voltage developed at the terminals of the magneto.

Main Crank Pin. Fig. 1138. The crank pin to which the main rod is attached.

Main Reservoir (Air Brake). See **Reservoir,** 156, Figs. 77-124; Fig. 2463.

Main Reservoir Cut-out Cock (Air Brake). Fig. 2532. A special form of cut-out cock placed in the reservoir pipe near the main reservoir in the Westinghouse ET locomotive brake equipment. It is arranged for pipe connection to the duplex pump governor, and when closed to bleed off the pressure in the reservoir pipe when it is desired to remove the brake valves or feed valves.

Main Rod. Figs. 1155-1156, etc. Called also connecting rod, particularly in Great Britain. A large iron or steel rod of rectangular or I section, pivoted at one end to the crosshead wrist pin, and at the other to the main crank pin. It transmits the motion of the piston and piston rod to the driving wheels.

Main Rod Bearing. 9 and 12, Figs. 1155-1229. The brass and wedges inserted in the end of a main rod to form a bearing for the crank pin or the wrist pin.

Main Rod Brass. See **Main Rod Bearing** and **Bearing.**

Main Rod End. 11, Figs. 1155-1229. The enlargement on the end of a main rod which holds the brass or bearing. See **Stub End.**

Main Rod Oil Cup. Figs. 1286-1300; 1, Figs. 1155-1229. A receptacle for holding oil for lubricating a main rod bearing, frequently forged solid with and machined on the rod end. See **Oil Cup.**

Main Steam Valve (Air Pump.) 76, Figs. 2429-2435. A valve mechanism consisting of two main valve pistons of different diameter which operate the main slide valve to admit and exhaust steam above and below the steam piston. This valve mechanism is operated at the end of each stroke by alternately admitting and releasing steam pressure back of the larger main valve piston, through the medium of the reversing valve, 72, reversing valve rod, 71, and reversing valve plate, 69.

Major Pilot Coupler. Figs. 2362-2369.
Major Tender Coupler. Figs. 4019-4032.
Malleable Iron. Cast iron which has been annealed and the brittleness greatly decreased by packing the castings in iron pots containing forge scale, hematite ore or some other oxide of iron and subjecting them to a continued red heat for from four to six days. They are then allowed to cool slowly. The change which takes place is internal, and while little or no carbon is removed its physical condition is changed from graphite to amorphous or cement carbon and the iron is rendered less brittle. Malleable castings can be bent within moderate limits, but are not truly malleable like wrought iron. Many parts used in locomotive work are made of it, including couplers, brake levers, journal boxes and many small castings.

Mallet Articulated Compound Locomotive. Figs 22, 83-87. A system of compounding proposed by A. Mallet. The driving wheels are divided into two groups of two or three pairs of wheels each. The rear group is carried by the main frame of the engine, and is driven by two high-pressure cylinders. The forward group is carried by a supplementary frame and is driven by a pair of low-pressure cylinders; the frame and wheels of the low-pressure engine constituting a swiveling truck supporting the front end of the boiler. The object is to obtain a locomotive of great weight and power, but having a short rigid wheel base to permit its rounding sharp curves.

Mandrel. 1. (For Lathes.) A shaft serving as a temporary axis for objects to be turned.
2. (Foundry.) A plug around which a body of metal is cast.

Mandrel Pin or **Cross Bar** (Swing Link Hanger.) The bar which supports the spring plank. See **Swing Hanger.**

Manhole Cover. 1, Figs. 4067-4118. A plate or lid to close a **Tank Manhole,** which see.

Manhole Eye. 2, Figs. 4067-4118. A ring fastened to the lid of a **Tank Manhole,** which see.

Manhole Hinge. 3, Figs. 4067-4118. A hinge by which a tank manhole cover is attached to the manhole ring.

Mansell Retaining Ring. Fig. 4561. A mode of connecting steel tires to the wheel centers by a ring of an approximate L or U cross-section, which secures the tire to the wheel, so that every part of the tire is securely held, into however many pieces it may be ruptured.

Marker Lamp. Figs. 3317-3322. A Signal Lamp, which see, used on locomotives or trains to indicate the class of the train, whether first or second section of a regular train, helper engine or extra train. A classification lamp.

Marshaling (British). American equivalent, switching, or drilling. Arranging the cars of a freight train in proper station order.

Mason Reducing Valve. Figs. 3161-3162.

Master Mechanics Standards. The American Railway Master Mechanics' Association has adopted standards of practice as follows:
Screw Threads, Bolt Heads and Nuts.
Sheet Metal Gage.
Distance Between Backs of Wheel Flanges.
Limit Gages for Round Iron.
Driving Wheel Centers and Sizes of Tires.
Section of Steel Tires. Figs. 4882-4883.
Specifications for Boiler and Firebox Steel.
Method of Conducting Efficiency Tests of Locomotives.
Specifications for Iron Locomotive Boiler Tubes.
Specifications for Seamless Cold-Drawn Steel Locomotive Boiler Tubes.
Decimal Gage.
Briggs' Standard Wrought-Iron Pipe Threads.
Standard Pipe Unions.
Axles. Figs. 4878-4881.
Journal Box, Bearing and Pedestal. Figs. 4797-4877, 4884-4887.
Specifications for Locomotive, Driving and Engine Truck Axles.
Specifications for Locomotive Forgings.
Specifications for Steel Blooms and Billets for Locomotive Forgings.
The Association has further made recommendations as follows:
Specifications and Tests for Cast Iron Wheels.
Air Brake and Signal Instructions.
Apprenticeship Rules.

Mastodon Locomotive. A locomotive having a four-wheel front truck and ten coupled driving wheels, but no trailing truck. Not in general use.

Mears' Water Glass Shield. Figs. 3144-3145.

Melrose Pilot Coupler Head. Figs. 2404-2405.

Metal Screw Thread. A form of screw thread used when both the male and female screws are made of metal. Metal threads are made of the same size as the spaces between them, whereas the spaces between wood screw threads are made wider than the projections. See also **Sellers' System of Screw Threads.**

Metropolitan "1898" Locomotive Injector. Figs. 3088-3090. A double tube injector composed of a lifting set of tubes which lift the water and deliver it to the forcing set of tubes under pressure, which in turn force the water into the boiler. The lifting set of tubes act as a governor to the forcing tubes, delivering the proper amount of water required for the condensation of the steam, thus enabling the injector to work without adjustment under a great range of steam pressure, handle very hot water and admit of the capacity being regulated for light or heavy service under all conditions. This injector will start with 30 pounds to 35 pounds steam pressure and without adjustment of any kind will work at all steam pressures up to 300 pounds.

Middle of Axle. The portion of a car axle between the two sloping necks which come next to the wheel seat. See **Axle.**

Middle Connection. 3, Figs. 1371-1380. That part of a crank axle between the two cranks. It lies between the inner faces or webs of the two cranks.

Mikado Type Locomotive. Figs. 45, 99-100. A locomotive having a two-wheel front truck, eight coupled driving wheels and a two-wheel trailing truck. Used for heavy freight service. See **Whyte's Nomenclature.**

Milling Machine. Figs. 4963-4967. A machine in which a special form of cutting tool, known as a milling cutter, is used. These tools are circular in form and have upon their circumference a number of cutting edges or teeth. They are secured to arbors which are rotated by power. Milling machines are classed as plain milling machines, universal milling machines, planer type milling machines, etc.

Miner Draft Gear. Figs. 3953-3956.

Miner Gravity Side Bearing. Figs. 4513-4518.

Mineral Wool. A substance having much the appearance, which its name implies, manufactured from the slag of iron furnaces by throwing against it while in the molten state a strong blast of air. It is used largely as a non-conductor for coating steam pipes.

Minimum Thickness of Steel Tires. The thickness to which the steel tires of wheels are allowed to be worn. For tender wheels it is 1 inch, to be measured normal to the tread and radial to the curved portions of the flange through the thinnest part within 4¼ inches from the back of the flange; the thickness from the latter point to the outer edge of tread to be not less than ½ inch at thinnest part. A further practice has been adopted of cutting a small groove in the outer face of all tires when wheels are new, at a radius of ¼ inch less than that of the tread of tire when worn to the prescribed limit, to facilitate inspection.

Mining Locomotive. Fig. 8. A small locomotive operated by steam, compressed air or electricity for hauling cars in mines.

Mogul Locomotive. Figs. 32-35, 89-92. A locomotive having a two-wheel front truck and six coupled driving wheels, of which the middle pair is connected to the crosshead. It has no trailing truck. Used principally for fast freight service. See **Whyte's Nomenclature.**

Molding. "A mode of ornamentation by grooved or swelling bands or forms, following the line of the object."—Knight. Small moldings are often termed beads, and also fillets. A cove molding is one of concave section. There are a great variety of other special technical terms for different forms of moldings. Moldings are either straight or waved.

Monitor Injector. Fig. 3097.

Monkey Wrench. Fig. 4574. See **Wrench**.

Moran Flexible Steam Joint. Fig. 3779.

Morris Pressed Steel Journal Box Lid. Figs. 4502-4506.

Motion Plate (British). 56, Figs. 5077-5078. See **Guide Yoke**.

Motor (Electric Locomotives). Figs. 4589-4590, 4650, 4654, 4659-4660. A machine for converting electrical energy into mechanical energy in the form of rotary motion. It consists of a rotating **Armature**, which see, turning in a magnetic field produced by an electric current flowing through coils surrounding soft iron pole pieces. Motors for electric locomotives are built to operate with direct current and with either alternating or direct current. See **Electric Locomotive**.

Motor Armature. See **Armature**.

Motor Blower (Electric Locomotive). Fig. 4667. A motor-driven fan on an electric locomotive for supplying a blast of air for the purpose of cooling the transformer, rheostat and motors.

Motor-Driven Air Compressor (Air Brakes). Figs. 2512-2515. An air compressor driven by a motor for use on electric locomotives.

Motormen's Brake Valve. See **Engineer's Brake Valve**.

Muck Bar. "Bar iron which has passed once through the rolls. It is usually cut into lengths, piled and rerolled."—Knight. Certain grades of iron axles are made directly from muck bars and contain no scrap. See **Axle**.

Mud Door (British). See **Hand Hole**.

Mud Drum. 60, Figs. 151-206. A shallow cylindrical receptacle in the bottom of the shell of a boiler near the smokebox, closed by a cast iron cover or plate bolted to a ring that is riveted to the plate forming the drum. Its purpose is to facilitate the removal of mud and sediment that accumulates in that part of the boiler. See **Hand Hole**.

Mud Drum Plug. A plug cock or blow-off cock screwed into the mud drum cover.

Mud Ring. See **Firebox Ring**.

Muffler (Vacuum Brake). A device to render noiseless the emission of steam at the ejector when brakes are applied. It is simply a lot of beads or shot, through the interstices of which the steam forces its way.

Muley Axle. An axle without collars.

Multiple. A mode of connecting two or more motors to the supply circuit. Two motors are said to be in multiple or in parallel when the current divides and a part of it passes through each motor.

Multiple Control Switch. See **Westinghouse Unit Switch System of Control** and **Control System**.

N

Nail. "A small pointed piece of metal, usually with a head, to be driven into a board or other piece of timber, and serving to fasten it to the other timber."—Webster.

The common nails of commerce are divided into cut nails, and clinch nails, and wire nails. They are distinguished in size by the number of pennies, as 10d., 20d., etc., nails.

Name Plate. Fig. 454. A cast iron or brass plate, commonly fastened on each side of the smokebox, giving the name of the builder of the locomotive.

Narrow Firebox Boiler. Figs. 134-135, 138-139, 144-146, etc. A boiler having a deep firebox narrow enough to extend down between the frames. See **Firebox**.

Nathan Injector. Fig. 3098.

Nathan Lubricator. Figs. 3200-3202.

National Equalizing Wedge (Journal Box). Figs. 4480-4484.

National Hollow Brake Beam. Fig. 4440. A brake beam consisting of a hollow tube 2 or 2½ inches in diameter, trussed by a rod passing through cast end pieces and over a king post, through which the brake lever passes.

National Journal Box. Figs. 4471-4479.

National Pivoted Pilot Coupler. Figs. 2398-2402.

Neck of Axle. The sloping portion of a tender axle just inside of the hub of the wheel.

Nest Spring. Figs. 4533-4535. A spiral spring with one or more coils of springs inside of it.

Netting. See **Smokebox Netting**.

New York Air Brake. Figs. 2557-2614. Air brake apparatus sold by the New York Air Brake Company. The devices sold accomplish much the same ends as the Westinghouse equipment. The apparatus will work in the same train with Westinghouse equipment.

Nipple. 1. In mechanics "a small rounded perforated protuberance, as the nipple of a gun."—Knight. It is often used, however, in a more general sense.

2. (Pipe Fittings.) A short wrought iron pipe with a screw thread cut on each end, used for connecting couplings, tees, etc., together or with some other object, as a tank or heater. See **Hose Nipple**.

Non-Pressure Head (Brake Cylinder). 4, Fig. 2497. The cover for the end of the brake cylinder opposite to that having air pressure against it. It has an opening in the center for the piston rod.

Nose. See **Pilot Nose**.

Nosing. 1. An iron band fastened on the outside of the bottom pieces of a pilot frame, and on the edges of the running board.

2. (Of steps.) The part of a tread board which projects beyond the riser, hence the metallic moldings used to protect that part of the tread board. The nosings should be distinguished from the step facings.

Number Plate. Figs. 452-453; 138, Figs. 77-124. A round or square metal plate fastened to the smokebox door, with the number of the locomotive cast in raised figures upon it.

Nut. "A small block of metal or wood containing a concave or female screw."—Webster. Nuts take their names from the bolts, rods or other parts to which they are attached. They are usually either square or hexagonal. A spanner nut is one with eight or more sides. They are usually more truly couplings than nuts, properly so-called, which screw on to a bolt or rod. See **Screw Threads**.

Nut Tapping Machine. Fig. 4968. A machine for tapping or threading nuts.

O

O. B. Air Strainer (Train Air Signal System). Fig. 2543. A cylindrical casing having pipe connections at either end, its interior cavity lined with wire gauze and filled with pulled curled hair, through which the air supply to the train air signal system is made to pass, thus preventing dirt and dust from penetrating into the system.

Ohm. The unit of electrical resistance.

Oil Axle Box (British). A journal box in which oil is used instead of grease as a lubricant. See **Axle Box**.

Oil Box. A **Journal Box**, which see.

Oil Burner. Figs. 750-774. A device for burning crude oil in a locomotive firebox by vaporization in a nozzle to which a supply of air and steam can be admitted to effect complete combustion.

Oil Burning Fireboxes. Figs. 721-747; Details, Figs. 750-787.

Oil Can. A vessel for holding oil, consisting usually of a cylindrical receptacle having a long spout or tube to make it possible to reach any bearing or oil hole. Oil cans are commonly made of tin plate, brass or copper.

Oil Can Holder. 18, Figs. 340-342. A shelf on the boiler head for holding the oil cans used on an engine.

Oil Cellar. A cavity in the lower part of some exceptional forms of journal boxes for collecting the oil and dirt which run off the axle at the dust guard. The oil cellar is below the space occupied by the axle packing.

Oil Cock Plug. A brass fitting attached to the oil dash pot of an intercepting valve. See **Intercepting Valve.**

Oil Cup. Figs. 1288-1299. A receptacle, fitted with a cap screwed on, and a nut for tightening the same, used on parts of a locomotive. There are oil cups on all side and main rod bearings; on rocker boxes, eccentrics, and all other wearing parts of the valve gear, piston rods, guides, and crossheads.

Oil Dash Pot. A small cylinder with a piston and rod connected to the stem of an intercepting valve. The cylinder is partially filled with oil so as to form a cushion that allows the intercepting valve to open and close without sudden jar. A by-pass pipe connects the two ends of the dash pot to regulate the flow of oil from one side of the plunger to the other.

Oil Injector. Figs. 750-755. See **Oil Burner.**

Oil Lamp. A lamp for burning oil.

Oil Regulator. Figs. 776-777. A valve and extension handle, placed in the oil supply pipe to regulate the amount of oil supplied according to the demand for steam.

Oil Supply Valve. Figs. 778-779. A plug valve in the oil tank of the tender to close the mouth of the oil supply pipe leading to the locomotive. Also called tank valve.

Open Return Bend (Pipe Fittings). A short cast or malleable iron U-shaped tube for uniting two parallel pipes. It differs from a close return bend, in having the arms separated from each other.

Operating Valve (Westinghouse Traction Brake). See **Engineer's Brake Valve.**

Order Clip. 245, Figs. 76-124. A snap catch for holding train orders, placed in a conspicuous place in the cab.

Outside Admission Valve. A valve which admits steam to the cylinder through ports which are uncovered by the outside edges of its ends of the valve and opens the exhaust ports by the inside edges of its ends. See **Valve** and **Slide Valve.**

Outside Firebox Sheet. 9, Figs. 151-206. The outside plate of a boiler above the firebox and to which the crown sheet proper is secured by crown bars and stays or by radial stays. Also called roof sheet, and in Great Britain, wrapper plate.

Outside Lap (Valve). The extension of the outside edge of a slide valve beyond the outside edge of a steam port is the outside lap. Its effect on the steam distribution in a cylinder is to shorten the period of admission; in other words, to make the valve cut-off shorter. Sometimes called steam lap. See **Inside Lap.**

Outside Welt. 55, Figs. 151-206. A strip or narrow plate riveted on the outside of the abutting edges of two plates of a boiler to form a butt joint.

Over-Running Rail. See **Third-Rail.**

Overhang (Cab Roof). 21, Figs. 2787-2791. The rear of a cab roof which extends out over the apron.

P

Pacific Type Locomotive. Figs. 68-71, 123. A locomotive having a four-wheel front truck, six coupled driving wheels and a two-wheel trailing truck. Used for heavy fast passenger service. See **Whyte's Nomenclature.**

Packing. Figs. 1015-1021. 1. A device or arrangement for making a steam-tight fitting on the piston rod and valve stem where they pass through their stuffing boxes on cylinder and steam chest, respectively. Also used on air pump piston rods and throttle rods. Metallic packing, generally employed, consists of a set of soft metal rings, each cut in one place so as to take up the wear of a rod, and held in place by a spring. Asbestos, hemp, and other packings, are also used. The term is also applied to the rings used on pistons.

2. (Journal Boxes.) The waste, saturated with oil or other lubricant, used in journal box cellars to lubricate the bearing.

Packing Expander (Brake Cylinder). A spring wire ring for spreading out the leather packing of the brake piston so as to make it fit air tight. See **Piston Packing Expander.**

Packing Gland. See **Stuffing Box.**

Packing Leather. 1. (Of Journal Boxes.) A dust guard is sometimes called packing leather.

2. (Brake Cylinder.) A ring of leather used in connection with brake cylinder pistons to make an air-tight joint. When so used it is always accompanied with a packing leather expander. A packing leather for a piston rod is called a cup leather, and is compressed by a piston spring. See **Piston Packing Leather.**

Packing Ring (Air Brake). 67, Figs. 2429-2435. 1. A soft metal ring set in a groove in the pistons of the steam and air cylinders of an air pump, and in the triple valve, and engineer's brake valve, to make a steam-tight or air-tight fit in the respective cylinders. The rings are turned slightly larger than the cylinder and cut apart diagonally at one point so that when compressed they will tend to spring open.

2. (Hose Coupling.) An India rubber ring in a coupling case which makes a tight joint between the two parts of the coupling.

3. A term sometimes used to mean **Piston Ring,** which see.

Packing Tools. Special tools made for the purpose of removing and replacing journal-box packing.

Paint. The protective and coloring material applied to the outside of a locomotive and tender.

Pair of Trucks. A pair of trucks means two truck frames, each with two or more pairs of wheels, etc., complete for an entire tender, and does not mean one truck frame with wheels and axles for one end of a tender only.

Pair of Wheels. This term is used to designate two wheels fitted on one axle, including the axle.

Palm Stay (British). See **Throat Brace.**

Panel. 1. A board inserted in the space left between the stiles and rails of a frame or between moldings. Sometimes metal plates are used for this purpose.

2. (Of a Truss.) The space between two vertical posts or braces and the two chords of a truss.

Paper Wheel. More properly, **Allen Paper Wheel,** which see. Figs. 4538-4539. A wheel with a steel tire and a center formed of compressed paper held between two iron face plates. It is in limited use. The compressed paper can be turned and polished like wood.

Parallel. (Arrangement of Motors.) See **Multiple.**

Parallel Rods. See **Side Rod.**

Patch Bolt. Fig. 285. A small threaded plug with a square head and washer formed on it, used for plugging staybolt holes or applying temporary patch plates to boilers.

Patent Plate. A brass or iron plate, stamped or cast with the name of the maker of some special equipment used on a locomotive, such as an air pump, injector, compound cylinder arrangement, lubricator, etc.

Pawl. A short metal piece pivoted at the center and fitting into the ratchet of a hand-brake wheel on a tender. Knight's definition is "A pivoted bar adapted to fall into the notches or teeth of a wheel as it rotates in one direction, and to restrain it from back motion. Used in windlasses, capstans and similar machinery." See **Brake Pawl.**

Pedestal. 1. (Trucks.) 7, Figs. 3369-3380; Figs. 3386-3387. A casting of somewhat the form of an inverted letter U, bolted to the wheel piece of a truck frame to hold the journal box in its place, while permitting a vertical movement. The two projections of a pedestal are called pedestal horns, and the space between them a jaw, which is closed at the bottom by a **Pedestal Brace,** which see. In Great Britain pedestals are called axle guards on cars and hornplates on locomotives, and are there made of wrought iron.

2. (Locomotive.) 3, Figs. 1446-1476. The vertical legs of a locomotive frame that hold a driving box in place. The front leg of a pedestal is usually made vertical and the back leg sloping, and the opening between the legs into which the box fits is often called the pedestal jaw. British, hornblock, axlebox guide or hornplate.

Pedestal Binder. 4, Figs. 1446-1476. Called also pedestal cap and pedestal brace. A cast or wrought iron, or cast steel bar or filling piece fitted across the opening between the pedestal legs and held in place by bolts passing through the bottom rail or brace of the frame. See **Pedestal Thimble.** British, hornplate stay.

Pedestal Bolt. 5, Figs. 1446-1476; 9, Figs. 3369-3380. Bolts holding a pedestal cap or binder in place on either the main frame or a truck frame.

Pedestal Bolt Key. A key or cotter passed through an opening in the end of a pedestal bolt to prevent the nut from jarring loose and falling off.

Pedestal Box. A **Journal Box,** which see.

Pedestal Brace (Trucks). A diagonal bar or rod staying the lower end of a pedestal longitudinally. It is often combined into one piece with a pedestal tie bar to form a pedestal brace tie bar.

Pedestal Brace Tie Bar. A pedestal brace and a pedestal tie bar combined in one piece. See above.

Pedestal Cap (Engine Truck). 4, Figs. 1446-1476. A piece fitted in the opening of the truck pedestal jaw and held in place by a brace or binder. See **Pedestal Brace** and **Pedestal Binder.**

Pedestal Crosstie (Engine Truck). 8b, 3369-3380. Transverse braces bolted to the bottom of the truck pedestals or to the pedestal braces to strengthen them laterally.

Pedestal Horns. See **Pedestal.**

Pedestal Jaw. It is closed at the bottom by a jaw bit or a pedestal brace. See **Pedestal.**

Pedestal Spring. A **Journal Spring,** which see.

Pedestal Stay Rod. 8b, Figs. 3369-3380. A transverse rod connecting the pedestal tie bars on each side of a truck, so as to prevent them from spreading apart. Also called pedestal crosstie.

Pedestal Thimble. 4, Figs. 1446-1476. A cast-iron filling piece in the pedestal jaw or opening between the pedestal legs, held in place by a bolt passing through it longitudinally. Used on frames where the usual form of pedestal binder or cap would interfere with the wedge bolts. See **Frame Wedge Bolt.**

Pedestal Tie. A U-shaped bolt with nuts on the ends that passes around the outside of the pedestal legs and holds the cap in place. Not commonly used.

Pedestal Tie Bar. 8, Figs. 3369-3380. An iron bar or rod bolted to the bottom of two or more pedestals on the same side of a truck, thus holding or tying them together. The pedestal tie bar is used to get a low truck. Sometimes it is given a half turn for additional stiffness.

Pedestal Trucks. Figs. 4349-4354. Trucks so called because the journal boxes are held in jaws or pedestals which are an integral part of the truck frame as distinguished from trucks having pedestals bolted to the truck frames.

Perfecto Brake Shoe. Fig. 2782.

Petticoat Pipe. 40, Figs. 343-442. A pipe in the smokebox over or surrounding the exhaust pipe, for the purpose of causing a partial vacuum in the front end and tubes.

Phoenix Locomotive and Truck Springs. Figs. 1757-1758, 4522-4525.

Phosphor Bronze. "A term applied to an alloy of bronze or brass, or to a triple alloy of copper, tin and zinc, which has been given special purity and excellence by skilful fluxing with phosphorus. It is supposed that the presence of phosphorus gives the tin a crystalline character which enables it to alloy more completely and strongly with the copper. Whether for this reason or not, the phosphor bronzes, when skilfully made, are greatly superior to unphosphorated alloys."—Thurston.

Pilot. 144, Figs. 77-124; Figs. 2256-2327; Details, Figs. 2328-2409. An inclined pointed structure of wood or iron bars fastened to the front bumper of a locomotive to remove obstructions from the track. Formerly called cow catcher.

Pilot Angle. A right-angled piece of iron or steel bolted to the horizontal and vertical frames on each side of a pilot to stiffen and secure it. Called also pilot corner bracket.

Pilot Band. 15, Figs. 2256-2327. A strip of iron bolted on the outside of the bottom rail or frame of a pilot. Also called pilot nosing.

Pilot Bars. 14, Figs. 2256-2327. The wooden strips or iron rods which form the two inclined surfaces of a pilot.

Pilot Bottom Plate. A triangular plate of iron or steel bolted on the under side of the bottom frame of a pilot.

Pilot Bracket. A right-angled casting bolted to the vertical frame of a pilot on each side and to the under side of the bumper timber to strengthen the frame. Called also pilot knee.

Pilot Center Brace. 3, Figs. 2256-2327. One of two braces bolted to the back of a pilot frame near each corner and to the main frames or the cylinder saddles. Called also pilot middle brace.

Pilot Corner Bracket. See **Pilot Angle.**

Pilot Cross Braces. Two braces bolted to the inside of a pilot frame, crossing each other, and secured to the cylinder saddles.

Pilot Diagonal Brace. 3, Figs. 2256-2327. A rod secured to the bottom of a pilot near the nose and to the drawhead casting at the top. Two braces are commonly used, one on either side of the center timber.

Pilot Filling Piece. See **Bumper Plate.**

Pilot Frame. 1, Figs. 2256-2327. The framing or principal members on which a pilot is built.

Pilot Heel Brace. See **Pilot Center Brace.**

Pilot Knee. See **Pilot Bracket.**

Pilot Middle Brace. See **Pilot Center Brace.**

Pilot Nose. 15, Figs. 2256-2327. The tip, point or apex of a pilot.

Pilot Plate. A plate bolted on the back of a bumper timber between the frames. Called usually a pilot stiffening plate to distinguish it from the pilot bottom plate.

Pilot Shield. A name sometimes used for a small snow plow or scraper made of thin sheet steel and secured to the front of the pilot.

Pilot Shoe. A cup-shaped casting bolted to a bumper to receive the end of a push pole. A shoe is fastened on each end of the bumper timber. Called also push pole bracket or pilot pushing shoe, and sometimes, switching eye.

Pilot Step. 18 and 19, Figs. 2256-2327. A bracket secured on each side of a pilot to enable a man to mount the front bumper.

Pilot Strap. See **Pilot Band.**

Pin. "A peg or bolt of wood or metal having many uses."—Knight. In railroad service the word, when used alone, commonly means a coupling pin. See **Crank Pin.**

Pinch Bar. A lever with one end bent so as to form a fulcrum foot and a chisel point or nose, used to move a locomotive or tender a very short distance forward or backward by successive applications on the rail under the tread of a wheel.

Pinion. 1. The smaller cog wheel of two wheels in gear.

2. A small toothed wheel keyed to the armature shaft of an electric motor, and engaging with or meshing into a larger toothed wheel, called a gear wheel, fastened on the driving axle.

Pipe. "A tube for conveyance of water, air, or other fluids."—Knight. The wrought iron pipes used for conveying gas, steam, etc., and commonly called gas pipe, are usually meant by compound words beginning with pipe. See **Brake Pipe, Discharge Pipe, Dry Pipe, Signal Pipe, Steam Pipe.**

Pipe Bending Machine. Fig. 4969. A machine for bending pipe.

Pipe Bracket. 1. A support for a pipe, as injector delivery pipe bracket.

2. (Air Brake.) That part of a valve device serving as its support, to which the pipe connections are made and from which it may be removed without breaking any pipe joints.

Pipe Bushing. See **Bushing.**

Pipe Clamp. Figs. 4731-4738. A clamp for the air brake pipe or train pipe under the engine or tender.

Pipe Clip or Strap. An iron band for fastening a pipe against or to some other object. They are usually single, but sometimes double, for two or more pipes.

Pipe Coupling. A short cast iron tube with a thread cut on the inside at each end, which is screwed on the ends of two pipes and used for uniting them together, or uniting one pipe with another object, as a cock or valve. In some couplings the thread at one end is right hand and the other left hand, but generally they are both right hand threads. See **Union.**

Pipe Fittings. The connections for systems of gas, water, and steam pipes. The more usual pipe fittings are bushings, elbows, tees, return bends (close or open), reducers, couplings, nipples, plugs, clips, etc.

Pipe Hanger. Figs. 3743-3744. A hanger for the brake pipe, train pipe or other pipe under a tender.

Pipe Reducer. See **Pipe Fittings.** Bushings, tees and couplings may be and are all so made as to serve as reducers.

Pipe Screw Threads. Screw threads used for connecting wrought iron pipes together. Such screws are cut "tapered"; that is, the end of the pipe, or the inside of the coupling where the thread is cut, forms part of a cone, so that in screwing up the pipe a tight joint can be made. Pipe threads are of a V-shape, sharp at the top and bottom, and their sides stand at the angle of 60 deg. to each other. The following is the number of threads per inch for pipes of different sizes. The size is given by the inside diameter, but the actual bore of the smaller sizes is considerably larger than the nominal. The exterior diameter of ordinary gas pipe is from .27 to .37 inches greater than the inside diameter.

AMERICAN STANDARD SYSTEM OF PIPE THREADS.

Size of pipe.	Outside diameter. Ins.	Inside diameter. Ins.	Inside diam. Extra strong. Ins.	Inside diam. Double extra strong. Ins.	Threads per inch.	Whitworth's thread.
1/8 in.	.405	.27	.205		27	28
1/4 "	.54	.364	.294		18	19
3/8 "	.675	.494	.421		18	19
1/2 "	.84	.623	.542	.214	14	14
3/4 "	1.05	.824	.736	.422	14	14
1 "	1.315	1.048	.915	.587	11½	11
1¼ "	1.66	1.38	1.272	.881	11½	11
1½ "	1.9	1.611	1.494	1.088	11½	11
2 "	2.375	2.067	1.933	1.491	11½	11
2½ "	2.875	2.468	2.315	1.755	8	
3 "	3.5	3.067	2.892	2.284	8	
3½ "	4.	3.548	3.358	2.716	8	
4 "	4.5	4.026	3.818	3.136	8	
4½ "	5.	4.508			8	
5 "	5.563	5.045			8	
6 "	6.625	6.065			8	
7 "	7.625	7.023			8	
8 "	8.625	7.982			8	
9 "	9.688	9.001			8	
10 "	10.075	10.019			8	

(The European standard is the Whitworth pipe thread, which is quite different.)

Taper of Thread ¾ in. per foot.

Pipe Threading and Cutting-off Machine. Figs. 4970-4972. A machine for threading and cutting off pipe.

Pipe Turnbuckle. See **Turnbuckle.**

Pipe Unions. In 1902 standard dimensions for pipe unions ⅛ to 4 inches, inclusive, were proposed for adoption by the American Railway Master Mechanics' Association, and, at the convention of 1903, the same were adopted as standard. These dimensions are shown in the table on opposite page.

"Pipeless" Triple Valves (Air Brake). Figs. 2494-2495. A triple valve arranged to have all pipe connections made in the cylinder head, reservoir, or bracket to which it is attached, these connections being completed to the triple valve through suitable ports.

DIMENSIONS FOR STANDARD PIPE UNIONS.

1	2	3	4	5	6	7	8	9	10	11	12	13	14	15	16	17	18	19	20	21	22
⅛-inch	.375	.270	.105	.59	.63	.78	.80	.85	89	1.06	.26	¼	27	.2225	.08	.5625	½	.59	.615	006	.05
¼ "	.496	.364	.132	.76	.80	.96	.98	1.06	1.09	1.29	.33	5/16	18	2625	.10	.6925	9/16	.78	76	006	.06
⅜ "	630	.494	.136	.90	.95	1.11	1.13	1.20	1.24	1.45	.34	⅜	18	2825	.11	.7325	⅝	.90	.905	006	.07
½ "	.783	.623	.160	1.16	1.21	1.38	1.40	1.49	1.54	1.78	.40	7/16	14	3025	.12	.8225	11/16	1.03	1.20	006	.08
¾ "	.992	.824	.168	1.38	1.43	1.61	1.63	1.72	1.77	2.02	.42	½	14	.3225	.13	.8725	¾	1.24	1.43	007	.09
1 "	1.246	1.048	.198	1.74	1.79	1.98	2.01	2.13	2.19	2.49	.49	9/16	11	.3625	.15	1.0025	13/16	1.565	1.76	.007	.10
1¼ "	1.592	1.380	.212	2.12	2.18	2.37	2.40	2.52	2.58	2.90	.53	.6	11	.3825	.16	1.0725	.9	1.91	2.15	007	11
1½ "	1.831	1.610	.221	2.40	2.46	2.66	2.69	2.81	2.87	3.20	.55	.7	11	.4025	.17	1.1225	1.0	2.18	2.40	007	13
2 "	2.306	2.067	.239	2.89	2.95	3.16	3.19	3.31	3.38	3.74	.60	.8	11	.4225	.18	1.2025	1.1	2.66	2.90	008	.14
2½ "	2.775	2.468	.307	3.39	3.45	3.67	3.70	3.86	3.93	4.39	.77	.9	8	.5225	.23	1.5225	1.2	3.16	3.41	008	.16
3 "	3.401	3.067	.334	4.07	4.13	4.36	4.40	4.56	4.63	5.13	.84	1.0	8	.5625	.25	1.6525	1.3	3.81	4.08	.008	.18
3½ "	3.901	3.548	.353	4.61	4.68	4.91	4.95	5.11	5.19	5.72	.88	1.1	8	.6025	.27	1.7325	1.4	4.31	4.63	.008	.20
4 "	4.4	4.026	.374	5.15	5.22	5.47	5.51	5.67	5.75	6.31	.94	1.2	8	.6725	.28	1.8425	1.5	4.81	5.19	.008	.22

DESCRIPTION ACCOMPANYING TABLE OF MALLEABLE PIPE UNIONS.

NUMBERS AT THE HEAD OF THE COLUMNS ABOVE ARE THOSE GIVEN IN THE DIMENSION LINES ON TABLE A.

Column No. 1 in table represents the nominal diameter of pipe.

Column No. 2 represents diameter of pipe at one-half the height of full thread nearest solid section of pipe.

Column No. 3 represents the internal diameter of the pipe.

Column No. 4 represents the difference between columns Nos. 2 and 3, and is equal to twice the thickness of metal in pipe measured from inside line to one-half the height of thread, as specified before.

Column No. 5 represents the outside diameter of end of pipe union and is taken as *No. 2, plus twice No. 4*, plus an arbitrary increment.

Column No. 6 is equal to No. 5 plus an increment varying from .04 to .07 of an inch. This increment was allowed for the purpose of being able to slip the nut over upper swivel end of union.

Column No. 7 is No. 6 plus an amount varying between .15 and .25. This lip created is considerably in excess of what exists on present pipe unions for the reason that we find the surface between the lip and the corresponding part of nut is often damaged, and the bearing surface, when the full strength of the man is used on the wrench, is sufficient. We assume that a man would pull about 30 pounds on a wrench, with a possibility of using less force on pipes of small diameters. For that reason we made a variation in the width of lip, which lip, theoretically, would be uniform for all sizes of pipe. The nut itself has been strengthened to prevent the lip from deflecting upward.

Column No. 8 is No. 7, plus an increment varying from .02 to .04 of an inch.

Column No. 9 is No. 8, plus twice the height of the thread.

Column No. 10 is No. 9, plus an increment varying between .04 and .08 of an inch.

Column No. 11 is No. 10, plus one and one-half times No. 4.

Column No. 12 is two and one-half times No. 4, and was figured especially for bearing surface, so that the thread would not wear away too rapidly when the nut is occasionally removed.

Column No. 13 has been assumed arbitrarily, but in all cases is greater than the length of full thread on standard pipe.

Column No. 14 represents the number of threads per inch in length of nut. This thread, we believe, should be United States Standard form and not sharp thread.

Column No. 15 is taken arbitrarily, but is based on the probable requirements of manufacturers for tapping out the nut.

Column No. 16 is three-fourths of No. 4.

Column No. 17 represents the full height of nut, and is equal to No. 12, plus No. 15, plus No. 16.

Column No. 18 is the amount of projection outside of nut.

Column No. 19 is No. 2, plus No. 4, plus an arbitrary increment.

Column No. 20 is No. 7, less No. 16, with slight modifications.

Column No. 21 represents the clearance at several points, as indicated on print.

Column No. 22 is assumed arbitrarily.

This arrangement admits of the valve being removed without breaking any pipe joints.

Piston. Figs. 879-911. A metal disk with packing, etc., made to fit air or steam tight and work back and forth in a cylinder. The piston consists of a piston head, attached to a piston rod. The piston follower or follower plate lies at the back of the piston head, inclosing between them the piston packing rings, or (in the Westinghouse brake cylinders) the piston packing leather, which latter is provided with a packing leather expander. The follower plate is secured to the piston with follower bolts. All these parts are essentially the same in all the various cylinders shown, and for distinctness should be designated with the name of the cylinder within which they work.

Piston Clearance. The distance between the surface of a piston and the cylinder head at the extreme end of the stroke. Usually it is from ¼ to ½ inch.

Piston Follower. A circular plate fitted on that face of a piston that is away from the rod and secured by bolts called follower bolts. By removing the follower it is possible to reach and adjust the packing springs by means of the bolts and nuts provided for that purpose.

Piston Follower Bolt. One of several bolts (with their heads countersunk in the follower) screwed into brass nuts let into the body of the piston.

Piston Key. A flat wedge-shaped key passing through the center of a piston and the end of a piston rod to fasten them together.

Piston Nut. A nut screwed on the end of a piston rod to secure it to the piston. The rod is tapered in that part that passes through the piston and has a filet or collar that is drawn tight against one face of the piston when the nut is tightened up against the other.

Piston Packing Expander (Air Brake). 12, Figs. 2497-2498. A spring wire ring for spreading out the leather packing of the piston so as to make it air tight.

Piston Packing Leather (Air Brake). 11, Figs. 2497-2498. A circular ring of leather used as a substitute for **Piston Packing Rings,** which see, pressed into the cylinder so as to have an L-section, which is attached to and surrounds the piston and bears against the inside surface of the cylinder, being pressed against it by a round steel rod called the piston packing expander.

Piston Packing Ring. See **Packing Ring.**

Piston Ring. 6, Figs. 907-910. A cast iron, brass or soft alloy ring, made slightly larger than the internal diameter of a cylinder and cut at one place so as to spring outwards and fit snugly against the cylinder, and thus make an air or steam-tight joint. Two such rings are commonly used.

Piston Rod. 1. 3, Figs. 907-910; Figs. 912-915. A wrought iron or steel rod secured at one end to the center of a piston and at the other to a crosshead. It is usually secured in place in the piston by a **Piston Nut,** which see, or by a key driven through the rod back of the piston, the manner described under **Piston Nut,** which see.

2. (Brake Cylinder.) A rod attached to the piston of a brake cylinder, by means of which the pressure against the piston is transmitted to the brake levers and shoes.

3. A tube attached to the piston of tender brake cylinders to act as a guide to the piston as it is forced outward by the air pressure. In this case a **Push Rod,** which see, is attached to the levers and is enclosed by the tube. The push rod transmits the pressure on the piston to the levers and brake shoes, while it allows an application of the brakes by hand without pulling out the piston.

Piston Rod Guide. A ring-shaped bearing or gland attached to the front cylinder head of a locomotive to form a support for a piston rod extending through the front cylinder head. Extended piston rods are used to prevent the weight of large pistons from wearing the cylinders unevenly. See **Extended Piston Rod.**

Piston Rod Jack. A small portable hydraulic or screw jack for handling a piston rod in case of a breakdown on the road.

Piston Rod Nut. 7, Figs. 1039-1086. A nut holding the outer end of a piston rod to a crosshead.

Piston Rod Packing. See **Packing.**

Piston Rod Stuffing Box. 2, Figs. 928-930; Figs. 1015-1021. A cylindrical, cup-shaped receptacle surrounding the piston rod on the head of an air or steam cylinder for the purpose of holding piston rod packing.

Piston Staybolt. A short rod or rivet used to strengthen a hollow cast piston.

Piston Stroke. The linear distance traversed by a piston from one end of a cylinder to the other.

Piston T-Ring. A cast iron ring of T-section, usually shrunk on a piston to hold the packing rings. Called also a bull ring. See Figs. 901-902.

Piston Travel (Air Brakes). The amount of movement of the piston when forced outward as the brakes are applied. Running piston travel is the piston travel obtained when the tender is in motion and is always greater than the travel obtained when the tender is at rest, due to the fact that the slack or lost motion in trucks and brake gear as well as the elasticity of the frame is more easily taken up by the brake shoe pressure when the tender is in motion. False travel is that due to some unevenness of the track or to some cause which occasions a momentary change.

Piston Valve. Figs. 2137-2192. A spool shaped casting of iron or steel, moving backwards and forwards in a cylindrical valve chamber formed in a steam chest, for admitting steam to and exhausting it from a locomotive cylinder. It is operated by valve gear in the same manner as a slide valve. Piston valves are made with disks or short cylindrical pieces secured to each end, with metal snap rings fitted on, to insure a steam tight fit in the bushing of the valve chamber. They are of either the inside or the outside admission types. An inside admission valve takes steam from the steam pipe into its central cavity, between the ends, and admits it to the steam passages leading to the ends of the cylinder; the exhaust steam from the cylinder being in contact with the ends of the valve. An outside admission piston valve uncovers the ports leading to the cylinder in the same manner as a slide valve, and the exhaust steam passes through the internal cavity of the valve before entering the exhaust pipe. The inside admission type is the more common, and is used instead of the slide valve on many recent locomotives. Its advantages over the slide valve are its better balancing, and consequently smaller resistance to being moved, and a better distribution of steam at high piston speeds. In four-cylinder compound locomotives, where one valve is employed for a high and a low-pressure cylinder on each side of the engine, a piston valve is the only kind of valve that experience has shown to be practicable.

Pitt Tender Coupler. Figs. 4055-4062.

Pivot. "A pin or short shaft on which anything turns."—Webster.

Pivot Pin (M. C. B. Coupler). Another name for the **Knuckle Pin**, which see. So called from the fact that the knuckle when opening swings about the pin as a pivot.

Planished Iron. One of the attempted substitutes for Russia iron. One of many processes consists of the formation of an oxidized surface on each sheet over and above the surface secured in ordinary working. The oxidized surface is then reconverted into metallic iron, which will enter readily into combination with an oxidizing agent applied throughout. The surface thus given to the sheet is fixed by planishing or hammering until the desired polish is secured. It is extensively used for the jackets of locomotive boilers.

Plain Triple Valve (Air Brake). Figs. 2496, 2574-2575. A triple valve which has no quick action feature for hastening the emergency application throughout the train. See **Triple Valve.**

Planer. Figs. 4973-4977. A machine tool for machining flat surfaces. It is composed of a bed having a reciprocating motion, two uprights, commonly known as the housings, and a cross rail. The cross rail is carried on, and generally has a vertical movement on the face of the uprights, and is fitted with one, or in many cases with two, tool heads in which the cutting tools are held.

Plank. "A broad piece of sawed timber, differing from a board only in being thicker. In America, broad pieces of sawed timber, which are not more than an inch or an inch and a quarter thick are called boards; like pieces from an inch and a half to three or four inches thick are called planks."—Webster. See **Spring Plank, Truss Plank.**

Plate (of a Cast Car Wheel). The central portion connecting the hub and tread, sometimes single plate, sometimes double plate. The plate is stiffened by brackets. See **Wheel** and **Face Plate** (Steel Tired Wheel).

Plate Washer. Usually a wrought iron cut washer, in distinction from a cast washer, but also used to designate many forms of large washers or plates serving as double or triple washers. See **Washer.**

Plate Wheel. Figs. 4547-4551, etc. A wheel of which the center portion is formed of a disk or plate instead of spokes. Varieties are the single, double, open and combination plate wheel. See **Wheel.**

Platform (British). See **Runboard.**

Platform Support (British). See **Runboard Bracket.**

Player Ash Pan. Figs. 510-511. An ash pan with double hoppers closed by slides suspended from links which are connected by self-locking toggle levers on an operating shaft running across under the hoppers.

Player Traction Increaser. Figs. 1793-1804. See **Traction Increaser.**

Plug. A cylindrical or conical piece, either smooth or threaded, fitting into a hole, tube, pipe, or valve body.

Plug Cock. Figs. 4156-4158. A stop cock having a plug or key with a hole or slot through it and a handle for turning it so as to allow a fluid to pass through.

Plugging Bar. A steel bar long enough to extend completely through a firebox, with one end so arranged as to hold a plug or stopper which may be inserted in one of the tube openings in the tube sheet to stop the escape of steam and water in case a tube leaks or bursts.

Pneumatic Blow-off Cock. Figs. 3334-3339.

Pneumatic Tools. Figs. 4978-4990. Tools operated by compressed air, including pneumatic chipping, calking, beading and riveting hammers, drills, flue welding machines, etc.

Point of Cut-off. 1. That fraction of the stroke of a piston at which the valve closes the steam port.

2. The linear distance traversed by a piston from either end of a cylinder before the valve closes the steam port.

Poker. A long bar used to stir a fire and break up the fuel.

Pony Truck. Figs. 3344-3368. A two-wheel swiveling truck used under the front end of mogul, prairie and consolidation locomotives. See **Truck.**

Pop Safety Valve. Figs. 3214-3225. A valve set with a spring so as to open suddenly with a wide opening at a fixed pressure; hence the name. They are frequently muffled to deaden the noise of escaping steam, by causing it to take a torturous passage over corrugated surfaces to the atmosphere.

Port. An opening, usually rectangular, in the face or chamber of a valve. In locomotive cylinder castings the ports opening into the steam passages leading to the cylinders and those opening into the exhaust passage are rectangular apertures in the valve seat or valve chamber, according as the locomotive has slide or piston valves. See **Steam Port** and **Exhaust Port.**

Port Cock. A faucet screwed into the bottom of a cylinder saddle to allow water to escape from the steam and exhaust passages. It is operated by an arm sometimes, but not always, connected to the cab by a rod. Also sometimes actuated by the cylinder cock rigging. See **Cylinder Cock.**

Port Cock Arm. A piece of metal attached to the shank of the port cock to open and close it.

Port Cock Lever. A lever placed in the cab to operate the rod attached to the port cock rigging.

Port Cock Shaft. A transverse shaft forming part of the port cock rigging.

Prairie Type Locomotive. Figs. 36-37, 93-94. A locomotive having a two-wheel front truck, six coupled driving wheels and a two-wheel trailing truck. Used for heavy fast passenger service. See **Whyte's Nomenclature.**

Pre-Admission. The opening of a steam port to admit steam to one end of a cylinder while the piston is still moving towards that end of the cylinder. See **Admission.**

Pre-Release. The opening of communication between either end of a cylinder and the exhaust port before the piston reaches the end of its stroke. See **Release.**

Pressure Gage. Figs. 3148-3160, 2483-2486. A device for indicating the pressure in a boiler or air reservoir. Usually placed in the cab and illuminated by a gage lamp. Three gages are commonly mounted in a locomotive cab to indicate boiler steam pressure, train line steam heat pressure, and brake pipe and main reservoir air pressure.

Pressure Head (Brake Cylinder). The head that covers the end of the brake cylinder into which air pressure is admitted when the brakes are applied.

Pressure Regulator (Gold's Car Heating). Fig. 3164. A valve designed to regulate the delivery pressure of steam. It depends entirely upon the elasticity of springs, the pressure of which can be gaged or regulated by screw studs that bear upon one end of the springs. In the Gold pressure regulator there is a spring on each side of the valve.

Pressure Retaining Valve (Air Brake). Figs. 2500-2502. A device by means of which a certain part of the brake cylinder pressure may be retained to aid in retarding the acceleration of a train in descending long grades while the brake pipe pressure is increased after one application to recharge the auxiliary reservoirs. It is controlled by a small handle, the position of which causes it to operate or not, as desired. There are four different types, the ordinary, Fig. 2500; the vestibule, the double pressure, Fig. 2501, and the driver brake, Fig. 2502. The first two types may be made to retain 0 to 15 pounds; the third is built in two sizes, one to retain 0, 15 or 30 pounds, the other to retain 0, 25 or 50 pounds; the fourth type to retain 0 or 15 pounds on all cylinder pressures. In descending grades the handle is turned to allow the air to escape to the atmosphere. Also called retaining valve.

Priest Snow Flanger. Figs. 2408-2409.

Priming (Painting). The first coat in tender or cab painting. Usually a pure thin oil. A thin drier, or red lead or borate of manganese, is used with it. The next coat is the scraping filling coat or rough stuff.

Pull Bars. See **Water Pull Bar Grate.**

Pull Rod. Any rod or slender bar used to connect an arm or lever with the cab for convenience of operation, as sand box rod, cylinder cock rod, etc.

Pump Governor (Air Brake). Figs. 2458-2462. 1. (Single-Pressure Governor). Figs. 2458-2459. A device to be attached to the steam inlet of the air pump, or placed in the steam pipe leading to the pump, to automatically cut off the supply of steam to the pump when the air pressure in the main reservoir reaches a fixed maximum, usually either 90 or 130 pounds. It obviates the unnecessary working of the pump after the desired air pressure has been attained.

2. (Duplex Governor.) Figs. 2460-2462. A device similar to the single pressure type, except that it has two regulating portions so as to stop the pump at either one of two pressures, depending on which regulating portion is brought into action. It also allows a higher main reservoir pressure to be obtained during brake applications than at other times, thereby insuring a prompt release and recharging of the brakes. See also **Electric Pump Governor.**

Punching and Shearing Machine. Figs. 4992, 4998. A combined machine for punching and shearing metal plates. Made in various sizes and capacities in either double or single design, and arranged for either punching or shearing, or both. In the double machine both ends may be arranged for punching or shearing, or one end can be arranged for punching and one end for shearing.

Punching Machine. Figs. 4991-4999. A machine for punching holes in boiler plates, structural shapes, etc.

Push Bar (Air Brake). Usually called push rod. A compression bar which bears against the piston of a brake cylinder, being guided by a hollow piston rod in such manner as to transmit the pressure of the piston when the air brake is used, but to simply move away from the piston, without moving the latter, when brakes are applied by hand.

Push Rod (Tender Brake). 14, Fig. 2498. A round steel bar which transmits the air pressure against the piston of the brake cylinder to the levers and to the brake shoes. It has a crosshead formed on one end by which it is attached to the cylinder lever. It is guided by the hollow piston rod and transmits the pressure when the air brake is used. When hand brakes are used it simply moves away from the piston without moving it.

Push Pole. A pole or wrought iron tube which is used as a strut to span diagonally the distance between the corners of a locomotive and a car, standing on two parallel tracks, and which is used to push such car without switching the locomotive onto the same track that the car occupies.

Push Pole Bracket. See **Pilot Shoe.**

Putty. A mixture of linseed oil with whiting, which latter is chalk finely pulverized. Water is sometimes added in adulteration, causing the putty to stick to the fingers, and making it hard and brittle when dry. Panel putty, used for filling nail holes, is an extra quality made from whiting, white lead in oil, Japan or varnish, and a small quantity of turpentine. The whiting is used merely to prevent the white lead from sticking to the fingers, and no more than necessary for this purpose is required. This putty forms a hard cement, which does not shrink. When dry it can be rubbed down with pumice stone or dusted with sandpaper. Glycerine putty is made of good thick glycerine and white lead or litharge. It hardens in 15 to 45 minutes, and stands water and acids.

Pyle-National Electric Headlight. Figs. 3267-3290.

Q

Quadrant. Figs. 1976-1988; 3049-3052. A notched sector along which the reverse lever moves and which, by means of a latch, holds the lever at any particular point to regulate the point of cut-off in the cylinders. Used also for a throttle lever.

Quartering Machine. Fig. 5000. A machine especially designed for locating and boring the crank pin holes in locomotive driving wheels. The machine derives its name from the fact that crank pins are set quartering, or at 90 degrees from each other.

Quick-Action Air Brake. Figs. 2412-2415. A system now almost universally used, equipped with quick-action triple valves to permit the rapid, successive application of brakes throughout the train. See **Westinghouse Air Brake** and **Triple Valve**.

Quick Action Triple Valve (Air Brake). See **Triple Valve**.

Quill. See **Armature Quill**.

R

Rack. 1. "A frame for receiving various articles."—Webster.
  2. "In machinery, a rectilineal sliding piece, with teeth cut on its edge for working with a wheel."—Brande. A **Ratchet**, which see.

Rack Locomotive. Figs. 126-129. A locomotive for climbing grades too steep for good adhesion. It runs on rails as other locomotives, and on moderate grades the adhesion of the driving wheels is sufficient, but on the steepest grades a rack rail is laid between the two running rails and engages with gears keyed on the center of the driving axle, thus giving a positive tractive effort. The boiler is mounted so as to preserve a uniform water level when the locomotive is climbing a steep grade. Rack locomotives are provided with powerful air, hand and water brakes to prevent runaways down grade.

Radial Stay. In many boilers the crown sheet of the firebox is supported by a number of rods or stays passing through the outside of the firebox and secured by nuts. These stays are set radially to the curvature of the crown sheet, hence the name.

Radial Stay Boiler. Figs. 159-172, etc. A boiler having a transversely arched crown sheet, supported from the outside sheet by stays or stay bolts set on lines that are radii of curvature of the inner and outer sheets. Boilers with flat crown sheets supported by similar stays are also designated as of the radial stay type.

Radial Truck. Figs. 3344-3348, 3407-3477. A two-wheel engine truck, either leading or trailing, which is free to turn about a pivot, to which it is attached by **Radius Bars**, which see.

Radius Bar. 1. 10, Figs. 3344-3348; Figs. 3363-3364. On locomotives having a two-wheel leading or trailing truck, one of two heavy beams forming a triangular frame, the apex of which is pivoted on a transverse brace secured to the frames back of the cylinder saddles or under the firebox. The outer ends of the radius bars are fastened to the side frames of the truck.
  2. The bar extending from the valve stem to the link of the Walschaerts valve gear, taking the place of the ordinary valve rod. See **Valve Gear**.

Radius Bar Brace. 11, Figs. 3344-3348. A brace riveted to the radius bar near its pivot and secured at its outer end to the bottom of the truck pedestal.

Radius Bar Clamp. A heavy piece of metal fastened across the two pieces that form the radius bar of a two-wheel truck to bind them firmly together.

Radius Bar Crosstie. 13, Figs. 3344-3348; Figs. 3357-3358. A heavy iron bar riveted across the frames back of the center line of the cylinders or under the firebox, and having a pivot or center pin on which the radius bar, and with it the truck, can swing.

Radius Bar Pin. The pivot on which the radius bar turns.

Radius Rod (Walschaerts Valve Gear). Fig. 1812. Also called radius bar. A steel bar or rod attached at one end by a pin to the upper end of the **Combination Lever**, which see, and at the other to the link lifter on the reverse shaft arm. It also carries the link block, at a point near to the point of attachment to the lifting link.

Radley & Hunter Diamond Stack. Figs. 472-473.

Rail Guard (British). 10, Figs. 5077-5078. A piece of metal fastened to the front bumper and curving slightly forward to within a few inches of the rail. Used on British and other foreign locomotives that have no pilots.

Railway Steel-Spring Co.'s Steel Tired Wheels. Figs. 4538-4546.

Ratchet. A serrated edge like that of a saw, sometimes straight and sometimes on a wheel, into which a pawl engages, for producing or (more commonly) restraining motion. See **Brake Ratchet Wheel**.

Ratchet Wheel. A wheel with teeth like a saw cut into the outer edge to engage with a **Pawl**, which see, which prevents the wheel from being turned in one direction while allowing it to turn in the opposite direction. See **Brake Ratchet Wheel**.

Reach Rod. Figs. 2007-2008; 126, Figs. 77-124. A bar reaching from the reverse lever to the reverse shaft arm. Sometimes made of pipe.

Reach Rod End. 14a, Figs. 1917-1988. The end of a reach rod fitted to take the reverse lever or the reverse shaft arm.

Receiver Pipe. Fig. 2222. In cross-compound locomotives, a pipe conveying exhaust steam from the high-pressure steam chest to the low-pressure steam chest.

Receiver Pipe Flange. An extension or edge around the end of a receiver pipe.

Receiver Pipe Ring. A metal ring fitted to the end of a receiver pipe and having one side ground to a hemispherical surface.

Receiver Pipe Support. A casting secured in the smokebox to hold a receiver pipe.

Reducer (Pipe Fittings). A means of decreasing the diameter of the pipe used. They are either **Bushings, Couplings or T's**, which see.

Reducing Tee or **T** (Pipe Fittings). See also **Reducer** and **T**. A pipe fitting having three openings, one of which is smaller or larger than the other two.

Reducing Valve. Figs. 3161-3162. A valve for air or steam that receives the fluid at a certain pressure and delivers it at a predetermined lower pressure. Used for the live steam connection to low pressure cylinders on compound locomotives, for the steam heat pipe for train; automatic reducing valve for high speed brake, and air signal reducing valve.

Reducing Valve Dash Head. A plunger fitting in a small cylinder, and attached to the stem of the intercepting valve on a compound locomotive to cause the intercepting valve and reducing valve to seat and unseat without jar when the engine is changed from compound to simple and vice versa.

Reducing Valve Pipe (Air Brake). The pipe which connects the reducing valve with the independent brake valve in the **Westinghouse ET Locomotive Brake Equipment,** which see.

Regulating Nut (Pump Governor). 40, Figs. 2458-2461. A cap nut in the top of an air pump governor which can be screwed up and down to alter the tension of the **Regulating Spring,** which see.

Regulating Spring (Pump Governor). 41, Figs. 2458-2461. A spiral spring in the upper part of an air pump governor, which by its tension, holds a piston to which the pin valve is attached on its seat until the main reservoir pressure rises to such a point that it forces the piston up, overcoming the tension of the spring, opening the pin valve, and as a result, closing the steam supply to the pump.

Regulator. 1. See **Reducing Valve.**
  2. The British term for **Throttle,** which see.

Regulator Head (British). 119, Figs. 5077-5078. See **Throttle Box.**

Regulator Lever (British). 117, Figs. 5077-5078. See **Throttle Lever.**

Regulator Rod (British). 120, Figs. 5077-5078. See **Throttle Rod.**

Regulator Valve (British). 121, Figs. 5077-5078. See **Throttle Valve.**

Release. The position of the valve in which either end of the cylinder is in communication with the exhaust port and thereby releases the steam from the cylinder.

Release Cock. See **Release Valve.**

Release Spring. 1. (Tender Trucks.) 17, Figs. 4294-4382. A spring attached to the end piece of a truck for the purpose of throwing the brakes out of contact with the wheels. The name is also applied to any spring used to throw the brake off from the wheels, either drivers or engine truck.
  2. (Brake Cylinder.) 6, Figs. 2497-2498. A spiral spring coiled around the piston rod and compressed when the piston moves out to apply the brakes. It moves the brake piston inward, and thus releases the brakes from the wheels after the compressed air is allowed to escape from the cylinders.

Release Valve (Air Brake). More properly an auxiliary reservoir bleeding valve. A cock attached to the auxiliary reservoir for permitting the air pressure to be reduced therein, when the locomotive is detached or when the apparatus is out of order, so as to release or "bleed" the brakes.

Release Valve Rod. A rod extending from the release valve on the auxiliary reservoir to the side of the tender to operate the release valve.

Relief Valve. Figs. 991-1014. A valve screwed into a cylinder head or steam chest, and having a disk held to its seat by a spring whose tension is so adjusted that the valve will lift in case an accumulation of water or an abnormal pressure of steam occurs. Also called cylinder head relief valve and water relief valve.

Reservoir. 156, Figs. 77-121; Figs. 2463, 2627-2633. A receptacle, usually cylindrical, in which air is compressed and stored for the air brake and signal system. A locomotive is generally, but not always, equipped with two main reservoirs, brake valve reservoir, and driver brake, truck brake, and tender brake auxiliary reservoirs. See **Air Brake.**

Reservoir Drain Cock (Air Brake). Fig. 2468. A cock for emptying the reservoir of any water condensed from the compressed air.

Reservoir Pipe (Air Brake). The pipe that conveys the compressed air from the main reservoirs to the brake apparatus.

Resistance. 1. The property of an electric conductor which opposes the passage of an electric current through it. The reciprocal of **Conductivity,** which see.
  2. A coil or length of metallic wire or ribbon or a volume of water or oil, having high relative resistance, interposed in an electric circuit to reduce the amount of current flowing through it. See **Rheostat.**

Retaining Ring (for Wheel Tires). Figs. 4559-4561. A ring securing the tire to the wheel. See **Mansell Retaining Ring** and **Tire Fastening.**

Retaining Valve. See **Pressure Retaining Valve.**

Return Bend (Pipe Fittings). A short cast-iron U-shaped tube for uniting the ends of two wrought-iron pipes. They are called close return bends, or open return bends, according as the section of the pipe is kept a distinct circle at all points. The close return bend has simply a partition dividing the two parts for a short distance.

Reverse Lever. 125, Figs. 77-121; Figs. 1917-2000. A lever pivoted to the frame or the foot plate and connected by means of the reach rod and reverse arm to the link of the valve gear for moving the link and thereby either reversing the motion of the engine or causing the valves to cut off steam at any desired point. It is arranged to move along a notched sector or quadrant, in any one of whose notches it can be latched. Sometimes made in two pieces, fastened together. On British locomotives the reversing mechanism commonly consists of a hand wheel on a shaft having a worm gear which moves an arm attached to the reach rod.

Reverse Lever Foot Rest. Figs. 1973-1975. An inclined step or brace attached to the reverse lever quadrant or other convenient place, against which the engineman can place his foot when moving the reverse lever.

Reverse Lever Fulcrum. Figs. 1999-2000. A casting having lugs or jaws and holding the lower end of a reverse lever by a pivot. The fulcrum is secured either to the deck plate or to the frame.

Reverse Lever Fulcrum Pin. Figs. 1997-1998. The pivot passing through the lower end of a reverse lever and holding it in place in the fulcrum.

Reverse Lever Handle. The upper end of a reverse lever, which is grasped by an engineman.

Reverse Lever Latch. 6, Figs. 1917-1951. A catch or detent having a tooth or bolt held in place by a latch box through which it passes, and forced into a notch in the reverse lever quadrant by means of a spring.

Reverse Lever Latch Box. A box-shaped piece fastened to the reverse lever to hold the latch bolt, which passes through it.

Reverse Lever Latch Gib. A steel wedge or strip in a reverse lever latch box, held in place by a set screw or thumb screw, to form a guide for the latch bolt.

Reverse Lever Latch Link. 7, Figs. 1917-1958. One of two small rods fastened to the reverse lever latch at one end and to the latch handle at the other for the purpose of lifting the latch bolt out of a notch in the quadrant when the latch handle is grasped and pressed up against the reverse lever handle.

Reverse Lever Quadrant. 1, Figs. 1917-1958. A steel bar or bars forming an arc of a circle, over or along which the reverse lever moves. It is secured to the frame or deck plate or to the side of the boiler, and has notches cut in its upper surface for the bolt of the reverse lever latch.

Reverse Lever Quadrant Bracket. Figs. 1966-1971. A lug secured to the side of the boiler to serve as a bracket to which the quadrant is bolted.

Reverse Lever Quadrant Stand. A standard secured to the deck plate and having a lug or projection on its upper end to which the quadrant is bolted.

Reverse Lever Slot Plate. A piece of metal having a narrow longitudinal opening in it fastened to the floor of a locomotive cab to allow the reverse lever to pass through. A slot plate is used in designs where the reverse lever fulcrum is attached to the frame and is below the cab floor.

Reverse Shaft. 12, Figs. 2001-2006. A transverse shaft resting at each end in bearings or boxes bolted to the frames. The upper reverse arm, secured to one end of this shaft, rotates it when the reverse lever and reach rod move. The reverse shaft carries also two arms, one near each end, from which the link lifters or hangers are suspended. Called also lift shaft and lifting shaft. British, weigh shaft.

Reverse Shaft Bearing. Figs. 2013-2017. A casting bolted on the frames on each side, with a cap bolted on, furnishing a bearing for the ends of the reverse shaft.

Reverse Shaft Bearing Bushing. A bushing or sleeve in the reverse shaft bearing, usually case hardened, and forming the actual bearing for the reverse shaft.

Reverse Shaft Bearing Cap. A cap or cover bolted on top of a reverse shaft bearing.

Reverse Shaft Box Bolt. A bolt holding the reverse shaft box or bearing in place on the frame.

Reverse Shaft Pin. A pivot or pin on the lower arm of a reverse shaft, and on which the upper end of the link lifter is secured.

Reverse Shaft Reach Rod. See **Reach Rod.**

Reverse Shaft Reach Rod Guide. A guide, strap or keeper through which the reach rod passes, to hold it in place. Usually secured to the running board or the side of the boiler.

Reverse Shaft Reach Rod Pin. A pin or pivot connecting the reach rod with the reverse shaft arm.

Reverse Shaft Spring. Figs. 2024-2025; 9, Figs. 2032-2037. A half elliptic or helical spring, attached to a lug or short arm on the reverse shaft. The tension of the spring balances the weight of the links and eccentric rods and assists the engineman in moving the reverse lever.

Reverse Shaft Spring Bracket. Figs. 2026-2031. A transverse iron brace bolted to the frames to hold the reverse shaft spring. Called also reverse spring bracket.

Reverse Shaft Spring Casing. 9a, Figs. 2032-2037. A cylindrical cover or housing for a coil or helical reverse spring.

Reverse Shaft Spring Lug. Figs. 2038-2039. A lug attached to the center of a reverse shaft for the attachment of the spring rod by means of a pin.

Reverse Shaft Spring Nut. A nut on the reverse spring rod to adjust the tension exerted by the spring on the reverse shaft.

Reverse Shaft Spring Pin. A bolt holding one end of the spring rod securely to the spring lug.

Reverse Shaft Spring Rod. 11a, Figs. 2032-2037. A rod fastened to a reverse shaft spring and connecting it with the lug on the shaft arm.

Reverse Spring. See **Reverse Shaft Spring.**

Reversing Cock (Air Brakes). Fig. 2531. A special form of cock used with the high-speed brake and double-pressure control equipments, for the purpose of throwing the control of brake pipe pressure on to either one of the two slide-valve feed valves attached to its sides. One feed valve is set for a low-brake pipe pressure, and the other for a high. The reversing cock is connected by piping to the brake valve in such a way that when feeding up the brake-pipe pressure the air must pass through the reversing cock and one of the feed valves before going to the brake pipe. The feed valve through which it passes depends on the position of the reversing-cock handle.

Reversing Cock Pipe Bracket (Air Brake). Fig. 2536. A bracket arranged for pipe connections, which bolts to the brake valve in place of the slide valve feed valve, and is connected by piping with the **Reversing Cock,** which see. Often called a feed-valve pipe bracket.

Reversing Valve (Air Pump). 72, Figs. 2429-2435. A slide valve operated by the reversing rod in a small cylinder in the top head, which controls the admission and exhaust of steam to the chamber back of the large main-valve piston, thereby causing the main valve mechanism to operate. See **Reversing Valve Rod.**

Reversing Valve Bush (Air Pump). 73, Figs. 2429-2435. The bushing which is inserted in the top head and forms the seat for the reversing valve. See **Bushing.**

Reversing Valve Chamber Cap (Air Pump). 74, Figs. 2429-2435. A screw plug by means of which access is had to the reversing valve chamber and reversing valve.

Reversing Valve Rod or Stem (Air Pump). 71, Figs. 2429-2435. A slender steel rod attached to the reversing valve of an air pump. It passes through the steam cylinder from top to bottom, inside the piston rod, which is made hollow to allow this. The reversing valve plate on the steam piston also fits loosely around the reversing valve rod, and at the top of the cylinder it strikes a lug on this rod, thereby lifting the rod when the piston has reached the end of its stroke. This movement causes the reversing valve to admit or release steam pressure back of the large main valve piston, and by this means move it and the main slide valve with it, thereby admitting steam above the piston and starting it on its downward stroke.

Rheostat (Electric Locomotive). Fig. 4663. A resistance used in connection with the controller for limiting the current taken by the motors during acceleration. Usually consists of a number of iron grids or strips of iron ribbon properly connected together and packed in a substantial frame, the whole being mounted in groups along the sides and near the ends of the cab of the locomotive.

Rib (of a Cast Iron Wheel). A **Bracket,** which see.

Richardson Balanced Slide Valve. Figs. 2122-2125. See **Allen Valve.**

Richmond Cross Compound Locomotive. Fig. 32. Details Figs. 2216-2221. See **Compound Locomotive.**

Right and Left Screw. A pair of screw threads cut turning in opposite directions, so that a common nut or pipe coupling tapped with similar threads will, according to the direction in which it is turned, draw the two rods nearer together or press them farther apart.

Rigid Trailing Truck. Figs. 3179-3181. See **Trailing Truck.**

Rim. 1. (Of a Car Wheel.) That portion of a car wheel outside of the plate. The face of the rim is the outside vertical edge or face.

2. (Of a Steel Tired Wheel.) 2, Figs. 1353-1367. The wrought ring which is welded or cast in the outer ends of the spokes and is surrounded by the tire.

Rivet. "A pin of iron or other metal, with a head drawn through a piece of timber or metal, and the point bent or spread and beaten down fast to prevent it being drawn out, or a pin or bolt clinched at both ends."—Webster.

Riveted Joints. Figs. 315-330.

Riveting Machine. Figs. 5001-5002. A machine for driving rivets; usually operated by hydraulic power, although sometimes operated by steam or compressed air. The riveting machines used for riveting locomotive fireboxes and boilers are commonly called gap riveting machines.

Rocker (Valve Gear). 20 and 21, Figs. 1813-1815; Figs. 2045-2056. A short shaft having two arms, one of which is pivoted to the valve rod and the other to the link block or to the transmission bar pin. Frequently called a rock shaft or rocker shaft.

Rocker Box. 22, Figs. 1813-1815; Figs. 2063-2068. A casting with bearings in which the rocker shaft rests. It is bolted to the frame on each side of the engines. British, rocker shaft carrier.

Rocker Box Cap. A cast iron cover secured to the box by bolts. It is provided with an oil cup, and when removed gives access to the rocker shaft.

Rocker Bushing. A cylindrical sleeve fitted inside the rocker box as a bearing for the shaft. Usually made of phosphor bronze or other anti-friction metal.

Rocker Pin. 1. (Bottom.) A hardened steel pin passing through the lower rocker arm and fastened to it. This pin carries the link block, or the forward end of the transmission bar. In locomotives having the transmission bar carried over the forward driving axle, the rocker is sometimes hung with both arms downward, in which case the inner arm would carry the transmission bar pin, while the outer one would connect with the valve rod.

2. (Top.) A similar pin secured to the upper rocker arm to the valve rod.

Rocker Shaft Carrier (British). See **Rocker Box**.

Rocker Trunnion Collar. An enlargement or fillet on the rocker shaft.

Rocking Grate. Figs. 528-545. A grate having grate bars carried in bearings on the side frame and revolved out of a horizontal position to drop the ashes by means of a system of crank arms and levers operated from the cab deck. See **Grate** and **Shaking Grate**.

Rocking Shaft (British). See **Rocker**.

Rod. 1. A slender bar of iron with a nut on each end, in distinction from a bolt which has a head on one end and a nut on the other. Very long bolts are often called rods. Rods in general take their name from the parts with which they are connected or the use which they serve.

2. On a locomotive the steel connecting bars between the crosshead and the several driving wheels. See **Main Rod, Side Rod, Eccentric Rod, Valve Rod, Brake Rod**.

Rod Bearing. The bearing secured in the end of a main or side rod where it is in contact with the journal of the crank pin or wrist pin. Called also rod brass.

Rod Oil Cup. Figs. 1286-1300. A holder for supplying oil to a crank pin. Sometimes screwed into the stub or strap, and frequently forged on the stub end.

Rolled Axle. An axle made of rolled iron. See **Axle**.

Roller. "That which rolls; that which turns on its own axis, particularly a cylinder of wood, stone, metal, etc."—Webster.

Roller Side Bearings, Body and Truck. Figs. 4519-4521. See **Anti-Friction Side Bearings**.

Roof. 1. (Cabs.) 162, Figs. 77-124. The cover or upper part of a cab with a surface sloping to the sides to shed water.

2. (Firebox.) See **Crown Sheet**.

Roof Sheet. See **Outside Firebox Sheet**.

Rope. "A large string or line composed of several strands twisted together."—Webster.

Runboard. 45, Figs. 77-124; 2231-2246. A narrow platform, made of wood or steel, placed on each side of the boiler to enable the engineman or fireman to go from the cab to the front end of the locomotive. Called also running board and run.

Runboard Angle. An angle secured to a steel runboard to stiffen it.

Runboard Bracket. 172, Figs. 77-124. A cast, malleable or wrought iron bracket fastened to the boiler and to the runboard to support it.

Runboard Edge A strip of iron or brass on the outer edge of a wooden runboard

Runboard Tee. A T-shaped support for a runboard.

Rushton Radial Trailing Truck. Figs. 3469-3477.

Russia Iron. A form of sheet iron manufactured in Russia, the exact process for making which has heretofore been kept secret, but which consists essentially in forming a chemical compound of iron upon its surface at the same time that it is highly polished, so that it is not likely to rust. Modern substitutes for this iron are also known as **Planished Iron**, which see. Used for boiler and cylinder jackets.

S

S., H. & H. Tender Truck. Figs. 4306-4310.

Saddle. 10, Figs. 77-124; 13, Figs. 788-1029; Figs. 800-803. That part of a cylinder casting on which the smokebox rests and containing the steam and exhaust passages is called a half saddle. In very large engines the saddle is sometimes cast separately and bolted to the cylinders through flanges on each. See **Driving Box Saddle, Link Saddle**.

Saddle Tank Locomotive. Figs. 76-77, 3, 5-6, etc. A locomotive having a water tank over the top of the boiler.

Safety Beam (Trucks). 17, Figs. 3369-3380. A longitudinal timber connecting the end piece and transom above the axles and inside of each wheel piece. Iron straps (axle safety bearings) are attached to the beam and pass under the axles so as to hold them in position in case of a breakage of axles or wheels on either side.

Safety Chain. Figs. 3768-3770. A chain fastened to each of the forward corners of a locomotive truck and to the bumper timber to prevent the truck from turning in case of derailment. Safety chains are also fastened to the four corners of both tender trucks to hold them to the tender frame, and in addition two are commonly used between the engine and tender in case a safeguard of a drawbar or drawhead breaks. Called also check chains.

Safety Chain Clevis. A holder or stirrup fastened to a locomotive or tender truck for the attachment of a safety chain.

Safety Chain Eye. 30, Figs. 3369-3380. An iron eye with a broad base bolted to the under side of the side sills of a tender or to the truck frame to receive the hook on the end of a truck safety chain.

Safety Chain Eye Bolt. Figs. 3768-3770. An eye bolt secured to an engine bumper, a tender sill or a truck frame to hold the end of a safety chain.

Safety Chain Hook. Figs. 3768-3770. A hook on the end of a safety chain or check chain to attach it to an eye on the truck or on the frame of an engine or tender.

Safety Chain Lug. A projection or eye for the attachment of a safety chain.

Safety Chain Pin. A pin put through the jaw of the safety chain clevis to secure the clevis to an eye bolt or lug.

Safety Steam Heating Apparatus. Figs. 3180-3194.

Safety Strap. 9a, Figs. 3344-3351. A bent piece of iron on a two-wheel front truck to support the end of the equalizer in case of breakage of a center pin. See also **Guide Safety Strap, Axle Safety Strap.**

Safety Valve. 1. Figs. 3214-3225; 153, Figs. 77-124. A valve screwed into an opening in the steam space of a boiler, arranged to open at a predetermined pressure, for which it has been set, in order to relieve the boiler pressure and prevent an explosion. It consists of a case with a circular opening having a conical seat on which a disk fits accurately and is held in place by a spiral spring, or by a lever which in turn is held by a spring. The lever type is little used now. The usual form has the spring inside the case and is provided with an adjusting nut for regulating the tension of the spring so that the valve will open and relieve the boiler at any pressure desired. Two and sometimes three safety valves are used on a locomotive boiler. They are screwed in the dome cap or in a turret on the boiler. See **Pop Safety Valve.**

2. (Air Brake.) Fig. 2511. A pop valve applied to the brake apparatus in various equipments so as to prevent an excessive pressure in the brake cylinders. The same valve is applied to the main reservoir on electric locomotives to prevent an excessive accumulation of pressure if the electric pump governor should fail to act.

Safety Valve Extension. A nipple or short piece of pipe screwed in the dome cap and to the lower part of a safety valve.

Safety Valve Extension Flange. A flanged fitting bolted to the body of a safety valve and having the safety valve extension screwed in it.

Safety Valve Turret. 102, Figs. 77-124. A stand or outlet screwed on the top of a boiler for holding the safety valves.

Safety Valve Turret Ring. A ring riveted to an opening in the boiler for the attachment of a safety valve turret.

Sand Box. 46, Figs. 77-124. A receptacle, usually cylindrical, with a dome-shaped top, placed on the boiler for carrying sand to prevent slipping of the driving wheels. It is operated by a rod from the cab to a valve or by a pneumatic sander which allows sand to run through the sand pipes to the rail in front of the drivers. The sand box is also sometimes located beneath the running board.

Sand Box Arm. A lever or rod connection to open or close the sand box valve.

Sand Box Base. An iron or steel casting secured to the shell of the boiler, and bolted to the body of the sand box.

Sand Box Bracket. A casting or projection secured to the top of a boiler to hold a sand box.

Sand Box Casing. Fig. 3235. The outside sheathing or cover of a sand box.

Sand Box Connection Pins. Short studs used to secure the links to the operating shaft and valve of a sand box.

Sand Box Cover. 47, Figs. 77-124. A dome-shaped casting or pressed steel shape having a hole in the top, and forming the upper part of a sand box.

Sand Box Lug. A projection forming part of a sand box base by which it is bolted to the sand box bracket.

Sand Box Pipe. 7, Figs. 3230-3231. An outlet pipe on each side of a sand box to connect with the sand pipes that lead down to the rail.

Sand Box Rod. A rod secured to the arm or lever of a sand box valve, and extending from the sand box to the cab.

Sand Box Rod Handle. That part of a sand box rod which is grasped by the engineman to operate the sand box valve.

Sand Box Shaft. A short shaft with links attached for operating the sand box valve. It has an arm fastened to one end for attaching the operating rod to the cab.

Sand Box Step. 48, Figs. 77-124; Figs. 3232-3234. A standing place secured to the side of a locomotive boiler to enable a man to reach the sand box.

PROPORTIONS FOR SELLERS' STANDARD SCREW-THREADS, NUTS AND BOLTS.

Screw-Threads.				Nuts.				Bolt Heads.			
Diameter of screw	Threads per inch.	Diameter at root of thread.	Width of flat.	Short diameter rough.	Short diameter finish.	Thickness rough.	Thickness finish.	Short diameter rough.	Short diameter finish.	Thickness rough.	Thickness finish.
1/4	20	.185	.0062	1/2	7/16	1/4	3/16	1/2	7/16	1/4	3/16
5/16	18	.240	.0074	11/16	5/8	5/16	1/4	11/16	5/8	5/16	1/4
3/8	16	.294	.0078	3/4	11/16	3/8	5/16	3/4	11/16	3/8	5/16
7/16	14	.344	.0089	13/16	3/4	7/16	3/8	13/16	3/4	7/16	3/8
1/2	13	.400	.0096	7/8	13/16	1/2	7/16	7/8	13/16	1/2	7/16
9/16	12	.454	.0104	1 1/16	15/16	9/16	1/2	1	15/16	9/16	1/2
5/8	11	.507	.0113	1 1/8	1	5/8	9/16	1 1/8	1	5/8	9/16
3/4	10	.620	.0125	1 1/4	1 3/16	3/4	11/16	1 1/4	1 3/16	3/4	11/16
7/8	9	.731	.0138	1 7/16	1 3/8	7/8	13/16	1 7/16	1 3/8	7/8	13/16
1	8	.837	.0156	1 5/8	1 1/2	1	15/16	1 5/8	1 1/2	1	15/16
1 1/8	7	.940	.0178	1 13/16	1 3/4	1 1/8	1 1/16	1 13/16	1 3/4	1 1/8	1 1/16
1 1/4	7	1.065	.0178	2	1 15/16	1 1/4	1 3/16	2	1 15/16	1	1 3/16
1 3/8	6	1.160	.0208	2 3/16	2 1/8	1 3/8	1 5/16	2 3/16	2 1/8	1 3/32	1 5/16
1 1/2	6	1.284	.0208	2 3/8	2 5/16	1 1/2	1 7/16	2 3/8	2 5/16	1 3/32	1 5/16
1 5/8	5 1/2	1.389	.0227	2 9/16	2 1/2	1 5/8	1 9/16	2 9/16	2 1/2	1 3/32	1 5/16
1 3/4	5	1.491	.0250	2 3/4	2 11/16	1 3/4	1 11/16	2 3/4	2 11/16	1 3/8	1 11/16
1 7/8	5	1.616	.0250	2 15/16	2 7/8	1 7/8	1 13/16	2 15/16	2 7/8	1 15/32	1 13/16
2	4 1/2	1.712	.0277	3 1/8	3 1/16	2	1 15/16	3 1/8	3 1/16	1 5/16	1 15/16

Sand Box Step Block. A bracket on the boiler to which the sand box step is fastened.

Sand Box Top. 47, Figs. 77-124. The lid or cap closing the opening in the cover of a sand box.

Sand Box Valve. 5, Figs. 3230-3231. A valve in the base of a sand box to allow sand to run out through the sand pipes to the rail.

Sand Pipe. 189, Figs. 77-124. The tubes leading down from the sand box outlets to the rails in front of the driving wheels.

Sand Plank. A common name for a **Spring Plank**, which see.

Sander. Figs. 3226-3231, 3253-3254. A device attached to a sand box, operated by compressed air and controlled by a valve in the cab, for delivering sand to the sand pipes.

Sash. The frame of a window or blind, in which the glass or slats are set, but commonly used, especially in compound words, as a substitute for window, meaning the window and sash complete.

Schenectady Compound Locomotive. Details Figs. 2222-2230. Compound locomotives built at the Schenectady works of the American Locomotive Co., including two-cylinder cross compounds, four-cylinder tandem compounds and Cole four-cylinder balanced compounds. See **Compound Locomotive**.

Schenectady Superheater. Figs. 486-495. See **Cole Superheater** and **Superheater**.

Schmidt Superheater. Figs. 483-485, 504-507. See **Superheater**.

Scotch Yoke. See **Valve Rod Block Yoke**.

Scotch Yoke Block. See **Valve Rod Block**.

Scoop Shovel. See **Shovel**.

Screw. "A cylinder surrounded by a spiral ridge or groove, every part of which forms an equal angle with the axis of the cylinder, so that if developed on a plane surface it would be an inclined plane. It is considered as one of the mechanical powers."—Knight. When used alone the term commonly means a wood screw, having a slotted head and gimlet point, for driving in with a screw driver. Machine screws are similar, except that they have no gimlet point and have a metal screw thread. They are used for uniting metallic parts. All ordinary forms of bolts have screw threads cut on them, but are not commonly called screws. A special form of wood screw is a lag screw, which is a large-sized screw with a head like a bolt, so that it may be inserted with a wrench instead of a screw driver. See **Screw Thread**.

Screw Coupling (British). The means by which the engines and vehicles of a train are coupled together. On the Continent it is used for both passenger and freight trains. It comprises a right and left-handed screw provided with a hinged weighted handle, which always hangs downward, so that it has no tendency to unscrew and slacken the coupling, and two nuts with gudgeons taking in the eyes of U-shaped coupling links or shackles. The screw coupling may be either loose, or one shackle may be attached to the drawbar.

Screw Gages. Instruments for measuring the diameter or size of screws. They are of two kinds: external, for measuring male screws, and internal, for measuring female screws.

Screw Jack. Figs. 4578-4579. A jack, the power of which depends upon a screw, turned by a lever. There are several such jacks in use, the bell base, ratchet screw jack, the differential screw jack which has two screws, one working within the other, and jacks with a capstan head, into which a bar may be inserted.

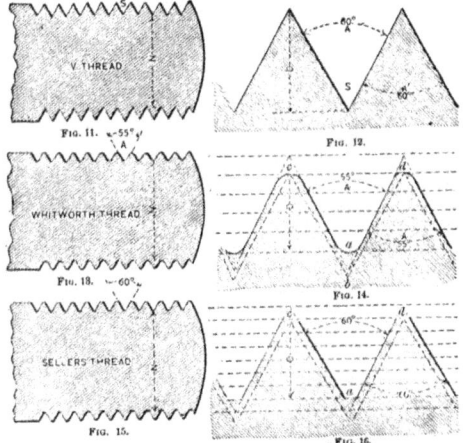

Screw Pitch Gage. "A gage for determining the number of threads to the inch on screws and taps. It consists of a number of toothed plates turning on a common pivot, so that the serrated edge of each may be applied to the screw until one is found which corresponds therewith. The figures stamped on the plate indicate the number of threads to the inch."—Knight. In the ordinary single thread screw the pitch is indicated by the number of threads to an inch.

Screw Thread. The groove, or the material between the grooves, which is cut on the outside surface of a cylinder to form a male screw, or on the inside screw. **Pipe Screw Threads**, which see, are usually V-shaped, but all other threads in common use for

PROPORTIONS FOR SELLERS' STANDARD NUTS AND BOLTS

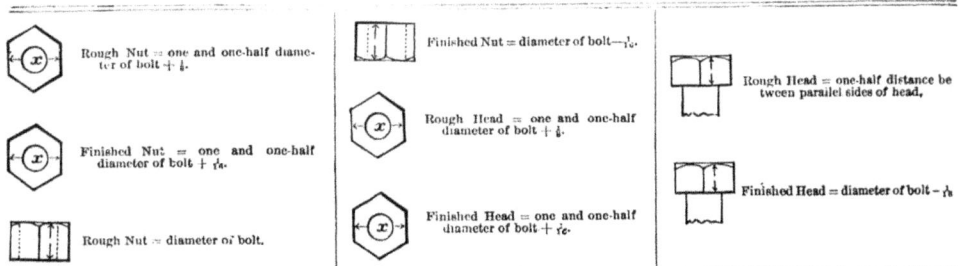

NOTE — In 1899 the following dimensions for square bolt heads were adopted as recommended practice: The side of the head shall be one and one-half times the diameter of the bolt, and the thickness of the head shall be one-half the side of the head.

ordinary purposes are made by the Whitworth or Sellers standard screw threads, the former being the European and the latter the American standard. The American Railway Master Mechanics' Association in 1870 adopted the report of a committee recommending the United States Standard screw thread. The forms and dimensions of the threads are shown below. It is also known as the Sellers surface of a cylindrical hole to form a nut or female and Franklin Institute Standard. This system of screw threads, bolt heads and nuts is the standard of the Association, and repeated action of the Association has deprecated the use of any other system, and encouraged the careful maintenance of these standards.

A set of gages for standard screw threads and a standard inch scale, 2 ft. long, are held in the office of the Secretary for reference.

Mr. Sellers, who proposed this system of screw threads, described it in an essay before the Franklin Institute of Philadelphia, April 21, 1864, as follows:

"The proportions for the proposed thread and its comparative relation to the sharp and rounded threads will be readily understood from the diagrams. The angle of the proposed thread is fixed at 60 degrees, the same as the sharp thread, it being more readily obtained than 55 degrees, and more in accordance with the general practice in this country. Divide the pitch, or, which is the same thing, the side of the thread into eight equal parts, take off one part from the top and fill in one part in the bottom of the thread, then the flat top and bottom will equal one-eighth of the pitch; the wearing surface will be three-quarters of the pitch, and the diameter of screw at bottom of the thread will be expressed by the formula:

$$\text{Diameter,} \frac{1,299}{\text{Number of threads per inch}}$$

The tables on the preceding pages are reprinted from Mr. Sellers' essay; they give the proportions of his standard screw threads, nuts and bolt heads.

The Sellers or Franklin Institute System is also called the United States Standard System. In 1892 the Association adopted as standard the United States Standard sizes of nuts and bolt heads.

In 1903 the arrangement of these standards was made to conform to the arrangement as adopted by the Master Car Builders' Association.

Screw Thread Gage. A steel plate with notches in the edge of the precise form of screw threads, used for giving the proper form to the edges of screw cutting tools.

Seam Lap. That portion of one edge of a boiler plate that is laid over the other edge of the same plate or an adjoining plate to rivet them together.

Second Course (Of Boiler Shell). 37, Figs. 151-206. That section of a boiler adjoining the first course. Made either straight or tapering.

Seibert Lubricator. Fig. 3205.

Sellers Injectors. Figs. 3102-3107. The improved self-acting injector of 1887, class P, Figs. 3105-3107, is a special form of self-acting injector designed for attachment to the back head of the locomotive boiler (Fig 3109). The feed to the boiler may enter through a check valve bolted to the back head and conveyed to the front end by means of an internal pipe, or the delivery pipe may be extended on each side of the boiler to the front end and connected to the usual form of main check valve. The former method is the more economical and has been adopted by some railroads.

The self-acting injector, class K, non-lifting, Figs. 3102-3103, is designed to receive the water supply under head, and should be placed below the running board of the locomotive. It will start promptly, even when the water supply is hot, and the capacity increases with the steam pressure from 30 pounds to 225 pounds, using the same set of tubes. It is of the self-adjusting and re-starting type.

The self-acting injector, class N, Figs. 3104, 3106, is applicable to all kinds of steam boilers. It will lift promptly even when the suction pipe is hot. At 10 pounds steam it can lift the supply water 2 feet; at 30 pounds steam, 5 feet, and at higher pressures, 12 feet to 20 feet. As the name self-acting implies, all the ordinary hand adjustments for re-starting or regulating the feed supply to suit changing steam pressures are entirely dispensed with; all adjustments are automatic. It is also re-starting; that is, if the water supply is temporarily interrupted, the injector will start automatically as soon as the supply is resumed. It is also self-adjusting, as it requires no regulation of the water supply to prevent overflow above 40 pounds steam pressure. The construction is such that the tubes and other parts can be easily taken out for cleaning or repairs. By unscrewing the jam nut the waste pipe sleeve can be removed and the body can then be placed through a round hole in the cab frame.

Sellers System of Screw Threads. A system of screw threads designed by William Sellers, of Philadelphia. Often called Franklin Institute or United States Standard thread. See **Screw Thread.**

Series. A mode of connecting two or more electric motors to the supply circuit. The motors are arranged or connected in series when the current passes first through one and then through the other.

Sessions-Standard Friction Draft Gear. Figs. 3935-3942. A form of friction draft gear in which the friction surfaces are triangular wedges forced together with gradually increasing pressure as they slide over each other.

Set (of Elliptic Springs). The amount of compression of which the spring is capable. The distance between the spring bands when unloaded. The arch is half the set, plus the thickness of the spring band.

Set of Springs. All the springs for carrying the weight of one tender, not including draw springs. A set of bolster springs consist of the springs which are placed between the truck frames and carry the weight of the body only. A set of equalizing bar springs means all the springs for a tender on the equalizing bars. A set of wheel or journal springs means all the springs which are placed directly over the journal boxes of one tender.

Set of Wheels. This term means a number of wheels sufficient for one car or tender. A set of wheels and axles means the requisite number of wheels fitted to axles complete for one car or tender. A pair of wheels means two wheels already fitted to an axle, including the axle; but a set of wheels does not include the axles unless specified.

Sextuple Riveting. Figs. 329-330. An arrangement of six rows of rivets, three on each side of the joint, to hold two abutting edges of a boiler plate and secure them to the inside and outside welts. See **Butt Joint.**

Shaking Grate. Figs. 525-527, 546-720. A grate with broad, flat or finger grate bars carried on eccentric bearings or links and arranged to move up and down relatively to each other to shake the ashes from the fire through to the ash pan below.

Shaper. Figs. 5003-5007. A machine tool intended for a similar but smaller class of work, as that done by the planer. It differs from the planer in that the cutting tool moves back and forth while the table or bed of the machine remains stationary. There are two types of shapers; one known as the crank shaper and the other as the geared shaper. In the crank shaper the ram is driven by a crank movement, while in the geared shaper the ram is driven by a gear meshing in a rack on the under side of the ram. A double head shaper consists of two complete single head shapers mounted on one bed.

Shay Geared Locomotive. Figs. 130-133. A locomotive for climbing steep grades which utilizes the entire weight of engine and tender for adhesion. A three-cylinder vertical engine is mounted on one side just in front of the firebox. It drives a horizontal shaft made in sections and joined with flexible couplings, which extends the entire length of the engine and tender and drives all the axles by means of bevel gears on the shaft and wheels. The wheels are grouped in four-wheel swiveling trucks to enable the locomotive to round sharp curves.

Shearing Machine. Figs. 4992-4998. A machine for shearing or cutting hot or cold metal.

Sheet Metal Gage. A gage, usually a micrometer, for measuring the thickness of thin sheets or plates of metal.

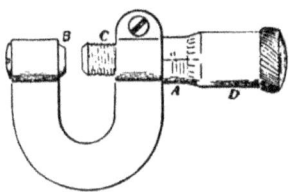

The American Railway Master Mechanics' Association in 1882 adopted the Brown & Sharpe micrometer gage shown below as standard for the measurement of sheet metal. Reaffirmed 1891.

Shell. See **Barrel**.

Shell Plate. The plate or plates composing that part of a locomotive boiler between the smokebox and firebox.

Shelled Out (Car Wheels). A term applied to wheels which become rough from circular pieces shelling out of the tread, leaving a rounded flat spot, deepest at the edge, with a raised center.

Sherburne Sander. Figs. 3226-3231.

Shield. See **Fire Door Shield**.

Shim. A thin piece of wood or metal used as a distance block to save more careful fitting. In track work shims are very largely used in order to remedy the heaving of the rails from frost. Shimming has been used in fitting on car wheels when the wheel seat of the axle was a little too small, but it is considered bad practice.

Shoe. A plate, block or piece of any material on or against which an object moves, usually to prevent the latter from being worn. See **Brake Shoe, Third-Rail Shoe, Pedestal Shoe**.

Shovel. Figs. 4572-4573. A steel tool slightly concave and provided with a wooden handle. Used for putting coal in the firebox. Called also scoop and scoop shovel.

Shunting (British). The act of moving cars from one track to another, as in making up or separating trains. In this country usually called switching. Sometimes the word drilling or regulating is used.

Side Bearing. 32, Figs. 3614-3656; 22, Figs. 4294-4382; Figs. 4511-4521. A support for the body of a tender on the bolster of a truck. The bearings may consist of two plates or of a plate resting on rollers, but in any case the upper half of the bearing is attached to the body bolster and the lower half to the bolster or side frame of the truck on each side. Usually the forward tender truck has a center bearing only, while the rear one has side bearings, in which case the center plate carries no load, and the weight of the tender being supported at three points, excessive rolling on rough or crooked track is prevented.

Side Rod. Figs. 1137-1285. A rolled or cast steel rod connecting the crank pins of any two adjoining driving wheels on the same side of a locomotive to distribute the power transmitted through the main rod to any number of driving wheels. Called also coupling rod and parallel rod.

Side Sheet. See **Firebox Side Sheet**.

Side Sheet Angle Iron. A steel angle bar or post to which one of the sides of a tender tank is riveted. See **Tank Angle**.

Side Sheet Step Support. A bracket secured to the side of a boiler for holding a step.

Side Sill. 1, Figs. 3614-3656. One of the longitudinal outside pieces or members of a tender frame, made of either wood or steel.

Side Water Space (Boilers). 64, Figs. 151-204. See **Water Space**.

Sight Feed Lubricator. Figs. 3195-3205. A device for supplying oil to the cylinders, steam chest and other moving parts surrounded by live steam by admitting drops of oil at regular intervals into small steam pipes which carry the lubricant to the wearing surfaces. The oil is forced through nozzles up through a body of condensed steam in the lubricator, and in rising through the water can be seen through a glass bull's-eye or short glass tube. The amount of oil flowing can thus be determined at all times and regulated according to need by needle valves under the nozzles. Commonly three or more nozzles are combined in one lubricator, one being used for the steam chest on each side and the third for the air pump, or held in reserve.

Signal Fixture. 194, Figs. 77-124. A bracket or holder on engine and tender for carrying lamps, flags or distinguishing markers of any kind. Called also signal lamp fixture and signal lamp holder.

Signal Lamp. See **Lamp**.

Signal Lamp Fixture. Figs. 3326-3328. A bracket on either side of the smokebox and on the two rear corners of the tender to hold signal lamps.

Signal Pipe (Train Air Signal Apparatus). A continuous pipe running from car to car through the train, substantially a duplicate of the brake pipe, but working with a much lower pressure of air. The signal pipe couplings are also similar to brake pipe hose couplings (Fig. 2539), but are arranged so that they will not couple with them.

Signal Pipe Cut-out Cock (Train Air Signal Apparatus). A cut-out cock placed in the signal pipe at each end of the locomotive for closing the signal pipe when the signal pipe hose coupling at that end is not in use. Similar to an **Angle Cock**, which see.

Signal Reservoir (Train Air Signal Apparatus). A small reservoir for storing air used by the train signal equipment. Its use is now altogether obsolete, but formerly it was carried on the locomotive and connected with the main reservoir through the signal reducing valve, which reduces the pressure to that used in the signal system viz., 40 or 45 pounds.

Signals. The lanterns, flags, torpedoes and fuses used for making signals, and carried as part of the equipment of a locomotive.

Signal Valve (Train Air Signal Apparatus). Fig. 2550. A valve attached to a branch from the signal pipe, which, on the opening of the car discharge valve in any car, and the consequent reduction of pressure in the signal pipe, permits the air to escape to blow the signal whistle. On motor cars this valve and whistle are placed in the cab at each end of the car.

Signal Whistle. (Train Air Signal Apparatus.) See **Signal Valve** and **Whistle**.

Sill. A piece of wood or steel forming part of a tender frame. Four or six longitudinal sills are commonly used in wooden frames, while with steel construction fewer may be employed. The center pieces are often called the draft sills. See **Center Sill, End Sill, Intermediate Sill** and **Side Sill**.

Simplex Bolster. Figs. 4113-4420. A type of bolster, both body and truck, using flat iron plates for the top and bottom members, and a cast center filling piece. The ends are lapped over and riveted. In the truck bolster the top member is a channel or I-beam, and a heavy malleable iron strut is used in the center.

Simplex Brake Beams. Figs. 4444-4455.

Simplex Injector. Figs. 3099-3101. An injector of the self-adjusting and re-starting type. It is also self-regulating, requiring no water valve regulation above 50 pounds steam pressure to prevent spilling at the overflow. When located outside of the cab this injector is operated from the cab by means of an extension rod attached to the lever.

Simplicity Bell Ringer. Figs. 3261-3262.

Single Plate Wheel. A cast iron wheel, in which the hub and tire are united by only a single plate, which is strengthened usually by ribs, called brackets, or sometimes by corrugations. See **Wheel**.

Siphon. 4, Figs. 4083-4085. 1. A steel pipe to which the water scoop of a tender is attached, passing through it and having the upper end bent over to deliver water into the tank. Also called siphon pipe.

2. A siphon is placed between a steam gage and the boiler to prevent the steam reaching the inside of the gage. With a siphon, only water can actually enter the bent tube of the gage. Figs. 3157-3158.

Siphon Pipe Support. A bracket fastened on the inside of a tender tank to hold the siphon pipe or siphon.

Six-Wheel Switcher. Figs. 13-16, 78-80. A locomotive having six driving wheels, but no front or trailing truck. Used for switching purposes.

Slab Frame. A locomotive frame forged with a deep and narrow section in order to give sufficient space for a firebox, valve gear, etc. See **Frame**.

Slash Bar. A long, heavy poker used for breaking up lumps of coal in a fire.

Slide Bar (British). 55, Figs. 5077-5078. See **Guide**.

Slide Valve. 1. (Triple Valve.) 3, Figs. 2490-2493. A plain slide valve, controlled in its motion by the piston, by means of which the air is admitted to and exhausted from the brake cylinder, applying and releasing the brake.

2. (High Speed Brake.) See **Reducing Valve**.

3. Figs. 2097-2136. A box-shaped iron casting with a semi-cylindrical cavity in it communicating with the bottom surface which forms the valve face. It is moved backward and forward in a steam chest by a valve rod and stem, and it admits steam to and exhausts it from a cylinder. The top of the valve has two transverse metal strips set in it that rub against a metal plate, called a balance plate, bolted to the under side of the steam chest cover. This device takes the excess pressure off the top of the valve when the engine is using steam, and thereby makes less resistance to be overcome by the valve gear. See **Steam Chest Balance Plate**. Slide valves are sometimes made with a passage through them from one end to the other for the purpose of admitting steam to either port from the opposite end of the valve and thereby getting more steam in the cylinder at short cut-offs than is possible with an ordinary slide valve. This type is called the **Allen Valve**, which see. Often called D valve.

Slide Valve Feed Valve (Air Brake). Figs. 2464-2467. Also called feed valve, reducing valve and slide valve reducing valve. A valve which automatically maintains the pressure of air supplied through the brake valve to the automatic brake system. It may be attached either to the brake valve or placed in the piping between the main reservoir and the brake valve.

Slide Valve Intermediate Spindle (British). 34, Figs. 5077-5078. See **Valve Rod**.

Slide Valve Reducing Valve. See **Feed Valve**.

Slide Valve Spindle (British). 33, Figs. 5077-5078. See **Valve Stem**.

Sliding Door. Figs. 2893-2916. A door opened by sliding sideways instead of swinging on hinges. Such doors are sometimes used at the back of cabs. They are hung by a hook called the door hanger, which slides on a top door track.

Sling Stay. 14, Figs. 151-204. A boiler stay attached at each end with a pin fitting through a hole in a tee or channel bracket on the boiler plates and a corresponding hole in the end of the stay. It gives some degree of flexibility and allows the plates to contract and expand freely and independently.

Sling Stay Channel. Figs. 251-252. See above.

Slotting Machine. Figs. 5008-5011. A machine tool in which the cutting tool is carried on a ram having an up and down movement. The table is usually provided with horizontal, cross and circular feeds. There are two general types of slotting machines, crank slotting machines and geared slotting machines. In the heavier type of slotting machines, such as special locomotive frame slotting machines, the beds are stationary and the heads of the machine are provided with variable power cross and longitudinal feeds.

Smokebox. 175, Figs. 77-124; Figs. 343-442. The forward portion of a boiler to which the products of combustion pass from the tubes before being discharged through the stack. Frequently called front end.

Smokebox Back Ring. 30, Figs. 343-442. A steel ring to which the back edge of a smokebox and the front tube plate or front edge of the boiler shell are secured.

Smokebox Brace. 203, Figs. 77-124. A heavy steel rod fastened to the smokebox at one end and to the bumper timber or frame front at the other. One is usually placed on each side of a smokebox.

Smokebox Crane. 165, Figs. 76-124. A swinging arm pivoted to the smokebox and carrying on it a chain hoist for conveniently handling parts around the front end of the locomotive in case of break downs.

Smokebox Door. 22, Figs. 343-442. A door hinged at the side of the smokebox front, and held in place by clamps held by nuts screwed on studs set in the smokebox front, or by hinged bolts fitting in radial slots in the edge of the door.

Smokebox Door Catch. A bent piece of metal used to fasten a smokebox door to a smokebox front.

Smokebox Door Clamp. See **Smokebox Door.**

Smokebox Door Handle. An arm attached to a smokebox door to operate the catch and to swing the door open.

Smokebox Door Hinge. 226, Figs. 343-442. One or two hinges riveted to a smokebox door and held by pivots passing through projections or lugs cast on the smokebox front.

Smokebox Door Liner. A metal plate or sheet riveted on the inside of a smokebox door to avoid overheating it by the accumulation of sparks in the front end.

Smokebox Extension. A cylindrical ring secured at the front of a smokebox, thus extending or lengthening it 20 or 30 inches and providing space for the accumulation of sparks or cinders which if thrown out of the stack might cause fires near the track. See **Extended Smokebox.**

Smokebox Front. 21, Figs. 343-442; Figs. 394-403. The cast iron or pressed steel front of a smokebox, usually somewhat convex. It has a large circular opening, closed by a hinged door, through which access can be had to the steam and exhaust pipes, draft appliances and tubes.

Smokebox Front Door Washer. A gasket of some heat resisting material placed under the edge of a smokebox door to make an air tight joint with the front.

Smokebox Front Ring. 20, Figs. 343-442. A heavy ring riveted inside the front edge of a smokebox to form a bearing for attaching the smokebox front.

Smokebox Middle Ring. A heavy ring inside a smokebox sometimes used to connect the two plates of which the smokebox is built up.

Smokebox Netting. 18, Figs. 343-442; Figs. 442-443, 446. A network of wire having meshes from ⅜ inch to ½ inch square, placed in the front end of the locomotive to prevent the sparks from entering the smokestack. The netting is usually provided with a door, so as to give ready access to the upper part of the steam pipes and exhaust nozzles. Sheet steel with perforations or meshes stamped out is frequently used. British, spark arrester.

Smokebox Netting Manhole. 31, Figs. 343-442. An opening, with a door, in the netting, to give access to the tubes or steam pipes without removing the whole netting.

Smokebox Ring. Any one of the three rings, back, front and middle, used in building up a smokebox.

Smokebox Spark Arrester (British). See **Smokebox Netting.**

Smokebox Superheater. See **Superheater.**

Smoke Stack. 4, Figs. 77-124; Figs. 455-478. A cast iron, sheet steel or pressed steel pipe or chimney secured to the top of a smokebox to convey the products of combustion and exhaust steam from the smokebox to the outer air. British, chimney.

Smoke Stack Barrel. 1, Figs. 455-482. The straight portion of a smoke stack. Called also smoke stack body. Diamond stacks, for wood burning, have the body conical in shape.

Smoke Stack Base. 4, Figs. 455-482. A plate or foundation casting secured to a smokebox to support the barrel of a stack which is fastened to it by bolts.

Smoke Stack Base Bolt. A bolt passing through a lug on the barrel of a stack and through a corresponding lug on the base.

Smoke Stack Casing. A cylindrical jacket or covering of thin iron or steel on the outside of a smoke stack.

Smoke Stack Cone (Diamond Stack). 12, Figs. 472-477. An inverted conical casting supported in the bell of a diamond stack over the barrel mouth to break up large sparks which are thrown out.

Smoke Stack Hood or **Smoke Deflector.** Figs. 479-482. A movable elbow attached to the top of a stack which can be thrown down clear when running in the open and can be raised to deflect the smoke and cinders back over the engine when running through tunnels.

Smoke Stack Lift Pipe. 5, Figs. 343-342. An extension of the smoke stack inside the smokebox and coming down close to the exhaust nozzle where no petticoat pipe is used.

Smoke Stack Liner. A cylindrical steel casing sometimes used inside a smoke stack to protect it from abrasion by sparks.

Smoke Stack Netting. 15, Figs. 472-477. A mesh of wires placed across the bell of a diamond stack to prevent large sparks from being thrown out.

Smoke Stack Opening. An aperture in the top of a smokebox around which the smoke stack base is fitted.

Smoke Stack Ring. 4, Figs. 455-482. A flange or collar around the base of a stack.

Smoke Stack Top. 7, Figs. 455-482. The upper portion of a stack on top of the barrel or body. British, chimney cap.

Snow Flanger. A plate of iron or steel attached to the pilot of a locomotive to scrape away snow and ice on the sides of the heads of the rails so as to make room for the flanges of the wheels. The term is sometimes applied to an adjustable plow fitted to a locomotive or car which extends low down on the track and has a plate or tool for cutting and scraping the snow and ice from the rail. Figs. 2408-2409.

Solid Wheel. See **Wheel.**

Soule Rawhide Lined Dust Guard. Fig. 4508.

Spanner Wrench. See **Wrench.**

Spark Cleaning Hole. See **Cleaning Hole.**

Spark Pocket. See **Cinder Pocket.**

Specifications for Axles (A. R. M. M. A. Standard). See **Axles.**

Specifications for Locomotive Forgings (A. R. M. M. A. Standard). See **Forgings.**

Specifications for Blooms and Billets (A. R. M. M. A. Standard). See **Blooms and Billets.**

Spectacle Plate. A common name for a **Guide Yoke**, which see.

Splash Plate (British). See **Swash Plate.**

Splasher (British). 86, Figs. 5077-5078. See **Wheel Cover.**

Splice. See **Frame Splice.**

Split Key. A form of pin which is self-fastening, consisting essentially of two parallel strips or bars of metal, which, when united, constitute one pin, but which tend to spring apart, so that the pin cannot be withdrawn without the use of considerable force.

Spoke. "One of the radial arms, which connect the hub with the rim of a wheel."—Knight, 7, Figs. 1353-1367.

Spoke Wheel. Figs. 4567-4568, etc. A wheel, the rim or tire of which is connected with the hub by spokes instead of one or more plates. These spokes are sometimes made of solid cast iron, in others they are cast hollow, and in still others are made of wrought iron or cast steel. All driving and trailing engine truck wheels are spoke wheels.

Spread Driver Brake. Figs. 2562, 2648-2649. See **Cam Driver Brake.**

Spring. Figs. 4522-4537. An elastic body to resist shocks. They are divided into two general groups, elliptic and spiral. Driving springs, or those that transmit the load to a driving axle, are made of flat steel plates from 3 to 5 inches wide and are half elliptic. Similar springs are used for engine and tender trucks, though on tender trucks full ellipties are frequent. Coil or spiral springs are used for driving axles at the end of an equalizer resting on the box. Also for coupler, draft springs and buffer springs.

Spring Band (Elliptic Springs). A wrought iron strap which embraces the plates at the center.

Spring Band Bracket (British). See **Spring Seat.**

Spring Block. A piece of wood or iron used as a stop or distance piece above or below a spring.

Spring Cap. A cup-shaped piece of cast or wrought iron for holding the top of a spring and against which the latter bears. They are further distinguished by the name of the spring, as bolster spring cap, etc. The spring seat comes below the spring, but both these parts are very commonly called spring plates, especially in large group springs.

Spring Hanger. 1. 2, Figs. 1605-1728. A bar or link attached to the frame or to one end of an equalizer for holding or suspending the end of a spring. Called also spring link.

2. (Engine Trucks.) 11, Figs. 3369-3380. A link or suspender fastened at one end by a pin or gib to the equalizer and at the other to a truck spring.

Spring Hanger Gib. 6, Figs. 1605-1728. A flat piece of steel passing through an opening near the end of a spring hanger to connect it with an equalizer.

Spring Hanger Link. 16, Figs. 1605-1728. A bar or link bolted to the end of a spring hanger to connect it with an equalizer above or below it; as when the spring is above and the equalizer below the frame. Also called equalizer hanger.

Spring Link Hanger. See **Spring Hanger Link.**

Spring Link Seat. A plate or block placed above or below a bar of the main frame, holding a pin that passes through a spring hanger or equalizer hanger.

Spring Plank. 20, Figs. 4294-4382. A transverse timber underneath a truck bolster and on which the bolster springs rest. Also called sand plank or sand board. In iron trucks, iron spring plank bars take the place of the wooden spring plank, and in other trucks they are very common. A swing spring plank is used in swing motion trucks. In rigid bolster trucks the spring plank is bolted to the lower arch bar of the truck frame.

Spring Plank Bearing. A casting on which a spring plank rests, and which is supported by the lower swing hanger pivot. Also called crossbar casting or spring plank carrier.

Spring Plate. 4c-4d, Figs. 4294-4382. A common term for spring seats and caps, especially those of considerable size, as for bolster springs. They are often provided with spring plate lugs to hold the spring in place.

Spring Rigging. Figs. 1605-1781. The arrangement of springs and equalizers in any particular design of locomotive.

Spring Seat. 4d, Figs. 4294-4382. A cup-shaped piece of cast or wrought iron, on which the bottom of a spring rests. See **Spring Plate.** They are further distinguished by the name of the spring for which they serve, as bolster spring seat, equalizer spring seat, etc.

Spring Seat Chafing Iron. A metal plate inserted between a spring and the frame to prevent undue wear or cutting by the relative motion of the two.

Sprinkler. A device consisting of a valve and hose connection tapped into the boiler below the water line for forcing water through a hose and thus wetting the coal. See Figs. 2963-2964.

Sprinkler Hose. A flexible rubber tube about 10 ft. long, attached to the sprinkler connection on the boiler head and having a nozzle on the other end for sprinkling coal in the tender.

Sprinkler Hose Nozzle. A perforated metal end attached to the sprinkler hose.

Sprinkler Saddle. The pipe connection to which the sprinkler hose is attached.

Square Bolt Heads. In 1899 the following dimensions for square bolt heads were adopted as Recommended Practice by the American Railway Master Mechanics' Association:

The side of the head shall be one and one-half times the diameter of the bolt, and the thickness of the head shall be one-half the side of the head.

In 1900 these dimensions were adopted as Standard.

Square Root Iron. A term applied by manufacturers to angle iron in which the corners are brought to a sharp angle and not rounded off. Square root iron is one form of angle iron, but is never meant when that term alone is used.

Stack. See **Smoke Stack.**

Staggered Riveting. Figs. 317-318, 327-330. A name applied to the mode of setting rivets in a boiler seam. Two parallel rows of rivets are put in, and each rivet in either row is opposite the space between two rivets in the other row. See **Chain Riveting.**

Standard. 1. A name sometimes applied to the **Column** or **Bolster Guide Bar,** which see.

2. (Of A. R. M. M. Assoc.). A number of standard details of locomotives and tenders adopted by the American Railway Master Mechanics' Association. See **Master Mechanics' Standards.**

Standard Gage. The most common distance between the rails of railroads, which is throughout the world 4 ft. 8½ ins. See **Gage.** This gage originated from the use of an even 5-ft. gage, with outside flanges. As inside flanges came to be preferred, and had to run on the same rails (then with much narrower heads than now), the present standard was of necessity used.

Standard Steel Works Steel Tired Wheels. Figs. 4559-4571.

Star Brass Mfg. Co. Cylinder relief valve, Figs. 991-992; water glass gage, Fig. 3146; pressure gage, Figs. 3148-3150; gage lamp, Fig. 3151; whistles, Figs. 3211-3212; safety valves, Figs. 3222-3223.

Star Headlight. Figs. 3298-3299.

Starting Valve. Figs. 2209-2214, 2227-2229. In compound locomotives, a valve operated manually by a rod from the cab to admit live steam or steam directly from the boiler to the steam passages of the low-pressure cylinder in order to obtain the maximum tractive effort in starting a train. When a moderate speed has been attained, the starting valve should be closed and communication opened between the high-pressure exhaust and the low-pressure steam chest, thus causing the engine to operate as a compound.

Stay Bolt. Figs. 278-305; 12, Figs. 151-206. A bolt with both ends threaded, used for staying the inner and outer plates of a firebox. The ordinary stay bolt is screwed through both plates and its projecting ends are hammered and riveted over the plates. Flexible stay bolts are used to afford some elasticity between the inner and outer firebox sheets, whose different rates or degrees of expansion cause numerous breakages of stay bolts. Hollow stay bolts are used for admitting air above the fire. It is usual to drill a ⅛-inch hole to a depth of about ¾ inch in the outer ends of stay bolts in order to more easily discover a broken stay bolt by the escape of steam and water.

Steam. The vapor of water formed by its ebullition when heat is imparted to it. The temperature of ebullition, or at which water boils depends upon the pressure to which it is subjected. At atmospheric pressure the boiling temperature is 212 deg. Fahr.; at 100 lbs. per square inch it is 338 deg., and at 200 lbs. 388 deg. The formation of steam in a locomotive boiler is a physical change caused by the application of heat; but there also occurs a chemical change, due to the same cause, which results in precipitating the mineral salts held in solution in the water when it entered the boiler and forming a hard crust or scale on the plates and tubes. This scale is a bad conductor of heat, and when it forms on a plate to a thickness of ⅛ in. more coal must be burned to transmit the same amount of heat to the water than before the scale formed, and the firebox, especially the crown sheet, is overheated to a dangerous extent.

Steam Chest. 11, Figs. 77-124; 31, Figs. 788-1029. A cast-iron chamber containing either a slide or a piston valve controlling the admission of steam to a cylinder. See **Slide Valve** and **Piston Valve**.

Steam Chest Balance Plate. 53, Figs. 2097-2118. A cast-iron plate bolted to the under side of the cover of a steam chest and against which transverse packing strips, set in the top of the slide valve, bear so as to make a steam-tight fit. The balance plate reduces the area of the top of the valve exposed to boiler pressure, and thus allows the valve to be moved more easily.

Steam Chest Casing. Figs. 956-963. A thin sheet steel jacket or sheathing placed on a steam chest.

Steam Chest Cover. Figs. 941-943. An iron casting covering the steam chest and secured to it by stud bolts and nuts.

Steam Chest Cover Gasket. Fig. 4760. Usually a thin strip of copper wire or ribbon put in between the steam chest and the steam chest cover to make a steam tight joint.

Steam Chest Head. Figs. 952-955. A circular casting similar in every respect to a **Cylinder Head**, which see, closing one end of a piston valve steam chest. The front head is solid and usually tapped for a water relief valve, while the back head has a hole in it through which the piston valve stem works in a stuffing box.

Steam Chest Oil Plug. Figs. 1004-1008. A brass fitting screwed into a steam chest cover and attached to the end of the cylinder oil pipe by a coupling nut or union.

Steam Chest Valve Seat. 31a, Figs. 788-1029. That part of a cylinder casting in which the steam and exhaust ports terminate and on which the slide valve moves. On locomotives having piston valves, the seat is a cylindrical bushing, with openings in it communicating with the steam and exhaust passages.

Steam Cylinder (Air Pump). 61, Figs. 2429-2435. The admission of steam to this cylinder is controlled by the reversing valve which operates the main slide valve. See **Cylinder**.

Steam Cylinder Gasket. See **Gasket**.

Steam Cylinder Head (Air Pump). 60, Figs. 2429-2435. The upper end or cover of the steam cylinder. The main steam valve and reversing valve are bolted to the top of it. Usually called the top head.

Steam Gage. Figs. 3148-3160. A device for showing the steam pressure in a boiler, consisting of a slightly flattened bent tube filled with steam or water from the boiler and which tends to alter its curvature with any change of pressure. The free end of the tube is connected by an arm to a toothed sector which meshes in a small pinion to which an index or hand is fastened. A very slight change in curvature is thus multiplied and is easily observable on the dial or face of the gage over which the hand or pointer moves.

Steam Gage Cock. Fig. 3017. A stop cock in the steam pipe between the boiler and the steam gage.

Steam Gage Fittings. The pipes, couplings, outlets, turrets, nuts, etc., used to attach a steam gage to a locomotive boiler.

Steam Gage Stand. Figs. 3014-3015. A bracket secured to the boiler inside the cab for the attachment of a steam gage.

Steam Gage Stand Block. A support secured to the boiler for the attachment of a steam gage stand.

Steam Head. See **Tee Head**.

Steam Heat Apparatus. Figs. 3161-3194. An arrangement of valves and pipes by means of which steam is taken from a locomotive boiler, through a reducing valve, and conducted through a pipe to each car of a passenger train.

Steam Heat Couplings. Figs. 3166-3167; 3176-3179; 3182-3185. A fitting attached to a short hose on the end of a steam pipe from the locomotive that couples with a similar fitting on a tender or car.

Steam Heat Gage. Figs. 3193-3194. A pressure gage connected to the pipe supplying steam for heating a train, to enable an engineman to ascertain the pressure of steam used for that purpose.

Steam Heat Reducing Valve. Figs. 3161-3162, 3164. A valve attached to the boiler head or to a turret on the boiler that can be set so as to supply steam for heating a train at moderate pressures according to the requirements of weather and length of train.

Steam Hose. A piece of tubing or hose for flexibly connecting the train heating pipes between engine and tender or between a tender and a car.

Steam Lap. See **Outside Lap**.

Steam Passage (Cylinders). 32, Figs. 788-1029. Cored openings in a cylinder saddle casting leading from the steam pipe in the smokebox to the steam chest.

Steam Pipe. 12, Figs. 343-442. One of two pipes that conduct steam from the dry pipe tee in the smokebox to the cylinder saddle. Usually made of cast iron. In order to permit a little adjustability in fitting and to allow for contraction and expansion steam pipes are made with ball joints or spherical ends where they fit into the tee pipe and cylinder saddles.

Steam Pipe (British). 123, Figs. 5077-5078. See **Dry Pipe**.

Steam Pipe Opening. The aperture in a cylinder saddle casting, to which the lower end of a steam pipe is attached by means of studs set around the opening and passing through a flange on the lower end of the pipe.

Steam Pipe Ring. 44, Figs. 343-442. An iron or brass ring, having one side flat and the other ground to a concave or convex spherical surface to form a flexible joint at either end of a steam pipe.

Steam Pipe T Piece (British). 30, Figs. 5077-5078. See **Tee Head**.

Steam Pipe Union (Air Pump). 130, Figs. 2423-2428.

The pipe coupling to which either the pump governor or steam pipe connection is made.

Steam Port. 35, Figs. 788-1029. An opening in a valve seat or valve chamber at the mouth of a cored passage leading to either end of a cylinder through which live steam enters. See **Exhaust Port.**

Steam Valve or **Main Steam Valve.** 1. (Air Pump.) 76, Figs. 2423-2428. A device for controlling the admission and exhaust of steam to and from the steam cylinder of the air pump by means of the **Reversing Valve,** which see. See **Main Steam Valve.**

2. (Pump Governor.) 26, Figs. 2458-2461. A disk valve in the steam pipe to the air pump. It is attached to the rod of a piston above which air pressure is admitted by the pump governor. A coil spring opens the steam valve as soon as the main reservoir pressure is sufficiently reduced, and thus starts the pump, which pumps up main reservoir pressure until it overcomes the tension of the spring and closes the valve.

Steel. "A variety of iron intermediate in composition and properties between wrought iron and cast iron (containing between one-half of 1 per cent. of carbon) and consisting of an alloy of iron with an iron carbide. Steel, unlike wrought iron, can be tempered and retains magnetism. Its malleability decreases and fusibility increases with an increase in carbon."—Webster.

Steel (Specifications for). The American Railway Master Mechanics' Association in 1894 adopted specifications for the steel entering into the construction of boilers and fireboxes. These specifications were revised in June, 1904, and are as follows:

SPECIFICATION FOR BOILER AND FIREBOX STEEL.
MADE BY THE OPEN HEARTH PROCESS.

1. *Special Requirements for Shell Sheets.*

This grade of steel is known to the trade as flange or boiler steel. The desired tensile strength is 60,000 pounds per square inch, with minimum and maximum limits 55,000 and 65,000 pounds. The elongation in eight inches shall not be less than twenty-five per cent. for sheets three-quarters of an inch thick or under. For thicker sheets, deduct one per cent. from specified elongation for each one-eighth inch additional thickness.

2. *Chemical Requirements for Shell Sheets.*

	Per cent.
Phosphorus shall not exceed (acid)	0.06
Phosphorus shall not exceed (basic)	0.04
Sulphur shall not exceed	0.05
Manganese	0.30 to 0.60

3. *Special Requirements for Firebox Steel.*

The desired tensile strength is 57,000 pounds per square inch, with minimum and maximum limits of 52,000 and 62,000 pounds. The elongation in eight inches shall not be less than twenty-six per cent.

4. *Chemical Requirements for Firebox Sheets.*

	Per cent.
Carbon	0.15 to 0.25
Phosphorus shall not exceed (acid)	0.04
Phosphorus shall not exceed (basic)	0.03
Sulphur shall not exceed	0.04
Manganese	0.30 to 0.50

GENERAL REQUIREMENTS.

5. *Bending Tests.*

Test specimens for this purpose shall be 1½ inches wide, and for material ¾ inch or less in thickness shall be of the same thickness as that of the finished sheet. For sheets more than ¾ inch thick, the bending-test specimen may be ½ inch thick. The sheared edges of bending-test specimens may be milled or planed. The cold bending test shall be made on the material in the condition in which it is to be used. The specimen for quench bending test shall be heated to a light cherry red, as seen in the dark, and quenched in water having a temperature between 80° and 90° F. Boiler steel and firebox steel, before and after quenching, shall bend cold 180° flat on itself without fracture on the outside of the bent portion. The bending test may be made by pressure or by blows. One cold bending specimen and one quenched bending specimen will be furnished from each plate as it is rolled. The homogeneity tests for firebox steel shall be made on one of the broken tensile test specimens.

6. *Specimens for Tensile Test.*

Two tensile test specimens will be furnished from each plate as it is rolled. The standard test specimen of 8-inch gaged length shall be used for the tensile test. The standard shape of the test specimens shall be as shown by the following sketch:

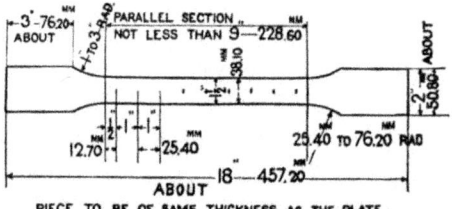

PIECE TO BE OF SAME THICKNESS AS THE PLATE.

7. *Homogeneity Test.*

The homogeneity test for firebox steel is made as follows: A portion of the broken tensile test specimen is either nicked with a chisel or grooved on a machine, transversely about a sixteenth of an inch deep, in three places about two inches apart. The first groove should be made on one side, two inches from the square end of the specimen; the second, two inches from it on the opposite side, and the third, two inches from the last and on the opposite side from it. The test specimen is then put in a vise, with the first groove about a quarter of an inch above the jaws, care being taken to hold it firmly. The projecting end of the test specimen is then broken off by means of a hammer, a number of light blows being used, and the bending being away from the groove. The specimen is broken at the other two grooves in the same way. The object of this treatment is to open and render visible to the eye any seams due to failure to weld up, or to foreign interposed matter, or cavities due to gas bubbles in the ingot. After rupture, one side of each fracture is examined, a pocket lens being used if necessary, and the length of the seams and cavities is determined. The broken specimen shall not show any single seam or cavity more than ¼ inch long in either of the three fractures.

8. *Variation in Weight.*

The variation in cross section or weight of more than two and one-half per cent. from that specified will be sufficient cause for rejection, except in the case of sheared plates, which will be covered by the following permissible variations:

Plates 12½ pounds per square foot or heavier, up to 100 inches wide, when ordered to weight, shall not average more than 2½ per cent. variation above or 2½ per cent. below the theoretical weight. When 100 inches wide and over 5 per cent. above or below the theoretical weight.

Plates under 12½ pounds per square foot, when ordered to weight, shall not average a greater variation than the following:

Up to 75 inches wide, 2½ per cent. above or 2½ per cent. below the theoretical weight. Seventy-five inches wide up to 100 inches wide, five per cent. above or three per cent. below the theoretical weight. When 100 inches wide and over, ten per cent. above or three per cent. below the theoretical weight.

For all plates ordered to gage there will be permitted an average excess of weight over that corresponding to the dimensions on the order equal in amount to that specified in the following table:

9. *Table of Allowances for Overweight for Rectangular Plates When Ordered to Gage.*

Plates will be considered up to gage if measuring not over 1-100 inch less than the ordered gage. The weight of 1 cubic inch of rolled steel is assumed to be 0.2833 pound.

PLATES ¼ INCH AND OVER IN THICKNESS.

Thickness of plate. Inch.	Up to 75 inches. Per cent.	75 to 100 inches. Per cent.	Over 100 inches. Per cent.	Over 115 inches. Per cent.
¼	10	14	18	..
5/16	8	12	16	..
⅜	7	10	13	17
7/16	6	8	10	13
½	5	7	9	12
9/16	4½	6½	8½	11
⅝	4	6	8	10
Over ⅝	3½	5	6½	9

PLATES UNDER ¼ INCH IN THICKNESS.

Thickness of plate. Inch.	Up to 50 inches. Per cent.	50 inches and above. Per cent.
⅛ up to 5/32	10	15
5/32 up to 3/16	8½	12½
3/16 up to ¼	7	10

10. *Branding.*

Each sheet shall be stamped with the melt number and maker's name, and the test specimens cut from it shall be stamped with separate identifying marks or numbers, as may be specified by the purchaser.

11. *Inspection.*

The inspector, representing the purchaser, shall have all reasonable facilities afforded to him by the manufacturer to satisfy him that the finished material is furnished in accordance with these specifications.

Steel Back Brake Shoe. 2765-2786. A brake shoe having a thin steel strip cast into the back of it which holds the parts together in case they break when the shoe is worn down thin.

Steel Tired Wheel. Figs. 4538-4546, 4553-4571. A wheel with a steel tire. The tire is shrunk on, bolted, or fastened with retaining rings.

Step. A foot piece for ascending to or descending from an engine or tender or for standing in certain places or positions. Steps take their distinguishing names from their position or use, as bumper step or headlight step.

Step Hanger. A vertical board or metal plate by which the steps are supported from the corner of a tender or from the locomotive frame.

Step Riser. The vertical portion of a step.

Stephenson Valve Motion. Figs. 1813-1815. See **Valve Gear**.

Stiffening Liner (Boiler Shell Support). 62, Figs. 151-206. A steel plate, riveted on the bottom of a boiler and to the angle piece to which the waist brace or shell brace is riveted. It reinforces that part of the boiler shell.

Stirrup. 1. A ring or bent bar of iron resembling somewhat the stirrup of a saddle.

2. A drawbar carry iron is sometimes called a stirrup.

3. The support placed on a driving box and spanning the frame to carry a driving spring. 11a, Figs. 1605-1728.

Stop Cock (Air Brake). See **Angle Cock, Cut-out Cock**.

"Straight-Air" (Air Brake). A term applied to the original form of the Westinghouse air brake, which is still used on engines and tenders. See **Westinghouse Air Brake**.

Straight Top Boiler. Figs. 148, 177-196. A locomotive boiler having the shell of uniform diameter and with its top level with the top of the outside firebox sheet.

Straightening Rolls. Figs. 5012-5013. A machine for straightening iron or steel plates. It generally consists of four top rolls and three lower rolls supported in housings. The upper rolls can be raised or lowered to allow for different thicknesses of plates. The lower rolls are driven by gearing and are fixed in position.

Strainer. 1. Fig. 4151. A perforated metal cover or plate on the end of a water or air pipe to exclude dirt or foreign particles. A large brass strainer is used in the tender water tank over the end of each suction pipe, so as to exclude foreign matter from the injector feed pipes.

2. In the air brake system strainers are used on air inlet of pump, on pipe from main reservoir to engineer's brake valve, in triple valve on engine and tender, in high speed brake automatic reducing valve and on train air signal pipe. Figs. 2541-2543.

Strap. 1. A long narrow piece or strip of metal usually bent or curved so as to enclose another piece.

2. On main and side rods, a U-shaped strip bolted and keyed to a rod to hold the brass in place. 20, Figs. 1155-1229.

Strap Bolt or **Lug Bolt**. A round bolt with a flat bar of iron welded to it, and usually with a hook on the end which serves the purpose of a head. The flat bar has holes in it, by which it is attached to a piece of timber or other object by one or more separate bolts or screws.

Streeter Brake Shoe. Figs. 2772, 2785.

Stroke. See **Piston Stroke**.

Stub Back Block. A distance piece or spacing piece fitted into the forked back end of a main rod and secured by a bolt and nut.

Stub Brass. 9 and 12, Figs. 1155-1229. A brass bearing, made in halves, fitted to the end of a main or side rod and held in place by a strap. It is called back or front stub brass, according to the end of the rod in which it is used. The two halves are also called front or back, according to their location in the strap. Thus the front stub back brass is the back half of the brass bearing at the front or cylinder end of the main rod.

Stub Bushing. 2, Figs. 1155-1229. A sleeve or cylindrical liner bearing on a crank pin in a rod having a solid stub end, in contrast to one having brasses held by a strap fitted with bolts and keys.

Stub End (Main and Side Rods). 11, Figs. 1155-1229. The enlargement on the end of a main or side rod to which the bearing for the crank pin or wrist pin is attached by a strap.

Stub Key. 7 and 14, Figs. 1155-1229. A key passing through the fork of a main rod for adjusting the brass, in connection with a gib or liner holding the brass in place. Known as front or back stub key, according to the end of the rod on which they are used.

Stub Key Washer. 14a, Figs. 1155-1229. A ring placed on the threaded end of a stub key and having a nut screwed on it. Used on strap end main or side rods.

Stub Liner. 13, Figs. 1155-1229. A thin piece of metal inserted between a stub brass and the key by which it is set out or adjusted.

Stub Plate. Another name for a strap used on main and side rods.

Stub Strap. 20, Figs. 1155-1229. The strap holding the brass in the end of a side or main rod. Called front or back stub strap, according to its location.

Stub Wedge. 14 and 16, Figs. 1155-1229. A tapering piece of steel, a wedge, or gib bearing against the brass in a main or side rod.

Stub Wedge Bolt. A bolt through the side of a rod stub end to bind against the wedge and prevent it from loosening.

Stuffing Box. Figs. 1015-1021. A cylindrical projection cast on a cylinder head or steam chest forming a cup to hold the packing around a piston rod or valve stem. It has a gland or flanged ring bolted on and surrounding the rod, thus holding the packing in place.

Suction Pipe. 9, Figs. 2958-2959. A pipe conveying water from the tender tank to the injector feed pipe by means of a hose connection between engine and tender.

Suction Pipe Clamp. Figs. 2965-2966. A clamp or clasp for coupling the suction hose to the goose neck of a tender.

Superheater. Figs. 483-507. An arrangement of tubes and headers placed in a locomotive boiler to impart heat to the steam in addition to that which it already holds as saturated steam, and thereby giving it power to do more work. This additional heat is imparted after the steam leaves the dry pipe and before it enters the steam chests. Superheaters are placed in the smokebox or in the tubes with headers or connections in the smokebox. Steam from the boiler, passing into the dry pipe, is a saturated vapor. If its temperature be raised by the addition of heat, it will become less saturated, that is, more like a gas, in which condition it will have more available energy. The addition of heat does not, under the circumstances, increase the pressure of the steam, but for any given pressure increases its temperature. When this additional heat can be obtained from the waste gases and smoke, there is apparently an advantage gained. The usual form of superheater consists of small tubes from ⅞ inch to 1½ inch in diameter, connected at one end to a box or header in the smokebox, and into which the dry pipe passes. Steam from the dry pipe goes through the small tubes to the end near the firebox, and returns through another set of small tubes to the steam pipes in the smokebox, taking up on the way the heat from the products of combustion passing through the fire tubes in which the superheater tubes are placed. In order to accommodate the superheater tubes, from 30 to 60 fire tubes, 5 inches in diameter, are used in boilers 70 inches diameter of shell. The degree of superheat varies with the conditions, but from 100 degrees to 200 degrees may be added to the heat in steam by the devices now in use. It is said that the use of a superheater in service effects a saving of coal of 10 per cent. The Schmidt, the Vaughan and the Schenectady, or Cole, types of superheater are those now in use.

Supply Pipe (Air Compressor). A pipe sometimes connected to the air inlet of an air compressor by means of which the air supply is drawn from a point away from the compressor.

Susemihl Roller Side Bearing. Figs. 4519-4521.

Suspension Link (British). See **Link Lifter**.

Swash Plate. 31, Figs. 4067-4118. One of several transverse plates secured in a tender tank to prevent any violent surge or rush of water caused by stopping or starting suddenly. British, splash plate.

Swing Bolster. Figs. 3369-3375, 4315-4318. A cross beam or transverse member of a truck carrying the center plate and suspended by bars or links, called swing links, from a transom or crosstie attached to and resting on the truck frame. It is intended to relieve lateral strains due to the weight of the locomotive, and to absorb lateral shocks that would otherwise be transmitted to the locomotive. Called swing bolster to distinguish it from a rigid bolster. Swing bolster trucks for tenders are built with a wood or steel bolster resting on springs which bear at the bottom on a transverse timber called a spring plank, which is in turn suspended by swing links from the truck frame, thus furnishing the desired lateral flexibility. See **Bolster**.

Swing Frame. 19, Figs. 4315-4318. A casting secured to a truck bolster by short links, and on top of which the center plate rests. See **Swing Bolster**.

Swing Link. 19a, Figs. 4315-4318. One of four short bars or hangers pivoted to a swing bolster and to a transverse member or transom of a truck frame, and forming a flexible connection between the truck and the center casting or center plate. Also called swing hanger or swing link hanger.

Swing Link Pin. 19b, Figs. 4315-4318. A pivot or bolt holding the top or bottom end of a swing link on an engine truck with swing bolster.

Swing Link Pin Key. A small piece of steel holding the end of a swing link pin to prevent it from pulling out.

Swing Motion. A term applied to an arrangement of hangers and other supports for the springs and truck bolster which enables a tender frame to swing laterally on the truck.

Swing Motion Spring. 1. A **Bolster Spring**, which see. 2. A lateral motion spring.

Swing Motion Truck. Figs. 3369-3375, 4315-4318. A truck with a bolster and spring plank suspended on swing hangers so that they can swing laterally to the truck frame. Also called swing bolster truck in distinction from a rigid bolster truck.

Swing Spring Plank. A transverse timber underneath the bolster of a four-wheel truck, on which the bolster springs rest. A swing spring plank differs from an ordinary spring plank in being supported by hangers or links. See **Spring Plank**.

Switch (Air Brake). Fig. 2548. A single-throw, double-break, indicating, snap switch used to make and break the circuit to the motor-driven air compressor and electric pump governor.

Switching. The act of moving cars from one track to another by means of switches, as in making up or separating trains, and placing the cars on the tracks and in places where they are needed. Also occasionally called drilling or regulating, and in Great Britain shunting or marshaling.

Switching Engine Mileage. The American Railway Master Mechanics' Association in 1872 adopted the following recommendations:

"In the matter of cost of keeping up repairs of engines engaged in switching service exclusively, that an allowance of six miles per hour for the time that such engines are in actual use be allowed:

"That for engines running local freight trains an allowance of six per cent. to the train mileage be added for switching:

"That where engines run empty to exceed one-half mile between where the trains are taken or left and the roundhouse, such mileage should be computed, and that for engines running through freight or passenger trains no computation should be made by switching."

Switching Eye. More commonly **Push Pole Corner Iron** or **Pilot Shoe**, which see. A cast iron socket usually attached to the lower corner plate of a tender and at the ends of the front bumpers of a locomotive, to which a push bar or push pole can be attached, to move the car by an engine on an adjoining track. A roping staple or pull iron is sometimes called a switching eye.

Switching Locomotive. Figs. 2-7, 13-16, 19-21, 75-80. A locomotive used for shifting or switching cars in yards and terminals. Sometimes termed switcher.

Symington Journal Box. Figs. 4490-4495. A journal box with a machined joint on the lid and box and with a spring exerting its entire pressure in the center of the lid. The interior of the box is arranged to prevent settling and rolling of waste and to facilitate packing and maintenance.

T

Tail Lamp or **Tail Light.** A signal lamp attached to the rear end of a train. When used on a locomotive running light they are attached to brackets on the rear corners of the tender tank. They often have two or more lenses of different colors.

Tail Piece. See **Back Bumper.**

Tank. Figs. 4063-4226; 256, Fig. 77. That part of a locomotive tender, or of a tank locomotive, that contains the water. Tender tanks for large modern locomotives hold from 4,000 to 9,000 gallons of water.

Tank Angle. A piece of steel bent at right angles, used to brace or secure any of the plates or sheets of which a tender tank is built.

Tank and Coal Bunker. The coal box and water tank on an extension of the main frames of a tank locomotive. In some designs a water tank is placed on each side of the boiler.

Tank Back. The plate that forms the back wall of a tender tank.

Tank Bottom. The plates forming the bottom of a tender tank.

Tank Brace. 18 and 19, Figs. 4067-4118; Figs. 4139-4140, 4159-4176. A steel rod, flat bar or tee or angle riveted to two tank plates to serve as a brace or stiffening piece.

Tank Bracing. The system of rods, bars, tees or angles used to strengthen and secure the various plates composing a tender tank.

Tank Coal Board. A gate or partition composed of several boards sliding in vertical ways riveted to the legs of a tender tank for the purpose of holding back the coal or allowing only a little at a time to slide to the most convenient point to be reached by a fireman.

Tank Coal Bracket. A narrow plate of metal riveted longitudinally to the top of a tender tank to prevent the coal from falling off.

Tank Coal Gate. A door for holding back the coal on a tender.

Tank Coal Gate Hinge. One of two hinges on which a gate for holding back coal in a tender turns.

Tank Coal Rack Slide. 30, Figs. 4067-4118; Figs. 4187-4192. A vertical channel or slide formed by steel angle strips riveted to the inner sides of a tender for a sliding gate or rack that keeps the coal in place. See **Tank Coal Board.**

Tank Collar. Called also tank wings and tank dashboard. A vertical or slightly inclined strip of metal secured around the sides and back end of a tender tank to prevent coal from spilling off.

Tank Dashboard Bracket. Metal strips or holders riveted to the sides and end of a tender tank to hold the projecting edge or dashboard.

Tank Drain Pipe. A piece of pipe open at both ends, screwed into a flange riveted to the tank top near the manhole and passing down through the tank bottom to allow any water spilled on the top plate when filling the tank to run off.

Tank End. See **Tank Back.**

Tank Filling Hole. 5, Figs. 4067-4118. A large opening closed by a flap or lid in the top of a tank near the back end through which water is poured from a water crane alongside the track to fill the tank. Also called tank manhole or tank funnel.

Tank Filling Hole Lid. 1, Figs. 4067-4118. A cover on a tank filling hole or manhole, usually hinged for convenience in opening.

Tank Filling Hole Lid Handle. 2, Figs. 4067-4118. A curved piece of metal fastened to a filling hole lid to serve as a handle for raising or lowering it.

Tank Filling Hole Lid Hinge. 3, Figs. 4067-4118. A hinge fastened to the edge of a filling hole and to its lid.

Tank Fire Tools Bracket. Figs. 4204-4205. A bent piece of metal riveted to a side frame or tank collar of a tender to hold the poker, hoe, or any other long-handled tools used in firing.

Tank Funnel. A term used instead of **Tank Manhole** or **Tank Filling Hole,** which see.

Tank Goose Neck. 15, Figs. 4119-4120. A curved cast-iron pipe to convey water from the front end of a tender tank to a hose which couples to the injector feed pipe. One goose-neck is placed in the bottom of the tank leg on each side of a tender. British, swan neck.

Tank Hand Hold. Figs. 4209-4210; 7, Figs. 4067-4118. A piece of malleable or wrought iron or steel secured to the ends of a tender tank to assist a man in getting on or off.

Tank Handle Post. A short piece of metal riveted to a tender tank to hold one end of a tank handle.

Tank Hose Sleeve. A brass collar fitting loosely around the end of the tank goose neck and having lugs on it for a spanner wrench. It screws on the hose nipple of the suction pipe.

Tank Knee. A right-angled plate used as a brace or stiffening piece in the ends and corners of a tender tank.

Tank Ladder. A metal ladder fastened to the back end of a tender to give access to the tank top from the back bumper.

Tank Legs. 17, Figs. 4067-4118. The front portions of a tender tank, or those nearest the engine and forming the sides of the coal space.

Tank Locomotive. Figs. 2-3, 5-7, etc. One having a water tank and coal box on the extension of the main frames. See **Saddle Tank Locomotive.**

Tank Lug. An angle or bracket riveted to the sides or top of a tender tank for securing the collar or dashboard.

Tank Manhole. 5, Figs. 4067-4118. A round or oblong opening in the top of a tender tank near the back end fitted with a collar to raise it somewhat above the top plate, for filling the tank with water from a crane or stand pipe. Also called tank filling hole and tank funnel.

Tank Side. One of the steel plates forming either side of a tender tank.

Tank Side Bracket. A right-angled casting riveted to a tender side sill and to the bottom plate of the tank, to secure the tank to the frame.

Tank Step. See **Tender Step.**

Tank Support. See **Tank Brace, Tank Angle.**

Tank Swash Plate. See **Swash Plate.**

Tank Tee. A T-shaped piece of metal used inside a tender tank to strengthen and support the sides or top.

Tank Throat. The back part of a tender tank where the two legs join.

Tank Top. The upper or roof sheet or plate of a tender tank.

Tank Valve. Figs. 4119-4128. A valve placed in the bottom of a tender in the tank leg on each side, operated by a stem working in a nut and provided with a handle for opening or closing the valve. Its purpose is to admit water to the goose neck and thence to an injector suction pipe.

Tank Valve Cage. An open metal casting surrounding a tank valve and limiting the extent of its travel.

Tank Valve Chamber. A cast-iron receptacle in the bottom of a tank leg containing one of the tank valves.

Tank Valve Cover. A metal casting, fitted over a tank valve, inside the strainer.

Tank Valve Handle. 8, Figs. 4119-4128. A handle on the upper end of the rod that opens and shuts a tank valve.

Tank Valve Rack. A spiral piece surrounding a tank valve rod and provided with notches or steps to engage with a piece attached to the valve rod for holding the rod at any particular point.

Tank Valve Seat. 2, Figs. 4119-4128. A brass casting with an opening, coned to fit a correspondingly coned piece which forms the tank valve.

Tank Valve Strainer. Figs. 4131-4134. A perforated brass cylinder covering a tank valve to prevent dirt or any solid particles getting in the feed pipe.

Tate Flexible Stay Bolt. Figs. 286-291.

T or Tee (Pipe Fittings). A T-shaped cast iron tube for uniting one pipe at right angles to two others in the same line. The pipes are screwed into the arms of the T. A reducing tee has the arms of different diameters.

Tee Head. 10, Figs. 343-442. A T-shaped pipe attached to the front tube sheet in the smokebox and forming the connection between the dry pipe in the boiler and the steam pipes in the smokebox. Also called steam head and branch pipe, and in Great Britain, steam pipe tee piece.

Ten-Wheel Locomotive. Figs. 61-67, 119-122. Specifically a locomotive having ten wheels, but commonly applied only to locomotives having a four-wheel front truck and six coupled driving wheels. See **Whyte's Nomenclature.**

Ten-Wheel Switcher. Fig. 21. A locomotive having ten driving wheels, but no front or trailing truck. Used for heavy switching service.

Tender. Figs. 3614-3656. A vehicle built of sheet steel on a wood or steel frame, and carried on two four-wheel trucks. Used to carry a supply of fuel and water for an engine. In Great Britain, tenders are usually mounted rigidly on three axles.

Tender Axle. Figs. 4878-4881. (A. R. M. M. Standard.) A shaft made of wrought iron or steel to which a pair of wheels is attached. The wheels are both rigidly fastened to the axle by making a hydraulic press fit. The following are the names of the parts of an axle: Center of Axle, Neck of Axle, Wheel Seat, Dust Guard Bearing, Collar, Journal. See **Axle.**

Tender Back Bumper. 4, Figs. 3614-3656; Figs. 3637-3639. A transverse timber or steel shape forming an end sill at the back of a tender frame. See **Bumper.**

Tender Bolster. See **Bolster and Body Bolster.**

Tender Brake (Air Brake). The tender brake gear does not differ essentially from that used under cars, except that the plain triple valve is used on freight and switch engines instead of the quick-action triple valve.

Tender Buffer. Figs. 3820-3825. An iron or steel casting having a flat exterior face attached to the back bumper of a tender to absorb shocks and blows. In some designs the buffer is held out by springs, but with those having no springs, a style of coupler is commonly used which has side springs to provide the necessary elasticity.

Tender Bumper. 4, Figs. 3614-3656. A transverse piece forming the end sill at either end of a tender. Usually of cast steel in one piece or built up of shapes and angles.

Tender Bumper Push Pole Pocket. 18, Figs. 3614-3656. A cup-shaped casting fastened to the corners of a tender rear end sill by bolts or rivets to receive the end of a push pole. Also called a pushing shoe.

Tender Center Plate. 8, Figs. 3614-3656. A circular grooved plate or bearing attached to the under side of a tender body bolster and fitting into a corresponding plate on the truck bolster.

Tender Chafing Plate. 19, Figs. 3614-3656; Figs. 3802-3804. A metal plate fastened to the front end of the tender frame where it comes in contact with a similar plate fastened to the tail piece of the engine frame.

Tender Crosstie. 34, Figs. 3614-3656. A transverse beam to stiffen a tender frame.

Tender Deck. The floor at the front end of a tender between the legs.

Tender Drain Cup (Air Brake). Fig. 2528. A device located in the brake pipe on tenders, containing a chamber in which is an air strainer and from which the branch pipe leads to the triple valve. A drain cock is provided in the bottom of the chamber for removing any water that may collect in it.

Tender Draw Gear. The arrangement of coupler, spring, drawbar, etc., applied to either end of a tender.

Tender Drawhead. Figs. 3817-3819. A heavy casting secured to the center sills at the forward end of a tender frame to hold the drawbar that couples the engine and tender.

Tender Drawhead Bolt. A bolt used to secure a drawhead to the frame and sills of a tender.

Tender End Sill. 4, Figs. 3614-3656. A steel or wooden beam forming the transverse member of a tender frame at the end. Known as the back or front end sill according to its location. See **Tender Back Bumper.**

Tender Frame. Figs. 3614-3656. A horizontal skeleton or foundation built of wood or steel to support and carry the tank, and having two transverse bolsters with center plates that rest upon the truck center plates. Wood is now seldom used for tender frames, having been superseded by steel in the form of I beams or channel sections. The parts of a tender frame are the side, center and intermediate longitudinal sills, the transverse end sills, the bolsters and crossties and diagonal braces.

Tender Frame Angle. An angle used to stiffen or brace any portion of a tender frame.

Tender Frame Back Bumper Brace. 7a, Figs. 3637-3639. One of two flat or channelled steel struts or pieces riveted to the back bumper and to the body bolster to strengthen the bumper and distribute the shocks received by it to other parts of the frame.

Tender Frame Crosstie. 34, Figs. 3614-3656. A transverse tie bar holding the longitudinal sills of a tender frame together.

Tender Frame Diagonal Brace. 7 and 7a, Figs. 3614-3656; Figs. 3665-3669. One of several wrought iron or steel bars, flat or of angle section, riveted diagonally across a tender frame to stiffen it.

Tender Frame Knee. A casting, its arms at right angles, fastened to the corners of a tender frame, inside the sills to hold the frame square.

Tender Frame Spring Cap. A piece of metal fastened on the top of a semi-elliptic spring used with a certain type of tender truck, in which the ends of the spring rest on the axle boxes and the center bears against a cup or pocket secured to the tender frame. See **Tender Frame Spring Pocket.**

Tender Frame Spring Pocket. A piece of metal fastened to the under side of a tender frame to form a bearing for a semi-elliptic spring mounted longitudinally on the tender truck frame.

Tender Frame Truss Plate. A transverse metal piece secured to the sills above the body bolster. Commonly used with wooden tender sills.

Tender Frame Truss Rod. A long bar or metal piece used to truss a wooden tender frame.

Tender Floor Plate. A sheet of steel fastened to a tender frame and forming the bottom of the tank and coal bin.

Tender Front Bumper. 1, Figs. 3614-3656; Figs. 3643-3647. A transverse timber or steel shape forming an end sill at the forward end of a tender frame. See **Bumper.**

Tender Front Bumper Foot Plate. A piece of metal secured across the front bumper of a tender to form a standing place. The cab apron rests upon the front edge of this plate.

Tender Hose Thimble. A short brass tube fastened to the lower end of the injector feed pipe and provided with a sleeve nut or fitting for attachment to the fitting on the supply hose.

Tender Roof. A covering or roof built over the forward end of a tender to shelter the fireman on locomotives having very wide or Wootten fireboxes. These locomotives also have a short cab on the back head of the boiler overlapping the tender roof.

Tender Shovel Plate. A sheet or piece of metal secured to the floor of the coal bin to provide a wearing surface on which the shovel is constantly scraped.

Tender Side Sill. 1. Figs. 3614-3656. A steel or wooden beam, one of the outside longitudinal members of a tender frame.

Tender Side Sill Filling. Strips of wood bolted to the webs of the beams forming the side sills of a steel tender frame.

Tender Step. 9 and 10, Figs. 3614-3656; Figs. 3759-3767. A foot piece for ascending to or descending from a tender. Made of cast or wrought iron or cast steel. Steps are secured at each end of both front and back bumpers of a tender.

Tender Step Hanger. A piece of metal fastened to a tender frame by bolts or rivets and having its lower end bent at right angles for the purpose of holding a step to which it is riveted.

Tender Step Hanger Brace. A piece of metal fastened to a tender frame and to a step hanger, to strengthen the step and hold it rigidly in place.

Tender Tool Box. A receptacle on a tender for holding small tools and supplies. Usually placed on top of the tank leg.

Tender Truck. Figs. 4294-4354; Details Figs. 4355-4571. A rectangular frame built of wood or metal, having boxes for two axles, and a transverse piece called a bolster that carries a center plate. It is in effect a small four-wheel car, under each end of a tender, and carrying the latter as a dead load by means of two swiveling center plates connected by a center pin or king bolt. The purpose of a truck is to allow short wheel bases to be used under the long body of a tender. Wood is seldom used even for such parts as bolsters, transoms and spring planks, and when used is strengthened by steel plates. See **Truck, Arch Bar Truck** and **Pedestal Truck.**

Tender Water Scoop. See **Water Scoop.**

Tender Wheel. See **Wheel.**

Tension Bar. Any bar subjected to a tensile strain. The upper member of an iron body bolster is called the tension bar.

Tension Member (of a Frame, Truss, Beam or Girder). Truss rods, brake rods, etc., are tension members, in distinction from compression members, which resist crushing or compression stresses.

Thimble. 1. A bushing.
 2. A sleeve or tube through which a bolt passes and which may act as a distance piece. A thimble is usually round, but sometimes square. See **Crown Bar Thimble.**

Third-Rail (Electric Locomotive). A soft steel rail conductor, supported on insulators near and parallel to one of the track rails for the purpose of supplying electrical energy to a locomotive or motor car. It is sometimes installed so that the collecting shoe on the motor car or locomotive slides along its top surface and sometimes so that the shoe is pressed against the lower edge. In the one case it is called an over-running and in the other an under running third-rail. The rails for this purpose are not made so hard as track rails, as the wear on them is much less, but the chief object sought in their manufacture is a combination of high electrical conductivity with good wearing qualities.

Third-Rail Shoe (Electric Locomotive). Figs. 1632-1634. A metallic sliding contact, of cast iron or cast steel, mounted on the truck of a motor car or on the frame of an electric locomotive, and insulated therefrom, for collecting current from an insulated third-rail located alongside the running rails. Positive contact between shoe and rail is maintained by gravity or by a stiff spring. Four shoes are commonly used for a double truck car or locomotive, each being carried on a wooden beam, supported by the truck journal boxes.

Third-Rail Shoe Spring (Electric Locomotive). 5, Figs. 1632-1634. One of two spiral springs used to hold a third-rail shoe in position. Its tension is sufficient to hold the shoe firmly against either the upper or lower edge of a third-rail.

Three-way Cock. A metal faucet or valve used to connect an indicator with either end of a locomotive cylinder. The handle has three positions, one for admitting steam from each end of the cylinder and a cut-off position.

Throat. 1. (Car Wheel.) The interior angle of a flange where it joins the tread of the wheel. See **Flange**.
2. The part of a locomotive boiler where the firebox joins the cylindrical portion of the shell.

Throat Brace. 32, Figs. 151-206. A piece of metal fastened to the back tube sheet and to the shell of a boiler to brace the tube sheet below the bottom row of tubes, at the throat of the firebox. British, palm stay.

Throat Brace Eyebolt. An eye formed on a throat brace where it is connected to the waist of a boiler by means of a pin or rivet.

Throat Brace Pin. See **Throat Brace Eyebolt**.

Throat Sheet. 28a, Figs. 151-206. A piece or plate of a locomotive boiler bent or flanged to a shape suitable to connect the cylindrical portion of the boiler with the firebox.

Throttle. The whole arrangement of valve, operating lever, reach rod, etc., by which the engineman controls the amount of steam admitted to the cylinders. British, regulator.

Throttle Arm.—See **Throttle Lever**.

Throttle Base. See **Throttle Box**.

Throttle Bell Crank. See **Throttle Crank**.

Throttle Box. 24, Figs. 3043-5065. A chamber or space in the upper part of a throttle pipe into which steam passes directly from the throttle valve when the valve is opened.

Throttle Crank. 85, Figs. 3043-3065. A cast iron or steel piece shaped like a right angle, pivoted to a bracket cast on the throttle pipe and having one end connected to the stem of the throttle valve and the other to the throttle rod. It transfers the horizontal motion of the throttle rod to the throttle stem, which is in a vertical position.

Throttle Crank Bracket. A lug or projection cast on the side of a throttle pipe to form a bearing or support for the pivot or pin of the throttle crank.

Throttle Crank Pin. A bolt or pivot secured to a throttle crank bracket to hold the throttle crank.

Throttle Lever. 3, Figs. 3043-3065. An arm or bar for operating the throttle valve. It is pivoted to a link or bracket on the boiler head, and connected to the throttle rod which passes through a stuffing box and is connected to the throttle crank. British, regulator lever.

Throttle Lever Eyebolt. A connection sometimes used between a throttle rod and throttle stem.

Throttle Lever Handle. The outer end of a throttle lever, which is grasped by the hand in order to move the lever. The term handle is also applied to the locking latch or detent that engages with the rack or toothed quadrant.

Throttle Lever Intermediate Lever. An additional arm or bar to connect the throttle lever with the throttle rod on locomotives where the design does not permit the throttle lever to be placed on the boiler back head.

Throttle Lever Latch. 7, Figs. 3043-3065. A small piece of metal connected to the throttle lever link and engaging with the lever quadrant.

Throttle Lever Latch Link. 4, Figs. 3043-3065. A metal rod connecting the latch with the latch handle or handle of a throttle lever.

Throttle Lever Link. A short piece of metal secured at one end to a stud set in the boiler back head, and at the other holding a steel pin on which the throttle lever is pivoted.

Throttle Lever Nut. A square or hexagonal block of metal, threaded on the inside and screwed on the end of a bolt or pin which secures the throttle lever to the throttle rod.

Throttle Lever Quadrant. 1, Figs. 3043-3065. A plate of brass or steel, secured to the boiler back head, and having one edge, curved to the arc of a circle and with notches cut in it to engage with the lever latch and thus hold the lever in any position.

Throttle Lever Stud. A short rod tapped into the boiler back head and having a jaw or yoke at its outer end to secure the link connected to the throttle lever.

Throttle Lever Support. A metal standard attached to the boiler to hold a short shaft fastened to the throttle lever. Used where the lever is not located on the back head of the boiler.

Throttle Pipe. 25, Figs. 3043-3065. A vertical cast-iron tube or conduit with an elbow on its lower end, secured inside the dome of a locomotive boiler to convey steam from the throttle valve to the dry pipe. An hemispherical or ball joint is generally made at the connection with the dry pipe. Also called throttle stand pipe.

Throttle Pipe Ring. A sleeve or short piece of pipe having its edge ground to a spherical surface and secured on the end of a dry pipe to fit into a corresponding surface on the end of the throttle pipe elbow.

Throttle Pipe Saddle. See **Dry Pipe Bridle**.

Throttle Pipe U Bolt. 89, Figs. 77-124. A bolt bent so as to pass around the outside of a throttle pipe and fasten it securely to the dry pipe. See **Dry Pipe Bridle**.

Throttle Rod. 86, Figs. 3043-3065. A metal rod fitted steam tight through a stuffing box on the boiler back head and connecting the throttle lever with the throttle crank. Also called throttle stem.

Throttle Rod Jaw. A U-shaped or bifurcated piece of steel, either screwed or keyed on to the outer end of a throttle rod so as to connect it to the throttle lever by means of a pin or bolt passing through the forked end.

Throttle Rod Packing. See **Packing**.

Throttle Rod Socket. A short piece of metal hollow at one end and formed into a fork at the other. The hollow end is screwed on and then keyed to the outer end of the throttle rod, while the forked end is fastened to the throttle lever by a bolt.

Throttle Stand Pipe. See **Throttle Pipe**.

Throttle Stem. See **Throttle Valve Stem**.

Throttle Stem Jaw. A fork or bifurcation on the lower end of a throttle stem for the attachment of one arm of the throttle crank by means of a pin or bolt.

Throttle Stuffing Box. Figs. 3066-3069. A cast-iron tube or sleeve with a wide flange fastened to the boiler back head by studs tapped in. The throttle rod passes through this, and a gland on the rod holds the packing in place and prevents the escape of steam while allowing the rod to be moved back and forth.

Throttle Stuffing Box Gland. A short cylinder or tube with a wide flange holding the packing in place around the throttle rod, and secured to the stuffing box by nuts screwed on the ends of projecting studs.

Throttle Stuffing Box Ring. A metal ring inside a throttle stuffing box to hold the throttle rod packing in place.

Throttle Valve. 8, Figs. 3043-3065. An arrangement or device for admitting steam from the boiler to the dry pipe and thence to the steam chests. It is placed in the upper part of the steam dome, in order to secure dry steam, and consists of two disks of cast iron united by a central body or web. These fit into two circular openings in the upper part of the throttle pipe. The upper disk is slightly larger than the lower, and in consequence the unbalanced steam pressure on the disks tends to keep the valve closed. The disks have conical edges, and when the valve is closed they rest upon correspondingly coned circular seats, to which they are ground in with emery.

Throttle Valve Stem. 84, Figs. 3043-3065. A steel rod or shaft secured to one arm of the throttle crank by a bolt or pin, or by a key, and carrying the valve at its upper end. The valve rests upon a flange or collar forged on the stem, and is held fast to it by a nut screwed on to the upper end of the stem and binding down on the valve. Also called throttle stem.

Throttle Valve Stem Key. A thin, tapered piece of steel used to secure a throttle valve to the valve stem. See **Throttle Valve** and **Throttle Valve Stem.**

Tie. "A beam or rod which secures parts together and is subjected to a tensile strain. It is the opposite of a strut or straining piece, which acts to keep objects apart, and is subject to compressing force."—Knight.

Tie Rod. An iron or steel rod which acts as a tie.

Tire. 5, Figs. 1353-1367. A heavy band of steel forming the periphery of a wheel to impart strength and to resist wear. Many devices for fastening a tire to a wheel have been devised. In Great Britain the word is spelled tyre. The supposed derivation of the term is that iron bands were first used on wheels in the city of Tyre, Syria. Locomotive driving wheels are always equipped with steel tires, but for trucks, especially under tenders, chilled cast-iron wheels, and solid rolled steel wheels, are extensively used, as well as steel-tired wheels.

Tire Expander. Fig. 5014. A device for expanding driving wheel tires by means of heat. It usually consists of a series of burners placed so as to force a flame against the outer portion of the tire. As the tire becomes heated it expands and is thus easily removed from or placed on the wheel center.

Tire Bolt. A screw bolt for holding a tire on a wheel center. When retaining rings are used the bolts pass through the rings and hold them and the center and tire together. Fig. 4561.

Tire Fastening. Figs. 4559-4564 show the principal methods. The Mansell fastening, shown in Fig. 4561, etc., is the mode of securing the tire to the wheel which becomes operative when the shrinkage of the tire alone is insufficient to prevent the tire leaving the wheel.

Toe (of a Car Wheel Flange). The extreme outer point where the wheel has the largest diameter.

Tongs. A hinged metal tool for grasping an object forming part of the tool outfit on a locomotive.

Tools. Implements carried on a locomotive for use in the course of its regular operation or in breakdowns. They comprise the following:

Shovel	Hammers	Hand Saw
Pick	Chisels	Axe
Poker	Crow Bar	Oil Cans
Hoe	Pinch Bar	Wrenches
Pair of Jacks	Chains	Tube Plugs.

Tool Box. A case or cupboard for holding the tools and supplies carried on a locomotive. Commonly located on the tender.

Top Arch Bar. More properly, simply **Arch Bar,** which see.

Top Reservoir Journal Box. A journal box having a reservoir for oil or grease above the journal, from which the oil flows to the journal. Rarly used in this country, but common in Europe, with either oil or some form of grease as a lubricant.

Top Side Bearing. A body side bearing. **See Side Bearing.**

Torch. A portable illuminating device commonly made of brass and containing a reservoir for oil into which a wick extends. Used for inspecting and oiling a locomotive at night, or when examining dark inaccessible places underneath the engine or tender.

Torch Base. The lower portion or bottom of a torch on which it stands. Usually made flat to allow the torch to stand alone.

Torch Top. The outer end or tip of a torch. That part surrounding the wick and screwed on to the main body.

Torpedo. A cylindrical detonating cap provided with clips for folding under the head of the rail for the purpose of making a loud alarm as a signal when engines pass over them. The basis of the detonating compound is fulminate of mercury. The interior pieces of iron, to insure the explosion of the fulminate, are termed anvils.

Tower Pocket Pilot Coupler. Figs. 2387-2397.

Tower Tender Coupler. Figs. 3984-3998.

Track. A rail or bar which forms a path on which anything, as a locomotive or door, runs. Sliding doors have usually two door tracks, bottom and top door track.

Traction Increaser. Figs. 1793-1808. An arrangement for transferring a portion of the weight of a locomotive from the leading or trailing truck to the driving wheels in order to increase the tractive power in starting. It consists of a cylinder supplied with compressed air and containing a piston and piston rod which operates a set of levers and shifts the fulcrum of the equalizing beam that connects the driving and trailing truck springs on 4-4-2 type engines. Locomotives of the 2-6-2 type have the piston rod of one traction increaser cylinder applied to the equalizer that connects the forward truck with the front transverse equalizer, and that of the other applied to the trailing truck as stated above. The device is operated from the cab, and in some designs the air valve is so connected with the reverse lever that it is closed and the normal distribution of weight on the driving wheels restored as soon as the reverse lever is moved back to a certain point; say when giving a cut-off in the cylinders of about 60 per cent. of the stroke.

Traction Increaser Cylinder. 1, Figs. 1793-1808. A cast iron cylinder operated by compressed air and attached to the frame of a locomotive, for transferring additional weight to the driving wheels through a system of equalizing levers.

Traction Increaser Cylinder Head. A circular cast iron cover fitted on either end of a traction increaser cylinder.

Traction Increaser Cylinder Head Gland. A cylindrical projection or sleeve cast on the cylinder head of a traction increaser to hold the piston rod packing.

Traction Increaser Cylinder Support. A bracket or casting bolted to a locomotive frame to hold the traction increaser cylinder.

Traction Increaser Filling. A steel casting having lips or flanges by means of which it is bolted to a locomotive frame for the purpose of holding or supporting part of a traction increaser as well as stiffening the frame at that point.

Traction Increaser Lever. 11, Figs. 1793-1808. A pivoted arm to one end of which the traction increaser piston rod is attached and which is connected at its other end to a link or bar fastened to the equalizer. Also called lifting bar.

Traction Increaser Links and Pins. The short bars or levers and the pins or pivots used to connect the mechanism of a traction increaser.

Traction Increaser Piston. A disk fitted in the traction increaser cylinder and against which the air pressure acts to move it in the cylinder.

Tractive Power. The force exerted by a locomotive in turning its wheels and moving itself with or without a load along the rails. It depends upon the steam pressure, the diameter and stroke of the cylinders, and the ratio of the weight on the driving wheels to the total weight of the engine, not including the tender.

The formula for simple engines is

$$T = \frac{d^2 \times s \times .85 P}{D}$$

where T = tractive force in pounds.
where d = diameter of cylinders, in inches.
where s = stroke of piston, in inches.
where D = diameter of driving wheels in in.
where P = boiler pressure in lbs. per sq. in.

Trailing Axle. Figs. 3545-3548. The axle of a trailing truck.

Trailing Truck. Figs. 3393-3481. Usually a two-wheel Truck, which see, under the firebox of a locomotive, back of the driving wheels and carrying part of the weight of the engine. They are commonly designed to have some side motion. See **Radial Truck.**

Trailing Truck Box. 3, Figs. 3393-3468. A box-shaped casting of iron or steel, fitted to slide vertically in the jaws, legs or pedestals of the trailing truck, and holding a brass or bearing resting on the trailing axle journal.

Trailing Truck Box Shoe. A strip of metal having parallel sides secured on the inside face of one of the pedestals of a trailing truck to form a wearing surface for the box which slides vertically in the jaw between the pedestals.

Trailing Truck Pedestal. See **Pedestal.**

Trailing Truck Pedestal Tie Bolt. A heavy piece or rod of metal having a head on one end and a thread cut on the other, passing through the lower ends of the trailing truck pedestals and through the pedestal thimble or cap. Also called a pedestal tie or pedestal binder, as its function is to secure and strengthen the jaws of a trailing truck.

Trailing Truck Pedestal Wedge. A wedge shaped strip of metal secured on the inside face of one of the pedestals of a trailing truck to form a wearing surface for the box. The lower end of the wedge rests upon the end of a set screw, by turning which the wedge can be adjusted to any degree necessary to take up the wear or lost motion of the box.

Trailing Truck Spring Saddle. 19, Figs. 3393-3468 A bent piece of metal secured to the band of a trailing truck spring and resting on the top of the axle box.

Trailing Truck Spring Seat. That part of a spring saddle on which a trailing truck spring rests, and through which a portion of the weight of the locomotive is transmitted to a trailing axle box.

Trailing Wheel. The wheels of a trailing truck. Usually steel-tired and of larger diameter than the forward truck wheels. See **Wheel.**

Train Air Signal Apparatus. Figs. 2422, 2550-2556. A substitute for the bell cord arranged to give train signals by compressed air. A separate line of signal pipe, similar to the brake pipe, extends throughout the train, connected between the cars by hose and couplings. A car discharge valve, connected to this signal pipe is located in each car and attached to the bell cord in such manner that pulling on the cord releases air from the signal pipe. In the cab on the engine or motor car is a signal valve, which is also connected with the main signal pipe and a small signal whistle. The supply of air is received from the main reservoir through a reducing valve, which maintains a pressure of about 45 pounds per square inch in the signal apparatus. When the car discharge valve is opened by pulling on the cord and the air pressure in the signal pipe is reduced the diaphragm in the signal valve is operated so as to blow the whistle. Signals can be given in this way with rapidity and great certainty. If the train breaks in two, the whistle is blown loudly for a considerable time.

Train Air Signal Stop Cock. A stop cock in the air signal pipe. There is one at each end of a car and the back end of the tender.

Train Brake Pipe. See **Brake Pipe.**

Train Pipe (Air Brake). See **Brake Pipe.** The later and preferable name is brake pipe.

Train Signal Pipe. See **Signal Pipe.**

Transformer (Electricity). Fig. 4662. A device used with alternating currents for transforming a quantity of energy from one pressure or voltage to another, either higher or lower. It consists of a primary coil supplied with current from some source or generator; a secondary coil, in which the energy is utilized, and an iron core that connects the two coils magnetically. The periodical alternating induction caused by the current in the primary coil induces an electromotive force in the secondary coil; and the primary and secondary electromotive forces are directly proportional to the relative number of turns on the two coils, thus providing means of either raising or lowering the voltage. Electric locomotives built to operate with alternating current have a transformer whose primary coil receives current from the trolley wire at about 3,000 volts, and this is transformed to about 650 volts in the secondary coil from which the motors are supplied.

Transmission Bar. 1, 18, Figs. 1813-1852. A curved piece, usually made of cast steel, having one end connected to the link block pin and the other end to a pin on the rocker arm. It is used on locomotives having the eccentrics on the second or third driving axle, where eccentric rods long enough to reach the rocker and curved so as to pass above and below a driving axle would be objectionable. Also called extension bar.

2. (Walschaerts Valve Gear.) The radius bar or radius rod that connects the link block with the valve rod is sometimes called a transmission bar.

Transmission Bar Hanger. 19, Figs. 1813-1852. A link or arm pivoted at one end to a bracket bolted to the frame and at the other end to the transmission bar.

Transmission Bar Hanger Bearing. The sleeve or brass set in a transmission bar hanger in which the hanger pin or pivot turns.

Transmission Bar Hanger Bracket. 25, Figs. 1813-1852. A cast iron holder or support, bolted to a locomotive frame and having a brass or bearing for the hanger pin.

Transmission Bar Hanger Pin. 34-35, Figs. 1813-1852.

A steel pivot set in a bearing in the transmission bar hanger bracket and from which the hanger is suspended. Also applied to the pivot connecting the hanger with the transmission bar itself.

Transmission Bar Link. Another term for **Transmission Bar Hanger**, which see.

Transmission Bar Oil Cup. A receptacle for oil secured to a transmission bar for lubricating the pins.

Transmission Bar Pin. A steel pivot at that end of a transmission bar which is connected to the link block. It is a **Link Block Pin**, which see.

Transom. 1. Primarily a cross piece.

2. (Carpentry.) A horizontal piece framed across a door or double light window. The term is also applied in the general sense of a cross piece in other ways.

3. (Trucks.) The cross braces in the center of a truck frame between which the bolster is mounted.

Transom or **Bolster Chafing Plate.** Figs. 4397-4398. A plate attached to the side of a transom to protect it from abrasion by the movement of the bolster.

Transom Tie Bar. A wrought iron bar bolted to a pair of transoms, sometimes above and sometimes below the center to hold them together.

Transverse Equalizer. Figs. 1674-1675. An **Equalizer**, which see, connecting the spring suspensions on the two sides of a locomotive.

Tread. (Of a Step.) The part on which the foot is placed.

2. (Of a Car Wheel.) The exterior cylindrical surface of a car wheel inside of the flange which comes in contact with the rail. The usual width is about 4 inches, measured from the throat or inside of the flange to outside of wheel.

Triple Valve (Air Brake). 1. A valve device consisting of a body or case, called the triple valve body, which has connections to the brake pipe, the auxiliary reservoir and the brake cylinder, in which a slide valve is operated by a piston, so that when the pressure of the air in the brake pipe is increased the auxiliary reservoir is charged and the air in the brake cylinder is released to the atmosphere; and so that, when the air pressure in the brake pipe is reduced, air from the auxiliary reservoir is discharged into the brake cylinder for applying the brakes. A triple valve performing only these functions is now known as the plain triple valve. Fig. 2496.

2. The quick-action triple valve has all the features and performs all the functions of the plain triple valve, and has the additional function of causing a discharge of air from the brake pipe to the brake cylinder, when, in emergencies, the maximum force of the brake is instantly required. Fig. 2490.

3. The quick-service triple valve is one having the features of discharging a small quantity of air from the brake pipe to the brake cylinder during service applications similarly to that occurring in emergency, but in lesser degree and without any danger of causing undesired quick action or of interfering with the sensitiveness of the triple valve. This feature has the effect of (1) materially hastening the service application throughout the train by helping to reduce the brake pipe pressure at each triple valve; (2) increasing the brake cylinder pressure above that resulting from the ordinary flow of air from the auxiliary reservoir; (3) a higher brake cylinder pressure for a given brake pipe reduction. Fig. 2491.

4. The retarded-release feature of certain triple valves is one which makes the time of releasing the air pressure from the brake cylinder to depend on the position of the car in the train, holding back the release on the forward end until those in the rear have an opportunity to release, thus causing the brakes to release uniformly throughout long trains. It is generally applied to triple valves for freight service. This feature is usually accompanied by the retarded-recharge feature which holds back the recharging of the auxiliary reservoirs on the forward end of the train in the same manner and degree as the release is retarded. Fig. 2491.

5. The graduated release triple valves are so designed as to permit the brakes to be released in steps or graduations by increasing the brake pipe pressure in corresponding steps. This is accomplished by means of a "supplementary" reservoir which is similar to the auxiliary reservoir, but so connected to the triple valve that it charges to brake pipe pressure during release, remains at that pressure during a brake application, and is connected to that auxiliary reservoir again in release, in such a way as to cause the brake cylinder exhaust to be cut off whenever the auxiliary reservoir pressure exceeds that in the brake pipe. In this way a partial increase in brake pipe pressure causes only a partial decrease in brake cylinder pressure, and these graduations of the release may be continued until the brake pipe pressure is almost entirely reinstated. In electric railway service a "control pipe," which connects the main reservoir throughout the train, is connected to the triple valve in place of the supplementary reservoir. Figs. 2492-2493.

Triple Valve Branch Pipe (Air Brake). A short pipe by which the triple valve is connected with the brake pipe.

Triple Valve Gasket. A gasket placed in the joint between the triple valve and the brake cylinder.

Triple Valve Nipple. The short pipe nipple by which the plain triple valve is connected with the auxiliary reservoir.

Trolley (Electric Locomotive). Fig. 4631. A small wheel, or a carriage with journal, bearings, case, etc., usually attached to the end of a trolley pole, the latter being attached, pivoted and swiveled to the top of a motor car or locomotive, and so stayed by springs that it tends to stand in a vertical position. This tendency of the trolley pole to stand erect keeps the trolley wheel in contact (on the under side) of an electric conductor stretched above the car over the center of the tracks. A grooved shoe is often used instead of a trolley wheel to make contact with the overhead wire. A pantagraph trolley frame, Fig. 2649, consists of a number of arms connected so that the shoe carried on top may be raised or lowered from the trolley wire by an air cylinder.

Trolley Air Cylinder. 2, Fig. 4631. A cylinder actuated by compressed air, having its piston rod connected to the trolley frame or trolley shoe so that by admitting air to the cylinder, the trolley shoe may be pushed up in contact with the overhead wire.

Trolley Frame. See **Trolley**.

Trolley Pole. The pivoted pole carrying a trolley wheel or trolley shoe. See **Trolley**.

Trolley Shoe (Electric Locomotive). 6, Fig. 4631. A sliding metallic contact piece for collecting current from an overhead wire. Used instead of a trolley wheel.

Trolley Wheel. A small grooved wheel mounted in bearings at the end of a trolley pole and running on the under side of the overhead conductor or wire for collecting current to supply the motors of an electric locomotive.

Truck. A rectangular metal frame holding axle boxes, and having a transverse piece called a truck bolster that may carry a center plate or center pin guide, or an arrangement of pivots and springs to allow a slight radial action of the axles. Ordinarily, the term refers to the leading truck of a locomotive with either two or four wheels. The term is also applied to the frame that carries the radial trailing axle as well as to the tender trucks. In any case it is a swiveling frame having boxes or bearings for wheels that are merely bearers or carriers of a portion of the weight of a locomotive, as distinguished from driving wheels. In Great Britain it is called a bogie. Engine trucks are shown in Figs. 3344-3525, and tender trucks in Figs. 4294-4354.

Truck Arch Bar. 1 and 2, Figs. 4294-4382. A flat steel bar forming part of the side frame of a diamond tender truck. See **Arch Bar.**

Truck Arch Bar Truss. The side frame of a diamond tender truck built up of flat steel bars and posts or columns that together form a rigid structure for carrying the axle boxes, and in connection with the other members of the truck support one end of the tender.

Truck Bolster. 4, Figs. 4294-4382; Figs. 4399-4428. A cross timber or steel beam in the center of a truck, to which the lower center plate is fastened, and on which the body of a tender or the front or back end of a locomotive rests. On the front truck of a locomotive, a heavy casting, called a center casting, usually takes the place of the bolster used on trailing or tender trucks. See **Bolster.**

Truck Bolster End Plate. A metal cap secured over the end of a truck bolster, sometimes used to take the place of the truss rod washers used with a trussed wooden bolster.

Truck Bolster Filling Piece. A small casting or plate inserted between the upper and lower members of a built-up metal tender truck bolster.

Truck Bolster Flitch Plates. See **Bolster Flitch Plates.**

Truck Bolster Guide Bars (Diamond Truck). 5, Figs. 4294-4382; Figs. 4385-4387. More commonly called columns. Cast or malleable iron posts between the top and bottom arch bars, held in place by column bolts, which form a guide for the end of the truck bolster. They are frequently made with a projecting lug on the inside to form a support for the brake hangers of inside-hung brake beams.

Truck Bolster Truss Rod (Rigid Bolster Trucks). A rod attached near the end of a wooden truck bolster. In swing bolster trucks, rods of a similar nature are used, and are termed transom truss rods.

Truck Bottom Bar. 3, Figs. 4294-4382. A flat steel bar forming the lowest member of a diamond tender truck side frame. Also called pedestal tie and pedestal cap.

Truck Box. 7, Figs. 4294-4382; Figs. 4464-4495. A cast-iron box or case which encloses the journal of a truck axle, the journal bearing and key, and which holds the packing for lubricating the journal. Also called an axle box, grease box, housing journal box, oil box and pedestal box. See **Journal Box.**

Truck Brake. A system of levers actuated by compressed air or vacuum, for applying the brake shoes to the wheels of a four-wheel engine truck. The brake beams in this type of brake are inside hung, and the air cylinder is usually located between the frames and just back of the steam cylinder saddle. See **Air Brake.**

Truck Brake Lever. Figs. 2708-2710. A lever with one end attached to the crosshead of the truck brake cylinder, and the other end to the truck brake rod.

Truck Center Plate. 19, Figs. 4294-4382. One of a pair of plates made of cast or malleable iron or pressed steel that support a tender on the center of a truck. There are two, the body center plate and the truck center plate, that are sometimes also called the male and female center plates. The center pin or king bolt passes through them, but takes none of the strain except in emergencies. See **Center Plate.**

Truck Centering Arrangement (Electric Locomotive). Figs. 4607-4609. A device forming a flexible connection between the two-wheel truck of an electric locomotive and the frame. It consists of a stout rod or bar with a ball and socket joint at each end; the spherical head at one end of the bar fitting a socket in the end of a short transverse casting bolted to the frame; and the other spherical head fitting a similar socket cast in the side frame of the truck. One such rod, with ball and socket joints, is placed on each side of the truck, forming a check or restraint on the swinging of the truck on curves. The function of the device is to enable the truck to take sharp curves with safety.

Truck Check Chain Eye. 21, Figs. 4294-4382. See **Check Chain.** A body check chain eye is also used.

Truck Check Chain Hook. A hook on the end of a **Check Chain,** which see.

Truck Equalizer. Figs. 1666-1667; 14, Figs. 1605-1728. A beam whose ends rest upon the boxes of an engine or tender truck, and connected with a spring attached to the truck bolster. Its function is to distribute the weight of an engine or tender supported by the truck bolster equally to the two axles; hence its name.

Truck Frame. A structure composed of wooden beams, iron bars or cast steel, to which the journal boxes or pedestals, springs and other loose parts are attached, and which forms the skeleton of a truck.

Truck Frame Crosstie. 2b, Figs. 4294-4382. A transverse member of a truck frame, made of a flat bar or a pressed or rolled steel shape.

Truck Pedestal. 2a, Figs. 4294-4382. One of the vertical legs or jaws of a truck frame between which an axle box is placed. See **Pedestal.**

Truck Safety Beam. 17, Figs. 3369-3380. A longitudinal piece connecting the end piece and transom of a truck above the axles and inside of each wheel piece. Iron straps, called axle safety bearings, are attached to the beam and pass under the axles so as to hold them in position in case the axles or wheels on either side break.

Truck Safety Beam Plate. A flat piece of steel bolted to the side of a truck safety beam to strengthen it. See **Truck Safety Beam.**

Truck Safety Chain. See **Safety Chain** and **Check Chain.**

Truck Side. A Truck Side Frame, which see.

Truck Side Bearing. 22, Figs. 4294-4382; Figs. 4511-4521. A plate, block or roller or spring plate attached to the top of the truck bolster, on which a corresponding bearing fastened to the body bolster rests. Their purpose is to prevent the tender body from having too much rocking or rolling motion. They are made of various forms, such as a plain metal plate, to protect a wooden bolster from wear, a cup-shaped casting to hold oil or grease and waste, and various forms of rollers, rockers, studs, spring cases and the like.

Truck Side Frame. The longitudinal portion of a truck frame, on the outside of the wheels, which extends from one axle to the other, and to which the journal boxes and bolsters or transoms are attached.

Truck Spring. 4a and 7a, Figs. 4294-4382. A **Spring**, which see, supporting the truck bolster or the side frame over the journal boxes. Truck springs are either coil, half-elliptic or elliptic springs, according to the design of truck.

Truck Spring Cap. See **Spring Cap**.

Truck Spring Seat. 4d, Figs. 4294-4382. A hollow or cup-shaped piece of metal attached to a tender truck bolster or spring plank to form a bearing for a truck spring. See **Spring Seat**.

Truck Wheel. See **Wheel**.

Truss Rod. An inclined rod used in connection with a king or queen post truss, or trussed beam, to resist deflection. It is attached to the ends of the beam, and is supported in the middle by a king post, truss block, or two queen posts between the beams and the rod.

Truss Rod Bearing. A bearing used to furnish support to a truss rod, at an angle or bend in the latter.

Tube. 33, Figs. 151-206. Called also flue. One of the pipes or flues that convey the products of combustion from the firebox to the smokebox and stack. Tubes are fitted in holes in the sheets or plates at each end of a boiler, and where they enter the holes in the firebox tube plate copper ferrules or sleeves are placed over the ends of the tubes to make a tight joint. Generally made of charcoal iron or mild steel. In Europe, brass and copper tubes are frequently used. See **Ferrule and Flue**.

Tubes. (Specifications and Tests for Iron and Steel Locomotive Boiler Tubes). At the convention of the American Railway Master Mechanics' Association in 1895 the following specification and tests for iron and steel locomotive boiler tubes were adopted as standard. Modified in 1896. Revised, June, 1904.

1. Tubes are to be made of knobbled, hammered charcoal iron, lap welded.

2. Tubes must be of uniform thickness throughout, except at weld, where an additional thickness of .015 will be allowed. They must be circular within .02 inch, and the mean diameter must be within .015 inch of the size ordered. They must be within .01 inch of the thickness specified and not less than the length ordered, but may exceed this by .125 inch.

3. The minimum weights for tubes of various diameters and thicknesses are given in the following table:

Outside diameter.	Nominal B. W. G.	Thickness M. M. G. Inches.	Minimum weight per foot. Lbs.
1¾ inch	No. 13	.095	1.65
	" 12	.110	1.89
	" 11	.125	2.07
	" 10	.135	2.29
2 inch	" 13	.095	1.91
	" 12	.110	2.17
	" 11	.125	2.38
	" 10	.135	2.64
2¼ inch	" 13	.095	2.16
	" 12	.110	2.46
	" 11	.125	2.70
	" 10	.135	2.99
2½ inch	" 12	.110	2.73
	" 11	.125	3.02
	" 10	.135	3.37

SURFACE INSPECTION.

4. Tubes must have a smooth surface, free from all laminations, cracks, blisters, pits and imperfect welds. They must be free from bends, kinks and buckles, and from evidence of unequal contraction in cooling or injury in manipulation.

PHYSICAL TESTS.

5. *Bending Tests.*—Strips ½ inch in width by 6 inches in length, planed lengthwise from tubes, after having been heated to a cherry red and quenched in water at 80° F., shall bend in opposite directions at each end, as shown in sketch below, without cracks or flaws, and when nicked

```
   Outside Surface of Tube
   Inside Surface of Tube
```

and broken by slight blows, these strips must show a fracture wholly fibrous.

6. *Expanding Test.*—Sections of tubes 12 inches long shall be heated a length of 5 inches to a bright red in daylight and then placed in a vertical position and a smooth taper steel pin at blue heat will be driven into the end of the tube by light blows of a 10-pound hammer. Under this test the tube must stretch to 1⅛ times its original diameter without splitting or cracking. The pin used shall be of tool steel tapered 1½ inches to the foot. In making this test, care must be taken to see that the end of the tube is smoothly trimmed.

7. One tube is to be tested, as required in paragraphs 5 and 6, in each lot of 250 tubes or less.

8. *Crushing Test.*—A section of tube 2½ inches long, when placed vertically on the anvil of a steam hammer and subjected to a series of light blows, must crush to a height of 1⅜ inches without splitting in either direction and without cracking or bending at weld.

9. *Hydraulic Test.*—Before shipping, each tube must be tested by manufacturer to 500 pounds per square inch, and each tube must be plainly marked in the middle: "Knobbled charcoal, tested to 500 pounds pressure."

10. In addition to the above tests, tubes which, when inserted into boilers, split or break while being expanded or beaded, and also individual tubes which fail to pass surface inspection will be rejected and returned to the makers at their expense.

11. *Etching Test.*—In case of doubt as to the quality of material, the following test shall be made to detect the presence of steel. A section of tube, turned or ground to a perfectly true surface on the end, will be polished free from dirt or cracks, and the end of the tube will be suspended in a bath of nine parts water, three parts sulphuric acid and one part hydrochloric acid. The bath will be prepared by placing water in a porcelain dish, adding the sulphuric and then the hydrochloric acid. The chemical action must be allowed to continue until the soft parts are sufficiently dissolved so that the iron tube will show a decided ridged surface, with the weld very distinct, while the steel will show a homogeneous surface.

SPECIFICATION FOR SEAMLESS, COLD-DRAWN STEEL LOCOMOTIVE BOILER TUBES.

1. Tubes are to be cold drawn, seamless and made of open hearth steel. It is desired that the steel from which the tubes are manufactured should have the following chemical composition:

	Per cent.
Carbon	.15 to .20
Manganese	.45 to .55
Sulphur, below	.03
Phosphorus, below	.03

Tubes containing more than .03 phosphorus or sulphur will be rejected.

2. Tubes must be of uniform thickness throughout. They must be circular within .02 of an inch and the mean diameter must be within .015 inch of the size ordered. They must be within .01 inch of the thickness specified and not less than the length ordered, but may exceed this by .125 inch. They must be free from bends, kinks and buckles.

3. The minimum weights of the tubes of various diameters and thicknesses are given in the following table:

Outside diameter.	Nominal B. W. G.	Thickness M. M. G. Inches.	Minimum weight per foot. Lbs.
1¾ inch	No. 13	.095	1.69
	" 12	.110	1.92
	" 11	.125	2.15
	" 10	.135	2.29
2 inch	" 13	.095	1.91
	" 12	.110	2.19
	" 11	.125	2.47
	" 10	.135	2.65
2¼ inch	" 13	.095	2.16
	" 12	.110	2.48
	" 11	.125	2.80
	" 10	.135	3.01
2½ inch	" 12	.110	2.73
	" 11	.125	3.04
	" 10	.135	3.41

PHYSICAL TESTS.

4. *Bending Test.*—Strips ½ inch in width by 6 inches in length, planed lengthwise from tubes, after having been heated to a cherry red and quenched in water at 80 degrees F., shall bend in opposite directions at each end, as shown in sketch below without cracks or flaws.

5. *Expanding Test.*—Sections of tubes 12 inches long shall be heated a length of five inches to a bright cherry red in daylight and then placed in a vertical position and a smooth taper steel pin at blue heat will be driven into the end of the tube by light blows of a 10-pound hammer. Under this test the tube must stretch to 1⅛ times its original diameter without splitting or cracking. The pin used shall be of tool steel tapered 1½ inches to the foot. In making this test care must be taken to see that the end of the tube is smoothly trimmed.

6. *Crushing Test.*—A section of tube 2½ inches long, when placed vertically on the anvil of a steam hammer and subjected to a series of light blows, must crush to a height of 1⅛ inches without splitting in either direction.

7. *Flattening Test.*—A test piece of tube 6 inches long, when flattened lengthwise cold until the sides are separated by a distance equal to the gage of the tube, must not show any splits or cracks.

8. One tube is to be tested as required in paragraphs 4, 5, 6 and 7 in each lot of 250 tubes, or less.

9. Each tube must be subjected by the manufacturer to an internal pressure of 1,000 pounds to the square inch, and must be plainly stenciled, "Seamless Steel Tubes, tested to 1,000 pounds."

Tube Ferrule. See **Ferrule.**

Tube Opening. (Tube Sheet.) The apertures or holes in the front or back tube sheet in which the tubes are set and expanded.

Tube Plate (British). See **Tube Sheet.**

Tube Plug. A slightly conical piece of metal used to close a tube opening in a tube sheet in case a tube bursts or ruptures. It is inserted by means of a bar of special design called a **Plugging Bar**, which see.

Tube Sheet. 30 and 42, Figs. 151-206. A plate or sheet forming one end of a locomotive boiler shell, and having a large number of holes in which the ends of the tubes are inserted. The plate next the smokebox is called the front tube sheet, and that next the firebox the back tube sheet. In Great Britain copper is commonly used for back tube sheets.

Tube Sheet Brace. 39, Figs. 151-206; Figs. 245-250. A steel bar or rod fastened at one end to a bracket or lug on the front tube sheet and at the other to the waist or shell of the boiler. Its purpose is to strengthen the tube sheet.

Tube Sheet Brace Crow Foot. A triangular-shaped bracket of cast iron fastened to the front tube sheet and holding one of the front tube sheet braces by a pin or bolt passing through both.

Tube Sheet Brace Jaw. A fork or bifurcation formed on one end of a front tube sheet brace at the point of attachment to a crow foot or lug fastened to the front tube sheet.

Tube Sheet Brace Pin. A short rod or bolt passing through one end of a front tube sheet brace, to secure it to the lug or bracket.

Tube Sheet Stay. See **Throat Brace.**

Tube Superheater. See **Superheater.**

Turnbuckle. A device inserted in the middle of a long rod for changing its length. Right and left screw turnbuckles, or single screw turnbuckles are the most common.

Turret. 137, Figs. 77-124. A distributing stand screwed into the steam space of a boiler to supply steam to the auxiliary devices, whistle, injector, etc. See **Cab Turret.**

Turret Lathe. Figs. 5015-5019. A special design of lathe fitted with a hollow spindle through which the material to be machined is fed to the cutting tools, which are held in a revolving turret.

Twelve-Wheel Locomotive. Figs. 72-74, 124-125. Specifically a locomotive having 12 wheels, but commonly applied only to locomotives having a four-wheel front truck and eight coupled driving wheels. See **Whyte's Nomenclature.**

Tyre. (of a Wheel). See **Tire.** The spelling "tyre" is the British method, and corresponds with the supposed origin of the word, which is from the fact that iron bands were first used on wheels in the city of Tyre, Syria.

U

U-Bolt. A double bolt made of a bar of iron or steel, bent in the shape of the letter U, with a screw thread and nut on each end.

"U" Brake Shoe. Figs. 2774, 2786. A cast iron brake shoe with inclined ends chilled from the back.

U. S. Metallic Rod Packing. Figs. 1017-1019.

Uncoupling Lever. 192, Figs. 77-124; 21, Figs. 2256-2327. An iron rod with a bent handle forming a lever, usually attached to the end sill or front bumper by which the lock of the automatic coupler is opened and the uncoupling effected without going between the engine and cars. The lever and rod are in various forms, as the form of lock may require.

Uncoupling Lever Bracket. 20, Figs. 2256-2327. One of two or more small brackets attached to the back end of a tender and to the pilot bumper of an engine for holding the uncoupling lever of a coupler.

Uncoupling Lever Chain. 7, Figs. 2256-2327. A short chain fastened to a coupler locking pin and to the uncoupling rod. See **Uncoupling Lever**.

Uncoupling Rod. 6, Figs. 2256-2327. A rod connecting the uncoupling lever with the lock of an automatic coupler. It is usually forged in one piece with the lever.

Underframe. A stout framework, which receives the buffing and pulling stresses and carries the weight of the floor and body of the vehicle. Underframe includes all the framing below the floor, and includes the draft timbers, etc. Tenders are now usually built with pressed steel or structural steel underframes.

Under-Running Rail. See **Third-Rail**.

Union (Pipe Fittings). A means of uniting the ends of two pipes with a nut. This nut turns freely on one pipe, where it is held by a collar or ring, and is screwed on the other pipe, or on a thimble or sleeve attached to the pipe. Often called a union joint or coupling. They are used for many forms of pipe work, and take their distinctive names, if any, from the parts with which they are connected, as drain pipe union, reservoir union, etc., of air brakes.

United States Standard System of Screw Threads. This term is often used to designate the **Sellers System of Screw Threads**, which see.

Universal Joint. "A device for connecting the ends of two shafts so as to allow them to have perfect freedom of motion in every direction within certain defined limits."—Knight. An application in locomotive work which has not yet secured general use as a substitute for brake hose, in connection with air brake and steam apparatus and in the connections between the engine and tender.

V

V-shaped Screw Thread. A thread with a sharp edge at the top and sharp groove at the root. The Sellers (U. S.) standard thread is flat at the top and at the root, and the Whitworth is rounded at those points.

Vacuum Brake. Figs. 5127-5131. A system of continuous brakes which is operated by exhausting the air from some appliance under each car, by which the pressure of the external air is transmitted to the brake levers and shoes. So called in distinction from **Air Brakes**, which see, which are technically understood to refer only to brakes operating with compressed air, although in a literal sense the vacuum brake is also an air brake. An ejector on the engine is ordinarily used for exhausting the air, connected with the rest of the train by pipes and flexible hose between the cars. The latest type of vacuum brakes in general use in passenger service and to some extent for freight service in Great Britain is shown in Figs. 5127-5131. A continuous pipe is connected through the train between cars by rubber hose, wound with wire to prevent collapsing, and having suitable couplings. Under each car is a large cylinder with a piston and rod connected to the brake levers actuating the brake shoes. These cylinders are connected to the train pipe through a simple form of ball valve. An **Ejector**, which see, on the locomotive, maintains a vacuum of from 20 to 24 inches in the train pipe and in the cylinders under each car. In the release position the piston rests by its own weight in the bottom of the cylinder. To apply the brakes air is admitted to the train pipe and through the ball valve under each car to the space **below** the piston. The vacuum **above** the piston permits the atmospheric pressure below the piston to raise it and apply the brakes. A vacuum is always maintained above the piston and is available for applying the brakes at any time. In case the train parts the admittance of air to the broken train pipe applies the brakes in both sections of the train. A valve in the guard's van may also be used to admit air to the train pipe and apply the brakes in case of emergency. To release the brakes the vacuum is restored in the train pipe and under the pistons by working the ejector.

Vacuum Valve. Figs. 1009-1011. A poppet valve inserted in the steam chest or cylinder head of a locomotive to relieve the vacuum formed when the engine is drifting—i. e., running with the throttle valve closed.

Valve. "A lid, plug or cover, applied to an aperture so that by its movement, as by swinging, lifting and falling, sliding, turning or the like, it will open or close the aperture to permit or prevent passage, as of a fluid."—Webster.

Piston Valve	By-Pass Valve	Throttle Valve
Slide Valve	Distributing Valve	Intercepting Valve
Vacuum Valve	Triple Valve	Engineer's Brake
Relief Valve	Reducing Valve	Valve.

Valve Body. The shell, case or frame of a valve.

Valve Follower. D, Figs. 2167-2192. A circular cast iron or steel end piece fastened to the body of a piston valve.

Valve Gear. Figs. 1809-2096. The mechanism by means of which the slide valves or piston valves are operated for the purpose of admitting steam to and exhausting it from locomotive cylinders. Valve gears are so arranged as to allow steam to be cut off at any desired point of the stroke of the piston, and admit steam to either end of the cylinders in order to run the engine either forwards or backwards. The ordinary link motion or so-called Stephenson link motion uses two eccentrics for each valve, the eccentric rods imparting motion to a link having a sliding block to which one end of a rocker arm is connected. The other arm of this rocker is connected to and thus moves the valve rod and valve. The point of cut off as well as the direction in which the engine turns its wheels is determined by the position of the link block and rocker pin in the link. The link is suspended by a link lifter attached to an arm on the reverse shaft. When this shaft is turned by the operation of the reverse lever, reach rod and reverse shaft arms, the link is raised or lowered, thereby moving the link block and rocker pin either backwards or forwards and consequently causing the valve to move on its seat. Inside connected engines generally have the block directly connected to the valve rod without the interposition of any rocker.

The Walschaerts valve gear, Fig. 1812, differs from the ordinary link motion in having only one eccentric rod, in altering the position or travel of the valve by moving the end of a bar attached to the end of the valve rod up or down in the link, without moving the link, and in having the valve rod also attached to a lever that derives its motion from the crosshead. This last detail determines the **Lap** and the **Lead**, which see, of the valve, and gives them a fixed value; whereas the ordinary link motion gives a variable lap and lead, affected by the valve travel. The Walschaerts gear derives its motion from an eccentric crank or return crank on the main crank pin, or from one eccentric on the main axle. The eccentric rod is secured to one end of the link which is pivoted in the center on a pin held by a bracket bolted to the guide yoke. The link block is secured to a radius arm or bar, one end of which is attached to the end of the valve rod and the other end to the lifting arm of the reverse shaft. The motion imparted to the valve by the crosshead connection is small, as the crosshead arm and union link are attached to the lower end of the combining or combination lever while the radius arm and valve rod are connected close to the upper end, thus imparting only a slight motion to the valve rod. For large locomotives, Walschaerts gear is now generally used, because it has lighter moving parts, and these parts are more accessible for inspection or repair than those of the common form of link motion. In the Gooch valve motion, the link is hung with its curvature reversed to its usual position, and in some cases is driven by eccentrics on an axle ahead of it.

Valve Handle. A hand grip attached to the plug, stem or movable portion of a valve for the purpose of opening and closing it.

Valve Packing Ring. 40, Figs. 2140-2164. One of four or more cast iron or composition rings secured on the outside of a piston valve to cause it to fit steam tight in the bushing or valve chamber. They are usually made slightly larger than the internal diameter of the valve chamber bushing, cut, and sprung in place, in the same manner as the packing rings on a steam cylinder piston. See **Piston**, and **Piston Valve**.

Valve Rod. Figs. 2083-2094; 36, Figs. 1813-1815. A steel shaft attached to a rocker arm or link block at one end, and to a valve stem at the other, for communicating the motion of an eccentric rod to a valve. British, slide valve intermediate spindle.

Valve Rod Block. 44, Figs. 2069-2075. A rectangular piece of metal attached to a rocker pin, and fitted to slide vertically in a rectangular frame or yoke formed on the valve rod, thus allowing the rocker pin to travel in the arc of a circle while the valve rod moves in a straight line parallel to its own axis. Also called Scotch yoke block.

Valve Rod Block Yoke. 198, Figs. 77-124; 43, Figs. 2069-2075. See above.

Valve Rod Guide. A cast iron support commonly bolted to the guide yoke, and having a hole through it in line with the valve rod stuffing box to keep the rod in its proper place.

Valve Rod Guide Bushing. A cylindrical lining or sleeve fitted in a valve rod guide to form a wearing surface for the rod.

Valve Rod Key. 37, Figs. 2069-2075. A wedge-shaped piece of metal inserted in an enlargement on the inner end of a valve rod to secure it to the valve stem.

Valve Rod Knuckle. Figs. 2089-2094. A flexible joint connecting a valve stem to a valve rod. Since the rocker pin travels over an arc of a circle, and the valve stem in a straight line, some form of flexible connection must be used to permit each to move in its own path.

Valve Rod Knuckle Pin. 36b. Figs. 2089-2094. A bolt fitted through the two portions of the knuckle joint attached to the valve stem and valve rod, respectively, and forming a pivot or flexible connection for them.

Valve Seat. "The flat or conical surface on which a valve rests."—Knight.

Valve Seat Facing Machine (Portable). Fig. 5020. A portable machine, designed to be attached to a locomotive cylinder casting for truing worn valve seats.

Valve Setting Machine. Fig. 5021. A portable device for raising and revolving the driving wheels of locomotives while adjusting or setting up the eccentrics and valves.

Valve Stem. Figs. 2080-2082; 2, Figs. 2069-2075. A short shaft secured at one end to the valve rod and at the other to a piston valve, or to the yoke of a slide valve. British, slide valve spindle.

Valve Stem Oil Cup Bracket. A holder fastened to the casing of a steam chest and holding an oil cup for the lubrication of the valve stem.

Valve Stem Packing. See **Packing**.

Valve Stem Stuffing Box. See **Stuffing Box**.

Valve Tee Ring. A metal ring, whose cross section has the shape of the letter T shrunk on to the body of a piston valve.

Valve Travel. The linear distance traversed by a valve on its seat in a steam chest or valve chamber. The travel of a valve depends upon the throw of the eccentric and on the position of the link or link block.

Valve Yoke. 45, Figs. 2097-2118. A rectangular shaped steel frame fitted over a slide valve, and to one end of which the valve stem is welded.

Valve Yoke Guide. A rod attached to the front of a slide valve yoke and extending through the front of the steam chest to serve as a guide to keep the valve in line on its seat.

Valve Yoke Guide Bushing. A sleeve fitted around the extension rod of a valve yoke in the front end of a steam chest. Seldom used.

Vanderbilt Boiler. Figs. 151-156. A locomotive boiler having a corrugated cylindrical firebox requiring no staying. See **Stayless Boiler** and **Lentz Boiler**.

Vanderbilt Tender Tank. Figs. 4070-4073. A cylindrical tank mounted on a tender instead of the more common form of square flat tank.

Vanderbilt Truck Bolster. Figs. 4426-4428.

Varnish. A limpid fluid composed of resinous matter and solvents, capable of hardening without losing its transparency, and of adhering to wood, metal and other materials. The resins commonly used are amber, anim, copal, mastic, rosin, sandarac and shellac. In oil varnishes the solvents used are linseed oil or spirits of turpentine, or adulterants. In spirit varnishes alcohol or methylated spirits are used as solvents. Ordinarily, two coats of varnish are applied to paint work on locomotives, at least 24 hours being allowed to elapse between the first and second applications.

Vauclain Compound Locomotive. Figs. 25, 58, 88, 99-100, etc. A four-cylinder compound locomotive having a high and low pressure cylinder on each side outside the frames and placed one above the other with the two pistons attached to a common crosshead. See **Compound Locomotive**.

Vaughan Superheater. Figs. 496-503. See **Superheater**.

Ventilator. Figs. 2928-2957. A hinged flap or door placed in the roof of a locomotive cab, to cause a circulation of air through it and by carrying off some of the heat, to make the temperature more endurable to the engine crew in hot weather. See **Cab Ventilator**.

Vogt Crosshead. Figs. 1092-1102. A **Crosshead**, which see, working in a solid guide. Used on the Pennsylvania Railroad.

Volt. The unit of electric pressure or electromotive

force. The term voltage is sometimes used to describe the amount of electric pressure.

Voltage. See **Volt.**

Vulcanized Fiber. A leathery material of great durability and toughness, made by subjecting vegetable fiber to the action of acids. It is insoluble in all ordinary solvents, such as oil, alcohol, ammonia, ether, etc. It is made in two classes, hard and flexible, the hard kind being used for dust guards of journal boxes on locomotive tenders.

W

Wagon Top Boiler. Figs. 149-150. A boiler having the steam dome over the firebox and a sloping course from in front of the firebox to the cylindrical shell. See **Extended Wagon Top Boiler.**

Waist (of Boiler). That part of the boiler shell immediately in front of the firebox. See **Waist Sheet.**

Waist Brace. 11, Figs. 77-124. A vertical steel plate riveted to the waist sheet crosstie and to an angle piece which is also fastened to the waist of a boiler to secure that part to the frame, and at the same time allow a small amount of expansion and contraction. See **Expansion Knee.**

Waist Brace Angle. 42, Figs. 77-124. A steel strip riveted to the shell of a boiler and having its edge bent to a right angle, and to which a plate or strut is fastened for the purpose of bracing the waist of a boiler to the frames.

Waist Sheet. The plate forming that portion of a boiler directly ahead of the outside firebox sheet. It is sometimes made cylindrical in shape and sometimes tapering or conical.

Waist Sheet Crosstie. 13, Figs. 1524-1525. A transverse brace or casting binding the frames together in front of the firebox and usually having a plate fastened to it and to the boiler to support the waist of the boiler at this point.

Waist Sheet Wearing Plate. A steel strip riveted to the waist sheet of a boiler and to the angle of the waist sheet brace or expansion plate, to reinforce the bearing or support of the boiler at this point.

Walschaerts Valve Gear. Fig. 1812. A valve gear so-called from its inventor, largely in use in Europe and being rapidly introduced in the United States. It has no eccentric and is entirely outside of the frames. See **Valve Gear.**

Washburn Tender Coupler. Figs. 3999-4004.

Washburn Friction Draft Gear. Figs. 3931-3933.

Washburn Pilot Coupler and Buffer. Fig. 2403.

Washer. A plate of metal or other material, usually annular, which is placed under a nut or bolt head to give it a better bearing. Two or more washers are sometimes combined and called washer plates, strap washers, double or twin washers, triple washers, etc. They are sometimes made beveled or triangular for a rod or bolt, which is oblique, with reference to the bearing surface. A socket washer or flush washer is one provided with a recess for the bolt head, so as to leave it flush with the adjoining parts. Cut or wrought washers are those stamped out of rolled iron plates. Cast washers are made from cast iron. Both kinds are used.

Wash-out Plug. A short, solid metal cylinder with a screw thread cut on the outside and a square or hexagonal head for convenience in applying a wrench, screwed into the water leg and above the crown sheet of a locomotive boiler. Wash-out plugs are usually located near the bottom of a water leg, a little above the mud ring, or above the crown sheet, and from four to eight are provided in order to allow mud to be thoroughly washed out.

Waste. The spoiled bobbins of cotton or woolen mills, used for wiping machinery and for **Journal Packing,** which see.

Waste Cock or **Waste Valve.** 93, Fig. 3102. An arrangement attached to and forming part of the body of an injector, consisting of a valve provided with a handle or lever. If this valve is left open when the steam and water supply valves to the injector are also open, steam passes back through the injector feed pipe and may thus be used to prevent the water in the tender tank from freezing.

Water. A liquid composed of two gases, hydrogen and oxygen in the proportion of 8 to 1 by weight, colorless and transparent in the pure state. It is never obtained pure for locomotive use, always holding in solution a quantity of solid matter such as sulphates and carbonates of lime and magnesia that may form objectionable quantities of scale in a boiler. See **Steam.** Boilers fed with water that forms much scale must be washed out at frequent intervals; in some districts even at the completion of every trip. The best practice at present is to instal water-treating plants at water stations, by means of which the scale forming matters in the water are chemically treated and removed before the water reaches the locomotives.

Water Brake. An arrangement, consisting of a set of pipes and valves connected to a locomotive boiler below the water line, for admitting water to the cylinders to retard the motion of the pistons and thus act as a brake on the locomotive, which is run with the reverse lever back of the center. It is used on lines having long, steep grades.

Water Brake Valve. A globe valve with its connecting pipe screwed in the boiler back head below the water line, for operating the water brake.

Water Cooler. Figs. 1216-1219. A tank or vessel for carrying drinking water which is usually cooled with ice. The sides are generally made double, and the space between filled with some non-conducting substance. When used on locomotives they are commonly located on the tender tank.

Water Gage or **Water Glass.** Figs. 3130-3147. A device to enable an engineman or fireman to observe the height of water in a locomotive boiler. It consists of two brass fittings screwed into the back head, one above the other, and connected by a stout glass tube which communicates, through the fittings, with the water and steam in the boiler. The water level showing in the glass tube must be the same as that inside the boiler.

Water Gage Casing. Figs. 3144-3145, 3147. A covering or protector around a water gage glass. The casing prevents the glass from flying about in case of breakage.

Water Gage Cock. One of two brass fittings screwed into a locomotive boiler head, having a valve or plug cock for opening or closing communication between the boiler and the water gage glass. The end of the glass tube rests in an opening in the gage cock and is held in place by a coupling nut which is screwed down on an elastic washer surrounding the tube.

Water Gage Cock Extension. A piece of pipe leading from an opening in a boiler to one of the water gage cocks.

Water Gage Cock Gland. A neck or extension formed on a water gage cock to receive the end of the glass tube, or the stem of the cock or plug.

Water Gage Lamp. See **Gage Lamp.**

Water Gage Nut. A hexagonal brass nut surrounding a water gage glass near the end and holding an elastic washer so as to prevent leakage of water or steam around it.

Water Grate. See **Grate** and **Water Pull Bar Grate.**

Water Leg. 99, 100, 101, Figs. 151-124. The space between the inner and outer sheets of a firebox. At the bottom, where the two sheets are riveted to the mud ring, the width of the water leg is from three to five inches, increasing more or less rapidly, according to the design and size of the firebox.

Water Pull Bar Grate. A grate designed for burning anthracite coal, consisting of tubes running longitudinally through the bottom of the firebox and communicating with the front and back water legs, usually screwed into the tube sheet and expanded into the back sheet, a copper ferrule being used to insure a tight joint. Between the water tubes, iron pull bars, enclosed in short tubes, pass completely through the back water leg and project a short distance outside the back head. These outer ends have slots in them, into which a rod can be put, and the bars pulled out for the purpose of dumping or cleaning the fire. Midway of the length of the firebox is a bearer or bridge that supports both the tubes and bars that form the grate. A similar bearer is placed at the front end of the box to hold the bars. See **Grate.**

Water Scoop. Figs. 4227-4293. A device for putting water in a locomotive tender, while it is in motion, from a trough laid between the rails, and sometimes called a track tank. It consists of a cast-iron or steel plate conduit of rectangular cross section, about 8 x 12 inches, passing up through the tender tank and turned over at the top so as to discharge the water downward. The lower end, underneath the tender frame, is fitted with a scoop or dipper that can be lowered into the trough by a lever worked by hand, or by compressed air applied in a cylinder whose piston rod is connected to the mechanism for raising and lowering the scoop. Owing to its inertia, the water is forced up through the siphon pipe into the tender tank when the scoop moves through the trough at a speed of from 25 to 40 miles per hour.

Water Scoop Air Cylinder. A small cast-iron cylinder fastened underneath a tender for operating the water scoop. Compressed air is conveyed to it from the main air reservoir through a valve, thus moving the piston. The piston rod is connected to the levers that lower the dipper into the water trough between the rails. To insure the rapid raising of the dipper, when the locomotive reaches the end of the track tank, a coil spring is fastened to the scoop mechanism.

Water Scoop Air Cylinder Piston. A metal disk fitted inside a water scoop air cylinder and having attached to it a rod connected to the operating mechanism of the scoop.

Water Scoop Arm. A bent lever or bell crank, to one end of which the air cylinder piston rod is attached, while to the other the links for raising and lowering the dipper are bolted.

Water Scoop Body. 2, Figs. 4227-4232. That portion of a water scoop shaped like the frustum of a pyramid that is lowered into the track trough and to the lower end of which the dipper or nozzle is attached. It is usually made of cast iron.

Water Scoop Cylinder Connecting Rod. A short rod attached to the end of the piston rod of a water scoop cylinder, and with a coil spring attached to the end. This spring raises the scoop out of the water when the end of the track tank is reached and holds it in that position.

Water Scoop Cylinder Piston Rod. A wrought-iron or cast-steel rod attached to the piston of the air cylinder at one end, and to the bell crank for operating the water scoop at the other.

Water Scoop Cylinder Support. A metal carrier secured underneath a tender frame for the purpose of holding the water scoop air cylinder, which is bolted to it.

Water Scoop Delivery Pipe. Figs. 4249-4252. The square pipe which joins the scoop with the siphon pipe in the tender tank.

Water Scoop Delivery Pipe Brace. A rod secured to the tender frame center sills to stiffen the delivery pipe.

Water Scoop Delivery Pipe Bracket. 4, Figs. 4227-4232. A cast-iron support riveted on to the end of the delivery pipe and having a hole or bearing in its outer end for one of the trunnions of the water scoop.

Water Scoop Dipper. 2. Figs. 4227-4232. A hinged extension or hood at the end of a water scoop. That portion of the scoop that goes into the water.

Water Scoop Dipper Adjusting Bracket. 12. Figs. 4227-4242. A support or holder fastened underneath a tender to limit the movement of the dipper arm and thus prevent the scoop from hanging too low and striking the ties or ballast.

Water Scoop Dipper Lifting Link. 3, Figs. 4227-4242. A short metal bar attached to the bell crank or arm of the scoop-lifting mechanism and to the dipper, for raising it out of the water.

Water Scoop End Support. 14, Figs. 4227-4242. A metal rod fastened to either side of the outer end of a water scoop, next to the dipper, and to the under side of the tender frame.

Water Scoop Hanger. The bracket or frame fastened underneath a tender frame to support a water scoop and the mechanism for raising and lowering it.

Water Scoop Lifter. 3, Figs. 4227-4242. One of two links or bars attached to a water scoop at one end and to the water scoop arm at the other.

Water Scoop Locking Cylinder. A small air cylinder whose function is to hold the water scoop in place and prevent it from dropping down on the track.

Water Scoop Neck. The upper end of a water scoop; that portion that joins the water scoop pipe directly under the tender tank.

Water Scoop Operating Lever. Figs. 4263-4264; 22, Figs. 4227-4242. The arm or lever by which the water scoop is raised or lowered by hand. It extends up through the tender deck alongside the tank leg.

Water Scoop Operating Lever Connecting Rod. 8, Figs. 4227-4242. A long piece of pipe or solid rod, attached to the water scoop operating lever at one end and the scoop lifting arm at the other.

Water Scoop Operating Lever Fulcrum. Figs. 4275-4277. A cast iron support fastened on a tender frame and holding a bolt or pin that passes through the water scoop operating lever.

Water Scoop Pipe. 5, Figs. 4227-4242; Figs. 4243-4245, 4249-4252. The cast iron or steel plate conduit passing up through a tender for conveying the water forced into the scoop to the top of the tank.

Water Scoop Pneumatic Valve. The valve for admitting compressed air to a water scoop cylinder.

Water Scoop Rod. 8, Figs. 4227-4242. The rod connecting the water scoop lever with the arm or bell crank.

Water Scoop Shaft. 7, Figs. 4227-4242. A pivot fastened at right angles to a water scoop arm and resting in bearings in supports or hangers attached to the tender frame by bolts or rivets.

Water Scoop Shaft Bracket. 10, Figs. 4227-4242. A carrier attached to a tender frame and holding the ends of the water scoop shaft.

Water Scoop Side Brace. A rod fastened on either side of a water scoop and to the side sill of a tender to give transverse stiffness to the scoop.

Water Scoop Spring. 19, Figs. 4227-4242. The spring used to assist in lowering or raising a water scoop.

Water Scoop Spring Rod. A shaft attached to a water scoop operating mechanism and to the coil spring which forms a part of it.

Water Space. That part of a locomotive boiler that is filled with water, in contrast with the part normally occupied by steam. A **Water Leg**, which see, is also called a water space.

Water Table. A device for improving the combustion of fuel in a locomotive firebox. The form invented by William Buchanan, of the N. Y. C. & H. R. R. R., consists of two flat, parallel plates, extending diagonally upward from the tube sheet to the back sheet of the firebox. These plates are about 4½ inches apart, are strengthened with staybolts in the same manner as are the inner and outer firebox sheets, and form an inclined water leg connecting the front and back legs of the firebox. A hole 18 or 20 inches in diameter is made through the center of the water table for the passage of the products of combustion to the upper part of the firebox on their way to the tubes. Not extensively used.

Water Tube. A pipe containing water and surrounded with hot gases in contrast to a fire tube surrounded by water and having hot gases passing through it. See below.

Water Tube Boiler. Figs. 5113-5115. A boiler in which water circulates through tubes surrounded by hot gases, the products of combustion in the firebox. Not extensively used for locomotives although tried on the London & South Western.

Watson & Stillman Hydraulic Jacks. Figs. 4575-4577.

Watt. An electrical unit expressing the rate at which energy is transformed, or work done. It is equal to 1/746 part of one horse-power, or 44.23 foot pound a minute. It is used to express the product of the voltage of an electric circuit and the current or amperage. As it is a very small unit, a multiple of it, 1,000 times as large, and called a kilowatt, is commonly used.

Waycott Brake Beam. Figs. 4435-4438.

Waycott Dust Guard. Fig. 4507.

Wedge. 1. A term in quite general use for a **Journal Bearing Key,** which see.

2. A **Pedestal Wedge,** which see, is a tapering liner for the jaws of a pedestal to adjust the position of the driving box and take up wear.

Wedge Bolt. Figs. 1403-1404. A bolt passing through the pedestal cap of a driving or trailing wheel for adjusting the pedestal wedge.

Weigh Shaft (British). See **Reverse Shaft.**

Weigh Shaft Balance Weight (British). A large mass of cast iron used on British locomotives in place of a reverse shaft spring.

Weigh Shaft Lever (British). See **Reverse Shaft Arm.**

Westinghouse Air Brake. Figs. 2410-2556. A system of continuous brakes invented and patented (the first patent in 1869) by Mr. George Westinghouse, which is operated by compressed air. The air is compressed, by a steam air pump on the locomotive or an electric motor compressor on the car, and is stored up in a tank called the main reservoir on the engine or tender. By the original form of brake the compressed air was conveyed from the tank by pipes connected together between the cars by flexible brake hose to brake cylinders under each car, by means of which the pressure of the air was communicated to the brake levers, and thence to the brake shoes. A later and improved form is the Westinghouse automatic air brake, commonly called simply Westinghouse brake, which is now in universal use. At the present time the Westinghouse brake, unless otherwise specified, is always understood to mean the automatic air brake. The change made from the original form of the Westinghouse air brake in order to make it automatic was to carry a full pressure of air at all times in the brake pipes and cause the brakes to be applied by a reduction of this pressure instead of by the admission of pressure, so that the breaking apart of the train or a reduction of pressure by escape of air at any point on the brake pipe would apply the brakes to the whole train at once. A further advantage was that the action of the brakes was made quicker by saving the appreciable interval of time required for the compressed air to flow from a single reservoir at one end of the train in sufficient quantities to fill all the brake cylinders. An auxiliary reservoir is placed under each car, containing air at the same pressure as in the brake pipes. An ingenious valve called the triple valve connects the brake pipe, auxiliary reservoir and brake cylinder together in such manner that any reduction of pressure in the brake pipe opens a passage for the air from the auxiliary reservoir to the brake cylinder, applying the brakes, and closes the connection between brake pipe and reservoir. To release the brakes, the pressure in the brake pipes is restored, when the triple valve closes the connection between the auxiliary reservoir and brake cylinder and opens one between the brake cylinder and the outer air and between the auxiliary reservoir and the brake pipe. In order that the train brakes may be applied from any car, each car is fitted with a valve called the conductor's valve, connected to the brake pipe so that the compressed air therein can be permitted to escape by opening the valve.

Westinghouse E-T Locomotive Brake Equipment (Air Brake). Figs. 2419-2420. A new arrangement of air brake apparatus as applied to a locomotive. It differs from previous locomotive brake schedules principally in that the details are centralized and simplified so as to reduce the total number required, occupy less space, and give the engineman a more certain and flexible control of the locomotive brakes. It has all the good features of any of the older equipment, besides a number of new ones, viz., uniform brake cylinder pressure on engine and tender, and a pressure-maintaining feature by which the brake-cylinder pressure is automatically held to that resulting from the brake application as long as such application lasts. See **Distributing Valve.**

Westinghouse Friction Draft Gear. Figs. 3905-3922. A form of draft gear in which the forces are absorbed and dissipated by friction. The friction device is encased in a malleable iron cylinder open at the front end. The front follower bears against a preliminary spring, the other end of which bears against the center wedge of the shape of the frustum of an octagonal pyramid. Surrounding the wedge are four pairs of segmental carriers having one rib each which lies in a groove in the cylinder.

The other grooves in the cylinder are filled by friction strips resting on the carriers. These strips are of wrought iron and have lugs formed on them which engage in corresponding cavities in the carriers so that the friction strips must move with the carriers. The function of the preliminary spring is to absorb the light shocks without bringing into action the friction parts. The main release spring, placed back of the carriers, forces the carriers to their normal position when the pressure is removed and also adds to the capacity of the device. When the follower plates are moved toward each other, the preliminary spring is compressed until its capacity of 20,000 pounds is exceeded, when the follower bears against the release pin and forces it forward, relieving the wedge from the pressure of the auxiliary release spring, thereby allowing the compression of the preliminary and auxiliary preliminary springs to force the wedge forward and press the segmental carriers and friction strips firmly into the cylinder grooves. The follower then strikes and forces the segmental carriers in, producing friction between the friction strips and the grooves. The complete movement gives a resistance of 160,000 pounds. In releasing, the preliminary spring is gradually restored, and the auxiliary release spring then forces the wedge out, while the release spring returns the friction strips and carriers, giving a complete release. Owing to the varying width of the slots and lugs on the friction strips and carriers the strips are released four at a time through successive small distances. The operations of buffing and pulling are exactly the same, except that the load comes on the front or rear follower first, as the case may be. See **Draft Gear**.

Westinghouse SWA-SWB Locomotive Brake Equipment. Figs. 2417-2421. See **Combined Automatic and Straight-Air Locomotive Brake**.

Westinghouse Traction Brake. Fig. 2419. The adaptation of the Westinghouse air brake equipments to electrically propelled cars or trains. The changed conditions of motive power and method of operating such cars or trains have necessitated various changes in the details of the equipments, while the general principles of the Westinghouse straight-air and automatic brakes, which are the foundation of all known air brake equipments, remains the same. A motor-driven air compressor furnishes the compressed air; an electric pump governor controls the operation of the same; the brake and triple valves are of different design to accord with the conditions for which they are required. Otherwise the description of the **Westinghouse Air Brake**, which see, covers the traction brake also.

Westinghouse Train Air Signal Apparatus. Figs. 2422, 2550-2556. A device for utilizing the supply of compressed air required for operating the Westinghouse brakes to transmit signals to the engine or motorman's cab instead of using the ordinary bell cord. See **Train Air Signal Apparatus**.

Westinghouse Unit Switch System of Control. Figs. 4663-4665. A system of control for railway and other motors by means of low potential train line circuits taken from a storage battery under the car which operate electro-magnets controlling pneumatic valves and cylinders operating the main controller circuits under each car by air taken from the brake pipe. The main controller under each car consists of a group of electro-pneumatic switches which give the desired combinations to the motor circuits. A reverse switch and auxiliary resistance are essential parts of the apparatus under each car. The apparatus is applicable for either direct current or alternating current motors. Also called Westinghouse electro-pneumatic system of control. See **Control System**.

Wheel. Figs. 1301-1367, 3526-3541, 4538-4571. 1. A circular frame or solid piece of wood or metal which revolves on an axis.

2. A circular frame or disk, revolving on an axle, serving to support a moving vehicle. Engine truck wheels are sometimes made of chilled cast iron, but more commonly have a cast iron or cast steel center with a steel tire fastened on, as are also tender truck wheels. See **Wheel Center**. Driving wheels and trailing wheels are always made with a spoke center of cast iron or cast steel with a steel tire shrunk on. In addition to shrinkage, driving wheel tires are held on by bolts through the rim and by retaining rings also held by bolts.

Wheels (Specification for Cast Iron, A. R. M. M. Recommended Practice). At the convention of 1888 the following specifications and tests for cast-iron wheels were adopted as standard. In 1891 these were changed to Recommendations.

The specifications and tests are as follows:

1. The chills in which the wheels of any one wheelmaker are cast shall be of equal diameters, and the same chill must not vary at different points more than one-sixteenth of an inch in diameter.

2. There shall not be a variation of more than one-half inch in the circumference of any given number of wheels of the same nominal diameter, furnished by any one maker, and the same wheel must not vary more than one-sixteenth of an inch in diameter. The body of the wheel must be smooth and free from slag or blow holes. The tread must be free from deep and irregular wrinkles, slag, chill cracks and sweat or beads in the throat which are one-eighth of an inch or over in diameter, or which occur in clusters of more than six inches in length.

3. The wheels broken must show clean, gray iron in the plates; the depth of pure white iron must not exceed seven-eighths of an inch or be less than three-eighths of an inch in the middle of the tread, and shall not be less than three-sixteenths of an inch in the throat. The depth of the white iron shall not vary more than one-fourth of an inch around the tread on the rail line in the same wheel.

4. Wheels shall not vary from the specified weight more than two per cent.

5. The flange shall not vary in the same wheel more than three thirty-seconds of an inch from its mean thickness.

6. The single plate part of a 33-inch wheel, known as the Washburn pattern, shall not be less than five-eighths of an inch in thickness in a wheel weighing from 550 to 575 pounds, and not less than three-fourths of an inch in thickness in a wheel weighing from 575 to 600 pounds.

Tests.—1. For each hundred wheels which pass inspection and are ready for shipment, one representative wheel shall be taken at random and subjected to the following test:

The wheel shall be placed flange downward on an anvil block weighing seventeen hundred (1,700) pounds, set on rubble masonry at least two feet deep, and having three supports not more than five inches wide for the wheel to rest upon. It shall be struck centrally on the hub by a weight of one hundred and forty (140) pounds, falling from a height of twelve (12) feet. Should this wheel stand five (5) blows without breaking into two or more pieces, the hundred wheels shall be accepted. Or, wheels must be of such strength that 550 to 575 pound wheels shall require twenty (20) blows, and 575 to 600 pound wheels shall require thirty (30) blows of a hundred (100) pound drop falling seven (7) feet on the plate close to the rim to break a piece out—the wheel resting upon a cast-iron plate weighing not less than one thousand (1,000) pounds.

2. Should in either case the test wheel break into two or more pieces with less than the required number of blows, then a second wheel shall be taken from the same lot and similarly tested. If the second wheel stands the test, it shall be optional with the inspector whether he shall test a third wheel or not. If he does not so elect, or if he does and the third wheel stands the test, the hundred wheels shall be accepted.

3. The above tests shall apply to standard weight wheels from 26 inches to 42 inches diameter, used on standard gage roads.

Form of Contract.—THIS INDENTURE, made this ......day of......19.., between ....party of the first part, and........party of the second part, WITNESSETH:

1. The party of the first part hereby agrees to furnish to the party of the second part, free on board cars at ......chilled cast-iron wheels, ... inches in diameter under the following conditions:

2. The party of the second part hereby agrees to pay to the party of the first part......dollars for each wheel furnished, and to keep an accurate record of the mileage made by the wheels placed in service under cars in passenger equipment and under locomotives and tenders, and an accurate record of the number of months of service of the wheels placed under cars in freight equipment.

3. The party of the second part hereby agrees when any wheel furnished under this contract is scrapped, to furnish to the party of the first part a statement which will show

1.—The wheel number.
2.—The service in which the wheel ran.
3.—The amount of service in months or miles.
4.—The cause of failure.
5.—A charge against the party of the first part of fifty-five per cent. (55 per cent.) of the price of the wheel mentioned above.
6.—A credit to the party of the first part of
....cents per 1,000 miles for 36 in. passenger equipment.
....cents per 1,000 miles for 33 in. passenger equipment.
....cents per 1,000 miles for 30 in. passenger equipment.
....cents per 1,000 miles for 36 in. locomotives and tenders.
....cents per 1,000 miles for 33 in. locomotives and tenders.
....cents per 1,000 miles for 30 in. locomotives and tenders.
....cents per 1,000 miles for 28 in. locomotives and tenders.
....cents per 1,000 miles for 26 in. locomotives and tenders.
....cents per month for 36 in. freight equipment.
....cents per month for 33 in. freight equipment.
....cents per month for 30 in. freight equipment except in the case of wheels made flat by sliding, or removal for sharp flanges or other unfair treatment, which have not made sufficient service to balance the charge against the party of the first part as above; in such case a service credit shall be made which shall balance the charge.

4. The party of the first part hereby agrees that on presentation of the statement to pay to the party of the second part any balance due from lack of sufficient service on the part of the wheels (with above exceptions) to balance the charge; and the party of the second part hereby agrees to pay to the party of the first part any balance due as shown by the aforesaid statement—settlements to be made quarterly. It is, however, understood and agreed that no credit shall be allowed for excessive mileage for time service on freight wheels beyond the time guaranteed.

5. The party of the second part hereby agrees to hold, subject to the inspection of the party of the first part, for a period of thirty days after the said statement has been rendered, any wheels (with above exceptions) which have not earned for themselves a credit equal to the amount charged against them.

Service Guarantee.

36 inch passenger wheels............. 70,000 miles
33 "   "   "   .... 60,000 "
36 inch engine and tender wheels...... 60,000 "
33 "   "   "   ...... 50,000 "
30 "   "   "   ...... 45,000 "
26 and 28 inch engine and tender wheels 40,000 "
Refrigerator, through line and cattle cars 24 months
All other freight cars.................. 48   "

Settlements of claims for non-performance of guaranteed service shall be made upon the basis of mileage and time guarantee as above.

Wheel Base. The horizontal distance between centers of the first and last axles of a locomotive or tender. It is usual, in stating locomotive dimensions, to give the rigid wheel base, the truck wheel base and the total wheel base.

Wheel Bore. 4, Figs. 1353-1367. The hole through the hub or central part of a wheel in which an axle is fitted. Also called axle seat.

Wheel Boss (British). American term hub. The center of the wheel, which is bored out to receive the axle.

Wheel Center. 1, Figs. 1353-1367. The portion of a wheel inside of the tire and between it and the hub or boss. The centers of engine and tender truck wheels are sometimes in one piece and sometimes made up of two parts, the hub or boss, and the central filling piece. Face plates, front and back, are also used. The term is seldom applied to chilled, cast or rolled steel wheels. Driving and trailing wheel centers are made of cast iron or cast steel. In Great Britain, wheel centers are frequently made of wrought iron.

Wheel Cover. A strip of thin steel plate, curved to a radius slightly greater than that of a wheel, to prevent mud and oil being spattered over the locomotive. Wheel covers are usually bolted to the engine truck frame for the truck wheels, and the under side of the running board for the driving wheels. British, splasher.

Wheel Cover Block. A small piece of metal fastened to a running board or engine truck frame for the attachment of a wheel cover.

Wheel Cover Bracket. A small cast iron post or holder, for the attachment of a wheel cover.

Wheel Cover Edge. A beading or molding formed on the outer edge of a wheel cover.

Wheel Fit. That part of a driving or truck wheel that is forced on an axle or crank pin.

Wheel Flange. 6, Figs. 1353-1367. The projecting edge or rim on the periphery of a car wheel for keeping it on the rail.

Wheel Hub. 3, Figs. 1353-1367. The center of a wheel

surrounding the axle on which it is mounted. British, boss. See **Hub**.

Wheel Hub Liner. 11, Figs. 1353-1367. A brass or bronze disk secured to the inside hub of a wheel to form a wearing surface between the hub and the outside face of the box. Such liners are used on engine truck wheels, driving and trailing wheels.

Wheel Key. A piece of steel slightly tapered, driven into a slot or keyway cut longitudinally in the wheel seat of a driving axle and a corresponding slot in the bore through a driving wheel hub to key or secure the wheel to the axle.

Wheel Plates. That part of a cast iron engine truck or tender truck wheel which connects the rim and the hub. It occupies the place and fulfils the same purpose as the spokes in an open or spoke wheel. On steel-tired wheels the plates connecting the tire and hub, and bolted or fastened to each, are called wheel plates. Distinguished as front and back face plates.

Wheel Press (Hydraulic). Figs. 5022-5023. An hydraulic press for forcing locomotive driving wheels on and off their axles. They are fitted with a pressure gage which is usually graduated for total tons pressure and for pounds per square inch on the rams. They are made with capacities up to 400 tons pressure.

Wheel Ribs (Cast Iron Wheels). More commonly, brackets. Projections cast usually on the inner side of plate car wheels to strengthen them. They are placed in a radial position and are often curved so as to permit the wheel to contract when it cools.

Wheel Rim Filling Piece. A flat steel strip inserted in one of the radial spaces left to allow for shrinkage in casting in the rim of a driving wheel center.

Wheel Seat. 1, Figs. 1368-1385. That portion of an axle that is forced into a driving wheel or truck wheel.

Wheel Tread. The exterior cylindrical surface of a wheel which bears on the rails. The usual width of wheel tread is about 4 inches, measured from outside of wheel tread to the throat or inside of flange. The standard width from outside of wheel tread to inside face of flange, i. e., including the entire thickness of flange, is $5\frac{1}{2}$ inches. For driving wheels the width varies from 6 to 7 inches.

Wheel Web. That portion of a cast iron truck wheel center between the hub and the rim.

Whistle. Figs. 3210-3213; 153, Figs. 77-121. A device for producing a loud sound to give warning and as a means of signaling to trainmen and others. It consists of an inverted brass bell or cup, against the edge of which steam is directed from an annular nozzle by means of a suitable valve. The sound is produced because the steam, striking the edge of the whistle bell with considerable force, sets the air within in vibration, and causes it to emit a tone the pitch of which depends upon the length of the whistle and the velocity with which the steam impinges upon it. A chime whistle is made with the bell divided into three compartments or chambers, of unequal length. Each chamber therefore sounds a different tone; and by giving the three chambers certain relative lengths, a powerful yet agreeable and harmonious note can be produced. The whistle is attached to the dome or turret on the boiler.

Whistle Bell. 4, Fig. 3210. A cylindrical brass chamber with flat or hemispherical top, for producing a sound by steam blown against the edge. It is screwed on a stem directly over the whistle bowl.

Whistle Bowl. A hemispherical brass cup with a cylindrical extension below it containing a valve for admitting steam. The bowl has a disk over it that does not come quite to the edge, thus leaving an annular opening through which the steam escapes, and in the center of which the steam passing up through the bell is secured.

Whistle Crank. A short metal arm attached to the whistle lever in the cab for imparting motion to the lever or bar that opens the whistle valve.

Whistle Crank Fulcrum. A cast-iron bracket fastened in the cab of a locomotive to form a bearing for the whistle shaft.

Whistle Extension. 11, Fig. 3210. The cylindrical pipe below the bowl of a whistle, containing the whistle valve.

Whistle Lever. An arm or bar in the cab of a locomotive for operating the whistle valve. It is attached to a crank that moves the lever on the whistle through the medium of a link or bar.

Whistle Lever Fulcrum. A small bracket attached to a whistle extension to hold the pin on which the whistle lever is pivoted.

Whistle Lever Rod. A link or bar connecting the whistle lever on the whistle with the operating lever in the cab.

Whistle Nut. 1, Fig. 3210. A square or hexagonal brass nut screwed on the upper end of a whistle stem to secure the whistle bell in place, and usually surmounted by an acorn-shaped top called the whistle ornament.

Whistle Post. See **Whistle Stem**.

Whistle Reservoir. (Train Air Signal.) A small steel reservoir sometimes installed for storing air to be used by an air whistle on electric locomotives.

Whistle Shaft. A short metal rod in the cab, supported by a hanger or fulcrum at each end, and having the whistle lever and whistle crank attached to it.

Whistle Stem. 2, Fig. 3210. A steel or malleable iron standard, screwed in the center of a whistle bowl, and supporting the whistle bell. The bell has a hole through the top, tapped with a thread to fit that cut on the upper end of the whistle stem, which allows the height of the bell above the bowl to be adjusted.

Whistle Valve. 13, Fig. 3210. A disk with a shank or stem attached, fitting in an opening in the whistle extension for admitting steam to the whistle to cause it to sound. It is operated by a set of levers in the cab.

Whyte Nomenclature. Fig. 1. A system of classifying locomotives suggested by F. M. Whyte, and based upon the wheel arrangement, grouping each set of truck and driving wheels by number, beginning at the pilot or head end of the engine. Thus, a locomotive commonly known as a mogul, is denoted in the Whyte system as a 2-6-0, a six-wheel switching engine as a 0-6-0, an Atlantic type as a 4-4-2, an eight-wheel American type as a 4-4-0 locomotive, and so on.

Wide Firebox Boiler. Figs. 136-137, 147, 169, etc. A boiler with a wide, shallow firebox resting on the frames and extending out beyond them at the sides. The **Wootten Firebox**, which see, is a wide firebox for burning anthracite coal.

Williams Headlight Burner. Fig. 3300.

Wilson Balanced Piston Valves. Figs. 2167-2192.

Wilson Balanced Slide Valve. Figs. 2119-2121, 2130-2133.

Window. "An opening in the wall of a building or cab for the admission of light and of air when necessary. This opening has a frame on the sides, in which are set movable sashes containing panes of glass."—Webster. Hence the window itself, especially in compound words, is often termed simply the sash.

Window Glass. Panes of glass used for windows. They are either plate or rolled glass, made by pouring the molten glass onto a table having the height of the desired thickness of the plate, and then passing a roller over the top; or blown, or common window glass, the latter being by far the cheapest and most widely used, but of very much inferior quality. It is made by blowing the glass into a large bulb, which is then slit open while still hot and flattened out.

Window Sill. A horizontal piece of wood or metal under a window, on which the cab sashes rest when down.

Wootten Firebox. Figs. 136-137, 197-204. A locomotive firebox, very wide and shallow and having a curved crown sheet of large radius, used for anthracite coal burning locomotives which require a large grate area.

Worn Flat (Car Wheels). Irregular wear under fair usage, due to unequal hardness of the tread of the wheel, and to be carefully distinguished from slid flat, which is a defect produced by the slipping of the wheels from excessive brake pressure.

Wrecking Chain. A heavy steel chain, carried on a locomotive for use in emergencies.

Wrecking Frog. Fig. 4581. A frog-like device with one end elevated to form an inclined plane by which derailed trucks can be replaced upon the track by pulling the car, tender, or engine in the direction of its length.

Wrench. 1. A contrivance for screwing and unscrewing a nut.

2. A socket wrench is one having a cavity to receive a square or hexagonal end. The wrenches for the Westinghouse brake are packing nut and cap screw wrenches, and the discharge valve seat wrench. 114, Figs. 2429-2435.

3. A spanner is a wrench for use on round or many sided nuts, like hose couplings, to which lugs or slots are added for engaging with the wrench. 113, Figs. 2429-2435.

4. An alligator wrench for use on pipe or other cylindrical surfaces has immovable jaws, one serrated and the other smooth, inclined to each other at an acute angle.

5. A monkey wrench has smooth, parallel jaws, one of which is fastened to the handle or stem, while the other can be moved up to or away from it by a sleeve nut working on a thread cut on the stem. Fig. 4574.

Wrist Pin. See **Crosshead Wrist Pin.**

Wrought Iron Wheel. A steel tired wheel, with a wrought iron center, either with spokes or with solid plates.

Y

Yoke. A bar or bent piece connecting two pieces of the same kind. See **Coupler Yoke, Bell Yoke, Guide Yoke, Valve Yoke.**

Yoke Knee. See **Guide Yoke Knee.**

Yoke Sheet. See **Guide Yoke Sheet.**

Fast and Unusual Runs—1880-1906.

Month, day, year.	Railroad.	From.	To.	Dist. Miles.	Time. h. m. s.	Speed miles. per H.	Cars. No.	Cars. Weight. Lbs.	Locomotives. Type.	Locomotives. Cyls.	Locomotives. Diam. drivers. In.	Locomotives. Weight on drivers. Lbs.	Locomotives. Weight of engine. Lbs.	Month, day, year.*
6-14-'80	P. R. R.	Philadelphia.	Jersey City.	90	1:33:00	58.06	2	....	4-4-0	....	..	....	....	6-25-'80
0- 0-'80	Gt. N. (Eng.)	London.	Grantham.	105.5	1:51:00	66.5	..	....	4-4-2	....	96	....	....	8- 6-'80
4-22-'82	W. Jersey.	Camden.	Cape May.	81.5	1:23:30	58.63	3	....	4-4-0	....	..	....	....	4-28-'82
7-12-'83	S. B. & N. Y.	Syracuse.	Binghamton.	79	1:23:00	57.11	2	....	4-4-0	....	..	....	....	7-20-'83
5- 9-'84	P. & R.	N. Y. Div.	M. P. 48.	14	0:11:19	74.2	4	....	4-4-0	....	..	....	....	1- 6-'84
5- 8-'85	L. S. and N. Y. C.	Chicago.	New York.	964	22:45:00	42.38	..	....	.....	....	..	....	....	5-15-'85
7- 9-'85	W. Shore.	Alabama.	Gen. Junc.	36.3	0:30:00	72.60	3	153,660	4-4-0	18x24	68	62,500	94,500	8-28-'85
6-17-'86	C., B. & Q.	Princeton.	Burlington.	170	2:58:00	57.3	..	....	4-4-0	....	..	....	....	7- 2-'86
7- 5-'86	Wabash.	K. City.	Peru.	563	13:45:00	41	..	....	.....	....	..	....	....	7-16-'86
8- 8-'86	N. Y. C. & H. R.	Syracuse.	Fairport.	70.25	1:01:20	68.73	2	....	4-4-0	....	..	....	....	8-13-'86
7-10-'88	L. & N. W.-Cal.	London.	Edinboro.	400	7:52:00	50.85	..	....	.....	....	..	....	....	......
8- 0-'88	L. & N. W.	Crewe.	Preston.	51	0:50:00	61.20	..	....	.....	....	..	....	....	8-24-'88
8- 0-'88	L. & N. W.	Preston.	Carlisle.	90	1:30:00	60	..	....	.....	....	..	....	....	8-24-'88
8-30-'88	N. E. (Eng.)	York.	Newcastle.	80.5	1:18:00	62	7	....	4-2-2	18x24	84	....	....	12-14-'88
8-31-'88	Gt. N. (Eng.)	London.	Edinboro.	392.5	7:26:45	52.7	..	....	.....	....	..	73,000	....	10- 5-'88
4- 8-'89	C. & N. W.	Chicago.	Council Bluffs.	490	12:30:00	39.2	4	....	4-4-0	18x24	63	59,850	....	......
5-19-'89	P., F. W. & C.	Ft. Wayne.	Chicago.	148.3	2:59:00	49.7	5	....	4-4-0	18x24	62	....	91,900	......
5-26-'89	Mich. C.	S. Bridge.	Chicago.	511	11:41:00	43.74	..	....	.....	....	..	....	....	6- 6-'90
3-10-'90	P. & R.	Philadelphia.	Jersey City.	90	1:25:00	63.53	1	....	.....	....	..	....	....	3-14-'90
3-10-'90	P. R. R.	J. City.	Washington.	226	4:18:00	52.56	3	....	.....	....	..	....	....	3-14-'90
3-10-'90	P. R. R.	Washington.	Jersey City.	226	4:19:00	52.35	3	....	.....	....	..	....	....	3-14-'90
6-22-'91	N. Y. C. & H. R.	New York.	Buffalo.	439.52	8:58:00	49.2	6	515,700	4-4-0	19x24	..	....	121,300	6-26-'91
8- 0-'91	Canadian Pac.	Vancouver.	Brockville.	2,792	76:31:00	36.49	3	....	.....	....	..	....	....	9-18-'91
9-14-'91	N. Y. C. & H. R.	New York.	E. Buffalo.	436.32	7:17:30	59.56	..	....	4-4-0	19x24	..	....	....	9-18-'91
10-16-'91	N. Ry. (France)	Paris.	Calais.	184	3:43:00	49.51	12	311,360	.....	13¼, 20¾x25	84	67,200	96,320	......
11-28-'91	P. R. R.	Jersey City.	Washington.	227	4:11:00	54.22	3	250,000	.....	....	..	....	....	12- 4-'91
12-22-'91	B. & O.	Philadelphia.	Canton.	91.6	1:41:00	54.41	..	....	.....	....	..	....	....	1- 1-'92
3-28-'92	N. Y. C. & H. R.	Oneida.	De Witt.	21.37	0:17:40	72.69	..	....	4-4-0	19x24	78	81,400	126,150	4- 7-'93
11-18-'92	Cent. N. J.	Fanwood.	......	1	0:00:37	97.3	4	228,800	.....	13, 22 x24	78	88,400	123,800	11-25-'92
11-18-'92	P. & R.	Jenkintown.	L'horne.	5	0:03:25	87.8	..	....	.....	....	..	....	....	......
12- 0-'92	L. & N. W.	Crewe.	Rugby.	76	1:11:00	64.23	3	....	.....	....	..	....	....	......
5- 9-'93	N. Y. C. & H. R.	Grimesville.	......	1	0:00:35	102.8	4	....	4-4-0	19x24	86	84,000	124,000	6- 2-'93
5-19-'93	N. Y. C. & H. R.	Syracuse.	E. Buffalo.	146	2:21:00	62.13	..	....	4-4-0	19x24	84	84,000	124,000	5-26-'93
5-19-'93	N. Y. C. & H. R.	Looneyville.	Grimesville.	5	0:03:00	100	..	....	4-4-0	19x24	84	84,000	124,000	5-26-'93
5-28-'93	N. Y. C. & H. R. / L. S. & M. S.	New York.	Chicago.	964	19:57:00	48.2	..	....	.....	17x24	72	65,100	104,600	6- 2-'93
8-28-'93	P., C., C. & St. L.	Seymour.	N. Tower.	42	0:35:34	70.96	5	....	4-4-0	....	68	....	....	8-15-'93
3-23-'94	C. & N. W.	C. Bluffs.	Chicago.	488	12:52:00	41.1	8	....	.....	....	..	....	....	4- 6-'94
4-17-'94	L. S. & M. S.	Cleveland.	Erie.	95.5	1:35:00	60.32	..	....	4-6-0	....	..	....	....	4-27-'94
8-26-'94	A. C. Line.	Jacksonville.	Washington.	780.8	15:49:00	49.36	..	....	.....	....	..	....	....	9-21-'94
4- 0-'95	C., B. & Q.	Chicago.	G'burg.	163	2:45:00	59.27	6	....	2-6-0	19x24	68	101,000	120,000	12-13-'95
4-21-'95	Camden & Atl.	Camden.	Atlantic City.	58.3	0:45:45	76.46	1	....	4-4-0	....	78	87,300	122,600	1- 3-'95
8-21-'95	West Coast.	London.	Aberdeen.	540	8:55:00	60.56	..	....	.....	....	..	....	....	9-13-'95
8-21-'95	East Coast.	London.	Aberdeen.	523	8:40:00	60.35	..	....	.....	....	..	....	....	9-13-'95
9-11-'95	N. Y. C. & H. R.	New York.	E. Buffalo.	436.32	6:51:56	63.54	..	....	4-4-0	....	..	....	....	9-27-'95
9-24-'95	N. Y. C. & H. R.	Albany.	Syracuse.	147.84	2:10:00	68.23	2	....	4-4-0	19x24	..	84,000	124,000	10- 4-'95
10-24-'95	L. S. & M. S.	Erie.	Buffalo.	86	1:10:46	72.91	..	....	4-6-0	17x24	66	88,500	113,500	11- 1-'95
10-24-'95	L. S. & M. S.	Chicago.	Buffalo.	510.1	8:01:07	63.61	..	....	.....	....	..	....	....	11- 1-'95
10-24-'95	P. R. R.	J. City.	Philadelphia.	89.6	1:33:21	57.6	6	548,657	4-4-0	18½x26	..	91,600	134,800	1-17-'96
5- 7-'96	Mich. C.	Windsor.	St. Thomas.	11.2	1:43:05	64.72	3	230,050	4-6-0	19x24	68	96,300	123,500	......
5- 7-'96	Mich. C.	St. Thomas.	Fort Erie.	118.2	1:47:15	66.13	3	230,050	4-6-0	19x24	68	96,300	123,500	......
6-10-'96	Atlantic City.	Camden.	Atlantic City.	55.5	0:48:00	69.4	6	....	4-4-2	13, 22 x26	84½	80,000	141,000	6-19-'96
6-20-'96	Atlantic City.	Camden.	Atlantic City.	55.5	0:57:00	58.42	11	701,450	4-4-2	13, 22 x26	84½	78,600	141,000	6-26-'96
7- 3-'96	C., M. & St. P.	Forest Glen.	Nat. Ave.	74.0	1:22:00	54.2	13	974,390	2-4-2	13, 22 x26	..	71,600	140,700	1-22-'97
11-21-'96	S. & R.	Weldon.	Shops.	76.8	1:12:30	63.56	3	....	4-4-0	19x24	68	75,000	118,500	......
2-15-'97	C., B. & Q.	Chicago.	Denver.	1,025	18:53:00	54.27	1	72,000	.....	....	..	....	....	2-26-'97
3-11-'97	Char. & Sav.	Cent. Junc.	Ashley J.	102	1:40:00	61.02	..	....	4-4-0	17x24	64	57,000	90,000	4- 2-'97
4- 9-'97	Atlantic Coast L.	Florence, S.C.	Rocky Mt.	172.2	3:00:00	57.70	5	....	4-4-2	19x24	72	76,000	129,620	......
4-21-'97	Lehigh V.	Alpine.	Geneva Junc.	44	0:33:00	80.0	4	....	4-4-0	....	..	....	....	......
7-14-'97	Atl. City (P. & R.)	Camden.	Atlantic City.	55.5	0:46:30	71.60	5	320,300	4-4-2	13, 22 x26	84	78,000	143,000	7- 9-'97
7-16-'97	P., Ft. W. & C.	G. R. & I. Jc.	Colehour.	132.5	2:15:00	58.8	6	628,587	4-4-0	18x24	68	65,400	103,600	8-27-'97
8- 3-'97	Union Pacific.	Evanston.	Omaha.	955.2	23:55:00	39.93	3	264,755	4-4-0	19x24	69	81,000	119,600	10-22-'97
8- 3-'97	Union Pacific.	N. Platte.	Omaha.	291.0	5:35:00	52.1	3							
11-29-'97	Union Pacific.	Cheyenne.	Council Bluffs.	519.0	9:19:00	55.7	..	....	.....	....	..	....	....	12-17-'97
12- 4-'97	Union Pacific.	Sydney.	Omaha.	414.2	7:12:00	57.5	3 3 6	276,000 276,000 546,000	4-6-0 4-4-0 4-6-0	20x24 19x24 20x24	69 69 69	103,000 81,000 103,000	131,200 119,600 131,200	12-17-'97
2-13-'98	Erie.	Jersey City.	Buffalo.	423.0	7:30:00	56.4	3	....	.....	....	..	....	....	2-18-'98
8-20-'98	Atlantic City.	Camden.	Atlantic City.	55.5	0:46:45	71.2	7	437,700	4-4-2	13, 22 x26	84	76,400 est.	143,000 est.	......
1- 2-'99	Chic., B. & Q.	Omaha.	Chicago.	500.2	8:43:00	57.38	..	....	.....	....	..	....	....	......
4-23-'99	Chic., B. & Q.	Clyde.	Burlington.	197.3	3:04:00	64.33	4	378,000	2-6-0	19x24	69	106,500	125,000	5- 5-'99
7- 9-'99	Del., L. & W.	Bath.	East Buffalo.	104.0	1:30:00	69.30	..	....	.....	....	..	....	....	8- 4-'99
7-19-'99	Vandalia.	Clayton.	Transfer.	18.0	0:14:00	77.00	8	....	4-4-0	20x26	78	85,800	....	7-28-'99
7-22-'99	Atlantic City.	Camden.	Atlantic City.	55.5	0:51:15	65.00	8	....	.....	....	..	....	....	......
7-31-'99	W. J. & S. (Penn.)	Camden.	Atlantic City.	58.3	0:50:30	69.30	8	....	.....	21.5x26	80	....	....	8-11-'99
10- 7-'99	Penn. W. Pittsbg..	Ft. Wayne.	Chicago.	148.3	2:50:00	52.30	6	688,857	.....	19x24	68	112,550	138,000	11-10-'99
10-14-'99	Wabash.	Tilton.	Granite City.	176.6	2:47:30	63.30	4	360,000	4-4-2	19x26	73	83,450	157,900	......
11-22-'99	L. S. & M. S.	Buffalo.	Cleveland.	183.0	3:25:00	....	8	....	4-6-0	20x28	80	133,000	....	12- 1-'99
3-27-'00	Atch., T. & S. F.	Los Angeles.	Chicago.	2,236	58:00:00	38.55	2	148,900	.....	....	..	....	....	4-13-'00
4-30-'00	Chic., B. & Q.	Burlington.	Chicago.	205.8	3:23:00	60.80	4	....	2-6-0	19x24	69	106,500	125,000	5-11-'00
7- 9-'00	N. Y. C. & H. R.	Rochester.	Syracuse.	80.7	1:25:00	56.70	7	689,400	4-4-0	19x24	84	84,000	124,000	......
7- 4-'00	Atlantic City.	Camden.	Atlantic City.	55.5	0:44:15	75.20	4	364,000	4-4-2	15, 25 x24	84	89,200	173,600	11- 2-'00
8-16-'00	Atlantic City.	Camden.	Atlantic City.	55.5	0:44:15	75.20	5	456,000	4-4-2					
9-30-'00	Penn. Lines.	Ft. Wayne.	Clarke J.	126.0	2:38:00	47.90	9	....	.....	....	..	....	....	10-26-'00
12-21-'00	Burlington.	Omaha.	Billings.	892.6	16:23:00	54.40	1	....	.....	....	..	....	....	1- 4-'01
3- 1-'01	Sav., F. & W.	M. P. 69.	M. P. 74.	4.8	0:02:40	107.90	3	....	4-6-0	19x28	73	108,000	146,000	3-22-'01
9- 5-'01	Mich. Cent.	Susp. Bridge.	Windsor.	229.0	3:40:00	62.45	5	430,000	4-4-2	21x26	79	95,000	176,000	11-22-'01
2- 9-'02	N. Y., N. H. & H.	Harlem R.	Boston.	228.0	4:12:00	54.30	..	....	.....	....	..	....	....	2-21-'02
3-24-'02	Penn.	Philadelphia.	Jersey City.	89.8	1:19:00	68.17	2	....	.....	....	..	....	....	3-28-'02
3-24-'02	Burlington.	Eckley.	Wray.	14.8	0:09:00	98.66	9	....	4-6-0	19x26	72	....	156,600	4-25-'02
6-21-'02	Penn.	Harrisburg	Altoona.	131.4	2:10:00	60.70	3	280,824	4-4-0	18½x26	80	93,100	134,500	7- 4-'02
5-25-'03	L. S. & M. S.	Toledo.	Elkhart.	133.4	1:54:00	70.20	4	500,000	4-4-0	20x28	80	133,000	172,000	5-29-'03
6-19-'03	L. & N. W.	London.	Carlisle.	299.2	5:58:00	50.14	12	Note.	Note.	....	..	....	....	7-17-'03
8- 8-'03	A. T. & S. F.	Chicago	Los Angeles.	2,267.0	52:49:00	42.80	2	....	.....	....	..	....	....	8-14-'03
4-27-'04	Mich. Cent.	Niagara Falls.	Windsor.	225.7	3:18:00	68.38	4	334,900	4-4-2	21x26	79	95,000	176,000	5-20-'04
6- 9-'04	Gt. Western.	Plymouth.	London.	246.8	3:46:48	65.30	..	300,000	4-2-2	Note.	92	....	....	6- 3-'04

*Date reported in Railroad Gazette.

FAST AND UNUSUAL RUNS.—Continued.

Month, day, year.	Railroad.	From.	To.	Dist. Miles.	Time. h. m. s.	Speed miles. per H.	Cars. No.	Cars. Weight. Lbs.	Type.	Cyls. In.	Diam. drivers. In.	Weight on drivers. Lbs.	Weight of engine. Lbs.	Month, day, year.*
7-20-'04	Atlantic City.	Camden.	Atlantic City.	55.5	0:43:00	77.40	5	....	....	....	....	....	....	8- 5-'04
5-14-'05	Atlantic City.	Atlantic City.	Camden.	55.5	0:42:33	78.26	5	460,000	4-4-2	21x24	..	99,000	....	12-15-'05
6- 8-'05	Penn.	E. Tolleston.	Donaldson.	50.0	0:38:00	79.00	3	....	4-4-2	20½x26	..	109,000	....	12-15-'05
6-13-'05	L. S. & M. S.	Chicago.	Buffalo.	525.0	7:33:00	69.53	3	350,000	....	....	..	....	....	12-15-'05
0- 0-'05	N. Y. C. / L. S. & M. S.	New York.	Chicago.	964.0	18:00:00	53.55	..	Note.	....	....	..	....	....	12-15-'05
7- 9-'05	A. T. & S. F.	Los Angeles.	Chicago.	2,246.0	44:54:00	50.00	3	338,000	....	....	..	....	....	12-15-'05
10-23-'05	Southern Pac. / Union Pac. / Chic. & No. West. / L. S. & M. S. / Erie.	Oakland.	Jersey City.	3,239.0	73:12:00	44.30	..	....	....	....	..	....	....	12-15-'05
10-24-'05	Penn.	Crestline.	Ft. Wayne.	131.4	1:41:20	77.81	} 4	520,000	....	....	..	....	....	12-15-'05
10-24-'05	Penn.	Crestline.	Clarke J.	257.4	3:27:20	74.55								
11- 3-'05	Penn.	Harrisburg.	Chicago.	717.0	12:49:00	56.00	3	....	4-4-2	....	..	....	Note.	12-15-'05
5- 5-'06	Southern Pac. / Union Pac. / Chic. & N. W. / L. S. & Mich So. / N. Y. Cent.	Oakland.	New York.	3,255.0	71:27:00	45.60	3	Note.	....	....	..	....	....	5-18-'06
6-19-'06	Atlantic City.	Camden.	Atlantic City.	55.5	0:43:30	76.70	6	Note.	4-4-2	20x27	86	110,000	210,000	6-22-'06

*Date reported in RAILROAD GAZETTE.

The foregoing table is severely condensed. The time in every case is from the beginning to the end of the run, including stops. In speeds alone, for moderate distances, there has been little change since 1895. For example the engines of the Atlantic City Railway make substantially the same time as was made over the same line ten years ago; but with the larger boilers and fireboxes now used, heavier trains are hauled without loss of speed. The Empire State express of the New York Central, which for years was limited to four cars, now usually has five cars, and still makes its trip of 440 miles at the scheduled speed of 53.3 miles an hour, and with remarkable punctuality.

Some of the records above 80 miles an hour lack the elements necessary to make them entirely credible.

March 1, 1901.—The record of 107.9 miles an hour is given by an officer of the road. The grade was descending, mostly at 30 ft. per mile.

March 24, 1902.—This run was made on a descending grade, which for some of the way was as much as 32 ft. per mile.

June 21, 1902.—This run is notable by reason of the rising grade. Altoona is 861½ ft. higher than Harrisburg.

June 19, 1903.—This run was made without a stop, but there were two engines. The weight of the train was 1,008,000 lbs. There are a number of long ascending grades in the line.

August 8, 1903.—On this and the later run between the same places there were, of course, many changes of engines. The record gives no data concerning the sizes of the engines, but most or all of them were of the most powerful types made in the United States at that time.

June 9, 1904.—On this run engines were changed at Bristol. The dimensions given are those of the engine used on the second stage of the journey. A car was left at Bristol and the weight given is the average weight for the whole journey. The first engine had drivers 6 ft. 8 in. in diameter, four-coupled; cylinders, 18 x 26 in. The train making this run was the regular mail train, scheduled to run regularly, *without a stop*, from Plymouth to London in 4 h. 25 min.

July 20, 1904.—This is the best record which has been made over this line. The run of June 19, 1906, was made with one more car.

1905.—Eighteen hours between New York and Chicago is the regular schedule time of one daily train each way over the New York Central lines, and one over the Pennsylvania; the latter line being about 60 miles shorter. There is no published record of less time through, though on many occasions the trains of both roads have made up much lost time. The run of November 3, 1905, is an example of what has been done in such cases. In this run the number of cars was three, except over portions of the road where a dining car was added, making four.

October 23, 1905.—This run and that of May 5, 1905, were not undertaken with a view of making the highest possible speed, and each of the divisions over which these trains traveled has been traversed, no doubt, in shorter time; but these transcontinental records are notable for the long distances covered, even though the time be not the very highest of which the engines are capable. Both of these runs were made by special trains throughout, except that in the run of May, 1906, the run east of Buffalo was that of the regular Empire State express.

June 19, 1906.—On this run a distance of 12 miles was traversed in 8 minutes (90 m.p.h.).

It will be observed that the notable performance of October 24, 1895, which made a number of records that stood unsurpassed for years, was set aside by another performance, equally remarkable, just ten years later—October 24, 1905.

The following table shows the best records for given distances. They are classified by speeds alone, no account being taken of the modifying effects of load, or grade, or size of engine. It will be borne in mind that these records are all those of steam locomotives. For distances under 15 miles, the electric locomotive which was tried on the Berlin-Zossen line, in Germany, in 1903, made speeds over 130 miles an hour, which have not yet been equalled by any steam locomotive.

BEST RECORDED SPEEDS OF STEAM LOCOMOTIVES.

	Distance, Miles.	Rate, Miles per hour.	Date.	Road.		Distance, Miles.	Rate, Miles per hour.	Date.	Road.
1.	3,255	45.80	May 5, 1906.	Various.	7.	131	77.81	Oct. 24, 1905.	Penn.
2.	2,246	50.00	July 9, 1905.	A., T. & S. F.	8.	55.5	78.26	May 14, 1905.	Atlantic City.
3.	1,025	54.27	Feb. 15, 1897.	C., B. & Q.	9.	50	79.00	June 8, 1905.	Penn.
4.	717	56.00	Nov. 3, 1905.	Penn.	10.	15	98.66	March 24, 1902.	C., B. & Q.
5.	525	69.53	June 13, 1905.	L. S. & M. S.	11.	4.8	107.90	March 1, 1901.	S. F. & W.
6.	257	74.55	Oct. 24, 1905.	Penn.					

Considering passenger service alone, the crowning achievement of the locomotive designers of the past twenty years has been not speed alone, nor speed and power combined; but speed, power and reliability. The Pennsylvania trains running daily between Jersey City and Chicago, 905 miles, at 50.9 miles an hour, were on time at destination during the year ending June 11, 1906, 328 times out of 365, or 89.8 per cent. of the trips of the year, westbound, and 85.2 per cent. of the trips eastbound. Of the 37 late arrivals at Chicago 14 were not over 10 minutes late. The New York Central reported for its similar trains a somewhat less favorable record; but the Central fast trains travel at a higher speed, the distance being greater, and the trains often were made up of five, six or seven cars, for a part of the distance.

From a table published in the *Railroad Gazette* of January 12, 1906, page 33, giving the speeds of a large number of regular scheduled trains between London and other English cities, the following examples are selected:

REGULAR ENGLISH EXPRESS TRAINS, 1905.

London to—		Miles.	Speed, M. p. h.
Bristol.	Great Western.	118	59.2
Exeter.	Great Western.	194	56.7
Plymouth.	Great Western.	246	55.7
Liverpool.	L. & N. W.	201	56.1
Nottingham.	Midland.	125	56.8
Nottingham.	Great Central.	125	57.5
Sheffield.	Great Central.	164	58.0
Sheffield.	Great Northern.	162	57.2

On the two important long lines of Great Britain, the West Coast and the East Coast routes to Scotland, the best schedules now in effect are as follows: London & North Western and Caledonian, London to Glasgow (midnight train), 401.5 miles; 8 hours; rate 50.2 miles an hour. Great Northern, North Eastern and North British, London to Aberdeen (day train), 523.5 miles; 11 hrs. 7 min.; rate 47.1 miles an hour.

The table below shows the best performances of American railroads. The fast trains between New York and Philadelphia, which for years were notable as the fastest trains in America, are now outclassed by the New York-Chicago trains. The Pennsylvania's Chicago train is regularly scheduled from Jersey City to North Philadelphia, 84 miles, in 83 minutes.

SCHEDULED SPEEDS OF FAST REGULAR TRAINS ON AMERICAN RAILROADS, AUGUST, 1906.

	From.	To.	Railroad.	Distance, Miles.	Time, Hrs. Mins.	Speed, Miles per hour.
1.	Oakland.	Chicago.	Southern Pacific, Union Pacific, Chicago & North Western.	2,274	67:30	33.7
2.	Los Angeles.	Chicago.	Atchison, Topeka & Santa Fe.	2,267	66:15	34.2
3.	New York.	Chicago.	New York Central & Hudson River and Lake Shore & Michigan Southern.	964	18:00	53.5
4.	Jersey City.	Chicago.	Pennsylvania.	905	17:46	50.9
5.	New York.	Buffalo.	New York Central.	440	8:15	53.3
6.	New York.	Boston.	New York, New Haven & Hartford.	232	5:00	46.4
7.	Washington.	Jersey City.	Pennsylvania.	224	4:46	47.0
8.	Jersey City.	Washington.	Central of New Jersey, Philadelphia & Reading, Baltimore & Ohio.	226	4:48	47.1
9.	Atlantic City.	Camden.	West Jersey & Seashore (Pennsylvania).	59.0	0:52	68.1
10.	Camden.	Atlantic City.	Atlantic City (Philadelphia & Reading).	55.5	0:50	66.6

INDEX TO ENGRAVINGS

The engravings on the following pages, 5,148 in all, are arranged under the 19 general heads given below. The page number is put at the bottom of the page on the inside corner, and the inclusive figure numbers at the top of the page on the outside corner.

	PAGE.	FIG. NO.		PAGE.	FIG. NO.
LOCOMOTIVES, General Views ....(34 *pages*, 74 *cuts*)	1	1	PILOTS ....(9 " 179 ")	230	2,231
LOCOMOTIVES, Elevations ....(41 " 59 ")	35	75	BRAKES ....(37 " 377 ")	239	2,410
BOILERS ....(25 " 109 ")	77	134	CABS AND CAB FITTINGS ....(34 " 421 ")	276	2,787
SMOKEBOXES ....(16 " 165 ")	102	343	ENGINE FITTINGS...(13 " 136 ")	310	3,208
GRATES AND ASHPANS (18 " 280 ")	118	508	ENGINE TRUCKS.....(21 " 270 ")	323	3,344
CYLINDERS ....(25 " 234 ")	136	788	TENDERS ....(68 " 971 ")	344	3,614
RODS AND PINS......(15 " 279 ")	161	1,022	ELECTRIC LOCOMOTIVES (24 *pages*, 107 *cuts*)	412	4,585
RUNNING GEAR......(27 " 508 ")	176	1,301	MASTER MECHANICS' STANDARDS (12 *pages*, 196 *cuts*)	436	4,692
VALVES AND VALVE MOTION ....(27 " 422 ")	203	1,809	MACHINE TOOLS.....(45 " 136 ")	448	4,888
			BRITISH LOCOMOTIVES (31 *pages*, 125 *cuts*)	493	5,024

If the above general arrangement be borne in mind there will be no difficulty in turning at once to any class of engravings desired. The following detailed index of titles and sub-titles is arranged according to the consecutive order of each sub-division. The page and figure numbers given are the first under which any of the classes of engravings appear.

	PAGE.	FIG.		PAGE.	FIG.
LOCOMOTIVES. *General Views.*			ELEVATIONS...2-8-2 *Type*	54	99
" 4-4-0 *Type,* " " 2	2		" 2-10-0 *Type*	56	101
" 0-4-2 *Type,* " " 5	9		" 4-4-0 *Type*	57	106
" 0-4-4 *Type,* " " 6	11		" 4-4-2 *Type*	60	110
" 0-6-0 *Type,* " " 7	13		" 4-6-0 *Type*	66	119
" 0-6-4 *Type,* " " 9	17		" 4-6-2 *Type*	70	123
" 0-8-0 *Type,* " " 10	19		" 4-8-0 *Type*	71	124
" 0-10-0 *Type,* " " 10	21		" Rack Locomotive........	73	126
" 0-6-6-0 *Type,* " " 11	22		" Geared Locomotive......	74	130
" 2-4-0 *Type,* " " 11	23		DIMENSIONS OF HEAVY LOCOMOTIVES	76	—
" 2-4-2 *Type,* " " 11	24		BOILERS, General Views................	77	134
" 2-4-4 *Type,* " " 13	28		" Sections, *Wagon Top*........	80	149
" 2-4-6 *Type,* " " 14	30		" " *Vanderbilt*	82	151
" 2-6-0 *Type,* " " 15	32		" " *Extended Wagon Top*	83	159
" 2-6-2 *Type,* " " 17	36		" " *Straight Top*	88	177
" 2-6-6 *Type,* " " 18	38		" " *Wootten*	91	197
" 2-8-0 *Type,* " " 18	39		" Details. *Miscellaneous*........	93	207
" 2-8-2 *Type,* " " 21	45		" " *Braces and Stay Bolts*	95	245
" 2-8-4 *Type,* " " 22	46		" " *Riveting*	99	315
" 2-10-0 *Type,* " " 22	47		" " *Fire Doors*	100	331
" 2-10-2 *Type,* " " 22	48		SMOKEBOXES. Sections................	102	343
" 4-4-0 *Type,* " " 23	49		" Details, *Exhaust Pipe.*	104	354
" 4-4-2 *Type,* " " 25	54		" " *Front Doors* ..	107	394
" 4-4-4 *Type,* " " 28	60		" " *Smoke Stacks.*	110	455
" 4-6-0 *Type,* " " 29	61		" " *Superheaters* ..	113	483
" 4-6-2 *Type,* " " 32	68		GRATES AND ASHPANS. *General Views*	118	508
" 4-8-0 *Type,* " " 34	72		" " " *Details*	123	546
ELEVATIONS...0-4-0 *Type*	35	75	" " " *Oil Burning..*	128	721
" 0-6-0 *Type*	38	78	CYLINDERS. General Views............	136	788
" 0-6-2 *Type*	41	81	" Details, *Pistons and Rods.*	148	879
" 0-6-6-0 *Type*	42	83	" " *Heads*	155	918
" 2-4-2 *Type*	43	88	" " *Fittings, Cocks, etc.*	157	973
" 2-6-0 *Type*	44	89	" " *Packing*	160	1015
" 2-6-2 *Type*	48	93	" " *Guides*	161	1022
" 2-8-0 *Type*	50	95	" " *Crossheads*	162	1039
			RODS AND PINS.....................	167	1126

INDEX TO ENGRAVINGS.

	PAGE.	FIG.
RUNNING GEAR. *Driving Wheels*	176	1301
" " " *Axles*	179	1368
" " " *Boxes*	181	1386
" " *Frames, Elevations*	184	1446
" " " *Details*	187	1477
" " *Spring Rigging, Elevations*	194	1605
" " " *Details*	197	1659
" " *Traction Increasers*	201	1703
VALVES AND VALVE MOTION:		
General Views	203	1809
Details, *Stephenson Motion*	205	1818
" *Eccentrics*	206	1853
" *Reverse Shaft*	210	1917
" *Slide Valves*	216	2097
" *Piston Valves*	219	2137
" *Compounds*	223	2193
PILOTS	230	2231
" *Couplers*	233	2328
Brakes, Air, *Westinghouse*	239	2410
" " *New York*	261	2557
" " *Foundation*	271	2648
CABS AND FITTINGS:		
General Views	276	2787
Details	280	2826
" *Miscellaneous Fittings*	285	2958
" *Throttle*	290	3043
" *Injectors*	293	3088
" *Water Gages*	301	3127
" *Pressure Gages*	302	3148
" *Steam Heat*	303	3161
" *Lubricators*	308	3195
ENGINE FITTINGS. *Whistles*	310	3208
" " *Safety Valves*	311	3214
" " *Sanders*	313	3226
" " *Bells*	315	3255
" " *Headlights*	316	3267
" " *Miscellaneous*	321	3317
ENGINE TRUCKS. Front, *Two-Wheel*	323	3344
" " *Four-Wheel*	325	3369
" " Trailing, *Two-Wheel*	327	3383
" " Rear, *Two-Wheel*	334	3482
" " " *Six-Wheel*	337	3500
" " " *Four-Wheel*	338	3507
" " Details	341	3526
TENDERS:		
Underframes, *General Views*	344	3614
" *Details*	350	3657
" *Draft Connections*	356	3789
Draft Gear	358	3820
" *Couplers*	366	3964
Tanks, *General Views*	370	4063
" *Details*	377	4113
" *Water Scoops*	382	4227
Trucks	386	4294
Truck Details, *Bolsters*	394	4399
" " *Brake Beams*	398	4429
" " *Journal Boxes*	403	4464
" " *Side Bearings*	406	4511
" " *Springs*	407	4522
" " *Wheels*	408	4538
Tools	411	4572

	PAGE.	FIG.
ELECTRIC LOCOMOTIVES:		
General Electric	412	4585
Westinghouse	424	4649
Baldwin	430	4669
RAILROAD STANDARDS. *Pennsylvania*	436	4692
MASTER MECHANICS' STANDARDS:		
Journal Boxes	440	4797
Axles	447	4878
Tire Sections	447	4882
Pedestal	447	4884
MACHINE TOOLS. *Bending Rolls*	448	4888
" " *Bolt Cutters*	448	4889
" " *Boring Machines*	449	4895
" " *Bushing Press*	453	4904
" " *Centering Machine*	453	4905
" " *Cold Saws*	454	4906
" " *Crank Pin Turning Machine*	454	4908
" " *Crank Pin Press*	455	4909
" " *Drills*	455	4910
" " *Flue Cleaner*	459	4925
" " *Flue Welder*	460	4926
" " *Forges*	460	4927
" " *Forging Machines*	461	4933
" " *Furnaces*	462	4935
" " *Grinding Machines*	463	4937
" " *Hammers*	464	4942
" " *Lathes*	465	4947
" " *Milling Machines*	471	4963
" " *Nut Tapping Machine*	474	4968
" " *Pipe Bending Machine*	474	4969
" " *Pipe Threading Machine*	475	4970
" " *Planer*	476	4973
" " *Pneumatic Tools*	477	4978
" " *Punches and Shears*	479	4991
" " *Quartering Machine*	482	5000
" " *Riveters*	483	5001
" " *Shapers*	483	5003
" " *Slotters*	485	5008
" " *Straightening Rolls*	487	5012
" " *Tire Expander*	488	5014
" " *Turret Lathes*	488	5015
" " *Valve Seat Planer*	490	5020
" " *Valve Setting Machine*	490	5021
" " *Wheel Presses*	491	5022
BRITISH LOCOMOTIVES:		
General Views	493	5024
Dimensions	506	—
Elevations	507	5063
Boilers	511	5079
Miscellaneous Details	519	5118
Vacuum Brakes	520	5127
Bogie	522	5137
Water Scoop	523	5141

CLASSIFICATION OF LOCOMOTIVES; Whyte's System.

Fig. 1

Symbol.	Wheel Arrangement.	Type.
0-4-0		4-Wheel Switcher.
0-4-2		4-Coupled and Trailing.
0-4-4		Forney 4-Coupled.
0-4-6		Forney 4-Coupled.
0-6-0		6-Wheel Switcher.
0-6-2		6-Coupled and Trailing.
0-6-4		Forney 6-Coupled.
0-6-6		Forney 6-Coupled.
0-8-0		8-Wheel Switcher.
0-8-2		8-Coupled and Trailing.
0-10-0		10-Wheel Switcher.
0-4-4-0		8-Wheel Articulated.
0-6-6-0		12-Wheel Articulated.
2-4-0		4-Coupled.
2-4-2		Columbia.
2-4-4		4-Coupled Double Ender.
2-4-6		4-Coupled Double Ender.
2-6-0		Mogul.
2-6-2		Prairie.
2-6-4		6-Coupled Double Ender.
2-6-6		6-Coupled Double Ender.
2-8-0		Consolidation.
2-8-2		Mikado.
2-8-4		8-Coupled Double Ender.
2-10-0		Decapod.
2-10-2		10-Coupled Double Ender.
2-12-0		Centipede.
4-4-0		8-Wheel American.
4-4-2		Atlantic.
4-4-4		4-Coupled Double Ender.
4-4-6		4-Coupled Double Ender.
4-6-0		10-Wheel.
4-6-2		Pacific.
4-6-4		6-Coupled Double Ender.
4-6-6		6-Coupled Double Ender.
4-8-0		12-Wheel.
4-10-0		Mastodon.

Fig. 1. Whyte's System of Locomotive Classification.

Figs. 2-4 LOCOMOTIVES, General Views; 0-4-0 Type.

Fig. 2. Four-Wheel (0—4—0) Tank Switching Locomotive. Built by the Baldwin Locomotive Works for the Philadelphia & Reading Coal & Iron Co. Cylinders 10 in. x 16 in., Working Steam Pressure 160 lbs. per sq. in., Heating Surface 325.95 sq. ft., Diameter of Drivers 30 in., Weight on Drivers 31,725 lbs., Total Weight 31,725 lbs.

Fig. 3. Four-Wheel (0—4—0) Tank Switching Locomotive. Built by the American Locomotive Co. for the Michigan Central. Cylinders 18 in. x 24 in., Working Steam Pressure 180 lbs. per sq. in., Heating Surface 1,308 sq. ft., Diameter of Drivers 52 in., Weight on Drivers 114,400 lbs., Total Weight 114,400 lbs.

Fig. 4. Four-Wheel (0—4—0) Switching Locomotive. Built by the Baldwin Locomotive Works for the Wheeling & Lake Erie. Cylinders 17 in. x 24 in., Working Steam Pressure 175 lbs. per sq. in., Heating Surface 1,254 sq. ft., Diameter of Drivers 50 in., Weight on Drivers 93,110 lbs., Total Weight 93,110 lbs.

Fig. 5. Four-Wheel (0—4—0) Tank Switching Locomotive. Built by the American Locomotive Co. for the Lykens Valley Coal Co. Cylinders 9 in. x 14 in., Working Steam Pressure 130 lbs. per sq. in., Diameter of Drivers 29 in., Weight on Drivers 21,500 lbs., Total Weight 21,500 lbs.

Fig. 6. Four-Wheel (0—4—0) Tank Switching Locomotive. Built by the Baldwin Locomotive Works for the Hoopes & Townsend Co. Cylinders 13 in. x 20 in., Working Steam Pressure 160 lbs. per sq. in., Heating Surface 414.74 sq. ft., Diameter of Drivers 42 in., Weight on Drivers 50,000 lbs., Total Weight 50,000 lbs.

Figs. 7-8   LOCOMOTIVES, General Views; 0-4-0 Type.

Fig. 7. Four-Wheel (0—4—0) Compound Switching Locomotive. Built by the Baldwin Locomotive Works for the Brooklyn Wharf & Warehouse Co. Cylinders 10 in. and 17 in. x 24 in., Working Steam Pressure 180 lbs. per sq. in., Heating Surface 676.56 sq. ft., Diameter of Drivers 44 in., Weight on Drivers 78,770 lbs., Total Weight 78,770 lbs.

Fig. 8. Four-Wheel (0—4—0) Mining Locomotive. Built by the H. K. Porter Co. for the Mount Pleasant Mining Co. Cylinders 5 in. x 8 in., Working Steam Pressure 140 lbs. per sq. in., Diameter of Drivers 20 in., Weight on Drivers 7,000 lbs., Total Weight 7,000 lbs.

Fig. 9. Four-Coupled (0—4—2) Tank Locomotive with Trailing Truck. Built by the Baldwin Locomotive Works for the Embreeville Estate. Cylinders 10 in. x 16 in., Working Steam Pressure 160 lbs. per sq. in., Heating Surface 340 sq. ft., Diameter of Drivers 36 in., Weight on Drivers 32,440 lbs., Total Weight 37,140 lbs.

Fig. 10. Four-Coupled (0—4—2) Tank Locomotive with Trailing Truck. Built by the American Locomotive Co. Cylinders 8 in. x 12 in., Working Steam Pressure 180 lbs., per sq. in., Heating Surface 226 sq. ft., Diameter of Drivers 28 in., Weight on Drivers 17,600 lbs., Total Weight 20,300 lbs.

Figs. 11-12   LOCOMOTIVES, General Views; 0-4-4 Type.

Fig. 11. Forney Four-Coupled (0—4—4) Locomotive with Four-Wheel Rear Truck. Built by the American Locomotive Co. Cylinders 17 in. x 24 in., Working Steam Pressure 165 lbs. per sq. in., Total Heating Surface 1,209 sq. ft., Diameter of Drivers 50 in., Weight on Drivers 80,500 lbs., Total Weight 113,500 lbs.

Fig. 12. Forney Four-Coupled (0—4—4) Locomotive with Four-Wheel Rear Truck. Built by the Baldwin Locomotive Works for the Emmitsburg Railroad. Cylinders 13 in. x 20 in., Working Steam Pressure 160 lbs. per sq. in., Total Heating Surface 592.4 sq. ft., Diameter of Drivers 44 in., Weight on Drivers 50,700 lbs., Total Weight 73,000 lbs.

LOCOMOTIVES, General Views; 0-6-0 Type. Figs. 13-14

Fig. 13. Six-Wheel (0—6—0) Tank Switching Locomotive. Built by the Baldwin Locomotive Works for the Brooklyn Dock & Terminal Co. Cylinders 19 in. x 24 in., Working Steam Pressure 180 lbs. per sq. in., Total Heating Surface 1,070 sq. ft., Diameter of Drivers 46 in., Weight on Drivers 132,210 lbs., Total Weight 132,210 lbs.

Fig. 14. Six-Wheel (0—6—0) Tank Switching Locomotive. Built by the American Locomotive Co. Cylinders 17 in. x 24 in., Working Steam Pressure 180 lbs. per sq. in., Diameter of Drivers 46 in., Weight on Drivers 96,000 lbs., Total Weight 96,000 lbs.

LOCOMOTIVES, General Views; 0-6-0 Type.

Fig. 15. Six-Wheel (0—6—0) Switching Locomotive. Built by the American Locomotive Co. for the Chesapeake & Ohio. Cylinders 20 in. x 28 in., Weight on Drivers 142,500 lbs, Total Weight 142,500 lbs., Tractive Power 30,600 lbs.

Fig. 16. Six-Wheel (0—6—0) Switching Locomotive. Built by the American Locomotive Co. for the Southern Railway. Cylinders 20 in. x 26 in., Working Steam Pressure 185 lbs. per sq. in., Total Heating Surface 2,486.3 sq. ft., Diameter of Drivers 50 in., Weight on Drivers 143,200 lbs., Total Weight 143,200 lbs.

(8)

LOCOMOTIVES, General Views; 0-6-4 Type. Figs. 17-18

Fig. 17. Six-Coupled (0—6—4) Tank Locomotive for Suburban Passenger Service. Built by the Baldwin Locomotive Works for the Orekhoff Railway of Russia. Cylinders 16 in. x 24 in., Working Steam Pressure 165 lbs. per sq. in., Total Heating Surface 770.06 sq. ft., Diameter of Drivers 56 in., Weight on Drivers 66,000 lbs., Total Weight 99,000 lbs.

Fig. 18. Six-Coupled (0—6—4) Tank Locomotive. Built by the American Locomotive Co. for the Murphy Lumber Co. Cylinders 13 in. x 18 in., Working Steam Pressure 150 lbs. per sq. in., Heating Surface 723 sq. ft., Diameter of Drivers 38 in., Weight on Drivers 56,200 lbs., Total Weight 69,400 lbs.

Figs. 19-21　　LOCOMOTIVES, General Views; 0-8-0 and 0-10-0 Types.

Fig. 19. Eight-Wheel (0—8—0) Switching Locomotive. Built by the Baldwin Locomotive Works for the Lehigh Valley. Cylinders 21 in. x 28 in., Working Steam Pressure 200 lbs. per sq. in., Heating Surface 2,248 sq. ft., Diameter of Drivers 55½ in., Weight on Drivers 172,450 lbs., Total Weight 172,450 lbs.

Fig. 20. Eight-Wheel (0—8—0) Switching Locomotive. Built by the American Locomotive Co. for the Chesapeake & Ohio. Cylinders 21 in. x 28 in., Working Steam Pressure 200 lbs. per sq. in., Heating Surface 2,705.1 sq. ft., Diameter of Drivers 51 in., Weight on Drivers 171,175 lbs., Total Weight 171,175 lbs.

Fig. 21. Ten-Wheel (0—10—0) Switching Locomotive. Built by the American Locomotive Co. for the Lake Shore & Michigan Southern. Cylinders 24 in. x 28 in., Working Steam Pressure 210 lbs. per sq. in., Heating Surface 4,625.4 sq. ft., Diameter of Drivers 52 in., Weight on Drivers 270,000 lbs., Total Weight 270,000 lbs.

LOCOMOTIVES, General Views; 0-6-6-0, 2-4-0 and 2-4-2 Types.   Figs. 22-24

Fig. 22. Twelve-Wheel (0—6—6—0) Mallet Articulated Compound Locomotive. Built by the American Locomotive Co. for the Baltimore & Ohio. Cylinders 20 in. and 32 in. x 32 in., Working Steam Pressure 235 lbs. per sq. in., Total Heating Surface 5,585.7 sq. ft., Diameter of Drivers 56 in., Weight on Drivers 334,500 lbs., Total Weight 334,500 lbs.

Fig. 23. Four-Coupled (2—4—0) Locomotive. Built by the Baldwin Locomotive Works for the Marcellus & Otisco Lake. Cylinders 17 in. x 24 in., Working Steam Pressure 160 lbs. per sq. in., Total Heating Surface 1,012.4 sq. ft., Diameter of Drivers 56 in., Weight on Drivers 71,160 lbs., Total Weight 84,460 lbs.

Fig. 24. Columbia (2—4—2) Type Locomotive. Built by the Baldwin Locomotive Works for the Atlantic Coast Line. Cylinders 19 in. x 24 in., Working Steam Pressure 180 lbs. per sq. in., Total Heating Surface 1,686.97 sq. ft., Diameter of Drivers 72 in., Weight on Drivers 75,800 lbs., Total Weight 124,500 lbs..

Figs. 25-26.   LOCOMOTIVES, General Views; 2-4-2 Type.

Fig. 25. Columbia (2—4—2) Type Compound Locomotive. Built by the Baldwin Locomotive Works for the Philadelphia & Reading. Cylinders 13 in. and 22 in. x 24 in., Working Steam Pressure 180 lbs. per sq. in., Diameter of Drivers 78 in., Weight on Drivers 78,000 lbs., Total Weight 125,000 lbs.

Fig. 26. Four-Coupled Double Ender (2—4—2) Tank Locomotive. Built by the H. K. Porter Co. for the New York & Brooklyn Bridge. Cylinders 14 in. x 18 in., Working Steam Pressure 160 lbs. per sq. in., Diameter of Drivers 42 in., Weight on Drivers 57,000 lbs., Total Weight 80,000 lbs.

Fig. 27. Four-Coupled Double Ender (2—4—2) Tank Locomotive. Built by the Baldwin Locomotive Works for the Hastings Lumber Co. Cylinders 16 in. x 22 in., Working Steam Pressure 160 lbs. per sq. in., Total Heating Surface 1,062 sq. ft., Diameter of Drivers 44 in., Weight on Drivers 62,000 lbs., Total Weight 86,000 lbs.

Fig. 28. Four-Coupled Double Ender (2—4—4) Locomotive. Built by the Baldwin Locomotive Works for the U. S. Government Sandy Hook Proving Grounds. Cylinders 15 in. x 22 in., Working Steam Pressure 160 lbs. per sq. in., Total Heating Surface 896 sq. ft., Diameter of Drivers 54 in., Weight on Drivers 58,426 lbs., Total Weight 111,940 lbs.

Fig. 29. Four-Coupled Double Ender (2—4—4) Locomotive. Built by the American Locomotive Co. for the Dominion Coal Co. Cylinders 17 in. x 24 in., Diameter of Drivers 62 in., Weight on Drivers 70,000 lbs., Total Weight 133,000 lbs.

Fig. 30. Four-Coupled Double Ender (2—4—6) Suburban Locomotive. Built by the Baldwin Locomotive Works for the Wisconsin Central. Cylinders 17 in. x 24 in., Working Steam Pressure 130 lbs. per sq. in., Heating Surface 1,284.5 sq. ft., Diameter of Drivers 62⅞ in., Weight on Drivers 61,275 lbs., Total Weight 121,090 lbs.

Fig. 31. Four-Coupled Double Ender (2—4—6) Inspection Locomotive. Built by the American Locomotive Co. for the Adirondack & St. Lawrence. Cylinders 16 in. x 22 in., Working Steam Pressure 160 lbs. per sq. in., Diameter of Drivers 60 in., Weight on Drivers 57,000 lbs., Total Weight 134,000 lbs.

Fig. 32. Mogul (2—6—0) Richmond Compound Locomotive. Built by the American Locomotive Co. for the Missouri, Kansas & Texas. Cylinders 19 in. and 30 in. x 24 in., Working Steam Pressure 170 lbs. per sq. in., Diameter of Drivers 56 in., Weight on Drivers 107,000 lbs., Total Weight 120,000 lbs.

Figs. 33-35   LOCOMOTIVES, General Views; 2-6-0 Type.

Fig. 33. Mogul (2—6—0) Two-Cylinder Compound Locomotive. Built by the Rogers Locomotive Works for the Illinois Central. Cylinders 20 in. and 29 in. x 26 in., Working Steam Pressure 200 lbs. per sq. in., Diameter of Drivers 56½ in., Weight on Drivers 107,000 lbs., Total Weight 129,000 lbs.

Fig. 34. Mogul (2—6—0) Locomotive. Built by the Baldwin Locomotive Works for the Akron & Barberton Belt Railroad. Cylinders 20 in. x 24 in., Working Steam Pressure 180 lbs. per sq. in., Heating Surface 1,829.3 sq. ft., Diameter of Drivers 56 in., Weight on Drivers 115,000 lbs., Total Weight 132,000 lbs.

Fig. 35. Mogul (2—6—0) Locomotive. Built by the American Locomotive Co. for the Vandalia Line. Cylinders 21 in. x 28 in., Working Steam Pressure 200 lbs per sq. in., Total Heating Surface 2,935 sq. ft., Diameter of Drivers 63 in., Weight on Drivers 156,500 lbs., Total Weight 182,500 lbs.

LOCOMOTIVES, General Views; 2-6-2 Type.   Figs. 36-37

Fig. 36. Prairie (2—6—2) Locomotive. Built by the American Locomotive Co. for the Pennsylvania Railroad. Cylinders 21½ in. x 28 in., Working Steam Pressure 200 lbs. per sq. in., Total Heating Surface 3,881.6 sq. ft., Diameter of Drivers 80 in., Weight on Drivers 166,800 lbs., Total Weight 234,500 lbs.

Fig. 37. Prairie (2—6—2) Locomotive. Built by the American Locomotive Co. for the Chicago, Burlington & Quincy. Cylinders 22 in. x 28 in., Working Steam Pressure 210 lbs. per sq. in., Total Heating Surface 3,513.9 sq. ft., Diameter of Drivers 69 in., Weight on Drivers 154,000 lbs., Total Weight 212,500 lbs.

Figs. 38-39   LOCOMOTIVES, General Views; 2-6-6 and 2-8-0 Types.

Fig. 38. Six-Coupled Double Ender (2—6—6) Locomotive. Built by the American Locomotive Co. for the New York Central & Hudson River. Cylinders 20 in. x 24 in., Working Steam Pressure 200 lbs. per sq. in., Total Heating Surface 2,425.3 sq. ft., Diameter of Drivers 63 in., Weight on Drivers 128,000 lbs., Total Weight 216,000 lbs.

Fig. 39. Consolidation (2—8—0) Locomotive. Built by the American Locomotive Co. for the Chicago, Rock Island & Pacific. Cylinders 22 in. x 30 in., Working Steam Pressure 200 lbs. per sq. in., Heating Surface 3,264 sq. ft., Diameter of Drivers 63 in., Weight on Drivers 182,000 lbs., Total Weight 202,500 lbs.

LOCOMOTIVES, General Views; 2-8-0 Type. Figs. 40-41

Fig. 40. Consolidation (2—8—0) Locomotive. Built by the American Locomotive Co. for the New York Central & Hudson River. Cylinders 23 in. x 32 in., Working Steam Pressure 200 lbs. per sq. in., Total Heating Surface 3,702.52 sq. ft., Diameter of Drivers 63 in., Weight on Drivers 197,500 lbs., Total Weight 221,500 lbs.

Fig. 41. Consolidation (2—8—0) Locomotive. Built by the American Locomotive Co. for the Delaware & Hudson. Cylinders 21 in. x 30 in., Working Steam Pressure 180 lbs. per sq. in., Total Heating Surface 3,407.8 sq. ft., Diameter of Drivers 57 in., Weight on Drivers 170,000 lbs., Total Weight 193,000 lbs.

LOCOMOTIVES, General Views; 2-8-0 Type.

Fig. 42. Consolidation (2—8—0) Locomotive. Built by the American Locomotive Co. for the Pennsylvania Railroad. Cylinders 23 in. x 32 in., Working Steam Pressure 200 lbs. per sq. in., Total Heating Surface 3,736 sq. ft., Diameter of Drivers 63 in., Weight on Drivers 198,000 lbs., Total Weight 220,000 lbs.

Fig. 43. Consolidation (2—8—0) Locomotive. Built by the American Locomotive Co. for the Baltimore & Ohio. Cylinders 22 in. x 30 in., Working Steam Pressure 205 lbs. per sq. in., Heating Surface 2,792.2 sq. ft, Diameter of Drivers 60 in., Weight on Drivers 185,900 lbs., Total Weight 208,500 lbs.

LOCOMOTIVES, General Views; 2-8-0 and 2-8-2 Types. Figs. 44-45

Fig. 44. Consolidation (2—8—0) Cross Compound Locomotive. Built by the American Locomotive Co. for the Minneapolis, St. Paul & Sault Ste. Marie. Cylinders 23 in. and 35 in. x 34 in., Working Steam Pressure 210 lbs. per sq. in., Heating Surface 2,965.3 sq. ft., Diameter of Drivers 63 in., Weight on Drivers 174,000 lbs., Total Weight 201,500 lbs.

Fig. 45. Mikado (2—8—2) Type Locomotive. Built by the American Locomotive Co. for the Northern Pacific. Cylinders 24 in. x 30 in., Working Steam Pressure 200 lbs. per sq. in., Heating Surface 4,067 sq. ft, Diameter of Drivers 63 in., Weight on Drivers 196,000 lbs., Total Weight 259,000 lbs.

Figs. 46-48 LOCOMOTIVES, General Views; 2-8-4, 2-10-0 and 2-10-2 Types.

Fig. 46. Eight-Coupled (2—8—4) Tank Locomotive. Built by the American Locomotive Co. for the Dominion Coal Co. Cylinders 22 in. x 28 in., Working Steam Pressure 200 lbs. per sq. in., Heating Surface 2,687.47 sq. ft., Diameter of Drivers 55 in., Weight on Drivers 170,000 lbs., Total Weight 239,000 lbs.

Fig. 47. Decapod (2—10—0) Tandem Compound Locomotive. Built by the Baldwin Locomotive Works for the Atchison, Topeka & Santa Fe. Cylinders 19 in. and 32 in. x 32 in., Working Steam Pressure 225 lbs. per sq. in., Total Heating Surface 5,390 sq. ft., Diameter of Drivers 57 in., Weight on Drivers 237,800 lbs., Total Weight 267,800 lbs.

Fig. 48. Ten-Coupled and Trailing Truck (2—10—2) Tandem Compound Locomotive. Built by the Baldwin Locomotive Works for the Atchison, Topeka & Santa Fe. Cylinders 19 in. and 32 in x 32 in., Working Steam Pressure 225 lbs. per sq. in., Total Heating Surface 4,796 sq. ft., Diameter of Drivers 57 in., Weight on Drivers 234,580 lbs., Total Weight 287,240 lbs.

LOCOMOTIVES, General Views; 4-4-0 Type. Figs. 49-50

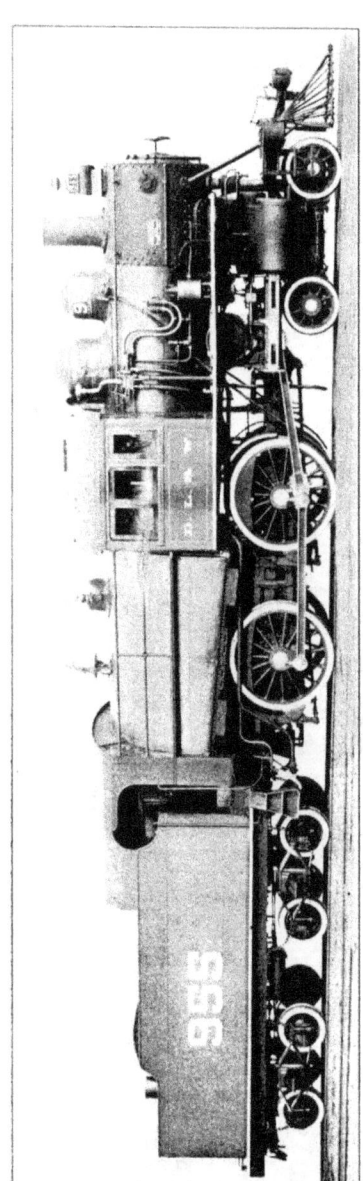

Fig. 49. Eight-Wheel American (4—4—0) Type Locomotive. Built by the American Locomotive Co. for the Delaware, Lackawanna & Western. Cylinders 20 in. x 26 in., Total Heating Surface 2,138.69 sq. ft, Diameter of Drivers 69 in., Weight on Drivers 100,000 lbs., Total Weight 151,200 lbs.

Fig. 50. Eight-Wheel American (4—4—0) Type Locomotive. Built by the Baldwin Locomotive Works for the Missouri Pacific. Cylinders 18 in. x 24 in., Working Steam Pressure 180 lbs. per sq. in., Total Heating Surface 1,715 sq. ft., Diameter of Drivers 68 in., Weight on Drivers 80,000 lbs., Total Weight 126,000 lbs.

Figs. 51-53   LOCOMOTIVES, General Views; 4-4-0 Type.

Fig. 51. Eight-Wheel (4—4—0) Inspection Locomotive. Built by the Baldwin Locomotive Works for the Central Railroad of New Jersey. Cylinders 17 in. x 20 in., Working Steam Pressure 200 lbs. per sq. in., Heating Surface 999 sq. ft., Diameter of Drivers 60 in., Weight on Drivers 62,340 lbs., Total Weight 97,920 lbs.

Fig. 52. Eight-Wheel (4—4—0) Inspection Locomotive. Built by the American Locomotive Co. for the New York Central Lines. Cylinders 15 in. x 24 in., Working Steam Pressure 200 lbs. per sq. in., Heating Surface 1,044.75 sq. ft., Diameter of Drivers 62 in., Weight on Drivers 66,500 lbs., Total Weight 99,500 lbs.

Fig. 53. Eight-Wheel (4—4—0) Inspection Locomotive. Built by the Baldwin Locomotive Works for the Philadelphia & Reading. Cylinders 17 in. x 20 in., Working Steam Pressure 200 lbs. per sq. in., Heating Surface 999 sq. ft., Diameter of Drivers 60 in., Weight on Drivers 65,000 lbs., Total Weight 99,400 lbs.

LOCOMOTIVES, General Views: 4-4-2 Type. Figs. 54-55

Fig. 54. Atlantic (4—4—2) Four-Cylinder Balanced Compound Locomotive. Built by the Baldwin Locomotive Works for the Pennsylvania Railroad. Cylinders 16 in. and 27 in. x 26 in., Working Steam Pressure 205 lbs. per sq. in. Total Heating Surface 2,864 sq. ft., Diameter of Drivers 80 in., Weight on Drivers 120,500 lbs., Total Weight 195,000 lbs.

Fig. 55. Atlantic (4—4—2) Locomotive. Built by the Baldwin Locomotive Works for the Central Railroad of New Jersey. Cylinders 19 in. x 26 in., Working Steam Pressure 200 lbs. per sq. in., Diameter of Drivers 84¼ in., Weight on Drivers 100,220 lbs., Total Weight 174,000 lbs.

Figs. 56-57　　LOCOMOTIVES, General Views; 4-4-2 Type.

Fig. 56. Atlantic (4—4—2) Four-Cylinder Balanced Compound Locomotive. Built by the Baldwin Locomotive Works for the Chicago, Rock Island & Pacific. Cylinders 15 in. and 25 in. x 26 in., Working Steam Pressure 220 lbs. per sq. in., Total Heating Surface 3,200 sq. ft., Diameter of Drivers 73 in., Weight on Drivers 105,540 lbs., Total Weight 199,400 lbs.

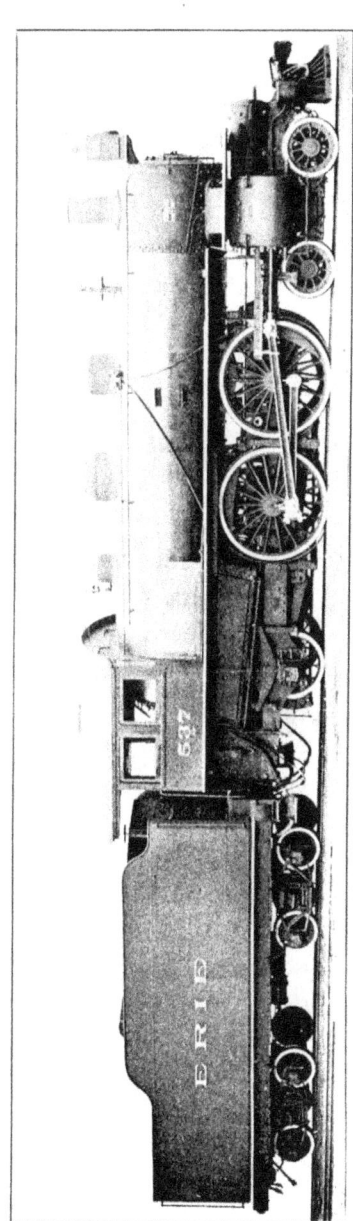

Fig. 57. Atlantic (4—4—2) Cole Four-Cylinder Balanced Compound Locomotive. Built by the American Locomotive Co. for the Erie Railroad. Cylinders 15½ in. and 26 in. x 26 in., Working Steam Pressure 220 lbs. per sq. in., Total Heating Surface 3,622.62 sq. ft., Diameter of Drivers 78 in., Weight on Drivers 115,000 lbs., Total Weight 206,000 lbs.

LOCOMOTIVES, General Views; 4-4-2 Type. Figs. 58-59

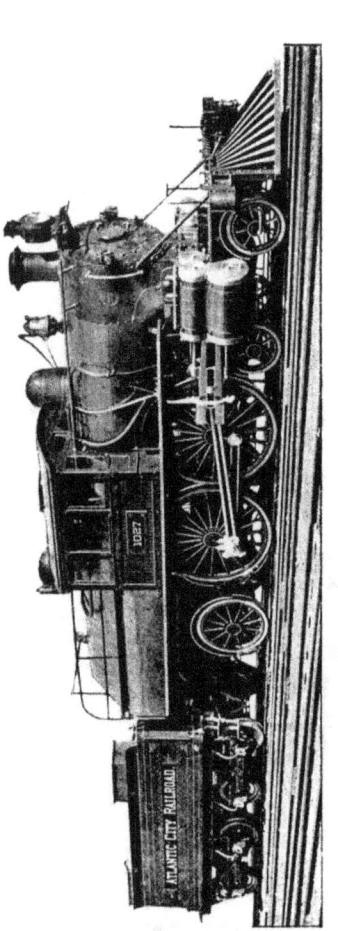

Fig. 58. Atlantic (4—4—2) Vauclain Compound Locomotive. Built by the Baldwin Locomotive Works for the Philadelphia & Reading. Cylinders 13 in. and 22 in. x 26 in., Working Steam Pressure 200 lbs. per sq. in., Diameter of Drivers 84¼ in., Weight on Drivers 79,000 lbs., Total Weight 143,000 lbs.

Fig. 59. Atlantic (4—4—2) Cole Four-Cylinder Balanced Compound Locomotive. Built by the American Locomotive Co. for the Pennsylvania Railroad. Cylinders 16 in. and 27 in. x 26 in., Working Steam Pressure 205 lbs. per sq. in., Total Heating Surface 2,861.57 sq. ft., Diameter of Drivers 80 in., Weight on Drivers 117,200 lbs., Total Weight 200,500 lbs.

Fig. 60 — LOCOMOTIVES, General Views; 4-4-4 Type.

Fig. 60. Four-Coupled Double Ender (4—4—4) Tank Locomotive. Built by the American Locomotive Co. for the Chicago & Northern Pacific (Chicago Terminal Transfer Co.). Cylinders 15 in. x 22 in., Working Steam Pressure 180 lbs. per sq. in., Diameter of Drivers 57 in., Weight on Drivers 56,000 lbs., Total Weight 100,000 lbs.

LOCOMOTIVES, General Views; 4-6-0 Type.   Figs. 61-63

Fig. 61. Ten-Wheel (4—6—0) Richmond Compound Locomotive. Built by the American Locomotive Co. for the Cleveland, Cincinnati, Chicago & St. Louis. Cylinders 19 in. and 30 in. x 24 in., Working Steam Pressure 180 lbs. per sq. in., Diameter of Drivers 56 in., Weight on Drivers 108,000 lbs., Total Weight 178,000 lbs.

Fig. 62. Ten-Wheel (4—6—0) Two-Cylinder Schenectady Compound Locomotive. Built by the American Locomotive Co. for the Pennsylvania Railroad. Cylinders 20 in. and 30 in. x 24 in., Working Steam Pressure 180 lbs. per sq. in., Diameter of Drivers 74 in., Weight on Drivers 106,000 lbs., Total Weight 143,000 lbs.

Fig. 63. Ten-Wheel (4—6—0) Vauclain Balanced Compound Locomotive. Built by the Baldwin Locomotive Works for the New York, New Haven & Hartford. Cylinders 15 in. and 25 in. x 26 in., Working Steam Pressure 200 lbs. per sq. in., Heating Surface 2,666 sq. ft., Diameter of Drivers 72 in., Weight on Drivers 123,100 lbs., Total Weight 160,600 lbs.

LOCOMOTIVES, General Views; 4-6-0 Type.

Fig. 64. Ten-Wheel (4—6—0) Locomotive. Built by the American Locomotive Co. for the New York Central & Hudson River. Cylinders 22 in. x 26 in., Working Steam Pressure 200 lbs. per sq. in., Total Heating Surface 3,305.5 sq. ft., Diameter of Drivers 69 in., Weight on Drivers 148,000 lbs., Total Weight 194,500 lbs.

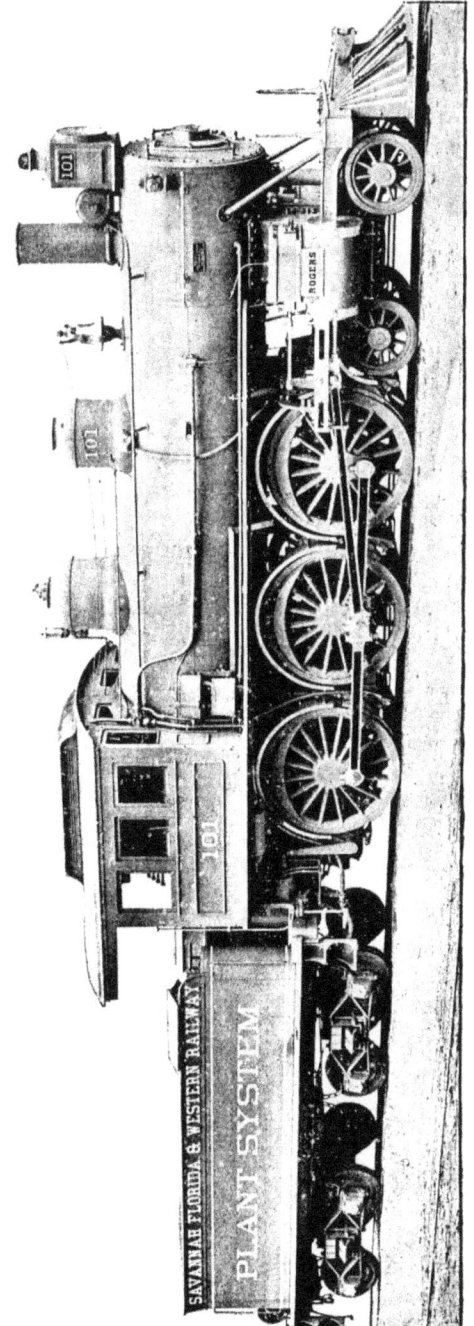

Fig. 65. Ten-Wheel (4—6—0) Locomotive. Built by the Rogers Locomotive Works for the Savannah, Florida & Western. Cylinders 20 in. x 24 in., Working Steam Pressure 200 lbs. per sq. in., Diameter of Drivers 72 in., Weight on Drivers 110,000 lbs., Total Weight 150,000 lbs.

LOCOMOTIVES, General Views; 4-6-0 Type. — Figs. 66-67

Fig. 66. Ten-Wheel (4—6—0) Locomotive. Built by the American Locomotive Co. for the Lehigh Valley. Cylinders 21 in. x 28 in., Working Steam Pressure 205 lbs. per sq. in., Total Heating Surface 3,284.24 sq. ft, Diameter of Drivers 68½ in., Weight on Drivers 150,200 lbs., Total Weight 199,200 lbs.

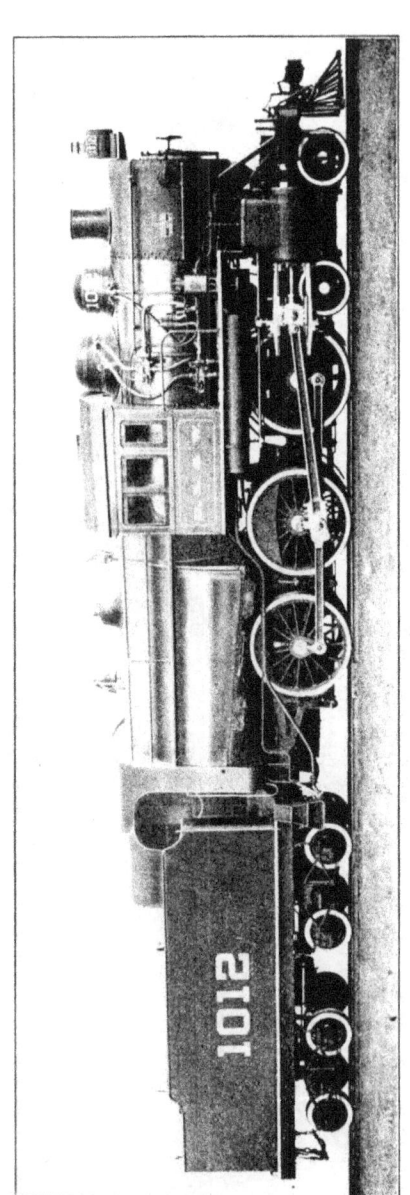

Fig. 67. Ten-Wheel (4—6—0) Locomotive. Built by the American Locomotive Co. for the Delaware, Lackawanna & Western. Cylinders 22½ in. x 26 in., Working Steam Pressure 215 lbs. per sq. in., Total Heating Surface 3,378 sq. ft, Diameter of Drivers 69 in., Weight on Drivers 154,000 lbs., Total Weight 201,000 lbs.

Figs. 68-69 LOCOMOTIVES, General Views; 4-6-2 Type.

Fig. 68. Pacific (4—6—2) Locomotive. Built by the Chicago, Milwaukee & St. Paul. Cylinders 23 in. x 26 in., Working Steam Pressure 200 lbs. per sq. in., Total Heating Surface, 3,381.6 sq. ft., Diameter of Drivers 72 in., Weight on Drivers 142,000 lbs., Total Weight 218,000 lbs.

Fig. 69. Pacific (4—6—2) Locomotive. Built by the American Locomotive Co. for the Michigan Central. Cylinders 22 in. x 26 in., Working Steam Pressure 200 lbs. per sq. in., Total Heating Surface 3,894.5 sq. ft., Diameter of Drivers 75 in., Weight on Drivers 140,500 lbs., Total Weight 221,000 lbs.

LOCOMOTIVES, General Views; 4-6-2 Type. Figs. 70-71

Fig. 70. Pacific (4—6—2) Locomotive. Built by the American Locomotive Co. for the Erie Railroad. Cylinders 22½ in. x 26 in., Total Heating Surface 3,321.91 sq. ft, Diameter of Drivers 74 in., Weight on Drivers 140,000 lbs., Total Weight 230,500 lbs.

Fig. 71. Pacific (4—6—2) Vauclain Balanced Compound Locomotive. Built by the Baldwin Locomotive Works for the Atchison, Topeka & Santa Fe. Cylinders 17 in. and 28 in. x 28 in., Working Steam Pressure 220 lbs. per sq. in., Total Heating Surface 3,595 sq. ft, Diameter of Drivers 73 in., Weight on Drivers 151,000 lbs., Total Weight 226,700 lbs.

Figs. 72-74 LOCOMOTIVES, General Views; 4-8-0 Type.

Fig. 72. Twelve-Wheel (4—8—0) Cross-Compound Locomotive. Built by the American Locomotive Co. for the Butte, Anaconda & Pacific. Cylinders 23 in. and 34 in. x 32 in., Working Steam Pressure 210 lbs. per sq. in., Total Heating Surface 3,866 sq. ft., Diameter of Drivers 56 in., Weight on Drivers 166,900 lbs., Total Weight 216,500 lbs.

Fig. 73. Twelve-Wheel (4—8—0) Locomotive. Built by the Baldwin Locomotive Works for the Duluth & Iron Range. Cylinders 22 in. x 26 in., Diameter of Drivers 54 in., Weight on Drivers 140,060 lbs., Total Weight 172,260 lbs.

Fig. 74. Twelve-Wheel (4—8—0) Locomotive. Built by the American Locomotive Co. for the Illinois Central. Cylinders 23 in. x 30 in., Working Steam Pressure 210 lbs. per sq. in., Heating Surface 3,494 sq. in., Diameter of Drivers 57 in., Weight on Drivers 193,200 lbs., Total Weight 232,200 lbs.

LOCOMOTIVES, Elevations; 0-4-0 Type. Fig. 75

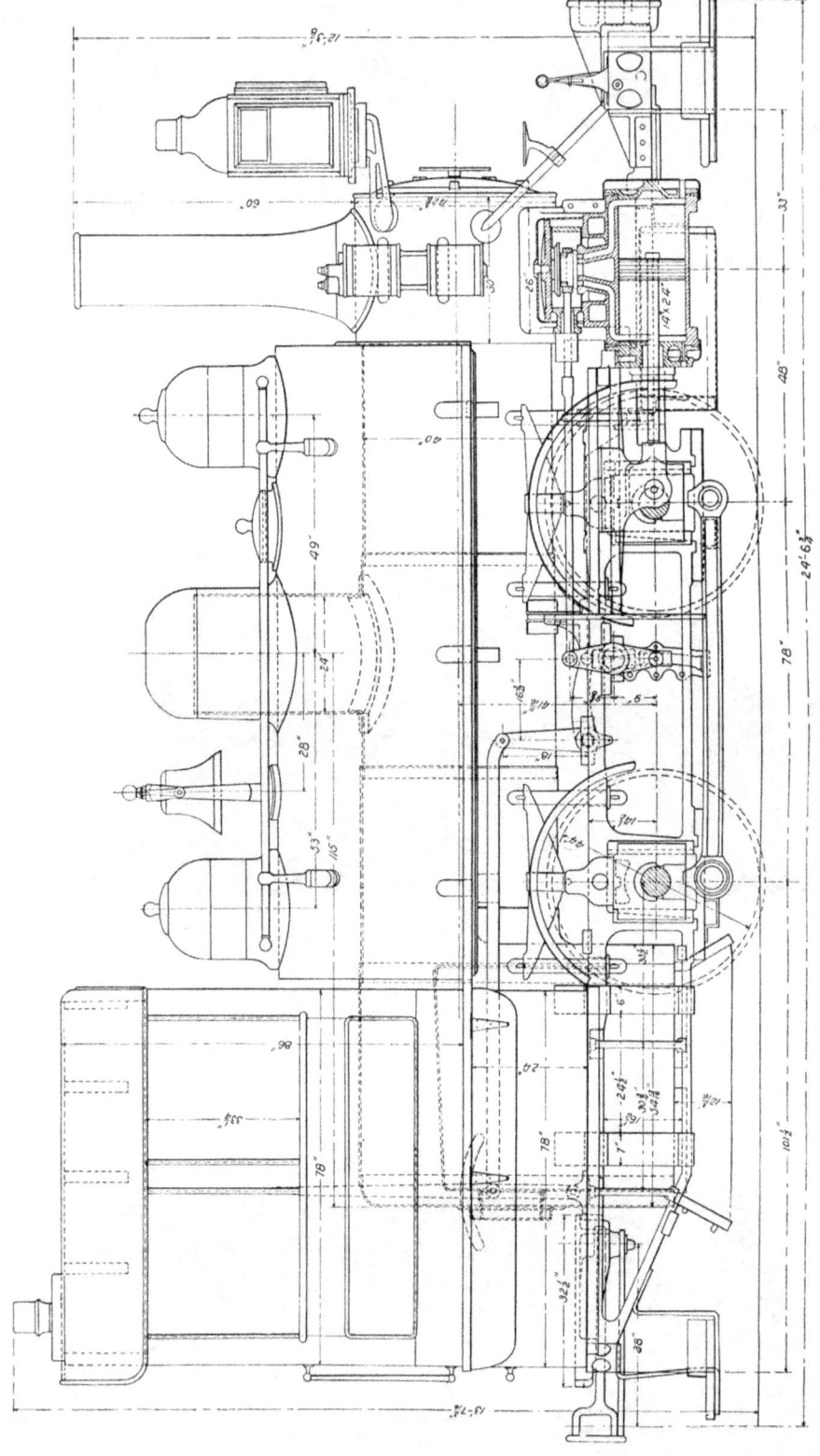

Fig. 75. Four-Wheel (0–4–0) Switching Locomotive. Built by the Baldwin Locomotive Works for the Baltimore & Ohio. Cylinders 14 in. x 24 in., Working Steam Pressure 170 lbs. per sq. in., Total Heating Surface 569.78 sq. ft., Diameter of Drivers 44 in., Weight on Drivers 68,000 lbs., Total Weight 68,000 lbs.

Figs. 76-77 — LOCOMOTIVES, Elevations; 0-4-0 Type.

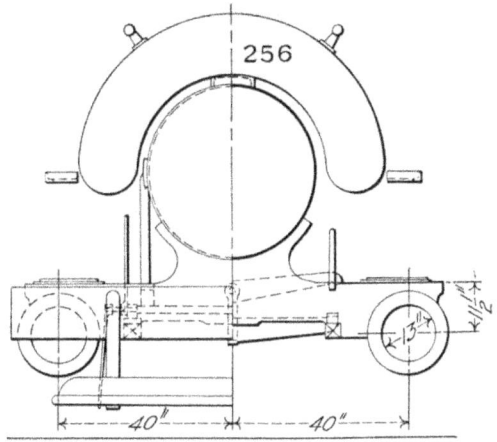

Fig. 76. Transverse Outline of Four-Wheel (0—4—0) Saddle Tank Switching Locomotive.
Built by the Baldwin Locomotive Works.

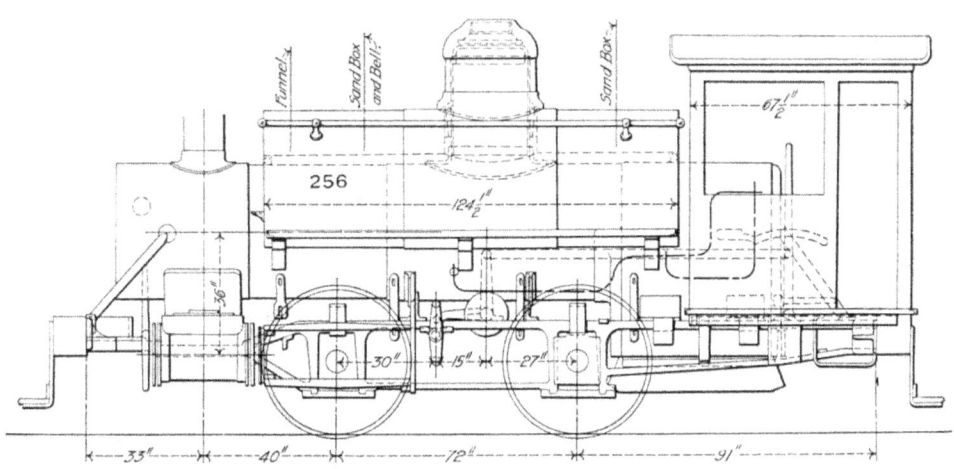

Fig. 77. Side Elevation of Four-Wheel (0—4—0) Tank Switching Locomotive.
Built by the Baldwin Locomotive Works.

Names of Parts of Locomotives.

1	Headlight	21	Front Truck Oil Box	41	Buckle Plate
2	Headlight Dynamo	22	Front Truck Oil Box Brass	42	Buckle Plate Angle
3	Headlight Bracket	23	Front Truck Axle	43	Cylinder Cock Bell Crank
4	Smokestack	24	Front Truck Pedestal Tie Bar	44	Cylinder Cock Bell Crank Bracket
5	Boiler Front	25	Front Truck Cross Tie		
6	Handrail	26	Front Truck Equalizer	45	Running Board
7	Spark Cleaning Hole Cap	27	Front Truck Spring	46	Sandbox
8	Spark Hole Chute	28	Front Truck Hanger	47	Sandbox Cap
9	Steam Pipe	29	Front Truck Spring Cap	48	Sandbox Step
10	Saddle	30	Valve Stem	49	Boiler Check
11	Steam Chest	31	Valve Rod	50	Feed Pipe
12	Steam Chest Head	32	Valve Stem Gland	51	Feed Pipe Bracket
13	Cylinder	33	Valve Rod Pin	52	Handrail Bracket
14	Cylinder Head Casing	34	Piston Rod	53	Front Tube Sheet
15	Front Bumper	35	Crosshead	54	Dry Pipe
16	Front Bumper Channel	36	Crosshead Shoe	55	Boiler Lagging
17	Front Frame	37	Rocker	56	Boiler Lagging Jacket
18	Front Truck Wheel	38	Rocker Pin	57	Bell
19	Front Truck Frame	39	Guide Yoke	58	Bell Stand
20	Front Truck Pedestal	40	Guide Yoke Angle	59	Bell Yoke

LOCOMOTIVES, Elevations.

Names of Parts of Locomotives (continued.)

60 Driver Brake Cylinder
61 Rocker Connection
62 Rocker Connection Hanger
63 Rocker Connection Hanger Bracket
64 Link
65 Link Hanger
66 Lifting Shaft Arm
67 Lifting Shaft Lever
68 Lifting Shaft
69 Lifting Shaft Bracket
70 Driving Axle Box
71 Driving Axle Box Brass
72 Driving Axle
73 Driving Axle Box Cellar
74 Frame Pedestal
75 Frame Pedestal Brace
76 Frame Brace
77 Top Frame Rail
78 Bottom Frame Rail
79 Driving Spring Hanger Stirrup
80 Driving Spring
81 Driving Spring Seat
82 Driving Spring Hanger
83 Driving Spring Hanger Bracket
84 Driver Equalizer
85 Driver Equalizer Bracket or Post
86 Driver Equalizer Safety Straps
87 Lifting Shaft Counterbalance Rod
88 Lifting Shaft Counterbalance Cylinder
89 Dry Pipe Hanger
90 Dome
91 Dome Lagging
92 Dome Casing
93 Dome Casing Cap
94 Dome Cover
95 Throttle Pipe
96 Throttle Casing
97 Throttle Valve
98 Throttle Stem
99 Throttle Bell Crank
100 Turret Pipe
101 Turret Stand Pipe
102 Safety Valve Dome
103 Back Tube Sheet
104 Air Pump
105 Outside Throat Sheet
106 Washout Plug Holes
107 Driver and Rear Truck Equalizer
108 Driver and Rear Truck Equalizer Bracket
109 Ashpan
110 Ashpan Hopper
111 Ashpan Hopper Slide
112 Ashpan Hopper Slide Hanger
113 Ashpan Hopper Slide Arm
114 Driving Wheel
115 Trailing Truck Wheel
116 Trailing Truck Axle Box

117 Trailing Truck Pedestal
118 Trailing Truck Spring
119 Trailing Truck Hanger
120 Trailing Truck Hanger Bracket
121 Rear Frame
122 Tail Piece
123 Back Chafing Plate
124 Reverse Lever Bracket
125 Reverse Lever
126 Reach Rod
127 Crownsheet
128 Backsheet of Firebox
129 Backhead of Boiler
130 Firedoor Opening
131 Foot Board
132 Reverse Lever Quadrant
133 Reverse Lever Quadrant Bracket
134 Cab
135 Cab Window Sash
136 Cab Ventilator
137 Turret
138 Number Plate
139 Headlight Step
140 Spark Cleaning Hole
141 Steam Chest Relief Valve
142 Low Pressure Cylinder
143 High Pressure Cylinder
144 Pilot
145 Front Bumper Brace
146 Pilot Bracket
147 Front Truck Radius Bar
148 Front Driver and Truck Equalizer
149 Guide
150 Manhole Cover
151 Driver Spring Stirrup
152 Driver Box Yoke
153 Safety Valve
154 Whistle
155 Intermediate Driver Spring
156 Main Air Reservoir
157 Expansion Bracket
158 Ashpan Slide Connection
159 Cab Hand Hold
160 Steam Gage Plate
161 Cab Window Opening
162 Cab Roof
163 Cab Roof Water Gutter
164 Ashpan Bell Crank
165 Smokebox Crane
166 Smokebox Crane Bracket
167 Smokebox Crane Traveler
168 Exhaust Nozzle
169 Exhaust Nozzle Damper
170 Back-Pressure Brake Exhaust Pipe
171 Cylinder Cock Lever
172 Running Board Brackets
173 Driver and Truck Equalizer Fulcrum
174 Driver and Truck Equalizer Pin
175 Smokebox
176 Boiler
177 Side Rod Crankpin
178 Main Crankpin

179 Eccentric
180 Main Reservoir Hanger
181 Cab Front Window
182 Cab Back Window
183 Throttle Lever
184 Suction Pipe Bracket
185 Suction Pipe
186 Injector
187 Injector Overflow
188 Sander
189 Sand Pipe
190 Pilot Coupler
191 Coupler Unlocking Chain
192 Coupler Unlocking Lever
193 Coupler Brace
194 Flag Staff
195 Flag Staff Base
196 Pilot Brace
197 Front Step
198 Valve Rod Block Yoke
199 Rear Cab
200 Gangway Chain
201 Tender Hand Hold
202 Tender Step
203 Front Boiler Brace
204 Driver Brake Lever
205 Driver Brake Head
206 Driver Brake Shoe
207 Driver Brake Pull Rod
208 Driver Spring Hanger Gib
209 Transverse Equalizer
210 Engine Step or Cab Step
211 Apron
212 Apron Hinge
213 Tee Head
214 Connecting Rod Safety Strap
215 Connecting Rod
216 Front Truck Box Yoke
217 Front Truck Pivot Pin
218 Front Truck Center Casting
219 Driver Box Wedge
220 Equalizer Safety Straps
221 Brick Arch
222 Footplate
223 Gage Cock
224 Blow-Off Cock
225 Handhold
226 Buffer
227 Bumper Angle
228 Cylinder Oil Pipe
229 Cab Step
230 Back Overhang of Cab
231 Whistle Lever
232 Whistle Lever Connection
233 Vertical Shaft for Ashpan Slide
234 Back Cab Braces
235 Engineer's Brake Valve
236 Firedoor Frame
237 Cylinder Cock Shaft
238 Boiler Front Door
239 Rocker Box
240 Cab Roof Carline
242 Steam Heat Valve
243 Steam Heat Pipe
244 Gage Glass Frame
245 Order Clip
246 Bell Cord Thimble
247 Reducing Valve
248 Steam Pipe to Injector
250 Blower Pipe
251 Cab Seat
252 Engineer's Valve
253 Train Pipe
254 Top Cab Bracket
255 Bottom Cab Bracket
256 Saddle Tank

Fig. 78 LOCOMOTIVES, Elevations; 0-6-0 Type.

Numbers Refer to List of Names of Parts with Figs. 76-77.

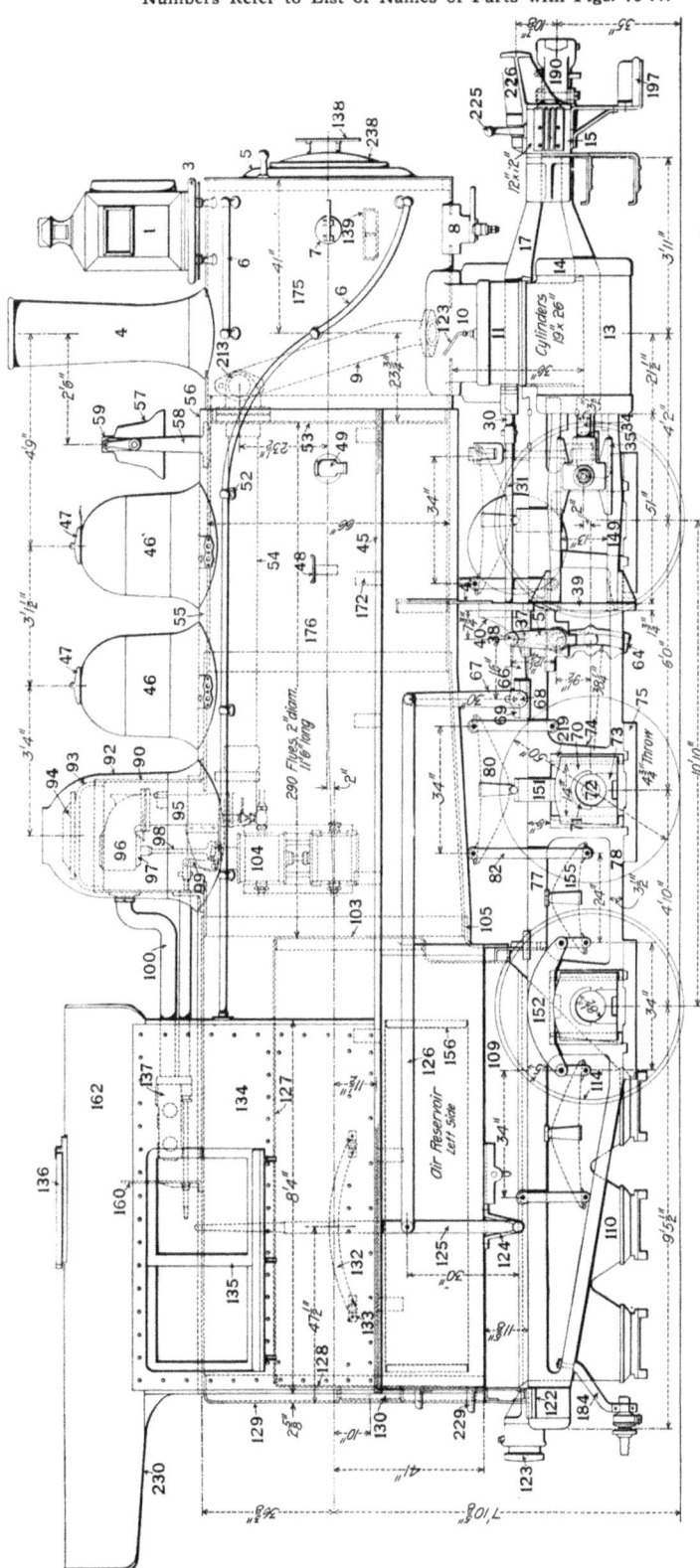

Fig. 78. Six-Wheel (0—6—0) Switching Locomotive. Built by the Baldwin Locomotive Works for the Erie Railroad. Cylinders 19 in. x 26 in., Working Steam Pressure 200 lbs. per sq. in., Total Heating Surface 1,879 sq. ft., Diameter of Drivers 50 in., Weight on Drivers 145,100 lbs., Total Weight 145,100 lbs.

LOCOMOTIVES, Elevations; 0-6-0 Type.

Fig. 79

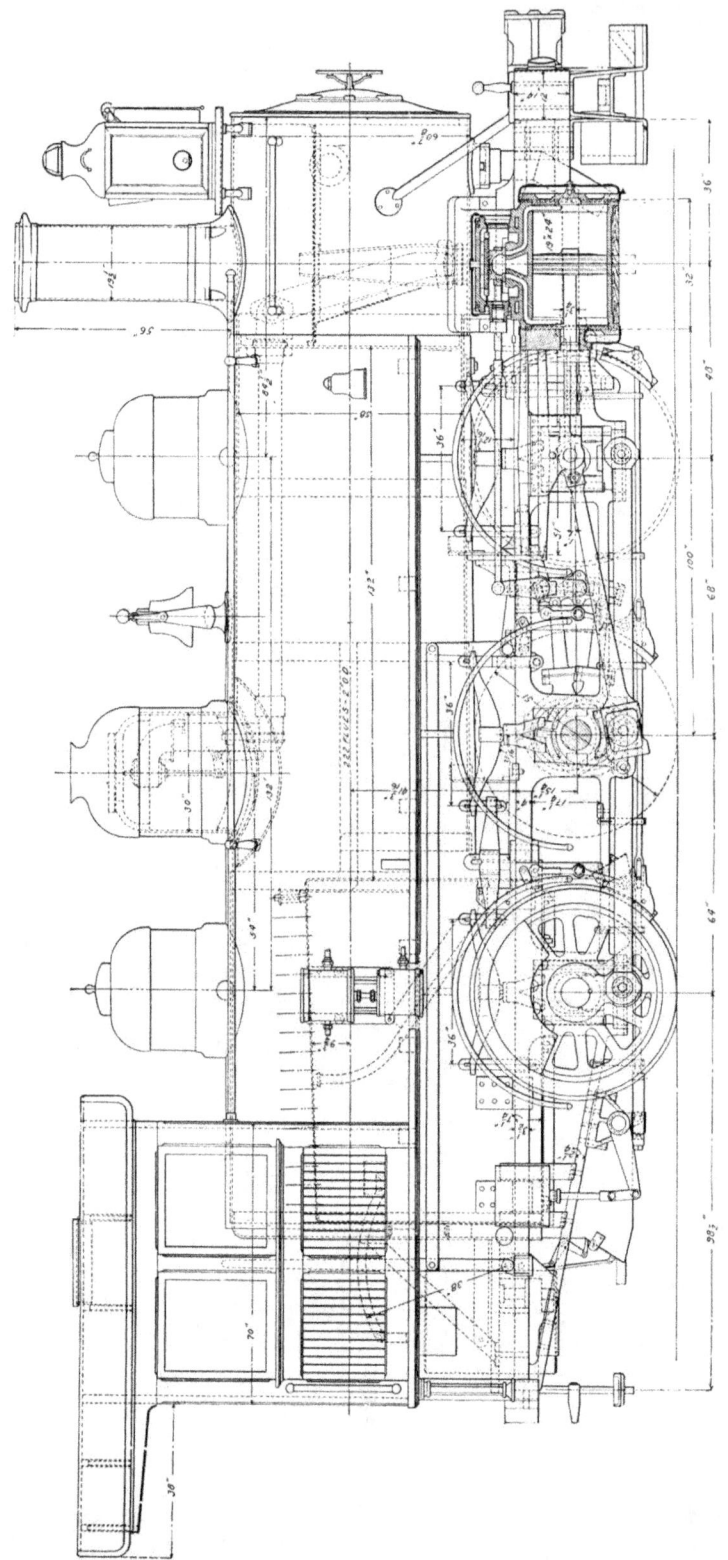

Fig. 79. Six-Wheel (0—6—0) Switching Locomotive. Built by the American Locomotive Co. for the Peoria & Pekin Union Railway. Cylinders 18 in. x 24 in., Working Steam Pressure 165 lbs. per sq. in., Total Heating Surface 1,520 sq. ft., Diameter of Drivers 50 in., Weight on Drivers 108,000 lbs., Total Weight 108,000 lbs.

Fig. 80 LOCOMOTIVES, Elevations; 0-6-0 Type.

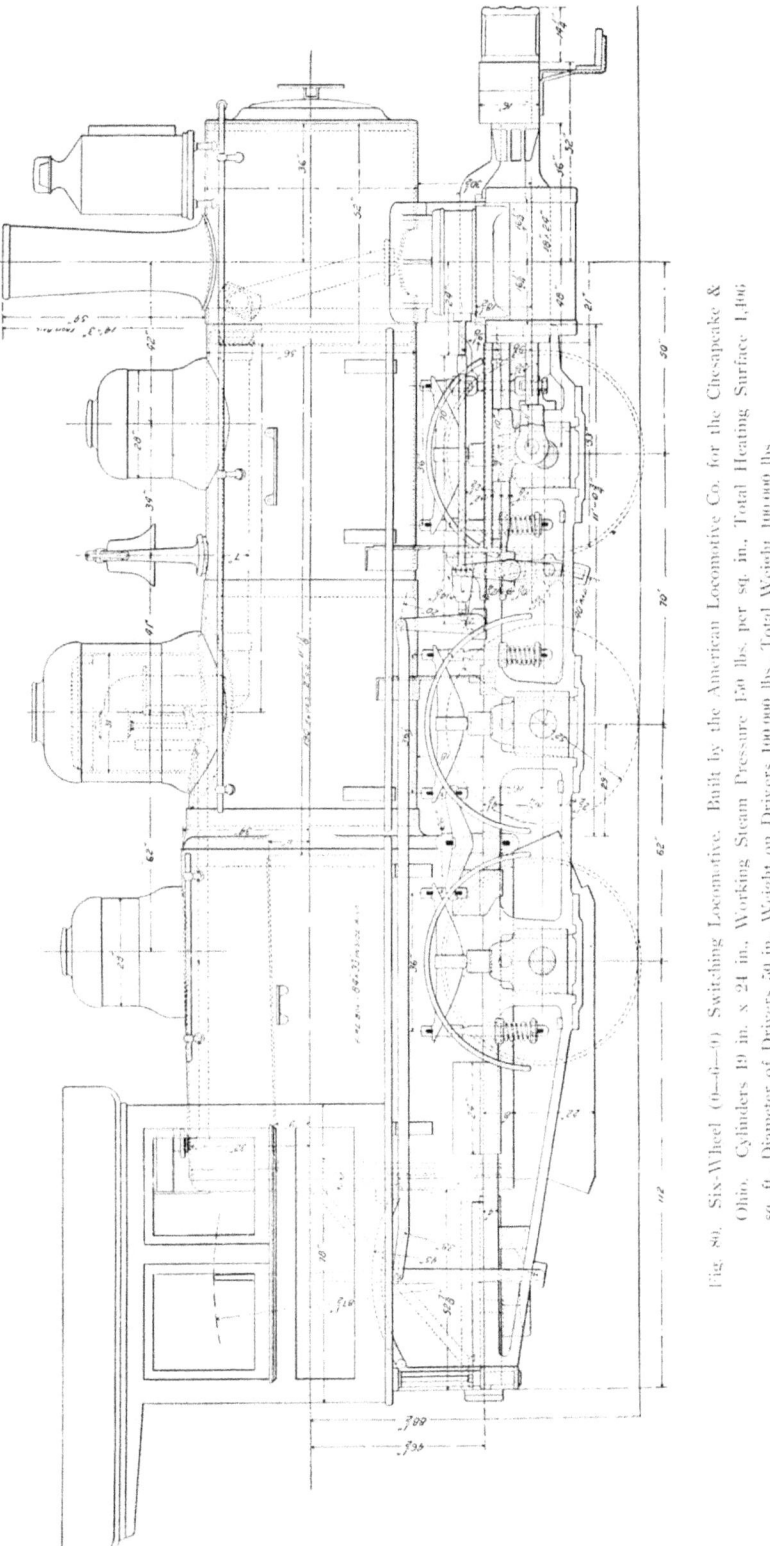

Fig. 80. Six-Wheel (0—6—0) Switching Locomotive. Built by the American Locomotive Co. for the Chesapeake & Ohio. Cylinders 19 in. x 24 in., Working Steam Pressure 150 lbs. per sq. in., Total Heating Surface 1,406 sq. ft., Diameter of Drivers 50 in., Weight on Drivers 100,000 lbs., Total Weight 100,000 lbs.

LOCOMOTIVES, Elevations; 0-6-2 Type. Figs. 81-82

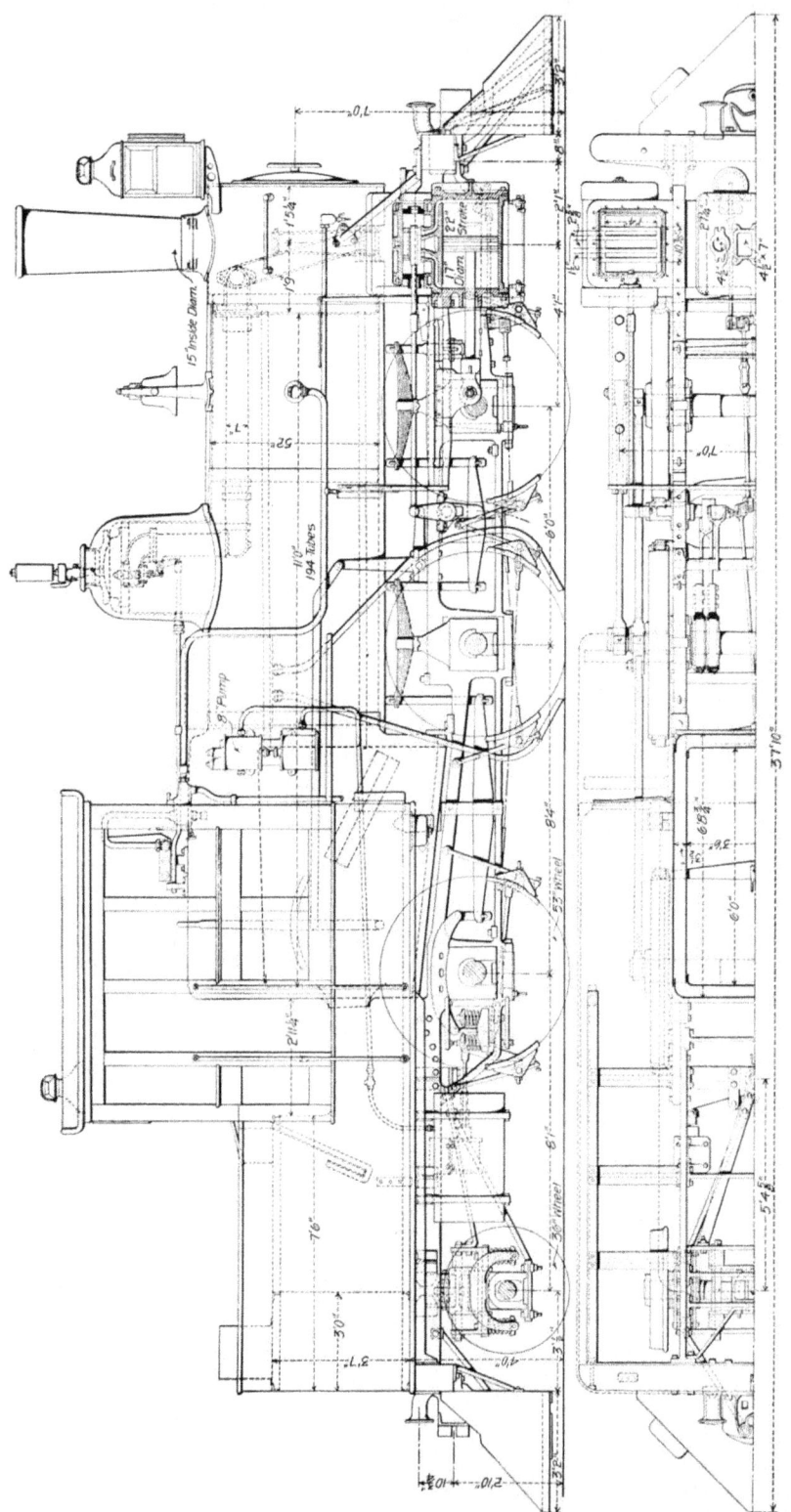

Figs. 81-82. Six-Coupled and Trailing (0—6—2) Suburban Tank Locomotive. Chicago, Burlington & Quincy. Cylinders 17 in. x 22 in., Diameter of Drivers 56 in., Weight on Drivers 94,000 lbs., Total Weight 113,000 lbs.

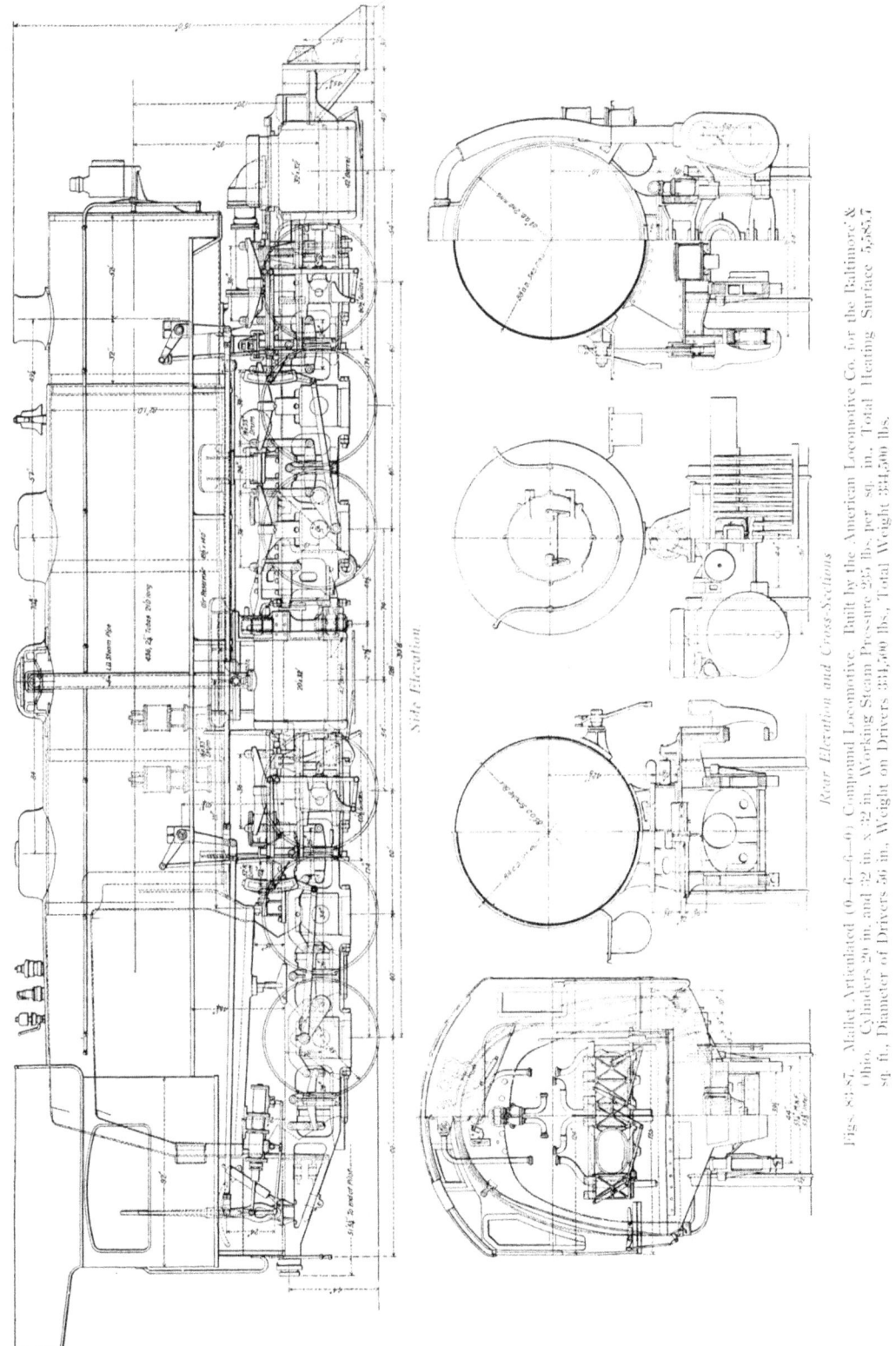

Figs. 83-87. Mallet Articulated (0—6—6—0) Compound Locomotive. Built by the American Locomotive Co. for the Baltimore & Ohio. Cylinders 20 in. and 32 in. x 32 in. Working Steam Pressure 235 lbs. per sq. in., Total Heating Surface 5,585.7 sq. ft., Diameter of Drivers 56 in., Weight on Drivers 334,500 lbs, Total Weight 334,500 lbs.

LOCOMOTIVES, Elevations; 2-4-2 Type.   Fig. 88

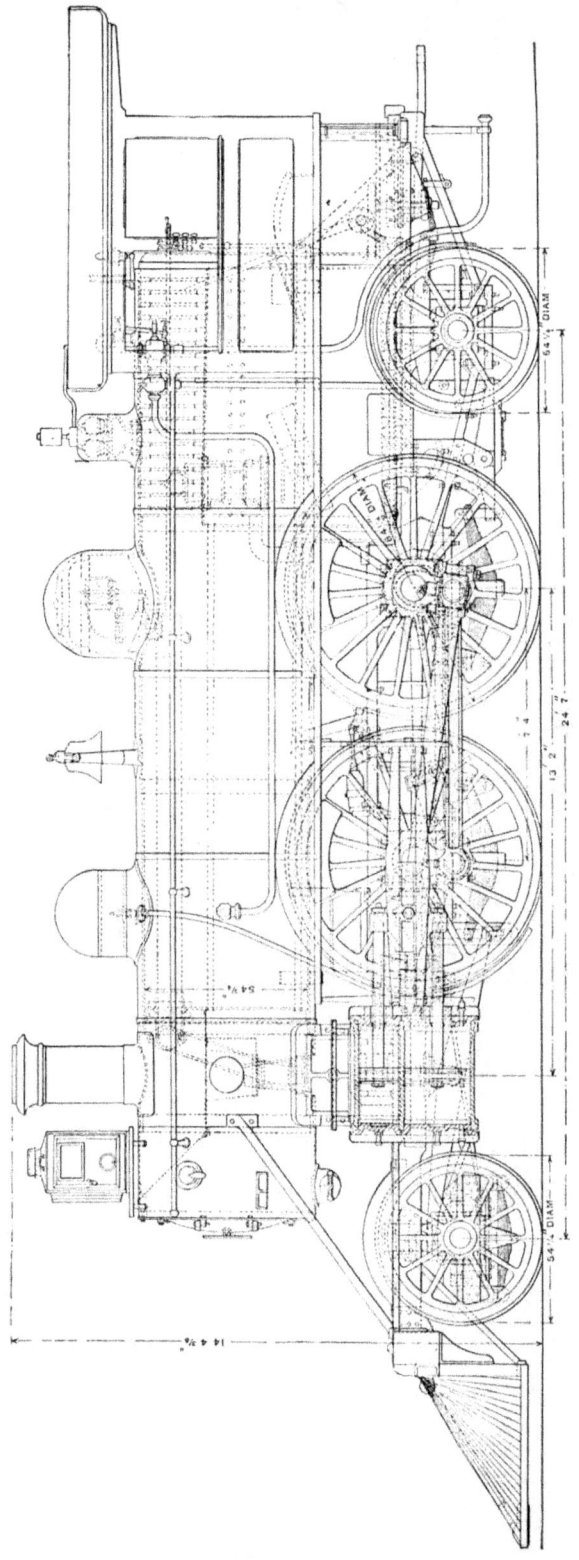

Fig. 88. Columbia (2—4—2) Compound Locomotive. Built by the Baldwin Locomotive Works. Cylinders 13 in. and 22 in. x 26 in., Working Steam Pressure 180 lbs. per sq. in., Total Heating Surface 1,478.13 sq. ft., Diameter of Drivers 81¼ in., Weight on Drivers 83,000 lbs., Total Weight 126,500 lbs.

Fig. 89　　LOCOMOTIVES, Elevations; 2-6-0 Type.

Numbers Refer to List of Names of Parts with Figs. 76-77.

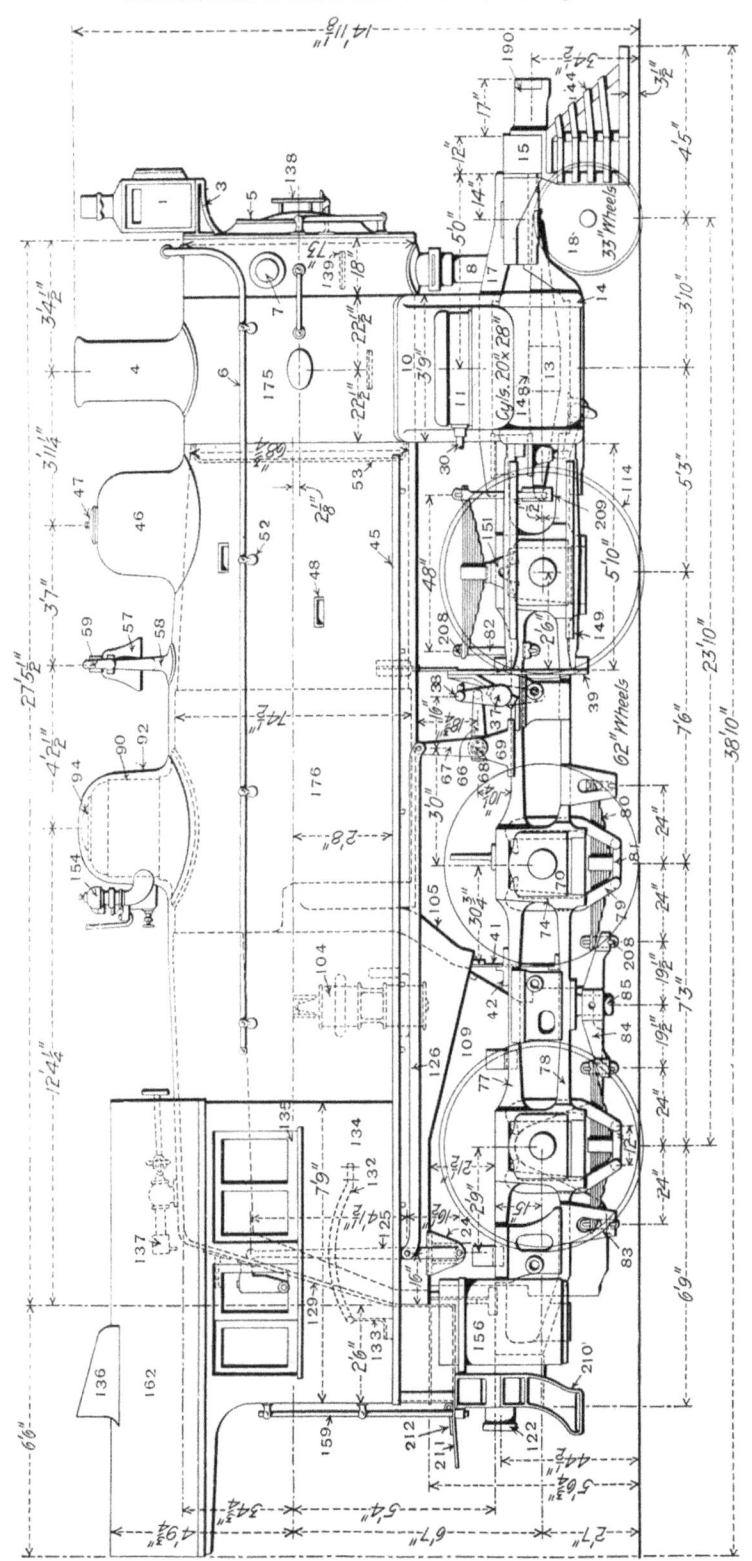

Fig. 89. Mogul (2-6-0) Locomotive. Pennsylvania Railroad. Cylinders 20 in. x 28 in. Total Heating Surface 2,431 sq. ft. Weight on Drivers 139,100 lbs. Total Weight 160,000 lbs.

LOCOMOTIVES, Elevations; 2-6-0 Type. Fig. 90

Numbers Refer to List of Names of Parts with Figs. 76-77.

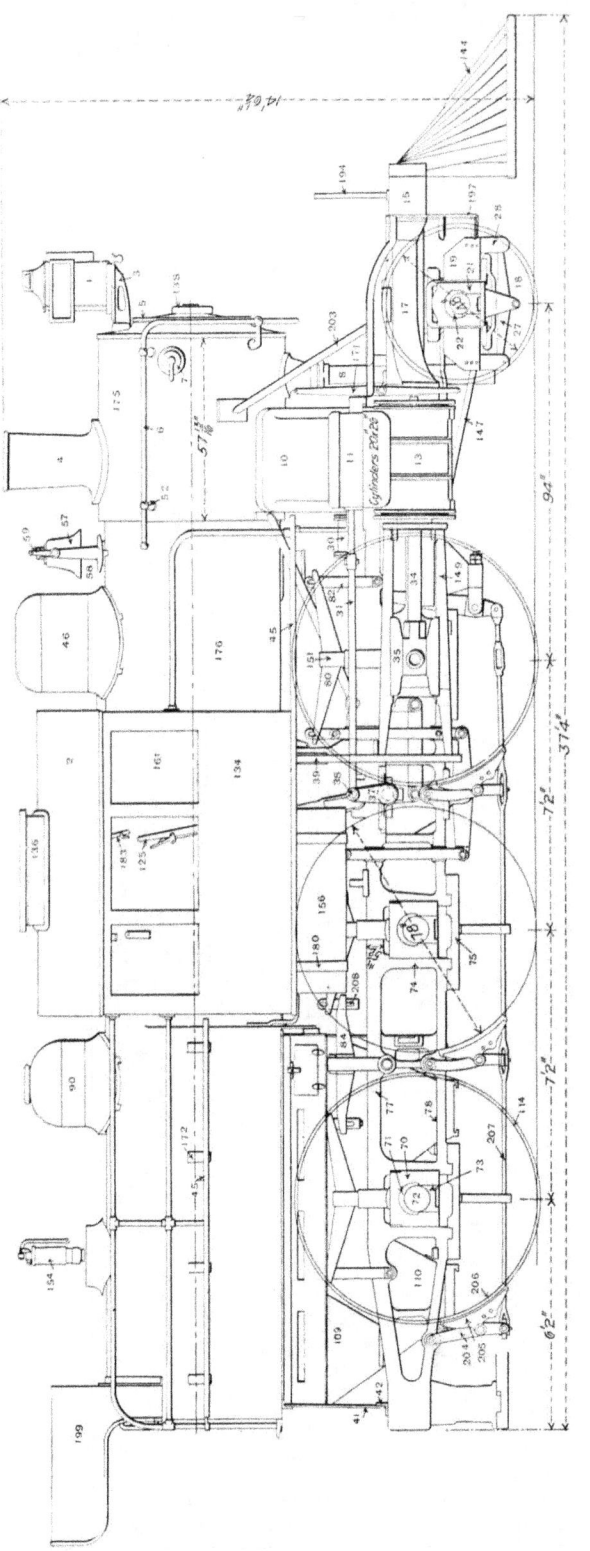

Fig. 90. Mogul (2—6—0) Locomotive. Built by the Philadelphia & Reading. Cylinders 20 in. x 26 in. Total Heating Surface 1,765 sq. ft. Weight on Drivers 131,400 lbs. Total Weight 159,300 lbs.

Fig. 91 — LOCOMOTIVES, Elevations; 2-6-0 Type.

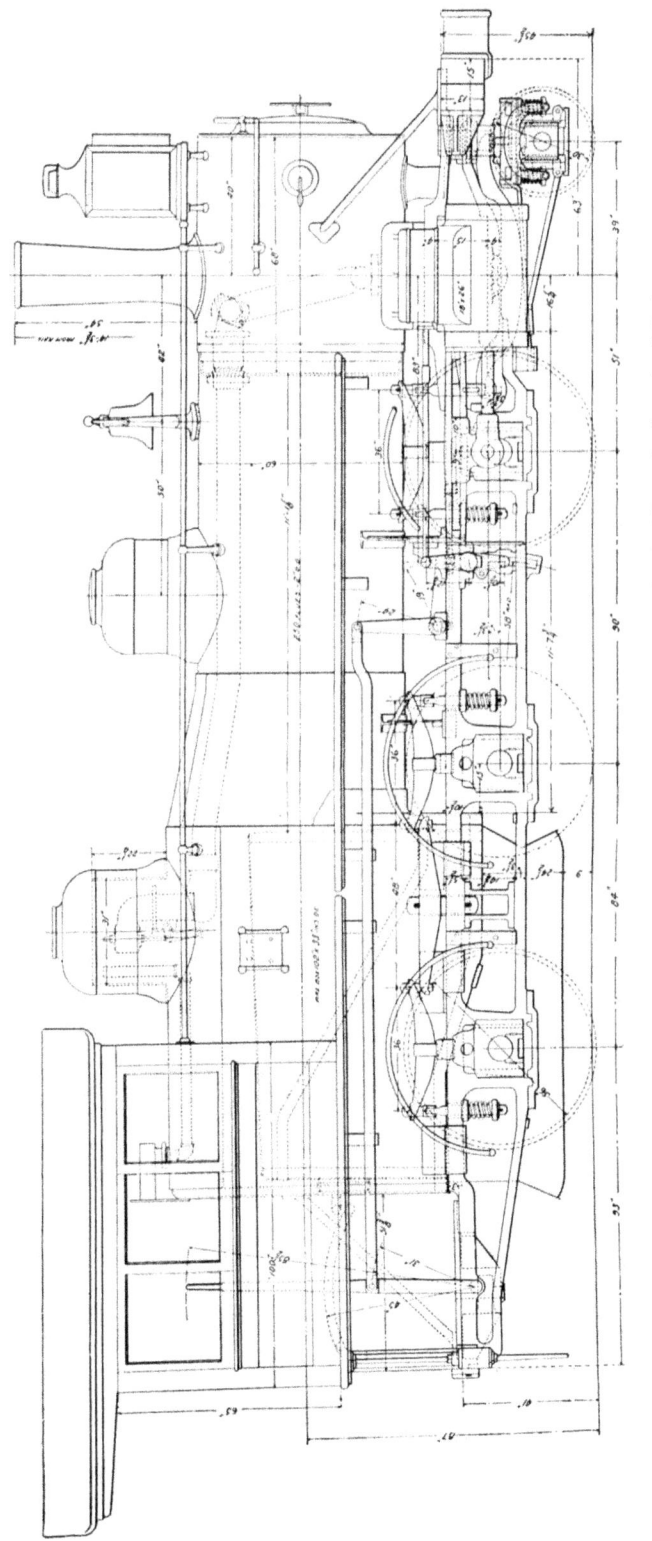

Fig. 91. Mogul (2—6—0) Locomotive. Built by the American Locomotive Co. for the Wisconsin Central. Cylinders 18 in. x 20 in., Working Steam Pressure 180 lbs. per sq. in., Total Heating Surface 1,610 sq. ft., Diameter of Drivers 56 in., Weight on Drivers 108,000 lbs., Total Weight 121,000 lbs.

LOCOMOTIVES, Elevations; 2-6-0 Type. Fig. 92

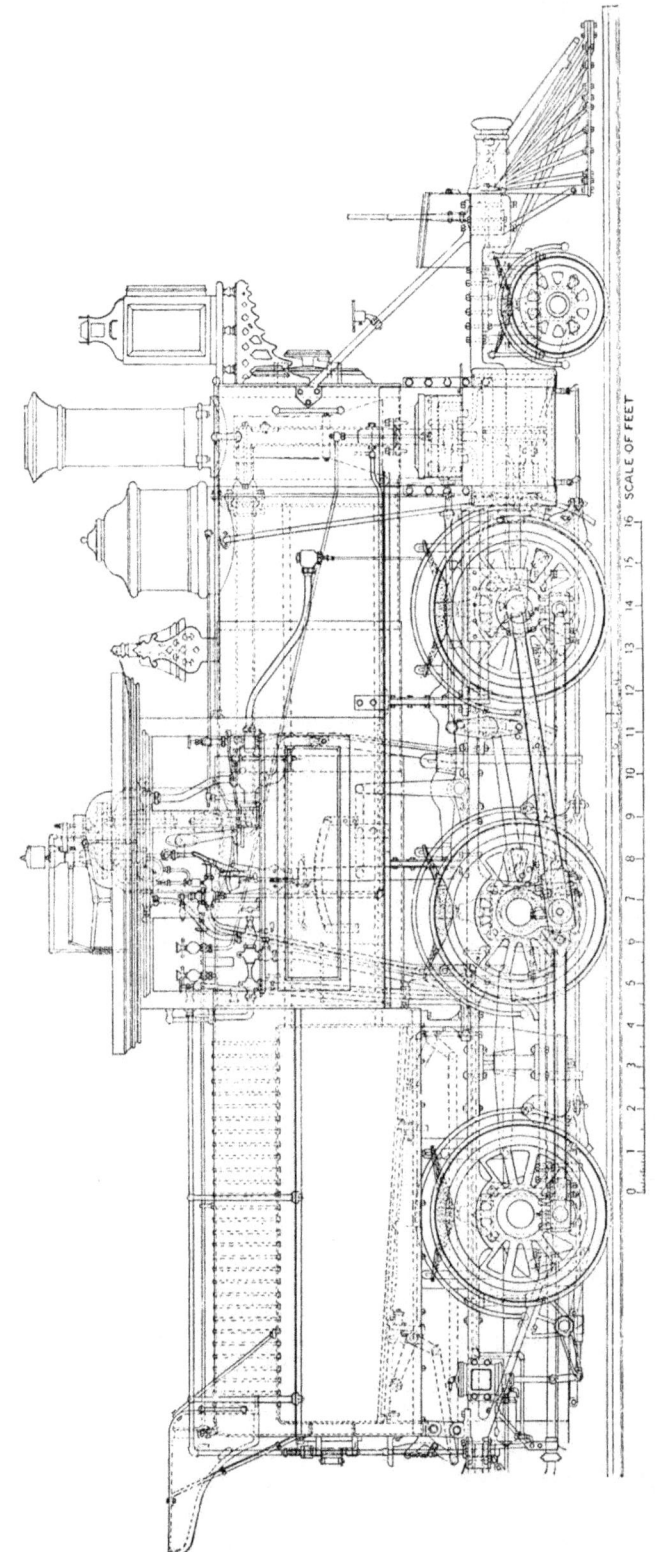

Fig. 92. Mogul (2—6—0) Locomotive. Built by the American Locomotive Co. for the Delaware, Lackawanna & Western. Cylinders 19 in. x 24 in., Working Steam Pressure 110 lbs. per sq. in., Total Heating Surface 1,469 sq. ft., Diameter of Drivers 57¾ in., Weight on Drivers 100,000 lbs., Total Weight 115,000 lbs.

Fig. 93　　　LOCOMOTIVES, Elevations; 2-6-2 Type.

Numbers Refer to List of Names of Parts with Figs. 76-77.

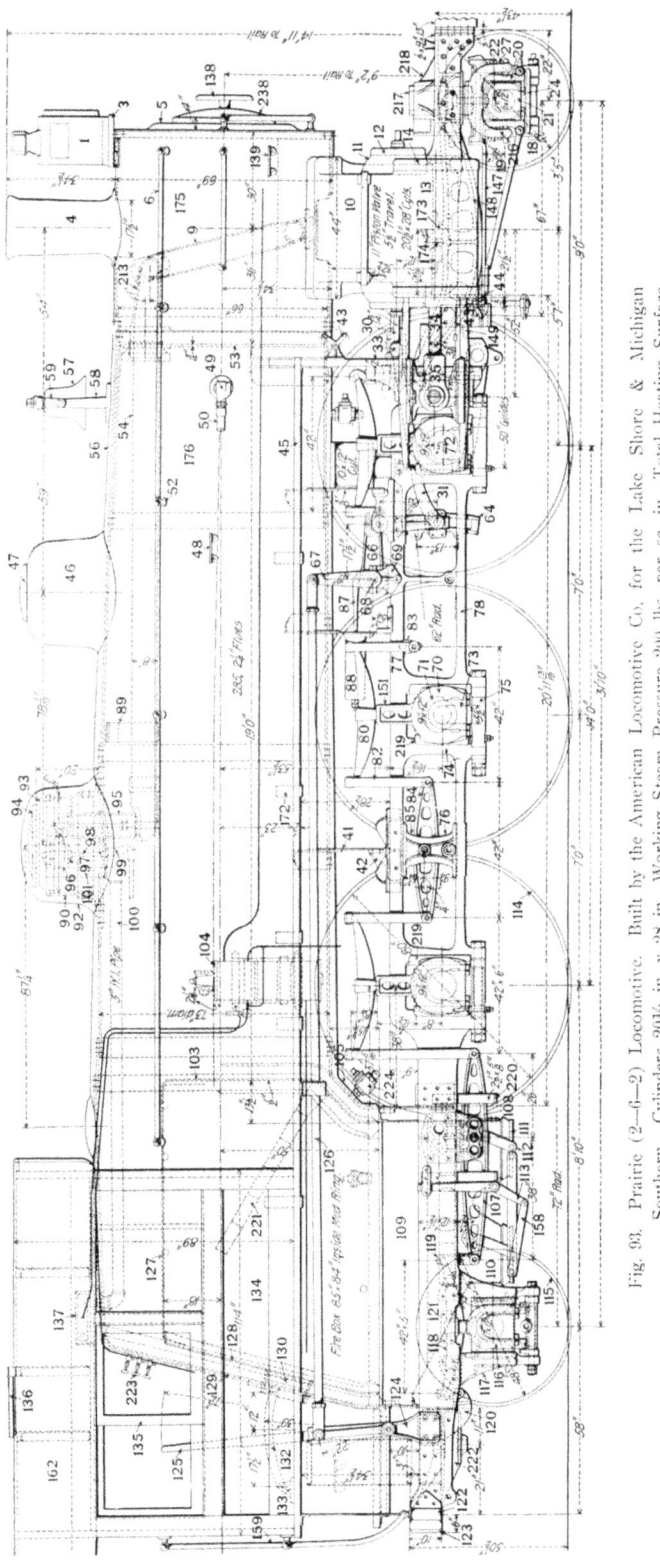

Fig. 93. Prairie (2—6—2) Locomotive. Built by the American Locomotive Co. for the Lake Shore & Michigan Southern. Cylinders 20½ in. x 28 in., Working Steam Pressure 200 lbs. per sq. in., Total Heating Surface 3,343 sq. ft., Diameter of Drivers 80 in., Weight on Drivers 130,000 lbs., Total Weight 174,500 lbs.

LOCOMOTIVES, Elevations; 2-6-2 Type.

Fig. 94

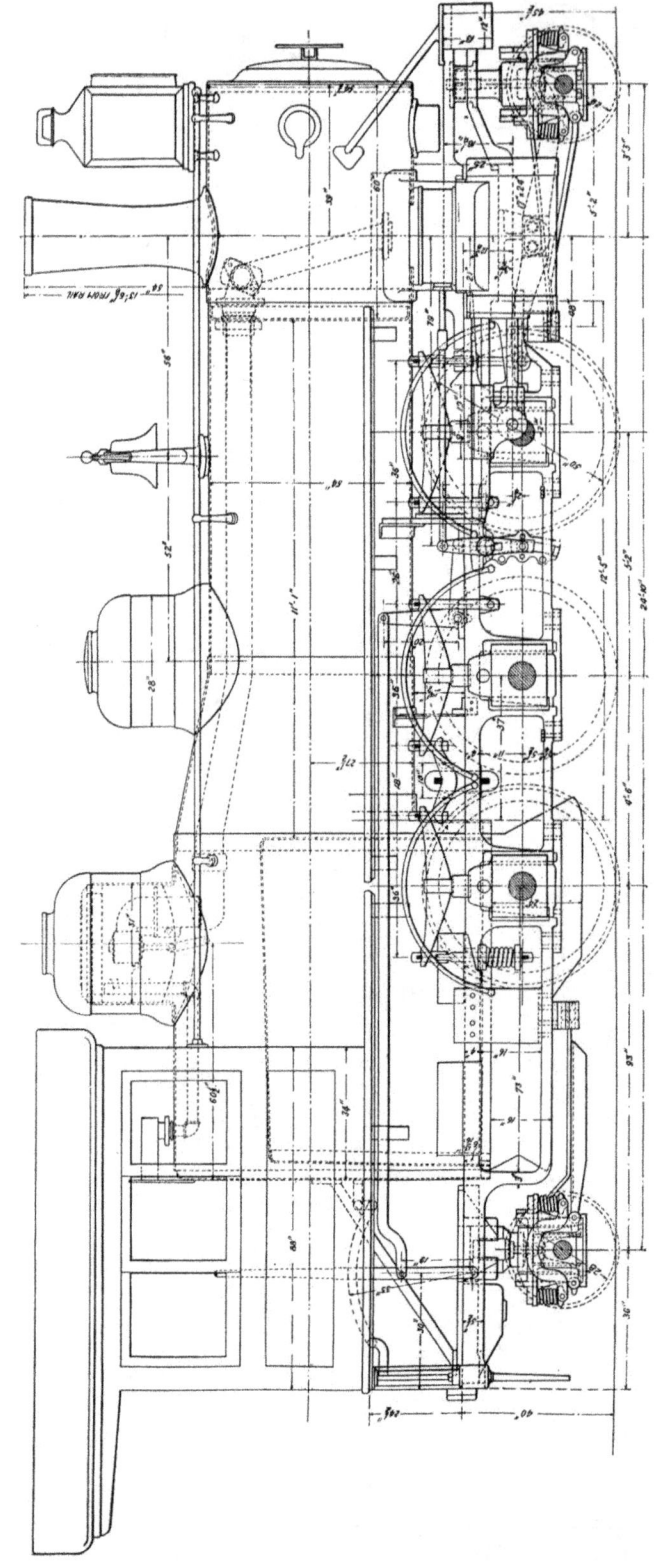

Fig. 94. Prairie (2—6—2) Locomotive. Built by the American Locomotive Co. for the Cincinnati, Lebanon & Northern. Cylinders 17 in. x 24 in., Working Steam Pressure 180 lbs. per sq. in., Total Heating Surface 1,292 sq. ft., Diameter of Drivers 50 in., Weight on Drivers 82,000 lbs., Total Weight 106,000 lbs.

Fig. 95 LOCOMOTIVES, Elevations; 2-8-0 Type.

Numbers Refer to List of Names of Parts with Figs. 76-77.

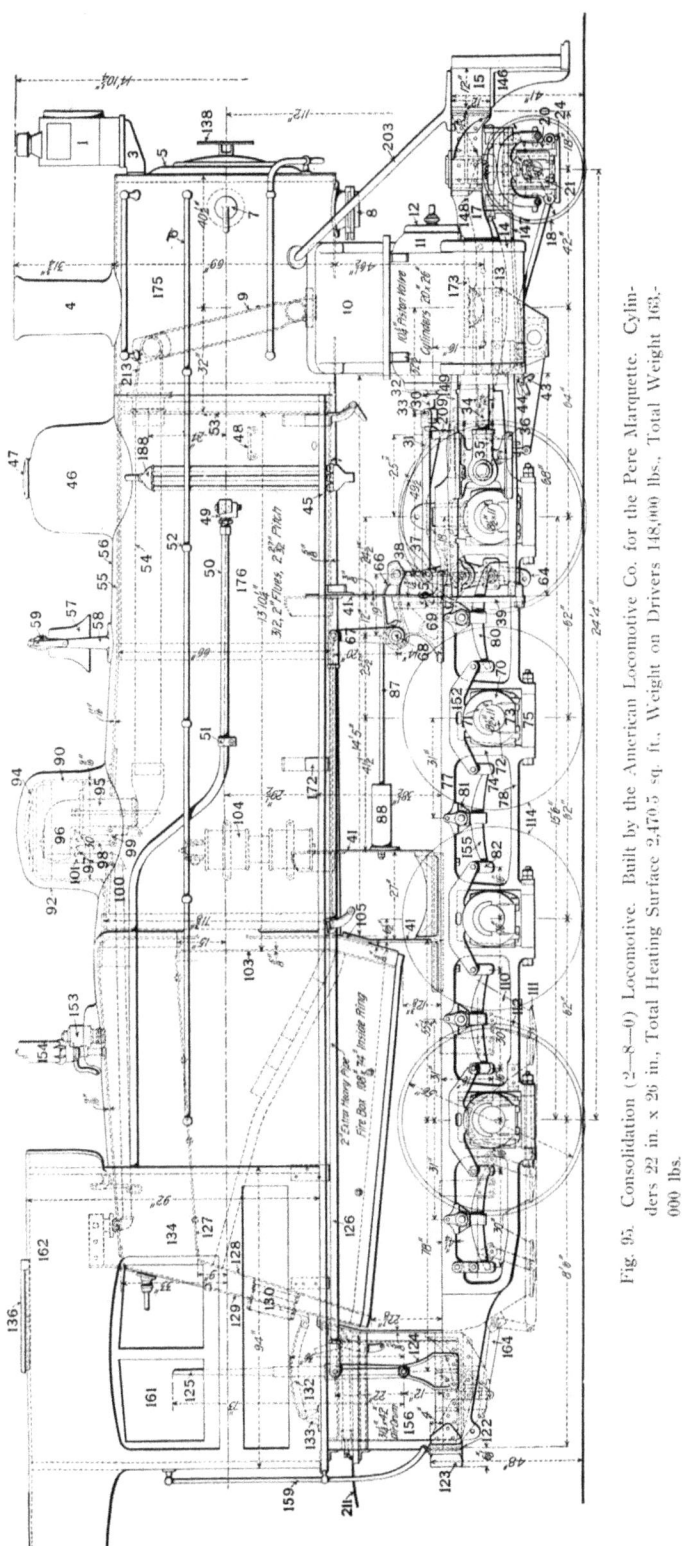

Fig. 95. Consolidation (2—8—0) Locomotive. Built by the American Locomotive Co. for the Pere Marquette. Cylinders 22 in. x 26 in., Total Heating Surface 2,470.5 sq. ft., Weight on Drivers 148,000 lbs., Total Weight 163,000 lbs.

LOCOMOTIVES, Elevations; 2-8-0 Type.

Fig. 96

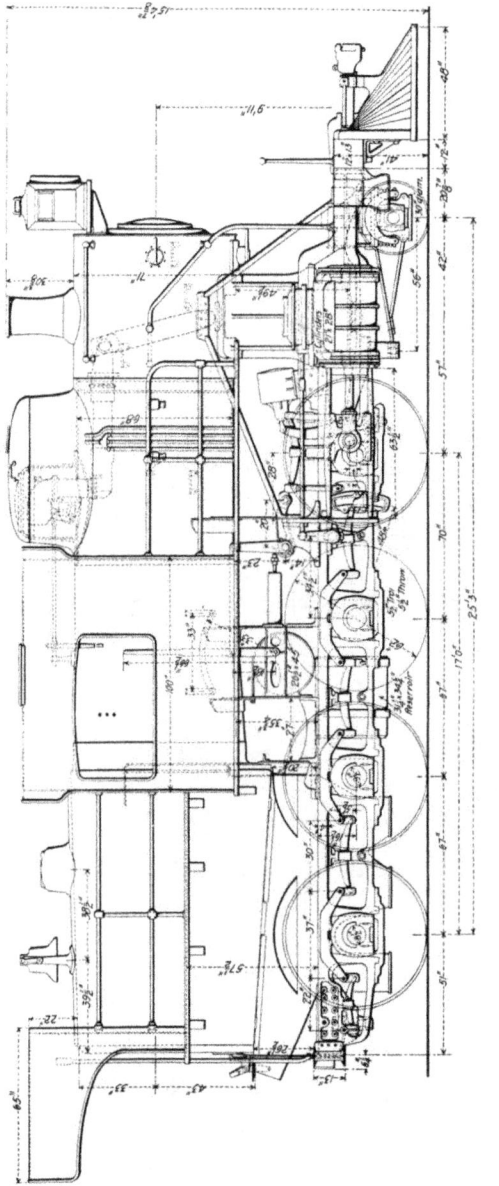

Fig. 96. Consolidation (2—8—0) Locomotive. Built by the American Locomotive Co. for the Erie Railroad. Cylinders 21 in. x 28 in., Working Steam Pressure 200 lbs. per sq. in., Total Heating Surface 2,391 sq. ft, Diameter of Drivers 63 in., Weight on Drivers 165,900 lbs., Total Weight 189,400 lbs.

Fig. 97 — LOCOMOTIVES, Elevations; 2-8-0 Type.

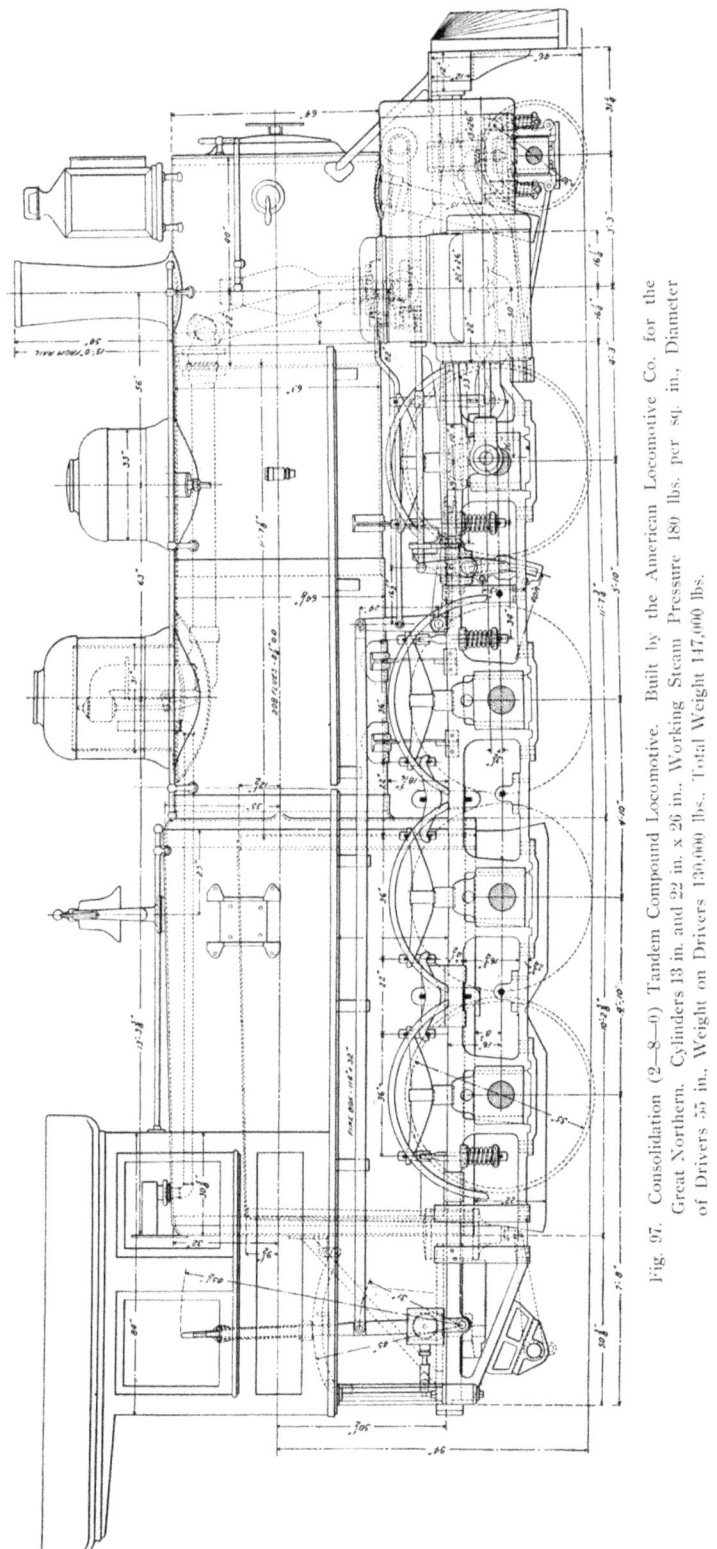

Fig. 97. Consolidation (2—8—0) Tandem Compound Locomotive. Built by the American Locomotive Co. for the Great Northern. Cylinders 13 in. and 22 in. x 26 in., Working Steam Pressure 180 lbs. per sq. in., Diameter of Drivers 55 in., Weight on Drivers 130,000 lbs., Total Weight 147,000 lbs.

LOCOMOTIVES, Elevations; 2-8-0 Type.

Fig. 98

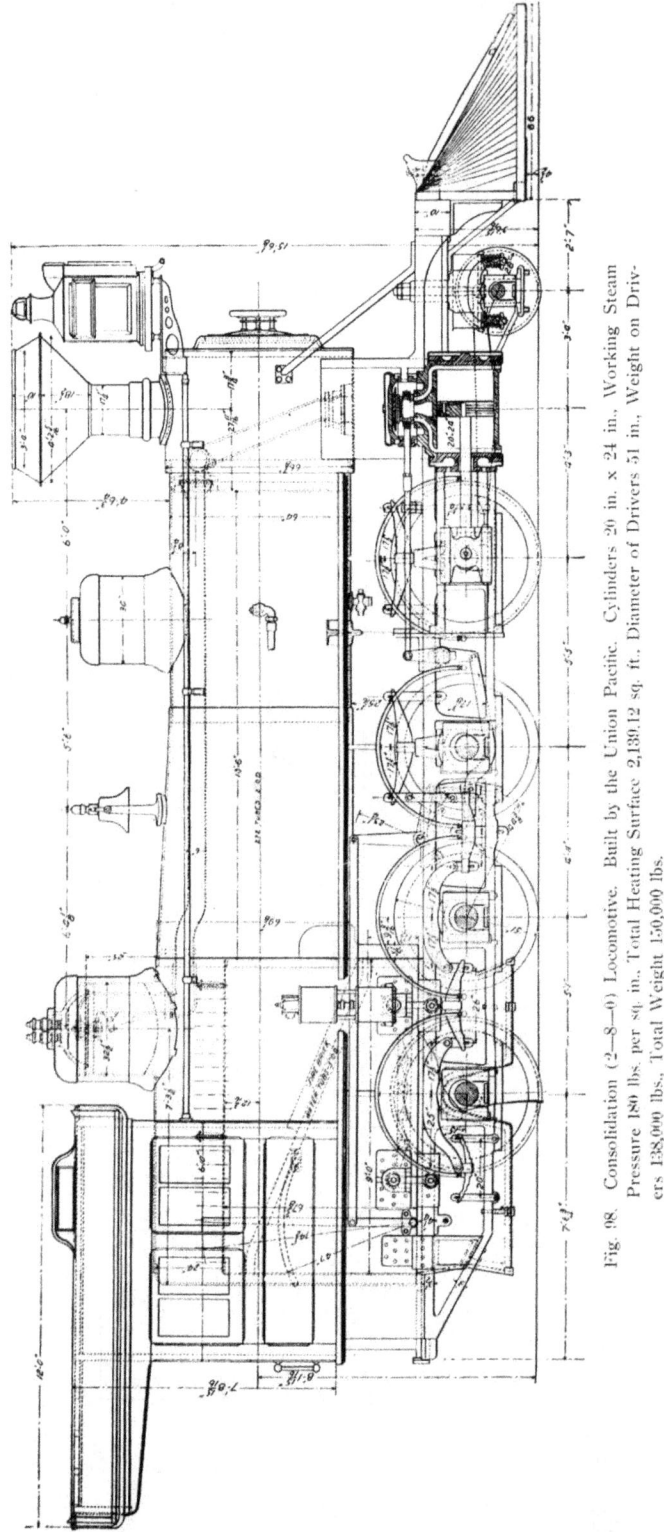

Fig. 98. Consolidation (2—8—0) Locomotive. Built by the Union Pacific. Cylinders 20 in. x 24 in., Working Steam Pressure 180 lbs. per sq. in., Total Heating Surface 2,130.12 sq. ft. Diameter of Drivers 51 in., Weight on Drivers 138,000 lbs., Total Weight 150,000 lbs.

Fig. 99 LOCOMOTIVES, Elevations; 2-8-2 Type.

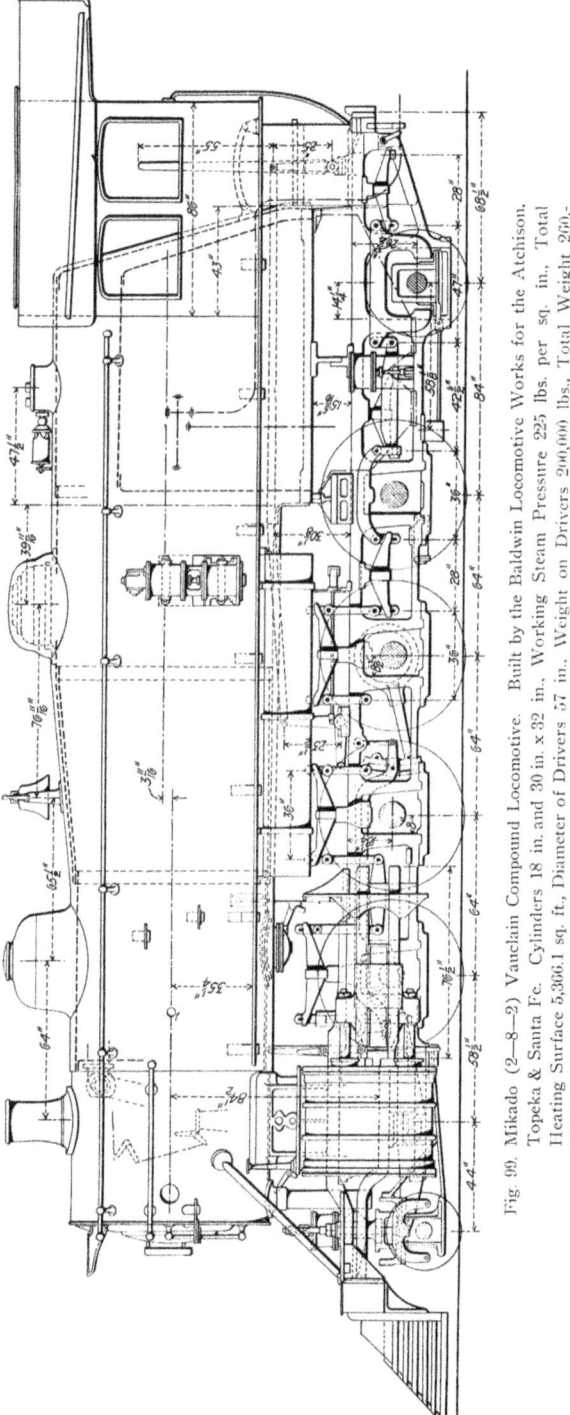

Fig. 99. Mikado (2—8—2) Vauclain Compound Locomotive. Built by the Baldwin Locomotive Works for the Atchison, Topeka & Santa Fe. Cylinders 18 in. and 30 in. x 32 in. Working Steam Pressure 225 lbs. per sq. in., Total Heating Surface 5,366.1 sq. ft, Diameter of Drivers 57 in. Weight on Drivers 200,000 lbs., Total Weight 260,000 lbs.

LOCOMOTIVES, Elevations; 2-8-2 Type.

Fig. 100

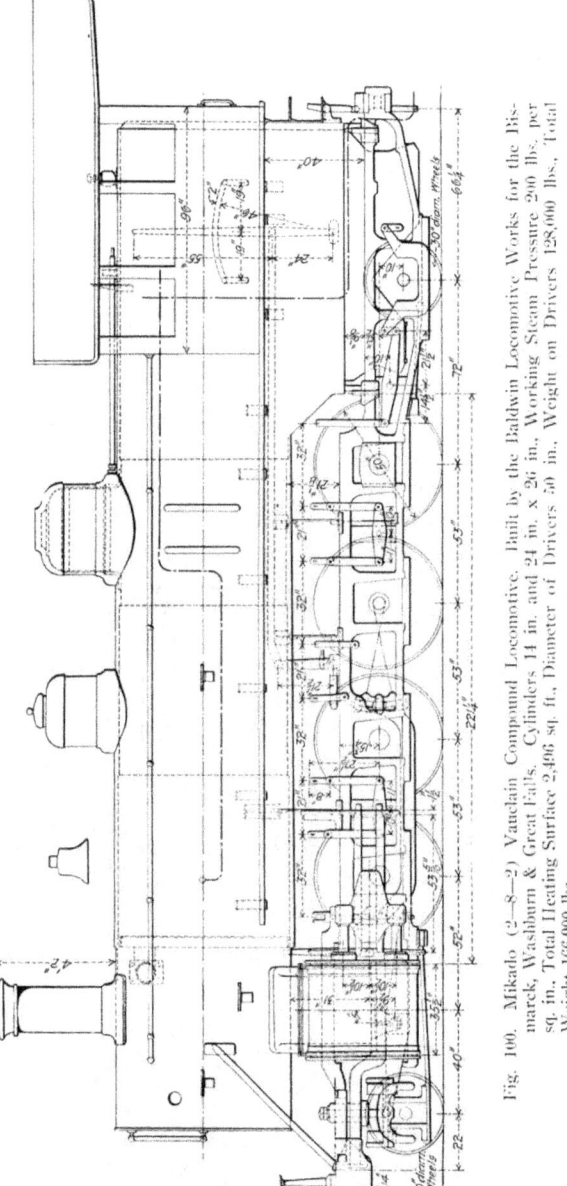

Fig. 100. Mikado (2—8—2) Vauclain Compound Locomotive. Built by the Baldwin Locomotive Works for the Bismarck, Washburn & Great Falls. Cylinders 14 in. and 24 in. x 26 in., Working Steam Pressure 200 lbs. per sq. in., Total Heating Surface 2,406 sq. ft., Diameter of Drivers 50 in., Weight on Drivers 128,000 lbs., Total Weight 166,900 lbs.

Numbers Refer to List of Names of Parts with Figs. 76-77.

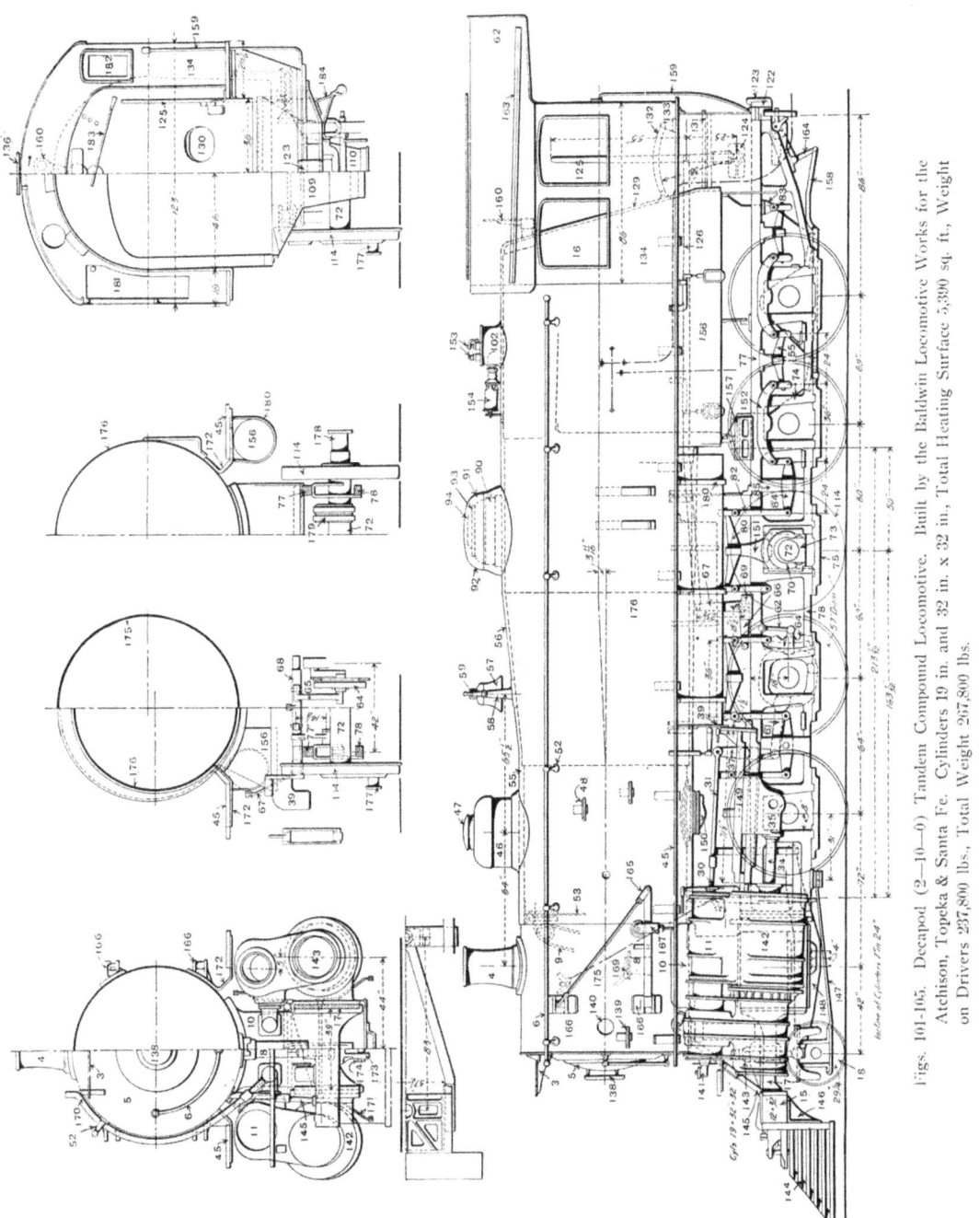

Figs. 101-105. Decapod (2—10—0) Tandem Compound Locomotive. Built by the Baldwin Locomotive Works for the Atchison, Topeka & Santa Fe. Cylinders 19 in. and 32 in. x 32 in., Total Heating Surface 5,300 sq. ft., Weight on Drivers 237,800 lbs., Total Weight 267,800 lbs.

LOCOMOTIVES, Elevations; 4-4-0 Type.

Fig. 106

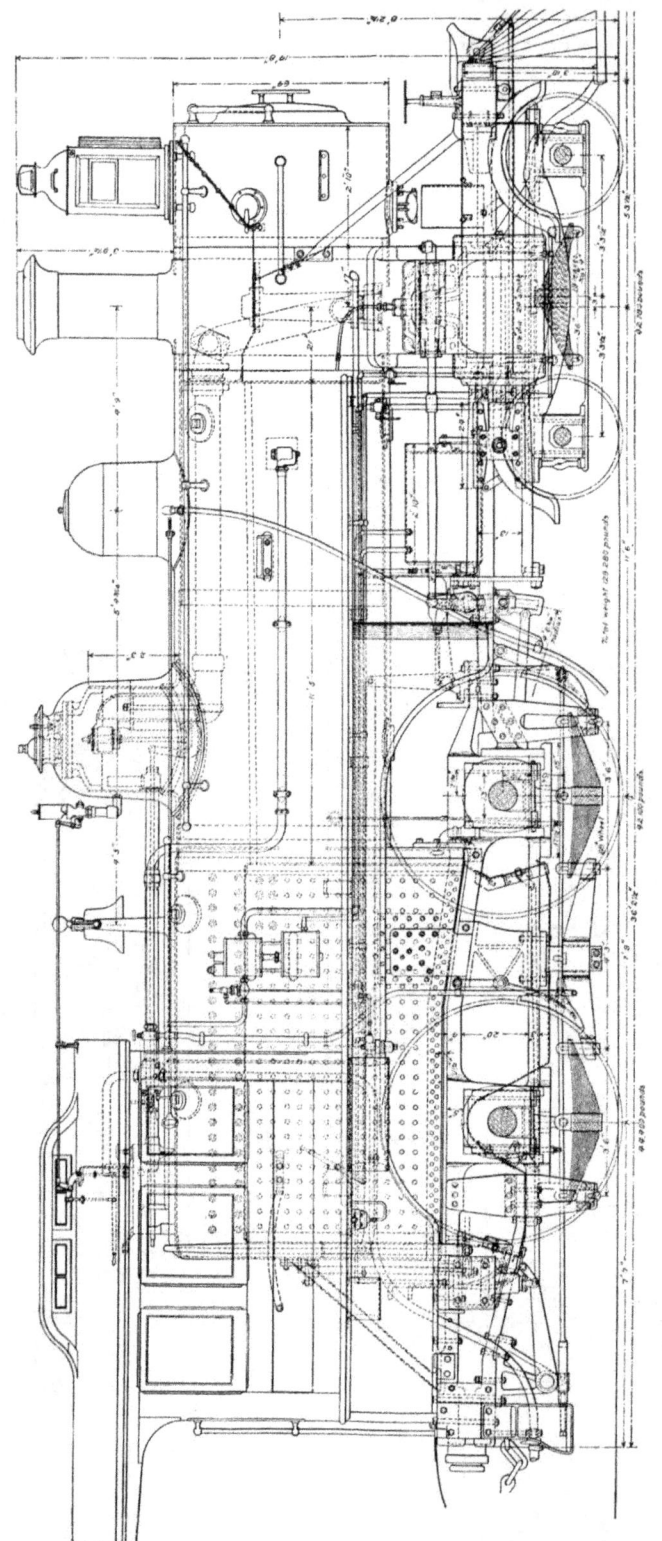

Fig. 106. Eight-Wheel American (4-4-0) Type Locomotive. Built by the American Locomotive Co. for the Cleveland, Cincinnati, Chicago & St. Louis. Cylinders 18½ in. x 24 in., Working Steam Pressure 175 lbs. per sq. in., Total Heating Surface 1,578 sq. ft., Diameter of Drivers 68 in., Weight on Drivers 90,000 lbs., Total Weight 139,000 lbs.

Fig. 107 — LOCOMOTIVES, Elevations; 4-4-0 Type.

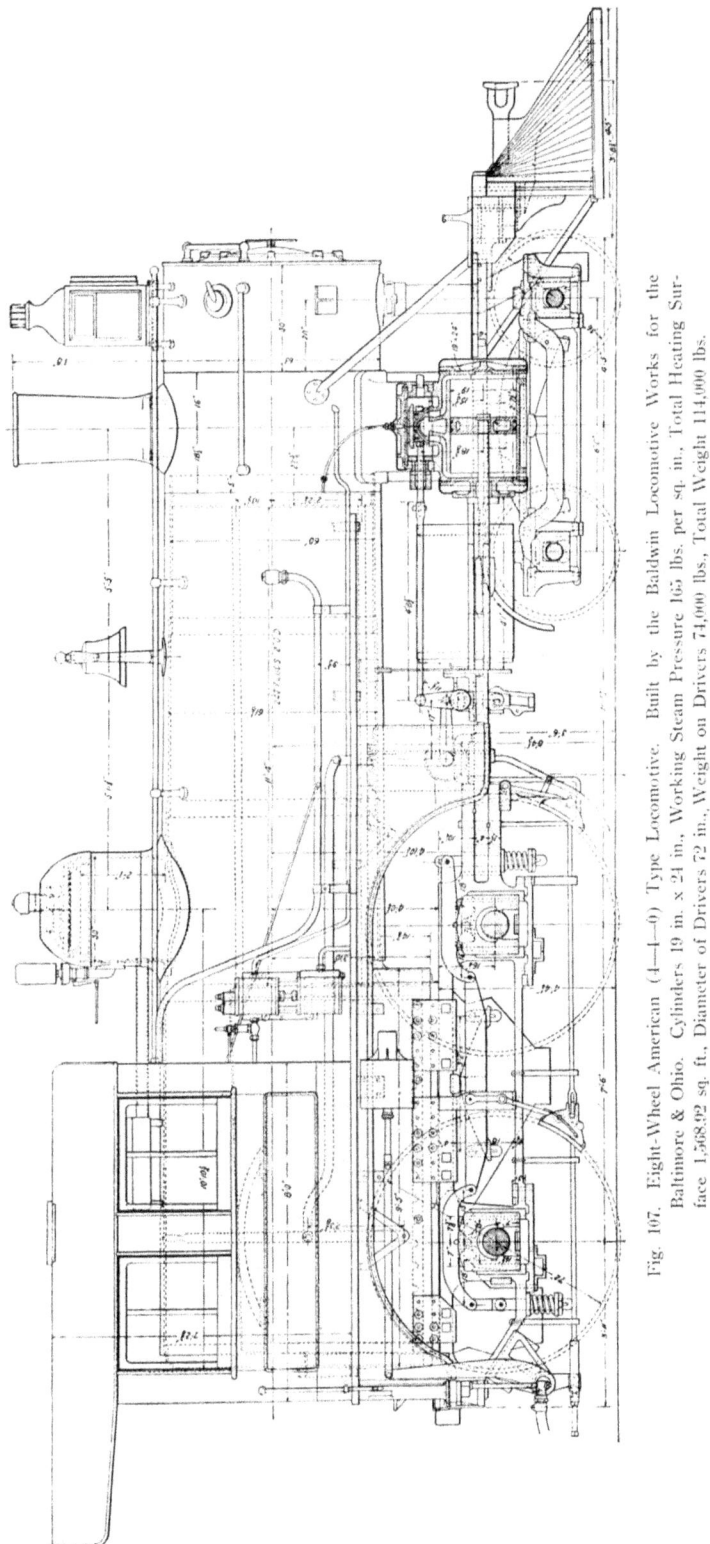

Fig. 107. Eight-Wheel American (4—4—0) Type Locomotive. Built by the Baldwin Locomotive Works for the Baltimore & Ohio. Cylinders 19 in. x 24 in., Working Steam Pressure 165 lbs. per sq. in., Total Heating Surface 1,568.92 sq. ft., Diameter of Drivers 72 in., Weight on Drivers 74,000 lbs., Total Weight 114,000 lbs.

LOCOMOTIVES, Elevations; 4-4-0 Type.

Fig. 108

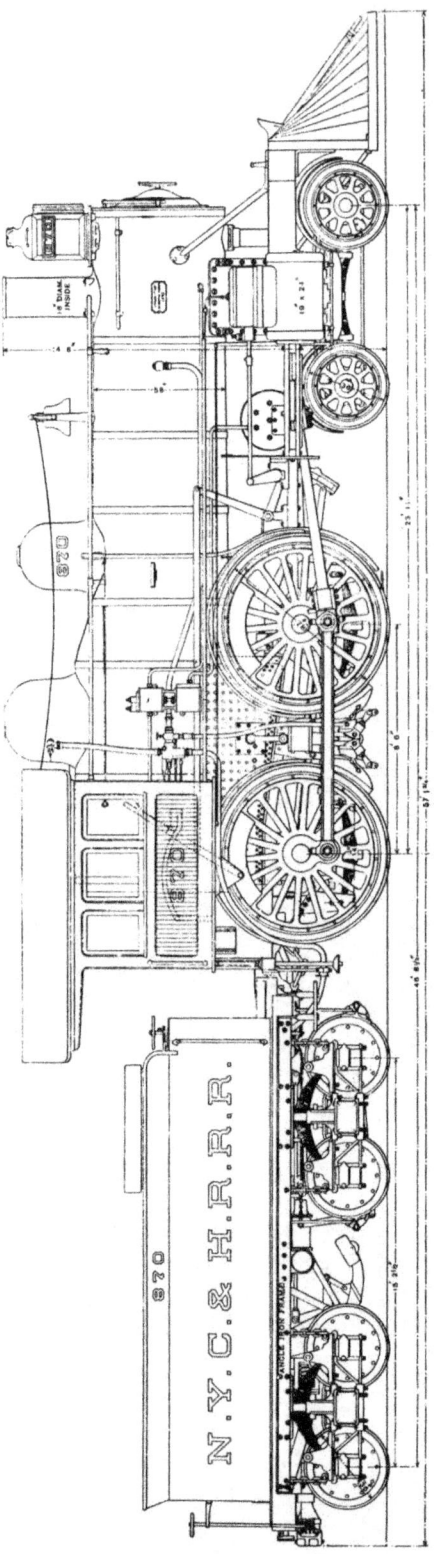

Fig. 108. Eight-Wheel American (4—4—0) Type Locomotive. Built by the American Locomotive Co. for the New York Central & Hudson River. Cylinders 19 in. x 24 in., Working Steam Pressure 180 lbs. per sq. in., Total Heating Surface 1,833.8 sq. ft., Diameter of Drivers 78 in., Weight on Drivers 82,000 lbs., Total Weight 126,000 lbs.

LOCOMOTIVES, Elevations; 4-4-0 and 4-4-2 Types.

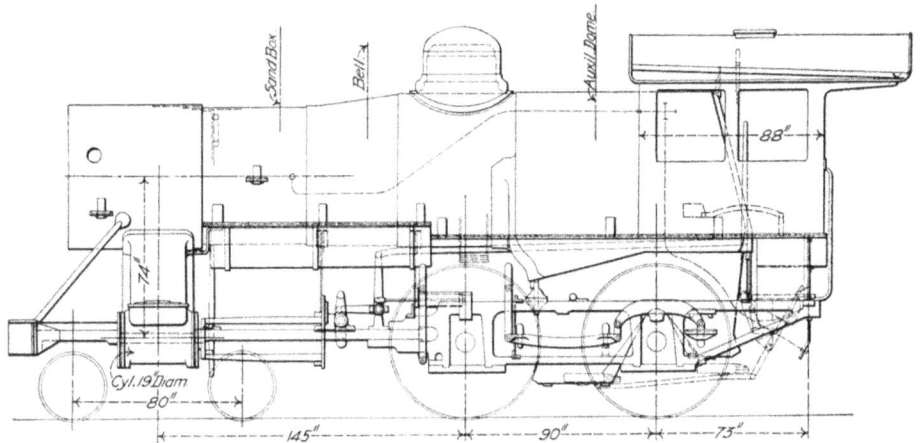

Fig. 109. Outline of Eight-Wheel American (4—4—0) Type Locomotive. Built by the Baldwin Locomotive Works.

Numbers Refer to List of Names of Parts with Figs. 76-77.

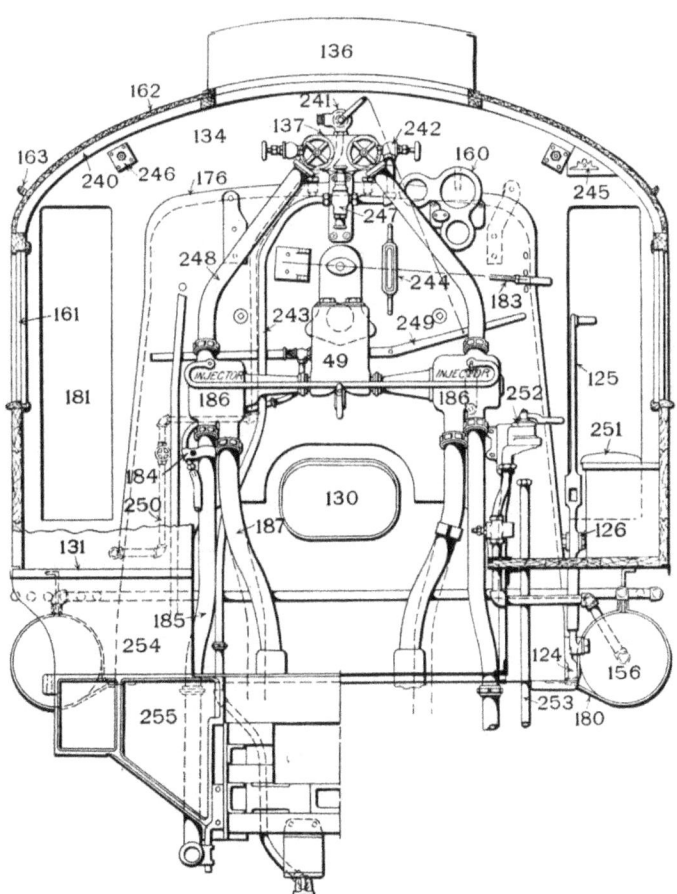

Fig. 110. Part Rear Elevation and Section Through Cab of Atlantic (4—4—2) Locomotive. Pennsylvania Railroad.

LOCOMOTIVES, Elevations; 4-4-2 Type. Fig. 111

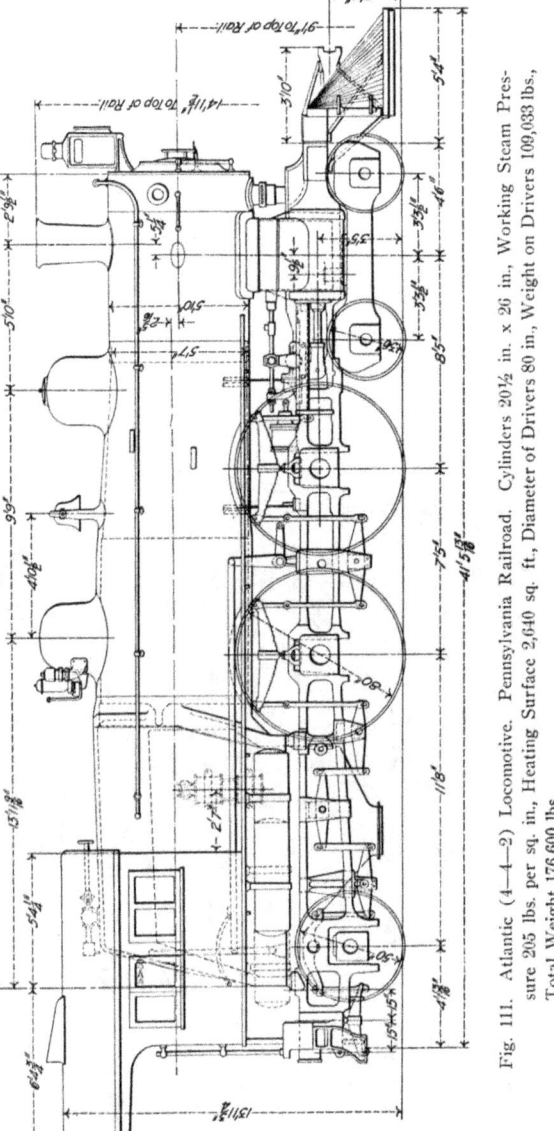

Fig. 111. Atlantic (4—4—2) Locomotive. Pennsylvania Railroad. Cylinders 20½ in. x 26 in., Working Steam Pressure 205 lbs. per sq. in., Heating Surface 2,640 sq. ft, Diameter of Drivers 80 in., Weight on Drivers 109,033 lbs., Total Weight 176,600 lbs.

LOCOMOTIVES, Elevations; 4-4-2 Type.

Numbers Refer to List of Names of Parts with Figs. 76-77.

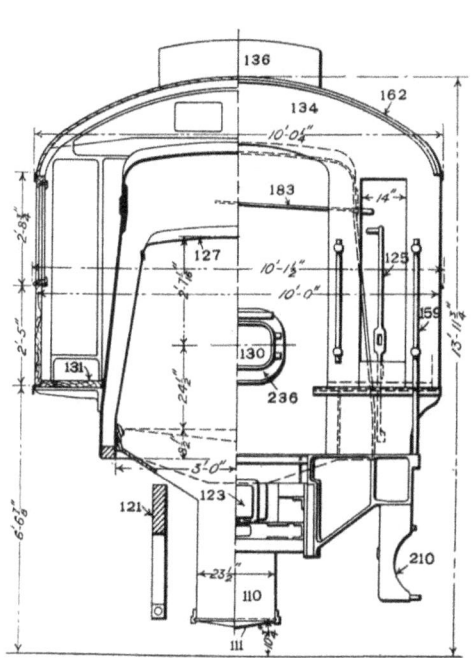

Fig. 112. Half Rear Elevation and Section at Fire-Box.

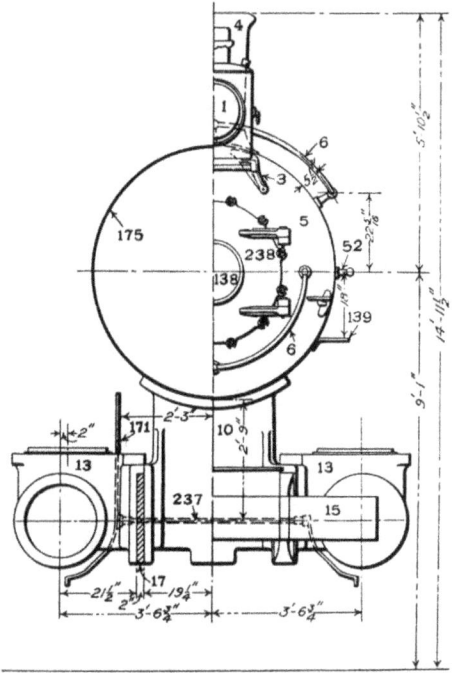

Fig. 113. Half Front Elevation and Section at Cylinders.

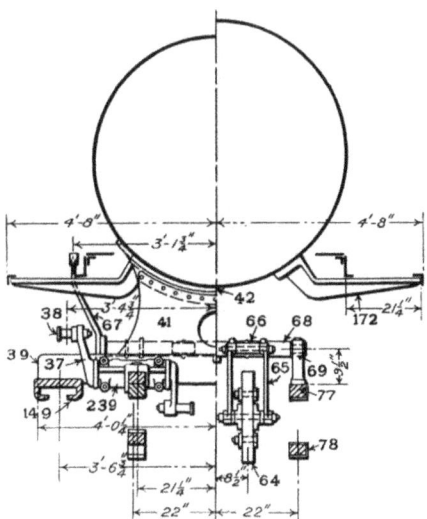

Fig. 114. Cross-Section at Link Motion.

Figs. 112-114. Sections of Atlantic (4—4—2) Locomotive. Pennsylvania Railroad.

LOCOMOTIVES, Elevations; 4-4-2 Type. Fig. 115

Numbers Refer to List of Names of Parts with Figs. 76-77.

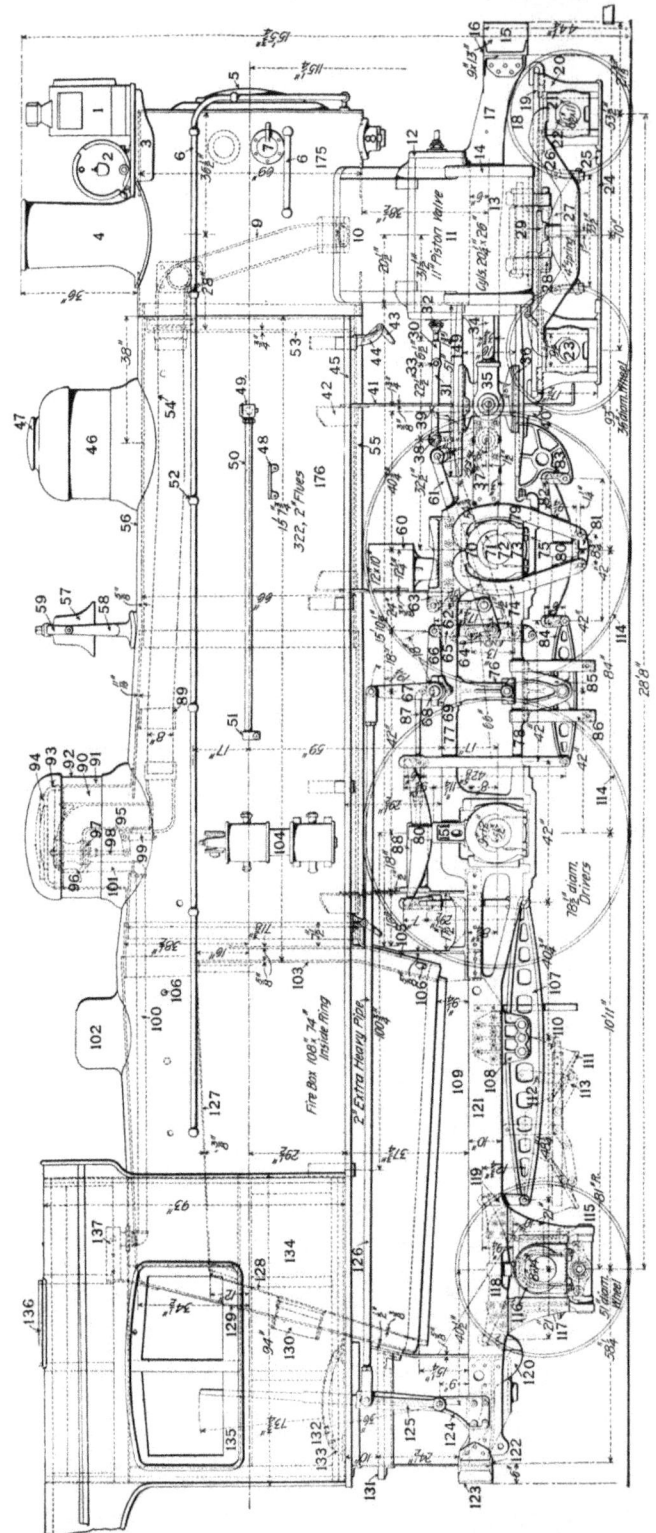

Fig. 115. Atlantic (4—4—2) Locomotive. Built by the American Locomotive Co. for the Chicago, Rock Island & Pacific. Cylinders 20¼ in. x 26 in., Total Heating Surface 2,806 sq. ft., Weight on Drivers 93,500 lbs., Total Weight 167,500 lbs.

Fig. 116 LOCOMOTIVES, Elevations; 4-4-2 Type.

Numbers Refer to List of Names of Parts with Figs. 76-77.

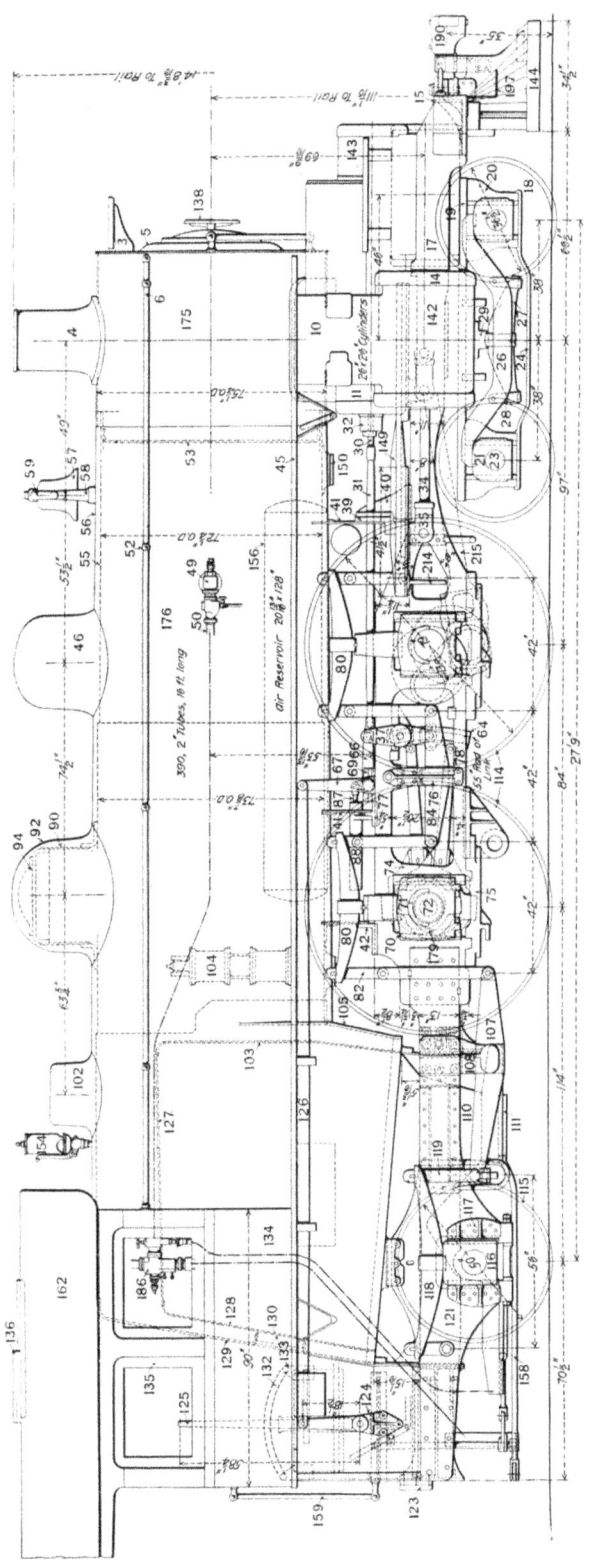

Fig. 116. Atlantic (4-4-2) Cole Four-Cylinder Balanced Compound Locomotive. Built by the American Locomotive Co. for the New York Central & Hudson River. Cylinders 15½ in. and 26 in. x 26 in., Heating Surface 3,416 sq. ft., Diameter of Drivers 79 in., Weight on Drivers 121,600 lbs., Total Weight 200,000 lbs.

LOCOMOTIVES, Elevations; 4-4-2 Type. Figs. 117-118

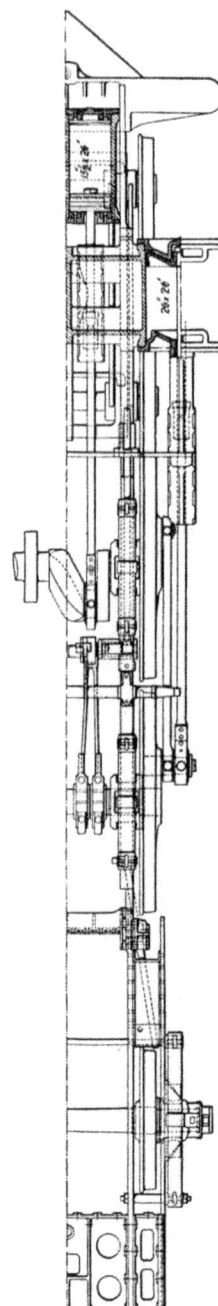

Fig. 117. Half Plan of Cylinders and Rods of Cole Four-Cylinder Balanced Compound Atlantic (4-4-2) Locomotive.

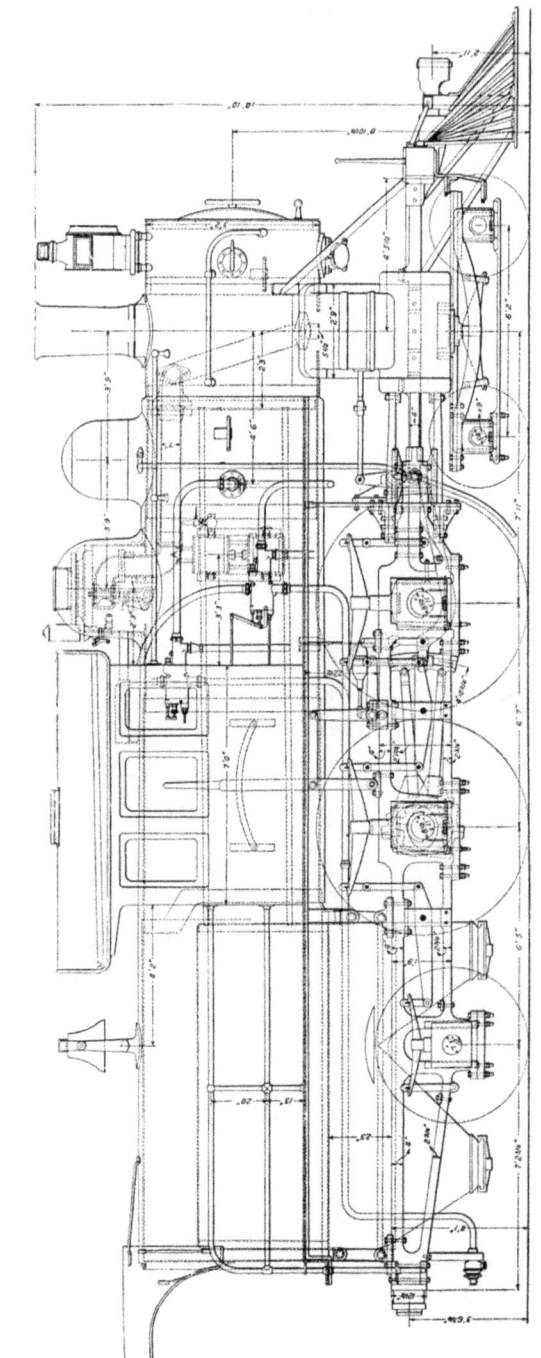

Fig. 118. Atlantic (4-4-2) Locomotive. Built by the Baldwin Locomotive Works for the Lehigh Valley. Cylinders 19 in. x 26 in., Working Steam Pressure 180 lbs. per sq. in., Diameter of Drivers 76 in., Weight on Drivers 82,000 lbs, Total Weight 141,000 lbs.

Fig. 119   LOCOMOTIVES, Elevations; 4-6-0 Type.

Numbers Refer to List of Names of Parts with Figs. 76-77.

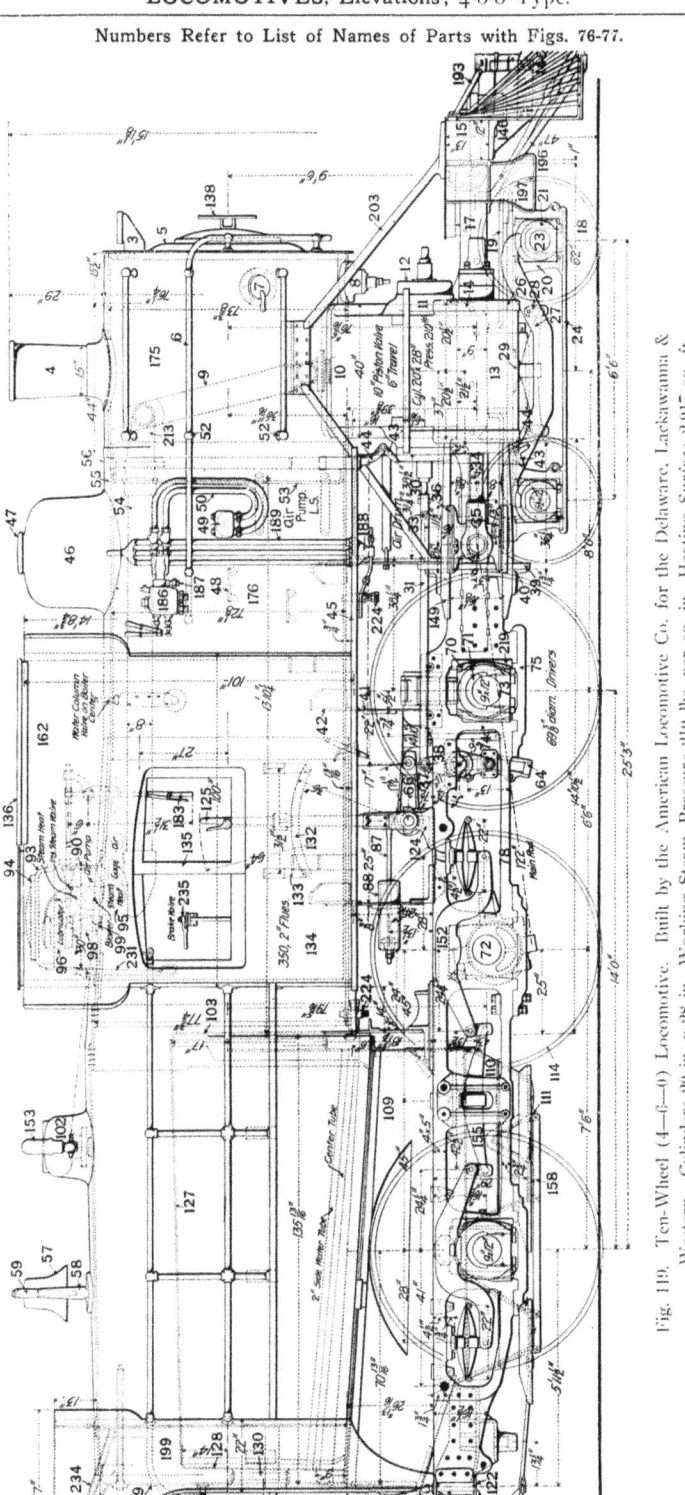

Fig. 119. Ten-Wheel (4—6—0) Locomotive. Built by the American Locomotive Co. for the Delaware, Lackawanna & Western. Cylinders 20 in. x 28 in., Working Steam Pressure 210 lbs. per sq. in., Heating Surface 2,917 sq. ft., Diameter of Drivers 80 in., Weight on Drivers 137,000 lbs., Total Weight 170,000 lbs.

LOCOMOTIVES, Elevations; 4-6-0 Type. Fig. 120

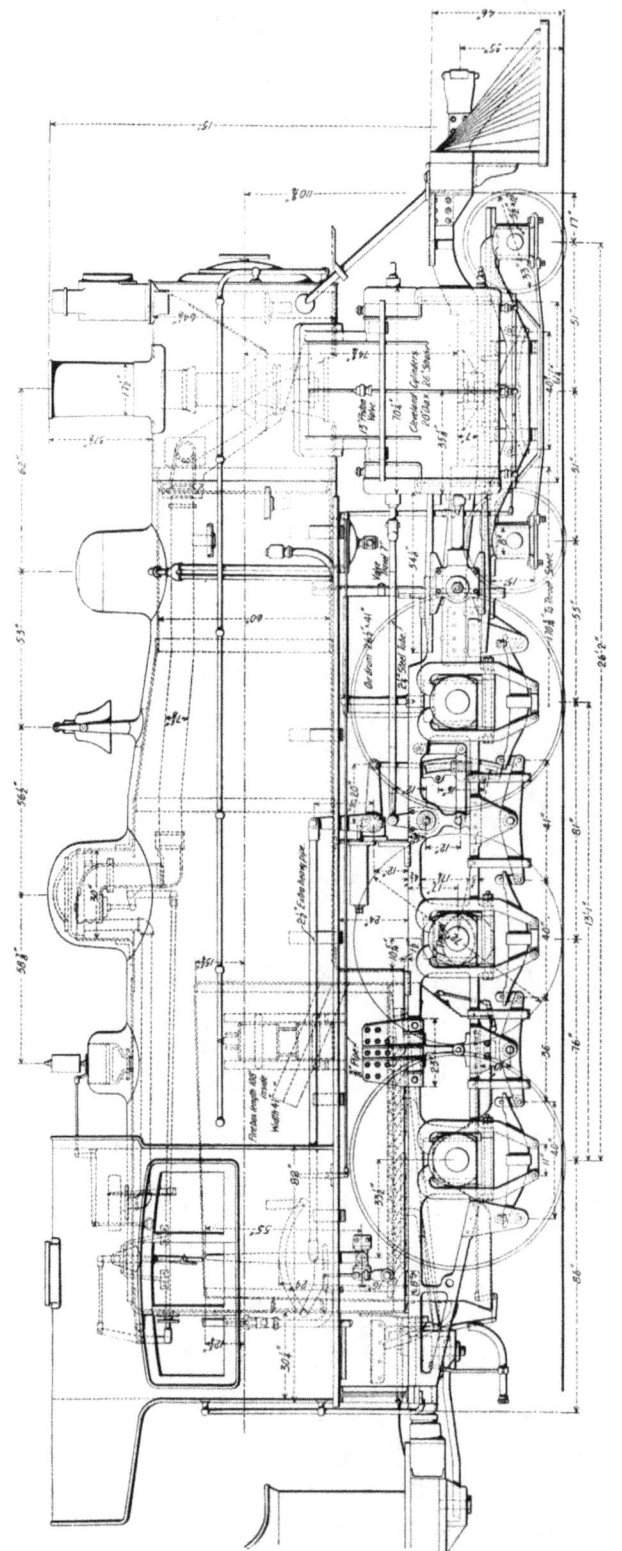

Fig. 120. Ten-Wheel (4—6—0) Locomotive with Cleveland Cylinders. Built by the American Locomotive Co. for the Intercolonial Railway. Cylinders 20 in. x 26 in., Working Steam Pressure 200 lbs. per sq. in., Heating Surface 2,200 sq. ft., Diameter of Drivers 72 in., Weight on Drivers 124,000 lbs., Total Weight 170,000 lbs.

Fig. 121 LOCOMOTIVES, Elevations; 4-6-0 Type.

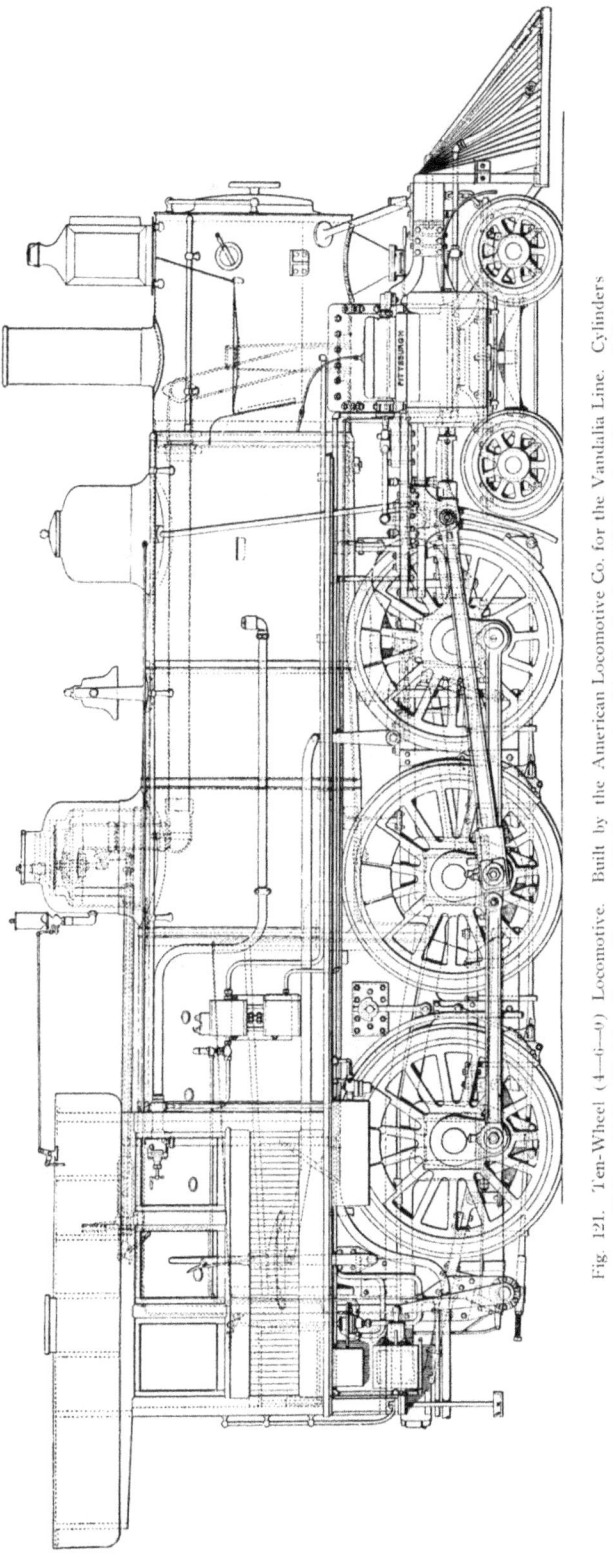

Fig. 121. Ten-Wheel (4—6—0) Locomotive. Built by the American Locomotive Co. for the Vandalia Line. Cylinders 20 in. x 26 in., Working Steam Pressure 180 lbs. per sq. in., Heating Surface 2,236 sq. ft, Diameter of Drivers 72 in., Weight on Drivers 110,000 lbs., Total Weight 138,000 lbs.

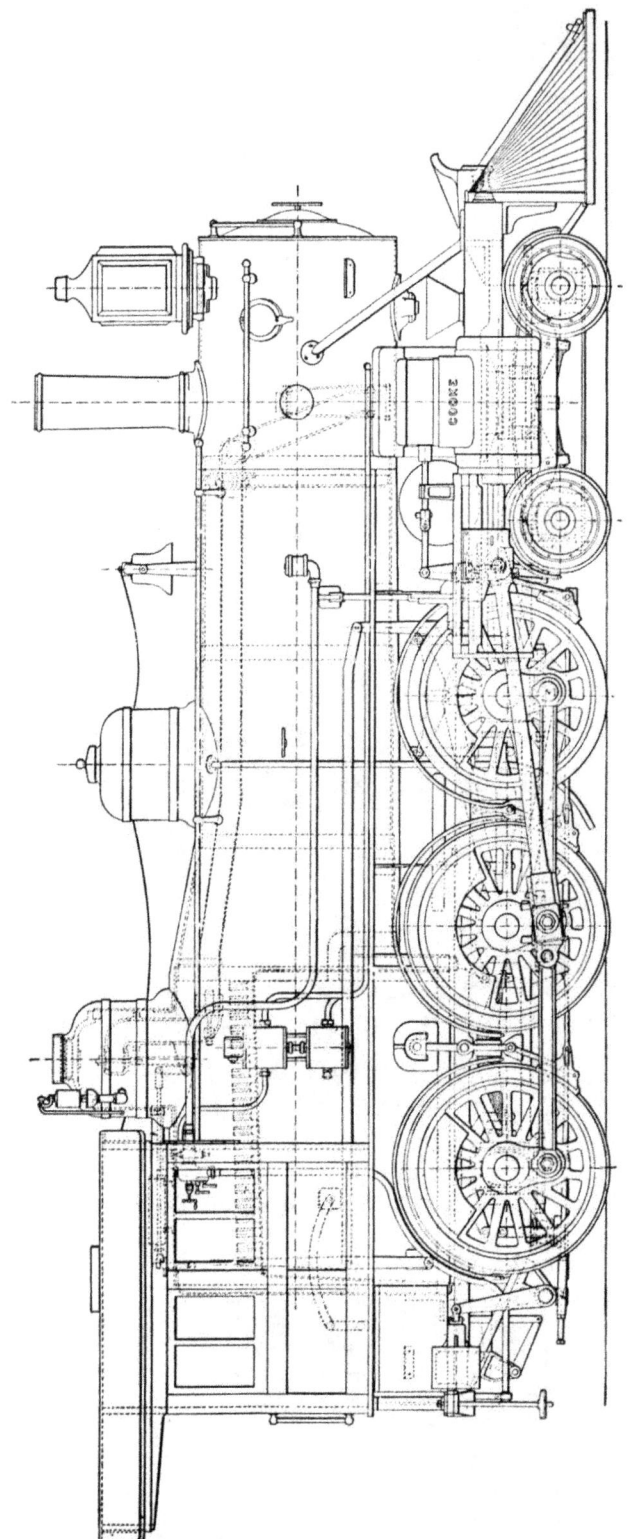

Fig. 122. Ten-Wheel (4—6—0) Locomotive. Built by the American Locomotive Co. for the Southern Pacific. Cylinders 20 in. x 26 in., Working Steam Pressure 180 lbs. per sq. in., Heating Surface 1,871.5 sq. ft., Diameter of Drivers 63 in., Weight on Drivers 100,000 lbs., Total Weight 140,000 lbs.

Fig. 123 LOCOMOTIVES, Elevations; 4-6-2 Type.

Numbers Refer to List of Names of Parts with Figs. 76-77.

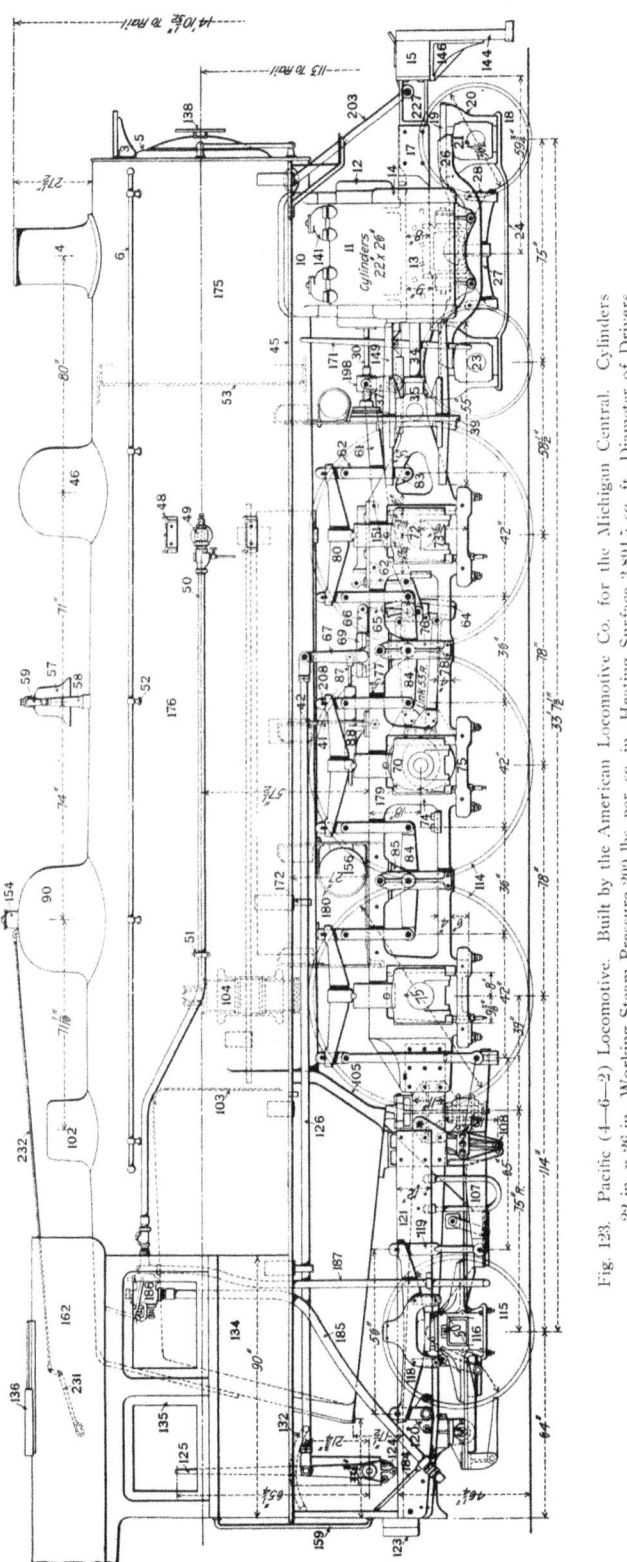

Fig. 123. Pacific (4-6-2) Locomotive. Built by the American Locomotive Co. for the Michigan Central. Cylinders 22 in. x 26 in., Working Steam Pressure 200 lbs. per sq. in., Heating Surface 3,894.5 sq. ft., Diameter of Drivers 75 in., Weight on Drivers 140,500 lbs., Total Weight 221,000 lbs.

LOCOMOTIVES, Elevations; 4-8-0 Type.

Fig. 124

Numbers Refer to List of Names of Parts with Figs. 76-77.

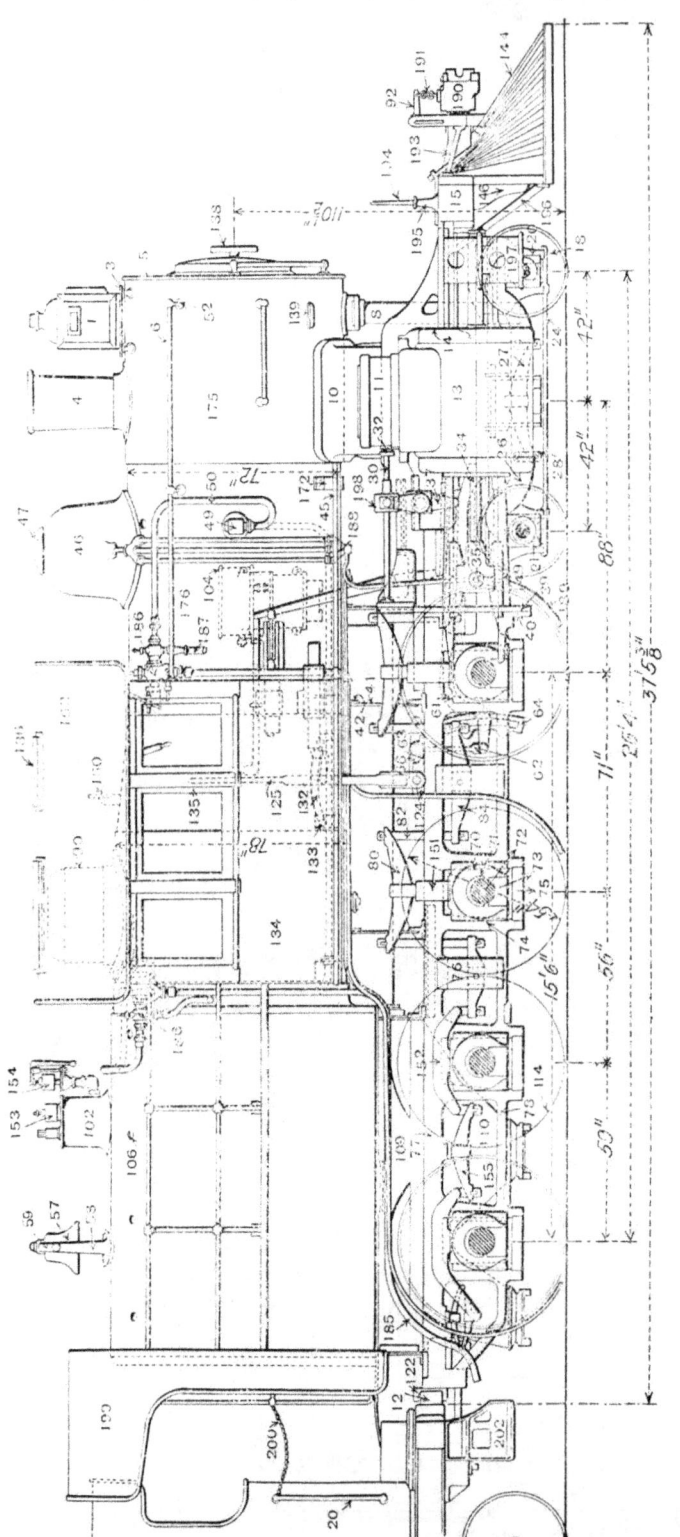

Fig. 124. Twelve Wheel (4-8-0) Compound Locomotive. Chicago & Eastern Illinois. Cylinders 21½ in. and 33 in. × 26 in. Heating Surface 2,417 sq. ft. Diameter of Drivers 51 in. Weight on Drivers 160,000 lbs. Total Weight 189,700 lbs.

(71)

Fig. 125 — LOCOMOTIVES, Elevations; 4-8-0 Type.

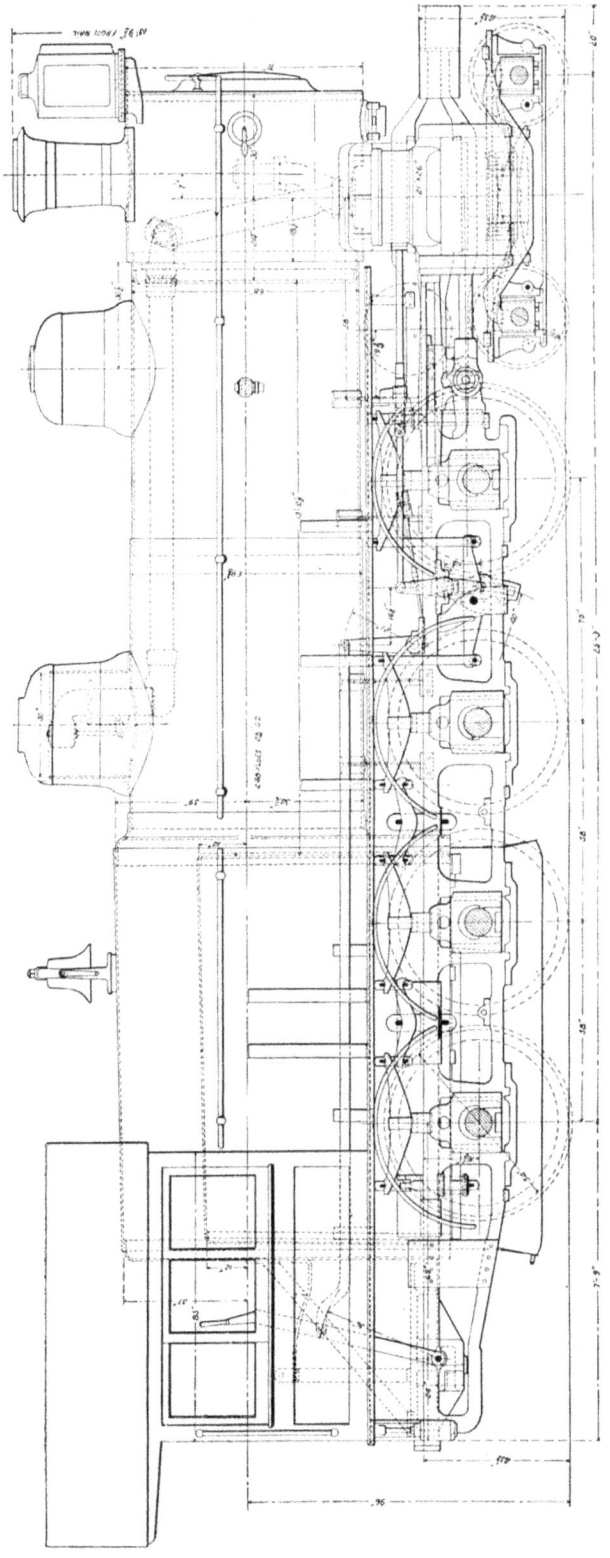

Fig. 125. Twelve-Wheel (4—8—0) Locomotive. Built by the American Locomotive Co. for the Central Railway of Brazil. Cylinders 21 in. x 26 in., Working Steam Pressure 180 lbs. per sq. in., Heating Surface 2,200 sq. ft., Diameter of Drivers 54 in., Weight on Drivers 139,000 lbs., Total Weight 169,000 lbs.

LOCOMOTIVES, Rack.

Figs. 126-129

Numbers Refer to List of Names of Parts Below.

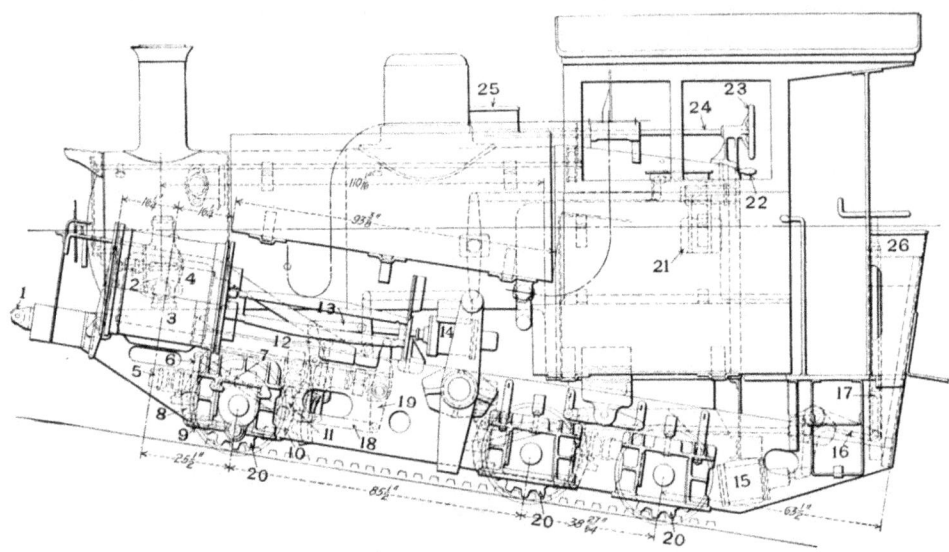

Fig. 126. Vauclain Compound Rack Locomotive. Built by the Baldwin Locomotive Works for the Manitou & Pike's Peak. Cylinders 10 in. and 15 in. x 24 in., Working Steam Pressure 210 lbs. per sq. in., Heating Surface 695 sq. ft., Weight 60,000 lbs., Tractive Effort 25,284 lbs.

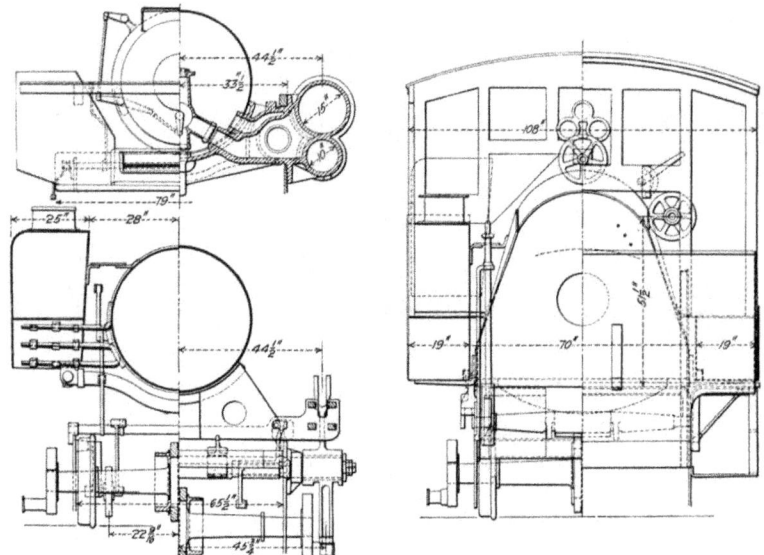

Figs. 127-129. Cross-Sections and Rear Elevation of Rack Locomotive.

Names of Parts of Rack Locomotive, Fig. 126.

1. Bumper Roller
2. Butterfly Valve
3. High Pressure Cylinder
4. Low Pressure Cylinder
5. Brake Crosstie, Front
6. Steam Brake Lever Link
7. Steam Brake Lever Connecting Rod
8. Front Steam Brake Lever
9. Steam Brake Jaw
10. Steam Brake Lever Rod
11. Back Steam Brake Lever
12. Steam Brake Shaft and Arm
13. Steam Brake Links
14. Rocking Lever
15. Steam Brake Cylinder, Back
16. Hand Brake Bell Crank
17. Hank Brake Shaft Jaw
18. Reverse Link Radius Rod
19. Rock Shaft
20. Rack Pinions
21. Reverse Screw Bearing
22. Reverse Screw Wheel
23. Throttle Valve Wheel
24. Throttle Valve Rod
25. Tank Funnel
26. Fender

Figs. 130-132   LOCOMOTIVES. Geared; Shay.

Fig. 130. Twelve-Wheel Shay Geared Locomotive. Built by the Lima Locomotive & Machine Co. for the Tioga Lumber Co.

Fig. 131. Sixteen-Wheel Shay Geared Locomotive. Built by the Lima Locomotive & Machine Co. for the Chesapeake & Ohio. Cylinders 3 Vertical 17 in. x 18 in., Working Steam Pressure 200 lbs. per sq. in., Heating Surface 2,332 sq. ft., Diameter of Drivers 46 in., Weight on Drivers 330,600 lbs., Total Weight 339,600 lbs.

Fig. 132. Front Truck of Shay Geared Locomotive.

LOCOMOTIVES, Geared; Shay.

Fig. 133

Names of Parts of Shay Geared Locomotive, Fig. 133.

1 Cylinder	6 Right Truck Box Cap	11 Crank Shaft
2 Exhaust Pipe	7 Gear	12 Crank Box Cap
3 Exhaust Pipe Elbow	8 Coupling Ring	13 Cylinder Frame
4 Exhaust Reducer	9 Square Shaft	14 Tumbling Shaft
5 Line Shaft	10 Sleeve Coupling	15 Truss Rod End, Back

16 Truss Rod End, Front
17 Reverse Lever Shaft Arm
18 Coal Bunk
19 Water Tank
20 Rear Sand Box

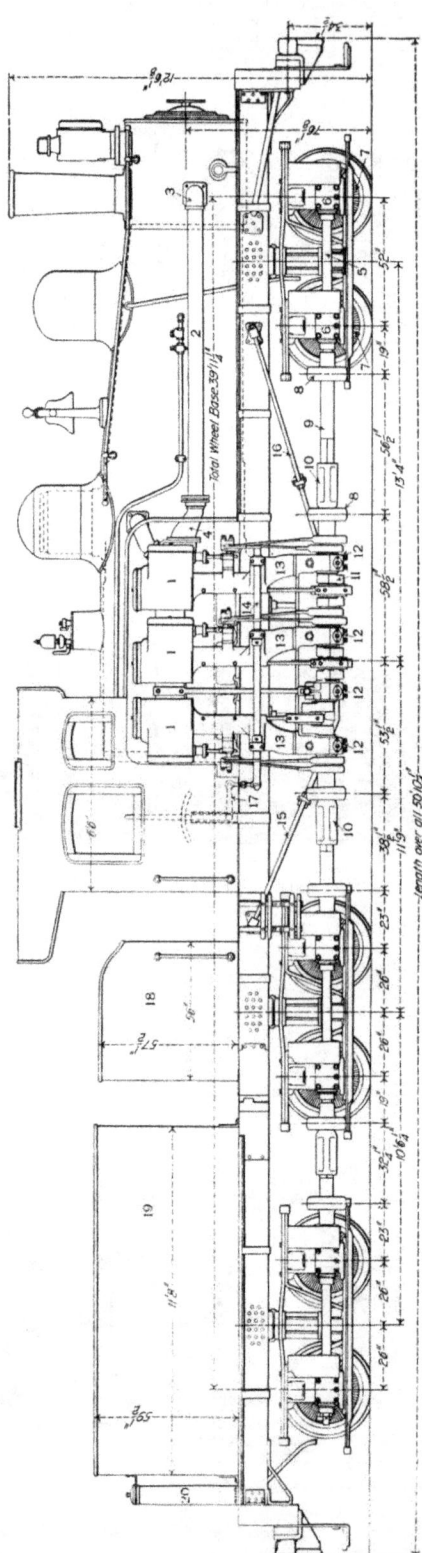

Fig. 133. Side Elevation of Twelve-Wheel Shay Geared Locomotive. Built by the Lima Locomotive & Machine Co. for the Tioga Lumber Co.

PRINCIPAL DIMENSIONS OF HEAVY AMERICAN LOCOMOTIVES.

Type.	Name of railroad.	When built.	Name of builder.	Simple or Compound.	Weight On dvrs. lbs.	Weight Total. lbs.	Diameter of cylinders. in.	Stroke of piston. in.	Diam. of drivers. in.	Type of boiler.	Working steam pressure. lbs.	Heating surface, total. sq. ft.	Tubes. No.	Tubes. Outside diam. in.	Tubes. Length. ft. in.	Firebox. Length. in.	Firebox. Width. in.	Grate area. sq. ft.	Tank capacity for water. gals.	Coal capacity. tons.
Six-wheel switcher 0-6-0	Pennsylvania	1904	Pennsylvania R. R.	Simple	170,000	170,000	22	24	56	Belpaire	205	2,495.1	325	2	13 10½	90	66	41.25	...	...
	Erie	1899	Erie Railroad	Simple	145,100	145,100	19	26	50	Straight top	180—200	1,879	290	2	11 6	113¾	66	52	4,500	6
Eight-wheel switcher 0-8-0	Ches. & Ohio	1903	American Loco. Co.	Simple	171,175	171,175	21	28	51	Wagon top	200	2,737	351	2	14 0	80	70	38.8	...	...
Ten-wheel switcher, 0-10-0	L. S. & M. S.	1905	American Loco. Co.	Simple	270,000	270,000	24	28	52	Radial wag. top	210	4,625	447	2	19 0	108	73	55	8,000	12
Mallet articulated, 0-6-6-0	Balto. & Ohio	1904	American Loco. Co.	Comp.	334,500	334,500	20—32	32	56	Straight top	235	5,585.7	436	2¼	21 0	108⅛	96¼	72.2	7,000	13
Mogul, 2-6-0	N. Y. C. & H. R.	1902	American Loco. Co.	Simple	128,000	166,000	20	24	63	Straight top	200	2,437	365	2	12 0	93	97⅛	63.2	...	...
Prairie, 2-6-2	L. S. & M. S.	1904	American Loco. Co.	Simple	166,000	233,000	21½	28	79	Ex'd wag. top, radial stay	200	3,905	322	2¼	19 6	109	74	55	7,800	15
	C., B. & Q.	1905	American Loco. Co.	Simple	154,000	212,500	22	28	69	Radial stay, straight top	210	3,513.9	301	2¼	19 0	109	73	54	6,000	16
	C., B. & Q.	1904	Baldwin Loco. Wks.	Simple	151,070	208,550	22	28	69	Straight top	210	3,575	301	2¼	19 0	108⅛	72¼	55	...	...
Consolidation, 2-8-0	Bess. & L. E.	1900	American Loco. Co.	Simple	225,200	250,300	24	32	54	Straight with slop'g b'k-end	220	3,805	406	2¼	15 0	132	40¼	36.8	7,500	14
	Lehigh Val.	1898	Baldwin Loco. Wks.	Vauclain comp.	205,232	228,082	18—30	30	55½	Wootten	200	4,145	502	2	15 0⅞	120	108	90	...	...
	Balto. & Ohio	1906	American Loco. Co.	Simple	185,900	208,500	22	30	60	Straight top	200	2,775.06	282	2¼	15 10	108⅛	75¼	56.5	7,000	12
	N. Y. C. & H. R.	1903	American Loco. Co.	Tandem comp.	200,000	225,000	16—30	30	51	Ext'd wag. top	200	4,142	507	2	14 9	105⅛	79⅝	58	...	...
Mikado, 2-8-2	No. Pacific	1904	American Loco. Co.	Tandem comp.	207,000	271,000	19—30	30	63	Radial ext'n'd wagon top	200	4,007	374	2	19 6	96	65	43.5	8,000	12
Decapod, 2-10-0	A., T. & S. F.	1902	Baldwin Loco. Wks.	Tandem comp.	237,800	267,800	19—32	32	57	Wagon top	225	5,390	463	2¼	19 0	108	78	58.5	7,000	10
Ten-coupled, 2-10-2	A., T. & S. F.	1903	Baldwin Loco. Wks.	Tandem comp.	234,580	287,240	19—32	32	57	Wagon top	225	4,796	391	2¼	20 0	108	78	58.5	...	...
Atlantic, 4-4-2	Erie	1905	American Loco. Co.	Cole bal. comp.	115,000	206,000	15½—26	26	78	Ex'd wag. top	220	3,622.02	388	2	17 0	108 1/16	75¼	56.3	8,500	16
	N. Y. C. & H. R.	1904	American Loco. Co.	Cole 4-cyl. bal. comp.	110,000	200,000	15½—26	26	79	Straight top	220	3,446	390	2	16 0	96⅛	75¼	50.3	6,000	10
	C., R. I. & P.	1905	Baldwin Loco. Wks.	Vauclain 4-cyl. bal. comp.	105,540	199,400	15—25	26	73	Ex'd wag. top	220	3,209	273	2¼	18 10	107 9/16	67¼	50.2	7,000	12
Ten-wheel, 4-6-0	D., L. & W.	1906	American Loco. Co.	Simple	154,000	201,000	22½	26	69	Straight top	215	3,378	398	2	15 3	126⅛	108¼	94.8	6,000	10
	Lehigh Val.	1905	American Loco. Co.	Simple	150,200	199,200	21	28	68½	Wootten	...	3,284.24	378	2	15 8	120⅛	102	85.08	7,500	12
	N. Y. C. & H. R.	1905	American Loco. Co.	Simple	148,000	194,500	22	26	69	Ex'd wag. top	200	3,305.5	400	2	14 11	105⅛	75¼	54.93	7,000	12
Pacific, 4-6-2	Oregon Ry. & Nav. Co.	1905	Baldwin Loco. Wks.	Vauclain 4-cyl. bal. comp.	143,600	231,300	17—28	28	77	Straight top	200	3,055	245	2¼	20 0	108	66	49.5	9,000	10
	A., T. & S. F.	1905	Baldwin Loco. Wks.	Vauclain 4-cyl.bal. comp.	151,900	226,700	17—28	28	73	Wagon top	220	3,595	290	2¼	20 0	108	71¼	...	8,500	*3,300
	Chic. & Alton	1904	Baldwin Loco. Wks.	Simple	135,510	221,500	22	28	77	Straight top	200	3,053	245	2¼	20 0	108	66	49.5	...	...
	Southern	1906	Baldwin Loco. Wks.	Simple	138,460	220,500	22	28	72½	Straight top	220	3,878.5	314	2¼	20 0	108¼	72½	54.25	7,500	12½
	N. Y. C. & H. R.	1904	American Loco. Co.	Simple	141,000	215,000	22	26	75	Straight top	200	3,776	303	2¼	20 0	96⅛	75¼	50.3	...	...
	C., R. I. & P.	1905	American Loco. Co.	Simple	133,800	206,000	22	26	69	Ex'd wag. top	200	3,354	328	2	18 7	96	67	44.8	7,500	13
Twelve-wheel, 4-8-0	Illinois Cent.	1899	American Loco. Co.	Simple	181,400	221,450	23	30	57	Belpaire	210	3,500	424	2	14 8¾	131	41¼	41.25	...	...

*Gals. oil.

BOILERS, General Views. Figs. 134-143

Numbers Refer to List of Names of Parts on Next Page.

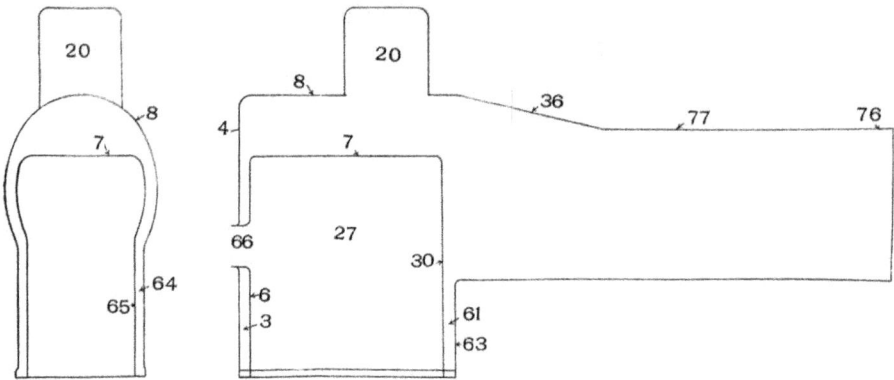

Figs. 134-135. Outline of Wagon Top Boiler with Narrow Firebox.

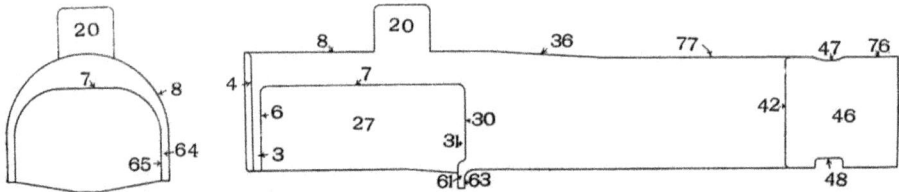

Figs. 136-137. Outline of Wagon Top Boiler with Wootten Firebox.

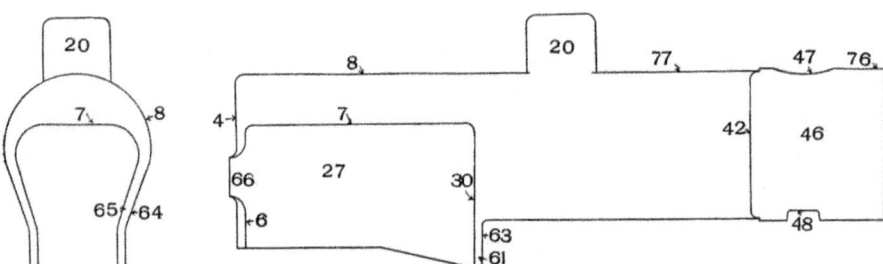

Figs. 138-139. Outline of Straight Top Boiler with Narrow Firebox.

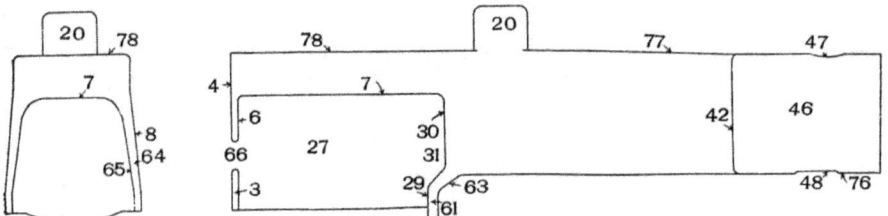

Figs. 140-141. Outline of Straight Top Boiler with Belpaire Firebox.

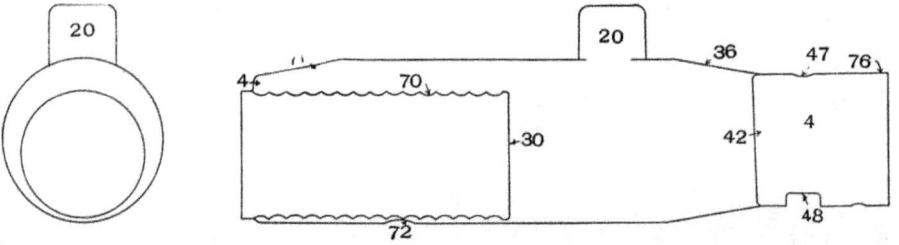

Figs. 142-143. Outline of Extended Wagon Top Boiler with Vanderbilt Corrugated Firebox.

Fig. 144   BOILERS, General Views.

Names of Parts of Boilers.

1 Foundation Ring
2 Grate Bar Thimble
3 Back Water Space
4 Back Head
5 Back Head Brace Angle
6 Back Sheet of Firebox
7 Crownsheet
7a Crownbar
8 Outside Firebox Sheet
9 Back Head Braces
10 Shell Feet for Back Head Braces
11 Back Head Brace Pins
12 Radial Stays for Crownsheet
13 Radial Stay Nuts
14 Sling Stay
15 Sling Stay T
16 Sling Stay Crownbar
17 Sling Stay Crownbar Bolts
18 Dome and Crown Stays
19 Dome Base or Flange
20 Dome
21 Dome Shell
22 Dome Cap
23 Dome Cover
23a Dome Casing
24 Throttle Case
25 Throttle Standpipe
26 Dry Pipe
27 Firebox
28 Staybolts
28a Throat Sheet
29 Inside Throat Sheet
30 Back Tubesheet
31 Combustion Chamber
32 Throat Brace
33 Tubes
34 Circumferential Riveting
35 Seam Lap
36 Conical Course of Shell
37 Second Course of Shell
38 First Course of Shell
39 Front Tube Sheet Brace
40 Shell Foot for Front Tubesheet Brace
41 Front Tubesheet Foot for Brace
42 Front Tubesheet
43 Dry Pipe Collar
44 Dry Pipe Stiffening Ring
45 Ball Joint for Tee Head
46 Smokebox
47 Smokebox Opening
48 Steam Pipe Opening
49 Smokebox Bottom Liner
50 Smokebox Ring
51 Front Smokebox Ring
52 Cinder Cleaning Hole
53 Cinder Hole
54 Sextuple Riveting
55 Outside Welt
56 Inside Welt
57 Shell Plate
58 Inside Injector Plate
59 Injector Hole
59a Injector Pipe
59b Injector Pipe Hanger
60 Washout or Handhole
60a Handhole Plate
60b Handhole Plate Bolt
60c Handhole Plate Gasket
60d Handhole Spider
60e Handhole Nipple
60f Handhole Nipple Cap
61 Front Water Space
62 Stiffening Liner for Shell Support
63 Outside Throat Sheet
64 Side Water Space
65 Side Sheet of Firebox
66 Firebox Door Opening
66a Firebox Door Ring
67 Tube Opening in Back Tubesheet
68 Tube Opening in Front Tubesheet
69 Steam Pipe Opening in Front Tubesheet
70 Corrugated Flue Firebox
71 Back Course of Stayless Boiler
72 Ash Dump in Stayless Boiler
73 Cleaning Plug for Combustion Chamber
74 Dome Stiffening Ring
75 Tubesheet Brace
76 Smokebox Shell
77 Barrel or Shell
78 Outside Crownsheet
79 Expansion Pad
80 Smokebox and Shell Ring
81 Feed Pipe
82 Feed Pipe Hanger
83 Firebox Cross Stays
84 Throttle Valve Stem
85 Throttle Bell Crank
86 Throttle Stem
86a Throttle Stem Bracket
87 Dry Pipe and Throttle Pipe Clamp Bolts
88 Throttle Valve
89 Fusible Plug
90 Furnace Head
91 Furnace Head Lining
92 Bridge Wall
93 Bridge Wall Support
94 Buckle Plate Tee
95 Brace for Front
96 Brick Arch
97 Brick Ashpan Floor
98 Ashpan
98a Ashpan Supporting Angles
99 Waterleg, Back
100 Waterleg, Front
101 Waterleg, Side

Fig. 144. Extended Wagon Top Boiler with Narrow Firebox, Mounted on Frames.

BOILERS, General Views.

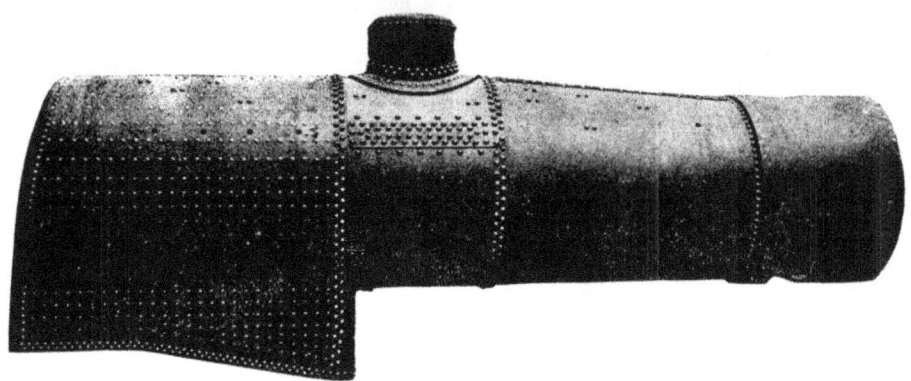

Fig. 145. Extended Wagon Top Boiler with Narrow Firebox.

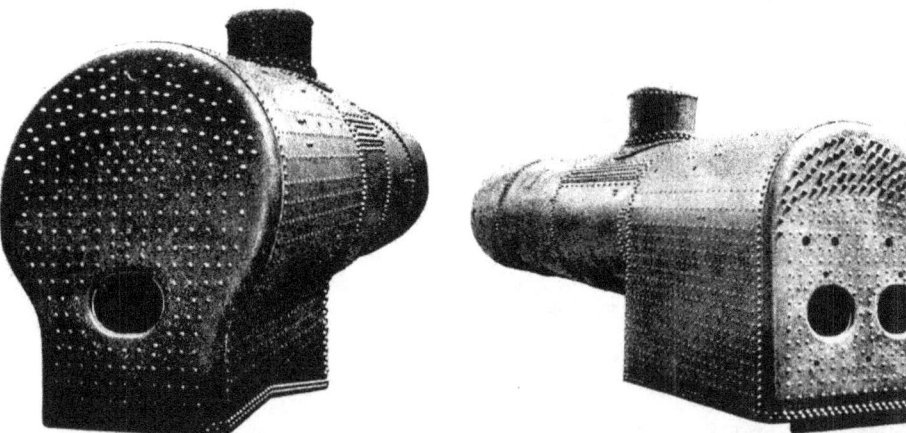

Fig. 146. Rear End View of Extended Wagon Top Boiler with Narrow Firebox.

Fig. 147. Rear End View of Extended Wagon Top Boiler with Wide Firebox.

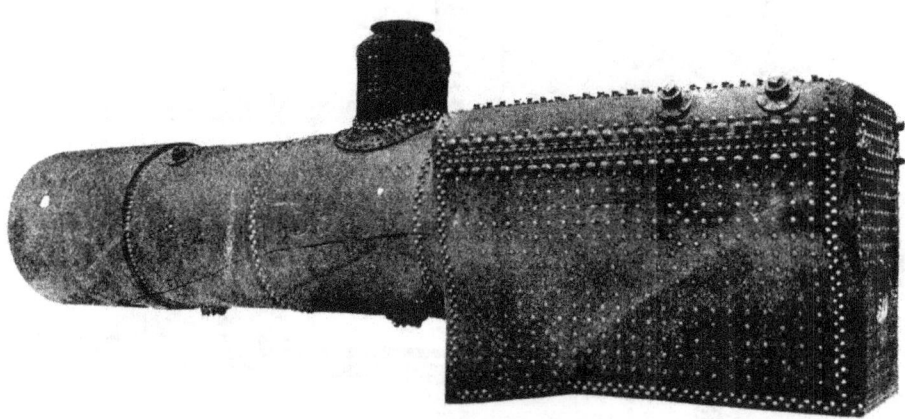

Fig. 148. Straight Top Boiler with Belpaire Firebox.

Fig 149   BOILERS, Sections; Wagon Top.

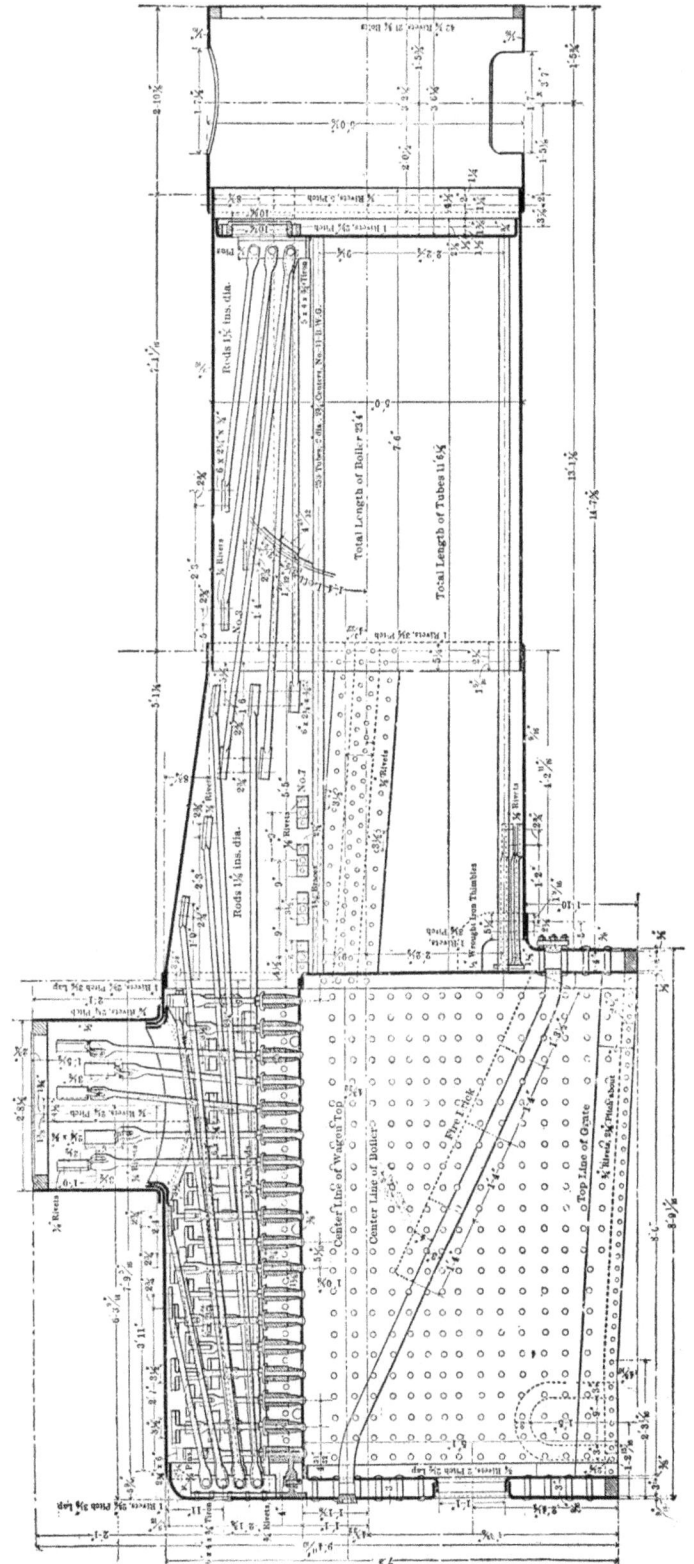

Fig. 149. Longitudinal Section Through Wagon Top Boiler with Narrow Firebox. Eight-Wheel (4—4—0) Locomotive. Union Pacific.

BOILERS, Sections; Wagon Top. Fig. 150

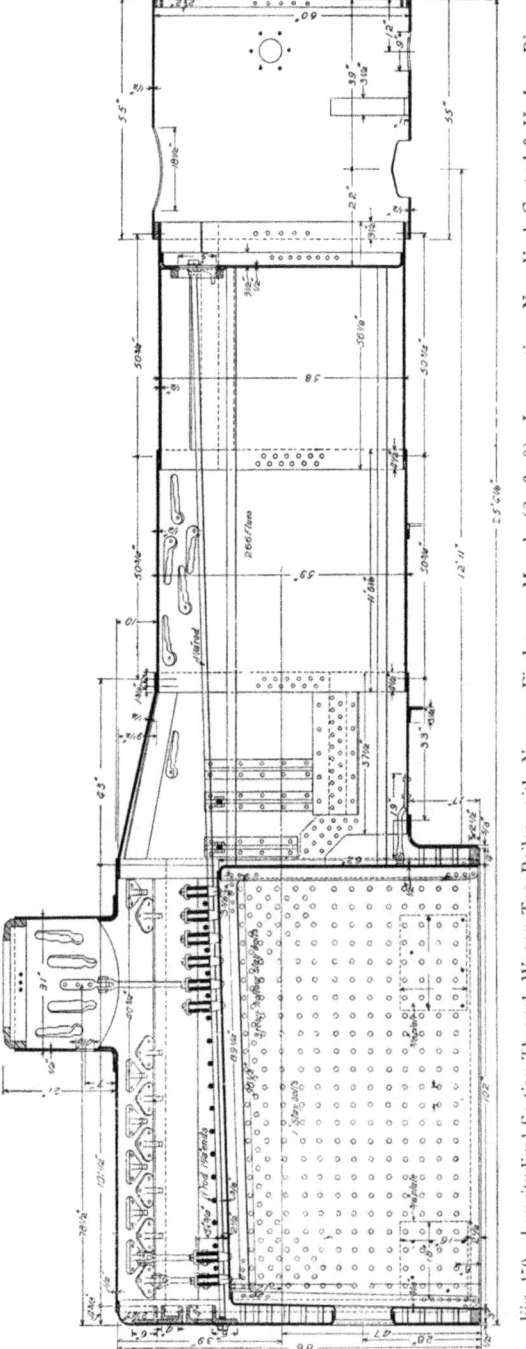

Fig. 150. Longitudinal Section Through Wagon Top Boiler with Narrow Firebox. Mogul (2—6—0) Locomotive. New York Central & Hudson River.

Figs. 151-156   BOILERS, Sections; Wagon Top and Extended Wagon Top.

Numbers Refer to List of Names of Parts with Fig. 144.

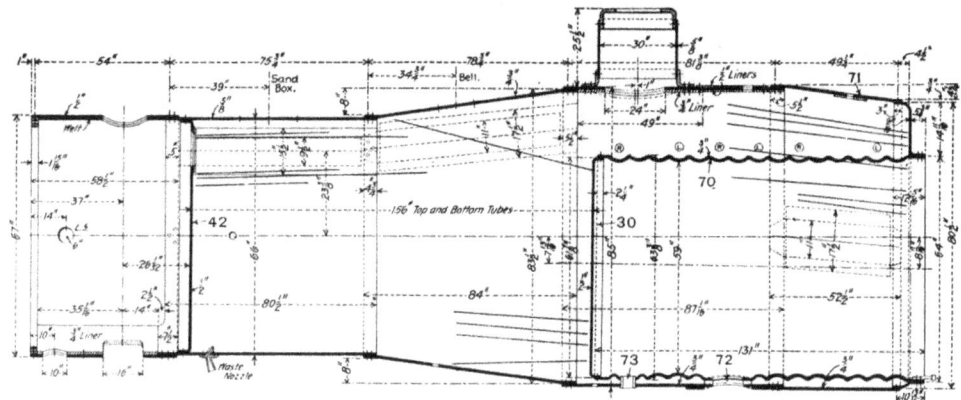

Fig. 151. Longitudinal Section Through Wagon Top Boiler with Vanderbilt Corrugated Firebox. **Ten-Wheel (4—6—0)** Locomotive. Illinois Central.

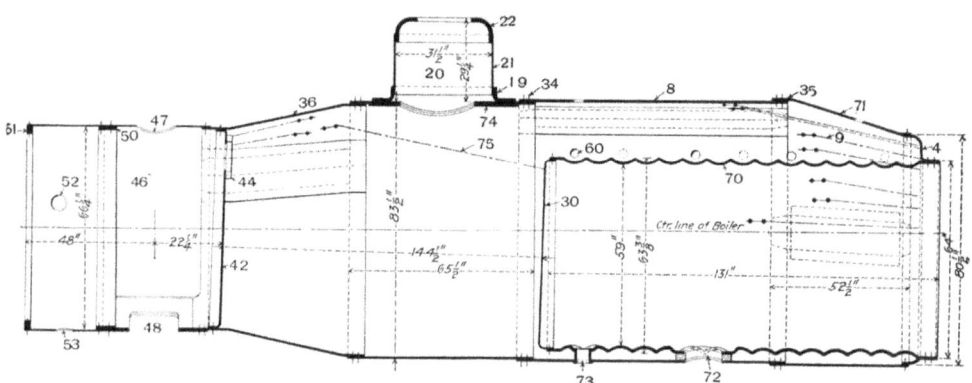

Fig. 152. Extended Wagon Top Boiler with Vanderbilt Corrugated Firebox.

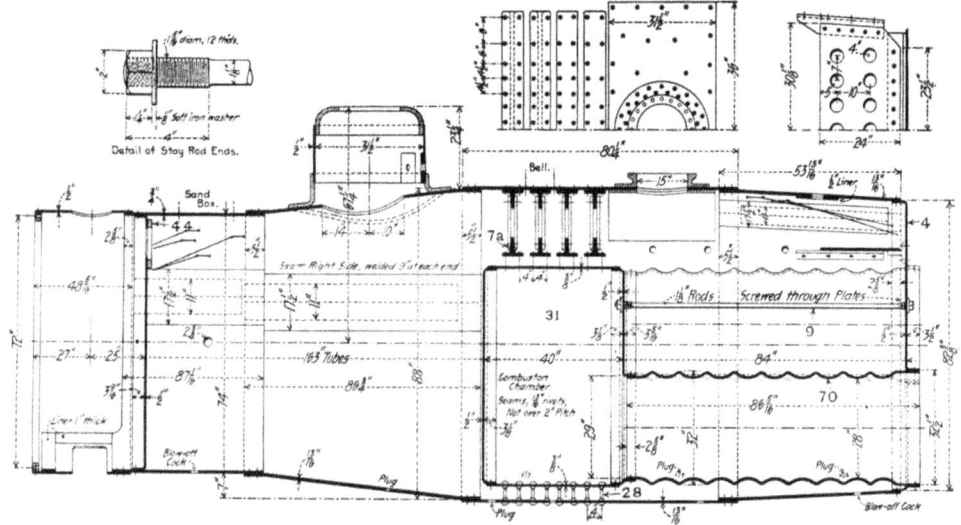

Figs. 153-156. Extended Wagon Top Boiler with Three Vanderbilt Corrugated Fireboxes and Internal Combustion Chamber. Consolidation (2—8—0) Locomotive. Atchison, Topeka & Santa Fe.

BOILERS, Sections; Extended Wagon Top. Figs. 157-159

Numbers Refer to List of Names of Parts with Fig. 144.

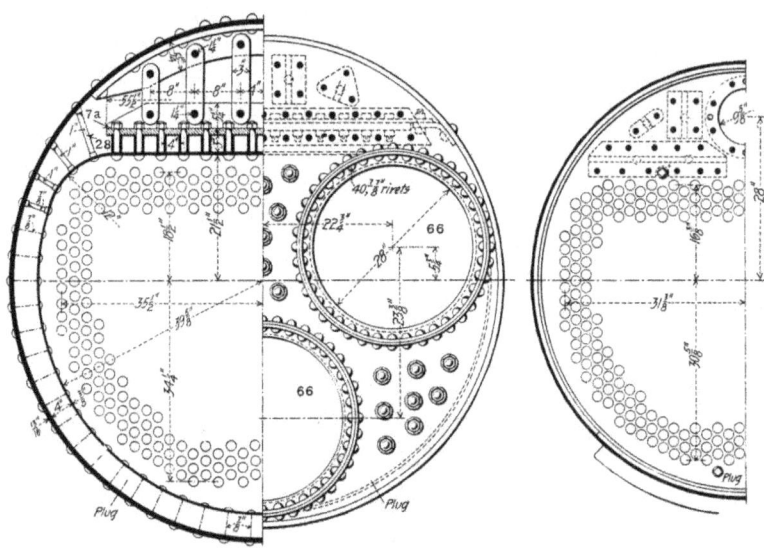

Figs. 157-158. Half Rear Elevation and Sections of Extended Wagon Top Boiler with Three Vanderbilt Corrugated Fireboxes and Internal Combustion Chamber. Consolidation (2—8—0) Locomotive. Atchison, Topeka & Santa Fe.

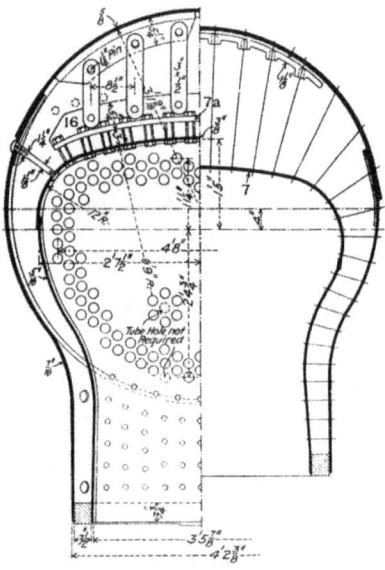

Fig. 159. Cross-Section Through Extended Wagon Top Boiler with Narrow Firebox. Ten-Wheel (4—6—0) Locomotive. Canadian Pacific.

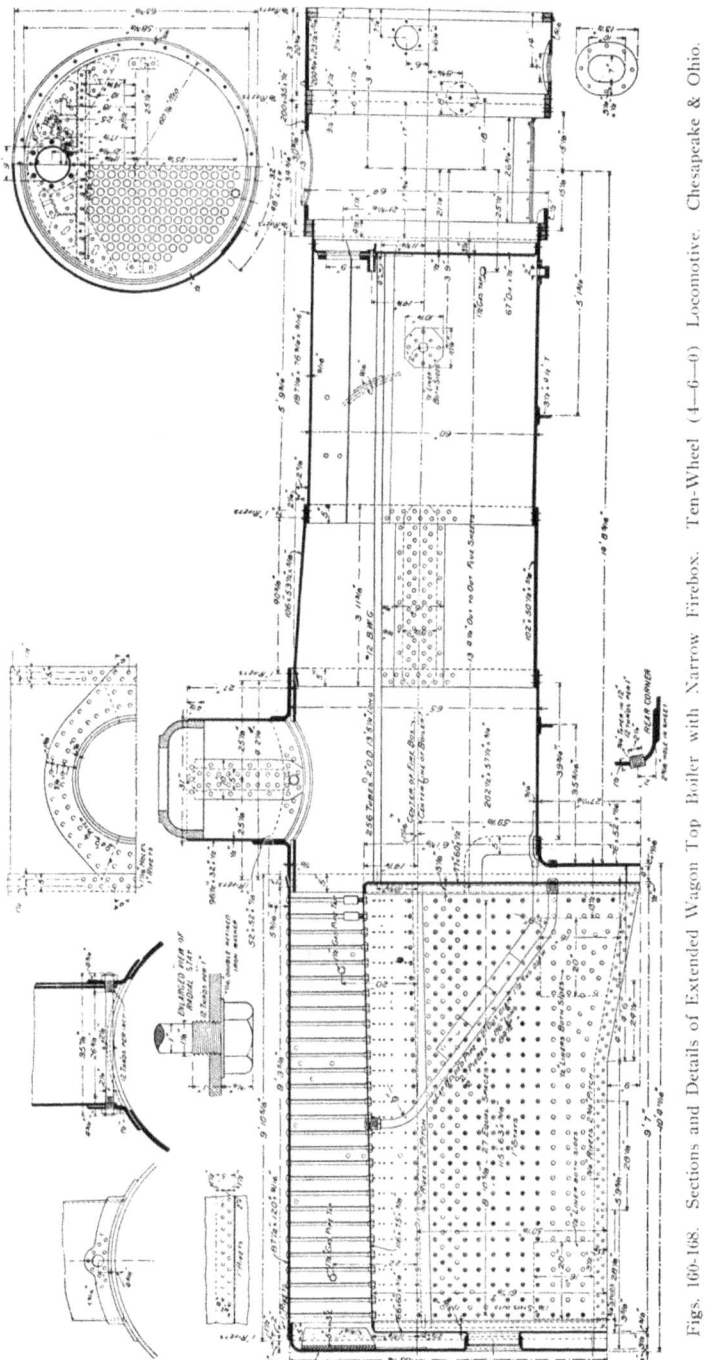

Figs. 160-168. Sections and Details of Extended Wagon Top Boiler with Narrow Firebox. Ten-Wheel (4—6—0) Locomotive. Chesapeake & Ohio.

BOILERS, Sections; Extended Wagon Top. Fig. 169

Numbers Refer to List of Names of Parts with Fig. 144.

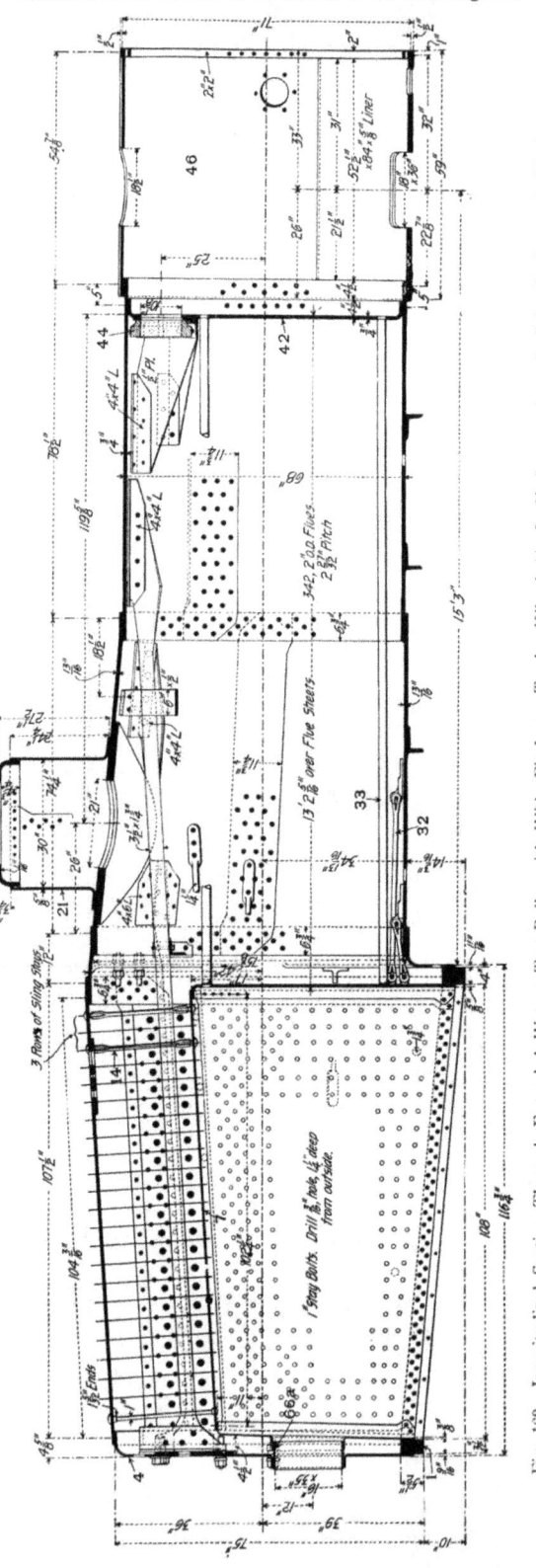

Fig. 169. Longitudinal Section Through Extended Wagon Top Boiler with Wide Firebox. Twelve-Wheel (4—8—0) Locomotive. Buffalo, Rochester & Pittsburg.

Figs. 170-172 — BOILERS, Sections; Extended Wagon Top.

Numbers Refer to List of Names of Parts with Fig. 144.

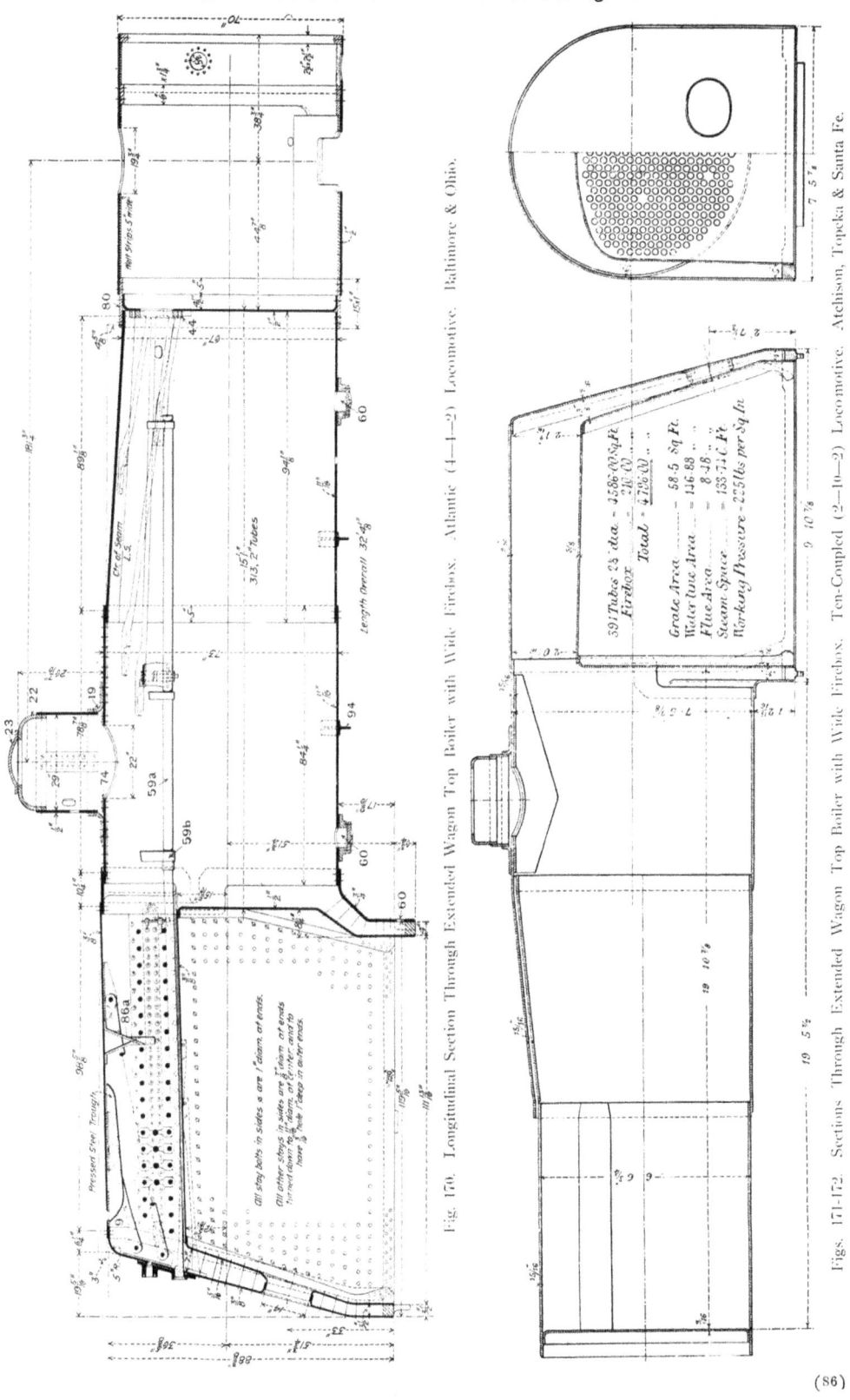

Fig. 170. Longitudinal Section Through Extended Wagon Top Boiler with Wide Firebox. Atlantic (4-4-2) Locomotive. Baltimore & Ohio.

Figs. 171-172. Sections Through Extended Wagon Top Boiler with Wide Firebox. Ten-Coupled (2-10-2) Locomotive. Atchison, Topeka & Santa Fe.

BOILERS, Sections; Extended Wagon Top. Figs. 173-176

Numbers Refer to List of Names of Parts with Fig. 144.

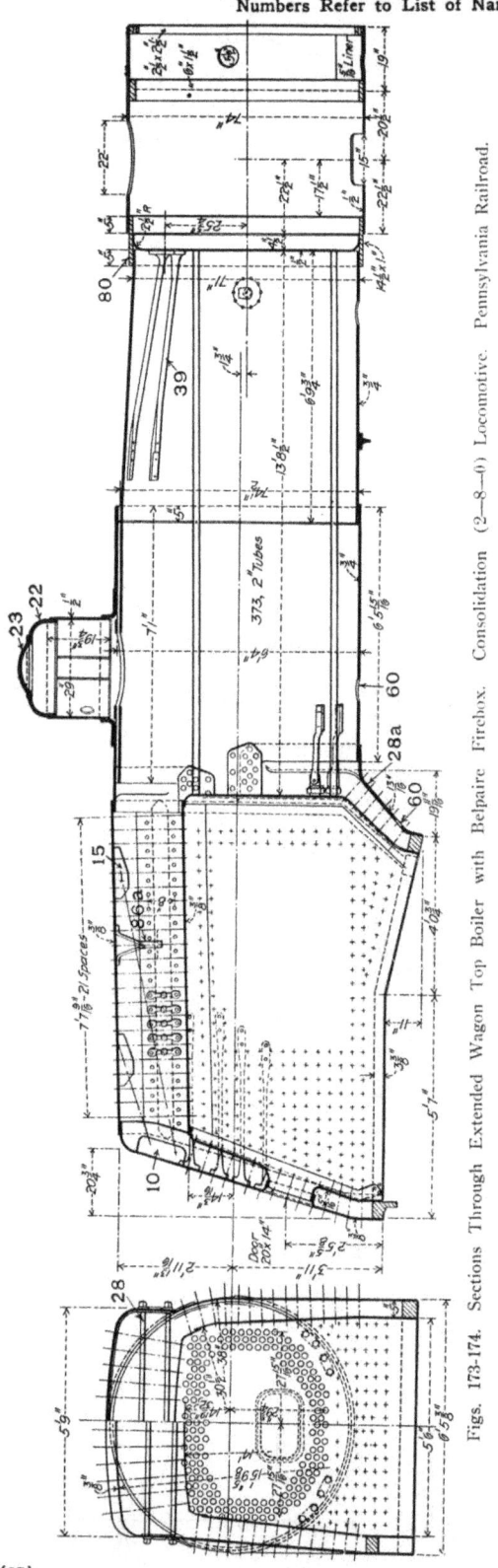

Figs. 173-174. Sections Through Extended Wagon Top Boiler with Belpaire Firebox. Consolidation (2—8—0) Locomotive. Pennsylvania Railroad.

Figs. 175-176. Sections Through Extended Wagon Top Boiler with Belpaire Firebox.

BOILERS, Sections; Straight Top.

Numbers Refer to List of Names of Parts with Fig. 144.

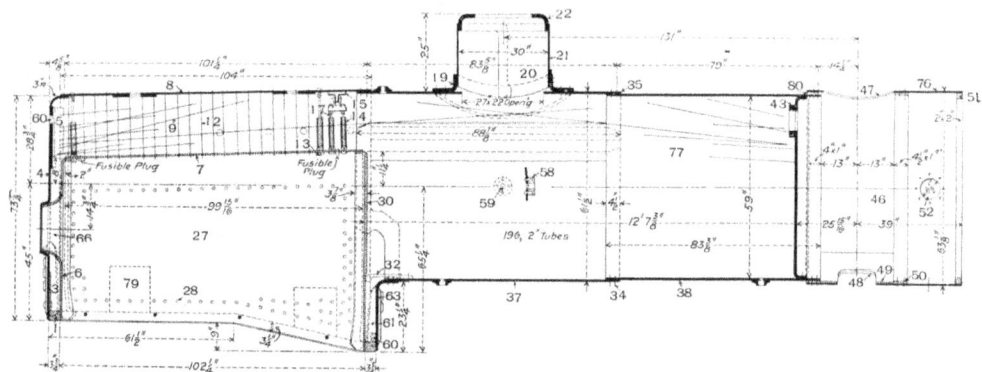

Fig. 177. Longitudinal Section Through Straight Top Boiler with Narrow Firebox.

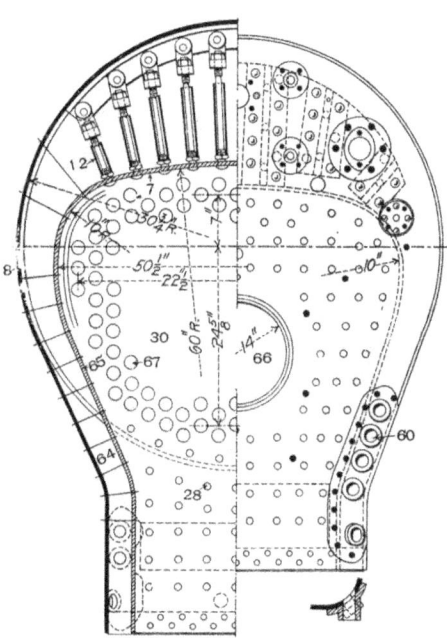

Fig. 178. Cross-Section Through Straight Top Boiler with Narrow Firebox.

BOILERS, Sections; Straight Top. Figs. 179-183

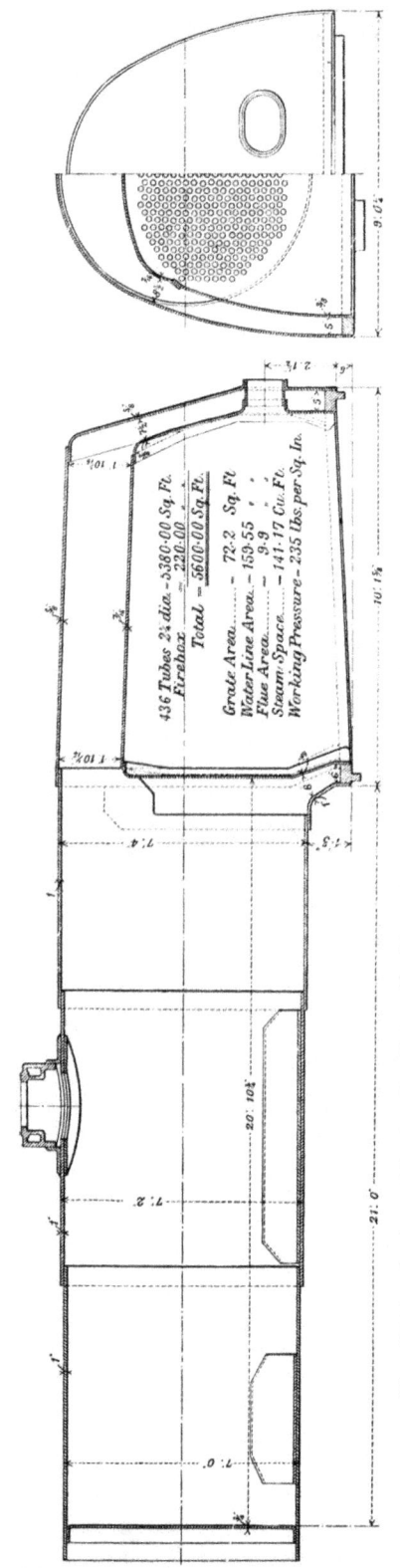

Figs. 179-180. Sections of Straight Top Boiler with Wide Firebox. Mallet Articulated (0—6—6—0) Compound Locomotive. Baltimore & Ohio.

436 Tubes 2¼ dia. = 5380.00 Sq. Ft.
Firebox = 220.00 Sq. Ft.
Total = 5600.00 Sq. Ft.

Grate Area .... 72.2 Sq. Ft.
Water-Line Area .... 159.55 „
Flue Area .... 9.9 „
Steam Space .... 141.17 Cu. Ft.
Working Pressure ... 235 lbs. per Sq. In.

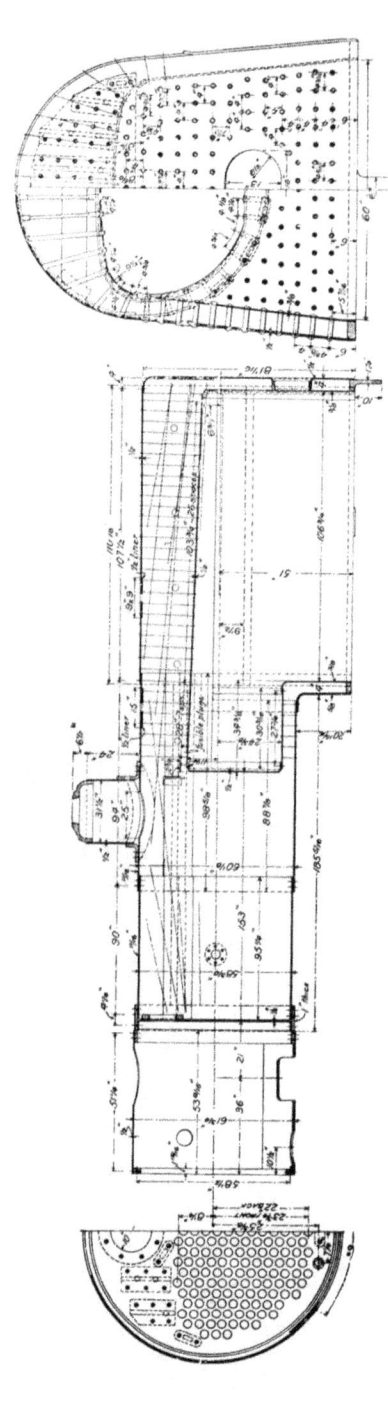

Figs. 181-183. Sections of Straight Top Boiler with Wide Firebox. Columbia (2—4—2) Locomotive. C. B. & Q.

Figs. 184-196   BOILERS, Sections; Straight Top.

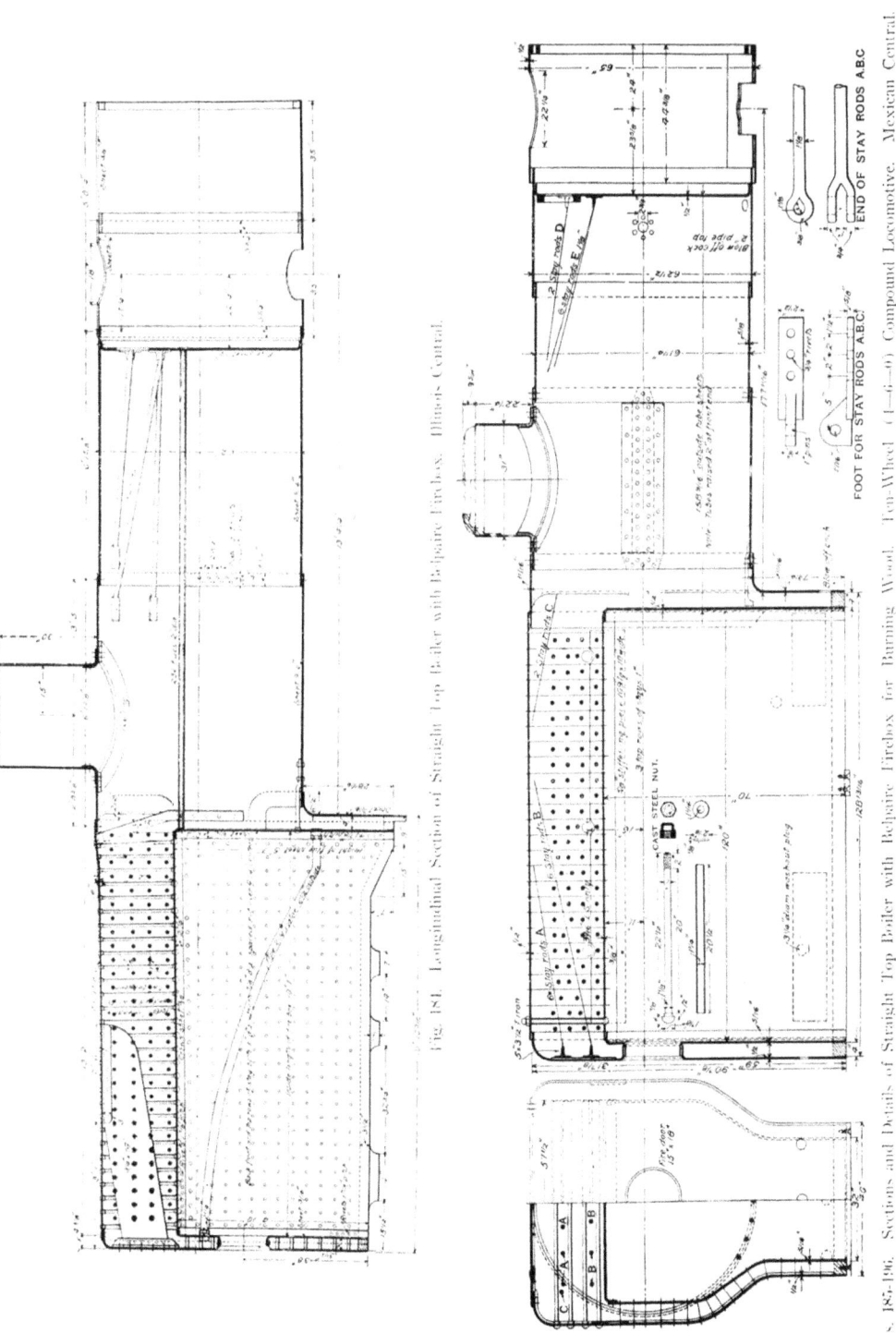

Fig. 184. Longitudinal Section of Straight Top Boiler with Belpaire Firebox. Illinois Central.

Figs. 185-196. Sections and Details of Straight Top Boiler with Belpaire Firebox for Burning Wood. Ten-Wheel (4-6-0) Compound Locomotive. Mexican Central.

(90)

BOILERS, Sections; Wootten. Figs. 197-201

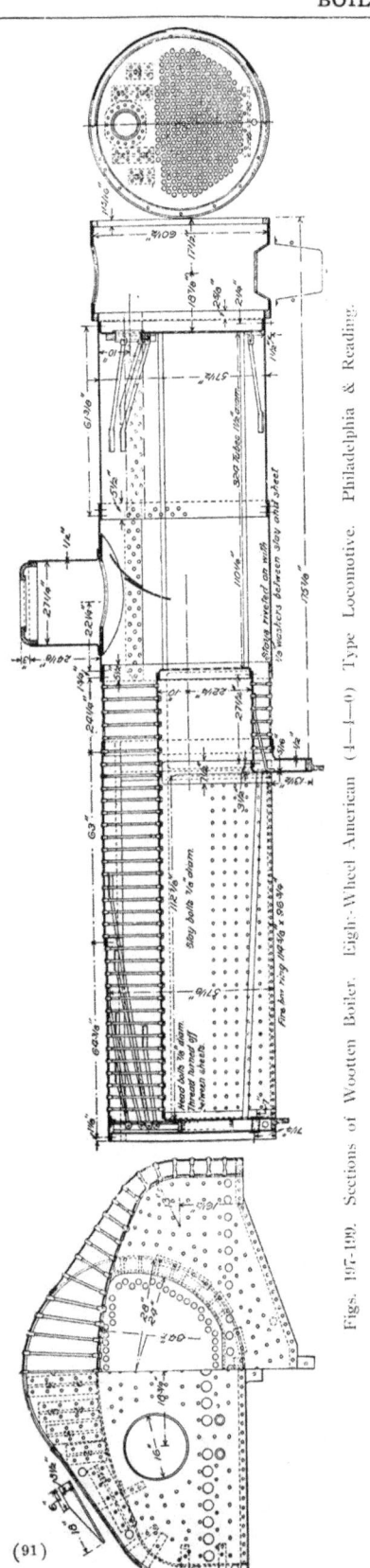

Figs. 197-199. Sections of Wootten Boiler. Eight-Wheel American (4-4-0) Type Locomotive. Philadelphia & Reading.

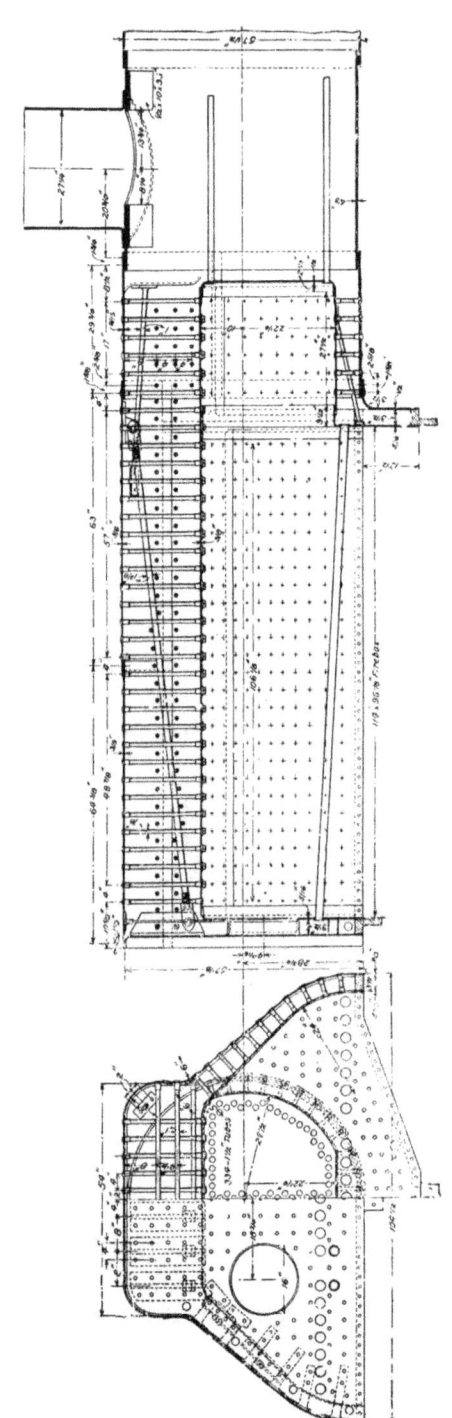

Figs. 200-201. Sections of Wootten Boiler with Belpaire Firebox.

Figs. 202-204   BOILERS, Sections; Wootten.

Numbers Refer to List of Names of Parts with Fig. 144.

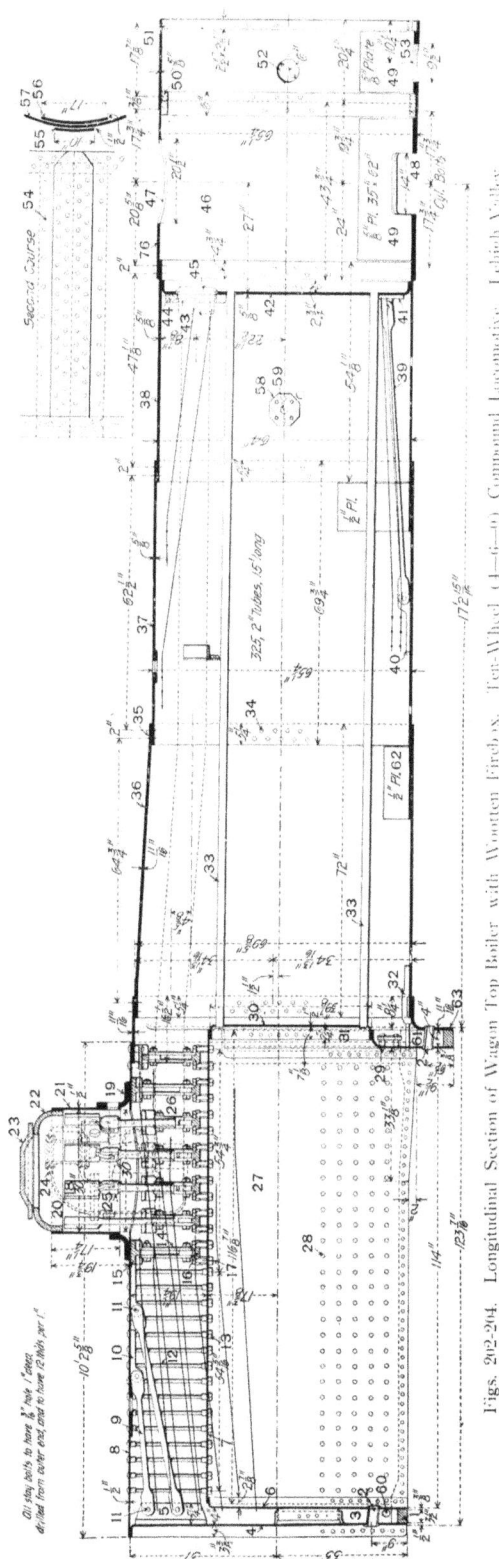

Figs. 202-204. Longitudinal Section of Wagon Top Boiler with Wootten Firebox. Ten-Wheel (4-6-0) Compound Locomotive. Lehigh Valley.

BOILERS, Sections; Wootten.   Figs. 205-220

Numbers Refer to List of Names of Parts with Fig. 144.

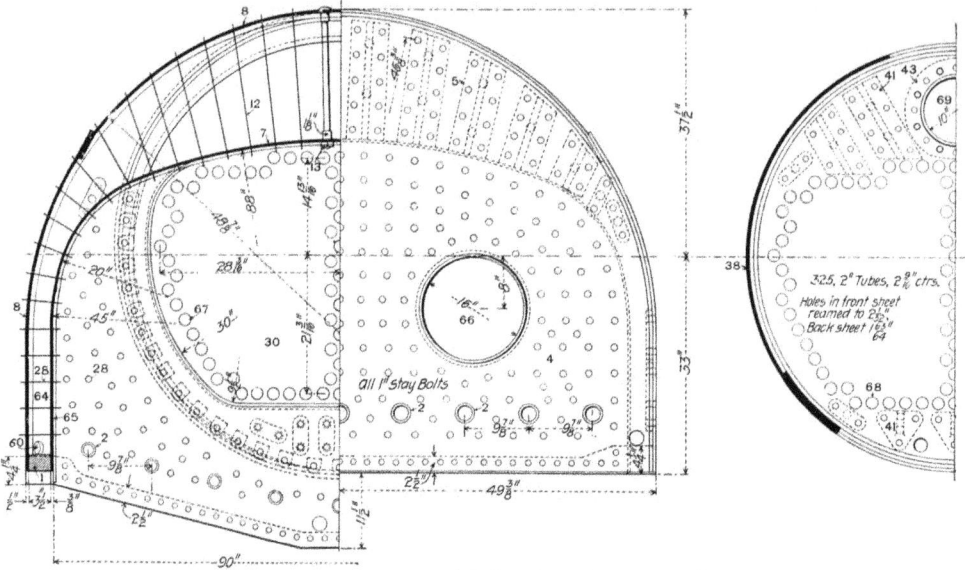

Figs. 205-206. Cross-Sections of Wagon Top Boiler with Wootten Firebox. Ten-Wheel (4—6—0) Compound Locomotive. Lehigh Valley.

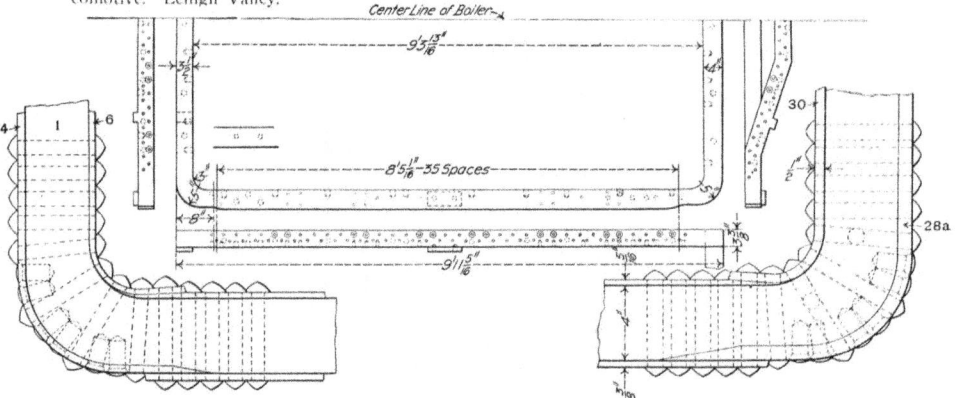

Figs. 207-212. Foundation Ring for Wide Firebox Boiler. Atlantic (4—4—2) Locomotive. Pennsylvania Railroad.

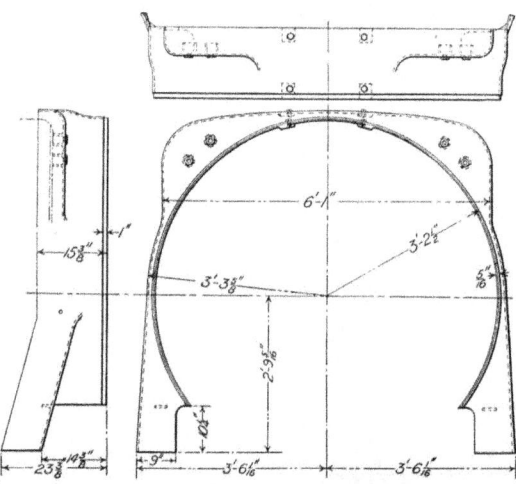

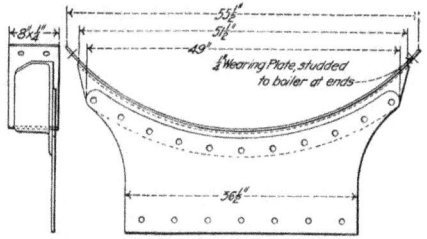

Figs. 216-217. Waist Sheet. Consolidation (2—8—0) Locomotive. American Locomotive Co.

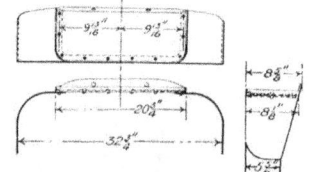

Figs. 218-220. Details of Firebox Hood. Atlantic (4—4—2) Locomotive. Pennsylvania Railroad.

Figs. 213-215. Details of Hip Joint Casing. Atlantic (4—4—2) Locomotive. Pennsylvania Railroad.

(93)

Figs. 221-244   BOILERS, Details; Miscellaneous.

Numbers Refer to List of Names of Parts with Fig. 144.

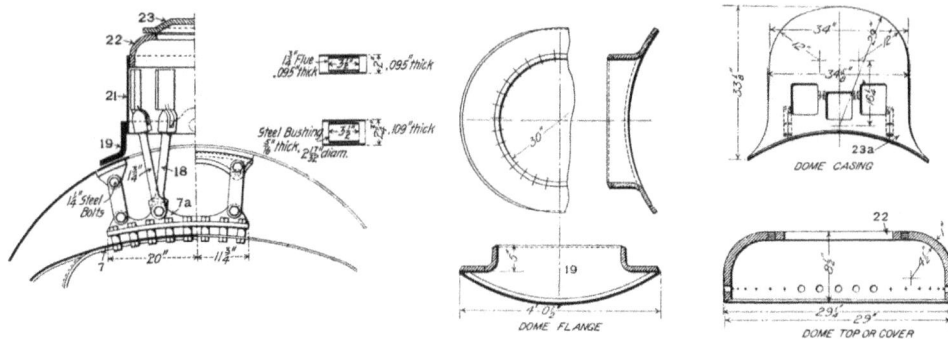

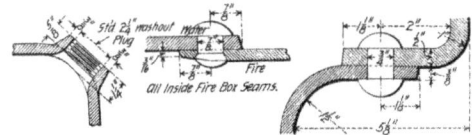

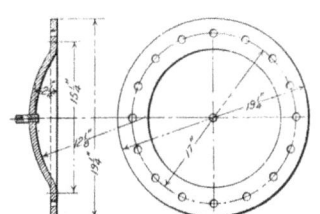

Figs. 227-231. Details of Dome. Atlantic (4—4—2) Locomotive. P. R. R.

Figs. 221-226. Details of Dome. Ten-Wheel (4—6—0) Locomotive. Lehigh Valley.

Figs. 232-233. Dome Lid. Atlantic (4—4—2) Locomotive. P. R. R.

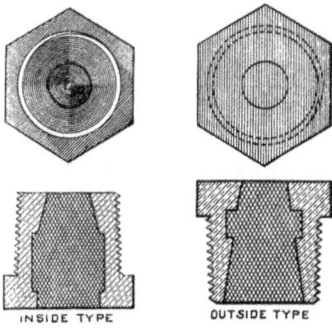

Figs. 234-236. Fusible Plugs.

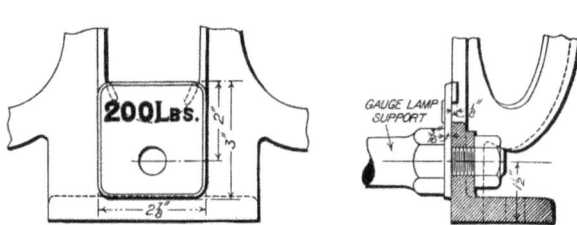

Figs. 237-238. Badge Plate for Boiler Pressure. Atlantic (4—4—2) Locomotive. P. R. R.

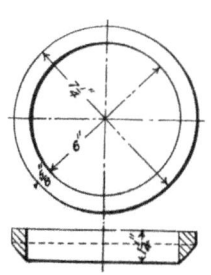

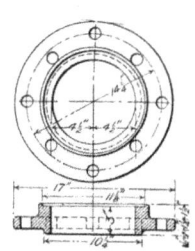

Figs. 239-240. Ground Washer for Dry Pipe Ball Joint.

Figs. 241-242. Collar for Fastening Dry Pipe.

Figs. 243-244. Badge Plate for Boiler Pressure. Atlantic (4—4—2) Locomotive. P. R. R.

BOILERS, Details; Miscellaneous.

Figs. 245-272

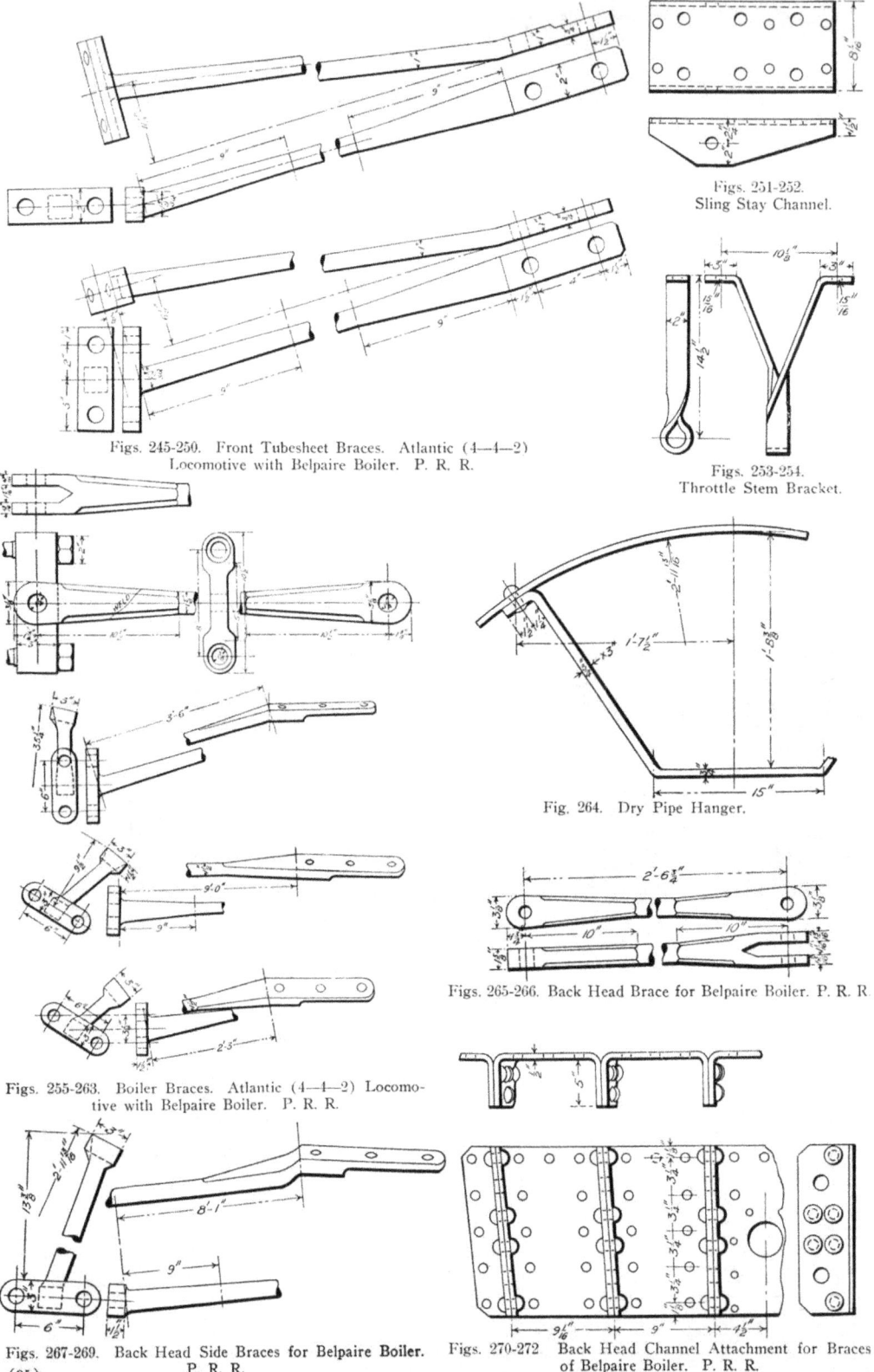

Figs. 245-250. Front Tubesheet Braces. Atlantic (4—4—2) Locomotive with Belpaire Boiler. P. R. R.

Figs. 251-252. Sling Stay Channel.

Figs. 253-254. Throttle Stem Bracket.

Fig. 264. Dry Pipe Hanger.

Figs. 255-263. Boiler Braces. Atlantic (4—4—2) Locomotive with Belpaire Boiler. P. R. R.

Figs. 265-266. Back Head Brace for Belpaire Boiler. P. R. R.

Figs. 267-269. Back Head Side Braces for Belpaire Boiler. P. R. R.

Figs. 270-272. Back Head Channel Attachment for Braces of Belpaire Boiler. P. R. R.

Figs. 273-291   BOILERS, Details; Miscellaneous.

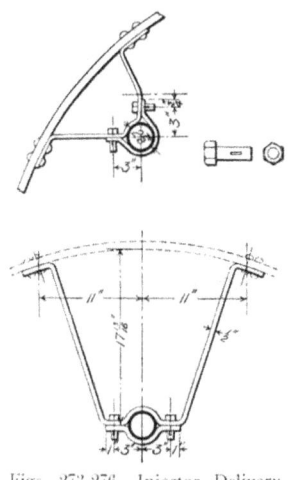

Names of Parts of Fig. 277.

2. Valve Stem
4. Valve Gland
6. Valve Case
10. Valve Stuffing Box
23. Plug
24. Plug Holder
25. Plug Holder Washer

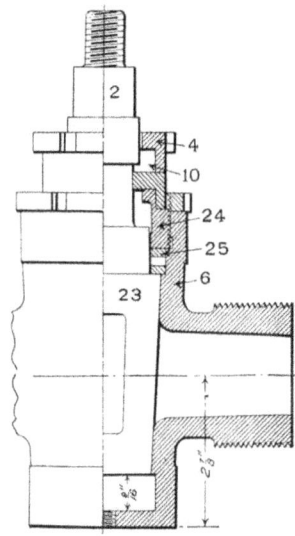

Figs. 273-276. Injector Delivery Pipe Hanger.

Fig. 277. Blow-off Cock.

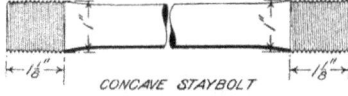

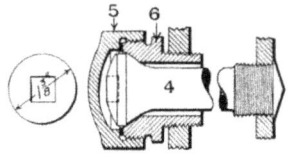
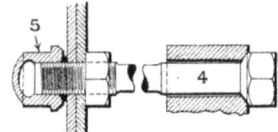
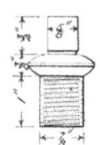

Fig. 285. Patch Bolt.

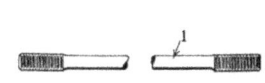
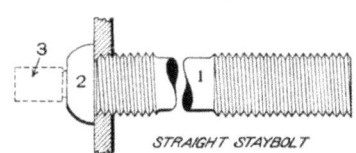

Figs. 278-284. Types of Staybolts.

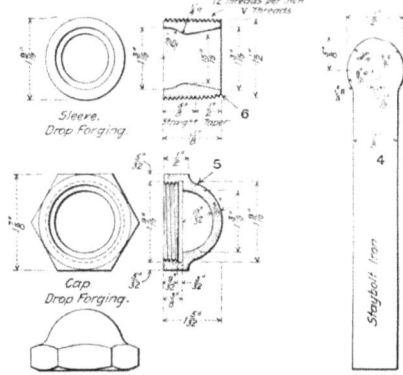

Figs. 286-291. Tate Flexible Staybolt. Flannery Bolt Co.

Names of Parts of Staybolts, Figs. 278-305.

1 Straight Staybolt
2 Cap
3 Screw Head
4 Staybolt Body
5 Seat Plug Cap
6 Seat Plug
7 Nut

(96)

BOILERS, Details; Miscellaneous. Figs. 292-309

Numbers Refer to List of Names of Parts with Figs. 286-291.

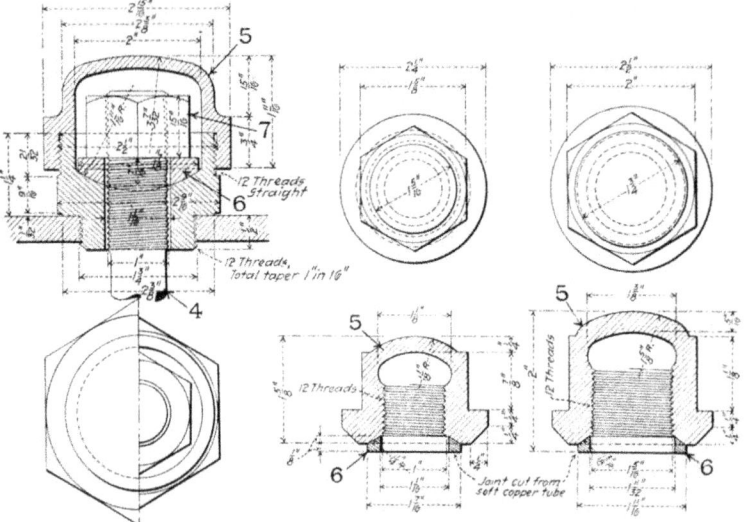

Figs. 292-297. Expansion Staybolts. Pennsylvania Railroad.

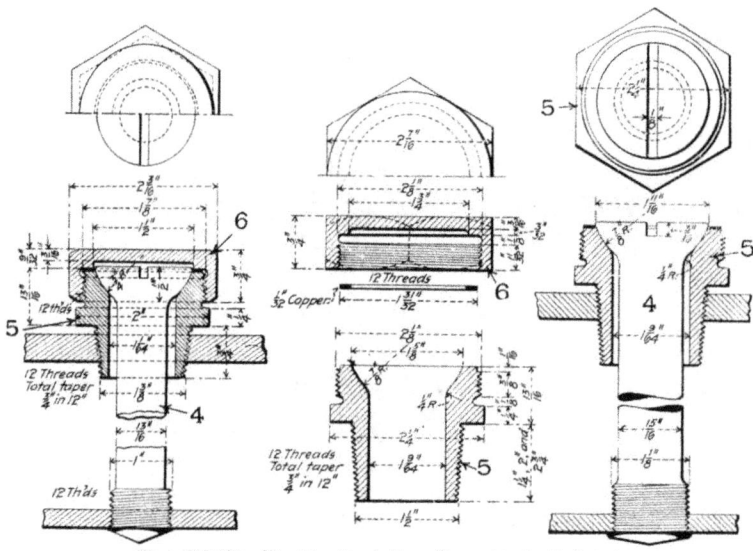

Figs. 298-305. Flexible Staybolts. Pennsylvania Railroad.

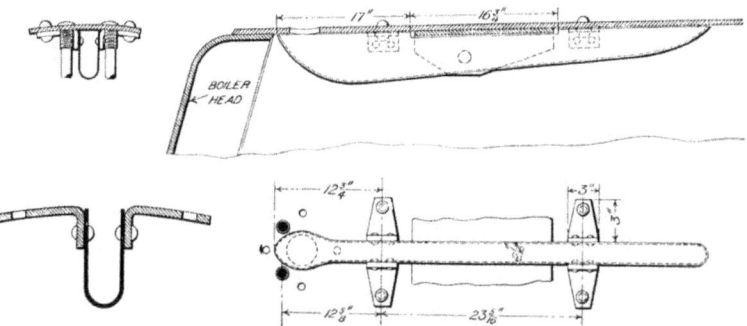

Figs. 306-309. Protecting Trough for Bridge Pipe. Atlantic (4—4—2) Locomotive, Pennsylvania Railroad.

(97)

Figs. 310-314 — BOILERS, Details; Miscellaneous.

Numbers Refer to List of Names of Parts Below.

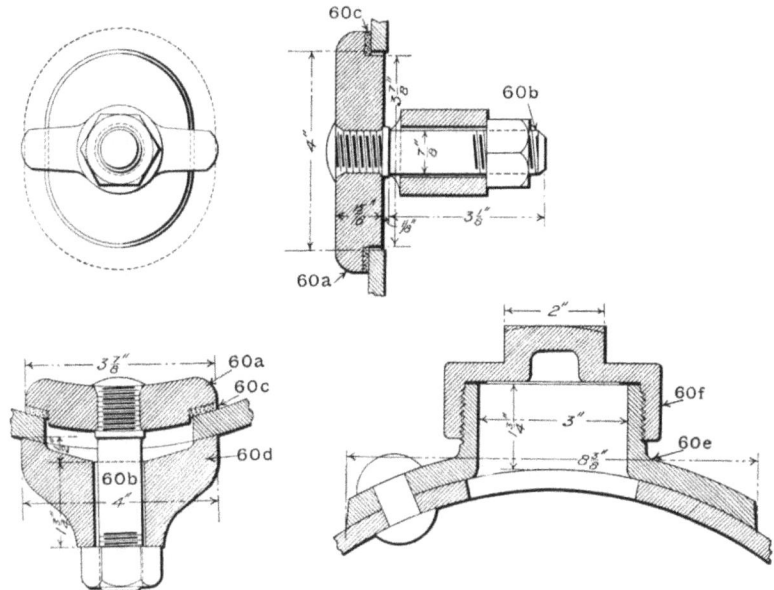

Figs. 310-313. Washout Handhole Plate. Atlantic (4—4—2) Locomotive. Pennsylvania Railroad.

Names of Parts of Figs. 310-313.

60a Handhole Plate
60b Handhole Plate Bolt
60c Handhole Plate Gasket
60d Handhole Spider
60e Handhole Nipple
60f Handhole Nipple Cap

Fig. 314. Application of K. & M. 85 per cent. Magnesia Sectional Boiler Lagging to Locomotive Boiler. Franklin Manufacturing Co.

BOILERS, Details; Riveting. Figs. 315-330

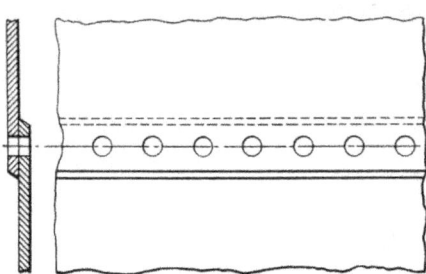

Figs. 315-316. Single Riveted Lap Joint.

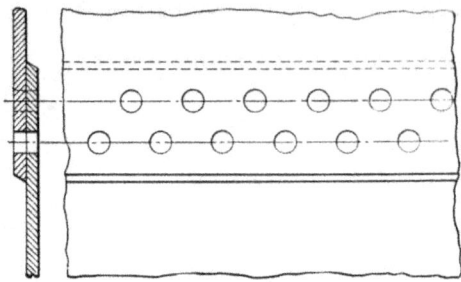

Figs. 317-318. Double Riveted Lap Joint with Staggered Rivets.

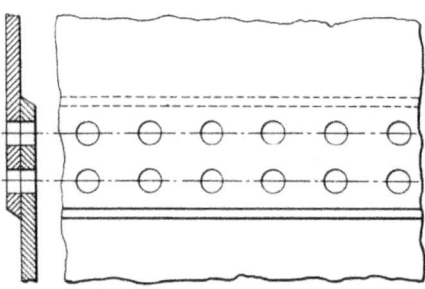

Figs. 319-320. Double Riveted Lap Joint, Chain Riveting.

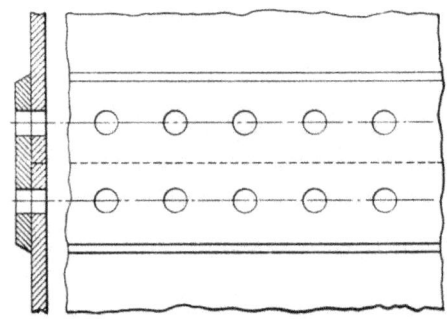

Figs. 321-322. Single Riveted Butt Joint with One Welt.

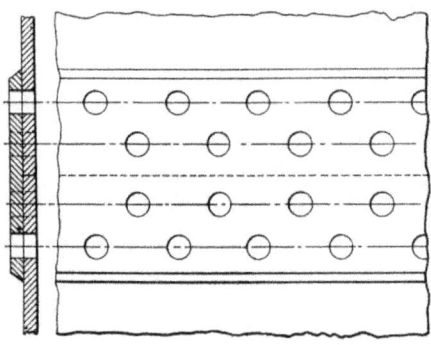

Figs. 323-324. Double Riveted Butt Joint with One Welt.

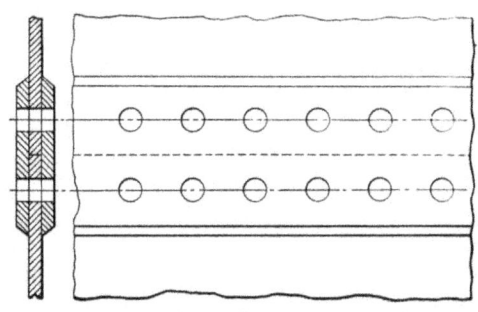

Figs. 325-326. Single Riveted Butt Joint with Two Welts.

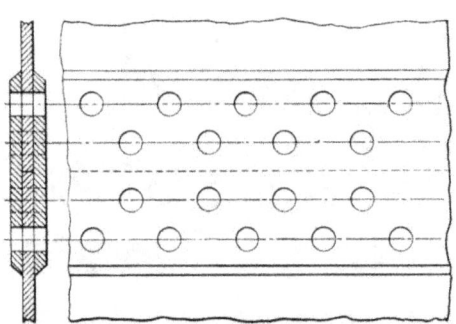

Figs. 327-328. Double Riveted Butt Joint with Two Welts.

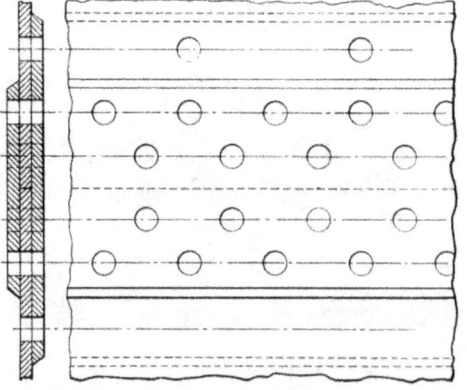

Figs. 329-330. Multiple Riveted Butt Joint with Two Welts.

Figs. 331-338 BOILERS, Details; Fire Doors.

Numbers Refer to List of Names of Parts on Opposite Page.

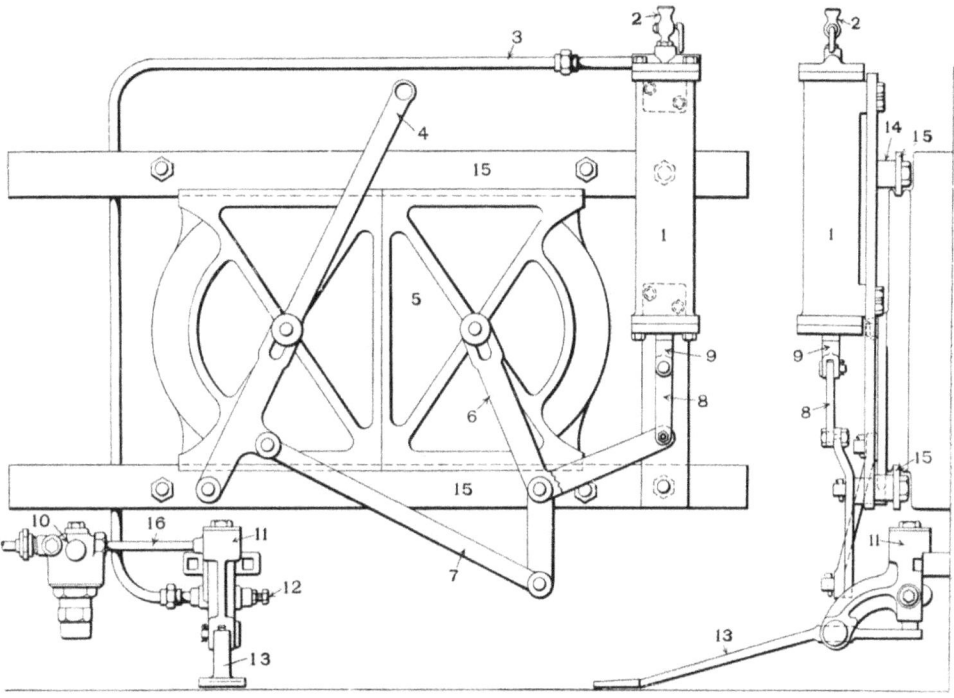

Figs. 331-332. Franklin Fire Door and Pneumatic Opening Device. Franklin Railway Supply Co.

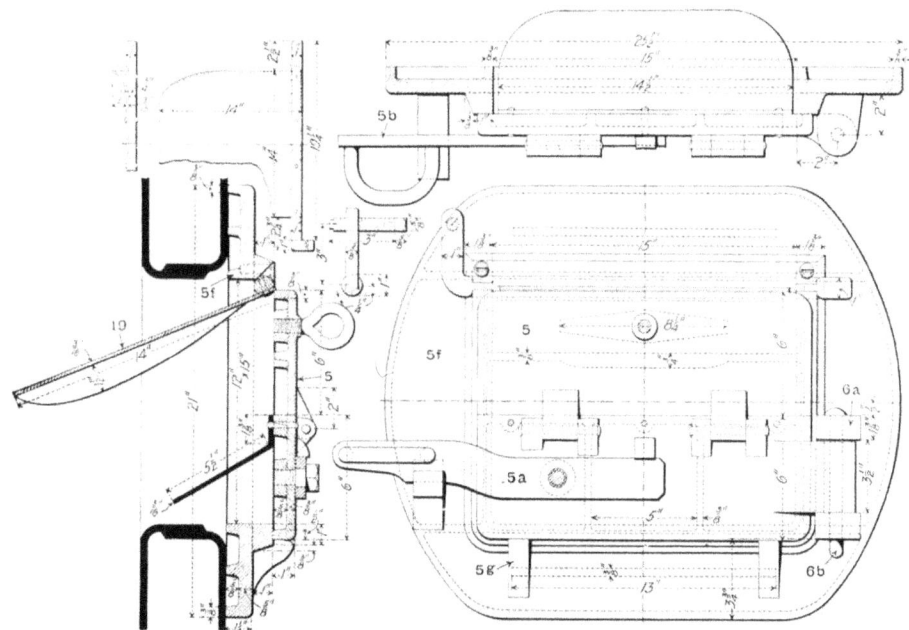

Figs. 333-338. Standard Fire Door. Southern Pacific.

BOILERS, Details; Fire Doors.   Figs. 339-342

Numbers Refer to List of Names of Parts Below.

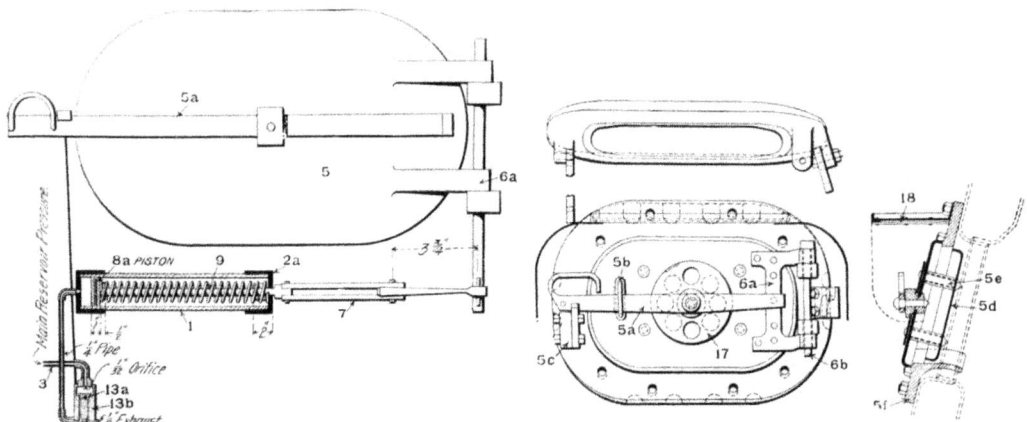

Fig. 339. Brewer's Pneumatic Fire Door Opener.

Figs. 340-342. Fire Door. Atlantic (4—4—2) Locomotive. Pennsylvania Railroad.

Names of Parts of Fire Doors, Figs. 331-342.

1 Operating Cylinder	5g Door Support	13a Operating Valve
2 Cylinder Lubricator	6 Door Bell Crank	13b Operating Valve Case
2a Cylinder Head	6a Door Hinge	14 Filling Piece
3 Steam or Air Pipe	6b Door Hinge Pintle	15 Door Slide
4 Door Lever	7 Operating Connection	16 Steam Pipe Connection for Reducing Valve
5 Door	8 Connecting Rod	
5a Door Latch	9 Piston Rod	17 Damper
5b Door Latch Guides	10 Westinghouse Reducing Valve	18 Oiler Stand
5c Door Latch Holder	11 Operating Valve Case	19 Deflector
5d Door Shield	12 Operating Valve Case Plug Screw	
5e Door Shield Bolt		
5f Door Ring	13 Operating Treadle	

Names of Parts of Smokeboxes, Figs. 343-442.

1 Spark Hopper Casting	20 Front Smokebox Ring	34 Diaphragm Stiffening Bar
2 Spark Hopper Slide	21 Boiler Front	35 Frame for Netting
3 Spark Hopper Pipe	22 Smokebox Door	36 Frame Angles
4 Smokestack	22a Smokebox Door Bolts	37 Horizontal Perforated Diaphragm Plate
5 Smokestack Lift Pipe	22b Smokebox Door Hinge	
6 Boiler Shell	23 Number Plate	38 Frame for Door Through Netting
7 Dry Pipe	24 Number Plate Studs	
8 Tubes	25 Cinder Hole	39 Diaphragm and Netting Studs
9 Stiffening Ring	25a Cleaning Hole Flange	40 Petticoat Pipe
10 Steam Head	25b Cleaning Hole Lid	41 Petticoat Pipe Bracket
11 Ball Joint Ring	25c Cleaning Hole Lid Handle	42 Headlight Bracket
12 Steam Pipe	25d Cleaning Hole Lid Latch	43 Auxiliary Steam Pipe
12a Steam Pipe Studs	25e Cleaning Hole Lid Chain	44 Ground Washer for Steam Pipe Ball Joint
13 Smokebox	26 Cleaning Hole	
14 Diaphragm	27 Hand Rail	45 Saddle
15 Exhaust Pipe	28 Hand Rail Bracket	46 Blower Connection to Exhaust Pipe
15a Exhaust Nozzle	29 Front Tubesheet	
15b Inner Exhaust Pipe	30 Smokebox and Boiler Connecting Ring	47 Blower Pipe Flange
16 Exhaust Muffler		48 Blower Pipe Flange Cap
17 Angle for Front Deflector	31 Diaphragm Door	49 Blower Pipe Union
18 Perforated Deflector	32 Diaphragm Door Studs	
19 Smokebox Ring	33 Diaphragm Apron	

(101)

Figs. 343-348   SMOKEBOXES. Sections.

Numbers Refer to List of Names of Parts with Figs. 339-342.

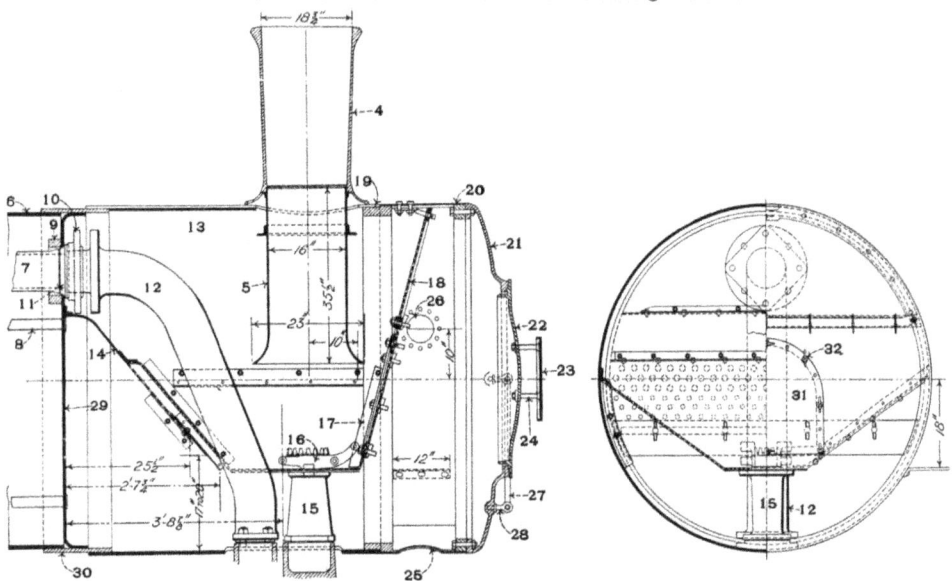

Figs. 343-344. Extended Smokebox. Atlantic (4—4—2) Locomotive. Pennsylvania Railroad.

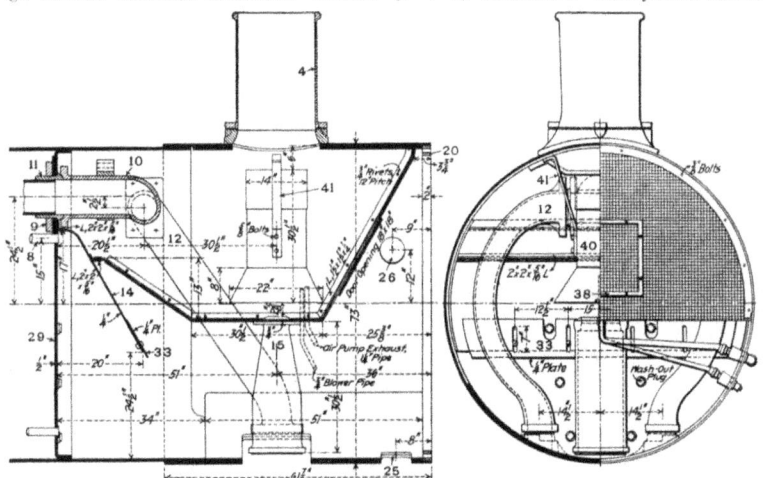

Figs. 345-346. Smokebox for Pacific (4—6—2) Locomotive. Chicago, Milwaukee & St. Paul.

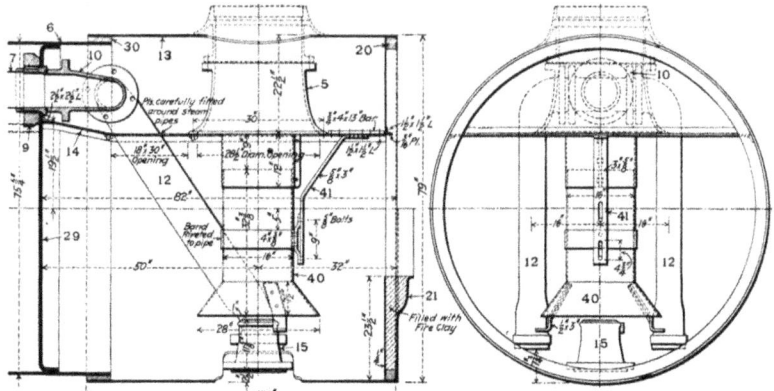

Figs. 347-348. Extended Smokebox. Mikado (2—8—2) Locomotive. Northern Pacific. Fitted with Diamond Stack for Burning Lignite.

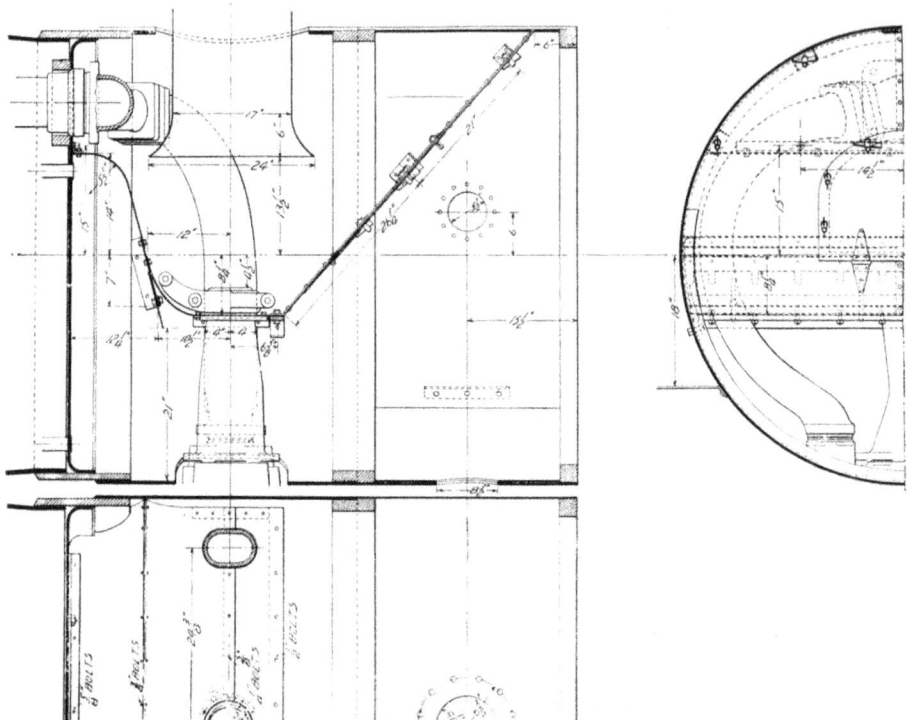

Figs. 349-351. Sections of Smokebox for Eight-Wheel American (4—4—0) Type Locomotive. Pennsylvania Railroad.

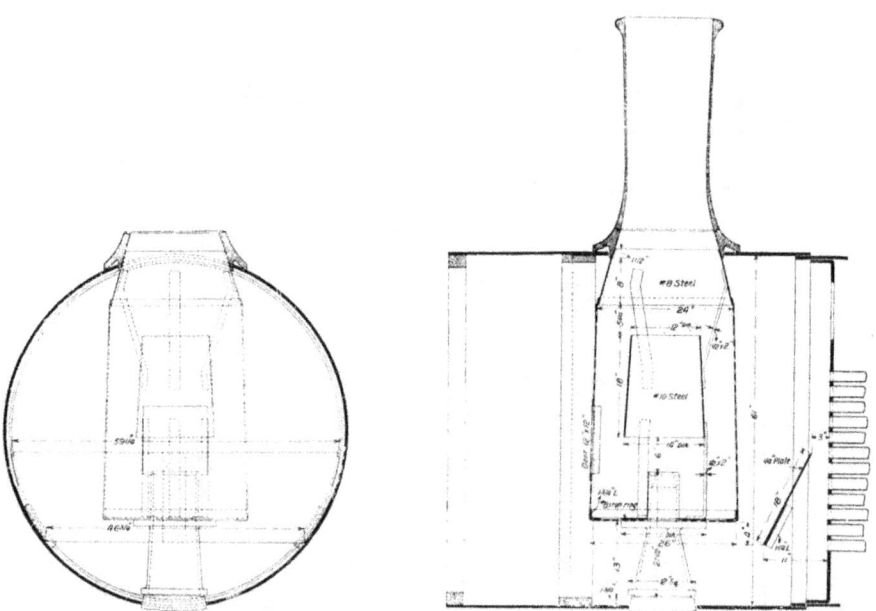

Figs. 352-353. Smokebox and Deflector Plate. Lehigh Valley.

Figs. 354–365 — SMOKEBOXES, Details; Steam Pipes.

Numbers Refer to List of Names of Parts with Figs. 339–342.

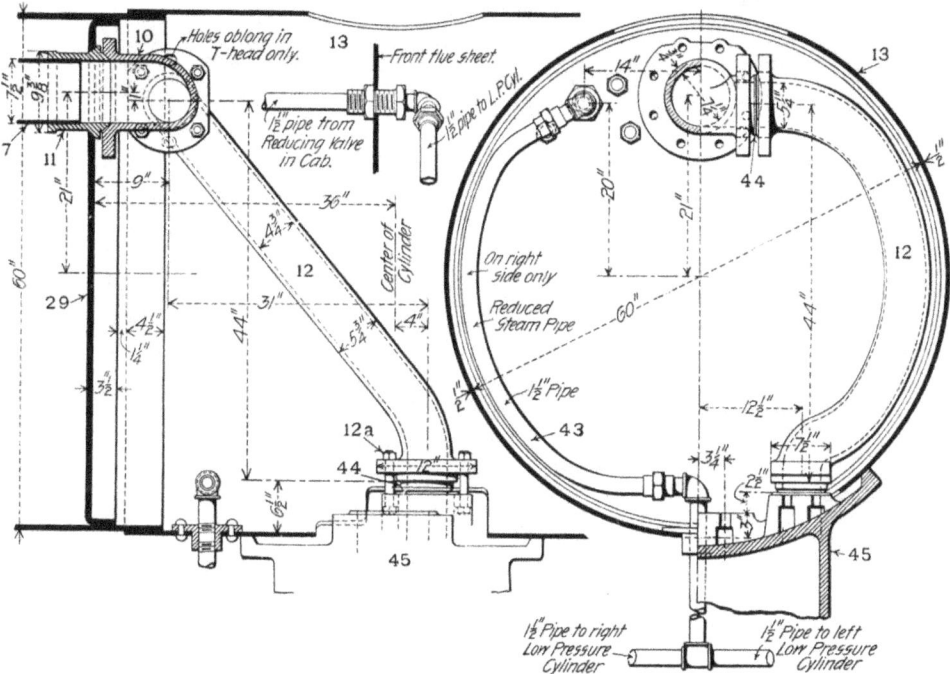

Figs. 354–356. Details of Steam Pipes of Tandem Compound Locomotive. Atchison, Topeka & Santa Fe.

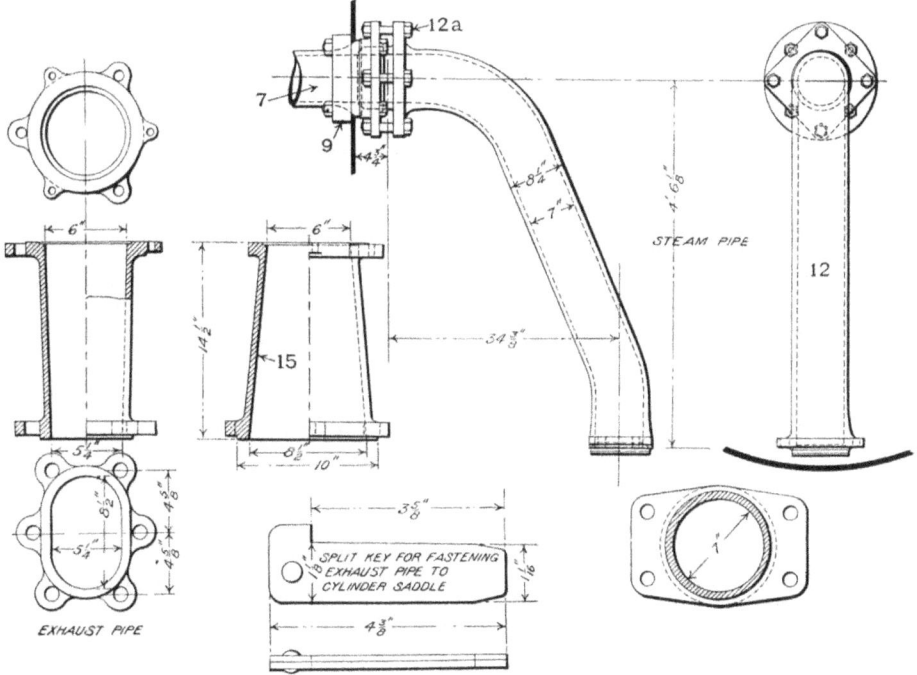

Figs. 357–365. Steam and Exhaust Pipe Details. Atlantic (4–4–2) Locomotive. Pennsylvania Railroad.

SMOKEBOXES, Details; Steam and Exhaust Pipes. Figs. 366-375

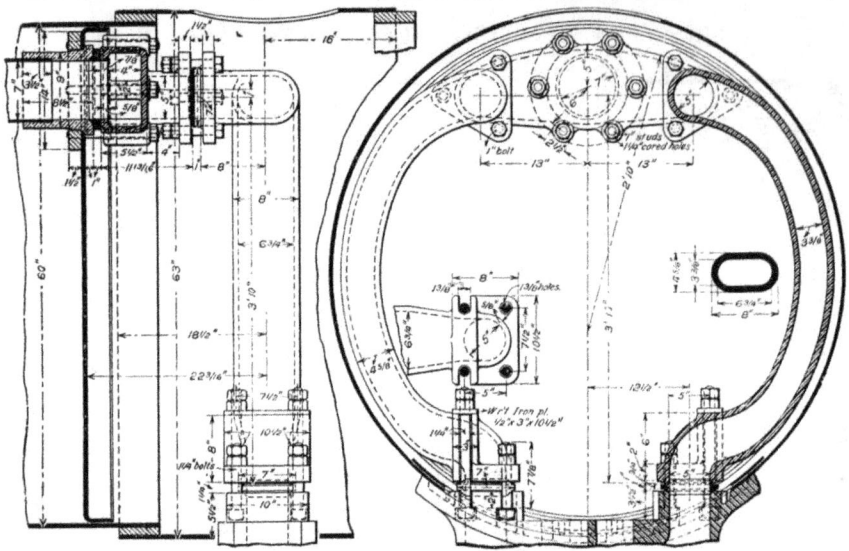

Figs. 366-367. Details of Steam Pipes of Eight-Wheel American (4—4—0) Type Locomotive. Baltimore & Ohio.
Numbers Refer to List of Names of Parts with Figs. 339-342.

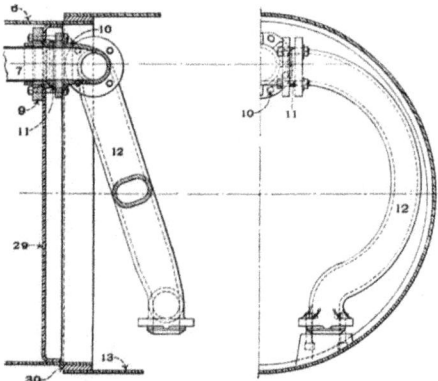

Figs. 368-369. Dry Pipe and Steam Pipe Connections.

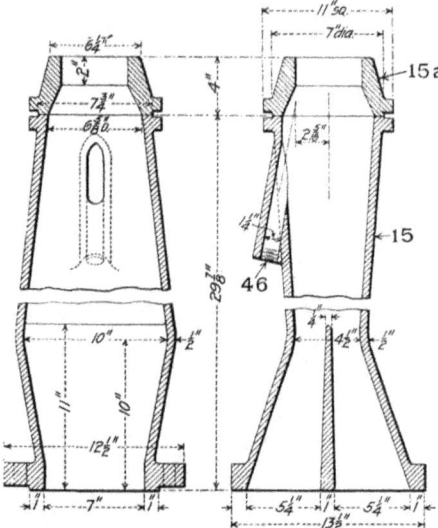

Figs. 370-372. Exhaust Pipe and Nozzle. Southern Pacific.

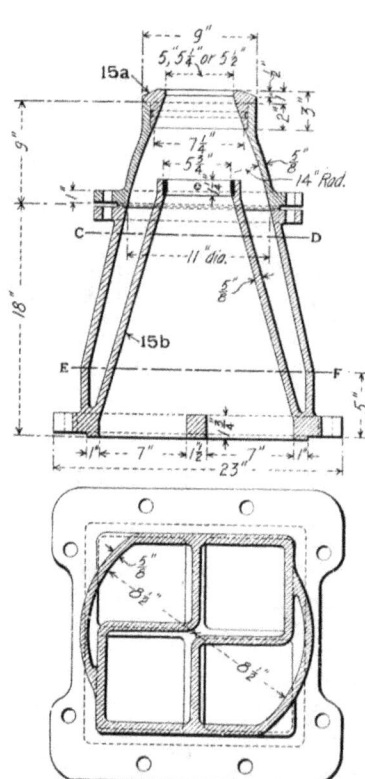

Figs. 373-375. Exhaust Pipe for Ten-Wheel (4—6—0) Locomotive with Cleveland Cylinders. Intercolonial Railway.

SMOKEBOXES, Details; Exhaust Pipes.

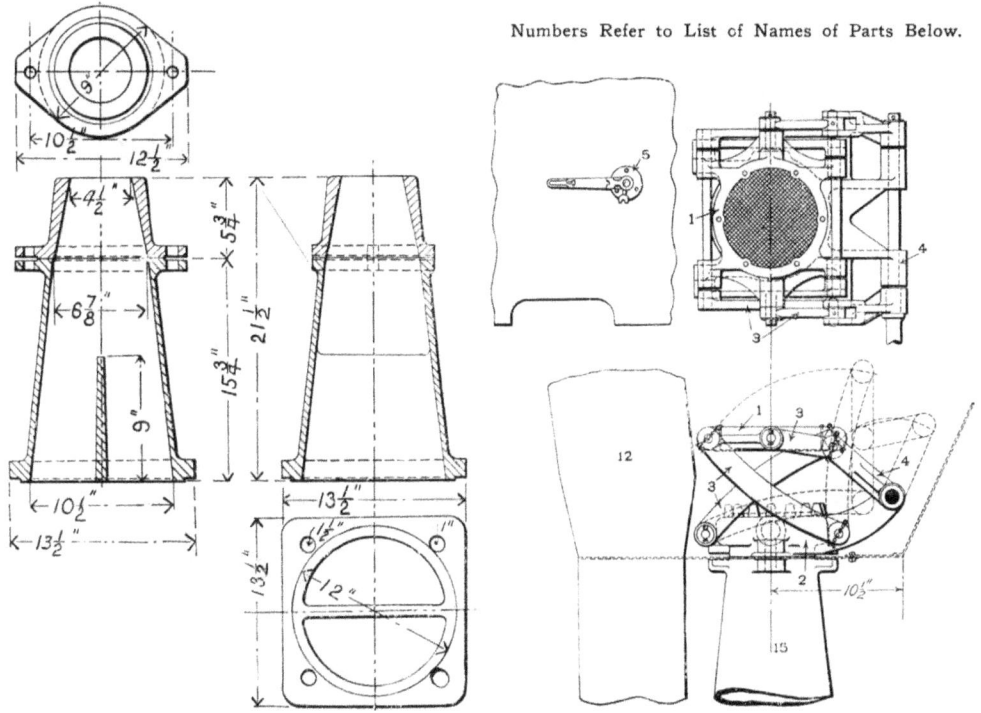

Figs. 376-379. Exhaust Nozzle. Baldwin Locomotive Works.

Figs. 380-382. Exhaust Muffler. Atlantic (4—4—2) Locomotive. Pennsylvania Railroad.

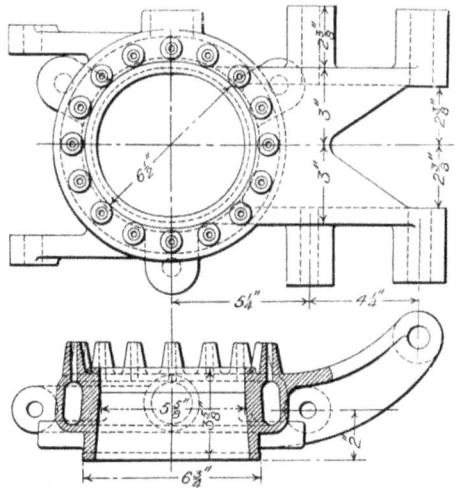

Figs. 383-384. Exhaust Nozzle with Muffler Attachment. Atlantic (4—4—2) Locomotive. P. R. R.

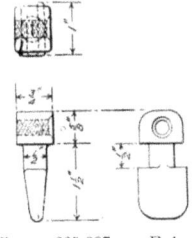

Figs. 385-387. Exhaust Muffler Trigger.

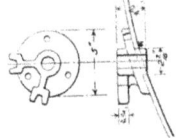

Figs. 388-389. Bearing for Muffler Shaft.

Names of Parts of Exhaust Muffler, Figs. 380-382.

1 *Frame for Muffler*
2 *Exhaust Nozzle with Muffler*
3 *Links*
4 *Crank Arm with Jaw*
5 *Bearing for Muffler Shaft*
12 *Steam Pipe*
15 *Exhaust Pipe*

SMOKEBOXES, Details; Miscellaneous.   Figs. 390-399

Numbers Refer to List of Names of Parts with Figs. 339-342.

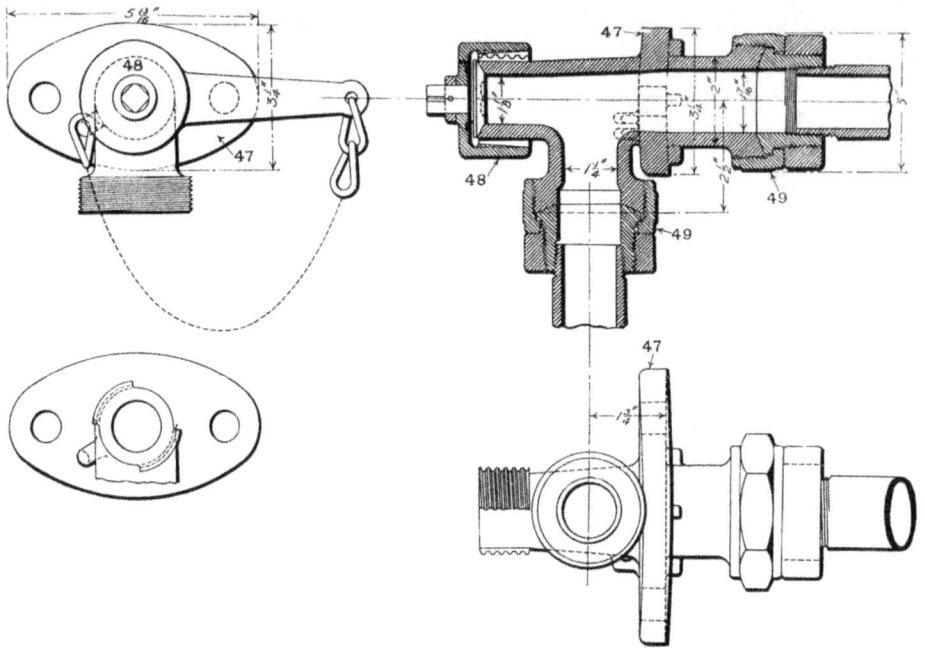

Figs. 390-393. 1¼-in. Blower Pipe Connection. Atlantic (4—4—2) Locomotive. Pennsylvania Railroad.

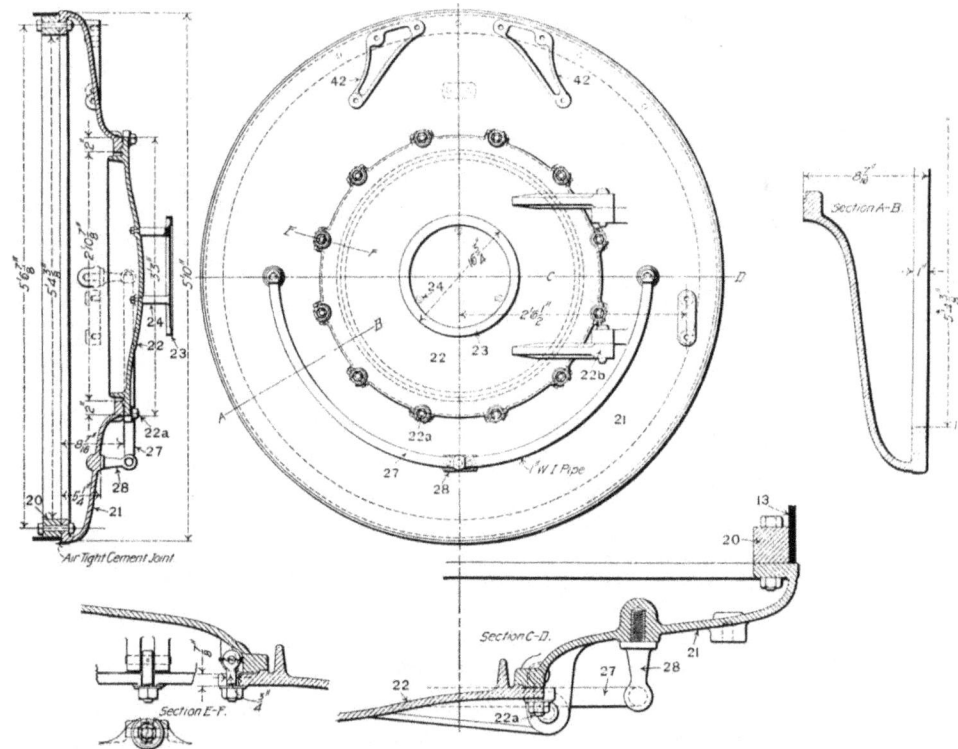

Figs. 394-399. Smokebox Front and Door. Atlantic (4—4—2) Locomotive. Pennsylvania Railroad.

Figs. 400-413 — SMOKEBOXES, Details; Miscellaneous.

Numbers Refer to List of Names of Parts with Figs. 339-342.

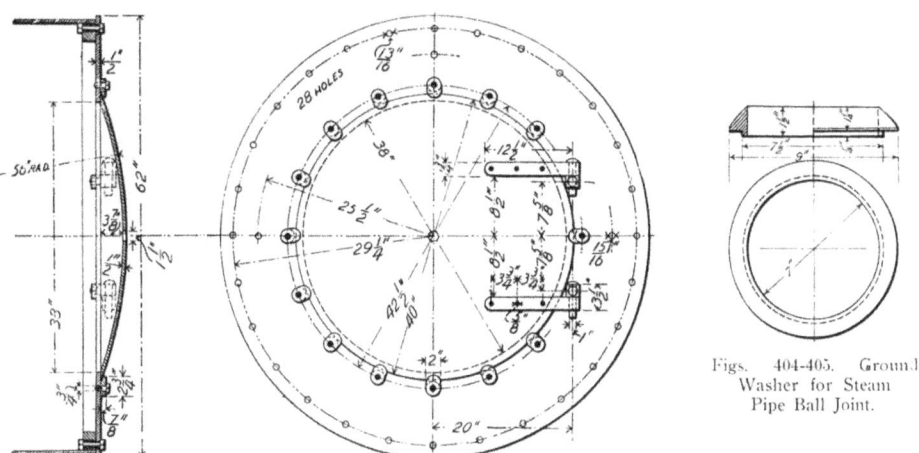

Figs. 400-401. Smokebox Front. Baldwin Locomotive Works.

Figs. 404-405. Ground Washer for Steam Pipe Ball Joint.

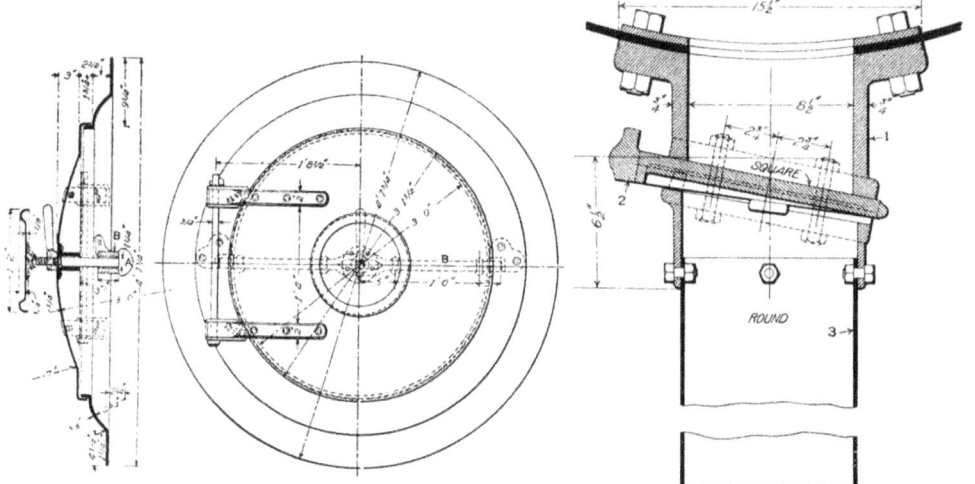

Figs. 402-403. Pressed Steel Smokebox Front.

Fig. 406. Hopper for Extended Smokebox. P. R. R.

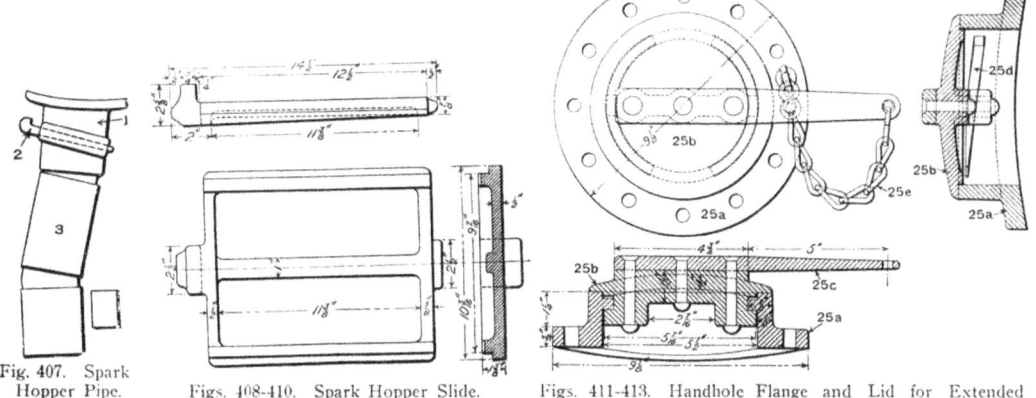

Fig. 407. Spark Hopper Pipe. P. R. R.

Figs. 408-410. Spark Hopper Slide. P. R. R.

Figs. 411-413. Handhole Flange and Lid for Extended Smokebox. P. R. R.

(108)

SMOKEBOXES, Details; Miscellaneous.   Figs. 414-454

Numbers Refer to List of Names of Parts with Figs. 339-342.

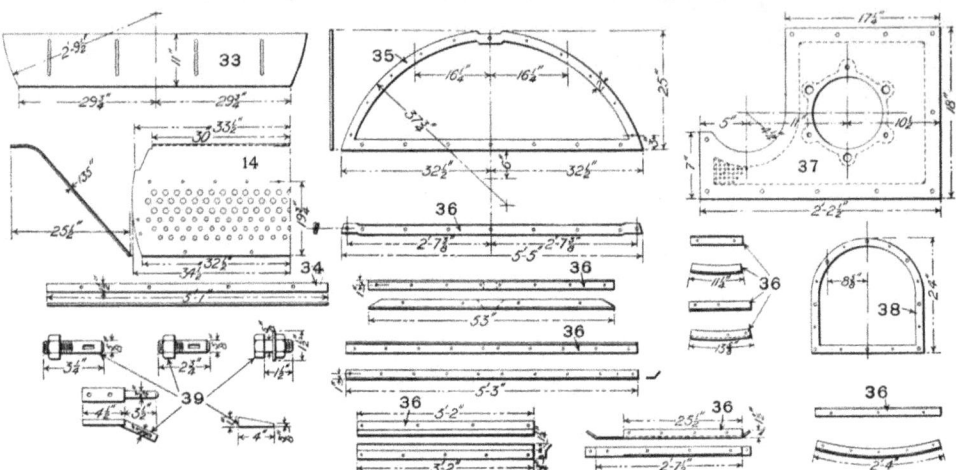

Figs. 414-441. Miscellaneous Details of Extended Smokebox. Atlantic (4—4—2) Locomotive. Pennsylvania Railroad.

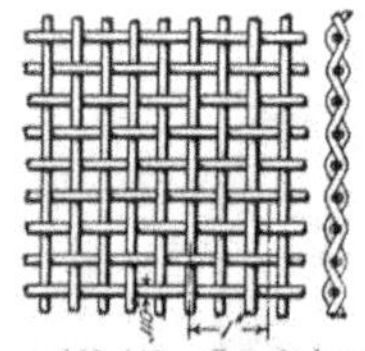

Figs. 442-443. Smokebox Netting.

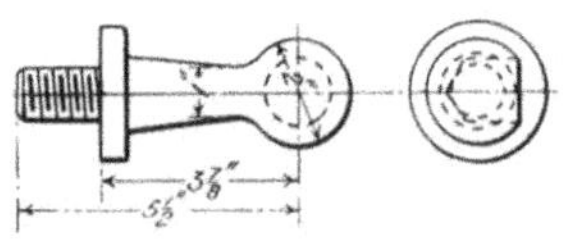

Figs. 444-445. End Hand Rail Column on Smokebox.

Fig. 446. Smokebox Netting, No. 10 Wire, 3 Mesh. W. S. Tyler Co.

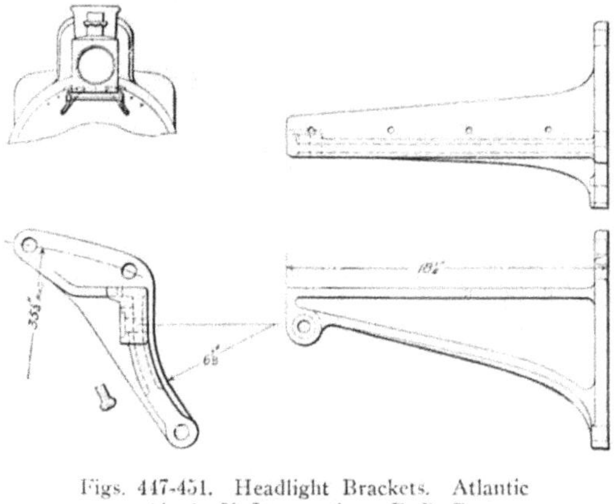

Figs. 447-451. Headlight Brackets. Atlantic (4—4—2) Locomotive. P. R. R.

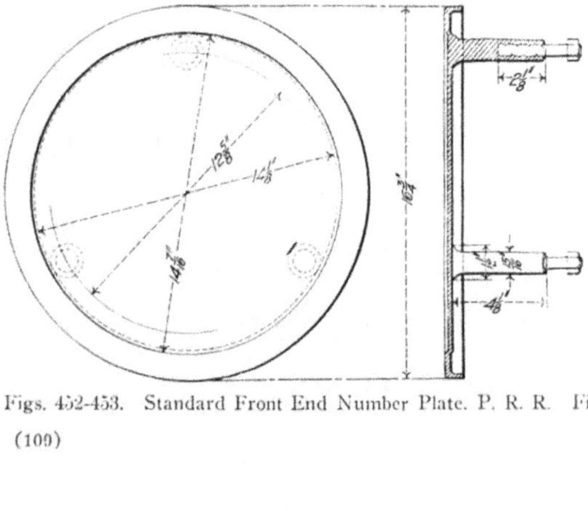

Figs. 452-453. Standard Front End Number Plate. P. R. R.    Fig. 454. Standard Badge Plate. Pennsylvania Railroad.

(109)

Figs. 455-471 SMOKESTACKS, Taper and Straight.

Numbers Refer to List of Names of Parts with Figs. 478-482.

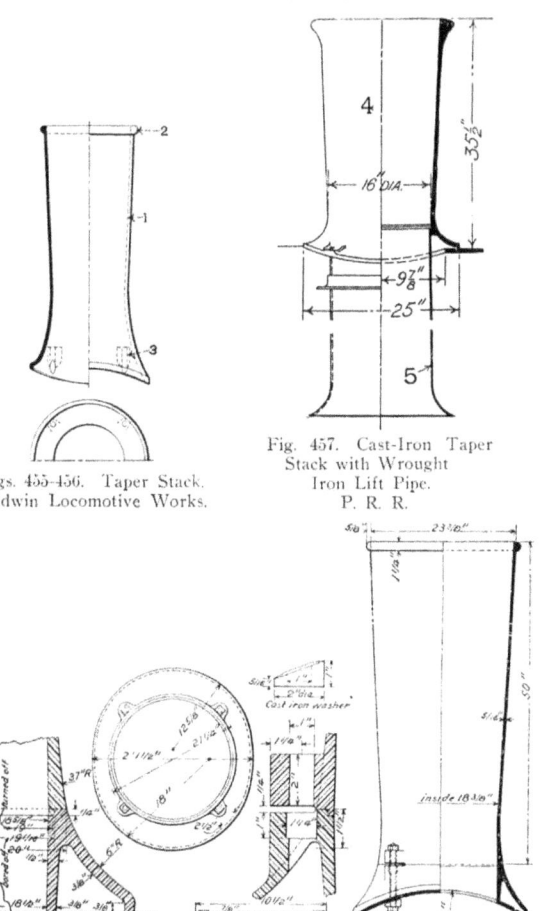

Figs. 455-456. Taper Stack. Baldwin Locomotive Works.

Fig. 457. Cast-Iron Taper Stack with Wrought Iron Lift Pipe. P. R. R.

Figs. 458-463. Cast-Iron Taper Stack. Six-Wheel (0—6—0) Switching Locomotive. Baltimore & Ohio.

Figs. 464-465. Taper Stack and Brace. Southern Pacific.

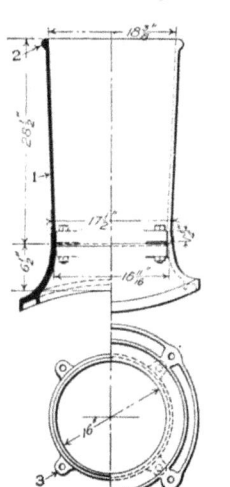

Figs. 466-467. Cast-Iron Taper Stack. American Loco. Co.

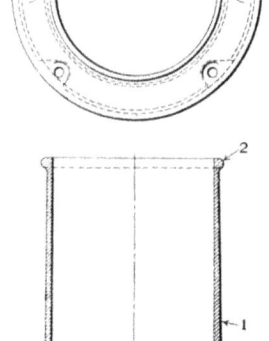

Figs. 468-469. Cast-Iron Straight Stack. American Loco. Co.

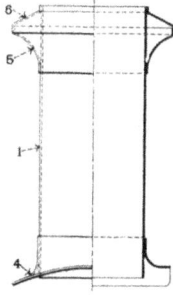

Fig. 470. Straight Stack. Baldwin Loco. Wks.

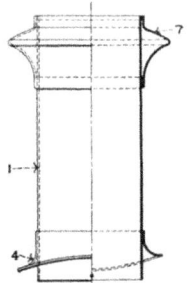

Fig. 471. Straight Stack. Baldwin Loco. Wks.

(110)

SMOKESTACKS, Diamond. Figs. 472-477

Numbers Refer to List of Names of Parts with Figs. 478-482.

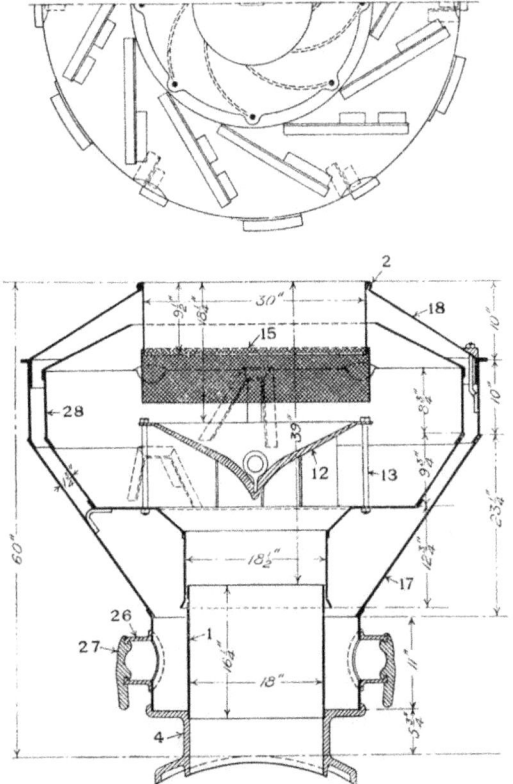

Figs. 472-473. Radley & Hunter Diamond Stack.

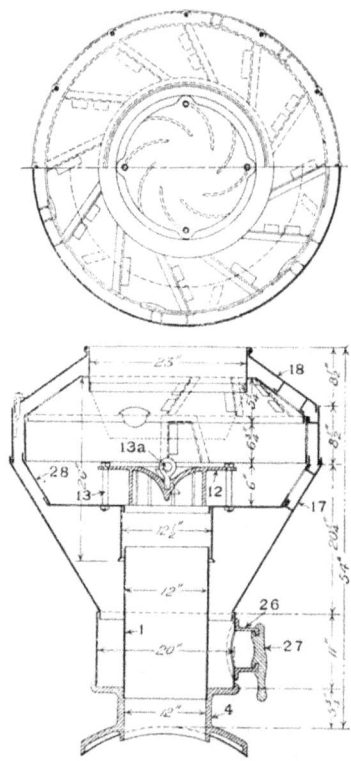

Figs. 474-475. Diamond Stack for Wood Burning Locomotive.

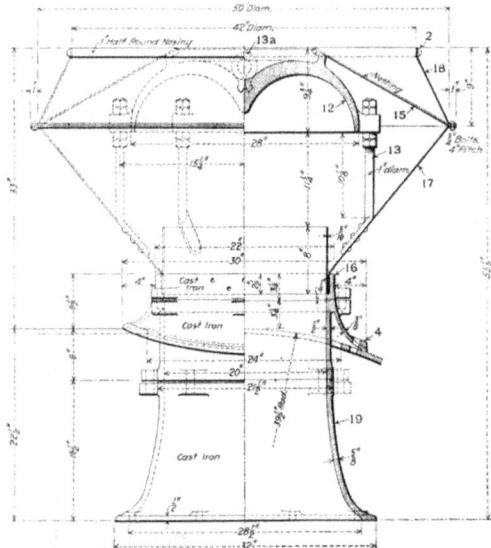

Fig. 476. Diamond Stack for Mikado (2—8—2) Locomotive, Northern Pacific, Burning Lignite.

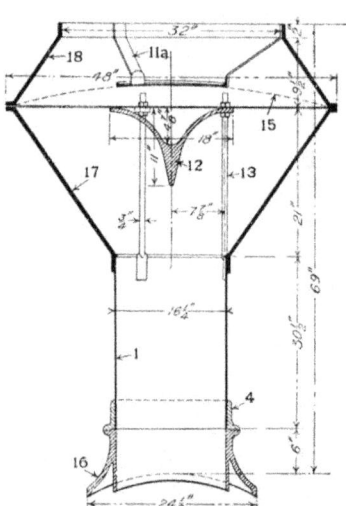

Fig. 477. Diamond Stack for Wood Burning Locomotive. American Locomotive Co.

(111)

Figs. 478-482   SMOKESTACKS, Details; Deflectors.

Numbers Refer to List of Names of Parts Below.

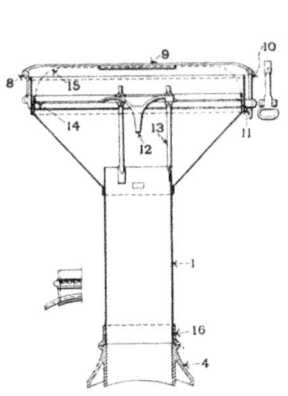

Fig. 478. Diamond Stack for Wood Burning Locomotive. Baldwin Locomotive Works.

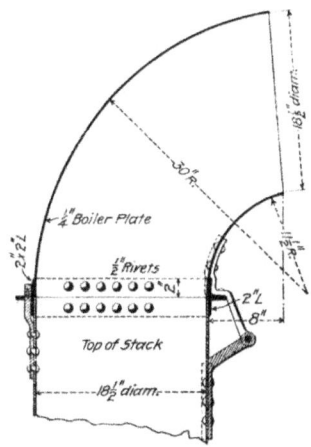

Fig. 479. Smokestack Hood. Great Northern.

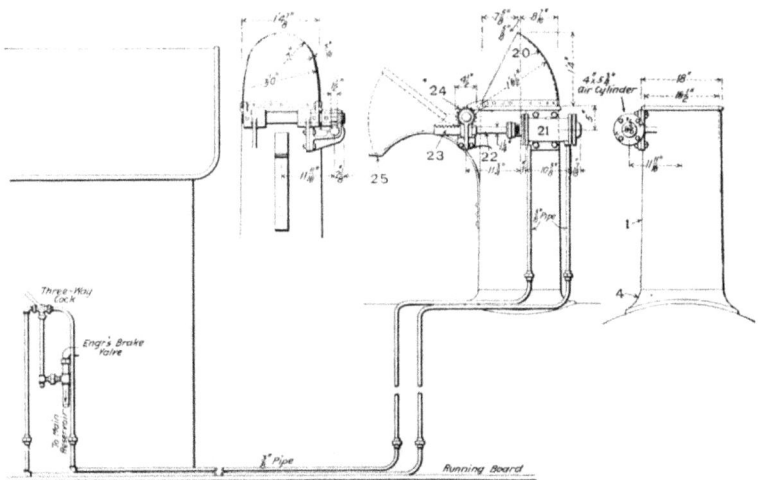

Figs. 480-482. Pneumatically Operated Smoke Deflector. Denver, Northwestern & Pacific.

Names of Parts of Smokestacks, Figs. 455-482.

1 Barrel	11 Netting Latch Staple	19 Lift Pipe
2 Bead or Nosing	11a Netting Support	20 Hood
3 Base Lug	12 Cone	21 Hood Operating Cylinder
4 Base	13 Cone Support	22 Hood Operating Piston Rod
5 Lower Cap	13a Cone Lift Ring	23 Hood Rack
6 Upper Cap	14 Netting Angle	24 Hood Pinion
7 Cap	15 Netting	25 Hood Support
8 Netting Brace Hinge	16 Base Ring	26 Cinder Cleaning Flange
9 Netting Brace	17 Bottom Flare	27 Cinder Cleaning Flange Cap
10 Netting Latch	18 Top Flare	28 Inner Flare

(112)

SUPERHEATERS, Smokebox; Schmidt. Figs. 483-484

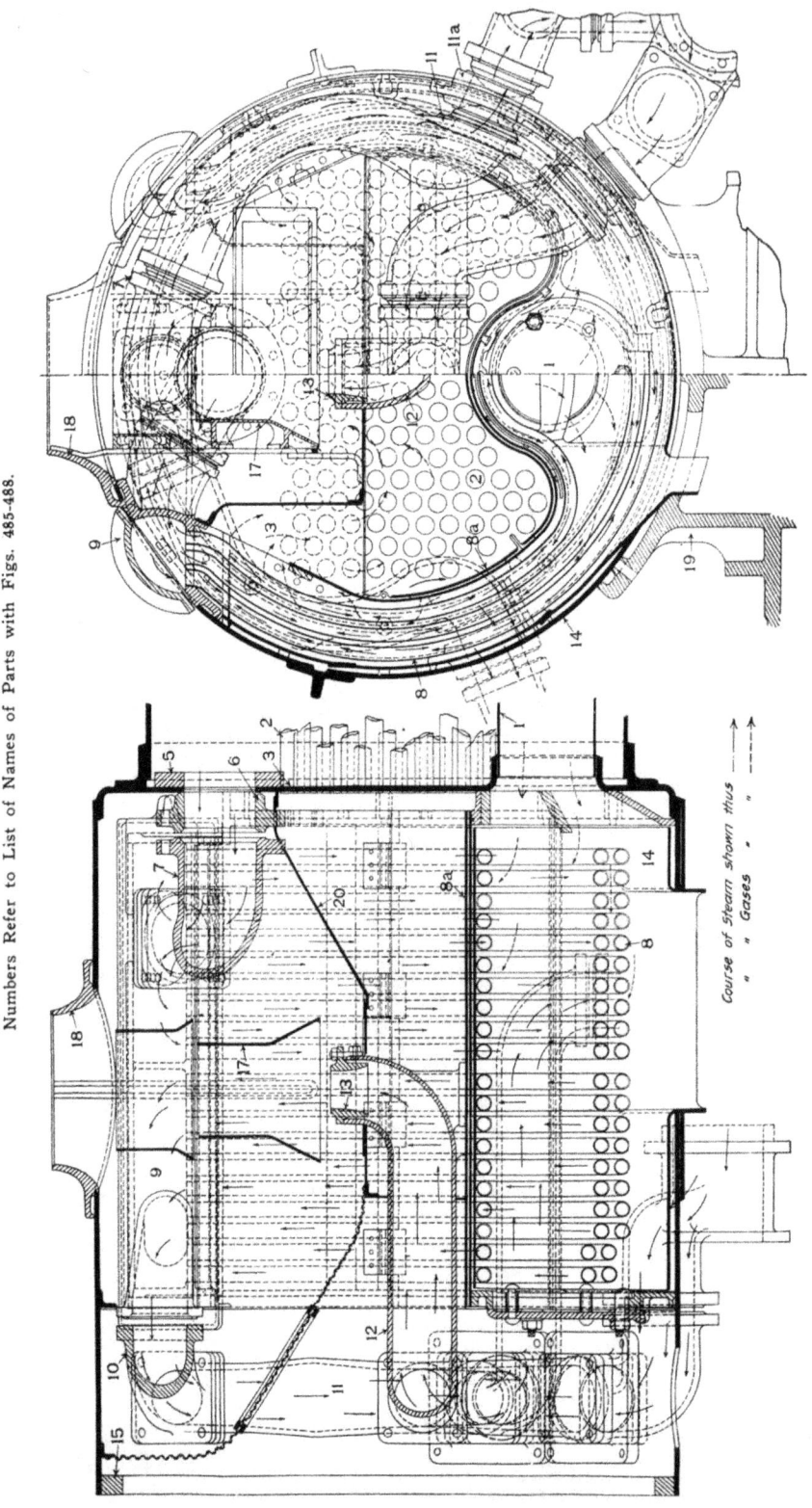

Figs. 483-484. Schmidt Smokebox Superheater as Applied to Locomotives on the Canadian Pacific. Numbers Refer to List of Names of Parts with Figs. 485-488.

Numbers Refer to List of Names of Parts Below.

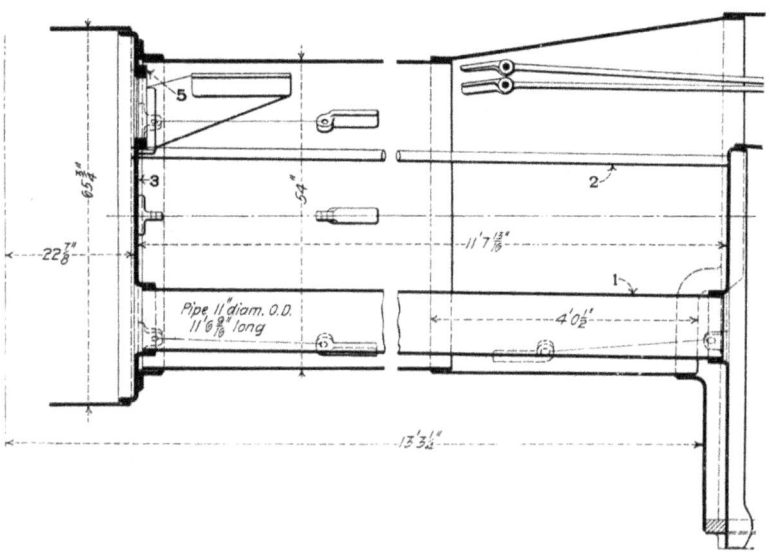

Fig. 485. Boiler Shell Used with Schmidt Smokebox Superheater. Canadian Pacific.

Names of Parts of Superheaters, Figs. 483-507.

1	Flue	8b	Superheater Tube Return Bend	16	Netting
2	Boiler Tubes	9	Headers	17	Petticoat Pipe
3	Front Tube Sheet	9a	Header Plugs	18	Smokestack Base
4	Dry Pipe	10	Connection to Steam Pipe	19	Saddle
5	Dry Pipe Stiffening Ring	11	Steam Pipe	20	Diaphragm
6	Dry Pipe Ball Joint	11a	Steam Pipe Ball Joint	21	Fire Tube for Superheater
7	Tee Head	12	Exhaust Pipe	22	Superheater Damper
8	Superheater Tubes	13	Exhaust Nozzle	23	Superheater Damper Rod
8a	Superheater Tube Shield	14	Smokebox	24	Superheater Damper Operating Cylinder
8b	Superheater Tube Holder	15	Smokebox Ring		

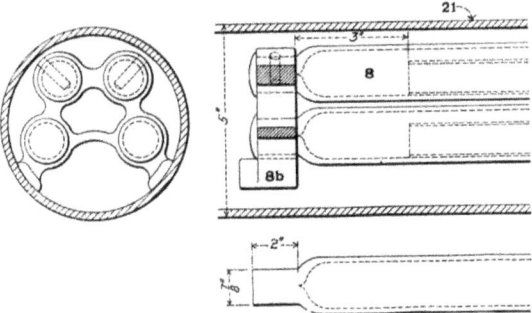

Figs. 486-488. Arrangement of Back End of Superheater Tubes for Cole Superheater. American Locomotive Co.

(114)

SUPERHEATERS, Fire Tube; Cole.

Figs. 489-495

Numbers Refer to List of Names of Parts with Figs. 485-488.

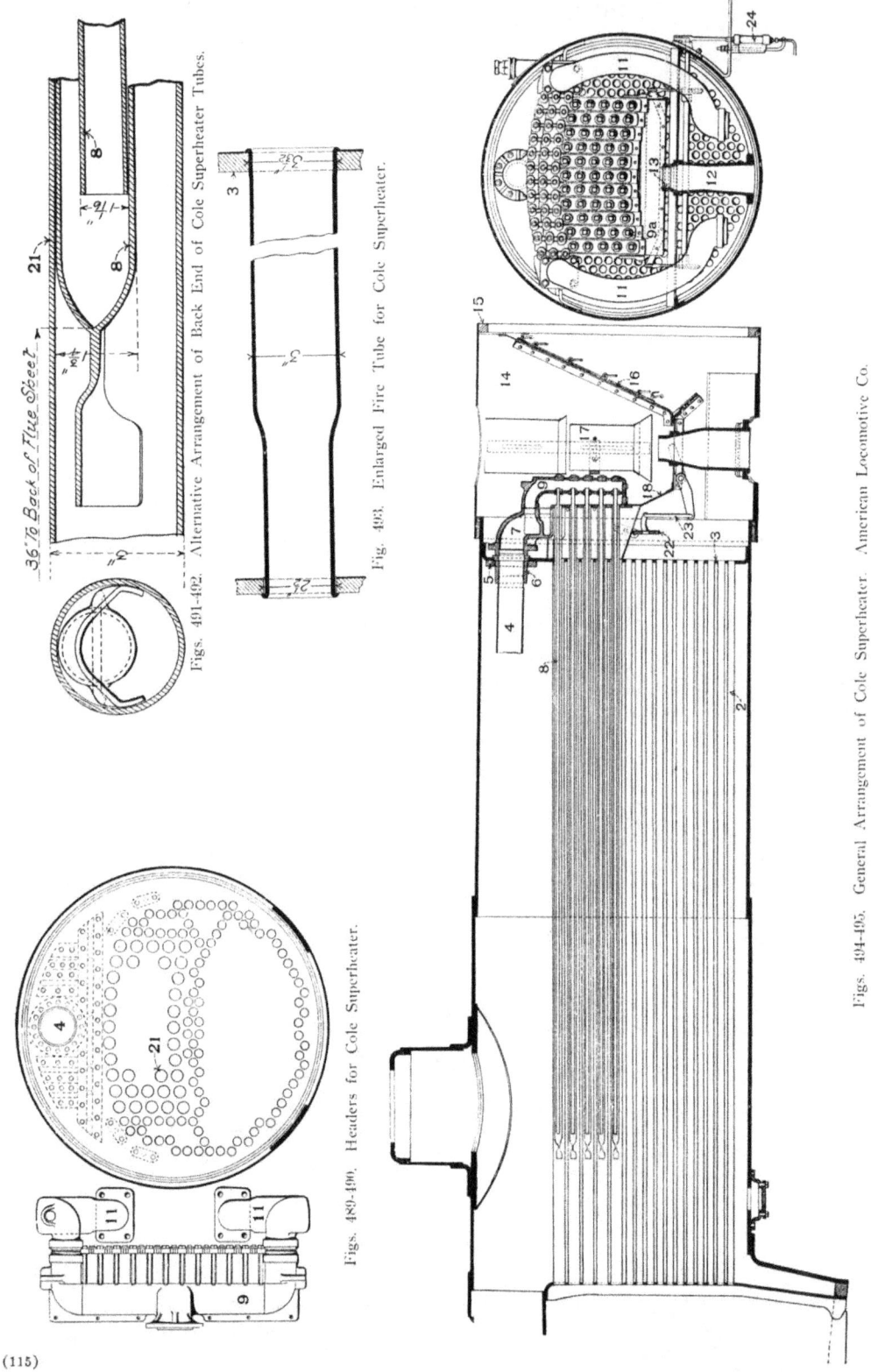

Figs. 491-492. Alternative Arrangement of Back End of Cole Superheater Tubes.
Fig. 493. Enlarged Fire Tube for Cole Superheater.
Figs. 489-490. Headers for Cole Superheater.
Figs. 494-495. General Arrangement of Cole Superheater. American Locomotive Co.

Figs. 496-503 SUPERHEATERS, Fire Tube; Vaughan.

Numbers Refer to List of Names of Parts with Figs. 485-488.

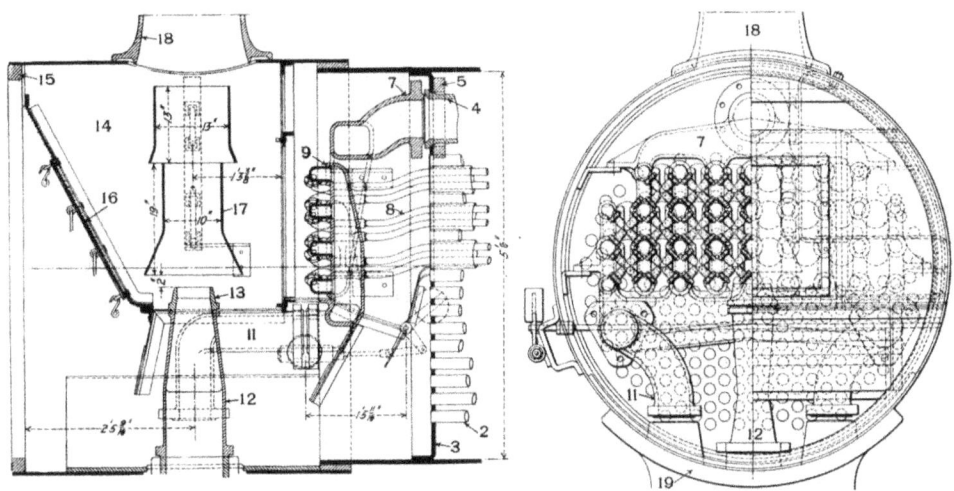

Figs. 496-497. General Arrangement of Vaughan Superheater as Applied to Locomotives on the Canadian Pacific.

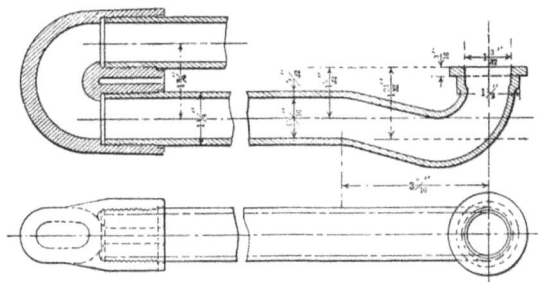

Figs. 498-499. Superheater Tubes with Upset Ends and Return Bend Connection.

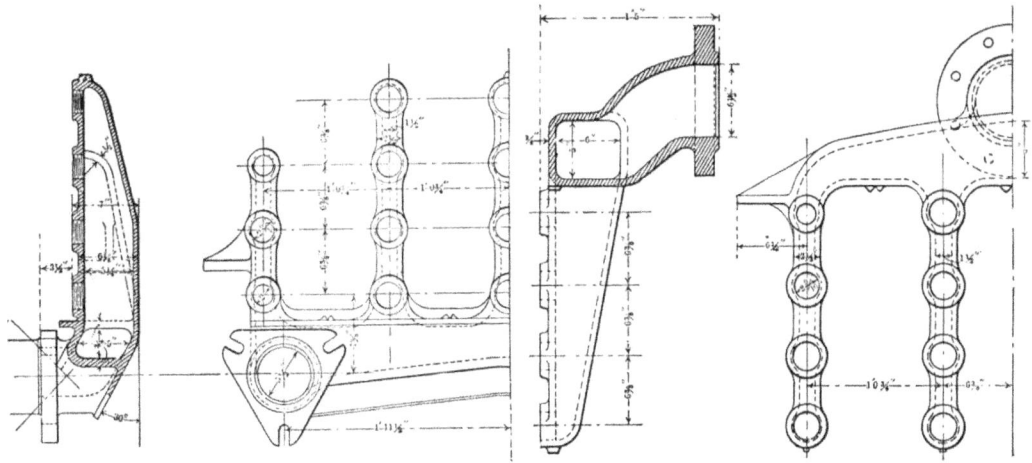

Figs. 500-501. Bottom or Superheated Steam Header for Vaughan Superheater.

Figs. 502-503. Top or Saturated Steam Header for Vaughan Superheater.

(116)

SUPERHEATERS, Fire Tube; Schmidt.

Figs. 504-507

Numbers Refer to List of Names of Parts with Figs. 485-488.

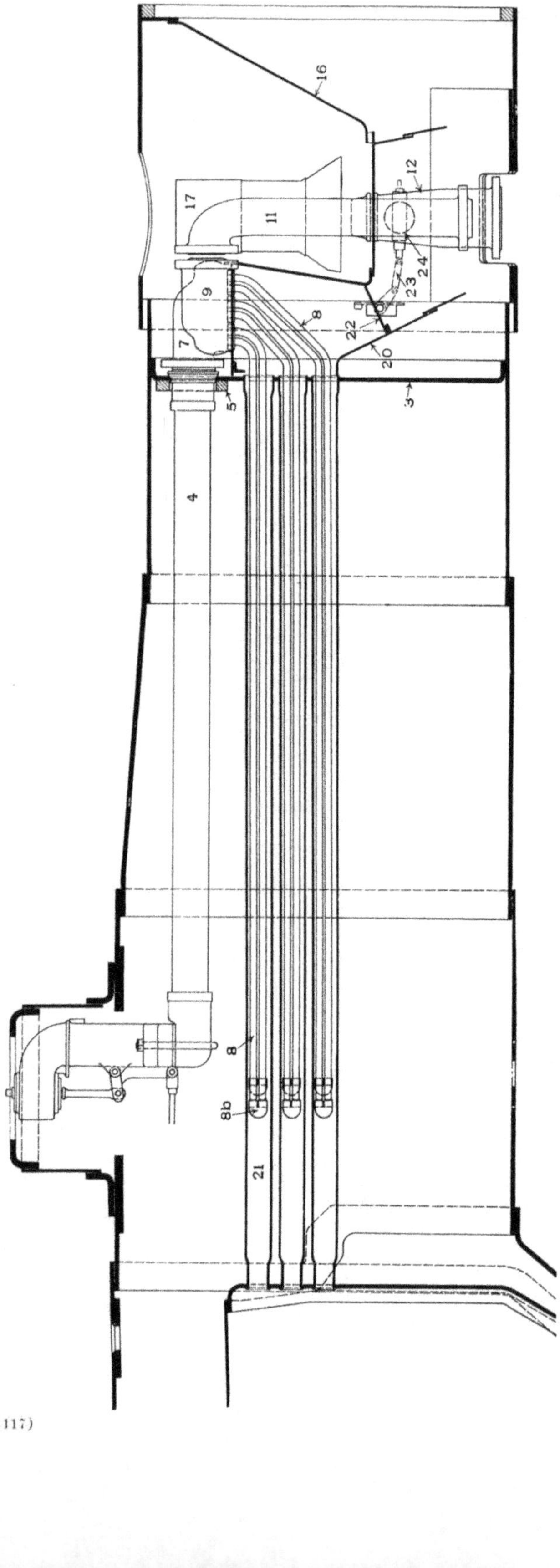

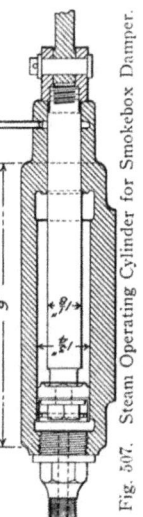

Fig. 504. General Arrangement of Schmidt Fire Tube Superheater as Applied to Locomotives on the Canadian Pacific.

Fig. 505-506. Back End of Superheater Tubes.

Fig. 507. Steam Operating Cylinder for Smokebox Damper.

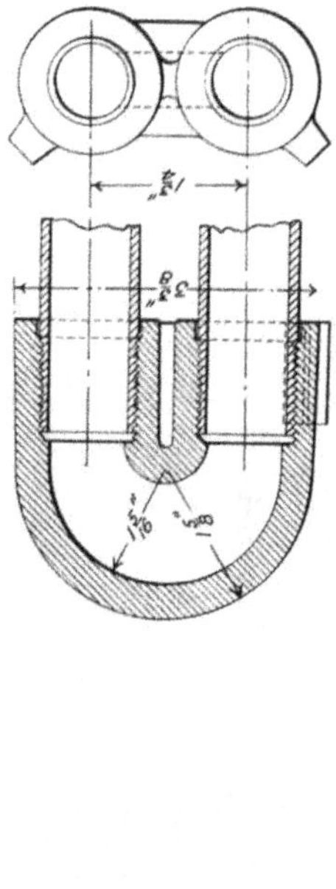

(117)

Figs. 508-511   ASHPANS, Assembled Views.

Numbers Refer to List of Names of Parts with Figs. 528-545.

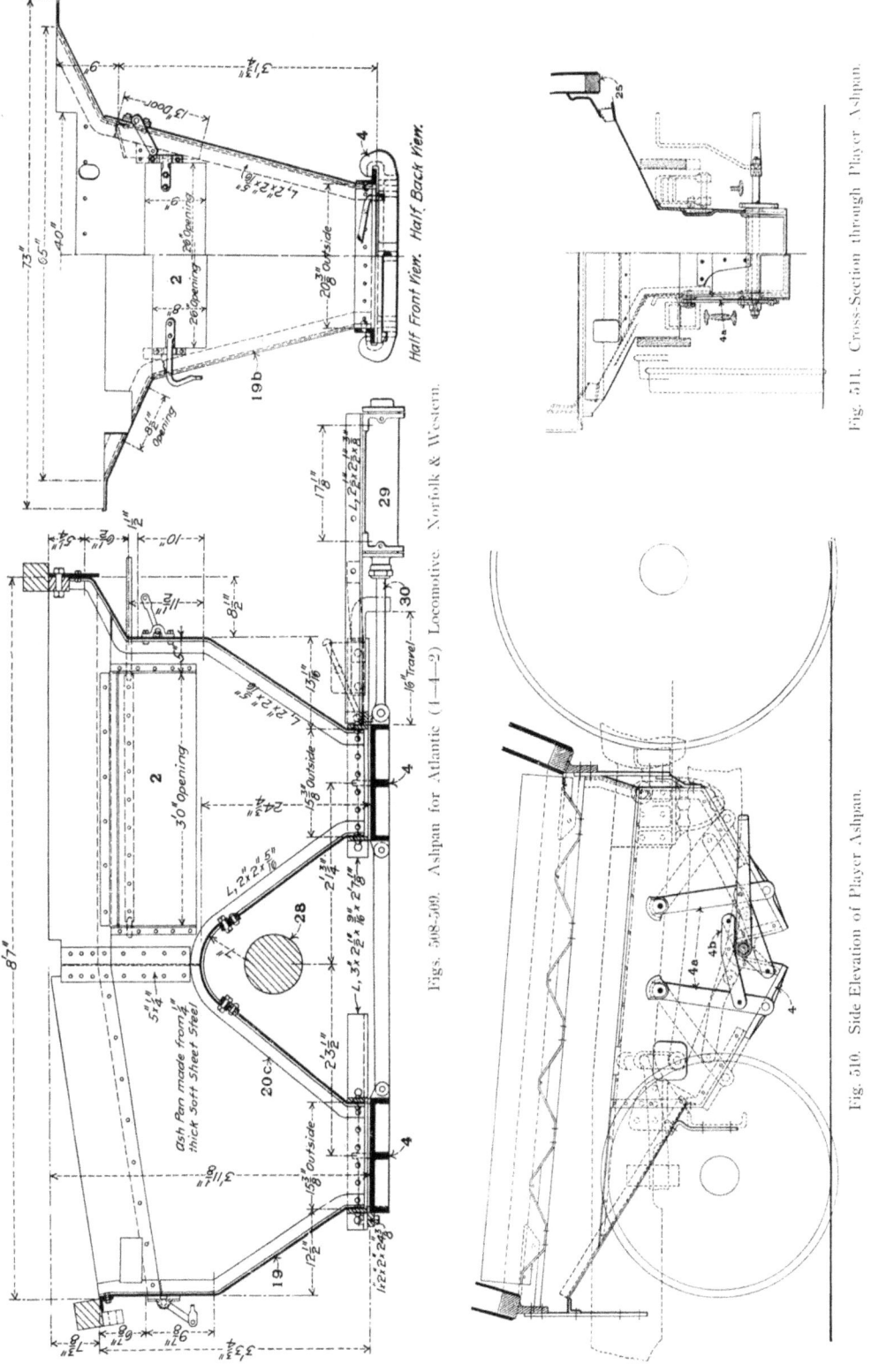

Figs. 508-509. Ashpan for Atlantic (4-4-2) Locomotive. Norfolk & Western.

Fig. 510. Side Elevation of Player Ashpan.

Fig. 511. Cross-Section through Player Ashpan.

Numbers Refer to List of Names of Parts with Figs. 528-545.

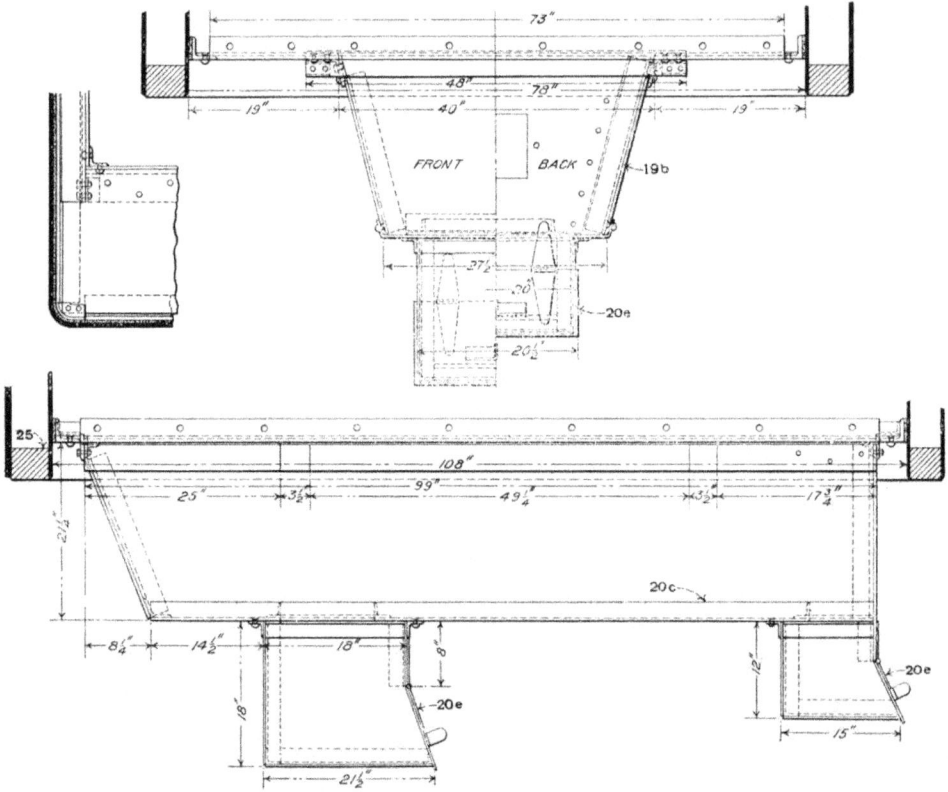

Figs. 512-514. Ashpan for Oil Burning Locomotive. Atchison, Topeka & Santa Fe.

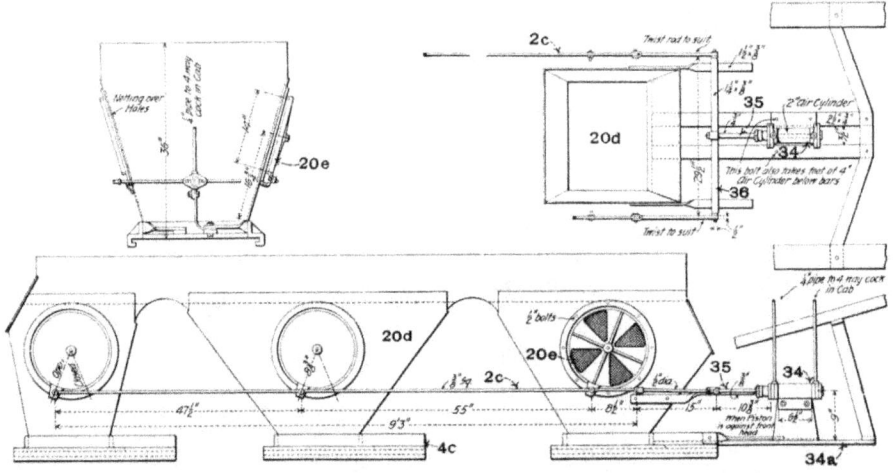

Figs. 515-517. Application of Pneumatically Operated Air Valves to Sides of Deep Hopper Ashpans. Southern Pacific.

ASHPANS, Assembled Views.

Numbers Refer to List of Names of Parts with Figs. 528-545.

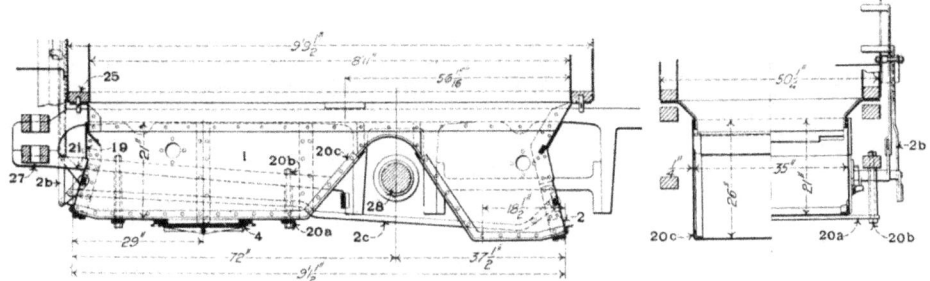

Figs. 518-519. Ashpan for Eight-Wheel (4—4—0) Locomotive. Pennsylvania Railroad.

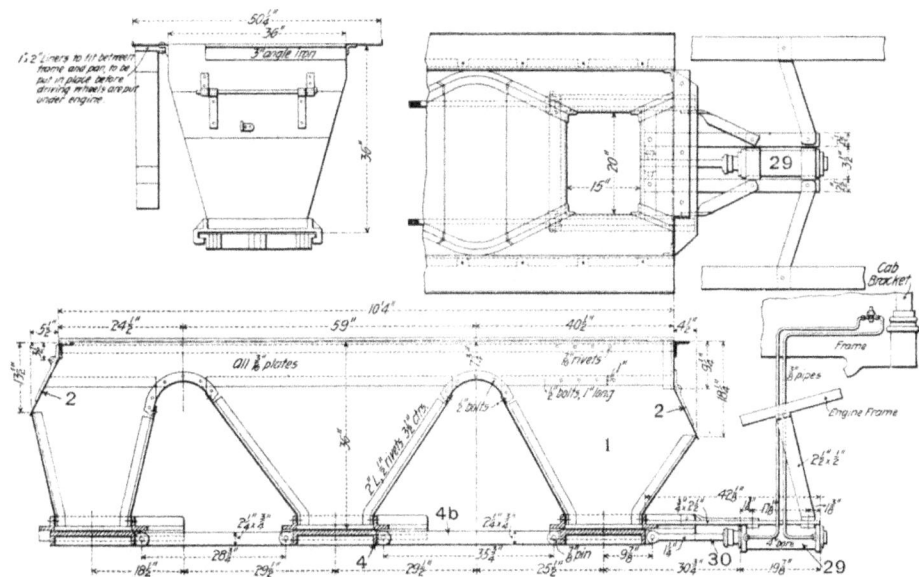

Figs. 520-522. Deep Hopper Ashpan Operated by Compressed Air. Southern Pacific.

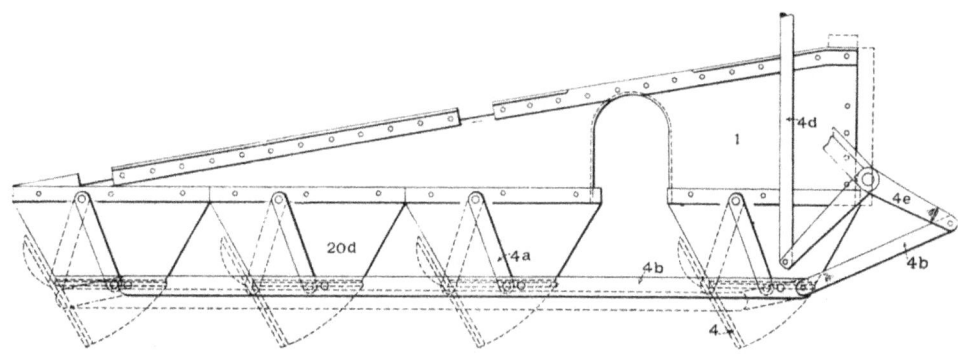

Fig. 523. Hale Ashpan as Applied to Locomotives on the New York, Ontario & Western.

ASHPANS AND GRATES, Assembled Views. Figs. 524-527

Numbers Refer to List of Names of Parts with Figs. 528-545.

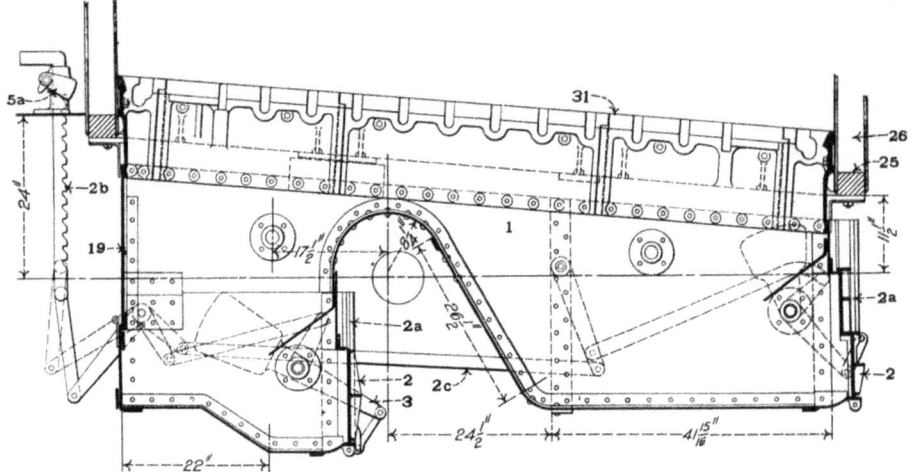

Fig. 524. Ashpan for Mogul (2—6—0) Locomotive. Pennsylvania Railroad.

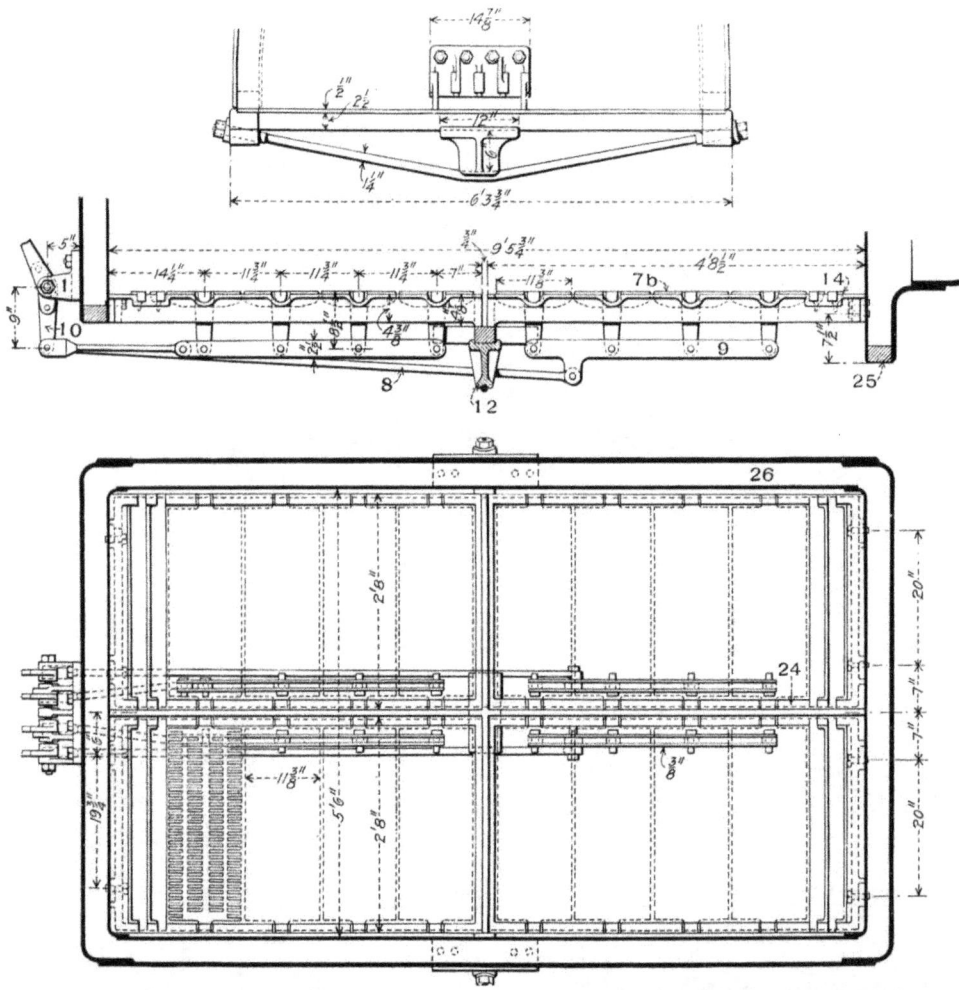

Figs. 525-527. Grate for Six-Wheel (0—6—0) Switching Locomotive with Wide Firebox. Erie Railroad.

ASHPANS AND GRATES, Assembled Views.

Numbers Refer to List of Names of Parts Below.

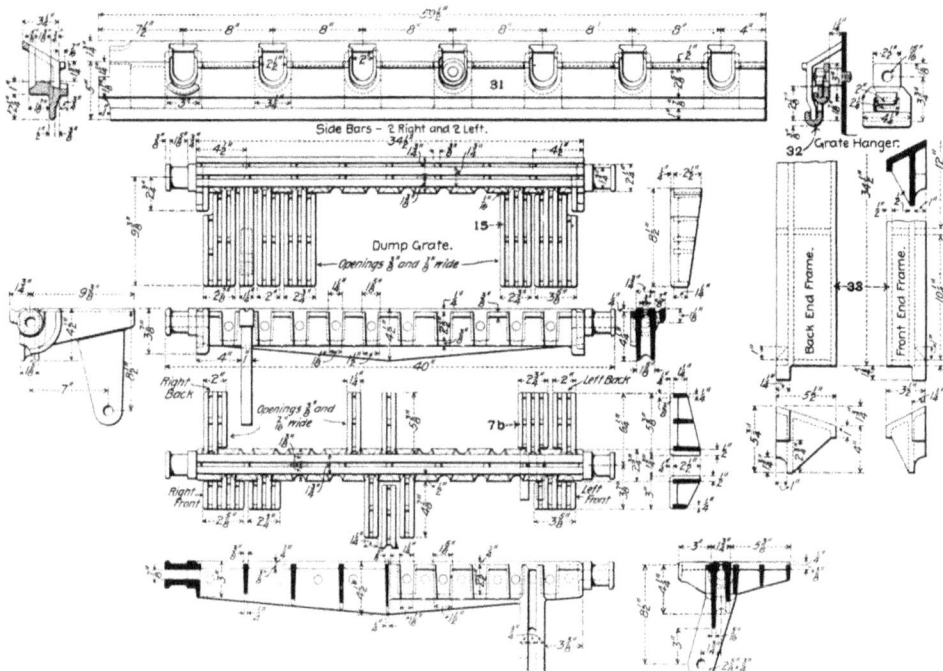

Figs. 528-545. Improved Finger Grates and Grate Bearings. Southern Pacific.

Names of Parts of Grates and Ashpans, Figs. 508-549.

- 1 Ashpan
- 2 Damper
- 2a Damper Guide
- 2b Damper Rigging Handle
- 2c Damper Rigging Rod
- 2d Damper Rigging Shaft
- 2e Damper Rigging Shaft Bearing
- 2f Damper Rigging Pin
- 2g Damper Hinge
- 2h Rear Damper
- 2i Damper Operating Arms
- 3 Damper Bell Crank with Counterweight
- 4 Slide for Drop
- 4a Slide Hanger
- 4b Slide Rod
- 4c Slide Guide
- 4d Slide Operating Handle
- 4e Slide Operating Bell Crank
- 5 Drop Cross Brace
- 5a Drop Latch
- 6 Ashpan Support and Injector Overflow
- 7 Front Side Grate and Ashpan Support
- 7a Fixed Grate
- 7b Shaking Grate
- 8 Shaking Grate Rod
- 9 Shaking Grate Connection Bar
- 10 Shaking Grate Lever
- 11 Shaking Grate Lever Fulcrum
- 12 Foundation Ring Cross Brace
- 13 Corner Grate
- 14 Dead Plate
- 15 Drop Grate
- 16 Drop Grate Operating Arm
- 17 Drop Grate Shaft Bearing
- 18 Same as 17
- 18a Drop Grate Tie Bolt
- 18b Drop Grate Shaft Center Bearing Bolt
- 19 Rear Ashpan Sheet
- 19a Side Ashpan Sheet
- 20 Ashpan Bracket
- 20a Ashpan Supporting Plate
- 20b Ashpan Supporting Bolt
- 20c Ashpan Corner Angle
- 20d Ashpan Hopper
- 20e Ashpan Hopper Damper
- 21 Brace for Operating Hopper
- 24 Grate Center Bearing
- 25 Mudring
- 26 Water Leg
- 27 Engine Frame
- 28 Axle
- 29 Slide Operating Cylinder
- 30 Slide Operating Piston Rod
- 31 Side Bars or Grate Frame
- 32 Grate Hanger
- 33 Grate End Frame
- 34 Damper Operating Cylinder
- 34a Damper Operating Cylinder Bracket
- 35 Damper Operating Piston Rod
- 36 Damper Operating Cross Bar

ASHPANS AND GRATES, Details.

Numbers Refer to List of Names of Parts on Opposite Page.

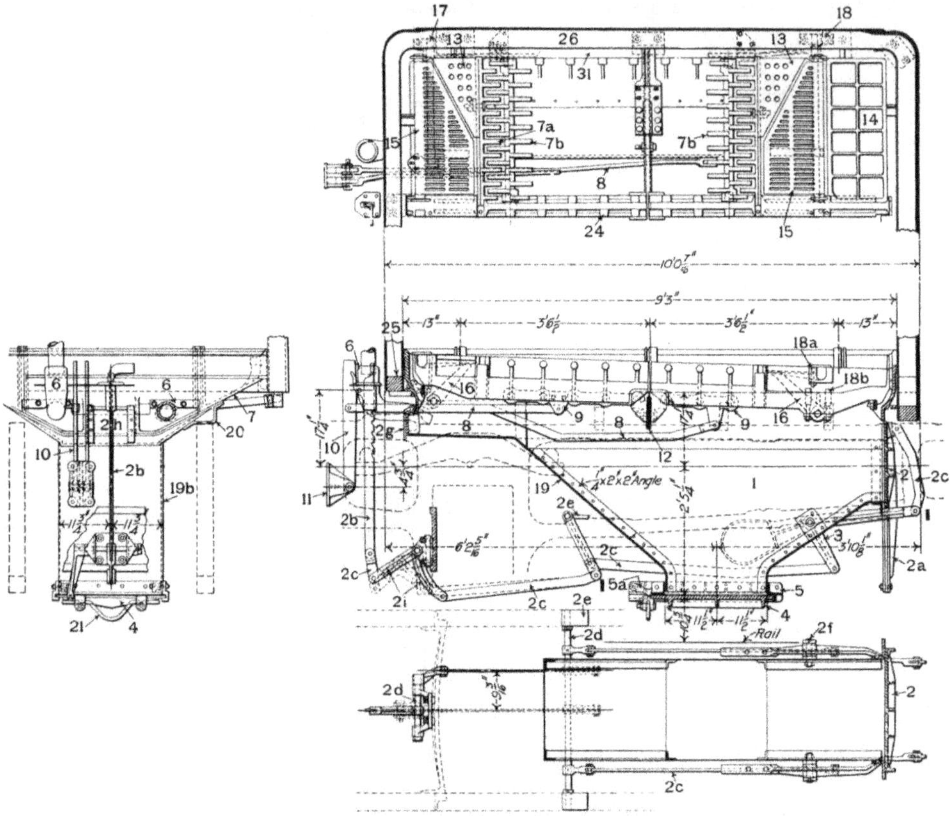

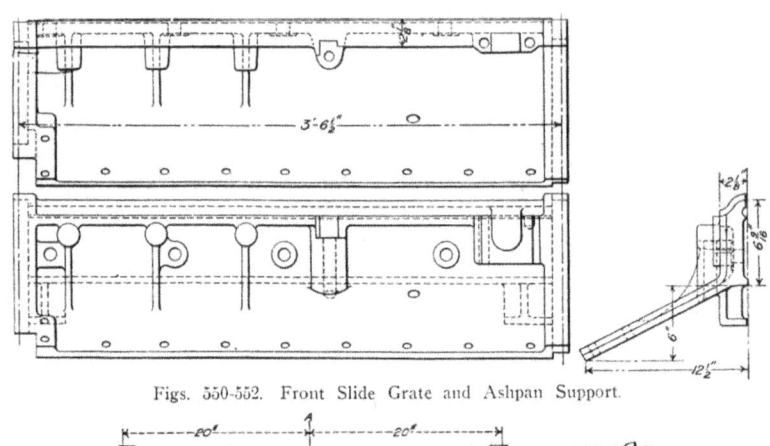

Figs. 546–549. General Arrangement of Ashpan and Shaking Grate. Atlantic (4—4—2) Locomotive. Pennsylvania Railroad.

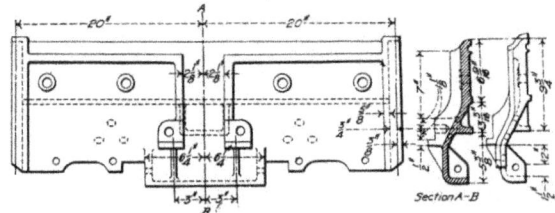

Figs. 550–552. Front Slide Grate and Ashpan Support.

Figs. 553–555. Back Intermediate Section Grate and Ashpan Support.

Figs. 546–555. Details of Ashpan and Shaking Grate. Atlantic (4—4—2) Locomotive. Pennsylvania Railroad.
(123)

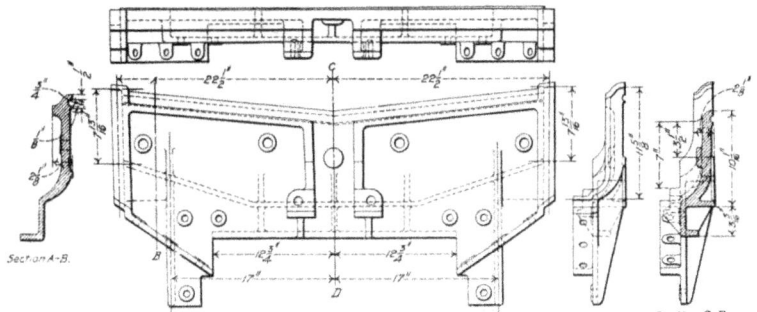

Figs. 556-560. Front Intermediate Section Grate and Ashpan Support.

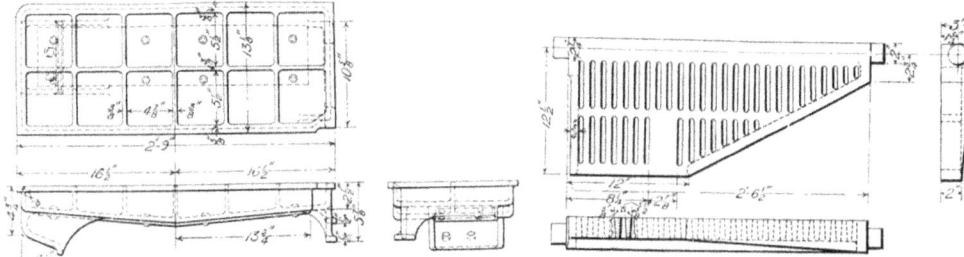

Figs. 561-563. Deal Plate for Grate. Figs. 564-566. Drop Grate.

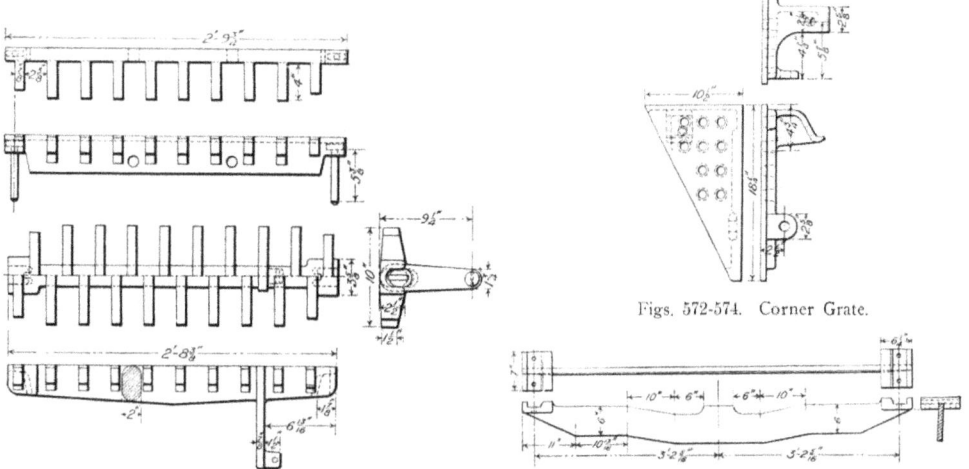

Figs. 567-571. Finger Grate Bars. Figs. 572-574. Corner Grate. Figs. 575-577. Foundation Ring Cross Brace.

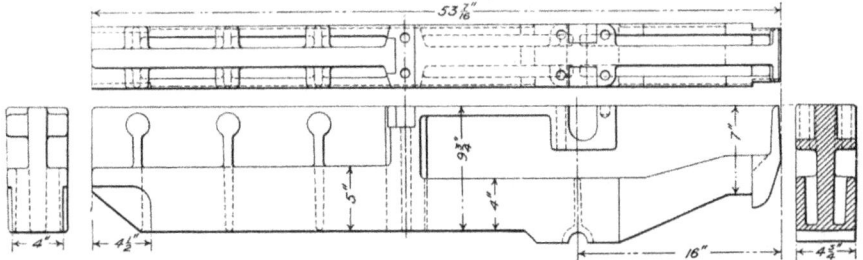

Figs. 578-581. Front Grate Center Support.
Details of Ashpan and Shaking Grate, Atlantic (4—4—2) Locomotive. Pennsylvania Railroad.

ASHPANS AND GRATES, Details.

Figs. 582-631

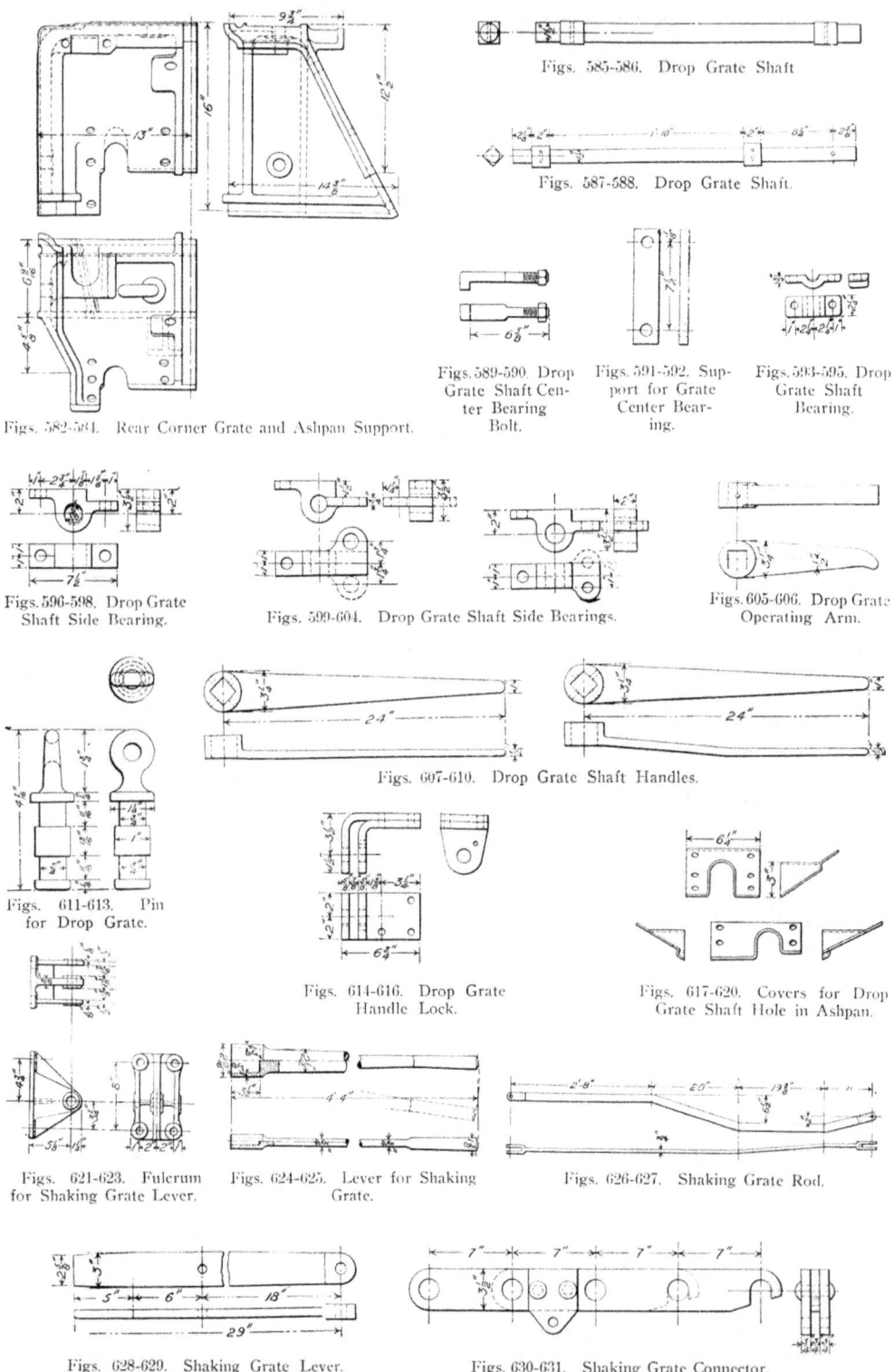

Figs. 582-584. Rear Corner Grate and Ashpan Support.
Figs. 585-586. Drop Grate Shaft
Figs. 587-588. Drop Grate Shaft.
Figs. 589-590. Drop Grate Shaft Center Bearing Bolt.
Figs. 591-592. Support for Grate Center Bearing.
Figs. 593-595. Drop Grate Shaft Bearing.
Figs. 596-598. Drop Grate Shaft Side Bearing.
Figs. 599-604. Drop Grate Shaft Side Bearings.
Figs. 605-606. Drop Grate Operating Arm.
Figs. 607-610. Drop Grate Shaft Handles.
Figs. 611-613. Pin for Drop Grate.
Figs. 614-616. Drop Grate Handle Lock.
Figs. 617-620. Covers for Drop Grate Shaft Hole in Ashpan.
Figs. 621-623. Fulcrum for Shaking Grate Lever.
Figs. 624-625. Lever for Shaking Grate.
Figs. 626-627. Shaking Grate Rod.
Figs. 628-629. Shaking Grate Lever.
Figs. 630-631. Shaking Grate Connector.

Details of Ashpan and Shaking Grate, Atlantic (4—4—2) Locomotive. Pennsylvania Railroad.

ASHPANS AND GRATES, Details.

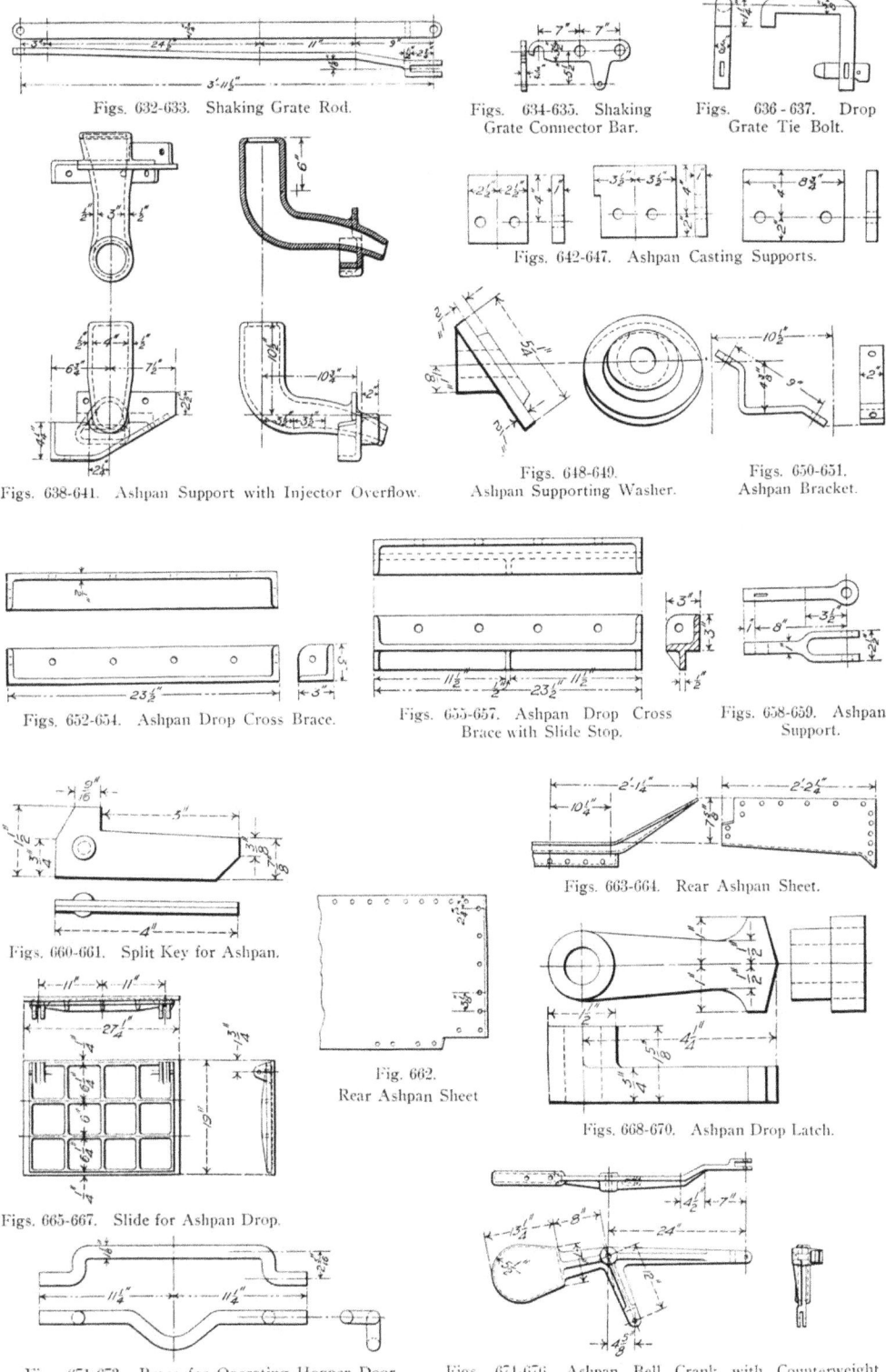

Figs. 632-633. Shaking Grate Rod.

Figs. 634-635. Shaking Grate Connector Bar.

Figs. 636-637. Drop Grate Tie Bolt.

Figs. 642-647. Ashpan Casting Supports.

Figs. 638-641. Ashpan Support with Injector Overflow.

Figs. 648-649. Ashpan Supporting Washer.

Figs. 650-651. Ashpan Bracket.

Figs. 652-654. Ashpan Drop Cross Brace.

Figs. 655-657. Ashpan Drop Cross Brace with Slide Stop.

Figs. 658-659. Ashpan Support.

Figs. 660-661. Split Key for Ashpan.

Fig. 662. Rear Ashpan Sheet.

Figs. 663-664. Rear Ashpan Sheet.

Figs. 665-667. Slide for Ashpan Drop.

Figs. 668-670. Ashpan Drop Latch.

Figs. 671-673. Brace for Operating Hopper Door.

Figs. 674-676. Ashpan Bell Crank with Counterweight.

Details of Ashpan and Shaking Grate. Atlantic (4—4—2) Locomotive. Pennsylvania Railroad.

ASHPANS AND GRATES, Details.

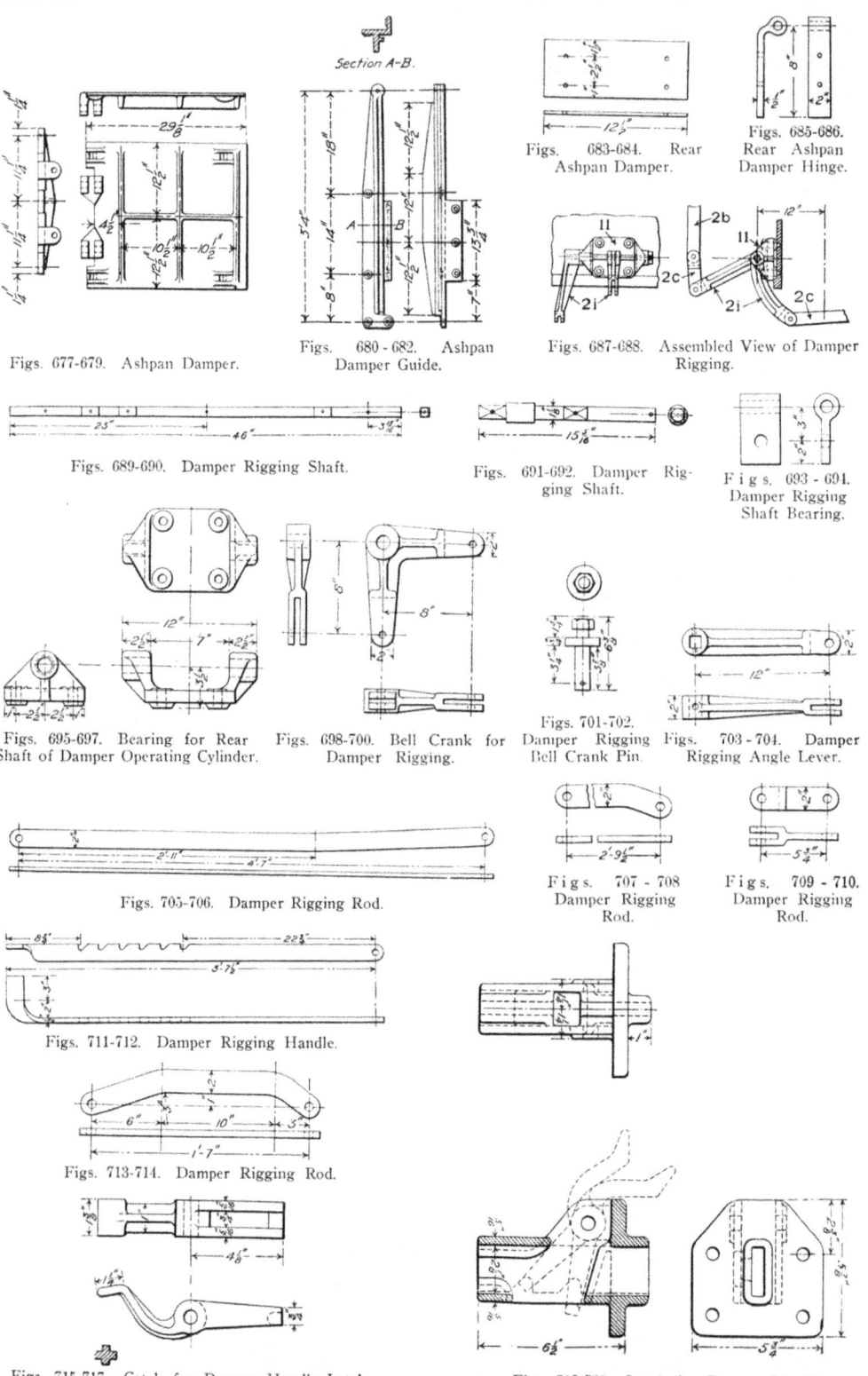

Figs. 677-679. Ashpan Damper.
Figs. 680-682. Ashpan Damper Guide.
Figs. 683-684. Rear Ashpan Damper.
Figs. 685-686. Rear Ashpan Damper Hinge.
Figs. 687-688. Assembled View of Damper Rigging.
Figs. 689-690. Damper Rigging Shaft.
Figs. 691-692. Damper Rigging Shaft.
Figs. 693-694. Damper Rigging Shaft Bearing.
Figs. 695-697. Bearing for Rear Shaft of Damper Operating Cylinder.
Figs. 698-700. Bell Crank for Damper Rigging.
Figs. 701-702. Damper Rigging Bell Crank Pin.
Figs. 703-704. Damper Rigging Angle Lever.
Figs. 705-706. Damper Rigging Rod.
Figs. 707-708. Damper Rigging Rod.
Figs. 709-710. Damper Rigging Rod.
Figs. 711-712. Damper Rigging Handle.
Figs. 713-714. Damper Rigging Rod.
Figs. 715-717. Catch for Damper Handle Latch.
Figs. 718-720. Latch for Damper Handle.

Details of Ashpan and Shaking Grate, Atlantic (4—4—2) Locomotive. Pennsylvania Railroad.

Figs. 721-729　　OIL BURNING FIREBOXES, Brickwork.

Numbers Refer to List of Names of Parts with Figs. 743-757.

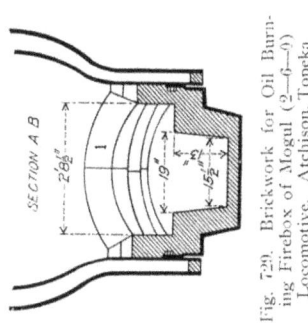

Fig. 729. Brickwork for Oil Burning Firebox of Mogul (2—6—0) Locomotive, Atchison, Topeka & Santa Fe.

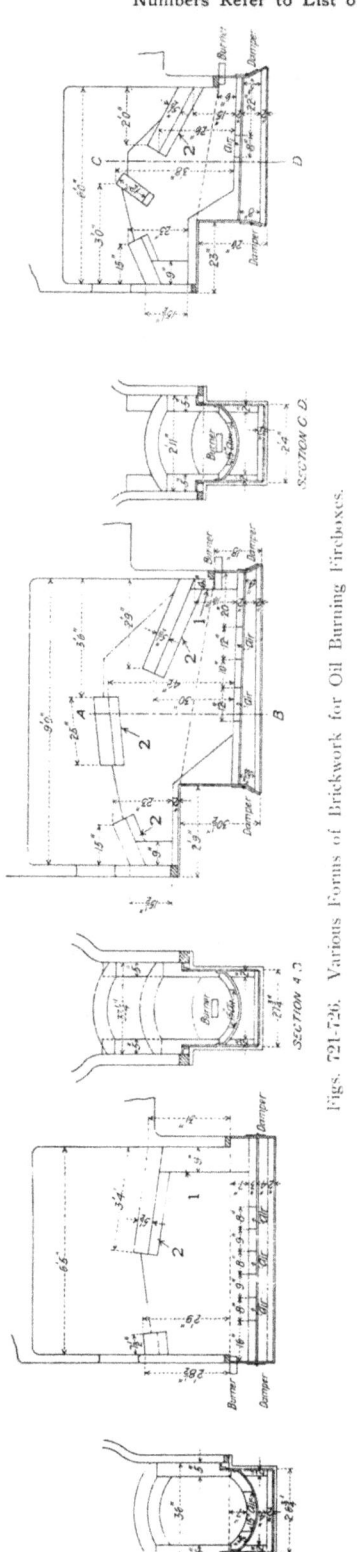

Figs. 721-726. Various Forms of Brickwork for Oil Burning Fireboxes.

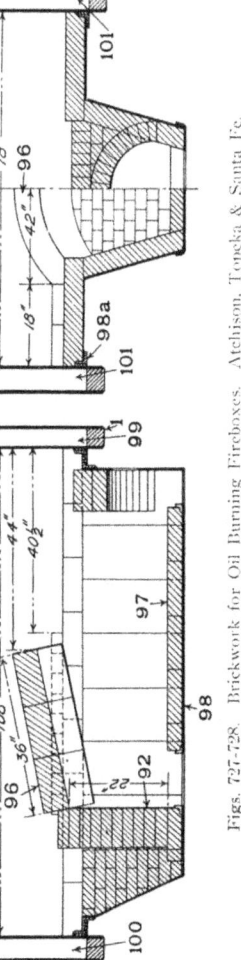

Figs. 727-728. Brickwork for Oil Burning Fireboxes, Atchison, Topeka & Santa Fe.

(128)

OIL BURNING FIREBOXES, General Arrangement. Figs. 730-736

Numbers Refer to List of Names of Parts with Figs. 743-757.

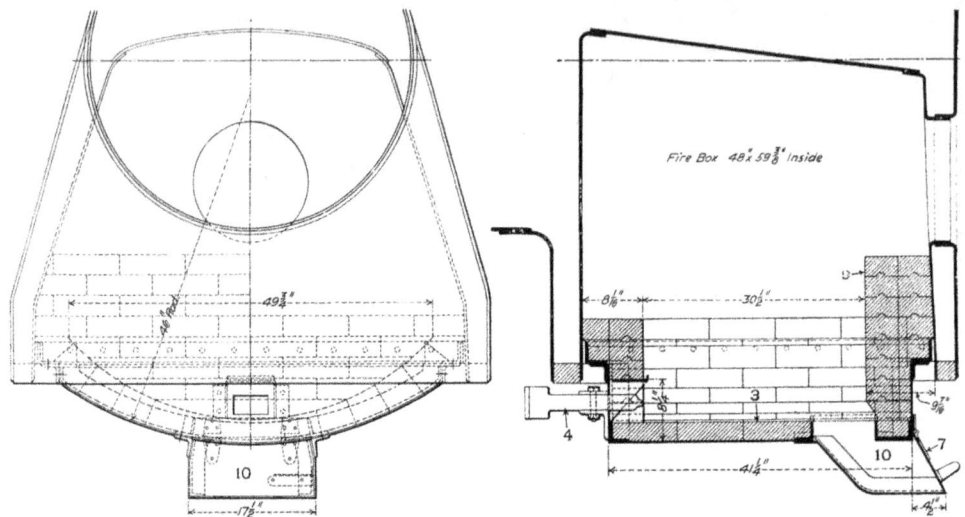

Figs. 730-731. General Arrangement of Oil Burning Firebox for Rack Locomotive. Manitou & Pike's Peak.

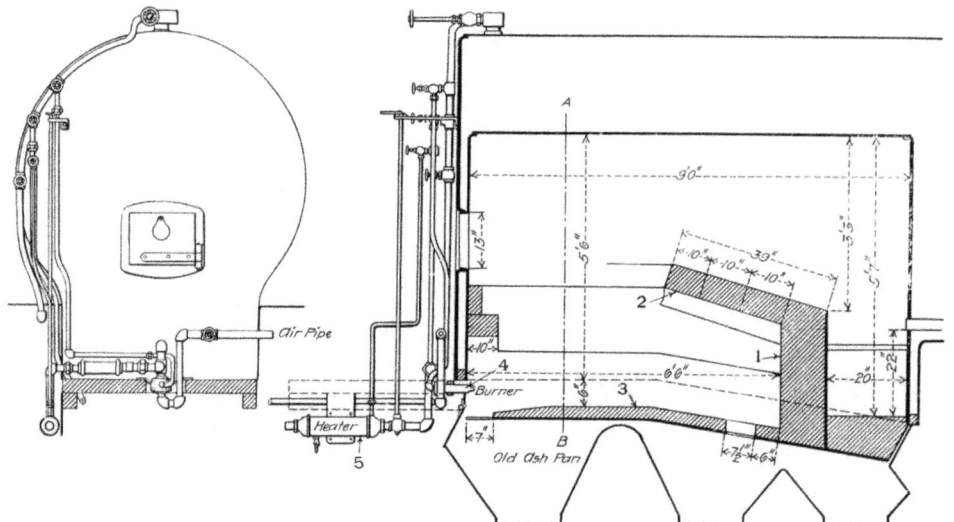

Figs. 732-733. General Arrangement of Oil Burning Firebox for Mogul (2—6—0) Locomotive. Southern Pacific.

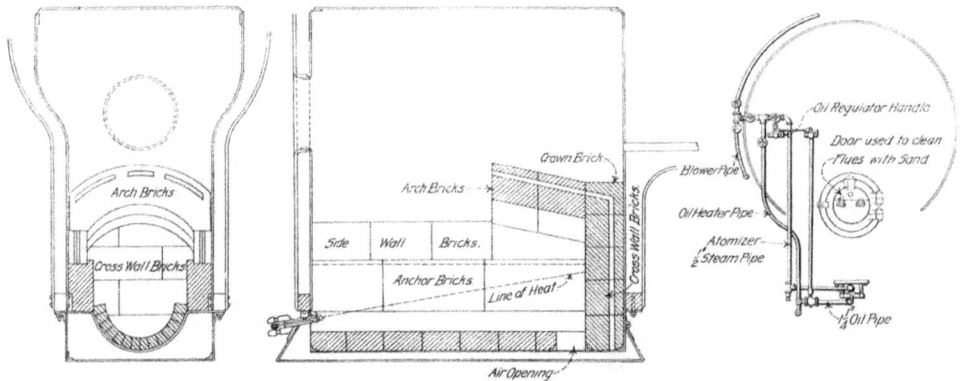

Figs. 734-736. General Arrangement of Oil Burning Firebox for Locomotives. W. N. Best American Calorific Co.

(129)

Figs. 737-742 OIL BURNING FIREBOXES, General Arrangement.

Numbers Refer to List of Names of Parts with Figs. 743-757.

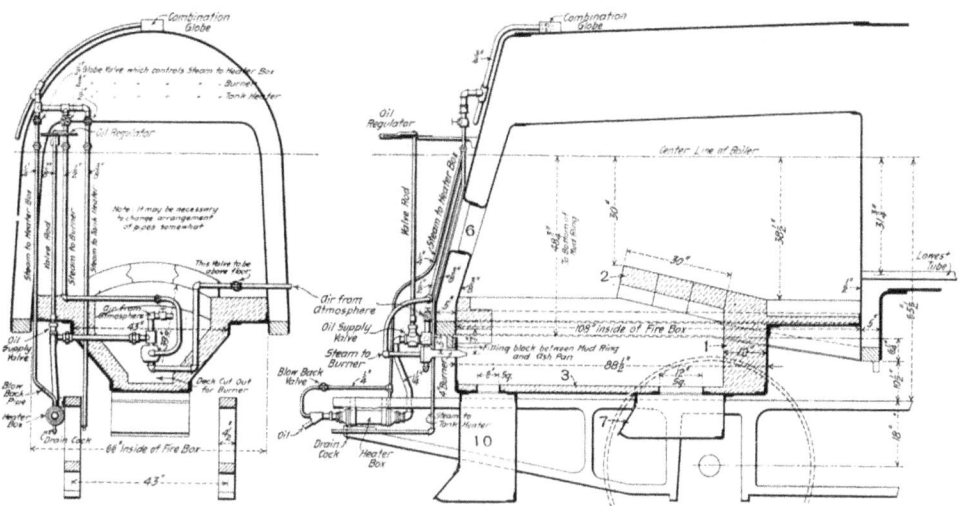

Figs. 737-738. General Arrangement of Oil Burning Firebox. Southern Pacific.

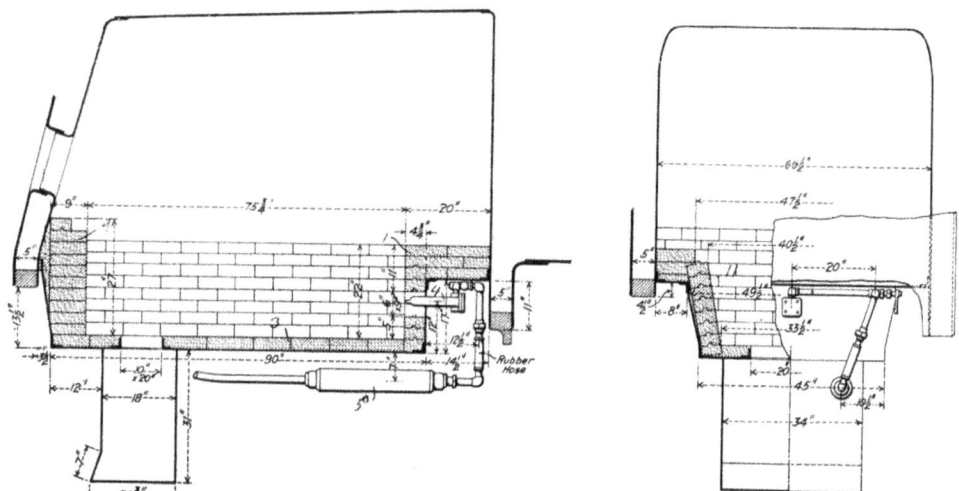

Figs. 739-740. Furnace of Oil Burning Locomotive. Southern Pacific.

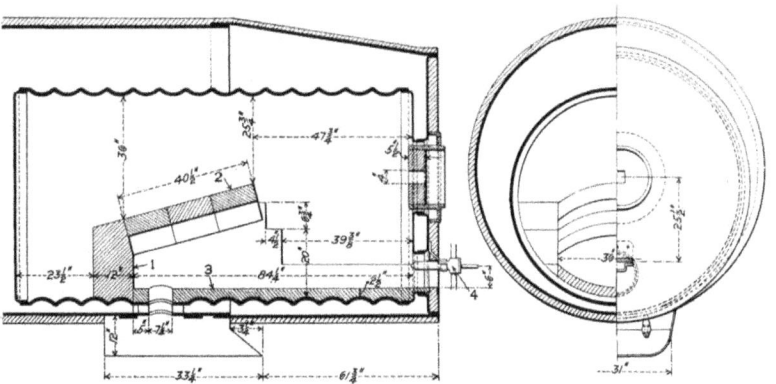

Figs. 741-742. Oil Burning Firebox for Vanderbilt Boiler. Southern Pacific.

OIL BURNING FIREBOXES, Details. Figs. 743-757

Numbers Refer to List of Names of Parts Below.

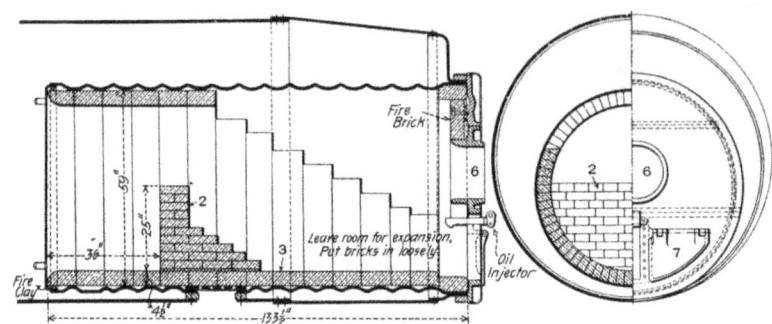

Figs. 743-744. Oil Burning Firebox for Vanderbilt Boiler. Atchison, Topeka & Santa Fe.

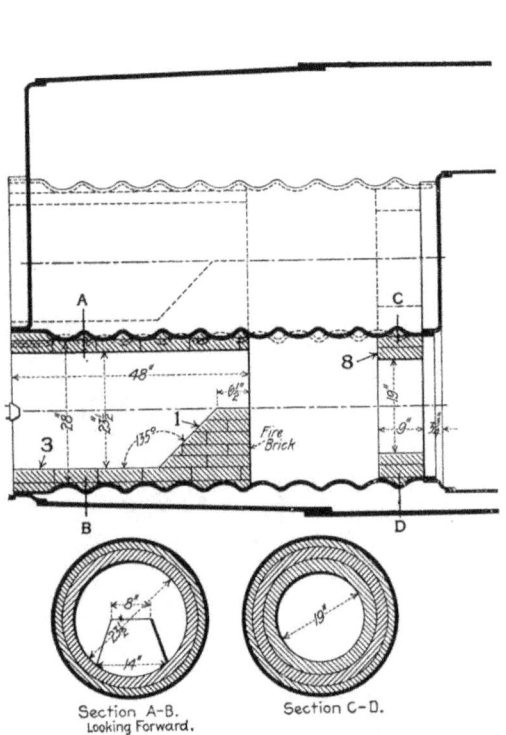

Figs. 745-747. Oil Burning Firebox for Vanderbilt Boiler with Internal Combustion Chamber. Atchison, Topeka & Santa Fe.

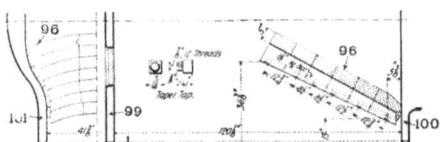

Figs. 748-749. Firebrick Arch for Oil Burning Locomotive. Southern Pacific.

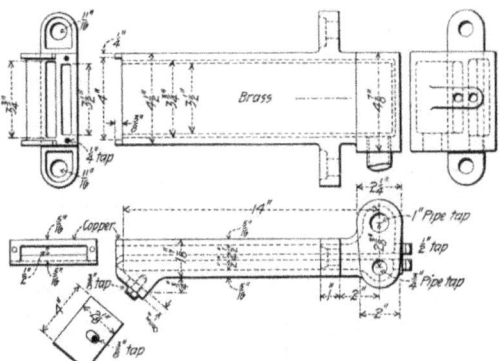

Figs. 750-755. Oil Injector for Oil Burning Vanderbilt Boiler. Atchison, Topeka & Santa Fe.

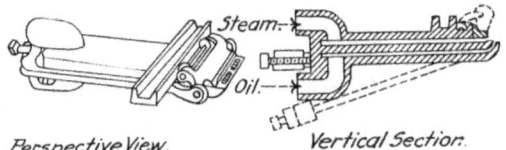

Figs. 756-757. Oil Burner for Locomotives. W. N. Best American Calorific Co.

Names of Parts of Oil Burning Fireboxes, Figs. 721-749.

1 Bridge Wall	9 Back Wall	96 Brick Arch
2 Brick Arch	10 Ashpan	97 Brick Firebox Floor
3 Firebox Floor	11 Side Wall	98 Firebox Floor Sheet
4 Oil Burner	12 Tank	98a Floor Supporting Angle
4a Oil Burner Nozzle	13 Tank Valve	99 Back Water Leg
5 Oil Heater	14 Tank Valve Stem	100 Front Water Leg
6 Firedoor	15 Tank Valve Handle	101 Side Water Leg
7 Damper	16 Tank Flange	
8 Tube Protection	92 Bridge Wall	

Figs. 758-771 — OIL BURNING FIREBOXES, Details; Burners.

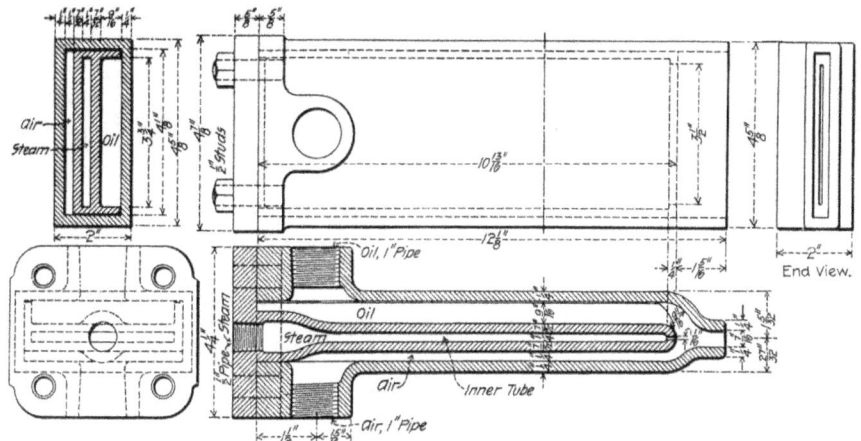

Figs. 758-762. Oil Burner for Locomotives. Southern Pacific.

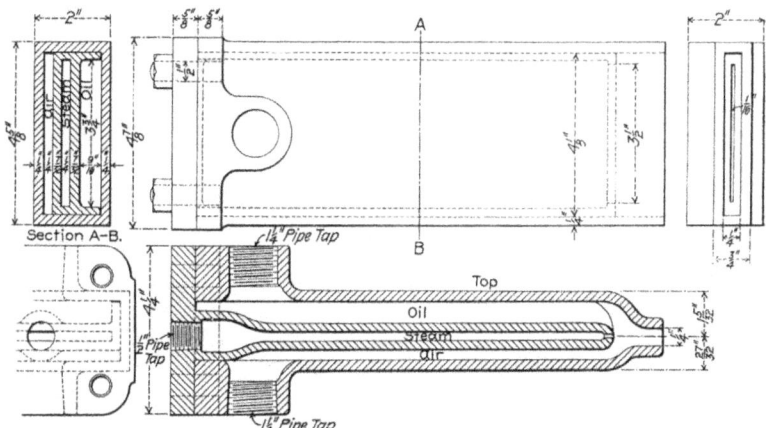

Figs. 763-767. Oil Burner for Locomotives. Southern Pacific.

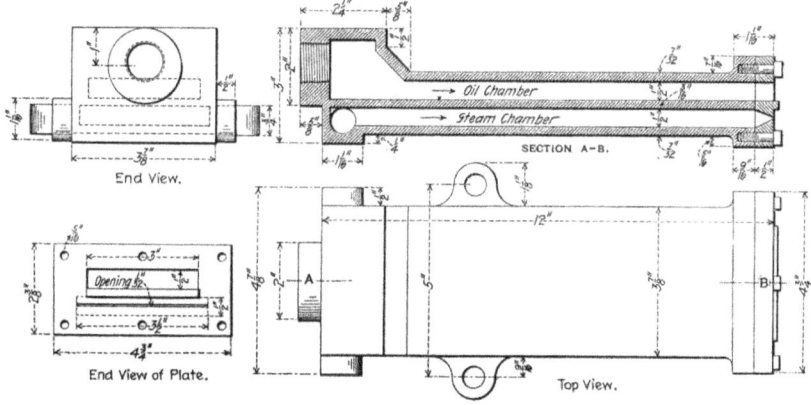

Figs. 768-771. Booth Fuel Oil Burner.

OIL BURNING FIREBOXES, Details; Miscellaneous.

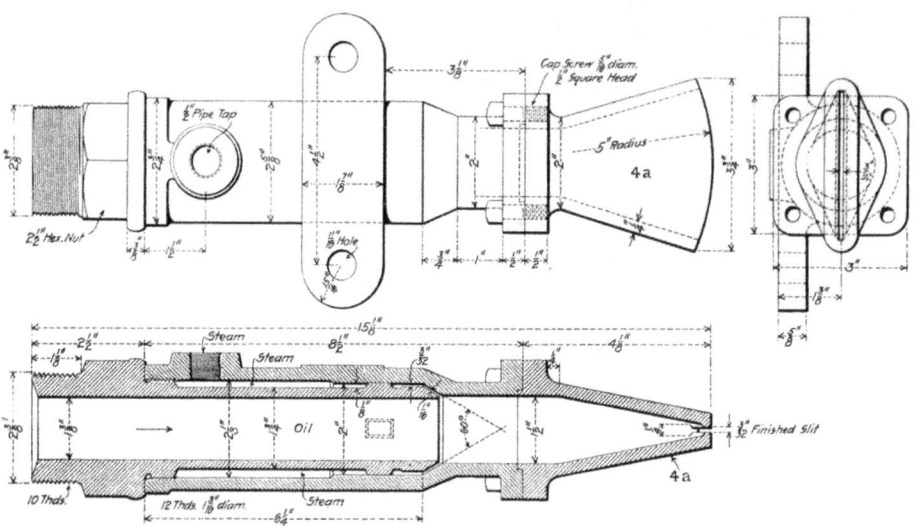

Figs. 772-774. Lundholm Fuel Oil Burner.

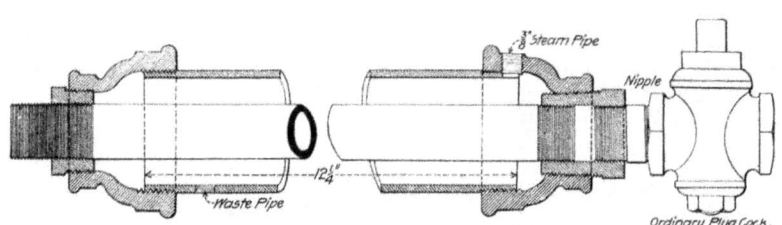

Fig. 775. Heater Box for Oil Burning Locomotive. Southern Pacific.

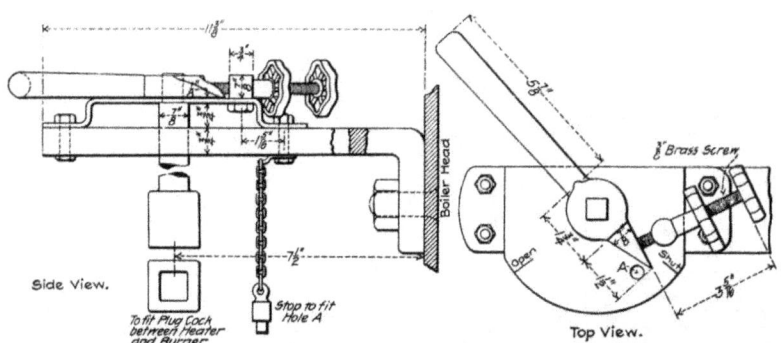

Figs. 776-777. Oil Regulator. Southern Pacific.

Numbers Refer to List of Names of Parts with Figs. 743-757.

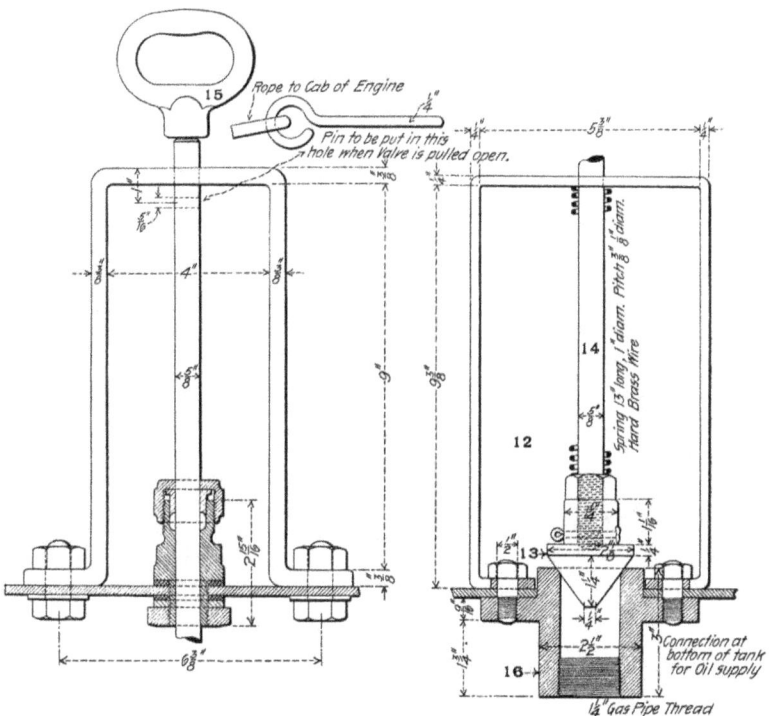

Figs. 778-779. Oil Supply Valve in Tank. Southern Pacific.

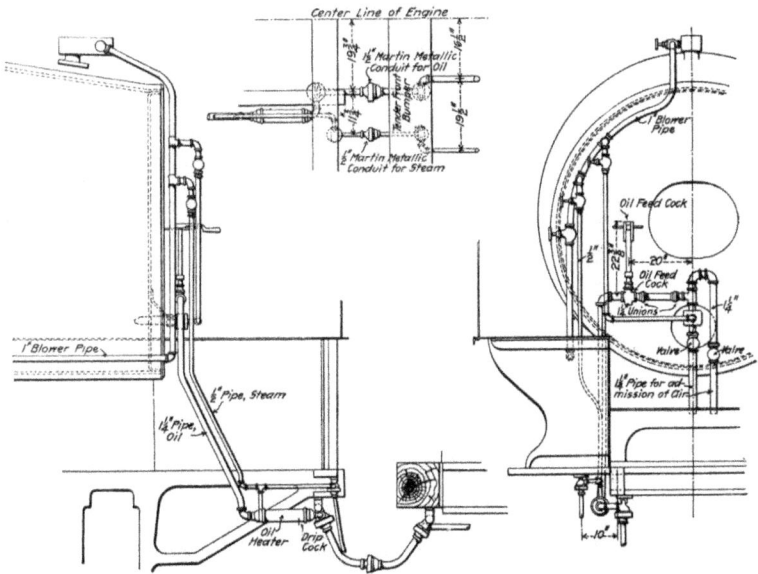

Figs. 780-782. Piping for Oil Burning Locomotive. Southern Pacific.

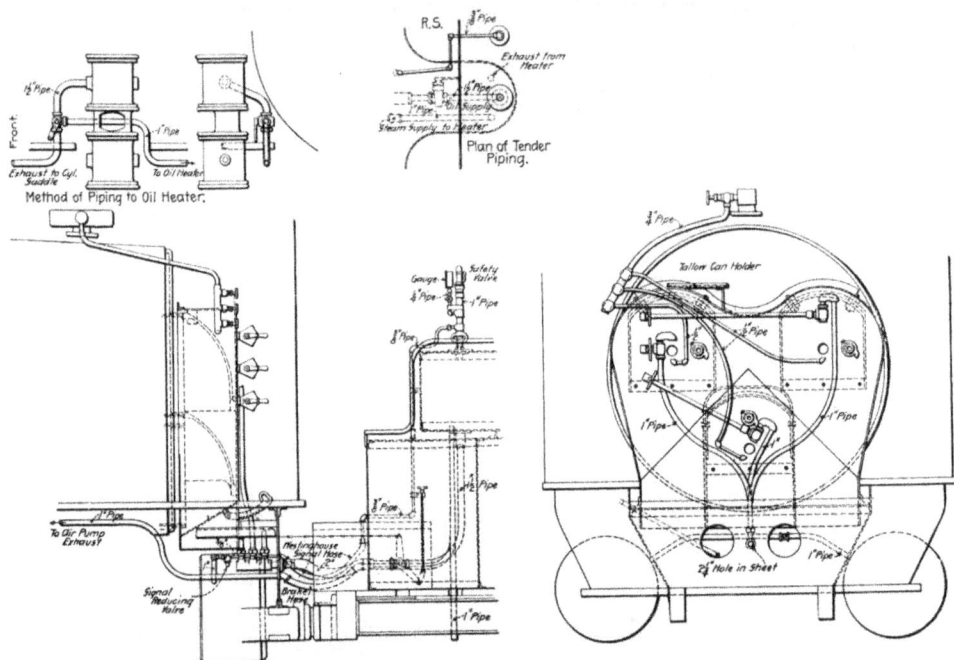

Figs. 783-786. Arrangement of Piping for Oil Burning Locomotive. Atchison, Topeka & Santa Fe.

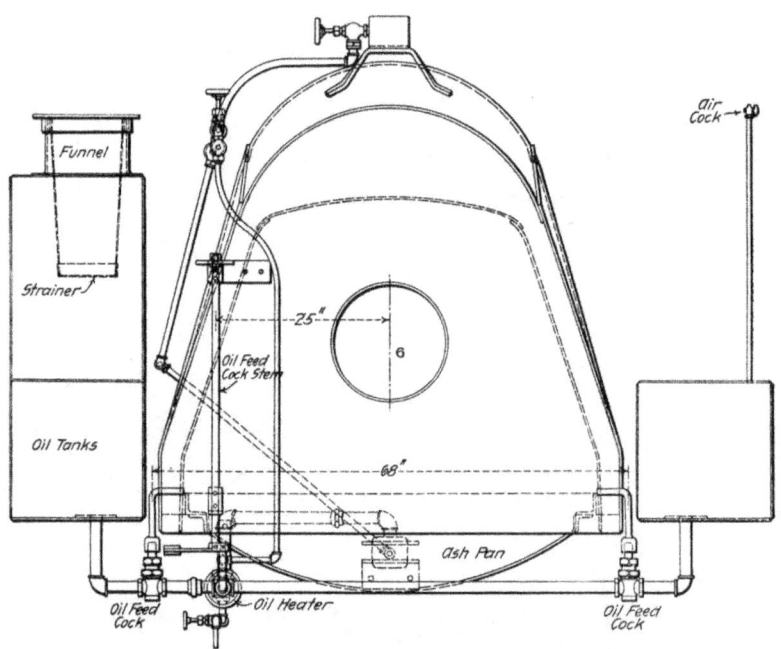

Fig. 787. Piping for Oil Burning Rack Locomotive. Manitou & Pike's Peak.

CYLINDERS, Simple; Slide Valve.

Numbers Refer to List of Names of Parts with Figs. 851-860.

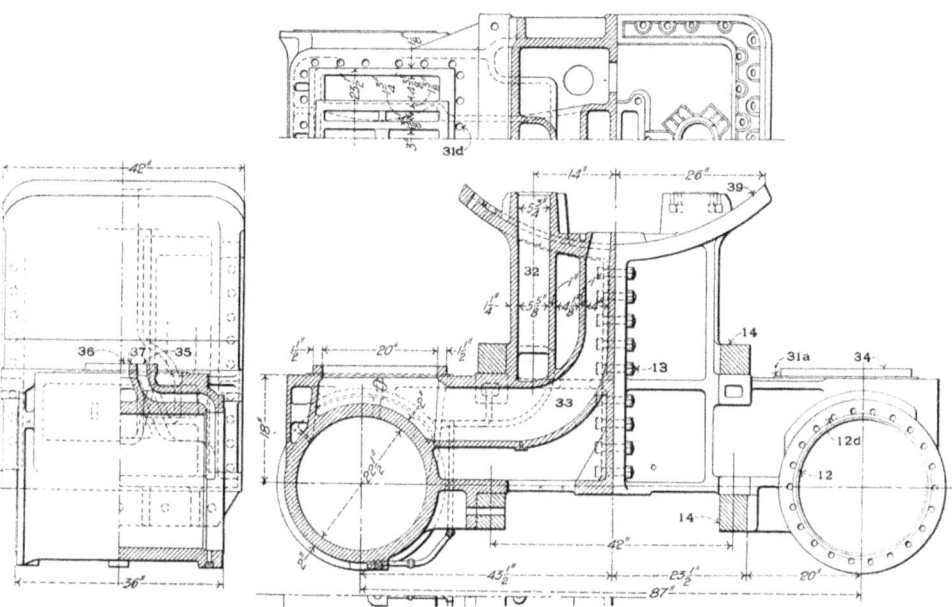

Figs. 788-790. Cylinders for Simple Locomotive with Slide Valves, Diameter 22½ in. American Locomotive Co.

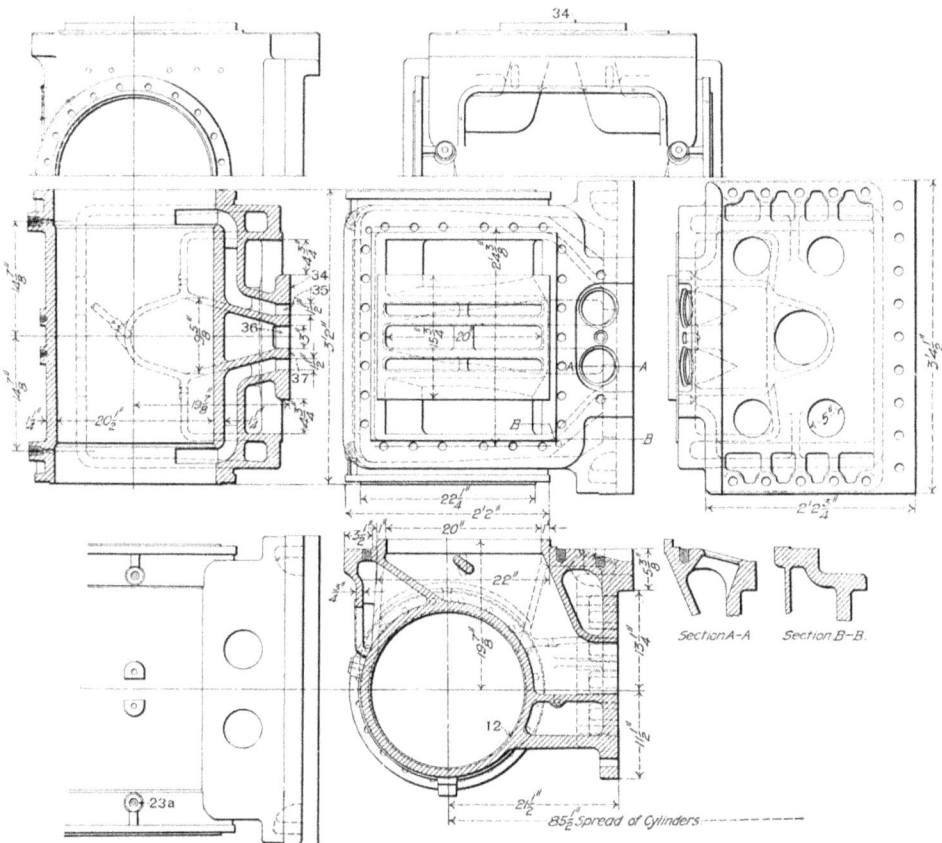

Figs. 791-799. Cylinders for Simple Atlantic (4—4—2) Locomotive with Slide Valves, Diameter 20½ in. Pennsylvania Railroad

CYLINDERS, Simple; Piston Valve.   Figs. 800-807

Numbers Refer to List of Names of Parts with Figs. 851-860.

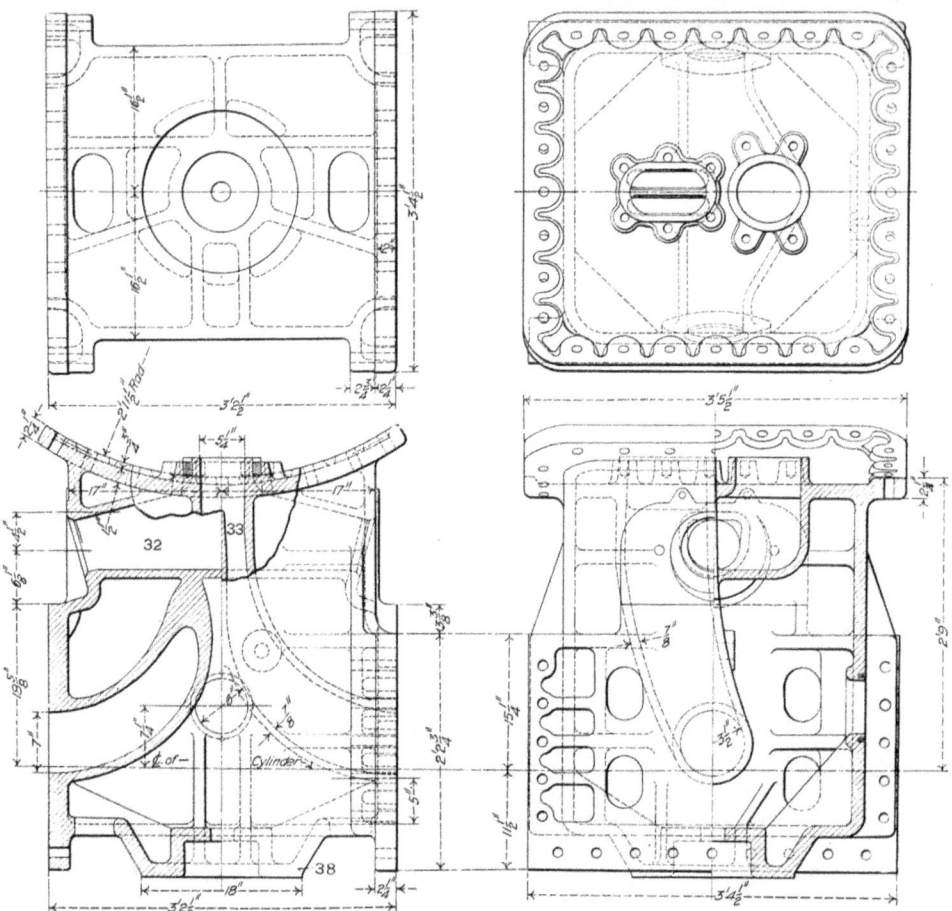

Figs. 800-803. Cylinder Saddle for Simple Atlantic (4—4—2) Locomotive. Pennsylvania Railroad.

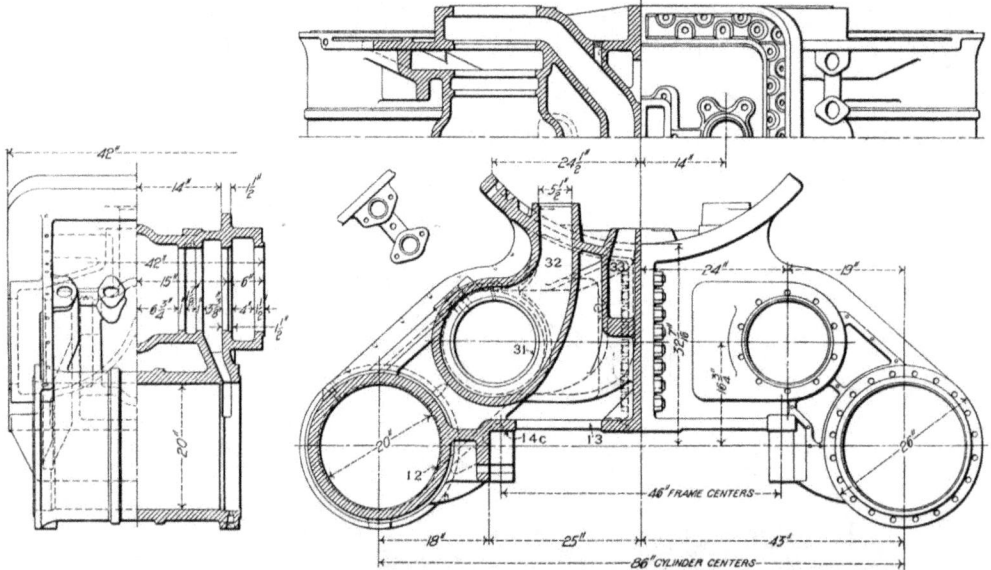

Figs. 804-807. Cylinders for Simple Locomotive with Piston Valves, Diameter 20 in. American Locomotive Co.

(137)

Figs. 808-818 CYLINDERS, Simple; Piston Valve.

Numbers Refer to List of Names of Parts with Figs. 851-860.

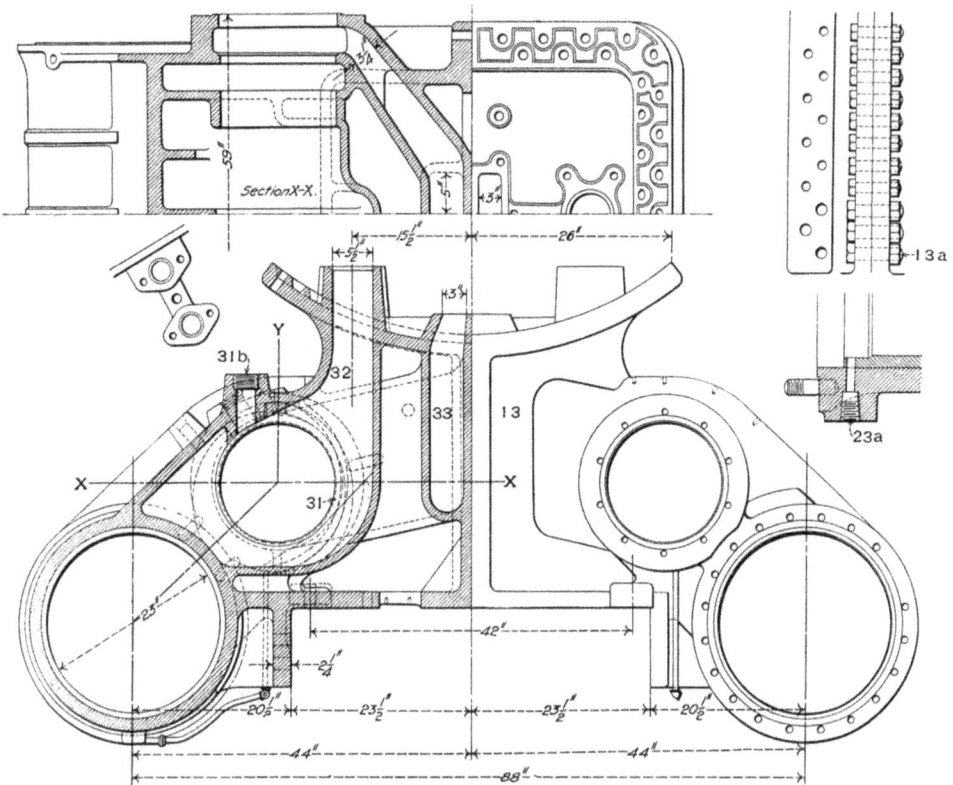

Figs. 808-813. Cylinders for Simple Locomotive with Piston Valves, Diameter 23 in. American Locomotive Co.

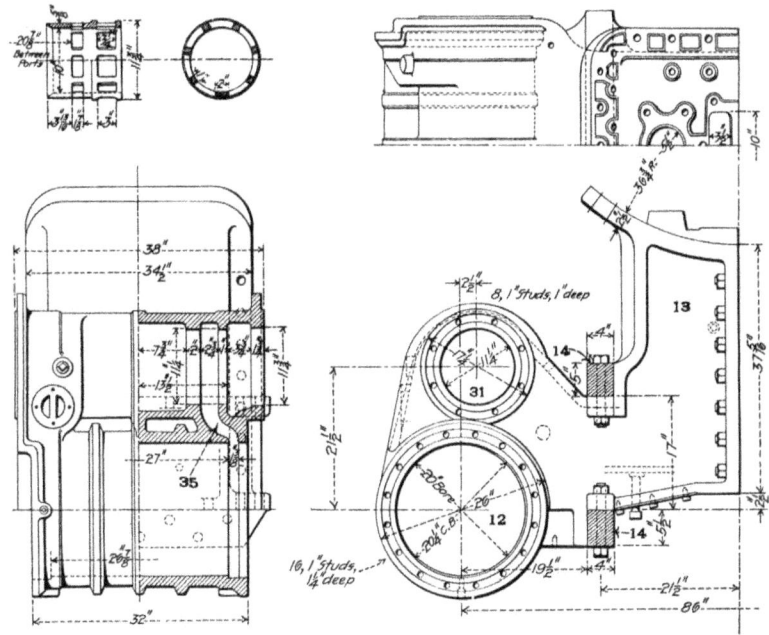

Figs. 814-818. Cylinders for Simple Suburban Locomotive with Piston Valves, Diameter 20 in. New York Central & Hudson River.

(138)

CYLINDERS, Simple; Piston Valve.   Figs. 819-826

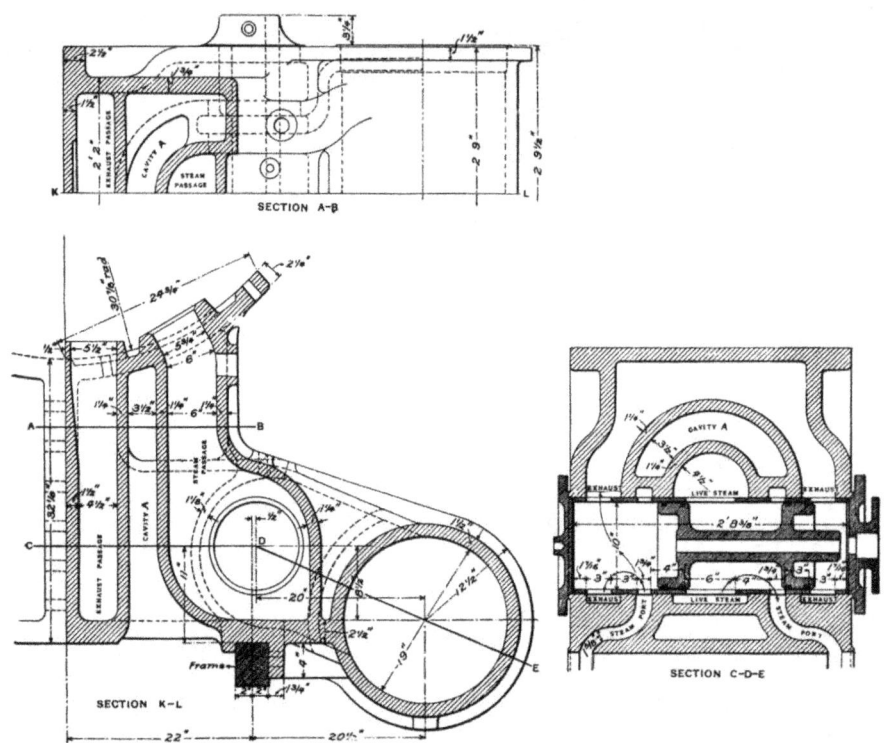

Figs. 819-821. Cylinders for Simple Ten-Wheel (4—6—0) Locomotive with Piston Valves, Diameter 19 in. Chicago, Burlington & Quincy.

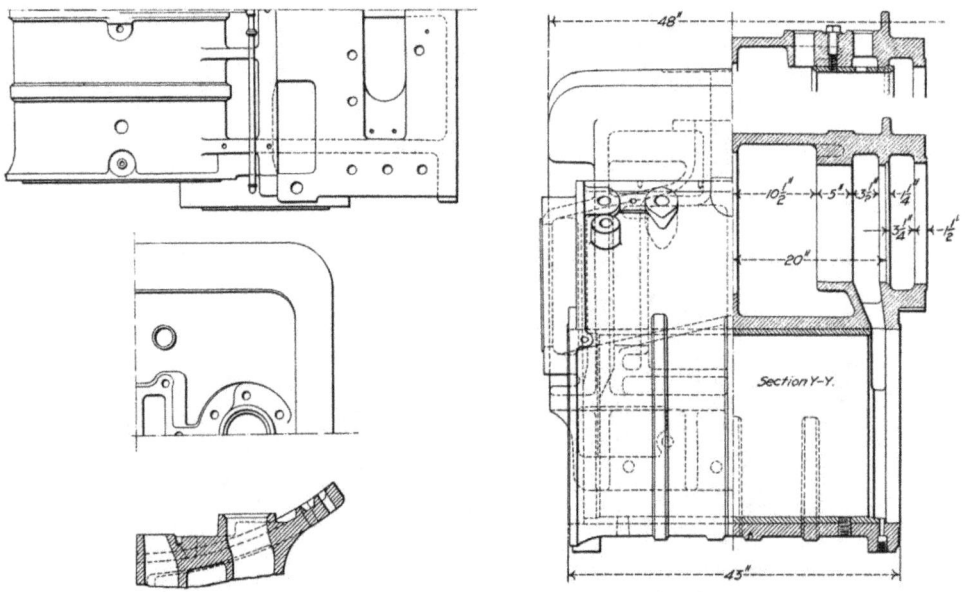

Figs. 822-826. Cylinders for Simple Locomotive with Piston Valves. American Locomotive Co.

Figs. 827-833 CYLINDERS, Compound.

Numbers Refer to List of Names of Parts with Figs. 851-860.

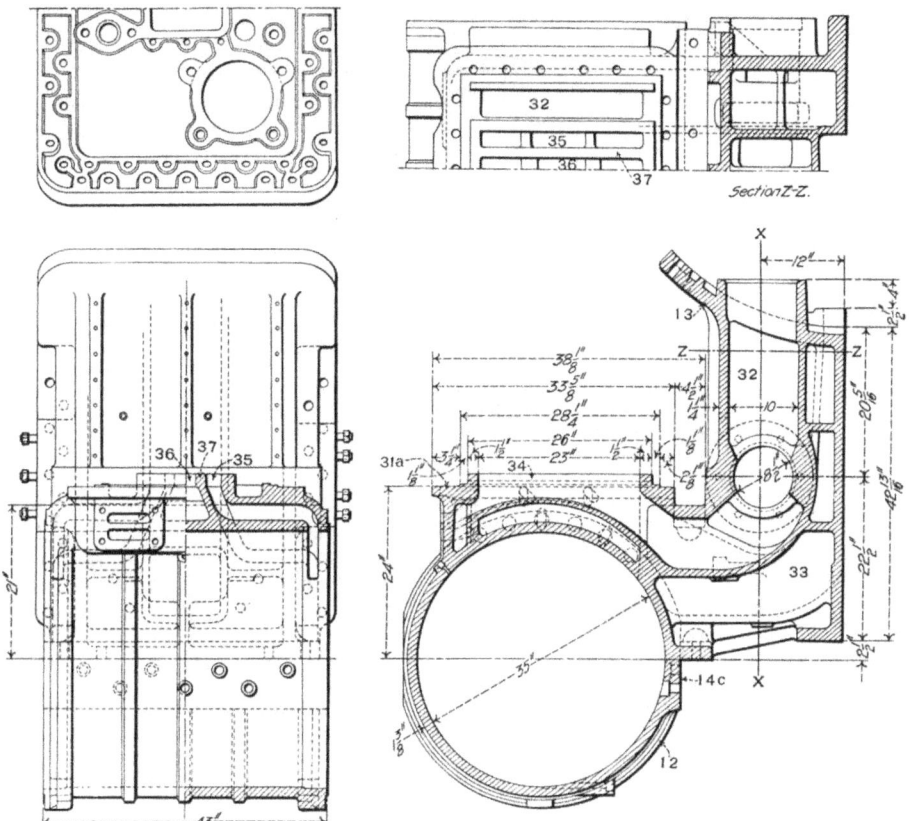

Figs. 827-830. Low Pressure Cylinder for Cross-Compound Locomotive with Slide Valves, Diameter 35 in. American Locomotive Co.

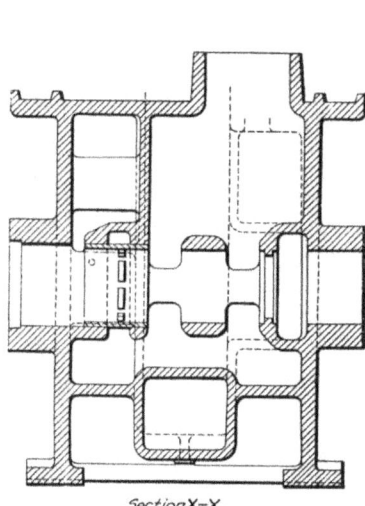

Fig. 831. Section Through Steam and Exhaust Passages.

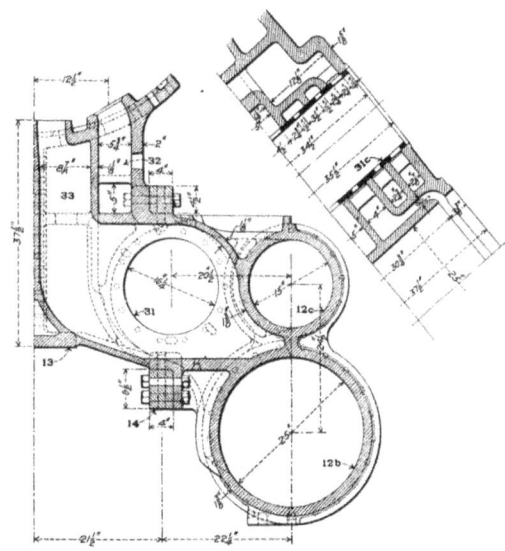

Figs. 832-833. Cylinders for Vauclain Compound Locomotive, Diameters 15 in. and 25 in. Baldwin Locomotive Works.

CYLINDERS, Compound.

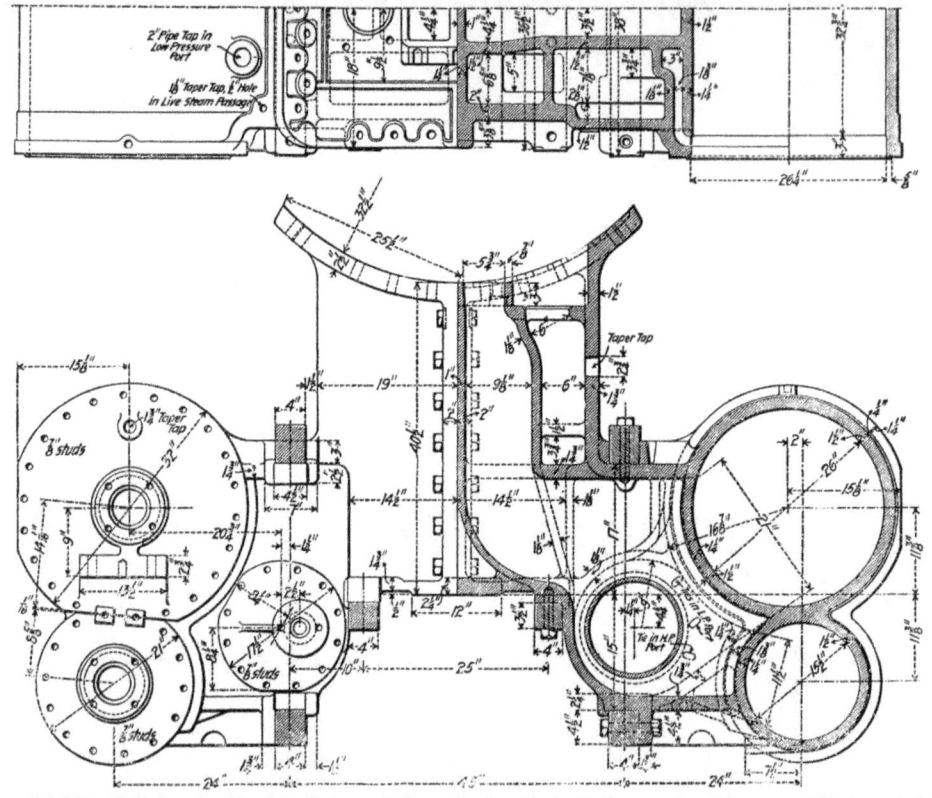

Figs. 834-835. Cylinders for Vauclain Compound Consolidation (2—8—0) Locomotive, Diameters 15½ in. and 26 in. Baldwin Locomotive Works.

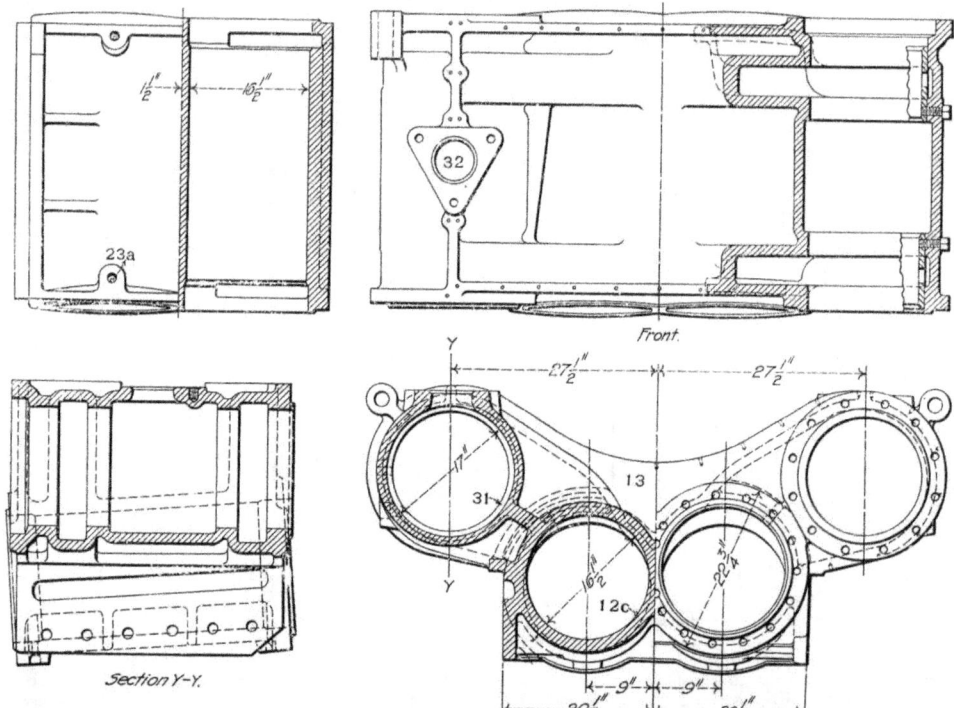

Figs. 836-839. High Pressure Cylinders of Cole Four-Cylinder Balanced Compound Locomotive, Diameter 16½ in. American Locomotive Co.

CYLINDERS, Compound.

Numbers Refer to List of Names of Parts with Figs. 851-860.

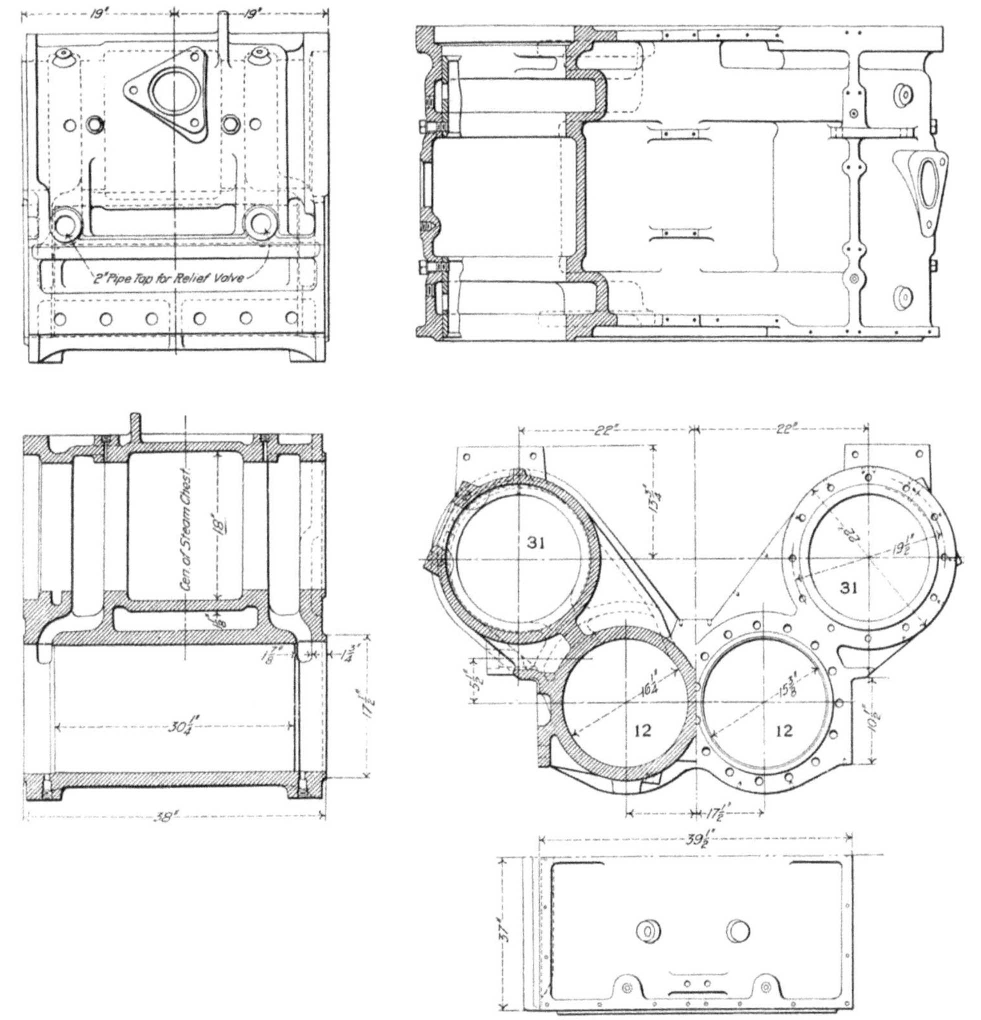

Figs. 840-844. High Pressure Cylinders and Steam Chests of Cole Four-Cylinder Balanced Compound Locomotive, Diameter 16¼ in. American Locomotive Co.

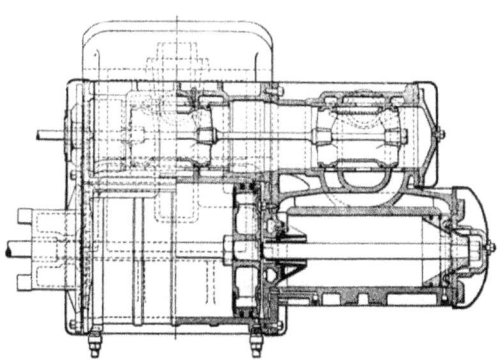

Fig. 845. Cylinders and Steam Chest for Schenectady Tandem Compound Locomotive. American Locomotive Co.

CYLINDERS, Compound. Figs. 846-850

Numbers Refer to List of Names of Parts with Figs. 851-860.

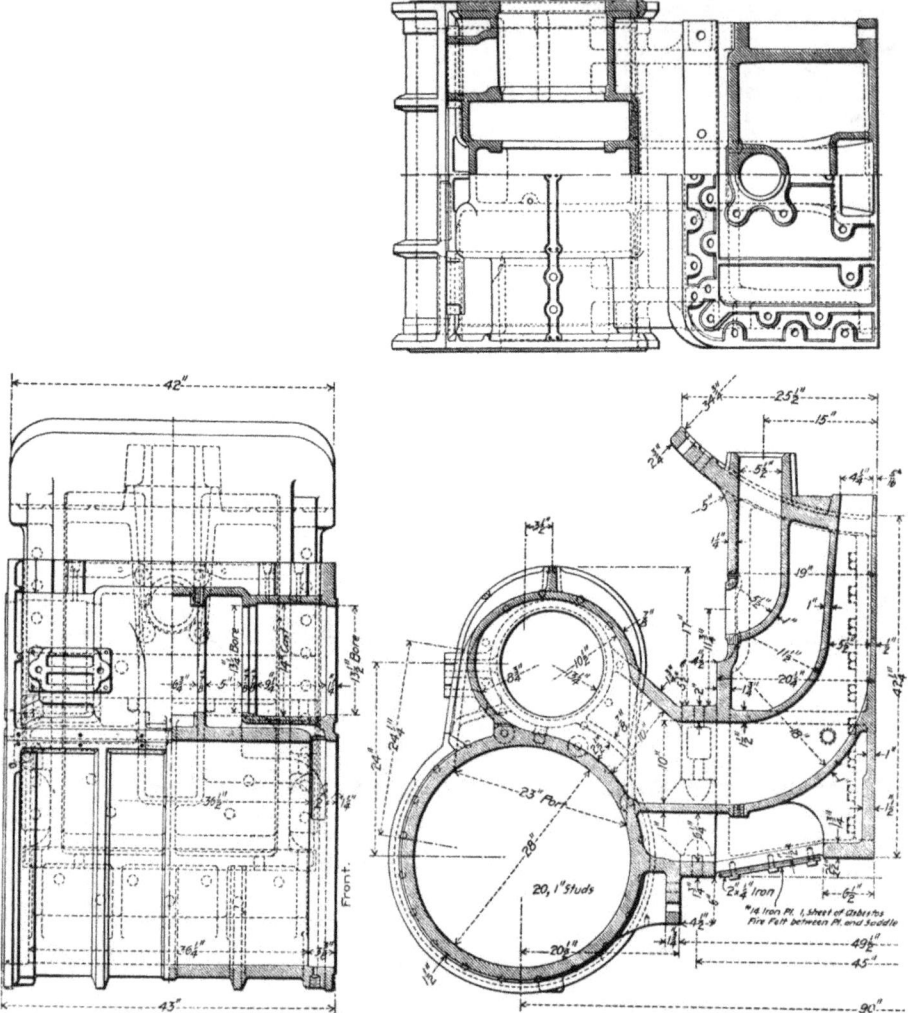

Figs. 846-848. Low Pressure Cylinder and Saddle for Schenectady Cross-Compound Locomotive with Piston Valves. Diameter 28 in. American Locomotive Co.

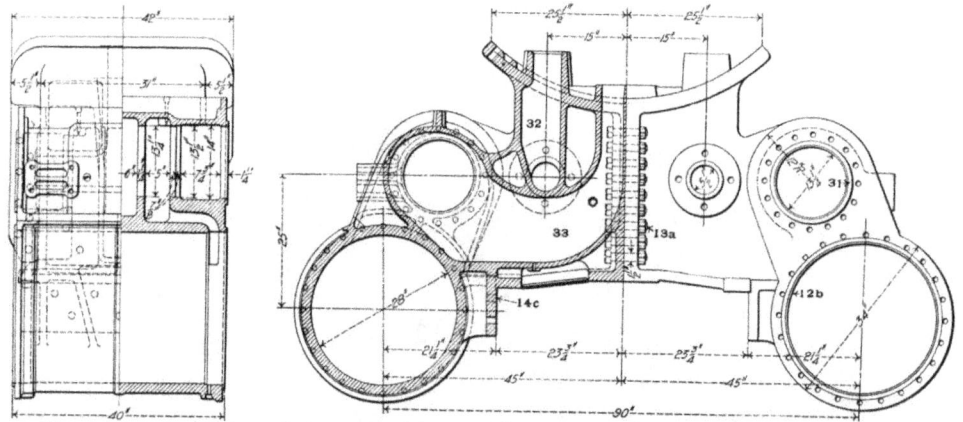

Figs. 849-850. Low Pressure Cylinders for Schenectady Tandem Compound Locomotive, Diameter 28 in. American Locomotive Co.

CYLINDERS, Compound.

Names of Parts of Cylinders, Pistons and Guides, Figs. 788-1029.

1 Guide Block
2 Packing Box in Cylinder Head
2a Packing Box Cover
2b Packing Box Gland
3 Piston Rod
3a Piston Rod Extension
3b Piston Rod Extension Carry Wheel
3c Piston Rod Extension Carry Wheel Bracket
4 Piston Head
5 Piston
6 Piston Ring
7 Piston Rod Check Nut
8 Cylinder Cock Valve
9 Cylinder Cock Stem
10 Cylinder Cock Casing
11 Cylinder Cock
12 Cylinder
12a Cylinder Head
12b Cylinder, Low Pressure
12c Cylinder, High Pressure
12d Cylinder Head Stud Holes
13 Saddle
13a Saddle Joint Bolts
14 Frame
14a Frame Brace
14c Frame Seat
15 Cylinder Cock Lever
16 Cylinder Cock Lever Shaft
17 Cylinder Cock Reach Rod
18 Cylinder Cock Reach Rod Bracket
19 Cylinder Cock Lifting Rod

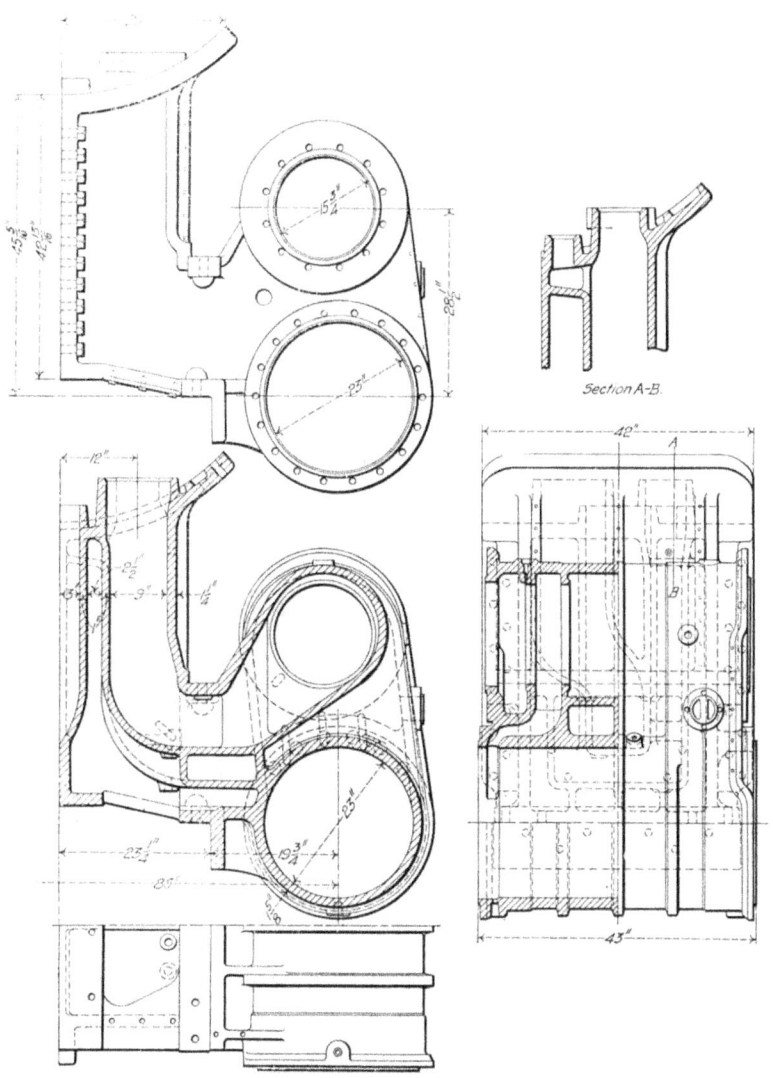

Figs. 851-855. Low Pressure Cylinders for Schenectady Tandem Compound Locomotive, Diameter 23 in. American Locomotive Co.

CYLINDERS, Compound. Figs. 856-860

Names of Parts of Cylinders, Pistons and Guides, Figs. 788-1029 (Continued).

20 Cylinder Cock Operating Lever	27 Bottom Guide	31d Steam Chest Stud Holes
21 Cylinder Cock Lever Bracket	28 Guide Yoke	32 Steam Passage
22 Cylinder Cock Operating Lever Shaft	29 Guide Block Bolt	33 Exhaust Passage
	29a Guide Step	34 Valve Seat
23 Cylinder Cock Reach Rod Carrier	30 Stuffing Box	35 Steam Port
	31 Steam Chest	36 Exhaust Port
23a Cylinder Cock Hole	31a Steam Chest Seat	37 Bridge
24 Piston Follower	31b Steam Chest Relief Valve Case	38 Center Plate
25 Piston Follower Stud	31c Steam Chest Bushing	39 Smokebox Seat
26 Top Guide		

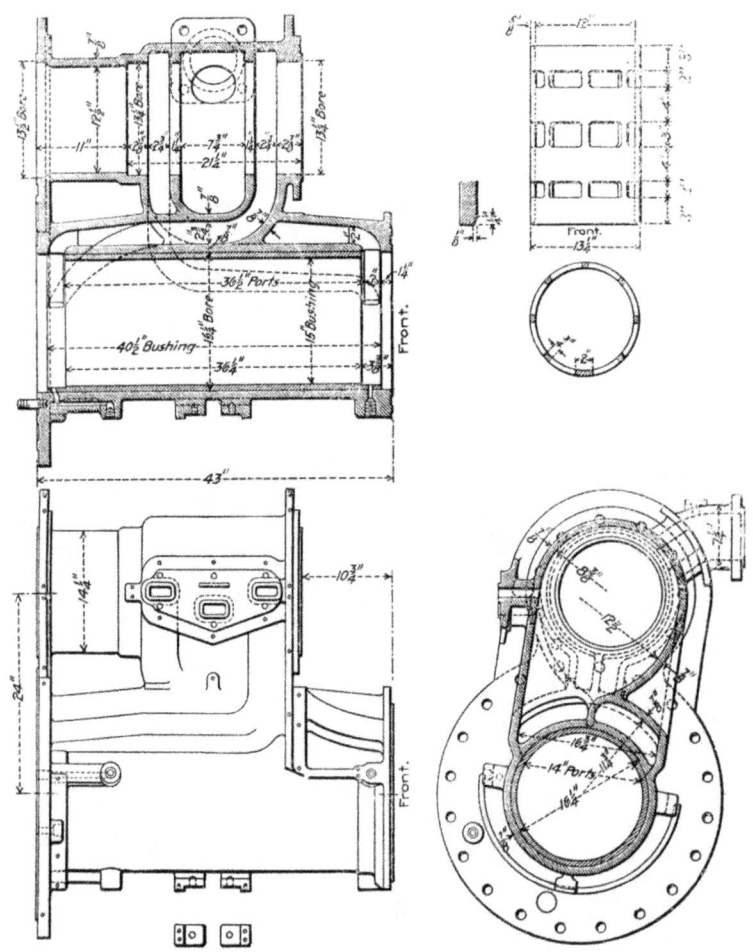

Figs. 856-860. High Pressure Cylinder for Schenectady Tandem Compound Locomotive, Diameter 15 in. American Locomotive Co.

Figs. 861-866 CYLINDERS, Compound.

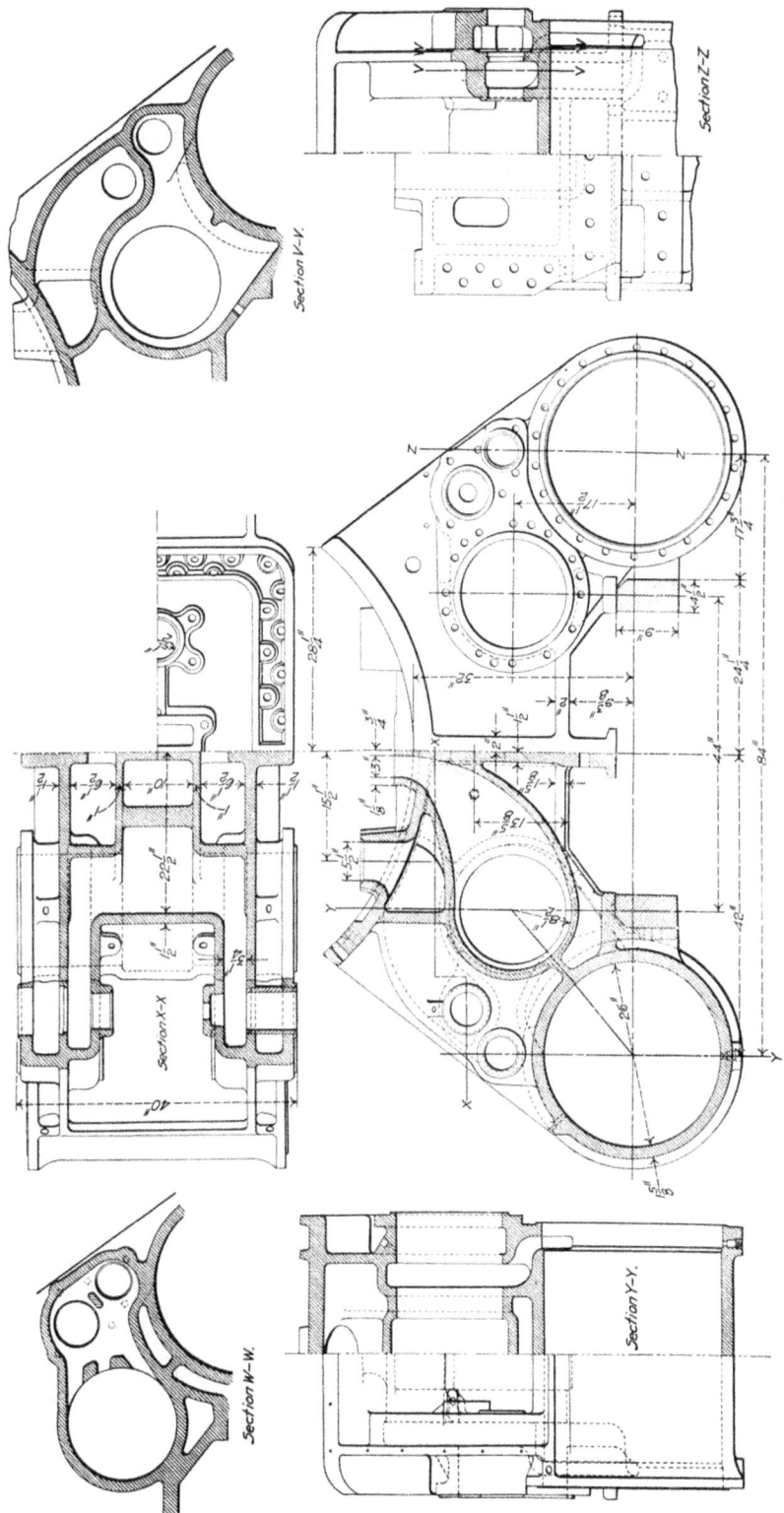

Figs. 861-866. Low Pressure Cylinders for Schenectady Tandem Compound Locomotive, Diameter 26 in. American Locomotive Co.

CYLINDERS, Compound. Figs. 867-873

Numbers Refer to List of Names of Parts with Figs. 851-860.

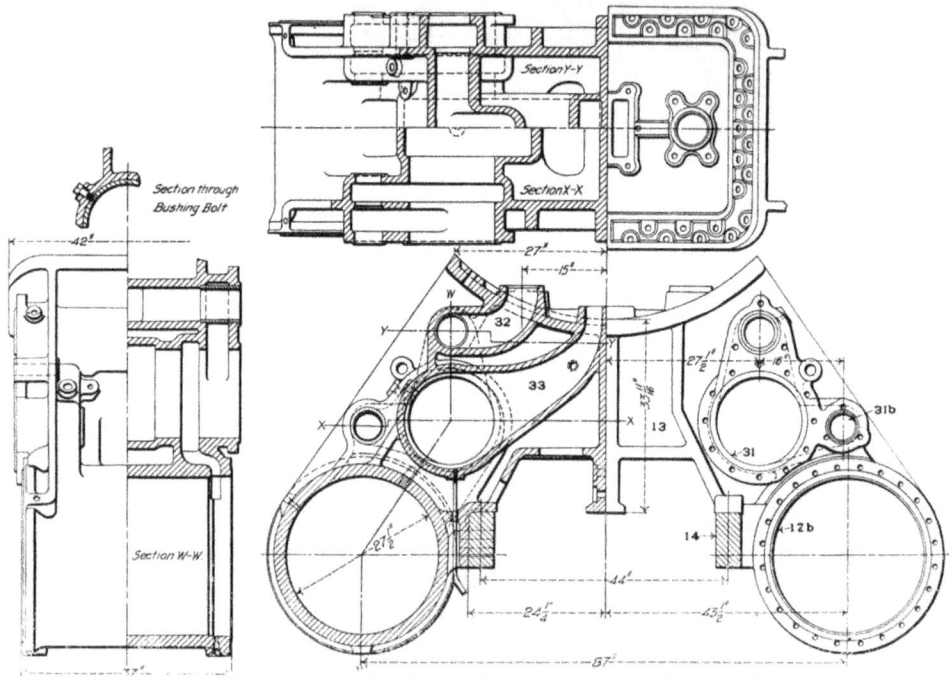

Figs. 867-870. Low Pressure Cylinders for Schenectady Tandem Compound Locomotive. Diameter 27½ in. American Locomotive Co.

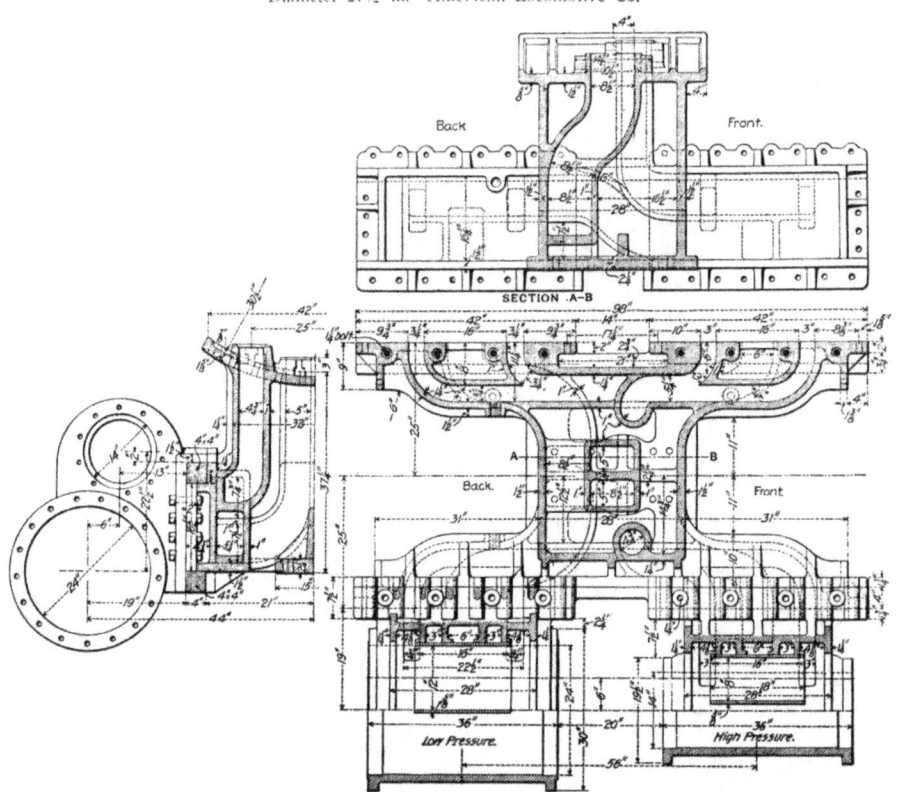

Figs. 871-873. Cylinder Saddle for Schenectady Tandem Compound Locomotive. American Locomotive Co.

CYLINDERS, Compound.

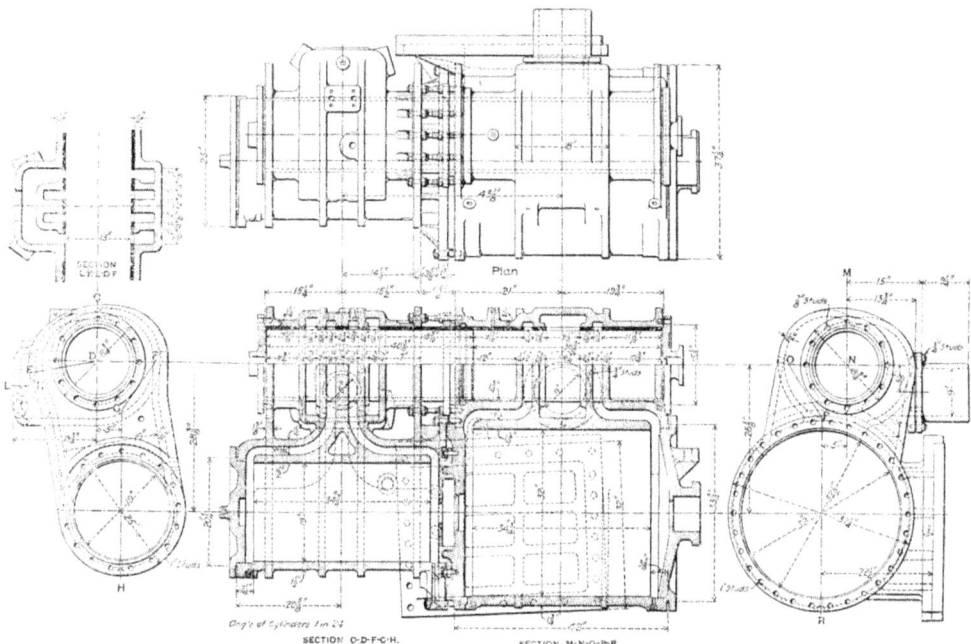

Figs. 874-878. Cylinders for Tandem Compound Decapod (2—10—0) Locomotive. Baldwin Locomotive Works.

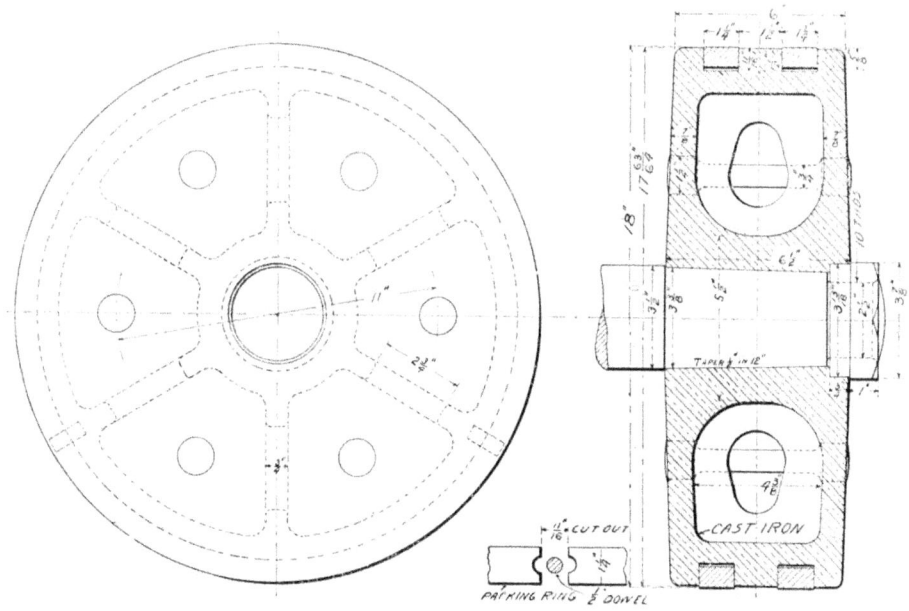

Figs. 879-880. Cast Iron Double Plate Piston, Diameter 18 in.

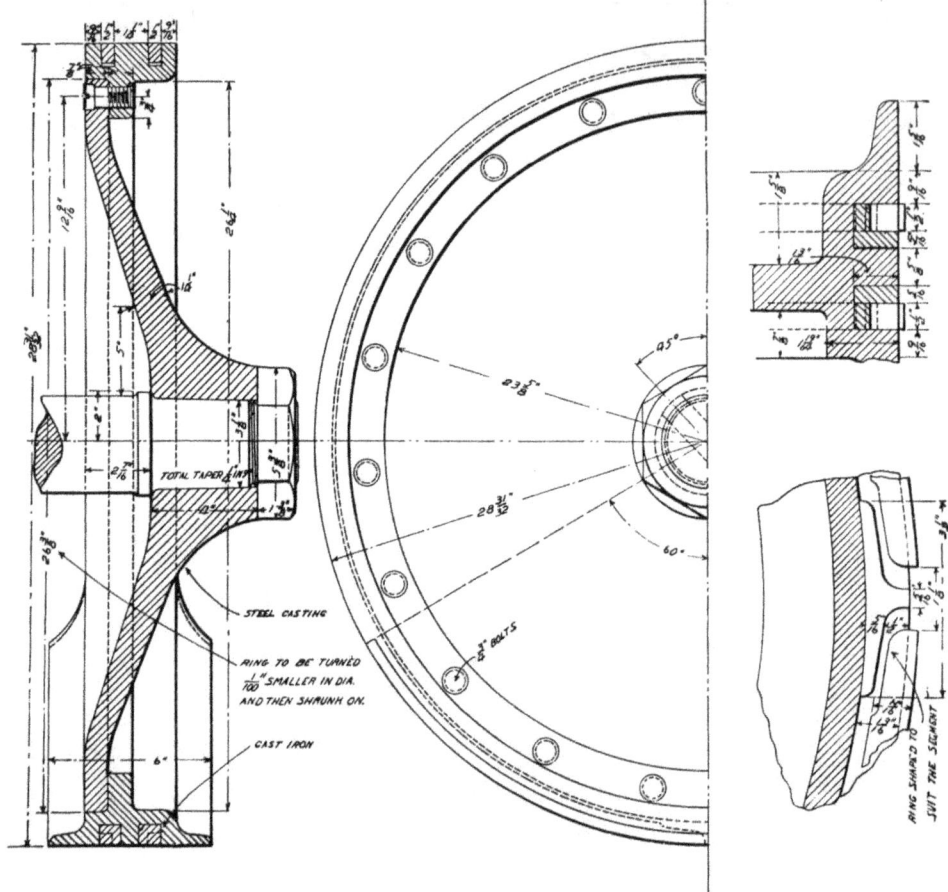

Figs. 881-884. 29-Inch Cast Steel Single Plate Piston. Pennsylvania Railroad.

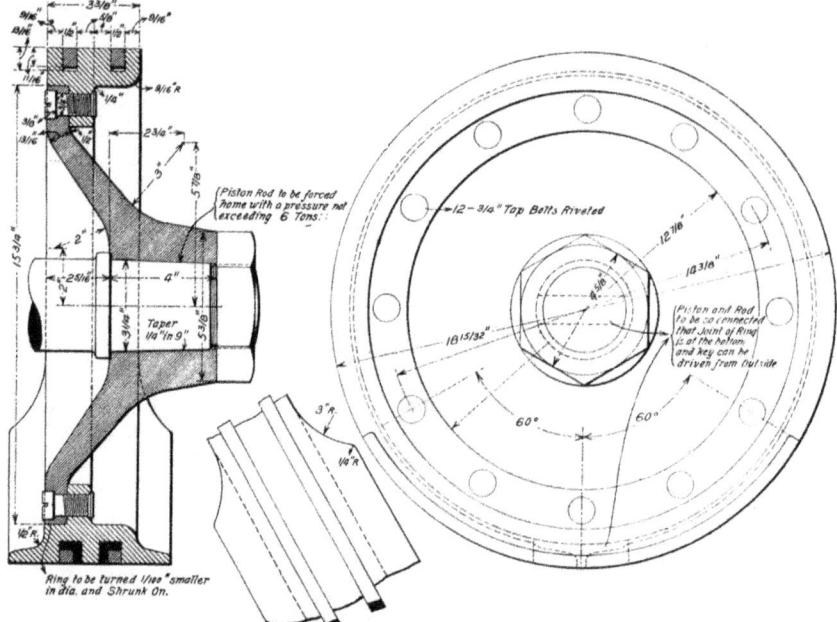

Figs. 885-887. 18½-Inch Cast Steel Single Plate Piston. Pennsylvania Railroad.

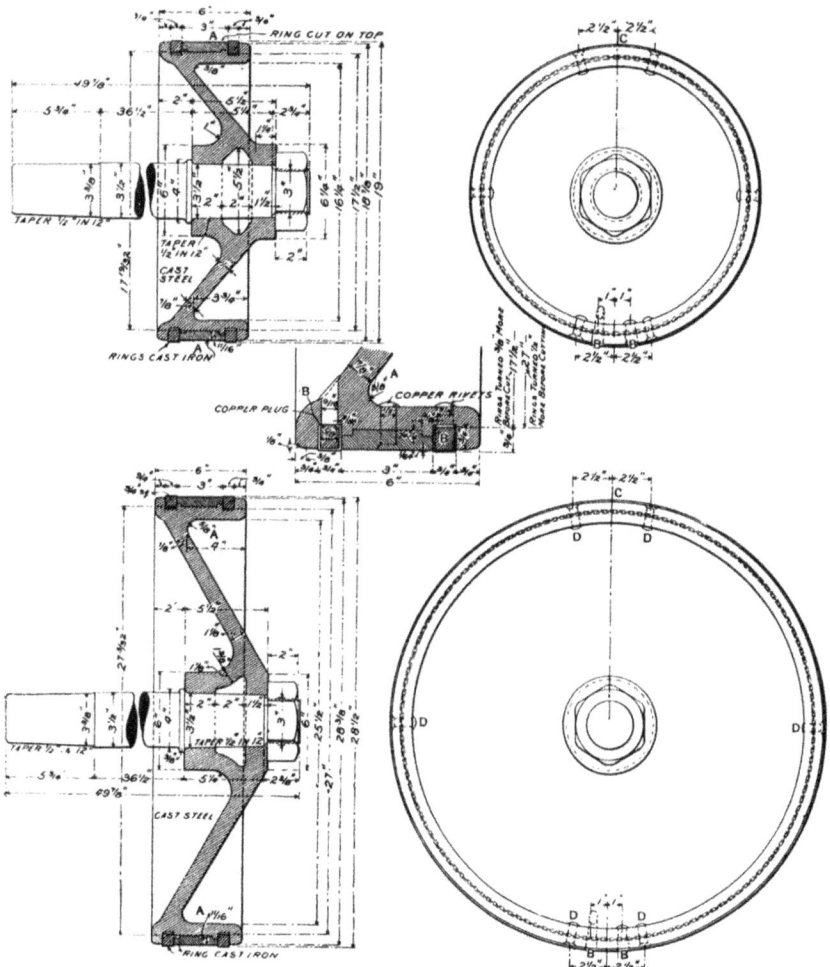

Figs. 888-892. 19-Inch and 28½-Inch Cast Steel Single Plate Pistons. Rogers Locomotive Works.

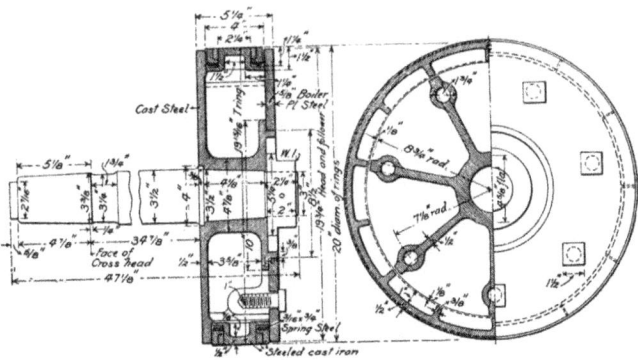

Figs. 893-894. 20-Inch Cast Steel Double Plate Piston.

CYLINDERS, Details; Pistons.

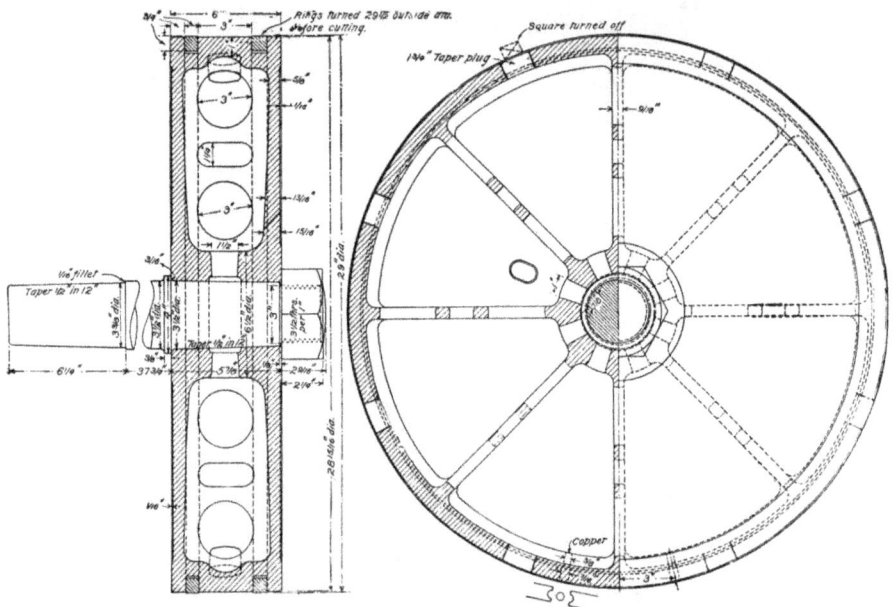

Figs. 895-896. 29-Inch Cast Iron Double Plate Piston for Compound Locomotive.

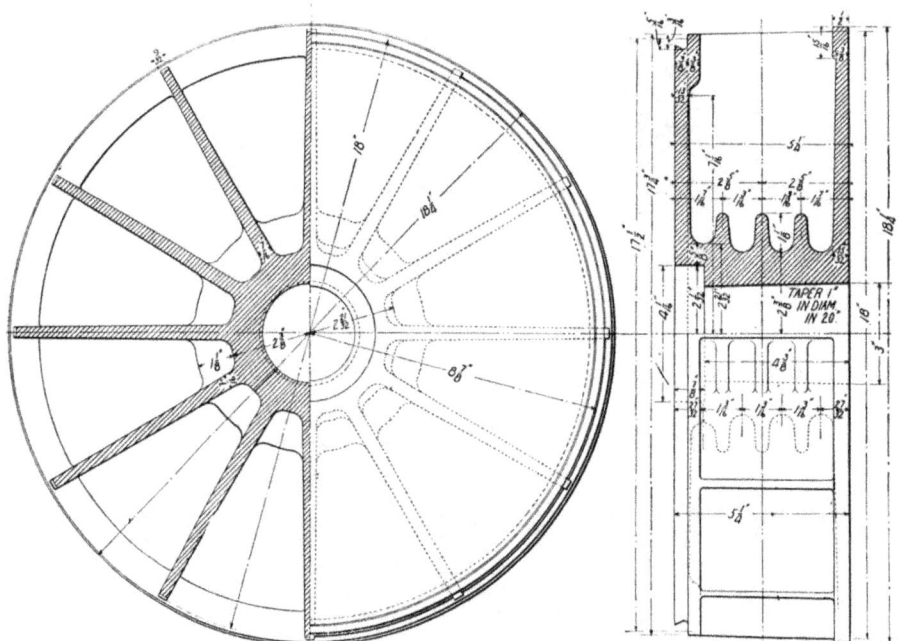

Figs. 897-898. Malleable Iron Double Plate Piston Center. Norfolk & Western.

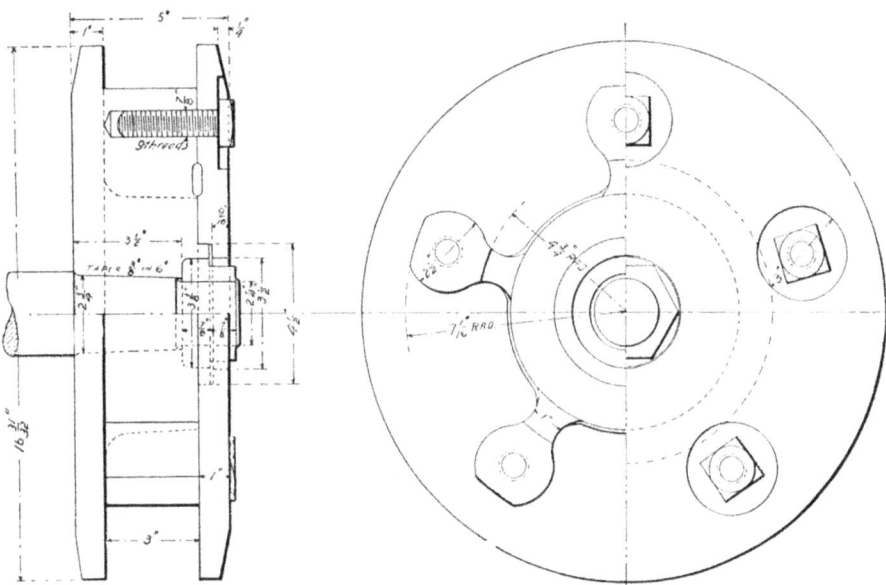

Figs. 899-900. Cast Iron Double Plate Center for 17-Inch Piston.

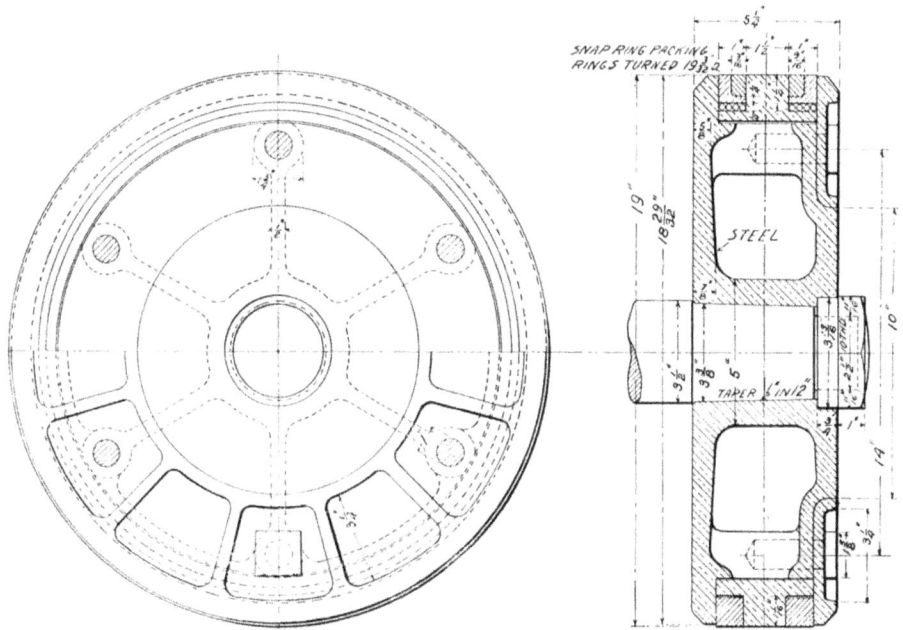

Figs. 901-902. Cast Steel Double Plate 19-Inch Piston. American Locomotive Co.

CYLINDERS, Details; Pistons.

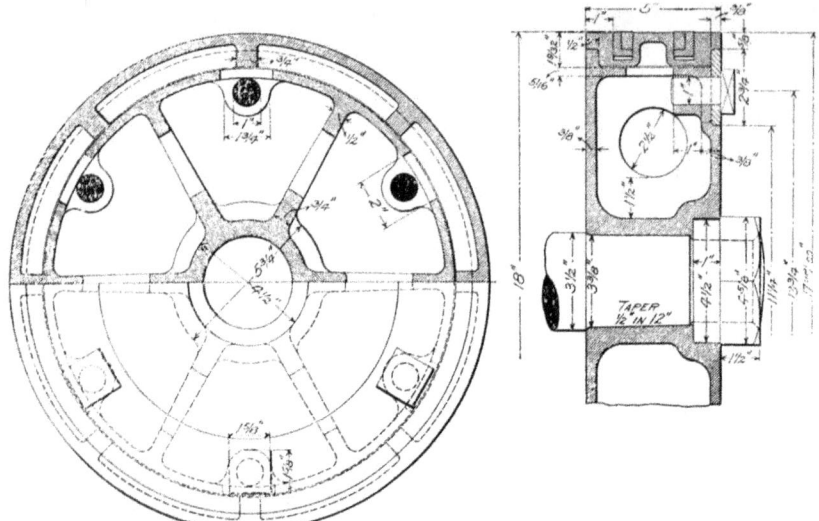

Figs. 903-904. Cast Iron Double Plate 18-Inch Piston. American Locomotive Co.

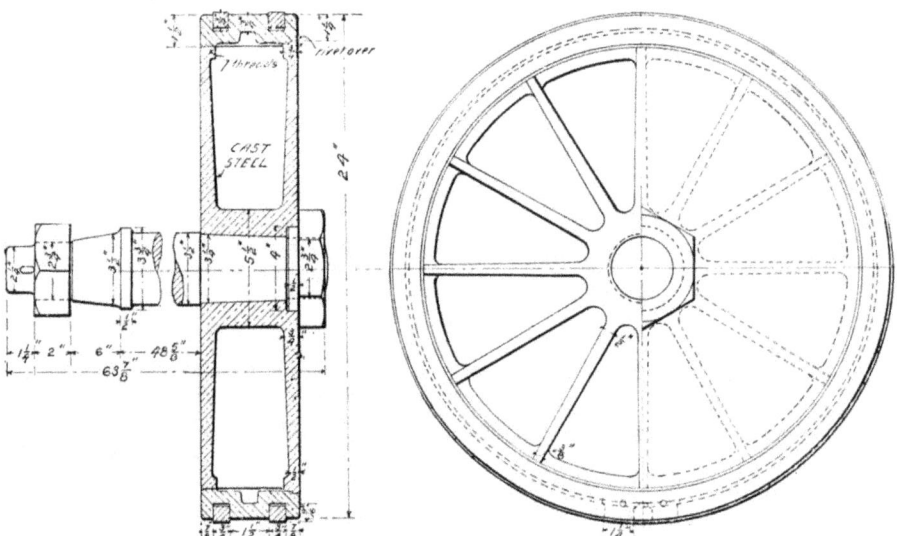

Figs. 905-906. Cast Steel Double Plate 24-Inch Piston. Baldwin Locomotive Works.

Numbers Refer to List of Names of Parts with Figs. 851-860.

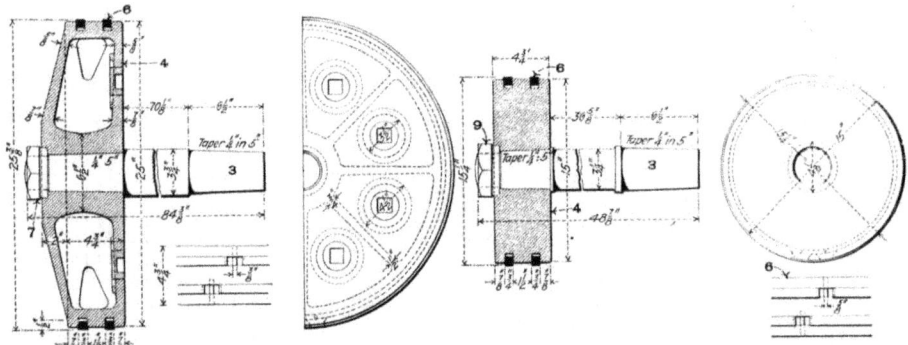

Figs. 907-910. High and Low Pressure Pistons and Rods for Baldwin Four-Cylinder Balanced Compound. Baldwin Locomotive Works.

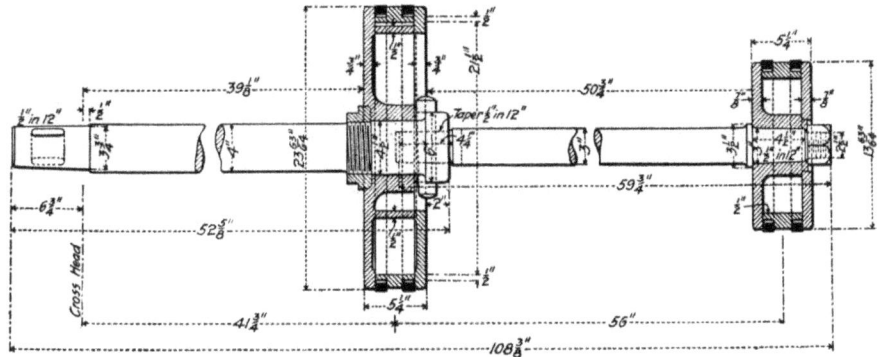

Fig. 911. Pistons and Rod for Tandem Compound Locomotive.

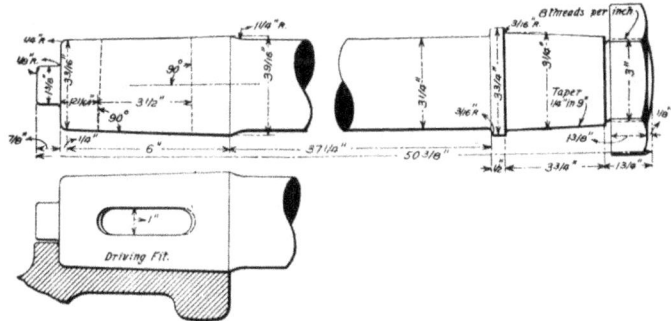

Figs. 912-913. Piston Rod for 18½-Inch x 26-Inch Cylinders. Pennsylvania Railroad.

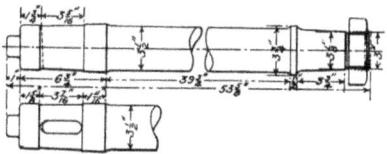

Figs. 914-915. Piston Rod for Atlantic (4—4—2) Locomotive. P. R. R.

Numbers Refer to List of Names of Parts with Figs. 851-860.

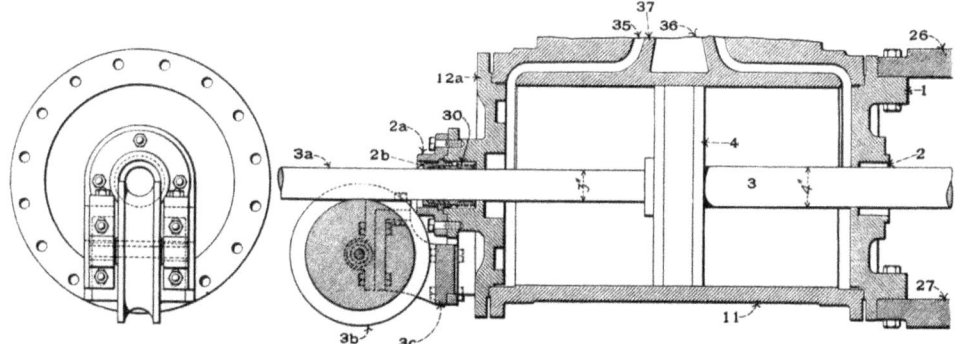

Figs. 916-917. Extension Piston Rod and Support.

CYLINDERS, Details; Heads.

Figs. 918-937

Numbers Refer to List of Names of Parts with Figs. 851-860.

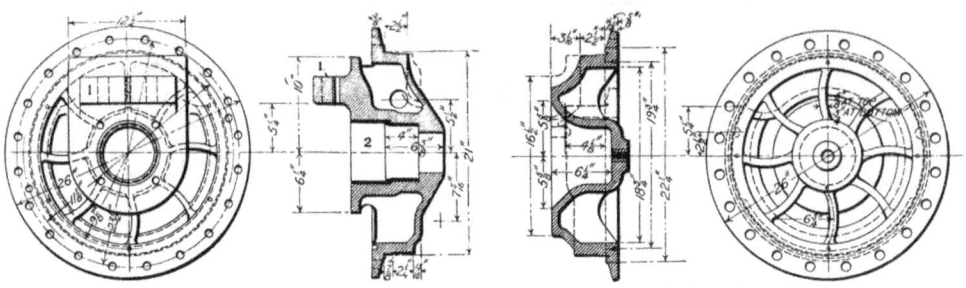

Figs. 918-919. Back Head.   Figs. 920-921. Front Head.
Cylinder Heads, Atlantic (4—4—2) Locomotive. Pennsylvania Railroad.

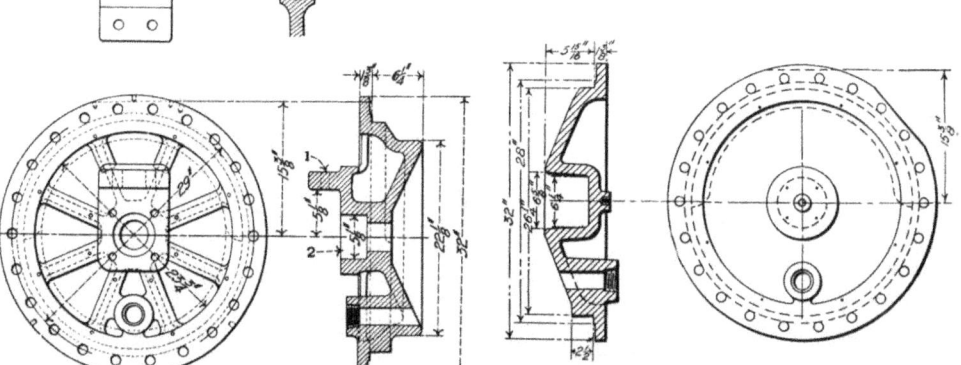

Figs. 922-925. Back Head.   Figs. 926-927. Front Head.
Cylinder Heads, Consolidation (2—8—0) Locomotive. American Locomotive Co.

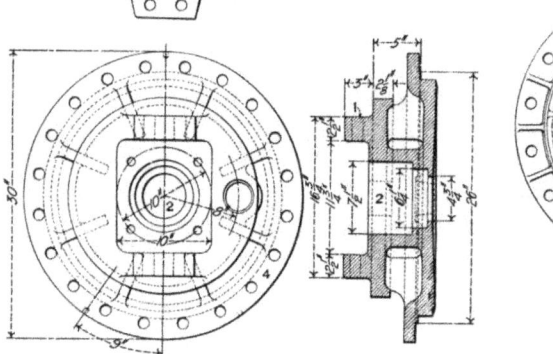
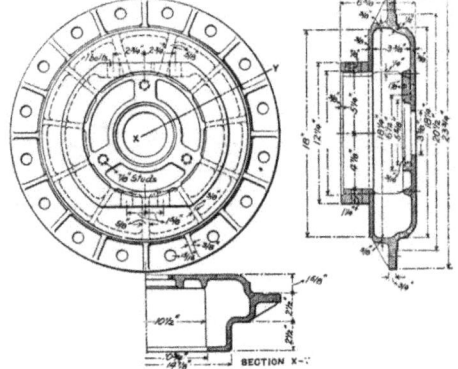

Figs. 928-930. Back Cylinder Head.   Figs. 931-933. Cast Steel Back Cylinder Head.
American Locomotive Co.

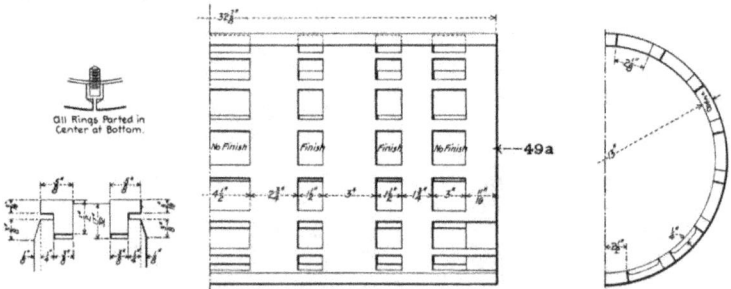

Figs. 934-937. Steam Chest Bushing for Consolidation (2—8—0) Locomotive with Piston Valves. Atchison, Topeka & Santa Fe.

Figs. 938-955 CYLINDERS, Details; Miscellaneous.

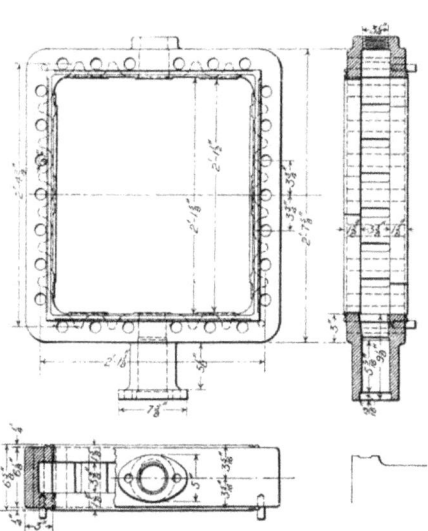

Figs. 938-940. Steam Chest for Slide Valve. Atlantic (4—4—2) Locomotive. Pennsylvania Railroad.

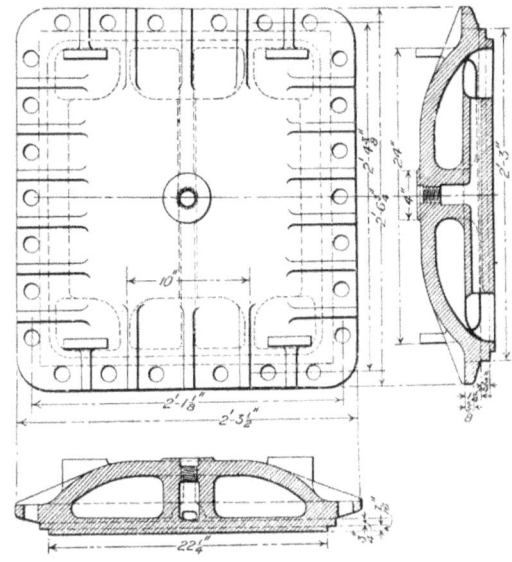

Figs. 941-943. Combined Steam Chest Lid and Balance Plate. Atlantic (4—4—2) Locomotive. Pennsylvania Railroad.

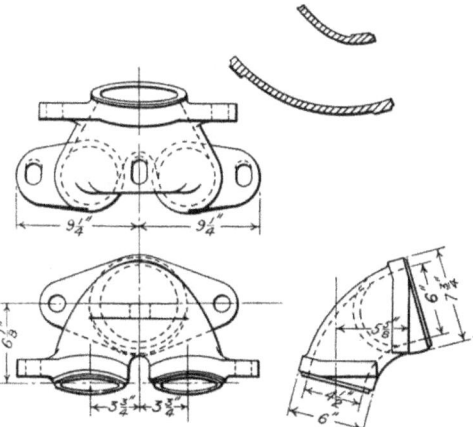

Figs. 944-948. Steam Connections Between Cylinders and Saddle. Atlantic (4—4—2) Locomotive. Pennsylvania Railroad.

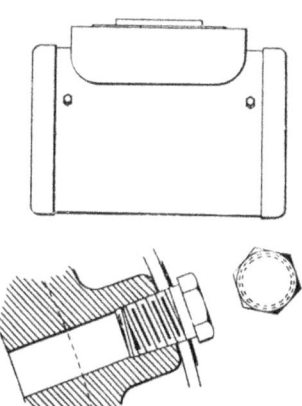

Figs. 949-951. Plugs for Indicator Connections.

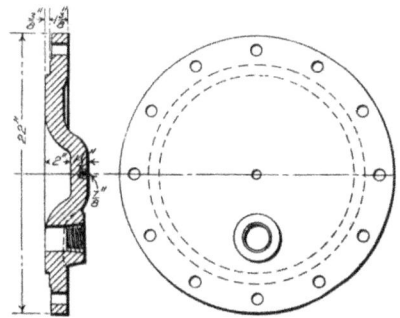

Figs. 952-953. Front Head.

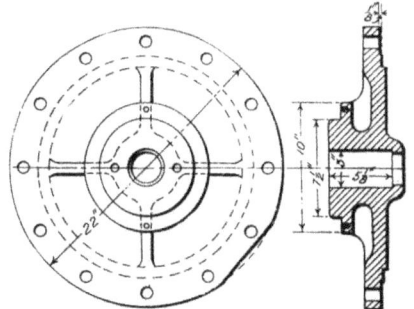

Figs. 954-955. Back Head.

Steam Chest Heads for Consolidation (2—8—0) Locomotive with Piston Valves. American Locomotive Co.

(156)

CYLINDERS, Details; Miscellaneous. Figs. 956-981

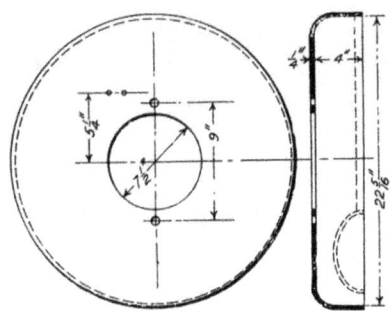

Figs. 956-957. Casing for Piston Valve Steam Chest Head. Consolidation (2—8—0) Locomotive. American Locomotive Co.

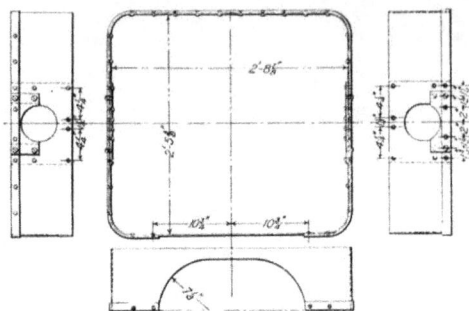

Figs. 958-961. Steam Chest Casing. Atlantic (4—4—2) Locomotive. Pennsylvania Railroad.

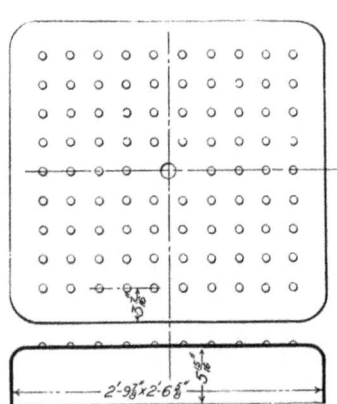

Figs. 962-963. Steam Chest Top Casing. Atlantic (4—4—2) Locomotive. Pennsylvania Railroad.

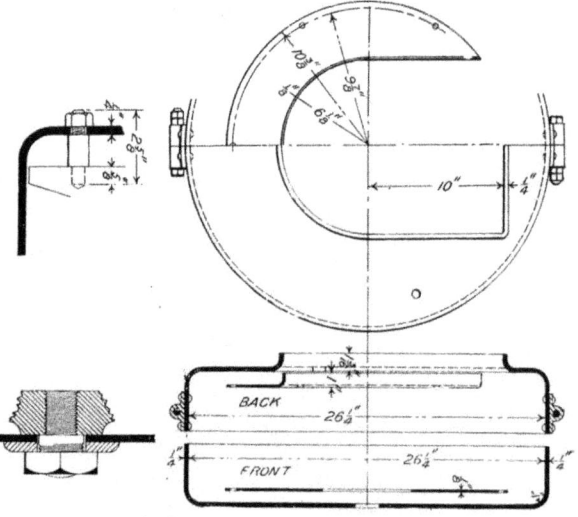

Figs. 964-968. Cylinder Head Casings. Atlantic (4—4—2) Locomotive. Pennsylvania Railroad.

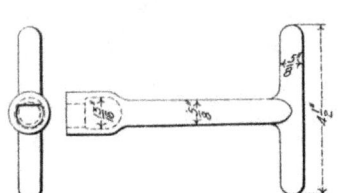

Figs. 969-970. Wrench for Cylinder Head Relief Valves.

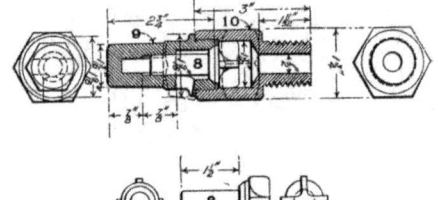

Figs. 973-978. Cylinder Cock. Pennsylvania Railroad.

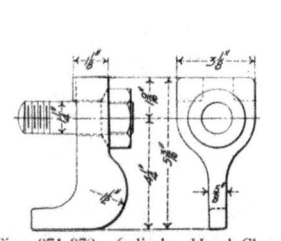

Figs. 971-972. Cylinder Head Clamp.

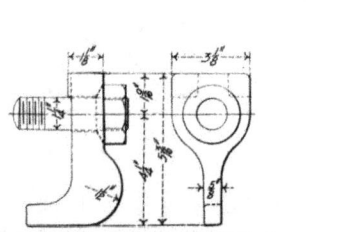

Figs. 979-981. Cylinder Cock Rigging Shaft Frame Bearing. Atlantic (4—4—2) Locomotive. P. R. R.

(157)

Figs. 982-994   CYLINDERS, Details; Cocks.

Numbers Refer to List of Names of Parts with Figs. 851-860.

Numbers Refer to List of Names of Parts on Opposite Page.

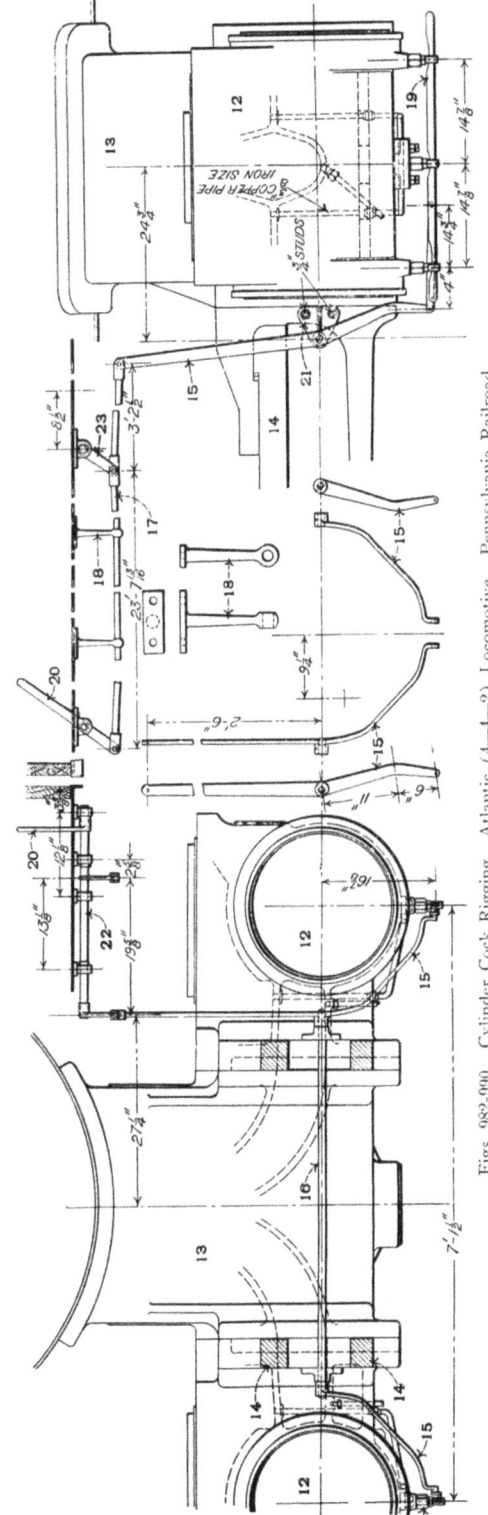

Figs. 982-990. Cylinder Cock Rigging. Atlantic (4-4-2) Locomotive. Pennsylvania Railroad.

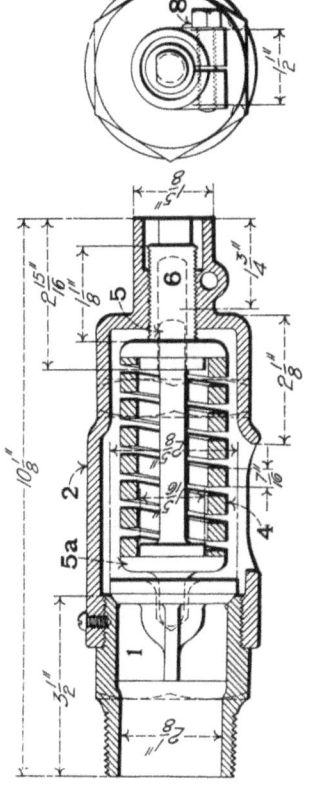

Figs. 993-994. Cylinder Head Relief Valve. American Locomotive Co.

Figs. 991-992. Cylinder Relief Valve and Nipple. Star Brass Mfg. Co.

(158)

CYLINDERS, Details; Relief Valves and Packing.   Figs. 995-1014

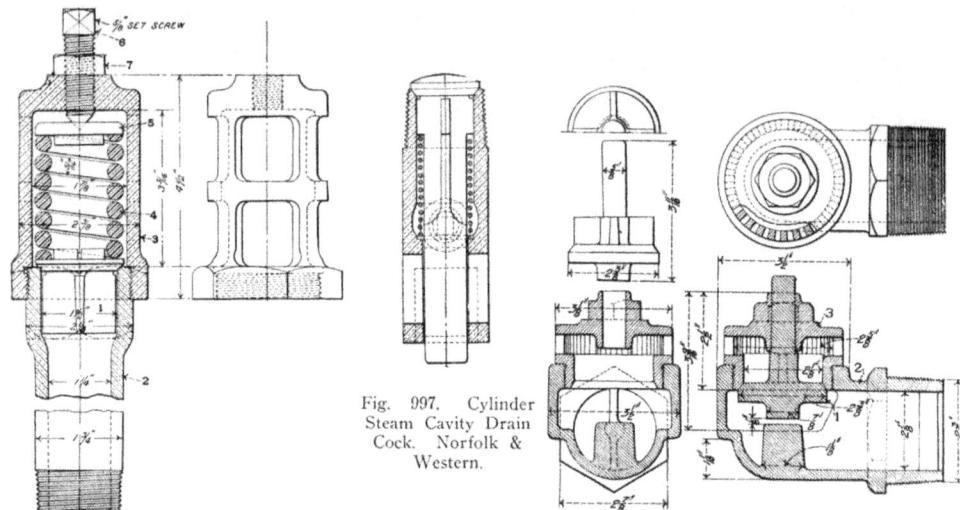

Figs. 995-996. Water Relief Valve for Cylinders with Piston Valves. Norfolk & Western.

Fig. 997. Cylinder Steam Cavity Drain Cock. Norfolk & Western.

Figs. 998-1003. Cylinder Relief Valve. American Locomotive Co.

Names of Parts of Relief Valves, Figs. 993-1003.

1	*Valve*	5	*Pressure Spring Cap*
2	*Casing*	5a	*Pressure Spring Seat*
3	*Cap*	6	*Adjusting Screw*
4	*Pressure Spring*	7	*Adjusting Screw Check Nut*
		8	*Adjusting Screw Clamp Bolt*

Names of Parts of Figs. 1004-1008.

1 *Steam Chest Plug*
2 *Steam Chest Plug Jam Nut*
3 *Steam Chest Plug Packing Collar*
4 *Lubricator Pipe*
5 *Lubricator Pipe Collar*

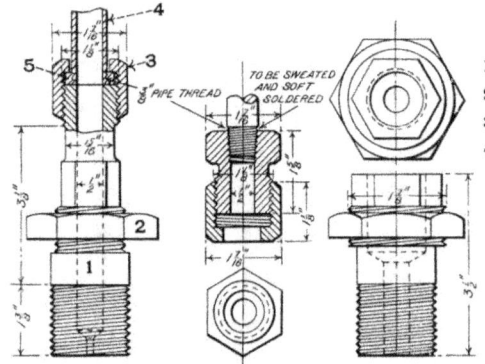

Figs. 1004-1008. Pipe Connections for Lubricator at Steam Chest. Atlantic (4—4—2) Locomotive. Pennsylvania Railroad.

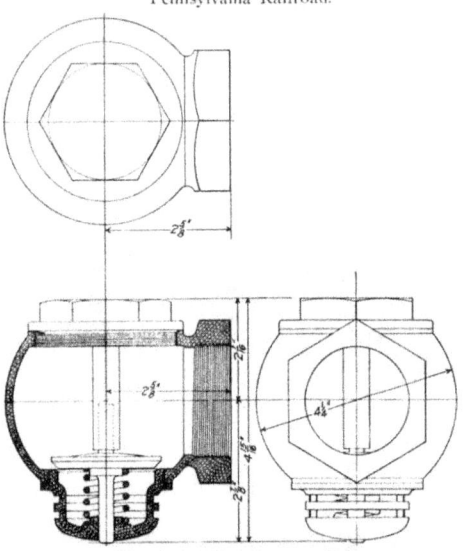

Figs. 1009-1011. Vacuum Valve. American Steam Gauge & Valve Co.

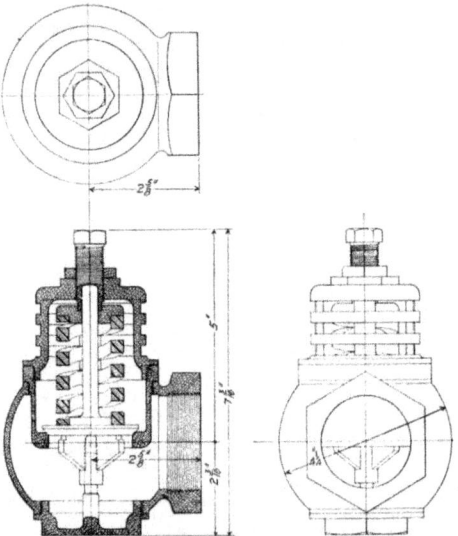

Figs. 1012-1014. Cylinder Relief Valve. American Steam Gauge & Valve Co.

CYLINDERS, Details; Rod Packing.

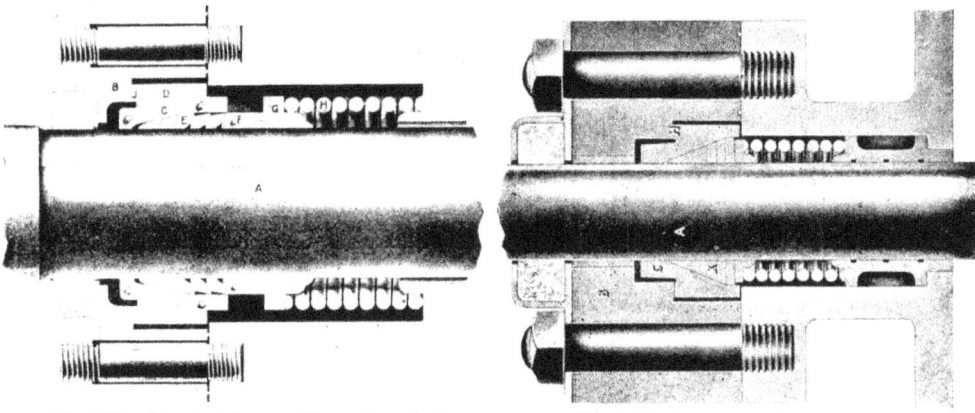

Fig. 1015. Standard Jerome Piston Rod Packing. Fig. 1016. Jerome Metallic Rod Packing.
Jerome & Elliot.

Fig. 1017. Standard Piston Rod Packing.
U. S. Metallic Packing Co.

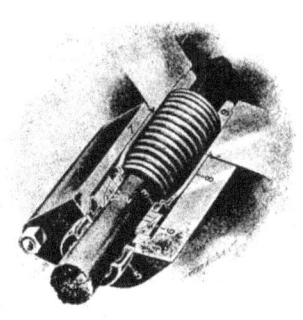

Fig. 1018. Valve Stem Packing.
U. S. Metallic Packing Co.

Names of Parts of Fig. 1017.

2	Babbitt Metal Ring	6	Vibrating Cup
3	Follower	7	Gland
4	Ball Joint	8	Preventer
5	Swab Cup		

Names of Parts of Fig 1018.

2	Babbitt Metal Ring	6	Vibrating Cup
3	Follower	7	Gland
4	Ball Joint	8	Preventer
5	Swab Cup	9	Support

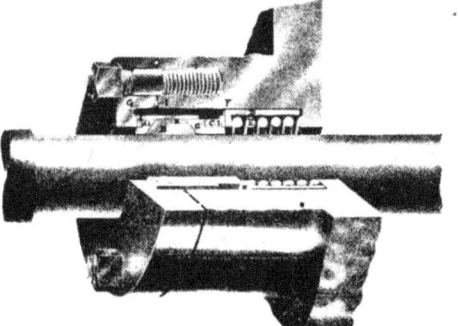

Fig. 1019. Piston Rod Packing with Gibbs Vibrating Cup.
U. S. Metallic Packing Co.

Fig. 1020. Hayden Segmental Metallic Piston Rod Packing.
N. L. Hayden Manufacturing Co.

Fig. 1021. Metallic Piston Rod Packing.
Aurora Metal Co.

(160)

CROSSHEAD GUIDES.

Figs. 1022-1029

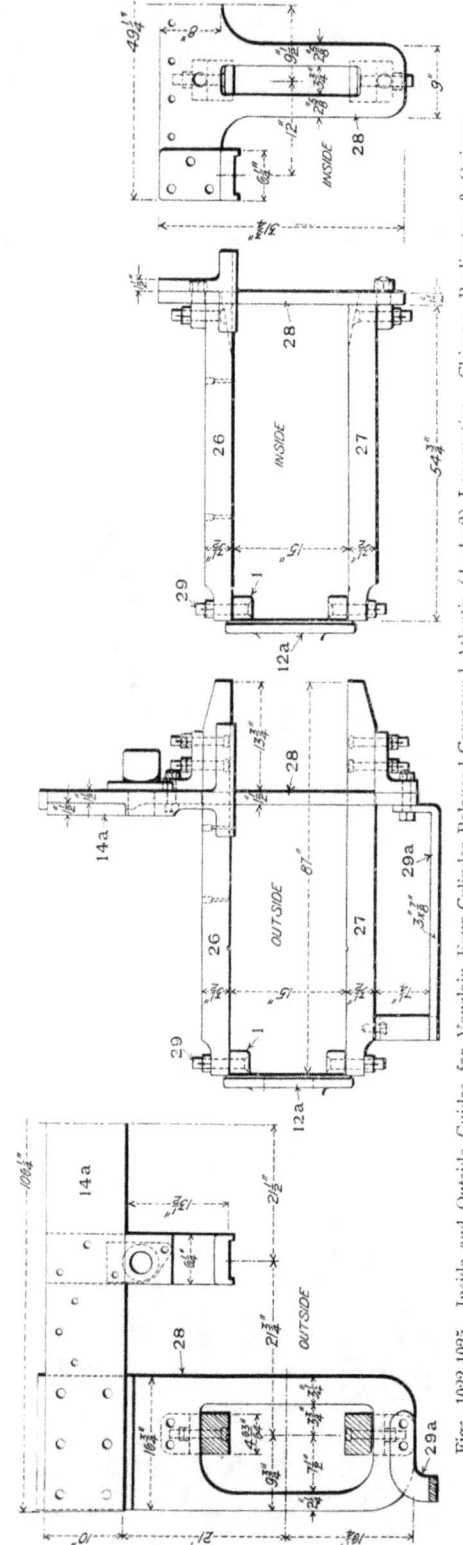

Figs. 1022-1025. Inside and Outside Guides for Vauclain Four-Cylinder Balanced Compound Atlantic (4–4–2) Locomotive. Chicago, Burlington & Quincy.

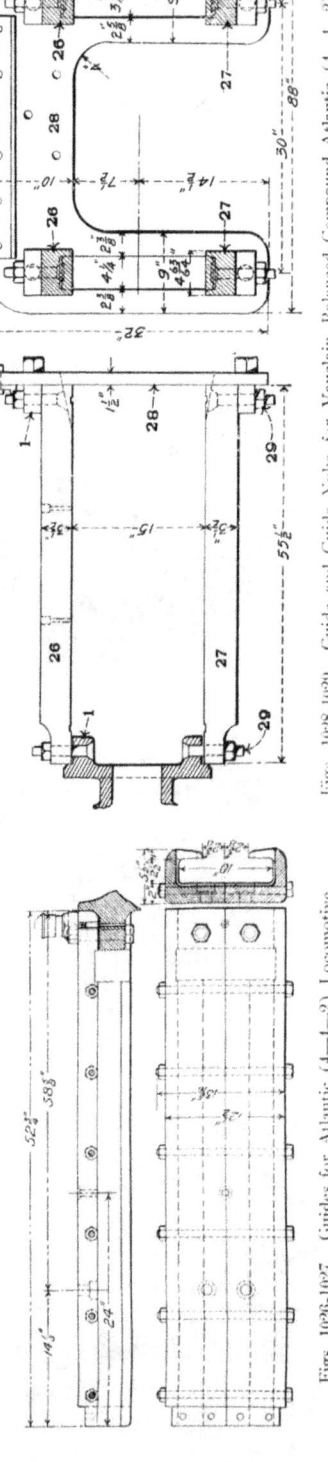

Figs. 1028-1029. Guide and Guide Yoke for Vauclain Balanced Compound Atlantic (4–4–2) Locomotive.

Figs. 1026-1027. Guides for Atlantic (4–4–2) Locomotive. Pennsylvania Railroad.

Numbers Refer to List of Names of Parts with Figs. 851-860.

CROSSHEADS.

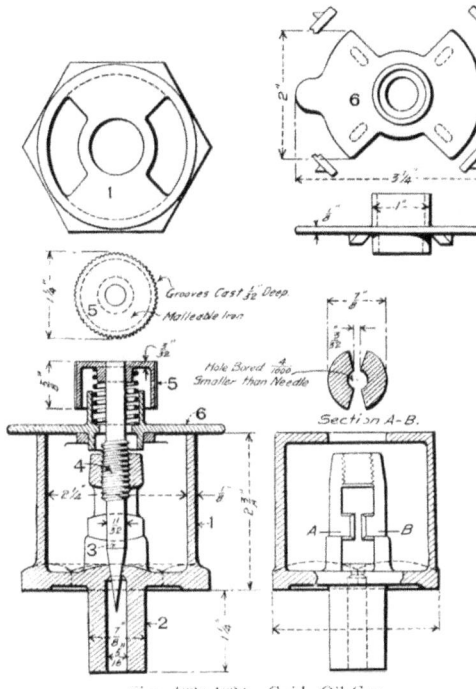

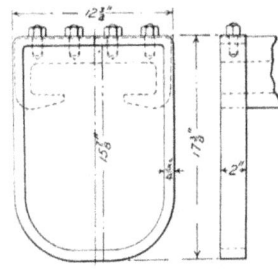

Figs. 1037-1038. Main Rod Guard. Atlantic (4—4—2) Locomotive. P. R. R.

Names of Parts of Crossheads, Figs. 1039-1086.

1. Body
2. Wrist Pin
3. Piston Rod Key
4. Lining
5. Piston Rod Boss
6. Piston Rod
7. Piston Rod Nuts
8. Lubricator
9. Gib
10. Oil Cup
11. Oil Cup Cover
13. Oil Cup Cover Spring
14. Arm for Combination Lever Link of Walschaert Valve Gear.

Figs. 1030-1036. Guide Oil Cup.

Names of Parts of Oil Cup, Figs. 1030-1036.

1. Body
2. Stem
3. Feeding Needle
4. Adjusting Screw
5. Adjusting Screw Cap
6. Cover

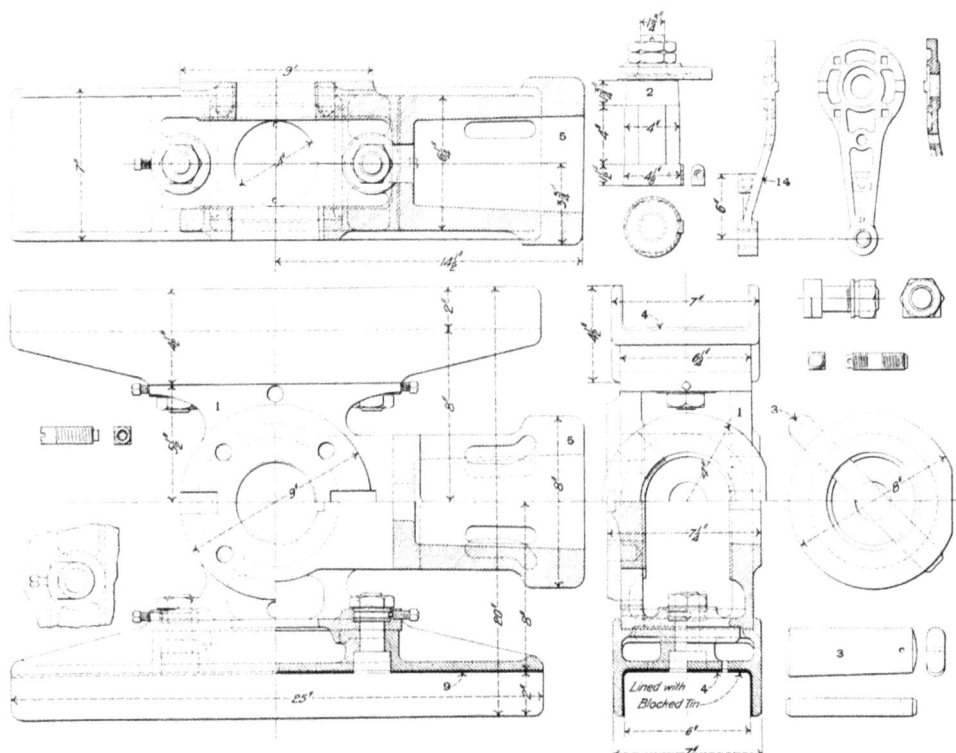

Figs. 1039-1058. Alligator Crosshead with Connection for Walschaert Valve Gear. Baldwin Locomotive Works.

CROSSHEADS.   Figs. 1059–1073

Numbers Refer to List of Names of Parts with Figs. 1030–1058.

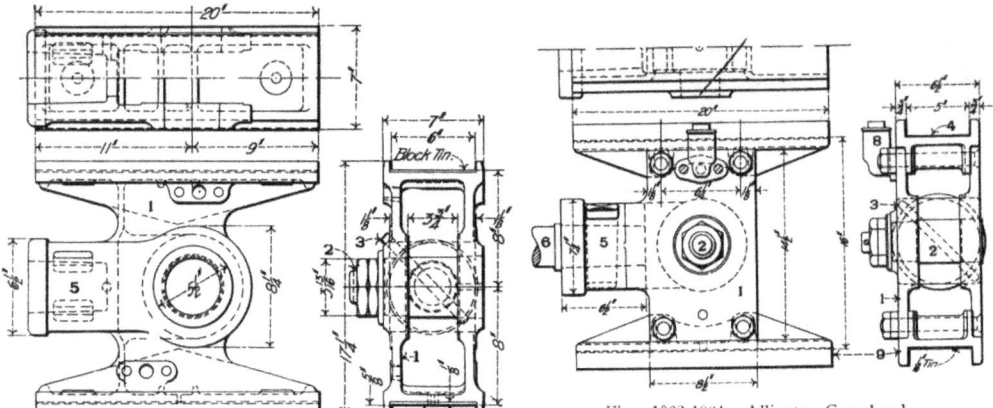

Figs. 1059-1061. Alligator Crosshead.
Baldwin Locomotive Works.

Figs. 1062-1064. Alligator Crosshead.
Baldwin Locomotive Works.

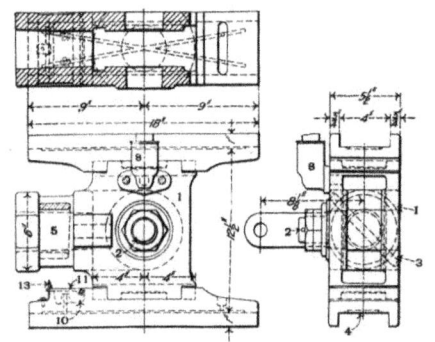

Figs. 1068-1069. Alligator Crosshead.
Baldwin Locomotive Works.

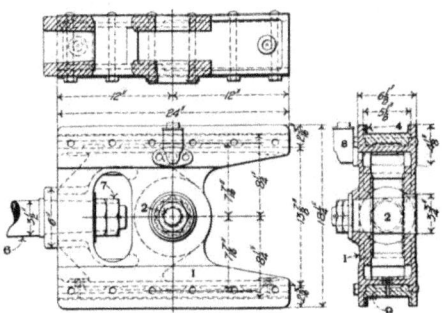

Figs. 1065-1067. Alligator Crosshead.
Baldwin Locomotive Works.

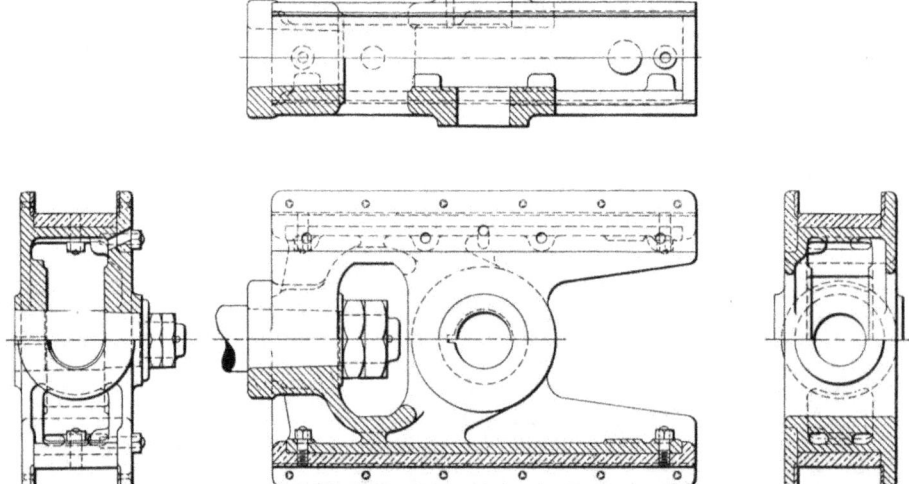

Figs. 1070-1073. Alligator Crosshead with Brass Gibs. Baldwin Locomotive Works.

CROSSHEADS.

Numbers Refer to List of Names of Parts with Figs. 1030-1058.

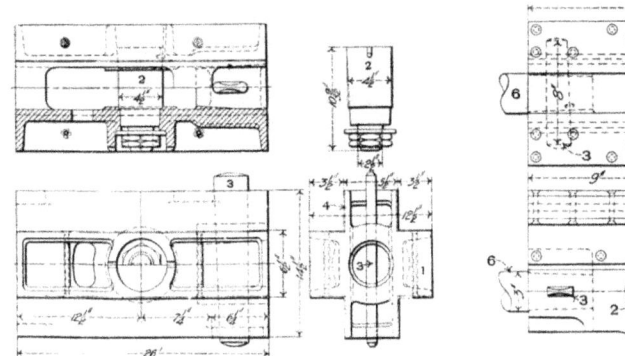

Figs. 1074-1077. Four-Guide Crosshead. Baldwin Locomotive Works.

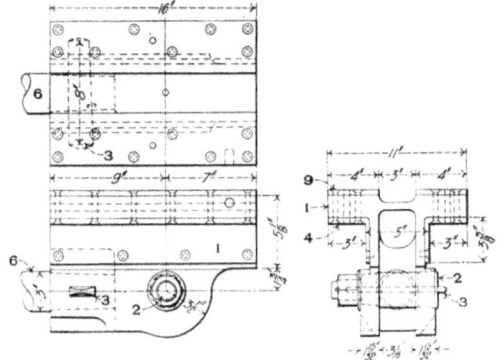

Figs. 1078-1080. Laird Crosshead. Baldwin Locomotive Works.

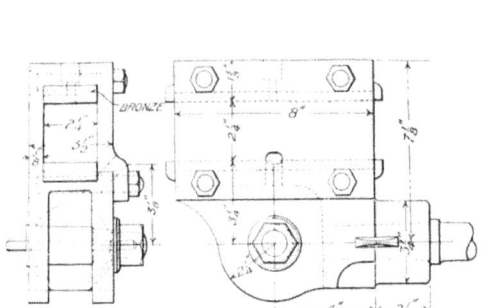

Figs. 1081-1083. Laird Crosshead. Baldwin Locomotive Works.

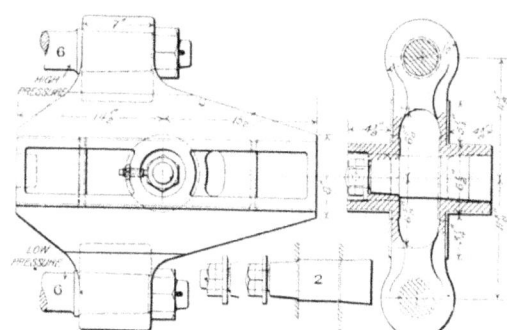

Figs. 1084-1086. Crosshead for Vauclain Compound Locomotive. Baldwin Locomotive Works.

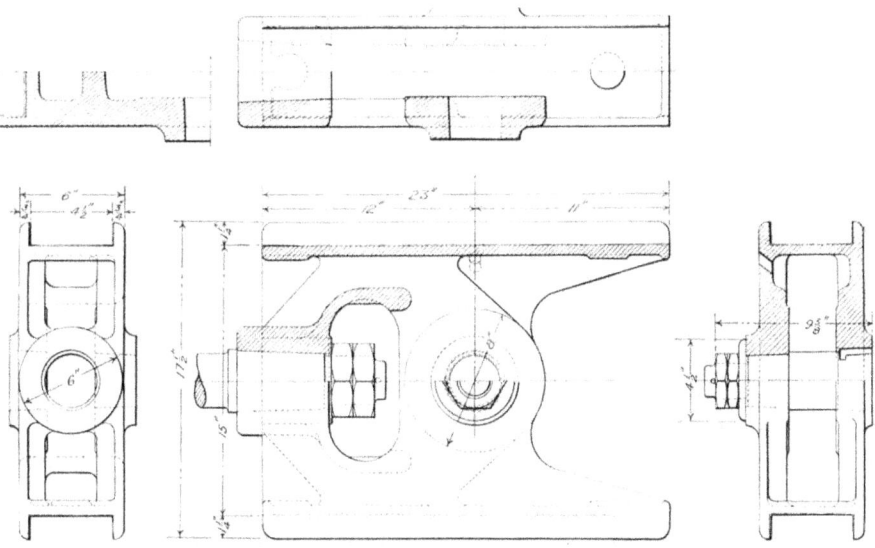

Figs. 1087-1091. Alligator Crosshead. Baldwin Locomotive Works.

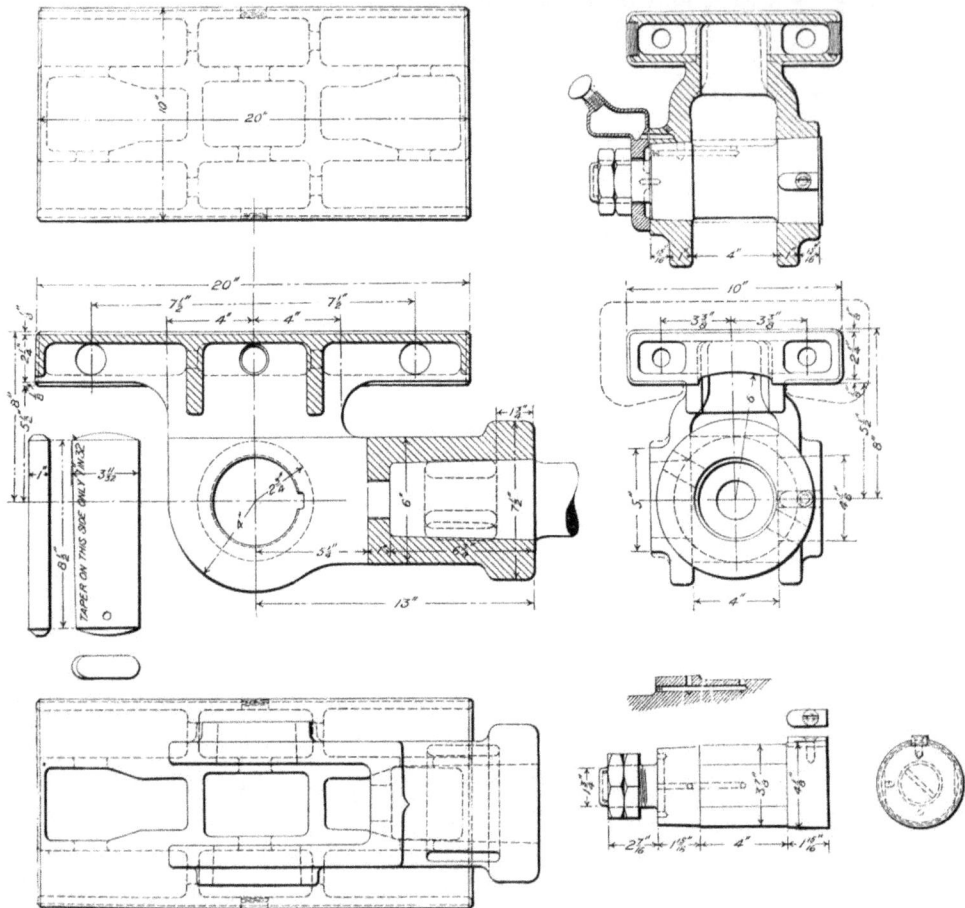

Figs. 1092-1102. Vogt Crosshead. Atlantic (4—4—2) Locomotive. Pennsylvania Railroad.

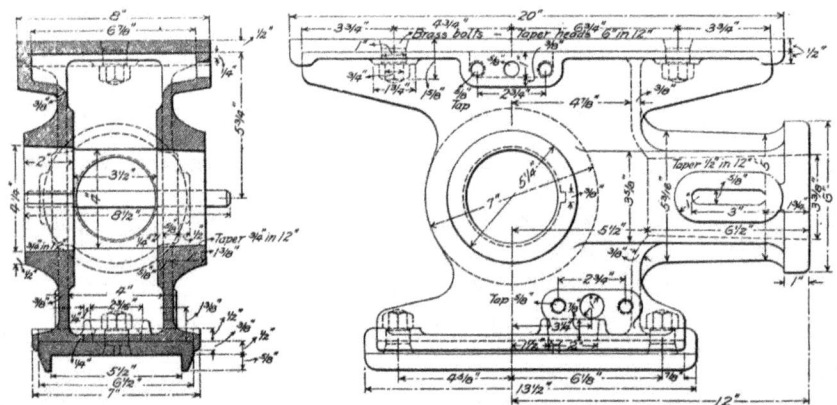

Figs. 1103-1104. Cast-Steel Alligator Crosshead.

CROSSHEADS.

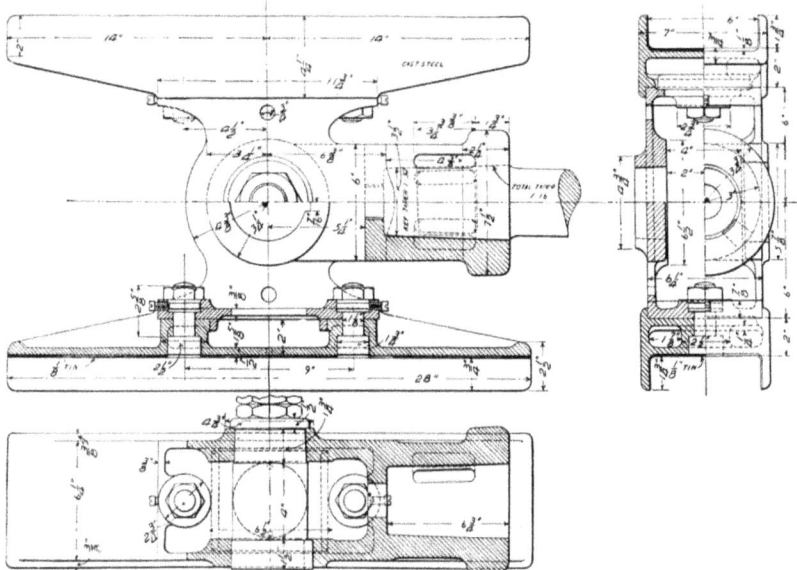

Figs. 1105-1107. Alligator Crosshead.

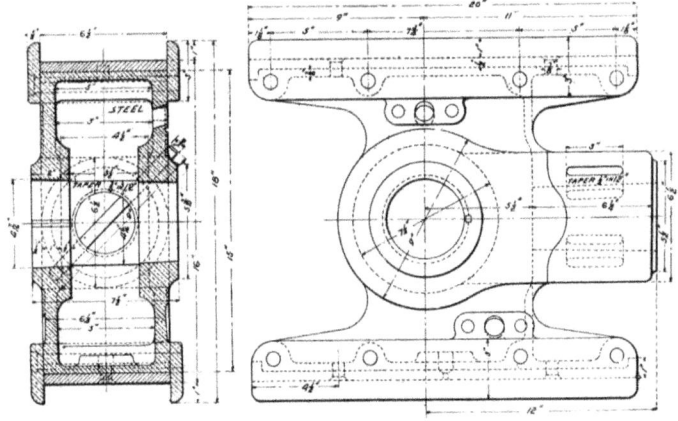

Figs. 1108-1109. Alligator Crosshead.

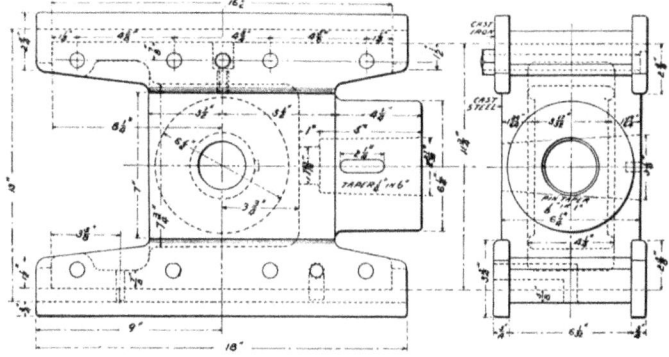

Figs. 1110-1111. Alligator Crosshead.

CROSSHEADS, Pins.

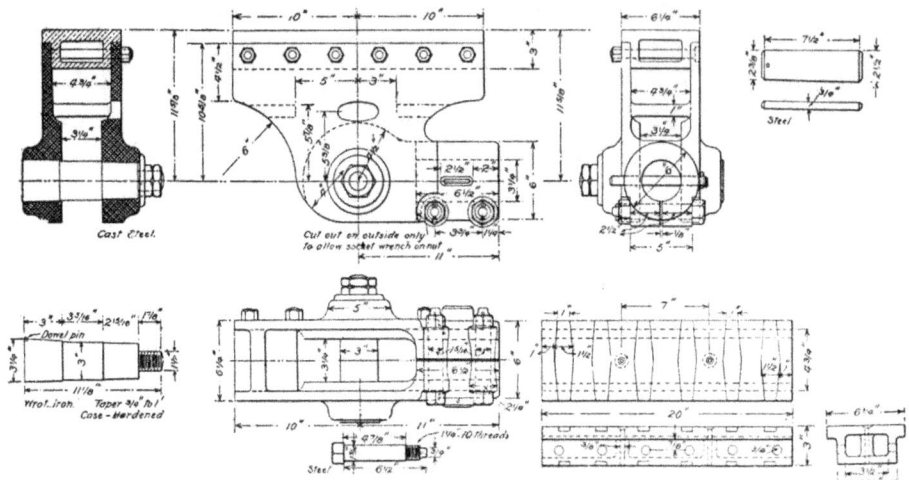

Figs. 1112-1122. Details of Laird Crosshead. Wabash Railroad.

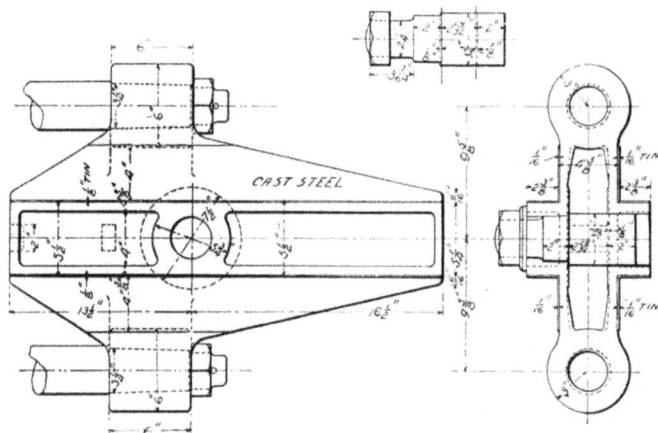

Figs. 1123-1125. Cast-Steel Crosshead for Vauclain Compound Locomotive. Baldwin Locomotive Works.

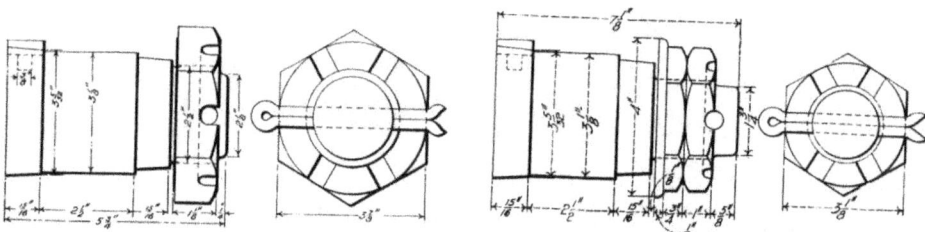

Figs. 1126-1127. Wrist Pin for Consolidation (2—8—0) Locomotive.

Figs. 1128-1129. Wrist Pin for Atlantic (4—4—2) Locomotive.

CRANK PINS.

Numbers Refer to List of Names of Parts Below.

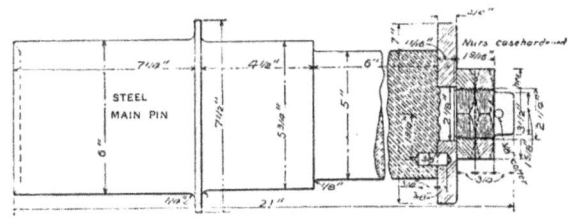

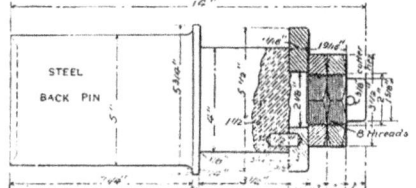
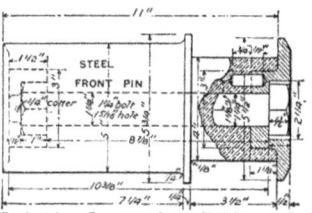

Figs. 1130-1134. Crank Pins for Six-Wheel (0—6—0) Switching Locomotive. Baltimore & Ohio.

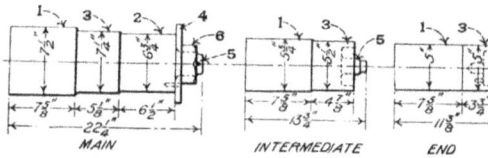
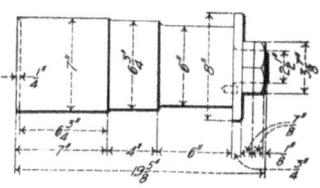

Figs. 1135-1137. Crank Pins for Consolidation (2—8—0) Locomotive.

Fig. 1138. Main Crank Pin for Consolidation (2—8—0) Locomotive.

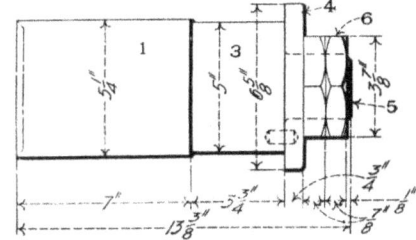
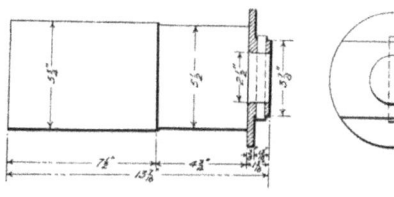

Fig. 1139. Back Crank Pin for Consolidation (2—8—0) Locomotive.

Figs. 1140-1141. Forward Crank Pin for Consolidation (2—8—0) Locomotive.

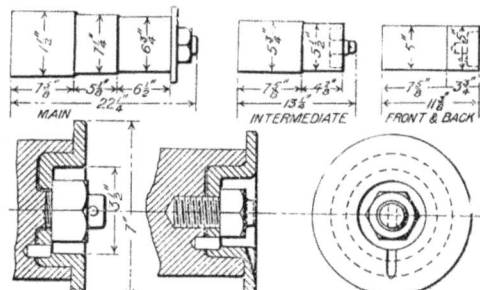
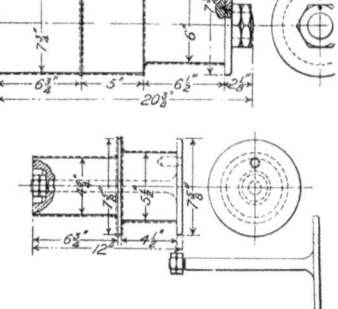

Figs. 1142-1147. Crank Pins for Consolidation (2—8—0) Locomotive.

Figs. 1148-1152. Crank Pins for Atlantic (4—4—2) Locomotive. P. R. R.

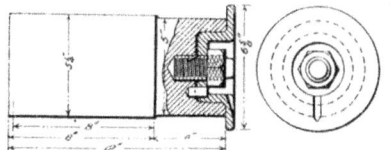

Figs. 1153-1154. Intermediate Crank Pin.

Names of Parts of Crank Pins, Figs. 1135-1139.

1 *Wheel Seat*
2 *Main Rod Bearing*
3 *Side Rod Bearing*
4 *Collar*
5 *Stud*
6 *Stud Nut*

MAIN AND SIDE RODS.

Figs. 1155-1171

Numbers Refer to List of Names of Parts with Figs. 1172-1183.

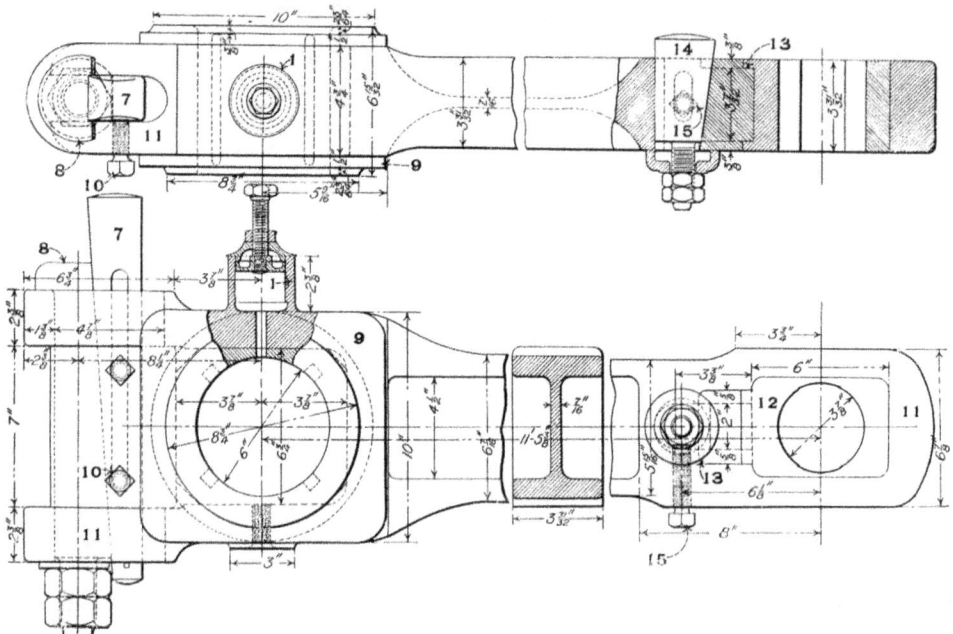

Figs. 1155-1156. Main Rod for Atlantic (4—4—2) Locomotive. Pennsylvania Railroad.

Figs. 1157-1158. Side Rods for Atlantic (4—4—2) Locomotive. P. R. R.

Figs. 1159-1163. Main Rod Fittings. Atlantic (4—4—2) Locomotive. P. R. R.

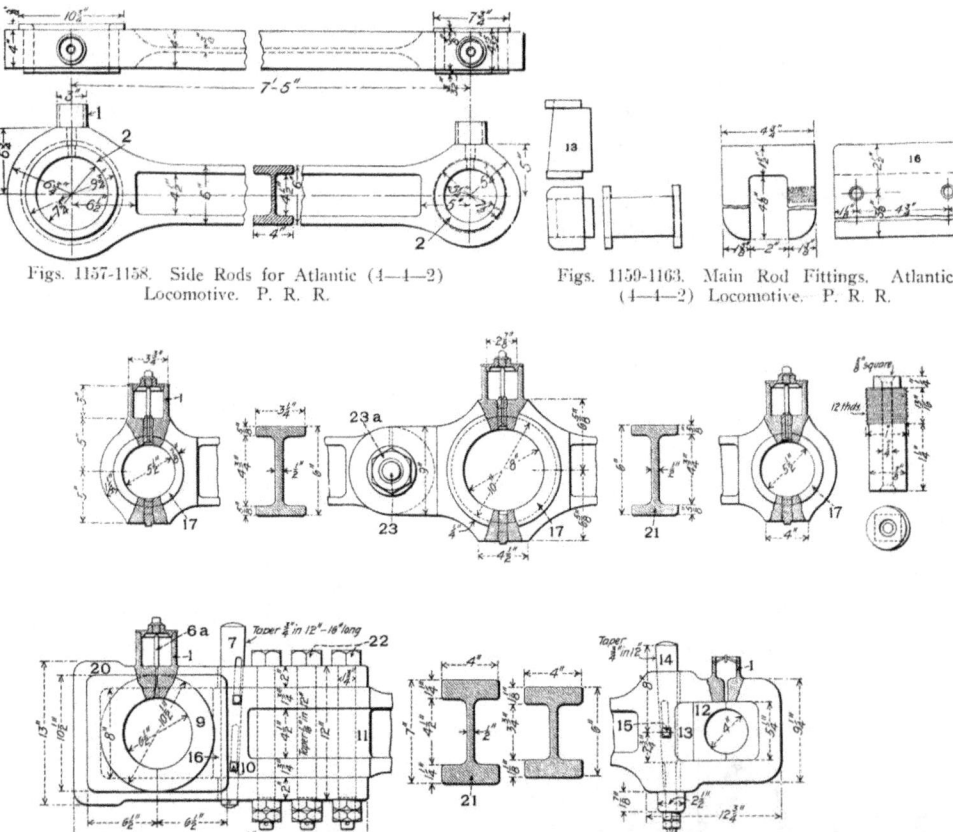

Figs. 1164-1171. Main and Side Rods for Ten-Wheel (4—6—0) Locomotive. Lehigh Valley.

MAIN AND SIDE RODS.

Numbers Refer to List of Names of Parts Below.

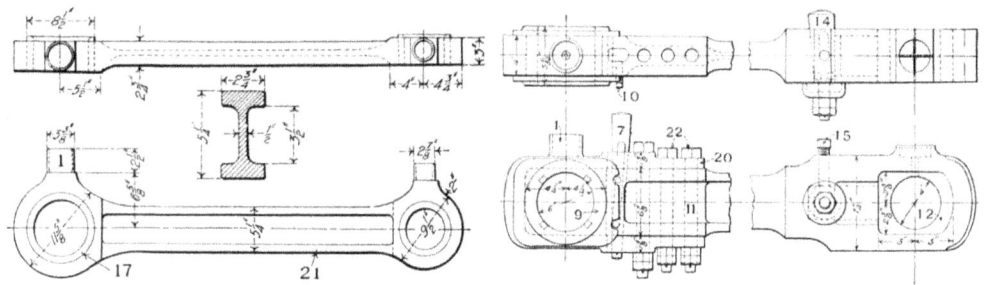

Figs. 1172-1174. Side Rod for Atlantic (4—4—2) Locomotive. American Locomotive Co.

Figs. 1175-1176. Stub Ends of Main Rod for Atlantic (4—4—2) Locomotive.

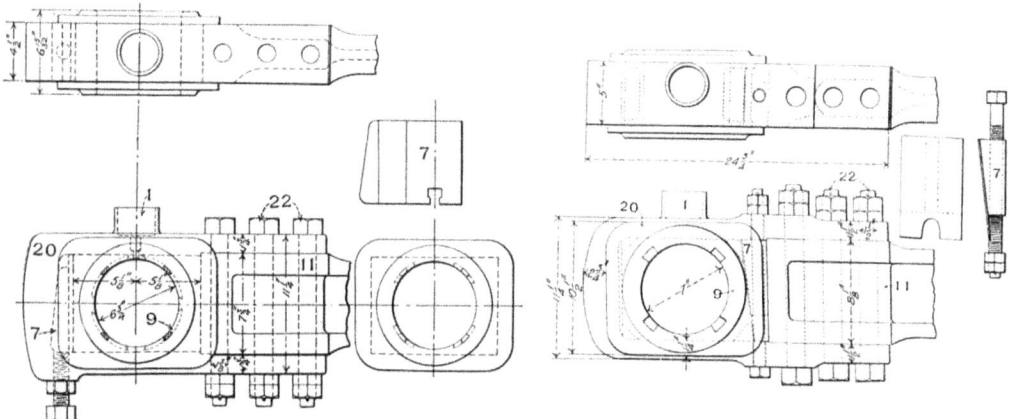

Figs. 1177-1179. Crank Pin Stub End of Main Rod.

Figs. 1180-1183. Stub Ends of Main Rod for Consolidation (2—8—0) Locomotive. American Locomotive Co.

Names of Parts of Rods, Figs. 1155-1229.

1 Oil Cup	10 Main Pin Brass Key Set Screw	17 Bushing
2 Crank Pin Bushing	11 Stub End of Main Rod	18 Stub End Fork
3 Oil Cup Check Nut	12 Wrist Pin Brass	19 Bushing Set Screw
6a Oil Cup Feeder Pin	13 Wrist Pin Brass Wedge Block	20 Rod Strap
7 Main Pin Brass Key	14 Wrist Pin Brass Key	21 Rod Body
8 Main Pin Brass Cotter	14a Wrist Pin Brass Key Washer	22 Rod Strap Bolts
9 Main Pin Brass	15 Wrist Pin Brass Key Set Screw	23 Knuckle Pin
	16 Main Rod Pin Wedge Block	23a Knuckle Pin Nut

MAIN AND SIDE RODS.

Figs. 1184-1213

Numbers Refer to List of Names of Parts on Opposite Page.

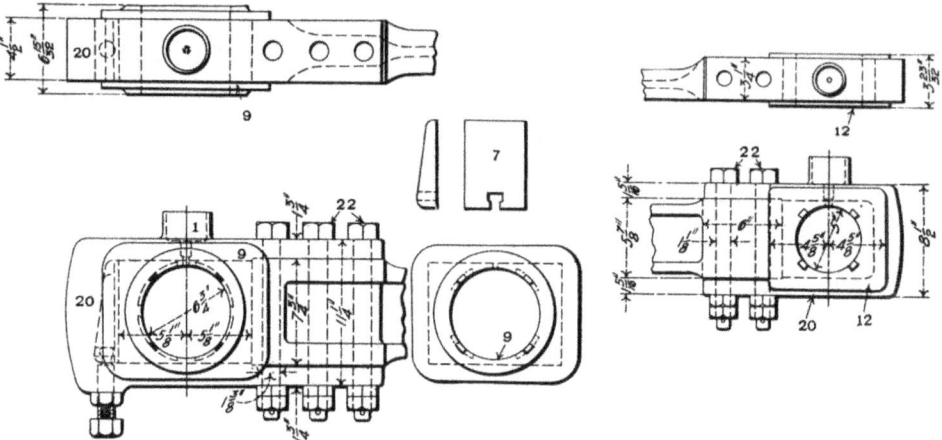

Figs. 1184-1190. Stub Ends of Main Rod for Consolidation (2—8—0) Locomotive. American Locomotive Co.

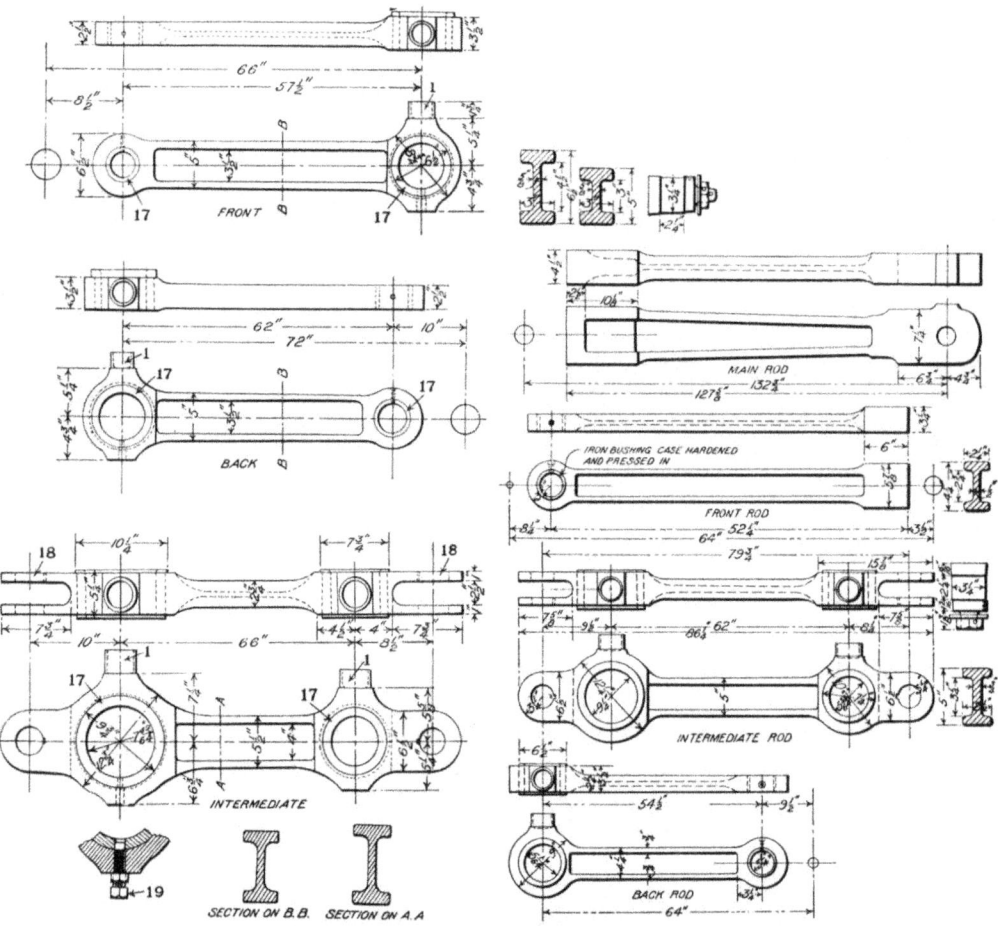

Figs. 1191-1199. Details of Side Rods for Consolidation (2—8—0) Locomotive. American Locomotive Co.

Figs. 1200-1213. Main and Side Rods for Consolidation (2—8—0) Locomotive. American Locomotive Co.

MAIN AND SIDE RODS.

Numbers Refer to List of Names of Parts with Figs. 1172-1183.

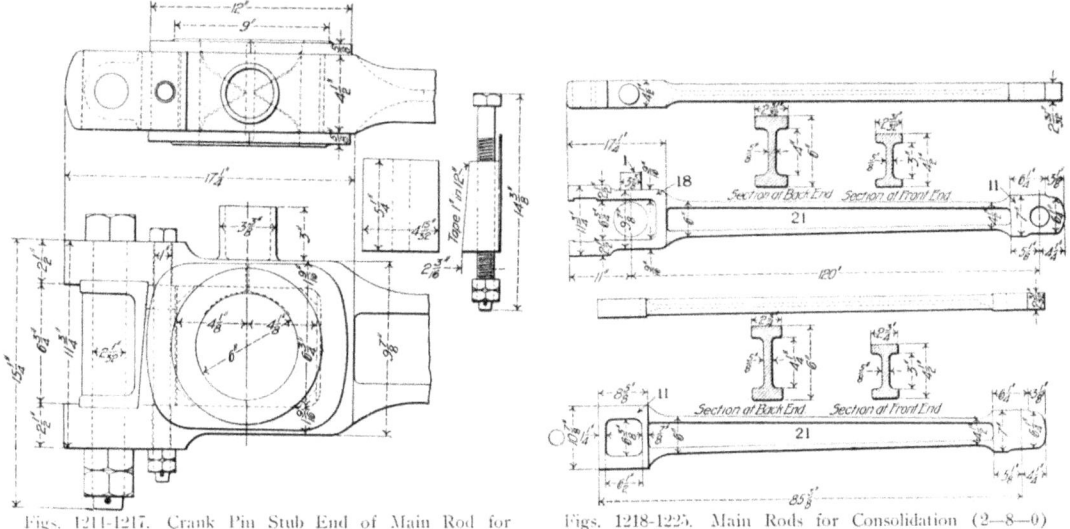

Figs. 1214-1217. Crank Pin Stub End of Main Rod for Consolidation (2—8—0) Locomotive. American Locomotive Co.

Figs. 1218-1225. Main Rods for Consolidation (2—8—0) Locomotives. American Locomotive Co.

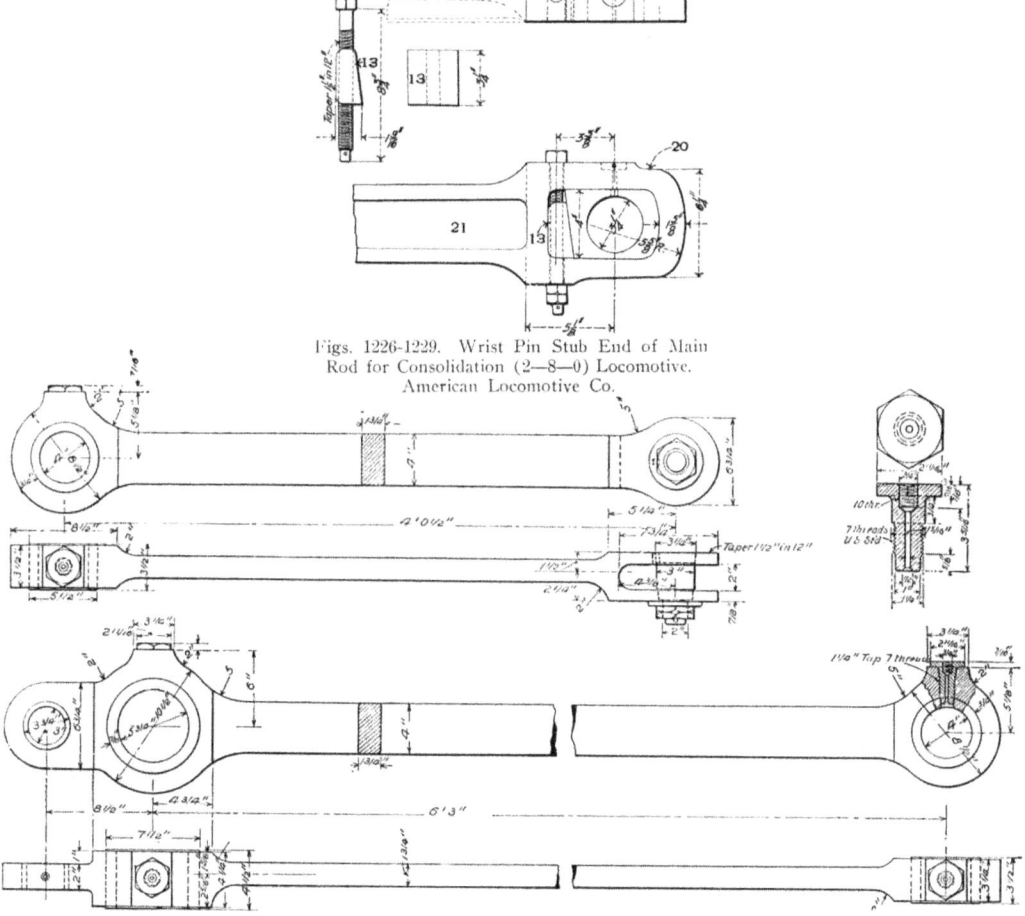

Figs. 1226-1229. Wrist Pin Stub End of Main Rod for Consolidation (2—8—0) Locomotive. American Locomotive Co.

Figs. 1230-1235. Side Rods for Six-Wheel (0—6—0) Switching Locomotive. Baltimore & Ohio.

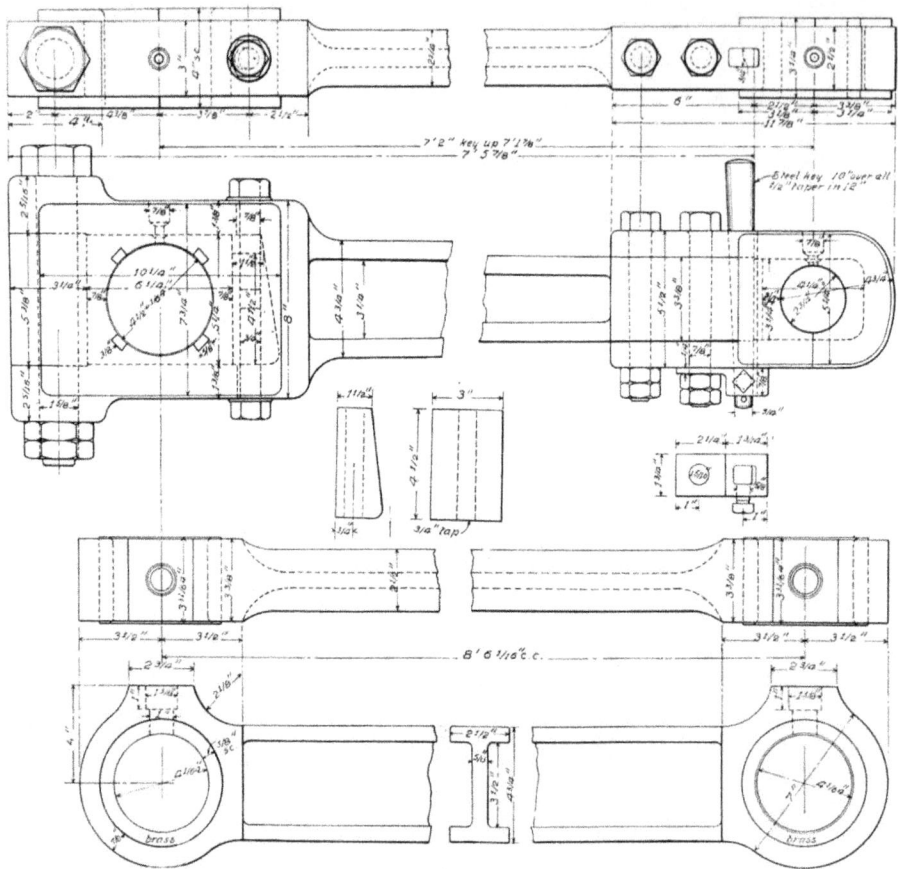

Figs. 1236-1242. Main and Side Rods for Eight-Wheel American (4—4—0) Type Locomotive. Chicago, Milwaukee & St. Paul.

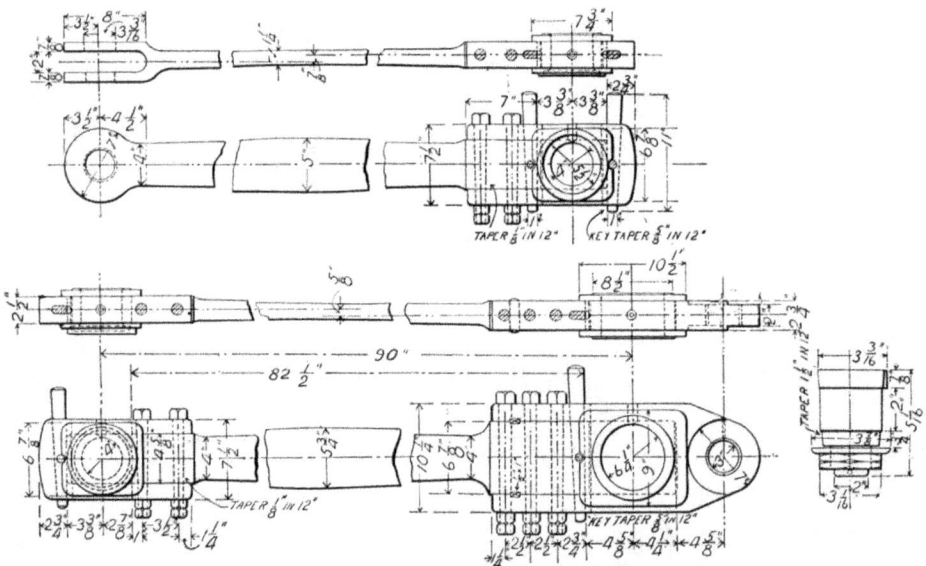

Figs. 1243-1247. Side Rods for Mogul (2—6—0) Locomotive.

MAIN AND SIDE RODS.

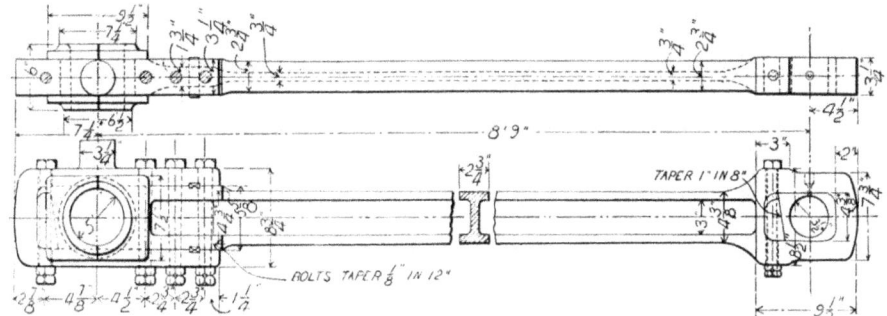

Figs. 1248-1249. Main Rod. American Locomotive Co.

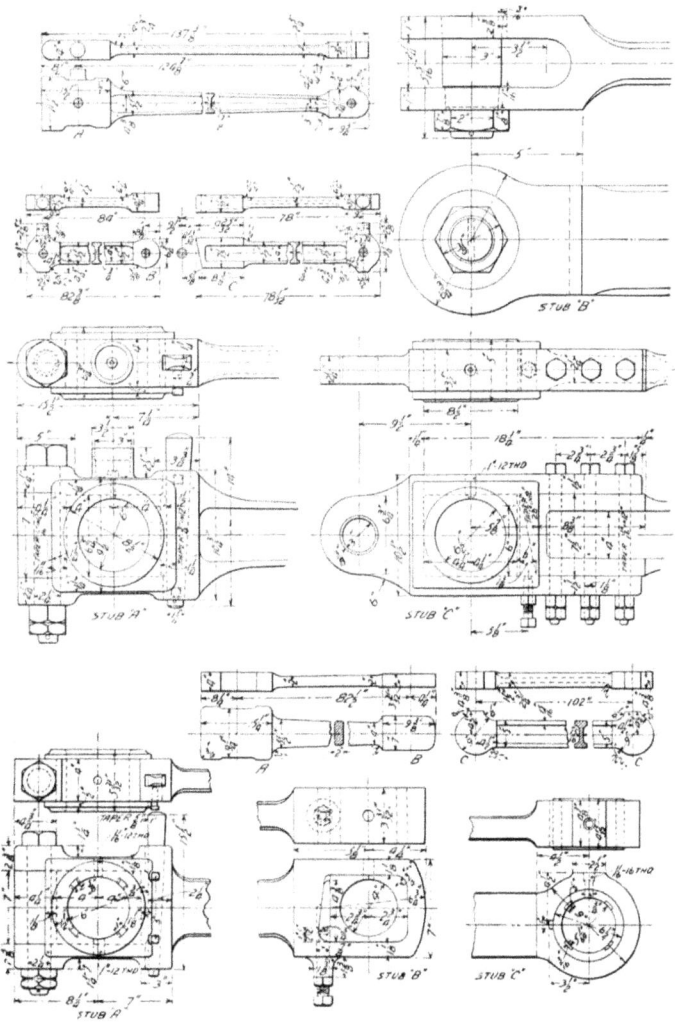

Figs. 1250-1271. Details of Rods for Ten-Wheel (4—6—0) Locomotive. Plant System.

MAIN AND SIDE RODS, Details; Oil Cups.   Figs. 1272-1300

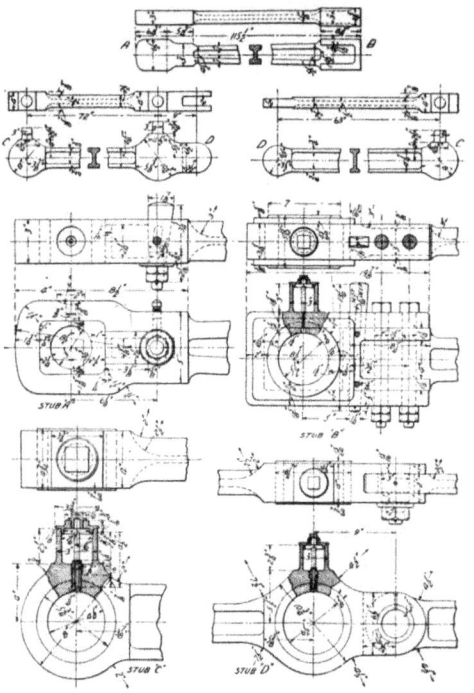

Figs. 1272-1285. Details of Connecting Rods. American Locomotive Co.

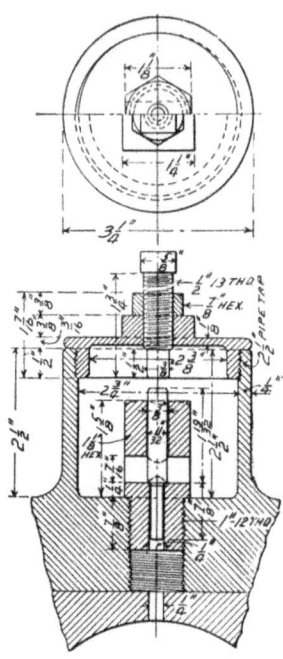

Figs. 1286-1287. Main Rod Oil Cup.

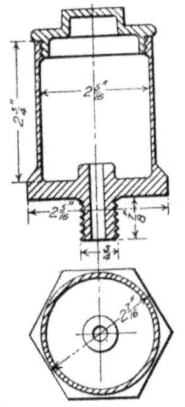

Figs. 1288-1289. Rod Oil Cup.

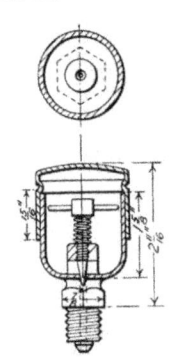

Figs. 1290-1291. Rod Oil Cup. U. S. Metallic Packing Co.

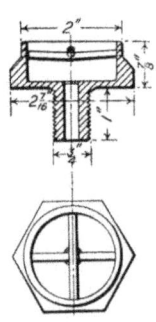

Figs. 1292-1293. Oil Cup Body.

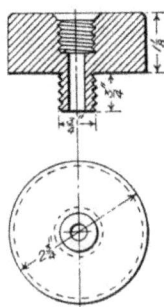

Figs. 1294-1295. Oil Cup Extension Nipple.

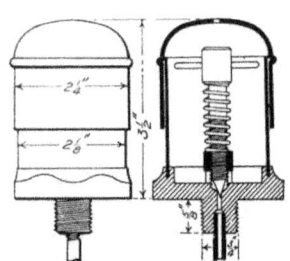

Figs. 1296-1297. Rod Oil Cup.

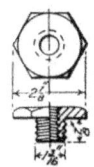

Figs. 1298-1299. Oil Cup Bushing.

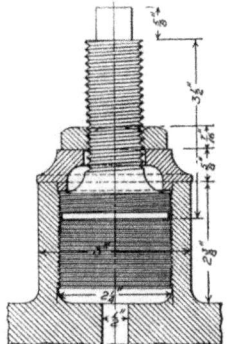

Fig. 1300. Main Rod Grease Cup.

(175)

WHEELS, Driving.

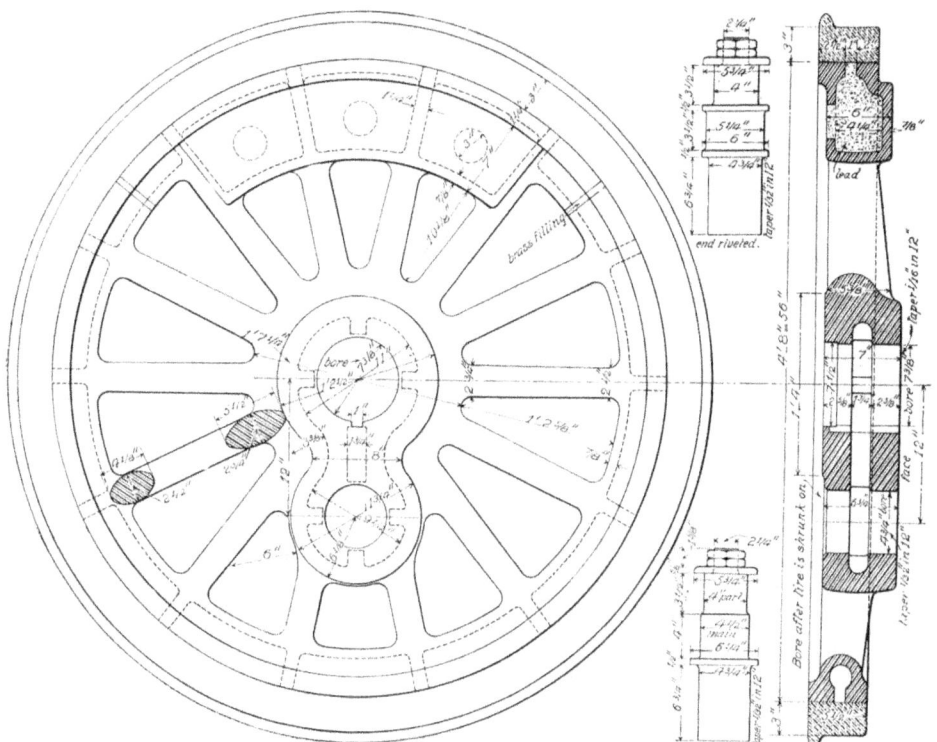

Figs. 1301-1304. 62-in. Driving Wheel for Eight-Wheel (4—4—0) Locomotive. Chicago, Milwaukee & St. Paul.

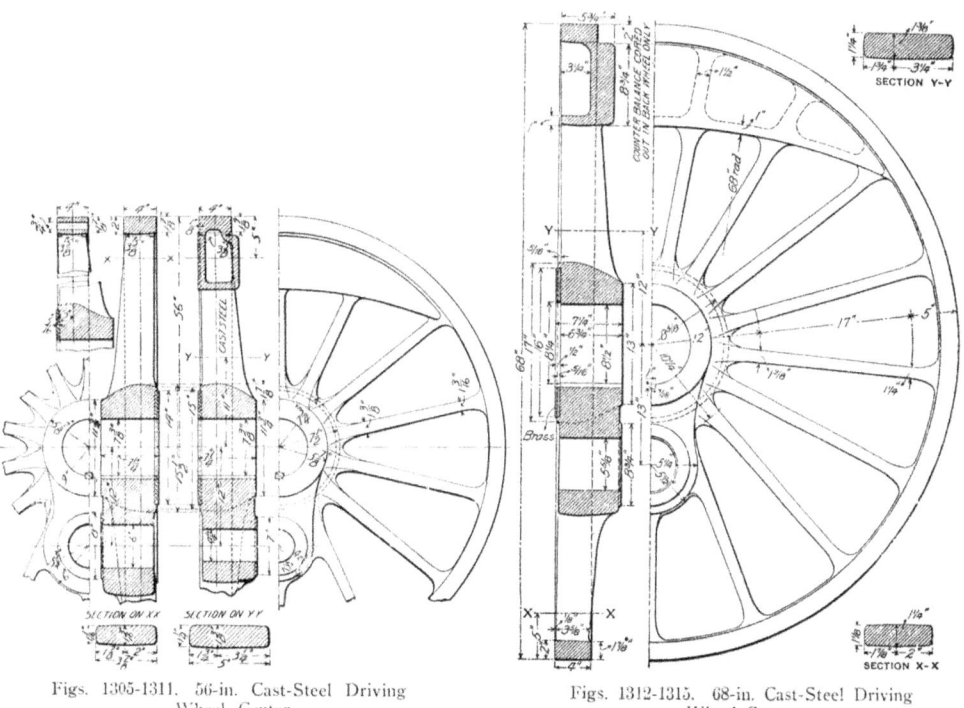

Figs. 1305-1311. 56-in. Cast-Steel Driving Wheel Center.

Figs. 1312-1315. 68-in. Cast-Steel Driving Wheel Center.

(176)

WHEELS, Driving.

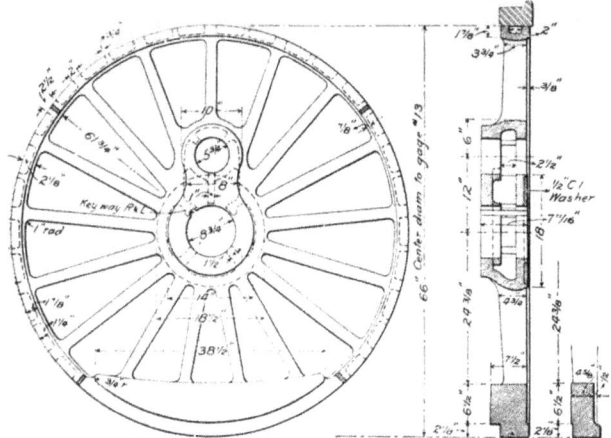

Figs. 1316-1318. 66-in. Driving Wheel Center.

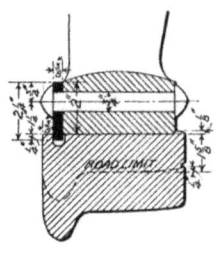

Fig. 1319. Flanged Driving Wheel Tire with Riveted Retaining Ring.

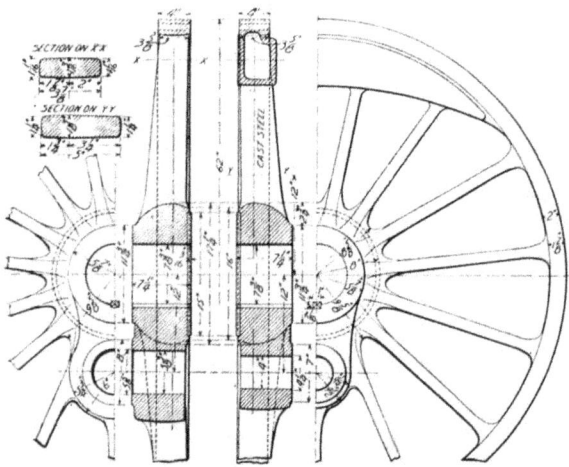

Figs. 1320-1325. 62-in. Cast-Steel Driving Wheel Center.

Fig. 1326. Cast-Steel Driving Wheel Center with Davis Counterbalance. Davis Loco. Wheel Co.

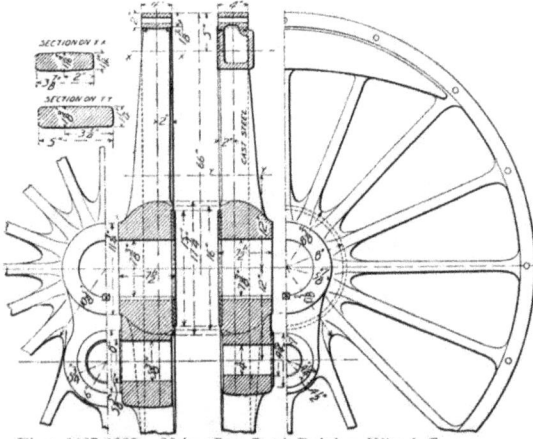

Figs. 1327-1332. 66-in. Cast-Steel Driving Wheel Center.

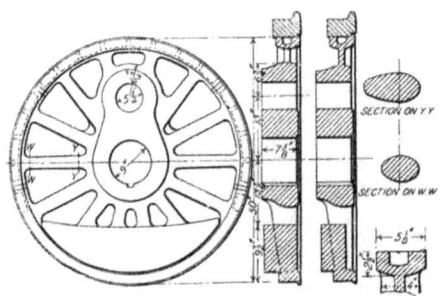

Figs. 1333-1338. Driving Wheel Center for Consolidation (2—8—0) Locomotive. American Locomotive Co.

(177)

WHEELS, Driving.

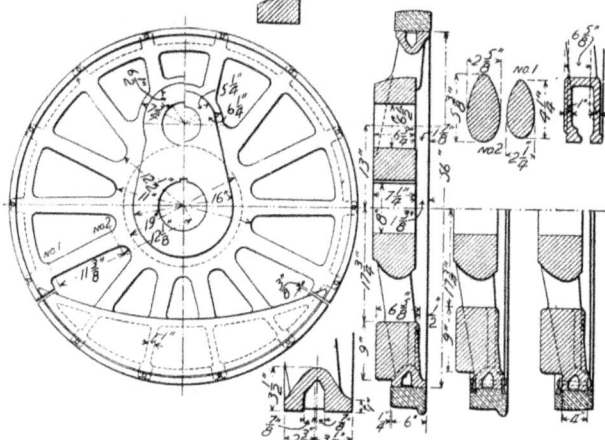

Figs. 1339-1347. 56-in. Driving Wheel Center.

Names of Parts of Driving Wheels, Figs. 1353-1367.

1. *Center*
2. *Rim*
2a. *Rim Slot*
3. *Hub*
4. *Axle Seat*
5. *Tire*
6. *Flange*
7. *Spoke*
8. *Counterbalance*
8a. *Counterbalance Cavity*
9. *Crank Hub*
10. *Crank Pin Seat*
11. *Hub Liner*
12. *Retaining Ring*
13. *Retaining Ring Lip*
14. *Retaining Ring Bolt*

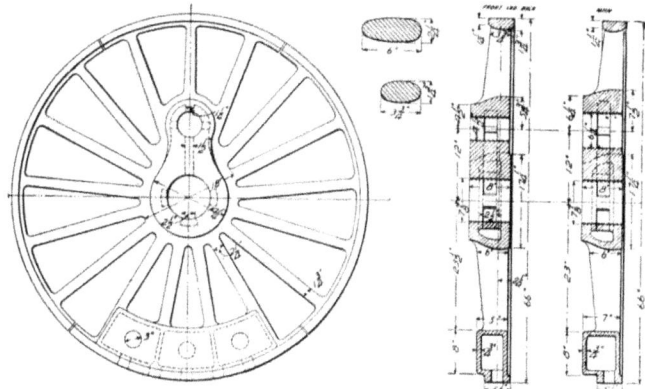

Figs. 1348-1352. 66-in. Cast-Steel Driving Wheel Center. Baldwin Locomotive Works.

Numbers Refer to List of Names of Parts Above.

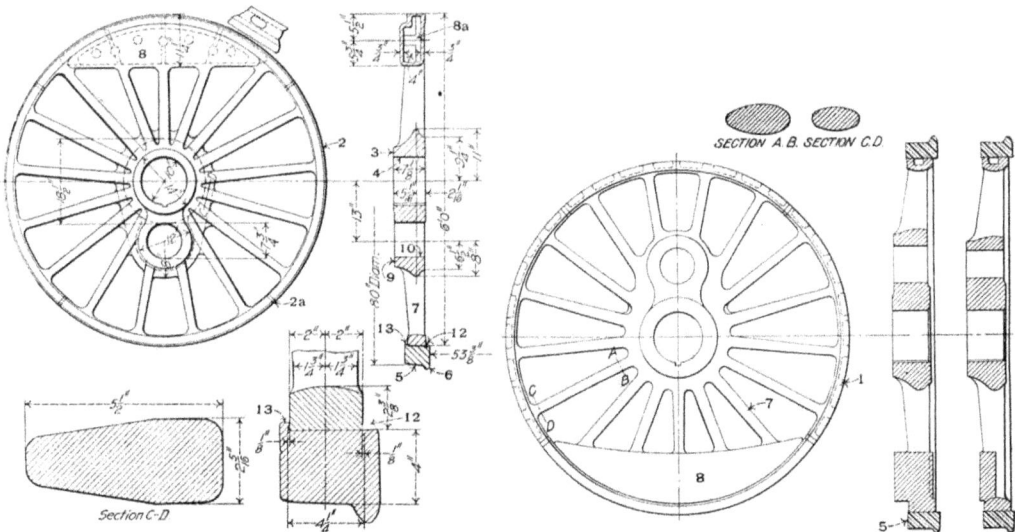

Figs. 1353-1357. 72-in. Cast-Steel Driving Wheel Center. Pennsylvania Railroad.

Figs. 1358-1362. Driving Wheel Center. American Locomotive Co.

(178)

WHEELS AND AXLES, Driving. — Figs. 1363-1376

Numbers Refer to List of Names of Parts of Wheels with Figs. 1339-1362.

Numbers Refer to List of Names of Parts of Axles with Figs. 1377-1385.

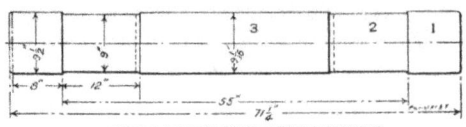

Fig. 1368. Driving Axle for Consolidation (2—8—0) Locomotive. American Locomotive Co.

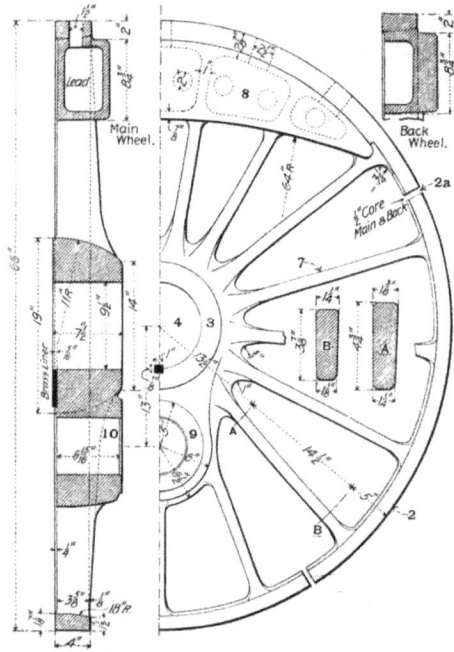

Figs. 1363-1367. 66-in. Driving Wheel Center. Chicago & Alton.

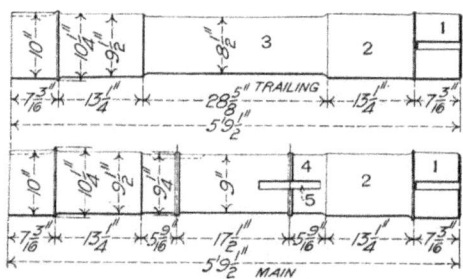

Figs. 1369-1370. Driving Axles. Pennsylvania Railroad.

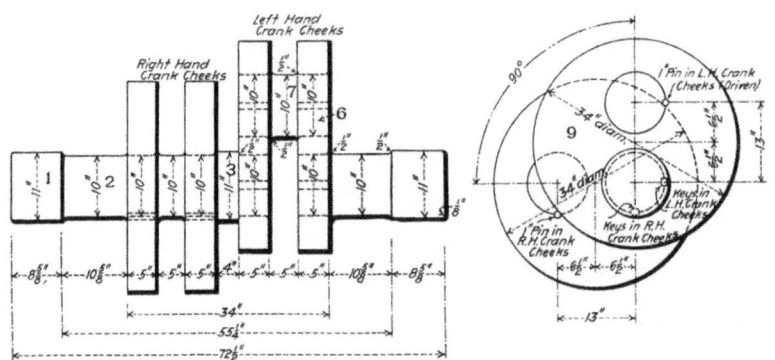

Figs. 1371-1372. Crank Axle for Four-Cylinder Balanced Compound Ten-Wheel (4—6—0) Locomotive. N. Y., N. H. & H. Baldwin Locomotive Works.

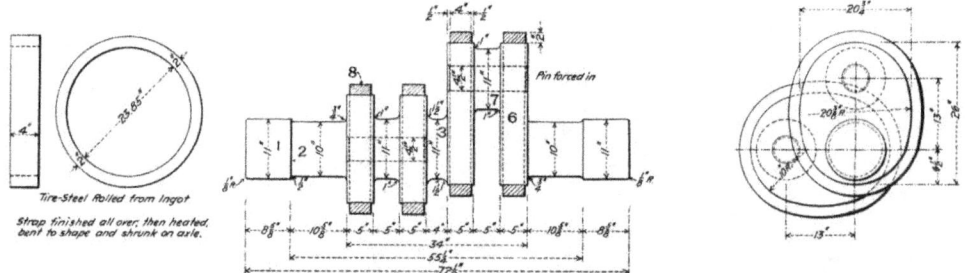

Figs. 1373-1376. Crank Axle for Four-Cylinder Balanced Compound Atlantic (4—4—2) Locomotive. C., B. & Q. Baldwin Locomotive Works.

(179)

Numbers Refer to List of Names of Parts Below.

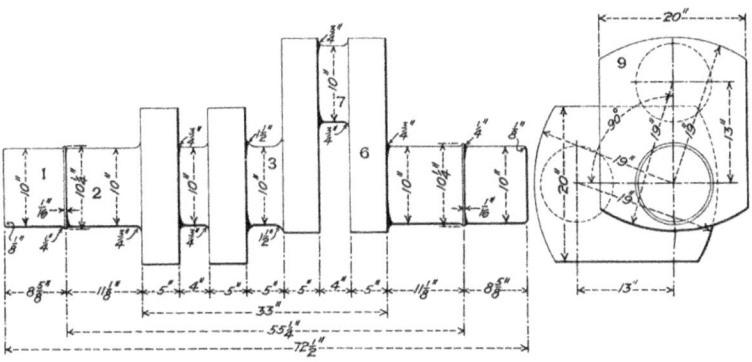

Figs. 1377-1378. Crank Axle for Four-Cylinder Balanced Compound Atlantic (4—4—2) Locomotive. Atchison, Topeka & Santa Fe. Baldwin Locomotive Works.

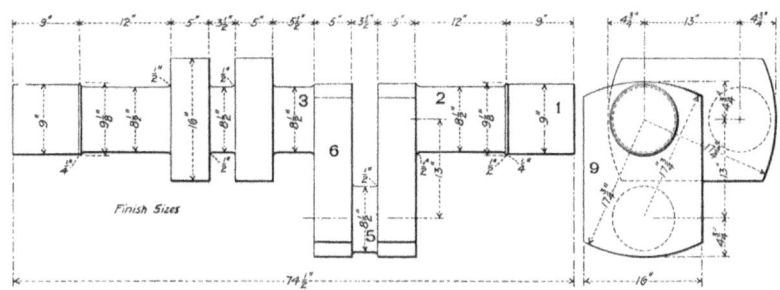

Figs. 1379-1380. Crank Axle for Four-Cylinder Balanced Compound Ten-Wheel (4—6—0) Locomotive. Plant System. Baldwin Locomotive Works.

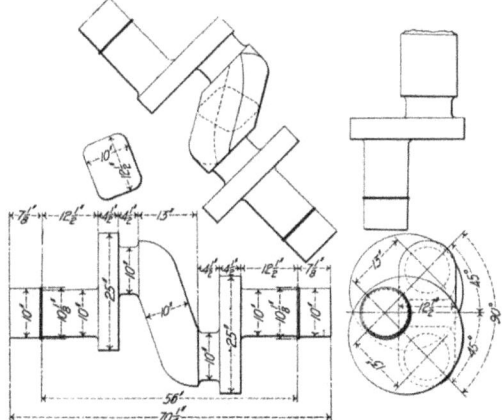

Figs. 1381-1385. Crank Axle for Cole Four-Cylinder Balanced Compound Locomotive. American Locomotive Co.

Names of Parts of Axles, Figs. 1368-1385.

1 *Wheel Seat*
2 *Bearing*
3 *Center*
4 *Eccentric Seat*
5 *Eccentric Keyway*
6 *Crank*
7 *Crank Pin*
8 *Crank Tire*
9 *Crank Disc*
10 *Collar*

BOXES, Driving. Figs. 1386-1404

Numbers Refer to List of Names of Parts with Figs. 1405-1424.

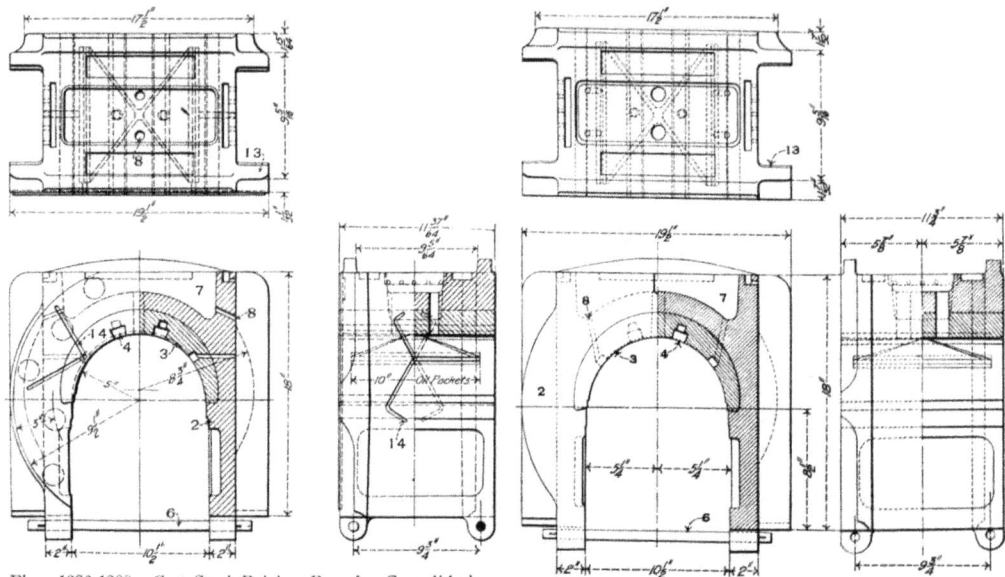

Figs. 1386-1388. Cast-Steel Driving Box for Consolidation (2—8—0) Locomotive. American Locomotive Co.

Figs. 1389-1391. Driving Box for Consolidation (2—8—0) Locomotive. American Locomotive Co.

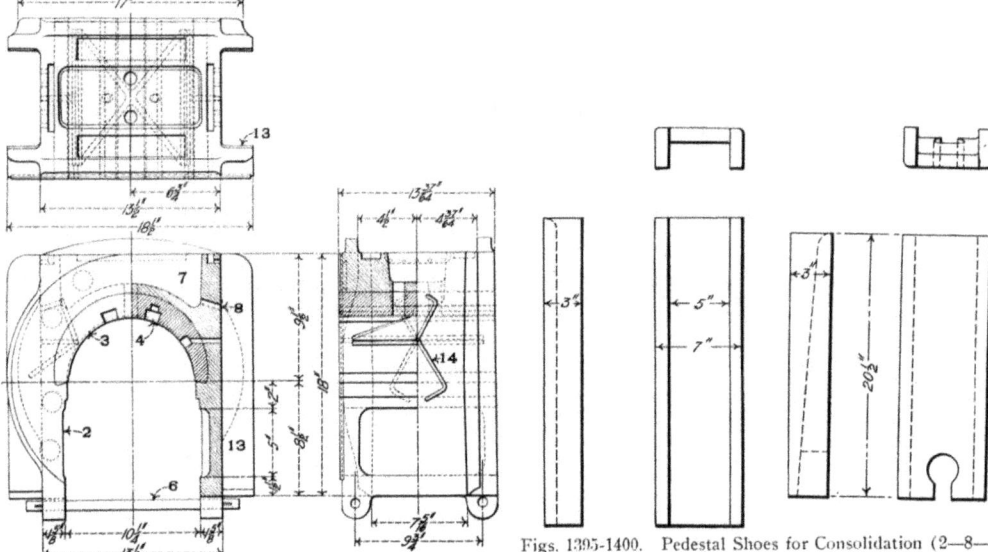

Figs. 1392-1394. Driving Box for Consolidation (2—8—0) Locomotive. American Locomotive Co.

Figs. 1395-1400. Pedestal Shoes for Consolidation (2—8—0) Locomotive. American Locomotive Co.

Figs. 1401-1402. Driving Box Cellar for Consolidation (2—8—0) Locomotive. American Locomotive Co.

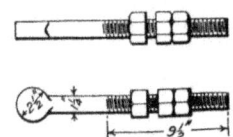

Figs. 1403-1404. Pedestal Wedge Adjusting Bolt.

(181)

BOXES, Driving.

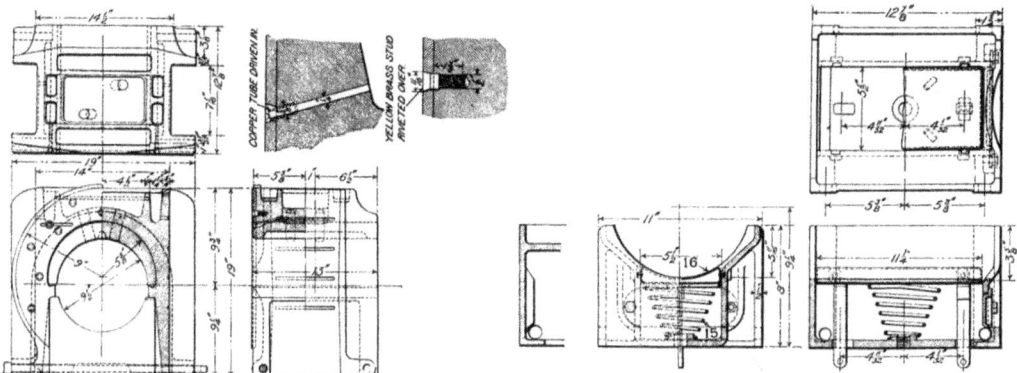

Figs. 1405-1409. Cast-Steel Driving Box for Journals 9½ in. x 13 in. Atlantic (4—4—2) Locomotive. Pennsylvania Railroad.

Figs. 1410-1413. Cellar for Journal Lubricating Device. Atlantic (4—4—2) Locomotive. Pennsylvania Railroad.

Names of Parts of Driving Boxes, Figs. 1386-1394.

- **2** *Box*
- **3** *Brass*
- **4** *Babbitt Lining*
- **6** *Cellar Wedge Bolts*
- **7** *Waste Cavity*
- **8** *Oil Hole*
- **13** *Box Flange*
- **14** *Oil Grooves*
- **15** *Lubricating Spring*
- **16** *Lubricating Pad*

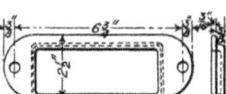

Figs. 1414-1415. Lid for Hand-Hole in Box Cellar. Atlantic (4—4—2) Locomotive. P. R. R.

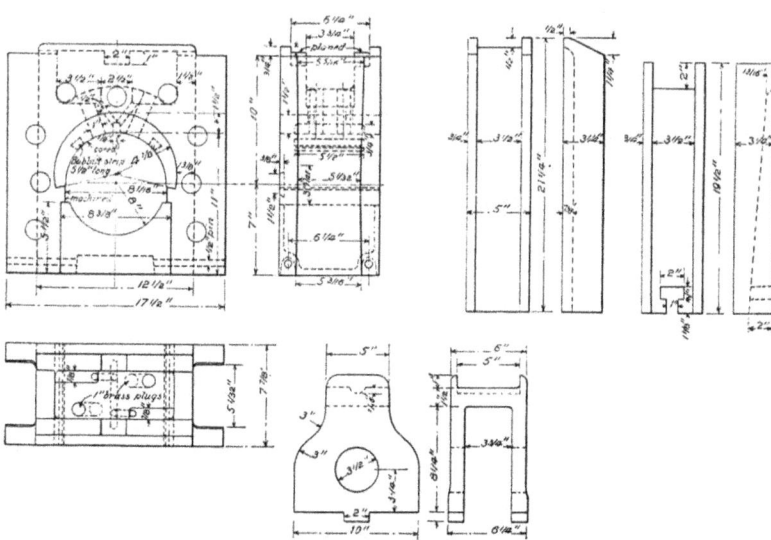

Figs. 1416-1424. Driving Box for Six-Wheel (0—6—0) Switching Locomotive. Baltimore & Ohio.

(182)

BOXES, Driving.

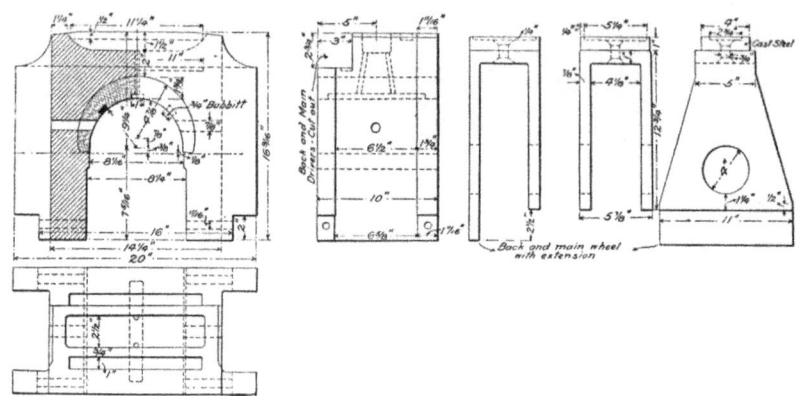

Figs. 1425-1430. Driving Box and Saddle for Ten-Wheel (4—6—0) Locomotive. Mexican Central.

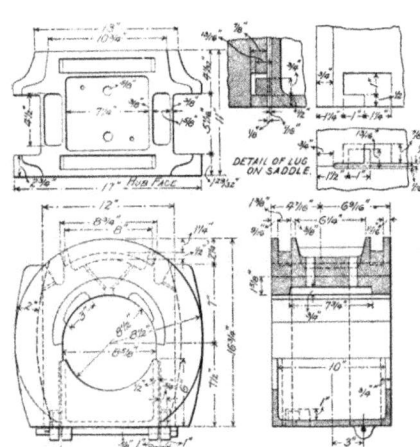

Figs. 1431-1436. Cast-Steel Driving Box for Journals 8½ in. x 11 in.

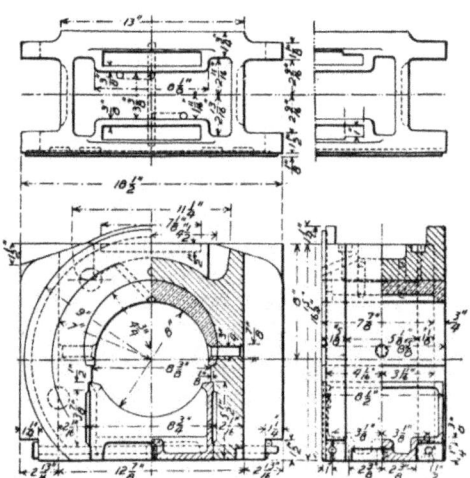

Figs. 1437-1440. Driving Box for Journals 8 in. x 8½ in.

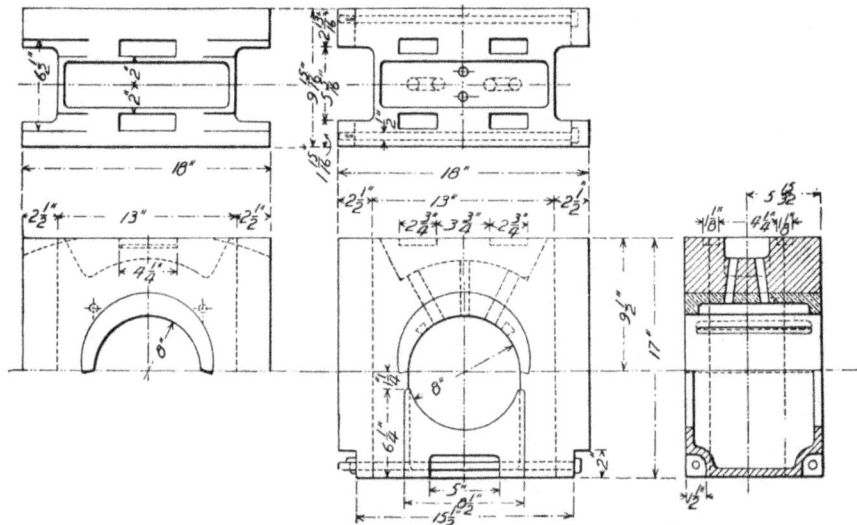

Figs. 1441-1445. Driving Box for Consolidation (2—8—0) Locomotive with Journals 8 in. x 10 in.

Figs. 1446-1460 — FRAMES, Elevations.

Numbers Refer to List of Names of Parts with Figs. 1461-1470.

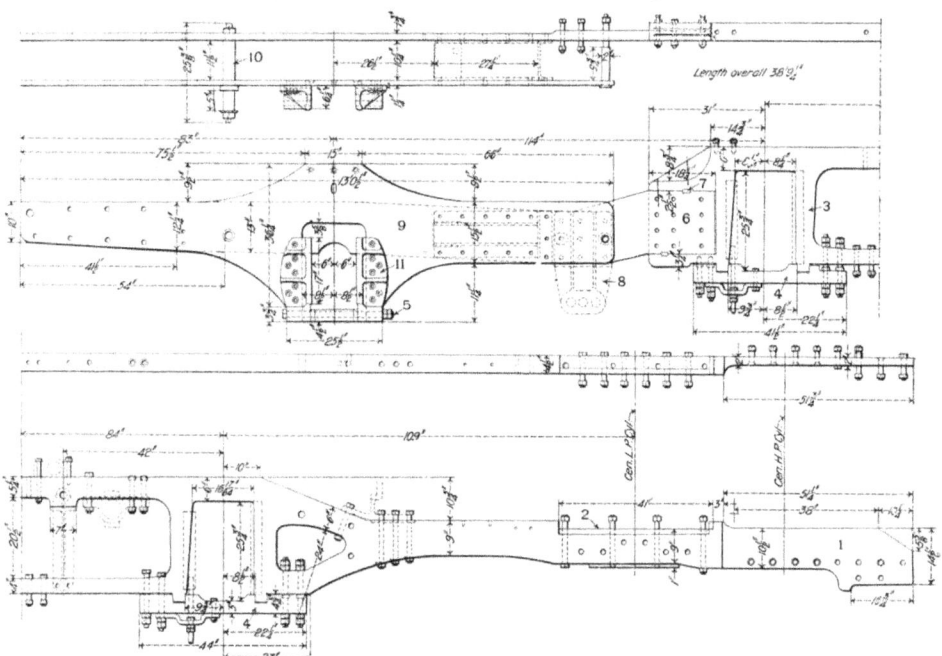

Figs. 1446-1447. Cast-Steel Frame for Atlantic (4—4—2) Locomotive. American Locomotive Co.

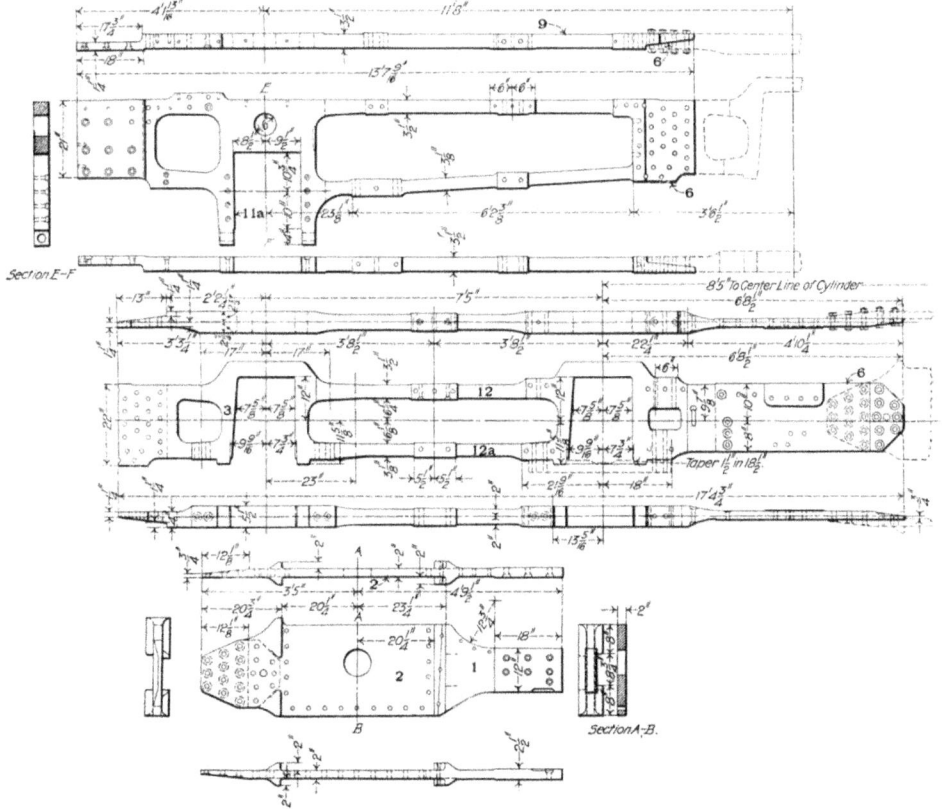

Figs. 1448-1460. Frame for Atlantic (4—4—2) Locomotive. Pennsylvania Railroad.

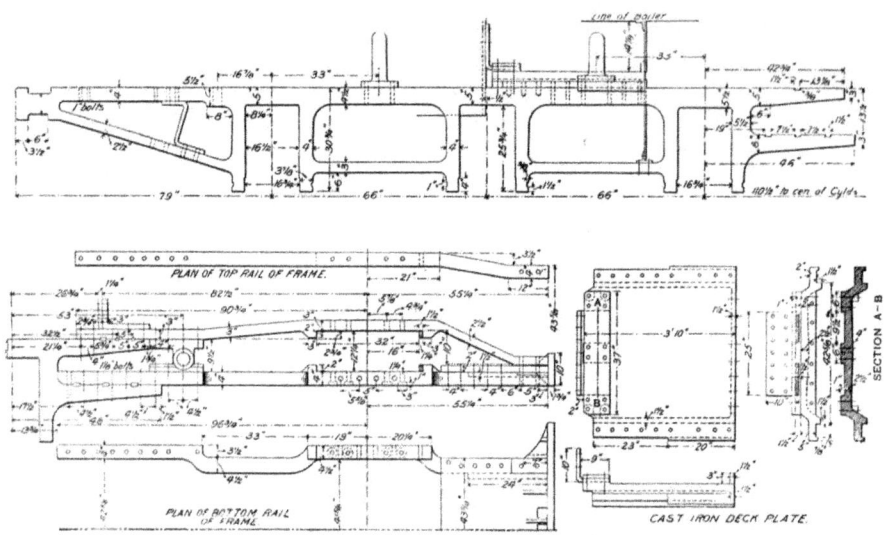

Figs. 1461-1468. Frame for Ten-Wheel (4—6—0) Locomotive. Mexican Central.

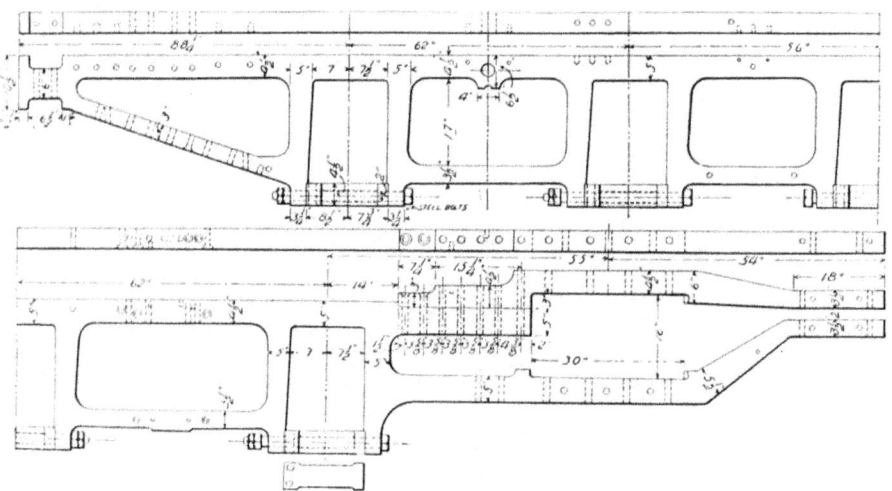

Figs. 1469-1470. Frame for Consolidation (2—8—0) Locomotive.

Names of Parts of Frames, Figs. 1446-1460, 1471-1476.

1 Front End Slab	8 Equalizer Fulcrum	13a Frame Brace
2 Cylinder Seat	9 Rear Frame	14 Waist Sheet
2a Cylinder Bolt	10 Rear Frame Separator	15 Waist Sheet Tee.
3 Pedestal	11 Trailing Truck Box Guide	16 Lifting Shaft Bearing
4 Pedestal Brace	11a Trailing Truck Box Pedestal	17 Brake Fulcrum Bracket
5 Pedestal Tie Bolt	12 Upper Frame Rail	18 Expansion Pad
6 Splice	12a Lower Frame Rail	19 Expansion Pad Clamp
7 Splice Key	13 Frame Crosstie	20 Expansion Pad Bearing Plate
		21 Expansion Plate

Figs. 1471-1476   FRAMES, Elevations.

Numbers Refer to List of Names of Parts with Figs. 1461-1470.

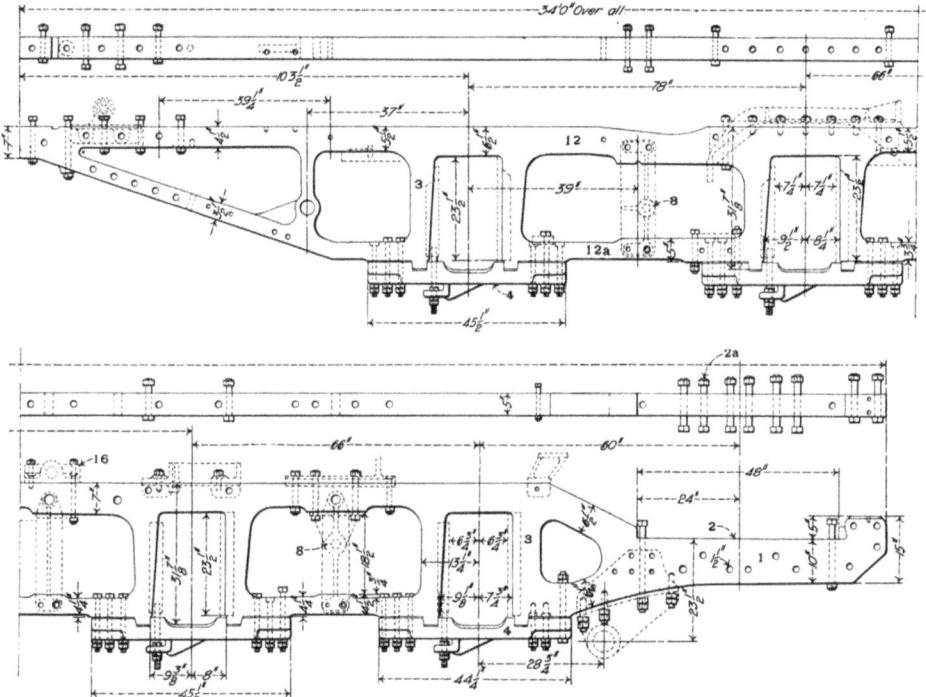

Figs. 1471-1472. Cast-Steel Frame for Consolidation (2—8—0) Locomotive. American Locomotive Co.

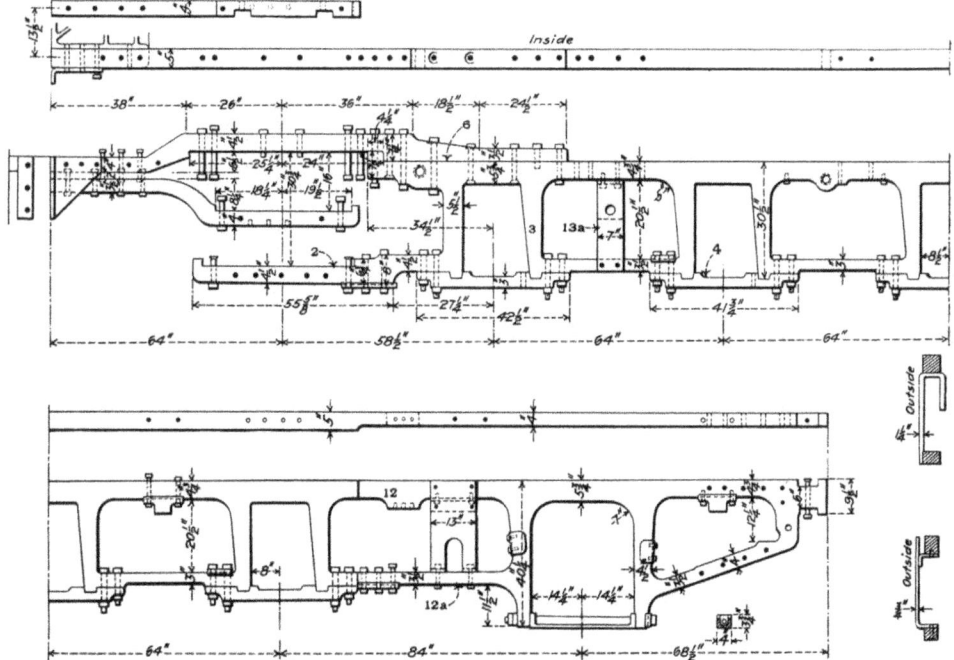

Figs. 1473-1476. Frame for Mikado (2—8—2) Locomotive. Atchison, Topeka & Santa Fe.

FRAMES, Details.

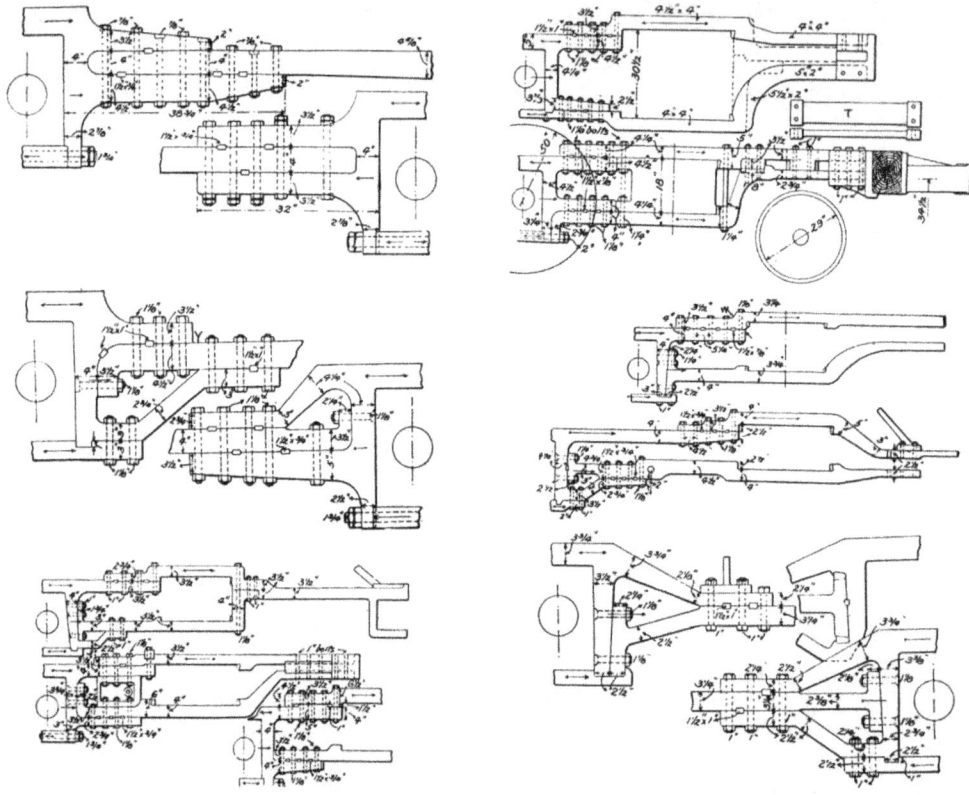

Figs. 1477-1489. Various Forms of Joints for Frames.

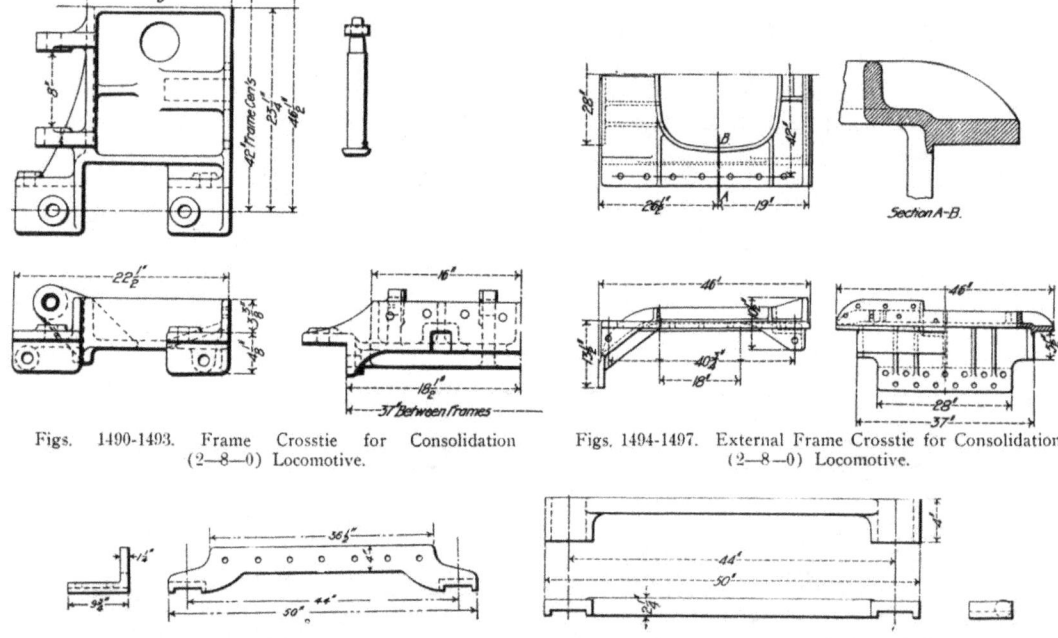

Figs. 1490-1493. Frame Crosstie for Consolidation (2—8—0) Locomotive.

Figs. 1494-1497. External Frame Crosstie for Consolidation (2—8—0) Locomotive.

Figs. 1498-1499. Frame Crosstie for Consolidation (2—8—0) Locomotive.

Figs. 1500-1502. Frame Crosstie for Consolidation (2—8—0) Locomotive.

Figs. 1503-1521. FRAMES, Details.

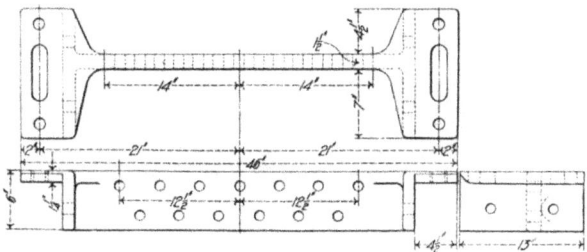

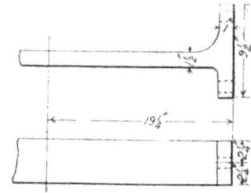

Figs. 1503-1505. Frame Crosstie for Consolidation (2—8—0) Locomotive.

Figs. 1506-1507. Lower Bar Frame Brace Back of Front Pedestal. Atlantic (4—4—2) Locomotive. P. R. R.

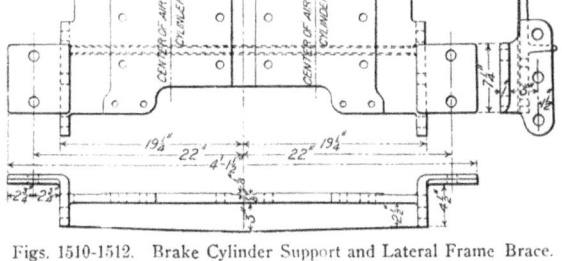

Figs. 1510-1512. Brake Cylinder Support and Lateral Frame Brace.

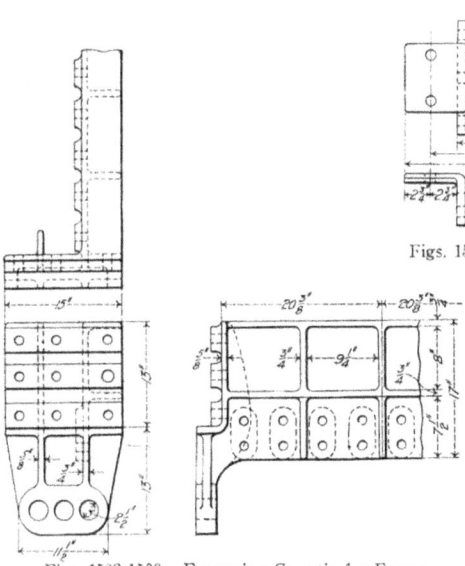

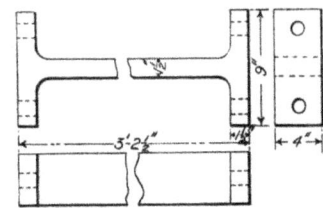

Figs. 1508-1509. Expansion Crosstie for Frame.

Figs. 1513-1515. Lower Frame Brace Ahead of Front Pedestal. Atlantic (4—4—2) Locomotive. P. R. R.

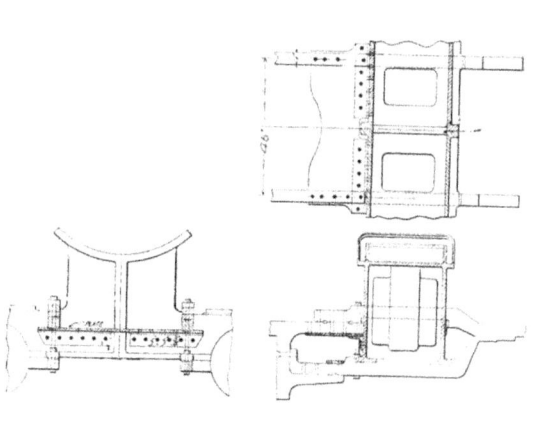

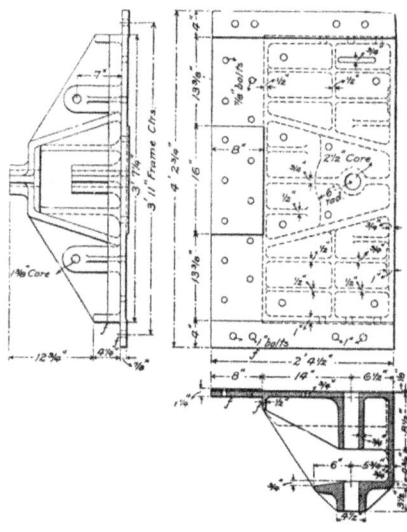

Figs. 1516-1518. Frame Plate Stiffener for Consolidation (2—8—0) Locomotive.

Figs. 1519-1521. Cast Deck Plate for Eight-Wheel (4—4—0) Locomotive. C., R. I. & P.

FRAMES, Details. Figs. 1522-1534

Numbers Refer to List of Names of Parts with Figs. 1461-1470.

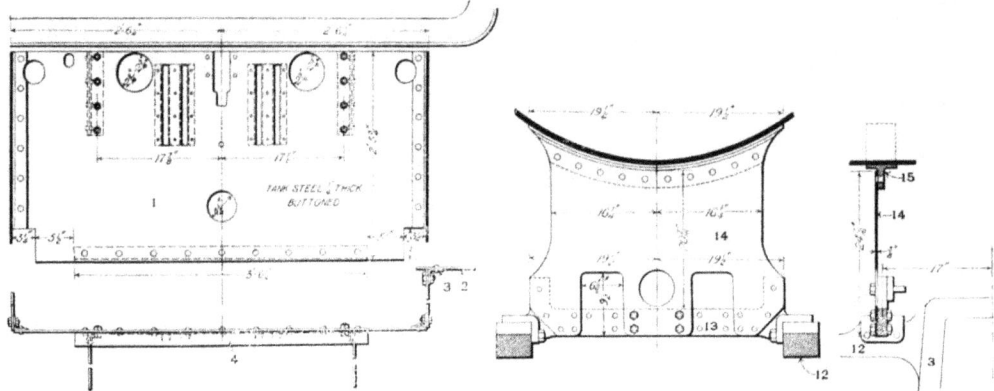

Figs. 1522-1523. Deck Plate for Atlantic (4—4—2) Locomotive. P. R. R.

Figs. 1524-1525. Waist Plate Over Front Drivers. Atlantic (4—4—2) Locomotive. P. R. R.

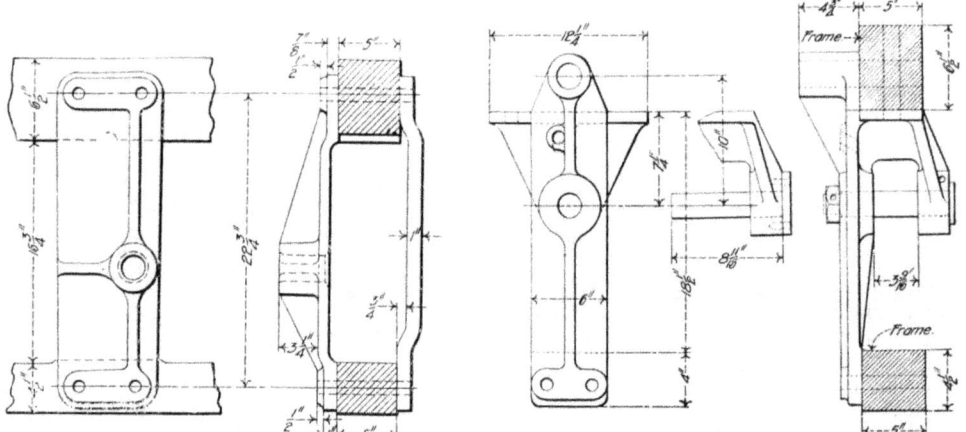

Figs. 1526-1527. Frame Filling Piece for Consolidation (2—8—0) Locomotive.

Figs. 1528-1530. Frame Filling Piece for Consolidation (2—8—0) Locomotive.

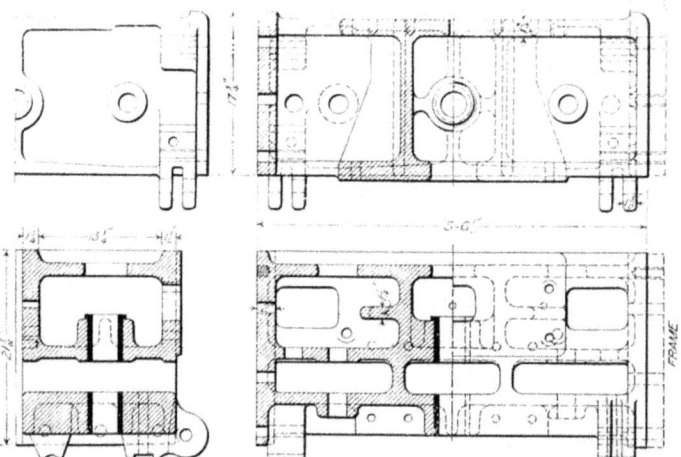

Figs. 1531-1534. Cast-Steel Foot Plate for Atlantic (4—4—2) Locomotive. P. R. R.

(189)

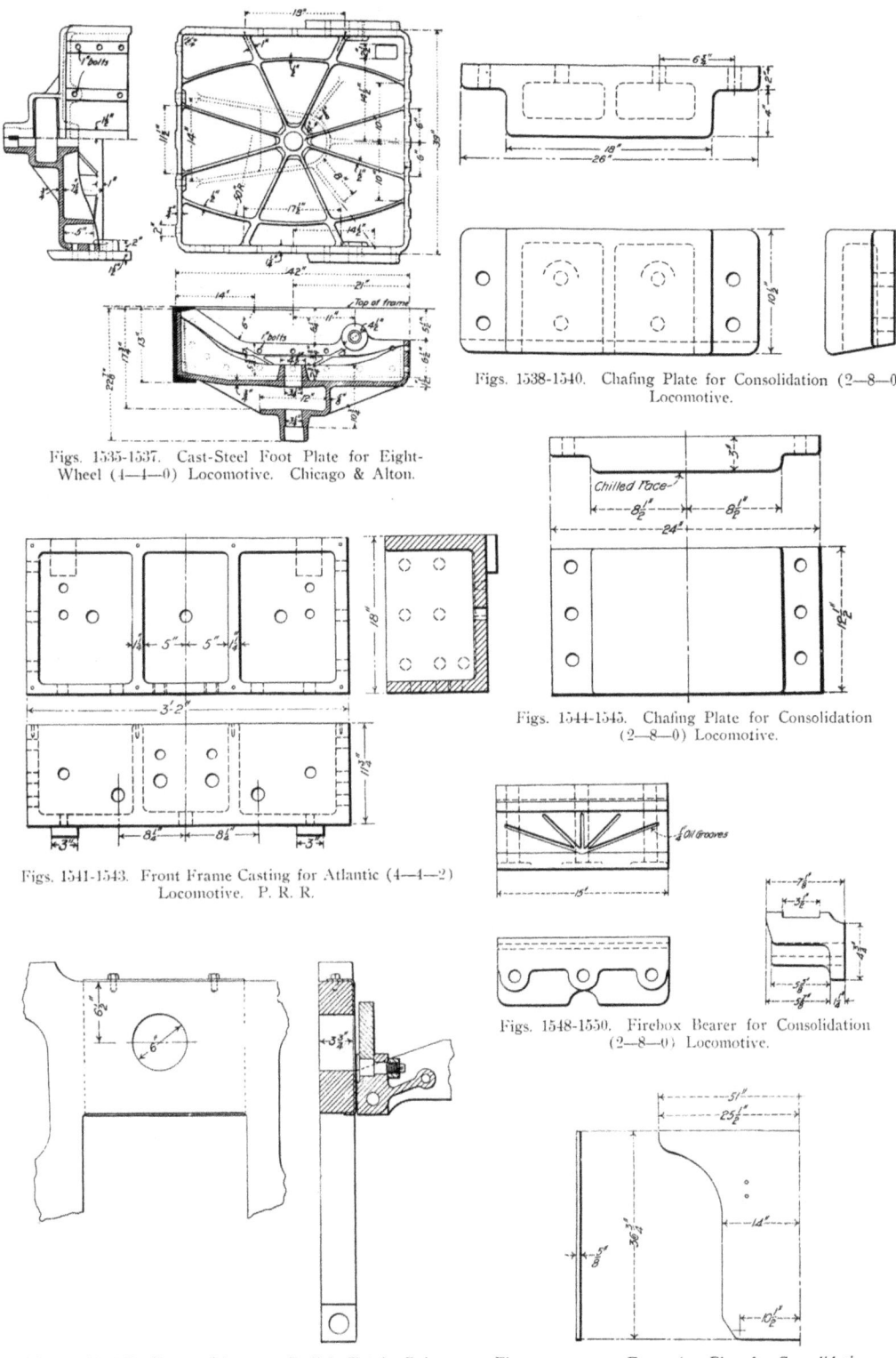

Figs. 1535-1537. Cast-Steel Foot Plate for Eight-Wheel (4—4—0) Locomotive. Chicago & Alton.

Figs. 1538-1540. Chafing Plate for Consolidation (2—8—0) Locomotive.

Figs. 1541-1543. Front Frame Casting for Atlantic (4—4—2) Locomotive. P. R. R.

Figs. 1544-1545. Chafing Plate for Consolidation (2—8—0) Locomotive.

Figs. 1548-1550. Firebox Bearer for Consolidation (2—8—0) Locomotive.

Figs. 1546-1547. Frame Liner at Radial Truck Bolster. Atlantic (4—4—2) Locomotive. P. R. R.

Figs. 1551-1552. Expansion Plate for Consolidation (2—8—0) Locomotive.

FRAMES, Details. Figs. 1553-1580

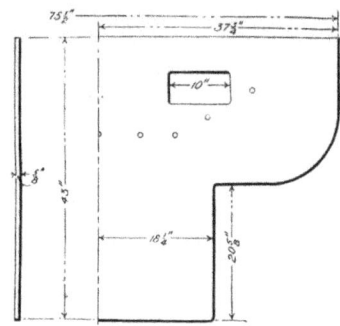

Figs. 1553-1554. Expansion Plate for Consolidation (2—8—0) Locomotive.

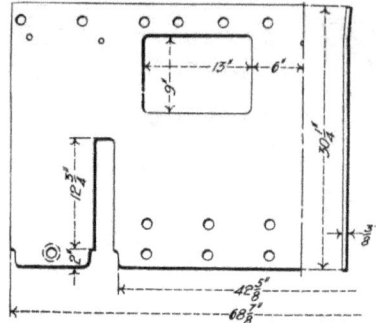

Figs. 1555-1556. Expansion Plate for Consolidation (2—8—0) Locomotive.

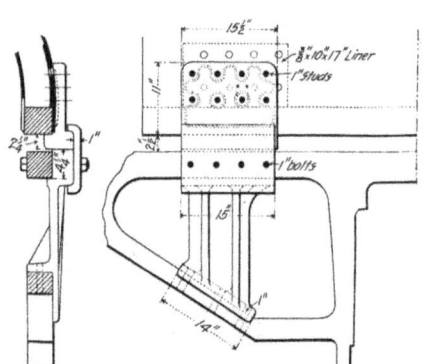

Figs. 1557-1558. Rear Expansion Pad for Eight-Wheel (4—4—0) Locomotive.

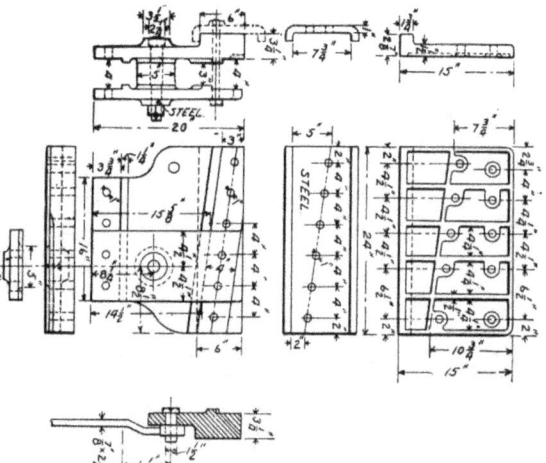

Figs. 1559-1567. Cast-Steel Expansion Pad.

Numbers Refer to List of Names of Parts with Figs. 1461-1470.

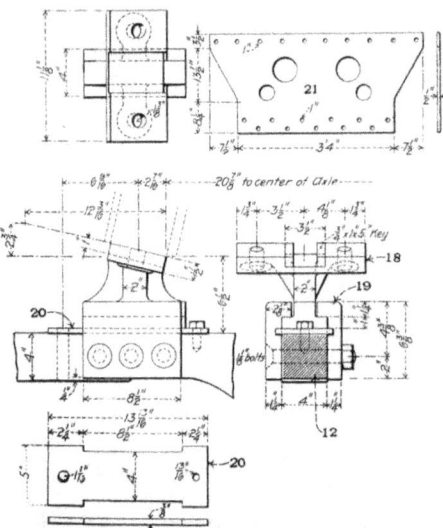

Figs. 1568-1574. Expansion Pad, Clamps and Plate for Ten-Wheel (4—6—0) Locomotive. P. R. R.

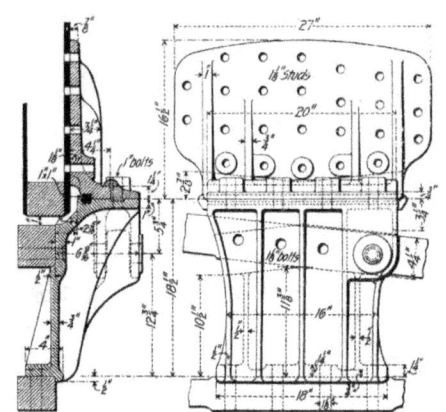

Figs. 1575-1576. Cast-Steel Side Bearer for Firebox for Eight-Wheel (4—4—0) Locomotive. Chicago & Alton.

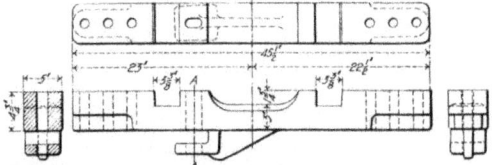

Figs. 1577-1580. Frame Pedestal Cap.

(191)

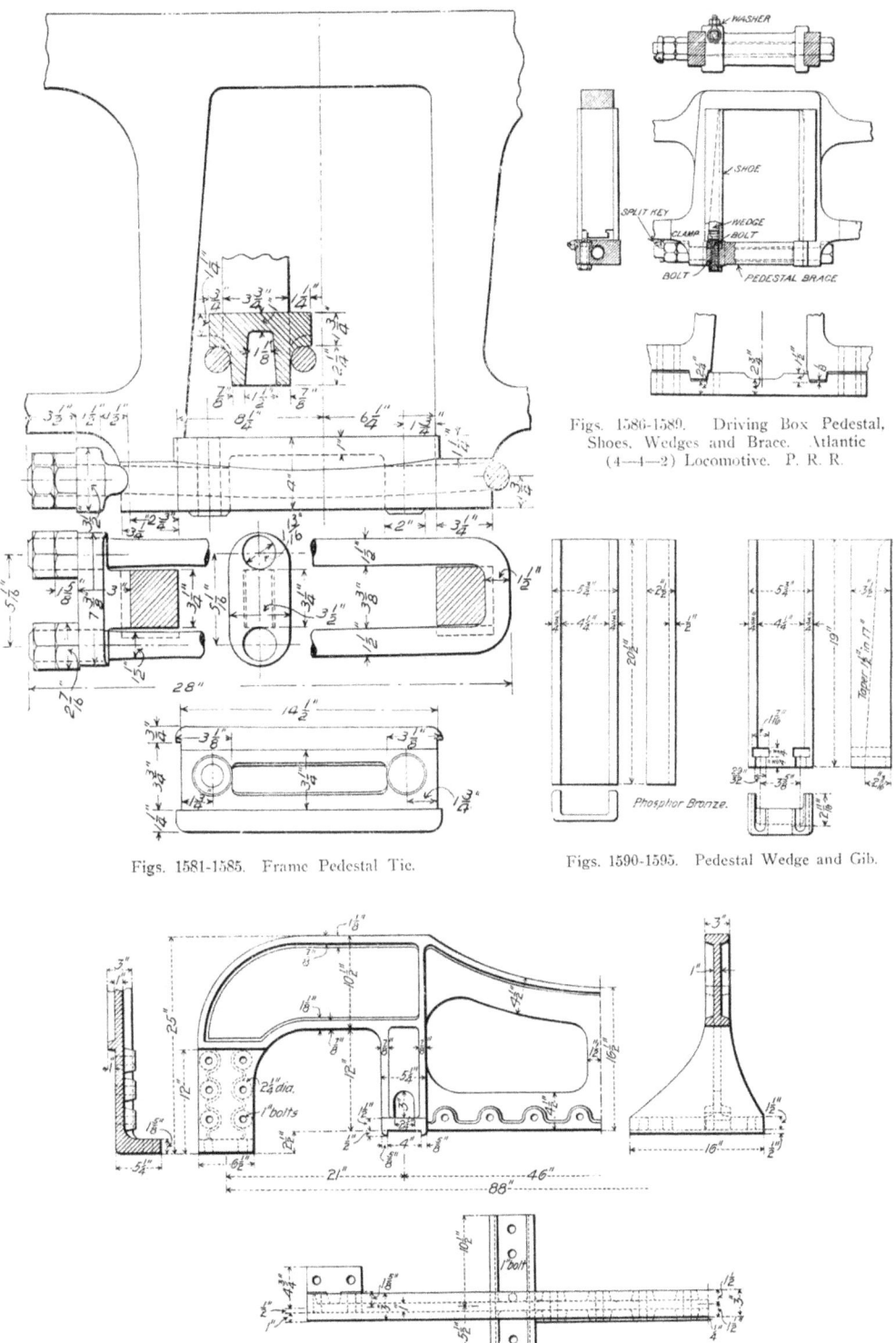

Figs. 1581-1585. Frame Pedestal Tie.

Figs. 1586-1589. Driving Box Pedestal, Shoes, Wedges and Brace. Atlantic (4—4—2) Locomotive. P. R. R.

Figs. 1590-1595. Pedestal Wedge and Gib.

Figs. 1596-1599. Cast-Steel Guide Yoke and Frame Crosstie. Ten-Wheel (4—6—0) Tandem Compound Locomotive. Atchison, Topeka & Santa Fe.

FRAMES, Details.

Figs. 1600-1604

Numbers Refer to List of Names of Parts Below.

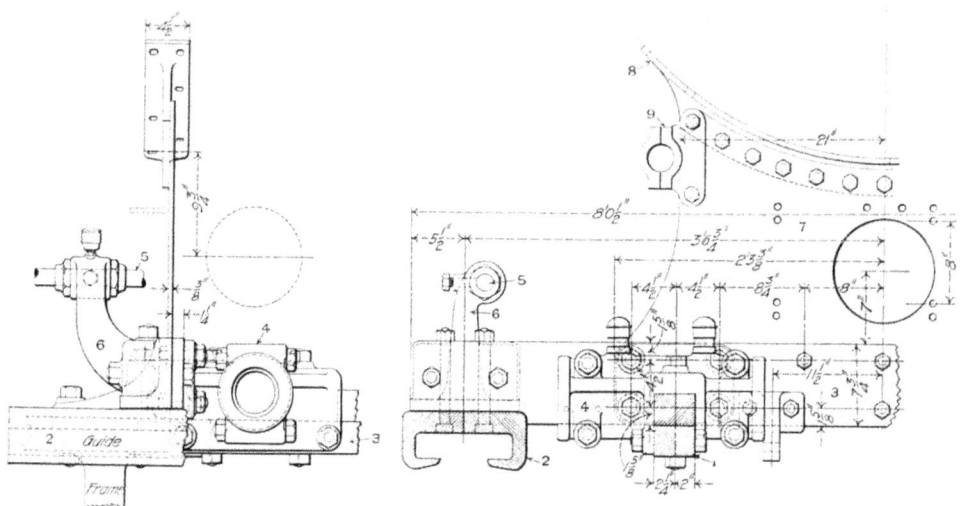

Figs. 1600-1601. Assembled View of Frame Rocker Box and Guide Yoke. Atlantic (4—4—2) Locomotive. Pennsylvania Railroad.

Names of Parts of Figs. 1600-1604.

- **1** *Frame*
- **2** *Guide*
- **3** *Guide Yoke*
- **4** *Rocker Box*
- **5** *Valve Rod*
- **6** *Valve Rod Guide*
- **7** *Waist Sheet*
- **8** *Waist Sheet Angle*
- **9** *Pipe Clamp*

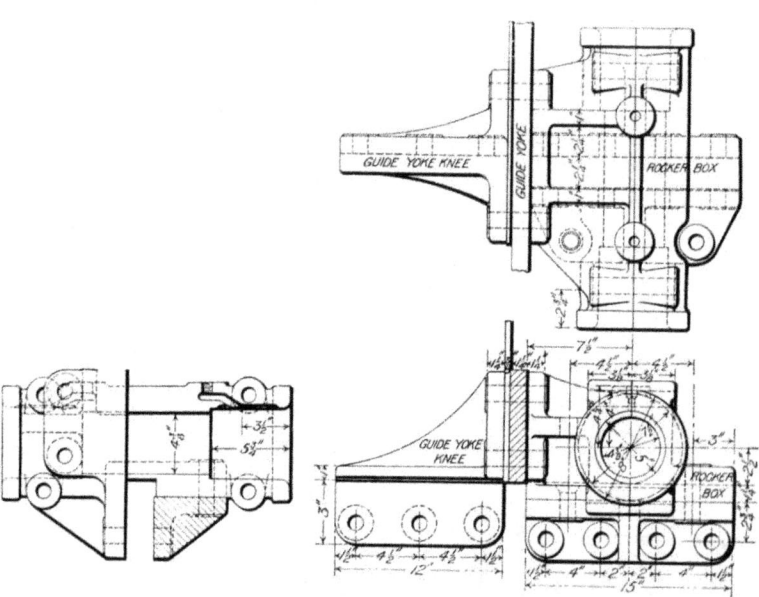

Figs. 1602-1604. Details of Rocker Box and Guide Yoke Knee. Atlantic (4—4—2) Locomotive. Pennsylvania Railroad.

(193)

SPRING RIGGING, Assembled Views.

Numbers Refer to List of Names of Parts with Figs. 1676-1728.

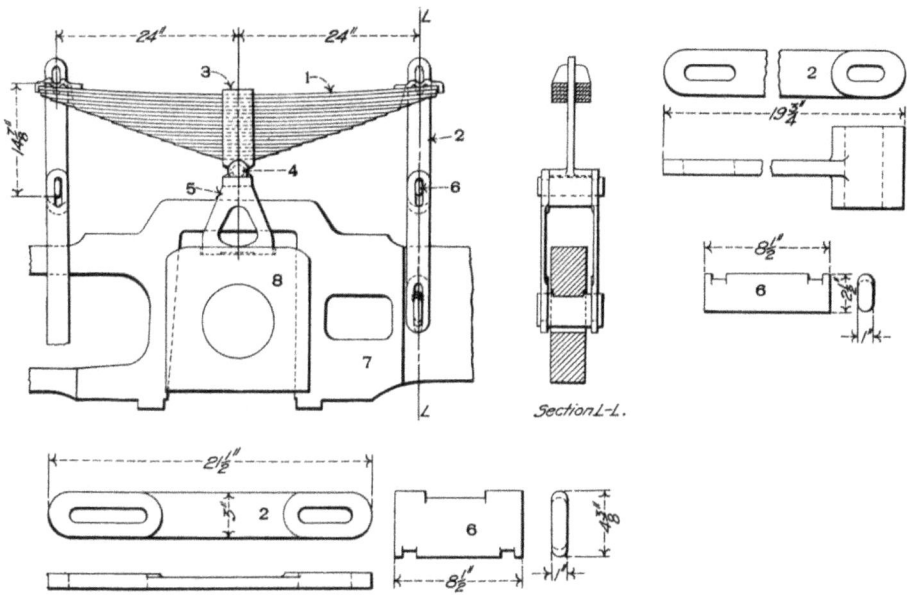

Figs. 1605-1614. Spring Rigging with Slab Front Frame. Atlantic (4—4—2) Locomotive. Pennsylvania Railroad.

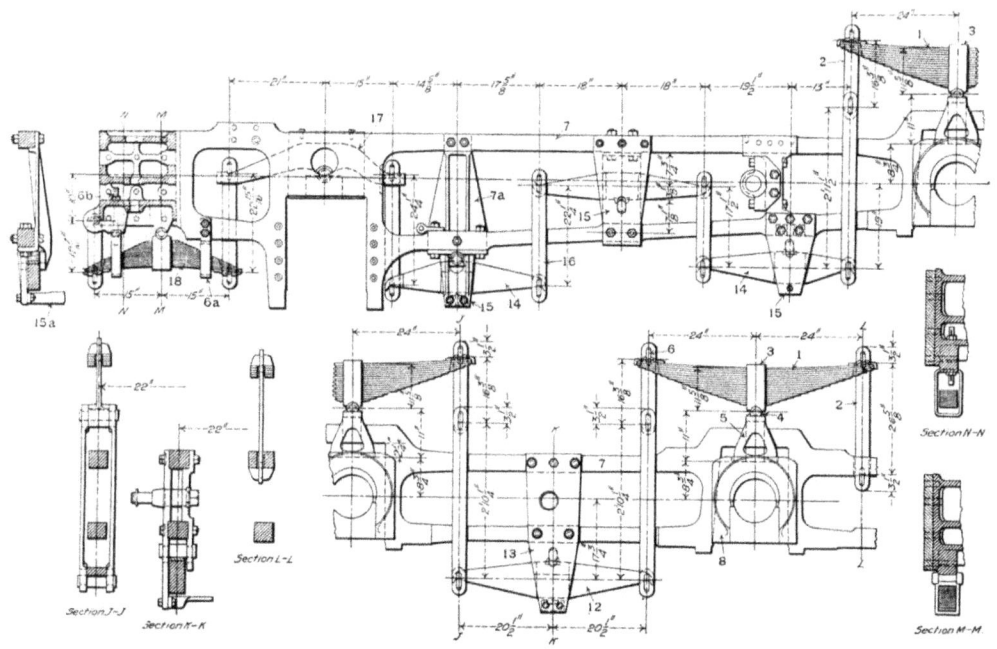

Figs. 1615-1621. Spring Rigging for Atlantic (4—4—2) Locomotive. P. R. R.

SPRING RIGGING, Assembled Views. Figs. 1622-1648

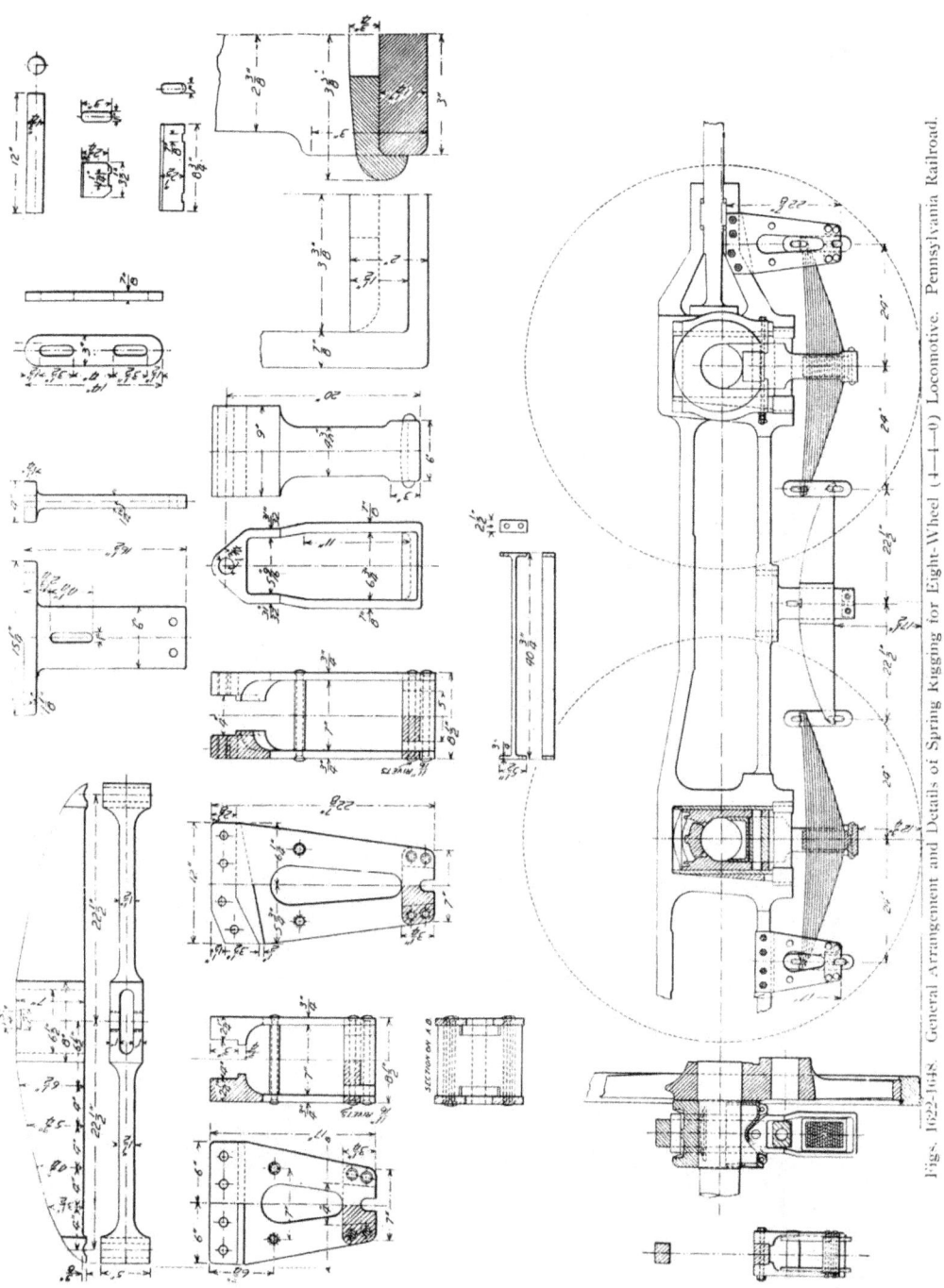

Figs. 1622-1648. General Arrangement and Details of Spring Rigging for Eight-Wheel (4-4-0) Locomotive. Pennsylvania Railroad.

Figs. 1649-1653. SPRING RIGGING, Assembled Views.

Numbers Refer to List of Names of Parts with Figs. 1676-1728.

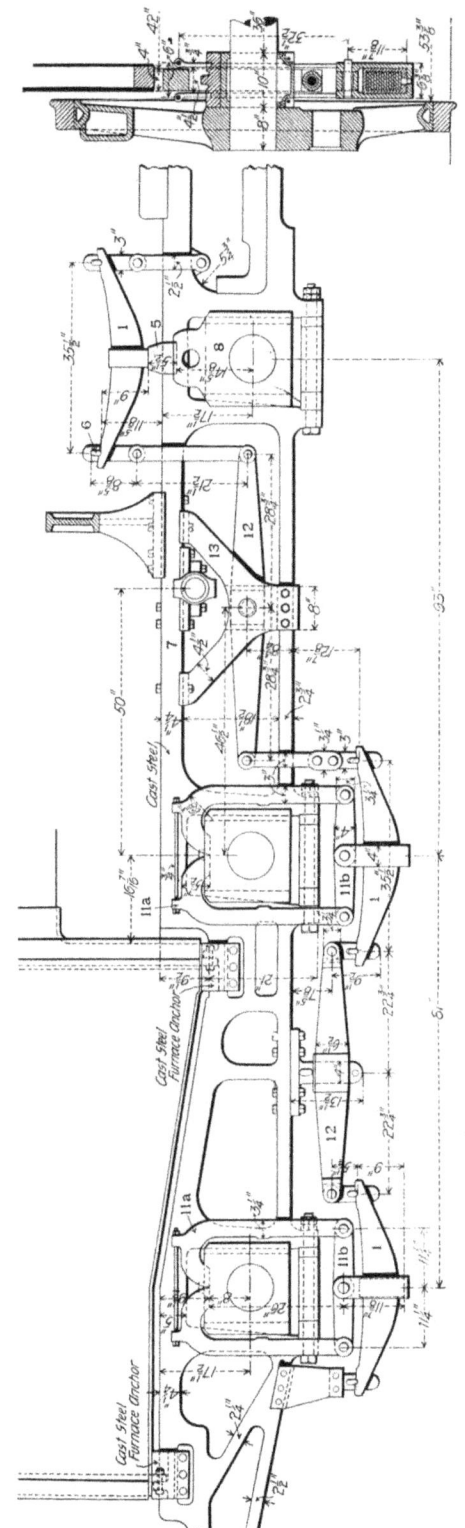

Figs. 1649-1650. Spring Rigging for Ten-Wheel (4—6—0) Tandem Compound Locomotive. Atchison, Topeka & Santa Fe.

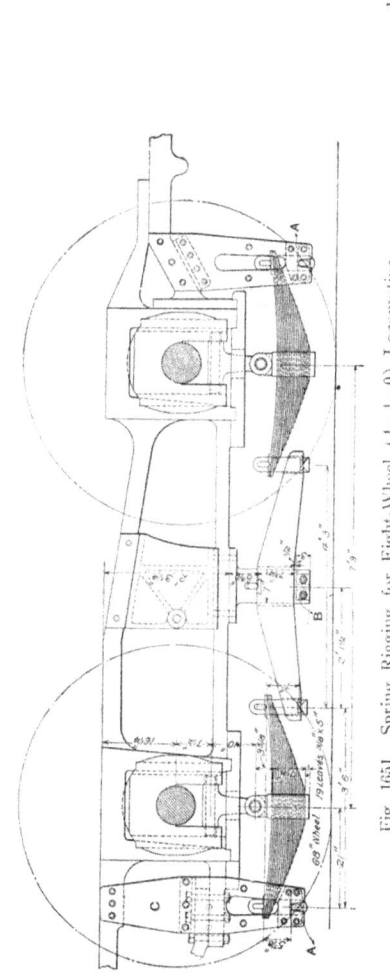

Fig. 1651. Spring Rigging for Eight-Wheel (4—4—0) Locomotive. Cleveland, Cincinnati, Chicago & St. Louis.

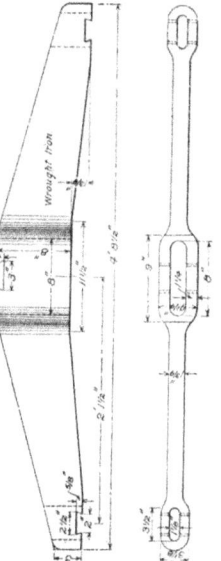

Figs. 1652-1653. Equalizer for Eight-Wheel (4—4—0) Locomotive. C., C., C. & St. L.

SPRING RIGGING, Details.

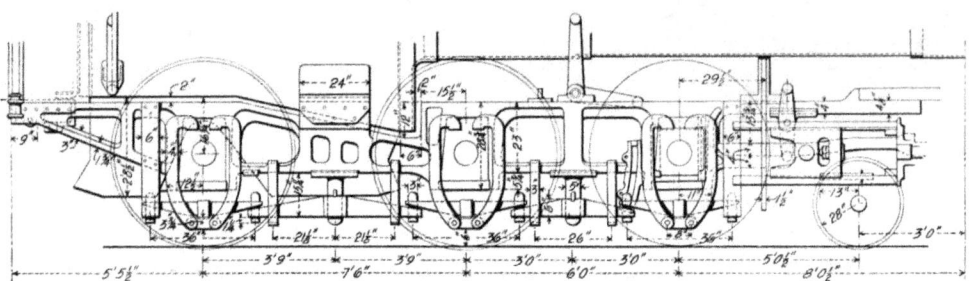

Fig. 1654. Spring Rigging for Ten-Wheel (4—6—0) Locomotive.

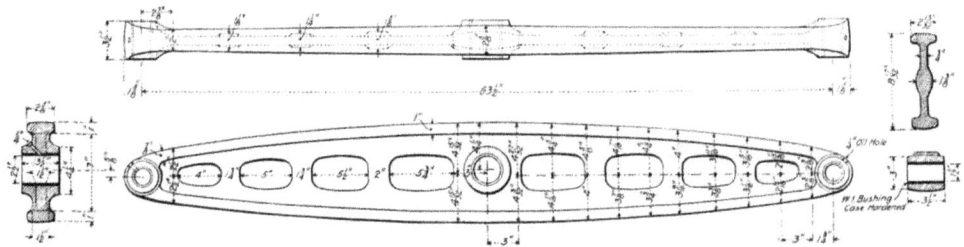

Figs. 1659-1663. Cast-Steel Equalizer. Eight-Wheel (4—4—0) Locomotive. Chicago & Alton.

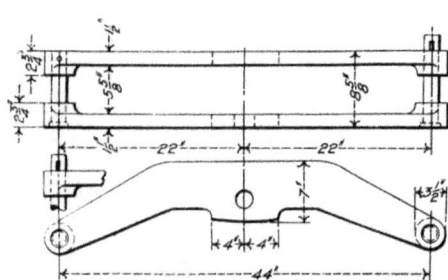

Figs. 1664-1665. Driving Box Equalizer.

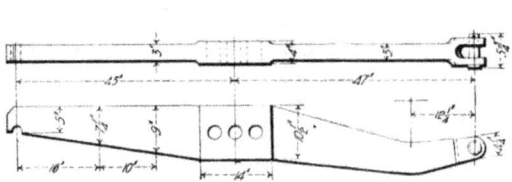

Figs. 1666-1667. Forward Driver and Truck Equalizer for Mogul (2—6—0) Locomotive. American Locomotive Co.

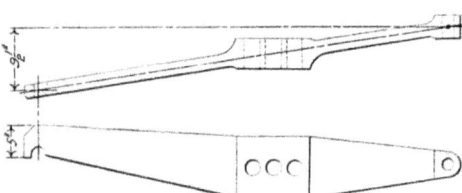

Figs. 1668-1669. Trailing Truck Equalizer for Atlantic (4—4—2) Locomotive. American Locomotive Co.

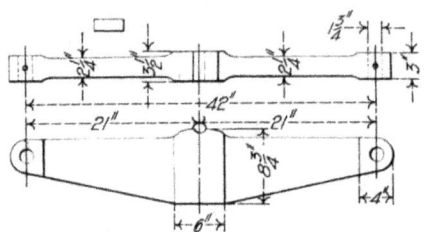

Figs. 1670-1671. Driver Equalizer for Atlantic (4—4—2) Locomotive. American Locomotive Co.

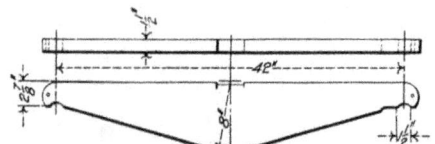

Figs. 1672-1673. Driver Equalizer for Consolidation (2—8—0) Locomotive. American Locomotive Co.

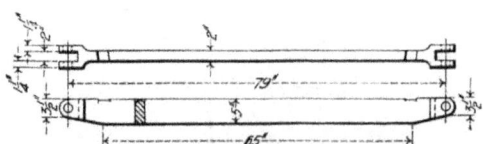

Figs. 1674-1675. Back Transverse Equalizer for Atlantic (4—4—2) Locomotive. American Locomotive Co.

SPRING RIGGING, Details.

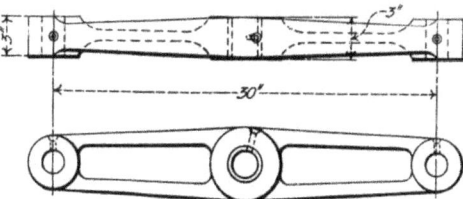

Figs. 1676-1677. Driver Equalizer for Twelve-Wheel (4—8—0) Locomotive. American Locomotive Co.

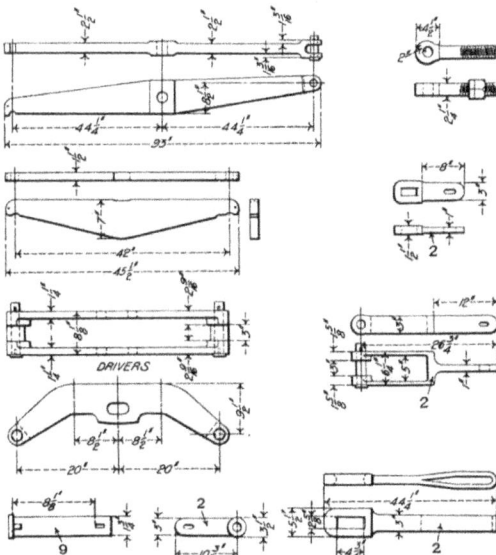

Figs. 1678-1694. Equalizers and Spring Hangers for Consolidation (2—8—0) Locomotive. American Locomotive Co.

Names of Parts of Spring Rigging.
Figs. 1605-1621, 1649-1650, 1695-1728.

1. Driver Spring
2. Spring Hanger
3. Spring Band
4. Spring Roller
5. Spring Stirrup
6. Spring Hanger Gib
6a. Spring Safety Strap
6b. Spring Safety Strap Bolt
7. Frame
7a. Frame Filler
8. Driver Box
9. Spring Hanger Pin
10. Driver Box Saddle
11. Driver Box Saddle Pin
11a. Driver Box Yoke Hanger
11b. Driver Box Yoke Hanger Cross-bar
12. Driver Equalizer
13. Driver Equalizer Fulcrum
14. Driver and Truck Equalizer
15. Driver and Truck Equalizer Fulcrum
15a. Driver and Truck Equalizer Fulcrum Brace
16. Equalizer Hanger
17. Truck Box Yoke
18. Rear Frame Supporting Spring

Numbers Refer to List of Names of Parts Above.

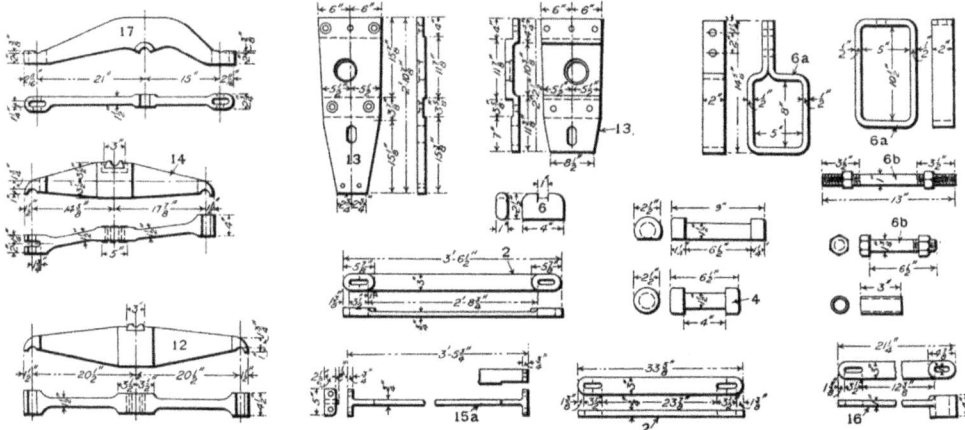

Figs. 1695-1728. Details of Spring Rigging for Atlantic (4—4—2) Locomotive. Pennsylvania Railroad.

SPRING RIGGING, Details.

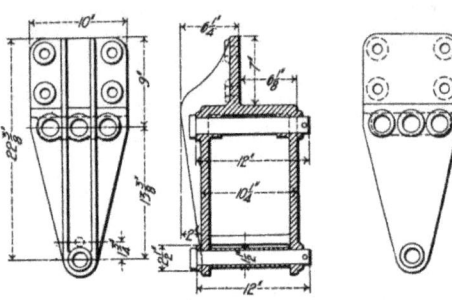

Figs. 1729-1731. Equalizer Fulcrum for Ten-Wheel (4—6—0) Locomotive. American Locomotive Co.

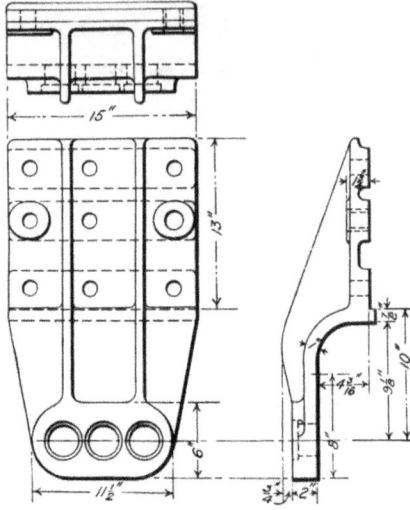

Figs. 1732-1734. Equalizer Fulcrum. American Locomotive Co.

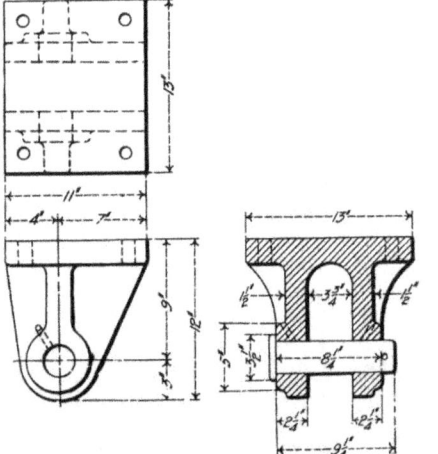

Figs. 1735-1737. Truck Equalizer Fulcrum for Ten-Wheel (4—6—0) Locomotive. American Locomotive Co.

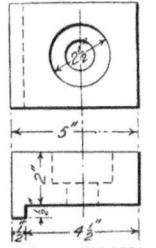

Figs. 1738-1739. Equalizer Safety Block for Consolidation (2—8—0) Locomotive.

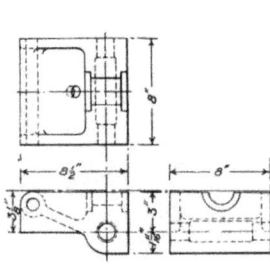

Figs. 1740-1742. Equalizer Seat. Atlantic (4—4—2) Locomotive. Pennsylvania Railroad.

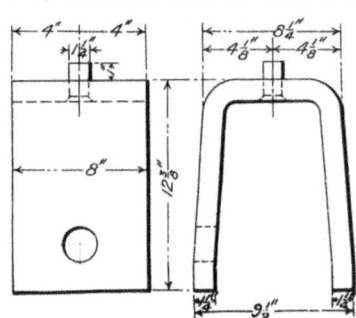

Figs. 1743-1744. Driving Box Saddle for Consolidation (2—8—0) Locomotive. American Locomotive Co.

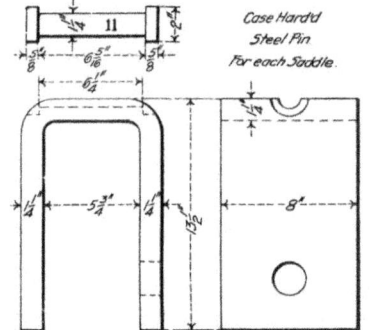

Figs. 1745-1747. Driving Box Saddle and Pin.

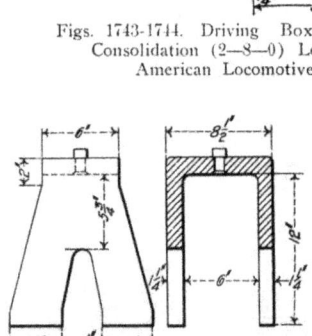

Figs. 1748-1749. Driving Box Saddle. American Locomotive Co.

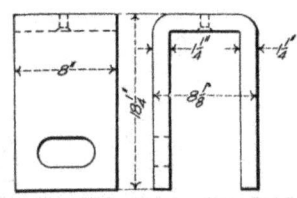

Figs. 1750-1751. Driving Box Saddle. American Locomotive Co.

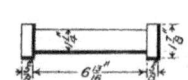

Fig. 1752. Driving Box Saddle Pin.

SPRING RIGGING, Details.

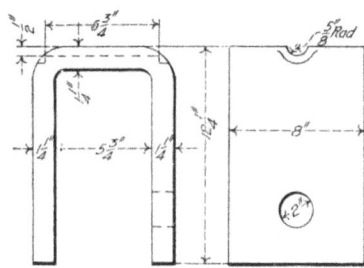

Figs. 1753-1754. Driving Box Saddle for Consolidation (2—8—0) Locomotive. American Locomotive Co.

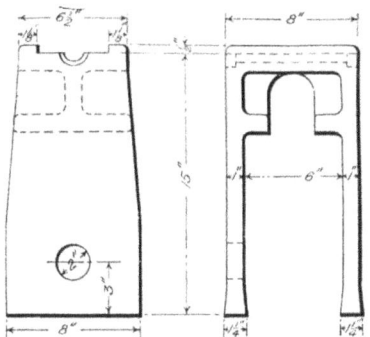

Figs. 1755-1756. Driving Box Saddle for Consolidation (2—8—0) Locomotive. American Locomotive Co.

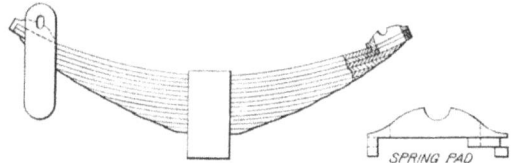

Figs. 1757-1758. Phoenix Driver and Truck Spring. Phoenix Car Spring Co.

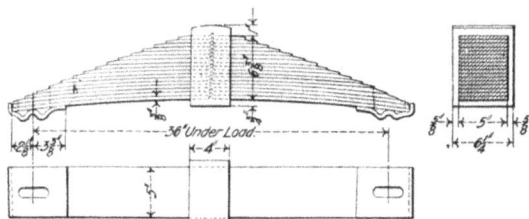

Figs. 1759-1761. Semi-Elliptic Engine Truck Spring for Atlantic (4—4—2) Locomotive. P. R. R.

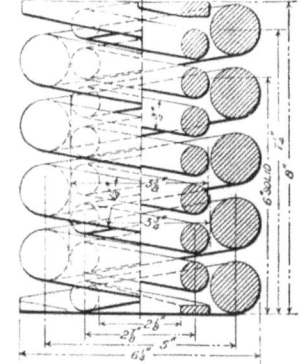

Fig. 1762. Helical Spring Class H24 for Atlantic (4—4—2) Locomotive. P. R. R.

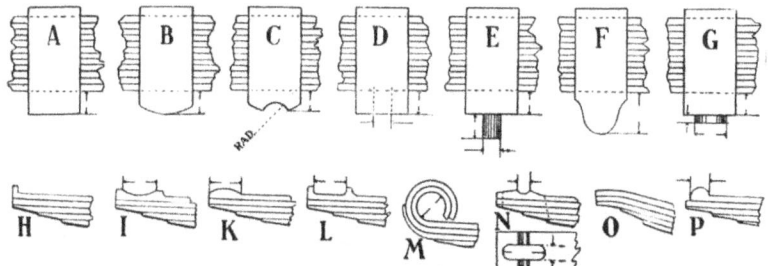

Figs. 1763-1778. Styles of Spring Ends and Spring Bands. Union Spring & Manufacturing Co.

Fig. 1779. Semi-Elliptic Driver Spring.

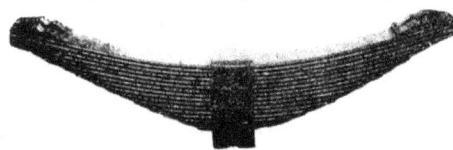

Fig. 1780. Semi-Elliptic Driver Spring.

Fig. 1781. Elliptic Engine Truck Spring.

Figs. 1779-1781. Locomotive Springs. American Steel Foundries.

SPRING RIGGING, Details; Traction Increasers. Figs. 1782-1804

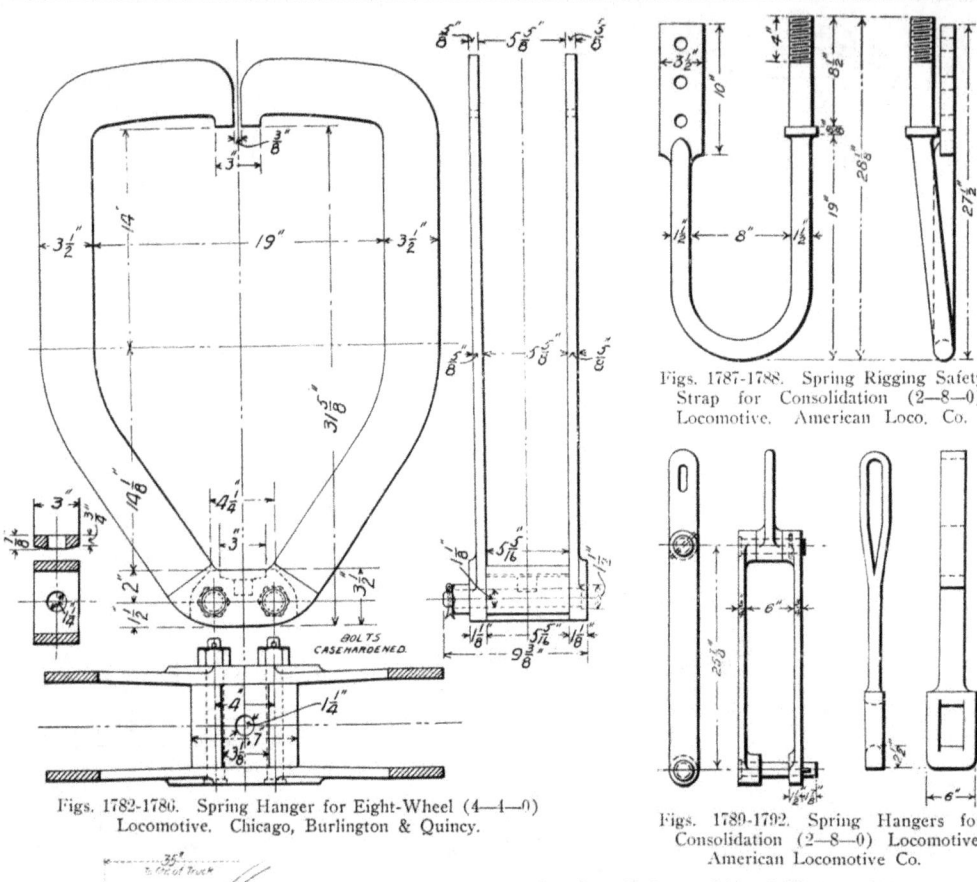

Figs. 1782-1786. Spring Hanger for Eight-Wheel (4—4—0) Locomotive. Chicago, Burlington & Quincy.

Figs. 1787-1788. Spring Rigging Safety Strap for Consolidation (2—8—0) Locomotive. American Loco. Co.

Figs. 1789-1792. Spring Hangers for Consolidation (2—8—0) Locomotive. American Locomotive Co.

Numbers Refer to List of Names of Parts with Figs. 1805-1808.

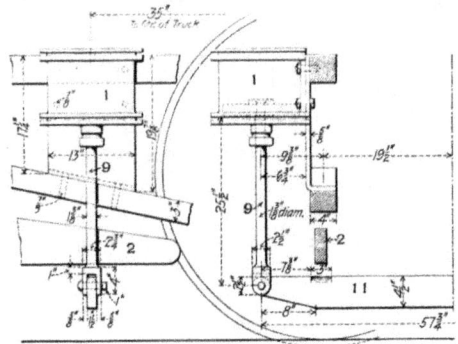

Figs. 1793-1794. Player Rear Traction Increaser. Atchison, Topeka & Santa Fe.

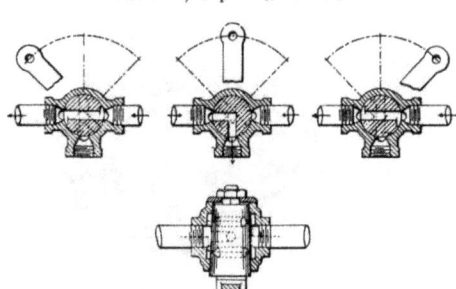

Figs. 1795-1798. Three-Way Cock for Player Traction Increaser. Atchison, Topeka & Santa Fe.

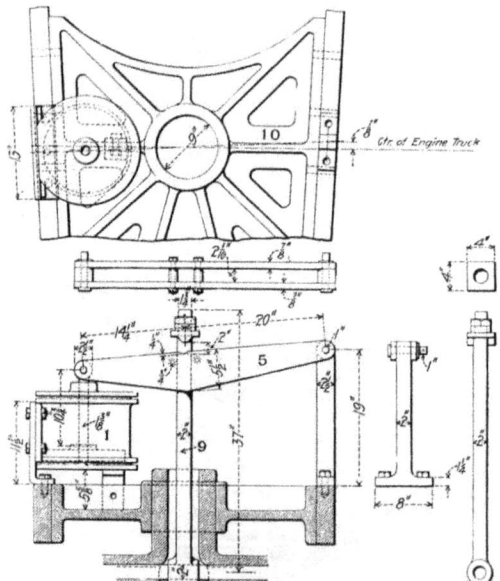

Figs. 1799-1804. Player Front Traction Increaser. Atchison, Topeka & Santa Fe.

(201)

TRACTION INCREASERS.

Numbers Refer to List of Names of Parts Below.

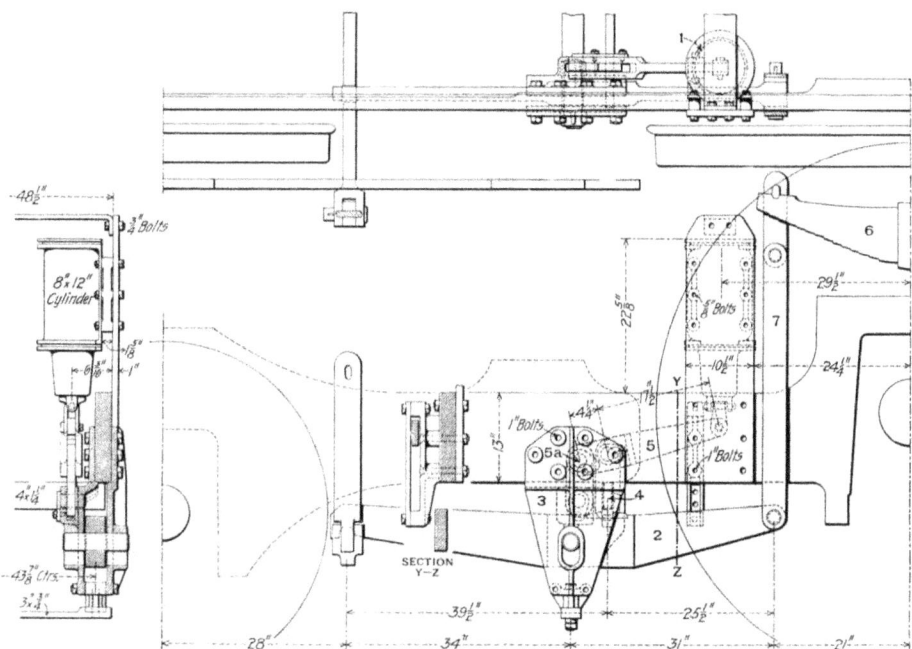

Figs. 1805-1807. Traction Increaser for Atlantic (4—4—2) Locomotive. American Locomotive Co.

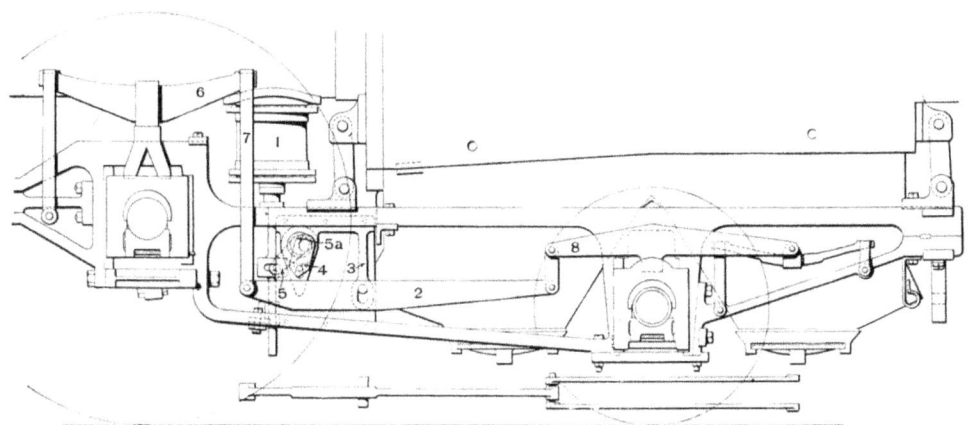

Fig. 1808. Traction Increaser. Baldwin Locomotive Works.

Names of Parts of Traction Increasers, Figs. 1793-1808.

1 Cylinder
2 Driver and Truck Equalizing Lever
3 Fixed Fulcrum
4 Adjustable Fulcrum
5 Adjustable Fulcrum Lever
5a Adjustable Fulcrum Lever Pin
6 Driver Spring
7 Driver Spring Hanger
8 Trailing Fulcrum Yoke
9 Equalizer Hanger
10 Engine Truck Center Plate
11 Lifting Bar

VALVE MOTION, Gooch and Walschaert. Figs. 1809-1812

Numbers Refer to List of Names of Parts Below.

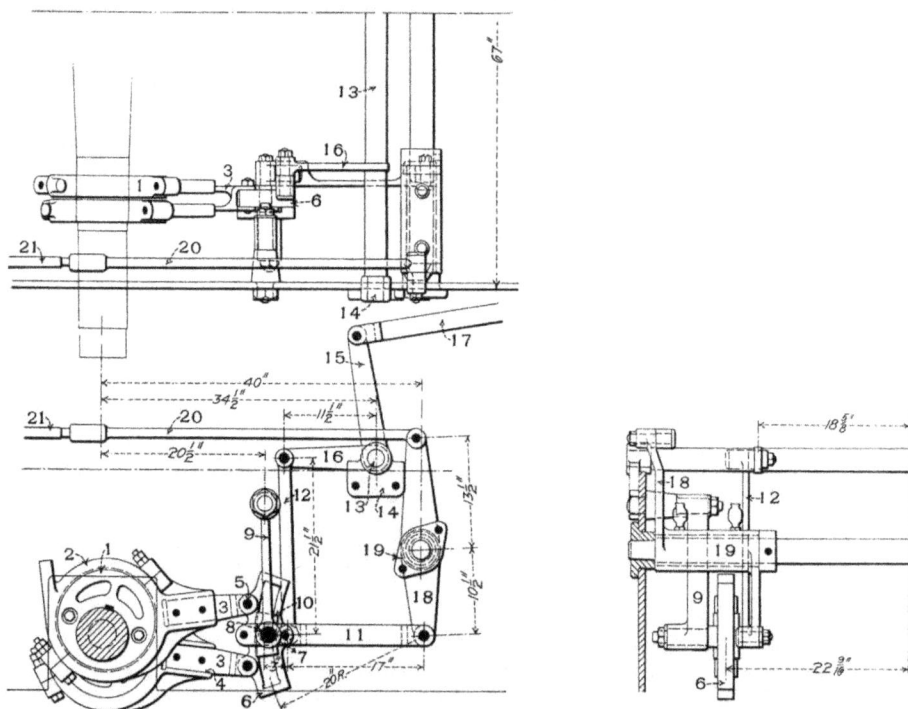

Figs. 1809-1811. Gooch Valve Motion as Applied to Rack Locomotive. Manitou & Pike's Peak.

Names of Parts of Gooch Valve Motion, Figs. 1809-1811.

1 Eccentric	8 Link Saddle Pin	15 Lifting Shaft Lever
2 Eccentric Strap	9 Link Hanger	16 Lifting Arm
3 Eccentric Rod	10 Link Block	17 Reach Rod
4 Eccentric Rod Seat	11 Radius Bar	18 Rocker
5 Eccentric Rod Pin	12 Radius Bar Hanger	19 Rocker Box
6 Link	13 Lifting Shaft	20 Valve Rod
7 Link Saddle	14 Lifting Shaft Bracket	21 Valve Stem

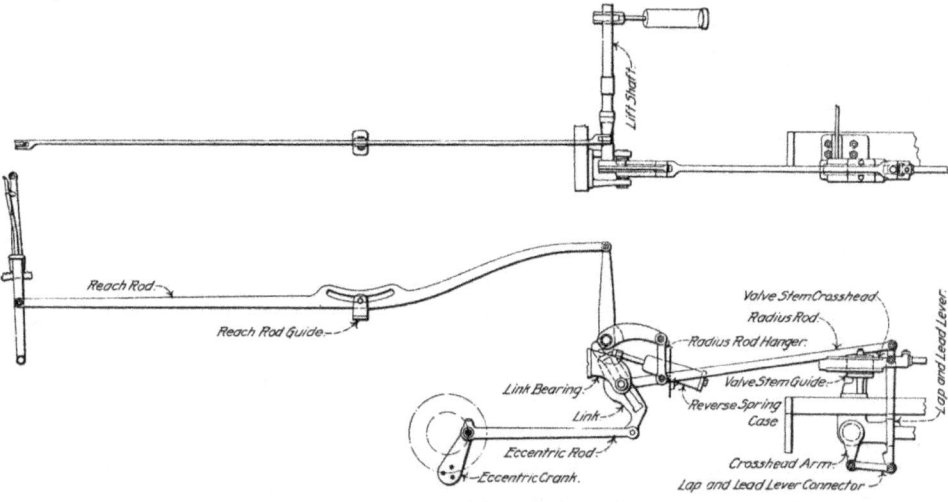

Fig. 1812. Diagram of Walschaert Valve Gear as Applied to Consolidation (2—8—0) Locomotives. Pennsylvania Railroad.

Numbers Refer to List of Names of Parts on Opposite Page.

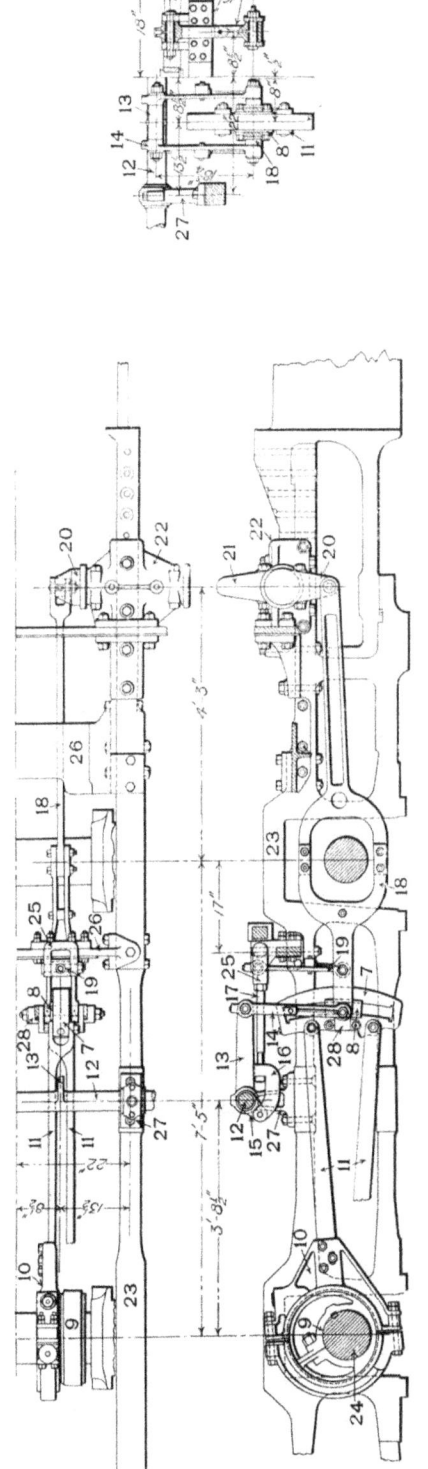

Figs. 1813-1815. Stephenson Link Valve Motion as Applied to Atlantic (4—4—2) Locomotive. Pennsylvania Railroad.

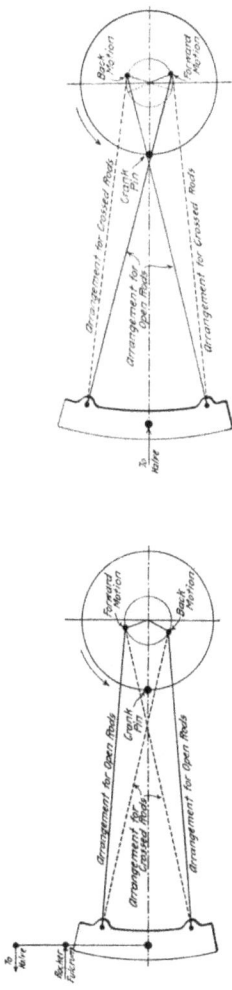

Figs. 1816-1817. Diagrams of Stephenson Link Motion with Open and Crossed Eccentric Rods.

VALVE MOTION, Stephenson; Details.   Figs. 1818-1852

Names of Parts of Valves and Valve Motion.

1 Guide Block	18 Transmission Bar	39 Valve Body
1a Valve	19 Transmission Bar Hanger	39a Valve Seat
2 Valve Stem	20 Lower Rocker Arm	40 Valve Packing Rings
3 Valve Stem Guide	21 Upper Rocker Arm	41 Valve Packing Spring Ring
4 Valve Stem Guide Bushing	21a Rocker Bearing	41a Valve Balance Strip
5 Valve Stem Guide Oil Cup	22 Rocker Box	41b Valve Balance Strip Groove
6 Valve Stem Guide Bushing Set Screw	23 Frame	41c Valve Balance Strip Spring
7 Link	24 Driving Axle	41d Valve Balance Rings
8 Link Block	25 Transmission Bar Hanger Bracket	42 Lifting Shaft Lever
9 Eccentric	26 Frame Brace	43 Scotch Yoke
10 Eccentric Strap	27 Lifting Shaft Bracket	44 Scotch Yoke Block
10a Eccentric Strap Rod	28 Link Saddle	45 Valve Yoke
11 Eccentric Rod	29 Link Saddle Pin	46 Piston Ring Pin
11a Eccentric Rod Seat	30 Transmission Bar Separator	47 Valve Spider
12 Lifting Shaft	31 Eccentric Rod Pin	48 Relief Hole
13 Lifting Shaft Arm	32 Lifting Shaft Arm Pin	49 Steam Chest
14 Link Hanger	33 Rocker Shaft Pin	49a Steam Chest Bushing
15 Lifting Shaft Counterbalance Arm	34 Transmission Bar Top Hanger Pin	50 Steam Chest Cover
16 Lifting Shaft Counterbalance Connection	35 Transmission Bar Bottom Hanger Pin	50a Steam Chest Cover Bolt
17 Lifting Shaft Counterbalance Rod	36 Valve Rod	51 Steam Chest Casing
	36b Valve Rod and Stem Pin	52 Steam Chest Cover Gasket
17a Lifting Shaft Counterbalance Spring	37 Valve Stem Key	53 Balance Plate
	38 Valve Rod Stub End	54 Steam Port
		55 Exhaust Port
		56 Bridge

Numbers Refer to List of Names of Parts Above.

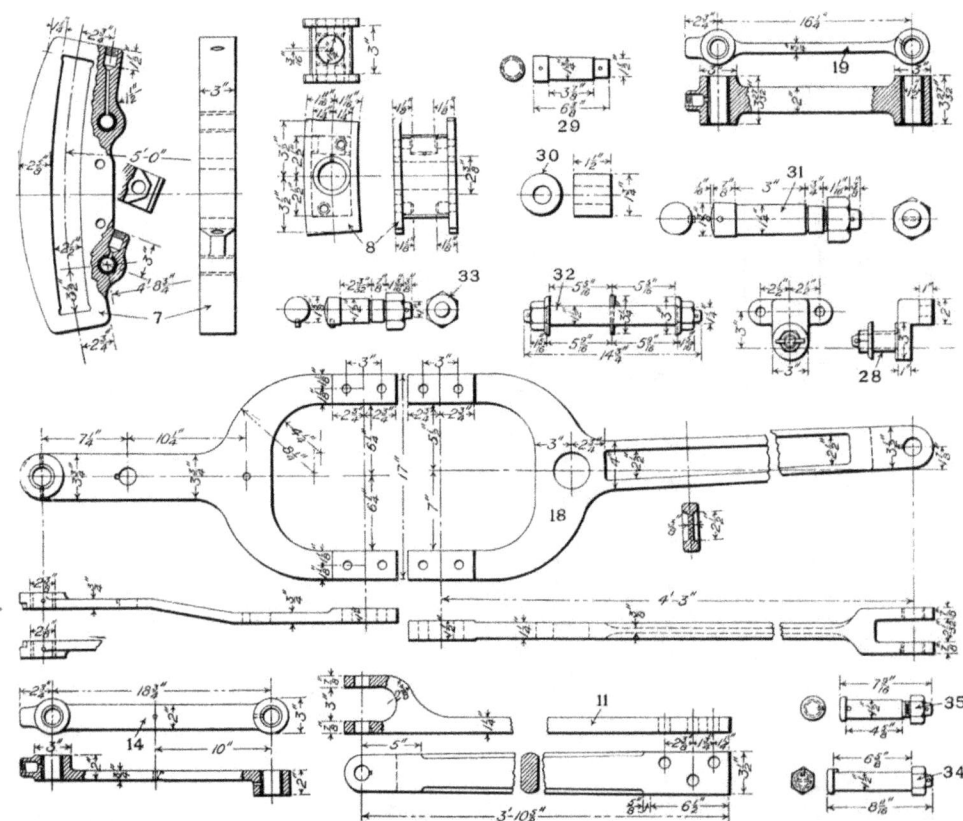

Figs. 1818-1852. Details of Valve Motion. Atlantic (4—4—2) Locomotive. Pennsylvania Railroad.

VALVE MOTION, Stephenson; Details.

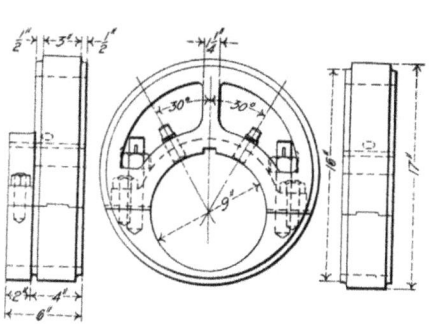

Figs. 1853-1855. Single Eccentric. American Locomotive Co.

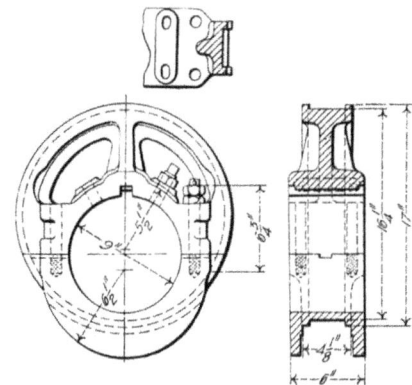

Figs. 1856-1858. Single Eccentric for Consolidation (2—8—0) Locomotive. American Locomotive Co.

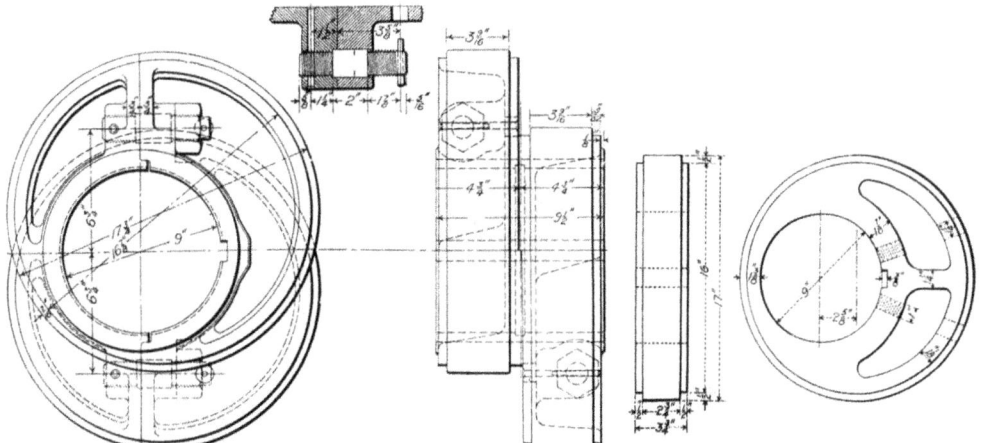

Figs. 1859-1861. Double Eccentric for Atlantic (4—4—2) Locomotive. P. R. R.

Figs. 1862-1863. Single Eccentric.

Numbers Refer to List of Names of Parts with Figs. 1818-1852.

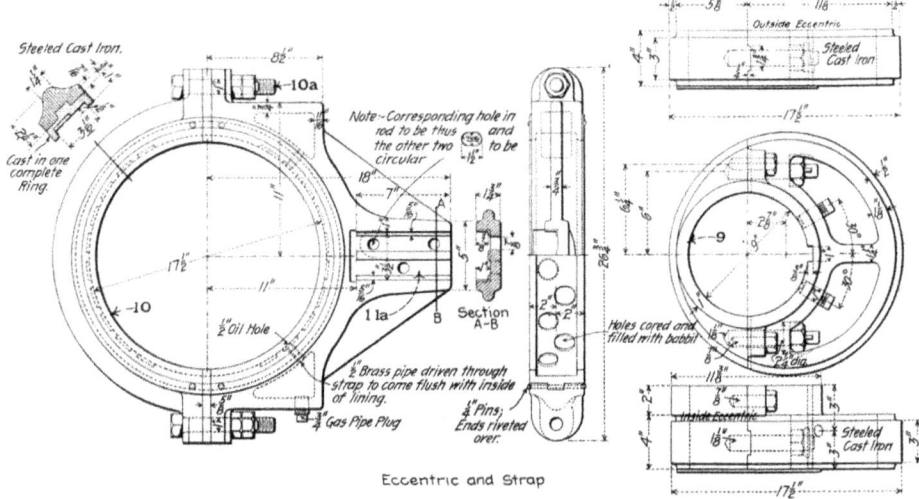

Figs. 1864-1870. Eccentric and Strap for Atlantic (4—4—2) Locomotive. Chicago & Northwestern.

VALVE MOTION, Stephenson; Details. Figs. 1871-1882

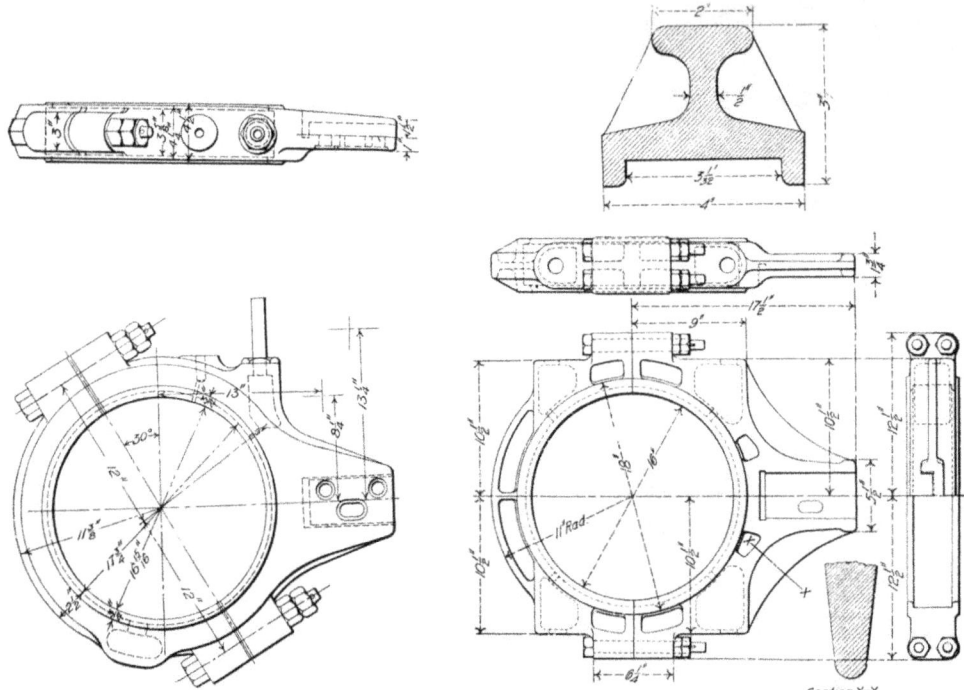

Figs. 1871-1872. Eccentric Strap for Atlantic (4—4—2) Locomotive. P. R. R.

Figs. 1873-1877. Eccentric Strap for Consolidation (2—8—0) Locomotive. American Locomotive Co.

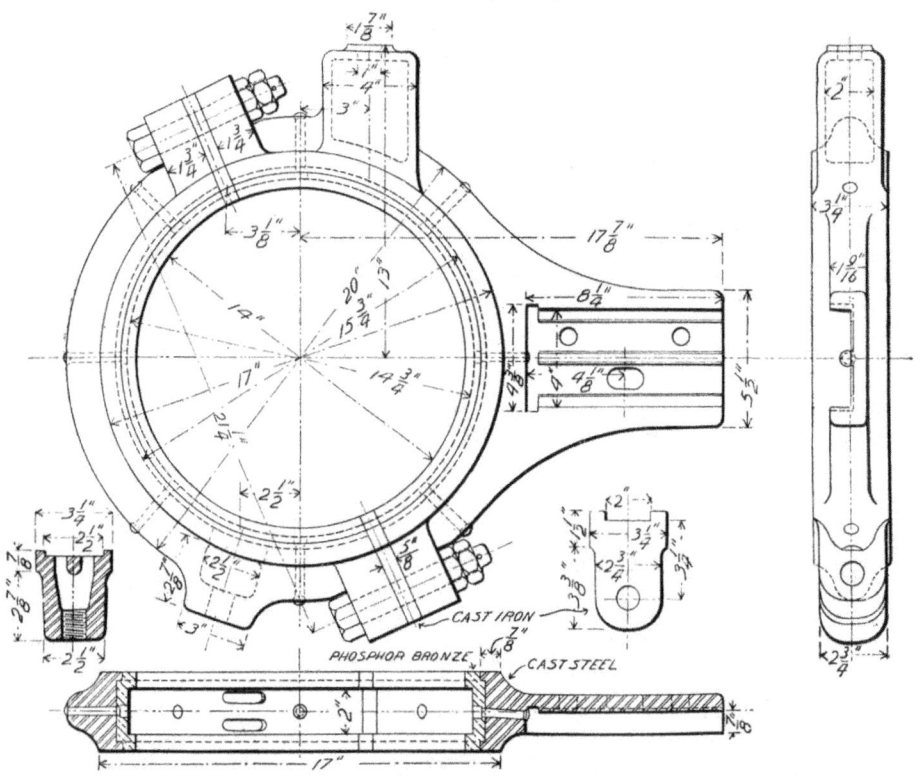

Figs. 1878-1882. Cast-Steel Eccentric Strap. Rogers Locomotive Works.

(207)

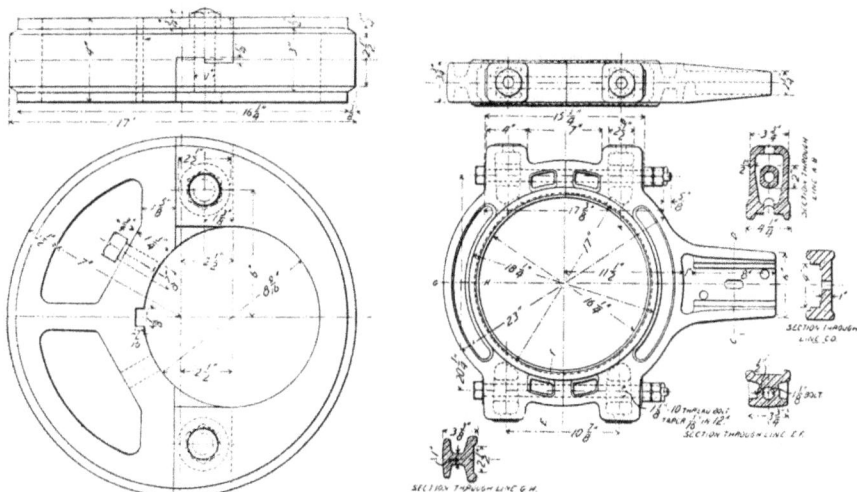

Figs. 1883-1890. Eccentric and Strap. American Locomotive Co.

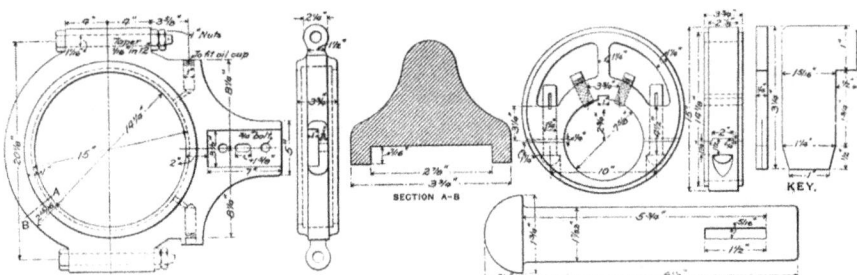

Figs. 1891-1898. Eccentric and Strap for Ten-Wheel (4—6—0) Locomotive. Mexican Central.

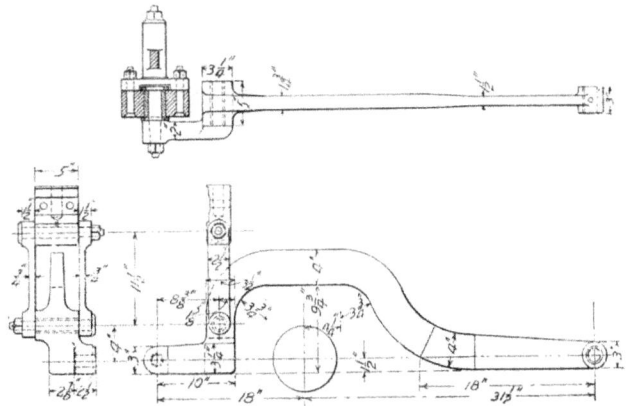

Figs. 1899-1901. Eccentric Rod for Consolidation (2—8—0) Locomotive.

VALVE MOTION, Stephenson; Details.   Figs. 1902-1916

Numbers Refer to List of Names of Parts Below.

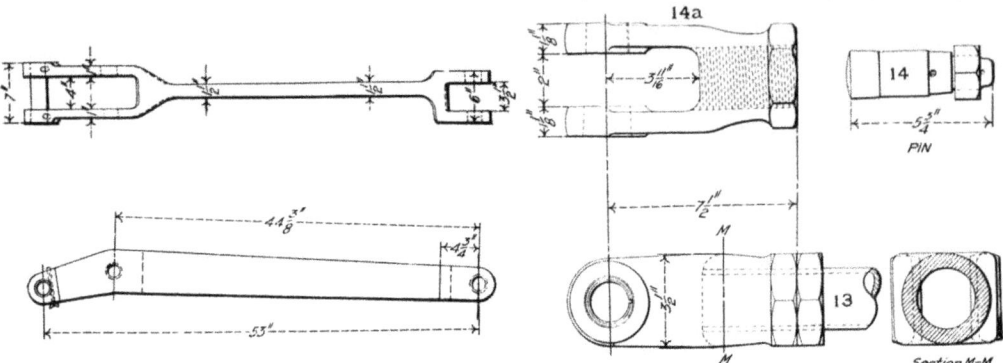

Figs. 1902-1903. Transmission Bar for Consolidation (2—8—0) Locomotive. American Locomotive Co.

Figs. 1904-1907. Reach Rod Jaw and Pin. American Locomotive Co.

Figs. 1908-1910. Transmission Bar Pins for Consolidation (2—8—0) Locomotive. American Locomotive Co.

Numbers Refer to List of Names of Parts with Figs. 1818-1852.

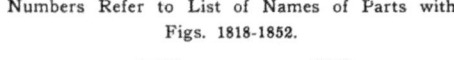

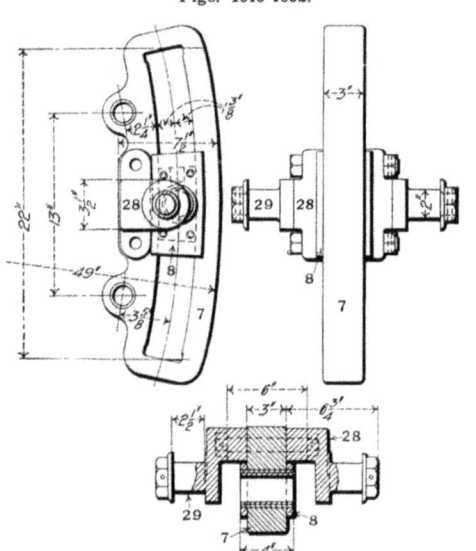

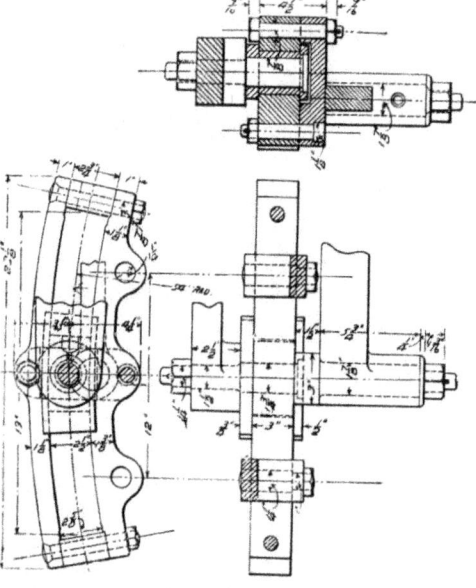

Figs. 1911-1913. Link for Consolidation (2—8—0) Locomotive. American Locomotive Co.

Figs. 1914-1916. Link. Baldwin Locomotive Works.

Names of Parts of Reverse Lever and Details, Figs. 1917-1988.

1 *Quadrant*
2 *Reversing Foot Rest*
3 *Quadrant Bracket*
4 *Quadrant Bracket Stud*
5 *Reverse Lever*
5a *Reverse Lever Guide*
6 *Reverse Lever Latch*
7 *Reverse Lever Latch Connection*
8 *Reverse Lever Latch Handle*
8a *Reverse Lever Latch Handle Bolt*
9 *Reverse Lever Latch Spring*
9a *Reverse Lever Latch Spring Casing*
10 *Reverse Lever Latch Stud Bolt*
11 *Reverse Lever Latch Equalizer*
11a *Reverse Lever Latch Spring Stem*
11b *Reverse Lever Latch Spring Stem Guide*
12 *Reverse Lever Latch Bolt*
12a *Reverse Lever Fulcrum*
13 *Reach Rod*
14 *Reach Rod Pin*
14a *Reach Rod Jaw*

Figs. 1917-1975   **VALVE MOTION, Stephenson; Reverse Lever Details.**

Numbers Refer to List of Names of Parts with Figs. 1902-1916.

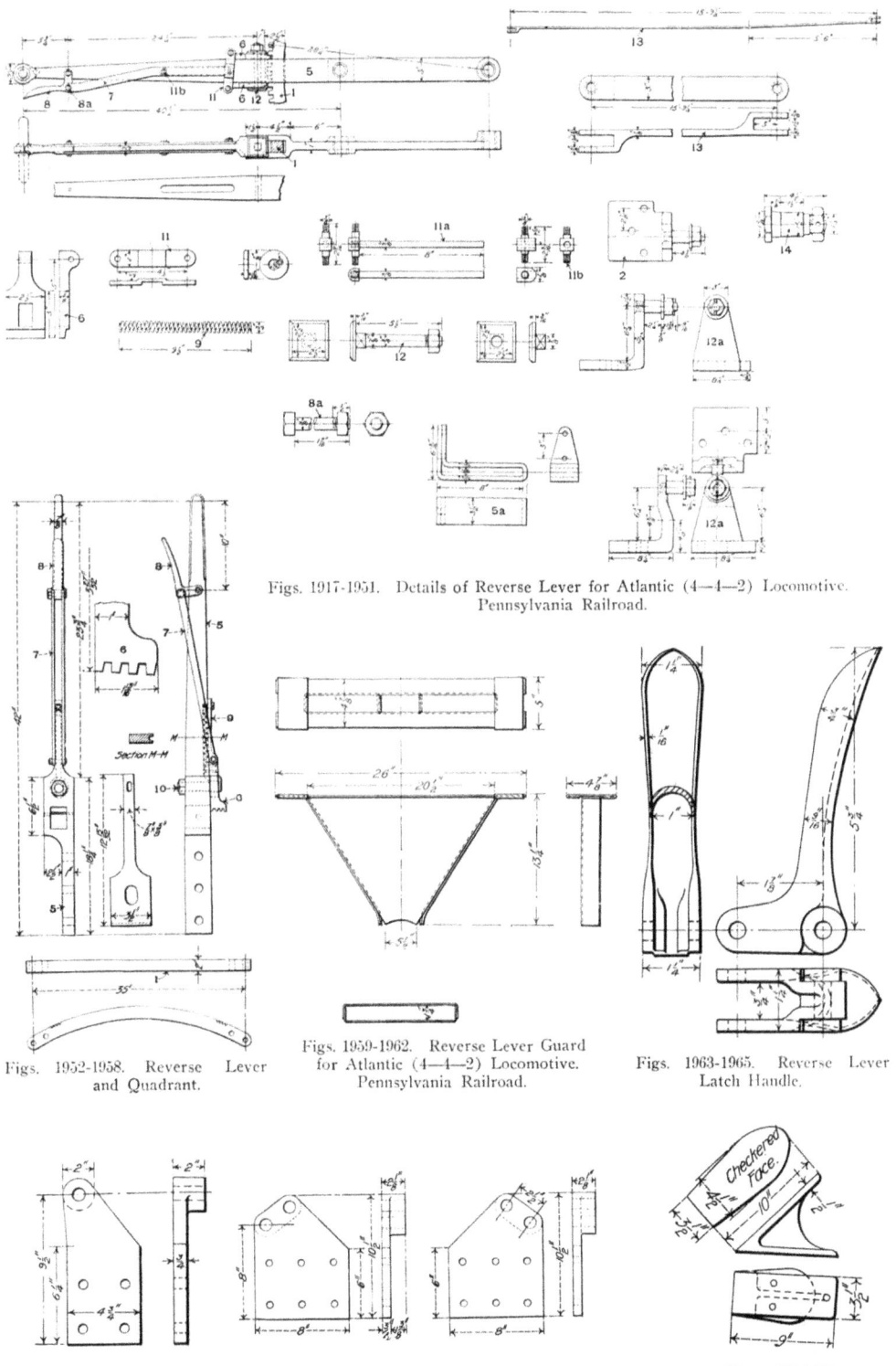

Figs. 1917-1951. Details of Reverse Lever for Atlantic (4—4—2) Locomotive. Pennsylvania Railroad.

Figs. 1952-1958. Reverse Lever and Quadrant.

Figs. 1959-1962. Reverse Lever Guard for Atlantic (4—4—2) Locomotive. Pennsylvania Railroad.

Figs. 1963-1965. Reverse Lever Latch Handle.

Figs. 1966-1971. Reverse Lever Quadrant Brackets for Consolidation (2—8—0) Locomotive. American Locomotive Co.

Figs. 1973-1975. Reverse Lever Foot Rest.

(210)

VALVE MOTION, Stephenson; Reverse Lever Details. Figs. 1976-2000

Numbers Refer to List of Names of Parts with Figs. 1902-1916.

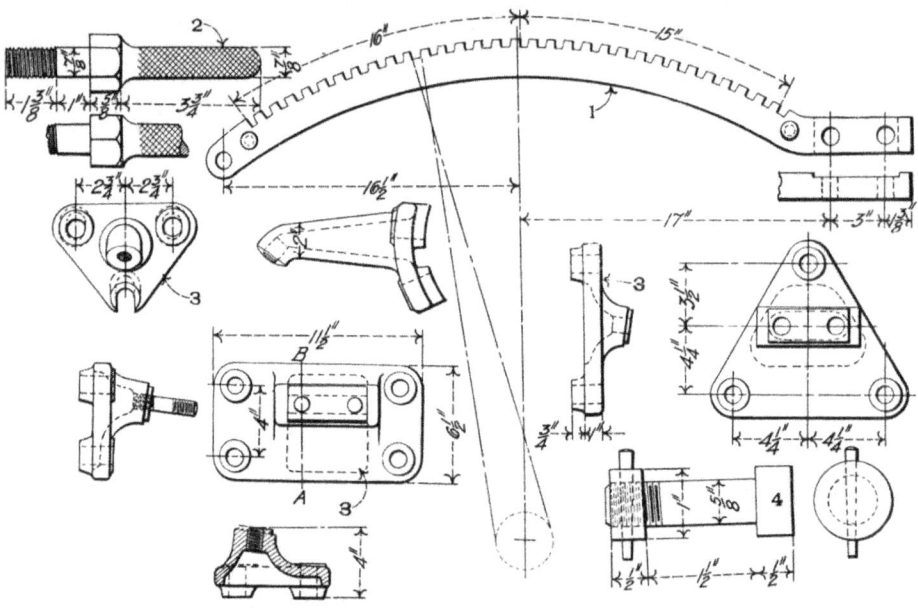

Figs. 1976-1988. Details of Reverse Lever Quadrant and Brackets for Atlantic (4—4—2) Locomotive. Pennsylvania Railroad.

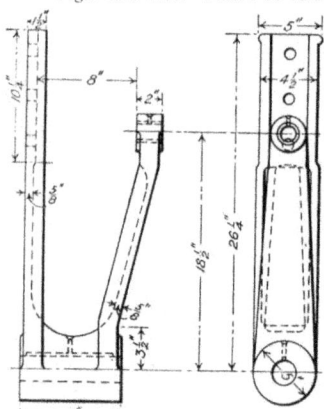

Figs. 1989-1990. Reverse Lever End. American Locomotive Co.

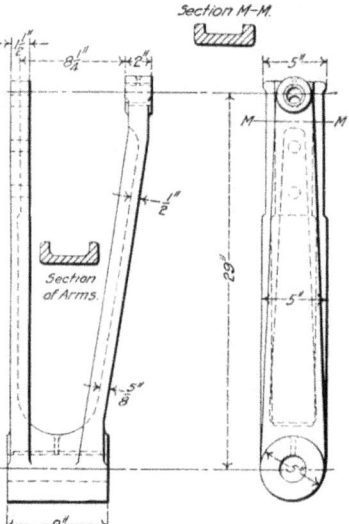

Figs. 1991-1993. Reverse Lever End. American Locomotive Co.

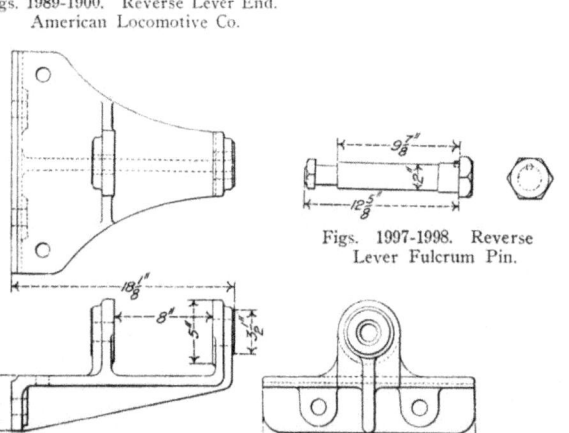

Figs. 1997-1998. Reverse Lever Fulcrum Pin.

Figs. 1994-1996. Reverse Lever Fulcrum. American Locomotive Co.

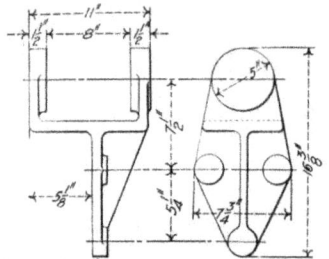

Figs. 1999-2000. Reverse Lever Fulcrum. American Locomotive Co.

(211)

Figs. 2001-2023. VALVE MOTION, Stephenson; Details.

Numbers Refer to List of Names of Parts with Figs. 1818-1852.

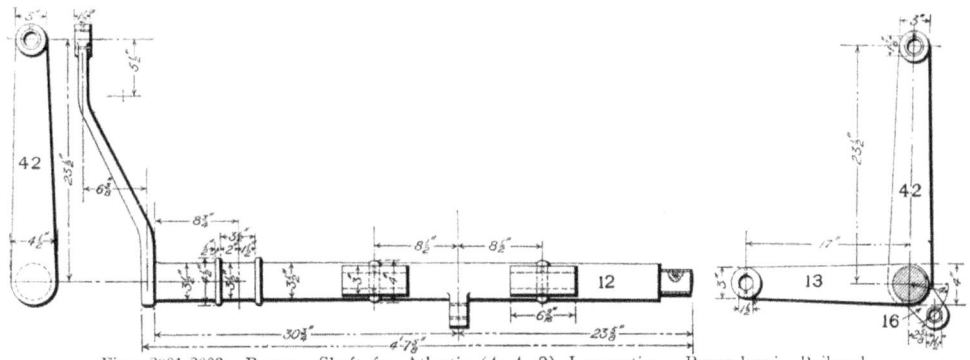

Figs. 2001-2003. Reverse Shaft for Atlantic (4—4—2) Locomotive. Pennsylvania Railroad.

Figs. 2004-2006. Reverse Shaft for Atlantic (4—4—2) Locomotive. Chicago & Northwestern.

Figs. 2007-2008. Reverse Shaft Reach Rod for Consolidation (2—8—0) Locomotive. American Locomotive Co.

Figs. 2009-2012. Cast-Steel Reverse Shaft Arm for Eight-Wheel (4—4—0) Locomotive. Chicago & Alton.

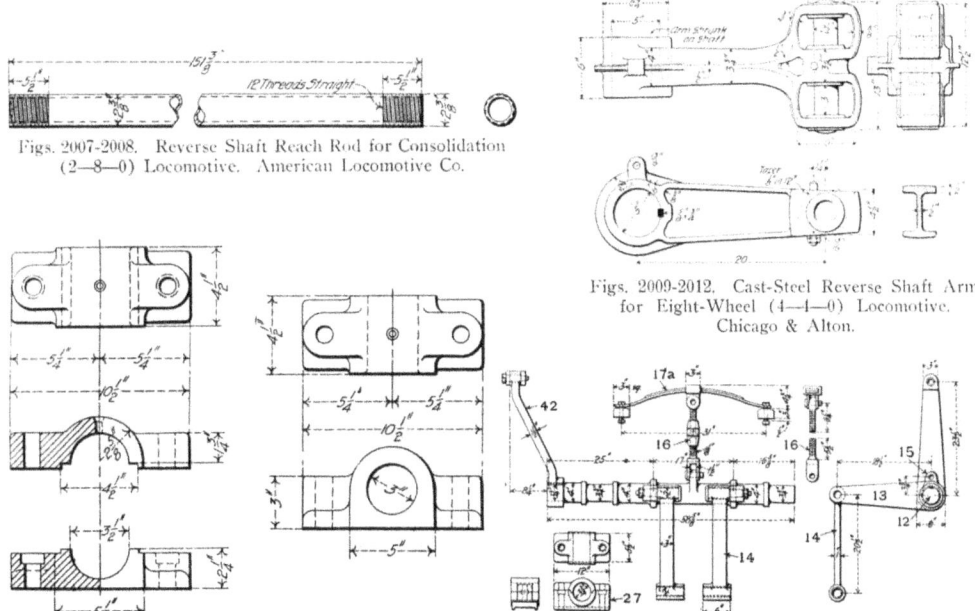

Figs. 2013-2017. Reverse Shaft Bearings for Consolidation (2—8—0) Locomotive. American Locomotive Co.

Figs. 2018-2023. Reverse Shaft and Spring. Atchison, Topeka & Santa Fe.

(212)

VALVE MOTION, Stephenson; Details. Figs. 2024-2056

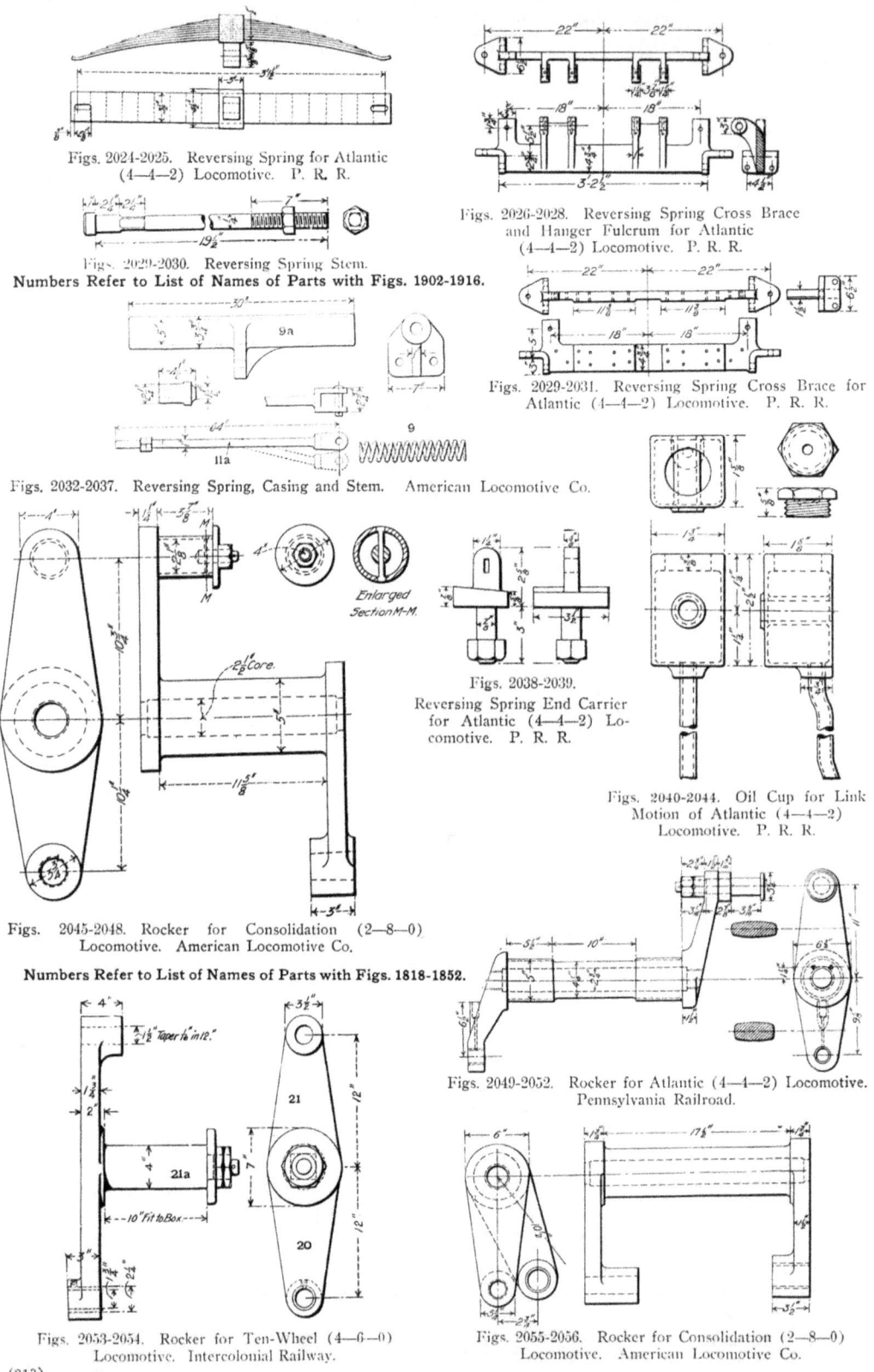

Figs. 2024-2025. Reversing Spring for Atlantic (4—4—2) Locomotive. P. R. R.

Figs. 2029-2030. Reversing Spring Stem.

Numbers Refer to List of Names of Parts with Figs. 1902-1916.

Figs. 2026-2028. Reversing Spring Cross Brace and Hanger Fulcrum for Atlantic (4—4—2) Locomotive. P. R. R.

Figs. 2029-2031. Reversing Spring Cross Brace for Atlantic (4—4—2) Locomotive. P. R. R.

Figs. 2032-2037. Reversing Spring, Casing and Stem. American Locomotive Co.

Figs. 2038-2039. Reversing Spring End Carrier for Atlantic (4—4—2) Locomotive. P. R. R.

Figs. 2040-2044. Oil Cup for Link Motion of Atlantic (4—4—2) Locomotive. P. R. R.

Figs. 2045-2048. Rocker for Consolidation (2—8—0) Locomotive. American Locomotive Co.

Numbers Refer to List of Names of Parts with Figs. 1818-1852.

Figs. 2049-2052. Rocker for Atlantic (4—4—2) Locomotive. Pennsylvania Railroad.

Figs. 2053-2054. Rocker for Ten-Wheel (4—6—0) Locomotive. Intercolonial Railway.

Figs. 2055-2056. Rocker for Consolidation (2—8—0) Locomotive. American Locomotive Co.

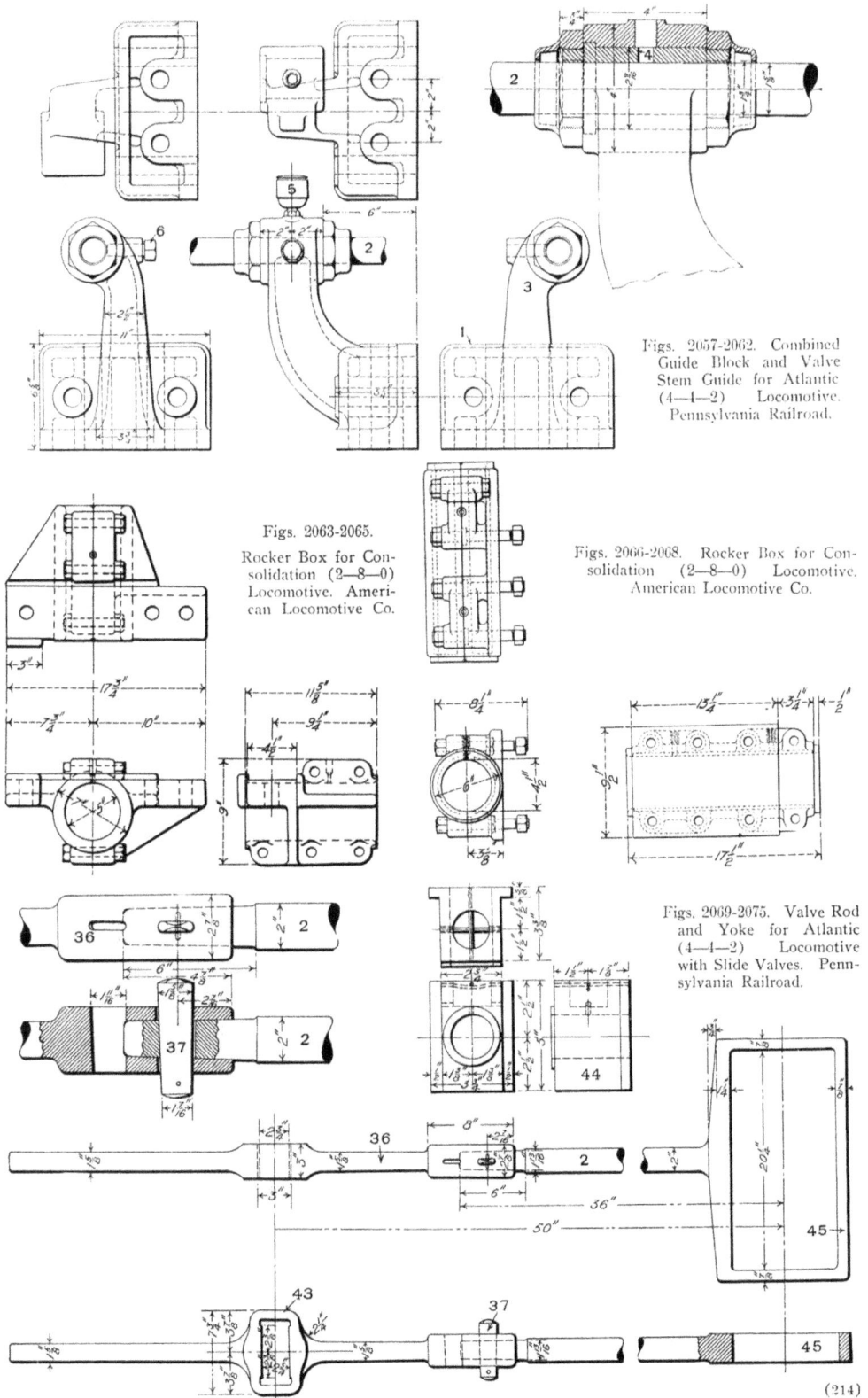

Figs. 2057–2062. Combined Guide Block and Valve Stem Guide for Atlantic (4—4—2) Locomotive. Pennsylvania Railroad.

Figs. 2063–2065. Rocker Box for Consolidation (2—8—0) Locomotive. American Locomotive Co.

Figs. 2066–2068. Rocker Box for Consolidation (2—8—0) Locomotive. American Locomotive Co.

Figs. 2069–2075. Valve Rod and Yoke for Atlantic (4—4—2) Locomotive with Slide Valves. Pennsylvania Railroad.

VALVE MOTION, Stephenson; Details.   Figs. 2076-2096

Numbers Refer to List of Names of Parts with Figs. 1818-1852.

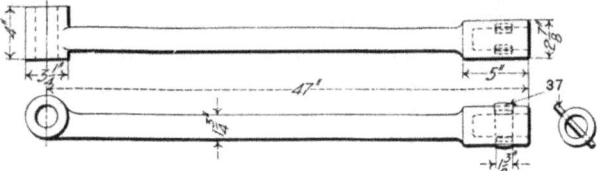

Figs. 2076-2078. Valve Rod for Consolidation (2—8—0) Locomotive. American Locomotive Co.

Fig. 2079. Valve Stem Pipe for Atlantic (4—4—2) Locomotive. P. R. R.

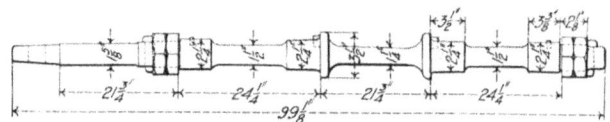

Fig. 2080. Valve Stem for Piston Valve of Tandem Compound Consolidation (2—8—0) Locomotive. American Locomotive Co.

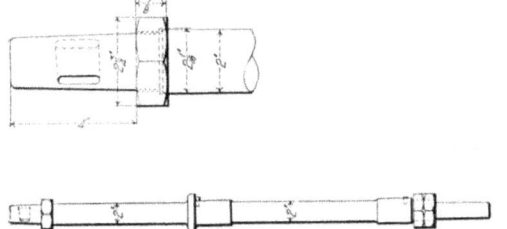

Figs. 2081-2082. Valve Stem for Piston Valve. American Locomotive Co.

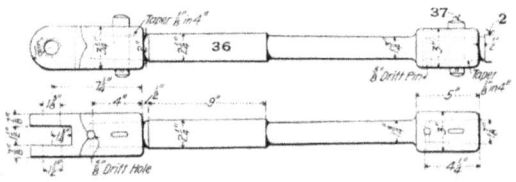

Figs. 2083-2084. Intermediate Valve Rod for Pacific (4—6—2) Type Locomotive. Oregon Short Line.

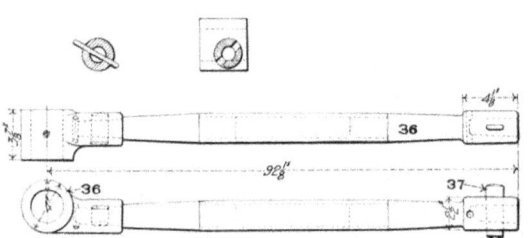

Figs. 2085-2088. Valve Rod for Consolidation (2—8—0) Locomotive. American Locomotive Co.

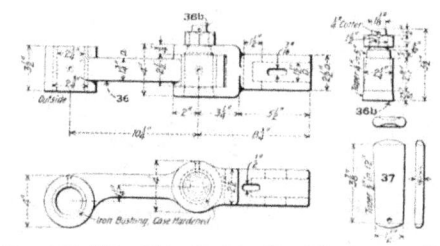

Figs. 2089-2094. Valve Rod for Ten-Wheel (4—6—0) Locomotive. Lehigh Valley.

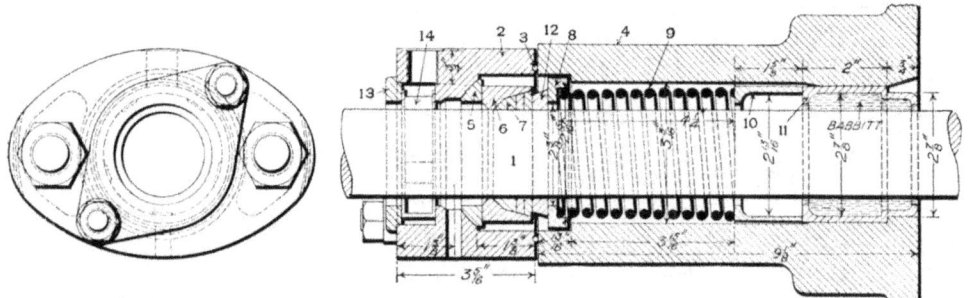

Figs. 2095-2096. Multiangular Packing for 2-in. Valve Stems on Atlantic (4—4—2) Locomotive. P. R. R.

Names of Parts of Valve Stem Packing, Figs. 2095-2096.

1 *Valve Stem*	6 *Vibrating Cup*	11 *Stem Support*
2 *Case*	7 *Packing Rings*	12 *Follower Cup*
3 *Copper Joint*	8 *Follower*	13 *Swab Cup Holder*
4 *Packing Cylinder*	9 *Spring*	14 *Swab Cup*
5 *Ball Joint*	10 *Extension Ring for Spring*	

(215)

Figs. 2097–2121 — VALVES, Slide.

Numbers Refer to List of Names of Parts with Figs. 1818–1852.

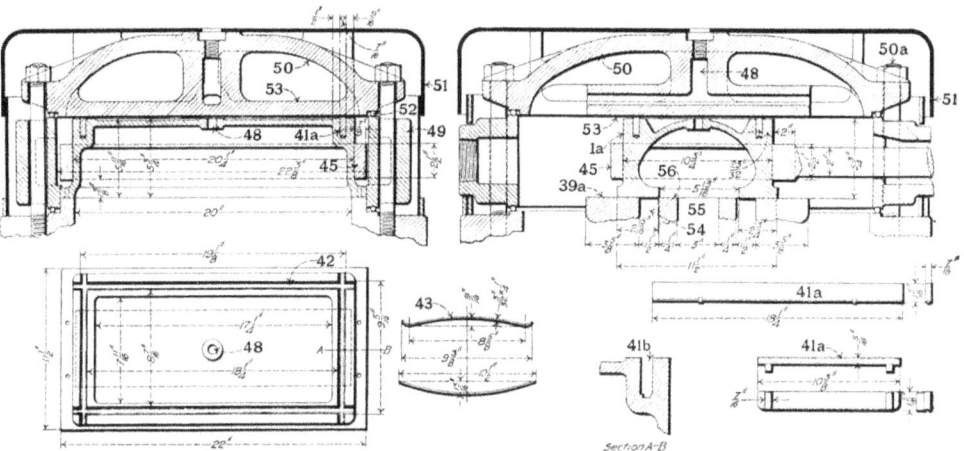

Figs. 2097–2107. Balanced Slide Valve for Atlantic (4–4–2) Locomotive. Pennsylvania Railroad.

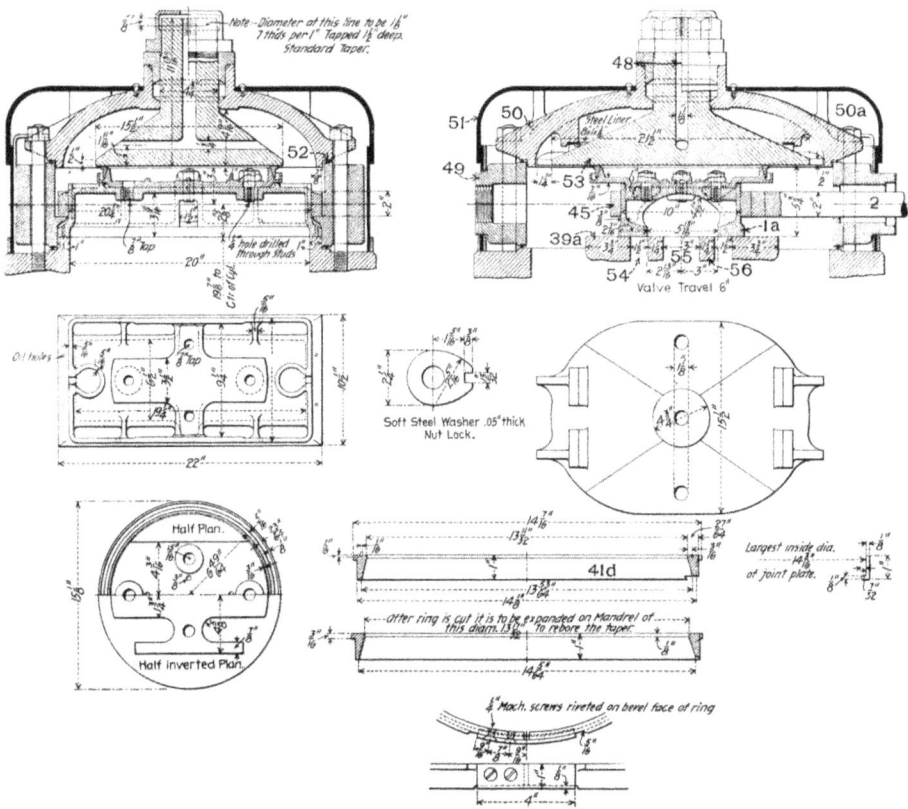

Figs. 2108–2118. American Balanced Slide Valve. American Balance Valve Co.

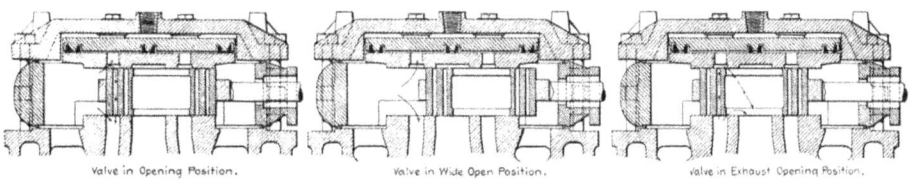

Valve in Opening Position.   Valve in Wide Open Position.   Valve in Exhaust Opening Position.

Figs. 2119–2121. Wilson High-Pressure Balanced Slide Valve. American Balance Valve Co.

VALVES, Slide.

Figs. 2122-2125

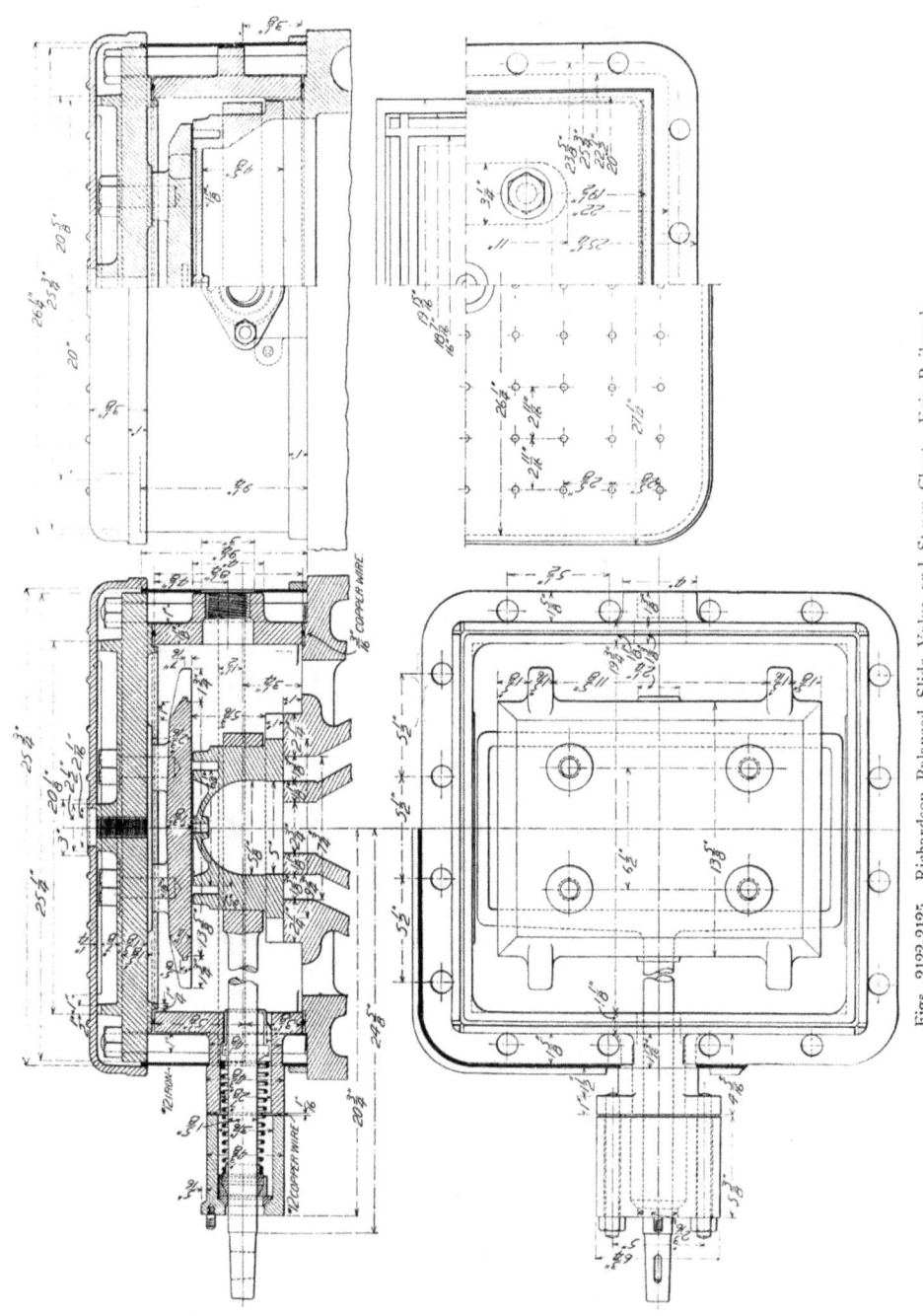

Figs. 2122-2125. Richardson Balanced Slide Valve and Steam Chest. Erie Railroad.

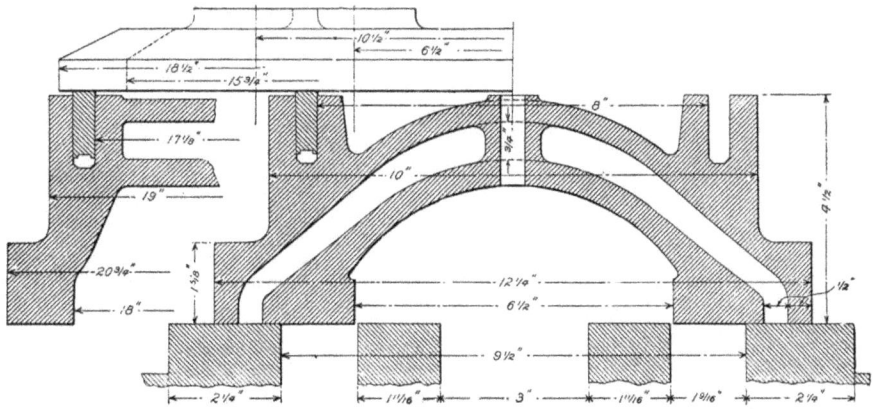

Figs. 2126-2127. Allen-Richardson Balanced Slide Valve for Eight-Wheel (4—4—0) Locomotive. Baltimore & Ohio.

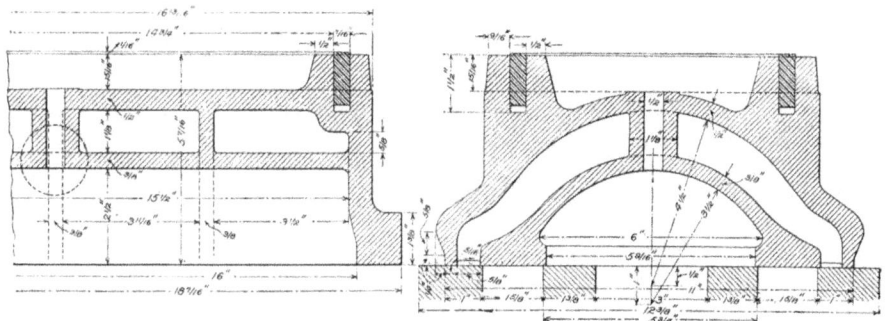

Figs. 2128-2129. Allen-Richardson Balanced Slide Valve for Eight-Wheel (4—4—0) Locomotive. Lake Shore & Michigan Southern.

Letters Refer to List of Names of Parts on Opposite Page.

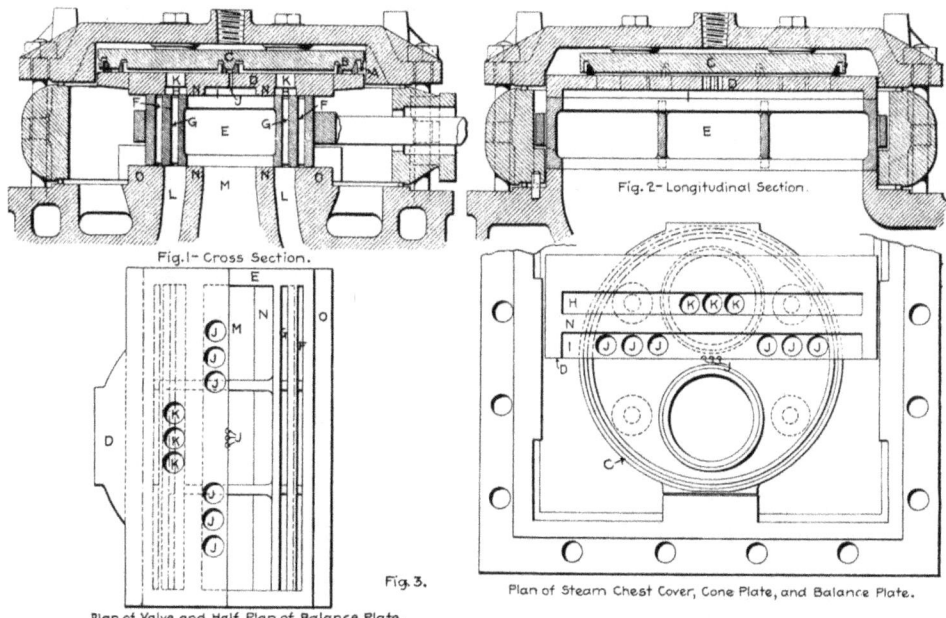

Figs. 2130-2133. J. T. Wilson High-Pressure Balanced Slide Valve. American Balance Valve Co.

(218)

VALVES, Piston.

Figs. 2134-2144

Numbers Refer to List of Names of Parts with Figs. 1818-1852.

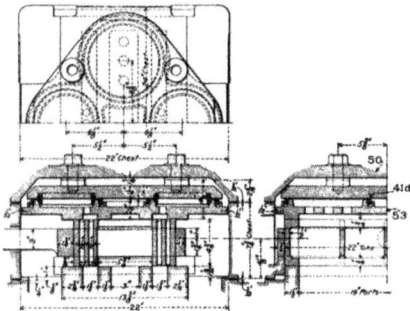

Figs. 2134-2136. Balanced Slide Valve. Northern Pacific.

Names of Parts of Figs. 2130-2133.

- **A** *Main Balancing Ring*
- **B** *Port Balancing Rings*
- **C** *Cone Plate for Rings A and B*
- **D** *Balance Plate*
- **E** *Main Valve*
- **F** *Double Admission Ports*
- **G** *Double Exhaust Ports*
- **H** *Pockets in Balancing Plate, Steam Ports*
- **I** *Pockets in Balancing Plate, Exhaust Ports*
- **J** *Steam Passage*
- **K** *Steam Passage*
- **L** *Steam Ports*
- **M** *Exhaust Ports*
- **N** *Bridge in Seat and Balancing Plate*
- **O** *Outer Edge of Valve Seat*

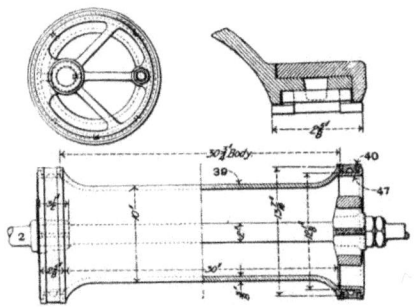

Figs. 2137-2139. Hollow Piston Valve for Consolidation (2—8—0) Locomotive. American Locomotive Co.

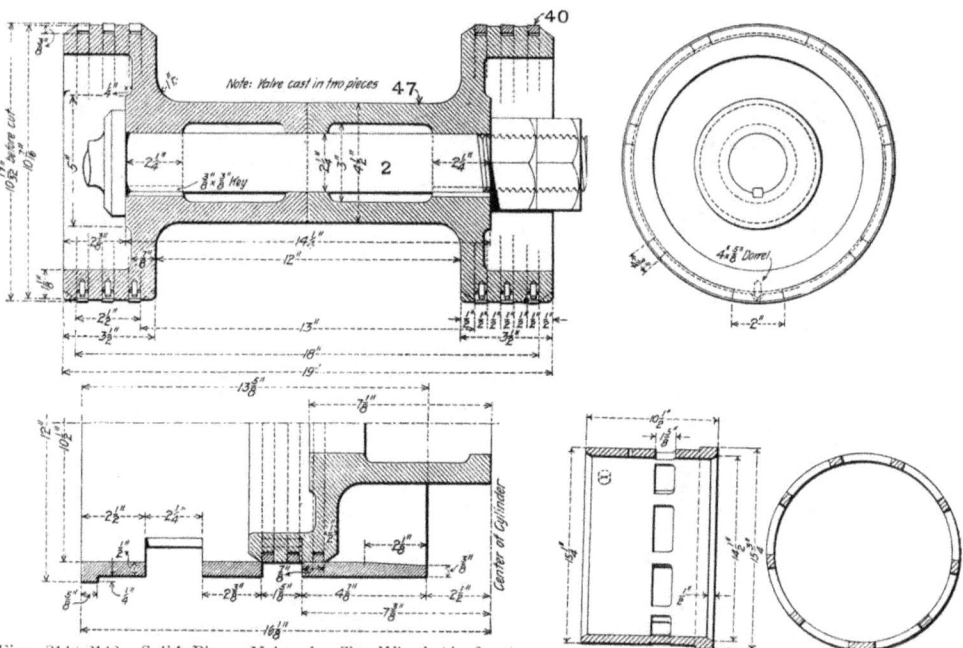

Figs. 2140-2142. Solid Piston Valve for Ten-Wheel (4—6—0) Locomotive with 20 in. x 28 in. Cylinders. Atchison, Topeka & Santa Fe.

Figs. 2143-2144. Piston Valve Steam Chest Bushing.

(219)

VALVES, Piston.

Numbers Refer to List of Names of Parts with Figs. 1818-1852.

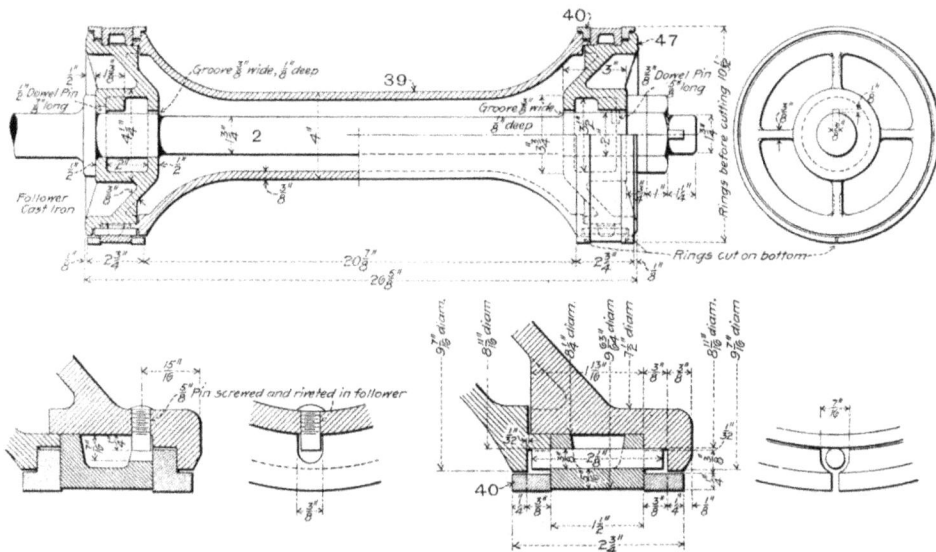

Figs. 2145-2150. Solid Piston Valve for Suburban Locomotive. New York Central & Hudson River.

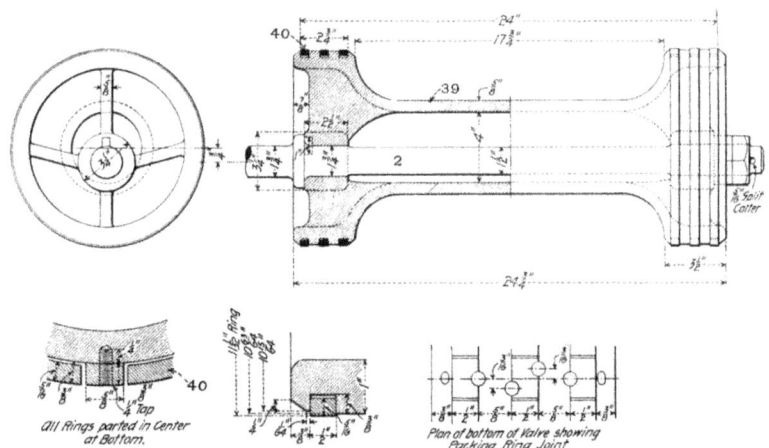

Figs. 2151-2155. 11-in. Piston Valve for Atlantic (4—4—2) Locomotive. Chicago & North-Western.

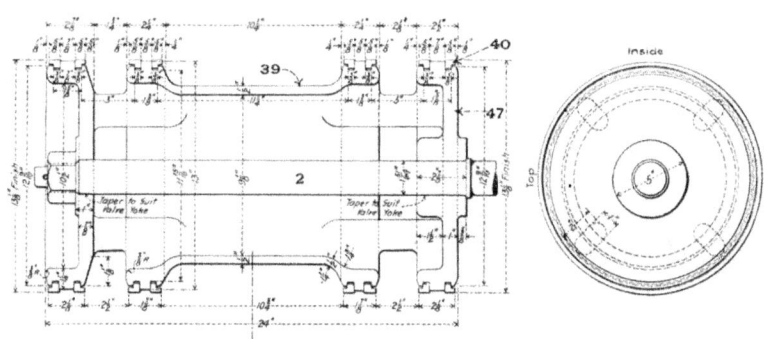

Figs. 2156-2157. Hollow Piston Valve for Consolidation (2—8—0) Locomotive. Atchison, Topeka & Santa Fe.

VALVES, Piston. Figs. 2158-2166

Numbers Refer to List of Names of Parts with Figs. 1818-1852.

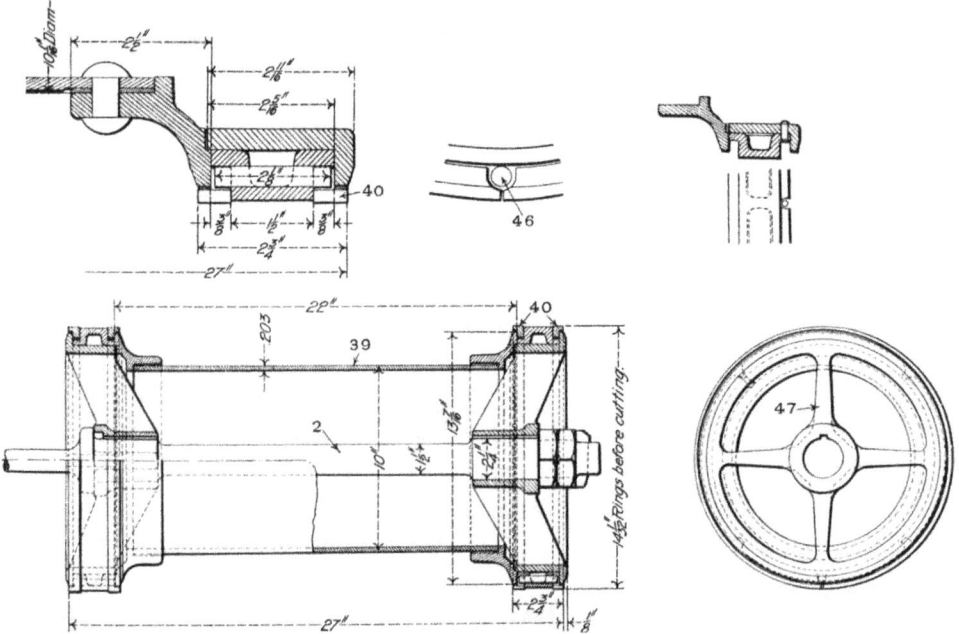

Figs. 2158-2162. Hollow Piston Valve for Consolidation (2—8—0) Locomotive. American Locomotive Co.

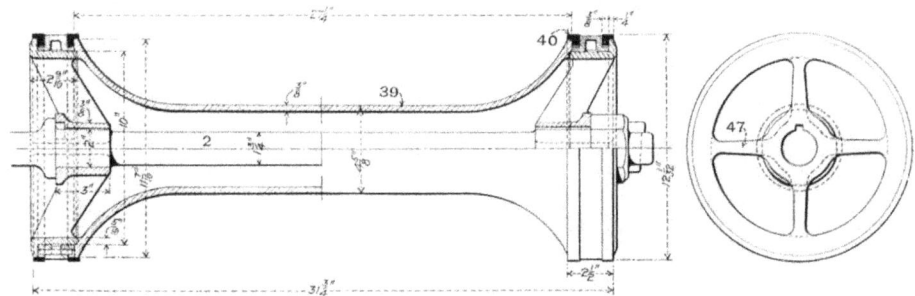

Figs. 2163-2164. Hollow Piston Valve. Northern Pacific.

Fig. 2165. Semi-Plug Piston Valve for Cylinders without Bridges in Steam Ports. American Balance Valve Co.

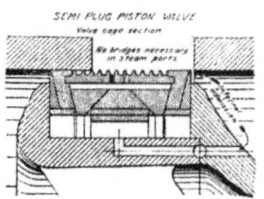

Fig. 2166. Packing Rings of Semi-Plug Valve.

Figs. 2167–2192 VALVES, Piston.

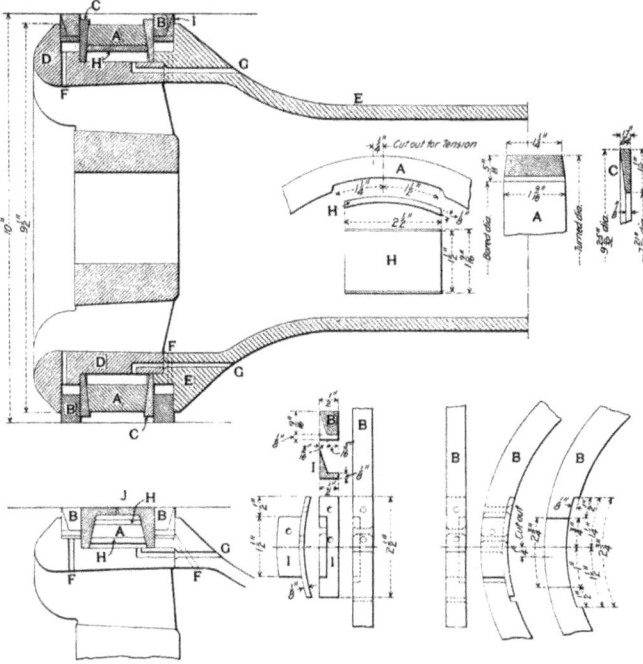

Names of Parts of Wilson Balanced Piston Valves, Figs. 2167–2192.

A *Wedge Ring*
B *Snap Rings*
C *Solid Rings*
D *Follower*
E *Valve Spool*
F *Relief Passage*
G *Steam Ports*
H *Joint Covering in Wedge Ring*
I *Joint Covering in Snap Rings*
J *Section of Solid Rings*

Figs. 2167–2181. Wilson Rigid Automatic Balanced Piston Valve with Narrow Rings. American Balance Valve Co.

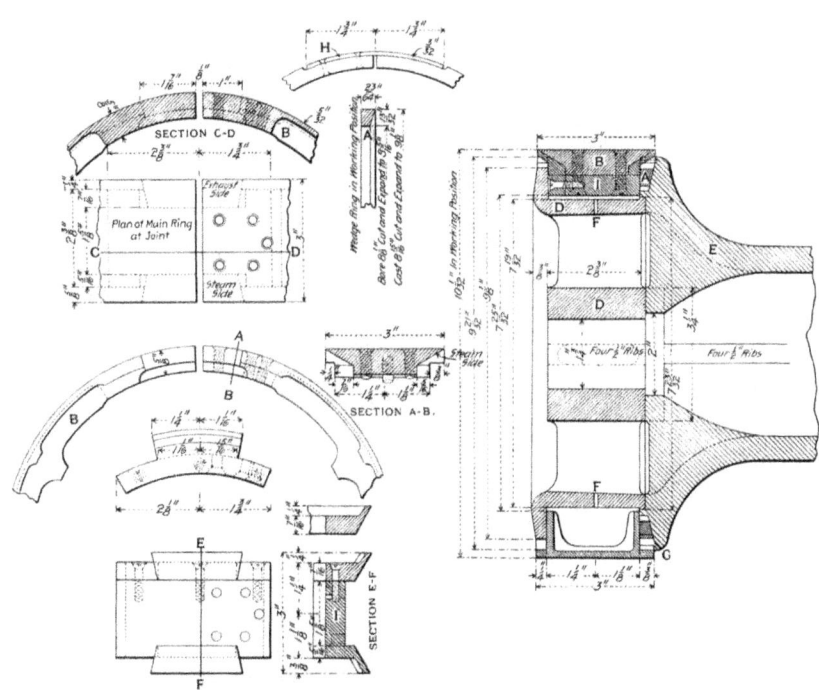

Figs. 2182–2192. Wilson Rigid Automatic Balanced Piston Valve with Wide Rings. American Balance Valve Co.

COMPOUND LOCOMOTIVES, Details; Baldwin. Figs. 2193-2194

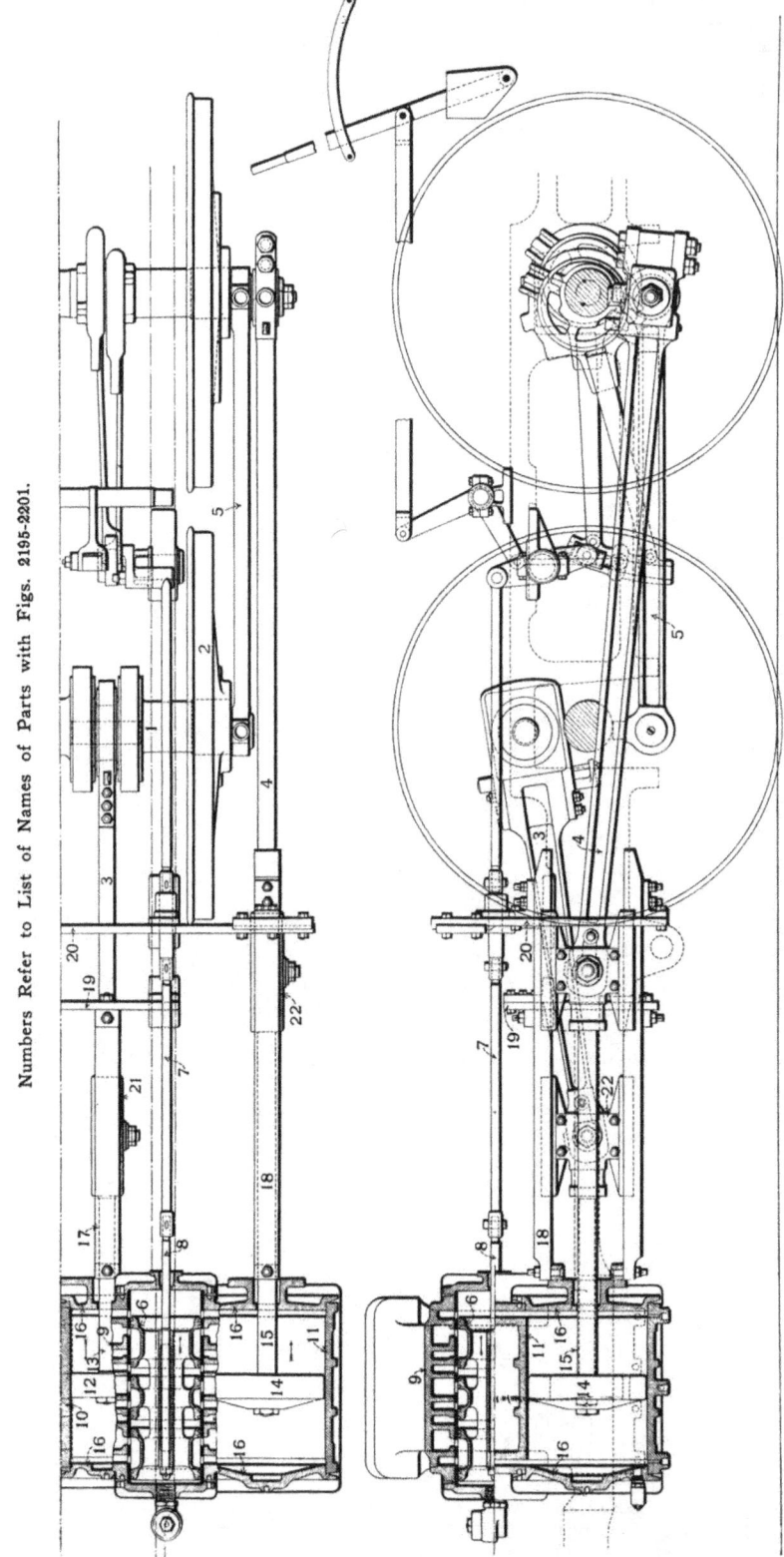

Numbers Refer to List of Names of Parts with Figs. 2195-2201.

Figs. 2193-2194. General Arrangement of Cylinders, Valves and Rods for Ten-Wheel (4—6—0) Baldwin Four-Cylinder Balanced Compound Locomotive. New York, New Haven & Hartford.

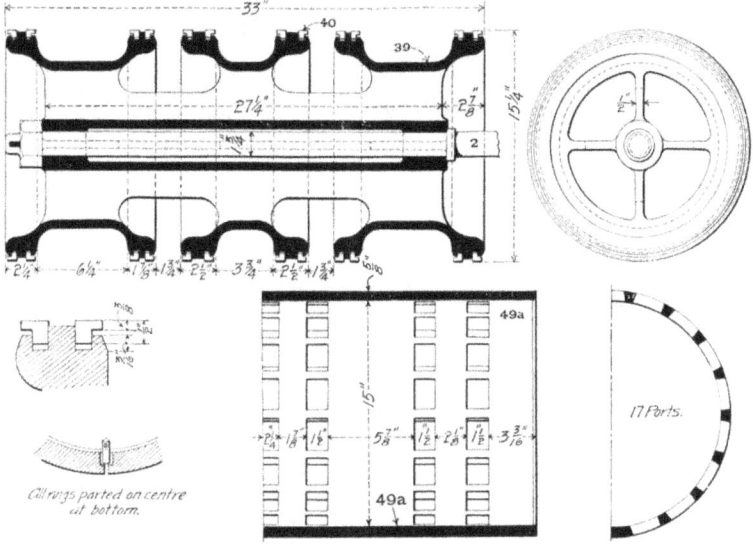

Figs. 2195–2200. Piston Valve and Steam Chest Bushing for Atlantic (4—4—2) Baldwin Four-Cylinder Balanced Compound Locomotive. Atchison, Topeka & Santa Fe.

Names of Parts of Baldwin Four-Cylinder Balanced and Tandem Compound Locomotives, Figs. 2193–2194 and Fig. 2707.

1. Crank Axle
2. Main Driving Wheel
3. High Pressure Connecting Rod
4. Low Pressure Connecting Rod
5. Side Rod
6. Valve
6a. High Pressure Valve
6b. Low Pressure Valve
7. Valve Rod
8. Valve Rod Stem
9. Steam Chest
10. High Pressure Cylinder
11. Low Pressure Cylinder
12. High Pressure Piston
13. High Pressure Piston Rod
14. Low Pressure Piston
15. Low Pressure Piston Rod
16. Cylinder Heads
16a. Intermediate Cylinder Heads
17. High Pressure Guide
18. Low Pressure Guide
19. High Pressure Guide Yoke
20. Low Pressure Guide Yoke
21. High Pressure Crosshead
22. Low Pressure Crosshead

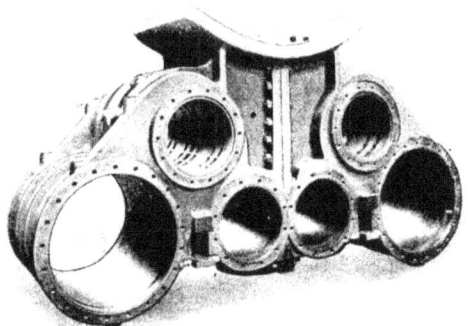

Fig. 2201. Cylinder Saddle for Baldwin Four-Cylinder Balanced Compound Locomotive. Baldwin Locomotive Works.

COMPOUND LOCOMOTIVES, Details; Baldwin.

Fig. 2202. Arrangement of Crossheads and Pistons of Baldwin Four-Cylinder Compound Locomotive.

Fig. 2203. Valve Bushing.

Fig. 2204. Piston Valve.

Fig. 2205. Built-up Crank Axle with Weights Balanced in Same Plane.

Fig. 2206. Built-up Disk Crank Axle.

Numbers Refer to List of Names of Parts on Opposite Page.

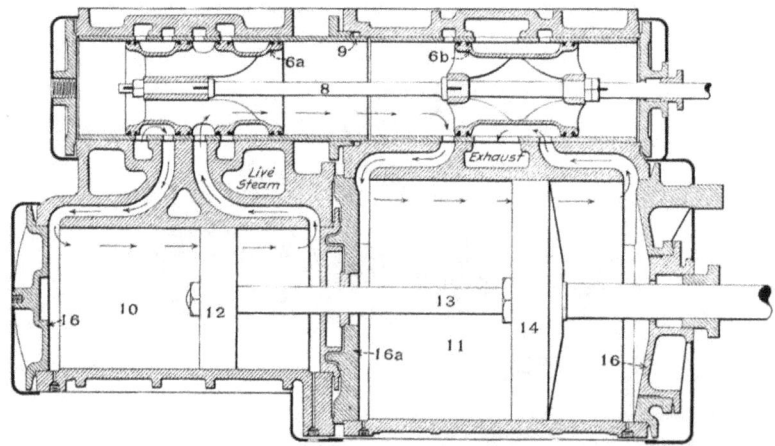

Fig. 2207. Arrangement of Cylinders and Valves of Baldwin Tandem Compound Locomotive. Baldwin Locomotive Works.

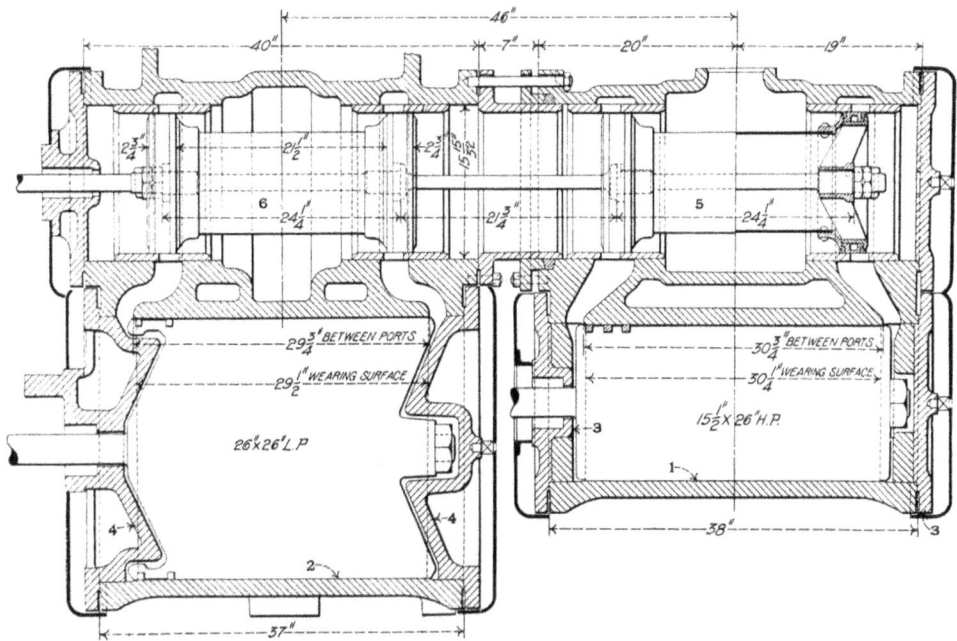

Fig. 2208. Arrangement of Cylinders and Valves of Cole Four-Cylinder Balanced Compound Locomotive. American Locomotive Co.

Names of Parts of Fig. 2208.

1 High Pressure Cylinder
2 Low Pressure Cylinder
3 High Pressure Cylinder Head
4 Low Pressure Cylinder Head
5 High Pressure Valve
6 Low Pressure Valve

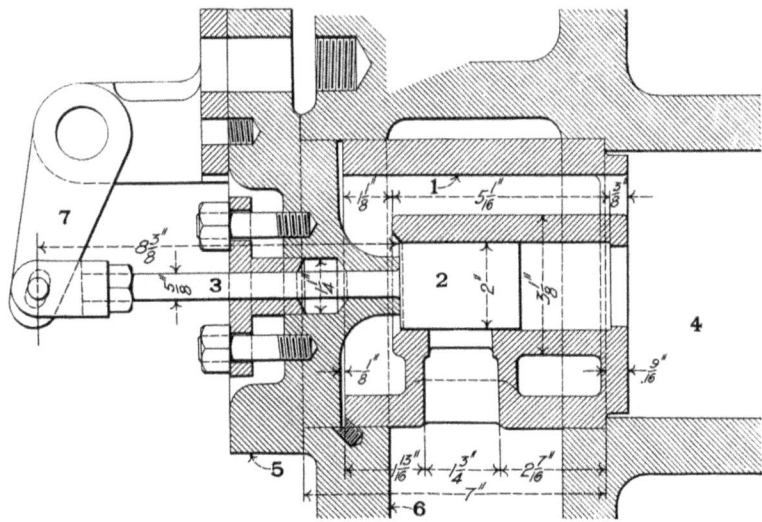

Fig. 2209. Starting Valve for Cole Four-Cylinder Balanced Compound Locomotive.

Names of Parts of Fig. 2209.

1 Bushing and Valve Seat
2 Valve
3 Valve Stem
4 Valve Chamber
5 Valve Chamber Head
6 Cylinder
7 Operating Arm

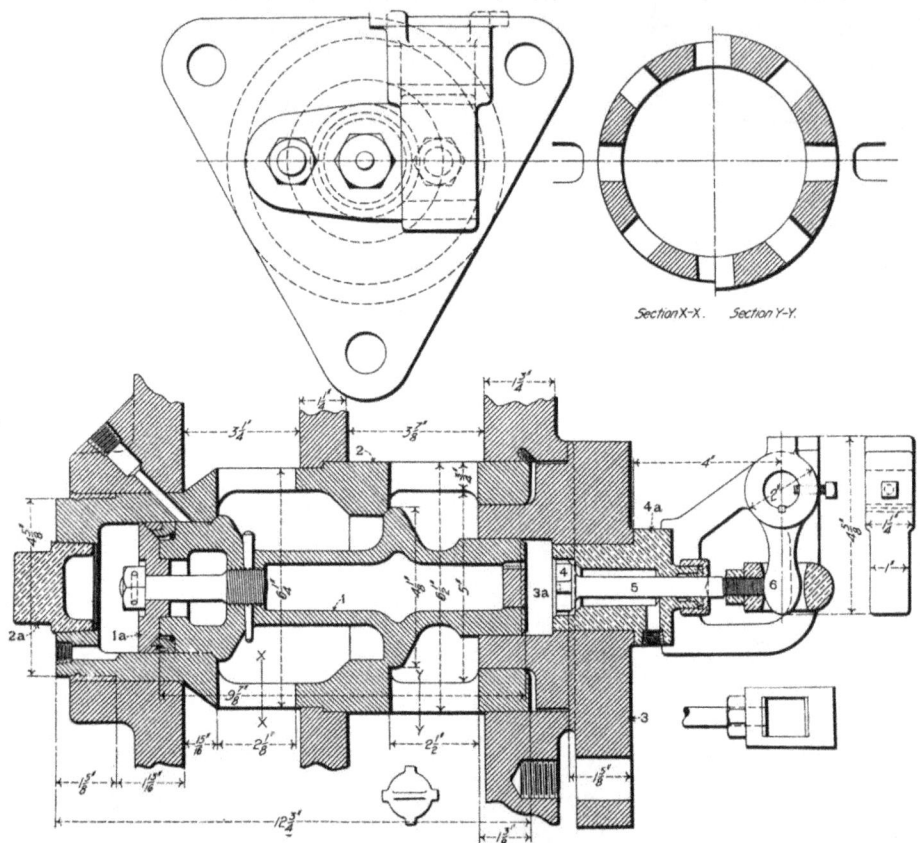

Figs. 2210-2214. Starting Valve for Cole Four-Cylinder Balanced Compound Locomotive.

Names of Parts of Figs. 2210-2214.

1 *Valve*
1a *Valve Follower*
2 *Starting Valve Chamber Bushing*
2a *Starting Valve Chamber Bushing Plug*
3 *Starting Valve Chamber Head*
3a *Operating Valve Chamber*
4 *Operating Valve*
4a *Operating Valve Chamber Plug*
5 *Operating Valve Stem*
6 *Operating Arm*

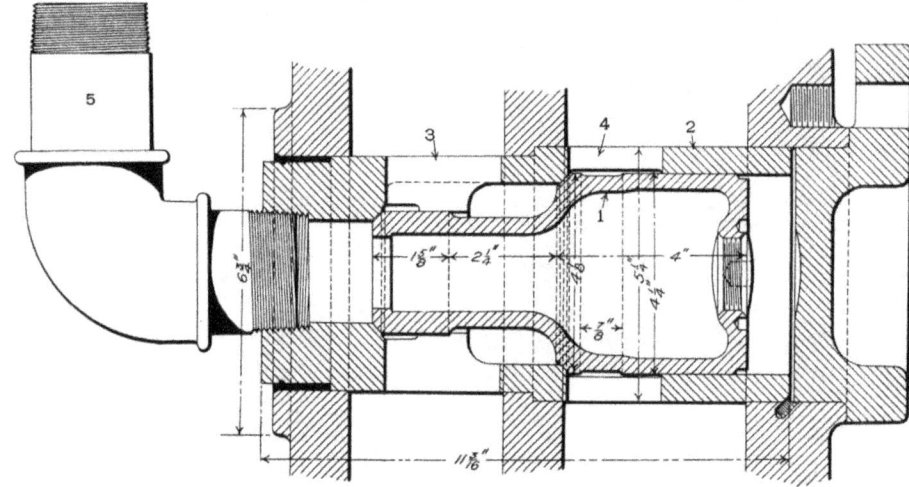

Fig. 2215. By-Pass Valve for Cole Four-Cylinder Balanced Compound Locomotive.

Names of Parts of Fig. 2215.

1 *Valve*
2 *Valve Bushing*
3 *Passage to Low Pressure Cylinder Port*
4 *Passage to Exhaust Port*
5 *Relief Pipe to Atmosphere*

Figs. 2216-2225 COMPOUND LOCOMOTIVES, Details; Richmond and Schenectady.

Numbers Refer to List of Names of Parts Below.

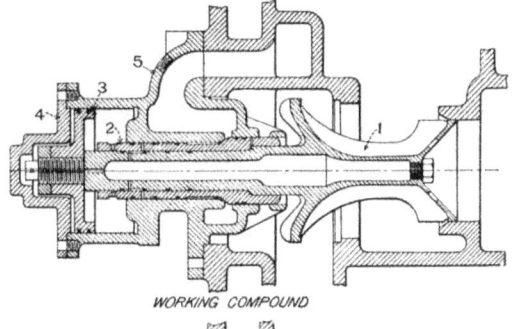
WORKING COMPOUND

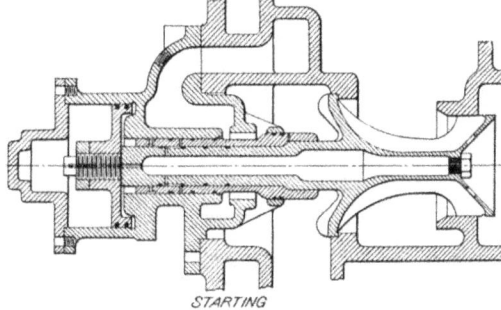
STARTING

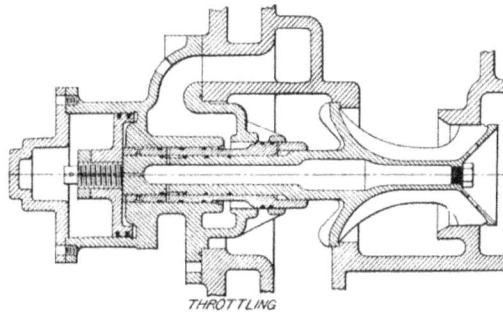
THROTTLING

Figs. 2216-2218. Intercepting Valve for Richmond Two-Cylinder Cross Compound Locomotive. American Locomotive Co.

Names of Parts of Figs. 2216 and 2219.

1. Intercepting Valve
2. Reducing Sleeve
3. Dashpot Piston
4. Dashpot Head
5. Valve Chamber Cap
6. Emergency Exhaust Valve Piston
7. Emergency Exhaust Valve
8. Emergency Exhaust Valve Spring
9. Emergency Exhaust Valve Stem

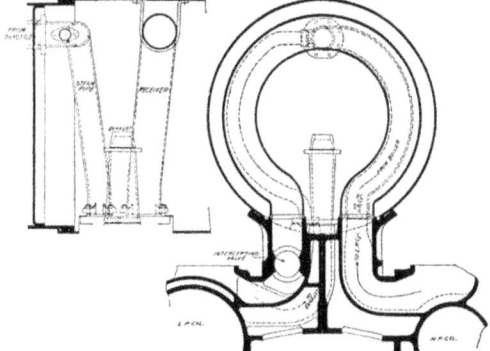
Fig. 2222. Location of Intercepting Valve for Schenectady Cross Compound Locomotives. American Locomotive Co.

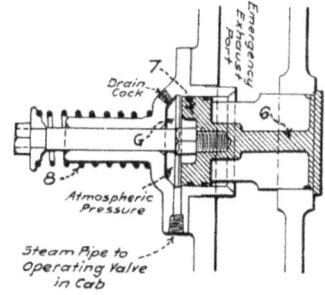
Fig. 2219. Emergency Exhaust Valve for Richmond Compound Locomotive.

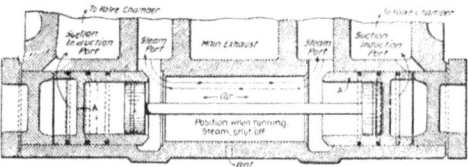
Position of Valve when Running with Steam Off.

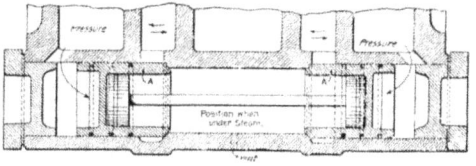
Position of Valve with Throttle Open.

Figs. 2220-2221. Over-Pass Valve of Low Pressure Cylinder of Richmond Compound Locomotive.

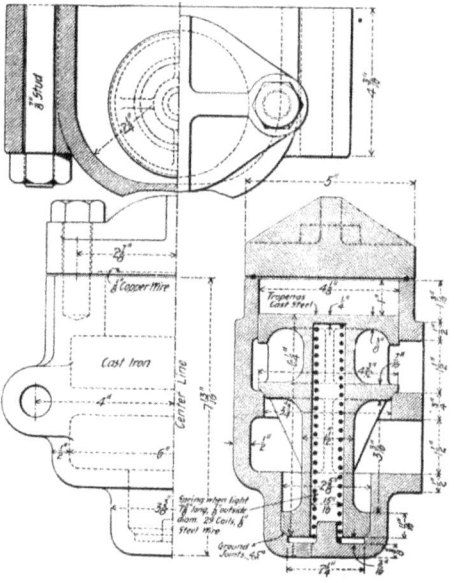
Figs. 2223-2225. Low Pressure By-Pass Valve for Schenectady Compound Locomotive.

(228)

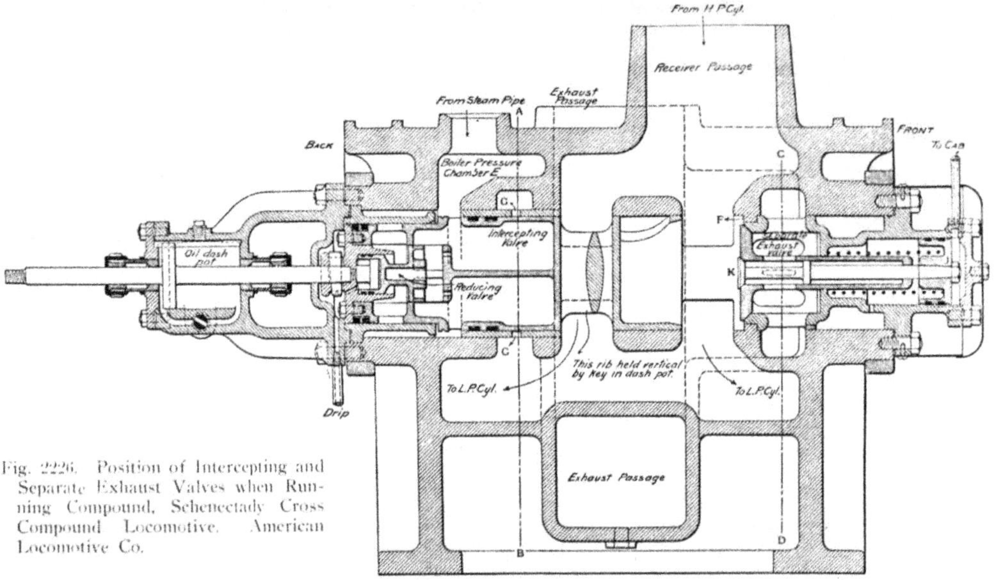

COMPOUND LOCOMOTIVES, Details; Schenectady. Figs. 2226-2230

Fig. 2226. Position of Intercepting and Separate Exhaust Valves when Running Compound, Schenectady Cross Compound Locomotive. American Locomotive Co.

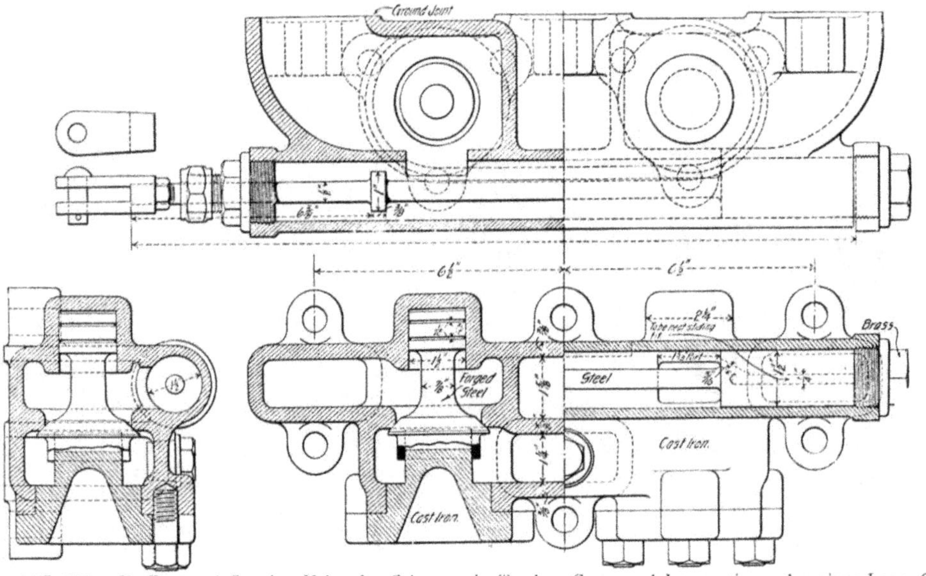

Figs. 2227-2229. By-Pass and Starting Valve for Schenectady Tandem Compound Locomotive. American Loco. Co.

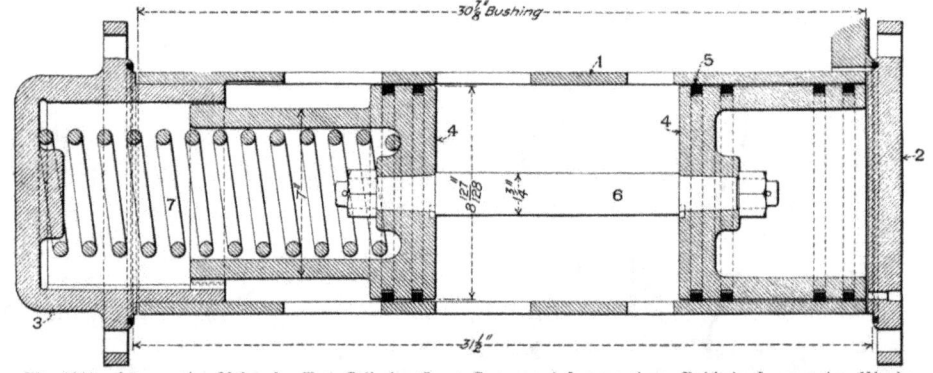

Fig. 2230. Intercepting Valve for Two-Cylinder Cross Compound Locomotive. Baldwin Locomotive Works.

Figs. 2231-2255 RUNNING BOARDS, Details.

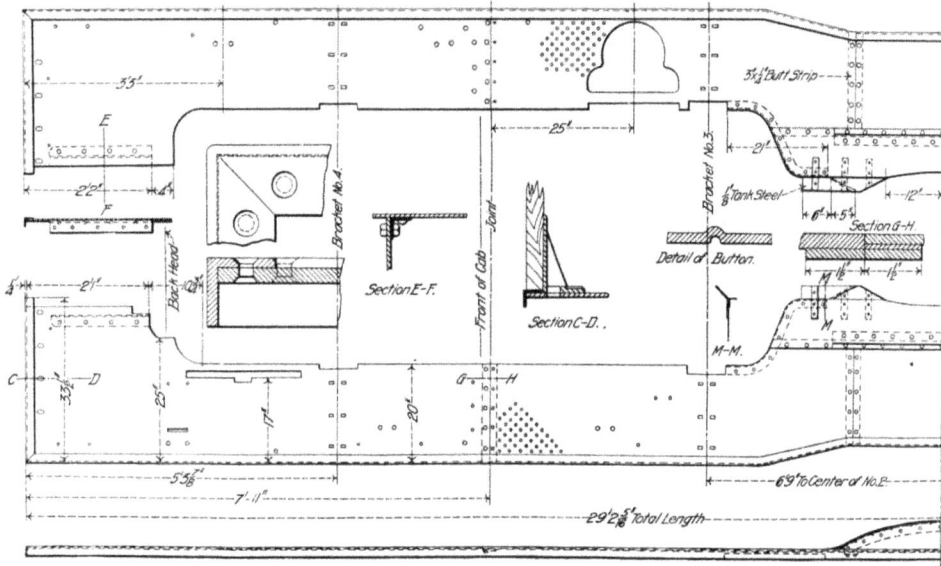

Figs. 2231-2240. Rear End of Running Board of Atlantic (4—4—2) Locomotive. Pennsylvania Railroad.

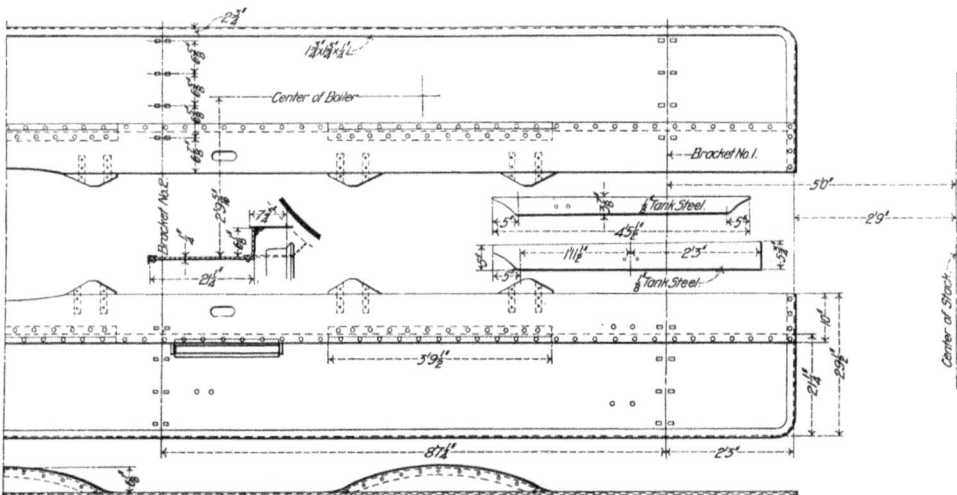

Figs. 2241-2246. Front End of Running Board of Atlantic (4—4—2) Locomotive. Pennsylvania Railroad.

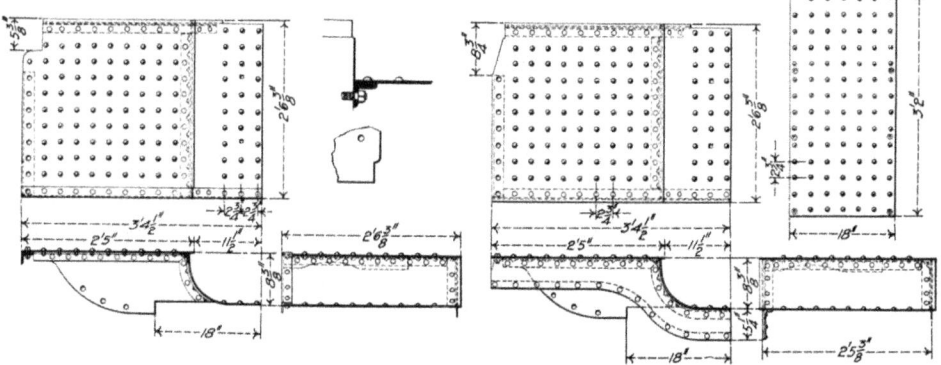

Figs. 2247-2255. Details of Front Platform of Atlantic (4—4—2) Locomotive. Pennsylvania Railroad.

PILOTS, Details. Figs. 2256-2272

Numbers Refer to List of Names of Parts with Figs. 2273-2315.

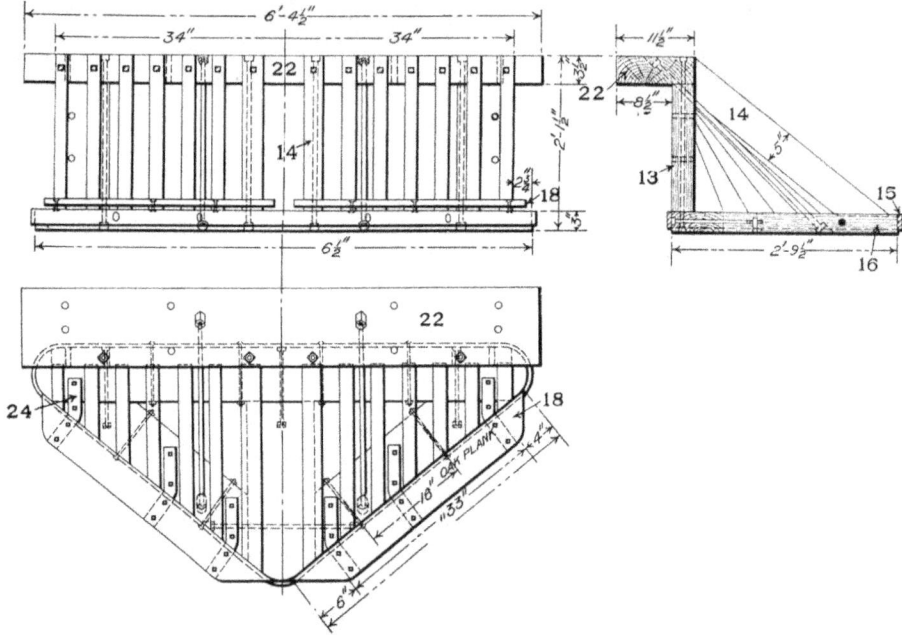

Figs. 2256-2258. Framing for Short Pilot of Atlantic (4—4—2) Locomotive. Pennsylvania Railroad.

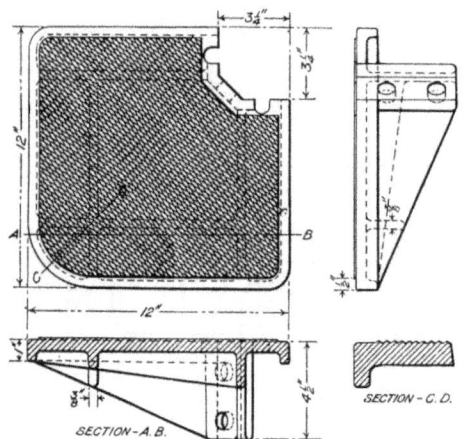

Figs. 2259-2262. Pilot Step, Atlantic (4—4—2) Locomotive. Pennsylvania Railroad.

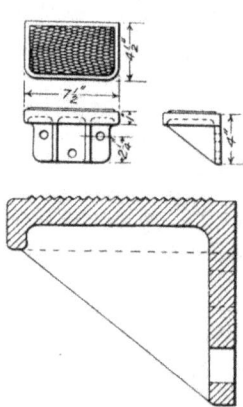

Figs. 2263-2266. Upper Pilot Step, Atlantic (4—4—2) Locomotive. P. R. R.

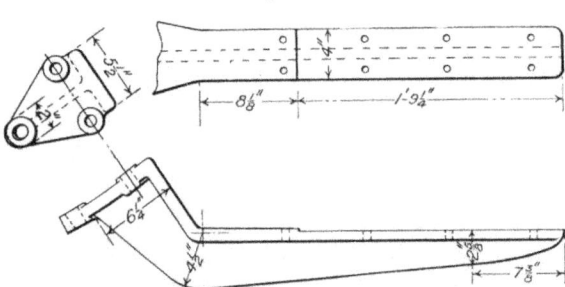

Figs. 2267-2269. Running Board Bracket, Atlantic (4—4—2) Locomotive. P. R. R.

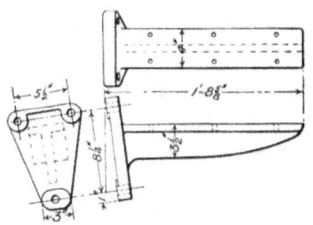

Figs. 2270-2272. Running Board Bracket, Atlantic (4—4—2) Locomotive. P. R. R.

(231)

Figs. 2273-2315   PILOTS, Details.

Numbers Refer to List of Names of Parts Below.

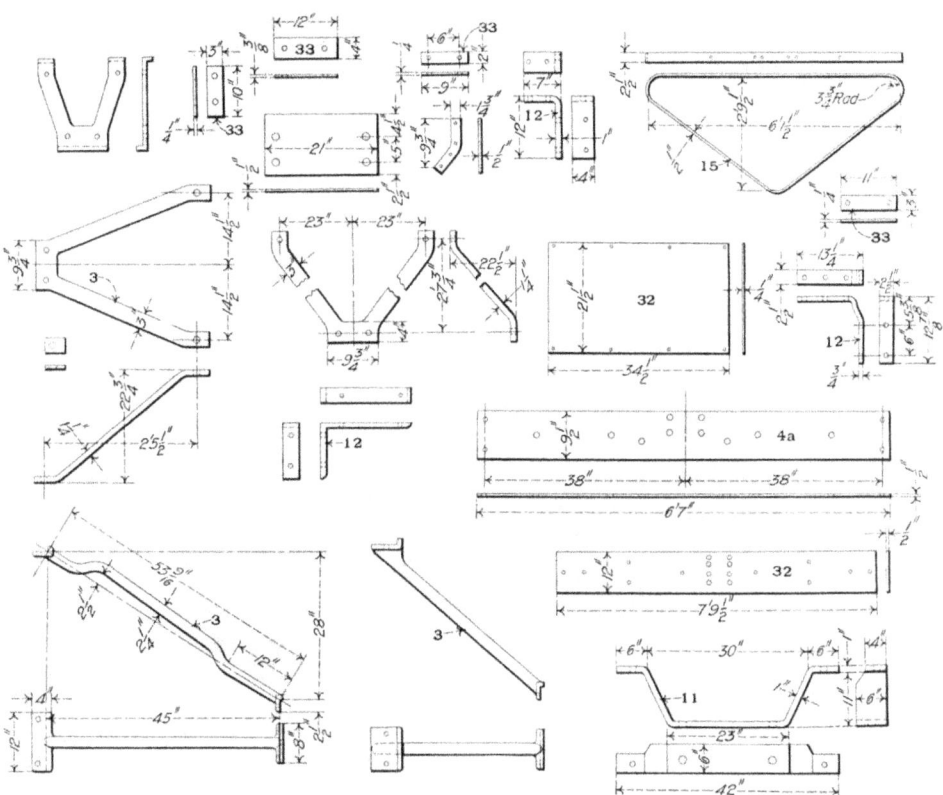

Figs. 2273-2315. Wrought Iron Details of Short Pilot for Atlantic (4-4-2) Locomotive. Pennsylvania Railroad.

Names of Parts of Pilots, Figs. 2256-2258, 2273-2318 and 2322-2327.

1 Frame	10 Coupler Knuckle Pin	19 Upper Pilot Step
2 Bumper Angle	11 Drawbar Carry Iron	20 Uncoupling Lever Shaft Bearing
3 Pilot Brace	12 Back Bar Bracket	21 Uncoupling Lever Shaft
4 Front Bumper Beam	13 Back Vertical of Pilot	22 Top Bar of Pilot
4a Front Bumper Beam Plate	14 Pilot Bars	23 Angle for Coupler and Pilot
5 Combined Bearing and Dog for Uncoupling Lever Shaft	15 Pilot Nosing	24 Pilot Step Bracket
	16 Pilot Base	28 Coupler Shank
6 Uncoupling Lever Arm	16a Pilot and Buffer Angle	29 Coupler Pivot Pin
7 Uncoupling Chain	16b Pilot Cross Tie	30 Coupler Brace
8 Coupler Head	17 Hand Hold	32 Front Platform Plate
9 Coupler Knuckle	18 Lower Pilot Step	33 Strap Washers

PILOTS, Details.

Numbers Refer to List of Names of Parts on Opposite Page.

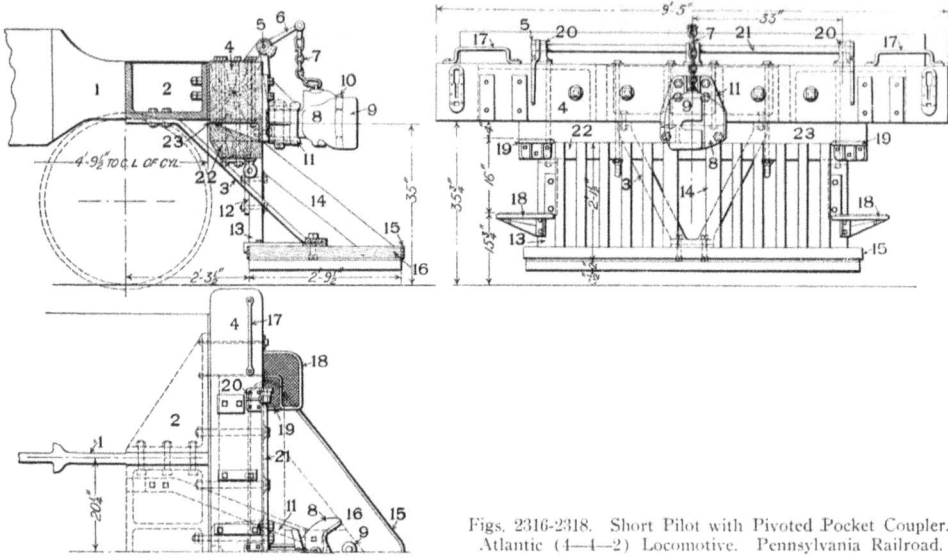

Figs. 2316-2318. Short Pilot with Pivoted Pocket Coupler. Atlantic (4—4—2) Locomotive. Pennsylvania Railroad.

Fig. 2319. Cast-Steel Pilot Beam. Davis Locomotive Wheel Co.

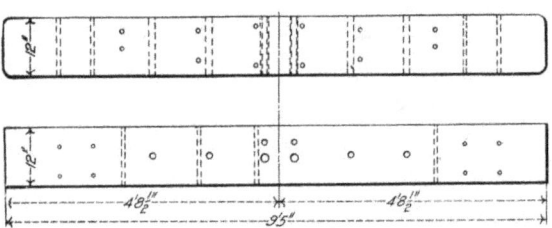

Figs. 2320-2321. Wooden Pilot Beam. Atlantic (4—4—2) Locomotive. P. R. R.

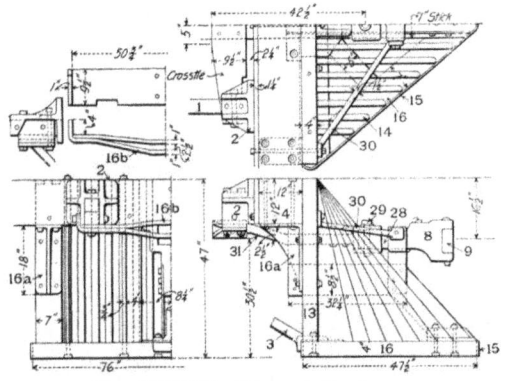

Figs. 2322-2327. Pilot and Coupler. New York Central & Hudson River.

Fig. 2328. Gould Pilot Coupler and Buffer. Gould Coupler Co.

Figs. 2329-2361 — PILOTS, Details; Couplers.

Numbers Refer to List of Names of Parts on Opposite Page

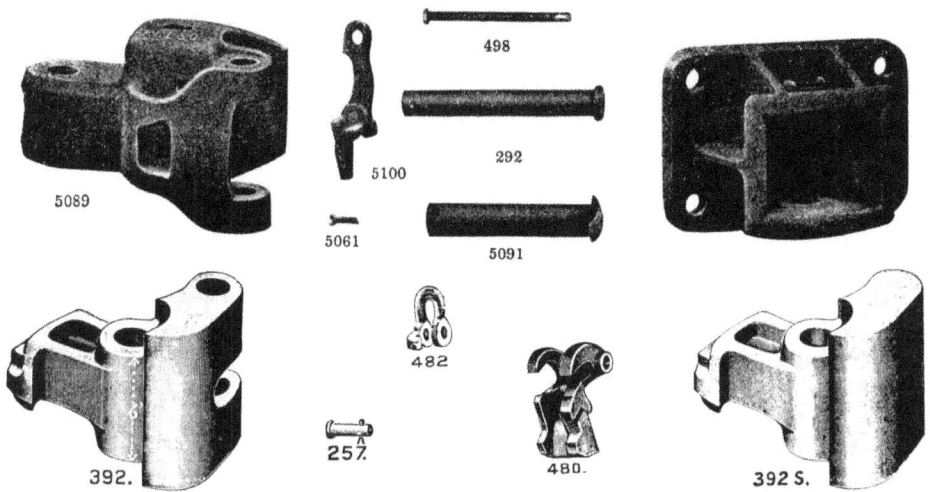

Figs. 2329-2340. Kelso Pivoted Pilot and Tender Coupler. McConway & Torley Co.

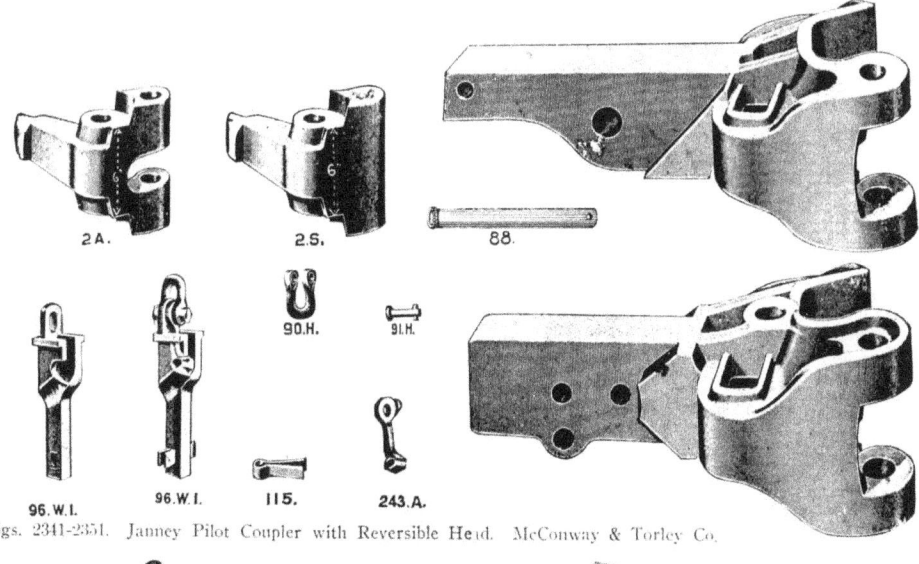

Figs. 2341-2351. Janney Pilot Coupler with Reversible Head. McConway & Torley Co.

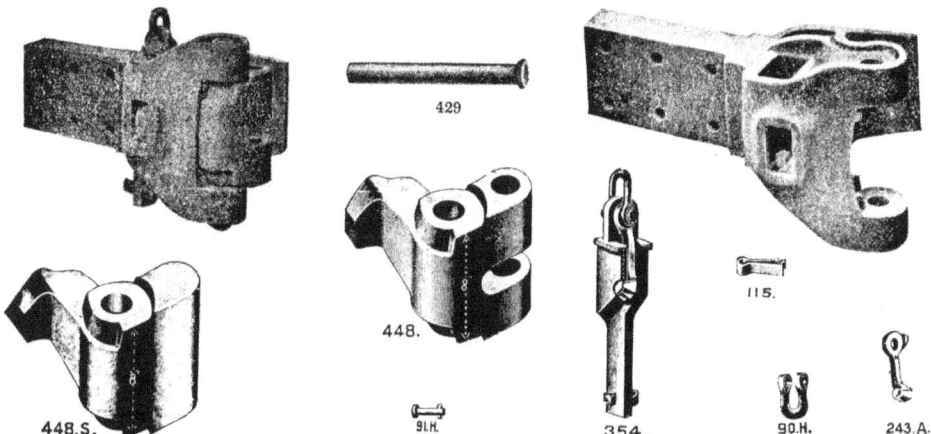

Figs. 2352-2361. Heavy Type Janney Pilot Coupler for Rigid Attachment. McConway & Torley Co.

(234)

PILOTS, Details; Couplers. Figs. 2362-2369

Names of Parts of Figs. 2329-2340.

257 *Clevis Pin*	480 *Locking Block*	5089 *Coupler Head*
292 *Knuckle Pin*	482 *Clevis*	5091 *Pivot Pin*
392 *Knuckle*	498 *Locking Block Pin*	5100 *Lock Lifter*
392S *Solid Face Knuckle*	5061 *Split Key*	

Names of Parts of Figs. 2341-2351.

2A *Wrought Knuckle*	90H *Clevis*	115 *Split Key*
2S *Solid Face Knuckle*	91H *Clevis Pin*	243A *Trigger*
88 *Knuckle Pin*	96WI *Locking Pin*	

Names of Parts of Figs. 2352-2361.

90H *Clevis*	243A *Trigger*	448 *Knuckle*
91H *Clevis Pin*	354 *Locking Pin*	448S *Solid Face Knuckle*
115 *Split Key*	429 *Knuckle Pin*	

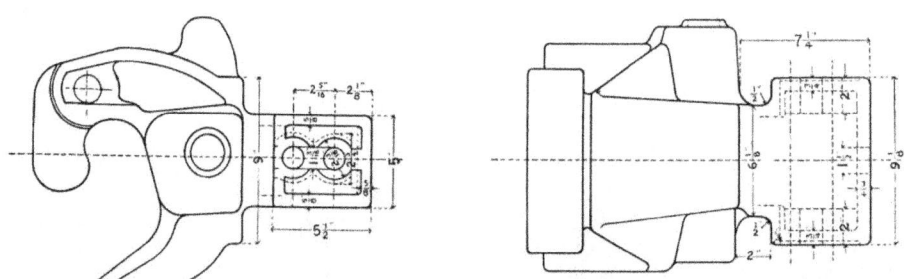

Figs. 2362-2363. Major Pilot Coupler Head for Rigid Attachment. Buckeye Steel Castings Co.

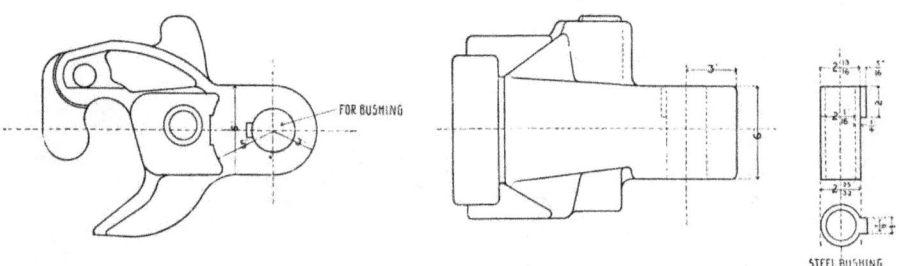

Figs. 2364-2367. Major Pilot Coupler Head for Pivoted Attachment. Buckeye Steel Castings Co.

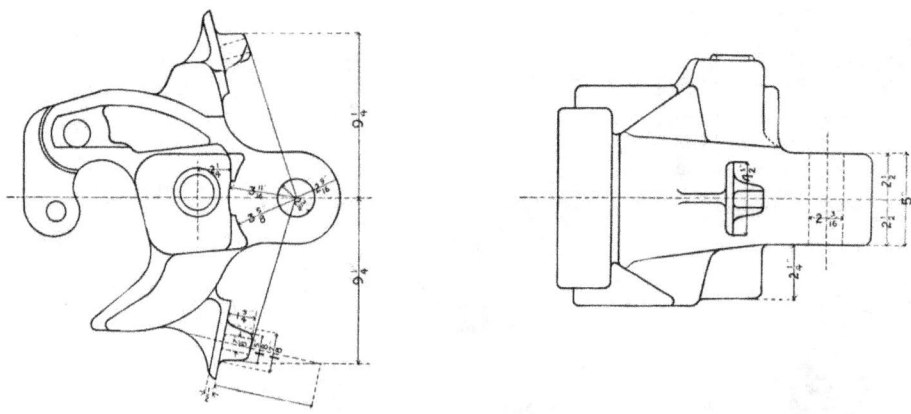

Figs. 2368-2369. Major Pilot Coupler Head for Pivoted Attachment with Side Springs. Buckeye Steel Castings Co.

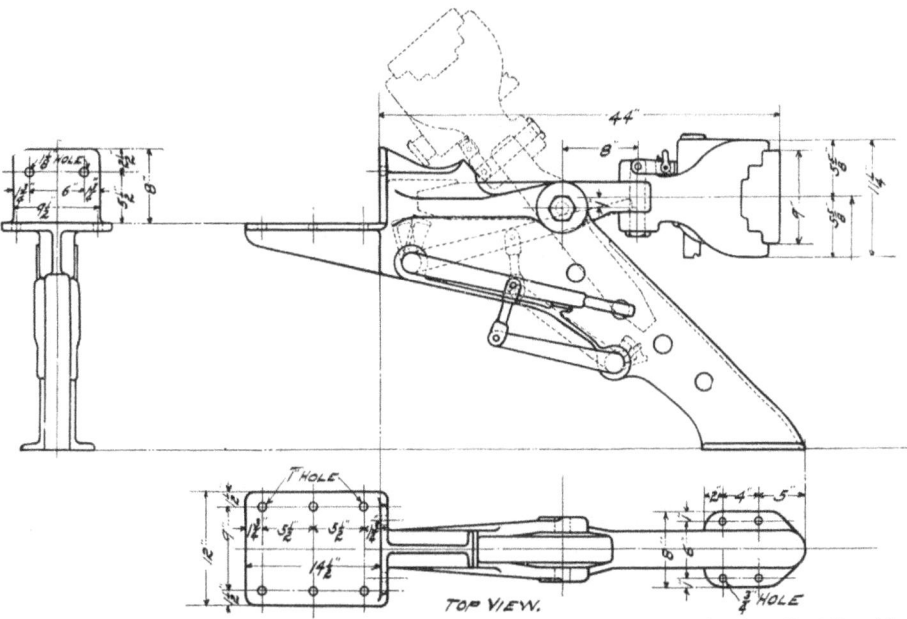

Figs. 2370-2372. Leeds Reversible Pilot Coupler with R. E. Janney Coupler Head. American Steel Foundries.

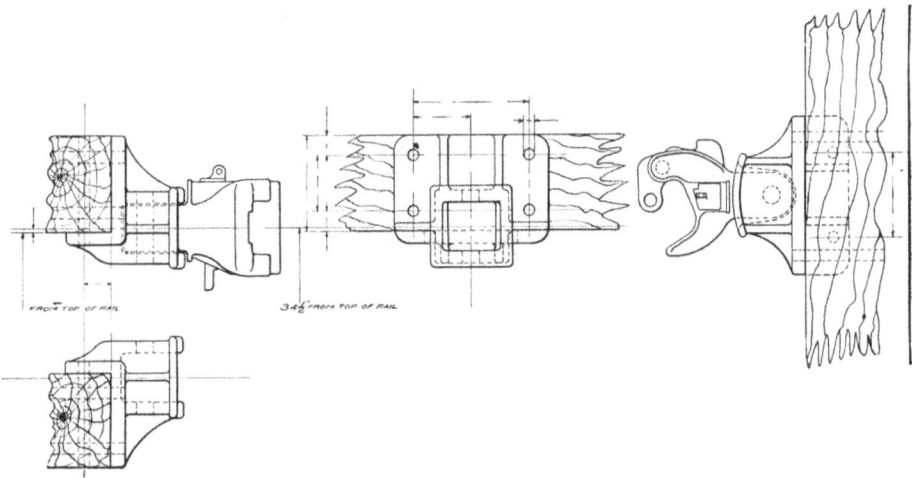

Figs. 2373-2376. R. E. Janney Pocket Coupler for Pilots or Tenders. American Steel Foundries.

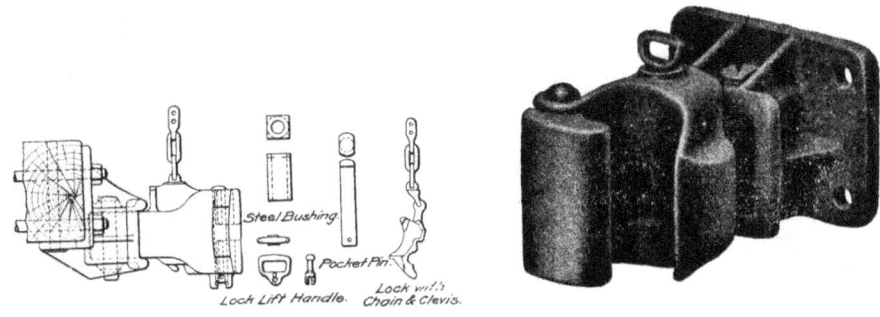

Figs. 2377-2386. Climax Pocket Coupler for Pilots or Tenders. National Malleable Castings Co.

PILOTS, Details; Couplers.   Figs. 2387-2405

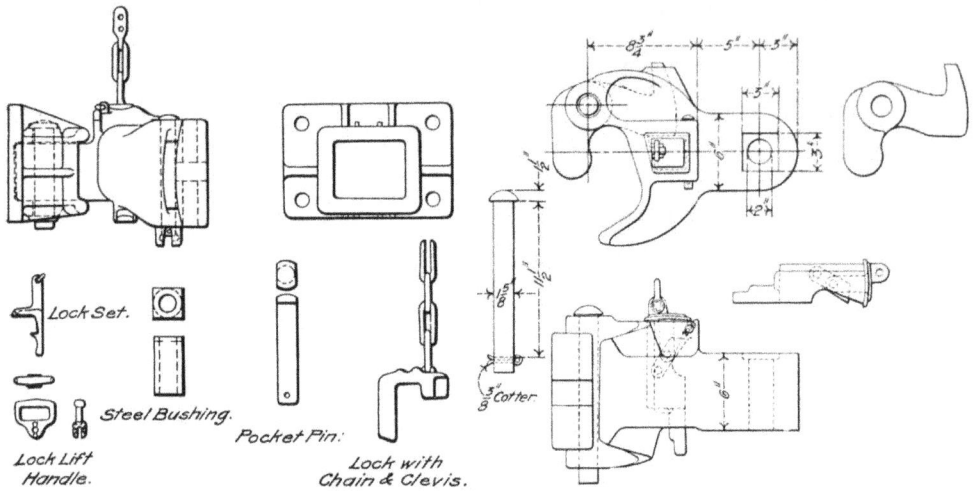

Figs. 2387-2397. Tower Pocket Coupler for Pilots or Tenders. National Malleable Castings Co.

Figs. 2398-2402. National Pivoted Pilot Coupler. National Car Coupler Co.

Fig. 2403. Washburn Pilot Coupler and Buffer. Washburn Coupler Co.

Figs. 2404-2405. Lewis-Seley Pilot Coupler and Buffer with Melrose Coupler Head. Latrobe Steel & Coupler Co.

(237)

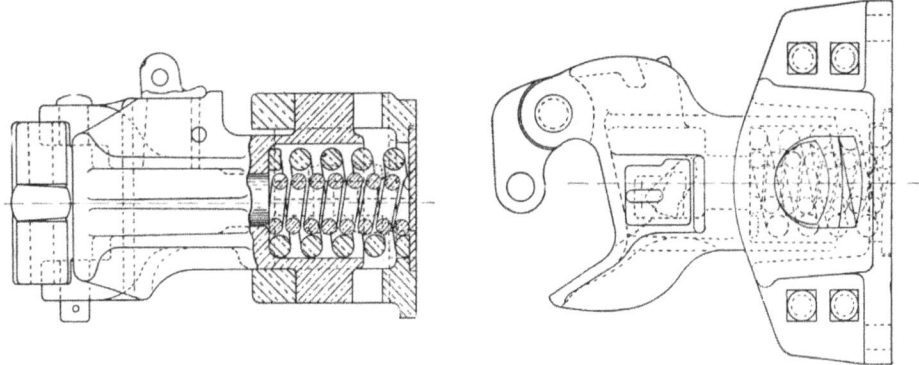

Figs. 2406-2407. Lewis-Seley Pilot Coupler and Buffer.
Latrobe Steel & Coupler Co.

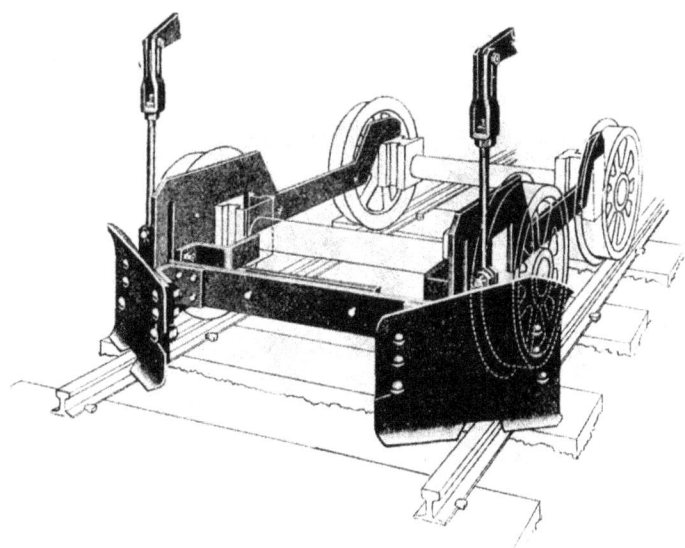

Fig. 2408. Priest Snow Flanger.
Quincy, Manchester, Sargent Co.

Fig. 2409. Priest Snow Flanger.
Quincy, Manchester, Sargent Co.

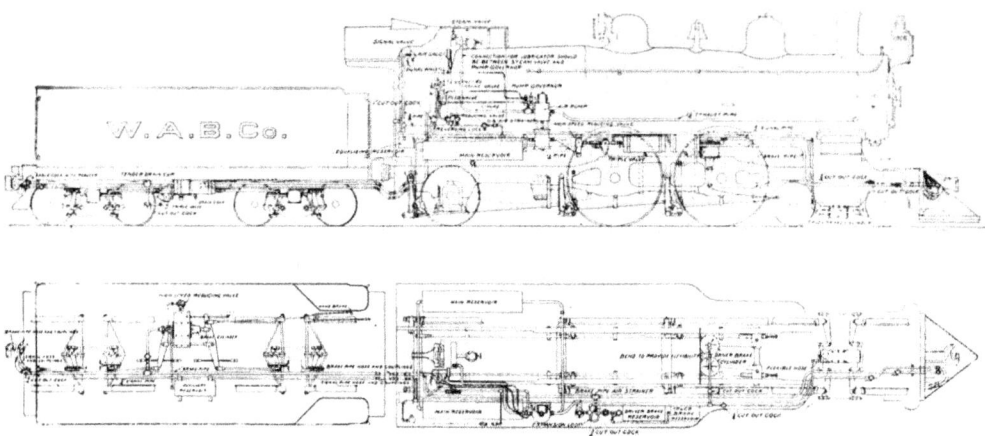

Figs. 2410-2411. General Arrangement of Westinghouse Air Brake on a High-Speed Passenger Locomotive.

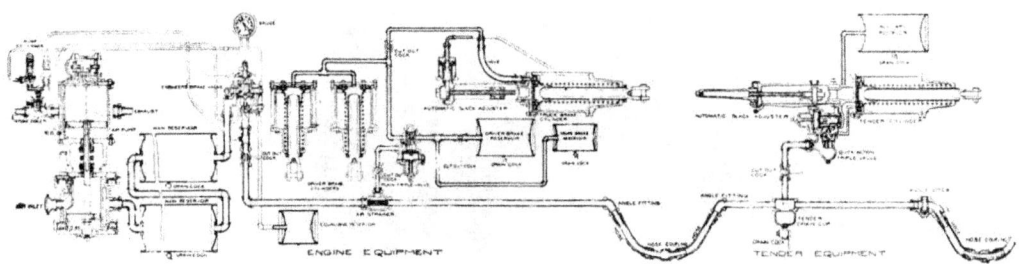

Fig. 2412. Diagram of Engine and Tender Equipment of Westinghouse Quick-Action Automatic Air Brake for Passenger Locomotives.

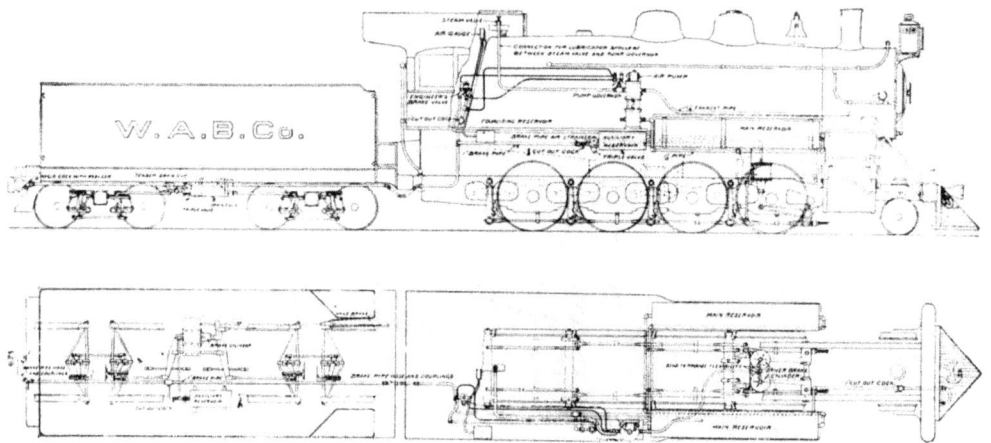

Figs. 2413-2414. General Arrangement of Westinghouse Air Brake with Double-Pressure Control on a Freight Locomotive.

BRAKE GEAR, Air; Westinghouse.

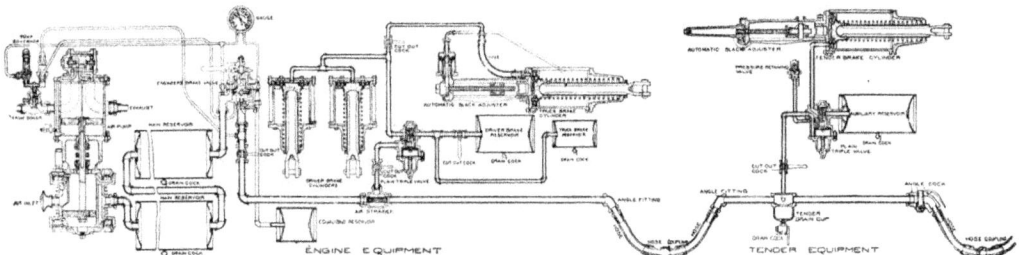

Fig. 2415. Diagram of Engine and Tender Equipment of Westinghouse Quick-Action Automatic Air Brake for Freight Locomotives.

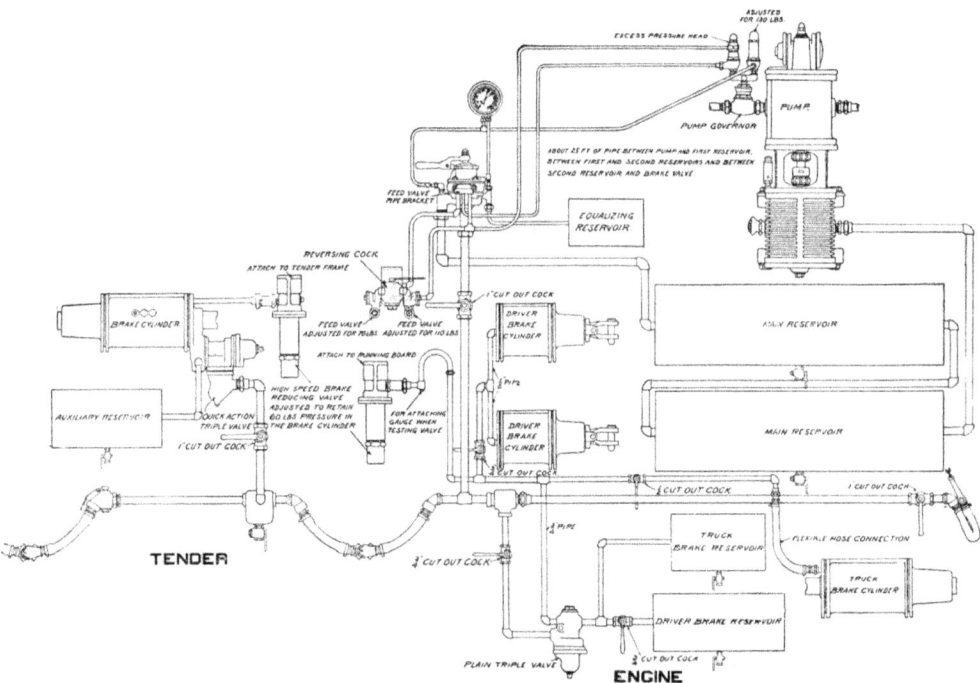

Fig. 2416. Diagram of Westinghouse High-Speed Locomotive Air Brake Equipment.

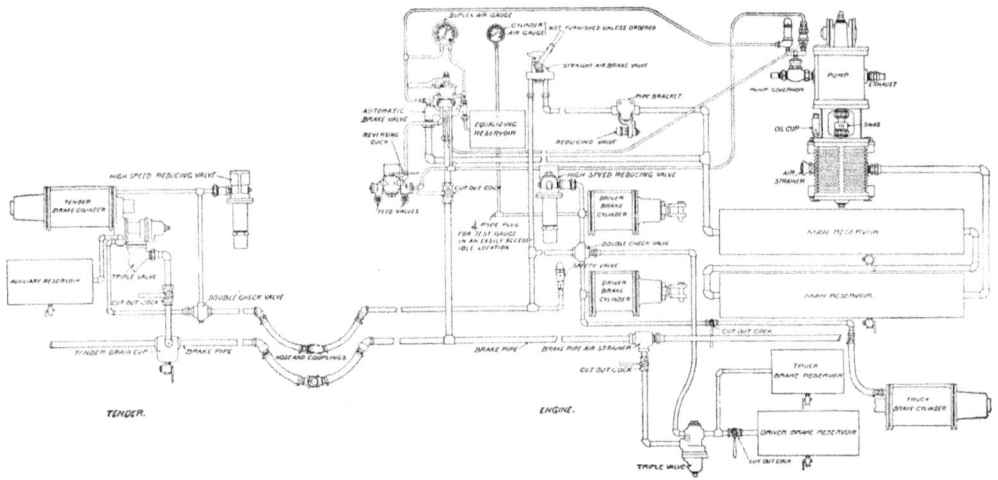

Fig. 2417. Diagram of Westinghouse Combined Automatic and Straight-Air Locomotive Brake Equipment for Passenger Locomotive with High-Speed Air Brake.

(240)

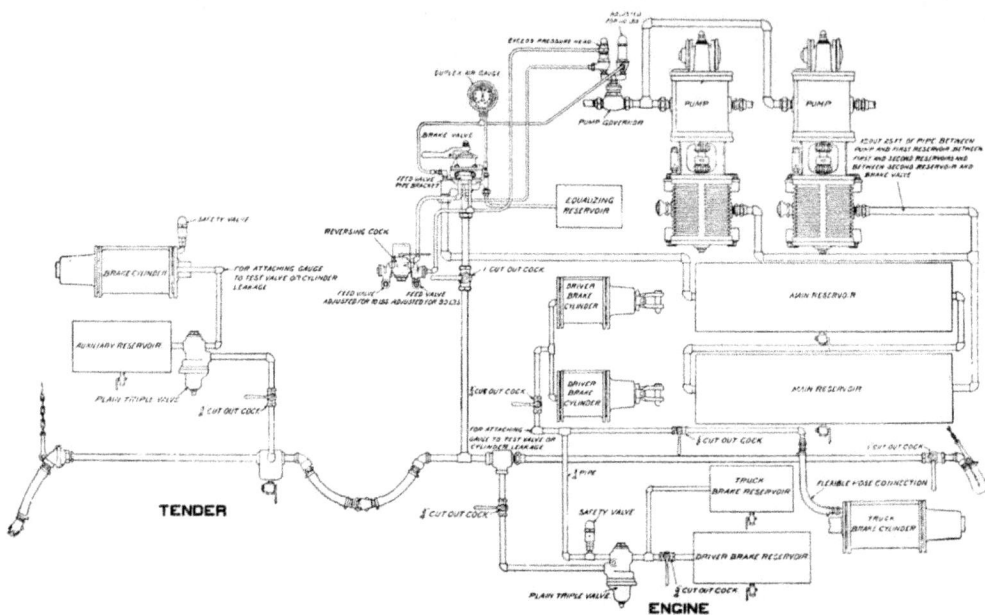

Fig. 2418. Diagram of Westinghouse Double-Pressure Control Locomotive Air Brake Equipment.

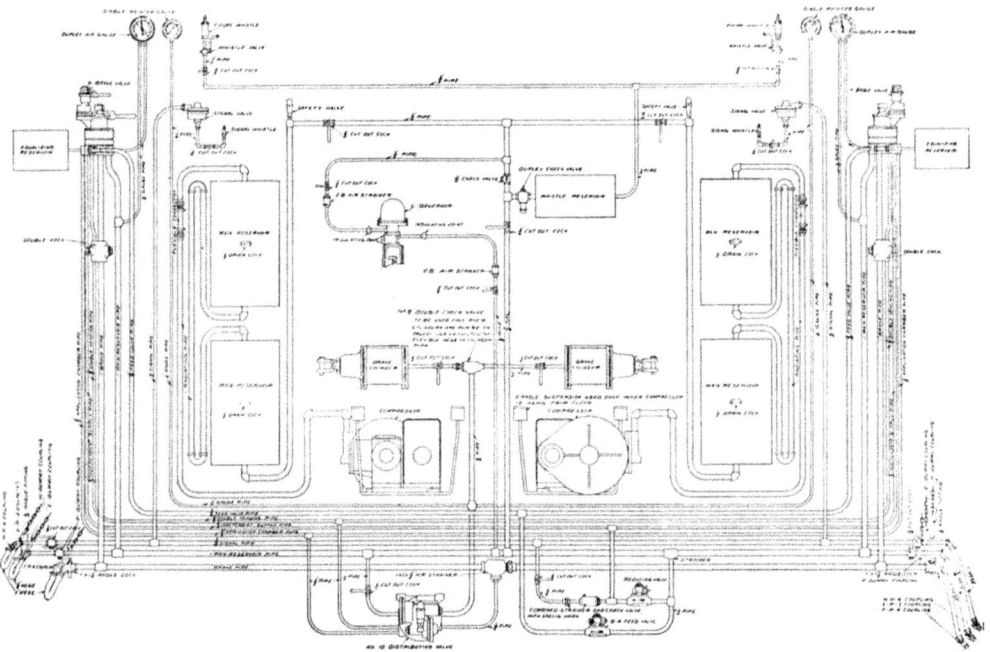

Fig. 2419. Diagram of Westinghouse E T Locomotive Air Brake Equipment for Double-End Electric Locomotive.

Figs. 2420-2422   BRAKE GEAR, Air; Westinghouse.

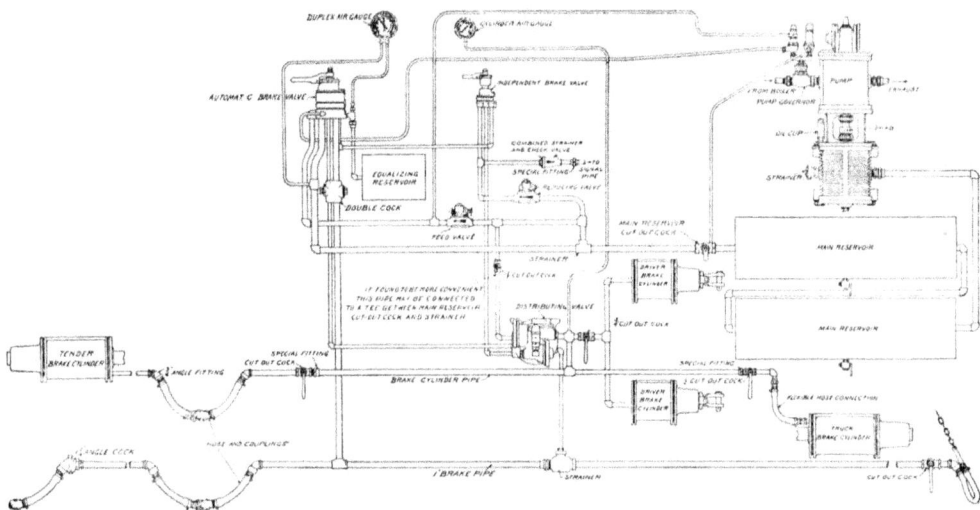

Fig. 2420. Diagram of Westinghouse E T Locomotive Air Brake Equipment.

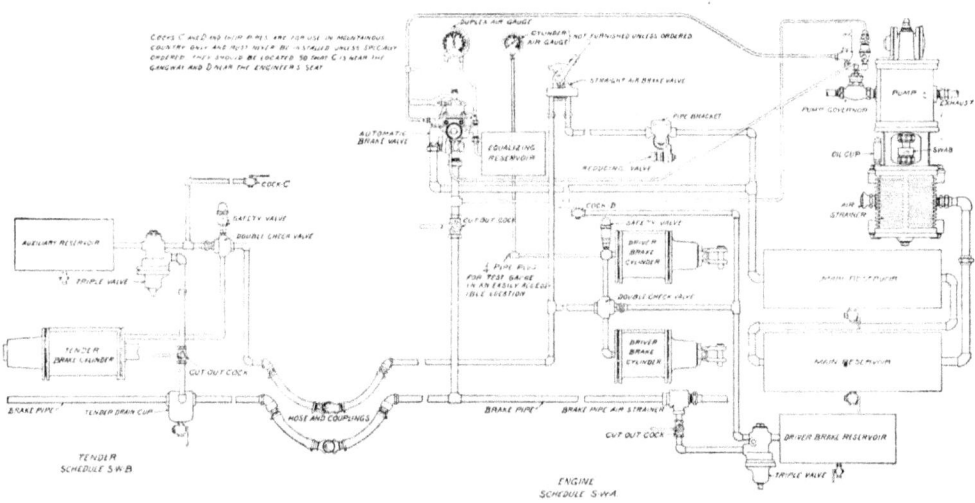

Fig. 2421. Diagram of Westinghouse Combined Automatic and Straight Air Locomotive Brake Equipment for Freight or Switching Locomotives.

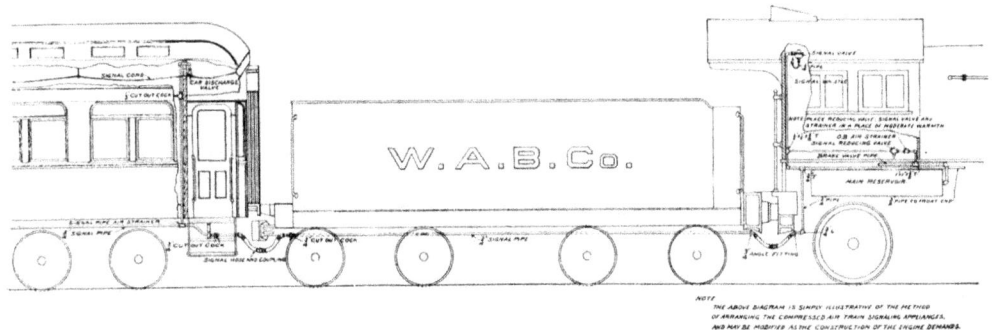

Fig. 2422. Diagram of Westinghouse Train Air Signal Equipment.

BRAKE GEAR, Air; Westinghouse. Figs. 2423-2428

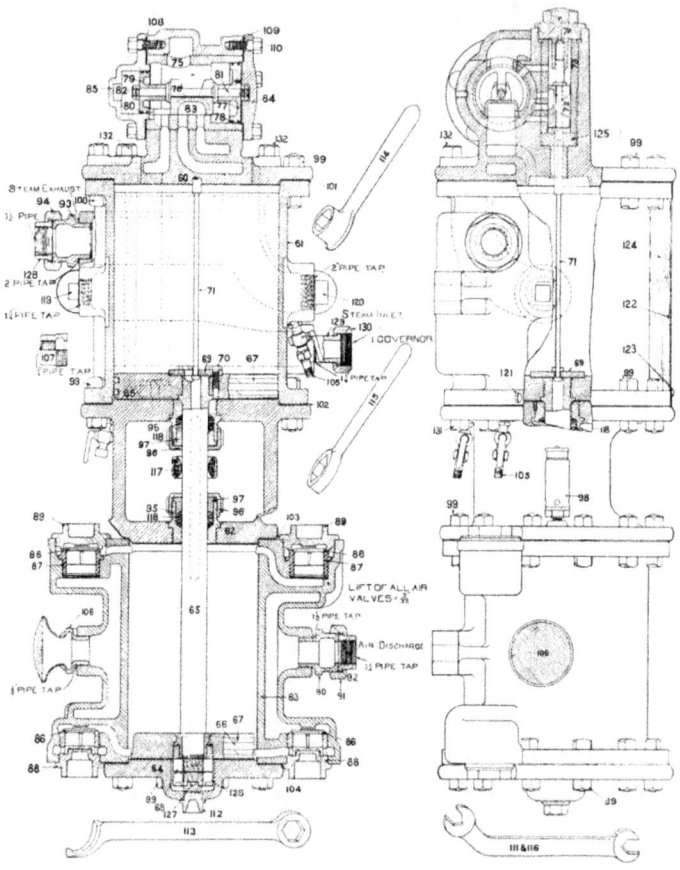

Figs. 2423-2428. Westinghouse 11-Inch Air Pump.

Names of Parts of Figs. 2423-2428.

60 Steam Cylinder Head
61 Steam Cylinder
62 Center Piece
63 Air Cylinder
64 Lower Head
65 Steam Piston and Rod
66 Air Piston
67 Piston Packing Ring
68 Piston Rod Nut
69 Reversing Valve Plate
70 Reversing Valve Plate Bolt
71 Reversing Valve Rod
72 Reversing Valve
73 Reversing Valve Chamber Bush
74 Reversing Valve Chamber Cap
75 Main Valve Bush
76 Main Valve
77 Large Main Valve Piston
78 Large Main Valve Piston Packing Ring
79 Small Main Valve Piston
80 Small Main Valve Piston Packing Ring
81 Main Valve Stem
82 Main Valve Stem Nut
83 Main Slide Valve
84 Right Main Valve Cylinder Head

85 Left Main Valve Cylinder Head
86 Air Valve
87 Air Valve Seat
88 Air Valve Cage
89 Valve Chamber Cap
90 Air Discharge Stud
91 Air Discharge Union Nut
92 Air Discharge Union Swivel
93 Steam Exhaust Stud
94 Steam Exhaust Union Nut
95 Stuffing Box
96 Stuffing Box Nut
97 Stuffing Box Gland
98 Automatic Air Cylinder Oil Cup
99 Short Cap Screw (⅜" x 2")
100 Long Tee Head Bolt (⅜" x 3⅜")
101 Upper Steam Cylinder Gasket
102 Lower Steam Cylinder Gasket
103 Upper Air Cylinder Gasket
104 Lower Air Cylinder Gasket
105 Drain Cock
106 Air Strainer
107 One-Inch Steam Pipe Sleeve
108 Left Main Valve Head Gasket
109 Right Main Valve Head Gasket

110 Main Valve Head Bolt (⅜" x 1½")
111 Cap Screw Wrench
112 Cylinder Head Plug
113 Spanner Wrench for Packing Nuts
114 Deep Socket Wrench
115 Socket Wrench
116 Cap Screw Wrench
117 Swab
118 Piston Rod Packing
119 One and One-Half Inch Pipe Plug
120 Two-Inch Pipe Plug
121 Drain Hole
122 Steam Cylinder Jacket
123 Steam Cylinder Jacket Screw
124 Steam Cylinder Lagging
125 Reversing Valve Chamber Valve Stem Bush
126 Piston Rod Jam Nut
127 Piston Rod Cotter Pin
128 Steam Exhaust Union Swivel
129 One-Inch Steam Pipe Stud
130 Governor Union Nut
131 Short Cap Screw (⅜" x 2")
132 Long Cap Screw (⅜" x 2⅞")

BRAKE GEAR, Air; Westinghouse.

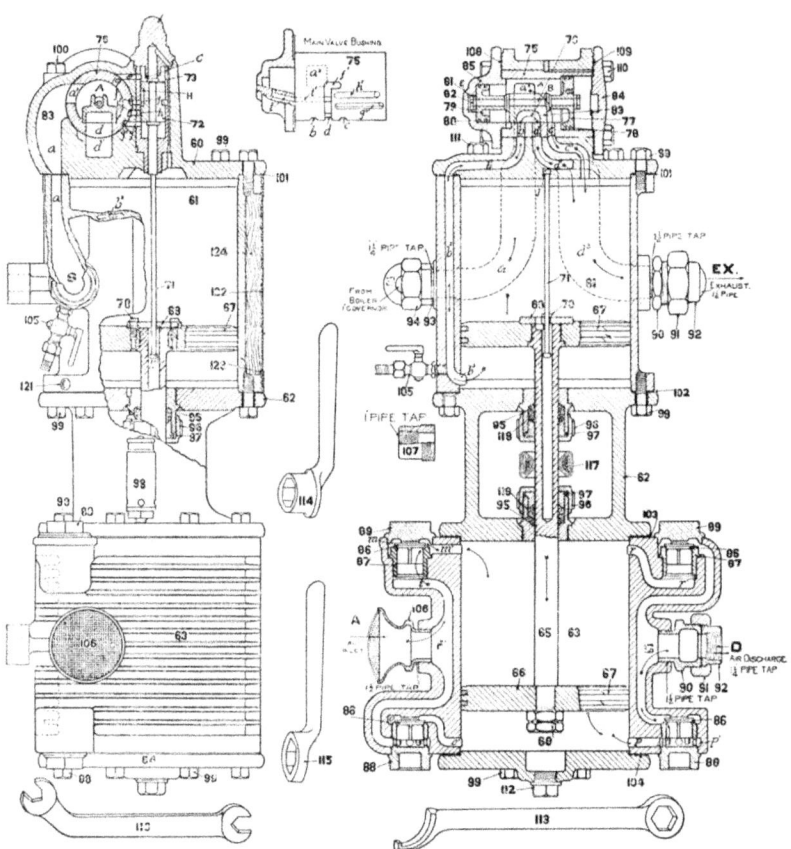

Figs. 2429-2435. Westinghouse 9½-Inch Air Pump.

Names of Parts of Figs. 2429-2435.

- 60 Steam Cylinder Head
- 61 Steam Cylinder
- 62 Center Piece
- 63 Air Cylinder
- 64 Lower Head
- 65 Steam Piston and Rod
- 66 Air Piston
- 67 Piston Packing Ring
- 68 Piston Rod Nut
- 69 Reversing Valve Plate
- 70 Reversing Valve Plate Bolt
- 71 Reversing Valve Rod
- 72 Reversing Valve
- 73 Reversing Valve Chamber Bush
- 74 Reversing Valve Chamber Cap
- 75 Main Valve Bush
- 76 Main Valve
- 77 Large Main Valve Piston
- 78 Large Main Valve Piston Packing Ring
- 79 Small Main Valve Piston
- 80 Small Main Valve Piston Packing Ring
- 81 Main Valve Stem
- 82 Main Valve Stem Nut
- 83 Main Slide Valve
- 84 Right Main Valve Cylinder Head
- 85 Left Main Valve Cylinder Head
- 86 Air Valve
- 87 Air Valve Seat
- 88 Air Valve Cage
- 89 Valve Chamber Cap
- 90 Air Discharge Stud
- 91 Air Discharge Union Nut
- 92 Air Discharge Union Swivel
- 93 Steam Exhaust Stud
- 94 Steam Exhaust Union Nut
- 95 Stuffing Box
- 96 Stuffing Box Nut
- 97 Stuffing Box Gland
- 98 Automatic Air Cylinder Oil Cup
- 99 Short Cap Screw (⅝" x 2")
- 100 Main Valve Cylinder Stud Nut
- 101 Upper Steam Cylinder Gasket
- 102 Lower Steam Cylinder Gasket
- 103 Upper Air Cylinder Gasket
- 104 Lower Air Cylinder Gasket
- 105 Drain Cock
- 106 Air Strainer
- 107 One-Inch Steam Pipe Sleeve
- 108 Left Main Valve Head Gasket
- 109 Right Main Valve Head Gasket
- 110 Main Valve Head Bolt (⅝" x 1½")
- 112 Cylinder Head Plug
- 113 Spanner Wrench for Packing Nuts
- 114 Deep Socket Wrench
- 115 Socket Wrench
- 116 Cap Screw Wrench
- 117 Swab
- 118 Piston Rod Packing
- 121 Drain Hole
- 122 Steam Cylinder Jacket
- 123 Steam Cylinder Jacket Band
- 124 Steam Cylinder Lagging

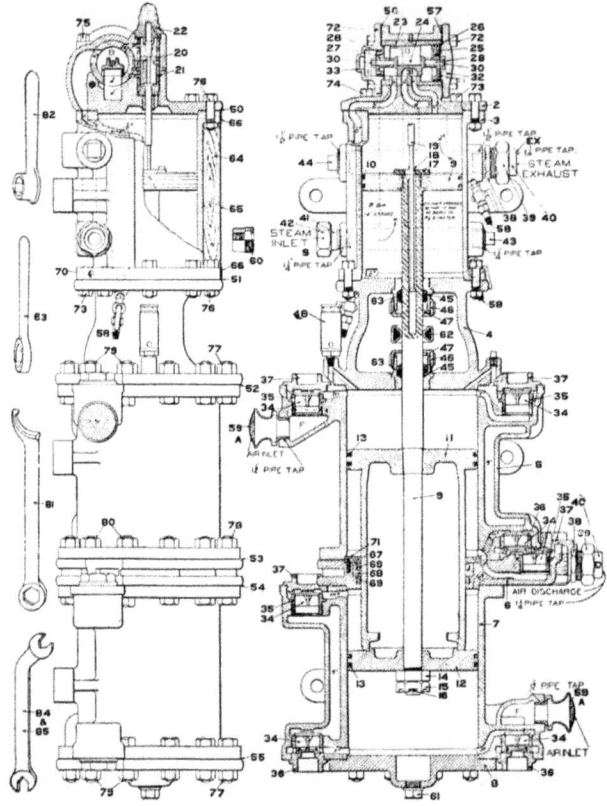

Figs. 2436-2441. Westinghouse 8-Inch Tandem Compound Air Pump.

Names of Parts of Figs. 2436-2441.

2 Steam Cylinder Head
3 Steam Cylinder
4 Center Piece
5 Low Pressure Air Cylinder
6 Air Discharge Valve Chamber
7 High Pressure Air Cylinder
8 Lower Head
9 Steam Piston and Rod
10 Steam Piston Packing Ring
11 Low Pressure Air Piston
12 High Pressure Air Piston
13 Air Piston Packing Ring
14 Piston Rod Nut
15 Piston Rod Jam Nut
16 Piston Rod Cotter Pin
17 Reversing Valve Plate
18 Reversing Valve Plate Bolt
19 Reversing Valve Rod
20 Reversing Valve
21 Reversing Valve Chamber Bush
22 Reversing Valve Chamber Cap
23 Main Valve Bush
24 Main Valve
25 Large Main Valve Piston
26 Large Main Valve Piston Packing Ring
27 Small Main Valve Piston
28 Small Main Valve Piston Packing Ring
29 Main Valve Stem
30 Main Valve Stem Nut
31 Main Slide Valve
32 Right Main Valve Cylinder Head
33 Main Valve Cylinder Cap

34 Air Valve
35 Air Valve Seat
36 Air Valve Cage
37 Valve Chamber Cap
38 Steam Exhaust Stud
39 Union Nut on Exhaust Outlet
40 Union Swivel on Exhaust Outlet
41 Steam Inlet Stud
42 Steam Inlet Union Nut
43 One and One-Quarter-Inch Pipe Plug
44 One and One-Half-Inch Pipe Plug
45 Stuffing Box
46 Stuffing Box Nut
47 Stuffing Box Gland
48 Automatic Air Cylinder Oil Cup
50 Upper Steam Cylinder Head Gasket
51 Lower Steam Cylinder Head Gasket
52 Low Pressure Air Cylinder Upper Gasket
53 Low Pressure Air Cylinder Lower Gasket
54 High Pressure Air Cylinder Upper Gasket
55 High Pressure Air Cylinder Lower Gasket
56 Left Main Valve Head Gasket
57 Right Main Valve Head Gasket
58 Drain Cock

59 Air Inlet
60 Steam Inlet Swivel Bushing
61 Cylinder Head Plug
62 Piston Rod Swab
63 Piston Rod Packing
64 Steam Cylinder Lagging
65 Steam Cylinder Jacket
66 Steam Cylinder Jacket Band
67 Diaphragm Ring Between High and Low Pressure Air Cylinders
68 Gland Between High and Low Pressure Air Cylinders
69 Packing Ring for Gland
70 Drain Hole
71 Diaphragm Ring Screw
72 Left Main Valve Cylinder Head
73 Steam Cylinder Head Short Cap Screw
74 Long Cap Screw
75 Main Valve Cylinder Stud Nut
76 Steam Cylinder Head Cap Screw
77 Air Cylinder Head Short Cap Screw
78 Air Cylinder Head Long Cap Screw
79 Air Inlet Valve Chamber Bolt
80 Air Valve Chamber Bolt
81 Spanner Wrench for Packing Nut
82 Deep Socket Wrench
83 Socket Wrench
84 Cap Screw Wrench
85 Cap Screw Wrench

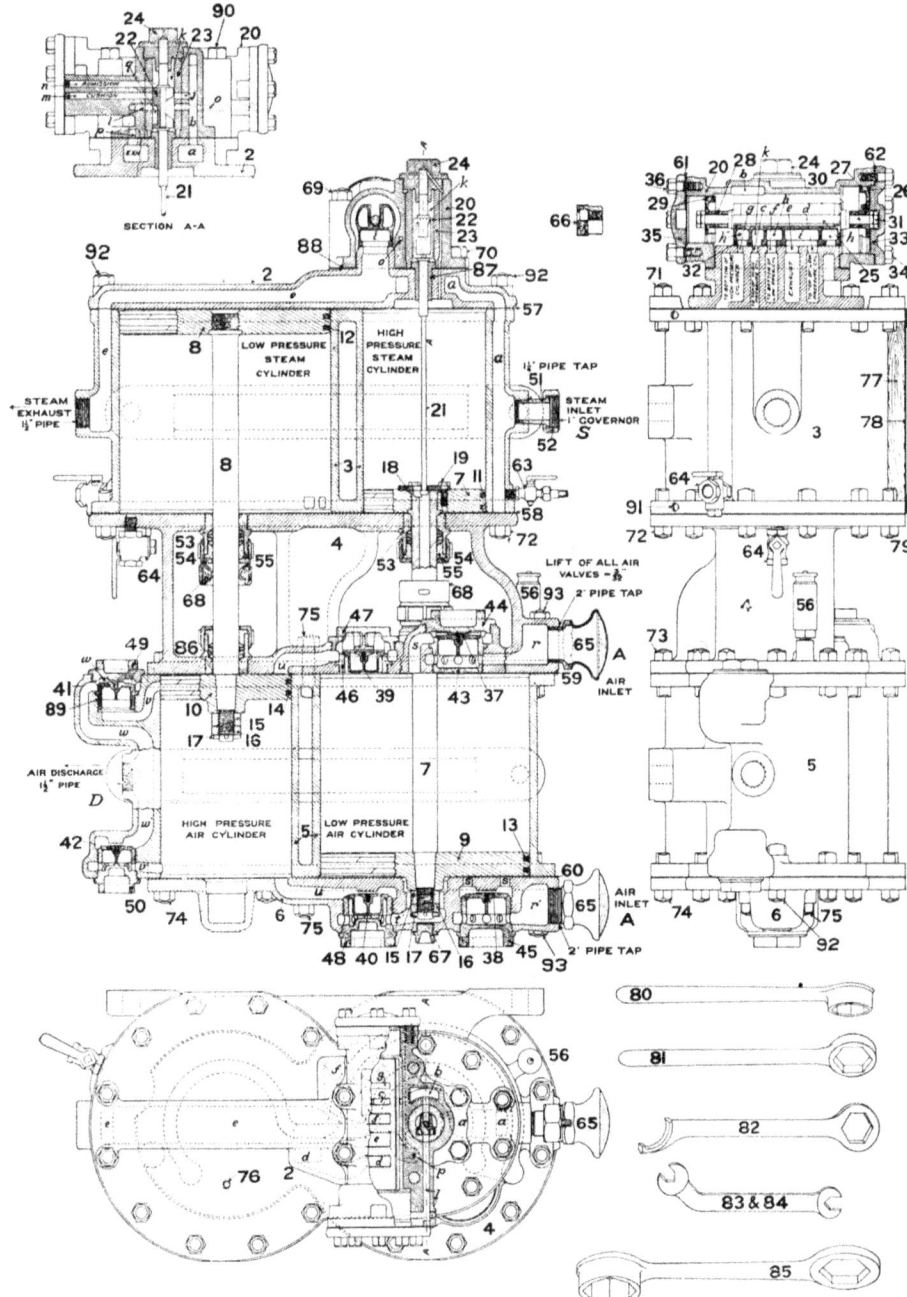

Figs. 2442-2450. Westinghouse 8½-Inch Cross-Compound Air Pump.

Names of Parts of Figs. 2442-2450.

- 2 *Steam Cylinder Top Head*
- 3 *Low Pressure Steam Cylinder*
- 4 *Center Piece*
- 5 *High Pressure Air Cylinder*
- 6 *Bottom Head of Air Cylinders*
- 7 *High Pressure Steam Piston and Rod*
- 8 *Low Pressure Steam Piston and Rod*
- 9 *Low Pressure Air Piston*
- 10 *High Pressure Air Piston*
- 11 *High Pressure Steam Piston Packing Ring*
- 12 *Low Pressure Steam Piston Packing Ring*
- 13 *Low Pressure Air Piston Packing Ring*
- 14 *High Pressure Air Piston Packing Ring*
- 15 *Air Piston Rod Nut*
- 16 *Air Piston Rod Jam Nut*
- 17 *Air Piston Rod Cotter Pin*
- 18 *Reversing Valve Plate*
- 19 *Reversing Valve Plate Bolt*
- 20 *Reversing Valve Cylinder*
- 21 *Reversing Valve Rod*
- 22 *Reversing Valve*
- 23 *Reversing Valve Chamber Bush*
- 24 *Reversing Valve Chamber Cap*
- 25 *Main Valve*

Names of Parts of Figs. 2442-2450 (Continued).

26 Large Main Valve Piston	45 Air Inlet Valve Cage	62 Right Main Valve Head Gasket
27 Large Main Valve Piston Packing Ring	46 Low Pressure Air Discharge Valve Seat	63 Drain Cock
28 Small Main Valve Piston	47 Low Pressure Air Discharge Valve Cap	64 Drain Cock
29 Small Main Valve Piston Packing Ring	48 Low Pressure Air Discharge Valve Cage	65 Air Inlet
30 Main Valve Stem	49 High Pressure Air Discharge Valve Cap	66 Steam Pipe Union Swivel Bushing
31 Main Valve Stem Nut	50 High Pressure Air Discharge Valve Cage	67 Cylinder Head Plug
32 Main Slide Valve	51 Steam Pipe Union Stud	68 Piston Rod Swab
33 Right Main Valve Cylinder Head	52 Steam Pipe Union Nut	69 Main Valve Cylinder Stud
34 Right Main Valve Cylinder Head Bolt	53 Stuffing Box	70 Reversing Valve Chamber Stud
35 Left Main Valve Cylinder Head	54 Stuffing Box Nut	71 Steam Cylinder Head Cap Bolt
36 Left Main Valve Cylinder Head Bolt	55 Stuffing Box Gland	72 Steam Cylinder Head Cap Bolt
37 Low Pressure Air Inlet Valve	56 Automatic Air Cylinder Oil Cup	73 Air Cylinder Head Cap Bolt
38 Air Inlet Valve	57 Upper Steam Cylinder Head Gasket	74 Air Cylinder Head Cap Bolt
39 Low Pressure Air Discharge Valve	58 Lower Steam Cylinder Head Gasket	75 Air Cylinder Head Stud Bolt
40 Low Pressure Air Discharge Valve	59 Upper Air Cylinder Head Gasket	76 Pipe Plug
41 High Pressure Air Valve	60 Lower Air Cylinder Head Gasket	77 Steam Cylinder Lagging
42 High Pressure Air Valve	61 Left Main Valve Head Gasket	78 Steam Cylinder Jacket
43 Air Inlet Valve Cage		79 Steam Cylinder Jacket Band
44 Air Inlet Valve Cap		80 Socket Wrench
		81 Socket Wrench
		82 Spanner Wrench for Stuffing Box Nut
		83 Cap Nut Wrench
		84 Cap Nut Wrench
		85 Double End Socket Wrench

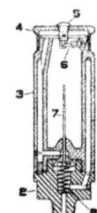

Fig. 2451. Westinghouse Automatic Air-Cylinder Oil Cup.

Names of Parts of Fig. 2451.

2 Oil Cup Base
3 Oil Cup Body
4 Oil Cup Cap
5 Oil Cup Cap Pin
6 Cap Hinge Chain
7 Feed Spindle
8 Feed Spring

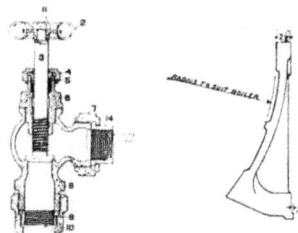

Fig. 2452. Steam Valve for Westinghouse Air Pump.

Names of Parts of Fig. 2452.

2 Valve Stem Handle
3 Valve Stem
4 Valve Stem Gland Nut
5 Valve Stem Gland
6 Valve Stem Cap
7 Union Nut
8 Valve Body
9 Bushing
10 Coupling Nut
11 Valve Stem Nut
14 Union Swivel

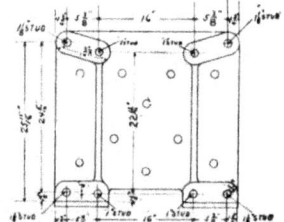

Figs. 2453-2454. Pump Bracket for 11-Inch Standard and 8½-Inch Cross-Compound Air Pumps.

Fig. 2455. Air Pump Lubricator.

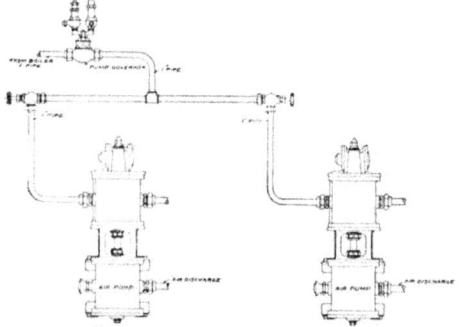

Fig. 2456. Arrangement of Two Air Pumps with One Air Pump Governor.

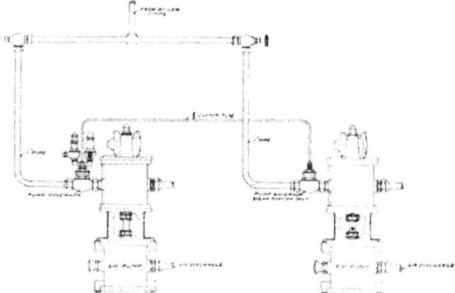

Fig. 2457. Arrangement of Two Air Pumps with One Complete Air Pump Governor and Steam Portion of Pump Governor.

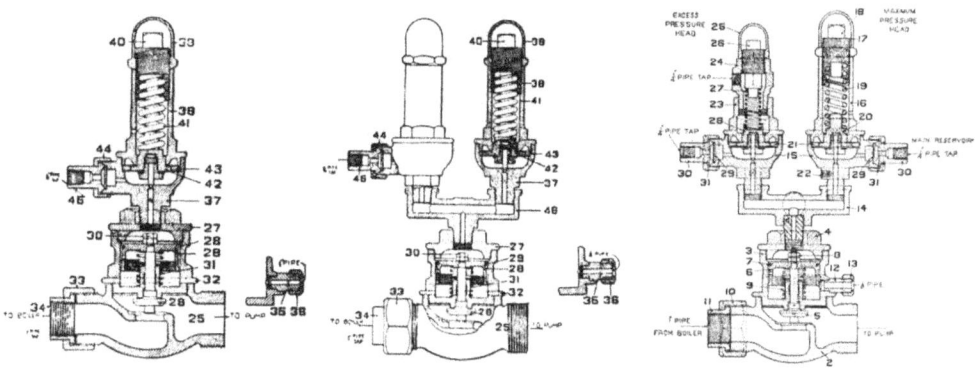

Figs. 2458-2459. One-Inch Single Pump Governor, S-4.

Figs. 2460-2461. Duplex Pump Governor, S D-4.

Fig. 2462. Duplex Pump Governor, S F-4.

Names of Parts of Figs. 2458-2459.

25 Steam Valve Body
26 Steam Valve
27 Cylinder Cap
28 Governor Piston
29 Piston Packing Ring
30 Governor Piston Nut
31 Governor Piston Spring
32 Steam Valve Cylinder
33 One-Inch Union Nut
34 One-Inch Union Swivel
35 Waste Pipe Stud
36 Waste Pipe Union Nut
37 Diaphragm Body
38 Spring Box
39 Check Nut
40 Regulating Nut
41 Regulating Spring
42 Diaphragm, Complete
43 Diaphragm Ring
44 Union Nut
45 Union Swivel

Names of Parts of Figs. 2460-2461.

25 Steam Valve Body
26 Steam Valve
27 Cylinder Cap
28 Governor Piston
29 Piston Packing Ring
30 Governor Piston Nut
31 Governor Piston Spring
32 Steam Valve Cylinder
33 One-Inch Union Nut
34 One-Inch Union Nut
35 Waste Pipe Stud
36 Waste Pipe Union Nut
37 Diaphragm Body
38 Spring Box
39 Check Nut
40 Regulating Nut
41 Regulating Spring
42 Diaphragm, Complete
43 Diaphragm Ring
44 Union Nut
45 Union Swivel
46 Siamese Fitting

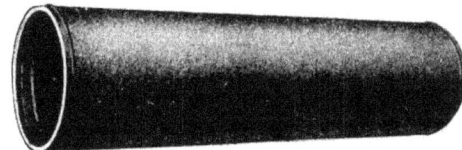

Fig. 2463. Main Reservoir.

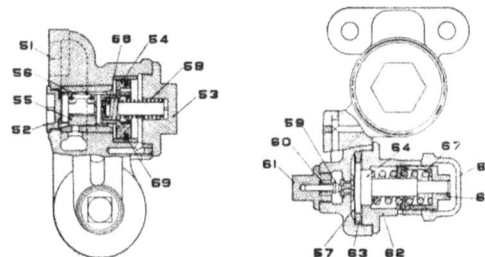

Figs. 2464-2465. Slide-Valve Feed Valve, B-3.

Names of Parts of Figs. 2464-2465.

51 Valve Body
52 Flush Nut
53 Supply Valve Cap Nut
54 Supply Valve Piston
55 Supply Valve
56 Supply Valve Spring
57 Diaphragm
58 Supply Valve Piston Spring
59 Regulating Valve
60 Regulating Valve Spring
61 Regulating Valve Cap Nut
62 Regulating Spring Case
63 Diaphragm Ring
64 Diaphragm Spindle
65 Regulating Nut
66 Cap Check Nut
67 Adjusting Spring

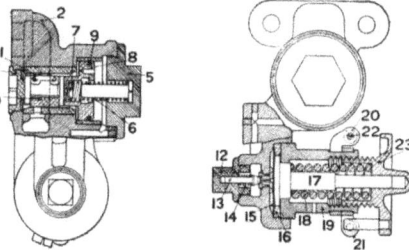

Figs. 2466-2467. High and Low Pressure Slide-Valve Feed Valve, B-4.

Names of Parts of Figs. 2466-2467.

2 Valve Body
4 Flush Nut
5 Cap Nut
6 Supply Valve Piston Spring
7 Supply Valve Spindle
8 Supply Valve Piston
9 Packing Ring
10 Supply Valve
11 Supply Valve Spring
12 Regulating Valve Cap Nut
13 Regulating Valve Spindle
14 Regulating Valve Spring
15 Diaphragm
16 Diaphragm Ring
17 Diaphragm Spindle
18 Adjusting Spring
19 Spring Box
20 Stud Bolt Bracket
21 Stud Bolt Bracket
22 Stud Bolt
23 Check Nut

BRAKE GEAR, Air; Westinghouse. Figs. 2468-2473

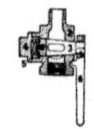

Fig. 2468.
Main Reservoir
Drain Cock.

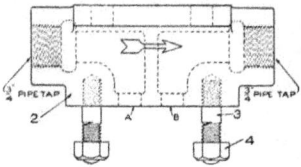

Fig. 2469. Feed Valve Pipe Bracket.

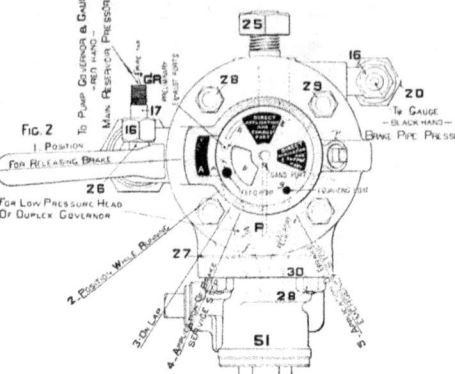

Fig. 2471. Plan.

Names of Parts of Fig. 2468.

2 Cock Body
3 Cock Key
4 Cock Cap Nut
5 Cock Key Spring
6 Cock Handle

Fig. 2470. Feed Valve Pipe Bracket Gasket.

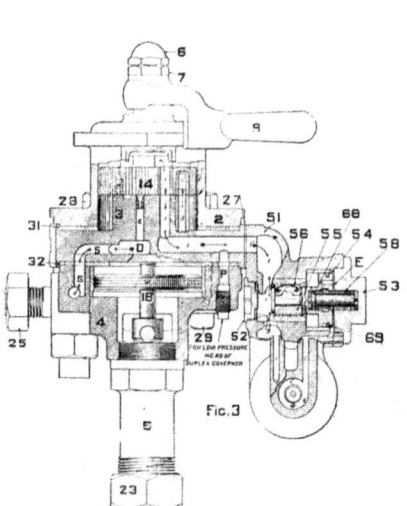

Fig. 2472. Section.   Fig. 2473. Section.

Figs. 2471-2473. Westinghouse G-6 Engineer's Brake Valve.

Names of Parts of Figs. 2471-2473.

2 Top Case	17 Small Union Swivel	30 Bolt or Stud
3 Upper Valve Body	18 Equalizing Piston	31 Upper Body Gasket
4 Lower Valve Body	19 Packing Ring	32 Lower Body Gasket
5 Union Nipple to Brake Pipe	20 Large Union Nut	33 Rotary Valve Spring
6 Top Nut, or Handle Lock Nut	21 Large Union Swivel	34 Oil Plug
7 Handle Nut	22 Train Pipe or Brake Pipe Exhaust	51 Feed Valve Body
8 Handle	23 Union Nut	52 Flush Nut
9 Handle Latch	24 Union Bushing	53 Cap Nut
10 Handle Latch Spring	25 Bracket Stud Nut	54 Supply Valve Piston
11 Handle Latch Screw	26 Elbow Nut for Pump Governor and Gage Connection	55 Supply Valve
12 Rotary Valve Key	27 Gasket	56 Supply Valve Spring
13 Reservoir Pressure Gasket	28 Stud Nut	58 Supply Valve Piston Spring
14 Rotary Valve	29 Stud Nut	68 Supply Valve Spindle
15 Brake Valve Tee		69 Packing Ring
16 Small Union Nut		

Names of Parts of Figs. 2474-2476.

2 Rotary Valve Seat	11 Housing Screw	20 Oil Plug
3 Valve Body	12 Return Spring Clutch	21 Upper Gasket
4 Pipe Bracket	13 Cover	22 Lower Gasket
5 Rotary Valve	14 Cover Screw	23 Holding Stud
6 Rotary Valve Key	15 Handle	24 Holding Stud Nut
7 Rotary Valve Spring	16 Top Nut	25 Bolt and Nut
8 Key Washer	17 Latch Spring	26 Cap Screw
9 Return Spring	18 Latch	
10 Return Spring Housing	19 Latch Screw	

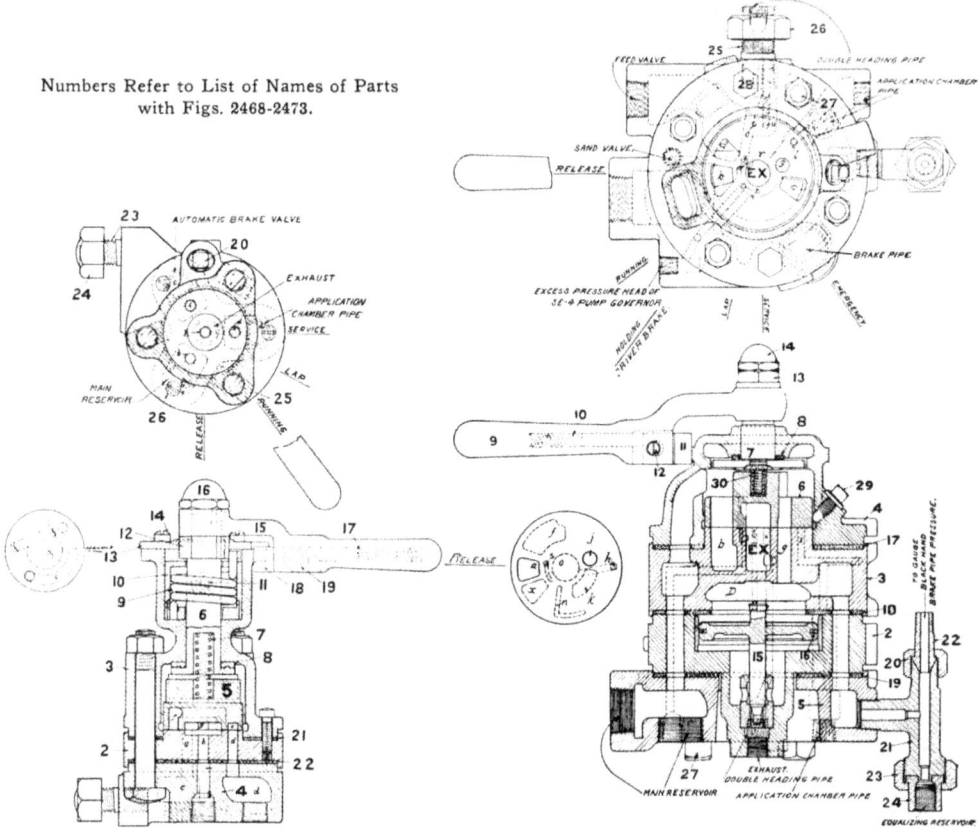

Figs. 2474-2476. Westinghouse S F Independent Engineer's Brake Valve.

Figs. 2477-2479. Westinghouse H-5 Automatic Engineer's Brake Valve.

Names of Parts of Figs. 2477-2479.

2	Bottom Case	12	Handle Latch Screw	22	Small Union Swivel
3	Rotary Valve Seat	13	Handle Nut	23	Large Union Nut
4	Top Case	14	Handle Lock Nut	24	Large Union Swivel
5	Pipe Bracket	15	Equalizing Piston	25	Bracket Stud
6	Rotary Valve	16	Equalizing Piston Packing Ring	26	Bracket Stud Nut
7	Rotary Valve Key	17	Valve Seat Upper Gasket	27	Bolt and Nut
8	Key Washer	18	Valve Seat Lower Gasket	28	Cap Screw
9	Handle	19	Pipe Bracket Gasket	29	Oil Plug
10	Handle Latch Spring	20	Small Union Nut	30	Rotary Valve Spring
11	Handle Latch	21	Brake Valve Tee		

Names of Parts of Fig. 2480.

2	Valve Seat Upper Gasket	12	Handle Latch Screw	26	Valve Seat Lower Gasket
3	Rotary Valve Seat	13	Valve	27	Pipe Bracket Gasket
4	Bottom Case	14	Gasket	34	Independent Brake Valve Handle
5	Pipe Bracket	15	Spring		
6	Rotary Valve	16	Cap Nut	38	Housing Screw
7	Rotary Valve Key	18	Key Screw	44	Handle Latch
8	Key Washer	19	Rotary Valve Spring	45	Latch Spring
9	Automatic Brake Valve Handle	20	Equalizing Piston	46	Latch Screw
10	Handle Latch Spring	21	Packing Ring	48	Cover Screw
11	Handle Latch	24	Plug	50	Bolt and Nut

Names of Parts of Figs. 2481-2482.

2	Valve Body	9	Spring Washer	16	Handle
3	Shaft Cap Nut	10	Shaft Spring	17	Latch Spring
4	Valve Cap	11	Valve	18	Latch
5	Quadrant	12	Valve Disk	19	Latch Screw
6	Quadrant Stud	13	Valve Packing Ring	20	Handle Stud
7	Valve Shaft	14	Check Valve Nut	21	Handle Screw
8	Shaft Washer	15	Check Valve Spring	22	Handle Stud Pin

BRAKE GEAR, Air; Westinghouse. Figs. 2480-2489

Numbers Refer to List of Names of Parts on Opposite Page.

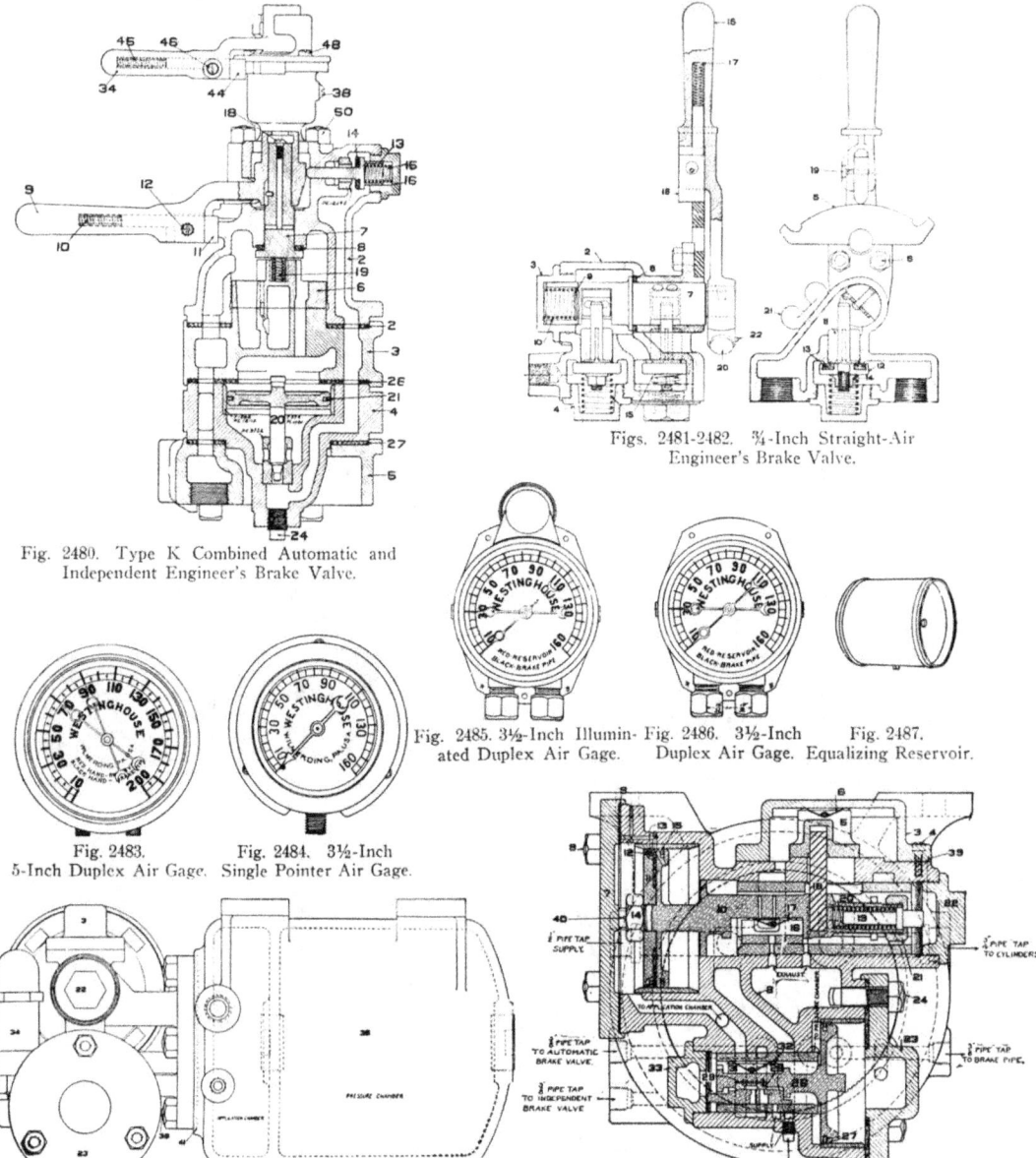

Fig. 2480. Type K Combined Automatic and Independent Engineer's Brake Valve.

Figs. 2481-2482. ¾-Inch Straight-Air Engineer's Brake Valve.

Fig. 2483. 5-Inch Duplex Air Gage.

Fig. 2484. 3½-Inch Single Pointer Air Gage.

Fig. 2485. 3½-Inch Illuminated Duplex Air Gage.

Fig. 2486. 3½-Inch Duplex Air Gage.

Fig. 2487. Equalizing Reservoir.

Fig. 2488. Distributing Valve and Double Chamber Reservoir.

Fig. 2489. Section Through Distributing Valve.

Names of Parts of Fig. 2489.

2 *Body*
3 *Supply Valve Cover*
4 *Supply Valve Cover Screw*
5 *Supply Valve*
6 *Supply Valve Spring*
7 *Cylinder Cover*
8 *Cylinder Cover Bolt and Nut*
9 *Cylinder Cover Gasket*
10 *Main Piston*
11 *Main Piston Follower*
12 *Packing Leather*
13 *Packing Leather Expander*
14 *Main Piston Nut*

15 *Main Piston Packing Ring*
16 *Exhaust Valve*
17 *Exhaust Valve Spring*
18 *Supply Valve Stem*
19 *Main Piston Graduating Stem*
20 *Main Piston Graduating Spring*
21 *Main Piston Graduating Stem Nut*
22 *Cap Nut and Piston Stop*
23 *Cylinder Cap*
24 *Cylinder Cap Bolt and Nut*
25 *Cylinder Cap Gasket*
26 *Equalizing Piston*

27 *Equalizing Piston Packing Ring*
28 *Equalizing Piston Graduating Valve*
29 *Graduating Valve Spring*
31 *Equalizing Slide Valve*
32 *Equalizing Slide Valve Spring*
33 *Cap Nut*
38 *Pipe Plug in Distributing Valve Body*
39 *Supply Valve Cover Gasket*
40 *Cotter for Main Piston*

(251)

BRAKE GEAR, Air; Westinghouse.

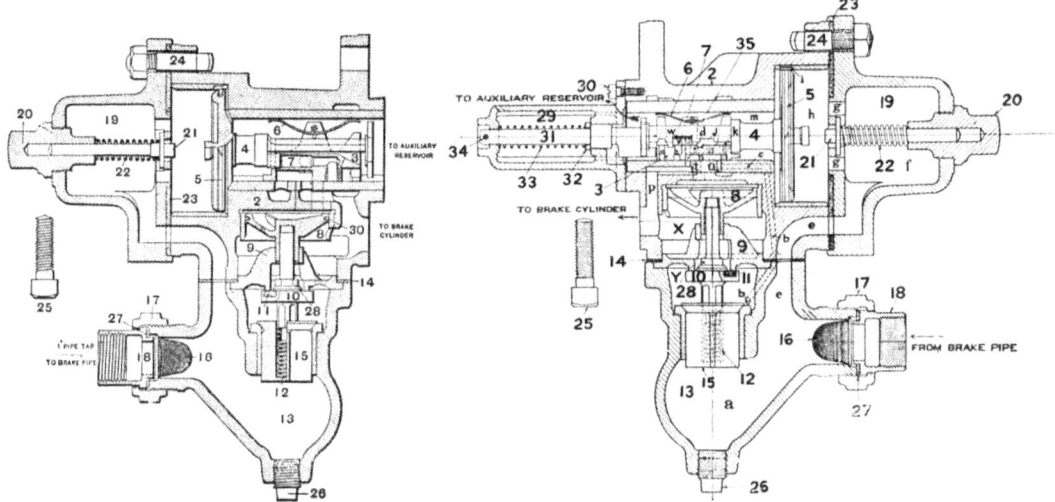

Fig. 2490. Quick-Action Triple Valve, Type P.

Fig. 2491. Quick-Service Triple Valve with Retarding Device, Type K.

Names of Parts of Fig. 2490.

#	Part	#	Part	#	Part
2	Triple Valve Body	12	Check Valve Spring	22	Graduating Spring
3	Slide Valve	13	Check Valve Case	23	Cylinder Cap Gasket
4	Piston	14	Check Valve Case Gasket	24	Bolt and Nut
5	Packing Ring	15	Check Valve	25	Half-Inch Cap Screw
6	Slide Valve Spring	16	Strainer	26	Half-Inch Plug
7	Graduating Valve	17	Union Nut	27	Union Gasket
8	Emergency Valve Piston	18	Union Swivel	28	Emergency Valve Nut
9	Emergency Valve Seat	19	Cylinder Cap	29	Cotter Pin
10	Emergency Valve	20	Graduating Stem Nut	30	Emergency Valve Piston Packing Ring
11	Rubber Seat	21	Graduating Stem		

Names of Parts of Figs. 2491-2493.

#	Part	#	Part	#	Part
2	Triple Valve Body	13	Check Valve Case	24	Bolt and Nut
3	Slide Valve	14	Check Valve Case Gasket	25	Half-Inch Cap Screw
4	Piston	15	Check Valve	26	Half-Inch Pipe Plug
5	Packing Ring	16	Strainer	27	Union Gasket
6	Slide Valve Spring	17	Union Nut	28	Emergency Valve Nut
7	Graduating Valve	18	Union Swivel	29	Retarding Device Body
8	Emergency Valve Piston	19	Cylinder Cap	30	Retarding Device Screw
9	Emergency Valve Seat	20	Graduating Stem Nut	31	Retarding Device Stem
10	Emergency Valve	21	Graduating Stem	32	Retarding Device Spring Collar
11	Rubber Seat	22	Graduating Spring	33	Retarding Device Spring
12	Check Valve Spring	23	Cylinder Cap Gasket	34	Retarding Device Spring Pin

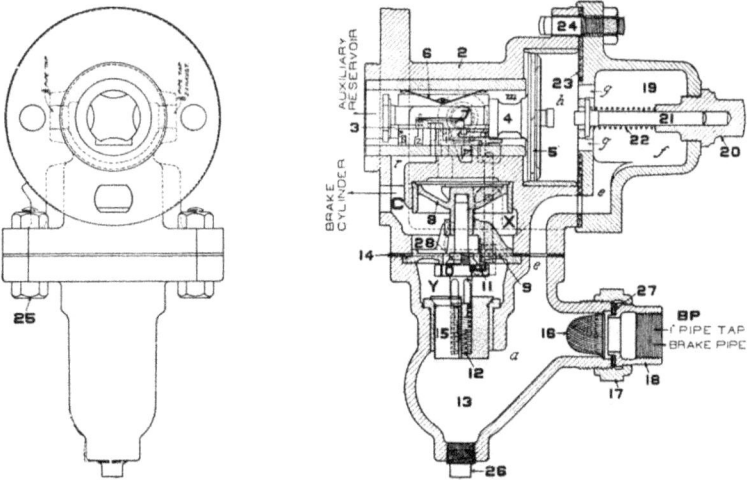

Figs. 2492-2493. Triple Valve with Graduated Release. Type Q.

(252)

BRAKE GEAR, Air; Westinghouse.

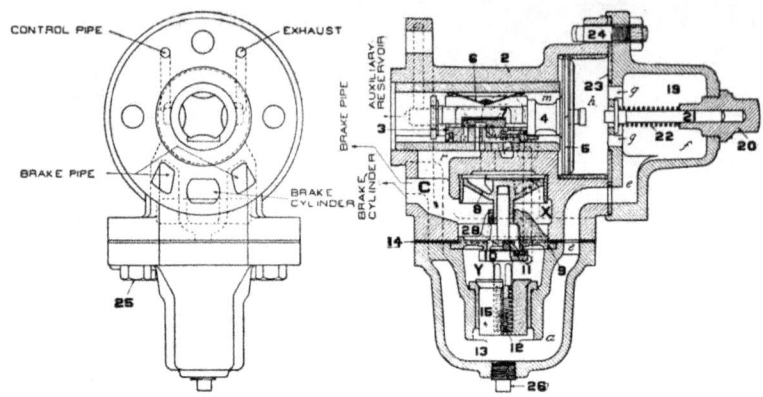

Figs. 2494-2495. "Pipeless" Triple Valve with Graduated Release, Type R.

Names of Parts of Figs. 2494-2495.

- 2 Triple Valve Body
- 3 Slide Valve
- 4 Piston
- 5 Packing Ring
- 6 Slide Valve Spring
- 7 Graduating Valve
- 8 Emergency Valve Piston
- 9 Emergency Valve Seat
- 10 Emergency Valve
- 11 Rubber Seat
- 12 Check Valve Spring
- 13 Check Valve Case
- 14 Check Valve Case Gasket
- 15 Check Valve
- 16 Strainer
- 17 Union Nut
- 18 Union Swivel
- 19 Cylinder Cap
- 20 Graduating Stem Nut
- 21 Graduating Stem
- 22 Graduating Spring
- 23 Cylinder Cap Gasket
- 24 Bolt and Nut
- 25 Half-Inch Cap Screw
- 26 Half-Inch Pipe Plug
- 27 Union Gasket
- 28 Emergency Valve Nut
- 30 Emergency Valve Piston Packing Ring

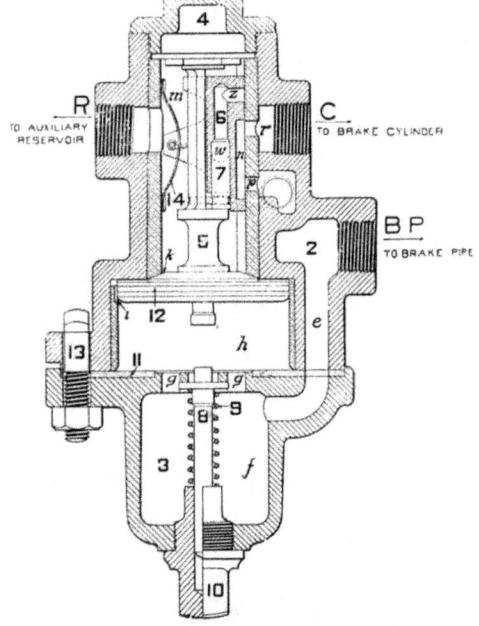

Fig. 2496. Plain Triple Valve, Type F.

Names of Parts of Fig. 2496.

- 2 Triple Valve Body
- 3 Lower Chamber
- 4 Triple Valve Cap
- 5 Triple Valve Piston
- 6 Slide Valve
- 7 Graduating Valve
- 8 Graduating Stem
- 9 Graduating Spring
- 10 Graduating Stem Nut
- 11 Gasket
- 12 Packing Ring
- 13 Bolt and Nut
- 14 Slide Valve Spring

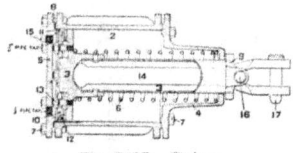

Fig. 2497. Driver Brake Cylinder.

Names of Parts of Fig. 2497.

- 2 Cylinder Body
- 3 Piston and Rod
- 4 Non-Pressure Head
- 5 Pressure Head
- 7 Cylinder Head Bolt and Nut
- 8 Gasket
- 6 Release Spring
- 9 Crosshead
- 10 Follower
- 11 Packing Leather
- 12 Packing Expander
- 13 Follower Stud and Nut
- 14 Push Rod
- 15 Oiling Plug
- 16 Crosshead Pin
- 17 Cylinder Lever Pin

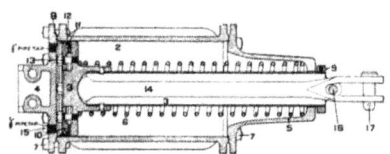
Fig. 2498. Engine Truck Brake Cylinder.

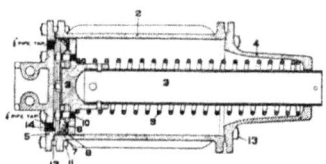
Fig. 2499. Tender Brake Cylinder.

Names of Parts of Fig. 2498.

2 Cylinder Body	8 Gasket	13 Follower Stud and Nut
3 Piston and Rod	9 Flange of Hollow Piston Rod	14 Push Rod
5 Non-Pressure Head	10 Follower	15 Oiling Plug
6 Release Spring	11 Packing Leather	16 Crosshead Pin
7 Cylinder Head Bolt and Nut	12 Packing Expander	17 Cylinder Lever Pin

Names of Parts of Fig. 2499.

2 Cylinder Body	7 Packing Leather	12 Gasket
3 Piston and Rod	8 Packing Expander	13 Non-Pressure Head Bolt and Nut
4 Non-Pressure Head	9 Release Spring	
5 Pressure Head	10 Follower Stud and Nut	14 Oiling Plug
6 Follower	11 Cylinder Head Bolt and Nut	

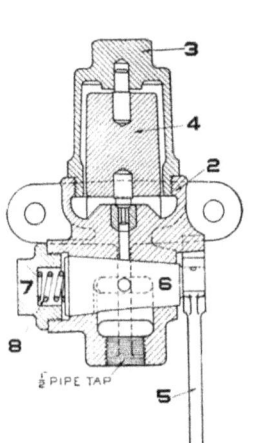

Fig. 2500. Pressure Retaining Valve for 12-Inch, 14-Inch and 16-Inch Cylinders.

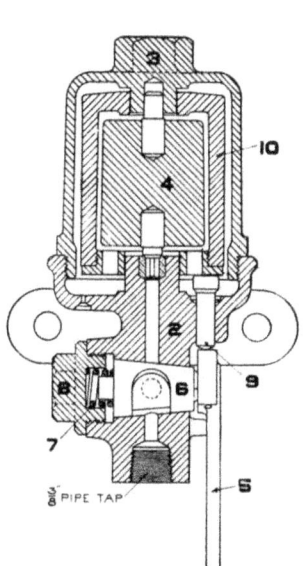

Fig. 2501. High and Low Pressure Retaining Valve.

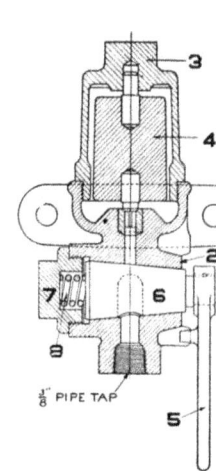

Fig. 2502. Driver Brake Pressure Retaining Valve.

Names of Parts of Fig. 2500.

2 Valve Body
3 Valve Case
4 Valve Weight
5 Valve Handle
6 Valve Cock Key
7 Valve Cock Cap Nut
8 Valve Cock Key Spring

Names of Parts of Fig. 2501.

2 Valve Body
3 Valve Case
4 Inside Valve Weight
5 Valve Handle
6 Valve Cock Key
7 Valve Cock Cap Nut
8 Valve Cock Key Spring
9 Valve Weight Lifting Rod
10 Outside Valve Weight

Names of Parts of Fig. 2502.

2 Valve Body
3 Valve Case
4 Valve Weight
5 Valve Handle
6 Valve Cock Key
7 Valve Cock Cap Nut
8 Valve Cock Key Spring

BRAKE GEAR, Air; Westinghouse. Figs. 2503-2507

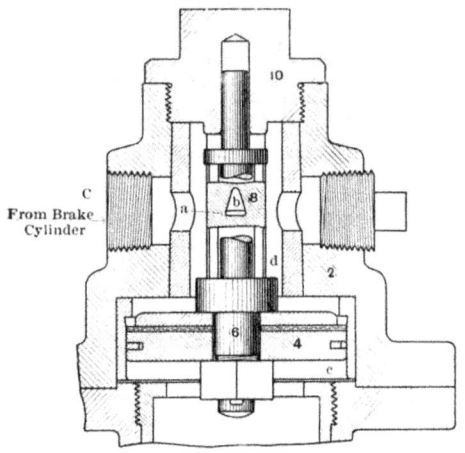

Service
Pressure Exceeding 60 Lbs.
in Brake Cylinder
Fig. 2503. High-Speed Reducing Valve. Service Position.

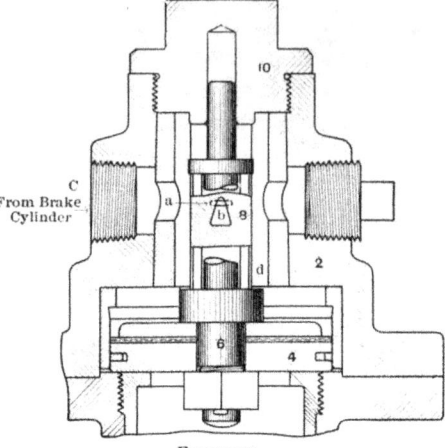

Emergency
Fig. 2504. High-Speed Reducing Valve. Emergency Position.

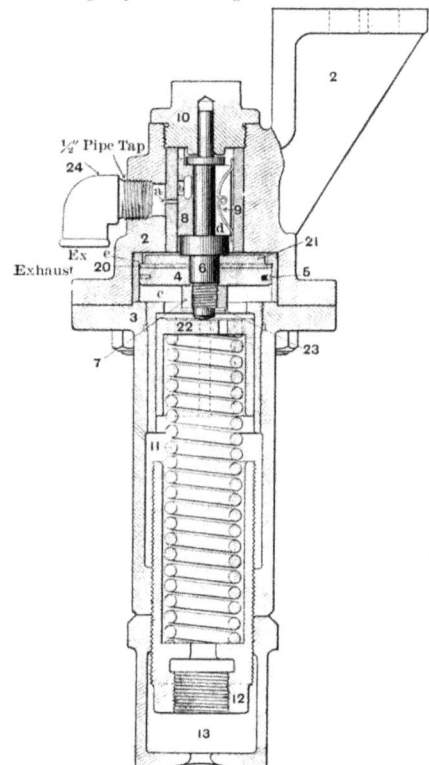

Fig. 2506. High-Speed Reducing Valve. Side View in Section.

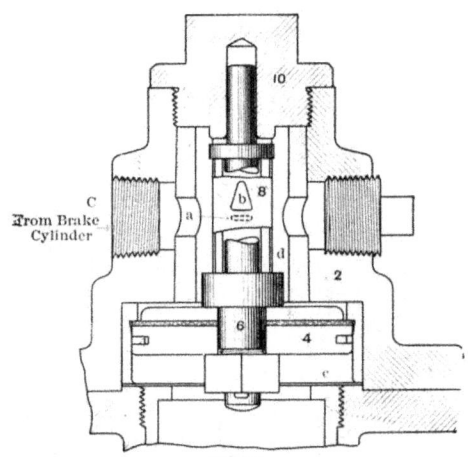

Release
Fig. 2505. High-Speed Reducing Valve. Release Position.

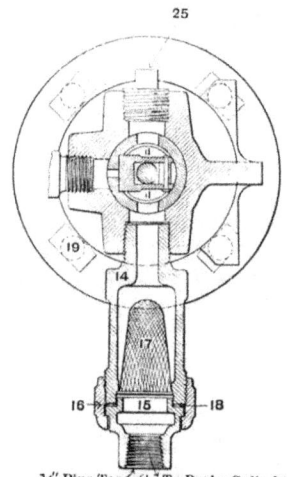

¾" Pipe Tap C To Brake Cylinder
Fig. 2507. High-Speed Reducing Valve. Top View in Section.

Names of Parts of Figs. 2503-2507.

2	Valve Body	14	Union Stud
3	Spring Box	15	Union Swivel
4	Valve Piston	16	Union Nut
5	Packing Ring	17	Air Strainer
6	Piston Stem	18	Union Gasket
7	Piston Stem Nut	19	Bolt and Nut
8	Slide Valve	20	Piston Seat
9	Slide Valve Spring	21	Piston Disc
10	Cap Nut	22	Spring Abutment
11	Regulating Spring	23	Cotter Pin
12	Regulating Nut	24	One-Half-Inch Galvanized Ell
13	Check Nut	25	Three-Quarter-Inch Pipe Plug

Figs. 2508-2515   BRAKE GEAR, Air; Westinghouse.

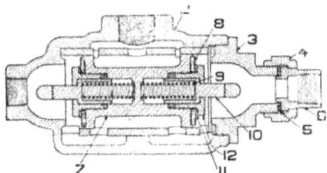
Fig. 2508. Special Double Check Valve.

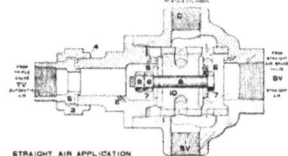
Fig. 2509. Double Check Valve.

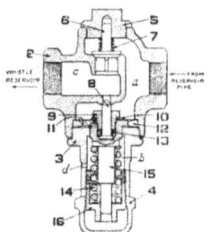
Fig. 2510. Duplex Check Valve.

Names of Parts of Fig. 2508.

- 2 *Check Valve Body*
- 3 *Valve Cap*
- 4 *Union Nut*
- 5 *Gasket*
- 6 *Union Swivel*
- 7 *Operating Valve*
- 8 *Valve Gasket*
- 9 *Valve Stem Spring*
- 10 *Valve Stem*
- 11 *Washer*
- 12 *Flange Nut*

Names of Parts of Fig. 2510.

- 2 *Check Valve Body*
- 3 *Check Valve Adjusting Spring Case*
- 4 *Lower Cap*
- 5 *Upper Cap Nut*
- 6 *Check Valve Stem*
- 7 *Check Valve Spring*
- 8 *Needle Valve*
- 9 *Bushing*
- 10 *Seat*
- 11 *Packing Ring*
- 12 *Sleeve*
- 13 *Packing Ring*
- 14 *Adjusting Spring*
- 15 *Lower Stem*
- 16 *Adjusting Nut*

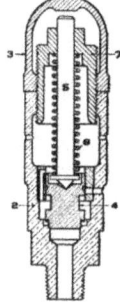

Fig. 2511. Safety Valve, Type E.

Names of Parts of Fig. 2511.

- 2 *Safety Valve Body*
- 3 *Cap Nut*
- 4 *Valve*
- 5 *Valve Stem*
- 6 *Safety Valve Spring*
- 7 *Regulating Nut*

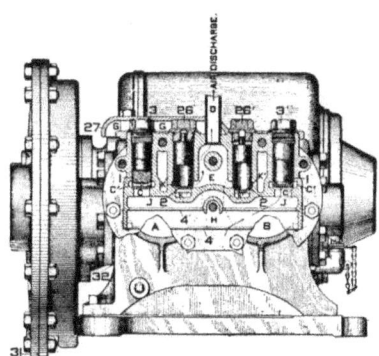
Fig. 2512. End View.

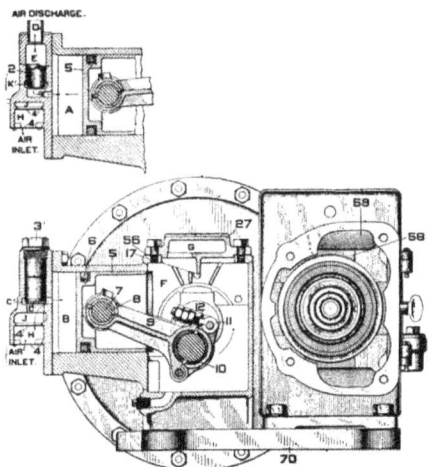
Figs. 2513-2514. Side View.

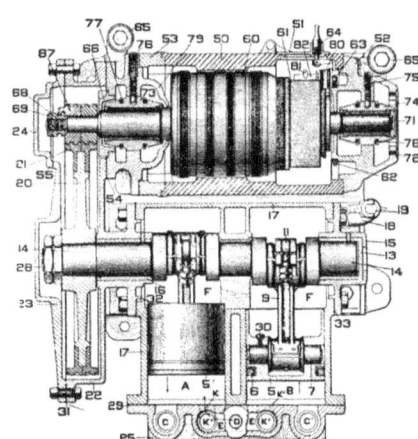
Fig. 2515. Top View.

Figs. 2512-2515. Motor-Driven Air Compressor.

Numbers Refer to List of Names of Parts on Opposite Page.

BRAKE GEAR, Air; Westinghouse. Figs. 2516-2519

Numbers Refer to List of Names of Parts with Figs. 2520-2524.

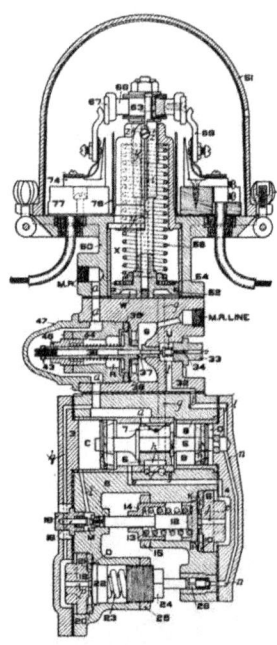

Fig. 2516. Electric Pump Governor, Type L.

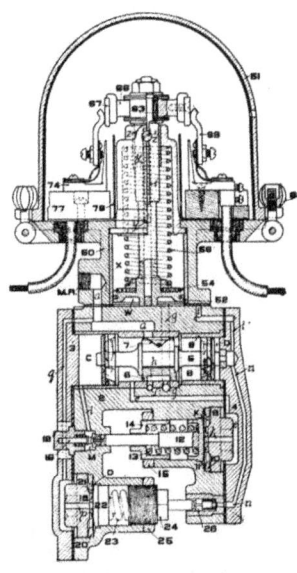

Fig. 2517. Electric Pump Governor, Type J.

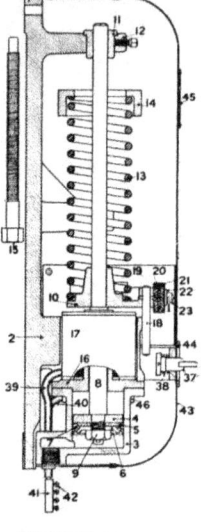
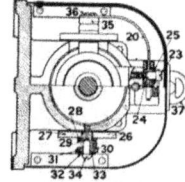

Figs. 2518-2519.
Electric Pump Governor, Type G-1-A.

Names of Parts of Motor-Compressor, Figs. 2512-2515.

1 Suction Valve
2 Discharge Valve
3 Suction Valve Chamber Cap
4 Perforated Plate for Suction Box
5 Piston
6 Piston Packing Ring
7 Wrist Pin with Special Dowel
8 Connecting Rod Bush
9 Connecting Rod
10 Connecting Rod Cap
11 Connecting Rod Eye Bolt
12 Connecting Rod Liners
13 Shaft Bearing Bush
14 Crank Shaft
15 Crank Case Cover and Shaft Bearing
16 Gear Case Shaft Bearing Bush
17 Cylinders and Crank Case
18 Crank Case Oil Fitting
19 Cap Nut for 18
20 Large Gear
22 Gear Case

23 Gear Case Cover
24 Gear Case Cover Cap
25 Cylinder Cover
26 Discharge Valve Chamber Cap
27 Crank Case Top Cover
28 Crank Shaft Nut
29 Cylinder Cover Gasket
31 Gear Case Cover Gasket
32 Shaft Bearing Gasket
33 Crank Case End Gasket
50 Field Yoke with Pole Pieces
51 Commutator Door
52 Front Bearing Housing
53 End Bell
54 Motor Gasket
55 Gear Case Cover Top Gasket
56 Crank Case Top Gasket
59 Field Coil
60 Armature
61 Commutator
62 Rocker Arm
63 Set Screw for Rocker Arm
64 Commutator Door Latch

65 Oil Filling Elbow Cap Nut
66 Nut for Rear Bearing Housing
67 Pinion for Motor Shaft
68 Nut for Removing Pinion
69 Motor Shaft Jam Nut
70 Bed Plate
71 Front Bearing Housing Dust Plate
72 Screw for Dust Plate
73 Rear Bearing
74 Front Bearing
75 Front Bearing Housing Headless Screw
76 Rear Bearing Housing Headless Screw
77 Rear Bearing Oil Ring
78 Front Bearing Oil Ring
79 Rear Bearing Housing
80 Carbon Holder
81 Carbon Holder Spring
82 Carbon Brush

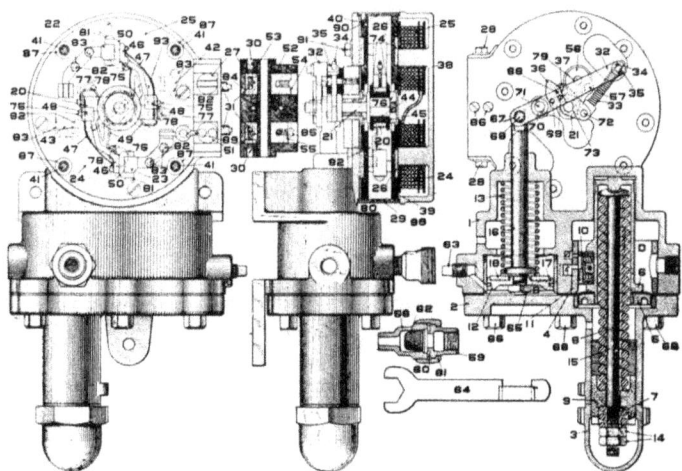

Figs. 2520-2524. Electric Pump Governor, Type E.

Names of Parts of Electric Pump Governor, Figs. 2518-2519.

1. Base
2. Cylinder
3. Piston
4. Packing Leather
5. Follower
6. Piston Rod
7. Piston Rod Nut
8. Piston Rod Guide
9. Set Screw for Piston Rod Guide
10. Armature
11. Pressure Spring
12. Spring Yoke
13. Adjusting Bolts
14. Adjusting Posts
15. Guide Posts
16. Magnet Shell
17. Magnet Coil
18. Magnet Core
19. Armature Guide Pin
20. Circuit Closer
21. Circuit Closer Insulator
22. Circuit Closer Insulator
23. Circuit Closer Screws
24. Circuit Closer Tips
25. Contacts
26. Contact Screws
27. Terminal Clips
28. Arc Shields
29. Cylinder Screws
30. Cover
31. Latch Plate
32. Thumb Latch
33. Latch Spring
34. Shield Insulator
35. Bushing for Leads
36. Positive Lead
37. Motor Lead
38. Packing Leather Expander
39. Contact Screw Insulator
40. Contact Insulator
41. Cover Insulation
44. Screws for Tips, No. 24

Names of Parts of Electric Pump Governor, Figs. 2520-2524.

1. Body
2. Cylinder Head
3. Lock Nut for Adjusting Nut
4. Diaphragm
5. Diaphragm Guide Nut
6. Diaphragm Guide
7. Retarding Spring
8. Regulating Spring
9. Adjusting Nut for Regulating Spring
10. Slide Valve
11. Bush with Slide Valve Seat
12. Operating Piston
13. Operating Piston Spring
14. Adjusting Nut for Retarding Spring
15. Regulating Spring Spindle
16. Operating Piston Rod
17. Packing Ring for Operating Piston
18. Leather Disc for Operating Piston
20. Switch Arm
21. Switch Rocker Shaft
22. Switch Terminal
23. Switch Terminal
24-25. Blow-out Coils, complete
26. Pole Piece for Blow-out
27. Main Terminal
28. Bolt and Nut for Switch Case Band
29. Switch Case Band, complete
30. Binding Screw for Terminal Block
32. Operating Lever, complete
33. Quick Break Spring
34. Stem for Quick Break Spring
35. Guide Pin for Quick Break Spring Stem
36. Operating Lever Detent
37. Special Pin for Rocker Shaft Arm
38. Switch Cover
39. Insulating Disc on Switch Cover
40. Insulating Disc on Body
41. Stud and Nut for Switch Cover
42-43. Connector for Blow-out Coils
44. Insulating Bush for Switch Arm
45. Insulating Washer for Switch Arm
46. Contact Finger
47. Contact Finger Spring
48. Clamp for Contact Finger Spring
49. Contact Finger Shunt
50. Contact for Switch Terminal
51. Main Terminal
52. Terminal Block, complete
53. Insulating Tube for Switch Case Band Bolt

(258)

BRAKE GEAR, Air; Westinghouse. Figs. 2525-2543

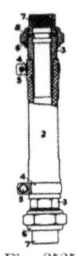

Fig. 2525. Flexible Hose Connection.

Names of Parts of Fig. 2525.

2 Hose
3 Hose Nipple
4 Hose Clamp
5 Hose Clamp Nut
6 Union Nut
7 Union Swivel
8 Washer

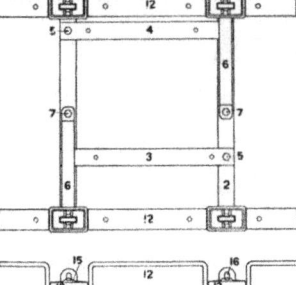

Figs. 2526-2527. Cradle for Westinghouse Motor-Driven Air Compressor.

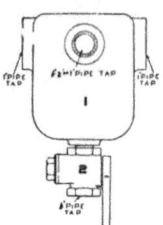

Fig. 2528. Tender Drain Cup.

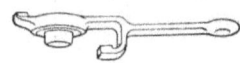

Fig. 2529. Dummy Coupling.

Names of Parts of Fig. 2530.

2 Cock Body
3 Cock Key
4 Cap Nut
5 Key Spring
6 Handle
7 Handle Lug
8 Handle Hinge Pin
9 Bushing

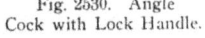

Fig. 2530. Angle Cock with Lock Handle.

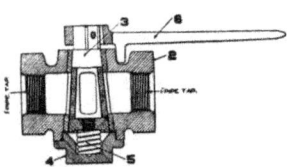

Fig. 2531. Cut-out Cock.

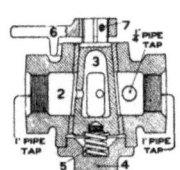

Fig. 2532. Main Reservoir Cut-Out Cock.

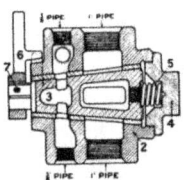

Fig. 2533. Double Cut-out Cock.

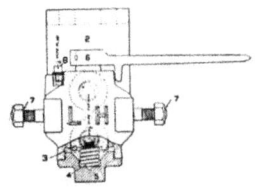

Fig. 2534. Reversing Cock.

Names of Parts of Fig. 2531.

2 Cock Body
3 Cock Key
4 Cock Cap Nut
5 Cock Key Spring
6 Handle

Names of Parts of Fig. 2532.

2 Cock Body
3 Cock Key
4 Cock Cap Nut
5 Cock Key Spring
6 Handle
7 Cock Stem Key

Names of Parts of Fig. 2533.

2 Cock Body
3 Cock Key
4 Cock Cap Nut
5 Cock Key Spring
6 Handle
7 Cock Stem Key

Names of Parts of Fig. 2534.

2 Reversing Cock Pipe Brackets
3 Reversing Cock Body
4 Cock Spring
5 Cock Cap
6 Handle
7 Bracket Studs

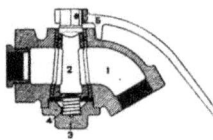

Fig. 2535. Angle Cock.

Names of Parts of Fig. 2535.

1 Angle Cock Body
2 Angle Cock Key
3 Angle Cock Cap
4 Angle Cock Key Spring
5 Angle Cock Handle

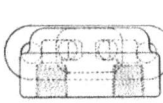

Fig. 2536. Reversing Cock Pipe Bracket.

Fig. 2537. Hose Clamp.

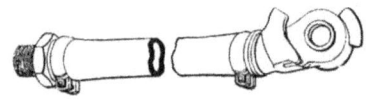

Fig. 2538. Brake Hose and Coupling.

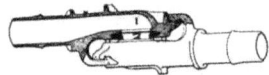

Fig. 2539. Hose Coupling.

Fig. 2540. Hose Nipple.

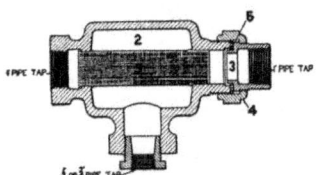

Fig. 2541. Brake Pipe Air Strainer.

Names of Parts of Fig. 2541.

2 Strainer Body
3 1-Inch Union Swivel
4 Union Nut
5 Union Gasket
6 Strainer

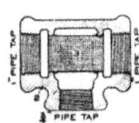

Fig. 2542. Tee with Strainer.

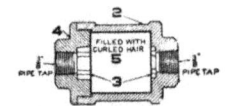

Fig. 2543. O. B. Air Strainer.

Names of Parts of Fig. 2543

2 Strainer Body
3 Perforated Metal Plate
4 Cap Nut
5 Straining Material

Figs. 2544-2556 BRAKE GEAR, Air; Westinghouse.

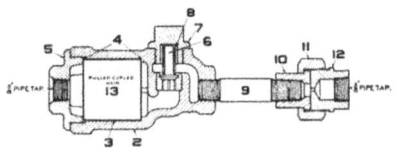

Fig. 2544. Combined Air Valve and Check Valve with Special Choke Union.

Names of Parts of Fig. 2544.

2	Air Strainer Body	8	Check Valve Spring
3	Bushing	9	Connecting Nipple
4	Perforated Metal Disc	10	Union Bushing
5	Cap Nut	11	Union Nut
6	Check Valve Stem	12	Union Swivel with Choke Hole
7	Check Valve Cap Nut		

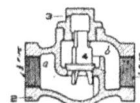

Fig. 2545. Check Valve.

Names of Parts of Fig. 2545.

2 Valve Body
3 Valve Cap Nut
4 Valve
a Feed Valve Chamber
b Brake Valve Chamber

Fig. 2546. Long Slotted Crosshead for Westinghouse Brake Cylinder.

Fig. 2547. Choke Fitting.

Fig. 2548. Snap Switch for Traction Brake Equipments.

Fig. 2549. Enclosed Fuse Block for Traction Brake Equipments.

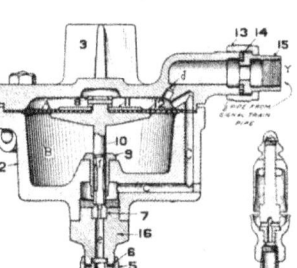

Fig. 2550. Train Air Signal Valve and Whistle.

Names of Parts of Fig. 2550.

2 Air Signal Valve Body
3 Valve Lug
4 Nipple
5 Sleeve Nut
6 Gasket
7 Lower Bushing
9 Valve Stem Bushing
10 Valve Stem
12 Diaphragm
13 Sleeve Nut
14 Gasket
15 Air Signal Pipe Connection
16 Cap

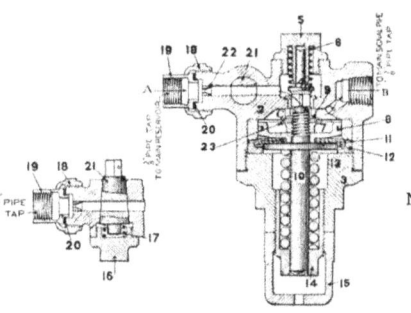

Figs. 2551-2552. Train Air Signal Reducing Valve.

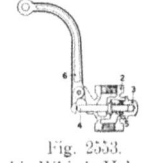

Fig. 2553. Air Whistle Valve.

Names of Parts of Fig. 2553.

2 Valve Body
3 Valve Cap
4 Valve Stem
5 Valve Stem Spring
6 Valve Handle

Names of Parts of Figs. 2551-2552.

2	Upper Valve Body	13	Regulating Spring
3	Lower Valve Body	14	Regulating Nut
4	Valve	15	Check Nut
5	Cap Nut	16	Plug Cock Cap Nut
6	Valve Spring	17	Plug Cock Key Spring
7	Adjusting Nut	18	Union Nut
8	Packing Ring	19	Union Swivel
9	Adjusting Nut	20	Union Washer
10	Regulating Stem	21	Plug Cock Key
11	Diaphragm	22	Taper Port
12	Seat for Regulating Disc	23	Diaphragm

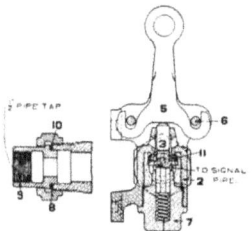

Figs. 2554-2555. Train Air Signal Car Discharge Valve.

Names of Parts of Figs. 2554-2555.

2 Discharge Valve Body
3 Valve Stem
4 Valve Stem Spring
5 Operating Handle
6 Stop Pin
7 Valve Cap Nut
8 Union Nut
9 Union Swivel
10 Gasket

Fig. 2556. Air Whistle.

(260)

BRAKE GEAR, Air; New York. Figs. 2557-2560

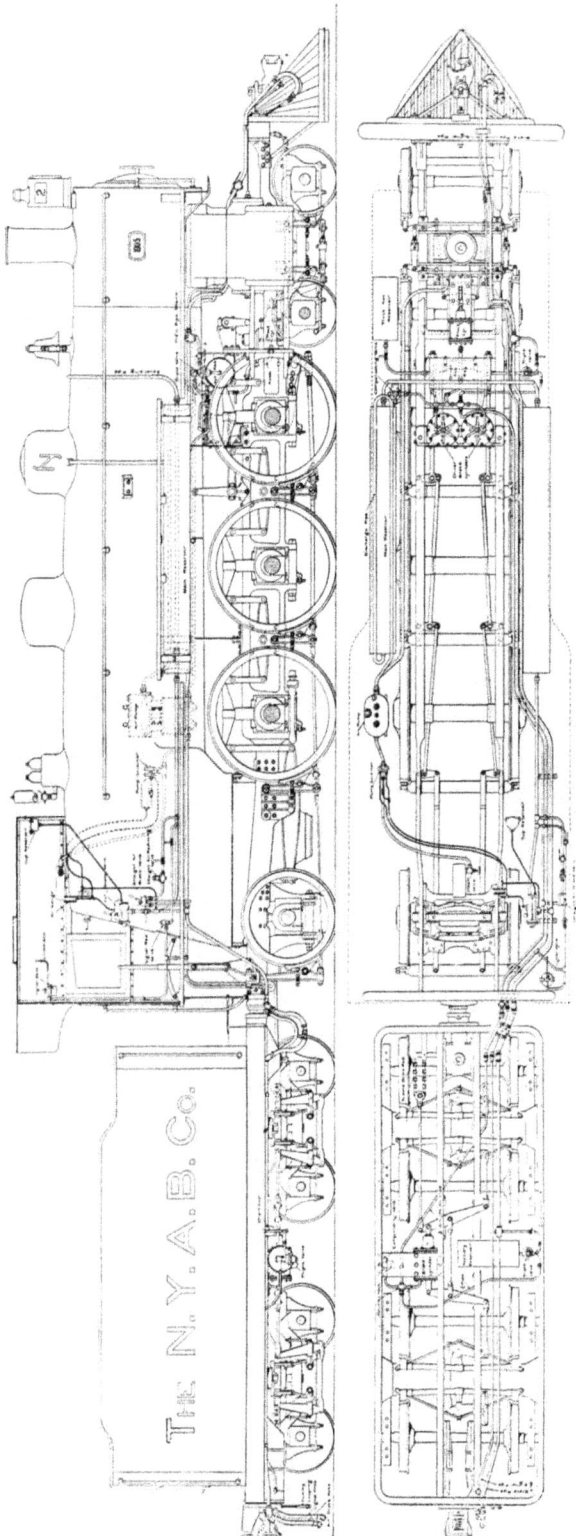

Figs. 2557-2558. Locomotive and Tender Equipment for Automatic and Straight-Air Brakes. New York Air Brake Co.

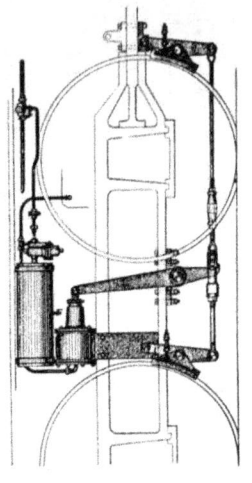

Fig. 2560. Equalized Driver Brake on Two Pairs of Wheels.

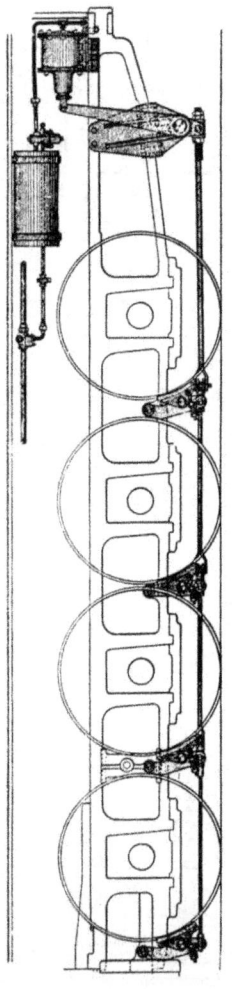

Fig. 2559. Arrangement of Equalized Driver Brake on Four Pairs of Wheels.

BRAKE GEAR, Air; New York.

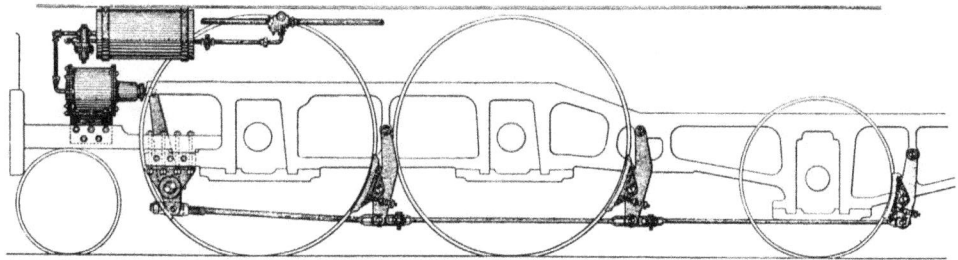

Fig. 2561. Arrangement of Equalized Driver Brake on Three Pairs of Wheels.

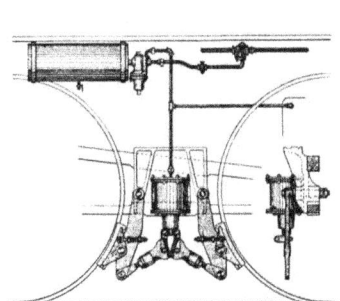

Fig. 2562. Cam or Spread Driver Brake Between Two Pairs of Wheels.

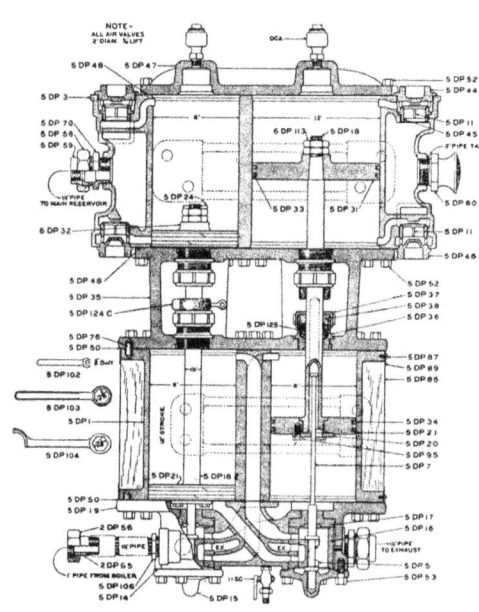

Fig. 2563. No. 5 Duplex Air Pump.
Made in 6 Sizes, Nos. 1, 2, 3, 4, 5 and 6.

Names of Parts of Fig. 2563.

1 8-Inch Steam Cylinders	47 Top Head
3 Air Cylinders	48 Air Cylinder Gasket
5 Slide Valve	50 8-Inch Steam Cylinder Gasket
7 Valve Stem	52 ⅝-Inch x 1⅞-Inch Tap Bolt
11 Air Valve	53 ⅝-Inch x 1½-Inch Tap Bolt
14 Steam Chest Gasket	55 Governor Union Stud
15 Steam Chest Cap	56 Governor Union Nut
16 Steam Chest Bush	58 1½-Inch Union Nut
17 Valve Stem Guide	59 1½-Inch Union Swivel
18 Piston Rod	60 Air Strainer
19 Steam Head	70 1½-Inch Union Stud
20 Tappet Plate	76 Dowel
21 8-Inch Steam Piston	85 Steam Cylinder Jacket
24 ¼-Inch x 1½-Inch Cotter	87 Jacket Screw
31 12-inch Air Piston	89 Steam Cylinder Jacket Band
32 8-Inch Air Piston	95 Tappet Plate Bolt
33 12-Inch Piston Ring	96 Tappet Plate Bolt Lock
34 8-Inch Piston Ring	102 Bolt Wrench
35 Center Piece	103 Upper Valve Seat Wrench
36 Stuffing Box	104 Packing Nut and Lower Valve Seat Wrench
37 Stuffing Box Nut	
38 Stuffing Box Gland	106 1½-Inch to 1¼-Inch Reducer
44 Upper Valve Cap	113 Piston Rod Nut
45 Upper Valve Seat	124c Piston Rod Swab, complete
46 Lower Valve Seat	125 Piston Rod Packing

BRAKE GEAR. Air; New York.

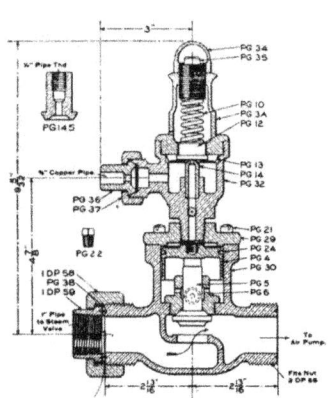

Fig. 2564. 1-Inch Single Pump Governor.

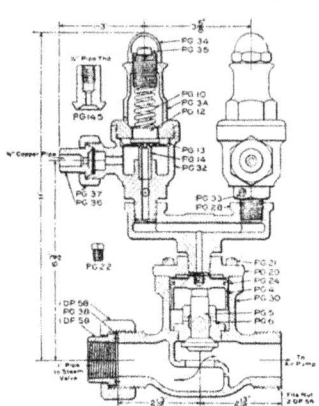

Fig. 2565. 1-Inch Duplex Pump Governor.

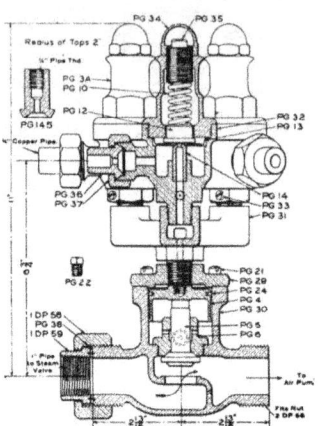

Fig. 2566. 1-Inch Triple Pump Governor.

Names of Parts of Fig. 2564.

- 3a Spring Casing
- 4 Piston
- 5 Steam Valve
- 6 Steam Valve Guide
- 10 Regulating Spring
- 12 Diaphragm Button
- 13 Diaphragm
- 14 Air Valve Seat
- 21 Screws
- 22 ⅛-Inch Drain Plug
- 24 2-Inch Piston Ring
- 29 Cylinder Cap
- 30 Steam Valve Body
- 32 Diaphragm Body
- 34 Cap
- 35 Regulating Nut
- 36 Air Union Swivel (⅜-inch copper pipe)
- 37 Air Union Nut
- 38 1-Inch Union Gasket
- 145 Air Union Swivel (¼-inch iron pipe)

Names of Parts of Fig. 2565.

- 3a Spring Casing
- 4 Piston
- 5 Steam Valve
- 6 Steam Valve Guide
- 10 Regulating Spring
- 12 Diaphragm Button
- 13 Diaphragm
- 14 Air Valve Seat
- 21 Screws
- 22 ⅛-Inch Drain Plug
- 24 2-Inch Piston Ring
- 28 Duplex Fitting
- 29 Cylinder Cap
- 30 Steam Valve Body
- 32 Diaphragm Body
- 33 Vent Plug
- 34 Cap
- 35 Regulating Nut
- 36 Air Union Swivel (⅜-inch copper pipe)
- 37 Air Union Nut
- 38 1-Inch Gasket
- 145 Air Union Swivel (¼-inch iron pipe)

Names of Parts of Fig. 2566.

- 3a Spring Casing
- 4 Piston
- 5 Steam Valve
- 6 Steam Valve Guide
- 10 Regulating Spring
- 12 Diaphragm Button
- 13 Diaphragm
- 14 Air Valve Seat
- 21 Screws
- 22 ⅛-Inch Drain Plug
- 24 2-Inch Piston Ring
- 29 Cylinder Cap
- 30 Steam Valve Body
- 31 Triplex Fitting
- 32 Diaphragm Body
- 33 Vent Plug
- 34 Cap
- 35 Regulating Nut
- 36 Air Union Swivel (⅜-inch copper pipe)
- 37 Air Union Nut
- 38 1-Inch Union Gasket
- 145 Air Union Swivel (¼-inch iron pipe)

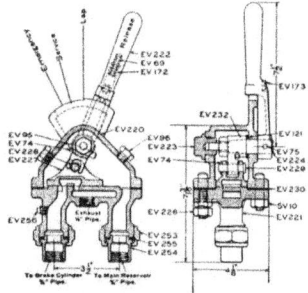

Figs. 2567-2568. ¾-Inch Straight-Air Brake Valve.

Names of Parts of Figs. 2567-2568.

- 69 Handle Spring
- 74 Cotter
- 75 Handle Pin
- 95 Lever Shaft Pin
- 96 Oil Plug
- 172 Quadrant Latch
- 173 Latch Screw
- 121 Lever Shaft Packing
- 220 Cover
- 221 Body
- 222 Handle
- 223 Lever Shaft Plug
- 224 Lever Shaft and Nut
- 226 Bracket Stud and Nut
- 227 Slide Valve
- 228 Slide Valve Thimble
- 229 Slide Valve Pin
- 230 Cover Gasket
- 232 Slide Valve Lever
- 253 ¾-Inch Union Nut
- 254 ¾-Inch Union Swivel
- 255 ¾-Inch Union Gasket
- 256 ¼-Inch Plug

Figs. 2569-2575   BRAKE GEAR, Air; New York.

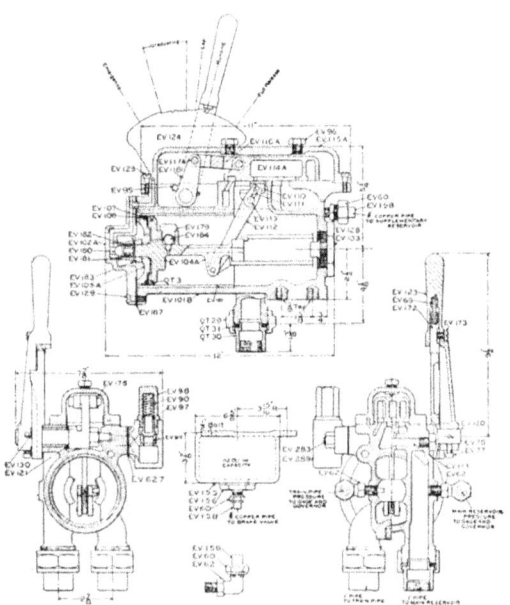

Names of Parts of Figs. 2569-2573.

3	Piston Ring	116a	Link
29	1-Inch Union Nut	117a	Link Pin
30	1-Inch Union Swivel	118	Slide Valve Lever
31	1-Inch Union Gasket	120	Lever Shaft
60	Small Union Nut	121	Lever Shaft Packing
62	Gage Union Ell	123	Handle
69	Handle Spring	124	Quadrant
75	Handle Pin	128	Small Union Stud
77	Handle Set Screw	129	Cover and Head Screw
90	Feed Valve Spring	130	Quadrant Screw
95	Lever Shaft Pin with Cotter	155	Supplementary Reservoir
		156	Reservoir Plug
96	¼-Inch Plug	158	Union Swivel (⅜-inch copper pipe)
97	Feed Valve		
98	Feed Valve Cap	167	Cap Gasket
101b	Body (bushed)	172	Latch
102a	Back Cap	173	Latch Pin
103	End Plug	175	Cotter
104a	Piston	179	Check Valve Cap
105a	Follower	180	Vent Valve
107	Packing Leather	181	Follower Cap Nut
108	Expander	182	Vent Valve Spring
110	Graduating Valve	183	Cotter Pin
111	Graduating Valve Spring	184	Ball Check Valve
112	Graduating Valve Lever	283	Feed Valve Stud and Nut
113	Fulcrum Pin	289	Feed Valve
114a	Main Slide Valve	627	Feed Valve Gasket
115a	Valve Cover		

Figs. 2569-2573. Engineer's Brake Valve, Type B-1, with Supplementary Reservoir, for Automatic Brake.

Names of Parts of Fig. 2574.

46	Plug	69	Cylinder Cap	82	Bushing
55	Graduating Valve	70	Cap Nut	84	Triple Valve Body (bushed)
56	Graduating Stem	72	Exhaust Valve	85	Bushing
57	Graduating Spring	77	Cap Gasket	86	Packing Ring (3⅜-inch)
58	Graduating Stem Nut	80	Exhaust Valve Spring	87	Piston

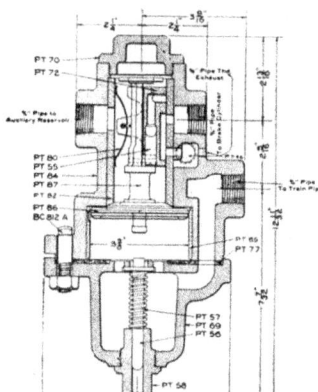

Fig. 2574. Plain Triple Valve, Type E, for 6-in., 8-in. and 10-in. Cylinders.

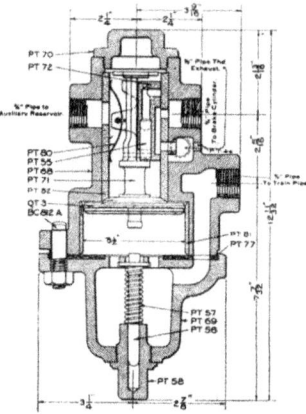

Fig. 2575. Plain Triple Valve, Type C, for 12-in., 14-in., and 16-in. Cylinders.

Names of Parts of Fig. 2575.

3	Piston Ring
46	Plug
55	Graduating Valve
56	Graduating Stem
57	Graduating Spring
58	Graduating Stem Nut
68	Triple Valve Body (bushed)
69	Cylinder Cap
70	Cap Nut
71	Piston
72	Exhaust Valve
77	Cap Gasket
80	Exhaust Valve Spring
81	Bushing
82	Bushing

BRAKE GEAR, Air; New York. Figs. 2576-2581

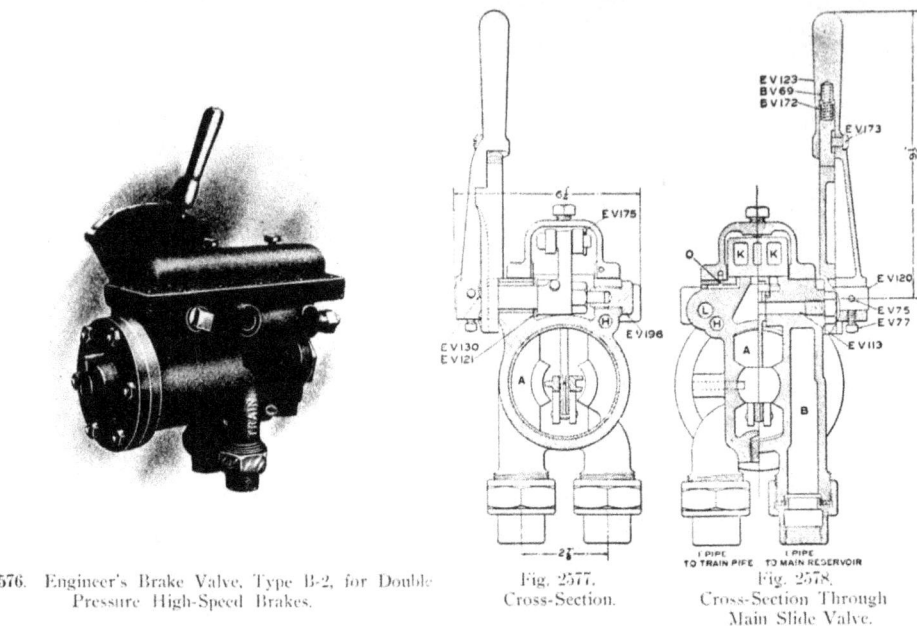

Fig. 2576. Engineer's Brake Valve, Type B-2, for Double Pressure High-Speed Brakes.

Fig. 2577. Cross-Section.

Fig. 2578. Cross-Section Through Main Slide Valve.

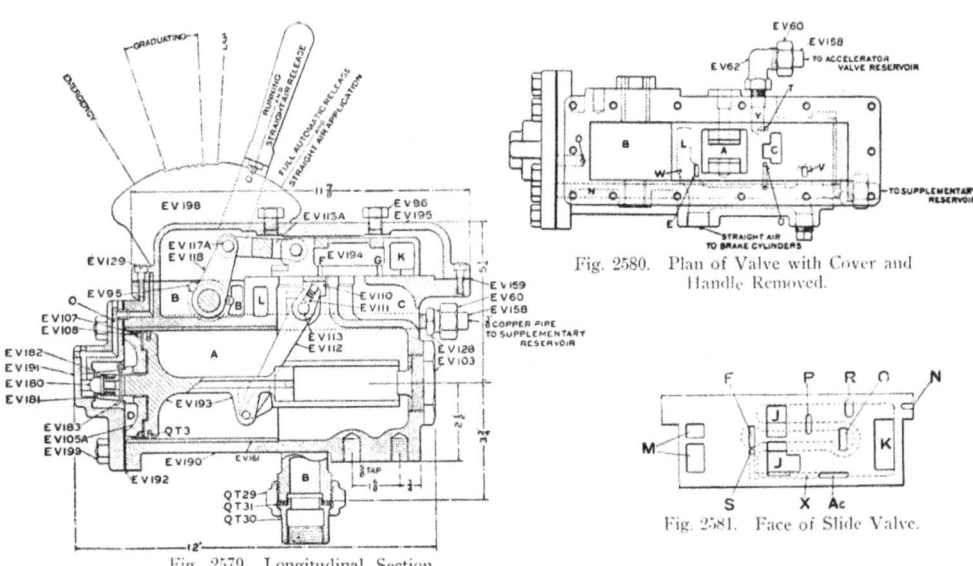

Fig. 2579. Longitudinal Section.

Fig. 2580. Plan of Valve with Cover and Handle Removed.

Fig. 2581. Face of Slide Valve.

Names of Parts of Figs. 2577-2579.

No.	Part	No.	Part	No.	Part
3	Piston Ring	111	Graduating Valve Spring	175	Link Pin Cotter
29	1-Inch Union Nut	112	Graduating Valve Lever	180	Vent Valve
30	1-Inch Union Swivel	113	Fulcrum Pin	181	Follower Cap Nut
31	1-Inch Union Gasket	116a	Link	182	Vent Valve Spring
60	Small Union Nut	117a	Link Pin	183	Piston Cotter
62	Small Union Ell	118	Slide Valve Lever	190	Body
69	Handle Spring	120	Lever Shaft	191	Back Cap
75	Handle Pin	121	Lever Shaft Packing	192	Cap Gasket
77	Handle Set Screw	123	Handle	193	Piston
95	Lever Shaft Pin and Cotter	128	Small Union Stud	194	Main Slide Valve
96	¼-Inch Plug	129	Cover Screw	195	Valve Cover
103	End Plug	130	Quadrant Screw	196	Lever Shaft Plug
105a	Follower	158	Small Union Swivel	198	Quadrant
107	Packing Leather	159	Cover Gasket	199	Back Cap Stud and Nut
108	Expander	172	Latch		
110	Graduating Valve	173	Latch Screw		

Fig. 2582. Supply Valve of Double Pressure Controller.

Fig. 2585. Regulator of Double Pressure Controller.

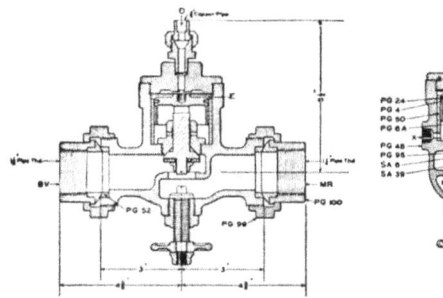
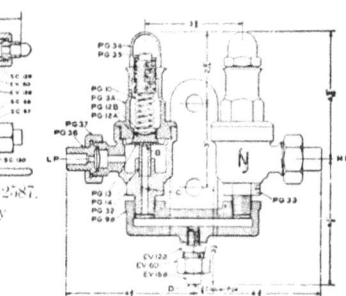

Figs. 2583-2584. Sections Through Supply Valve of Double Pressure Controller.

Figs. 2586-2587. Three-Way Cock for Double Pressure Controller.

Fig. 2588. Section Through Regulator of Double Pressure Controller.

Names of Parts of Figs. 2583-2584.

4	Piston	45	Hand Wheel	95	Valve
6	Leather Seat	46	Lifting Stem	99	1¼-Inch Union Nut
6a	Valve Guide	48	Body	100	1¼-Inch Union Swivel
24	2-Inch Piston Ring	49	Cap	128	Small Union Stud
28	Hand Wheel Nut	60	Small Union Nut	158	Union Swivel (⅜-inch copper pipe)
39	Valve Stem Nut	94	Guide		

Names of Parts of Fig. 2588.

3a	Spring Casing	33	Seat Plug	60	Small Union Nut
10	Regulating Spring	34	Cap	98	Duplex Bracket
12a	Diaphragm Button	35	Regulating Nut	128	Small Union Stud
13	Diaphragm	36	Air Union Swivel (⅜-inch copper pipe)	158	Small Union Swivel (⅜-inch copper pipe)
14	Air Valve Seat	37	Air Union Nut		
32	Diaphragm Body				

Names of Parts of Figs. 2586-2587.

57	Washer	60	Small Union Nut	158	Union Swivel (⅜-inch copper pipe)
58	Nut	129	Body		
		130	Plug		

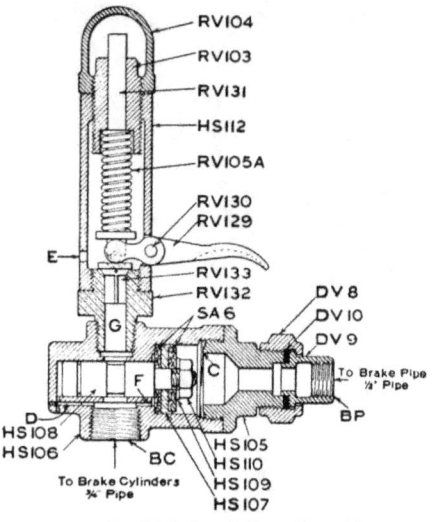

Fig. 2589. High Speed Controller with Lever Safety Valve.

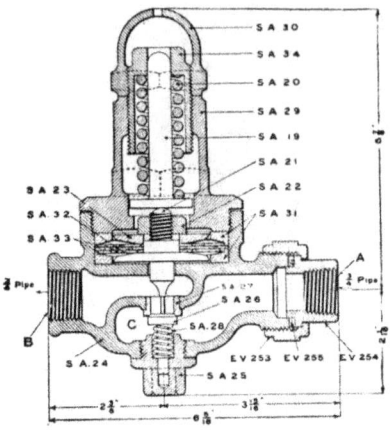

Fig. 2590. Straight-Air Reducing Valve.

Names of Parts of Fig. 2589.

- 6 *Leather Seat*
- 8 *½-in. Union Nut*
- 9 *½-in. Union Swivel*
- 10 *½-in. Union Gasket*
- 103 *Regulating Nut*
- 104 *Cap Nut*
- 105 *Cap*
- 105a *Regulating Spring*
- 106 *Base*
- 107 *Piston*
- 108 *Piston Valve*
- 109 *Washer*
- 110 *Nut*
- 112 *Body*
- 129 *Lever Handle*
- 130 *Lever Handle Pin and Cotter*
- 131 *Valve Stem*
- 132 *Valve Seat*
- 133 *Valve*

Names of Parts of Fig. 2590.

- 19 *Regulating Stem*
- 20 *Regulating Spring*
- 21 *Diaphragm Stem*
- 22 *Nut*
- 23 *Diaphragm Washer*
- 24 *Body*
- 25 *Feed Valve Cap Nut*
- 26 *Feed Valve*
- 28 *Feed Valve Spring*
- 29 *Spring Box*
- 30 *Check Nut*
- 31 *Diaphragm Ring*
- 32 *Diaphragm*
- 33 *Diaphragm Shield*
- 34 *Regulating Nut*
- 253 *¾-in. Union Nut*
- 254 *¾-in. Union Swivel*
- 255 *¾-in. Union Gasket*

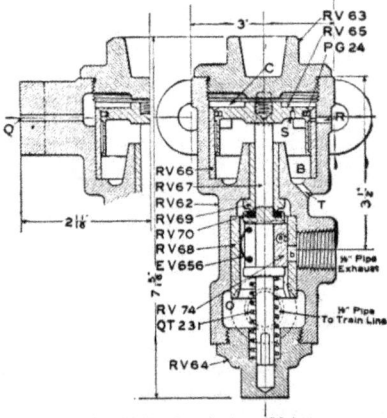

Fig. 2591. Accelerator Valve.

Names of Parts of Fig. 2591.

- 24 *Piston Ring*
- 62 *Body*
- 63 *Upper Cap*
- 64 *Lower Cap*
- 65 *Piston*
- 67 *Valve Stem*
- 68 *Slide Valve Bush*
- 69 *Valve Stem Bush*
- 70 *Leather Seat*
- 74 *Slide Valve*
- 231 *Spring*
- 656 *Slide Valve Spring*

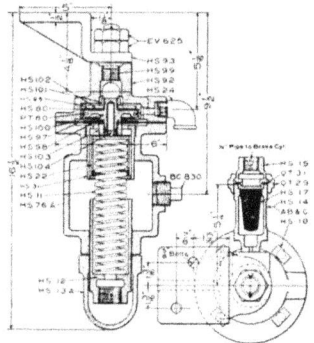

Figs. 2592-2593. Compensating Valve for High-Speed Brake Equipments.

Names of Parts of Figs. 2592-2593.

11	Regulating Spring	60	Packing Ring
12	Regulating Nut	76a	Spring Box (bushed)
13a	Check Nut	80	Leather Washer
14a	Union Stud for 10-inch and 12-inch Cylinders	92	Body (bushed)
		93	Bracket
14b	Union Stud for 14-inch and 16-inch Cylinders	97	Diaphragm
		98	Diaphragm Washer
14c	Union Stud for 6-inch and 8-inch Cylinders	99	Bracket Stud
		100	Piston
15	Union Swivel	101	Top Piston Nut
17	Union Strainer	102	Piston Disc
22	Spring Abutment	103	Bottom Piston Nut
24	½-Inch Street Ell	104	Rider Pin
29	1-inch Union Nut	830	1-inch plug
31	1-inch Union Gasket	625	Holding Nut

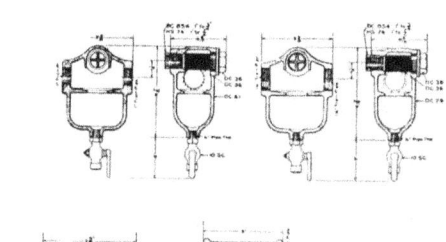
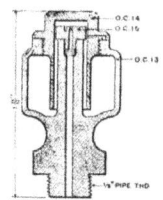
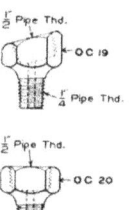
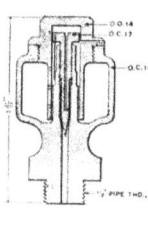

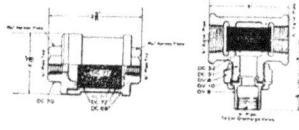

Figs. 2594-2600. Strainers and Drain Cups.

Names of Parts of Figs. 2611-2612.

2 Upper Case
3 Diaphragm
4a Diaphragm Stem
6 Lower Diaphragm Plate
7 Nut
8 Valve
10 ½-inch Tee Head Bolt
11 Cap
12 Upper Diaphragm Washer
22 Lower Case

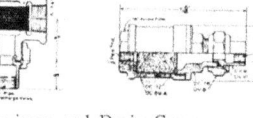

Figs. 2611-2612. Train Air Signal Valve.

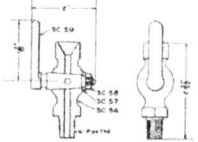
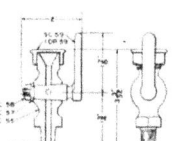
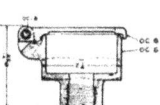
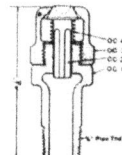

Figs. 2601-2610. Oil Cups for Pumps and Driver Brakes.

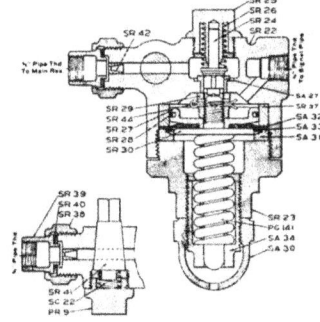

Figs. 2613-2614. Train Air Signal Reducing Valve.

Names of Parts of Figs. 2613-2614.

9	Cock Cap Nut	31	Diaphragm Ring
22	Body (bushed)	32	Diaphragm
23	Spring Box	33	Diaphragm Shield
24	Supply Valve	34	Regulating Nut
25	Supply Valve Cap	38	⅜-inch Union Nut
26	Supply Valve Spring	39	⅜-inch Union Swivel
27	Piston	40	⅜-inch Union Gasket
28	2½-inch Piston Ring	41	Cock Plug
29	Piston Nut	42	Choke
30	Piston Rod	141	Regulating Spring

BRAKE GEAR, Air; Miscellaneous. Figs. 2615-2621

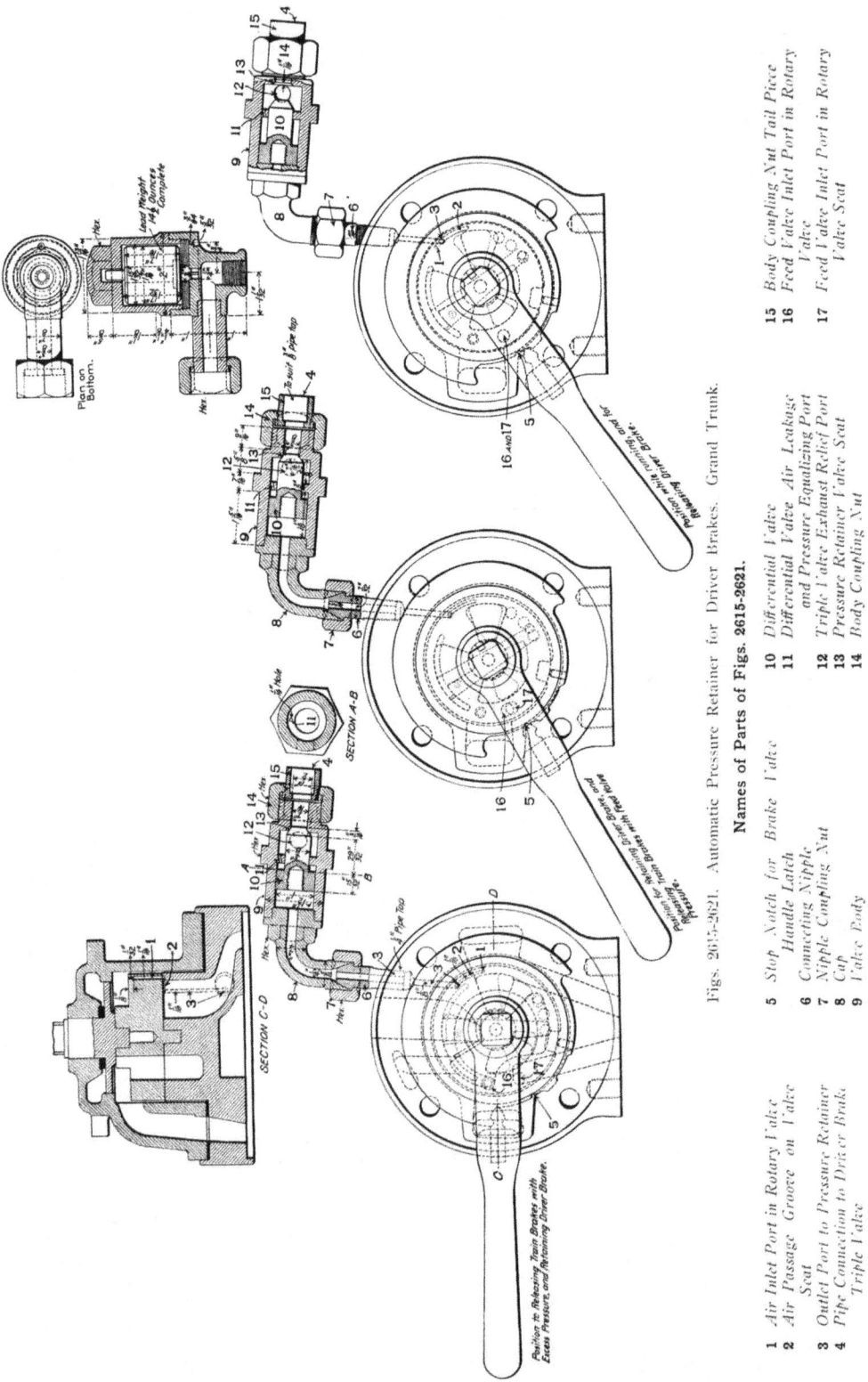

Figs. 2615-2621. Automatic Pressure Retainer for Driver Brakes. Grand Trunk.

Names of Parts of Figs. 2615-2621.

1 Air Inlet Port in Rotary Valve
2 Air Passage Groove on Valve Seat
3 Outlet Port to Pressure Retainer
4 Pipe Connection to Driver Brake
5 Stop Notch for Brake Valve Handle Latch
6 Connecting Nipple
7 Nipple Coupling Nut
8 Cap
9 Valve Body
10 Differential Valve
11 Differential Valve Air Leakage and Pressure Equalizing Port
12 Triple Valve Exhaust Relief Port
13 Pressure Retainer Valve Seat
14 Body Coupling Nut
15 Body Coupling Nut Tail Piece
16 Feed Valve Inlet Port in Rotary Valve
17 Feed Valve Inlet Port in Rotary Valve Seat

(269)

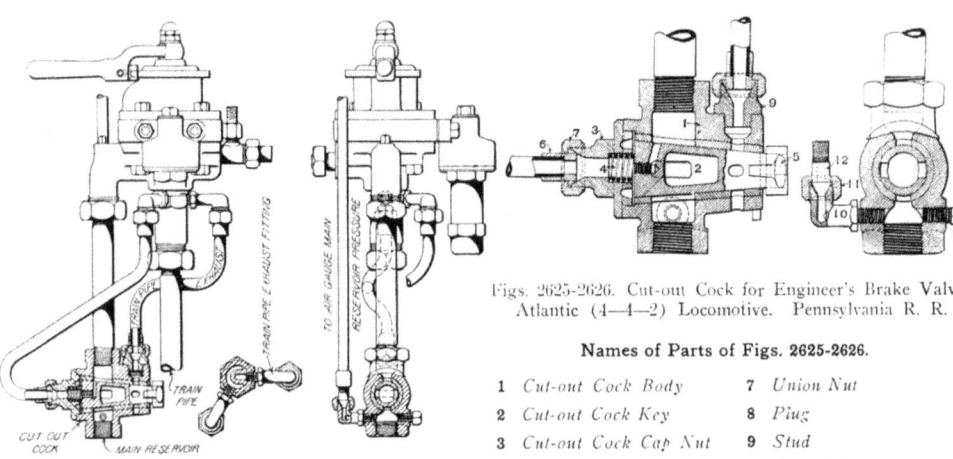

Figs. 2622-2624. Engineer's Brake Valve with Cut-out Cock for Double-Heading. Atlantic (4—4—2) Locomotive. Pennsylvania Railroad.

Figs. 2625-2626. Cut-out Cock for Engineer's Brake Valve. Atlantic (4—4—2) Locomotive. Pennsylvania R. R.

Names of Parts of Figs. 2625-2626.

1	Cut-out Cock Body	7	Union Nut
2	Cut-out Cock Key	8	Plug
3	Cut-out Cock Cap Nut	9	Stud
4	Cut-out Cock Key Spring	10	Gage Pipe Fitting
5	Cut-out Cock Handle	11	Gage Pipe Union Nut
6	Union Swivel	12	Gage Pipe Union Swivel

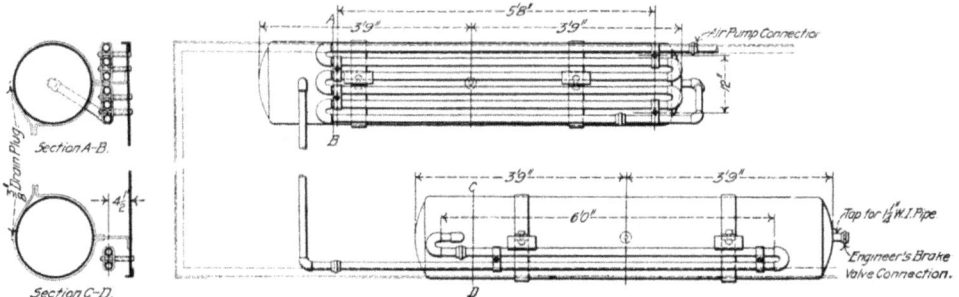

Figs. 2627-2630. Location and Arrangement of Main Reservoir. Atlantic (4—4—2) Locomotive. Pennsylvania R. R.

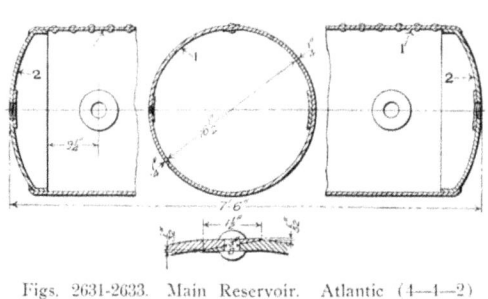

Figs. 2631-2633. Main Reservoir. Atlantic (4—4—2) Locomotive. Pennsylvania Railroad.

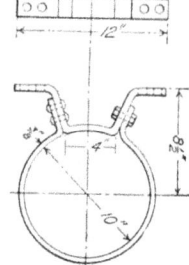

Figs. 2634-2635. Auxiliary Reservoir Hanger. Atlantic (4—4—2) Locomotive. P. R. R.

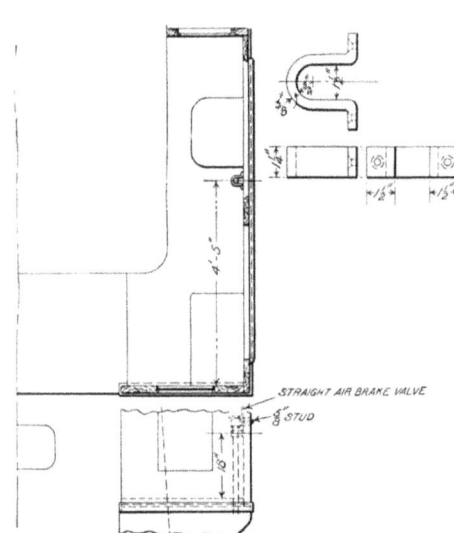

Figs. 2636-2640. Location and Method of Supporting Engineer's Brake Valve for Straight-Air Brake Equipments. Pennsylvania Railroad.

BRAKE GEAR, Foundation; General Arrangement.   Figs. 2641-2652

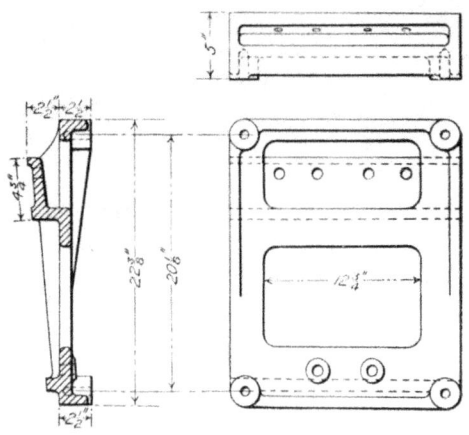

Figs. 2641-2643. Air Pump Bracket, Atlantic (4—4—2) Locomotive, P. R. R.

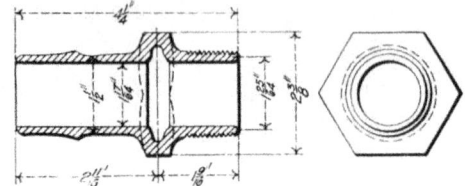

Figs. 2644-2645. Air Brake Hose Nipple.

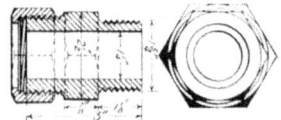

Figs. 2646-2647. 1¼-Inch Pipe Connection to Main Reservoir.

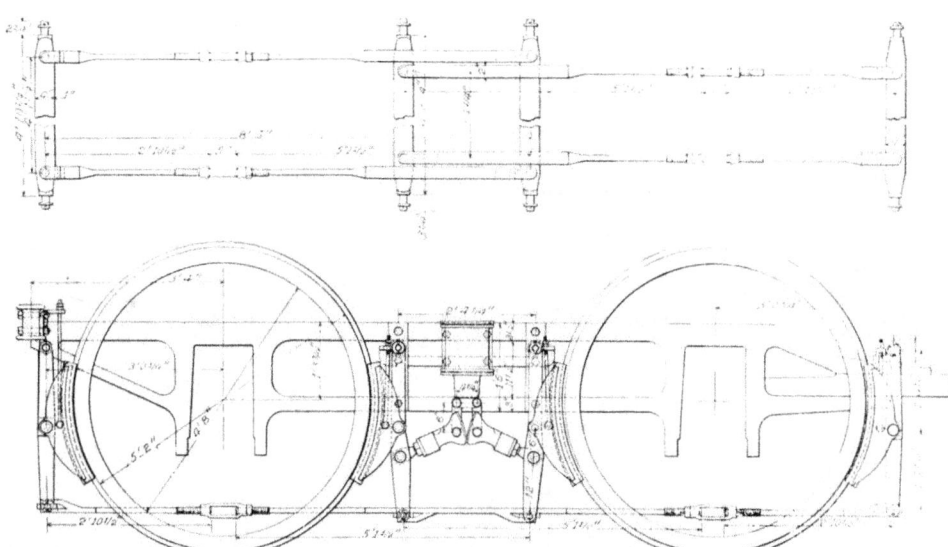

Figs. 2648-2649. Arrangement of Driver Brakes for Eight-Wheel (4—4—0) Locomotive, Chicago, Milwaukee & St. Paul.

Numbers Refer to List of Names of Parts with Figs. 2653-2704.

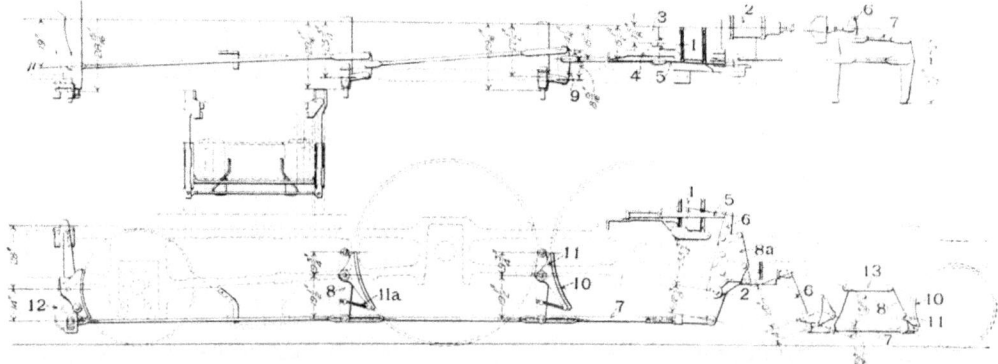

Figs. 2650-2652. General Arrangement of Foundation Brake Gear for Atlantic (4—4—2) Locomotive. Pennsylvania Railroad.

(271)

Figs. 2653–2704 BRAKE GEAR, Foundation; Details.

Names of Parts of Figs. 2650-2652.

1 Driver Brake Cylinder
2 Truck Brake Cylinder
3 Cylinder Equalizer
4 Cylinder Equalizer Guide
5 Cylinder Pull Rod
6 Cylinder Brake Lever
7 Pull Rod
8 Brake Lever
8a Brake Lever Fulcrum
9 Floating Lever
10 Brake Shoe
11 Brake Head
11a Brake Head Adjusting Spring
12 Retracting Spring
13 Brake Lever Coupling Rod

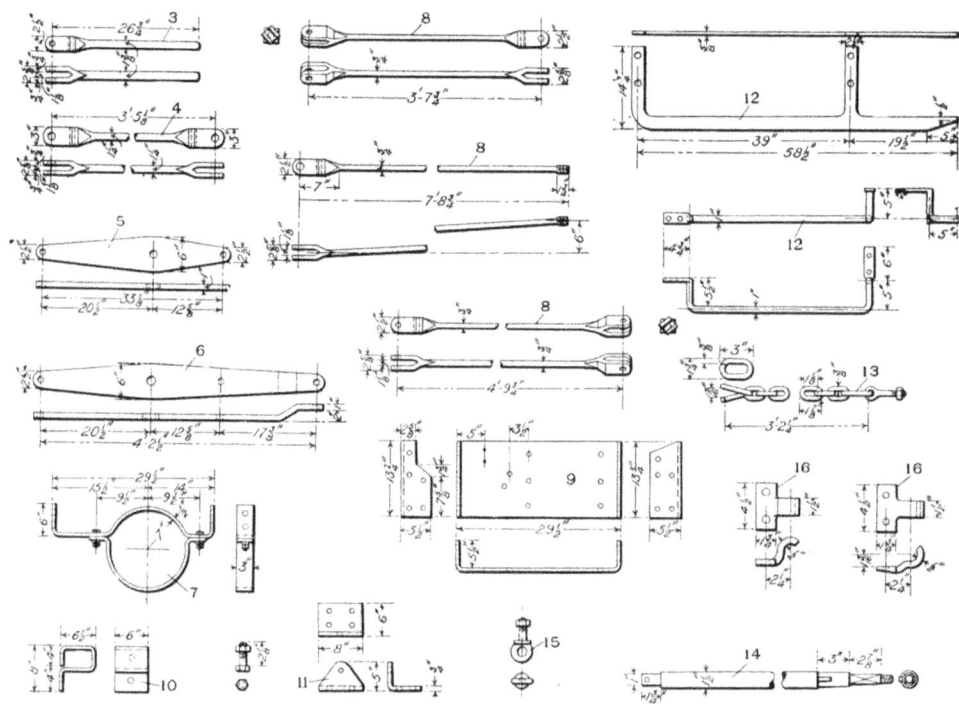

Figs. 2653–2696. Forged Details of Foundation Brake Gear for Tender of Atlantic (4—4—2) Locomotive. P. R. R.

Names of Parts of Figs. 2653-2696.

3 Brake Cylinder Push Rod
4 Cylinder Lever Connecting Rod
5 Dead Cylinder Lever
6 Live Cylinder Lever
7 Auxiliary Reservoir Support
8 Brake Rods
9 Cylinder Support
10 Chain Guard
11 Brake Mast Foot Step
12 Lever Guide
13 Brake Chain
14 Brake Mast or Shaft
15 Brake Chain Eye
16 Pipe Clamp

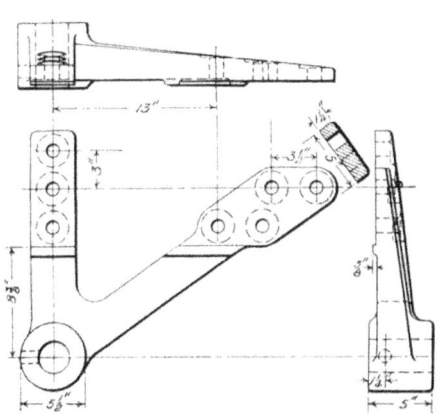

Figs. 2697–2700. Fulcrum for Driver Brake Lever. Atlantic (4—4—2) Locomotive. P. R. R.

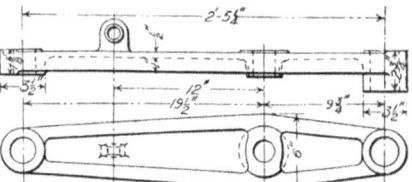

Figs. 2701–2702. Driver Brake Lever. Atlantic (4—4—2) Locomotive. P. R. R.

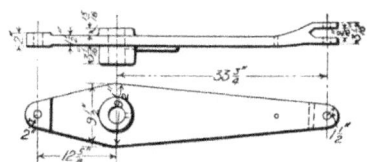

Figs. 2703–2704. Driver Brake Cylinder Lever. Atlantic (4—4—2) Locomotive. P. R. R.

BRAKE GEAR, Foundation; Details.

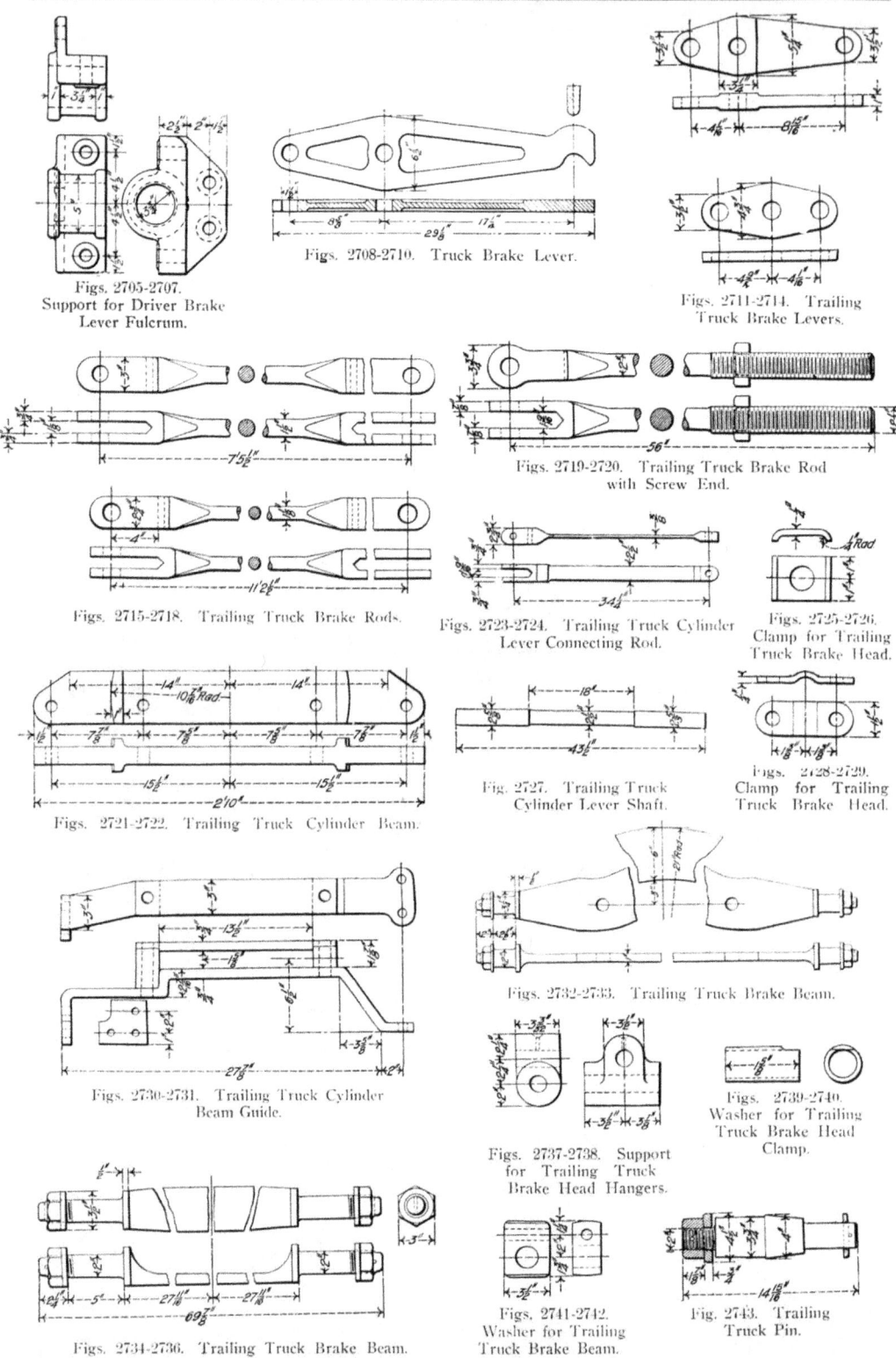

Figs. 2705-2707. Support for Driver Brake Lever Fulcrum.

Figs. 2708-2710. Truck Brake Lever.

Figs. 2711-2714. Trailing Truck Brake Levers.

Figs. 2719-2720. Trailing Truck Brake Rod with Screw End.

Figs. 2715-2718. Trailing Truck Brake Rods.

Figs. 2723-2724. Trailing Truck Cylinder Lever Connecting Rod.

Figs. 2725-2726. Clamp for Trailing Truck Brake Head.

Figs. 2721-2722. Trailing Truck Cylinder Beam.

Fig. 2727. Trailing Truck Cylinder Lever Shaft.

Figs. 2728-2729. Clamp for Trailing Truck Brake Head.

Figs. 2730-2731. Trailing Truck Cylinder Beam Guide.

Figs. 2732-2733. Trailing Truck Brake Beam.

Figs. 2737-2738. Support for Trailing Truck Brake Head Hangers.

Figs. 2739-2740. Washer for Trailing Truck Brake Head Clamp.

Figs. 2734-2736. Trailing Truck Brake Beam.

Figs. 2741-2742. Washer for Trailing Truck Brake Beam.

Fig. 2743. Trailing Truck Pin.

Figs. 2705-2743. Details of Foundation Brake Gear for Atlantic (4—4—2) Locomotive. Pennsylvania Railroad.

BRAKE GEAR, Shoes and Heads.

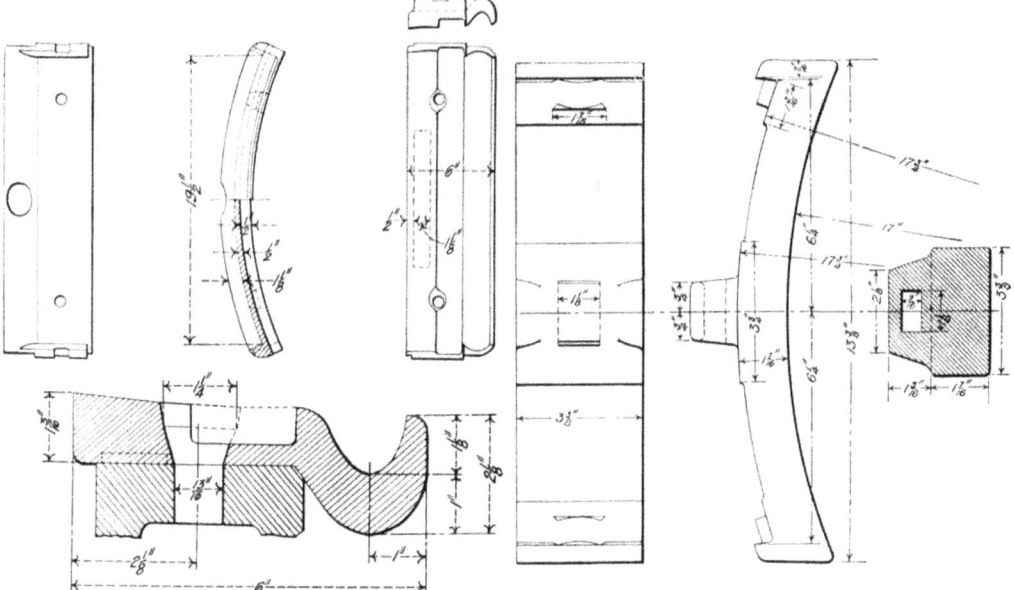

Figs. 2744-2748. Flanged Driver Brake Shoe. Atlantic (4—4—2) Locomotive. P. R. R.

Figs. 2749-2751. Christie Brake Shoe for Engine and Tender Trucks.

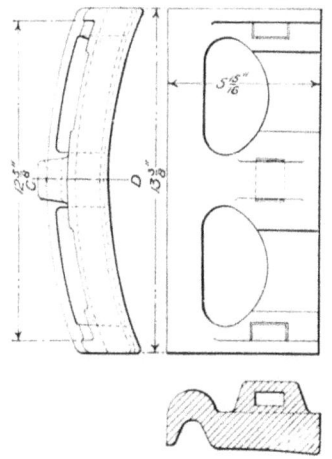

Figs. 2752-2754. Steel Flanged Brake Shoe for Engine Trucks. Pennsylvania R. R.

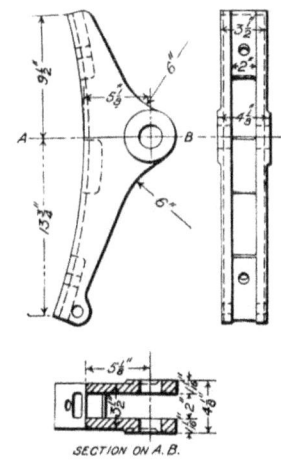

Figs. 2755-2757. Driver Brake Head. Atlantic (4—4—2) Locomotive. P. R. R.

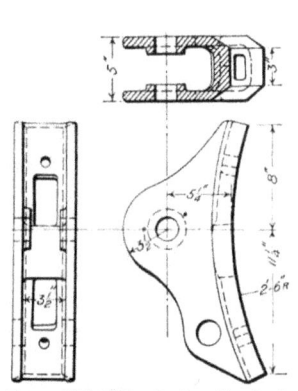

Figs. 2758-2760. Brake Head for Trailing Truck. Atlantic (4—4—2) Locomotive. P. R. R.

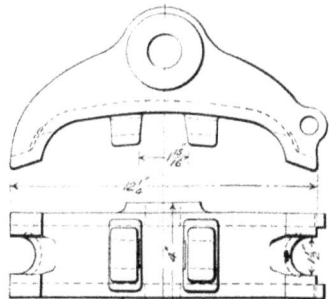

Figs. 2761-2762. Brake Head for Christie Brake Shoe.

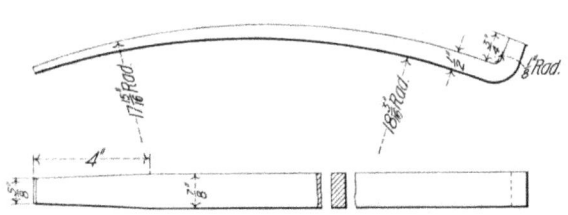

Figs. 2763-2764. Key for Christie Brake Head and Shoe.

(274)

BRAKE GEAR, Shoes. — Figs. 2765-2786

Figs. 2765-2766. Steel Back and Lug.   Fig. 2767. Steel Back Shoe, New.   Fig. 2768. Steel Back Shoe, Cracked but not Disabled.   Fig. 2769. Steel Back Shoe, Worn Out.

Unflanged Steel Back Engine and Tender Truck Brake Shoes.

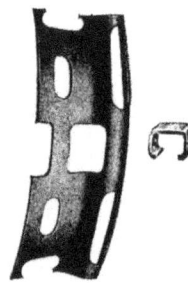    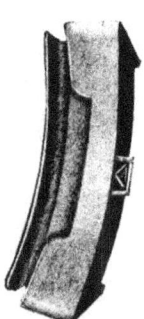

Fig. 2770. Flanged Steel Back and Lug.   Fig. 2771. Steel Back Shoe.   Fig. 2772. Streeter Type.   Fig. 2773. Diamond "S" Type.   Fig. 2774. "U" Type.

Flanged Steel Back Engine Truck and Tender Brake Shoes.

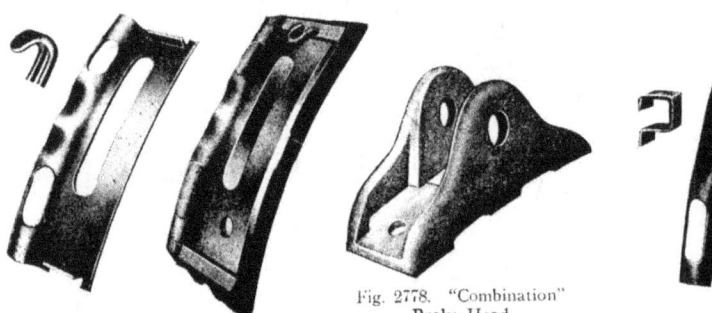 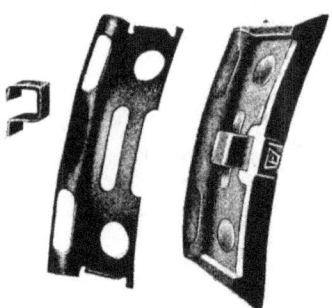

Figs. 2775-2777. Flanged Steel Back Driver Shoe.   Fig. 2778. "Combination" Brake Head.   Figs. 2779-2781. Flanged Steel Back Driver Shoe.

 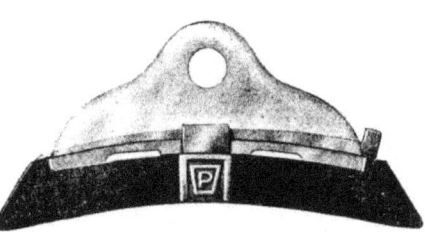 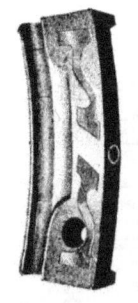 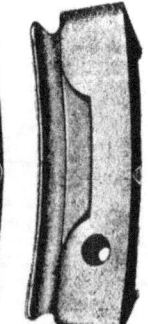

Fig. 2782. Perfecto Type.   Fig. 2783. Diamond "S" Type.   Fig. 2784. Combination Brake Head and Shoe.   Fig. 2785. Streeter Type.   Fig. 2786. "U" Type.

Steel Back Driver Brake Shoes. American Brake Shoe & Foundry Co.

Figs. 2787–2791 CABS, Details.

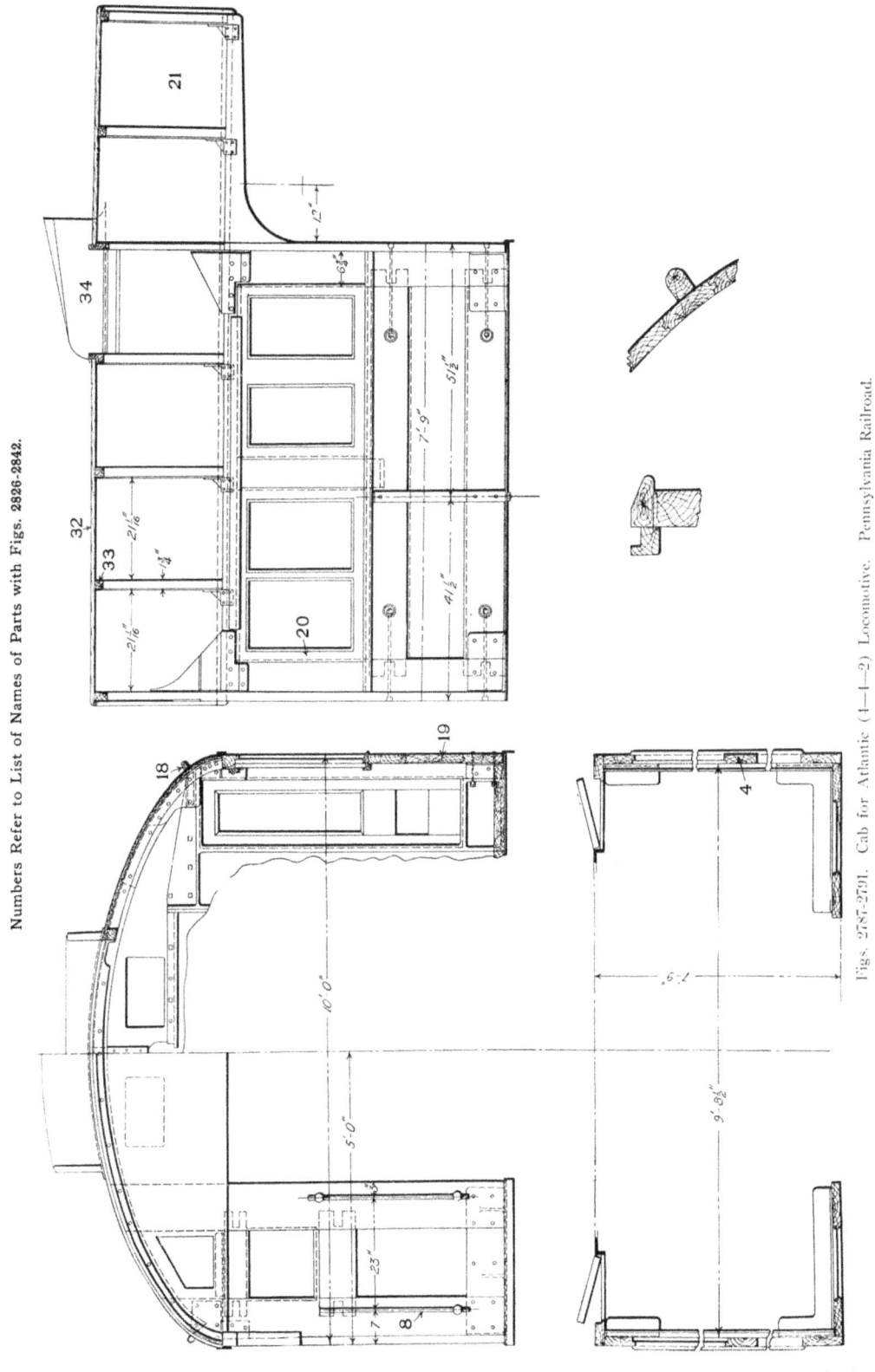

Figs. 2787–2791. Cab for Atlantic (4–4–2) Locomotive. Pennsylvania Railroad.

CABS, Details. Figs. 2792–2810

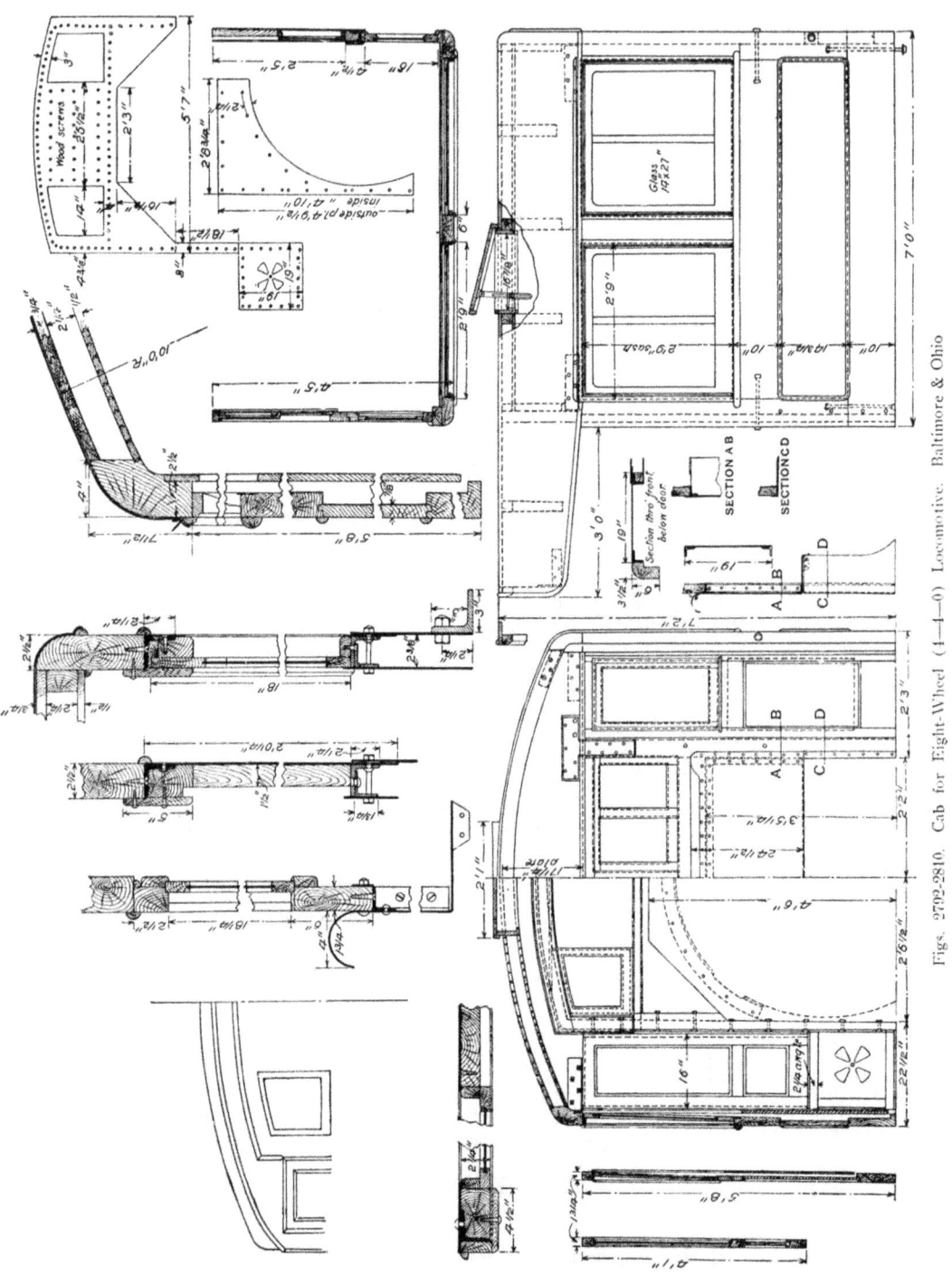

Figs. 2792–2810. Cab for Eight-Wheel (4–4–0) Locomotive. Baltimore & Ohio

CABS, Details.

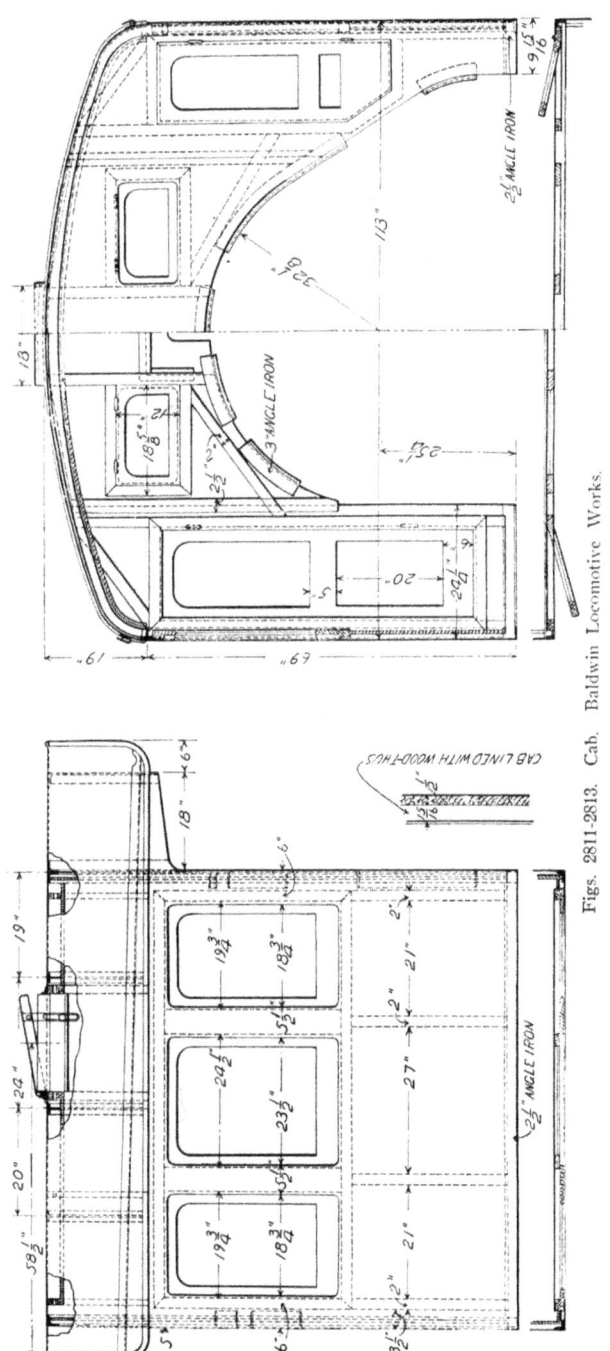

Figs. 2811-2813. Cab. Baldwin Locomotive Works.

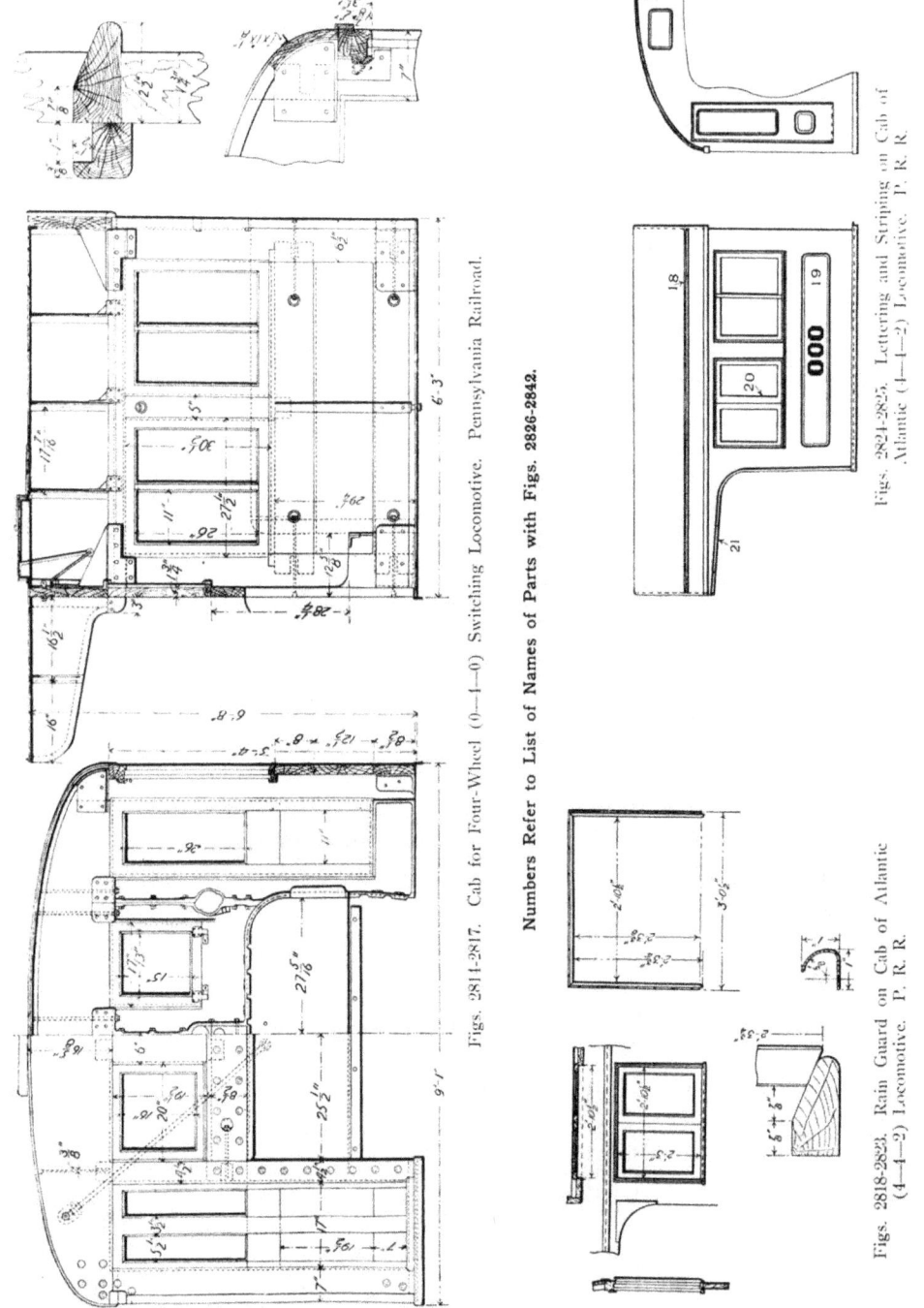

Figs. 2814-2817. Cab for Four-Wheel (0—4—0) Switching Locomotive. Pennsylvania Railroad.

Figs. 2818-2823. Rain Guard on Cab of Atlantic (4—4—2) Locomotive. P. R. R.

Figs. 2824-2825. Lettering and Striping on Cab of Atlantic (4—4—2) Locomotive. P. R. R.

Numbers Refer to List of Names of Parts with Figs. 2826-2842.

Names of Parts of Cabs, Figs. 2787-2791, 2824-2825, 2870-2871, 2874-2876, 2893-2896, 2946-2947.

1 *Seat*	12 *Hand Rail Column*	23 *Arm Rest Hinge*
2 *Back Window*	13 *Door Guides*	24 *Window Stile*
3 *Foot Boards*	14 *Door Handle*	25 *Ventilator Lever and Piece*
4 *Window Post*	15 *Back Sheet*	26 *Ventilator Lever Fulcrum Plate*
5 *Back Door*	16 *Bracket for Door Rail*	32 *Roof Boards*
6 *Back Door Rail*	17 *Axle for Door Wheels*	33 *Roof Carline*
7 *Back Door Roller*	18 *Eaves for Water Gutter*	34 *Ventilator*
8 *Handrail*	19 *Cab Side Panel*	35 *Ventilator Connection*
9 *Top Cab Bracket*	20 *Window Sash*	36 *Ventilator Lever*
10 *Protection Plate for Back Doors*	21 *Rear Overhang*	37 *Ventilator Lever Clamp*
11 *Door Hand Rails*	22 *Arm Rest*	

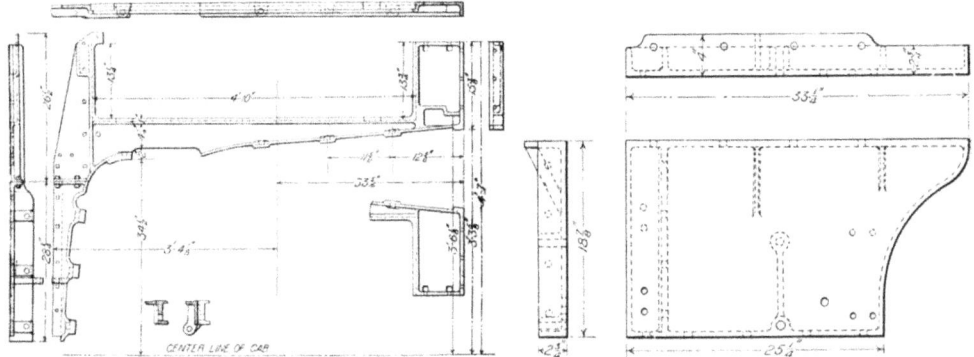

Figs. 2826-2832. Cab Saddle. Figs. 2833-2835. Top Cab Bracket.

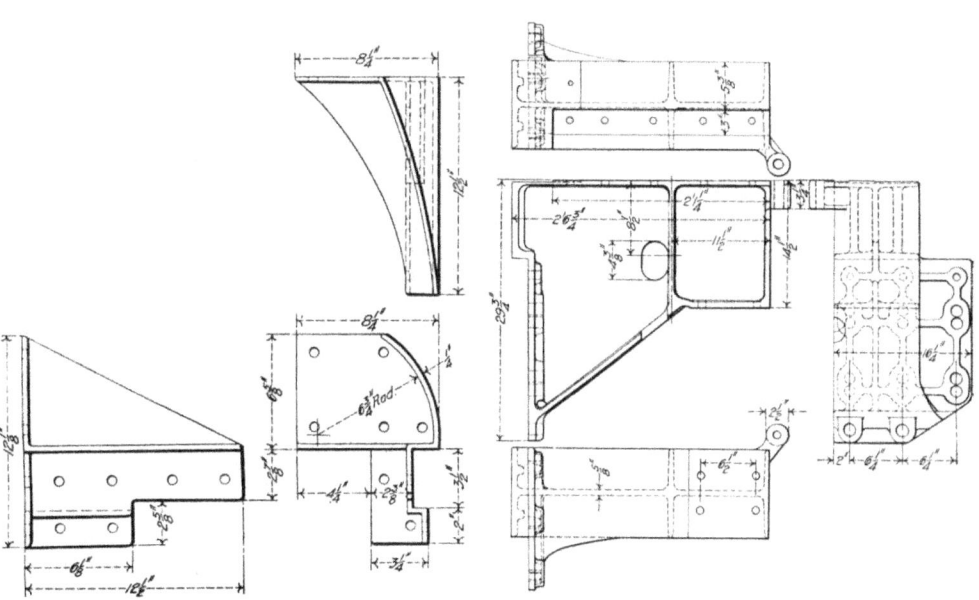

Figs. 2836-2838. Top Corner Cab Bracket. Figs. 2839-2842. Lower Cab Bracket.

Figs. 2826-2842. Details of Cab of Atlantic (4—4—2) Locomotive. Pennsylvania Railroad.

CABS, Details. Figs. 2843-2869

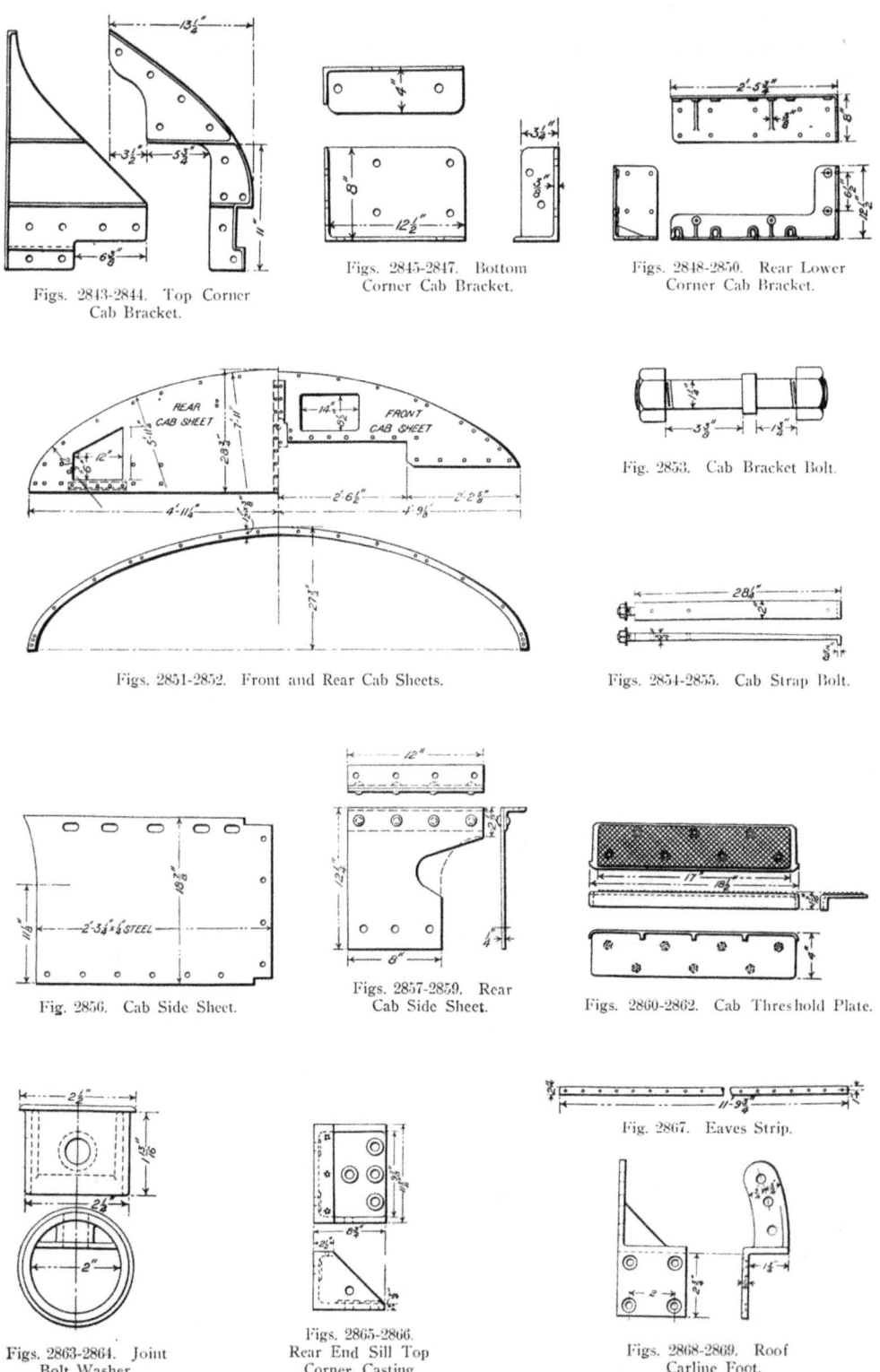

Figs. 2843-2844. Top Corner Cab Bracket.

Figs. 2845-2847. Bottom Corner Cab Bracket.

Figs. 2848-2850. Rear Lower Corner Cab Bracket.

Figs. 2851-2852. Front and Rear Cab Sheets.

Fig. 2853. Cab Bracket Bolt.

Figs. 2854-2855. Cab Strap Bolt.

Fig. 2856. Cab Side Sheet.

Figs. 2857-2859. Rear Cab Side Sheet.

Figs. 2860-2862. Cab Threshold Plate.

Figs. 2863-2864. Joint Bolt Washer.

Figs. 2865-2866. Rear End Sill Top Corner Casting.

Fig. 2867. Eaves Strip.

Figs. 2868-2869. Roof Carline Foot.

Figs. 2843-2869. Details of Cab of Atlantic (4—4—2) Locomotive. Pennsylvania Railroad.

Figs. 2870-2892. CABS, Details.

Numbers Refer to List of Names of Parts with Figs. 2826-2842.

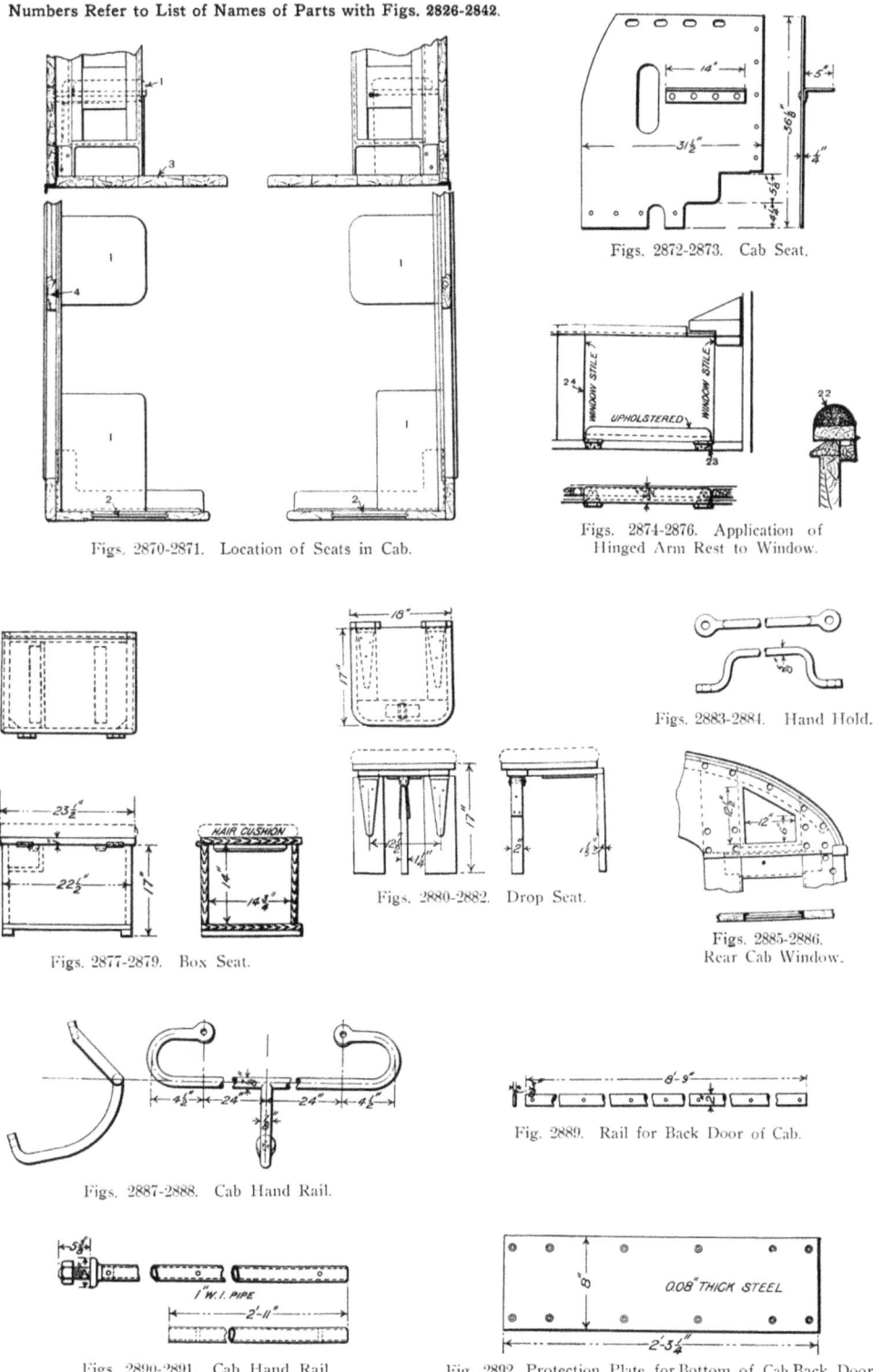

Figs. 2870-2871. Location of Seats in Cab.

Figs. 2872-2873. Cab Seat.

Figs. 2874-2876. Application of Hinged Arm Rest to Window.

Figs. 2877-2879. Box Seat.

Figs. 2880-2882. Drop Seat.

Figs. 2883-2884. Hand Hold.

Figs. 2885-2886. Rear Cab Window.

Figs. 2887-2888. Cab Hand Rail.

Fig. 2889. Rail for Back Door of Cab.

Figs. 2890-2891. Cab Hand Rail.

Fig. 2892. Protection Plate for Bottom of Cab Back Door.

Figs. 2870-2892. Details of Atlantic (4—4—2) Locomotive. Pennsylvania Railroad.

(282)

CABS, Details   Figs. 2893-2927

Numbers Refer to List of Names of Parts with Figs. 2826-2842

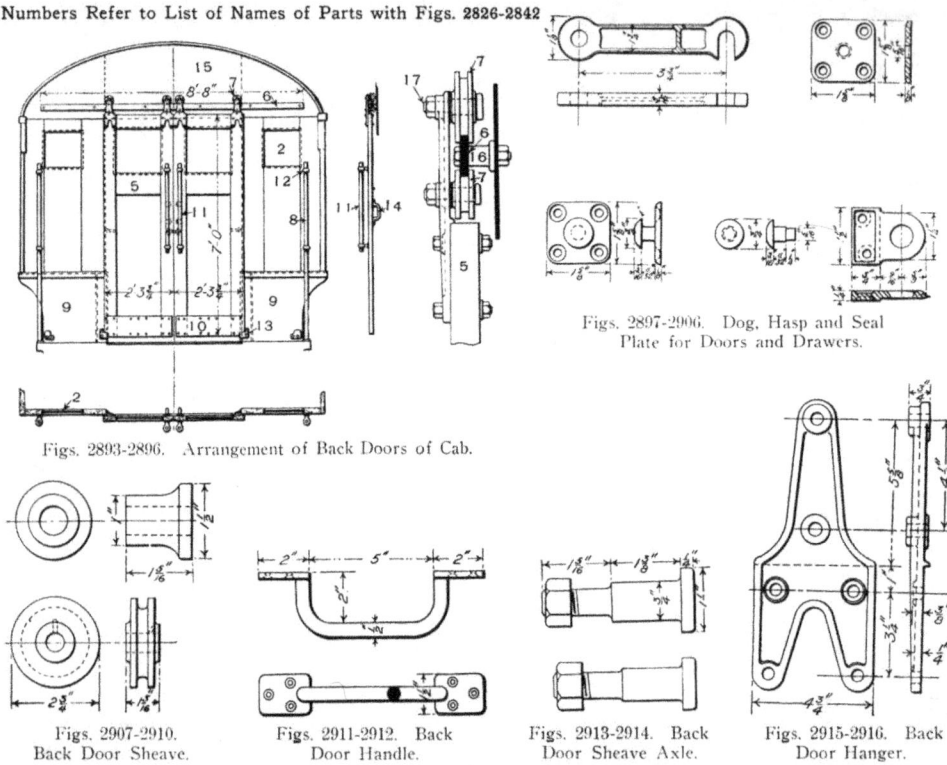

Figs. 2893-2896. Arrangement of Back Doors of Cab.

Figs. 2897-2906. Dog, Hasp and Seal Plate for Doors and Drawers.

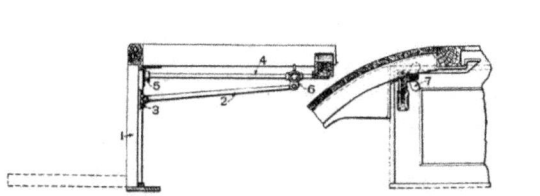

Figs. 2907-2910. Back Door Sheave.   Figs. 2911-2912. Back Door Handle.   Figs. 2913-2914. Back Door Sheave Axle.   Figs. 2915-2916. Back Door Hanger.

Numbers Refer to List of Names of Parts Below.

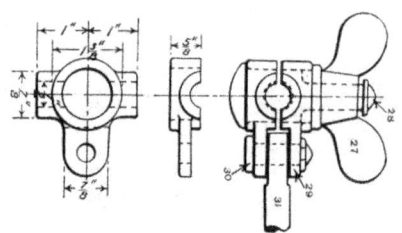

Figs. 2917-2918. Arrangement of Operating Device for Cab Front Door, Opening Outward.

Figs. 2919-2920. Clamp for Ventilator and Cab Front Door.

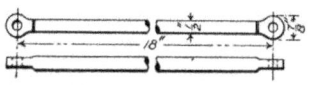

Figs. 2921-2922. Connecting Rod for Operating Device.

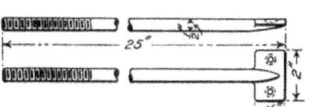

Figs. 2923-2924. Guide for Operating Device.

Names of Parts of Figs. 2917-2920.

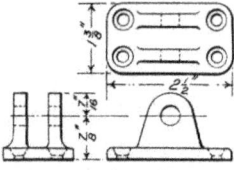

Figs. 2925-2927. Fulcrum for Operating Device.

1	*Door*	7	*Slide Thumb Screw*
2	*Door Rod*	27	*Thumb Screw*
3	*Door Rod Bracket*	28	*Thumb Screw Stem*
4	*Guide*	29	*Thumb Screw Clamp*
5	*Guide Bracket*	30	*Pin for Connecting Rod*
6	*Slide*	31	*Connecting Rod*

Figs. 2893-2927. Details of Cab Doors of Atlantic (4—4—2) Locomotive. Pennsylvania Railroad.

(283)

CABS, Details.

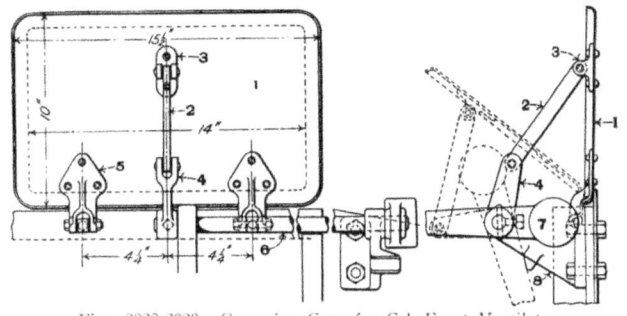

Figs. 2928-2929. Operating Gear for Cab Front Ventilator.

Names of Parts of Figs. 2928-2929.

1. *Ventilator Door*
2. *Link*
3. *Link Bracket*
4. *Operating Arm*
5. *Door Hinge*
6. *Operating Shaft*
7. *Counterbalance*
8. *Operating Shaft Bracket*

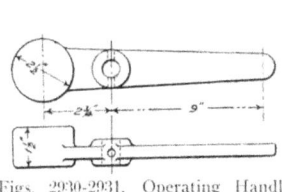
Figs. 2930-2931. Operating Handle.

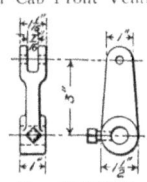
Figs. 2932-2933. Lever Arm.

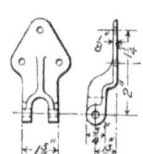
Figs. 2934-2935. Half Hinge.

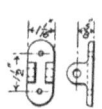
Figs. 2936-2937. Bracket.

Figs. 2938-2939. Operating Link.

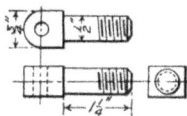
Figs. 2940-2942. Hinge Bolt.

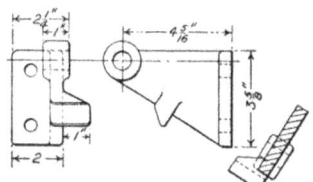
Figs. 2943-2945. Shaft Bearing.

Numbers Refer to List of Names of Parts with Figs. 2826-2842.

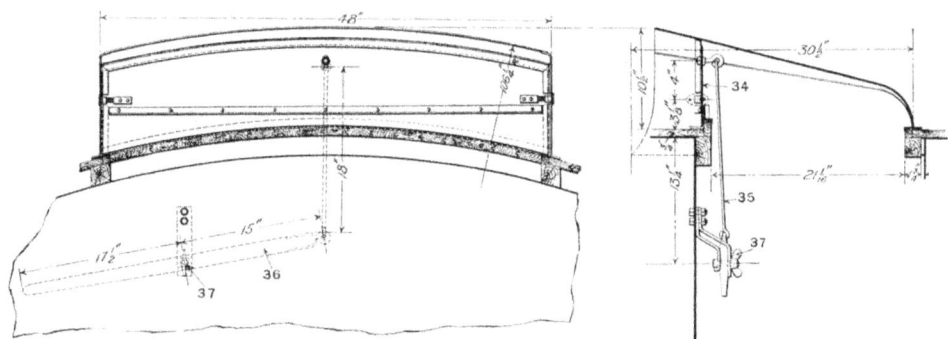
Figs. 2946-2947. General Arrangement of Cab Roof Ventilator.

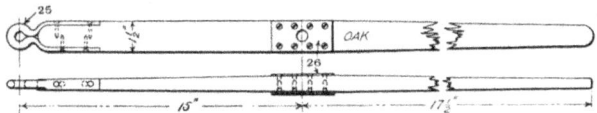
Figs. 2948-2949. Ventilator Lever.

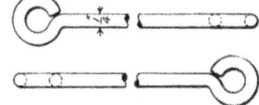
Figs. 2950-2951. Connecting Rod.

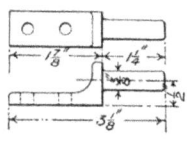
Figs. 2952-2953. Shutter Trunnion.

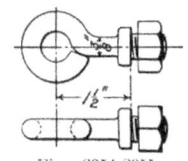
Figs. 2954-2955. Shutter Staple.

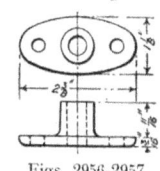
Figs. 2956-2957. Shutter Bearing.

Figs. 2928-2957. Details of Ventilators of Cab of Atlantic (4—4—2) Locomotive. Pennsylvania Railroad.

CAB FITTINGS, Miscellaneous.   Figs. 2958-2962

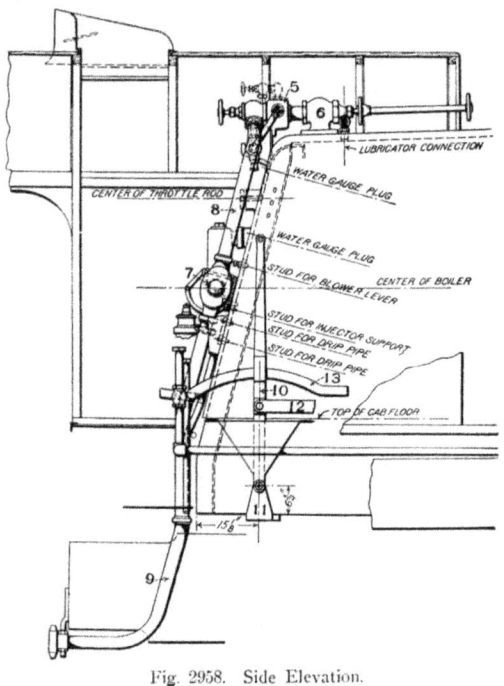

Fig. 2958. Side Elevation.

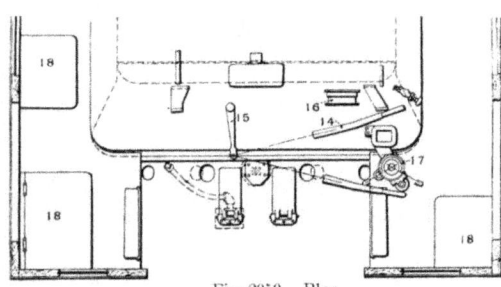

Fig. 2959. Plan.

Figs. 2958-2959. Arrangement of Cab Fittings on Atlantic (4—4—2) Locomotive. Pennsylvania Railroad.

Names of Parts of Figs. 2958-2959.

5 *Turret*
6 *Turret Valve*
7 *Injector*
8 *Injector Steam Pipe*
9 *Suction Pipe*
10 *Reverse Lever*
11 *Reverse Lever Bracket*
12 *Reach Rod*
13 *Quadrant*
14 *Throttle Lever*
15 *Throttle Lever Fulcrum Rod*
16 *Steam Gage*
17 *Engineer's Valve*
18 *Cab Seat*

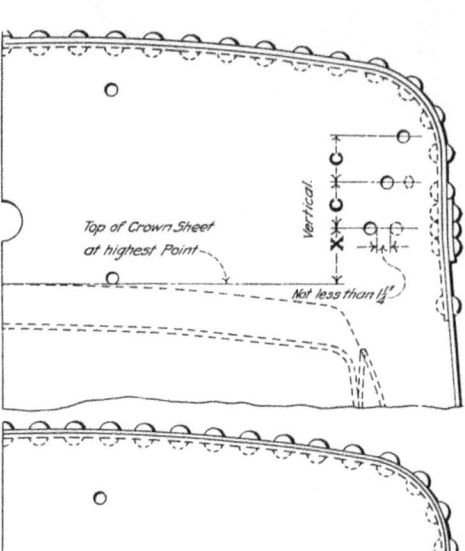

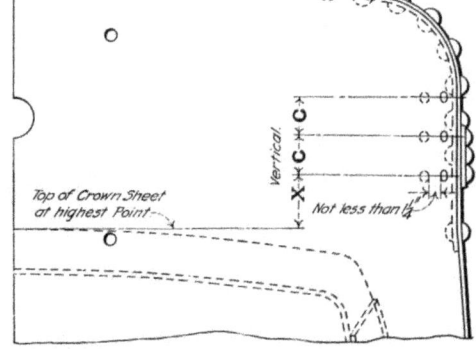

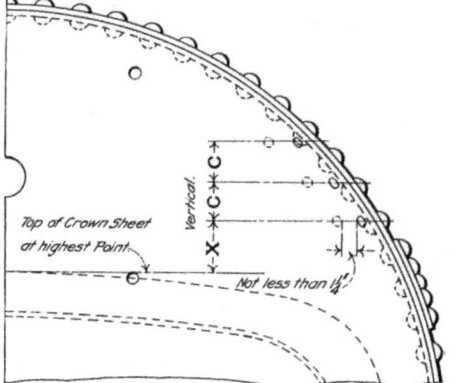

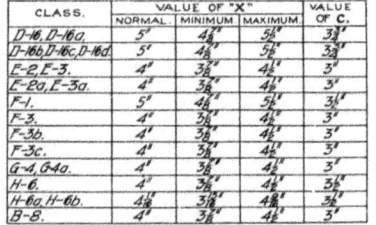

CLASS.	VALUE OF "X"			VALUE OF C.
	NORMAL.	MINIMUM.	MAXIMUM.	
D-16, D-16a.	5"	4½"	5½"	3½"
D-16b, D-16c, D-16d.	5"	4½"	5½"	3½"
E-2, E-3.	4"	3½"	4½"	3"
E-2a, E-3a.	4"	3½"	4½"	3"
F-1.	5"	4½"	5½"	3½"
F-3.	4"	3½"	4½"	3"
F-3b.	4"	3½"	4½"	3"
F-3c.	4"	3½"	4½"	3"
G-4, G-4a.	4"	3½"	4½"	3"
H-6.	4"	3½"	4½"	3½"
H-6a, H-6b.	4½"	3½"	4½"	3½"
B-8.	4"	3½"	4½"	3"

Figs. 2960-2962. Standard Location of Gage Cocks. Pennsylvania Railroad.

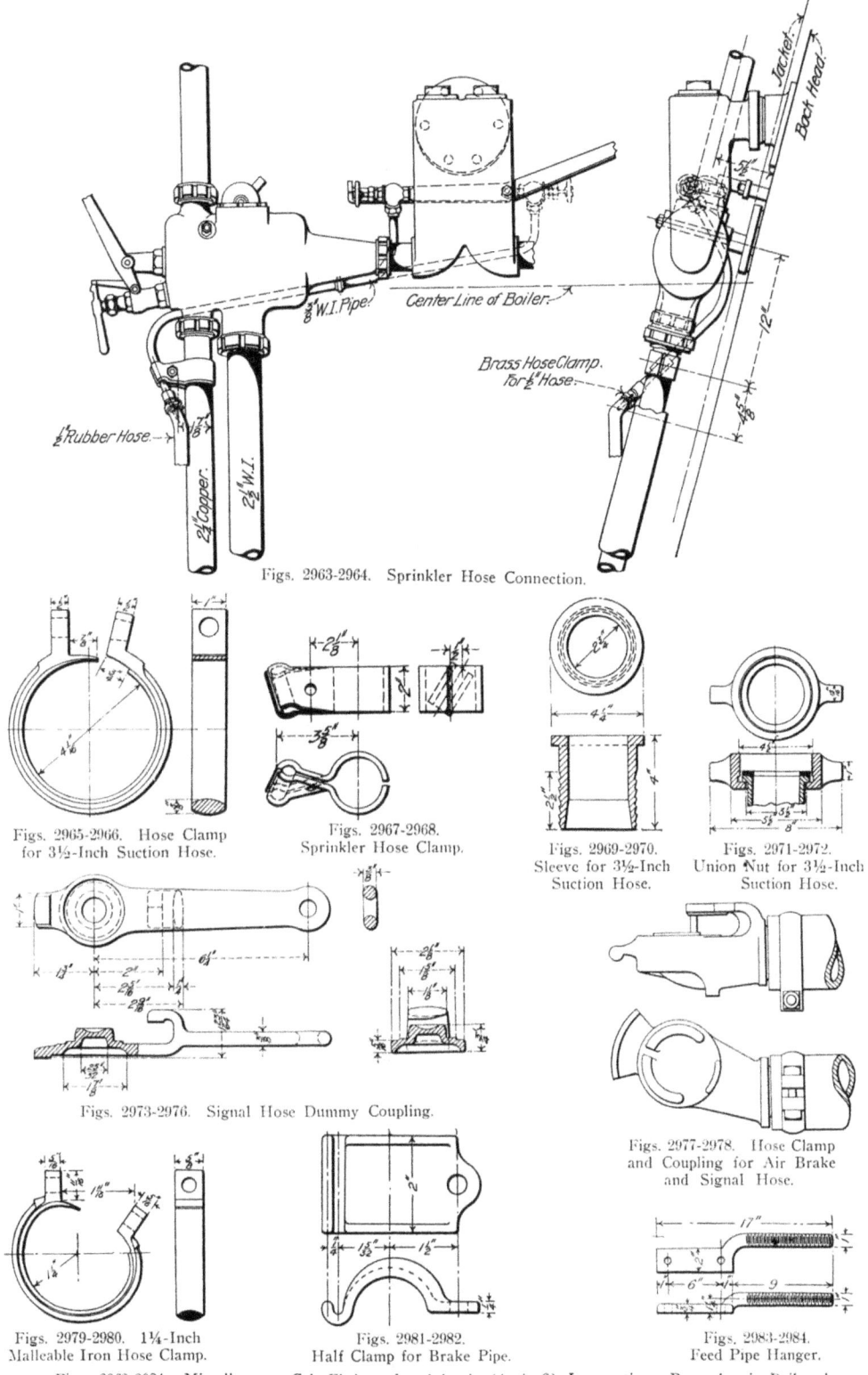

Figs. 2963-2964. Sprinkler Hose Connection.

Figs. 2965-2966. Hose Clamp for 3½-Inch Suction Hose.

Figs. 2967-2968. Sprinkler Hose Clamp.

Figs. 2969-2970. Sleeve for 3½-Inch Suction Hose.

Figs. 2971-2972. Union Nut for 3½-Inch Suction Hose.

Figs. 2973-2976. Signal Hose Dummy Coupling.

Figs. 2977-2978. Hose Clamp and Coupling for Air Brake and Signal Hose.

Figs. 2979-2980. 1¼-Inch Malleable Iron Hose Clamp.

Figs. 2981-2982. Half Clamp for Brake Pipe.

Figs. 2983-2984. Feed Pipe Hanger.

Figs. 2963-2984. Miscellaneous Cab Fittings for Atlantic (4—4—2) Locomotive. Pennsylvania Railroad.

CAB FITTINGS, Miscellaneous.

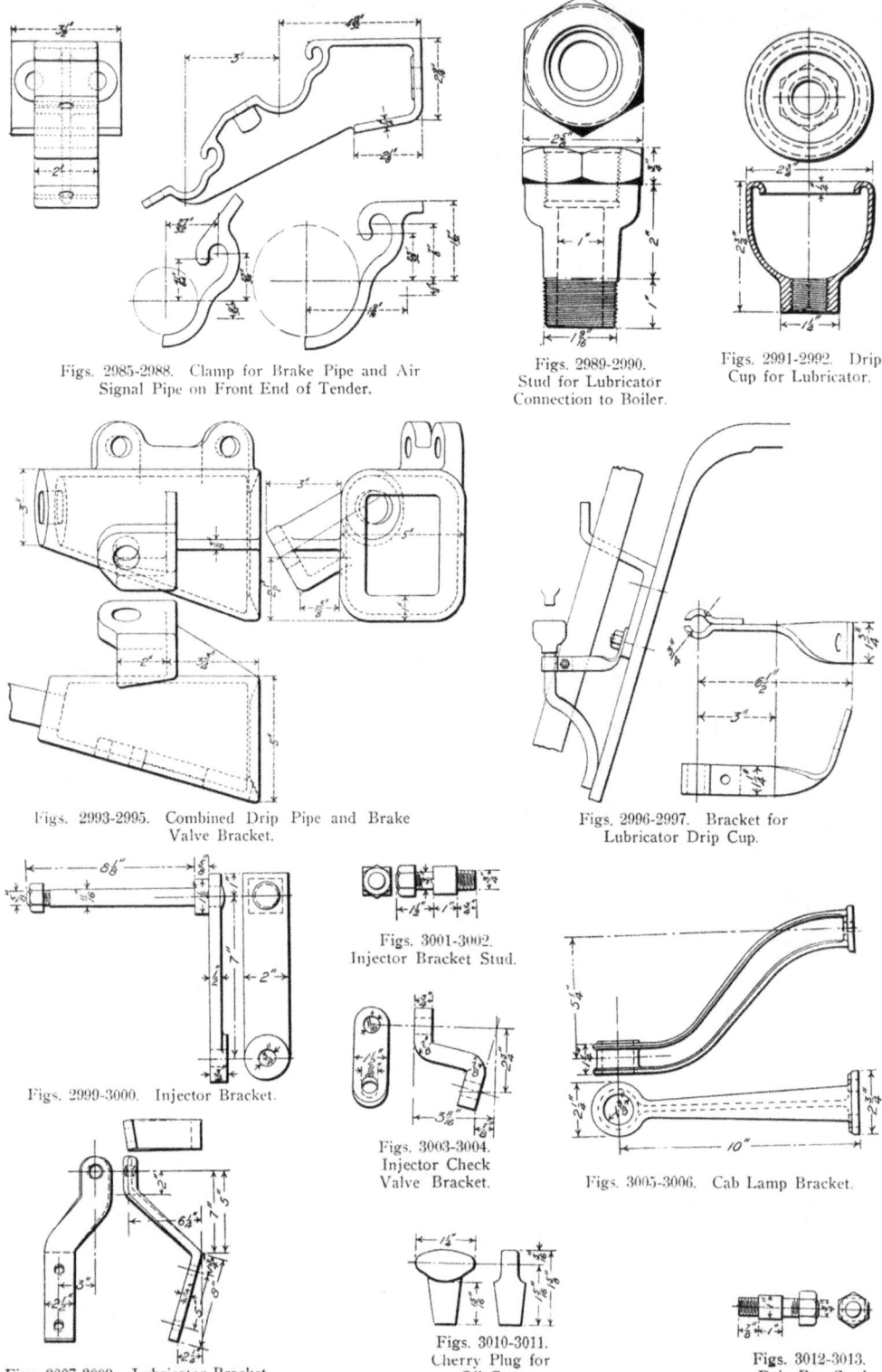

Figs. 2985-2988. Clamp for Brake Pipe and Air Signal Pipe on Front End of Tender.

Figs. 2989-2990. Stud for Lubricator Connection to Boiler.

Figs. 2991-2992. Drip Cup for Lubricator.

Figs. 2993-2995. Combined Drip Pipe and Brake Valve Bracket.

Figs. 2996-2997. Bracket for Lubricator Drip Cup.

Figs. 2999-3000. Injector Bracket.

Figs. 3001-3002. Injector Bracket Stud.

Figs. 3003-3004. Injector Check Valve Bracket.

Figs. 3005-3006. Cab Lamp Bracket.

Figs. 3007-3009. Lubricator Bracket.

Figs. 3010-3011. Cherry Plug for Oil Cup.

Figs. 3012-3013. Drip Pan Stud.

Figs. 2985-3013. Miscellaneous Cab Fittings for Atlantic (4—4—2) Locomotive. Pennsylvania Railroad.

CAB FITTINGS, Valves.

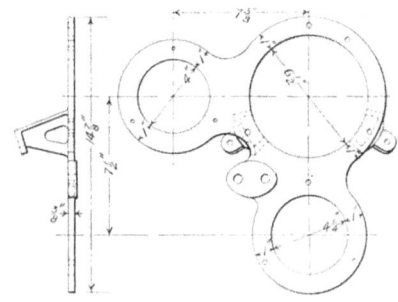

Figs. 3014-3015. Steam, Air and Steam Heat Gage Stand. Atlantic (4—4—2) Locomotive. P. R. R.

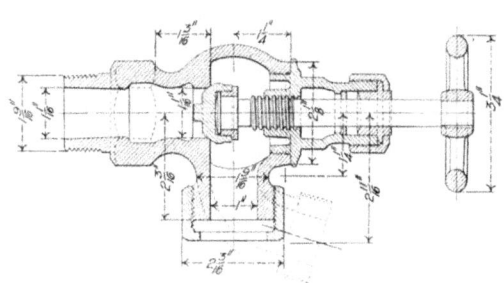

Fig. 3016. 1-Inch Angle Cock.

Numbers Refer to List of Names of Parts Below.

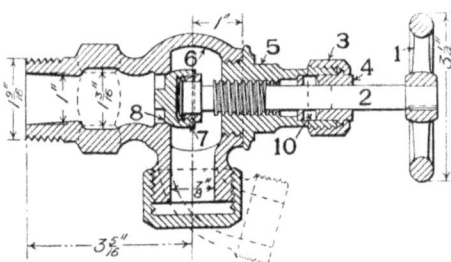

Fig. 3017. ¾-Inch Angle Valve.

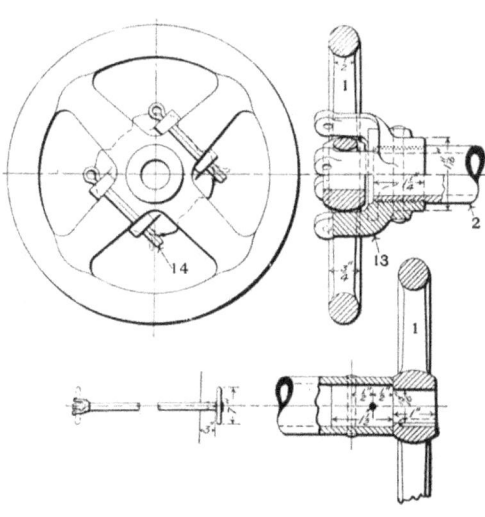

Figs. 3018-3021. Extension Stem and Hand Wheel for Bridge Pipe Valve.

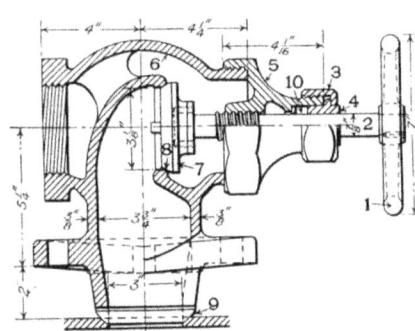

Fig. 3022. Bridge Pipe Valve.

Names of Parts of Figs. 3017-3022.

1 Valve Hand Wheel
2 Valve Stem
3 Valve Gland Nut
4 Valve Gland
5 Valve Stem Nut
6 Valve Case
7 Valve Adjustable Seat
8 Valve Seat
9 Valve Bearing Seat
10 Valve Stuffing Box
13 Valve Stem Head
14 Valve Stem Head Cotter

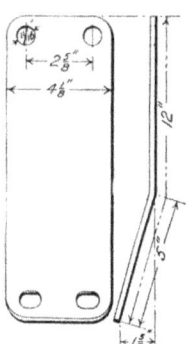

Figs. 3023-3024. Bridge Pipe Bracket.

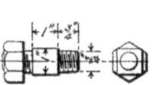

Figs. 3025-3026. Bridge Pipe Bracket Stud.

CAB FITTINGS, Blower Valves.

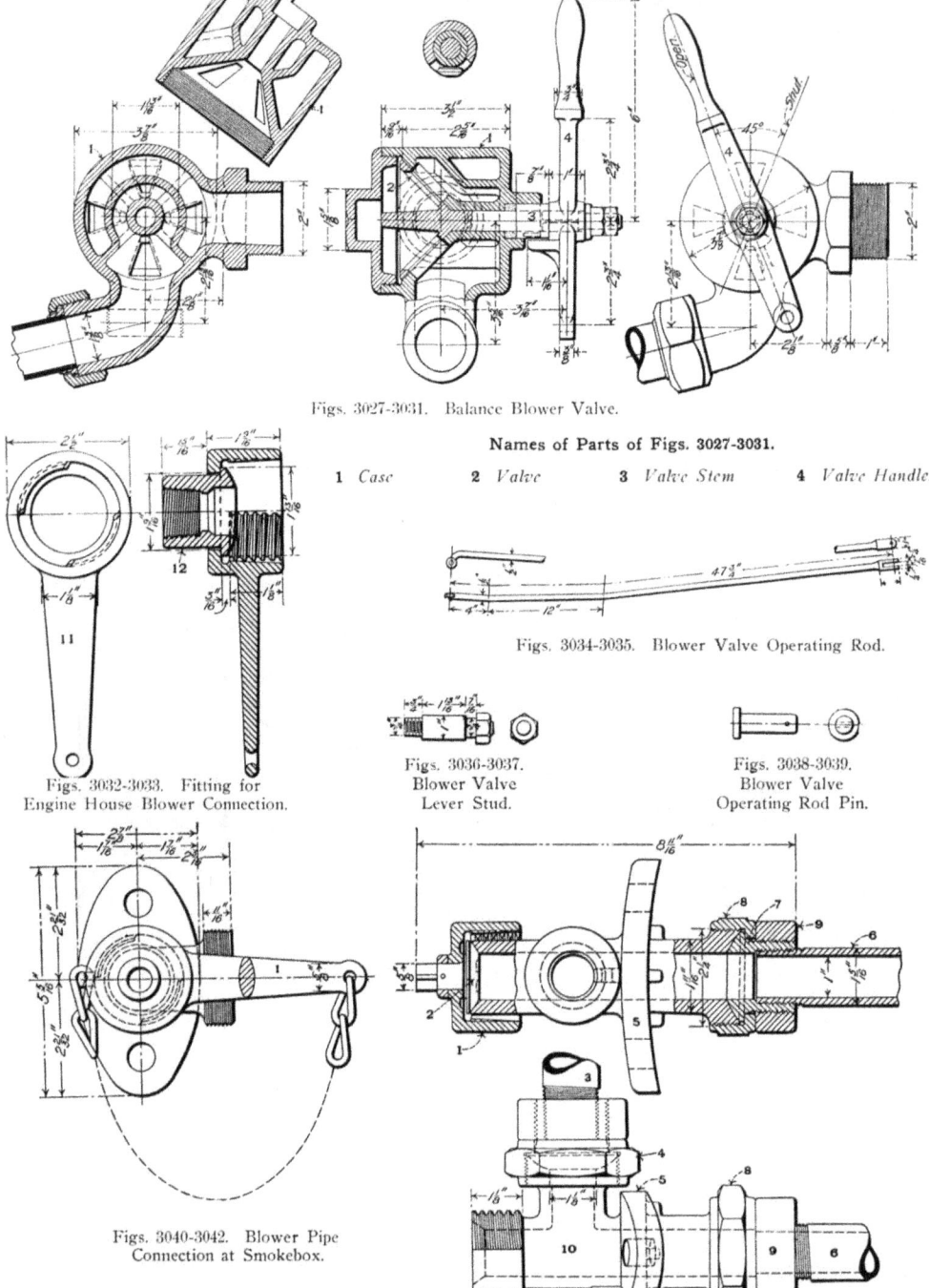

Figs. 3027-3031. Balance Blower Valve.

Names of Parts of Figs. 3027-3031.

1 *Case* 2 *Valve* 3 *Valve Stem* 4 *Valve Handle.*

Figs. 3032-3033. Fitting for Engine House Blower Connection.

Figs. 3034-3035. Blower Valve Operating Rod.

Figs. 3036-3037. Blower Valve Lever Stud.

Figs. 3038-3039. Blower Valve Operating Rod Pin.

Figs. 3040-3042. Blower Pipe Connection at Smokebox.

Names of Parts of Figs. 3040-3042.

1 *Handle Nut*
2 *Outside Valve*
3 *Blower Pipe*
4 *Blower Pipe Union*
5 *Smokebox Flange*
6 *Smokebox Blower Pipe*
7 *Smokebox Ball Joint*
8 *Smokebox Ball Joint Nut*
9 *Smokebox Ball Joint Check Nut*
10 *Casing*

Figs. 3027-3042. Details of Blower Valve and Connections for Atlantic (4—4—2) Locomotive. Pennsylvania Railroad.

Figs. 3043–3063   **CAB FITTINGS, Throttle Valve.**

Numbers Refer to List of Names of Parts on Opposite Page.

Figs. 3043–3045. Dry Pipe and Throttle Valve.   Fig. 3046. Throttle Valve and Chamber.

Figs. 3047–3048. Throttle Lever and Quadrant.

Figs. 3053–3055. Throttle Lever Fulcrum.

Figs. 3056–3057. Throttle Lever Latch Handle.

Figs. 3049–3052. Throttle Lever Quadrant.

Figs. 3058–3060. Throttle Lever Catch.   Figs. 3061–3063. Throttle Lever Bell Crank.

Figs. 3043–3063. Details of Throttle Valve and Lever for Atlantic (4–4–2) Locomotive. Pennsylvania Railroad.

(290)

CAB FITTINGS, Throttle Valve.

Figs. 3064-3072

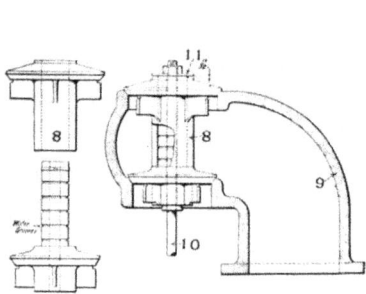

Figs. 3064-3065. Chamber's Compensating Throttle Valve.

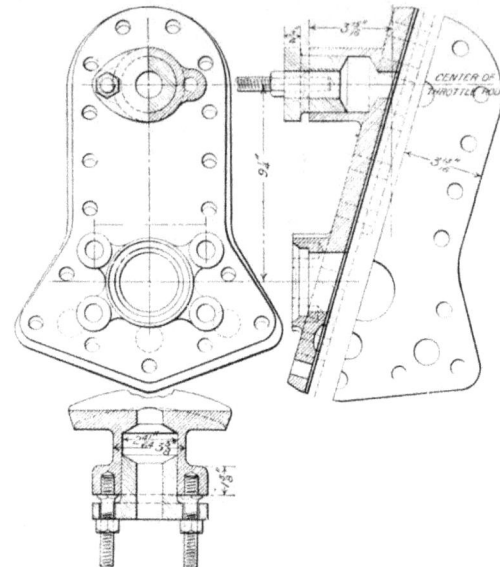

Figs. 3066-3069. Combined Throttle Rod Stuffing Box and Check Valve Flange.

Names of Parts of Throttle Valves, Figs. 3043-3065.

1. Throttle Lever Quadrant
2. Throttle Stem
3. Throttle Lever
4. Throttle Lever Latch Connection
5. Throttle Lever Latch Handle
6. Throttle Lever Latch Spring
7. Throttle Lever Latch
8. Throttle Valve
9. Throttle Valve Casing
10. Throttle Valve Stem
11. Compensating Valve
19. Dome Base or Flange
20. Dome
22. Dome Cap
24. Throttle Case
25. Throttle Standpipe
26. Dry Pipe
42. Front Tube Sheet
44. Dry Pipe Stiffening Ring
84. Throttle Valve Stem
85. Throttle Bell Crank
86. Throttle Stem
87. Throttle Pipe Clamp Bolt
88. Throttle Valve

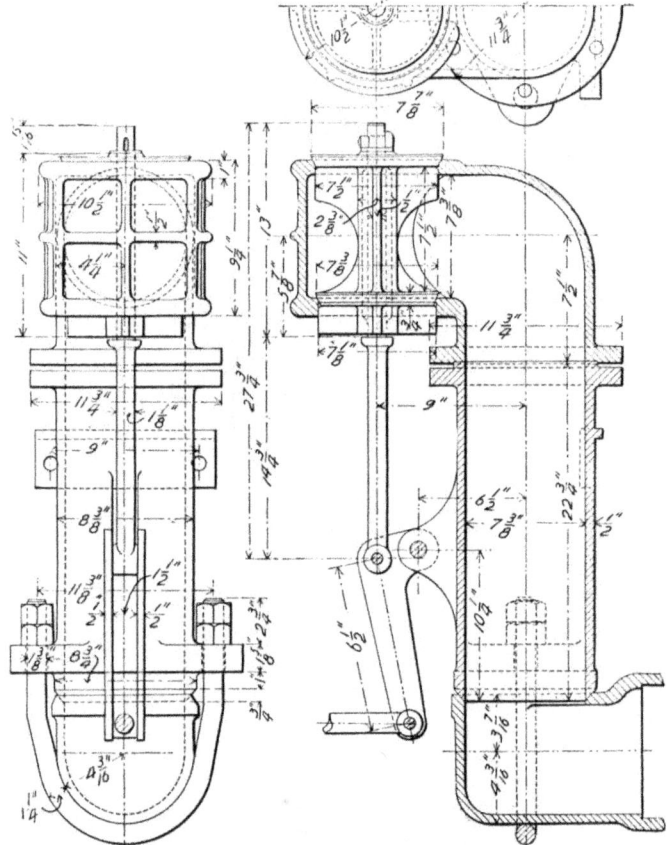

Figs. 3070-3072. Throttle Valve for Ten-Wheel (4—6—0) Locomotive. Plant System.

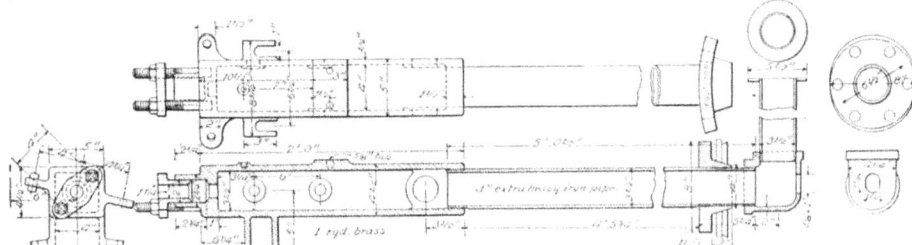

Figs. 3073-3078. Throttle Rod Pipe.

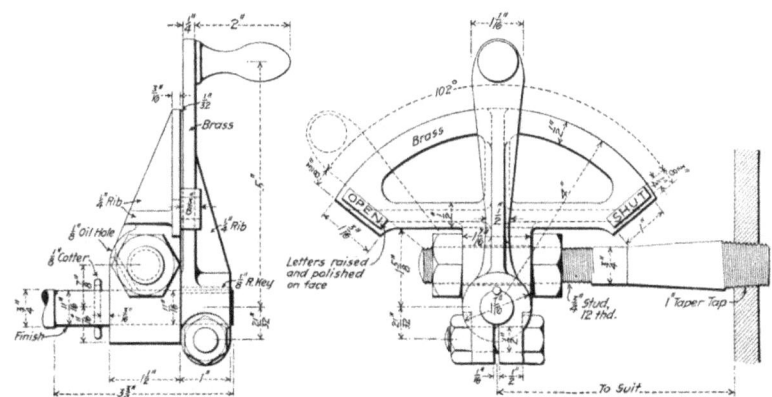

Figs. 3079-3080. Handle for Chamber's Drifting Valve. Wabash Railroad.

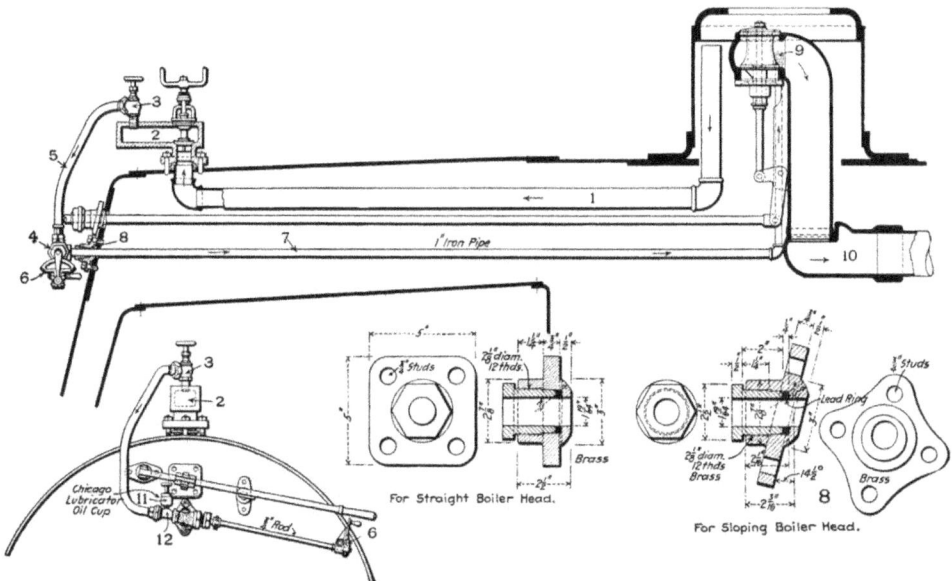

Figs. 3081-3087. Chamber's Drifting Valve. Wabash Railroad.

Names of Parts of Figs. 3079-3087.

1 *Steam Pipe*
2 *Turret*
3 *Globe*
4 *Drifting Valve*
5 *Drifting Valve Pipe*
6 *Drifting Valve Quadrant*
7 *Delivery Pipe*
8 *Delivery Pipe Stuffing Box*
9 *Delivery and Dry Pipe Connection*
10 *Dry Pipe*
11 *Oil Cup*
12 *Nipple*

CAB FITTINGS, Injectors; Metropolitan and Hancock. Figs. 3088-3091

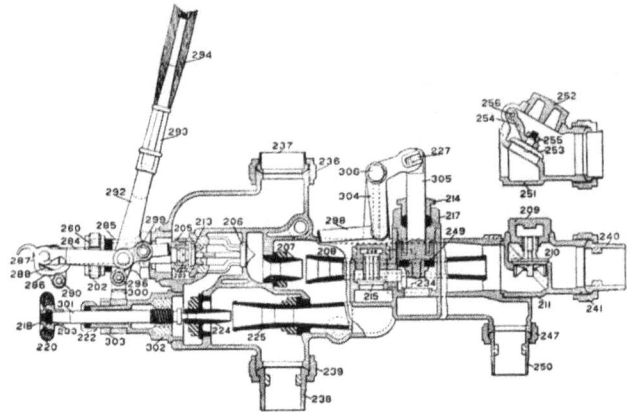

Figs. 3088-3089. Metropolitan "1898" Locomotive Injector, Models H and I.
Hayden & Derby Manufacturing Co.

Names of Parts of Figs. 3088-3099.

202 *Packing Nut*	236 *Union Nut, Steam End*	286 *Side Links*
203 *Champ Ring*	237 *Tail Pipe, Steam End*	287 *Pin for Steam Stem*
205 *Steam Swivel Ring*	238 *Tail Pipe, Suction End.*	288 *Spring*
206 *Steam Valve*	239 *Union Nut, Suction End*	289 *Outflow Valve Crank Bolt Nut*
207 *Forcing Steam Jet*	240 *Tail Pipe, Delivery End*	290 *Bolt for Side Links*
208 *Forcing Combining Tube*	241 *Union Nut, Delivery End*	291 *Nut for Bolt for Side Links*
209 *Check Valve Cap*	245 *Nut for Stud Bolts*	292 *Lever*
210 *Check Valve*	247 *Union Nut for Overflow Nozzle*	293 *Handle Rod*
211 *Check Valve Casing*	248 *Overflow Valve Cap*	294 *Wood Handle*
213 *Auxiliary Steam Valve*	249 *Disc for Overflow Valve*	295 *Handle Nut*
214 *Packing Gland*	250 *Tail Pipe for Overflow Nozzle*	296 *Fulcrum Bolt*
215 *Overflow Valve*	251 *Swing Check Valve Casing*	297 *Nut for Fulcrum Bolt*
217 *Overflow Center Piece*	252 *Swing Check Valve Cap*	298 *Connecting Bar*
218 *Regulating Valve Handle Nut*	253 *Swing Check Valve*	299 *Nut for Connecting Bar*
220 *Regulating Valve Wheel*	254 *Swing Check Valve Hinge*	300 *Fulcrum Collar*
222 *Packing Nut*	255 *Swing Check Valve Nut*	301 *Regulating Steam Stem*
224 *Lifting Steam Jet*	256 *Swing Check Valve Hinge Pin*	302 *Regulating Center Piece*
225 *Lifting Combining Tube*	257 *Swing Check Valve Hinge Pin Cap*	303 *Fulcrum Nut*
227 *Overflow Valve Pin*		304 *Overflow Valve Crank*
231 *Stud Bolt*	260 *Steam Packing Gland*	305 *Overflow Valve Stem*
233 *Regulating Valve Wheel Disc*	284 *Steam Valve Stem*	306 *Overflow Valve Crank Bolt*
234 *Nut for Overflow Disc*	285 *Steam Center Piece*	

Fig. 3090. Metropolitan "1898" Locomotive Injector, Models H and I.
Hayden & Derby Manufacturing Co.

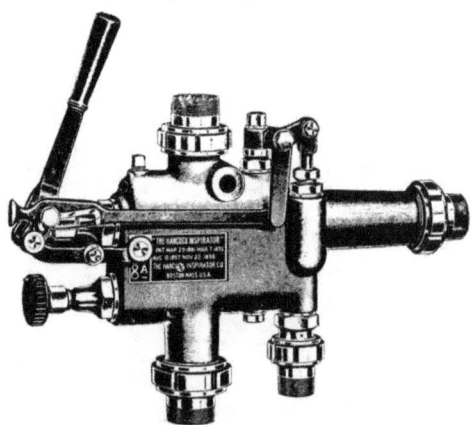

Fig. 3091. Hancock Inspirator, Type A.
Hancock Inspirator Co.

Figs. 3092-3094   CAB FITTINGS, Injectors; Hancock.

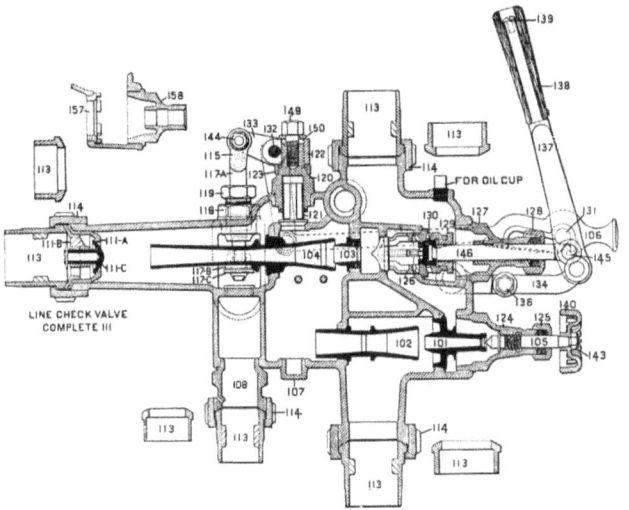

Fig. 3092. Hancock Inspirator, Types A, B and D. Hancock Inspirator Co.

Names of Parts of Fig. 3092.

101 Lifter Steam Nozzle
102 Lifter Tube
103 Forcer Steam Nozzle
104 Forcer Combining Tube
105 Regulating Valve Spindle
106 Connecting Rod
107 Clean-out Plug for Body
108 Overflow Nozzle
111 Line Check Valve, complete
111a Case for 111
111b Cage for 111
111c Valve for 111
113 Nipple for Steam Connection
113 Nipple for Suction Connection
113 Nipple for Delivery Connection
113 Nipple for Overflow Connection
114 Coupling Nut Steam Connection
114 Coupling Nut Suction Connection
114 Coupling Nut Delivery Connection
114 Coupling Nut Overflow Connection
115 Connecting Link for Final Overflow Valve
116 Steel Pin for 115
117 Final Overflow Valve, complete
117a Final Overflow Valve Stem
117b Nut for 117
117c Disc for 117
118 Bonnet for Final Overflow Valve
119 Packing Nut for Final Overflow Valve
120 Bonnet for Intermediate Overflow Valve
121 Intermediate Overflow Valve
122 Holder for Overflow Valve Crank
123 Adjusting Ring
124 Bonnet for Regulating Valve
125 Packing Nut for Regulating Valve
126 Forcer Steam Valve
127 Bonnet for Steam Valve
128 Packing Nut for Steam Valve
129 Coupling Nut for 126
130 Lifter Steam Valve
131 Steel Stud for Connecting Rod
132 Steel Stud for 122 and 133
133 Crank for Overflow Valve
134 Side Strap R. H.
135 Side Strap L. H.
136 Steel Bolt for 134 and 135
137 Lever
138 Wood Handle for 137
139 Screw for 137
140 Rubber Wheel for 105
141 Back Plate for 105
142 Brass Washer for 105
143 Steel Screw for 105
144 Steel Bolt for 115
145 Steel Pin Connecting 137 and 146
146 Steam Valve Stem
147 Spring for 106
148 Steel Nut for 144
149 Cap Screw for 120
150 Iron Washer for 120
151 Steel Nuts for 136
152 Name Plate
153 Name Plate Stud
154 Name Plate Screw
155 Spanner Wrench
156 Tube Wrench
157 Steam Valve Seat
158 Bonnet for Steam Valve

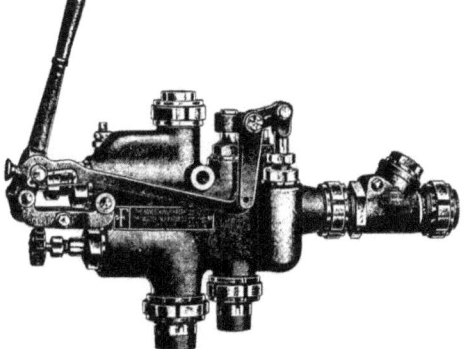

Fig. 3093. Hancock Inspirator, Type F.
Hancock Inspirator Co.

Fig. 3094. Hancock Inspirator, Type E.

Names of Parts of Fig. 3095.

401 Lifter Steam Nozzle
402 Lifter Tube
403 Forcer Steam Nozzle
404 Forcer Tube
405 Regulating Valve Spindle
406 Connecting Rod
411 Swing Check, complete
412 Swing Line Check Body
413 Threaded Nipple for Steam
413 Threaded Nipple for Delivery
413 Threaded Nipple for Overflow
414 Coupling Nut for Steam
414 Coupling Nut for Delivery
414 Coupling Nut for Swing Check
414 Coupling Nut for Overflow
415 Connecting Links for Final Overflow Valve
417 Final Overflow Valve Stem
418 Bonnet for Overflow Valve Stem
419 Packing Nut for Final Overflow Valve Stem
420 Bonnet for Intermediate Overflow Valve
421 Intermediate Overflow Valve
422 Holder for Overflow Valve Crank

(294)

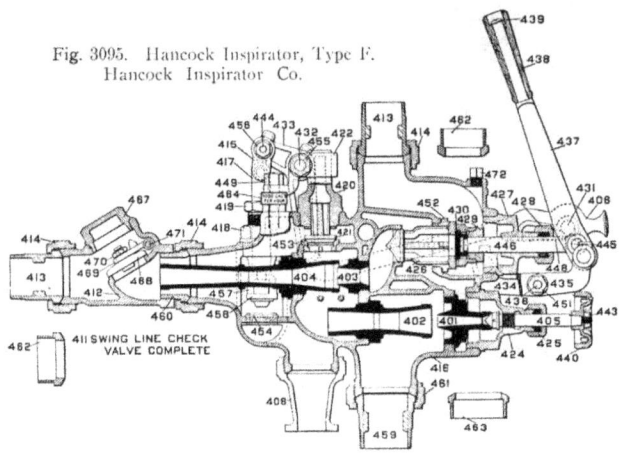

Fig. 3095. Hancock Inspirator, Type F.
Hancock Inspirator Co.

Names of Parts of Fig. 3095 (Continued).

424 Bonnet for Regulating Valve
425 Packing Nut for Regulating Valve
426 Forcer Steam Valve
427 Bonnet for Steam Valve Stem
428 Packing Nut for Steam Valve Stem
429 Coupling Nut for Forcer Steam Valve
430 Lifter Steam Valve
431 Steel Stud for Connecting Rod
432 Steel Stud for Overflow Valve Crank
433 Crank for Overflow Valve
434 Side Strap, right hand
435 Side Strap, left hand
436 Bolt for Side Straps
437 Lever
438 Wood Handle for Lever
439 Screw for Wood Handle
440 Wheel for Regulating Valve Spindle
443 Nut for Regulating Valve Spindle
444 Steel Bolt for Connecting Links
445 Steel Pin for Lever and Valve Stem
446 Steam Valve Stem
448 Connecting Rod Spring
449 Cap Screw for Overflow Valve Crank Holder
451 Nuts for Side Strap Bolts
452 Forcer Steam Valve Seat
453 Intermediate Overflow Valve Seat
454 Final Overflow Valve Seat
455 Nut for Overflow Valve Crank Stud
456 Nut for Connecting Link Bolt
457 Nut for Final Overflow Valve Stem
458 Disc for Final Overflow Valve Stem
459 Threaded Nipple for Suction
460 Threaded Nipple for Swing Check
461 Coupling Nut for Suction
462 Brazing Nipple for Steam
462 Brazing Nipple for Delivery
462 Brazing Nipple for Overflow
463 Brazing Nipple for Suction
464 Capacity Plate
465 Name Plate
466 Name Plate Screws
467 Swing Line Check Cap
468 Swing Line Check Disc
469 Swing Line Check Hinge
470 Swing Line Check Nut
471 Swing Line Check Stem
472 Oil Plug

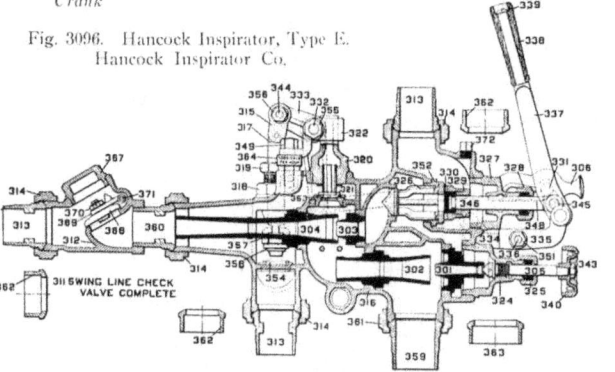

Fig. 3096. Hancock Inspirator, Type E.
Hancock Inspirator Co.

Names of Parts of Fig. 3096.

301 Lifter Steam Nozzle
302 Lifter Tube
303 Forcer Steam Nozzle
304 Forcer Tube
305 Regulating Valve Spindle
306 Connecting Rod
311 Swing Check, complete
312 Swing Line Check Body
313 Threaded Nipple for Steam
313 Threaded Nipple for Delivery
313 Threaded Nipple for Overflow
314 Coupling Nut for Steam
314 Coupling Nut for Delivery
314 Coupling Nut for Swing Check
314 Coupling Nut for Overflow
315 Connecting Links for Final Overflow Valve
317 Final Overflow Valve Stem
318 Bonnet for Overflow Valve Stem
319 Packing Nut for Final Overflow Valve Stem
320 Bonnet for Intermediate Overflow Valve
321 Intermediate Overflow Valve
322 Holder for Overflow Valve Crank
324 Bonnet for Regulating Valve
325 Packing Nut for Regulating Valve
326 Forcer Steam Valve
327 Bonnet for Steam Valve Stem
328 Packing Nut for Steam Valve Stem
329 Coupling Nut for Forcer Steam Valve
330 Lifter Steam Valve
331 Steel Stud for Connecting Rod
332 Steel Stud for Overflow Valve Crank
333 Crank for Overflow Valve
334 Side Strap, right hand
335 Side Strap, left hand
336 Bolt for Side Straps
337 Lever
338 Wood Handle for Lever
339 Screw for Wood Handle
340 Wheel for Regulating Valve Spindle
343 Nut for Regulating Valve Spindle
344 Steel Bolts for Connecting Links
345 Steel Pin for Lever and Valve Stem
346 Steam Valve Stem
348 Connecting Rod Spring
349 Cap Screw for Overflow Valve Crank Holder
351 Nuts for Side Strap Bolts
352 Forcer Steam Valve Seat
353 Intermediate Overflow Valve Seat
354 Final Overflow Valve Seat
355 Nut for Overflow Valve Crank Stud
356 Nut for Connecting Link Bolt
357 Nut for Final Overflow Valve Stem
358 Disc for Final Overflow Valve Stem
359 Threaded Nipple for Suction
360 Threaded Nipple for Swing Check
361 Coupling Nut for Suction
362 Brazing Nipple for Steam
362 Brazing Nipple for Delivery
362 Brazing Nipple for Overflow
363 Brazing Nipple for Suction
364 Capacity Plate
365 Name Plate
366 Name Plate Screws
367 Swing Line Check Cap
368 Swing Line Check Disc
369 Swing Line Check Hinge
370 Swing Line Check Nut
371 Swing Line Check Stem
372 Oil Plug

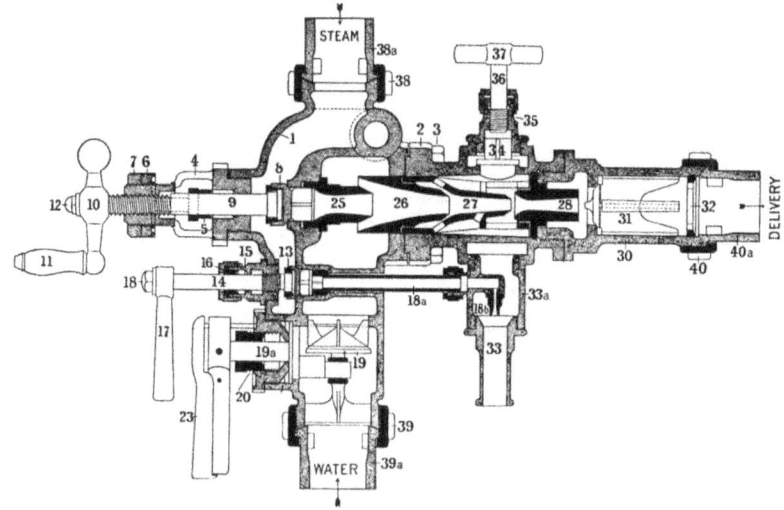

Fig. 3097. Monitor Injector. Nathan Manufacturing Co.

Names of Parts of Fig. 3097.

1 Body (back part)	16 Jet Valve Gland	32 Stop Ring
2 Body (front part)	17 Jet Valve Lever Handle	33 Overflow Nozzle
3 Body Screw	18 Jet Valve Top Nut	33a Overflow Chamber with Nut
4 Yoke	18a Jet Tube	34 Heater Cock Check
5 Yoke Gland	18b Lifting Nozzle	35 Heater Cock Bonnet and Nut
6 Yoke Packing Nut	19 Water Valve	36 Heater Cock Spindle
7 Yoke Lock Nut	19a Eccentric Spindle	37 Heater Cock T Handle
8 Steam Valve Disc and Nut	20 Water Valve Bonnet	38 Coupling Nut, Steam End
9 Steam Valve Spindle	23 Water Valve Lever Handle	39 Coupling Nut, Water End
10 Steam Valve Handle	25 Steam Nozzle	40 Coupling Nut, Delivery End
11 Steam Valve Rubber Handle	26 Intermediate Nozzle	38a Tail Piece, Steam End
12 Steam Valve Top Nut	27 Condensing Nozzle	39a Tail Piece, Water End
13 Jet Valve Disc and Nut	28 Delivery Nozzle	40a Tail Piece, Delivery End
14 Jet Valve Spindle	30 Line Check	
15 Jet Valve Bonnet and Nut	31 Line Check Valve	

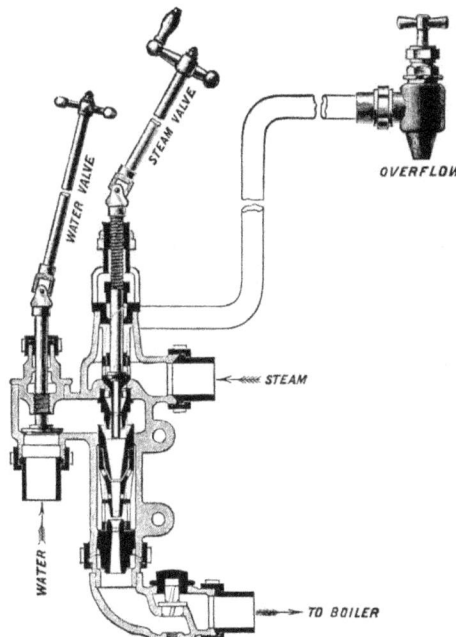

Fig. 3098. New "Nathan" Injector. Nathan Manufacturing Co.

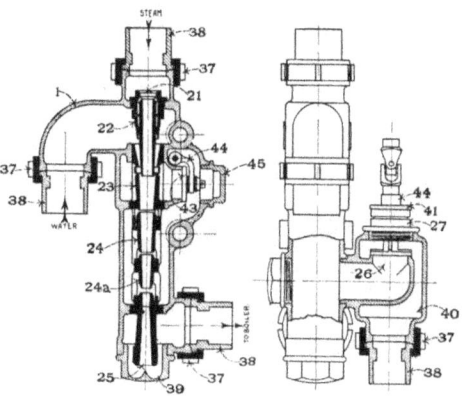

Fig. 3099. Simplex Non-Lifting Injector. Nathan Manufacturing Co.

Names of Parts of Fig. 3099.

1 Body	37 Coupling Nut
21 Steam Nozzle	38 Tail Piece
22 Jet Nozzle	39 Nozzle Cap
23 Intermediate Nozzle	40 Overflow Casing
24 Combining Nozzle	41 Overflow Cap
24a Combining Nozzle	42 Overflow Spindle
25 Delivery Nozzle	43 Hinge Check
26 Heater Cock Check	44 Hinge
27 Guide for Heater Cock Check	45 Hinge Cap

CAB FITTINGS, Injectors; Nathan and Sellers'. Figs. 3100-3103

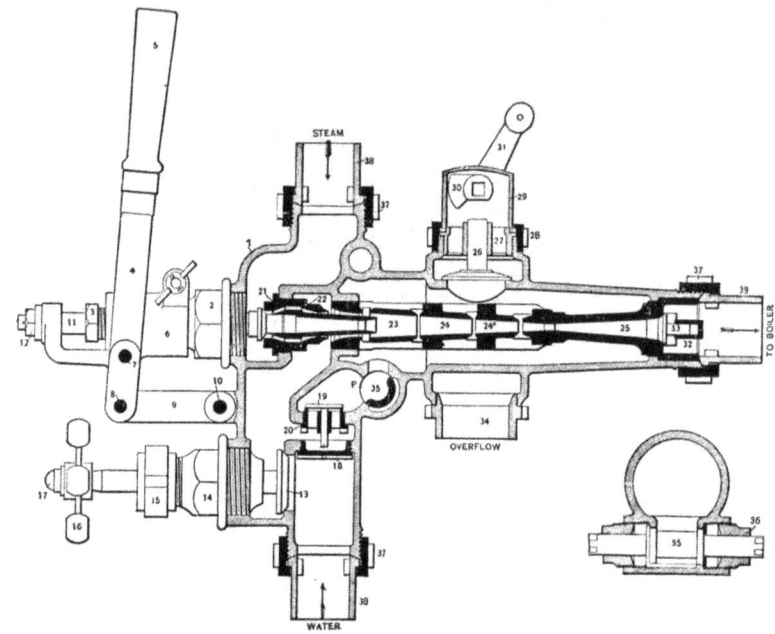

Figs. 3100-3101. Simplex Locomotive Injector. Nathan Manufacturing Co.

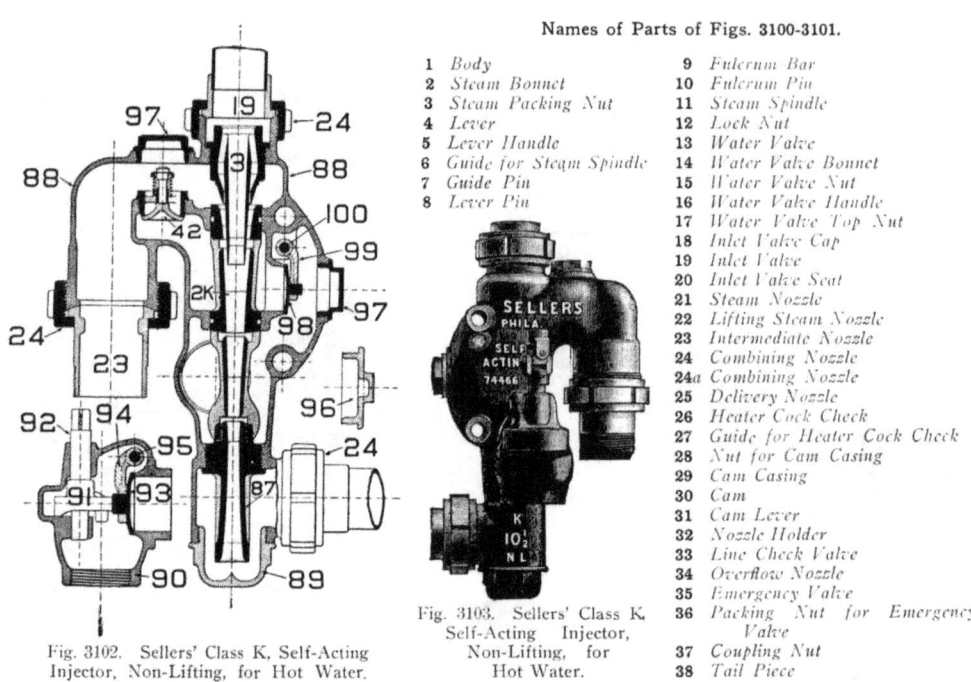

Fig. 3102. Sellers' Class K, Self-Acting Injector, Non-Lifting, for Hot Water.

Fig. 3103. Sellers' Class K Self-Acting Injector, Non-Lifting, for Hot Water.

William Sellers & Co. Inc.

Names of Parts of Figs. 3100-3101.

1. Body
2. Steam Bonnet
3. Steam Packing Nut
4. Lever
5. Lever Handle
6. Guide for Steam Spindle
7. Guide Pin
8. Lever Pin
9. Fulcrum Bar
10. Fulcrum Pin
11. Steam Spindle
12. Lock Nut
13. Water Valve
14. Water Valve Bonnet
15. Water Valve Nut
16. Water Valve Handle
17. Water Valve Top Nut
18. Inlet Valve Cap
19. Inlet Valve
20. Inlet Valve Seat
21. Steam Nozzle
22. Lifting Steam Nozzle
23. Intermediate Nozzle
24. Combining Nozzle
24a. Combining Nozzle
25. Delivery Nozzle
26. Heater Cock Check
27. Guide for Heater Cock Check
28. Nut for Cam Casing
29. Cam Casing
30. Cam
31. Cam Lever
32. Nozzle Holder
33. Line Check Valve
34. Overflow Nozzle
35. Emergency Valve
36. Packing Nut for Emergency Valve
37. Coupling Nut
38. Tail Piece

Names of Parts of Fig. 3102.

2k. Combining Tube
3. Steam Nozzle
19. Rings for Copper Pipe
23. Unions for Iron Pipe
24. Coupling Nuts
42k. Inlet Valve
87. Delivery Tube
88. Body
89. Body End Cap
90. Waste Pipe
91. Waste Valve Closing Cam
92. Cam Shaft
93. Waste Valve
94. Waste Valve Hinge
95. Waste Valve Hinge Pin
96. Cap
97. Inlet and Hot Water Valve Caps
98. Hot Water Valve
99. Hot Water Valve Hinge
100. Hot Water Valve Hinge Pin
101. Cap

Figs. 3104–3107 CAB FITTINGS, Injectors; Sellers'.

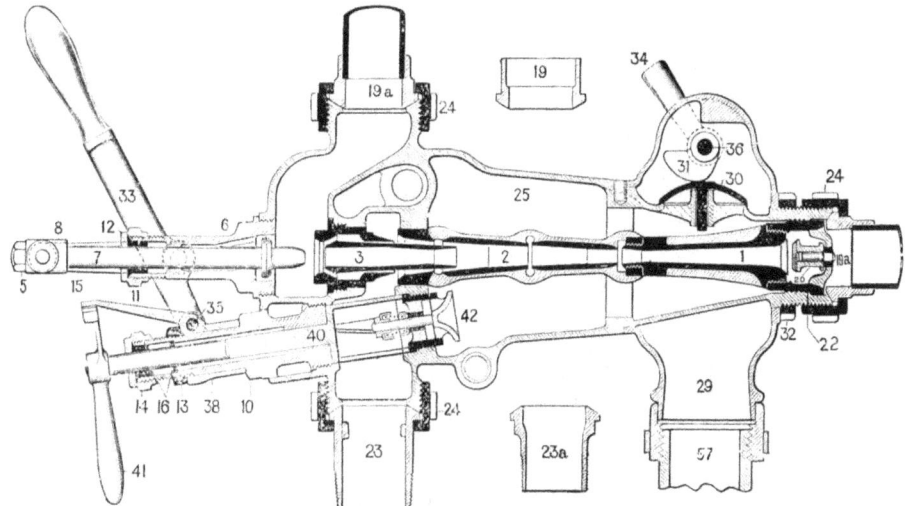

Fig. 3104. Sellers' Class N, Self-Acting Injector. William Sellers & Co., Inc.

Names of Parts of Fig. 3104.

1 Delivery Tube	13 Lock Nut	23 Plain ⎫ Unions for	33 Starting Lever
2 Combining Tube	14 Follower for No. 10	23a Reduc. ⎭ Iron Pipes	34 Cam Lever
3 Steam Nozzles	15 Links	24 Coupling Nuts	35 Pin, Nos. 38 and 33
5 Spindle Nut	16 Packing Ring	25 Injector Body	36 Cam Shaft
6 Steam Stuffing Box	17 Water Valve	26 Hand Wheel	37 Washer on 36
7 Spindle	18 Ring in No. 17	27 Wrench	38 Collar and Index
8 Crosshead	19 Plain ⎫ Rings for	29 Waste Pipe	40 Plug Water Valve
9 Collar on No. 10	19a Reduc. ⎭ Copper Pipe	30 Waste Valve	41 Regulating Handle
10 Water Stuffing Box	20 Check Valve	31 Waste Valve Cam	42 Inlet Valve
11 Follower	21 Valve Stem	32 Jam Nut for No. 29	57 Overflow Pipe Connection
12 Packing Ring	22 Guide for No. 20		

Numbers Refer to List of Names of Parts on Opposite Page.

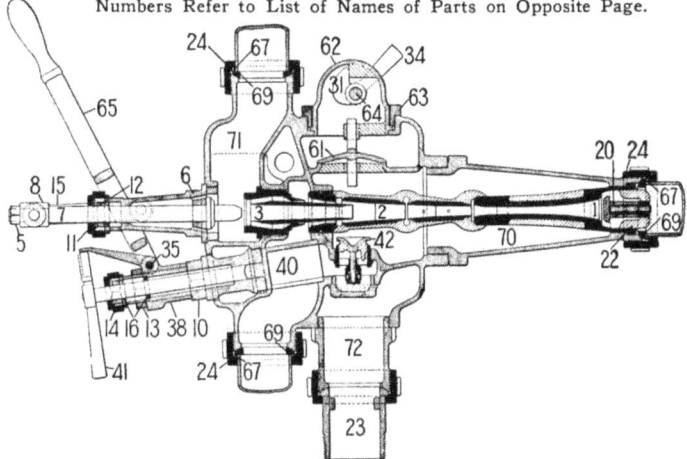

Fig. 3105. Sellers' Class P, Self-Acting Injector for Back Head of Boiler. William Sellers & Co., Inc.

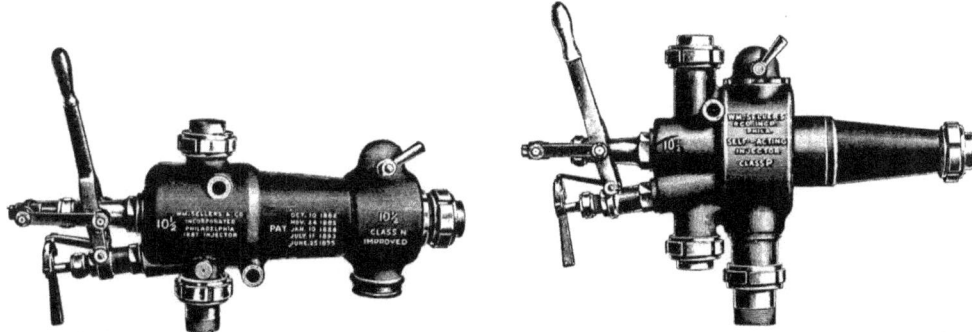

Fig. 3106. Sellers' Class N, Self-Acting Injector. Fig. 3107. Sellers' Class P, Self-Acting Injector for Back Head of Boiler.

(298)

CAB FITTINGS, Injectors; Check Valves.

Names of Parts of Fig. 3105.

1	Delivery Tube	25	Wrench
2	Combining Tube	31	Waste Valve Cam
3	Steam Nozzles	34	Cam Lever
5	Spindle Nut	35	Pin, Nos. 38 and 33
6	Steam Stuffing Box	37	Washer on 36
7	Spindle	38	Collar and Index
8	Crosshead	40	Plug Water Valve
10	Water Stuffing Box	41	Regulating Handle
11	Follower	42	Inlet Valve
12	Packing Ring	61	Waste Valve
13	Lock Nut	62	Hood over 61
14	Follower for No. 10	63	Jam Nut on 61
15	Links	64	Pin Through 62 and 31
16	Packing Ring	65	Starting Lever
19	Plain Rings for	67	Seat Ring
19a	Reduc. Cop'r Pipe	68	Steam and Delivery
20	Check Valve		Pipe Ring
22	Guide for No. 20	69	Suction Pipe Ring
23	Plain Unions for	70	Lower Cylinder
23a	Reduc. Iron Pipes	71	Upper Cylinder
24	Coupling Nuts	72	Waste Pipe

Fig. 3108. Sellers' Combined Main Check and Stop Valve. William Sellers & Co., Inc.

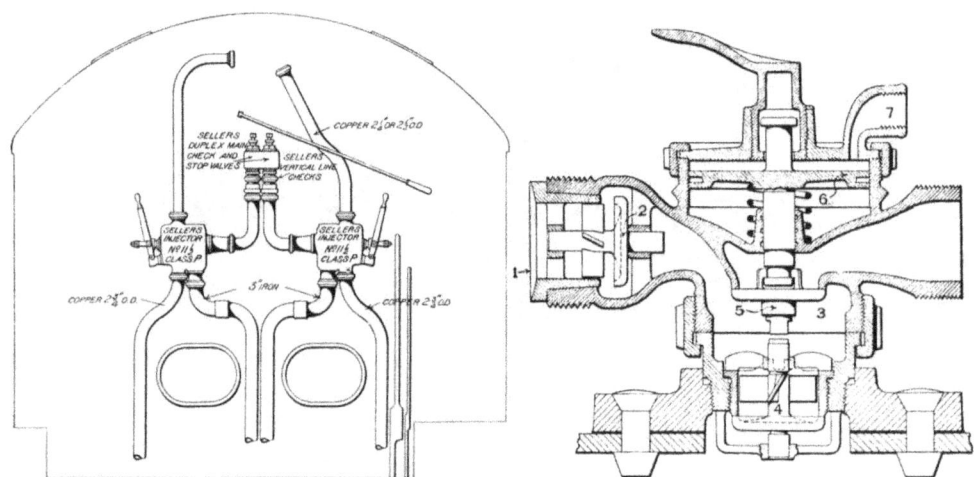

Fig. 3109. Arrangement of Sellers' Injectors on Back Head of Boiler of Atlantic (4—4—2) Locomotive. P. R. R.

Fig. 3110. Quadruple Safety Boiler Check. Central Railroad of New Jersey.

Names of Parts of Fig. 3110.

1	Delivery Connection	5	Blow-off Valve
2	Check Valve	6	Blow-off Operating Piston
3	Pressure Chamber	7	Blow-off Outlet
4	Delivery Check		

CAB FITTINGS, Check Valves; Water Glass Gages.

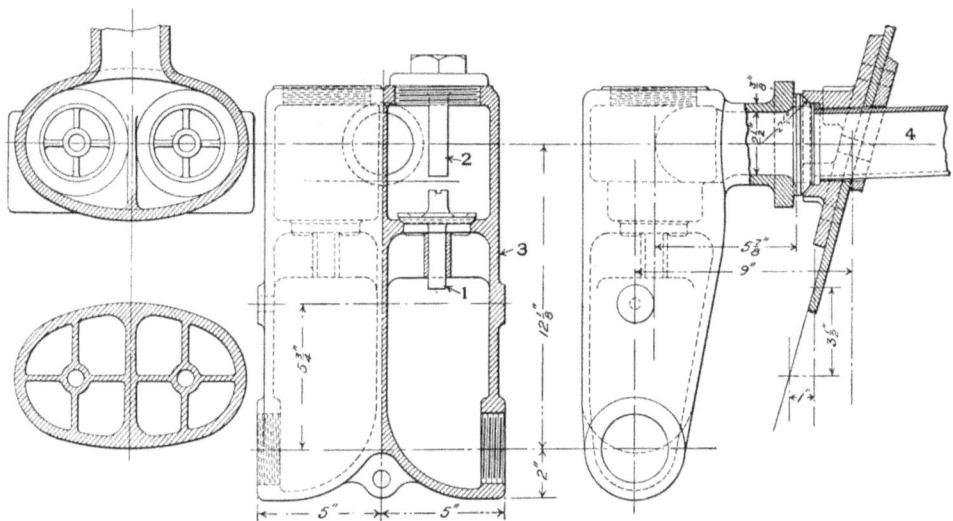

Figs. 3111-3114. Injector Check Valve for Back Head of Boiler of Atlantic (4—4—2) Locomotive. P. R. R.

Names of Parts of Figs. 3111-3114.

1 Valve   **2** Stop   **3** Case   **4** Inside Boiler Delivery Pipe

Numbers Refer to List of Names of Parts on Opposite Page.

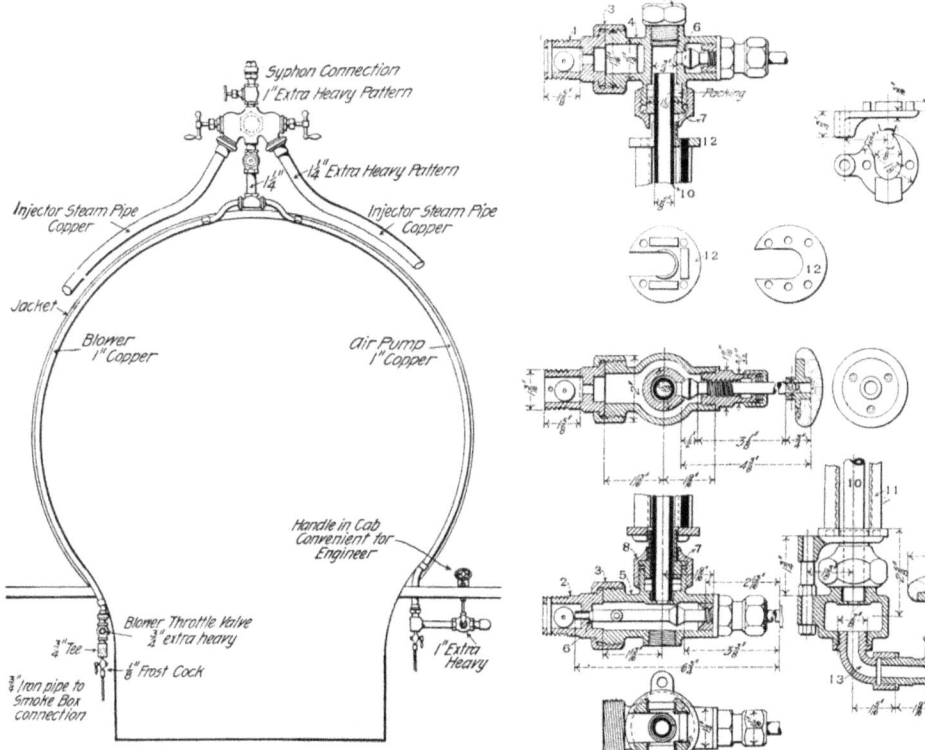

Fig. 3115. Steam Turret Arrangement. Oregon Short Line.

Figs. 3116-3126. Water Glass Gage. Pennsylvania Railroad.

(300)

CAB FITTINGS, Water Glass Gages. Figs. 3127-3147

Names of Parts of Figs. 3116-3126.

1 *Top Boiler Connection*	8 *Gland Nut*
2 *Bottom Boiler Connection*	9 *Body Plug*
3 *Union*	10 *Water Glass*
4 *Top Body*	11 *Water Glass Bar*
5 *Bottom Body*	12 *Water Glass Bar Ring*
6 *Valve*	13 *Drain*
7 *Packing Gland*	14 *Drain Valve*

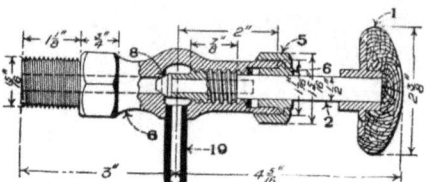

Fig. 3127. Gage Cock. P. R. R.

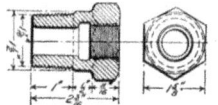

Figs. 3128-3129. Gage Cock Plug.

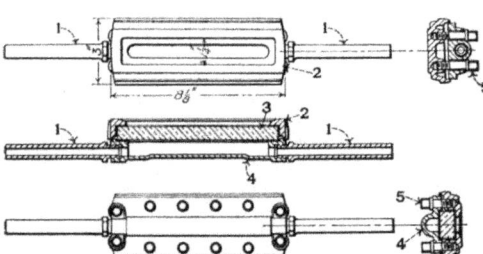

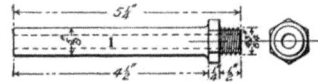

Figs. 3130-3140. Klinger Reflex Water Gage.

Names of Parts of Figs. 3130-3140.

1 *Pipe to Boiler*
2 *Casing*
3 *Glass*
4 *Shield*
5 *Fastening Bolts*

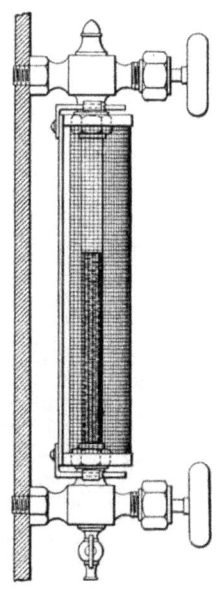

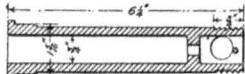

Fig. 3141. Top Plug for Klinger Reflex Water Gage.

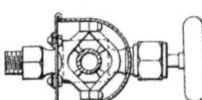

Figs. 3144-3145. Mears Water Glass Shield. Boyer Safety Device & Equipment Co.

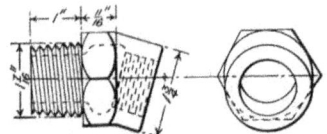

Figs 3142-3143. Plug for Water Glass Gage.

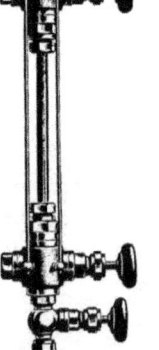

Fig. 3146. Water Glass Gage. Star Brass Mfg. Co.

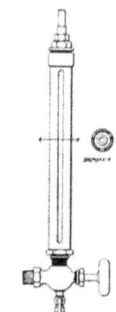

Fig. 3147. Casey Water Gage. Ashton Valve Co.

CAB FITTINGS, Steam Gages.

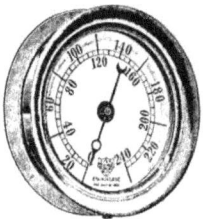  

Figs. 3148-3150. Star Improved Double Spring Bourdon Pressure Gage. Star Brass Mfg. Co.

Fig. 3151. Star Locomotive Gage Lamp. Star Brass Mfg. Co.

Figs. 3152-3153. Ashcroft Auxiliary Spring Locomotive Steam Gage. Ashcroft Mfg. Co.

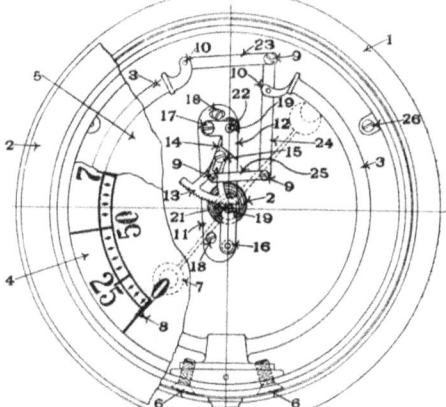

Fig. 3154. Locomotive Steam Gage. American Steam Gauge & Valve Mfg. Co.

Names of Parts of Fig. 3154.

1 Case	8 Escutcheon Pin	14 Adjusting Slide	20 Hair Spring
2 Ring	9 Lane Connection Screws	15 Screw for Adjusting Slide	21 Pinion
3 Gage Tube	10 Lane Connection Pins	16 Movement Post	22 Sector Shaft
4 Dial	11 Bottom Plate	17 Top Plate Screw	23 Lane Connection Link
5 Glass	12 Top Plate	18 Bottom Plate Screw	24 Lane Connection Link
6 Socket Screws	13 Sector	19 Bushing	25 Lane Connection Link
7 Hand			26 Dial Screw

Numbers Refer to List of Names of Parts on Opposite Page.

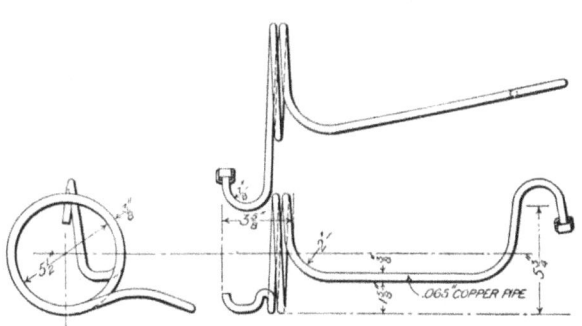

Figs. 3157-3158. Steam Gage Pressure Pipe. Atlantic (4—4—2) Locomotive. P. R. R.

Figs. 3155-3156. Steam and Air Gage Stand. Atlantic (4—4—2) Locomotive. Pennsylvania Railroad.

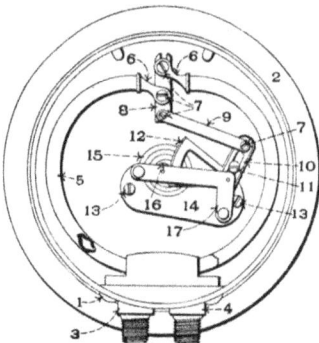

Fig. 3159. Ashton Improved Duplex Air Gage. Ashton Valve Co.

(302)

CAB FITTINGS, Gages; Steam Heat Apparatus. Figs. 3160-3162

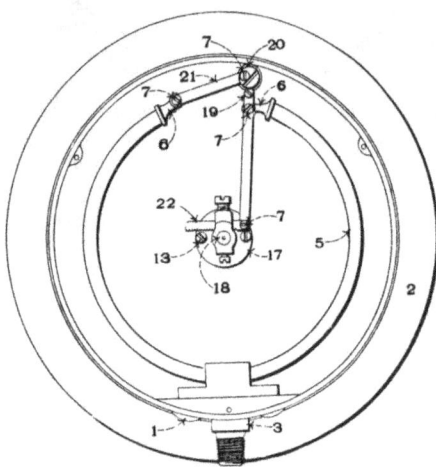

Fig. 3160. Ashton Improved Lane Gage.
Ashton Valve Co.

Names of Parts of Figs. 3159-3160.

1. Socket Screw
2. Case
3. Socket
4. Train Line Socket
5. Spring
6. Spring Tip
7. Connection Screws
8. Spring Connection Arm
9. Movable Connection Arm
10. Adjusting Slide
11. Adjusting Slide Lock Screw
12. Train Line Segment
13. Screws Holding Movement in Case
14. Bottom Plate of Movement
15. Pinion Hair Spring
16. Pinion
17. Movement Plate
18. Bushing Holding in Pinion
19. Lock Screw
20. Hub
21. Connection Arm
22. Rack

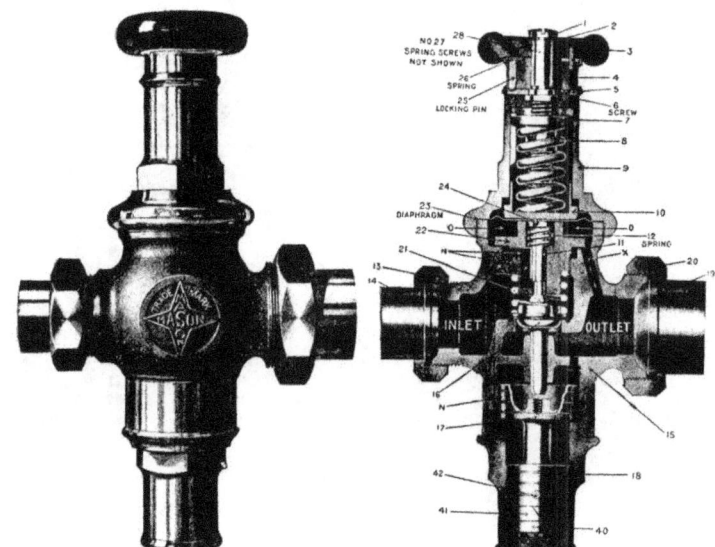

Figs. 3161-3162. Mason Locomotive Reducing Valve for Steam Heat.
Mason Regulator Co.

Names of Parts of Fig. 3162.

1. Wheel Screw
2. Wheel Plate
3. Wheel
4. Wheel Hub
5. Locking Plate
6. Locking Plate Screw
7. Compression Nut
8. Diaphragm Spring
9. Spring Case
10. Diaphragm Button
11. Auxiliary Valve
12. Auxiliary Valve Spring
13. Inlet Union Nut
14. Inlet Tail Piece
15. Body
16. Main Valve
17. Piston
18. Dash Pot
19. Outlet Tail Piece
20. Outlet Union Nut
21. Main Valve Spring
22. Auxiliary Valve Seat
23. Diaphragm
24. Auxiliary Valve Nut
25. Locking Pin
26. Locking Spring
27. Locking Spring Screws
28. Compression Screw

(303)

CAB FITTINGS, Steam Heat; Gold's.

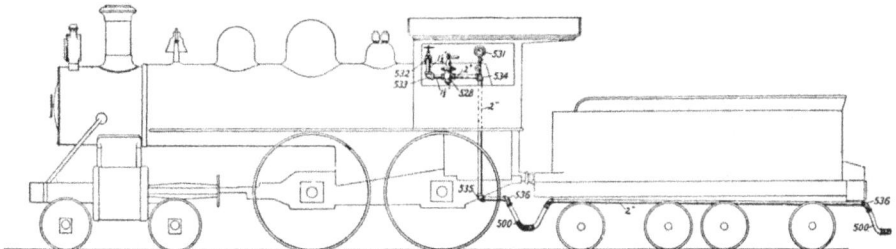

Fig. 3163. Gold's Improved Heating Apparatus for Locomotives.

Names of Parts of Fig. 3163.

- 500 Gold Steam Coupler
- 528 Gold Improved Pressure Regulator
- 531 Steam Gage
- 532 Starting Valve
- 533 1½-Inch Ell
- 534 2-Inch x ¼-Inch x 2-Inch Tee
- 535 2-Inch Ell
- 536 2-Inch x 1½-Inch 65 deg. Ell
- 552 2-Inch R. & L. Coupling

Names of Parts of Fig. 3164.

- A 1½-Inch Inlet Union Nipple
- B 2-Inch Outlet Union Nipple
- C Bolts and Nuts for Dome and Body
- D Balance Spindle with Hard Seats
- E Oscillating Washer
- F Bottom Spring
- G Body of Regulator
- H Bottom Plug
- I Handle
- J Top Nut
- K Hollow Screw
- L Top Spring
- M Dome of Regulator
- N Lock Nut
- O Top Flange
- P Bottom Flange
- Q Top Spindle
- R Set Screw
- T 1½-Inch Inlet Union Nut
- U 2-Inch Outlet Union Nut

Fig. 3164. Gold's Improved Balance Valve Pressure Regulator.

Fig. 3165. Locomotive Starting Valve.

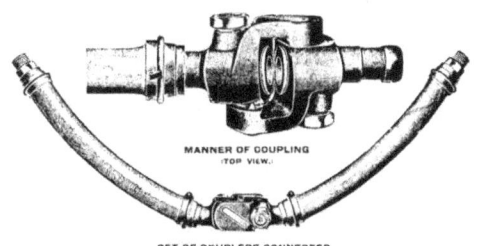

Figs. 3166-3167. Gold's Universal Straight Port Steam Coupler.

Gold Car Heating & Lighting Co.

CAB FITTINGS, Steam Heat; Consolidated.

Figs. 3168-3175

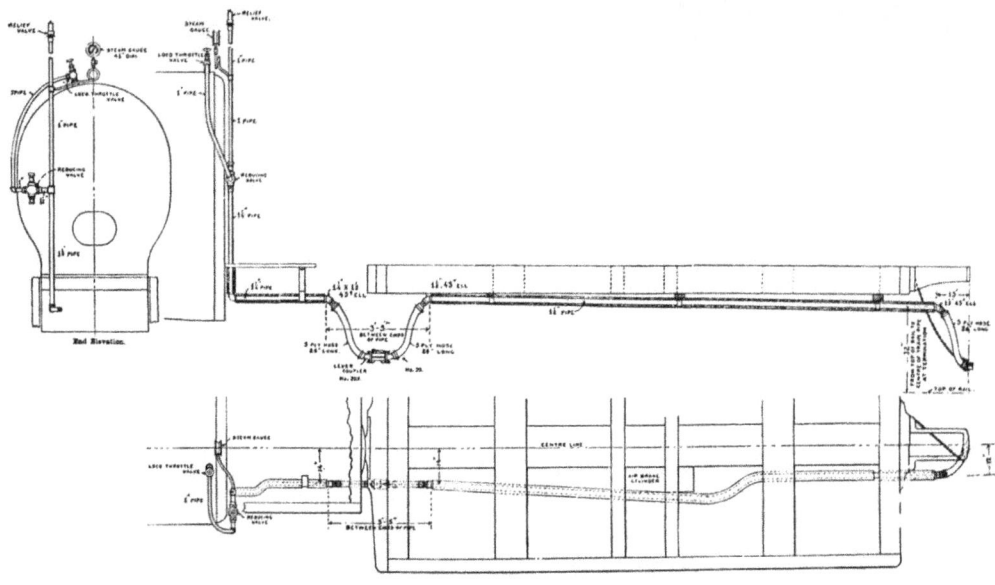

Figs. 3168-3170. Consolidated Steam Heat Locomotive Equipment.

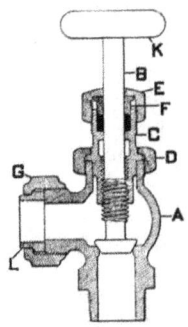

Fig. 3171. Throttle Valve, No. 11.

Names of Parts of Fig. 3171.

- A *Body*
- B *Stem*
- C *Bonnet*
- D *Bonnet Nut*
- E *Stuffing Box Nut*
- F *Stuffing Box Gland*
- G *Union Nut*
- K *Valve Handle*
- L *Union Collar*

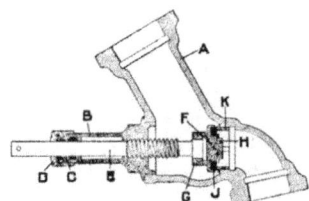

Fig. 3172. Section of End Train Pipe Valve, No. 200.

Names of Parts of Fig. 3172.

A	*Body Casting*	F	*Swivel Head*
B	*Bonnet*	G	*Swivel Head Nut*
C	*Gland*	H	*Gasket Nut*
D	*Gland Nut*	J	*Gasket*
E	*Stem*	K	*Brass Seat*

Fig. 3173. Throttle Valve, No. 11.

Fig. 3174. Special Relief Valve No. 16.

Fig. 3175. Clamp Lock for Steam Couplers.

Consolidated Car Heating Co.

Fig. 3176. Sewall Steam Coupler, No. 20 AF.

Fig. 3177. Consolidated Steam Coupler, No. 9 C.

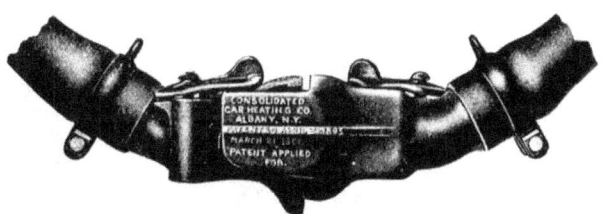

Fig. 3178. Pair of Consolidated Steam Couplers, No. 9 C (Locked).

Fig. 3179. Pair of Sewall Steam Couplers, No. 20 AF (Locked). Consolidated Car Heating Co.

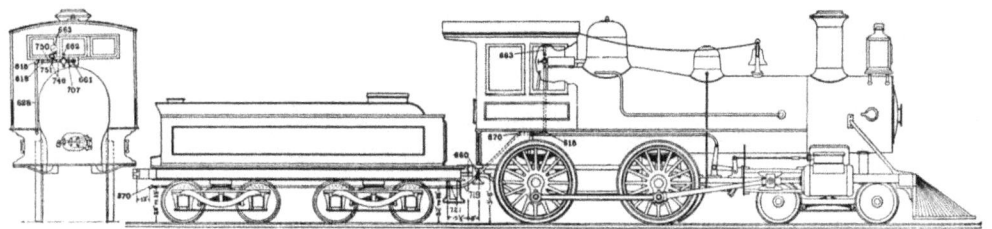

Figs. 3180-3181. Locomotive Equipment (L-8a). Safety Car Heating & Lighting Co.

Names of Parts of Figs. 3180-3181.

- 615 1½-Inch Ell
- 618 1½-Inch R. & L. Coupling
- 628 1½-Inch Standard Pipe
- 660 1½-Inch Union
- 661 1-Inch Angle Valve (Extra Heavy)
- 662 1-Inch x 1¼-Inch Reducing Valve
- 663 Steam Gage
- 664 ¼-Inch x 1⅛-Inch Bolt (Hex. Nut)
- 670 1½-Inch, 45-deg. Ell
- 674 Link
- 677 Covering for 1½-Inch Pipe
- 678 Covering for 1½-Inch Ell
- 707 1-Inch Close Nipple
- 719 Steam Hose, 1¼-Inch
- 721 Nipple, 1¼-Inch Hose, 1½-Inch Pipe Thread.
- 722a Hose Band, 1¼-Inch
- 746 1¼-Inch Nipple, 3 Inches Long
- 750 1½-Inch x ¼-Inch Reducer
- 751 1¼-Inch x 1¼-Inch x ¼-Inch Tee

CAB FITTINGS, Steam Heat; Safety Co.   Figs. 3182-3194

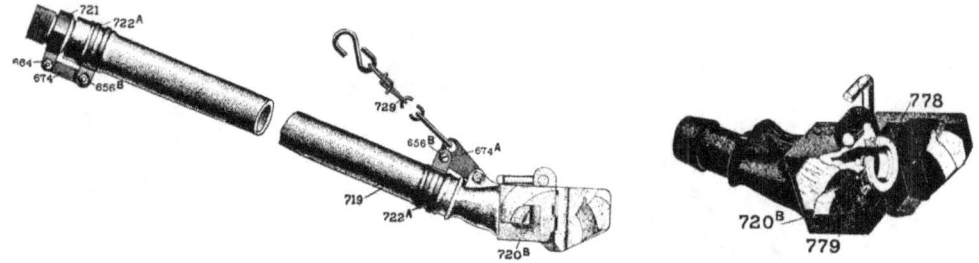

Figs. 3182-3183. Safety Straight Port Steam Hose Coupler, No. 720b. For 1¼-Inch Hose, S-5 Type.

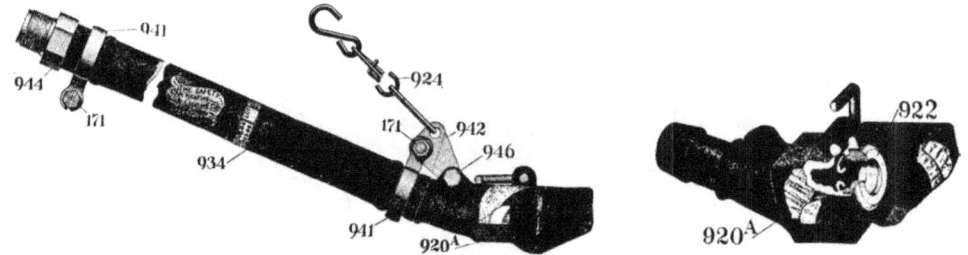

Figs. 3184-3185. Safety Straight Port Steam Hose Coupler, No. 920a. For 1½-Inch Hose, S-4 Type.

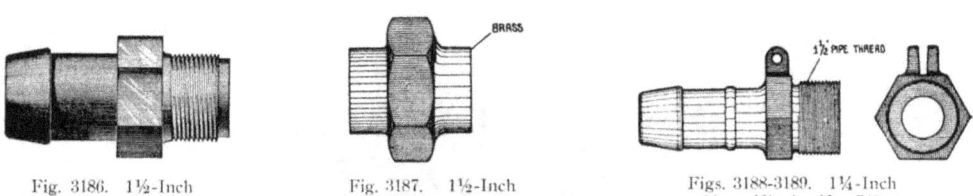

Fig. 3186. 1½-Inch Hose Nipple, No. 944.

Fig. 3187. 1½-Inch Brass Union, No. 660.

Figs. 3188-3189. 1¼-Inch Hose Nipple, No. 721.

Names of Parts of Figs. 3190-3192.

D Cap Nut	I Stem Nut	Z Gasket
E Gland	J Valve	142a Retaining Screw
F Bonnet	K Union Nut	150 Bonnet Screw
G Stem	L Union Nipple	
H Body	X Hand Wheel	

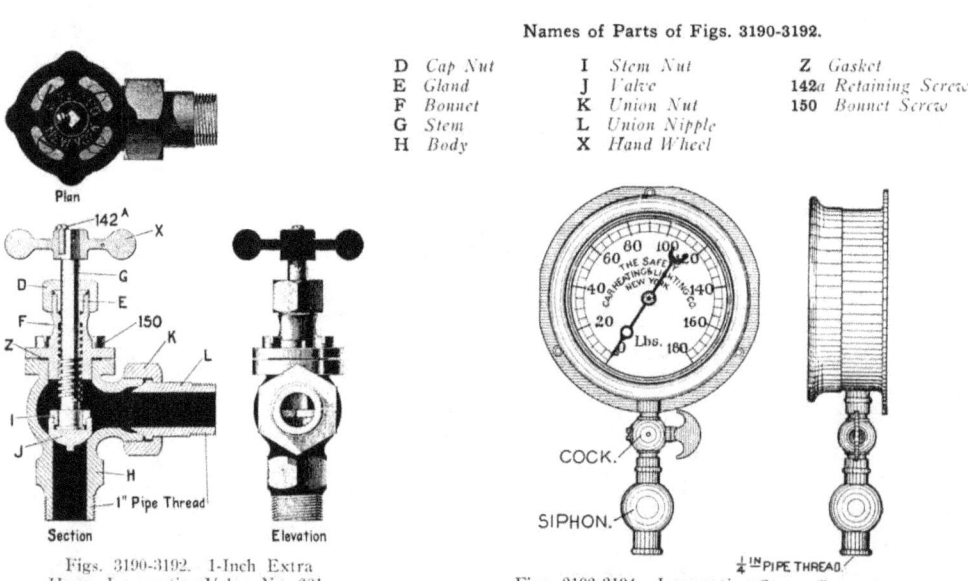

Figs. 3190-3192. 1-Inch Extra Heavy Locomotive Valve, No. 661.

Figs. 3193-3194. Locomotive Steam Gage.

Safety Car Heating & Lighting Co.

(307)

CAB FITTINGS, Lubricators; Detroit.

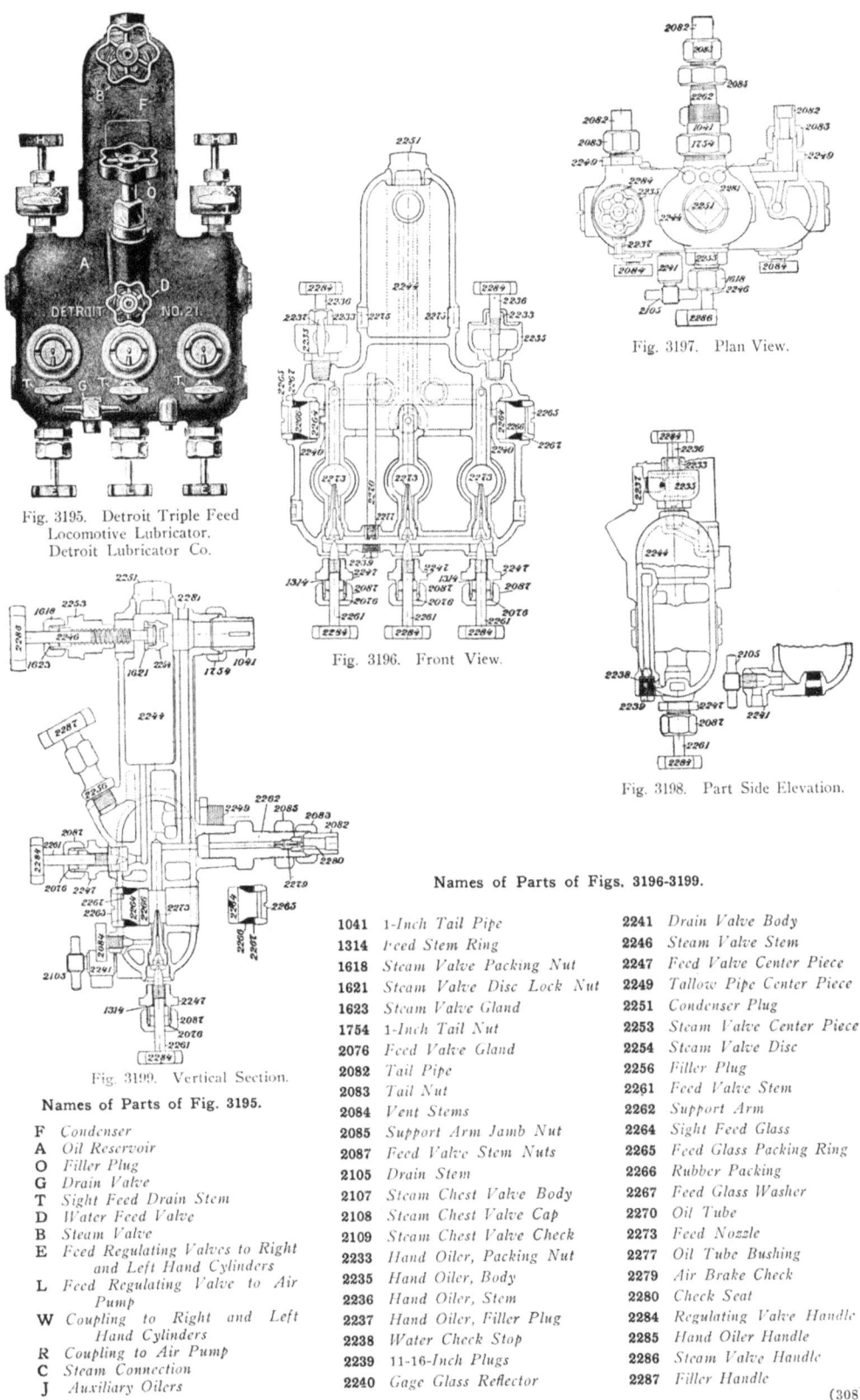

Fig. 3195. Detroit Triple Feed Locomotive Lubricator. Detroit Lubricator Co.

Fig. 3196. Front View.

Fig. 3197. Plan View.

Fig. 3198. Part Side Elevation.

Fig. 3199. Vertical Section.

Names of Parts of Fig. 3195.

- **F** Condenser
- **A** Oil Reservoir
- **O** Filler Plug
- **G** Drain Valve
- **T** Sight Feed Drain Stem
- **D** Water Feed Valve
- **B** Steam Valve
- **E** Feed Regulating Valves to Right and Left Hand Cylinders
- **L** Feed Regulating Valve to Air Pump
- **W** Coupling to Right and Left Hand Cylinders
- **R** Coupling to Air Pump
- **C** Steam Connection
- **J** Auxiliary Oilers

Names of Parts of Figs. 3196–3199.

1041	1-Inch Tail Pipe	2241	Drain Valve Body
1314	Feed Stem Ring	2246	Steam Valve Stem
1618	Steam Valve Packing Nut	2247	Feed Valve Center Piece
1621	Steam Valve Disc Lock Nut	2249	Tallow Pipe Center Piece
1623	Steam Valve Gland	2251	Condenser Plug
1754	1-Inch Tail Nut	2253	Steam Valve Center Piece
2076	Feed Valve Gland	2254	Steam Valve Disc
2082	Tail Pipe	2256	Filler Plug
2083	Tail Nut	2261	Feed Valve Stem
2084	Vent Stems	2262	Support Arm
2085	Support Arm Jamb Nut	2264	Sight Feed Glass
2087	Feed Valve Stem Nuts	2265	Feed Glass Packing Ring
2105	Drain Stem	2266	Rubber Packing
2107	Steam Chest Valve Body	2267	Feed Glass Washer
2108	Steam Chest Valve Cap	2270	Oil Tube
2109	Steam Chest Valve Check	2273	Feed Nozzle
2233	Hand Oiler, Packing Nut	2277	Oil Tube Bushing
2235	Hand Oiler, Body	2279	Air Brake Check
2236	Hand Oiler, Stem	2280	Check Seat
2237	Hand Oiler, Filler Plug	2284	Regulating Valve Handle
2238	Water Check Stop	2285	Hand Oiler Handle
2239	11-16-Inch Plugs	2286	Steam Valve Handle
2240	Gage Glass Reflector	2287	Filler Handle

CAB FITTINGS, Lubricators. Figs. 3200-3207

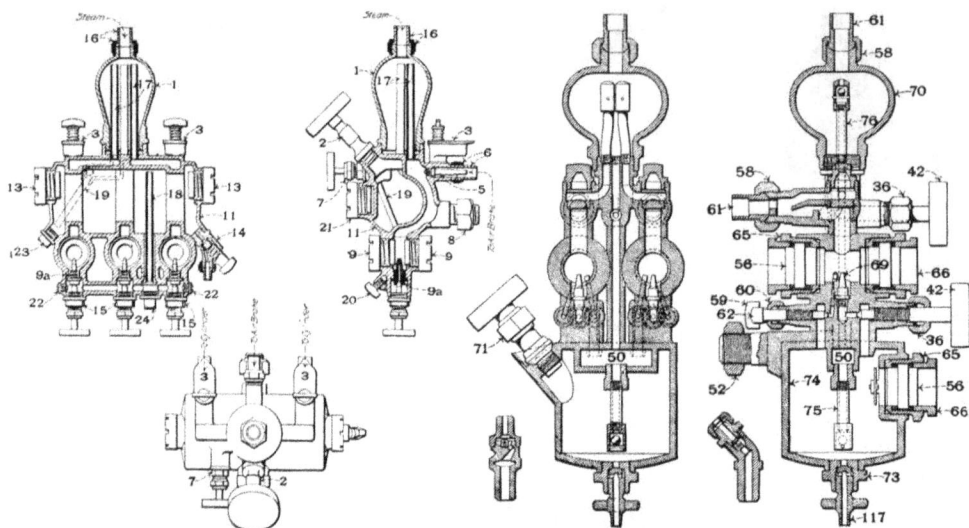

Figs. 3200-3202. Nathan Triple Feed Locomotive Lubricator. Nathan Manufacturing Co.

Figs. 3203-3204. "Bull's Eye" Locomotive Lubricator. Michigan Lubricator Co.

Names of Parts of Figs. 3200-3202.

1 Condenser
2 Filling Plug
3 Hand Oiler
5 Reducing Plug
6 Delivery Nut and Tailpiece
7 Water Valve
8 Stud Nut
9 Sight-Feed Glass and Casing
9a Feed Nozzle
11 Body
13 Gage Glass and Casing
14 Waste Cock
15 Regulating Valve
16 Top Connection
17 Equalizing Pipe
18 Oil Pipe
19 Water Pipe
20 Sight-Feed Drain Valve
21 Reserve Glass and Casing
22 Cleaning Plug
23 Body Plug
24 Oil Pipe Plug

Names of Parts of Figs. 3203-3204.

36 Feed and Water Stem Packing Nut
42 Water Valve Stem
42a Cylinder Feed Stem
50 Heating Chamber
56 Gage Glass
56a Sight-Feed Glass
57 Gage Glass Gasket
57a Sight-Feed Glass Gasket
58 Condenser Tail Pipe Nut
58a Cylinder Oil Pipe Union Nut
59 Sight-Feed Glass Drain Valve
60 Auxiliary Packing Nut
61 Condenser Tail Pipe
61a Cylinder Oil Pipe Union Tail Pipe
62 Auxiliary Oiler Stem
65 Sleeve for Gage Glass
65a Sleeve for Bull's Eye Glass
66 Sight-Feed Glass Packing Nut
66a Gage Glass Packing Nut
69 Sight-Feed Nozzle
70 Condenser
71 Filler Plug
73 Drain Valve Body
74 Oil Reservoir
75 Water Tube
76 Steam Tubes
117 Drain Valve Stem

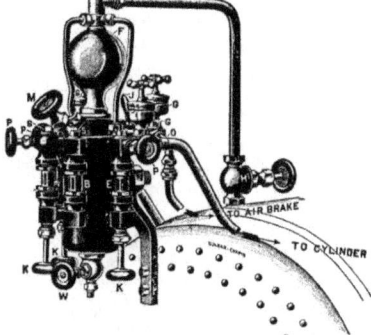

Fig. 3205. Seibert Triple Sight-Feed Locomotive Lubricator. Star Brass Manufacturing Co.

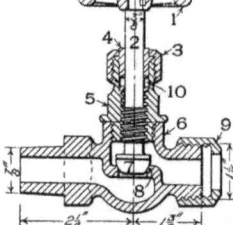

Fig. 3206. ⅝-Inch Globe Valve for Lubricator.

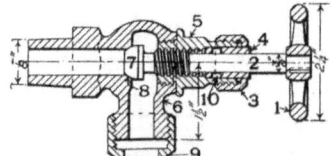

Fig. 3207. ⅝-Inch Angle Globe Valve for Lubricator.

ENGINE FITTINGS, Whistles.

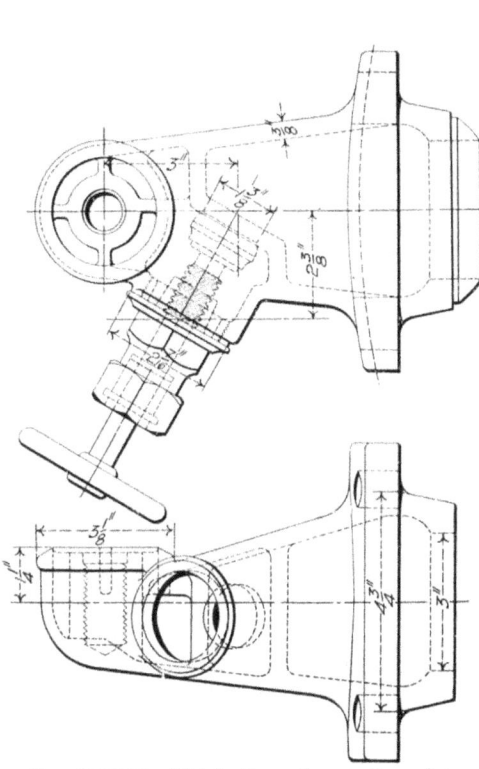

Figs. 3208-3209. Whistle Connection at Dome for Atlantic (4—4—2) Locomotive. Pennsylvania Railroad.

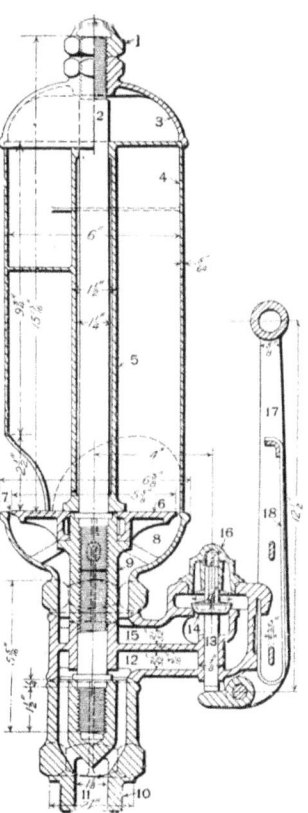

Fig. 3210. Chime Whistle. Pennsylvania Railroad.

Names of Parts of Fig. 3210.

1	Cap Nut	10	Base Screw
2	Stem	11	Steam Inlet
3	Cap	12	Steam Passage
4	Bell	13	Valve
5	Stem Casing	14	Valve Seat
6	Lip	15	Steam Port
7	Outlet	16	Valve Cap
8	Steam Chamber	17	Lever
9	Riser	18	Lever Spring

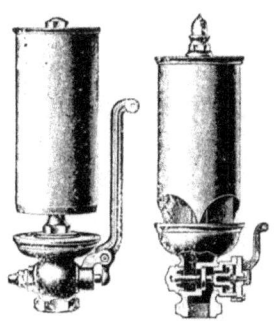

Fig. 3211. Plain Whistle. Fig. 3212. Chime Whistle.
Star Brass Manufacturing Co.

Names of Parts of Fig. 3213.

1 Cap Nut
2 Cap
3 Bell
4 Body
5 Disc
6 Fulcrum
7 Lever
8 Valve
9 Adjusting Nut
10 Body Nut
11 Lever Pin
12 Spring

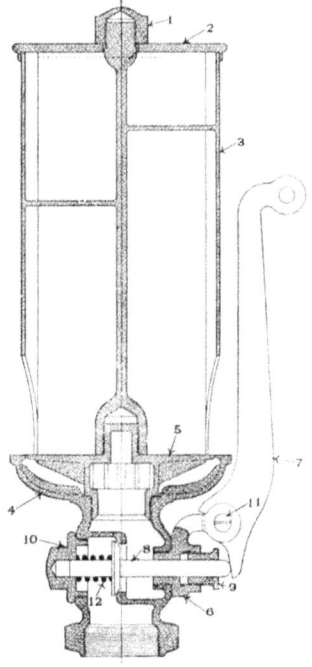

Fig. 3213. Whistle. American Steam Gauge & Valve Mfg. Co.

ENGINE FITTINGS, Safety Valves.

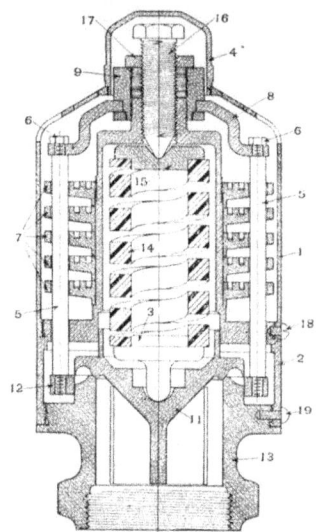

Fig. 3214. Muffled Pop Safety Valve. American Steam Gauge & Valve Mfg. Co.

Names of Parts of Fig. 3214.

1 Muffler Casing
2 Top
3 Bottom
4 Cap
5 Standards
6 Standard Nuts
7 Muffler Discs
8 Yoke
9 Swivel Nut
10 Ring for Swivel Nut
11 Valve
12 Relief Ring
13 Spindle
14 Spring
15 Follower
16 Compression Screw
17 Lock Nut
18 Muffler Case Screw
19 Top Screw

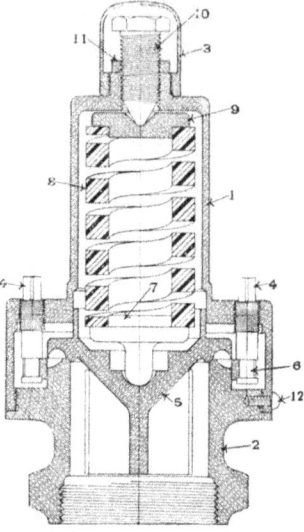

Fig. 3215. Open Pop Safety Valve. American Steam Gauge & Valve Mfg. Co.

Names of Parts of Fig. 3215.

1 Top
2 Bottom
3 Cap
4 Relief Screws
5 Valve
6 Relief Ring
7 Spindle
8 Spring
9 Follower
10 Compression Screw
11 Lock Nut
12 Top Screw

Numbers Refer to List of Names of Parts with Figs. 3218-3225.

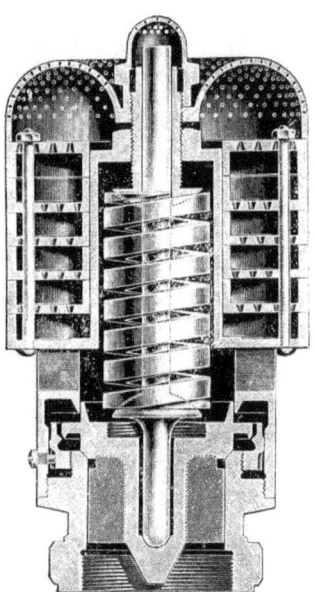

Fig. 3216. Muffled Pop Safety Valve. Consolidated Safety Valve Co.

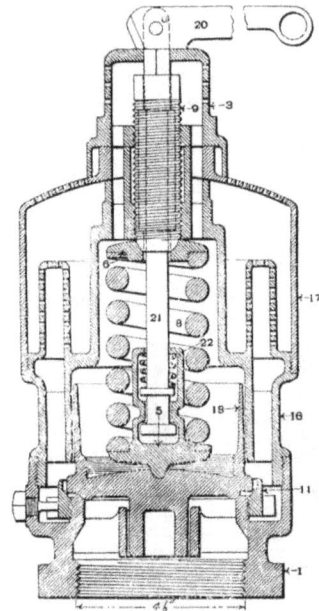

Fig. 3217. Coale Improved Muffled Safety Valve. Pennsylvania Railroad.

ENGINE FITTINGS, Safety Valves.

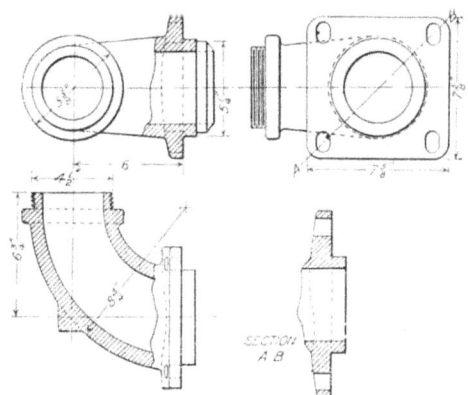

Figs. 3218-3221. Elbow for Attaching Coale Safety Valve.

Pennsylvania Railroad.

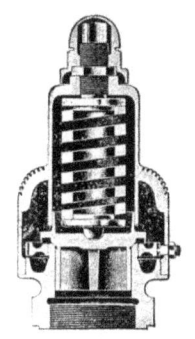

Figs. 3222. Star Improved Pop Safety Valve.

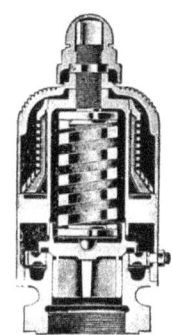

Fig. 3223. Star Improved Muffled Pop Safety Valve.

Star Brass Manufacturing Co.

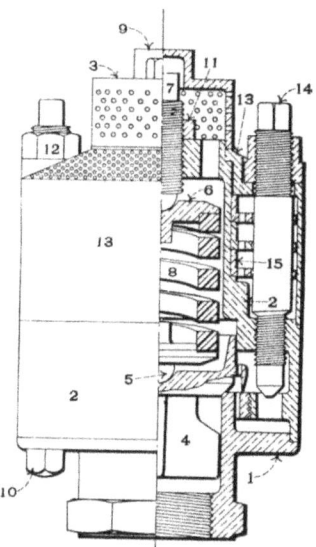

Fig. 3224. Ashton Muffled Safety Valve.

Ashton Valve Co.

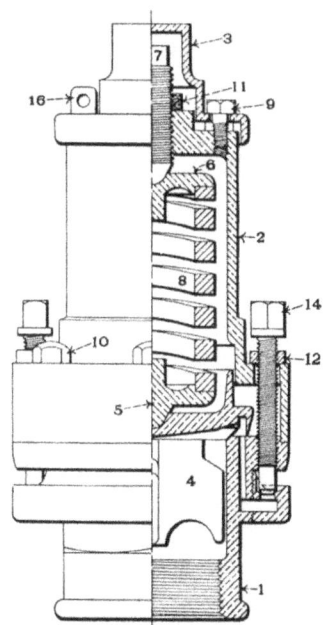

Fig. 3225. Ashton Improved Open Pop Safety Valve.

Ashton Valve Co.

Names of Parts of Safety Valves, Figs. 3217, 3224-3225.

1 *Bottom or Base*
2 *Head*
3 *Cap*
4 *Wing Valve*
5 *Lower Disc*
6 *Upper Disc*
7 *Pressure Screw*
8 *Spring*
9 *Cap Bolt*
10 *Body Screw*
11 *Pressure Screw Check Nut*
12 *Pop Regulator Check Nut*
13 *Dome Top*
14 *Pop Regulator*
15 *Muffler Plate*
16 *Lock Staple*
16 *Spring Case*
17 *Muffler Dome*
18 *Valve*
19 *Adjusting Ring*
20 *Relief Lever*
21 *Relief Spindle*
22 *Relief Spindle Spring*

(312)

ENGINE FITTINGS, Sanders. Figs. 3226-3235

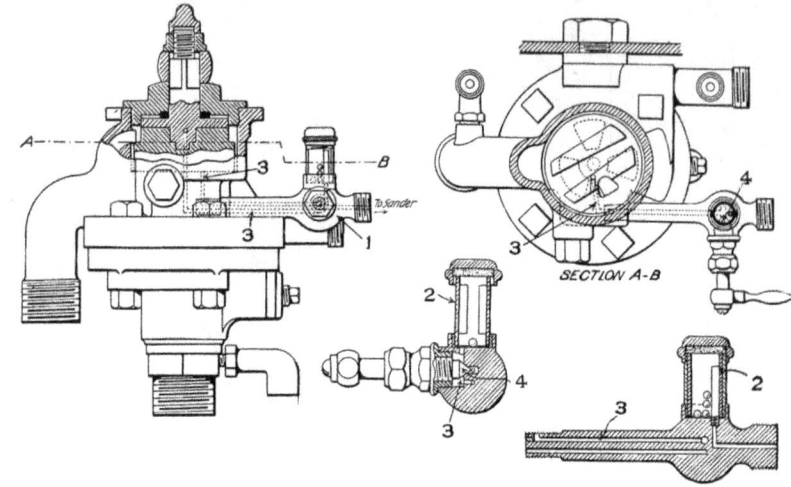

Figs. 3226-3229. Sherburne Brake Valve Attachment for Operating Pneumatic Sander. American Locomotive Sander Co.

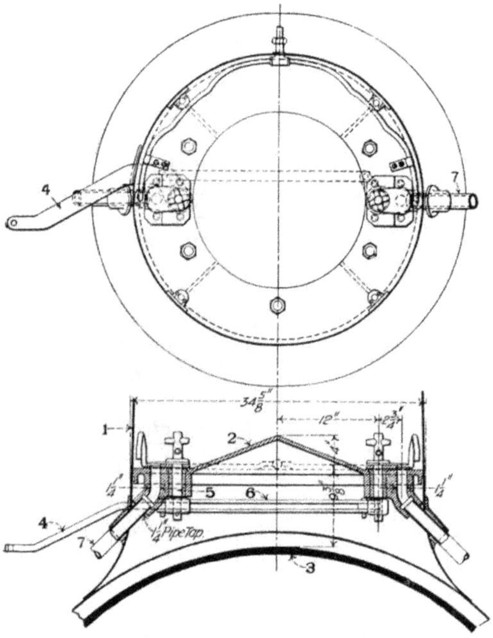

Names of Parts of Figs. 3226-3229.

1. *Attachment Casing*
2. *Indicator Case*
3. *Air Ports*
4. *Valve*

Names of Parts of Figs. 3230-3231.

1. *Sandbox*
2. *Sandbox Bottom*
3. *Boiler Shell*
4. *Sand Lever*
5. *Sand Valve*
6. *Sand Valve Connection*
7. *Sand Pipe*

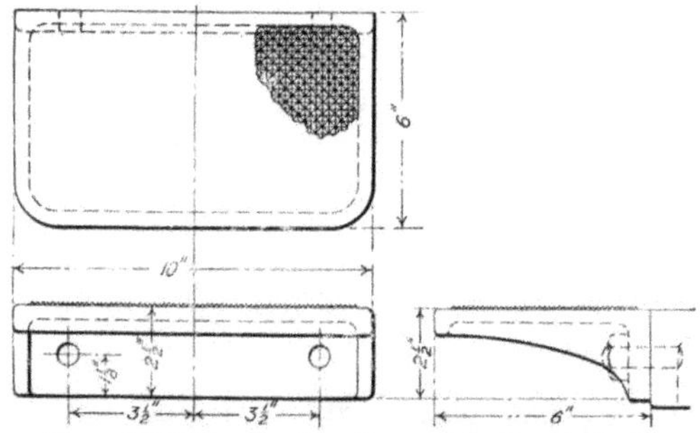

Figs. 3230-3231. Combined Gravity and Sherburne Sander Arrangement. Pennsylvania Railroad.

Figs. 3232-3234. Sandbox Step. Atlantic (4—4—2) Locomotive. Pennsylvania Railroad.

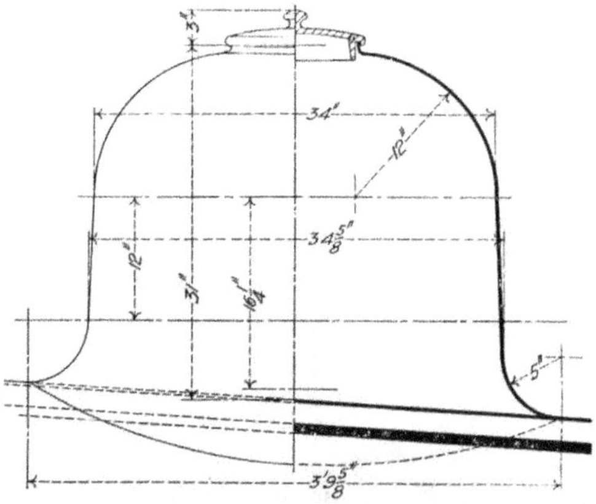

Fig. 3235. Sandbox Casing. Atlantic (4—4—2) Locomotive. Pennsylvania Railroad.

(313)

ENGINE FITTINGS, Sanders.

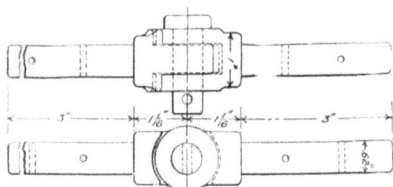

Figs. 3236-3237. Knuckle Joint for Sandbox Rod.

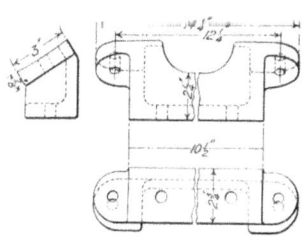

Figs. 3238-3240. Base for Upper Sandbox Step.

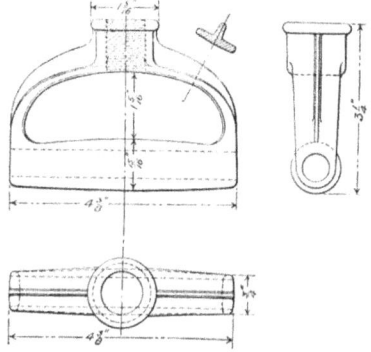

Fig. 3241. Handle for Sandbox Rod.

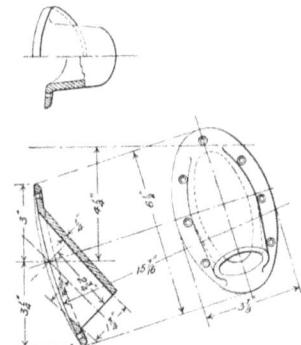

Figs. 3242-3244. Sand Pipe Cover on Sandbox Casing.

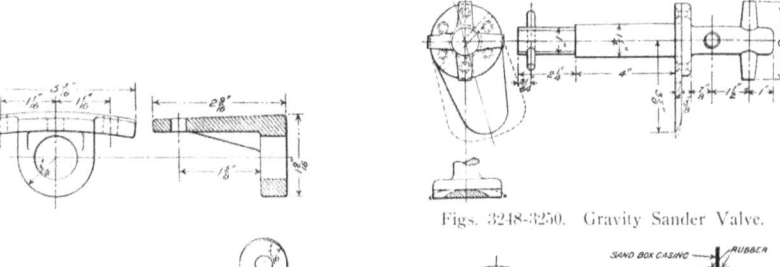

Figs. 3245-3247. Sandbox Base Bracket.

Figs. 3248-3250. Gravity Sander Valve.

Figs. 3251-3252. Air Pipe Connection to Sandbox.

Figs. 3236-3252. Details of Sander for Atlantic (4—4—2) Locomotive. Pennsylvania Railroad.

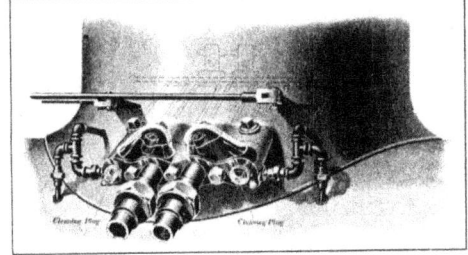

Fig. 3253. Leach Pneumatic Double Sander. Fig. 3254. Valve of Leach Pneumatic Double Sander.
American Locomotive Sander Co.

(314)

ENGINE FITTINGS, Bells. Figs. 3255-3264

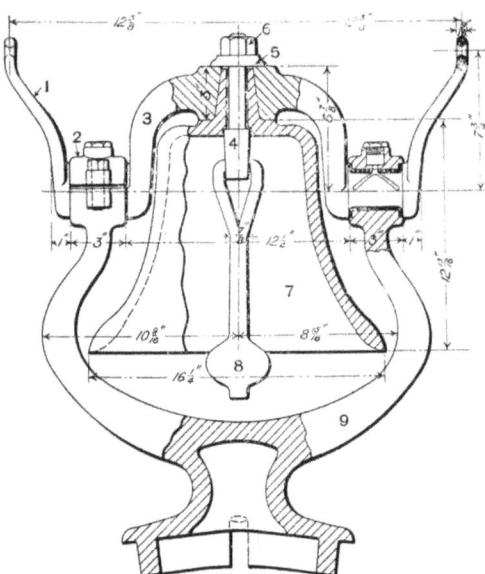

Fig. 3255. Standard Bell and Stand. Pennsylvania Railroad.

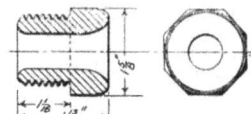

Figs. 3256-3257. Glass Bell Rope Bushing. P. R. R.

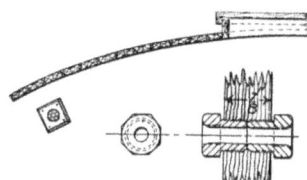

Figs. 3258-3260. Location of Bell Rope Bushing in Cab. P. R. R.

Names of Parts of Fig. 3255.

1. Lever
2. Yoke Bearing Cap
3. Yoke
4. Tongue Hanger
5. Tongue Hanger Washer
6. Tongue Hanger Nut
7. Bell
8. Tongue
9. Stand

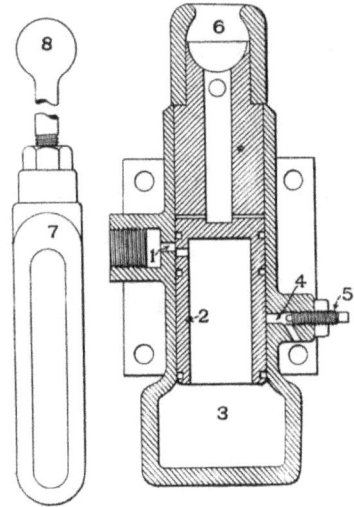

Figs. 3261-3262. Simplicity Bell Ringer. Adreon & Co.

Names of Parts of Figs. 3261-3262.

1. Air Inlet
2. Piston
3. Compression Chamber
4. Exhaust Port
5. Adjustable Choke
6. Bearing Socket and Oiler
7. Bell Crank Yoke
8. Adjustable Connecting Rod

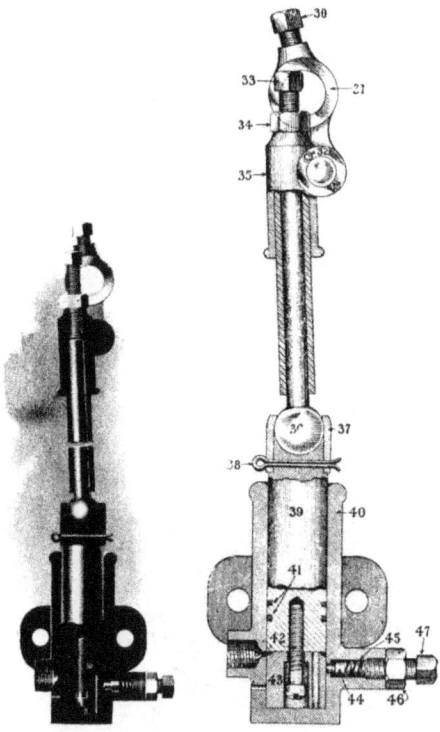

Figs. 3263-3264. Gollmar Bell Ringer. United States Metallic Packing Co.

(315)

ENGINE FITTINGS, Headlights; Pyle Electric.

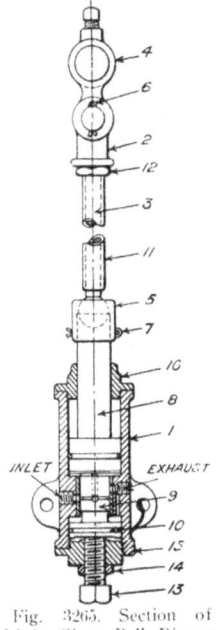

Fig. 3265. Section of Little Giant Bell Ringer. Chicago Pneumatic Tool Co.

Names of Parts of Fig. 3265.

1. *Cylinder*
2. *Connecting Rod Button*
3. *Ball Socket Rod*
4. *Crank*
5. *Ball Socket Collar*
6. *Crank Cotter Pin*
7. *Piston Cotter Pin*
8. *Piston*
9. *Valve*
10. *Packing Rings*
11. *Adjustable Reach Rod*
12. *Adjustable Reach Rod Lock Nut*
13. *Valve Adjusting Screw*
14. *Valve Adjusting Screw Lock Nut*
15. *Lower Cylinder Head*
16. *Upper Cylinder Head*

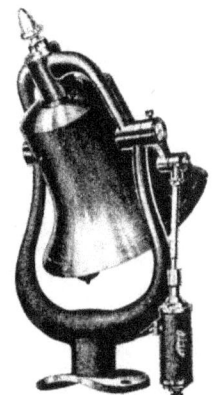

Fig. 3266. Little Giant Bell Ringer.

Numbers Refer to Lists of Names of Parts on Opposite Page.

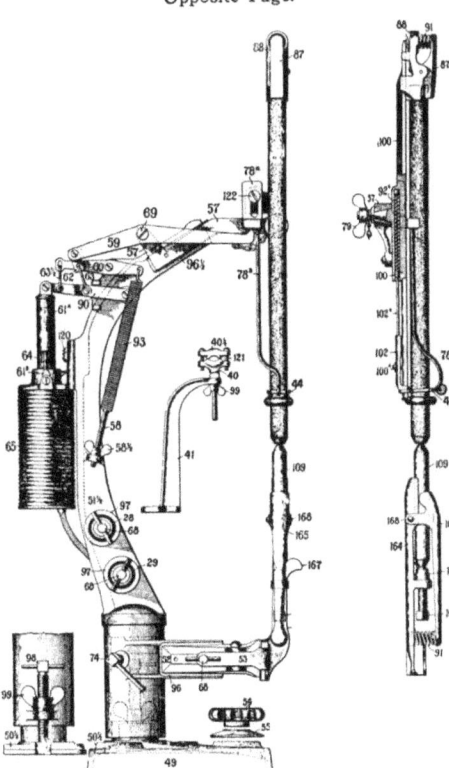

Figs. 3267-3270. Arc Lamp of Pyle-National Electric Headlight, Type D.

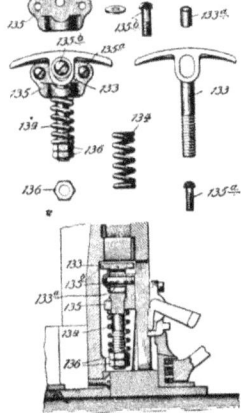

Figs. 3271-3280. Centrifugal Brake for Electric Headlight.

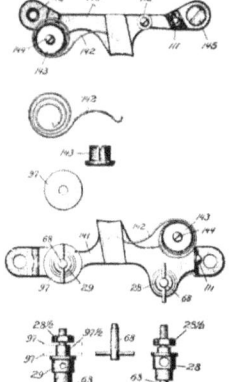

Figs. 3281-3288. Improved Brush Holders.
Pyle-National Electric Headlight Co.

ENGINE FITTINGS, Headlights; Pyle Electric.   Figs. 3289-3290

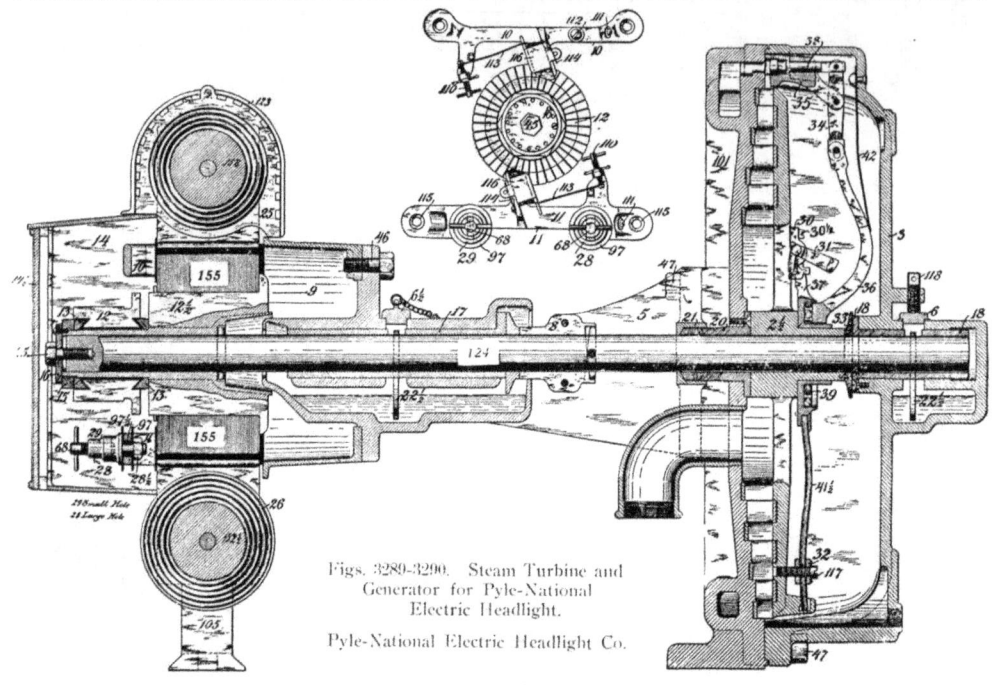

Figs. 3289-3290. Steam Turbine and Generator for Pyle-National Electric Headlight.
Pyle-National Electric Headlight Co.

Names of Parts of Figs. 3267-3270.

28	Binding Post, large hole	61a	Dash Pot	96	Insulation Fibre
28½	Binding Post Nut	61b	Dash Pot Plunger	97	Insulation Washer
29	Binding Post, small hole	62	Magnet Insulation	98	Vertical Adjusting Screw
40	Reflector Clamp, bottom	63	Magnet Long Link	99	Vertical Adjusting Nut
40½	Reflector Clamp, top	63½	Magnet Short Link	100	Upper Carbon Holder
41	Reflector Support	64	Magnet	102	Clutch Foot
44	Clutch	65	Solenoid	102a	Clutch Foot Rod
49	Extension Base	68	Binding Post Screw	109	Copper Electrode
50½	Lamp Base	69	Top Lever Screw	120	Solenoid Screw
51½	Lamp Column	74	Set Screw	121	Reflector Clamp Screw
52	Bottom, large clamp	78a	Clutch Rod Weight	122	Clutch Weight Screw
53	Bottom, small clamp	78b	Clutch Rod	164	Electrode Support
54	Hand Nut	79	Thumb Nut	165	Electrode Lever
55	Hand Washer	87	Carbon Clamp, male	166	Electrode Set Screw
57	Top Bracket	88	Carbon Clamp, female	167	Electrode Lock Nut
58	Spring Tension Screw	90	Magnet Yoke	168	Electrode Escutcheon Pin
58½	Spring Tension Nut	91	Carbon Holder Spring	200	Electrode Holder, complete
59	Top Lever	92a	Top Clutch Spring	300	Top Carbon Holder, complete
60	Small Lever	93	Tension Spring		

Names of Parts of Figs. 3289-3290.

1	Main Casting, 4 rows buckets	22½	Oil Ring	68	Binding Post Screw
2	Wheel, 5 rows buckets	25	Top Field Washer	97	Insulation Washer
2½	Wheel, 3 rows buckets	26	Bottom Field Washer	97½	Insulation
3	Engine Cap	27	Dynamo Feet, old style	101	Main Casting
5	Box Yoke	28	Binding Post, large hole	105	Dynamo Foot
6	Oil Cover, outside	28½	Binding Post Nut	110	Brush Spring Adjusting Screw
6½	Oil Cover, inside	29	Binding Post, small hole	111	Connecting Screw for Inc. Wire
7	Pole Pieces	30	Governor Weight Clamp		
8	End Thrust	30½	Governor Saddle Screw	112	Connecting Screw for Upper Field
9	Brass Yoke	31	Governor Weight		
10	Top Brush Holder	32	Spring Clamp	113	Brush Spring
11	Bottom Brush Holder	33	Cast Iron Washer	114	Brush Clamp Spring
12	Commutator	34	Connecting Link	115	Insulating Bushing
12½	Armature Spider	35	Governor Stand	116	Brush Clamp
13	Commutator Ring	36	Cross Arm	117	Governor Spring Adjusting Screw
14	Dynamo Door	37	Center Piece		
14½	Name Plate	38	Bronze Plunger	118	Oil Cover Set Screw
15	Commutator Nut	39	Graphite Ring	123	Top Field Cover
16	side Washer	41½	Governor Springs	124	Main Shaft
17	Long Bushing	42	Cap Spring	152	Top Field, complete
18	Short Bushing	45	Armature Lock Screw	152½	Bottom Field, complete
20	Stuffing Box	46	Cap Screw	155	Armature
21	Gland Nut	47	Cap Screw		

(317)

ENGINE FITTINGS, Headlights.

Fig. 3291. Electric Headlight.
General Electric Co.

Fig. 3292. Electric Headlight.
General Electric Co.

Fig. 3293. Electric Headlight.
General Electric Co.

Fig. 3294. Curtis Turbo-Generator for Electric Headlight.
General Electric Co.

Fig. 3295. Steel Bottom Oil Headlight.

Fig. 3296.
Dressel Headlight
Burner.

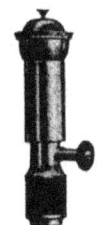

Fig. 3297.
Hull Headlight
Burner.

Dressel Railway Lamp Works.

ENGINE FITTINGS, Headlights.

Figs. 3298-3305

Fig. 3298. 23-Inch Square Case Star Standard Headlight.

Fig. 3299. Interior of 23-Inch Square Case Headlight.

Star Headlight Co.

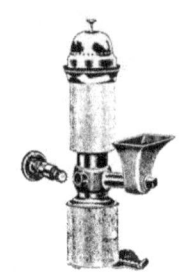

Fig. 3300. Williams' Headlight Burner with Wilder Stuffing Box.

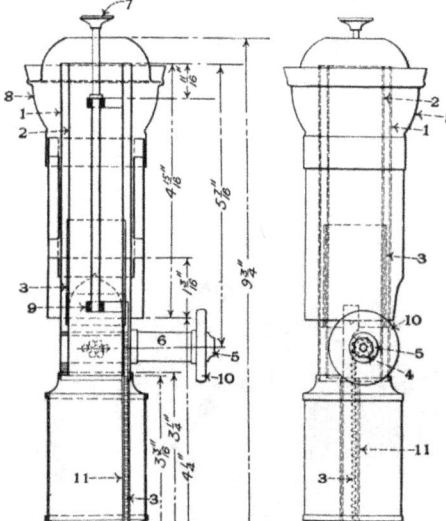

Figs. 3301-3302. Standard Headlight Burner. Pennsylvania Railroad.

Names of Parts of Figs. 3301-3302.

1 *Outside Tube*
2 *Inside Tube*
3 *Thimble and Rack*
4 *Pinion and Shaft*
5 *Slotted Nut*
6 *Stuffing Box*
7 *Button*
8 *Gallery*
9 *Spider*
10 *Hand Wheel*
11 *Rack Casing*

Numbers Refer to List of Names of Parts with Figs. 3306-3316.

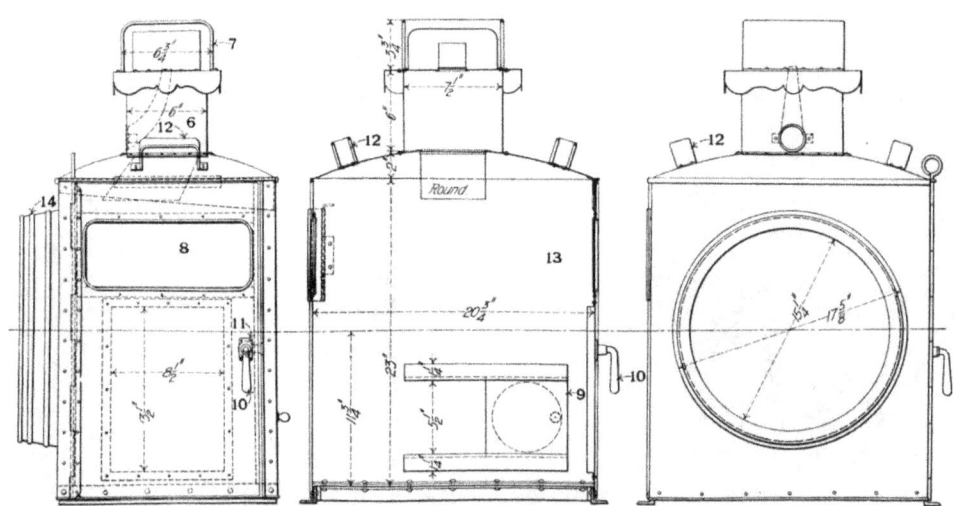

Figs. 3303-3305. Standard 16-Inch Oil Headlight. Pennsylvania Railroad.

Figs. 3306-3316 — ENGINE FITTINGS, Headlights.

Numbers Refer to List of Names of Parts Below.

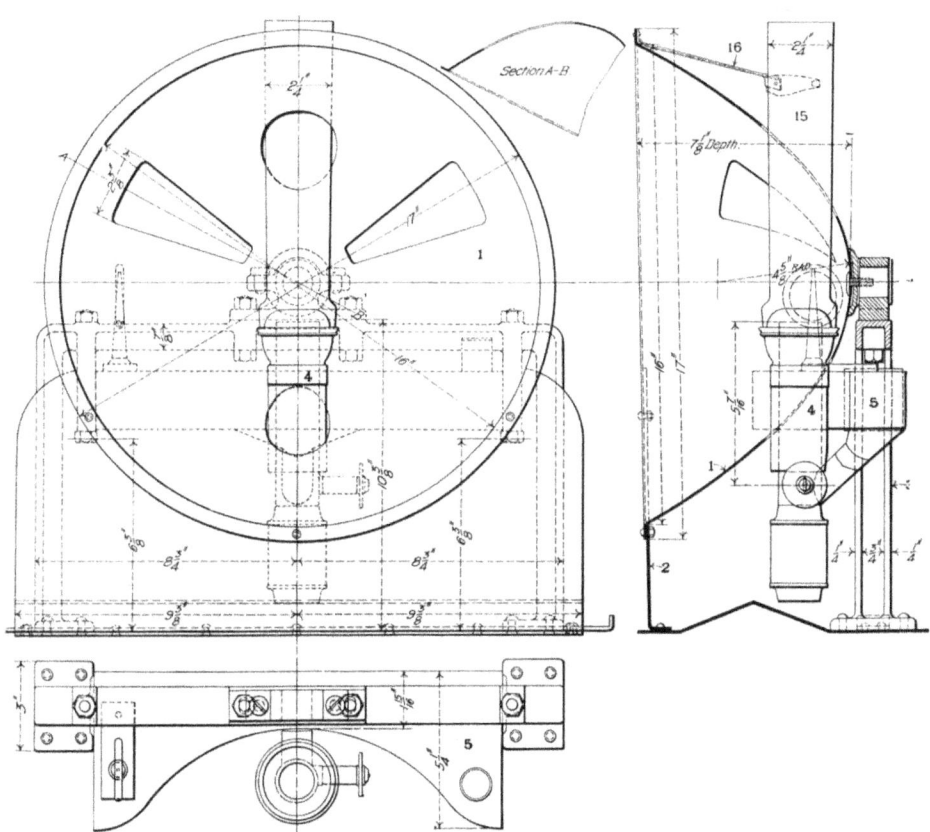

Figs. 3306-3308. Details of Standard 16-Inch Oil Headlight. Pennsylvania Railroad.

Names of Parts of Figs. 3303-3308.

1. Reflector
2. Reflector Casing
3. Reflector Stand
4. Burner
5. Oil Reservoir
6. Ventuator
7. Ventilator Cap
8. Number Slide
9. Lighting Hole Slide
10. Door Handle
11. Door Plate
12. Lifting Handle
13. Casing
14. Front Glass Casing
15. Chimney
16. Chimney Holder

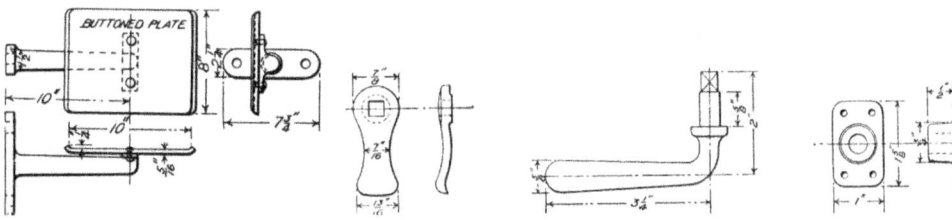

Figs. 3309-3311. Headlight Step on Smokebox Front.   Figs. 3312-3313. Headlight Door Latch.   Fig. 3314. Headlight Door Handle.   Figs. 3315-3316. Headlight Door Plate.

(320)

ENGINE FITTINGS, Lamps. Figs. 3317–3328

Names of Parts of Figs. 3317-3323.

1. Lamp Chimney Shield
2. Lamp Chimney
3. Cab Lamp
4. Lamp Chimney Setting
5. Lamp Base
6. Lamp Chimney Holder
7. Lamp Bracket
8. Lamp Base Fastening Screw
9. Lense
10. Lense Holder
11. Oil Reservoir
12. Oil Reservoir Filling Hole Cap
13. Ventilator
14. Ventilator Cap
15. Bail
16. Side Opening Hinge
17. Side Opening Fastening
18. Burner
19. Wick Adjusting Screw

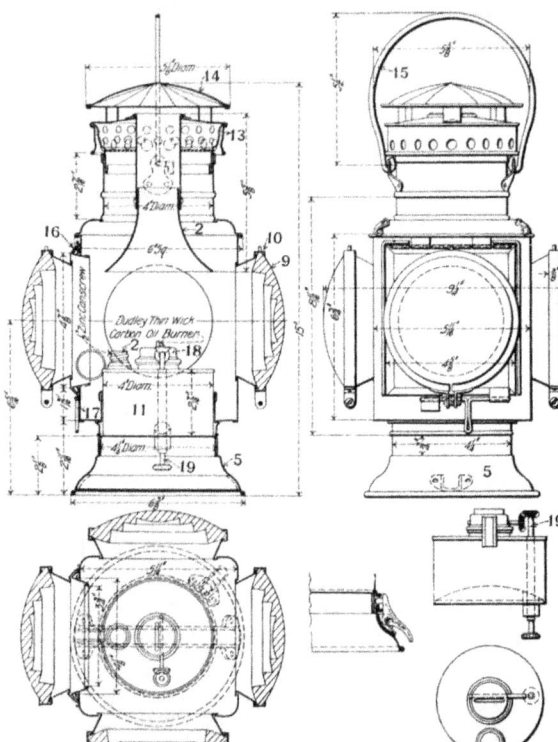

Figs. 3317-3322. Standard Front End Locomotive Classification Lamp. Pennsylvania Railroad.

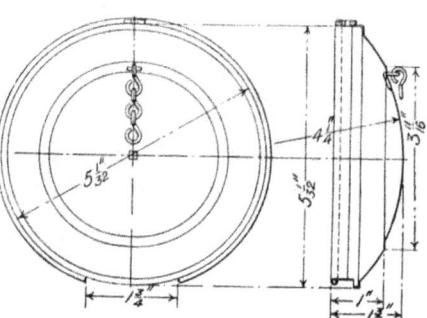

Figs. 3324-3325. Cover for Lense of Classification Lamp.

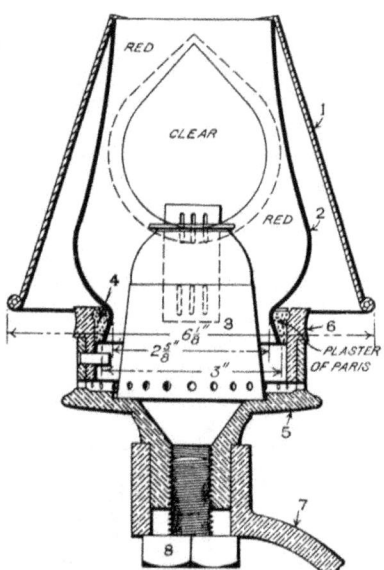

Fig. 3323. Locomotive Cab Lamp. Pennsylvania Railroad.

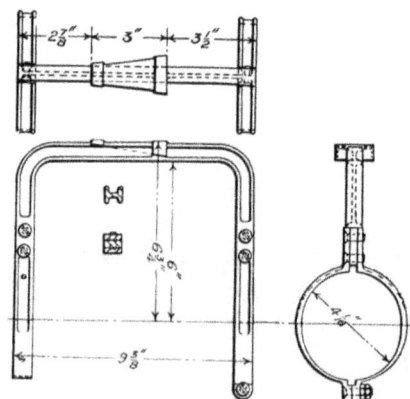

Figs. 3326-3328. Classification Lamp Bracket.

(324)

ENGINE FITTINGS, Miscellaneous.

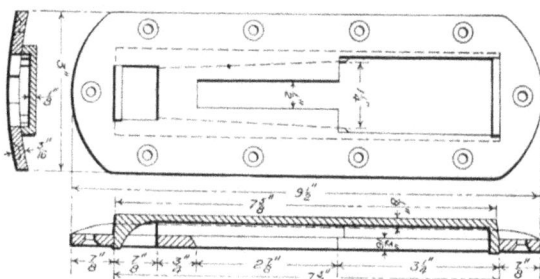

Figs. 3329-3331. Lamp and Flag Holder Socket.

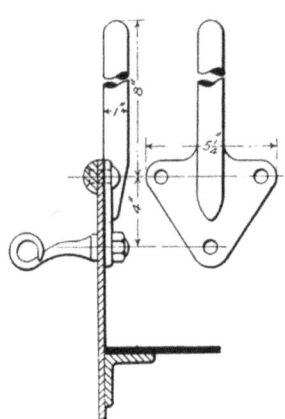

Figs. 3332-3333. Lamp Hanger Bracket.

Fig. 3334. Little Giant Pneumatic Blow-off Cock.   Fig. 3335. Pneumatic Blow-off Cock, Yoke Type.

Fig. 3336. Engineer's Valve for Operating Pneumatic Blow-off Cock.

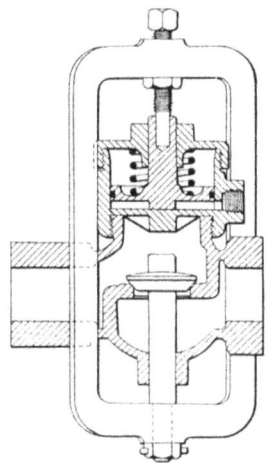

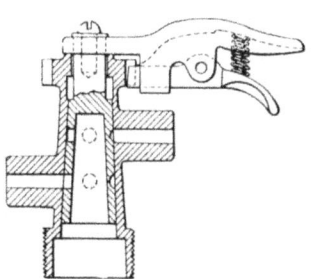

Fig. 3337. Little Giant Pneumatic Blow-off Cock.   Fig. 3338. Pneumatic Blow-off Cock, Yoke Type.   Fig. 3339. Engineer's Valve for Operating Pneumatic Blow-off Cock.

Pneumatic Blow-off Cocks. Chicago Pneumatic Tool Co.

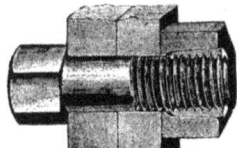
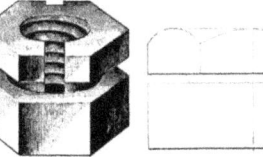 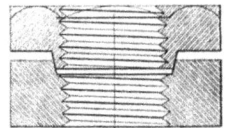

Figs. 3340-3341. Columbia Lock Nut. U. S. Metal & Mfg. Co.   Figs. 3342-3343. McLaughlin Lock Nut. Franklin Railway Supply Co.

(322)

ENGINE TRUCKS, Pony. Figs. 3344-3351

Numbers Refer to List of Names of Parts Below.

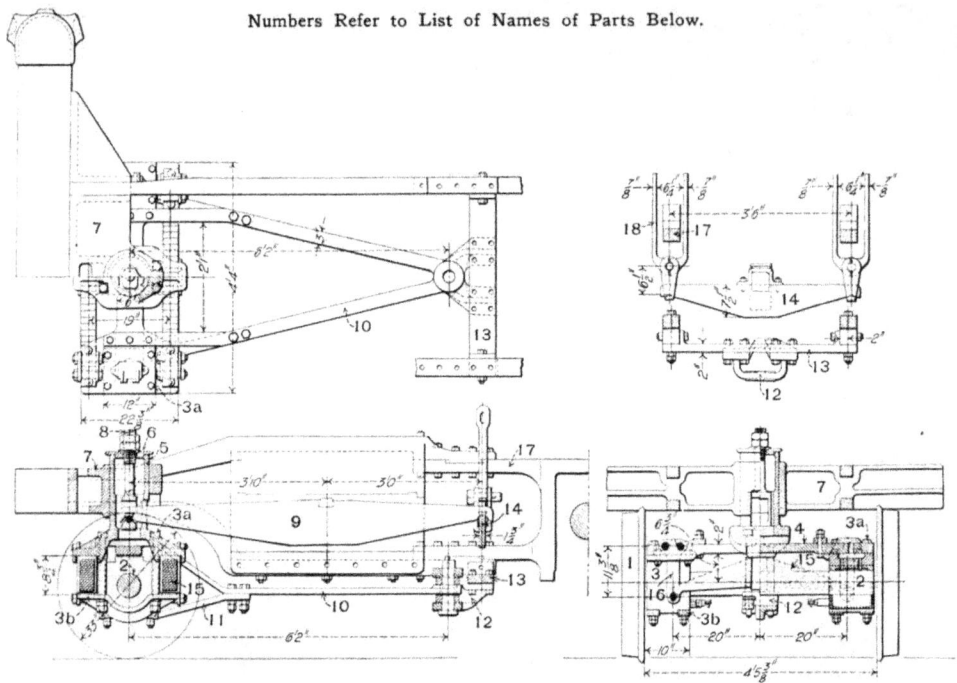

Figs. 3344-3348. Pony Truck for Mogul (2—6—0) Locomotive. Pennsylvania Railroad.

Names of Parts of Figs. 3344-3351.

1 Wheel
2 Axle
3 Journal Box
3a Journal Box Bolt
3b Journal Box Bolt Tie Bar
3c Journal Box Yoke
3d Journal Box Spring
4 Truck Frame
5 Center Pin
6 Center Pin Cap
7 Center Pin Guide
8 Center Bolt
9 Driver and Truck Equalizer
9a Equalizer Safety Strap
10 Radius Bar
11 Radius Bar Brace
12 Radius Bar Bearing
13 Radius Bar Bearing Support
14 Transverse Equalizer
15 Truck Spring
16 Truck Spring Hanger
17 Engine Frame
18 Driver Spring Hanger
19 Front Buffer beam
20 Center Plate
21 Center Plate Hanger
21a Center Plate Hanger Pin
22 Transom
23 Pedestal
24 Pedestal Tie Bar
24a Pedestal Cross Brace

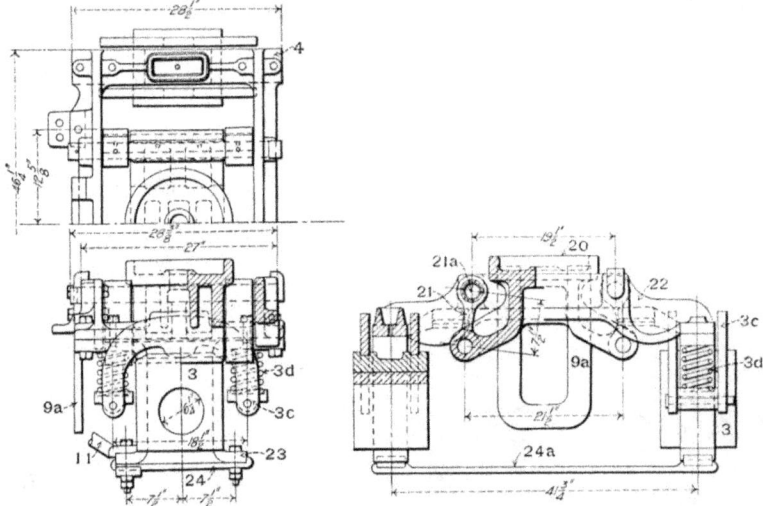

Figs. 3349-3351. Pony Truck for Mogul (2—6—0) Locomotive. American Locomotive Co.

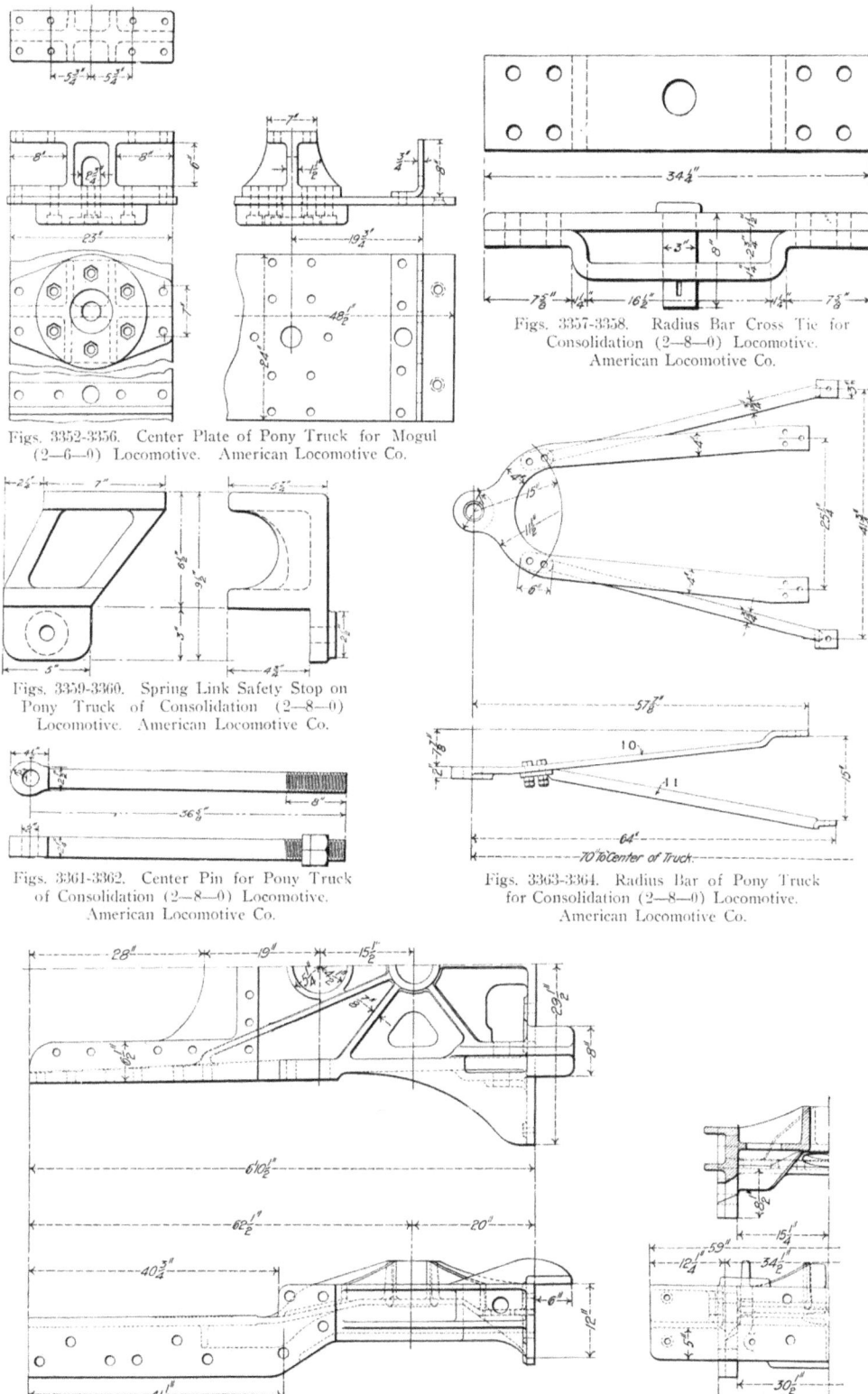

Figs. 3352–3356. Center Plate of Pony Truck for Mogul (2—6—0) Locomotive. American Locomotive Co.

Figs. 3357–3358. Radius Bar Cross Tie for Consolidation (2—8—0) Locomotive. American Locomotive Co.

Figs. 3359–3360. Spring Link Safety Stop on Pony Truck of Consolidation (2—8—0) Locomotive. American Locomotive Co.

Figs. 3361–3362. Center Pin for Pony Truck of Consolidation (2—8—0) Locomotive. American Locomotive Co.

Figs. 3363–3364. Radius Bar of Pony Truck for Consolidation (2—8—0) Locomotive. American Locomotive Co.

Figs. 3365–3368. Center Pin Guide for Pony Truck of Consolidation (2—8—0) Locomotive. American Locomotive Co.

ENGINE TRUCKS, Front; Four-Wheel.   Figs. 3369-3375

Numbers Refer to List of Names of Parts Below.

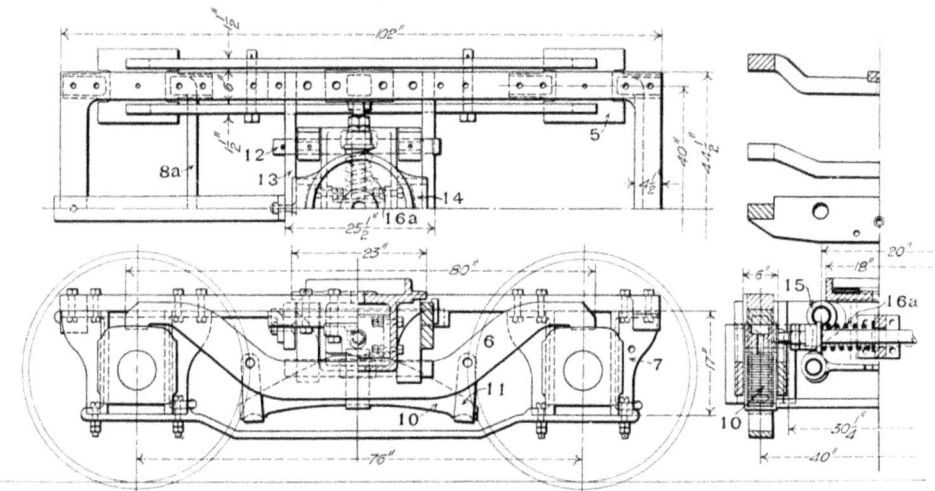

Figs. 3369-3372. Four-Wheel Front Engine Truck. American Locomotive Co.

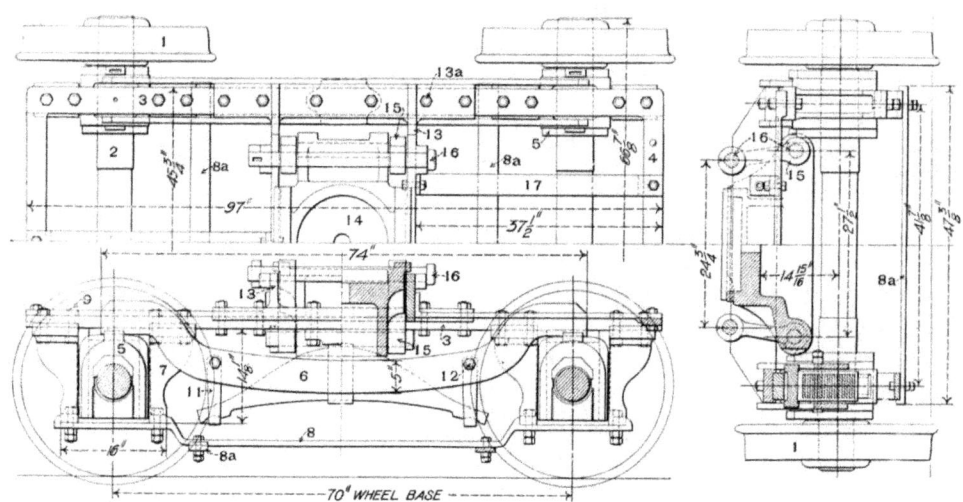

Figs. 3373-3375. Four-Wheel Front Engine Truck. Boston & Maine.

Names of Parts of Figs. 3369-3380.

1 Wheel	12 Spring Hanger Pin	21 Brake Equalizer
2 Axle	13 Transom	22 Brake Rod
3 Side Frame	13a Transom Bolt	23 Floating Brake Lever
4 End Frame	14 Center Plate	24 Floating Brake Lever Connection
5 Axle Box	15 Center Plate Hanger	
6 Equalizer	15a Center Plate T Hanger	25 Brake Hanger Lever
7 Pedestal	16 Center Plate Hanger Pin	25a Brake Hanger Lever Bracket
8 Pedestal Tie Bar	16a Centering Spring	26 Brake Shoe
8a Pedestal Tie Bar Cross Tie	17 Safety Beam	27 Brake Head
8b Pedestal Cross Brace	18 Brake Cylinder	28 Brake Head Adjusting Spring
9 Pedestal Bolt	18a Brake Cylinder Bracket	29 Brake Head Adjusting Spring Rod
10 Semi-Elliptic Spring	19 Brake Lever	
11 Spring Hanger	20 Brake Lever Fulcrum	30 Check Chain Eye

ENGINE TRUCKS, Front; Four-Wheel.

Numbers Refer to List of Names of Parts with Figs. 3369-3375.

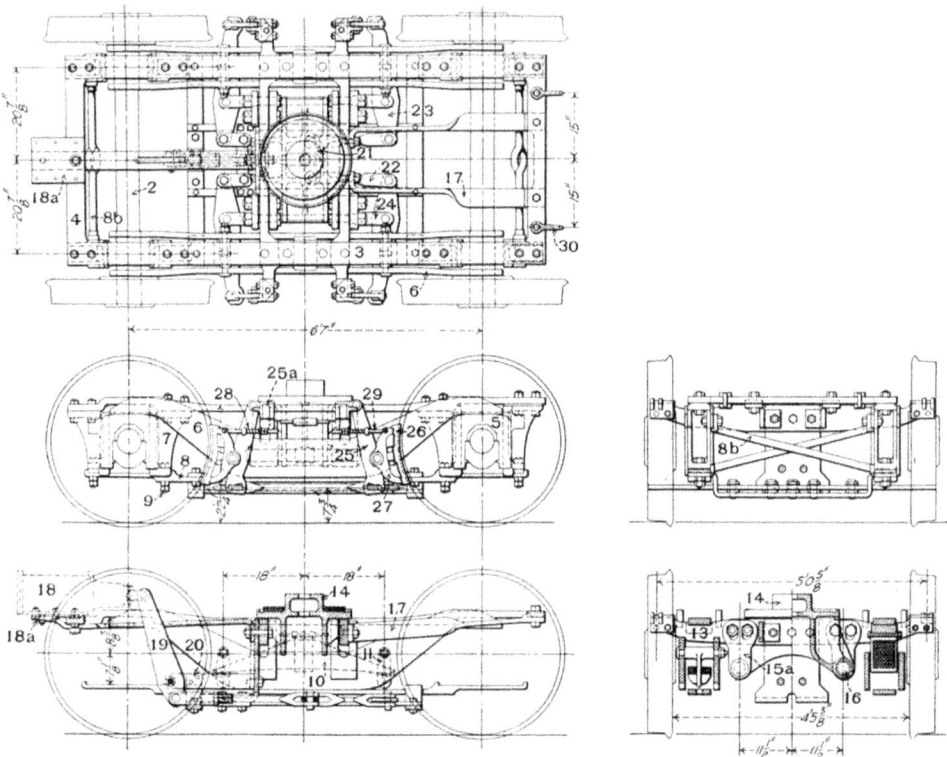

Figs. 3376-3380. Swing Motion Four-Wheel Front Engine Truck with T Hangers. Atlantic (4—4—2) Locomotive. Pennsylvania Railroad.

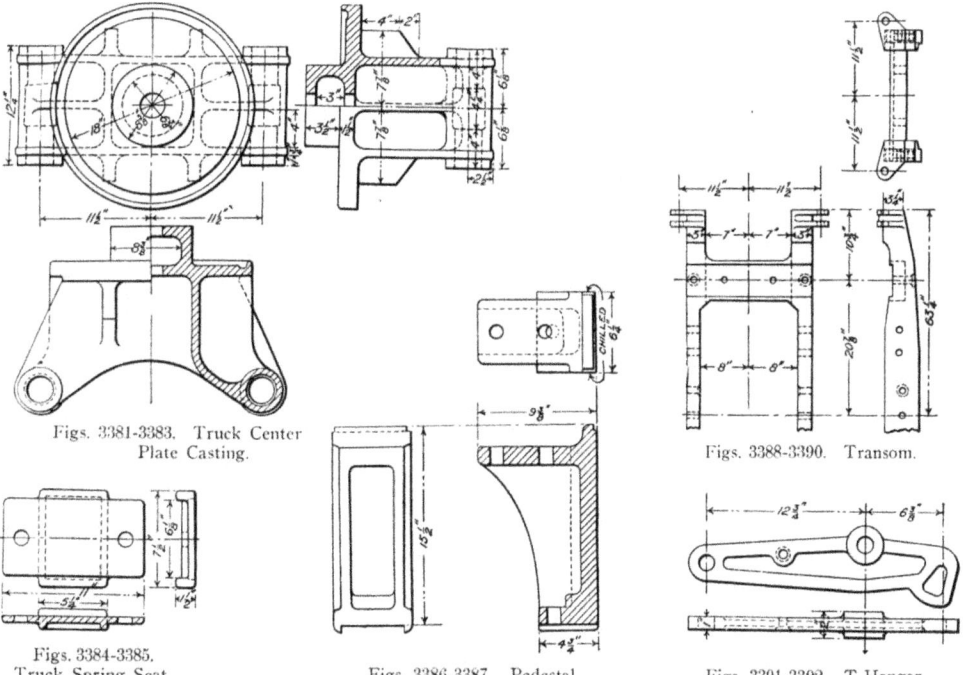

Figs. 3381-3383. Truck Center Plate Casting.

Figs. 3384-3385. Truck Spring Seat.

Figs. 3386-3387. Pedestal.

Figs. 3388-3390. Transom.

Figs. 3391-3392. T Hanger.

Figs. 3381-3392. Details of Swing Motion Four-Wheel Front Engine Truck. Atlantic (4—4—2) Locomotive. Pennsylvania Railroad.

(326)

ENGINE TRUCKS, Trailing. Figs. 3393-3403

Numbers Refer to List of Names of Parts with Figs. 3414-3424.

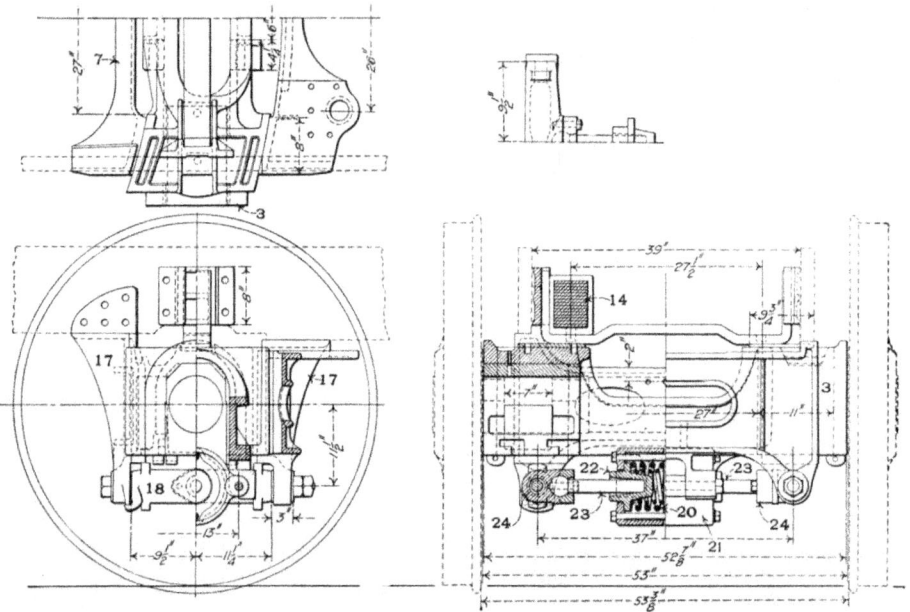

Figs. 3393-3396. Radial Trailing Truck for Atlantic (4—4—2) Locomotive. Baldwin Locomotive Works.

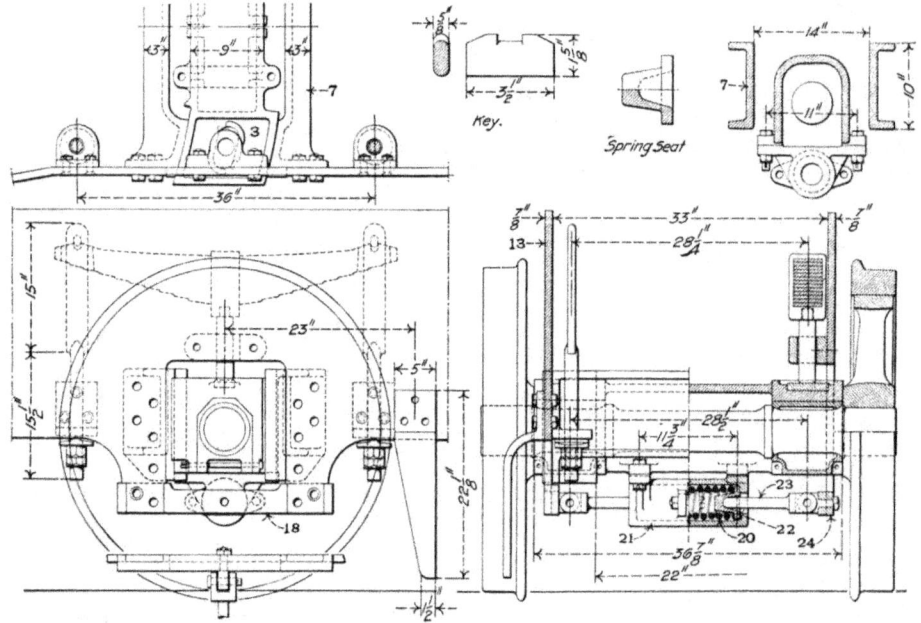

Figs. 3397-3403. Radial Trailing Truck for Six-Coupled (0—6—2) Locomotive. Baldwin Locomotive Works.

ENGINE TRUCKS, Trailing.

Numbers Refer to List of Names of Parts with Figs. 3414-3424.

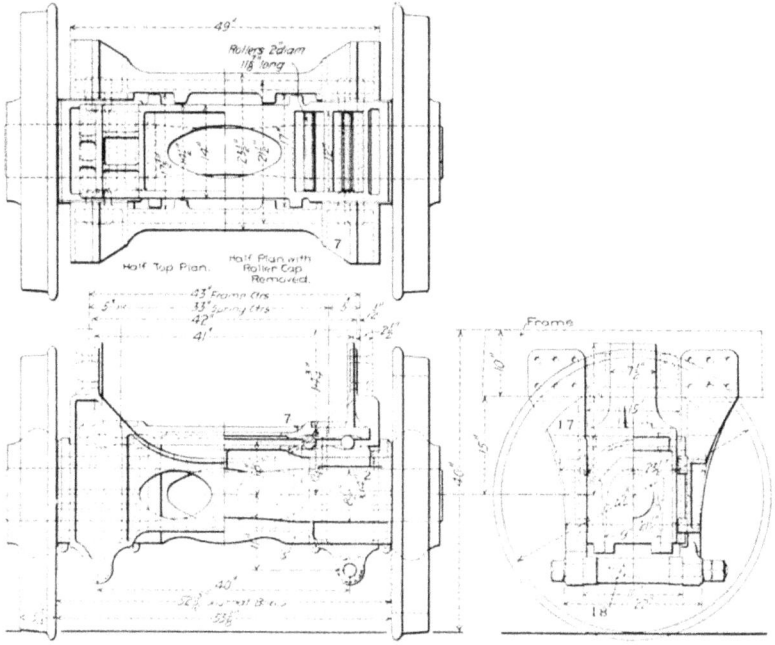

Figs. 3404-3406. Radial Trailing Truck for Atlantic (4—4—2) Locomotive. Chicago, Milwaukee & St. Paul.

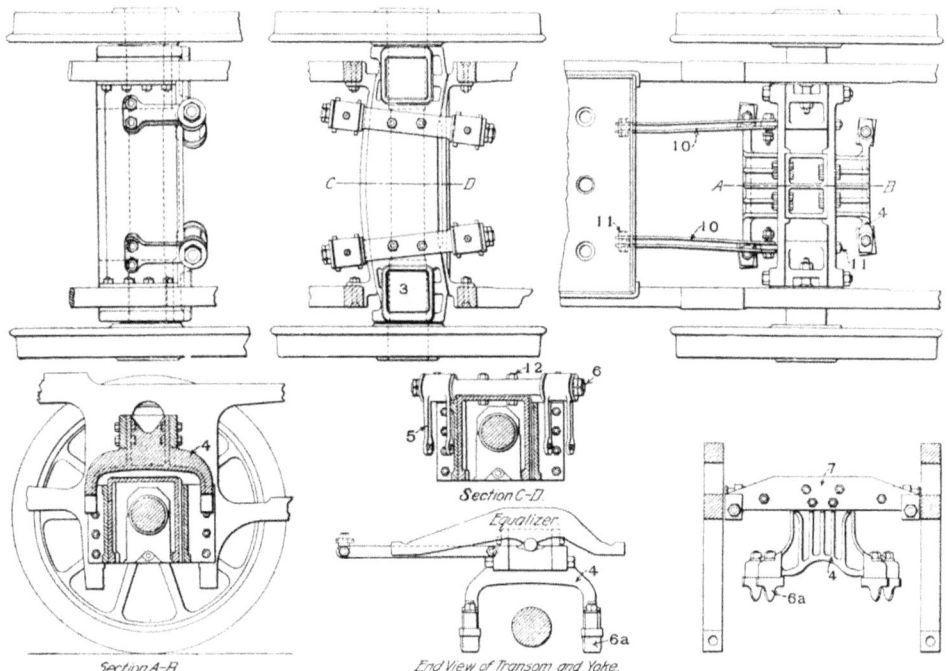

Figs. 3407-3413. Radial Trailing Truck for Atlantic (4—4—2) Locomotive. Pennsylvania Railroad.

ENGINE TRUCKS, Trailing.

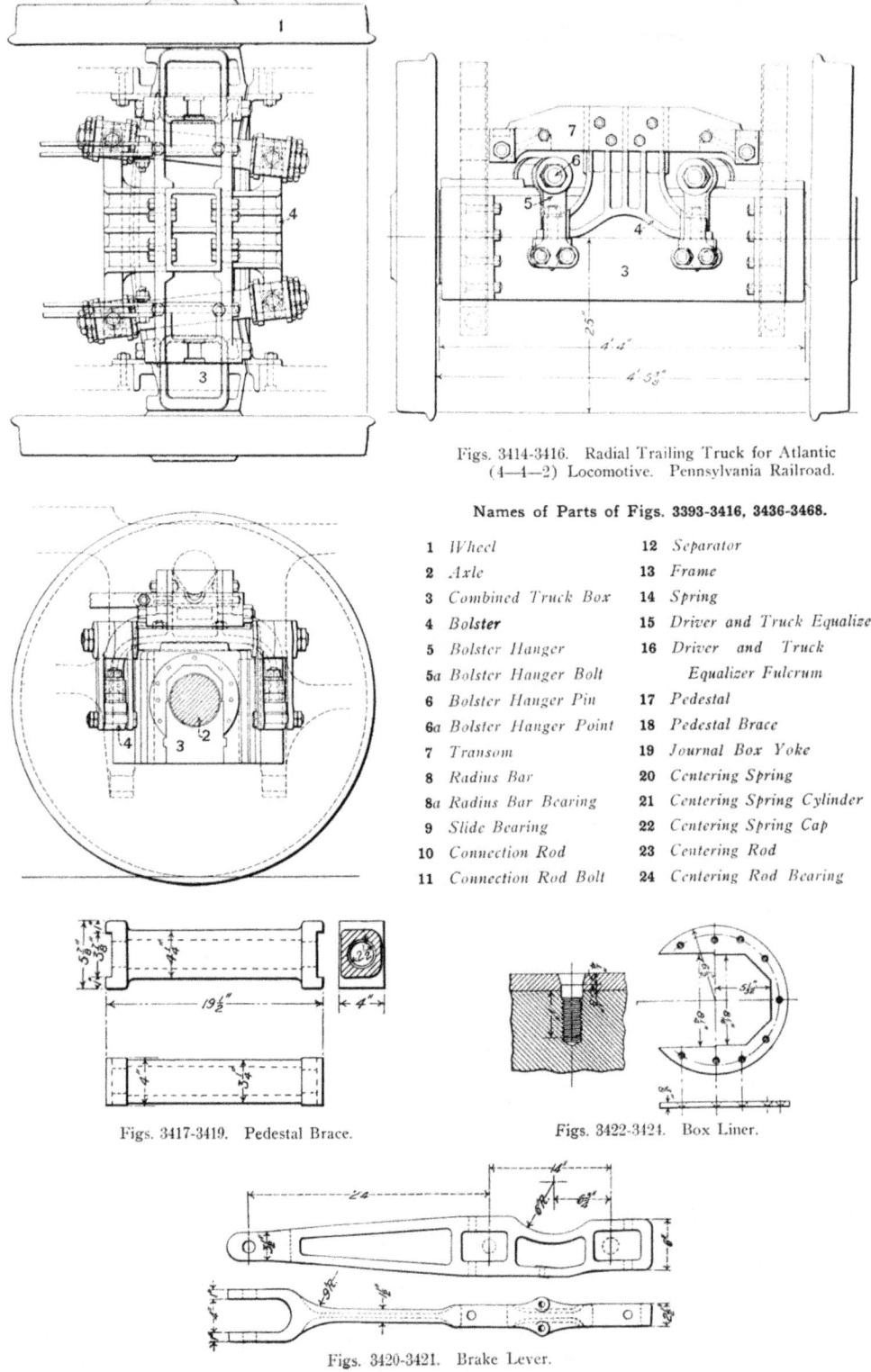

Figs. 3414-3416. Radial Trailing Truck for Atlantic (4—4—2) Locomotive. Pennsylvania Railroad.

Names of Parts of Figs. 3393-3416, 3436-3468.

1	Wheel	12	Separator
2	Axle	13	Frame
3	Combined Truck Box	14	Spring
4	**Bolster**	15	Driver and Truck Equalizer
5	Bolster Hanger	16	Driver and Truck Equalizer Fulcrum
5a	Bolster Hanger Bolt		
6	Bolster Hanger Pin	17	Pedestal
6a	Bolster Hanger Point	18	Pedestal Brace
7	Transom	19	Journal Box Yoke
8	Radius Bar	20	Centering Spring
8a	Radius Bar Bearing	21	Centering Spring Cylinder
9	Slide Bearing	22	Centering Spring Cap
10	Connection Rod	23	Centering Rod
11	Connection Rod Bolt	24	Centering Rod Bearing

Figs. 3417-3419. Pedestal Brace.   Figs. 3422-3424. Box Liner.

Figs. 3420-3421. Brake Lever.

Figs. 3417-3424. Details of Radial Trailing Truck for Atlantic (4—4—2) Locomotive. Pennsylvania Railroad.

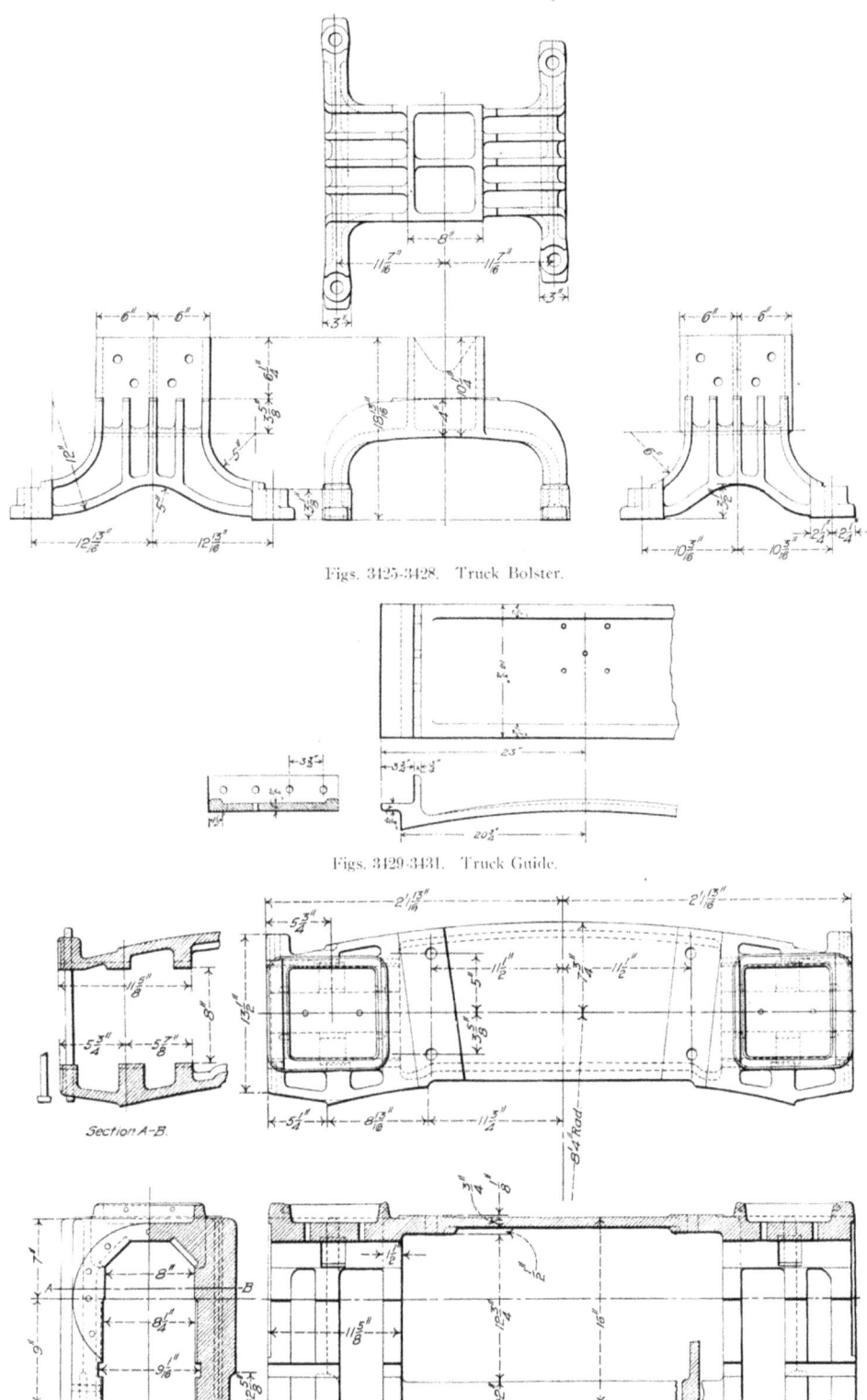

Figs. 3425-3428. Truck Bolster.

Figs. 3429-3431. Truck Guide.

Figs. 3432-3435. Combined Truck Box.

Figs. 3425-3435. Details of Radial Trailing Truck for Atlantic (4—4—2) Locomotive. Pennsylvania Railroad.

ENGINE TRUCKS, Trailing.

Numbers Refer to List of Names of Parts with Figs. 3414-3424.

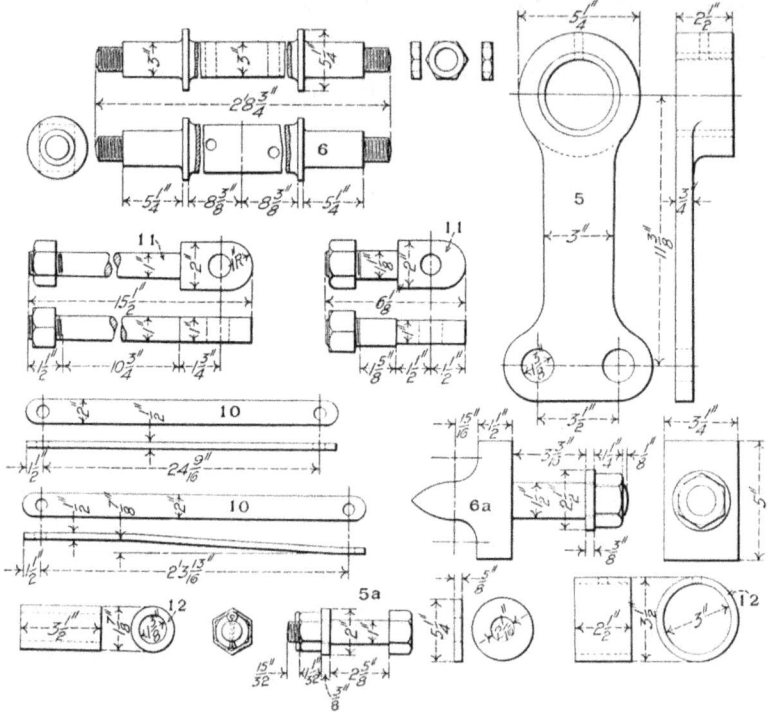

Figs. 3436-3461. Details of Radial Trailing Truck for Atlantic (4—4—2) Locomotive. Pennsylvania Railroad.

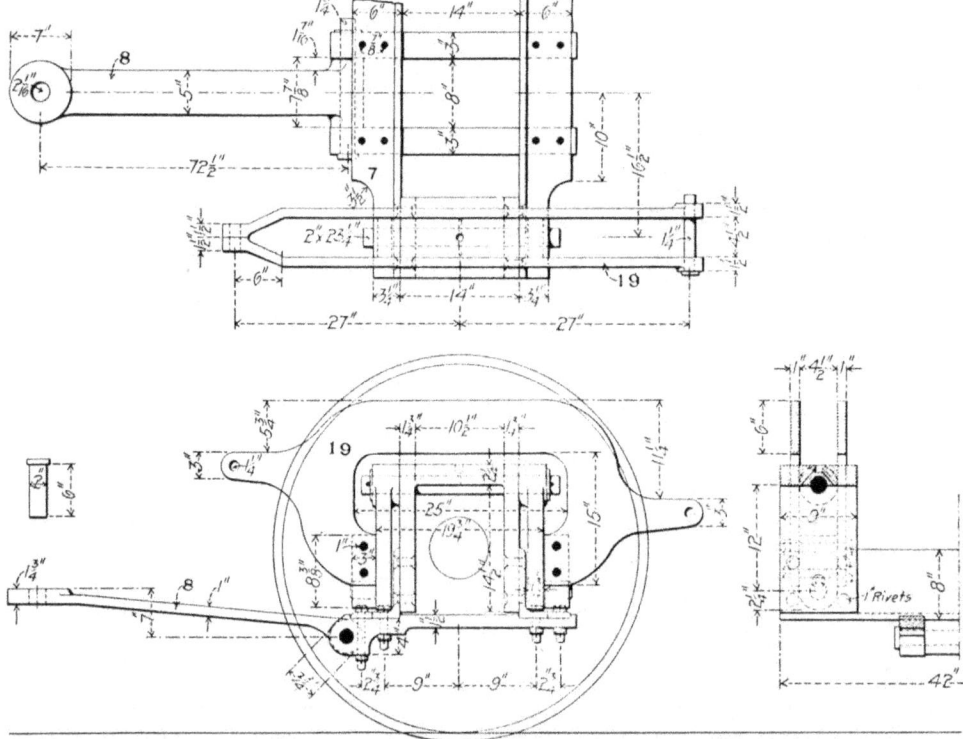

Figs. 3462-3465. Trailing Truck for Suburban Locomotive. Central Railroad of New Jersey.

ENGINE TRUCKS, Trailing.

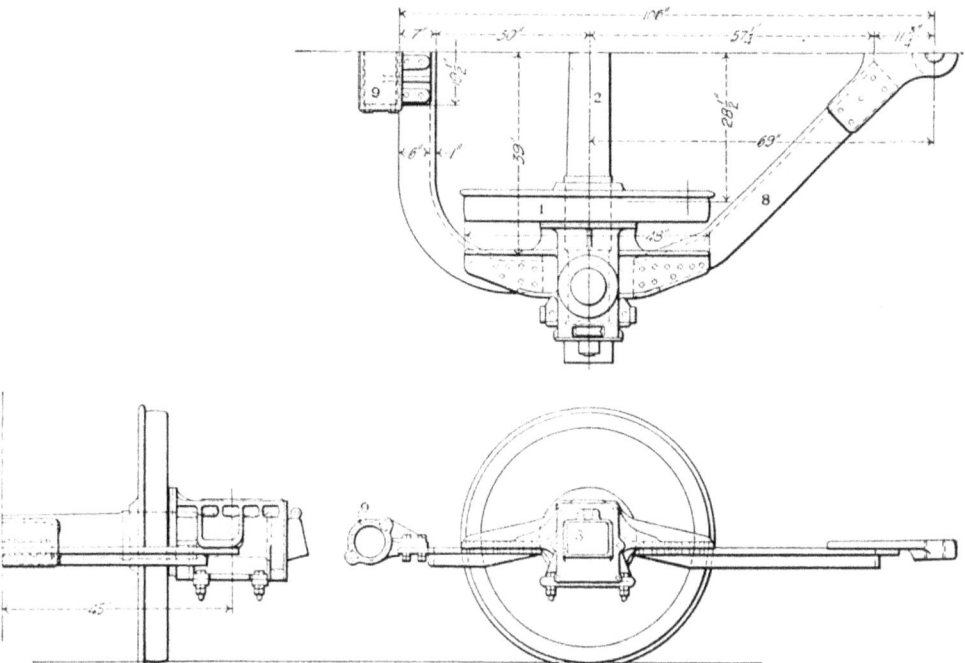

Figs. 3466-3468. Radial Trailing Truck for Atlantic (4—4—2) Locomotive. American Locomotive Co.

Names of Parts of Figs. 3469-3477.

1 *Transom*
2 *Box Yoke and Frame*
3 *Box Yoke Hinge*
4 *Box Yoke Hinge Pin*
5 *Pedestal*
6 *Pedestal Brace*
7 *Guide Bars*

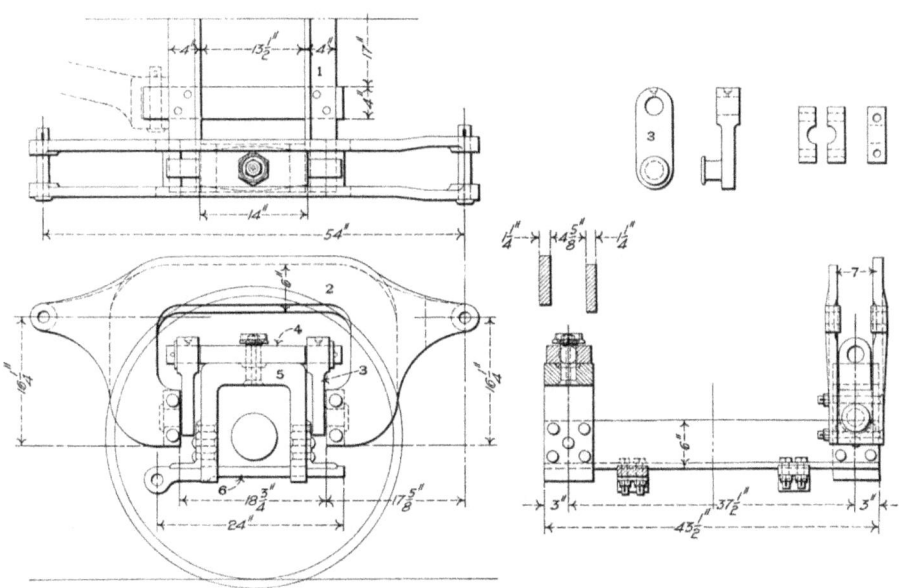

Figs. 3469-3477. Rushton Radial Trailing Truck for Pacific (4—6—2) Locomotive. Baldwin Locomotive Works.

ENGINE TRUCKS, Trailing.   Figs. 3478-3481

Numbers Refer to List of Names of Parts with Figs. 3414-3424.

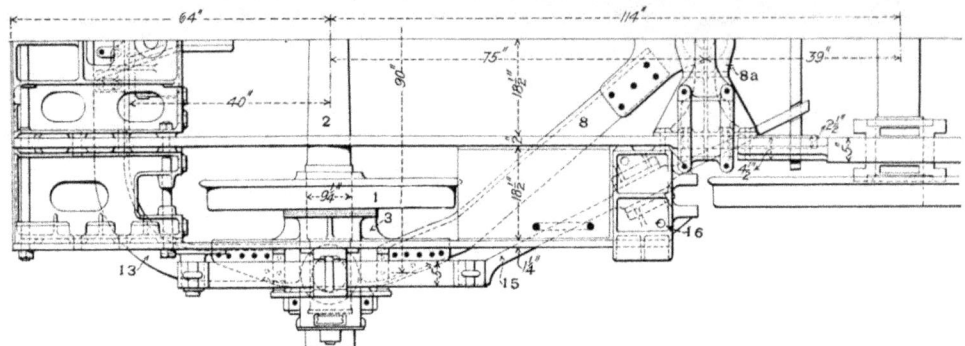

Fig. 3478. Radial Trailing Truck for Atlantic (4—4—2) Locomotive.
American Locomotive Co.

Numbers Refer to List of Names of Parts Below.

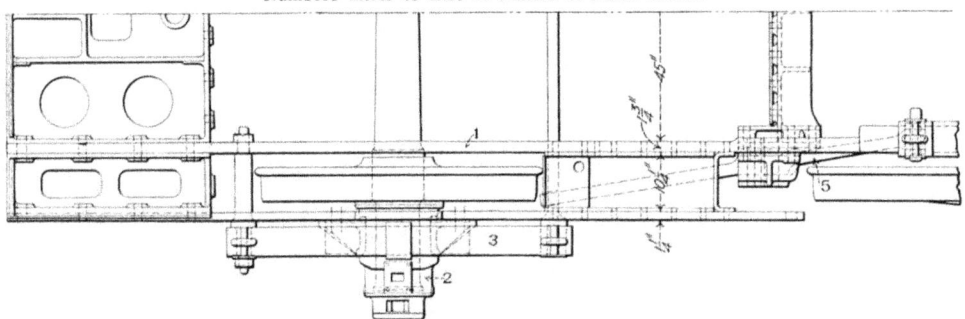

Fig. 3479. Plan of Rigid Trailing Truck with Outside Bearings for Atlantic (4—4—2) Locomotive.
American Locomotive Co.

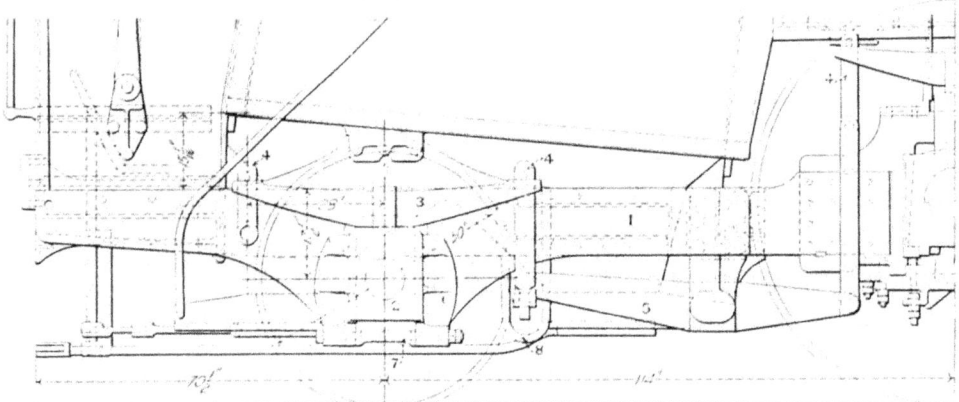

Fig. 3480. Side Elevation of Rigid Trailing Truck.

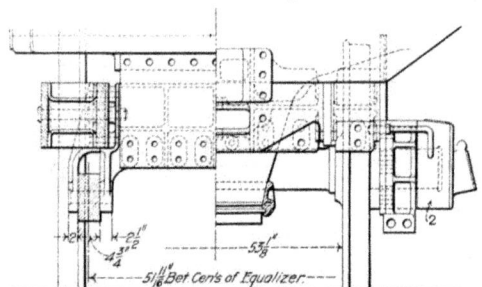

Fig. 3481. Half End Elevation and Cross-Section.

Names of Parts of Figs. 3479-3481.

1. *Rear Engine Frame*
2. *Journal Box*
3. *Journal Box Spring*
4. *Journal Box Spring Hanger*
5. *Driver and Truck Equalizer*
6. *Pedestal*
7. *Pedestal Brace*
8. *Equalizer Safety Strap*

Figs. 3482-3487 — ENGINE TRUCKS, Rear; Two-Wheel.

Numbers Refer to List of Names of Parts with Figs. 3500-3506.

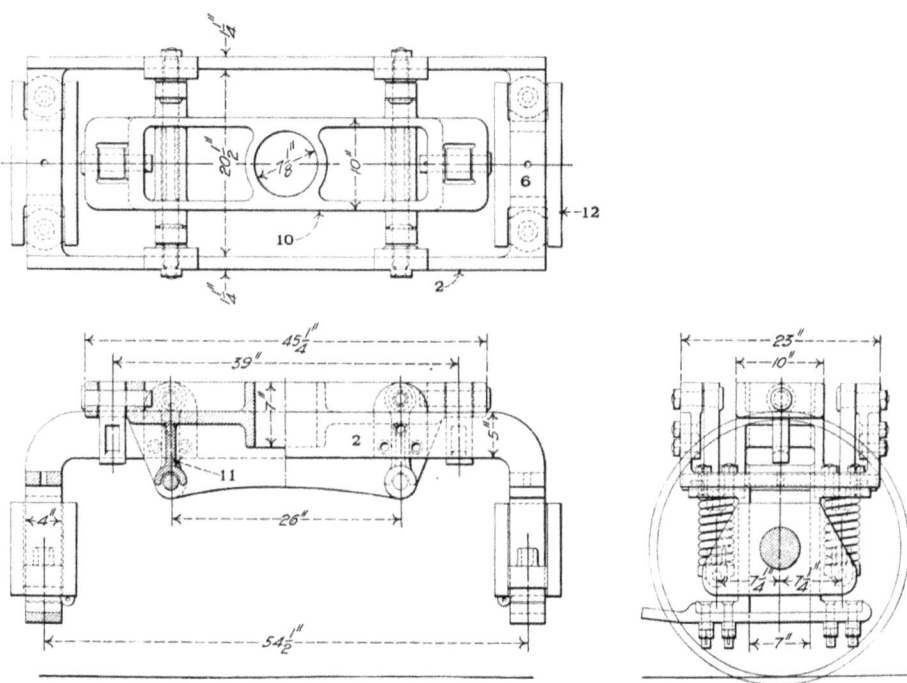

Figs. 3482-3484. Rear Truck for Six-Coupled (0—6—2) Locomotive with Side Bearings.
Baldwin Locomotive Works.

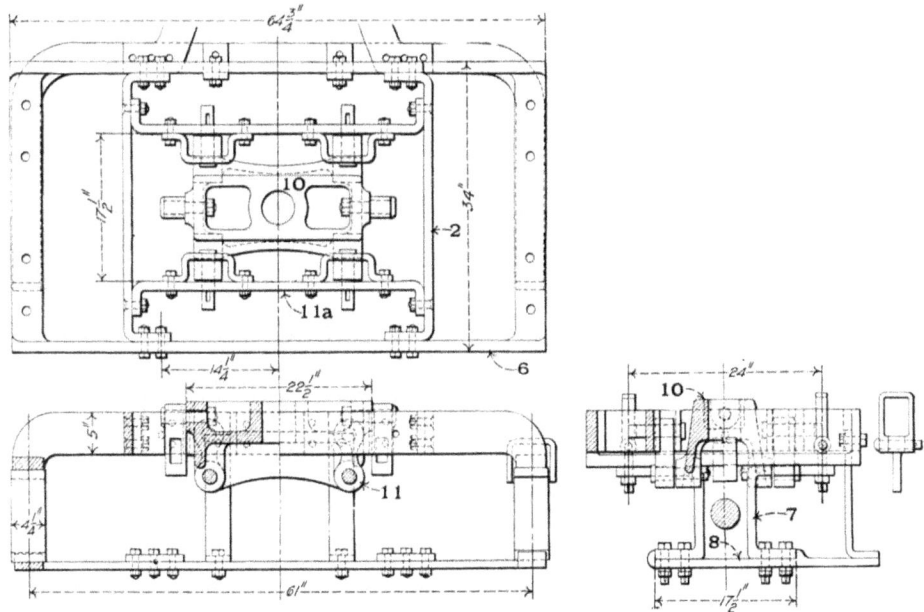

Figs. 3485-3487. Rear Engine Truck for Six-Coupled (2—6—2) Narrow Gage Locomotive.
Baldwin Locomotive Works.

(334)

ENGINE TRUCKS, Rear; Two-Wheel. Figs. 3488-3493

Numbers Refer to List of Names of Parts with Figs. 3500-3506.

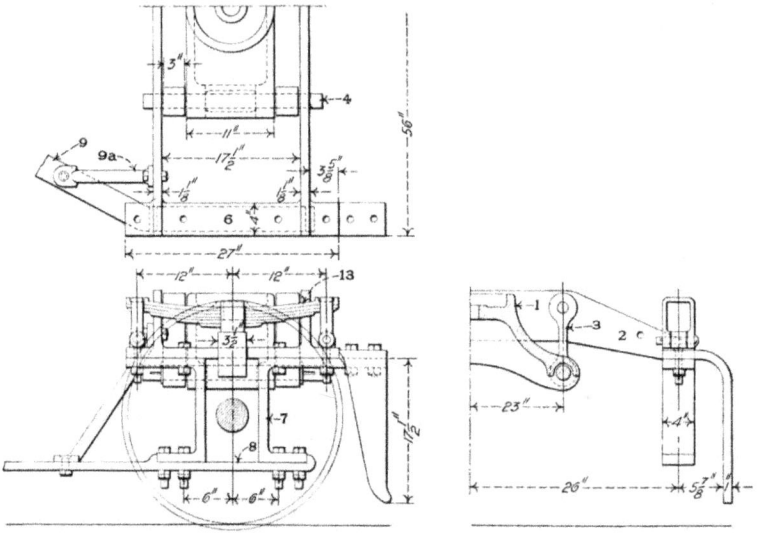

Figs. 3488-3490. Rear Truck with Outside Bearings for Six-Coupled (0—6—2) Narrow Gage Locomotive. Baldwin Locomotive Works.

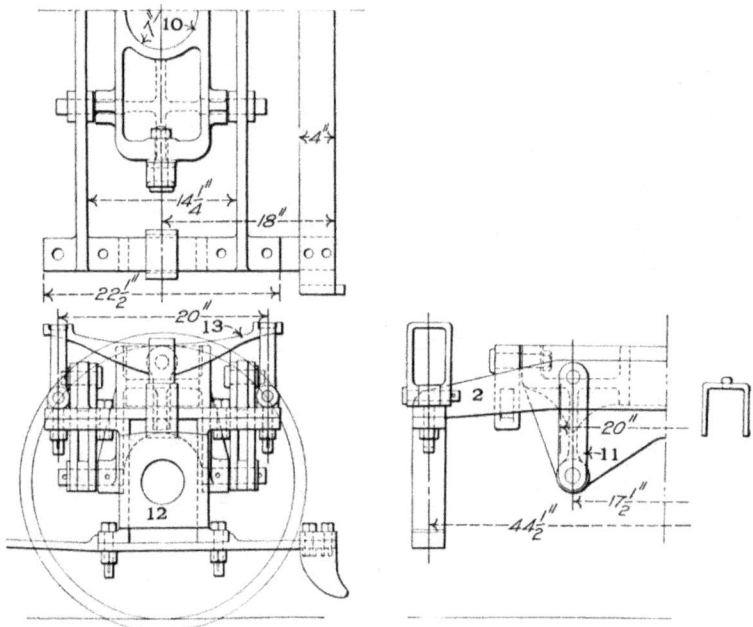

Figs. 3491-3493. Rear Truck for Four-Coupled (2—4—2) Locomotive. Baldwin Locomotive Works.

Numbers Refer to List of Names of Parts with Figs. 3500-3506.

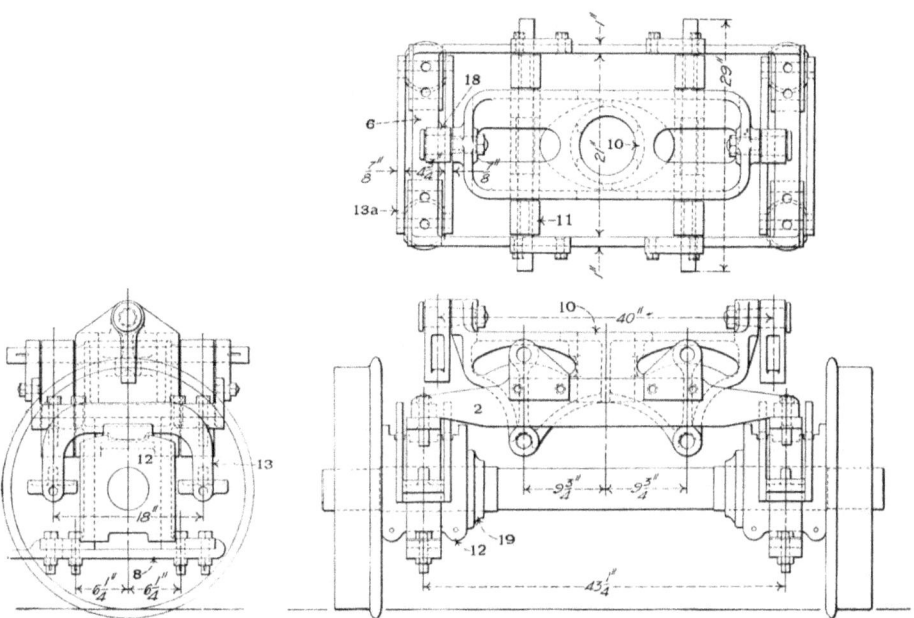

Figs. 3494-3496. Rear Truck with Side Bearings for Six-Coupled (2—6—2) Locomotive. Baldwin Locomotive Works.

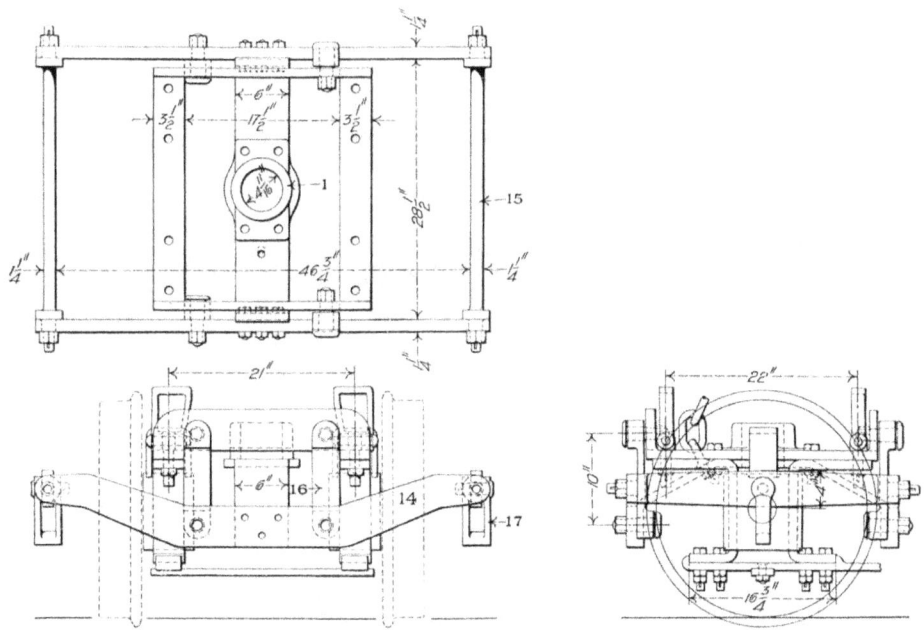

Figs. 3497-3499. Rear Truck with Inside Bearings and Outside Equalization for Narrow Gage Four-Coupled (2—4—2) Locomotive. Baldwin Locomotive Works.

ENGINE TRUCKS, Rear; Six-Wheel. Figs. 3500-3506

Names of Parts of Figs. 3482-3499.

1 Center Plate
2 Transoms
3 Center Plate Hanger
4 Center Plate Hanger Pin
5 Center Plate Hanger Pin Bracket
6 Side Frame
7 Pedestal
8 Pedestal Brace
9 Radius Bar
9a Radius Bar Brace
10 Center Pin Guide
11 Center Pin Guide Hanger
11a Center Pin Guide Hanger Bracket
12 Journal Box
13 Journal Box Spring
13a Journal Box Yoke
14 Equalizer
15 Equalizer Cross Tie
16 Equalizer Hanger
17 Spring Hanger
18 Side Bearing
19 Axle Collar

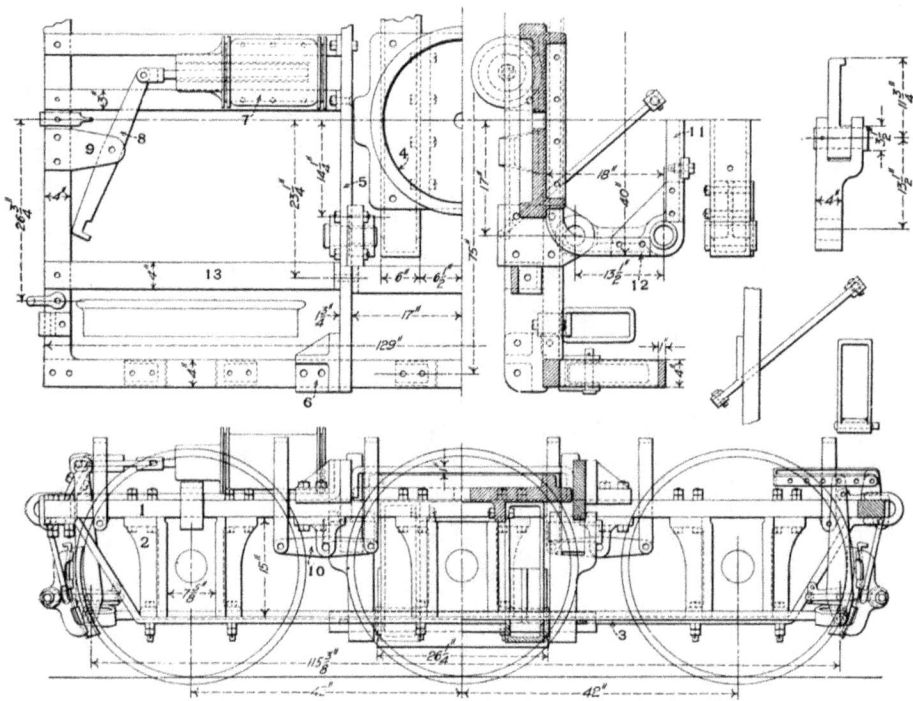

Figs. 3500-3506. Six-Wheel Rear Truck for Six-Coupled (0—6—6) Suburban Locomotive. Baldwin Locomotive Works.

Names of Parts of Figs. 3500-3506.

1 Frame
2 Pedestal
3 Pedestal Tie Bar
4 Center Plate
5 Transom
6 Transom Bracket
7 Brake Cylinder
8 Cylinder Lever
9 Cylinder Lever Bracket
10 Equalizer
11 Spring Plank
12 Spring Plank Hanger
13 Safety Beam

Figs. 3507-3512 ENGINE TRUCKS, Rear; Four-Wheel.

Numbers Refer to List of Names of Parts with Figs. 3519-3525.

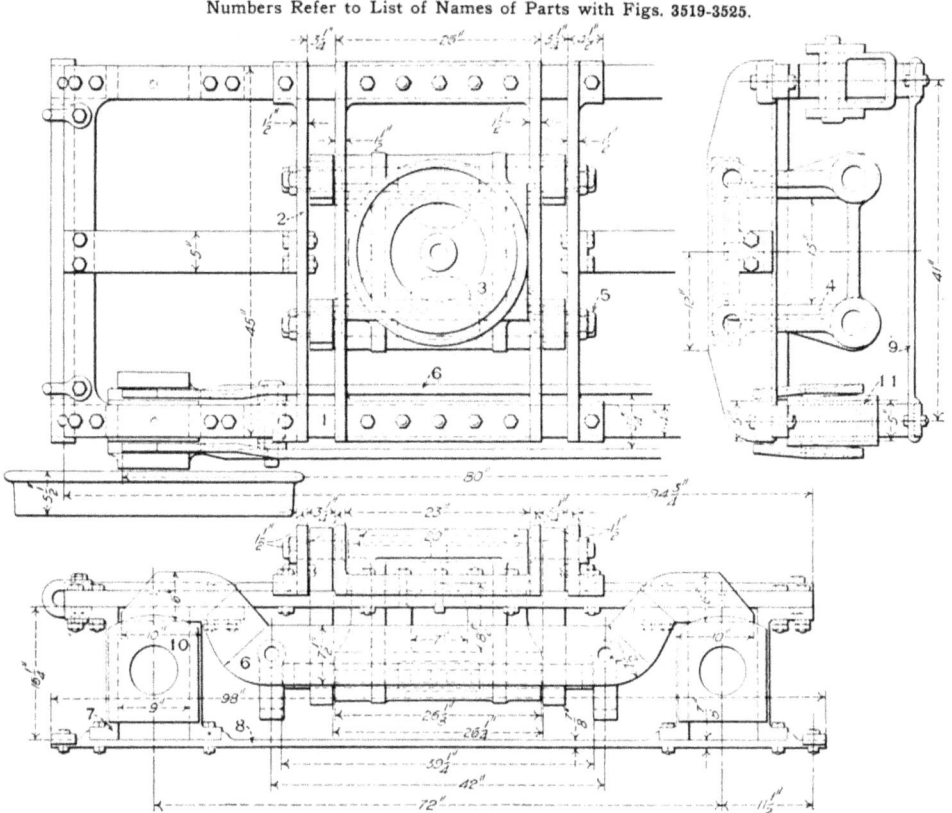

Figs. 3507-3509. Rear Truck for Heavy Six-Coupled (2—6—4) Suburban Locomotive. Baldwin Locomotive Works.

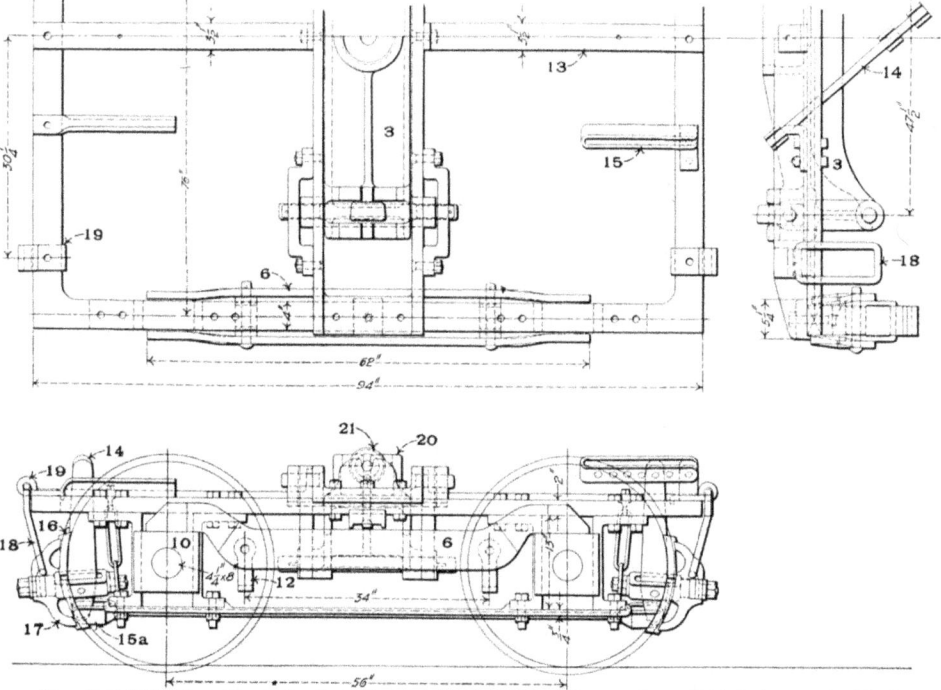

Figs. 3510-3512. Rear Truck for Four-Coupled (2—4—4) Tank Locomotive. Baldwin Locomotive Works.

ENGINE TRUCKS, Rear; Four-Wheel. Figs. 3513-3518

Numbers Refer to List of Names of Parts with Figs. 3519-3525.

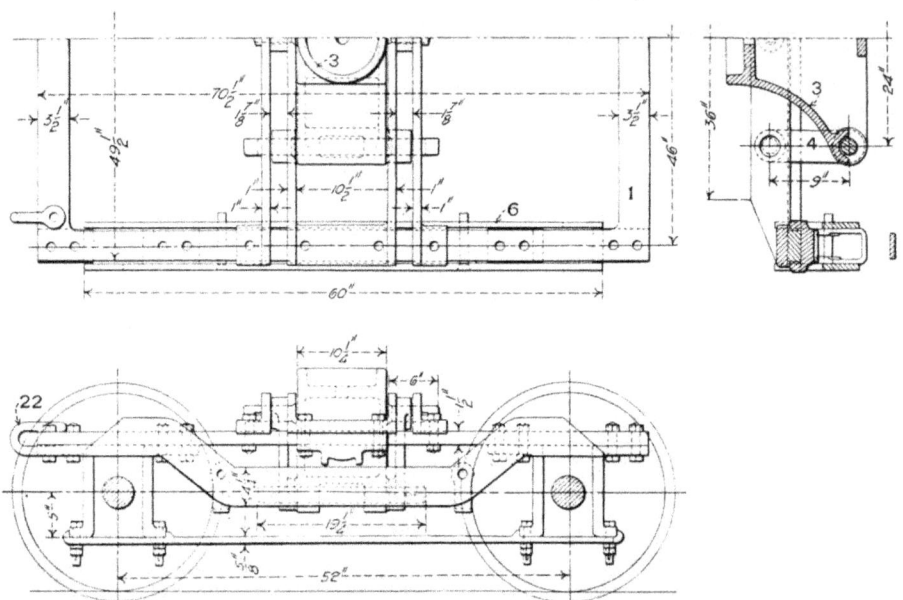

Figs. 3513-3515. Rear Truck for Forney (0—4—4) Type Locomotive. Baldwin Locomotive Works.

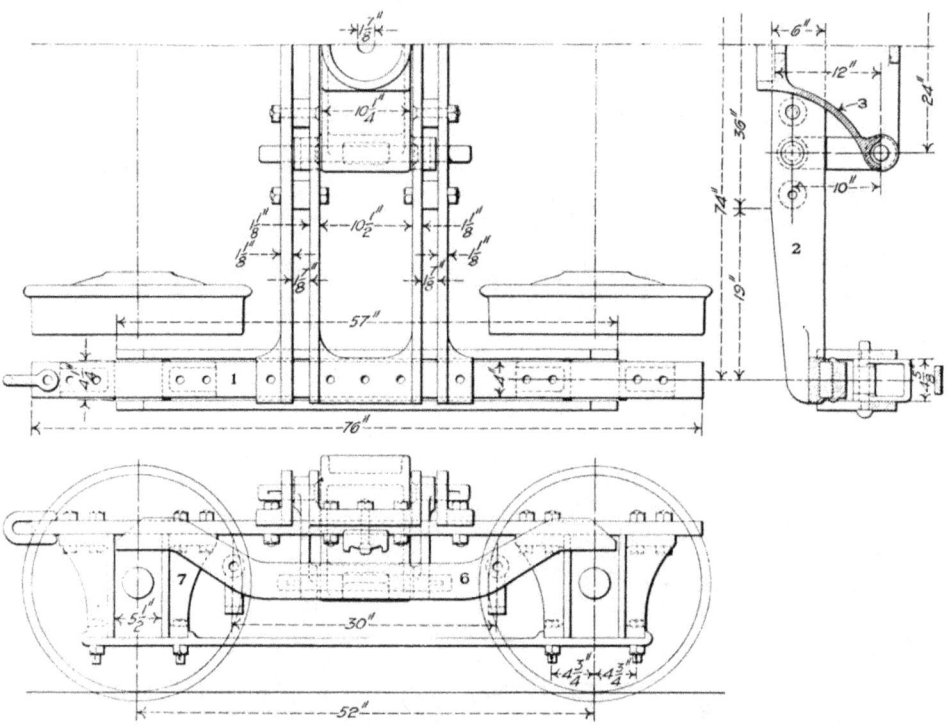

Figs. 3516-3518. Rear Truck for Forney (0—4—4) Type Locomotive. Baldwin Locomotive Works.

ENGINE TRUCKS, Rear; Four-Wheel.

Figs. 3519–3525

Numbers Refer to List of Names of Parts Below.

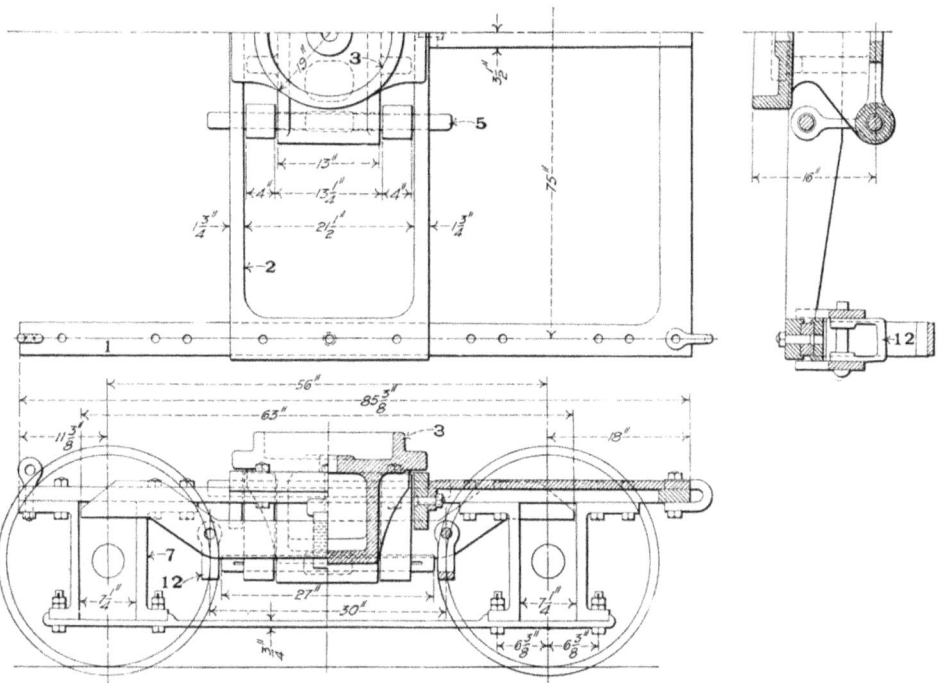

Figs. 3519-3521. Rear Truck for Four-Coupled (2—4—4) Tank Locomotive. Baldwin Locomotive Works.

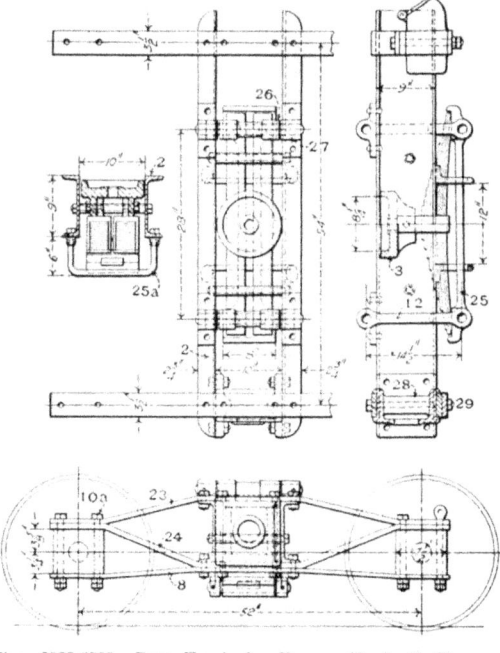

Figs. 3522-3525. Rear Truck for Forney (0—4—4) Type Locomotive. Baldwin Locomotive Works.

Names of Parts of Figs. 3507-3525.

1 Frame
2 Transom
3 Center Plate
4 Center Plate Hanger
5 Center Plate Hanger Pin
6 Equalizer
7 Pedestal
7a Pedestal Bolt
8 Pedestal Tie Bar
8a Pedestal Tie Bar Bolt
9 Pedestal Cross Tie
10 Journal Box
10a Journal Box Bolt
11 Semi-Elliptic Spring
12 Spring Hanger
13 Safety Beam
14 Brake Lever
15 Brake Lever Guide
15a Brake Lever Coupling Bar
16 Brake Shoe
17 Brake Head
18 Brake Hanger
19 Brake Hanger Bracket
20 Side Bearing Casting
21 Side Bearing Roller
22 Check Chain Eye
23 Upper Arch Bar
24 Lower Arch Bar
25 Spring Plank
25a Spring Plank Safety Strap
26 Bolster Chafing Plate
27 Transom Chafing Plate
28 Column
29 Column Bolt

(340)

ENGINE TRUCKS, Details; Wheels.   Figs. 3526-3544

Numbers Refer to List of Names of Parts Below.

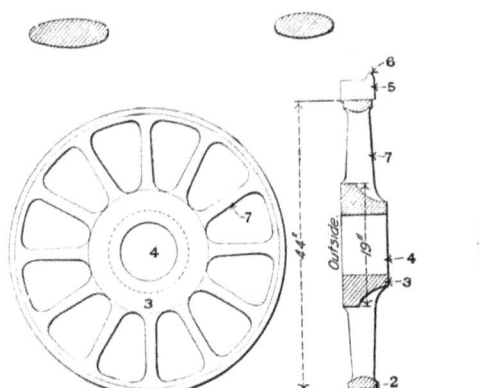

Figs. 3526-3529. 44-Inch Trailing Truck Wheel Center. American Locomotive Co.

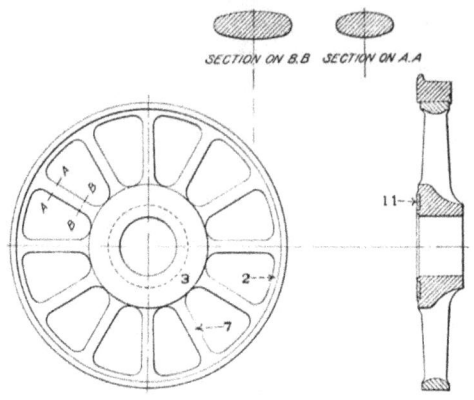

Figs. 3530-3533. Trailing Truck Wheel Center. American Locomotive Co.

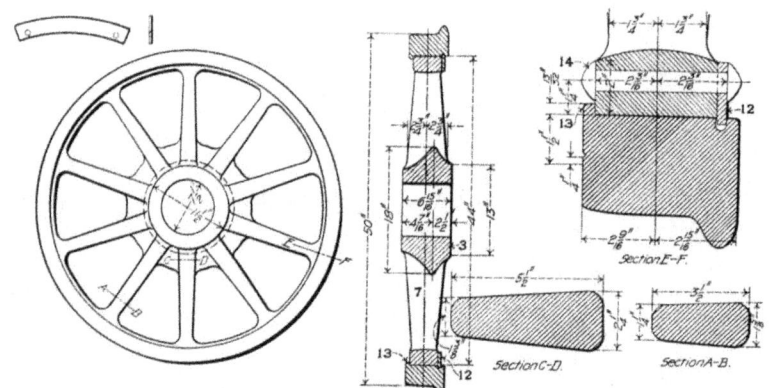

Figs. 3534-3540. Cast-Steel Center for 50-Inch Trailing Truck Wheel. Atlantic (4—4—2) Locomotive. Pennsylvania Railroad.

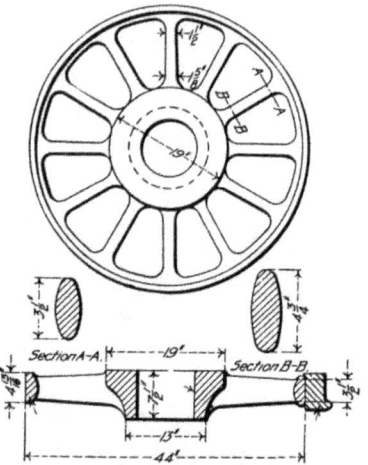

Figs. 3541-3544. 44-Inch Trailing Truck Wheel Center. American Locomotive Co.

Names of Parts of Figs. 3526-3540.

- 2 *Rim*
- 3 *Hub*
- 4 *Axle Seat*
- 5 *Tire*
- 6 *Flange*
- 7 *Spoke*
- 11 *Hub Liner*
- 12 *Retaining Ring*
- 13 *Retaining Ring Lip*
- 14 *Retaining Ring Bolt*

Names of Parts of Fig. 3545.

- 1 *Wheel Seat*
- 2 *Journal*
- 3 *Center*
- 10 *Collar*

Figs. 3545–3589 ENGINE TRUCKS, Details; Axles and Boxes.

Numbers Refer to List of Names of Parts with Figs. 3526–3544.

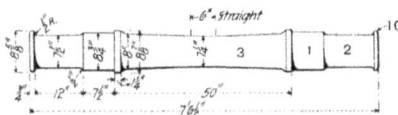

Fig. 3545. Trailing Truck Axle. Norfolk & Western.

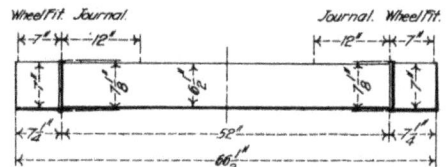

Fig. 3546. Pony Truck Axle for Consolidation (2—8—0) Locomotive. American Locomotive Co.

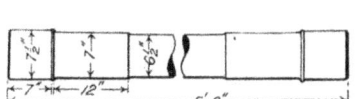

Fig. 3547. Trailing Truck Axle for Atlantic (4—4—2) Locomotive. Pennsylvania Railroad.

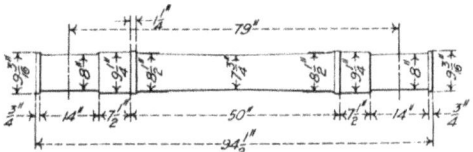

Fig. 3548. Trailing Truck Axle for Atlantic (4—4—2) Locomotive. American Locomotive Co.

Numbers Refer to List of Names of Parts with Figs. 3590-3613.

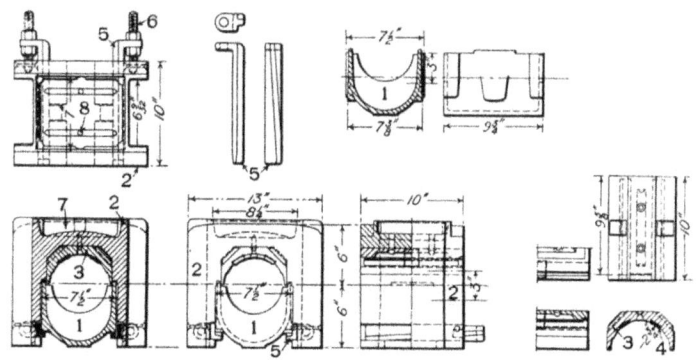

Figs. 3549-3561. Journal Box for Front Engine Truck of Atlantic (4—4—2) Locomotive, Journals 5½ x 10 in. Pennsylvania Railroad.

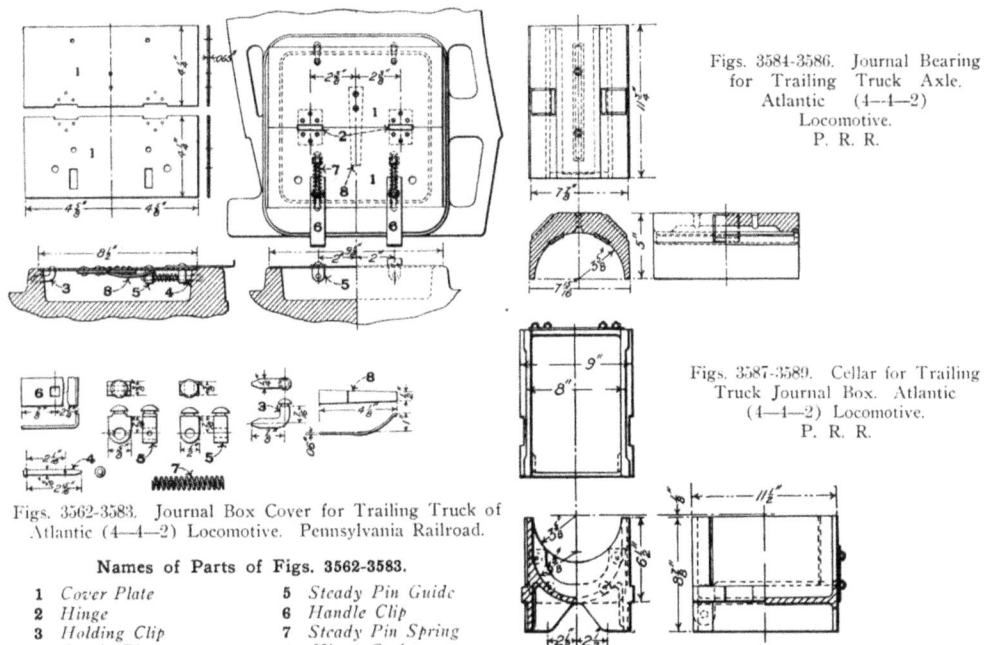

Figs. 3584–3586. Journal Bearing for Trailing Truck Axle. Atlantic (4—4—2) Locomotive. P. R. R.

Figs. 3587–3589. Cellar for Trailing Truck Journal Box. Atlantic (4—4—2) Locomotive. P. R. R.

Figs. 3562–3583. Journal Box Cover for Trailing Truck of Atlantic (4—4—2) Locomotive. Pennsylvania Railroad.

Names of Parts of Figs. 3562-3583.

1. Cover Plate
2. Hinge
3. Holding Clip
4. Steady Pin
5. Steady Pin Guide
6. Handle Clip
7. Steady Pin Spring
8. Hinge Spring

(342)

ENGINE TRUCKS, Details; Boxes.   Figs. 3590-3613

Names of Parts of Boxes, Figs. 3549-3561, 3590-3596.

1. *Cellar*
2. *Box*
3. *Brass*
4. *Babbitt Lining*
5. *Cellar Wedge*
6. *Cellar Wedge Bolt*
7. *Waste Cavity*
8. *Oil Hole*
13. *Box Flange*

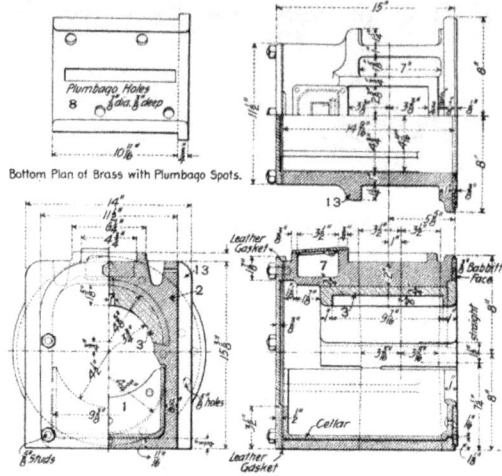

Figs. 3590-3593. Cast-Steel Journal Box for Trailing Truck of Atlantic (4—4—2) Locomotive. Chicago & North-Western.

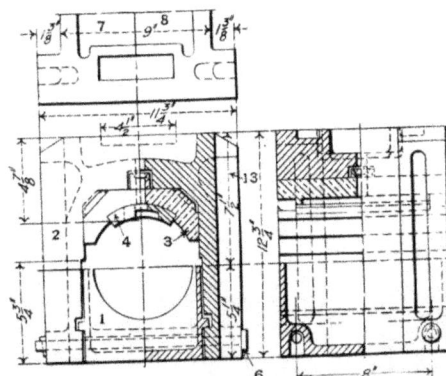

Figs. 3594-3596. Front Engine Truck Journal Box. American Locomotive Co.

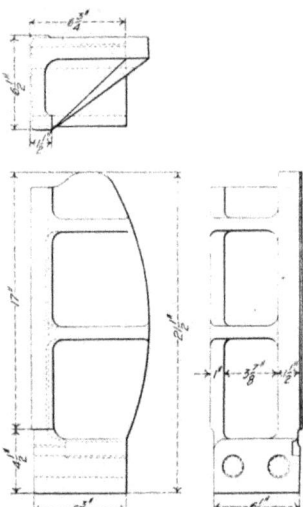

Figs. 3611-3613. Trailing Truck Journal Box Shoe. American Locomotive Co.

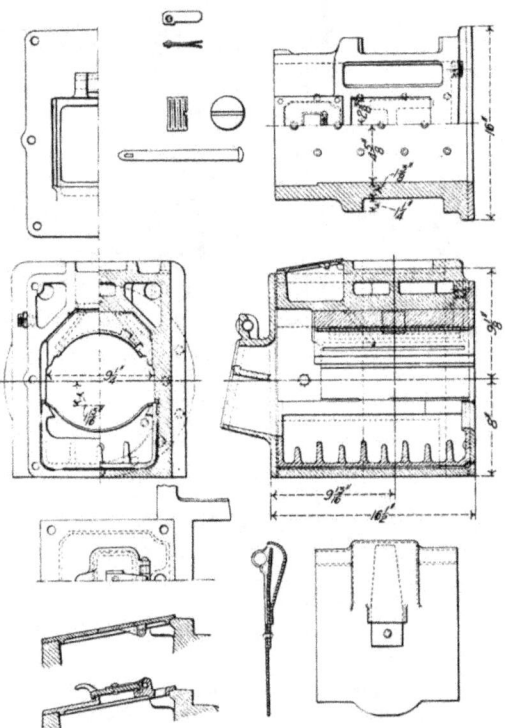

Figs. 3597-3610. Trailing Truck Journal Box. American Locomotive Co.

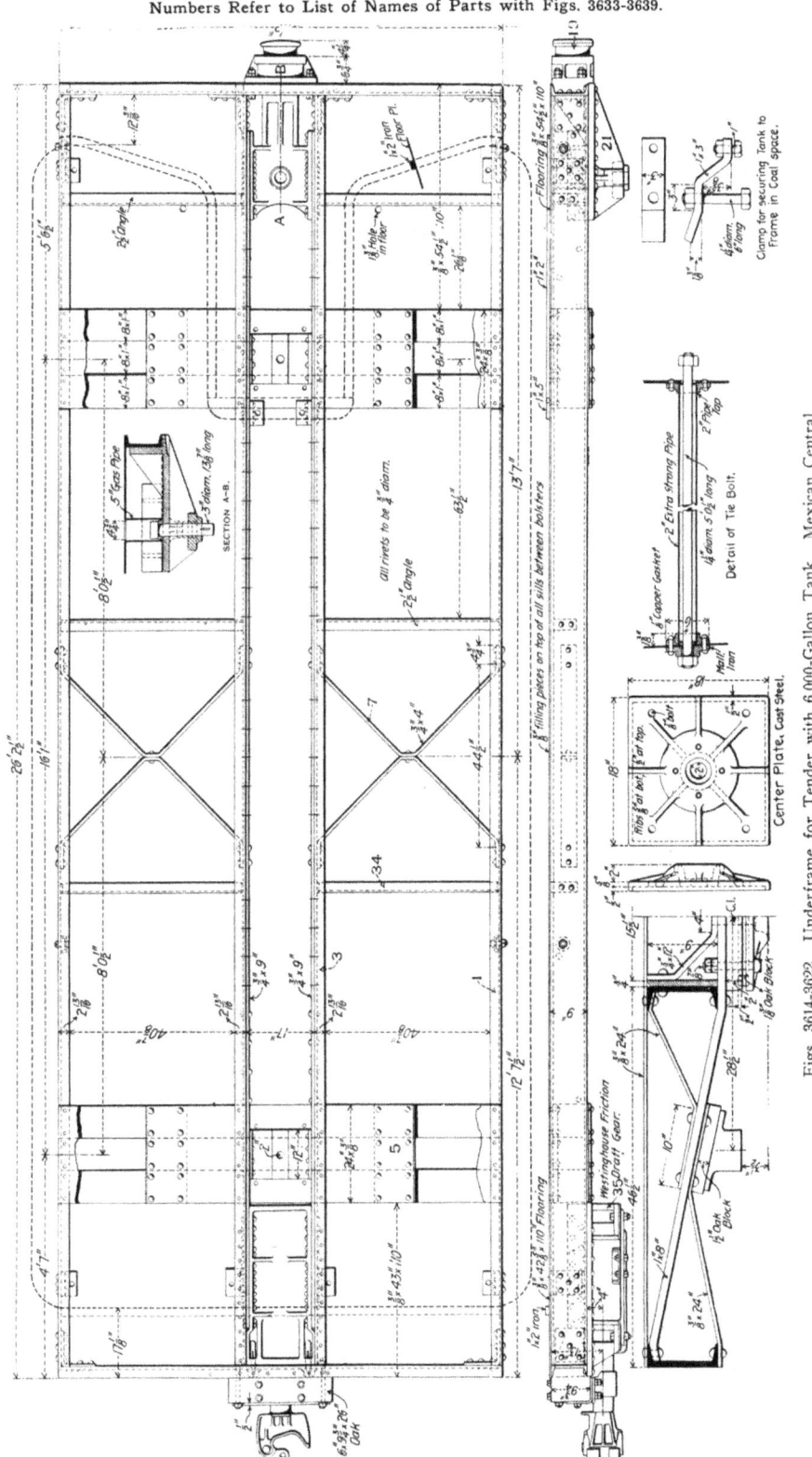

Figs. 3614-3622. Underframe for Tender with 6,000-Gallon Tank. Mexican Central.

TENDERS, Underframes. Figs. 3623–3629

Numbers Refer to List of Names of Parts with Figs. 3633–3639.

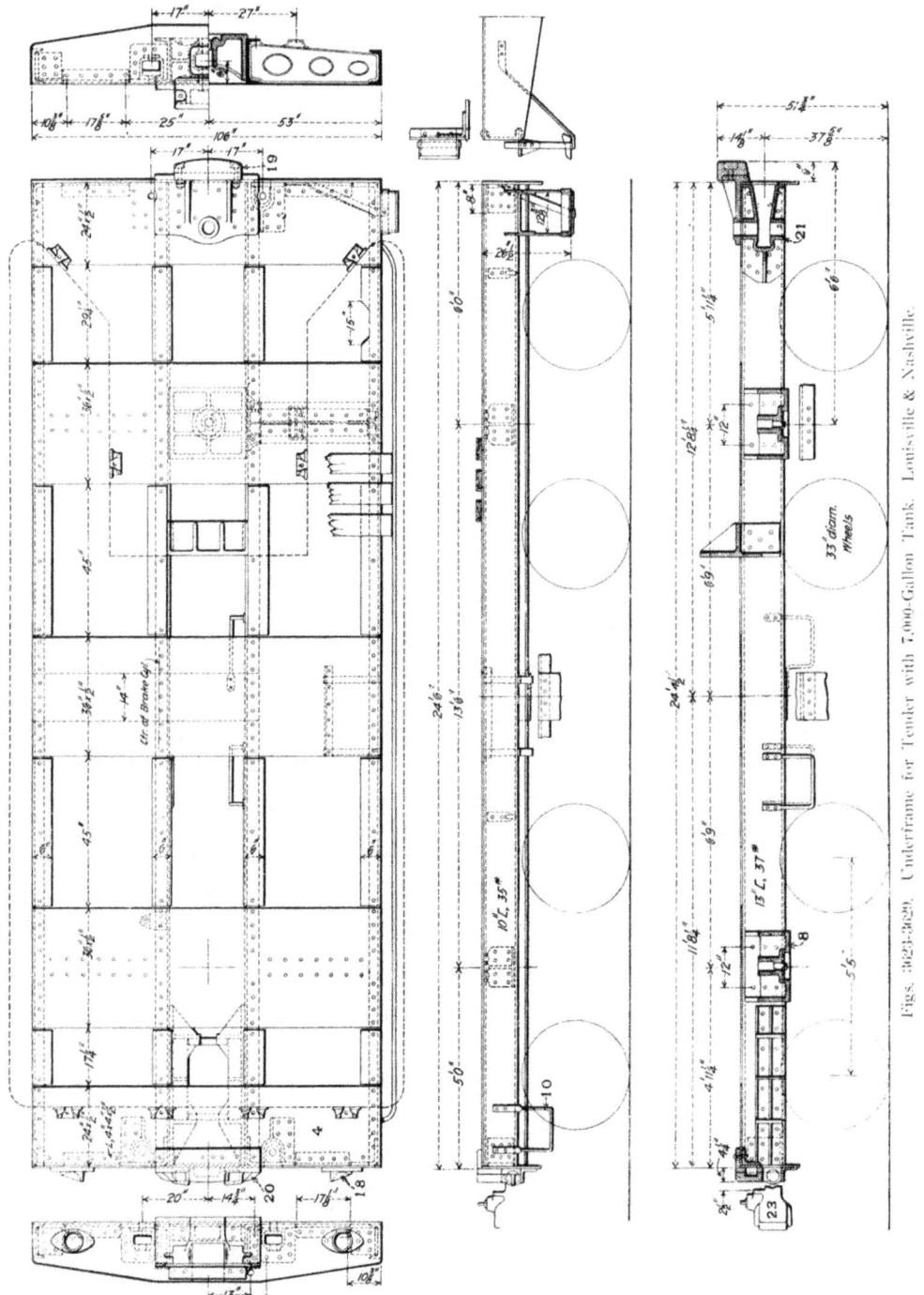

Figs. 3623–3629. Underframe for Tender with 7,000-Gallon Tank. Louisville & Nashville.

Figs. 3630-3632 — TENDERS, Underframes.

Numbers Refer to List of Names on Opposite Page.

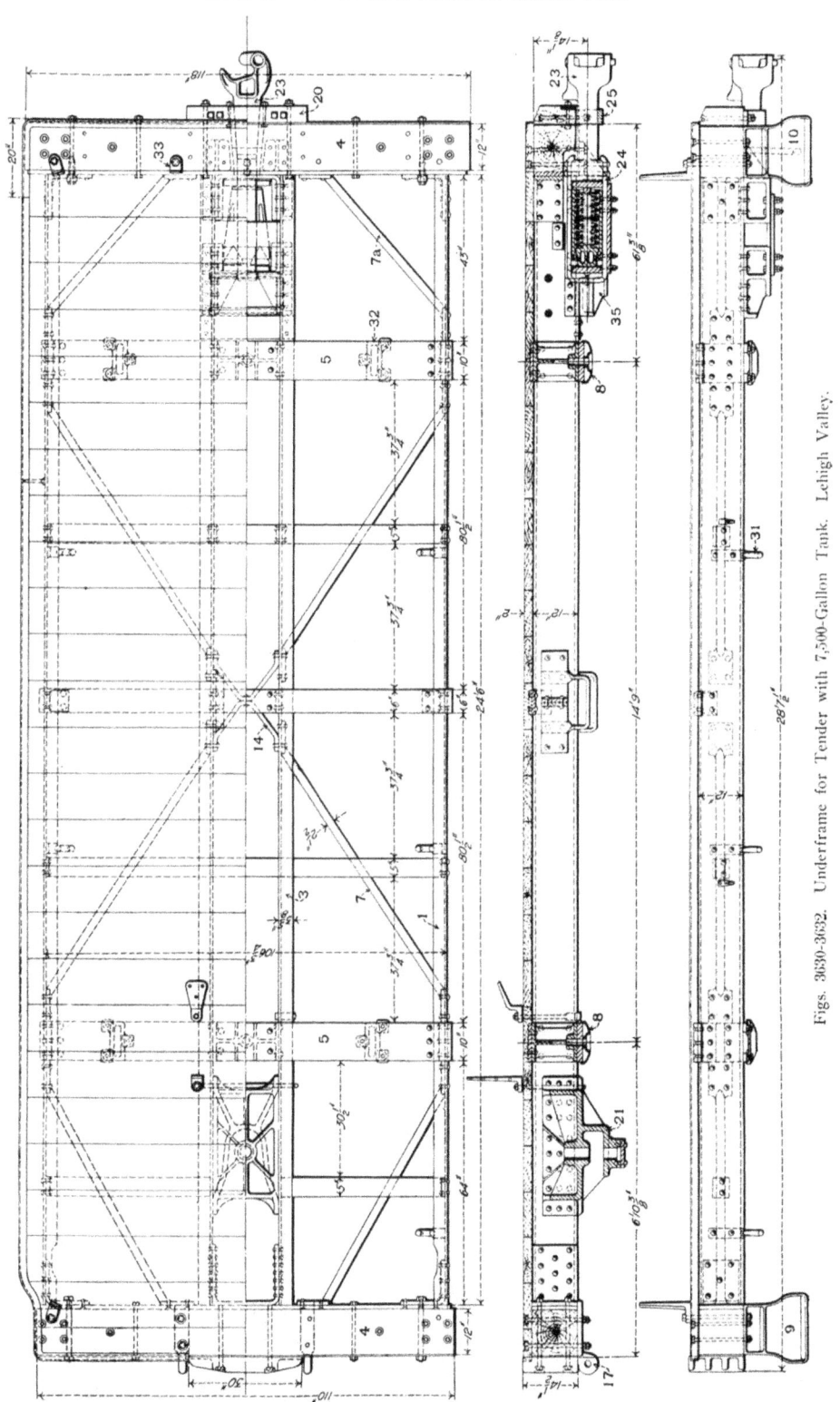

Figs. 3630-3632. Underframe for Tender with 7,500-Gallon Tank. Lehigh Valley.

TENDERS, Underframes. Figs. 3633-3639

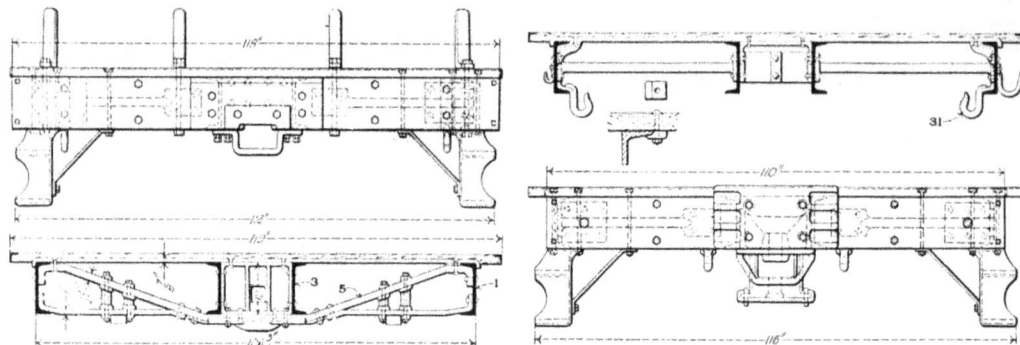

Figs. 3633-3636. Cross-Sections and End Elevations of Underframe for Tender with 7,500-Gallon Tank. Lehigh Valley.

Names of Parts of Tender Underframes, Figs. 3614-3656.

1 *Side Sill*
2 *Intermediate Sill*
3 *Center Sill*
4 *End Sill*
4a *End Sill Top Plate*
4b *End Sill Bottom Plate*
4c *End Sill Facing Plate*
5 *Bolster*
6 *Sill and Bolster Brace*
7 *Diagonal Frame Brace*
7a *Diagonal Rear Brace*
8 *Center Plate*
9 *Front Step*
10 *Rear Step*

11 *Bracket for Water Scoop Shaft*
12 *Side Bracket for Tank*
13 *Central Gusset for Side Channels*
14 *Center Sill Brace*
15 *End Gusset Plate for Bolster*
16 *Bolster Diaphragm*
17 *Safety Chain Eye*
18 *Poling Pocket*
19 *Chafing Plate*
20 *Rear Buffing Plate*
21 *Draft Casting*
22 *Draft Lugs*
23 *Drawbar*

24 *Drawbar Strap*
25 *Drawbar Carrier*
25a *Drawbar Pin*
26 *Corner Gusset*
27 *Handhold*
28 *Uncoupling Shaft*
29 *Uncoupling Shaft Handle*
30 *Uncoupling Shaft Bracket*
31 *Check Chain Hook*
32 *Side Bearings*
33 *Tank Holding Angle*
34 *Frame Crosstie*
35 *Cheek Plate*

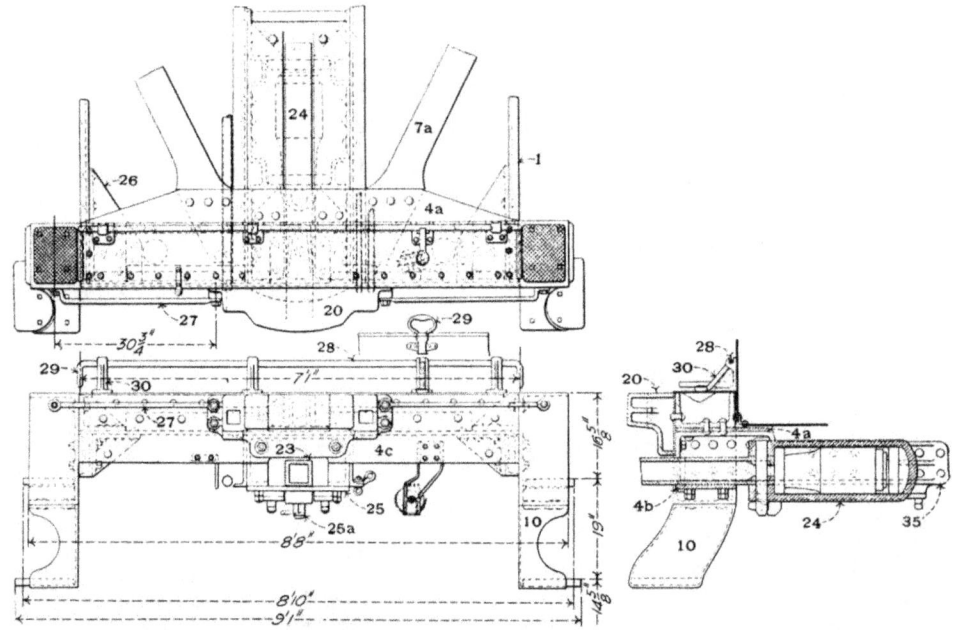

Figs. 3637-3639. Rear End Sill of Steel Tender for Atlantic (4—4—2) Locomotive. Pennsylvania Railroad.

(347)

Figs. 3640-3642 — TENDERS, Underframes.

Numbers Refer to List of Names of Parts with Figs. 3633-3639.

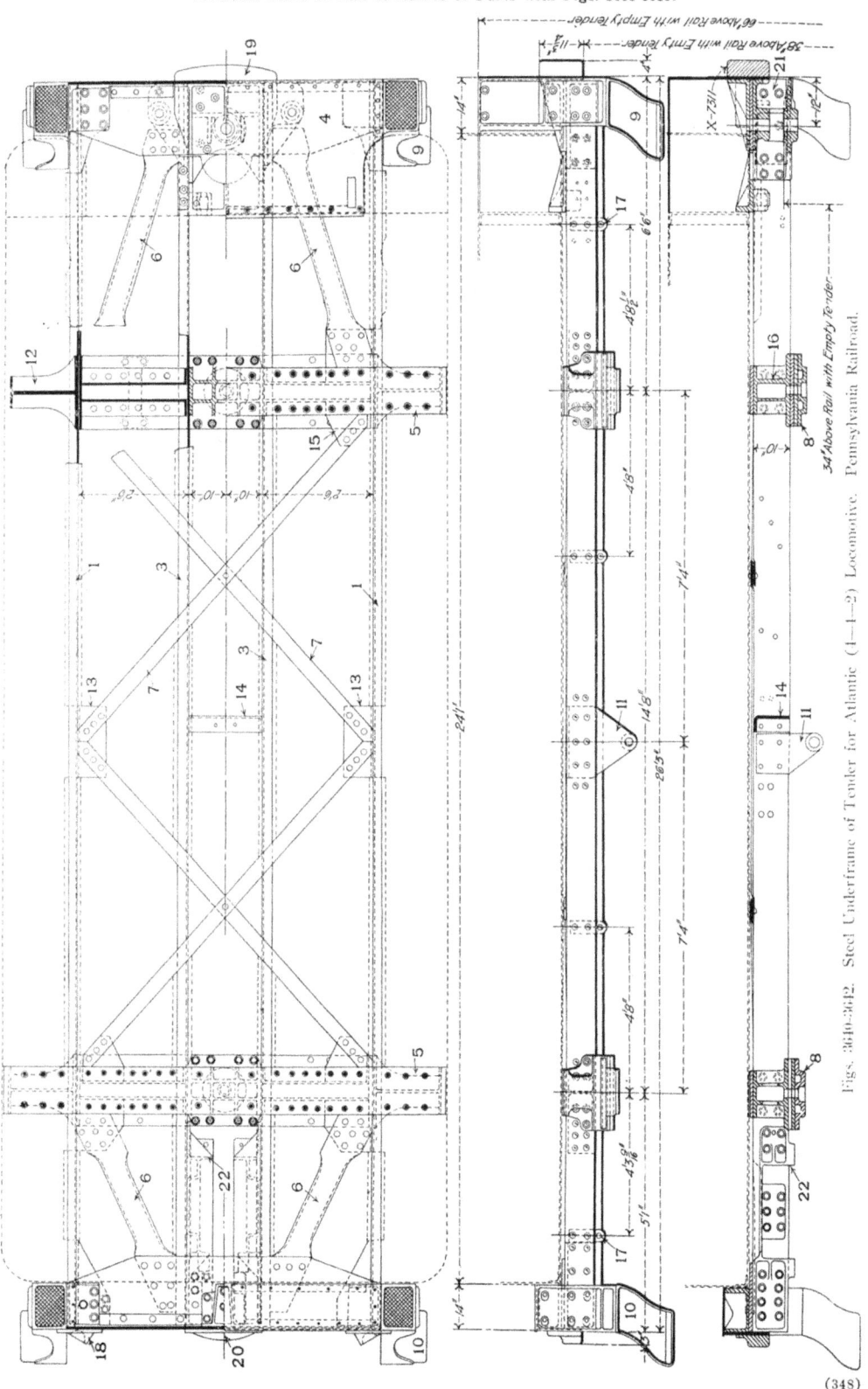

Figs. 3640-3642. Steel Underframe of Tender for Atlantic (4-4-2) Locomotive. Pennsylvania Railroad.

Numbers Refer to List of Names of Parts with Figs. 3633-3639.

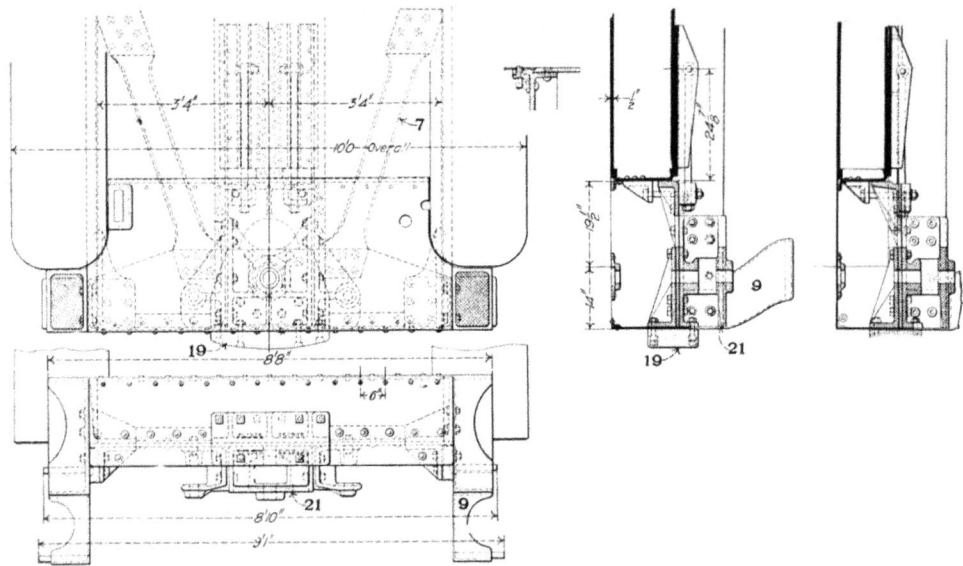

Figs. 3643-3647. Front End Sill of Steel Tender for Atlantic (4—4—2) Locomotive. Pennsylvania Railroad.

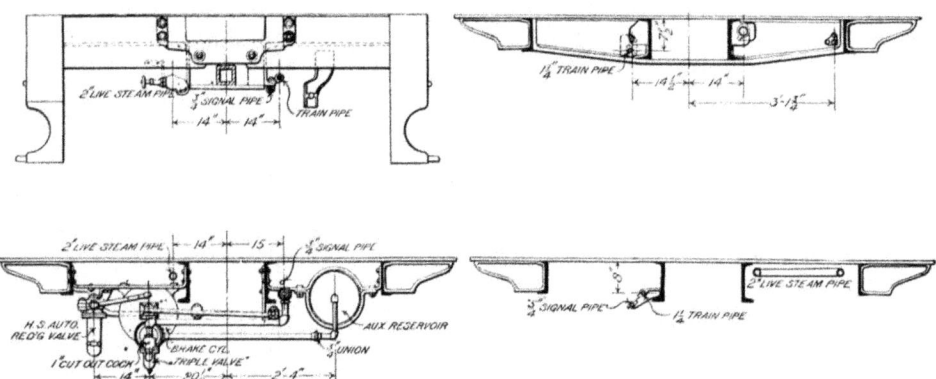

Figs. 3648-3651. End Elevations and Cross-Sections of Underframe of Steel Tender for Atlantic (4—4—2) Locomotive. Pennsylvania Railroad.

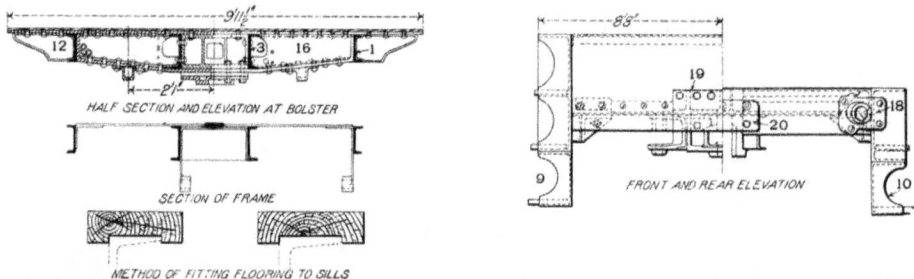

Figs. 3652-3656. Sections Through Underframe of Steel Tender for Atlantic (4—4—2) Locomotive. P. R. R.

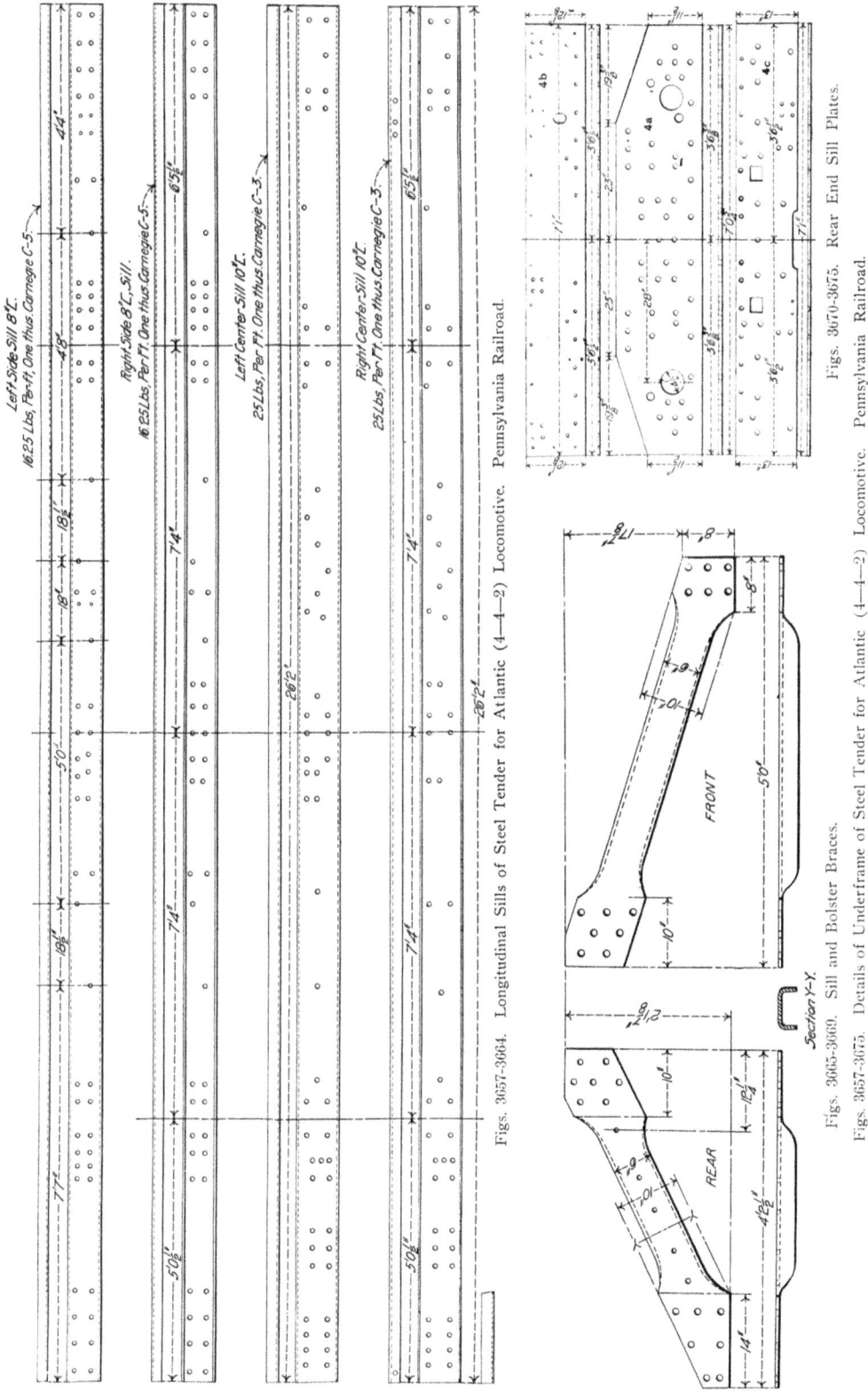

Figs. 3657-3664. Longitudinal Sills of Steel Tender for Atlantic (4—4—2) Locomotive. Pennsylvania Railroad.

Figs. 3670-3675. Rear End Sill Plates.

Figs. 3665-3669. Sill and Bolster Braces.

Figs. 3657-3675. Details of Underframe of Steel Tender for Atlantic (4—4—2) Locomotive. Pennsylvania Railroad.

TENDERS, Underframes; Details.

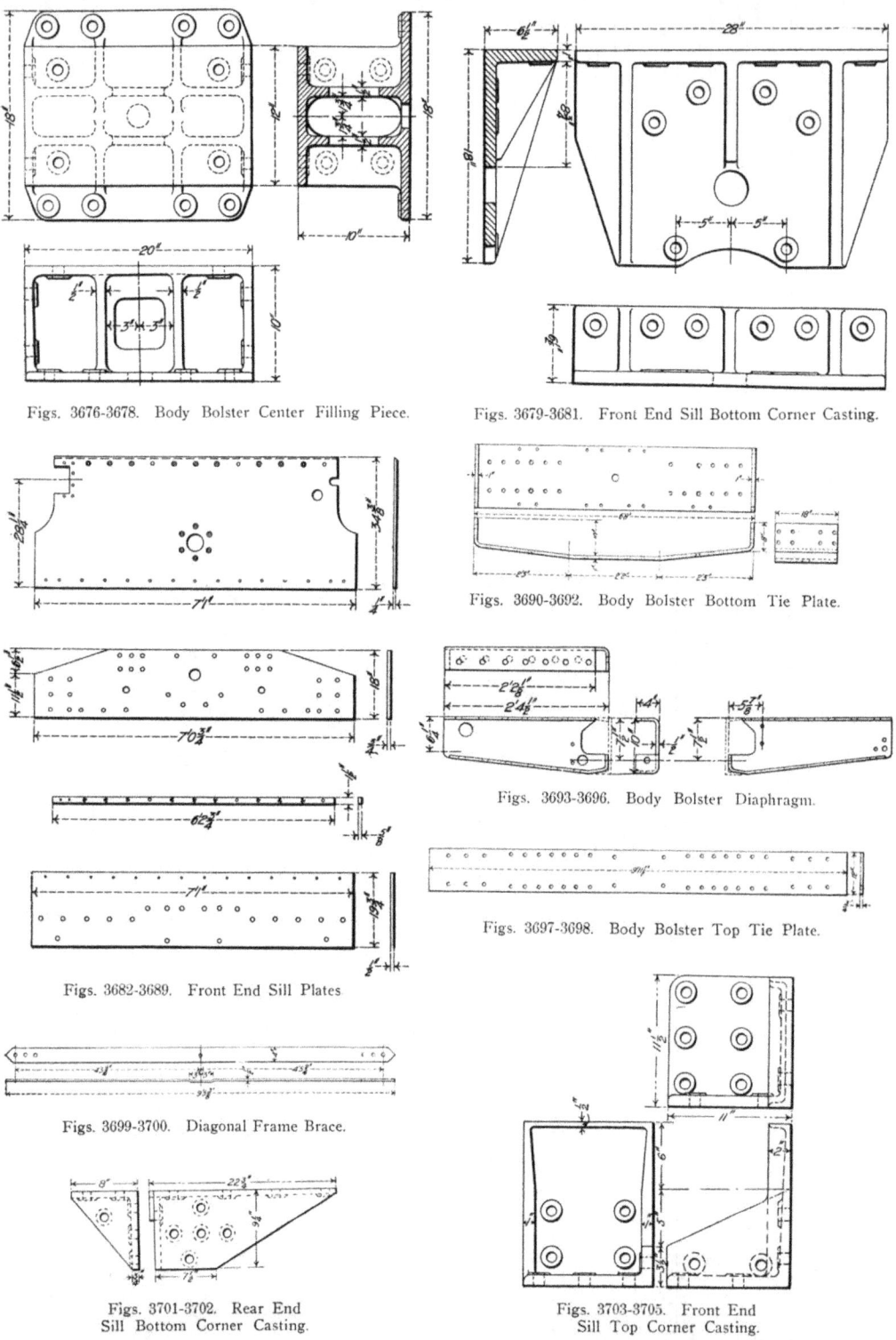

Figs. 3676-3678. Body Bolster Center Filling Piece.

Figs. 3679-3681. Front End Sill Bottom Corner Casting.

Figs. 3682-3689. Front End Sill Plates

Figs. 3690-3692. Body Bolster Bottom Tie Plate.

Figs. 3693-3696. Body Bolster Diaphragm.

Figs. 3697-3698. Body Bolster Top Tie Plate.

Figs. 3699-3700. Diagonal Frame Brace.

Figs. 3701-3702. Rear End Sill Bottom Corner Casting.

Figs. 3703-3705. Front End Sill Top Corner Casting.

Figs. 3676-3705. Details of Underframe of Steel Tender for Atlantic (4—4—2) Locomotive. Pennsylvania Railroad.

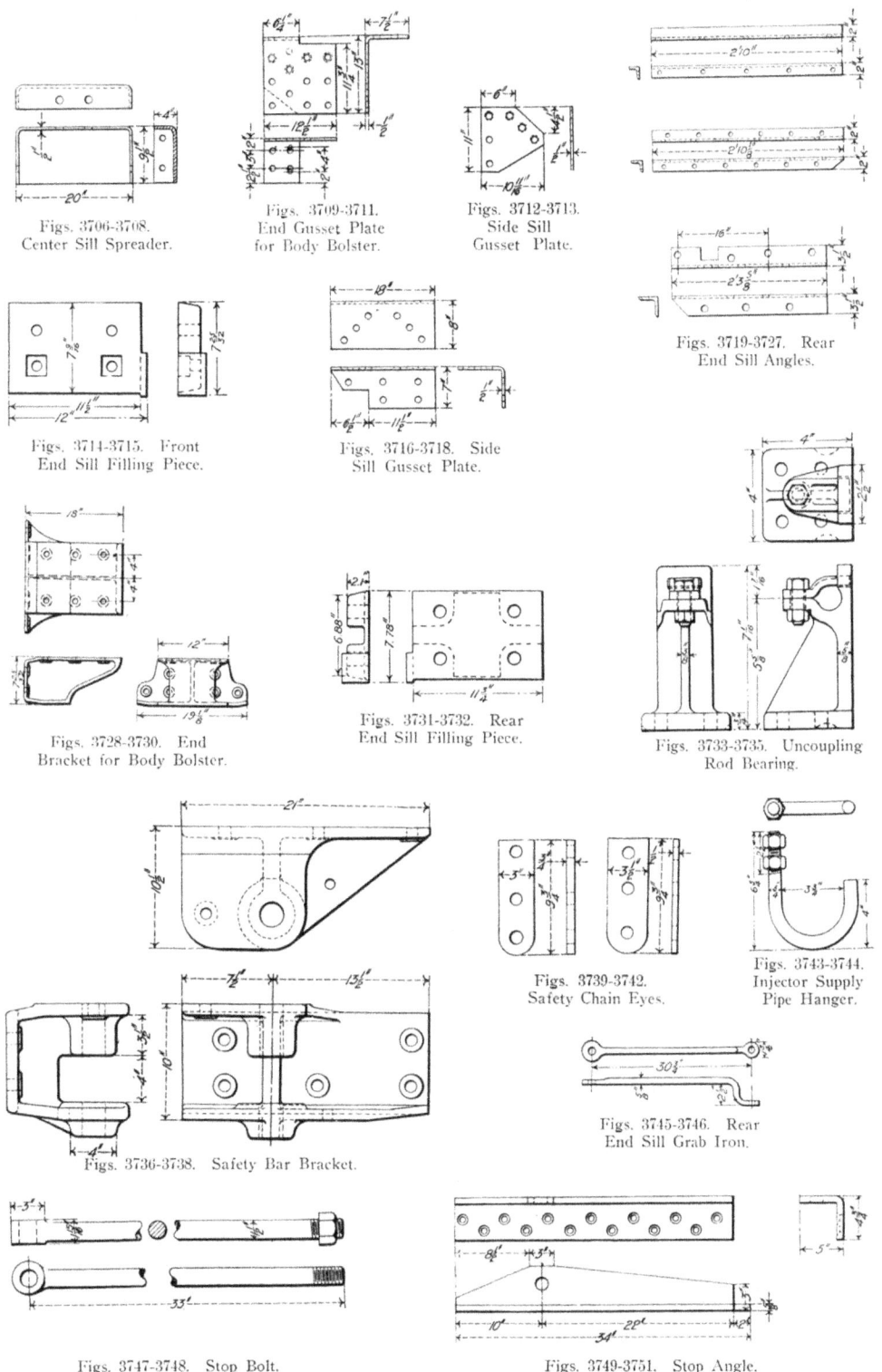

Figs. 3706-3751. Details of Underframe of Steel Tender for Atlantic (4—4—2) Locomotive. Pennsylvania Railroad

TENDERS, Underframes; Details.

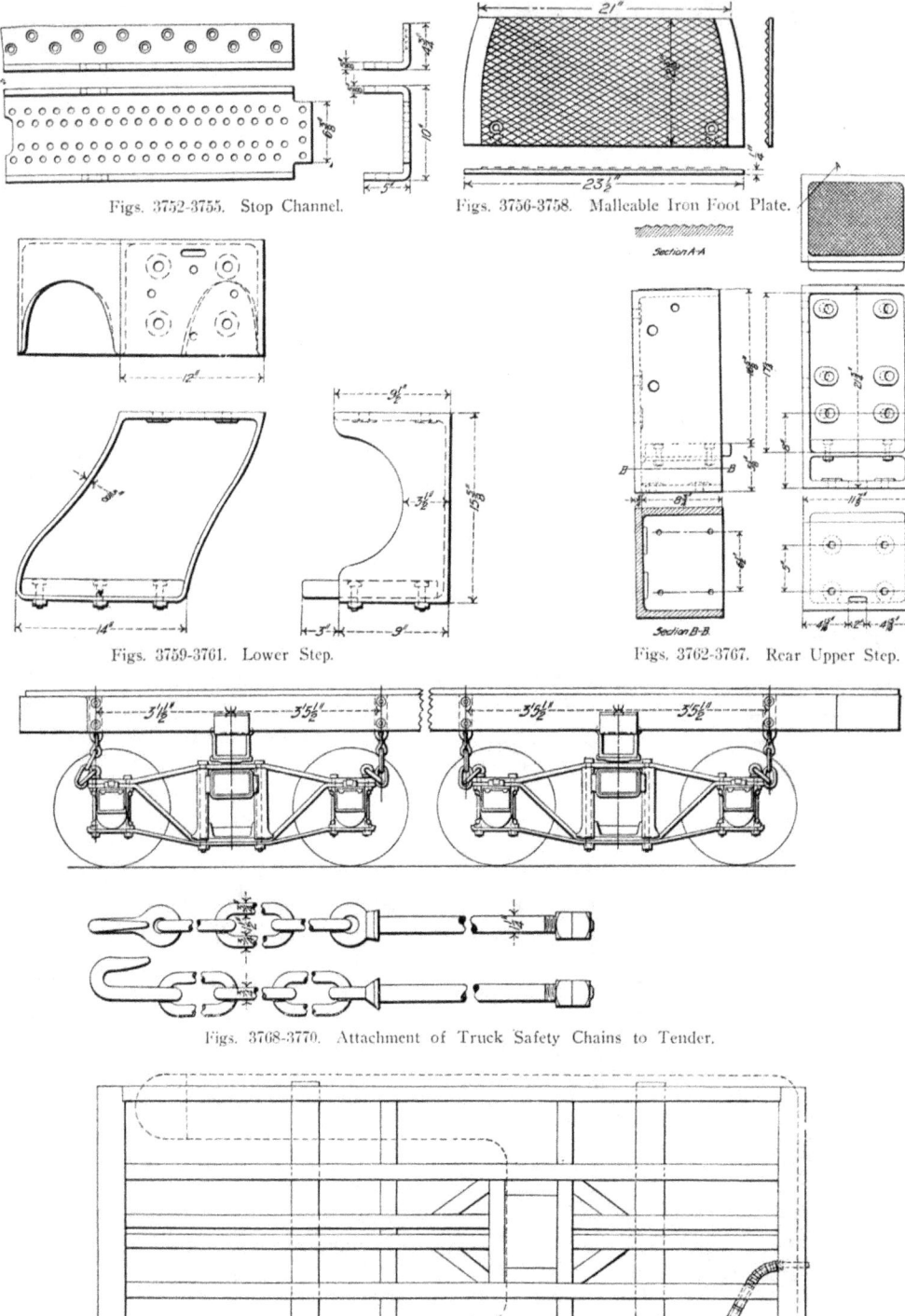

Figs. 3752-3755. Stop Channel.

Figs. 3756-3758. Malleable Iron Foot Plate.

Figs. 3759-3761. Lower Step.

Figs. 3762-3767. Rear Upper Step.

Figs. 3768-3770. Attachment of Truck Safety Chains to Tender.

Fig. 3771. Arrangement of Steam Pipe Covering Under Tender.

Figs. 3752-3771. Details of Underframe of Steel Tender for Atlantic (4—4—2) Locomotive. Pennsylvania Railroad.

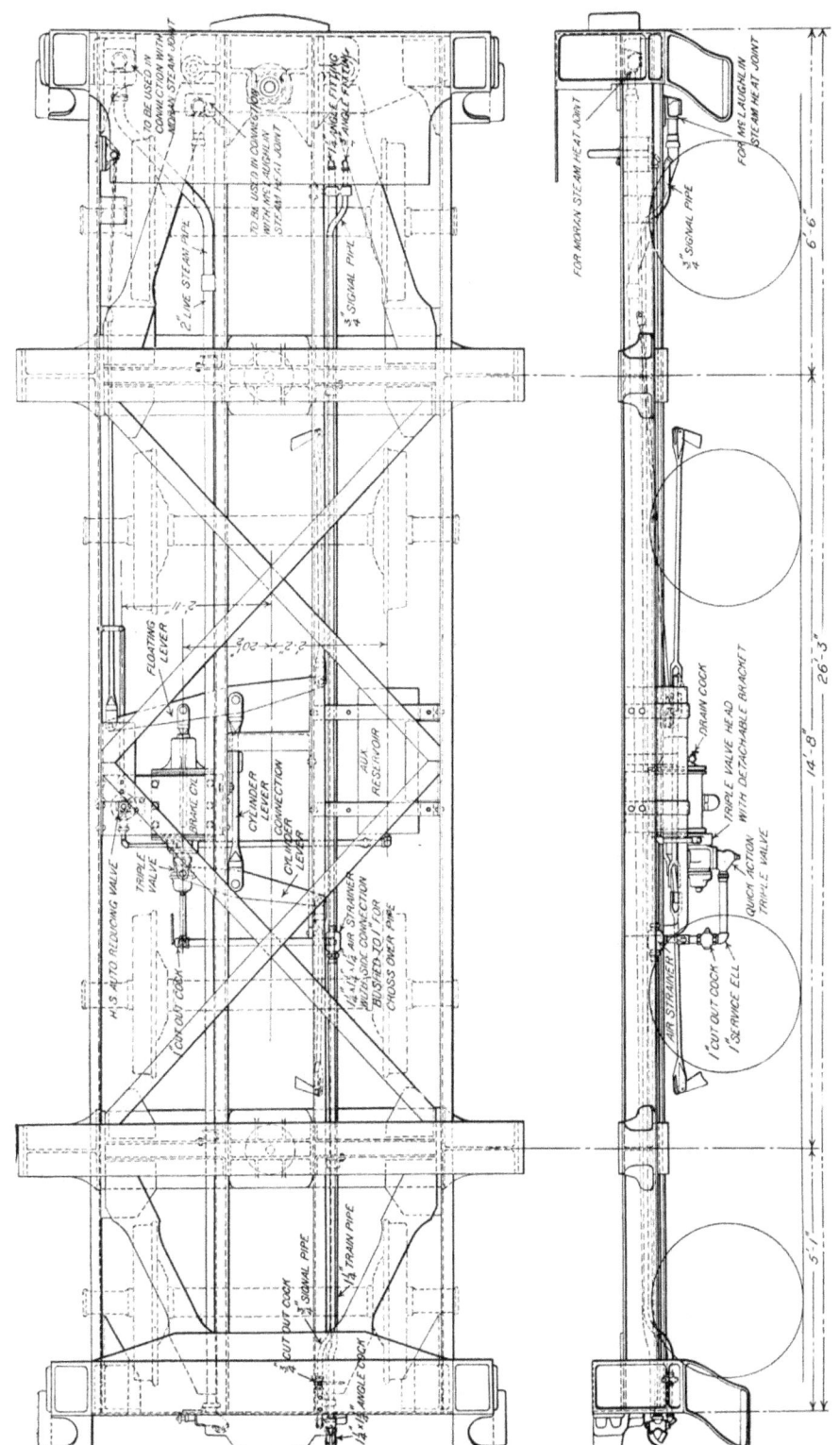

Figs. 3772-3773. Arrangement of Piping and Air Brake Apparatus Under Steel Tender for Atlantic (4-4-2) Locomotive. Pennsylvania Railroad.

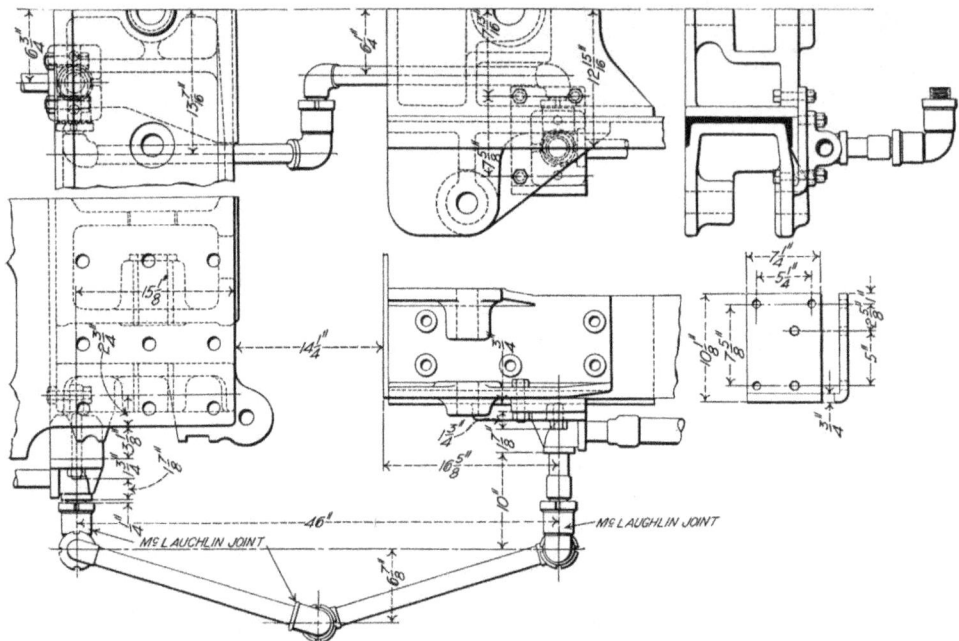

Figs. 3774-3778. McLaughlin Flexible Joint Steam Heat Connection. Franklin Railway Supply Co.

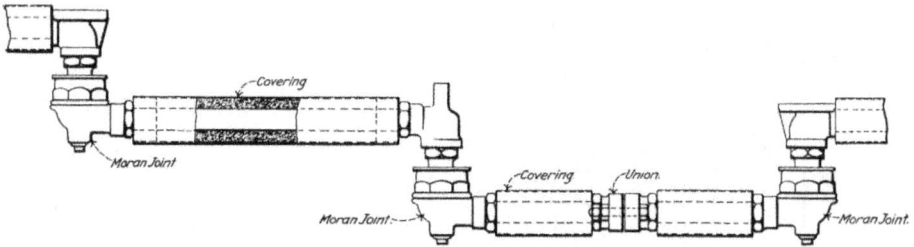

Fig. 3779. Lagging for Steam Heat Connections with Moran Flexible Joint. Atlantic (4—4—2) Locomotive, Pennsylvania Railroad.

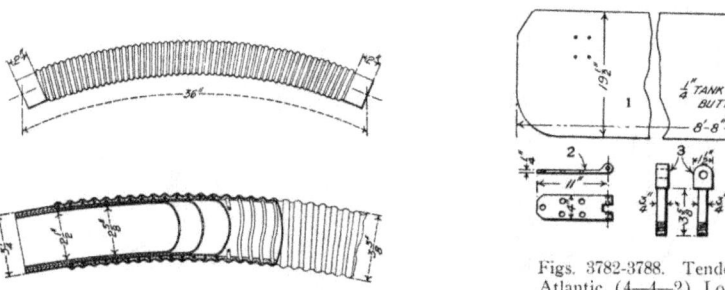

Figs. 3780-3781. Injector Supply Hose.

Figs. 3782-3788. Tender Apron. Atlantic (4—4—2) Locomotive. Pennsylvania Railroad.

Names of Parts of Figs. 3782-3788.

1 *Apron*   2 *Apron Hinge*   3 *Apron Hinge Bolt*

TENDERS, Draft Connections.

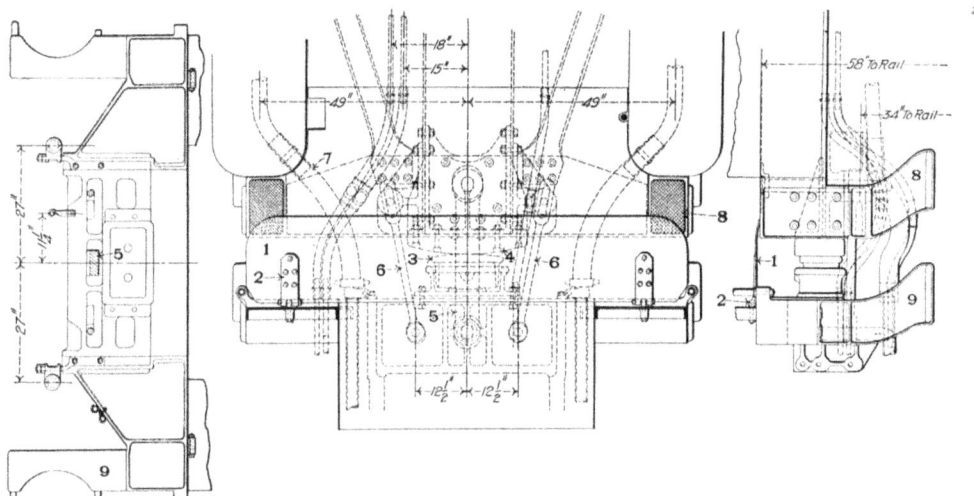

Figs. 3789-3791. Draft Connection Between Engine and Tender. Atlantic (4—4—2) Locomotive. Pennsylvania R. R.

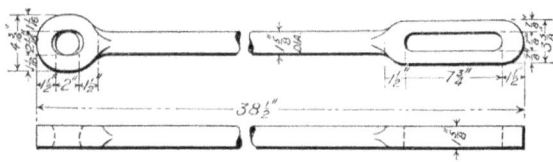

Figs. 3792-3793. Safety Bar.

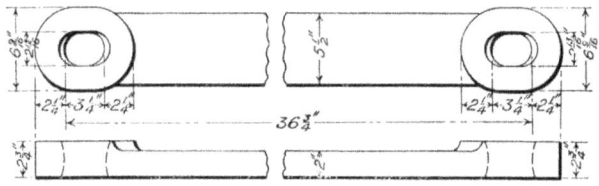

Figs. 3794-3795. Drawbar or Draft Iron.

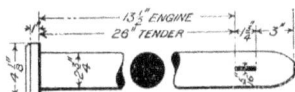

Fig. 3796. Drawbar Pin.

Names of Parts of Figs. 3789-3791.

1 *Apron*
2 *Apron Hinge*
3 *Engine Chafing Plate*
4 *Tender Chafing Plate*
5 *Drawbar*
6 *Safety Bar*
7 *Injector Suction Pipe*
8 *Tender Step*
9 *Engine Step*

Figs. 3792-3796. Details of Draft Connection Between Engine and Tender. Atlantic (4—4—2) Locomotive. P. R. R.

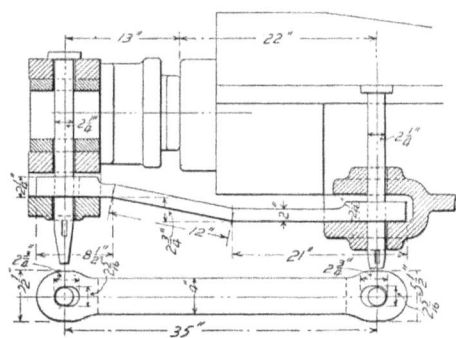

Figs. 3797-3798. Drawbar and Spring Buffer Between Engine and Tender.

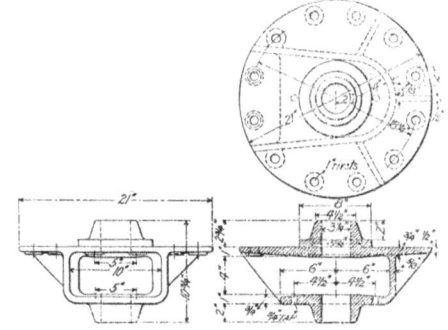

Figs. 3799-3801. Drawbar Pocket. Under Tender.

TENDERS, Draft Connections. Figs. 3802-3819

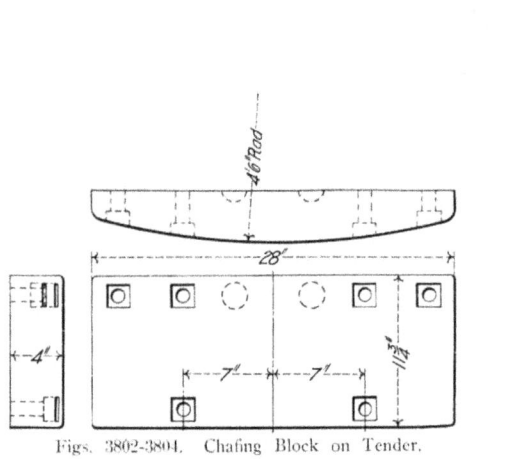
Figs. 3802-3804. Chafing Block on Tender.

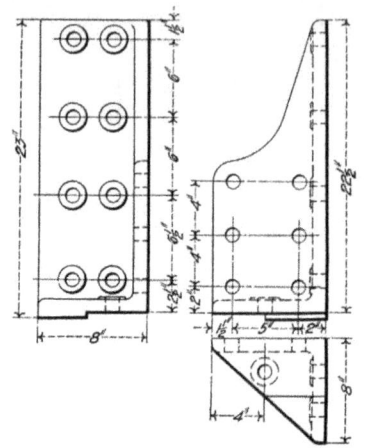
Figs. 3805-3807. Back Stop Casting for Chafing Block.

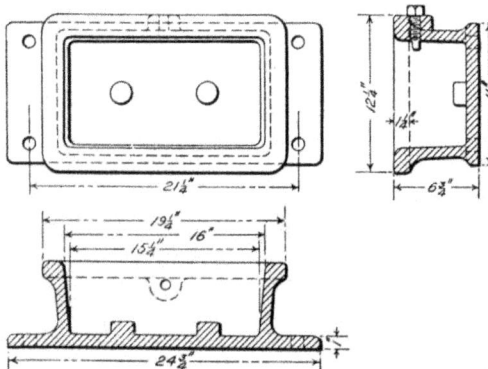
Figs. 3808-3810. Spring Buffer Chamber for Two Springs.

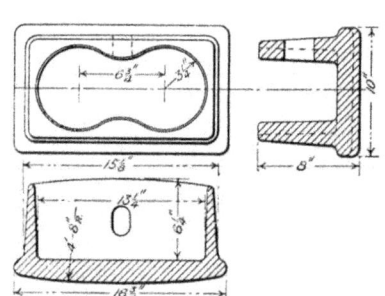
Figs. 3811-3813. Spring Buffer Cap for Two Springs.

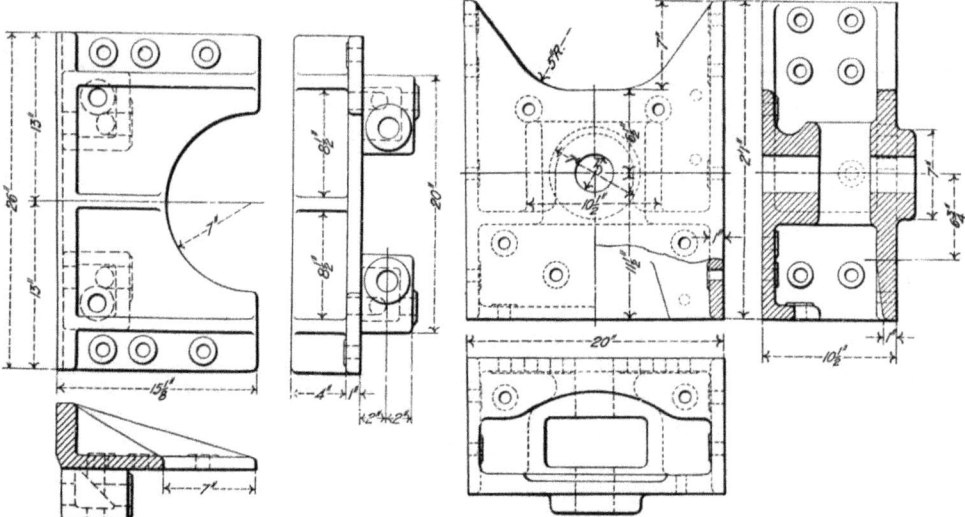
Figs. 3814-3816. Stop Block. Figs. 3817-3819. Drawbar Pocket Under Tender.

Figs. 3802-3819. Details of Draft Connection Between Engine and Tender, Atlantic (4—1—2) Locomotive. Pennsylvania Railroad.

TENDERS, Draft Gear.

Numbers Refer to List of Names of Parts Below.

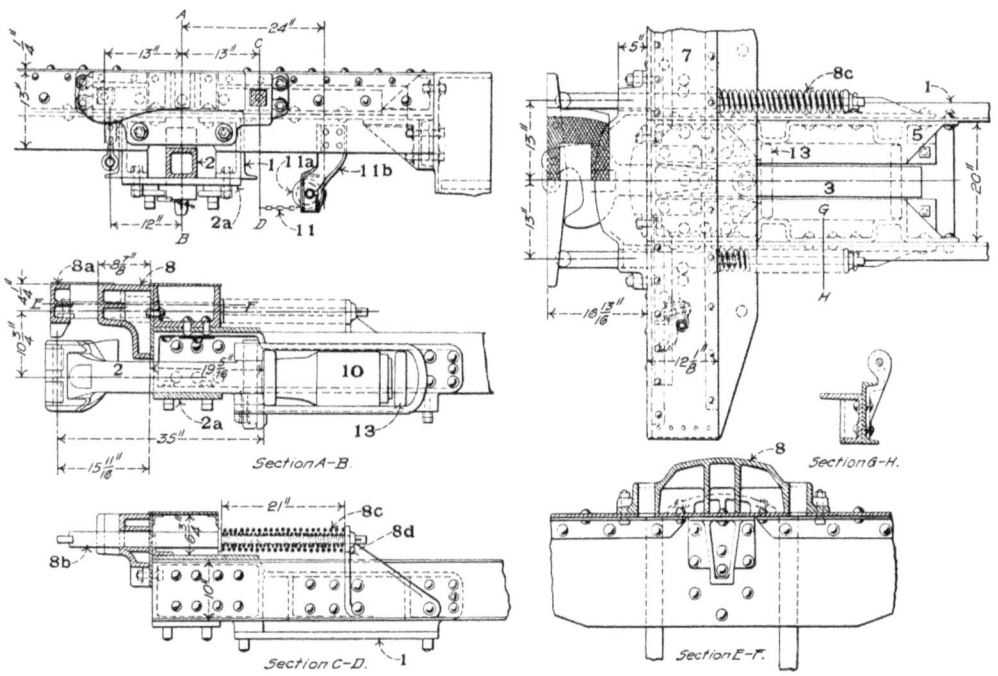

Figs. 3820–3825. Rear Buffer Arrangement for Steel Tenders. Pennsylvania Railroad.

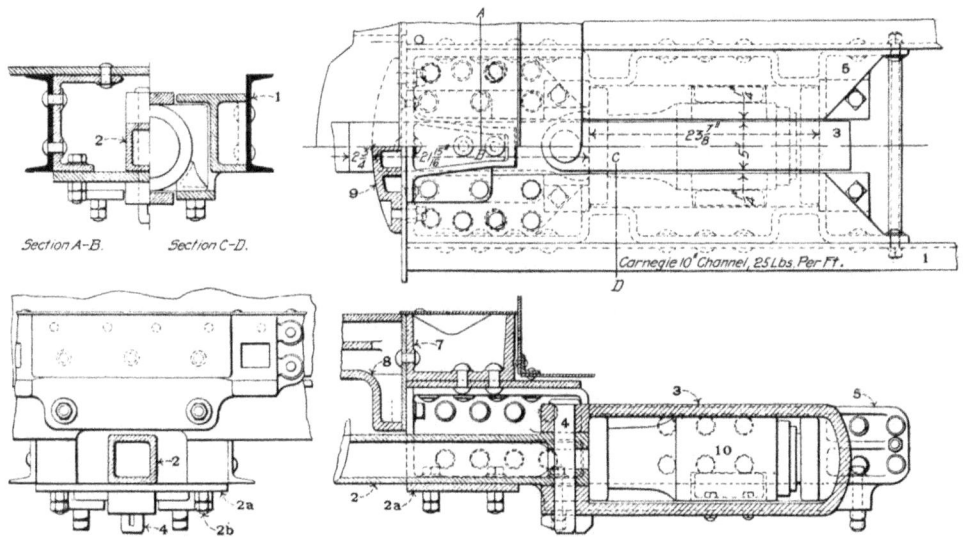

Figs. 3826–3829. Attachment of Westinghouse Friction Draft Gear to Steel Tenders. Pennsylvania Railroad.

Names of Parts of Figs. 3820-3854.

1 *Center Sill*
2 *Drawbar*
2a *Drawbar Carrier*
2b *Drawbar Carrier Bolt*
3 *Drawbar Yoke*
4 *Drawbar Yoke Pin*
4a *Drawbar Yoke Pin Cotter*
5 *Drawbar Cheek Casting*
7 *End Sill*
8 *Buffer Casting*
8a *Buffer Plate*
8b *Buffer Stem*
8c *Buffer Spring*
8d *Buffer Spring Stop*
8e *Buffer Spring Follower*
9 *Chafing Plate*
10 *Westinghouse Friction Draft Gear*
11 *Uncoupling Chain*
11a *Uncoupling Chain Sheave*
11b *Uncoupling Chain Sheave Bracket*
12 *Uncoupling Rod*
13 *Follower Plate*
14 *Follower Plate Strap*

TENDERS, Draft Gear. Figs. 3830-3875

Numbers Refer to List of Names of Parts with Figs. 3820-3829.

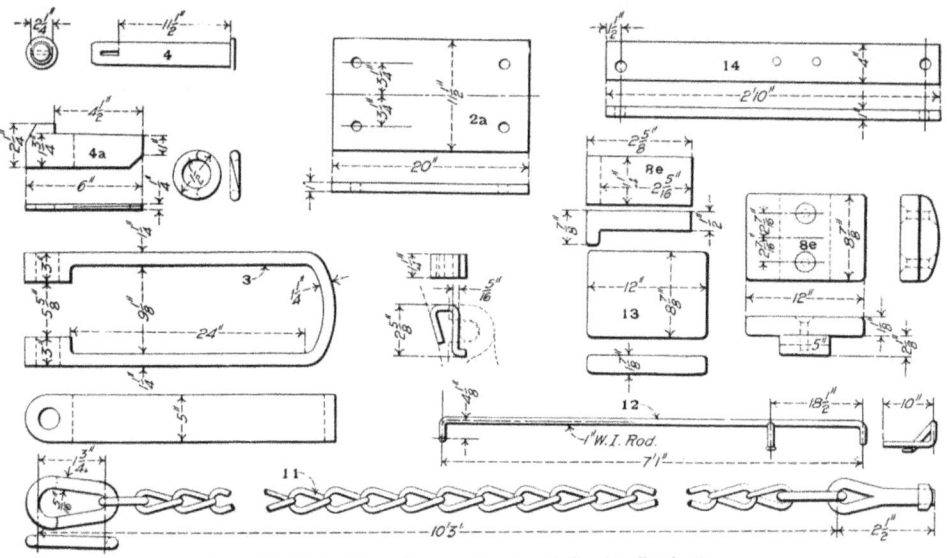

Figs. 3830-3854. Wrought Iron Details of Tender Draft Gear.

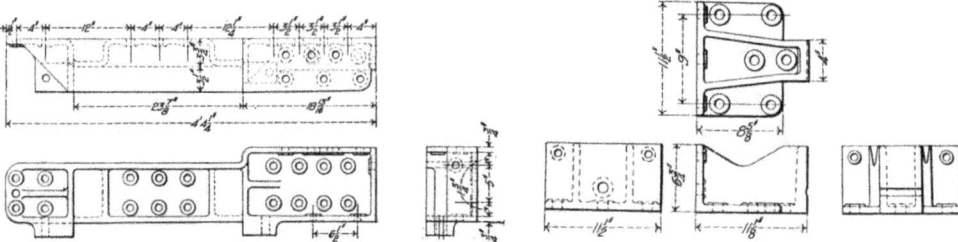

Figs. 3855-3857. Cheek Casting. Figs. 3858-3861. Buffer Casting.

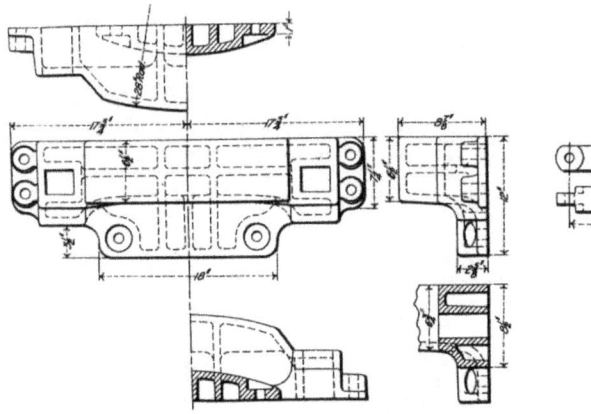

Figs. 3862-3866. Buffer Casting. Figs. 3867-3868. Buffer Stem.

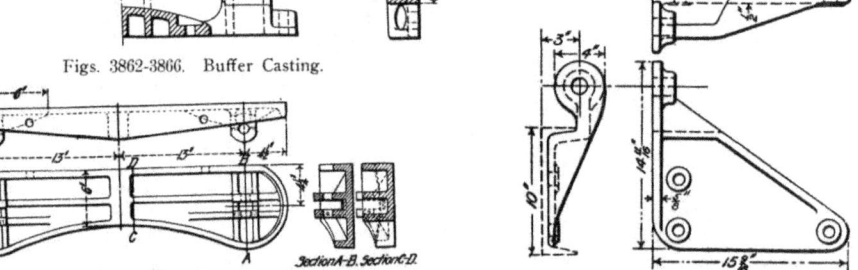

Figs. 3869-3872. Buffer Plate. Figs. 3873-3875. Buffer Spring Stop.

Figs. 3830-3875. Details of Draft Gear for Tender of Atlantic (4—4—2) Locomotive. Pennsylvania Railroad.

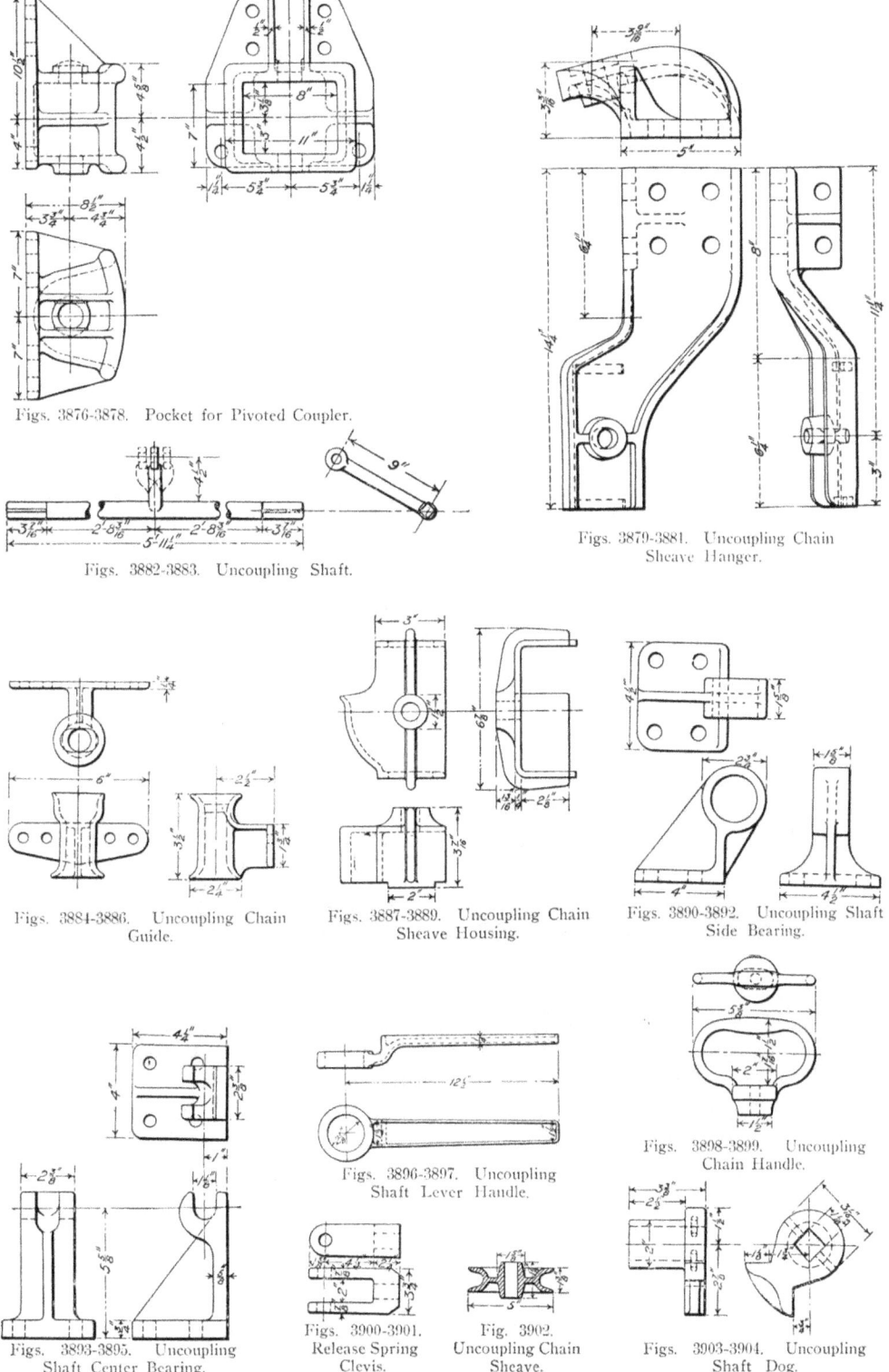

Figs. 3876-3878. Pocket for Pivoted Coupler.
Figs. 3879-3881. Uncoupling Chain Sheave Hanger.
Figs. 3882-3883. Uncoupling Shaft.
Figs. 3884-3886. Uncoupling Chain Guide.
Figs. 3887-3889. Uncoupling Chain Sheave Housing.
Figs. 3890-3892. Uncoupling Shaft Side Bearing.
Figs. 3893-3895. Uncoupling Shaft Center Bearing.
Figs. 3896-3897. Uncoupling Shaft Lever Handle.
Figs. 3898-3899. Uncoupling Chain Handle.
Figs. 3900-3901. Release Spring Clevis.
Fig. 3902. Uncoupling Chain Sheave.
Figs. 3903-3904. Uncoupling Shaft Dog.

Figs. 3876-3904. Details of Draft Gear for Tender of Atlantic (4—4—2) Locomotive. Pennsylvania Railroad.

TENDERS, Draft Gear. Figs. 3905-3922

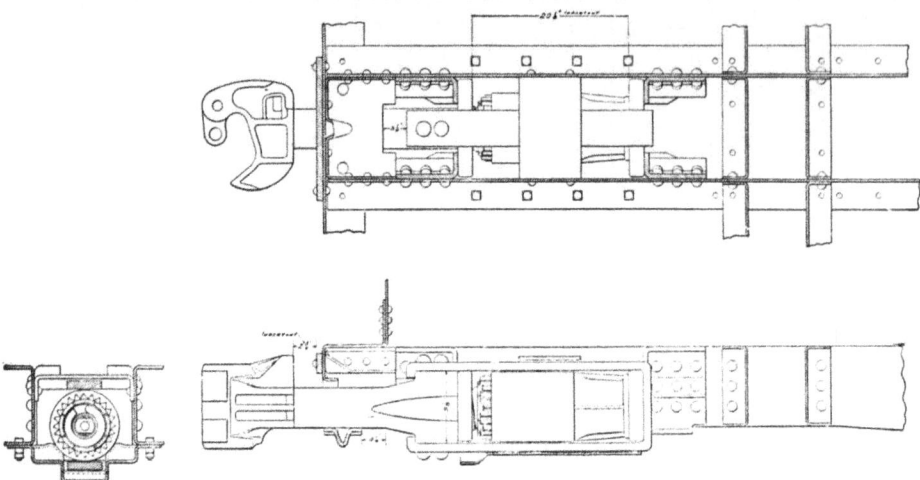

Figs. 3905-3907. Application of Westinghouse Friction Draft Gear to Tenders with Steel Underframe.

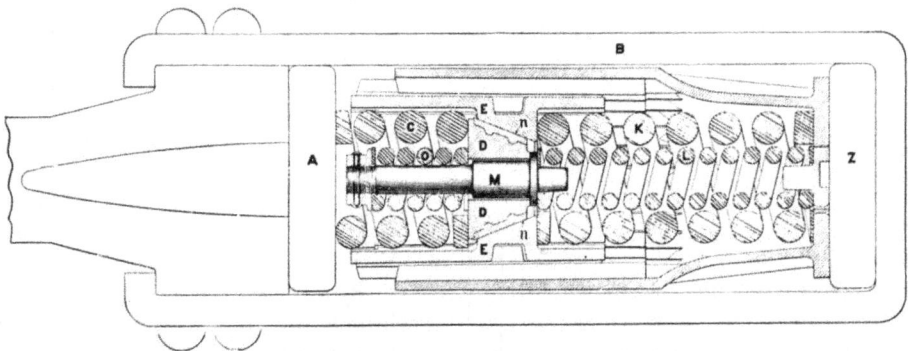

Fig. 3908. Sectional View of Westinghouse Friction Draft Gear.

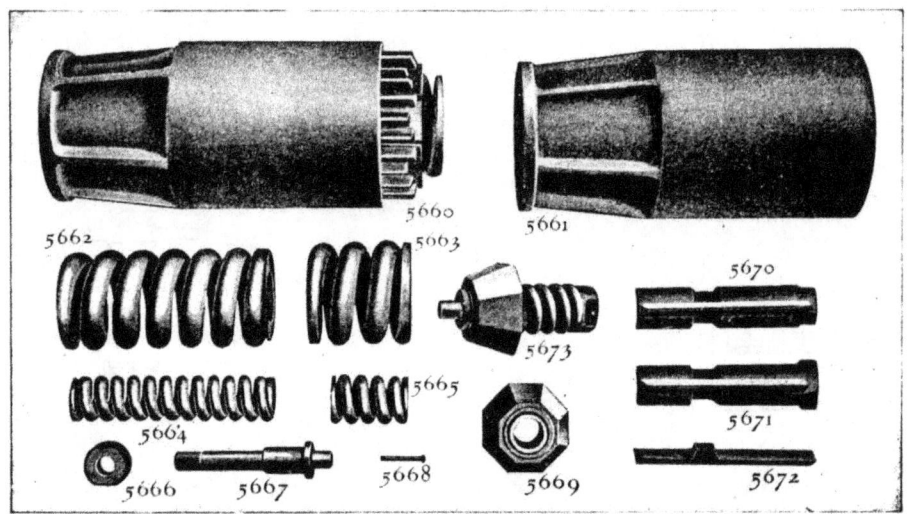

Figs. 3909-3922. Parts of Westinghouse Friction Draft Gear. Westinghouse Air Brake Co.

Names of Parts of Figs. 3909-3922.

5660 Friction Draft Gear, Complete	5666 Nut for Release Pin	5671 Male Segment
5661 Draft Gear Cylinder Body	5667 Release Pin	5672 Friction Strip
5662 Release Spring	5668 Rivet for Securing Release Pin Nut	5673 Wedge and Release Pin with Auxiliary Preliminary Spring, Complete
5663 Preliminary Spring	5669 Wedge	
5664 Auxiliary Release Spring	5670 Female Segment	
5665 Auxiliary Preliminary Spring		

TENDERS, Draft Gear.

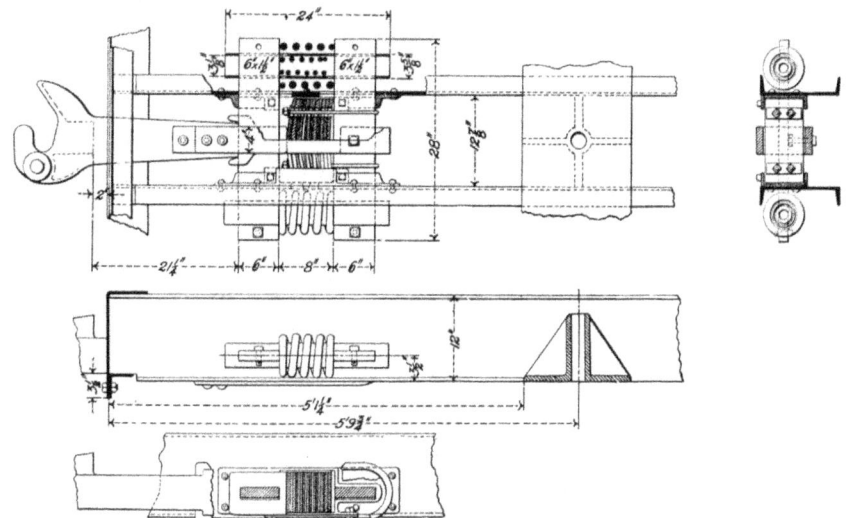

Figs. 3923-3926. Bradford Draft Gear with Plate Spring. Bradford Draft Gear Co.

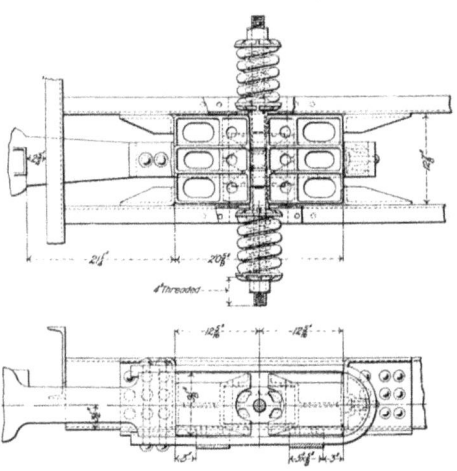

Figs. 3927-3928. Cardwell Friction Draft Gear. Type C-1.

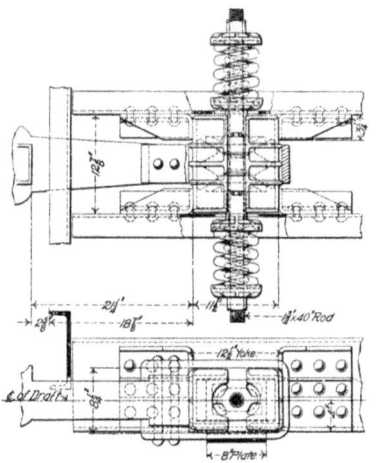

Figs. 3929-3930. Cardwell Friction Draft Gear, Type B-1.

Cardwell Manufacturing Co.

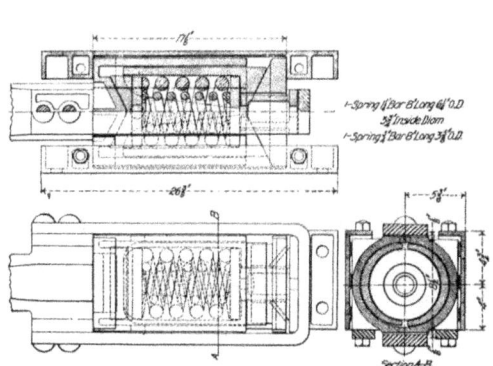

Figs. 3931-3933. Washburn Friction Draft Gear, Type FE. Washburn Coupler Co.

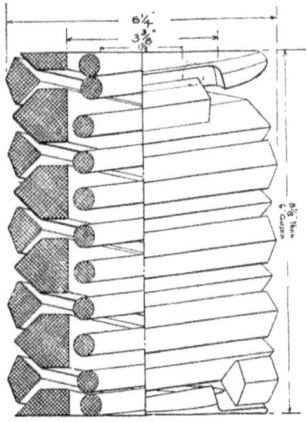

Fig. 3934. Harvey Friction Draft Spring. Frost Ry. Supply Co.

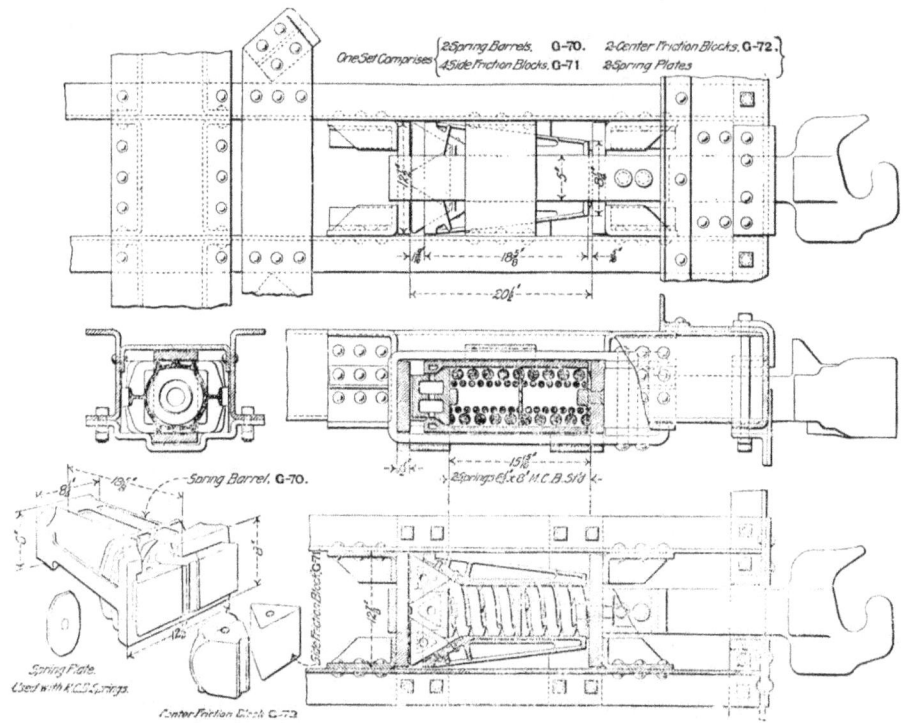

Figs. 3935-3942. Sessions-Standard Friction Draft Gear, Type C, Applied to Tender with Steel Underframe. Standard Coupler Co.

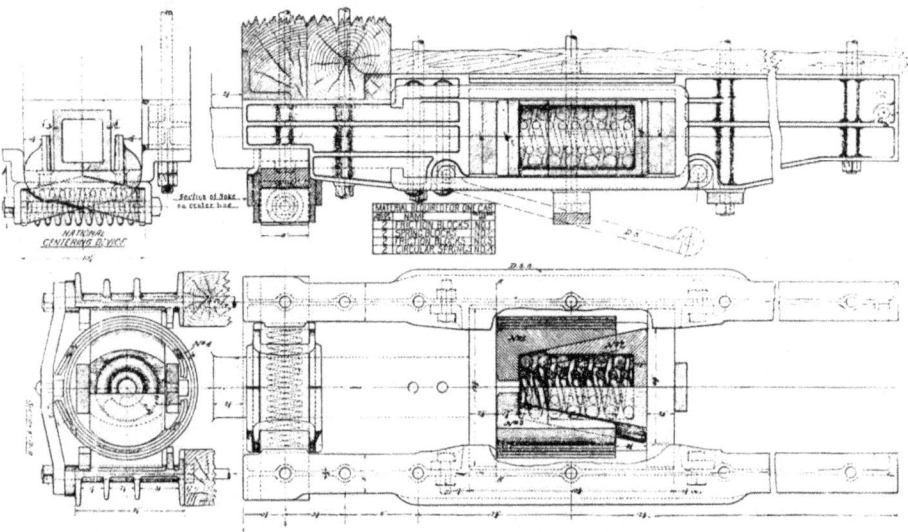

Figs. 3943-3946. Hinson Friction Draft Gear. National Car Coupler Co.

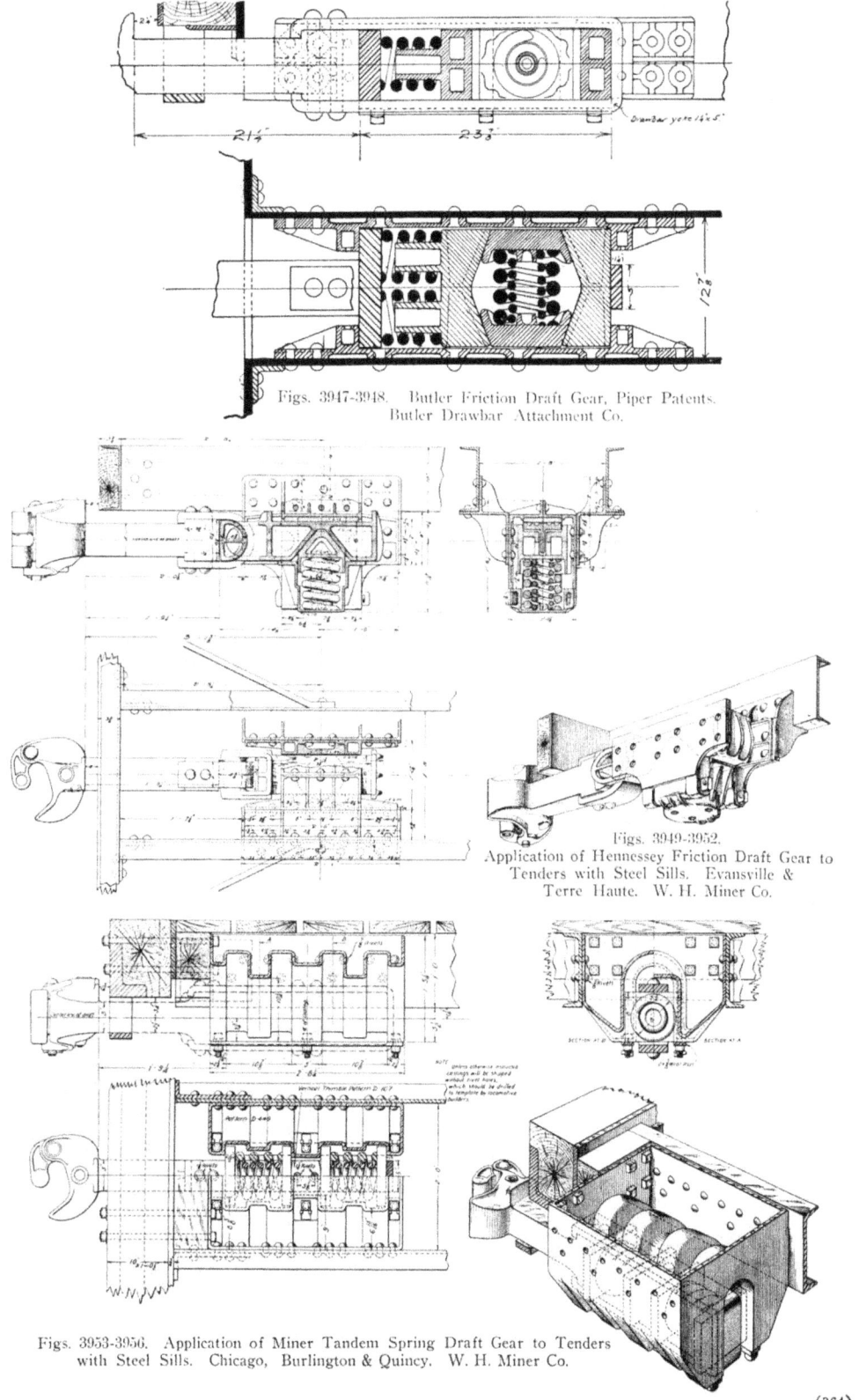

Figs. 3947-3948. Butler Friction Draft Gear, Piper Patents. Butler Drawbar Attachment Co.

Figs. 3949-3952. Application of Hennessey Friction Draft Gear to Tenders with Steel Sills. Evansville & Terre Haute. W. H. Miner Co.

Figs. 3953-3956. Application of Miner Tandem Spring Draft Gear to Tenders with Steel Sills. Chicago, Burlington & Quincy. W. H. Miner Co.

TENDERS, Draft Gear. Figs. 3957-3963

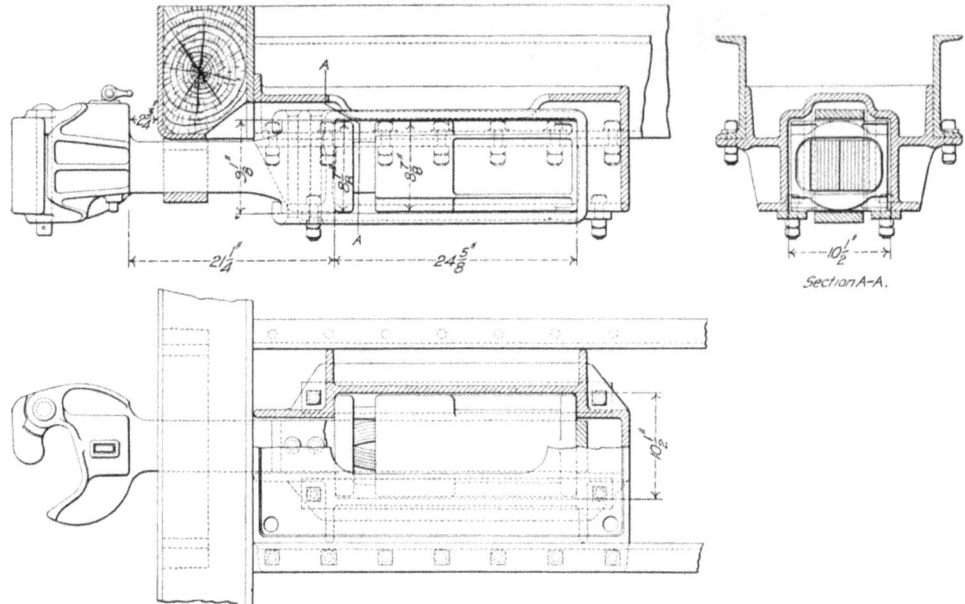

Figs. 3957-3959. Application of Gould Friction Draft Gear to Tenders with Steel Sills. Gould Coupler Co.

Fig. 3962. Gould Spring Buffer Plate.

Fig. 3960. Gould Friction Draft Gear, Dismantled.

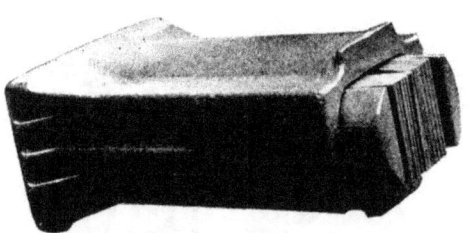

Fig. 3961. Gould Friction Draft Gear, Assembled.

Fig. 3963. Gould Tender Vestibule.

Gould Coupler Co.

Figs. 3964-3973 — TENDERS, Draft Gear; Couplers.

Fig. 3964. Gould Pivoted Tender Coupler.

Fig. 3965. Gould Tender Coupler and Plate.

Gould Coupler Co.

Fig. 3966. Gould Tender Coupler.

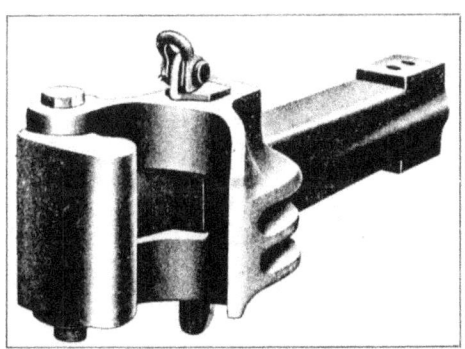
Fig. 3967. R. E. Janney Coupler.

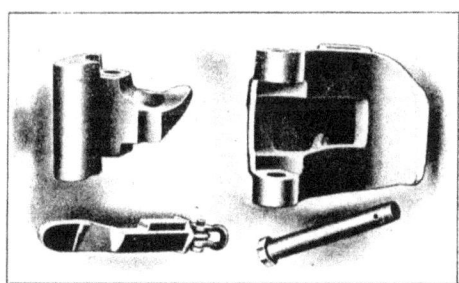
Figs. 3968-3971. Parts of R. E. Janney Coupler.

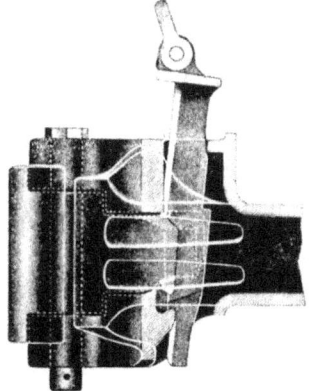
Fig. 3972. R. E. Janney Coupler, Unlocked.

Fig. 3973. R. E. Janney Coupler, Locked.

American Steel Foundries.

(366)

TENDERS, Draft Gear; Couplers.   Figs. 3974-4004

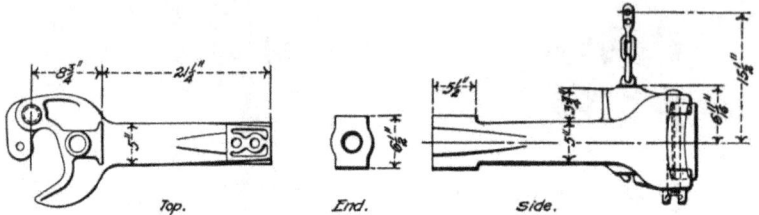

Figs. 3974-3976. Climax Coupler. National Malleable Castings Co.

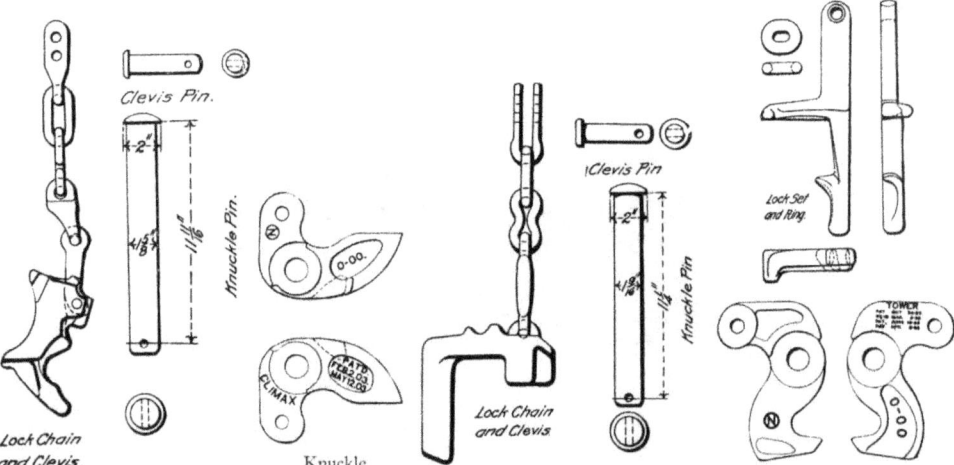

Figs. 3977-3983. Parts of Climax Coupler.   Figs. 3984-3995. Parts of Tower Coupler.

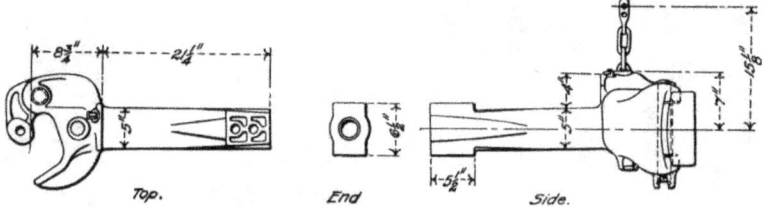

Figs. 3996-3998. Tower Coupler. National Malleable Castings Co.

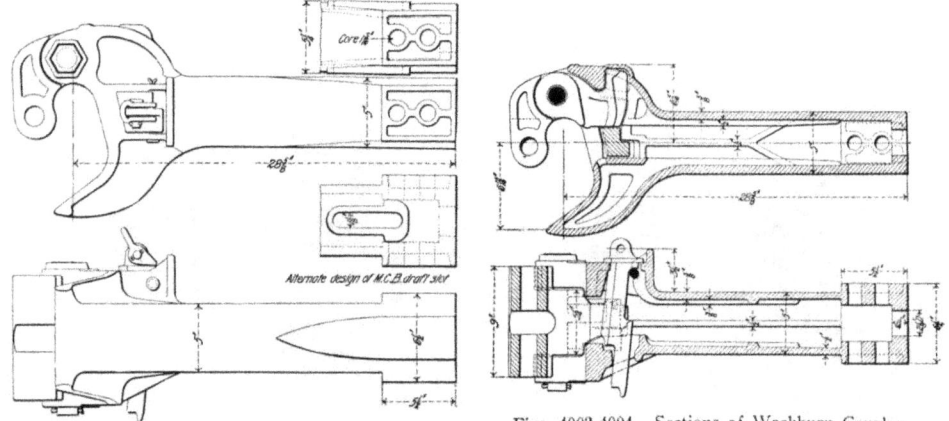

Figs. 3999-4002. Washburn Coupler, Type A.   Figs. 4003-4004. Sections of Washburn Coupler, Type A.

Washburn Coupler Co.

TENDERS, Draft Gear; Couplers.

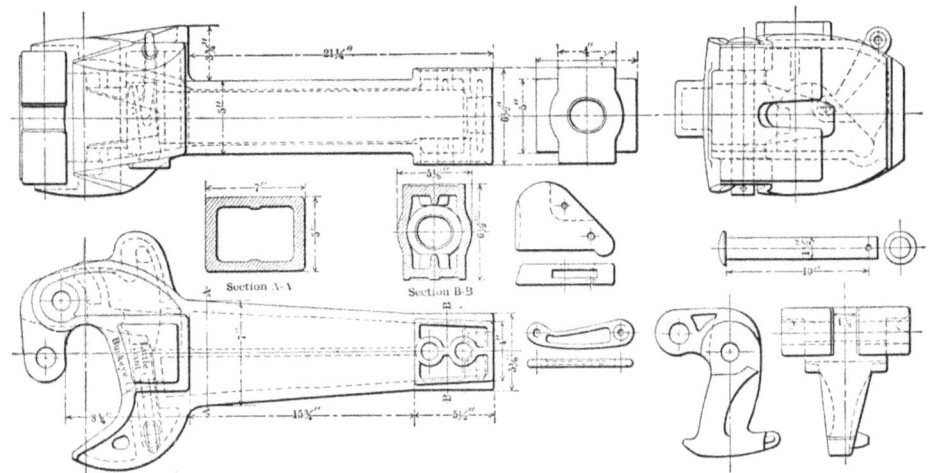

Figs. 4005-4018. Buckeye "Little Giant" Coupler and Parts, 5-in. x 7-in. Shank. Buckeye Steel Castings Co.

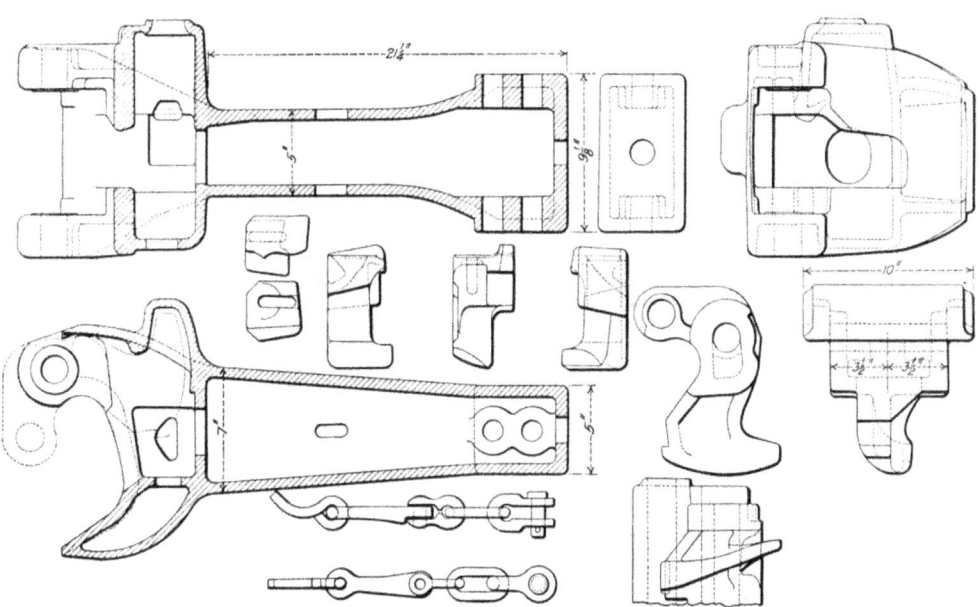

Figs. 4019-4032. Major Coupler and Parts, 5-in. x 7-in. Shank. Buckeye Steel Castings Co.

Names of Parts of Figs. 4033-4045.

90H Clevis	219C Coupler Spring	429 Knuckle Pin
91H Clevis Pin	243A Trigger for Locking Pin	448 Knuckle
115 Split Key	354 Locking Pin	448S Solid Face Knuckle
211 Pivot Pin	380 Coupler Head	

Names of Parts of Figs. 4046-4054.

15 Catch Spring Bolt	138 Catch	5080 Coupler Casting
23 Catch Spring Washer	294 Catch Lever	5081 Knuckle
25 Catch Spring	295 Thimble	5082 Knuckle Pin

Names of Parts of Figs. 4055-4062.

292 Knuckle Pin	5073 Knuckle Opener	5153 Locking Pin
5061 Split Key	5077 Knuckle Opener Pin	5154 Locking Pin Trigger
5071 Knuckle	5103 Coupler Casting	

TENDERS, Draft Gear; Couplers. Figs. 4033-4062

Numbers Refer to List of Names of Parts on Opposite Page.

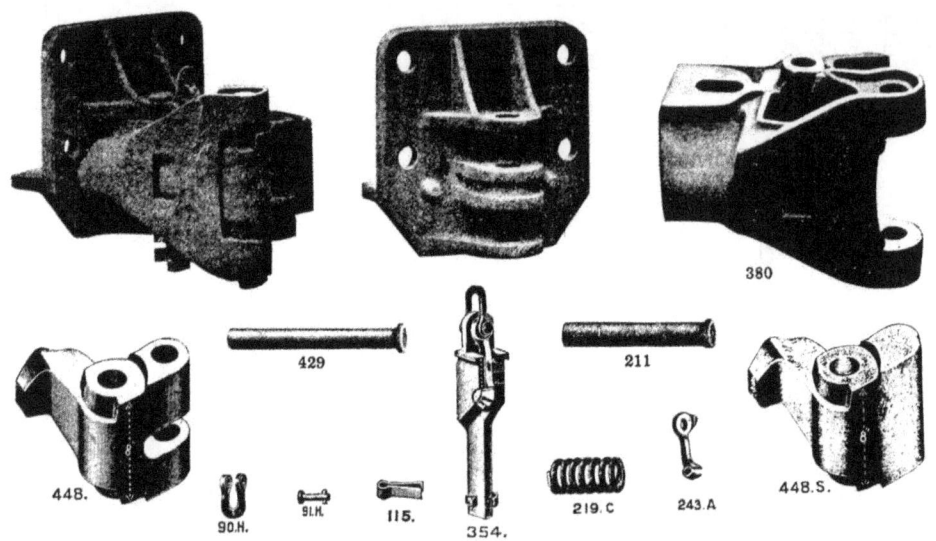

Figs. 4033-4045. Janney Tender Coupler, Curtis Pivoted Design. McConway & Torley Co.

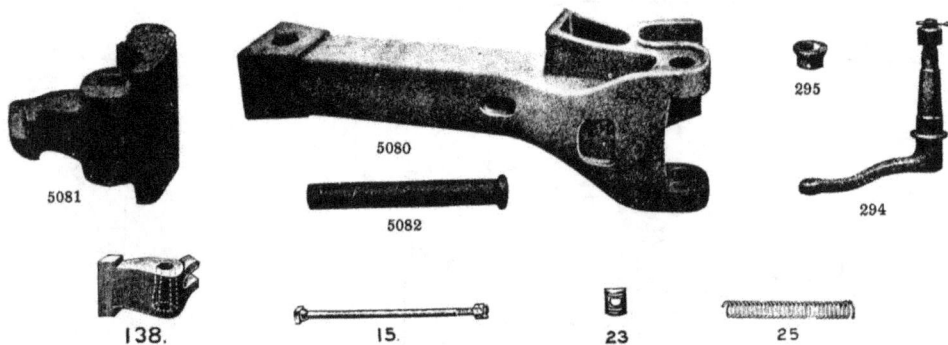

Figs. 4046-4054. Janney Tender Coupler for Attachment with Westinghouse Friction Draft Gear. McConway & Torley Co.

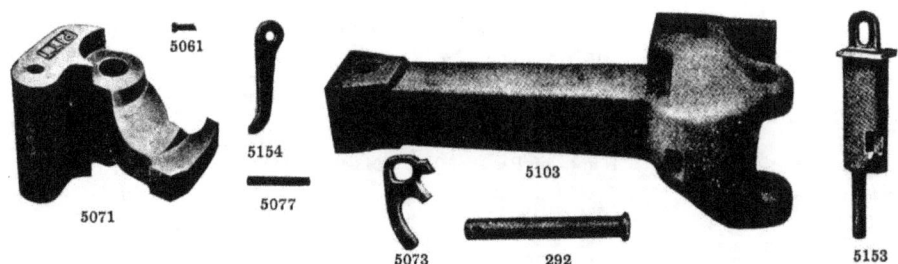

Figs. 4055-4062. Pitt Tender Coupler for Attachment with Westinghouse Friction Draft Gear. McConway & Torley Co.

Figs. 4063-4064 TENDERS, Tanks.

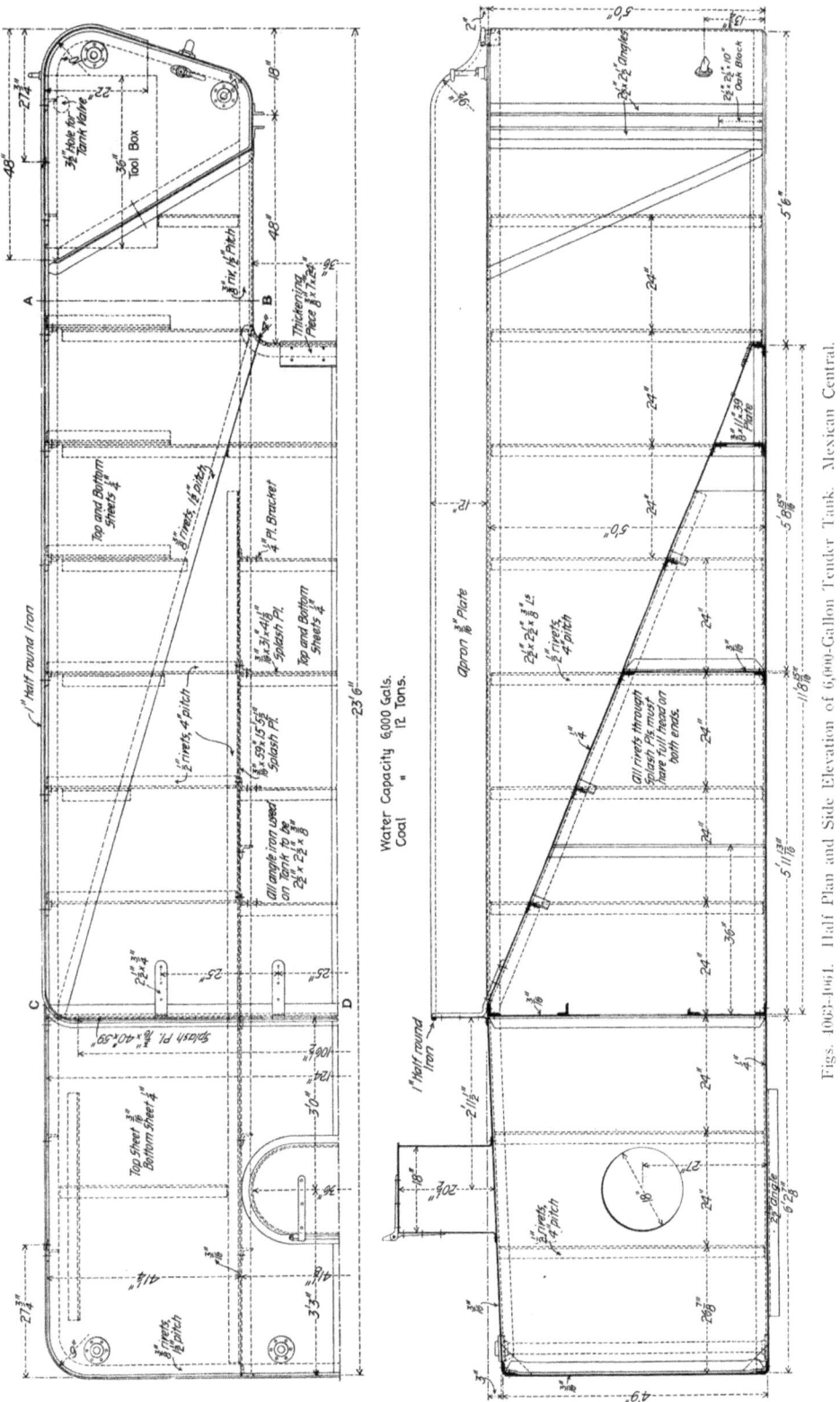

Figs. 4063-4064. Half Plan and Side Elevation of 6,000-Gallon Tender Tank. Mexican Central.

Numbers Refer to List of Names of Parts with Figs. 4081-4082.

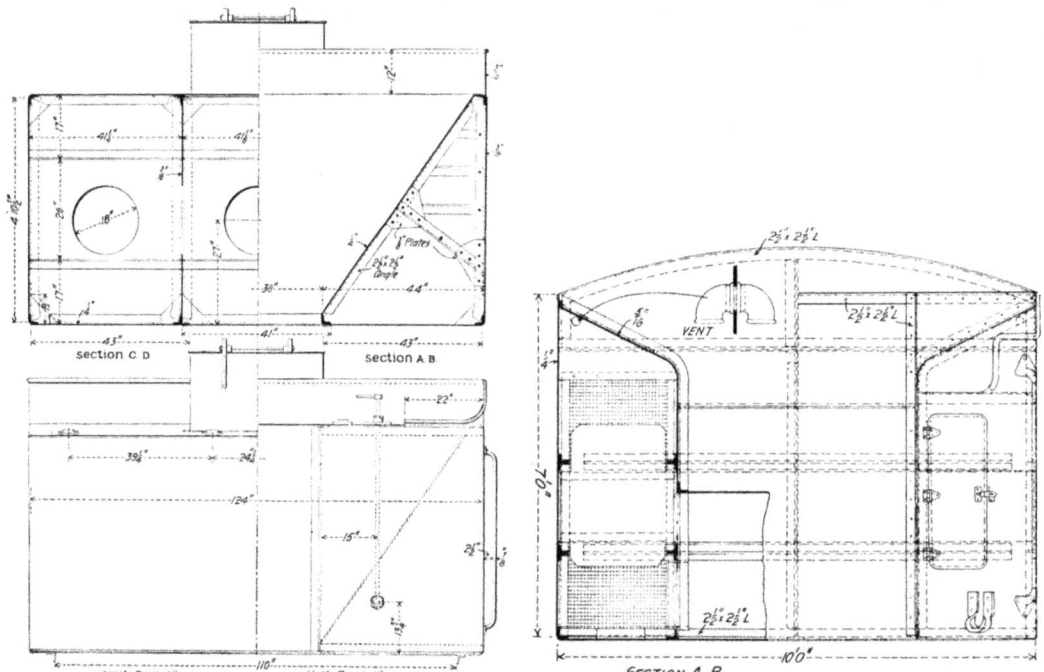

Figs. 4065-4066. Part End Elevations and Cross-Sections of 6,000-Gallon Tender Tank. Mexican Central.

Fig. 4067. Cross-Section of 7,000-Gallon Tender Tank. Louisville & Nashville.

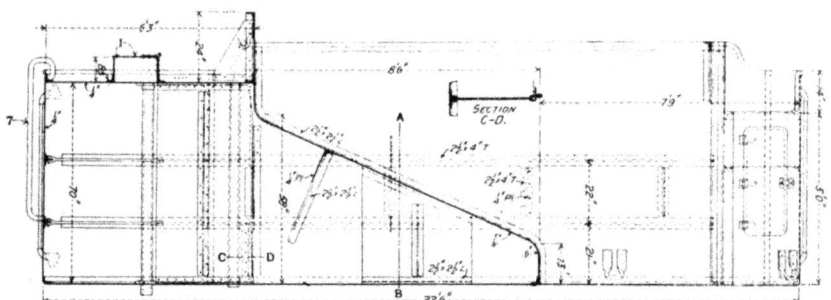

Fig. 4068. Longitudinal Section Through 7,000-Gallon Tender Tank. Louisville & Nashville.

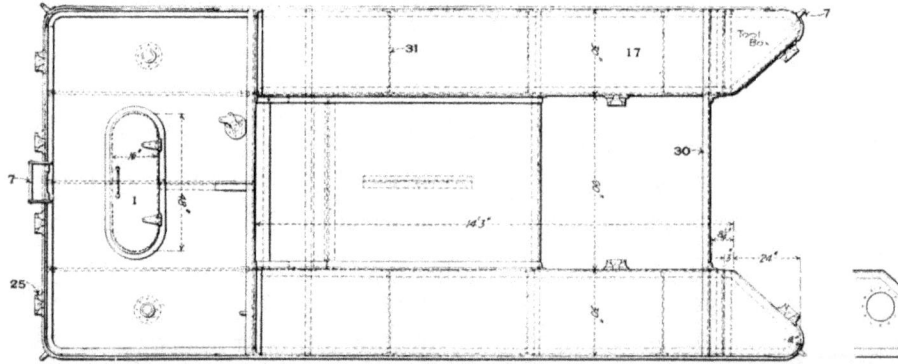

Fig. 4069. Plan of 7,000-Gallon Tender Tank. Louisville & Nashville.

Numbers Refer to List of Names of Parts with Figs. 4081-4082.

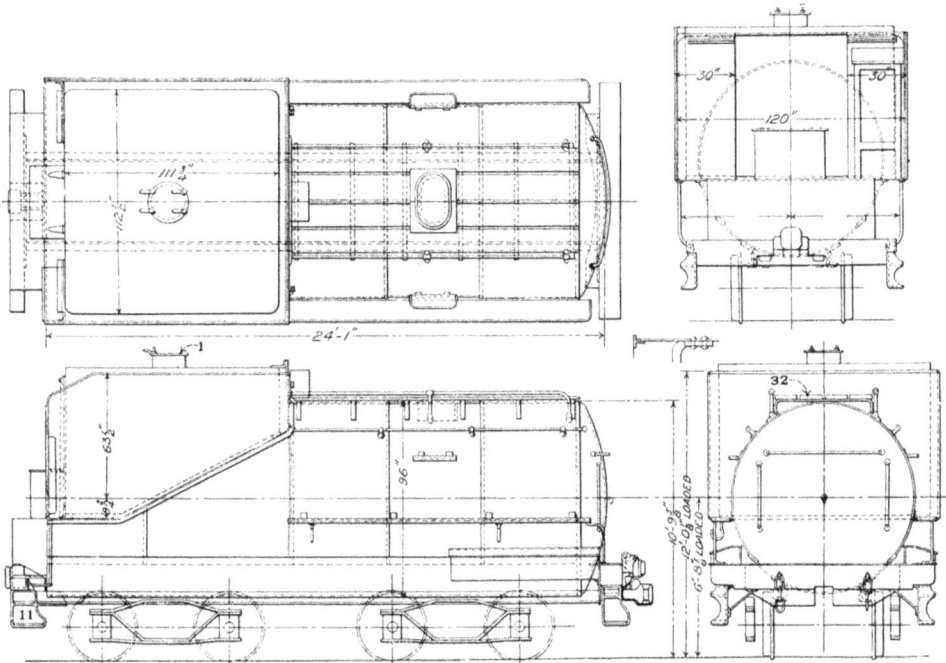

Figs. 4070-4073. Vanderbilt Tender and Cylindrical Tank for Oil Burning Locomotive.

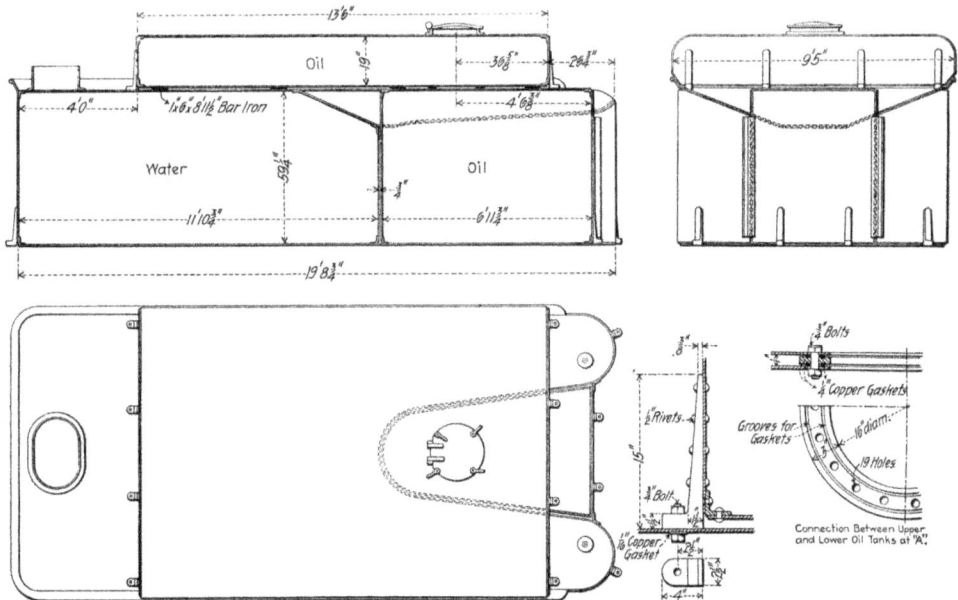

Figs. 4074-4080. Application of Oil Tanks to Standard 5,000-Gallon Tenders. Southern Pacific.

TENDERS, Tanks. Figs. 4081-4082

Numbers Refer to List of Names of Parts Below.

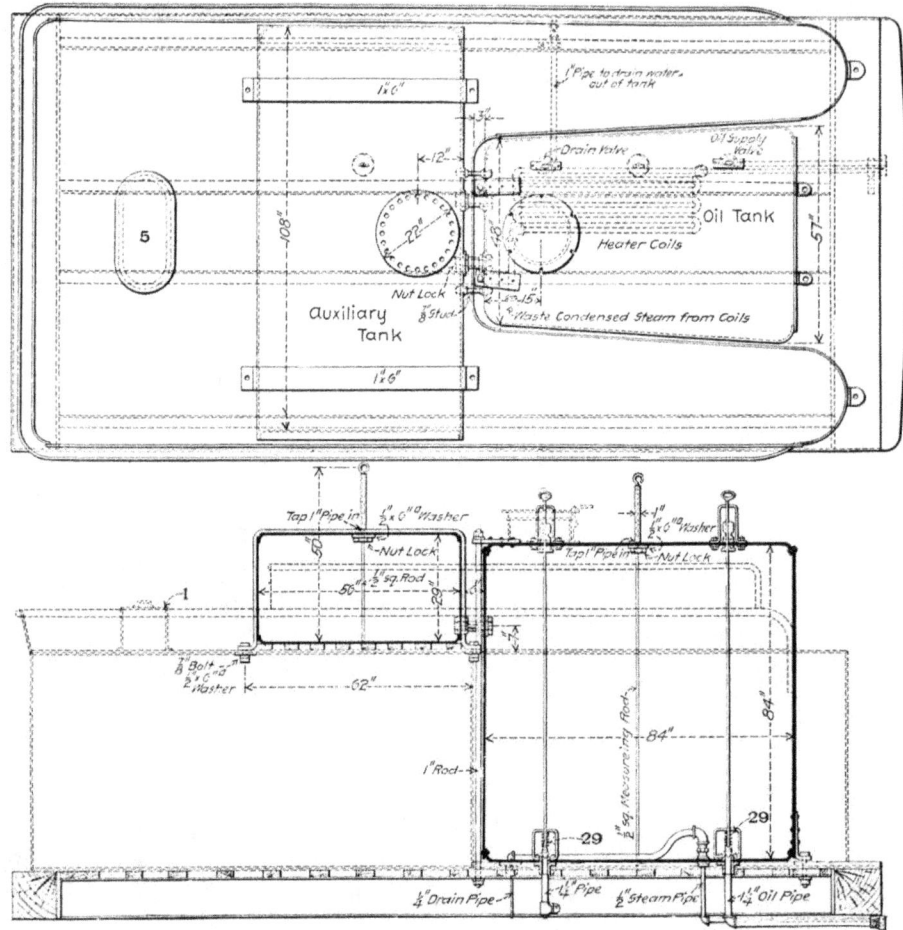

Figs. 4081-4082. Arrangement of Oil Tanks on 4,500-Gallon Tenders. Southern Pacific.

Names of Parts of Tender Tanks, Figs. 4067-4118.

1 Manhole Cover	12 Water Cock	23 Vertical Brace Plate
2 Manhole Cover Handle	13 Tender Body Bolster	24 Tank Corner Brace Plates
3 Manhole Cover Hinge	14 Chafing Plate	25 Back Lug for Tank
4 Internal Water Scoop Pipe	15 Tender Frame Diagonal Braces	26 Stop Angle
5 Manhole	16 Air Brake Cylinder	27 Tank Cock
6 Shield for Manhole	17 Water Leg of Tender	28 Water Bottom
7 Tank Hand Hold	18 Tank Cross Brace	29 Oil Valve
8 Guide for Coal Boards	19 Tank Diagonal Brace	30 Coal Board Slides
9 Operating Lever for Water Scoop	20 Tank Screen	31 Splash Plate
10 Tender Side Sills	21 Tank Screen Angle	32 Running Board
11 Tender Step	22 Buffer Spring Pocket	
	22a Vertical Brace	

(373)

Figs. 4083-4085   TENDERS, Tanks.

Numbers Refer to List of Names of Parts with Figs. 4081-4082.

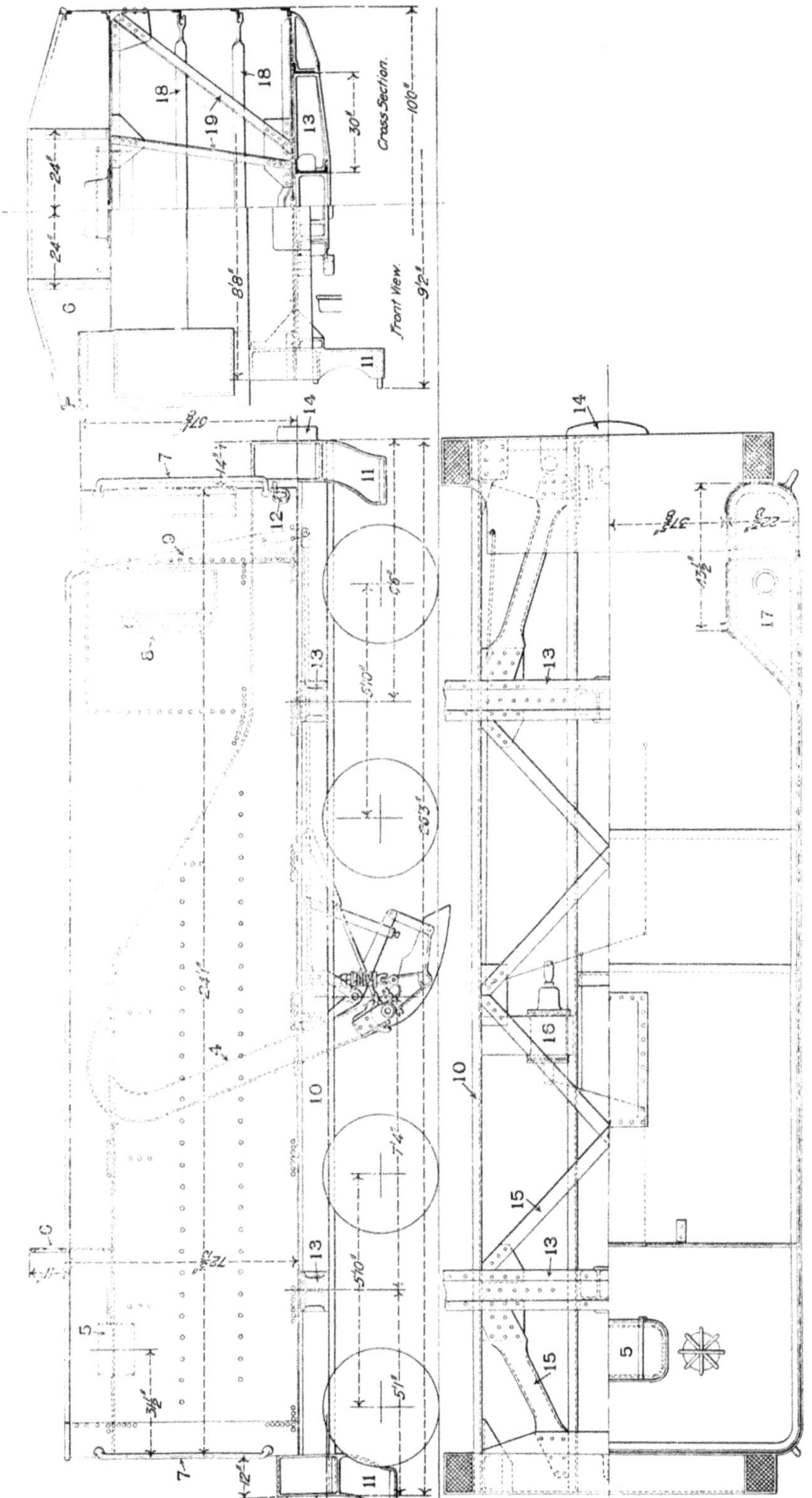

Figs. 4083-4085. General Arrangement of 5,500-Gallon Tender Tank for Atlantic (4-4-2) Locomotive. Pennsylvania Railroad.

TENDERS, Tanks. Figs. 4086-4093

Numbers Refer to List of Names of Parts with Figs. 4081-4082.

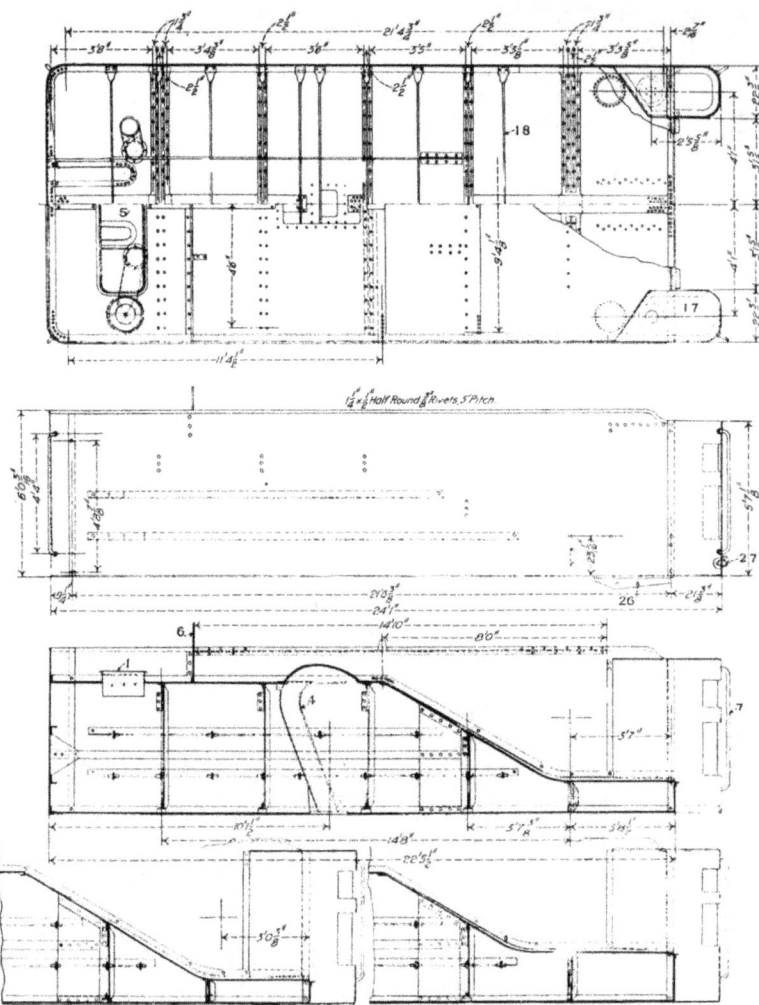

Figs. 4086-4090. Plan, Side Elevation and Sections of 5,500-Gallon Tender Tank for Atlantic (4—4—2) Locomotive. Pennsylvania Railroad.

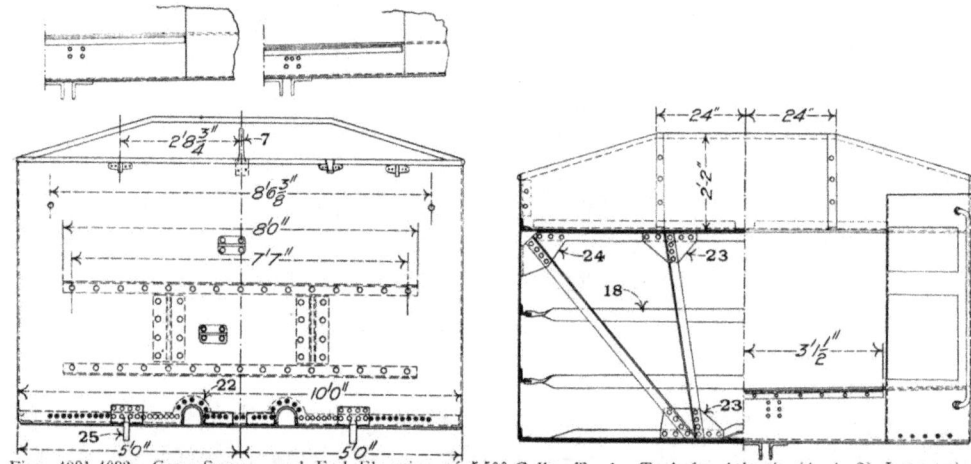

Figs. 4091-4093. Cross-Sections and End Elevation of 5,500-Gallon Tender Tank for Atlantic (4—4—2) Locomotive. Pennsylvania Railroad.

Figs. 4094-4112 — TENDERS, Tanks.

Numbers Refer to List of Names of Parts with Figs. 4081-4082.

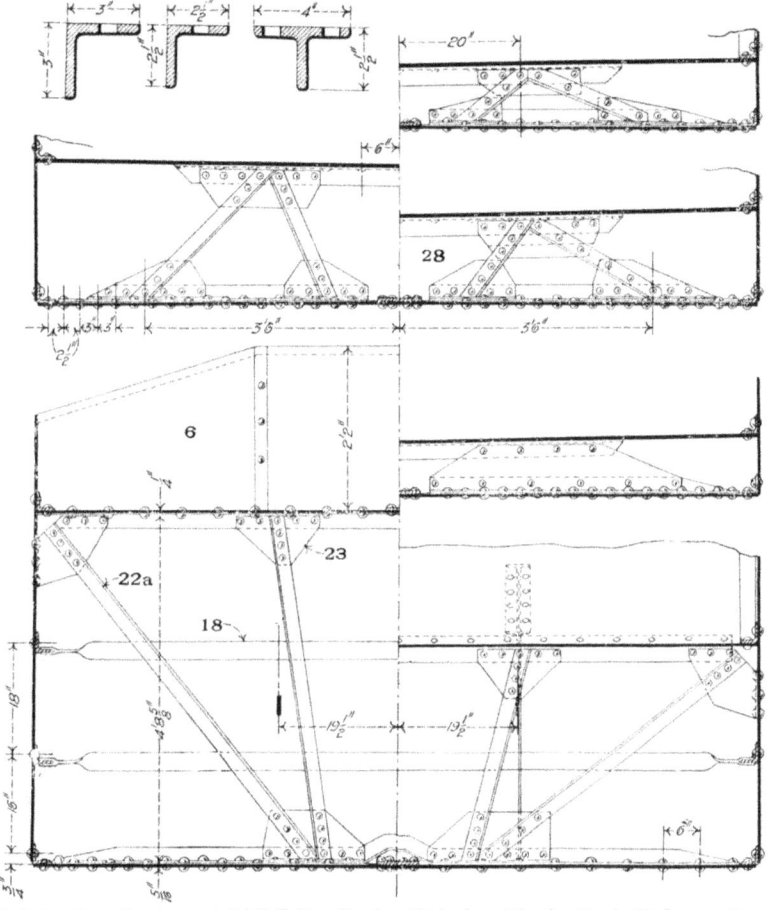

Figs. 4094-4100. Cross-Sections of 5,500-Gallon Tender Tank for Atlantic (4—4—2) Locomotive. P. R. R.

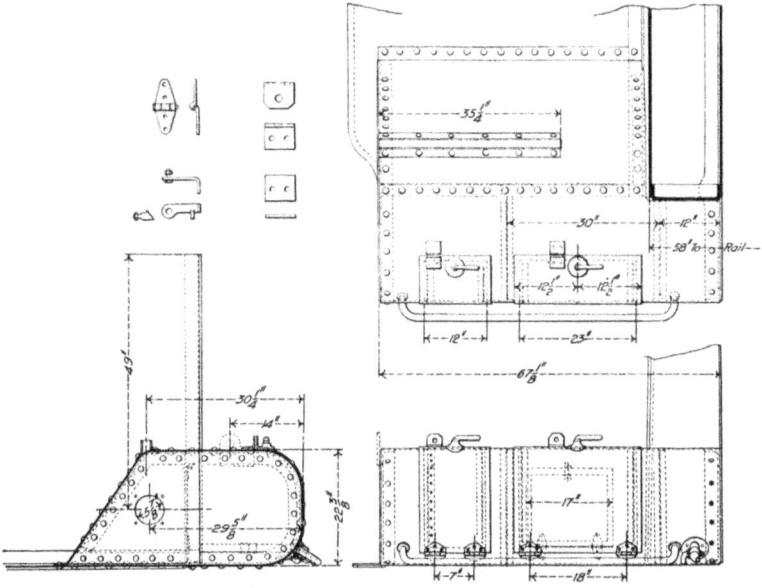

Figs. 4101-4112. Arrangement of Closets on Tender for Atlantic (4—4—2) Locomotive. P. R. R.

TENDERS, Tanks; Details.   Figs. 4113-4122

Numbers Refer to List of Names of Parts with Figs. 4081-4082.

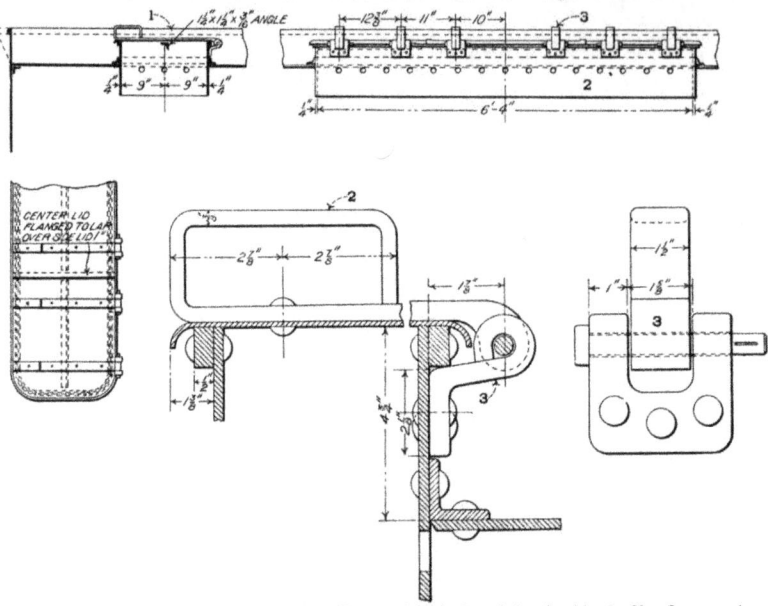

Figs. 4113-4118. Tank Manhole for 5,500-Gallon Tender Tank for Atlantic (4—4—2) Locomotive. P. R. R.

Numbers Refer to List of Names of Parts Below.

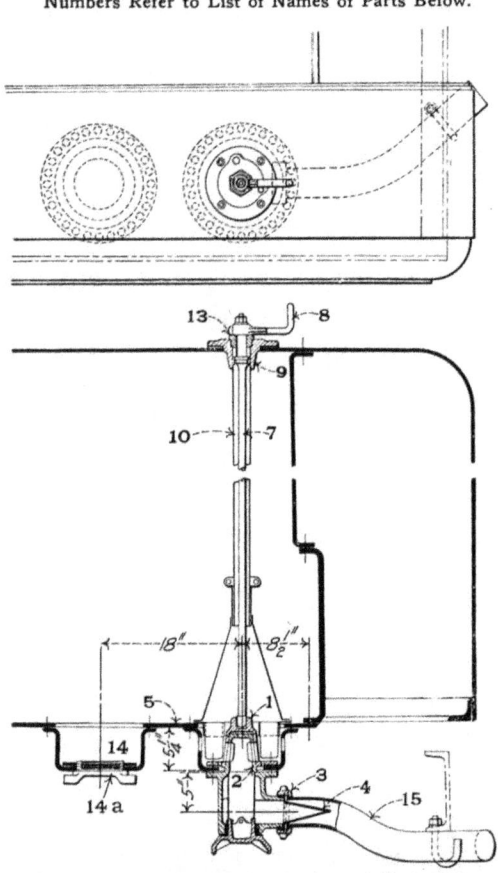

Figs. 4119-4120. General Arrangement of Tank Valve. Pennsylvania Railroad.

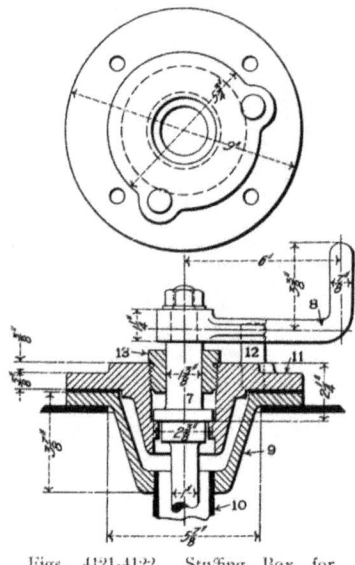

Figs. 4121-4122. Stuffing Box for Tank Valve. P. R. R.

Names of Parts of Figs. 4119-4128.
1 *Valve*
2 *Valve Seat and Body*
3 *Cap to Support Screen*
4 *Strainer*
5 *Tank Floor Sheet*
6 *Ring for Tank Valve on Floor*
7 *Tank Valve Shaft*
8 *Tank Valve Handle*
9 *Tank Valve Stuffing Box Case*
10 *Tank Valve Shaft Casing*
11 *Tank Valve Plate*
12 *Tank Valve Handle Stop*
13 *Tank Valve Shaft Gland*
14 *Tank Well*
14a *Tank Well Cap*
15 *Suction Pipe*

Figs. 4123-4140   TENDERS, Tanks; Details.

Numbers Refer to List of Names of Parts with Figs. 4113-4122.

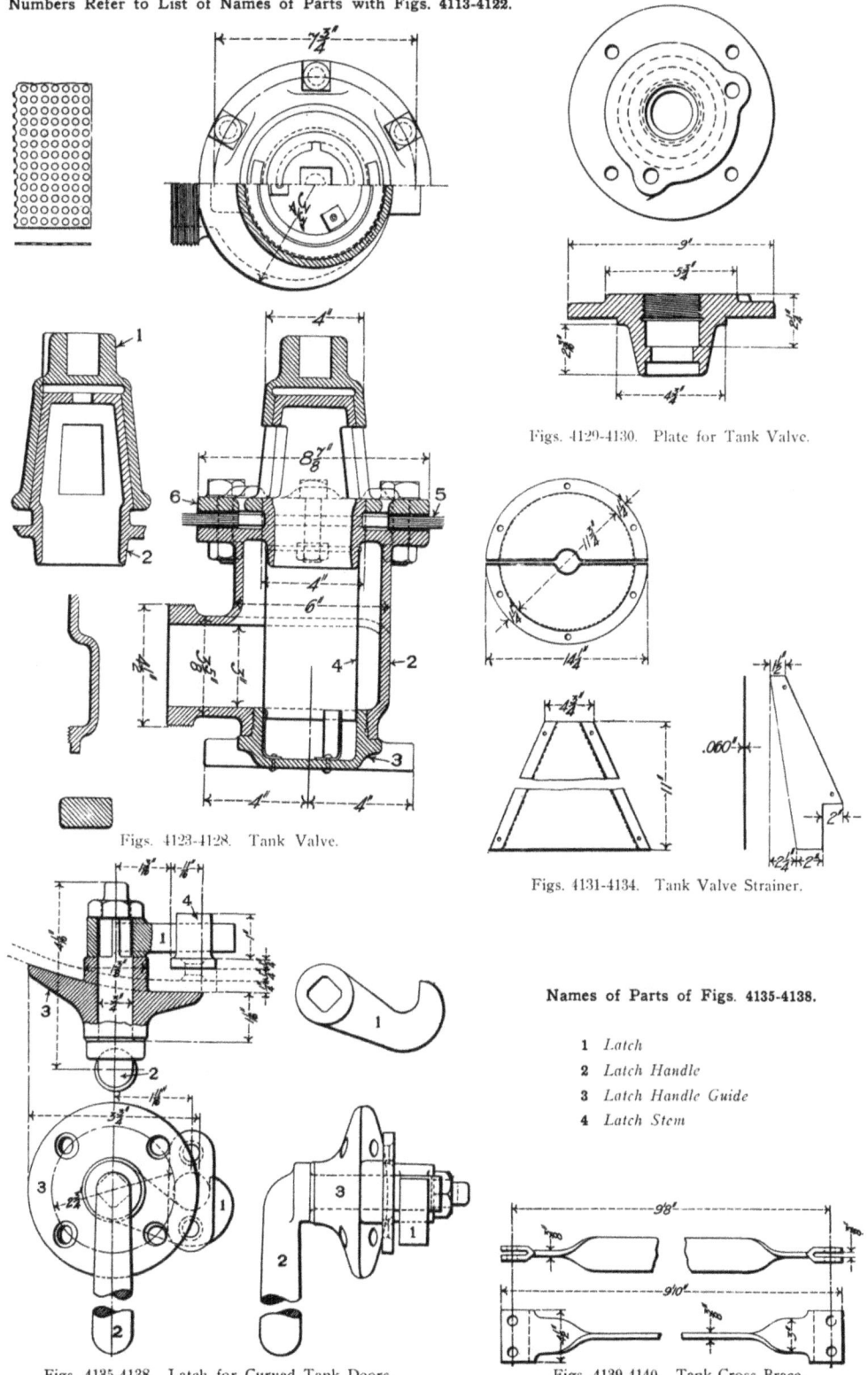

Figs. 4129-4130. Plate for Tank Valve.

Figs. 4123-4128. Tank Valve.

Figs. 4131-4134. Tank Valve Strainer.

Names of Parts of Figs. 4135-4138.

1   *Latch*
2   *Latch Handle*
3   *Latch Handle Guide*
4   *Latch Stem*

Figs. 4135-4138. Latch for Curved Tank Doors.   Figs. 4139-4140. Tank Cross Brace.
Figs. 4123-4140. Details of 5,500-Gallon Tender Tank for Atlantic (4—4—2) Locomotive. Pennsylvania Railroad.

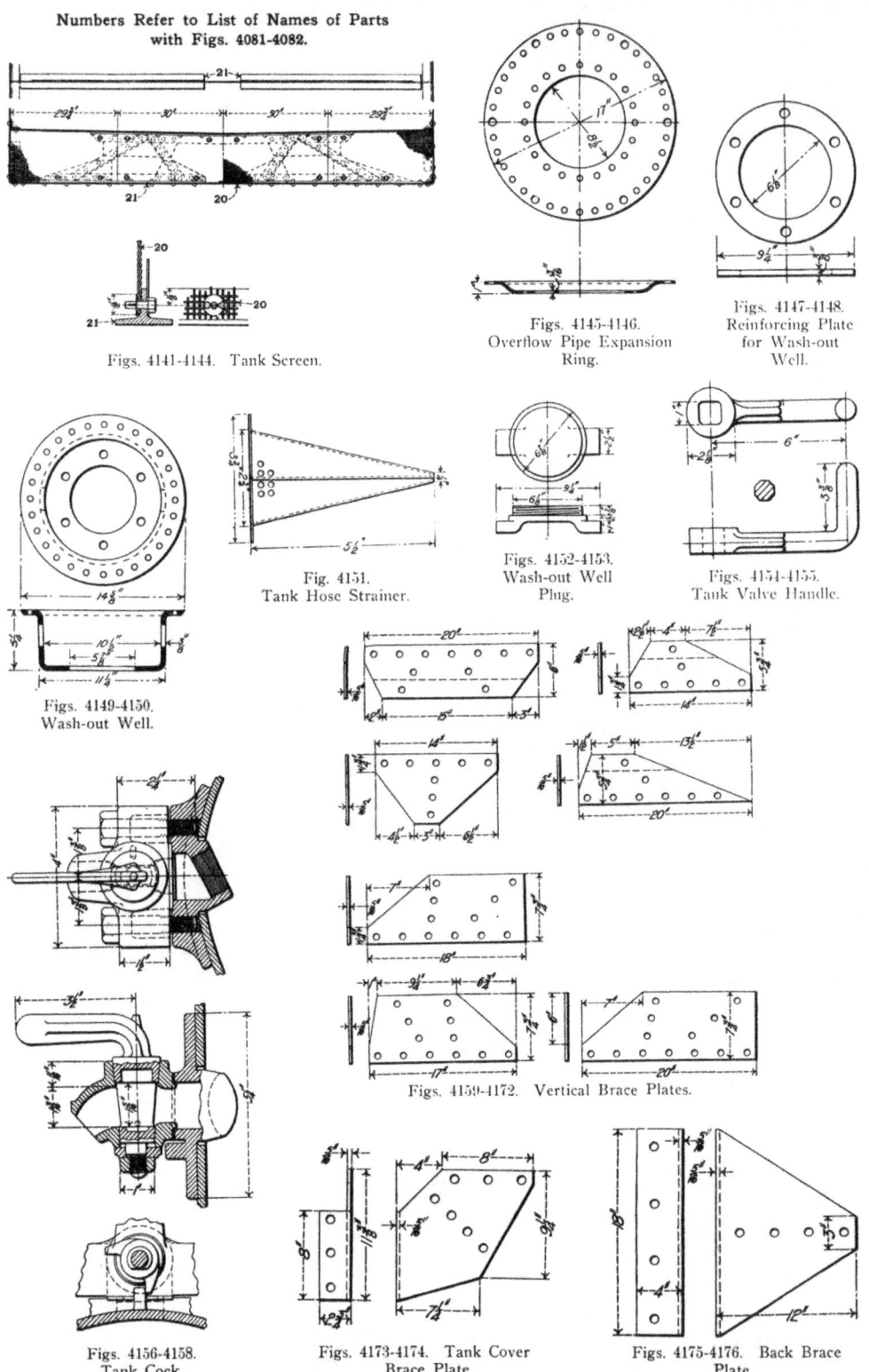

Figs. 4141-4176. Details of 5,500-Gallon Tender Tank for Atlantic (4—4—2) Locomotive. Pennsylvania Railroad.

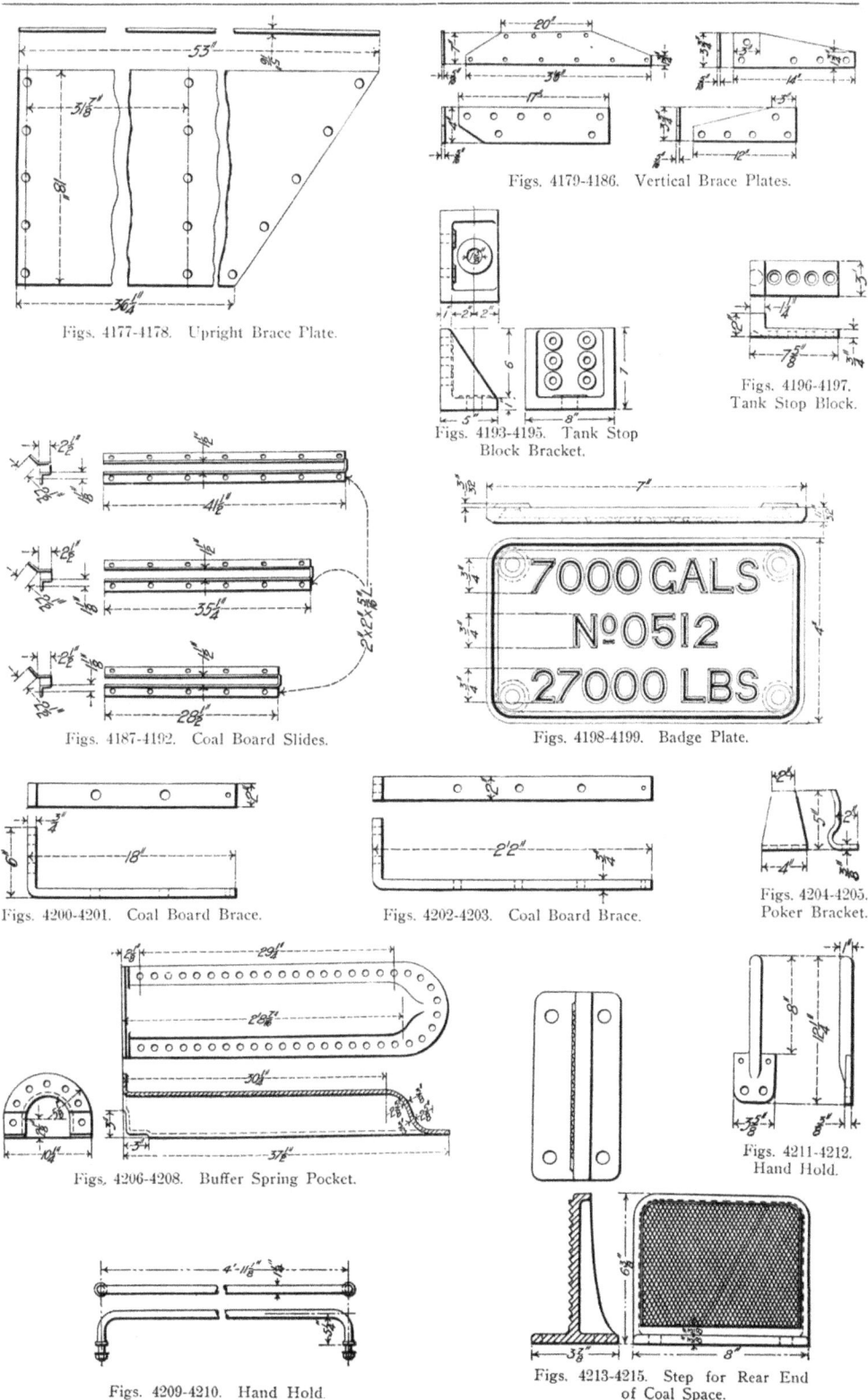

Figs. 4177–4178. Upright Brace Plate.
Figs. 4179–4186. Vertical Brace Plates.
Figs. 4193–4195. Tank Stop Block Bracket.
Figs. 4196–4197. Tank Stop Block.
Figs. 4187–4192. Coal Board Slides.
Figs. 4198–4199. Badge Plate.
Figs. 4200–4201. Coal Board Brace.
Figs. 4202–4203. Coal Board Brace.
Figs. 4204–4205. Poker Bracket.
Figs. 4206–4208. Buffer Spring Pocket.
Figs. 4211–4212. Hand Hold.
Figs. 4209–4210. Hand Hold.
Figs. 4213–4215. Step for Rear End of Coal Space.

Figs. 4177–4215. Details of 5,500-Gallon Tender Tank for Atlantic (4—4—2) Locomotive. Pennsylvania Railroad.

TENDERS, Tanks; Details. Figs. 4216-4226

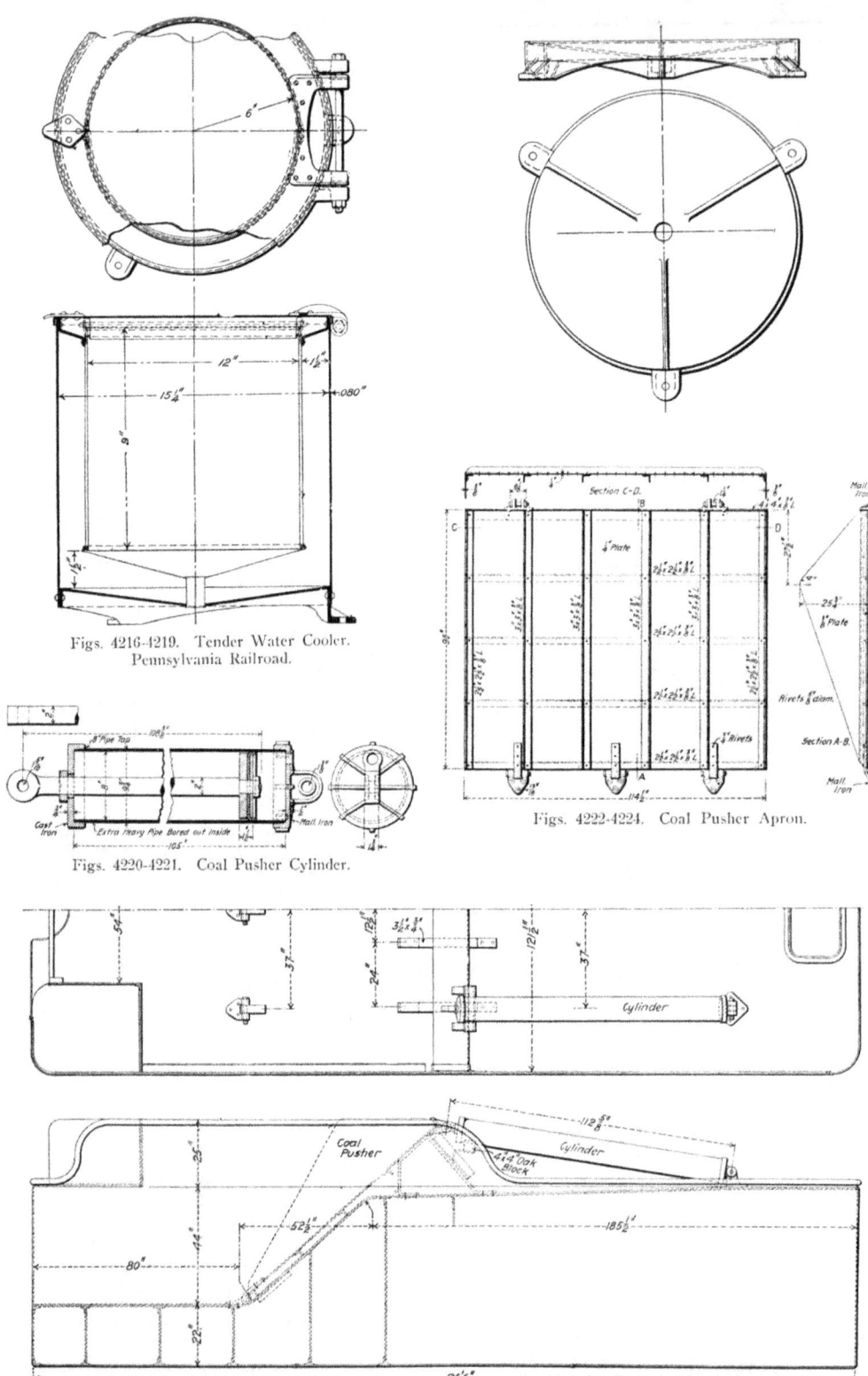

Figs. 4216-4219. Tender Water Cooler. Pennsylvania Railroad.

Figs. 4220-4221. Coal Pusher Cylinder.

Figs. 4222-4224. Coal Pusher Apron.

Figs. 4225-4226. Pneumatic Coal Pusher for Large Tenders. Atchison, Topeka & Santa Fe.

TENDERS, Water Scoops.

Numbers Refer to List of Names of Parts Below.

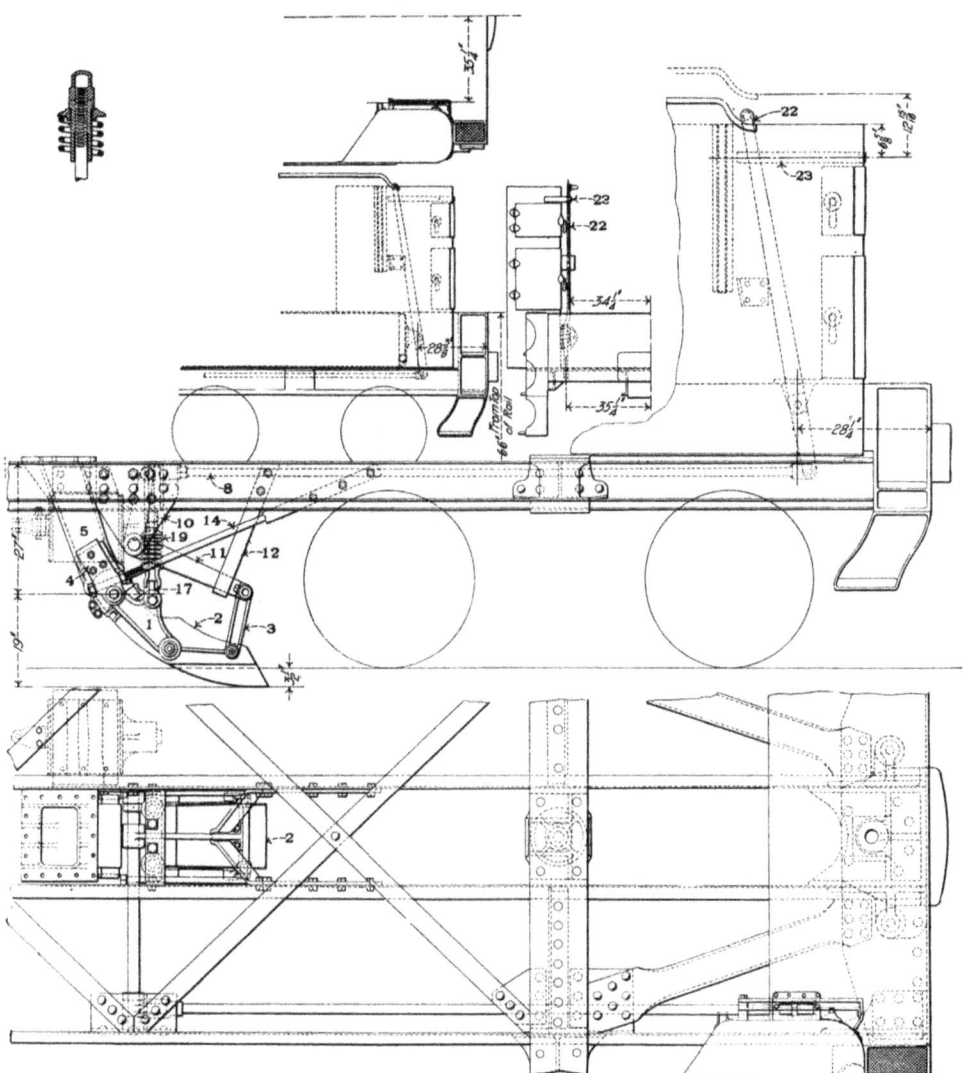

Figs. 4227-4232. Arrangement of Water Scoop on Tender of Atlantic (4—4—2) Locomotive. Pennsylvania Railroad.

Names of Parts of Water Scoops, Figs. 4227-4242.

1. Half Knuckle Joint with Arm or Cradle
2. Dipper
3. Dipper Link
4. Draft or Fulcrum Casting
5. External Scoop Pipe
6. Short Operating Crank Arm
7. Operating Shaft
8. Reach Rod
9. Reach Rod Jaw
10. Bearing for Operating Shaft
11. Long Operating Crank Arm
12. Crank Arm Guard
13. Bracket for Crank Arm Guard
14. Brace for External Scoop Pipe
15. Protection Shield
16. Protection Shield Brace
17. Spring Hanger
18. Yoke
19. Dipper Spring
20. Scoop Heater Pipe
21. Spring Hanger Cap
22. Operating Lever
23. Operating Lever Guide

Numbers Refer to List of Names of Parts with Figs. 4227-4232.

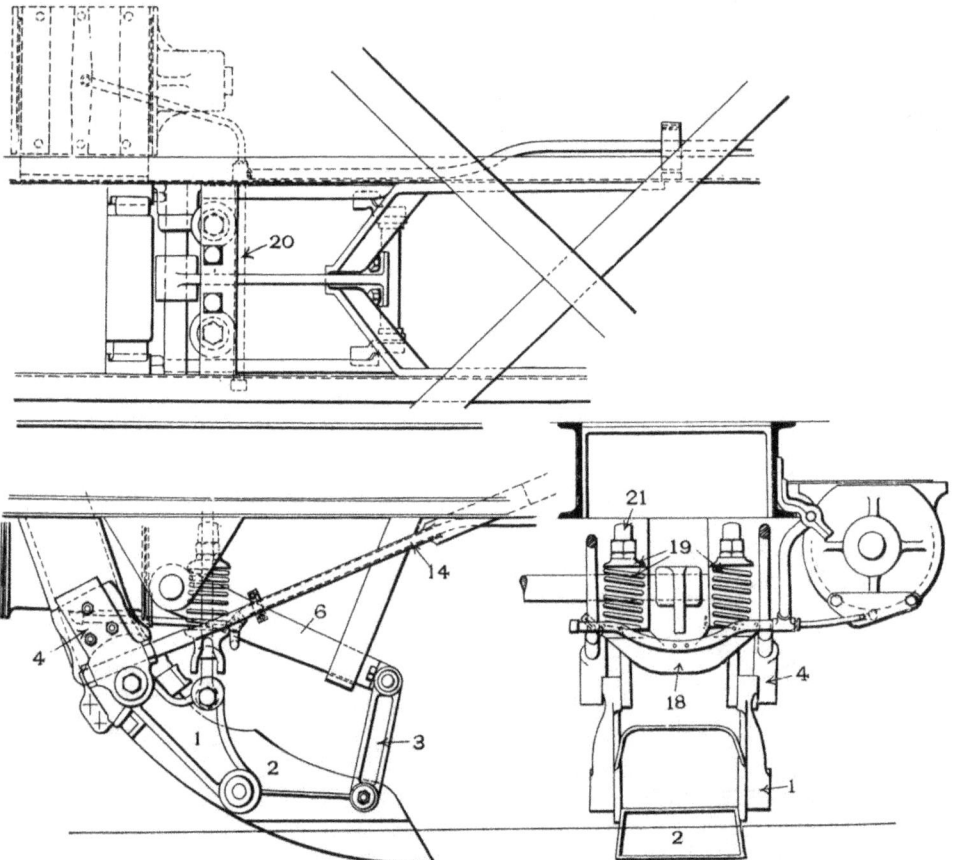

Figs. 4233-4235. Application of Heater Pipes to Water Scoop. Pennsylvania Railroad.

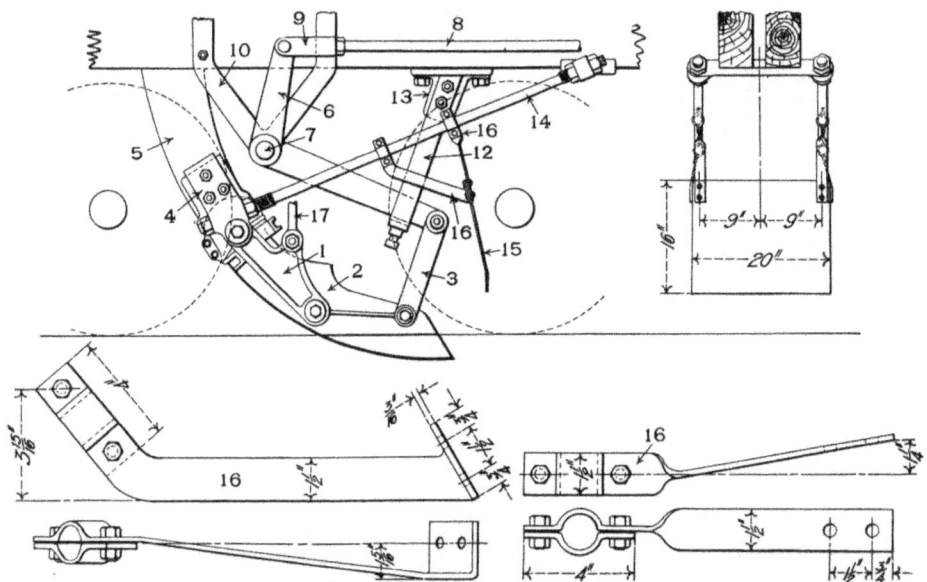

Figs. 4236-4241. Application of Protection Shield to Mouth of Water Scoop. Pennsylvania Railroad.

TENDERS, Water Scoops; Details.

Figs. 4242-4264

Numbers Refer to List of Names of Parts with Figs. 4227-4232.

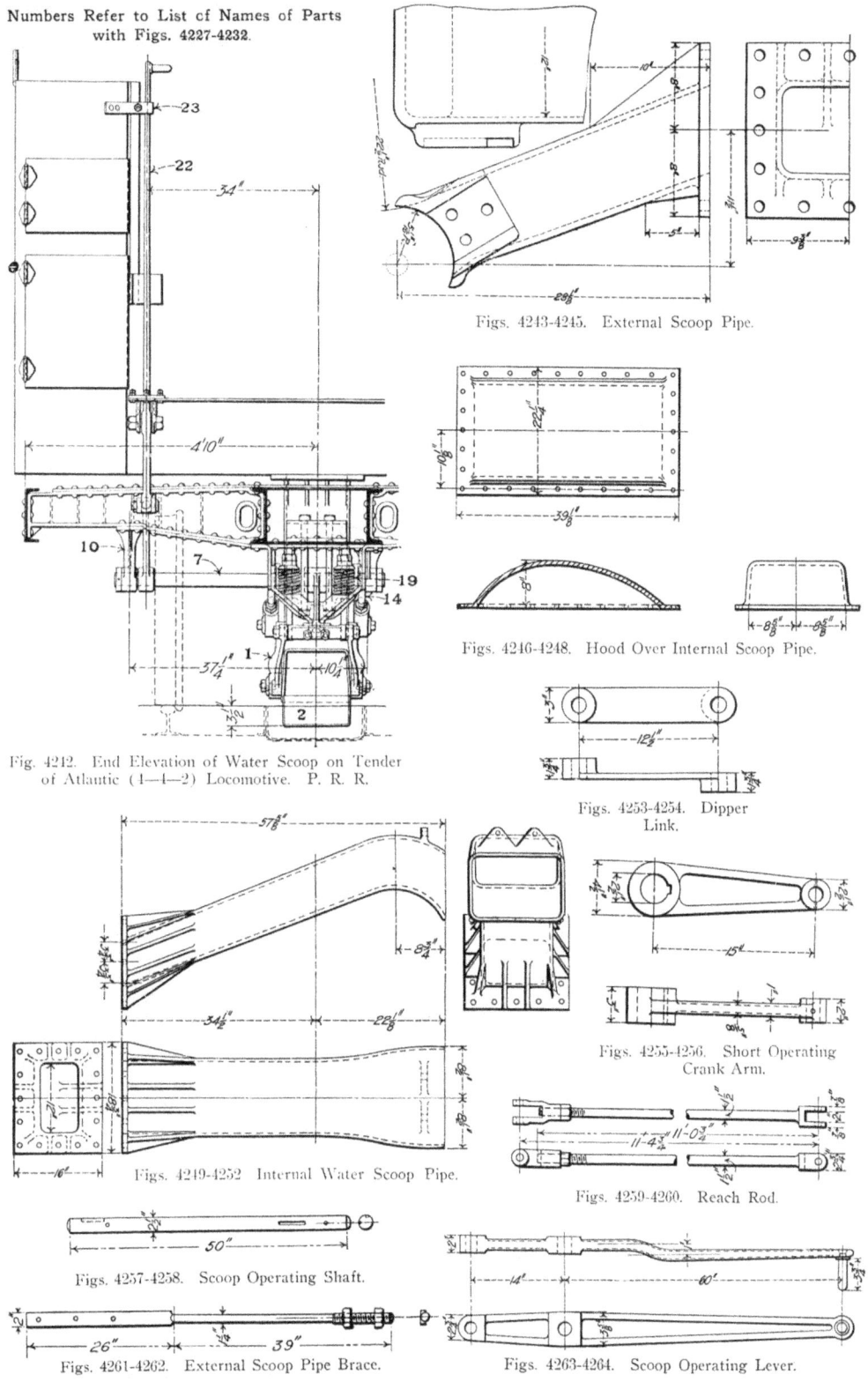

Fig. 4242. End Elevation of Water Scoop on Tender of Atlantic (4—4—2) Locomotive. P. R. R.

Figs. 4243-4245. External Scoop Pipe.

Figs. 4246-4248. Hood Over Internal Scoop Pipe.

Figs. 4249-4252. Internal Water Scoop Pipe.

Figs. 4253-4254. Dipper Link.

Figs. 4255-4256. Short Operating Crank Arm.

Figs. 4257-4258. Scoop Operating Shaft.

Figs. 4259-4260. Reach Rod.

Figs. 4261-4262. External Scoop Pipe Brace.

Figs. 4263-4264. Scoop Operating Lever.

Figs. 4243-4264. Details of Water Scoop on Tender of Atlantic (4—4—2) Locomotive. Pennsylvania Railroad.

(384)

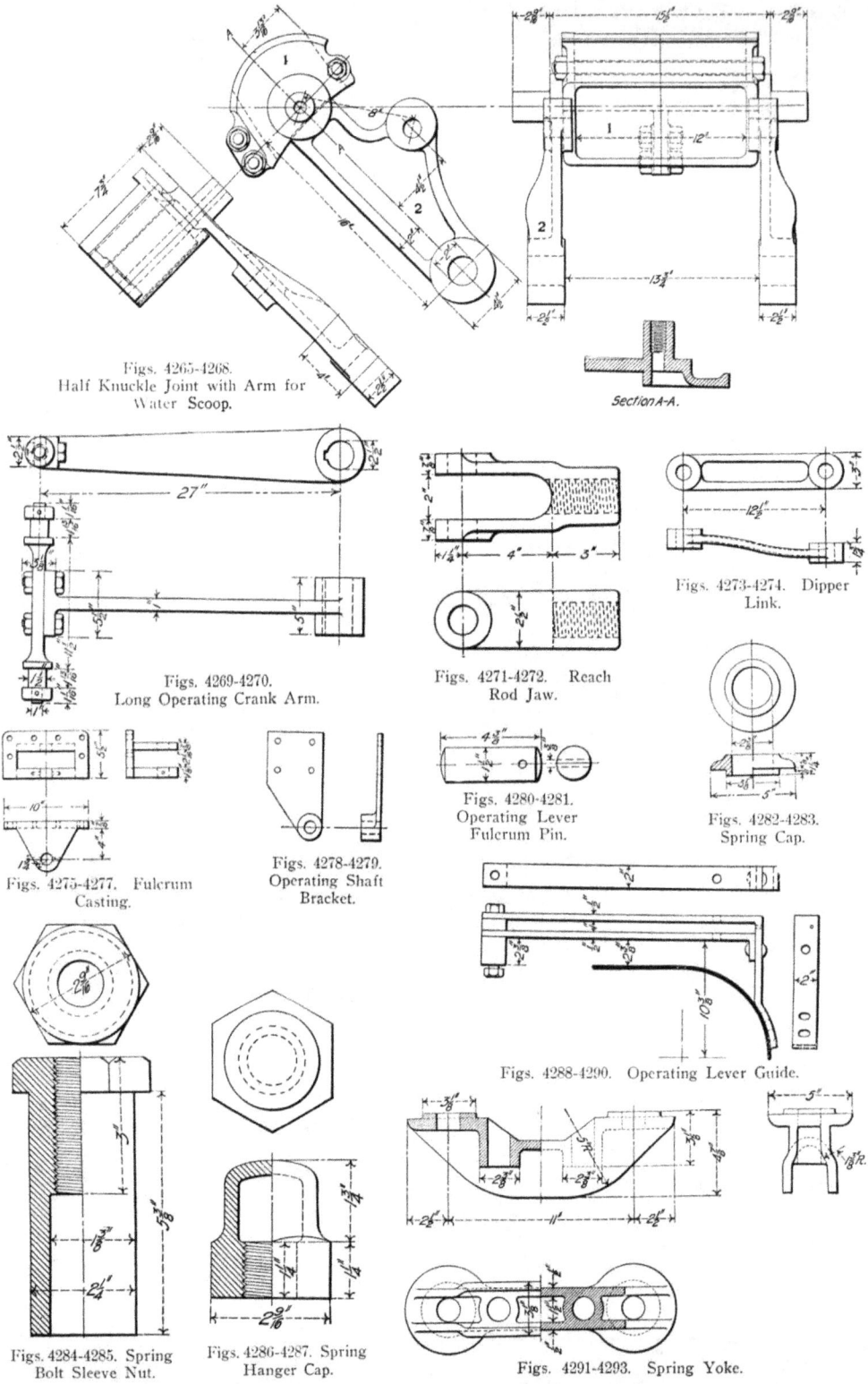

Figs. 4265-4268. Half Knuckle Joint with Arm for Water Scoop.

Figs. 4269-4270. Long Operating Crank Arm.

Figs. 4271-4272. Reach Rod Jaw.

Figs. 4273-4274. Dipper Link.

Figs. 4275-4277. Fulcrum Casting.

Figs. 4278-4279. Operating Shaft Bracket.

Figs. 4280-4281. Operating Lever Fulcrum Pin.

Figs. 4282-4283. Spring Cap.

Figs. 4288-4290. Operating Lever Guide.

Figs. 4284-4285. Spring Bolt Sleeve Nut.

Figs. 4286-4287. Spring Hanger Cap.

Figs. 4291-4293. Spring Yoke.

Figs. 4265-4293. Details of Water Scoop on Tender of Atlantic (4—4—2) Locomotive. Pennsylvania Railroad.

Figs. 4294-4314   TENDERS, Trucks.

Numbers Refer to List of Names of Parts on Opposite Page.

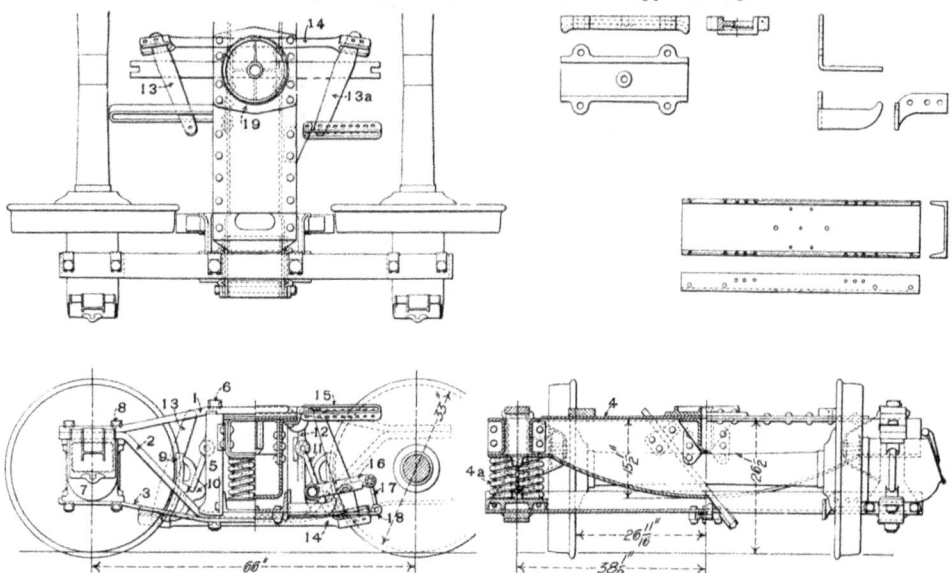

Figs. 4294-4305. Diamond Arch Bar Tender Truck with Pressed Steel Bolster. Pennsylvania Railroad.

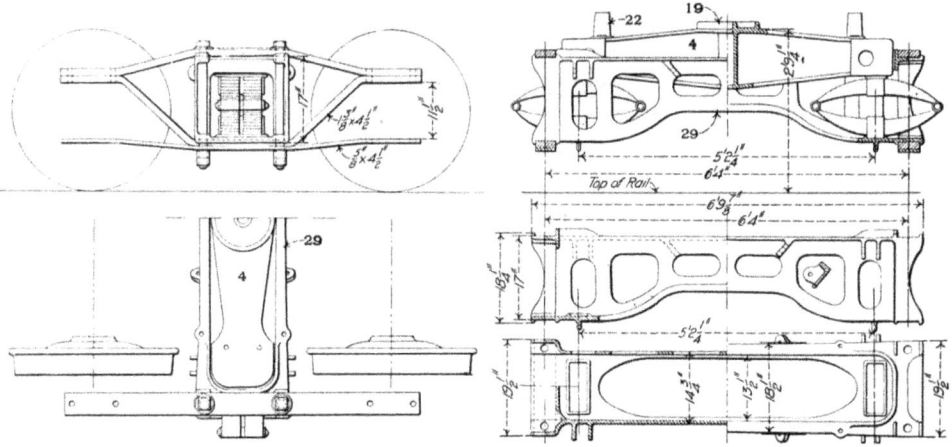

Figs. 4306-4310. S, H. & H. Diamond Arch Bar Tender Truck with Cast Steel Bolster and Transoms. American Steel Foundries.

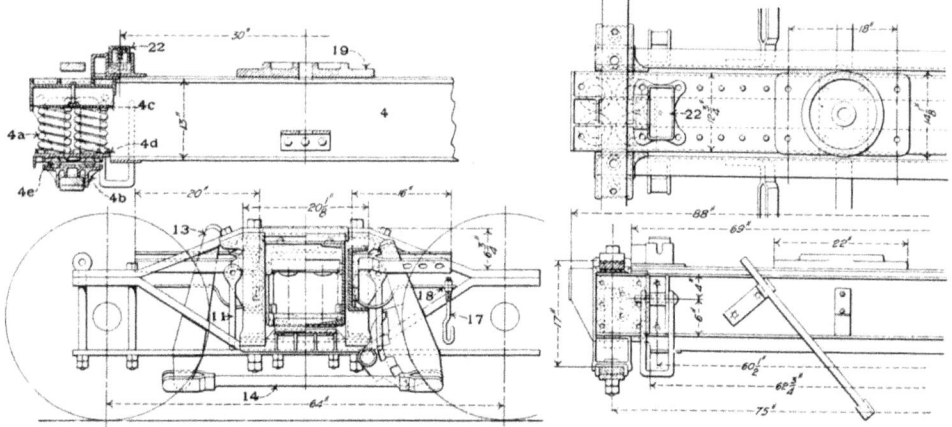

Figs. 4311-4314. Barber Tender Truck. Standard Car Truck Co.

TENDERS, Trucks.   Figs. 4315-4318

Numbers Refer to List of Names of Parts Below.

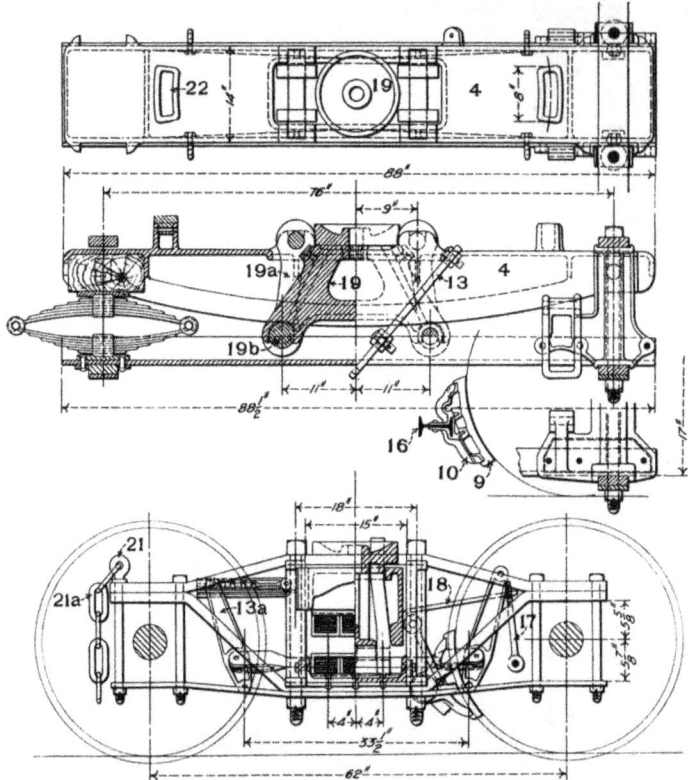

Figs. 4315-4318. Diamond Arch Bar Tender Truck with Swing Center and Cast-Steel Bolster. Baldwin Locomotive Works.

Names of Parts of Tender Trucks, Figs. 4294-4382.

1 Upper Arch Bar	8 Journal Box Bolt	19 Center Plate
2 Lower Arch Bar	9 Brake Shoe	19a Center Plate Hanger
2a Pedestal	9a Brake Shoe Key	19b Center Plate Hanger Pin
2b Pedestal Cross Tie	10 Brake Head	20 Spring Plank
2c Pedestal Liner	11 Brake Hanger	20a Spring Hanger
2d Pedestal Brace	11a Brake Hanger Pin	21 Check Chain Eye
3 Pedestal Tie Bar	12 Brake Hanger Bracket	21a Check Chain
4 Bolster	13 Live Brake Lever	22 Side Bearing
4a Bolster Spring	13a Dead Brake Lever	23 Equalizer
4b Bolster Compression Bar	13b Brake Lever Fulcrum Pin	24 Bolster Truss Rod
4c Bolster Spring Cap	14 Brake Lever Coupling Rod	25 Bolster Truss Rod Block
4d Bolster Spring Seat	15 Brake Lever Guide	26 Bolster Truss Rod Washer
4e Bolster Spring Roller	15a Brake Lever Guide Bracket	27 Frame
4f Roller Seat	15b Brake Lever Guide Bracket Pin	28 Flitch Plate
5 Column	16 Brake Beam	29 Transom
6 Column Bolt	17 Brake Beam Adjusting Hanger	29a Spring
7 Journal Box	18 Brake Beam Adjusting Hanger Carrier	30 Spring Support
7a Journal Box Spring		31 Column Guide
7b Journal Box Spring Cap	18a Brake Beam Safety Chain	32 Column Guide Bolt
7c Journal Box Spring Casing	18b Brake Beam Safety Chain Eye	

Numbers Refer to List of Names of Parts with Figs. 4315-4318.

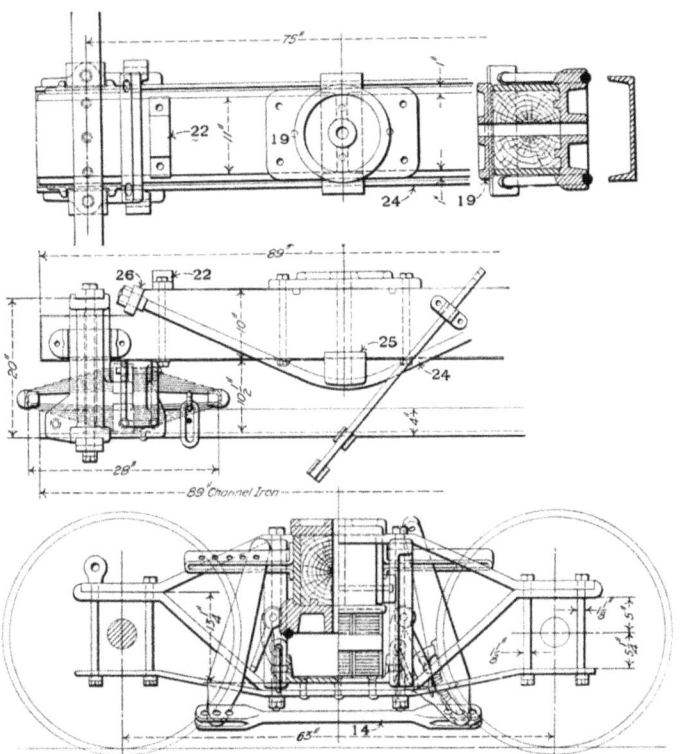

Figs. 4319-4323. Diamond Arch Bar Tender Truck with Trussed Wooden Bolster. Baldwin Locomotive Works.

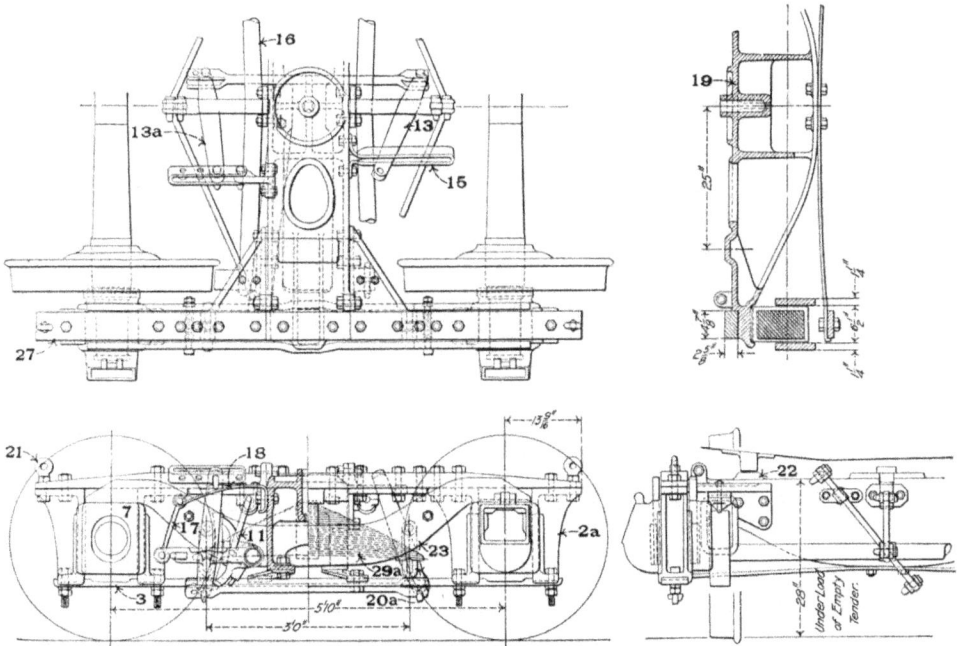

Figs. 4324-4327. Equalized Pedestal Truck for Tender of Atlantic (4—4—2) Locomotive. Pennsylvania Railroad.

TENDERS, Trucks. Figs. 4328-4333

Numbers Refer to List of Names of Parts with Figs. 4315-4318.

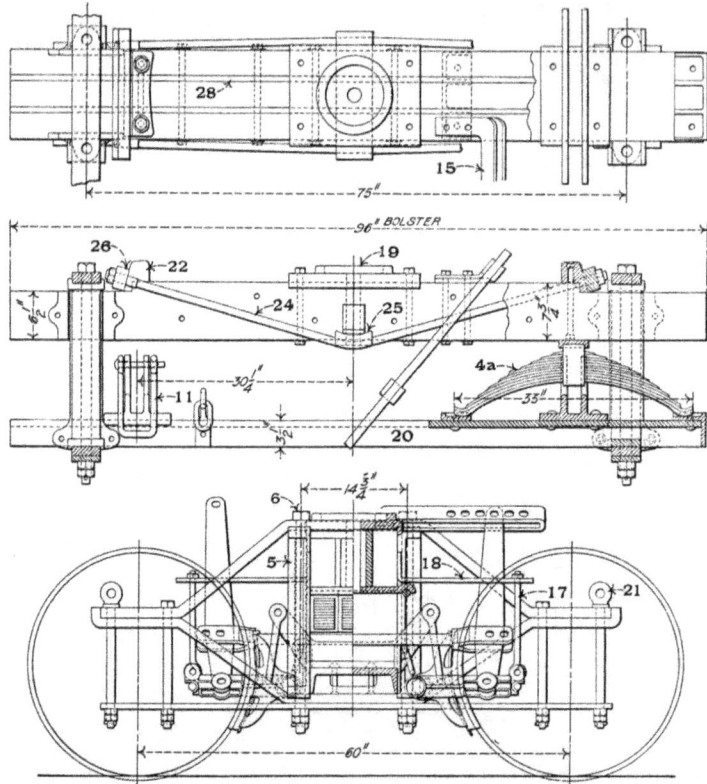

Figs. 4328-4330. Diamond Arch Bar Tender Truck, with Flitch Plate Bolster and Inverted Semi-Elliptical Springs. Baldwin Locomotive Works.

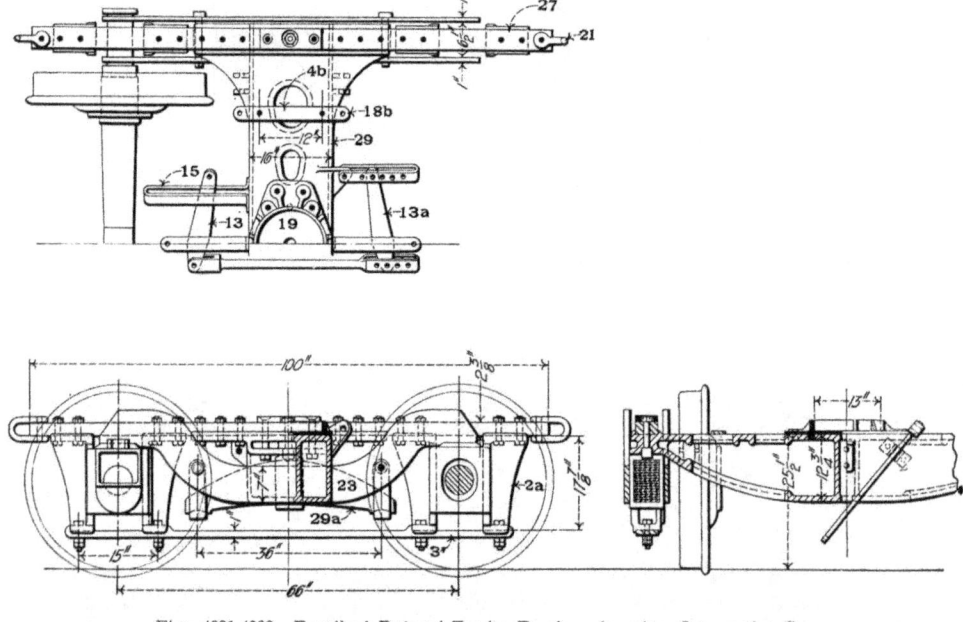

Figs. 4331-4333. Equalized Pedestal Tender Truck. American Locomotive Co.

(389)

TENDERS, Trucks.

Numbers Refer to List of Names of Parts with Figs. 4315-4318.

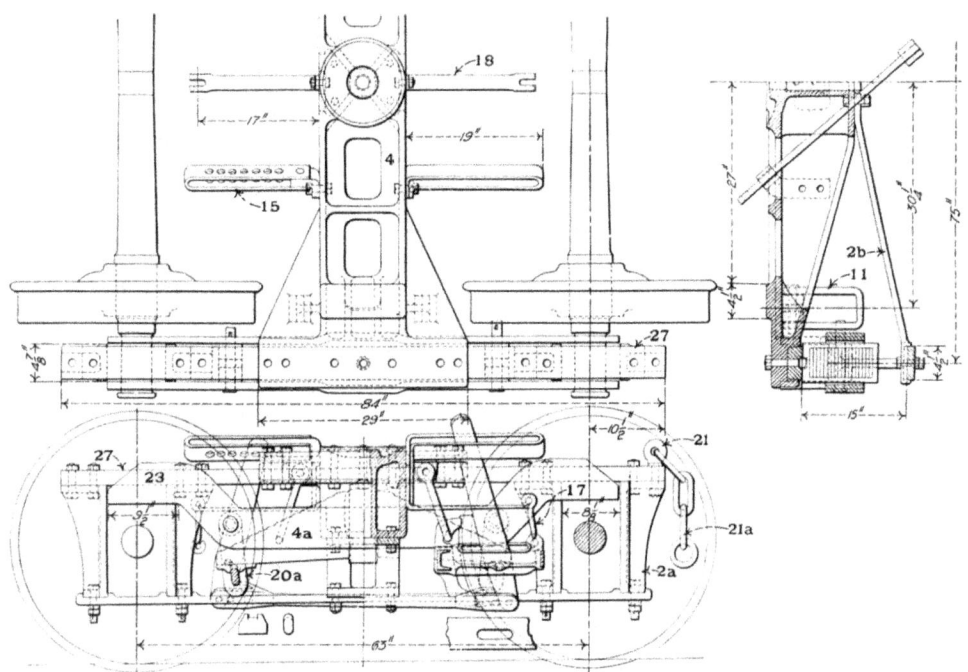

Figs. 4334-4336. Equalized Pedestal Tender Truck with Cast-Steel Bolster. Baldwin Locomotive Works.

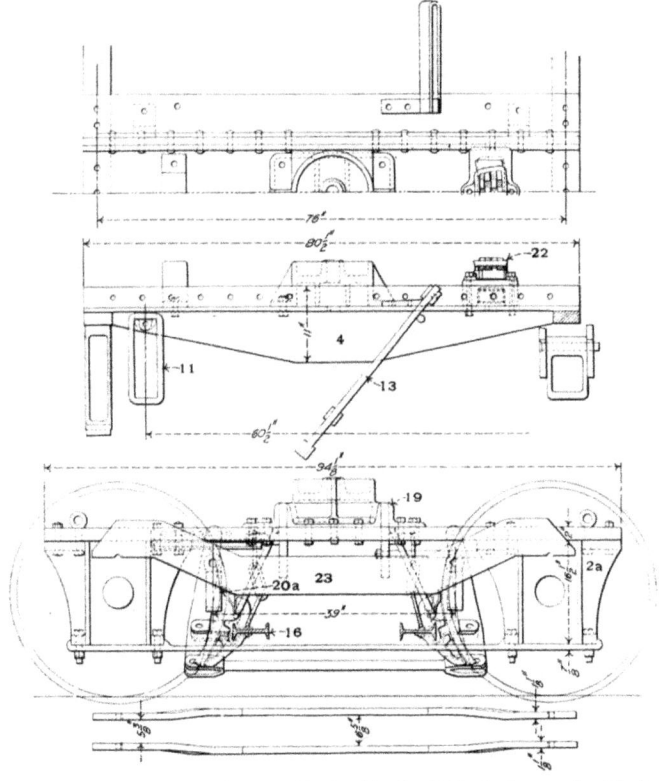

Figs. 4337-4341. Equalizer Pedestal Tender Truck. Baldwin Locomotive Works.

TENDERS, Trucks.

Figs. 4342-4348

Numbers Refer to List of Names of Parts with Figs. 4315-4318.

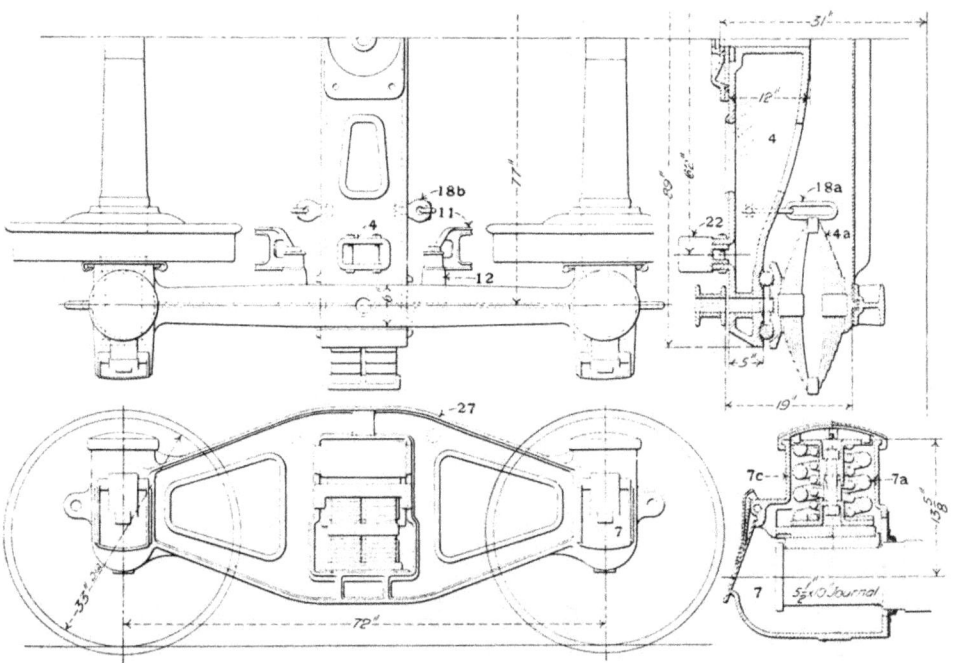

Figs. 4342-4345. Bettendorf Cast-Steel Tender Truck. Bettendorf Axle Co.

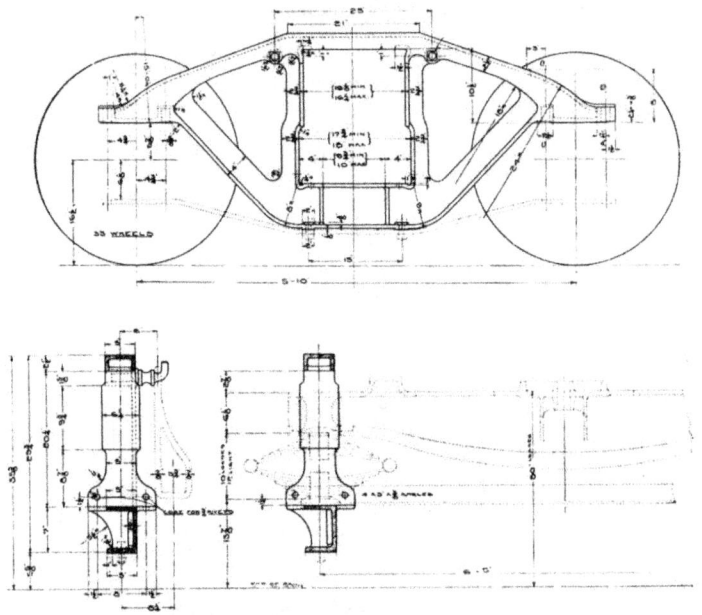

Figs. 4346-4348. Andrews Cast-Steel Truck Side Frame. American Steel Foundries.

Figs. 4349-4354 — TENDERS, Trucks.

Numbers Refer to List of Names of Parts with Figs. 4315-4318.

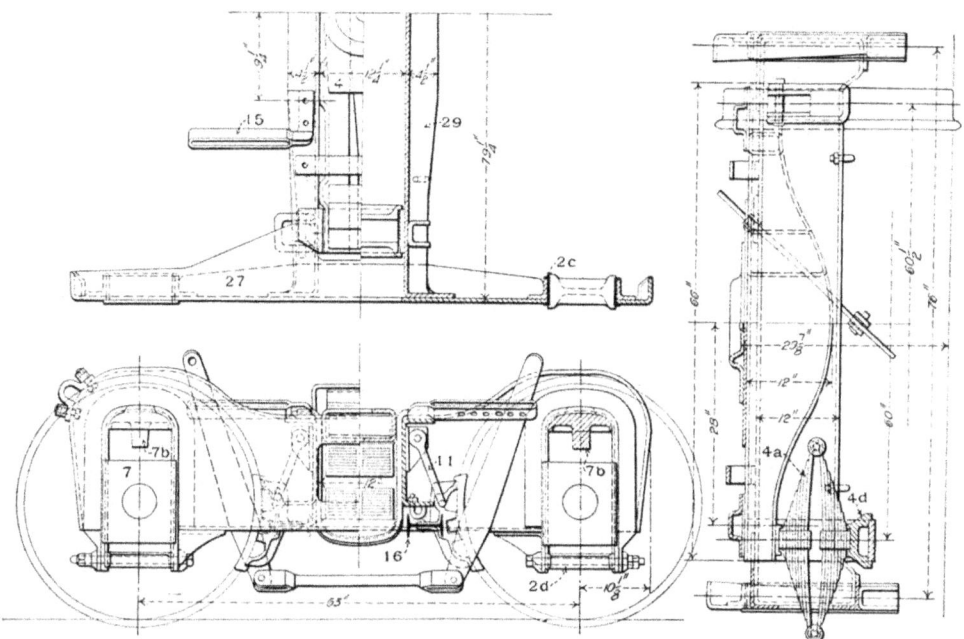

Figs. 4349-4351. Fox Pressed Steel Tender Truck. Pressed Steel Car Co.

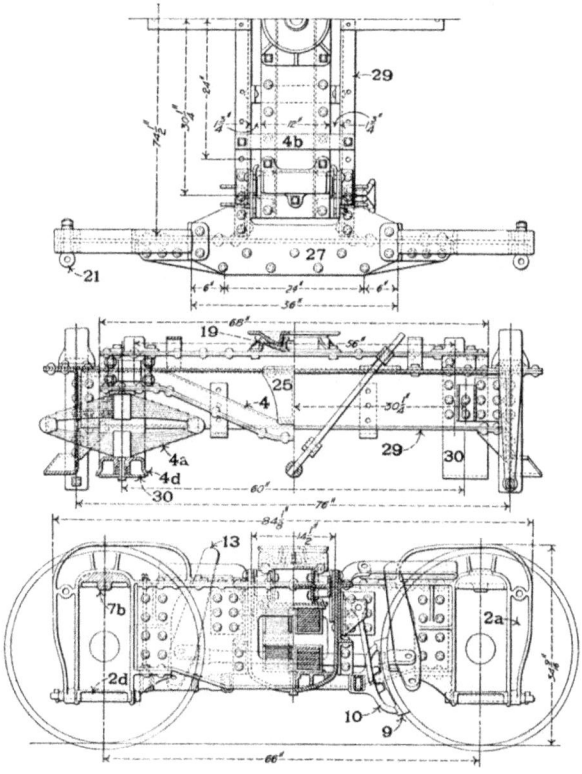

Figs. 4352-4354. Pedestal Tender Truck. Standard Steel Car Co.

TENDERS, Trucks; Details. Figs. 4355-4398

Numbers Refer to List of Names of Parts with Figs. 4315-4318.

Figs. 4355-4382. Wrought Iron Details of Diamond Arch Bar Tender Truck.

Figs. 4383-4384. Cast-Steel Center Plate Support for Pressed Steel Bolster.

Figs. 4385-4387. Combined Column Casting and Brake Hanger Carrier.

Figs. 4388-4390. Channel Spring Plank.

Figs. 4391-4393. Dead Lever Fulcrum Bracket.

Figs. 4394-4396. Brake Beam Adjusting Hanger Carrier Bracket.

Figs. 4397-4398. Bolster Chafing Plate.

Figs. 4355-4398. Details of Diamond Arch Bar Tender Truck Shown in Figs. 4294-4305. Pennsylvania Railroad.

(393)

Figs. 4399-4412 — TENDERS, Truck Details; Bolsters.

Numbers Refer to List of Names of Parts Below.

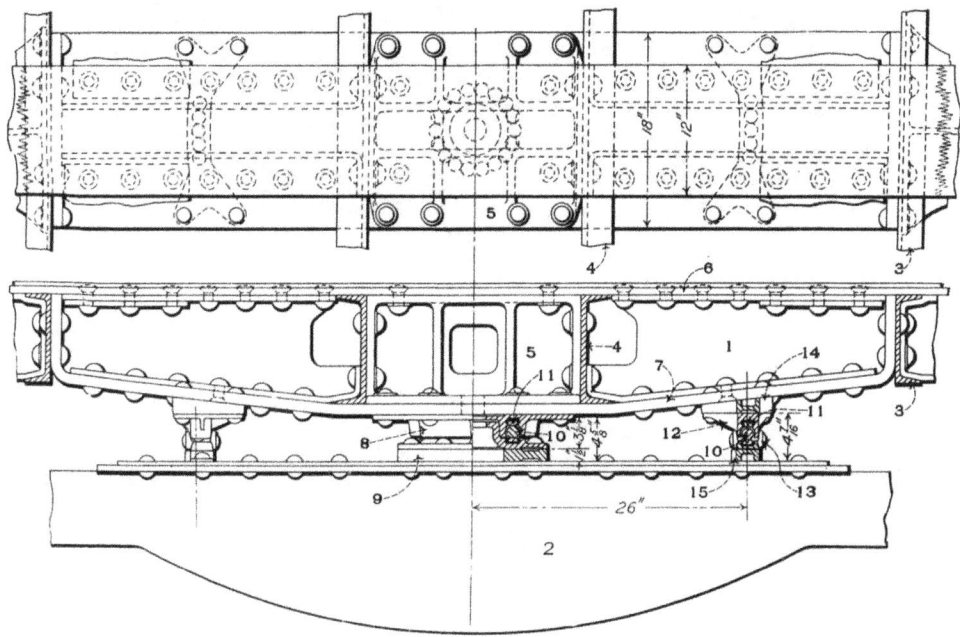

Figs. 4399-4400. Body and Truck Bolster for Tender Truck of Atlantic (4—4—2) Locomotive. Pennsylvania Railroad.

Names of Parts of Bolsters, Figs. 4399-4412.

1. Body Bolster
2. Truck Bolster
3. Side Sill
4. Center Sill
5. Body Bolster Center Casting
6. Top Plate of Body Bolster
7. Bottom Plate of Body Bolster
8. Body Center Plate
9. Truck Center Plate
10. Ball Bearing
11. Ball Runway
12. Body Side Bearing
13. Truck Side Bearing
14. Body Side Bearing Seat
15. Truck Side Bearing Seat
16. Same as 8
17. Same as 13
18. Column Guide

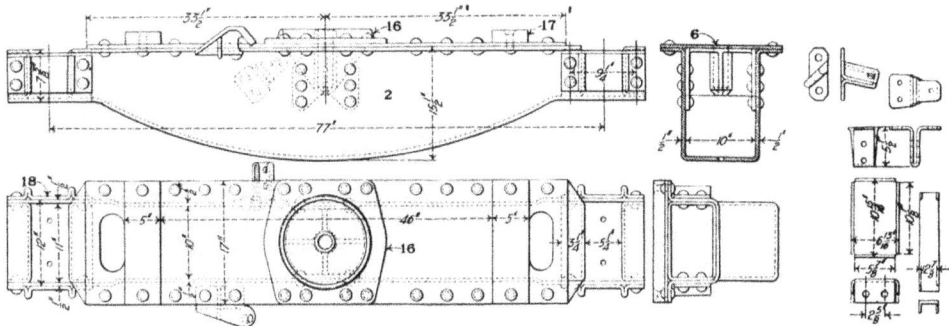

Figs. 4401-4412. Pressed Steel Truck Bolster for Tender Truck of Atlantic (4—4—2) Locomotive. Pennsylvania Railroad.

(394)

TENDERS, Truck Details; Bolsters.

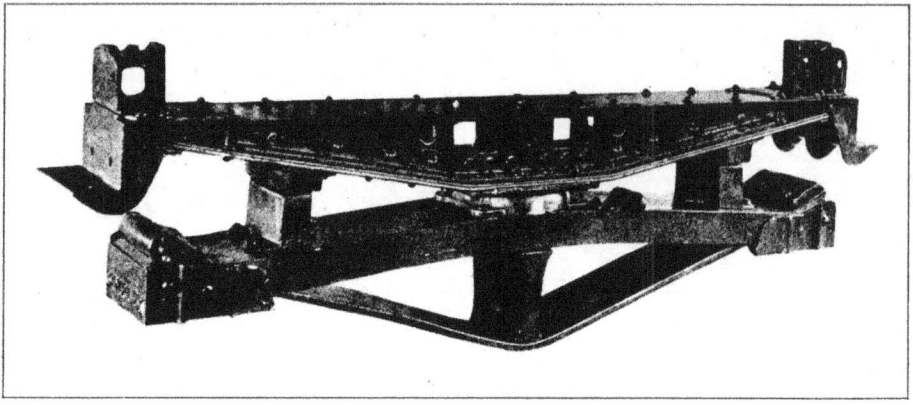

Fig. 4413. Simplex Body and Truck Bolster with Solid Side Bearings. Simplex Railway Appliance Co.

Fig. 4414. Simplex Body Bolster with Plate Web. Simplex Railway Appliance Co.

Fig. 4415. Simplex Truck Bolster. Simplex Railway Appliance Co.

Fig. 4416. Simplex Body and Truck Bearings with Susemihl Side Bearings. Simplex Railway Appliance Co.

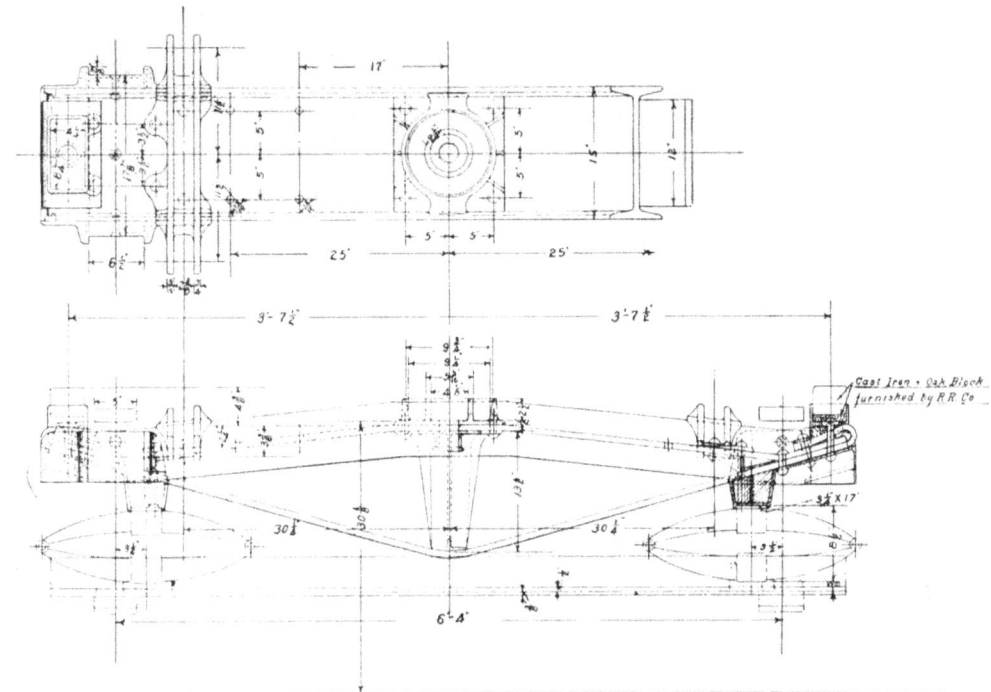

Figs. 4417-4418. Simplex I-Beam Truck Bolster. Simplex Railway Appliance Co.

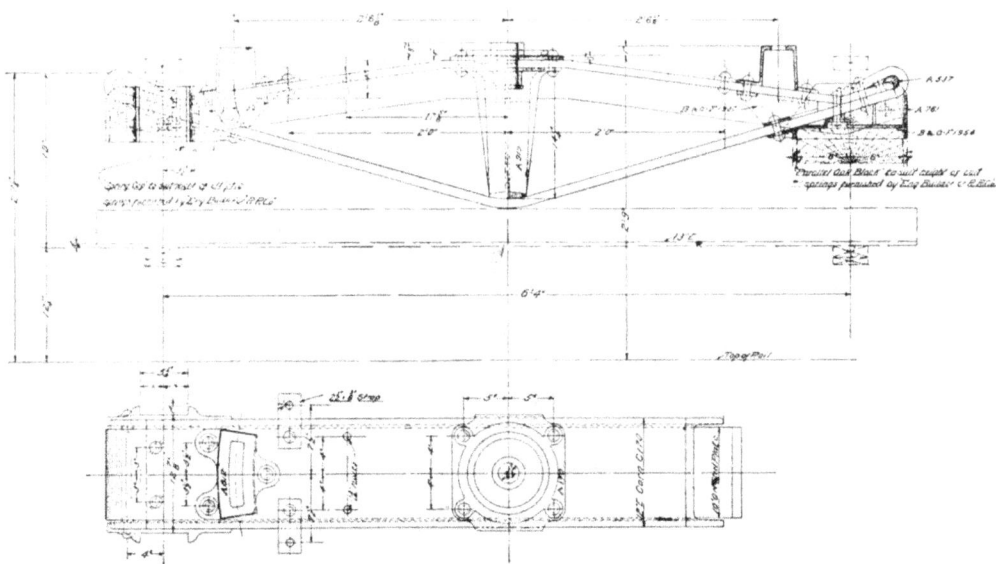

Figs. 4419-4420. Simplex Channel Truck Bolster. Simplex Railway Appliance Co.

Fig. 4421. Cast-Steel Truck Bolster, Box Section. American Steel Foundries.

TENDERS, Truck Details; Bolsters. Figs. 4422-4428

Fig. 4422. Cast-Steel Truck Bolster. Benjamin Atha & Co.

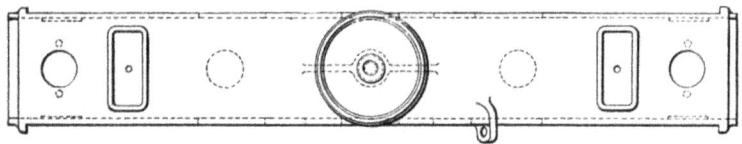

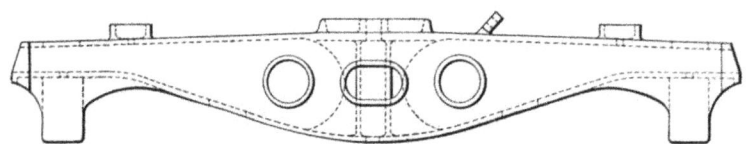

Figs. 4423-4424. Cast-Steel Truck Bolster for Tenders. Benjamin Atha & Co.

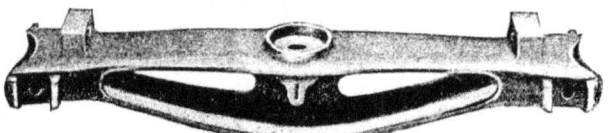

Fig. 4425. Commonwealth Cast-Steel Truck Bolster. Commonwealth Steel Co.

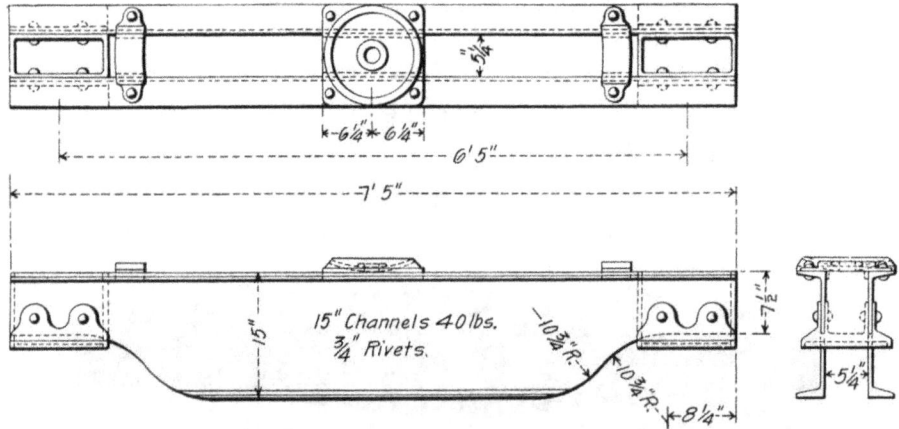

Figs. 4426-4428. Twin Channel Truck Bolster. Vanderbilt Patent.

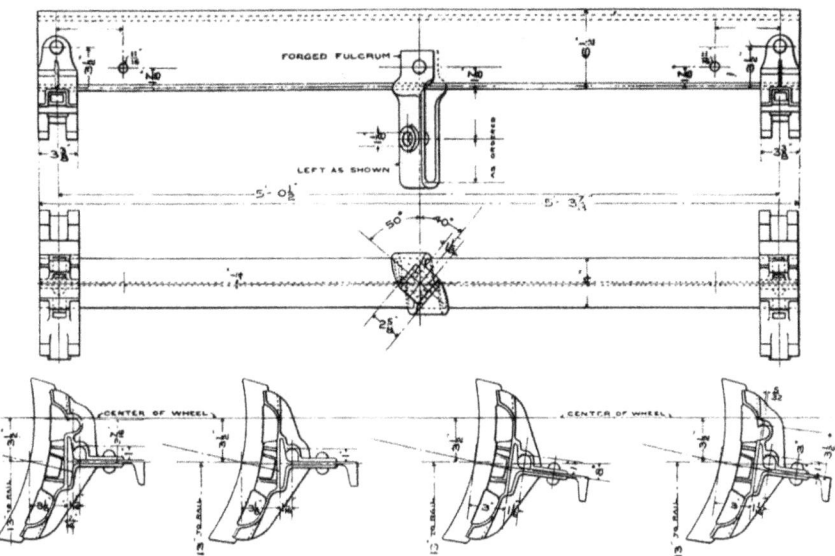

Figs. 4429-4434. Buffalo Special Brake Beam for Tenders. Buffalo Brake Beam Co.

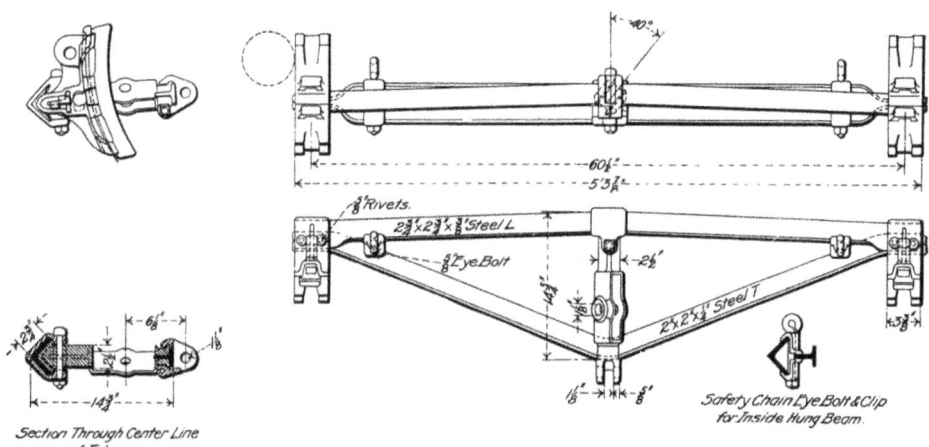

Figs. 4435-4438. Waycott Brake Beam. Damascus Brake Beam Co.

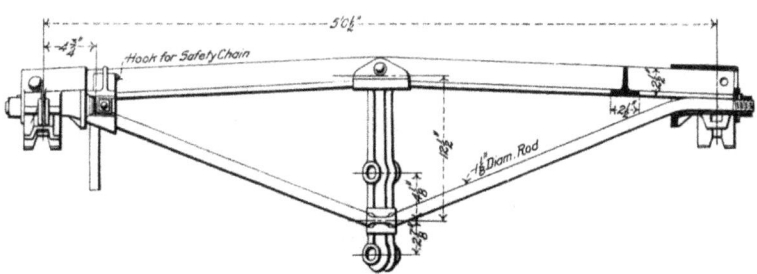

Fig. 4439. T-Iron Brake Beam. Standard Railway Equipment Co.

TENDERS, Truck Details; Brake Beams. Figs. 4440-4444

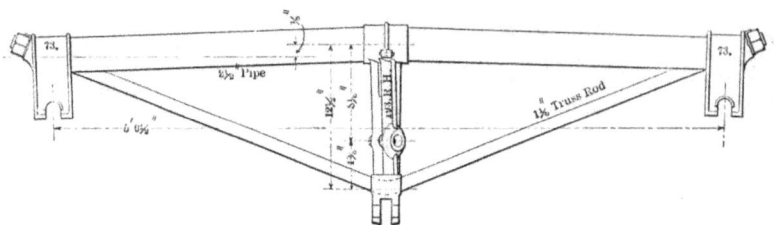

Fig. 4440. Special 2½-Inch National Hollow Brake Beam with Rigid Heads. Chicago Railway Equipment Co.

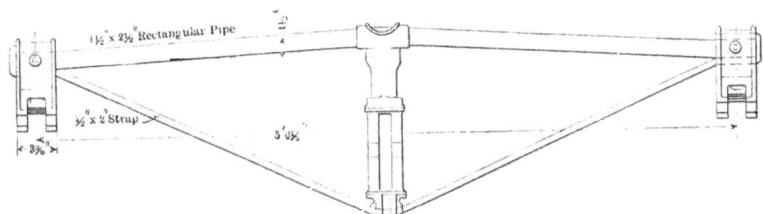

Fig. 4441. Kewanee Tender Brake Beam with Reversible Struts. Chicago Railway Equipment Co.

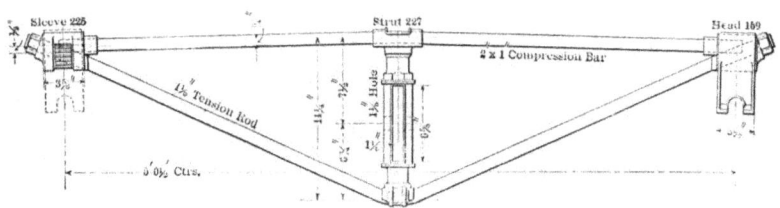

Fig. 4442. "Diamond" Adjustable Brake Beam. Chicago Railway Equipment Co.

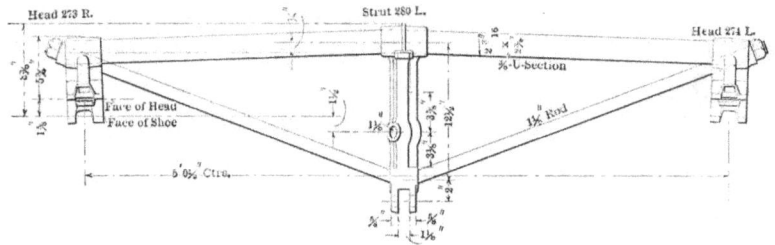

Fig. 4443. "Creco" Heavy Brake Beam. Chicago Railway Equipment Co.

Fig. 4444. 3-Inch Channel Trussed Brake Beam. Simplex Railway Appliance Co.

Figs. 4445-4449   TENDERS, Truck Details; Brake Beams.

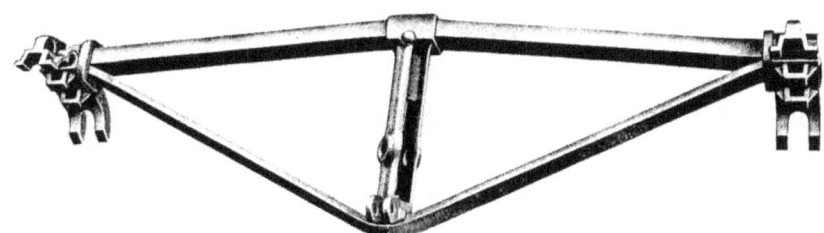

Fig. 4445. Trussed Brake Beam. Simplex Railway Appliance Co.

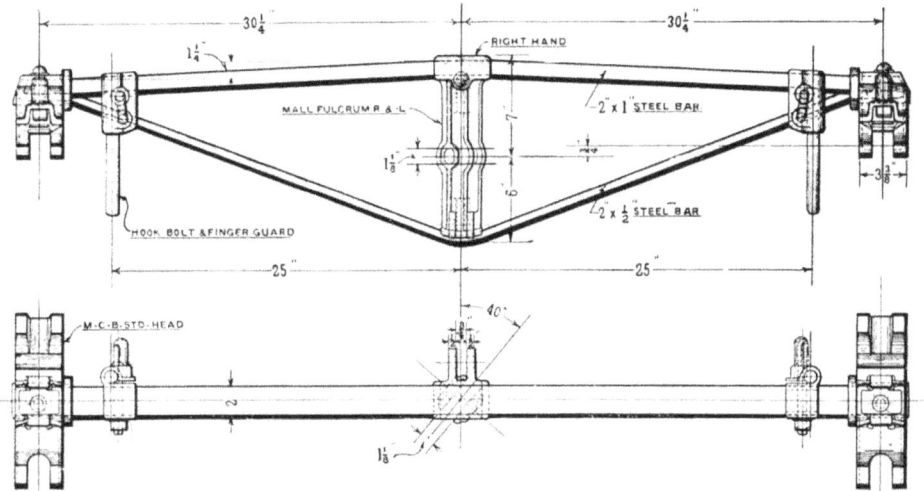

Figs. 4446-4447. Trussed Brake Beam. Simplex Railway Appliance Co.

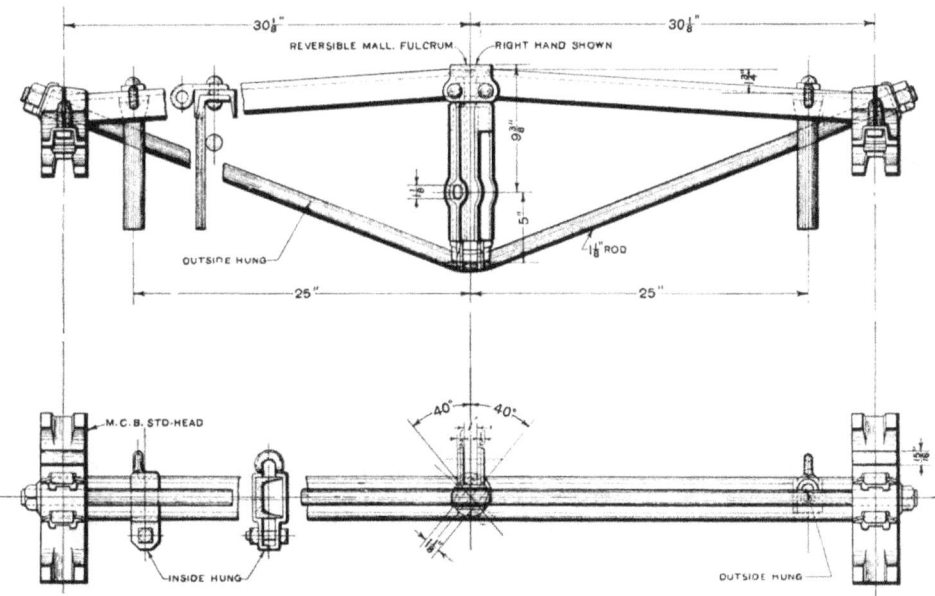

Figs. 4448-4449. Trussed Channel Brake Beam. Simplex Railway Appliance Co.

TENDERS, Truck Details; Brake Beams.   Figs. 4450-4454

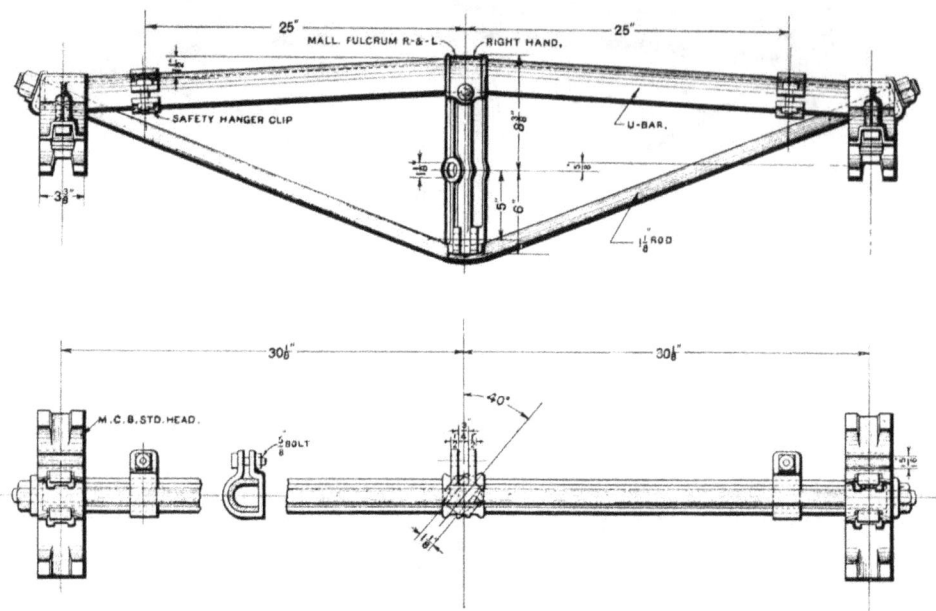

Figs. 4450-4451. Trussed U-Section Brake Beam. Simplex Railway Appliance Co.

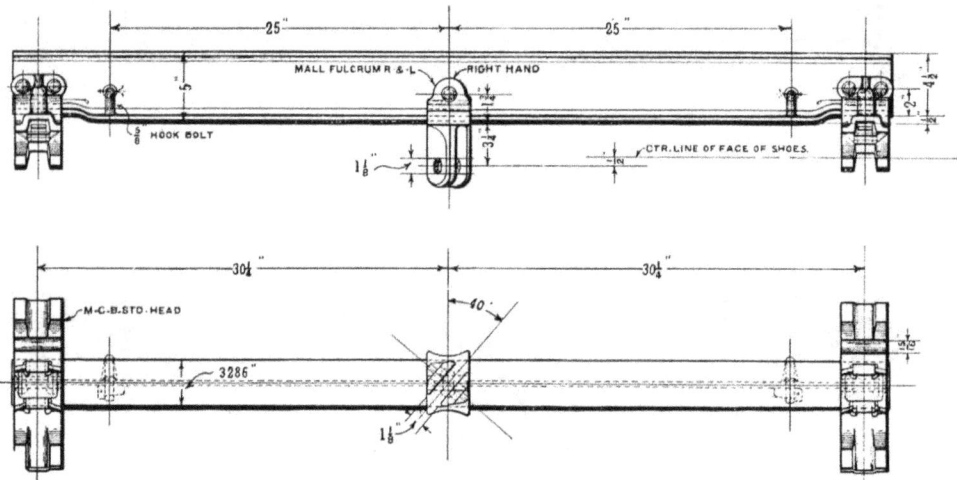

Figs. 4452-4453. 5-Inch I-Beam Brake Beam with Compressed Ends. Simplex Railway Appliance Co.

Fig. 4454. 5-Inch, 12¼-lb., I-Beam Brake Beam, Inside Hung. Simplex Railway Appliance Co.

Fig. 4455. 6-Inch, 12¼-lb., I-Beam Brake Beam, Outside Hung. Simplex Railway Appliance Co.

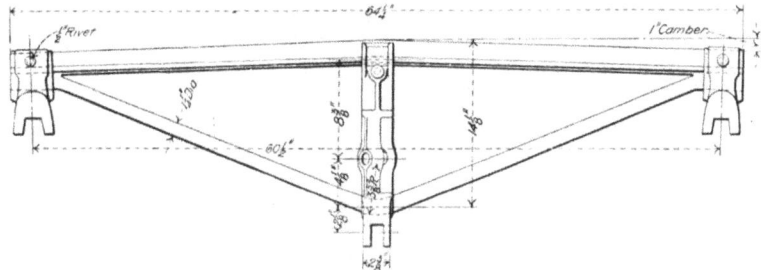

Fig. 4456. Davis Solid Truss Brake Beam. Davis Pressed Steel Co.

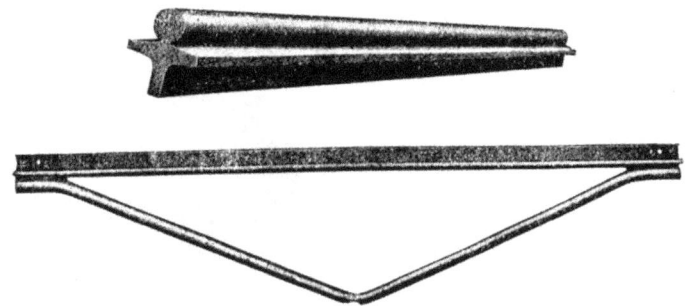

Figs. 4457-4458. Section for Davis Solid Truss Brake Beam and Finished Truss. Davis Pressed Steel Co.

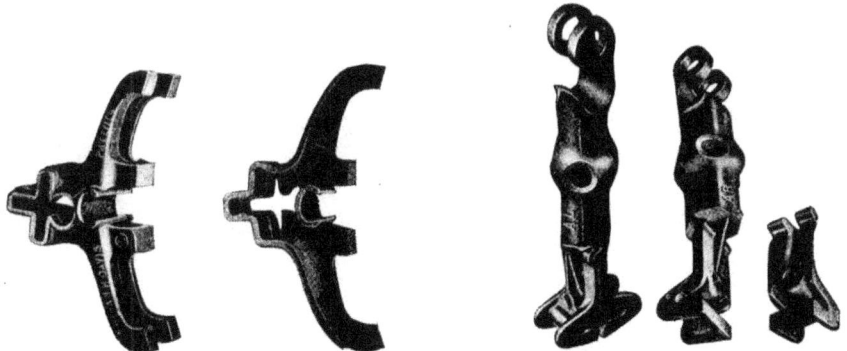

Figs. 4459-4460. Davis Brake Beam Heads.   Figs. 4461-4463. Davis Brake Beam Struts.
Davis Pressed Steel Co.

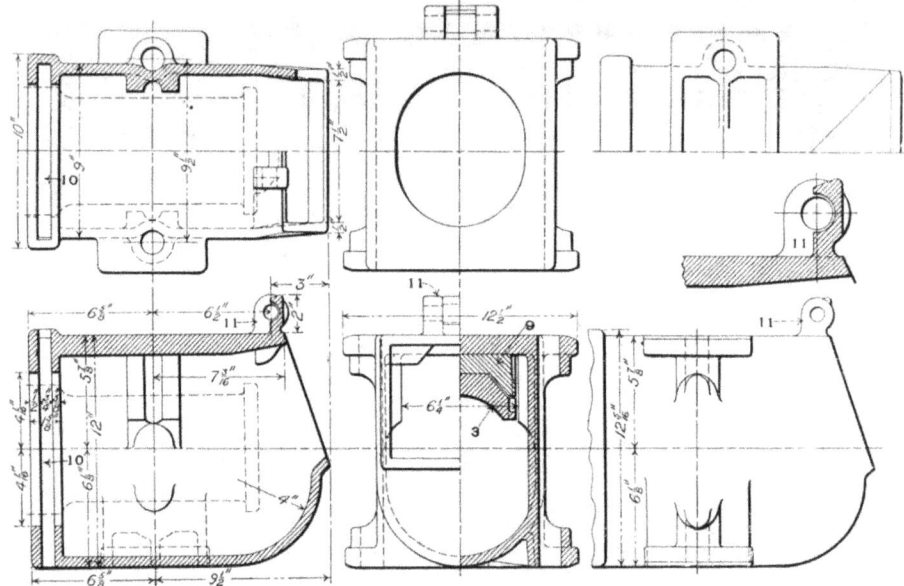

Figs. 4464-4470. Journal Box for 5½-Inch x 10-Inch Journals. Pennsylvania Railroad.

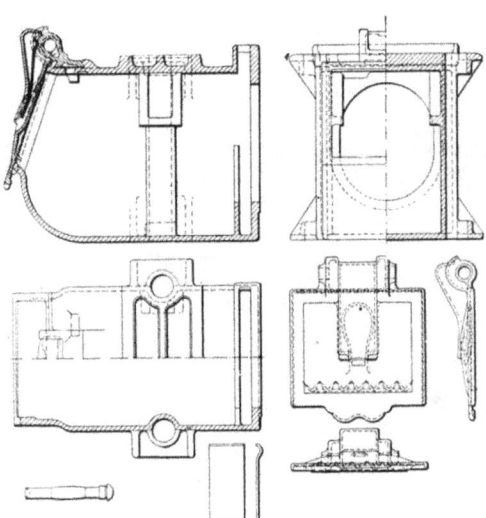

Figs. 4471-4479. National Journal Box for Arch Bar Truck.
National Malleable Castings Co.

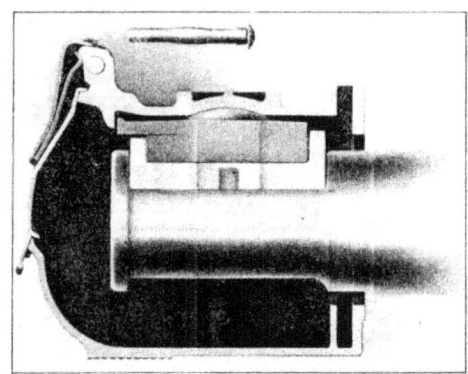

Fig. 4483. National Equalizing Wedge.

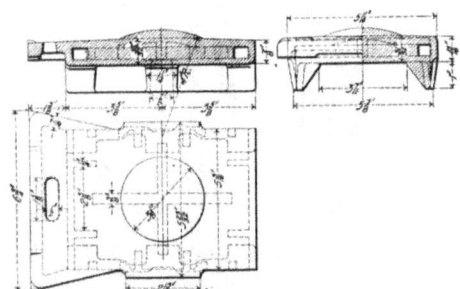

Figs. 4480-4482. National Journal Box Equalizing Wedge for Journals 5 in. x 9 in.
National Malleable Castings Co.

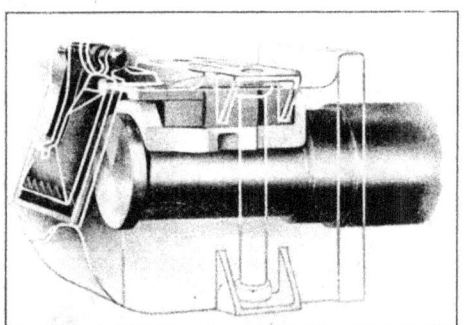

Fig. 4484. National Journal Box and Equalizing Wedge.
National Malleable Castings Co.

Figs. 4485-4489　　TENDERS, Truck Details; Journal Boxes.

Fig. 4485. Gould Journal Box with Inset Lid and Dust Guard, Type M-P, for Diamond Arch Bar Trucks.

Fig. 4486. Gould Journal Box with Inset Lid and Dust Guard, Type M-O, for Pedestal Trucks.

Gould Coupler Co.

Fig. 4487. McCord Journal Box with Coil Spring Lid and Outside Dust Guard.

Fig. 4488. McCord Journal Box with Coil Spring Lid and Inside Dust Guard.

Fig. 4489. McCord Journal Box and Outside Dust Guard, Removed.
McCord & Co.

TENDERS, Truck Details; Journal Boxes. Figs. 4490-4506

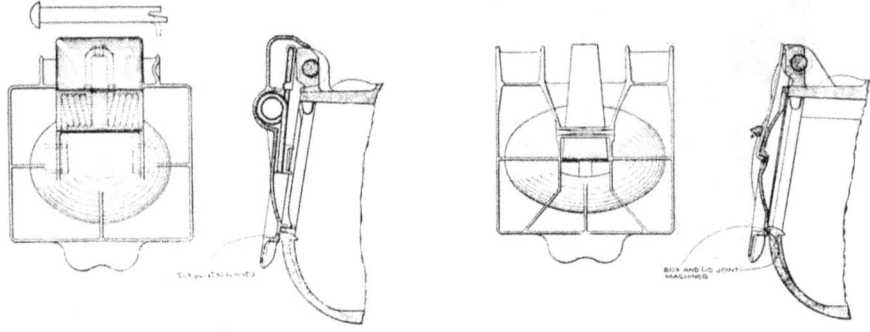

Figs. 4490-4491. Symington M. C. B. Journal Box Lid with Torsion Spring.

Figs. 4492-4493. Symington M. C. B. Journal Box Lid with Flat Spring.

T. H. Symington Co.

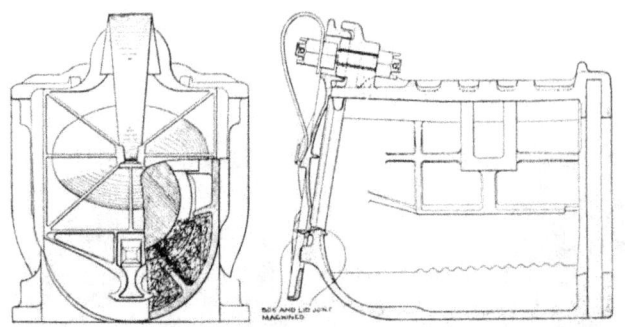

Figs. 4494-4495. Symington Journal Box with Pivot Lid and Central Spring Pressure. T. H. Symington Co.

Fig. 4496. "A. B. C." Journal Bearing and Wedge. Atlantic Brass Co.

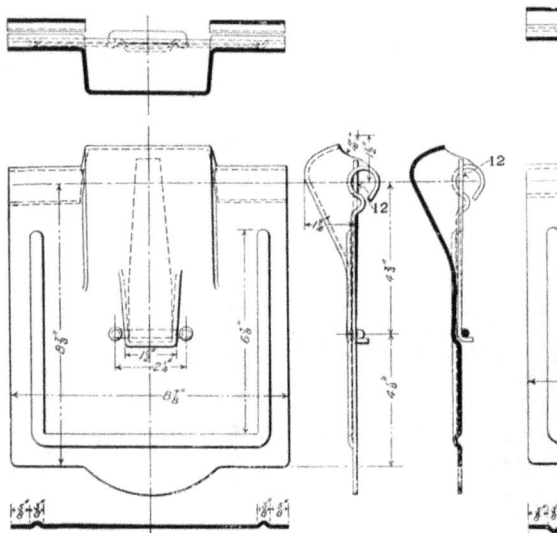

Figs. 4497-4501. Davis Pressed Steel Journal Box Lid. Davis Pressed Steel Co.

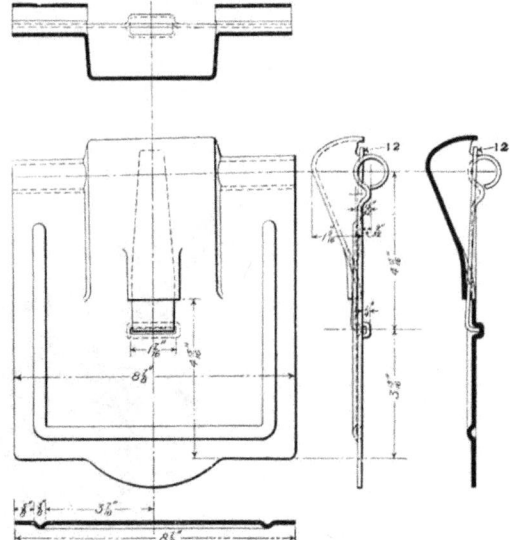

Figs. 4502-4506. Morris Pressed Steel Journal Box Lid.

Figs. 4507-4521 TENDERS, Truck Details; Dust Guards and Side Bearings.

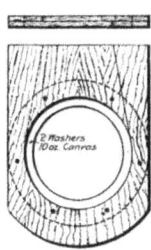

Fig. 4507.
Waycott Dust Guard.
Waycott Supply Co.

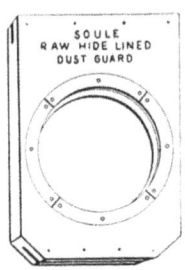

Fig. 4508.
Soule Rawhide Lined Dust Guard.
Soule Rawhide Lined Dust Guard Co.

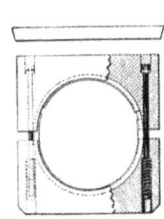

Fig. 4509.
Harrison Dust Guard.
Harrison Dust Guard Co.

Fig. 4510. Asbestos Dust Guard.
Franklin Mfg. Co.

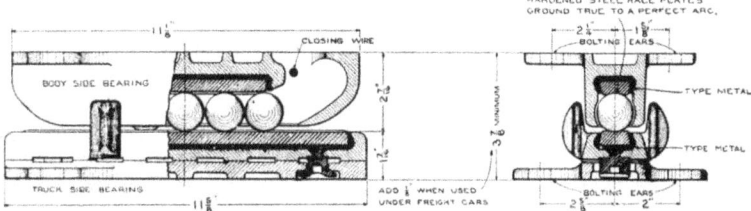

Figs. 4511-4512. Baltimore Ball Bearing Side Bearings. Baltimore Railway Specialty Co.

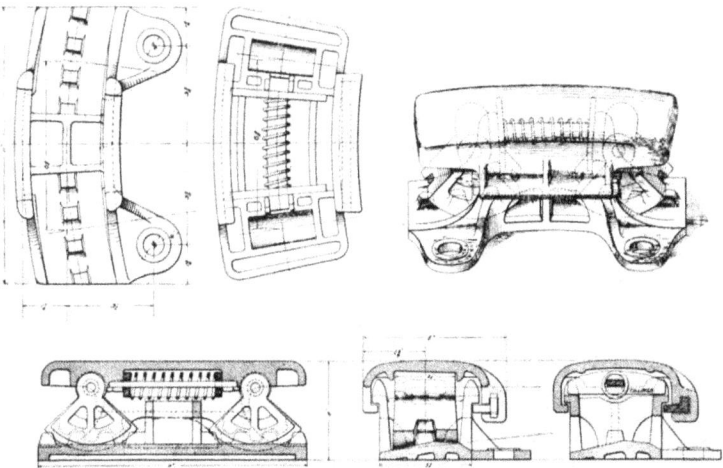

Figs. 4513-4518. Miner Gravity Side Bearing. W. H. Miner Co.

Figs. 4519-4521. Susemihl Roller Side Bearing
American Steel Foundries.

TENDERS, Truck Details; Springs. Figs. 4522-4537

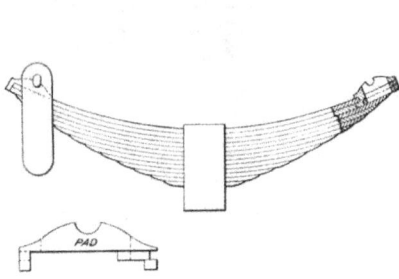

Figs. 4522-4523. Phoenix Semi-Elliptic Truck Spring and Pad. Phoenix Car Spring Co.

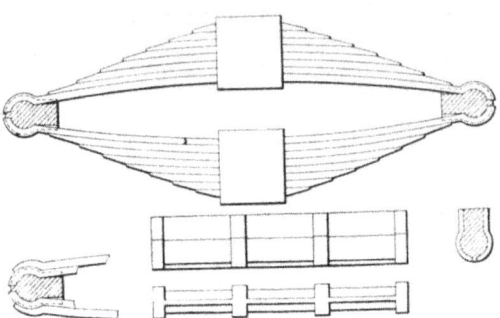

Figs. 4526-4530. Elliptic Truck Spring. Union Spring & Mfg. Co.

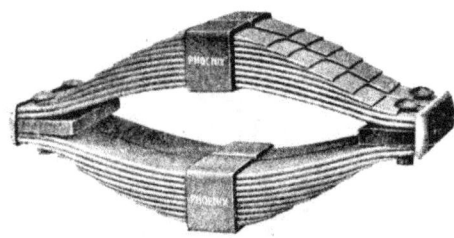

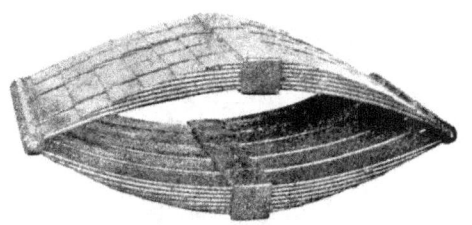

Fig. 4531. Quintuple Elliptic Truck Spring. American Steel Foundries.

Figs. 4524-4525. Phoenix Double Elliptic Truck Spring. Phoenix Car Spring Co.

Fig. 4532. American Controller Spring. American Steel Foundries.

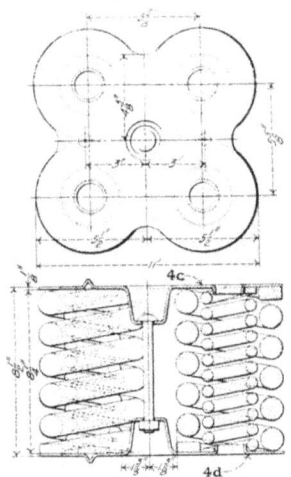

Figs. 4534-4535. Four-Coil Truck Bolster Spring.

Fig. 4533. Four-Coil Bolster Spring.

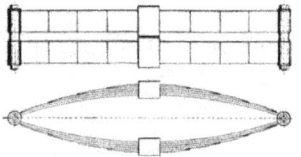

Figs. 4536-4537. Double Elliptic Spring.

Figs. 4538-4552   TENDERS, Truck Details; Wheels.

  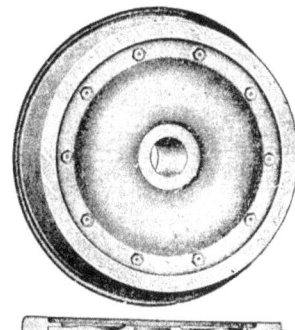

Figs. 4538-4539.
Allen Wheel with Paper Center.
Tire Secured by Plates and Bolts.

Figs. 4540-4541.
Cast Iron Spoke Center. Tire is Fastened with One Retaining Ring.

Figs. 4542-4543.
Wheel with Cast Iron Double Plate Center. Tire Secured by One Retaining Ring.

Fig. 4544.
Cross-Section of Wrought Iron Pressed Plate Wheel.

Fig. 4545.
Cross-Section of Cast Iron Double Plate Wheel.

Fig. 4546.
Cross-Section of Cast Iron Spoke Wheel.

Steel Tired Wheels. Railway Steel-Spring Co.

  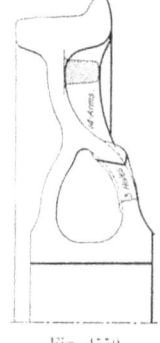

Figs. 4547-4548. 700-lb. Double Plate Cast Iron Wheel. Griffin Wheel Co.

Fig. 4550.
650-lb. Cast Iron Wheel, M. C. B. Pattern. Lobdell Car Wheel Co.

Figs. 4551-4552. Davis Rolled Steel Wheel. American Steel Foundries.

(408)

TENDERS, Truck Details; Wheels. Figs. 4553-4564

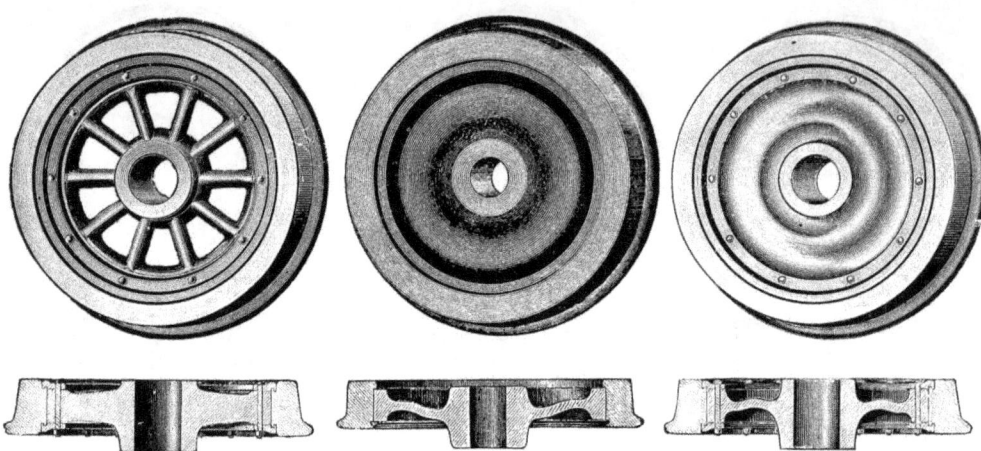

Figs. 4553-4554. No. 3 Krupp Wheel. Cast Iron Spoke Center. Tire Secured by Wrought Iron Retaining Rings.

Figs. 4555-4556. No. 14 Krupp Wheel. Patent Wrought Iron Disc Center. Steel Tire Secured with Bute Fastening.

Figs. 4557-4558. No. 1 Krupp Wheel. Wrought Iron Coil Disc Center. Tire Secured by Wrought Iron Retaining Rings.

Thomas Prosser & Son.

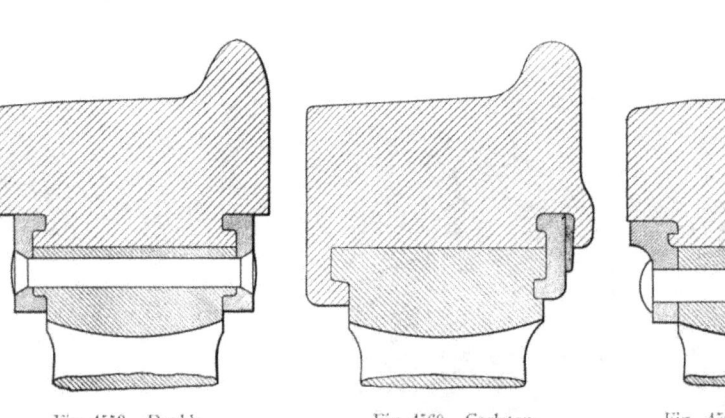

Fig. 4559. Double Lip Retaining Ring. 4 1-16-in. Shrink Base.

Fig. 4560. Carleton-Stroudley Fastening.

Fig. 4561. Mansell Retaining Ring with Bolt and Nut.

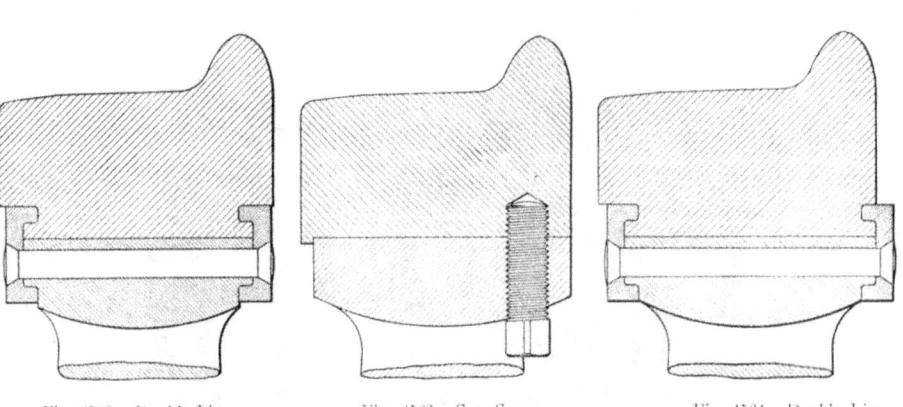

Fig. 4562. Double Lip Retaining Ring with 4⅞-in. Shrink Base.

Fig. 4563. Set Screw Fastening.

Fig. 4564. Double Lip Retaining Ring with 5-in. Shrink Base.

Figs. 4559-4564. Types of Steel Tire Fastenings. Standard Steel Works.

Figs. 4565-4571 TENDERS, Truck Details; Wheels.

Fig. 4565. Steel Tired Wheel with Wrought Iron or Cast Steel Plate Center. Double Lip Retaining Ring.

Fig. 4566. Steel Tired Wheel with Cast Iron Plate Center. Double Lip Retaining Ring.

Fig. 4567. Steel Tired Wheel with Cast Iron Spoke Center. Tire Shrunk On.

Fig. 4568. Steel Tired Wheel with Wrought Iron or Cast Steel Spoke Center. Double Lip Retaining Ring.

Fig. 4569. Steel Tired Wheel with Wrought Iron or Cast Steel Solid Plate Center. Bolted Fastening.

Fig. 4570. Steel Tired Wheel with Cast Steel or Wrought Iron Spoke Center. Bolted Fastening.

Fig. 4571. Solid Forged and Rolled Steel Wheel.

Steel Tired Wheels. Standard Steel Works.

ENGINE TOOLS.

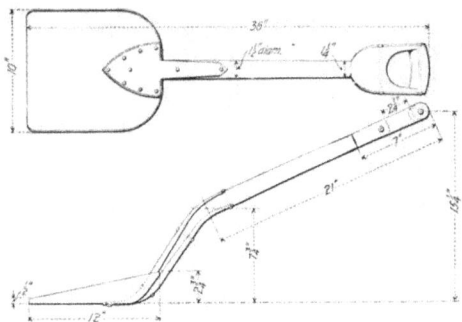

Figs. 4572-4573. Fireman's Shovel. Pennsylvania Railroad.

Fig. 4574. Coes' Steel Handle Railroad Monkey Wrench. Coes Wrench Co.

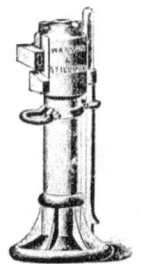

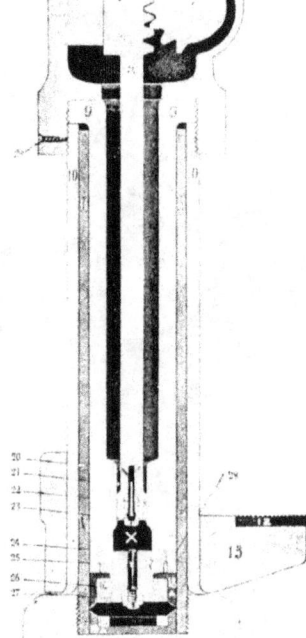

Fig. 4575. Broad Base Jack.

Fig. 4576. Journal Box Jack.

Fig. 4577. Claw Jack.

Hydraulic Jacks. Watson & Stillman Co.

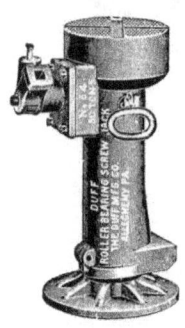

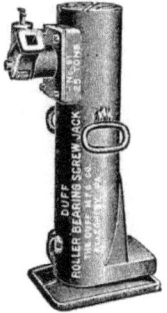

Figs. 4578-4579. Duff Roller Bearing Ratchet Screw Jacks. Duff Manufacturing Co.

Fig. 4580. Hydraulic Claw Jack. A. L. Henderer's Sons.

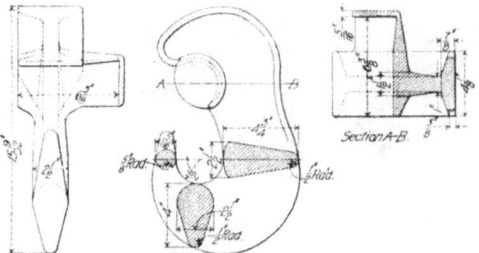

Fig. 4581. Alexander Car Replacer. Alexander Car Replacer Manufacturing Co.

Figs. 4582-4584. Goodman Wrecking Hook. Latrobe Steel & Coupler Co.

(411)

Fig. 4585 — ELECTRIC LOCOMOTIVES, General Electric.

Numbers Refer to List of Names of Parts on Opposite Page.

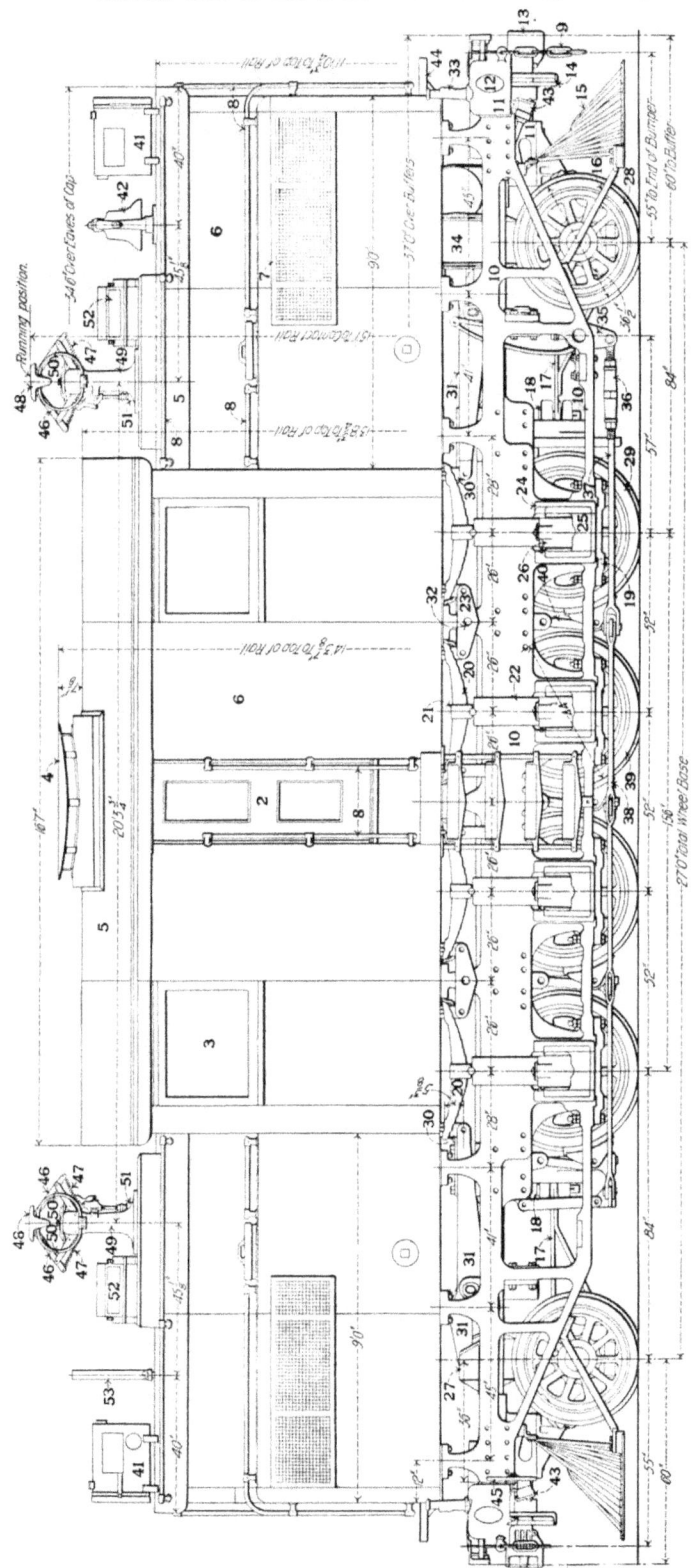

Fig. 4585. Side Elevation of Electric Locomotive for the New York Central & Hudson River. Built by the General Electric and American Locomotive Companies.

ELECTRIC LOCOMOTIVES, General Electric.

Fig. 4586. Electric Locomotive for the New York Central & Hudson River. Built by the General Electric and American Locomotive Companies.

Names of Parts of Fig. 4585.

- 2 Cab Door
- 3 Cab Window
- 4 Cab Ventilator
- 5 Cab Roof
- 6 Cab
- 7 Ventilating Grating for Rheostats
- 8 Hand Rail
- 9 Safety Chain
- 10 Frame
- 11 Bumper
- 12 Push Pole Socket
- 13 Coupler
- 14 Bumper Step
- 15 Pilot
- 16 Pilot Brace
- 17 Radius Bar
- 18 Radius Bar Pin
- 19 Pedestal Cap
- 20 Driver Spring
- 21 Driver Spring Band
- 22 Driver Spring Saddle
- 23 Equalizing Beam
- 24 Pedestal Shoe
- 25 Driving Box
- 26 Driving Box Lid
- 27 Center Pin Guide
- 28 Truck Wheel
- 29 Driving Wheel
- 30 Spring Hanger
- 31 Truck Equalizer
- 32 Equalizing Fulcrum Pin
- 33 Flag Fixture
- 34 Brake Cylinder
- 35 Brake Lever
- 36 Brake Rod Adjusting Sleeve
- 37 Forward Driver Brake Rod
- 38 Second Driver Brake Rod
- 39 Brake Head and Shoe
- 40 Brake Hanger
- 41 Headlight
- 42 Bell
- 43 Conductor Terminal Socket
- 44 End Door Sill
- 45 Hand Wheel to Unlock Coupler
- 46 Trolley
- 47 Trolley Spring
- 48 Trolley Shoe
- 49 Trolley Stand
- 50 Trolley Leads
- 51 Trolley Air Cylinder
- 52 Lightning Arrester
- 53 Whistle

Fig. 4587. End Elevation of New York Central Electric Locomotive.

ELECTRIC LOCOMOTIVES, General Electric.

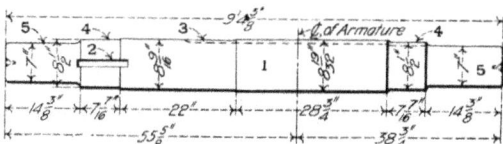

Fig. 4588. Driving Axle for New York Central Electric Locomotive.

Names of Parts of Fig. 4588.

1. Center
2. Key Slot for Wheel
3. Key Slot for Armature
4. Wheel Seat
5. Journal

Names of Parts of Fig. 4589.

1. Commutator
2. Armature
3. Brush Holder
4. Brush Holder Support
5. Brush Holder Support Bolt
6. Field Magnet Coil
7. Frame Crosstie and Field Magnet Core
8. Side Frame
9. Driving Wheel
10. Oil Guard
11. Driving Axle Journal
12. Driving Axle Box
13. Small Lid on Box Cover
14. Field Coil Bolt
15. Driving Axle
16. Wheel Seat
17. Hub Liner
18. Armature Sleeve

Fig. 4589. Longitudinal Section Through Motor of New York Central Electric Locomotive.

Names of Parts of Fig. 4590.

1. Longitudinal Frame Member
2. Frame Crosstie and Field Magnet Core
3. Soft Iron Pole Face
4. Field Magnet Coil
5. Commutator
6. Armature
7. Armature Coil
8. Brush Holder
9. Brush Holder Support
10. Motor Lead or Conductor
11. Brush Holder Support Bolt
12. Exterior of Field Magnet Coil
13. Field Coil Bolt
14. Driving Axle
15. Driving Wheel

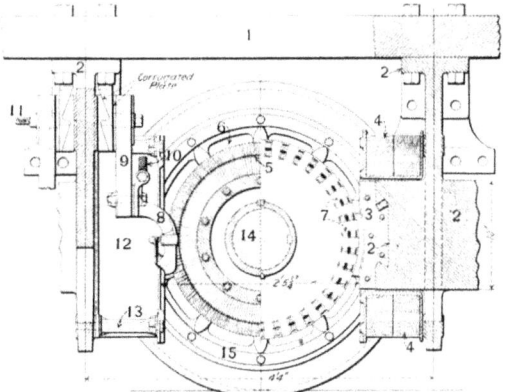

Fig. 4590. Transverse Section Through Motor of New York Central Electric Locomotive.

(414)

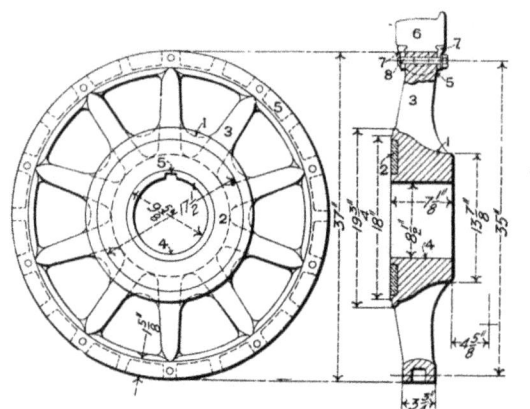

Figs. 4591-4592. Cast-Steel Driving Wheel Center for New York Central Electric Locomotive.

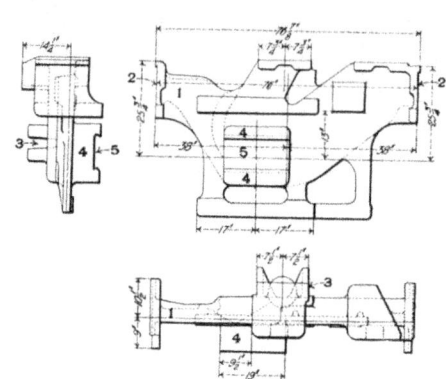

Figs. 4593-4595. Forward Transom and Field Magnet Core of New York Central Electric Locomotive.

Names of Parts of Figs. 4591-4592.
1. Hub
2. Brass Hub Washer or Liner
3. Spoke
4. Wheel Fit for Axle
5. Key Way
6. Tire
7. Retaining Ring
8. Retaining Ring Bolt

Names of Parts of Figs. 4593-4595.
1. Transom Casting
2. Frame Fit
3. Socket for Radius Bar
4. Field Magnet Core
5. Recess for Soft Iron Pole Face

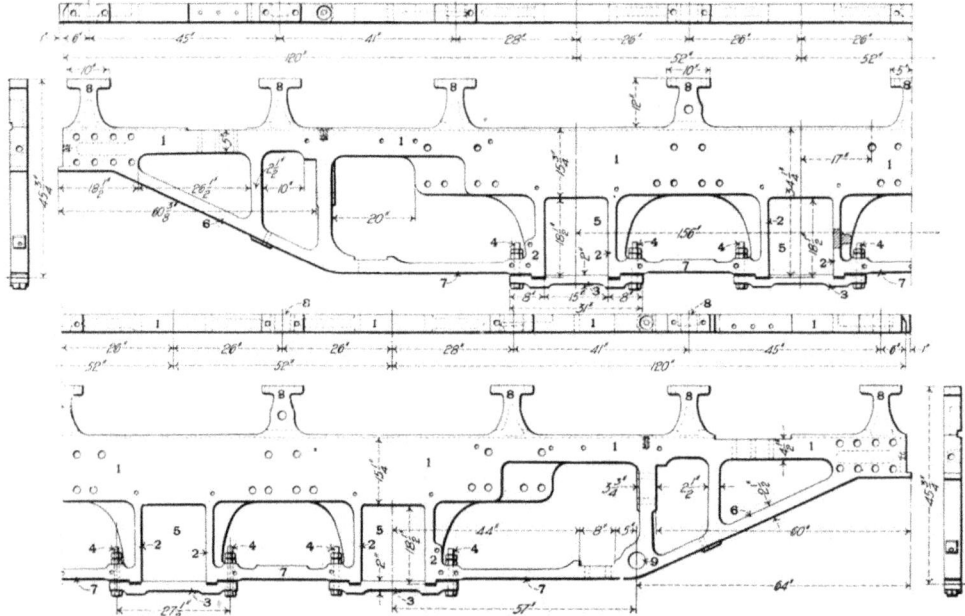

Figs. 4596-4600. Side Frame for New York Central Electric Locomotive.

Names of Parts of Figs. 4596-4600.
1. Top Rail of Frame
2. Pedestal
3. Pedestal Cap
4. Pedestal Bolt
5. Jaw
6. Frame Brace
7. Intermediate Frame Braces
8. Cab Support
9. Brake Lever Pin Hole

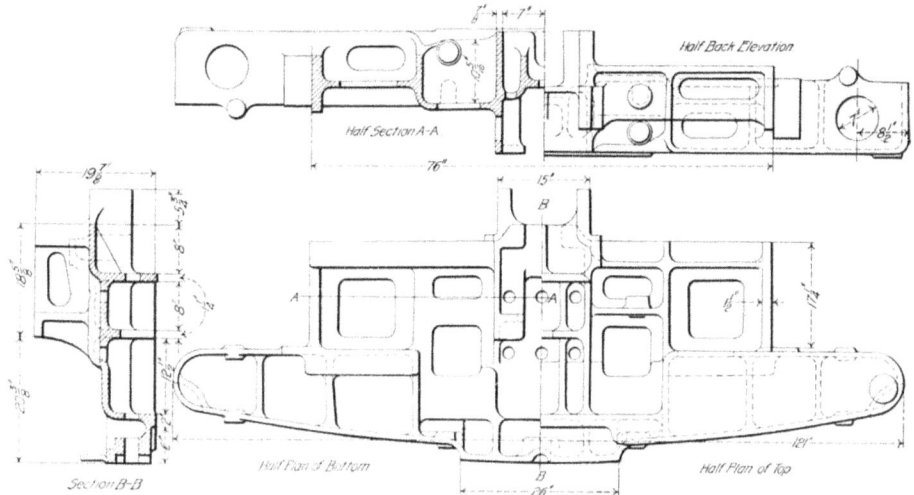

Figs. 4601-4603. Cast-Steel End Frame or Bumper for New York Central Electric Locomotive.

Names of Parts of Figs. 4604-4606.

1 *Cast-Steel Truck Bolster*
2 *Center Plate*
3 *Center Pin*
4 *Center Pin Guide*
5 *Truck Wheel*
6 *Truck Pedestal*
7 *Pedestal Cap or Thimble*
8 *Pedestal Tie Bolt*
9 *Truck Box*
10 *Brass*
11 *Axle*
12 *Swing Link Socket*
13 *Truck Spring*
14 *Oil Cup*

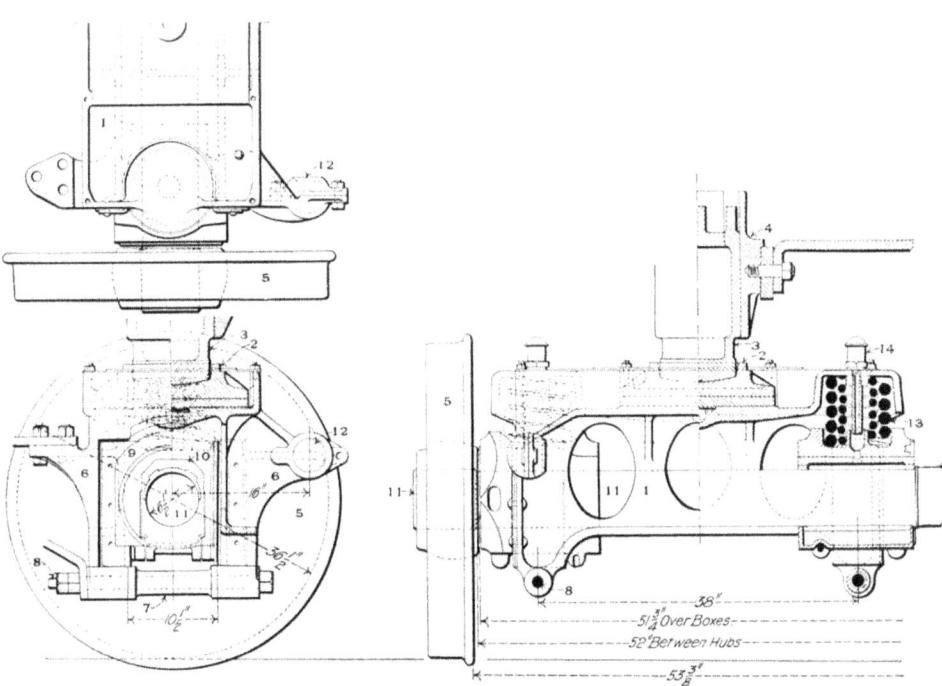

Figs. 4604-4606. Pony Truck for New York Central Electric Locomotive.

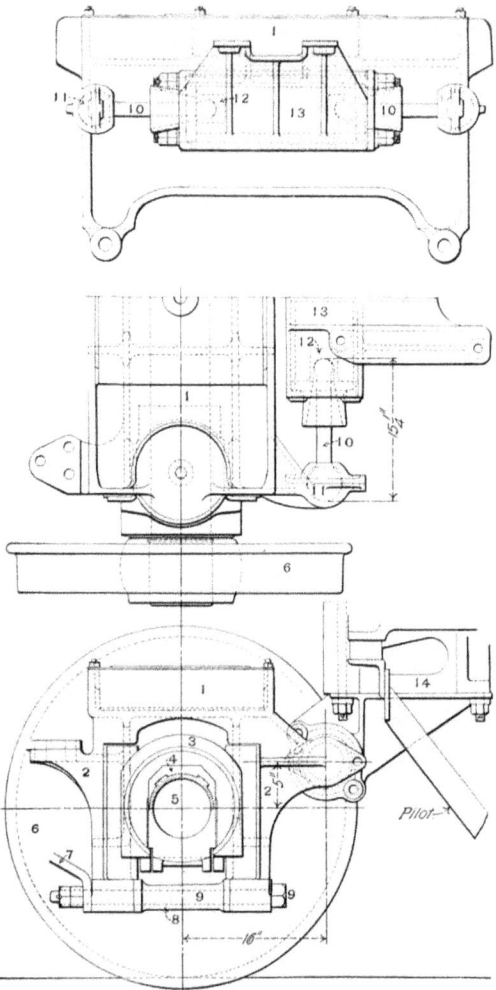

Figs. 4607-4609. Pony Truck Centering Device for New York Central Electric Locomotive.

Names of Parts of Figs. 4607-4609.

1 Truck Frame or Bolster
2 Pedestal
3 Box
4 Brass
5 Axle
6 Wheel
7 Radius Bar Brace
8 Pedestal Tie or Thimble
9 Pedestal Tie Bolt
10 Swing Link
11 Outer Swing Link Socket
12 Inner Swing Link Socket
13 Frame Transom
14 Bumper Casting

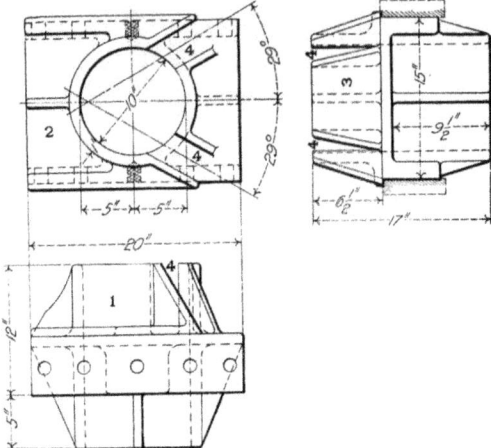

Figs. 4610-4612. Pony Truck Center Pin Guide for New York Central Electric Locomotive.

Names of Parts of Figs. 4610-4612.

1 Side Elevation
2 Plan
3 Rear Elevation
4 Slots for Equalizing Beams

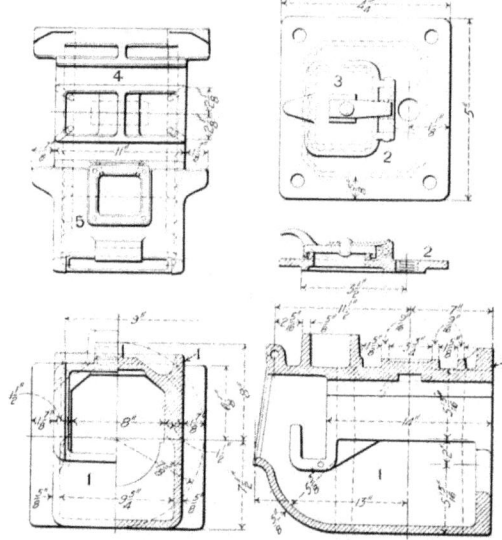

Figs. 4613-4617. Driving Axle Journal Box for New York Central Electric Locomotive.

Names of Parts of Figs. 4613-4617.

1 Box
2 Cover
3 Lid on Cover
4 Plan of Top
5 Front

Figs. 4618-4623   ELECTRIC LOCOMOTIVES, General Electric.

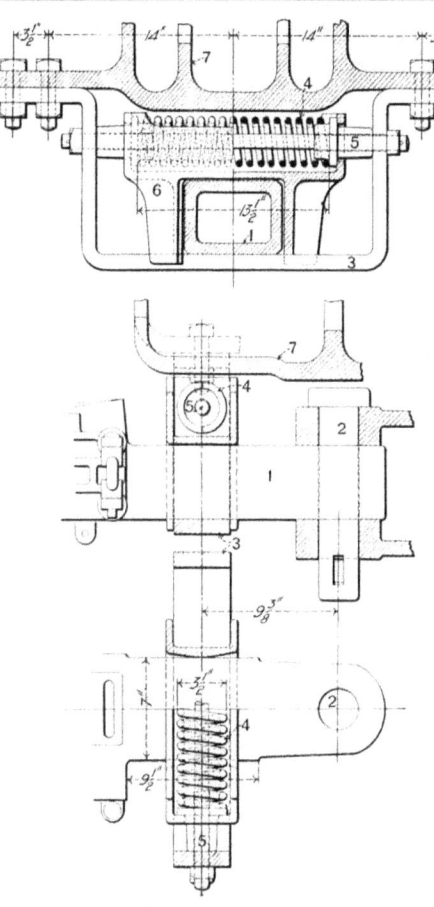

Names of Parts of Figs. 4618-4620.

1. *Coupler Shank or Drawbar*
2. *Draw Pin*
3. *Drawbar Carry Iron*
4. *Centering Spring*
5. *Centering Spring Pin*
6. *Centering Spring Yoke*
7. *Bumper Casting*

Names of Parts of Figs. 4621-4623.

1. *Drawbar*
2. *Yoke*
3. *Draw Pin*
4. *Drawbar Follower Plate*
5. *Twin Draft Springs*
6. *Bumper Casting*
7. *Draw Pin Key*

Figs. 4618-4620. Drawbar Centering Device for New York Central Locomotive.

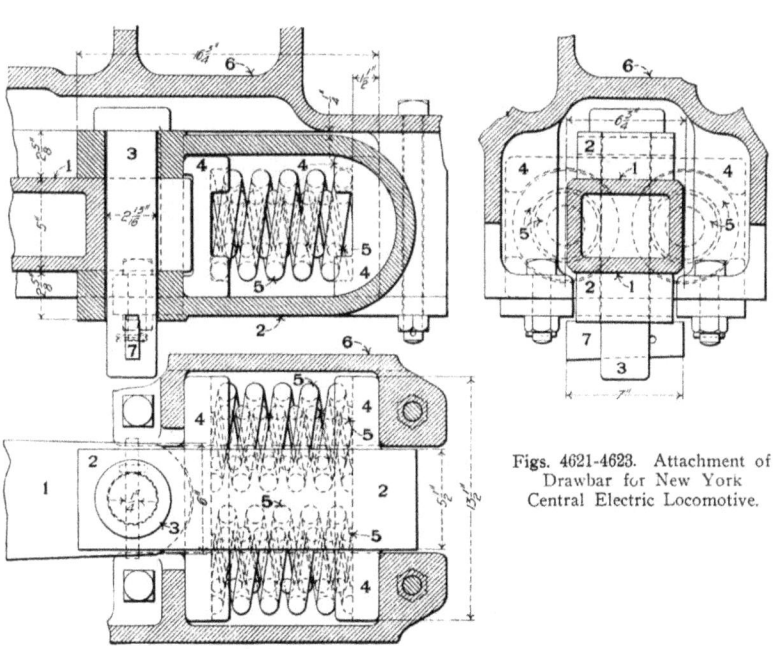

Figs. 4621-4623. Attachment of Drawbar for New York Central Electric Locomotive.

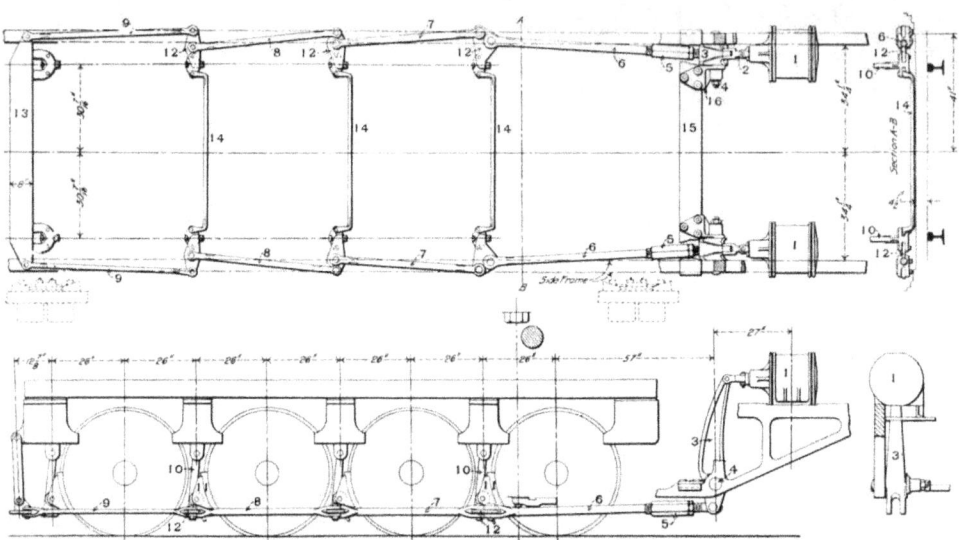

Figs. 4624-4627. Arrangement of Equalized Brakes for New York Central Electric Locomotive.

Names of Parts of Figs. 4624-4627.

1. Driver Brake Cylinder
2. Driver Brake Cylinder Push Rod
3. Driver Brake Lever
4. Brake Lever Pin Hole
5. Brake Rod Adjusting Sleeve
6. Forward Driver Brake Rod
7. Second Driver Brake Rod
8. Third Driver Brake Rod
9. Rear Driver Brake Rod
10. Driver Brake Hangers
11. Brake Head and Shoe
12. Intermediate Equalizing Lever
13. Rear Brake Equalizing Lever
14. Brake Shoe Tie Rods
15. Frame Crosstie
16. Brake Lever Bracket

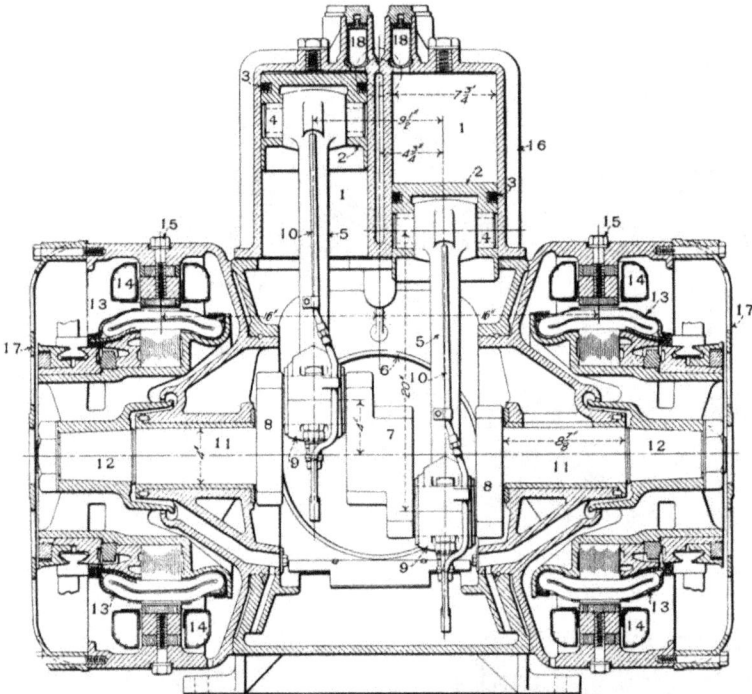

Fig. 4628. Section Through Motor-Driven Air Compressor for New York Central Electric Locomotive.

Names of Parts of Fig. 4628.

1. Air Cylinder
2. Trunk Piston or Plunger
3. Piston Packing Ring
4. Piston Wrist Pin
5. Driving Rod
6. Crank Case
7. Crank Middle Section
8. Crank Web
9. Stub Strap of Driving Rod
10. Oil Pipe
11. Main Shaft Journal
12. Armature Seat on Shaft
13. Armature
14. Field Magnet
15. Bolt for Field Magnet Pole Face
16. Air Cylinder Rib or Corrugation
17. Casing Over Commutator

ELECTRIC LOCOMOTIVES, General Electric.

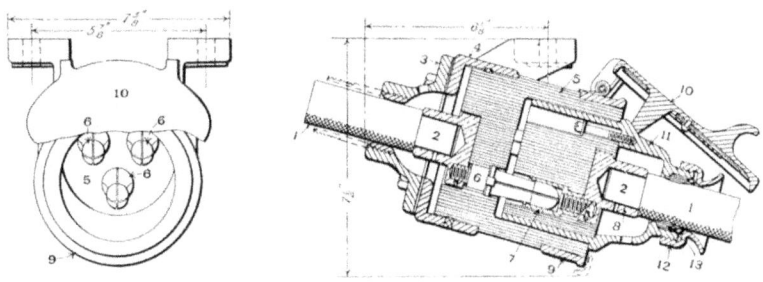

Figs. 4629-4630. Conductor Terminals for New York Central Electric Locomotive.

Names of Parts of Figs. 4629-4630.

1. Flexible Conducting Cable or Jumper
2. Cable Terminal
3. Socket Cap
4. Socket Flange
5. Insulation
6. Locomotive Terminal Plug
7. Jumper Socket
8. Terminal Head
9. Rim
10. Terminal Lid
11. Insulation on Jumper Terminal
12. Flange on Jumper Terminal
13. Insulation

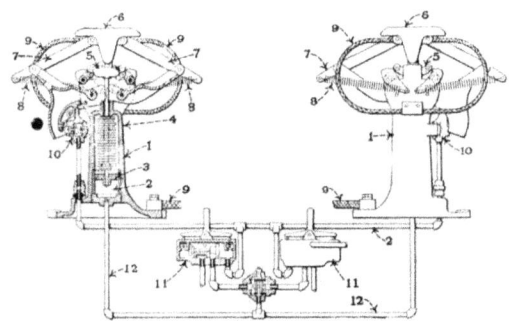

Fig. 4631. Overhead Trolley Connections for New York Central Electric Locomotive.

Names of Parts of Fig. 4631.

1. Trolley Stand
2. Trolley Air Cylinder
3. Trolley Air Cylinder Piston
4. Trolley Cylinder Spring
5. Crosshead on Trolley Piston Rod
6. Trolley Shoe
7. Trolley
8. Trolley Spring
9. Trolley Leads
10. Trolley Poppet Valve
11. Trolley Operating Valve
12. Air Pipe

Numbers Refer to List of Names of Parts on Opposite Page.

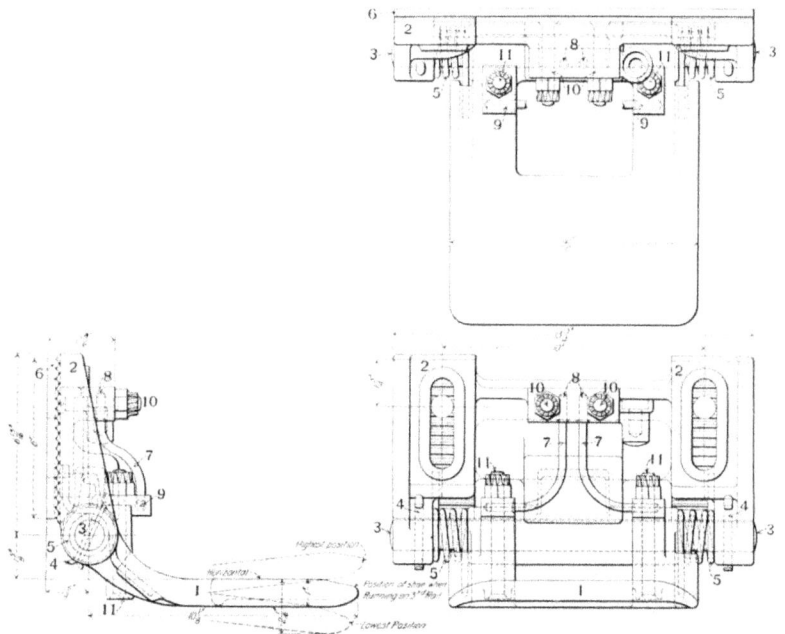

Figs. 4632-4634. Third-Rail Shoe for New York Central Electric Locomotive.

(420)

ELECTRIC LOCOMOTIVES, General Electric.   Fig. 4635

Names of Parts of Figs. 4632-4634.

1. *Shoe*
2. *Shoe Carrier or Bracket*
3. *Shoe Pin*
4. *Key for Shoe Pin*
5. *Spring*
6. *Corrugated Back Plate*
7. *Conductor*
8. *Connection to Locomotive Circuits*
9. *Connection to Shoe*
10. *Bracket Bolt*
11. *Lower Bracket Bolt*

Names of Parts of Figs. 4635-4637.

1. *Air Compressor*
2. *Main Reservoir*
3. *Equalizing Reservoir*
4. *Driver Brake Cylinder*
5. *Engineer's Brake Valve*
6. *Distributing Valve*
7. *Feed Valve*
8. *Feed Valve*
9. *Combined Strainer and Check Valve*
10. *Strainer in Brake Pipe*
11. *Strainer for Feed Valve*
12. *Cock for Main Reservoir*
13. *Double Cock for Engineer's Valve*
14. *Cock for Distributing Valve*
15. *Duplex Air Gage*
16. *Single Pointer Gage*
17. *Signal Valve*
18. *Signal Whistle*
19. *Drain Cock for Main Reservoir*
20. *Cut-out Cock for Whistle Pipe*
21. *Trolley Operating Valve*
22. *Double Check Valve for Trolley*
23. *Whistle*
24. *Whistle Valve*
25. *Bell*
26. *Bell Ringer*
27. *Governor*
28. *Sanding Valve*
29. *Globe Valve*
30. *Check Valve*
31. *Three-way Cock*

Names of Parts of Figs. 4638-4639.

1. *Steam Outlet from Heater Boiler*
2. *Steam Hose Connection*
3. *Pipe Hanger*
4. *Train Air Pipe*
5. *Reservoir Air Pipe*
6. *Air Signal Pipe*
7. *Frame of Locomotive*
8. *Brake Lever*

Names of Parts of Figs. 4647-4648.

1. *Air Compressor*
2. *Main Reservoir*
3. *Whistle*
4. *Bell*
5. *Brake Valve*
6. *Straight-Air Brake Valve*
7. *Driver Brake Cylinder*
8. *Trolley Operating Valve*
9. *Equalizing Reservoir*
10. *Duplex Air Gage*
11. *Feed Valve*

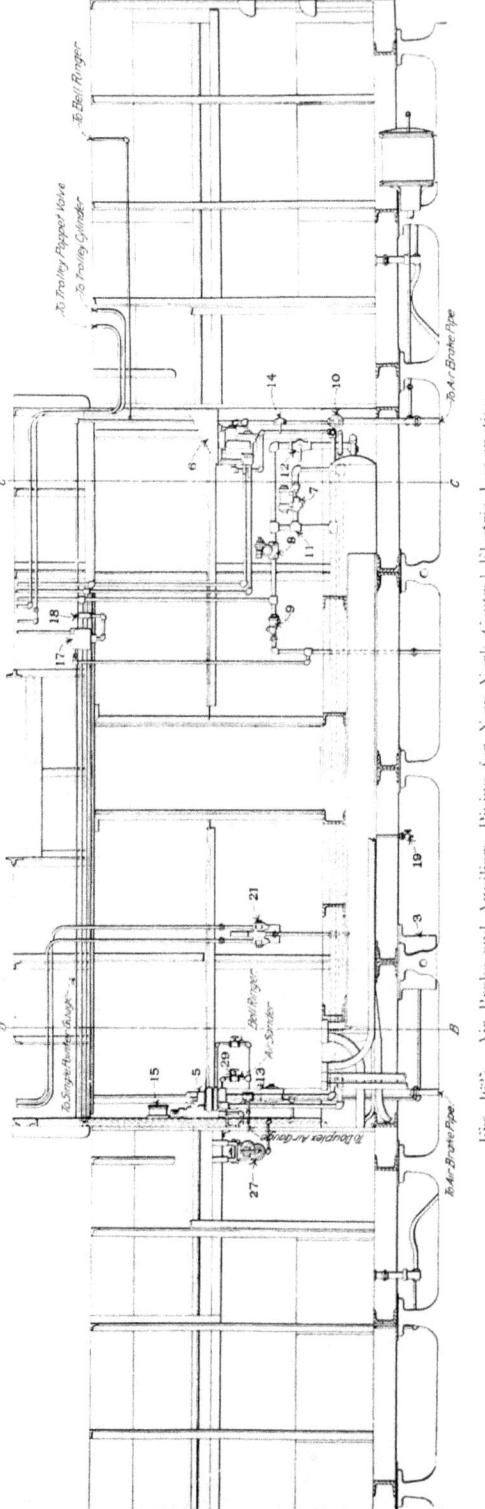

Fig. 4635. Air Brake and Auxiliary Piping for New York Central Electric Locomotive.

Numbers Refer to List of Names of Parts with Fig. 4635.

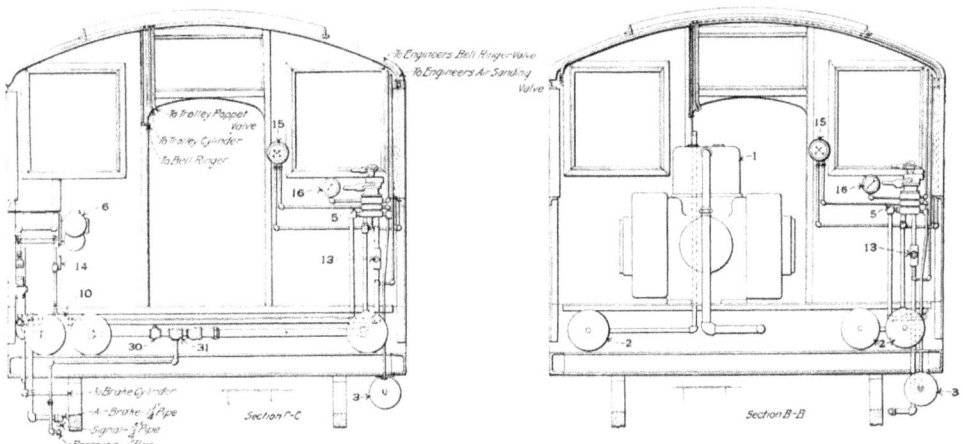

Figs. 4636-4637. Air Brake and Auxiliary Piping for New York Central Electric Locomotive.

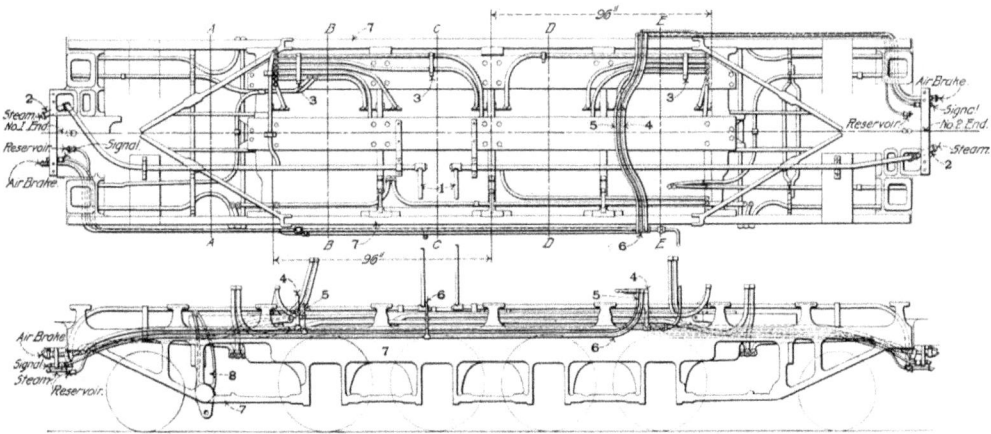

Figs. 4638-4639. General Arrangement of Piping for New York Central Electric Locomotive.

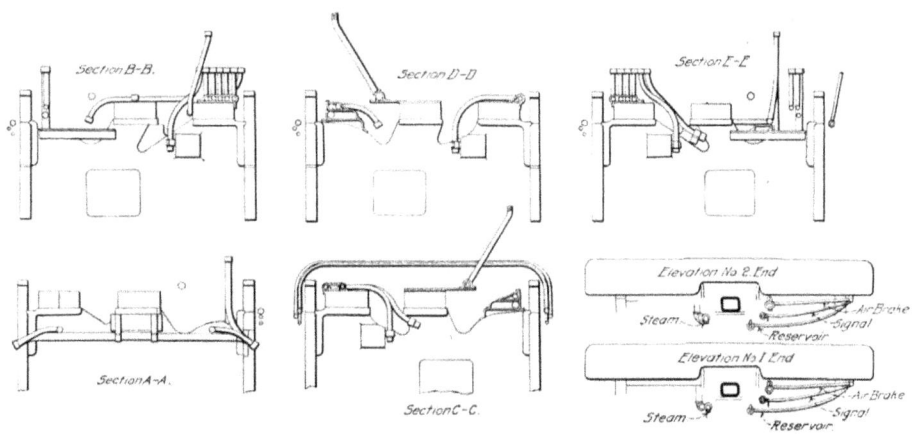

Figs. 4640-4646. General Arrangement of Piping for New York Central Electric Locomotive.

ELECTRIC LOCOMOTIVES, General Electric.   Figs. 4647-4648

Numbers Refer to List of Names of Parts with Fig. 4635.

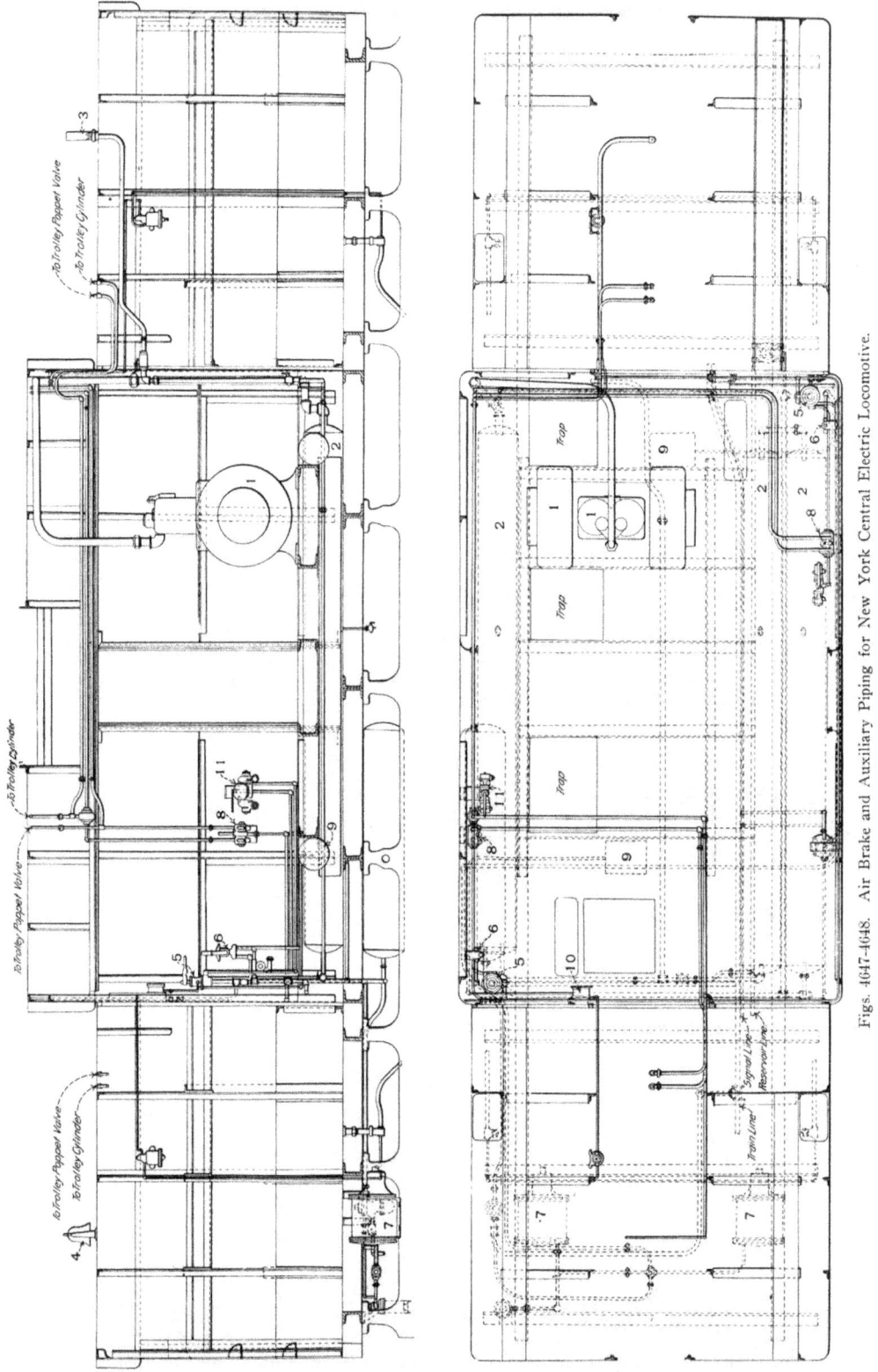

Figs. 4647-4648. Air Brake and Auxiliary Piping for New York Central Electric Locomotive.

(423)

ELECTRIC LOCOMOTIVES, Westinghouse.

Fig. 4649. Electric Locomotive for Single-Phase Alternating or Direct Current Operation. New York, New Haven & Hartford.
Built by the Westinghouse Electric & Mfg. Co. and the Baldwin Locomotive Works.

Fig. 4650. Motor Mounted on Axle. Westinghouse A. C. Electric Locomotive.

Fig. 4651. Top View of Truck Without Motors. Westinghouse A. C. Electric Locomotive.

Fig. 4652. Side View of Truck Without Motors. Westinghouse A. C. Electric Locomotive.

Fig. 4653. Truck Complete with Motors and Wiring. Westinghouse A. C. Electric Locomotive.

Fig. 4654. Motor Armature and Quill. Westinghouse A. C. Electric Locomotive.

Fig. 4655. Interior View of Cab. Westinghouse A. C. Electric Locomotive.

Fig. 4656. Outside View of Driving Wheel. Westinghouse A. C. Electric Locomotive.

Fig. 4658. Inside View of Driving Wheel Showing Pockets for Driving Pins on Quill. Westinghouse A. C. Electric Locomotive.

Fig. 4657. Driving Wheel with Caps Removed Showing Pockets for Driving Pins on Quill. Westinghouse A. C. Electric Locomotive.

ELECTRIC LOCOMOTIVES, Westinghouse. Figs. 4659-4663

Fig. 4659. Interior of Gearless Motor Field.
Westinghouse A. C. Electric Locomotive.

Fig. 4660. Skeleton Field Frame for Gearless Motor.
Westinghouse A. C. Electric Locomotive.

Fig. 4661. Brush Holder for Gearless Motor. Westinghouse A. C. Electric Locomotive.

Fig. 4662. 350-K. W. Air Blast Auto-Transformer.
Westinghouse A. C. Electric Locomotive.

Fig. 4663. Grid Resistance.
Westinghouse A. C. Electric Locomotive.

Fig. 4664. Unit Switch Group for Electro-Pneumatic System of Multiple Control. Westinghouse A. C. Electric Locomotive.

Fig. 4665. Master Controller with Cover Removed. Westinghouse A. C. Electric Locomotive.

Fig. 4666. 14-H. P. Motor-Driven Air Compressor with 600-Volt A. C. Series Motor.
Westinghouse A. C. Electric Locomotive.

Fig. 4667. 9½-H. P. Motor-Driven Blower for
Auto-Transformer.
Westinghouse A. C. Electric Locomotive.

Fig. 4668. Magneto Speed Indicator.
Westinghouse A. C. Electric Locomotive.

ELECTRIC LOCOMOTIVES, Baldwin-Westinghouse.

Fig. 4669. Baldwin-Westinghouse Electric Locomotive for the Dominion Phosphate Co. Weight, 12,000 lbs.; Diameter of Drivers, 30 in.; Wheel Base, 5 ft.; Drawbar Pull, Starting, 2,400 lbs.; Drawbar Pull, Running, 1,300 lbs.; No. of Motors, 2.

Fig. 4670. Baldwin-Westinghouse Electric Locomotive for the American Dock & Trust Co. Weight, 36,000 lbs.; Wheel Base, 5 ft. 6 in.; Drawbar Pull, Starting, 9,000 lbs.; Drawbar Pull, Running, 6,000 lbs.; No. of Motors, 2.

Fig. 4671. Baldwin-Westinghouse Electric Locomotive for the Hoboken Shore Road. Weight, 120,000 lbs.; Diameter of Drivers, 36 in.; Wheel Base, 19 ft.; Drawbar Pull, Starting, 24,000 lbs.; Drawbar Pull, Running, 14,500 lbs.; No. of Motors 4.

ELECTRIC LOCOMOTIVES, Baldwin-Westinghouse.   Figs. 4672-4677

Fig. 4672. Baldwin-Westinghouse Electric Locomotive for the Pennsylvania Steel Co. Weight, 28,000 lbs.; Diameter of Drivers, 30 in.; Wheel Base, 5 ft. 6 in.; Drawbar Pull, 5,600 lbs.; No. of Motors, 2.

Numbers Refer to List of Names of Parts with Figs. 4678-4679.

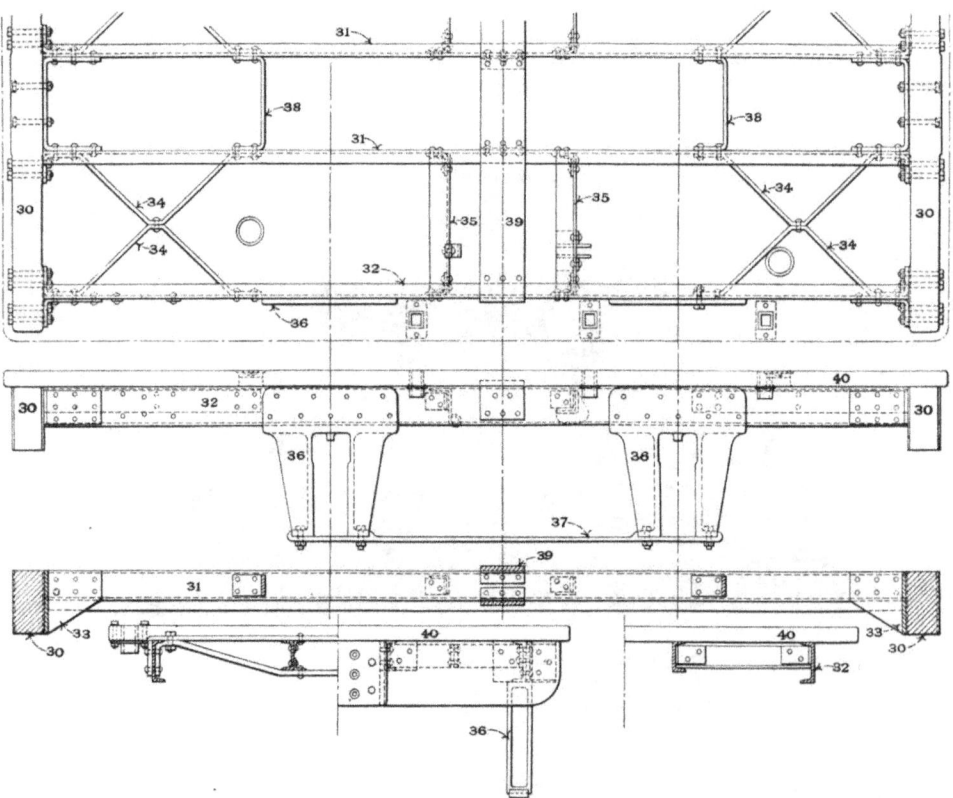

Figs. 4673-4677. Underframe of Baldwin-Westinghouse Electric Locomotive.

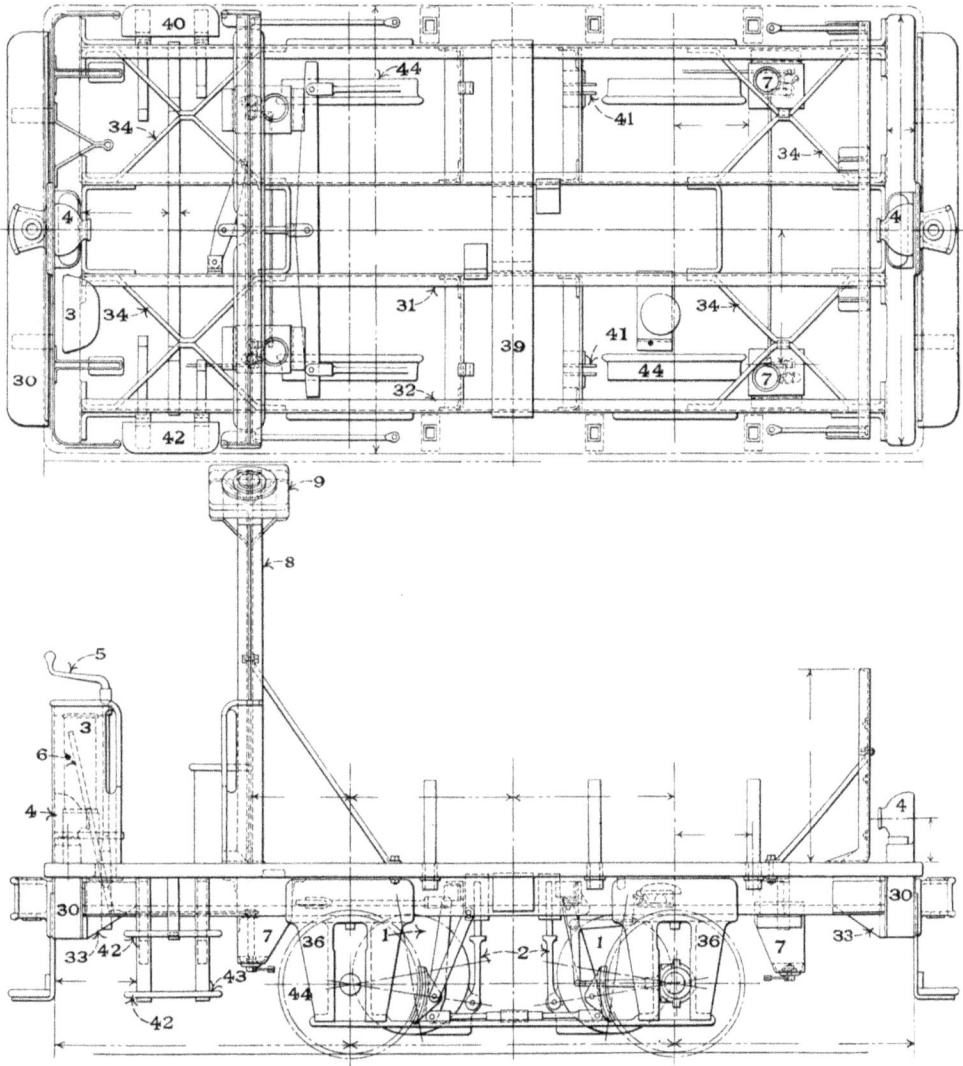

Figs. 4678-4679. Plan and Side Elevation of Baldwin-Westinghouse Electric Locomotive.

Names of Parts of Figs. 4673-4679.

1 *Motor*	9 *Cab Roof and Trolley Base*	37 *Pedestal Tie*
2 *Motor Suspender*	30 *Bumper*	38 *Center Sill Cross Tie*
3 *Controller*	31 *Center Sill*	39 *Transom*
4 *Headlight*	32 *Side Sill*	40 *Cab Floor*
5 *Brake Handle*	33 *Center Sill Gusset Plate*	41 *Brake Hanger Bracket*
6 *Sand Box Valve Handle*	34 *Diagonal Braces for Sills*	42 *Step*
7 *Sand Box*	35 *Transverse Angle Braces*	43 *Step Hanger*
8 *Cab Frame and Trolley Support*	36 *Pedestal*	44 *Wheel*

ENGINE TRUCKS, Details; Boxes.

Names of Parts of Boxes, Figs. 3549-3561, 3590-3596.

1. Cellar
2. Box
3. Brass
4. Babbitt Lining
5. Cellar Wedge
6. Cellar Wedge Bolt
7. Waste Cavity
8. Oil Hole
13. Box Flange

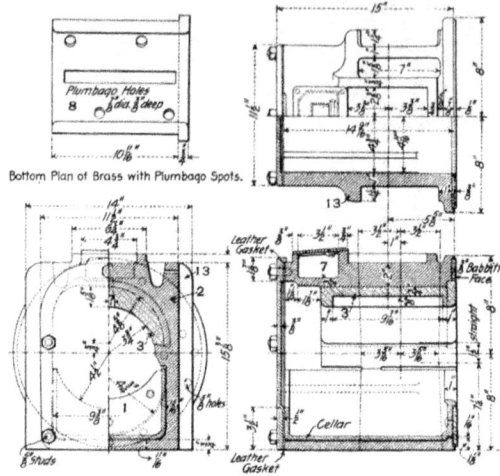

Figs. 3590-3593. Cast-Steel Journal Box for Trailing Truck of Atlantic (4—4—2) Locomotive. Chicago & North-Western.

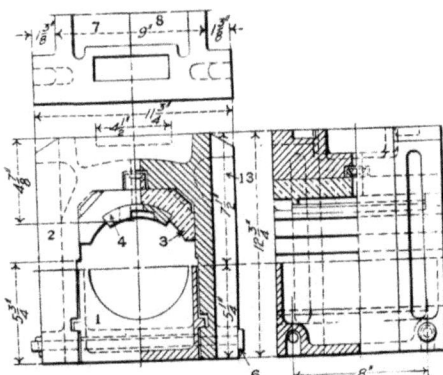

Figs. 3594-3596. Front Engine Truck Journal Box. American Locomotive Co.

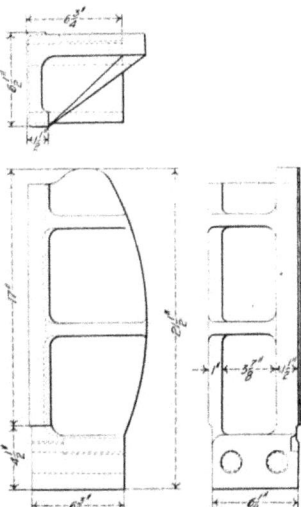

Figs. 3611-3613. Trailing Truck Journal Box Shoe. American Locomotive Co.

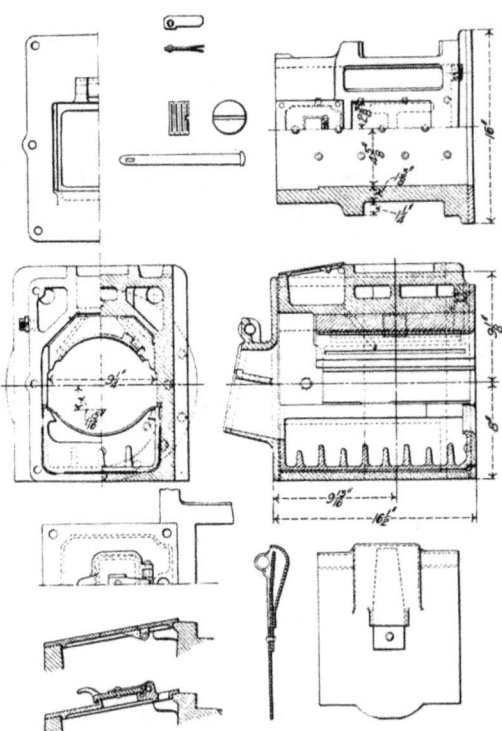

Figs. 3597-3610. Trailing Truck Journal Box. American Locomotive Co.

Names of Parts of Figs. 4680-4685.

1 Motor	13 Lower Brake Rod	25 Wheel
2 Controller	14 Pedestal Tie	26 Coupler
3 Hand Brake Shaft	15 Cab	27 Coil Spring
4 Brake-Handle	16 Cab Roof	28 Side Sill
5 Sand Box	17 Headlight	29 Intermediate Sill
6 Sand Pipe	18 Trolley Board	30 Intermediate Sill Corner Knee
7 Sand Box Valve Operating Rod	19 Hand Rail	31 Side Sill Cover Piece
8 Sand Box Valve Handle	20 Step	32 Intermediate Sill Stiffening Angle
9 Upper Brake Rod	21 Step Hanger	
10 Brake Lever	22 Bumper	33 Pedestal Spring Cap
11 Brake Head and Shoe	23 Pedestal	34 Transom
12 Rheostats for Motor	24 Journal Box	35 Side Sill Cross Ties

Numbers Refer to List of Names of Parts on Opposite Page.

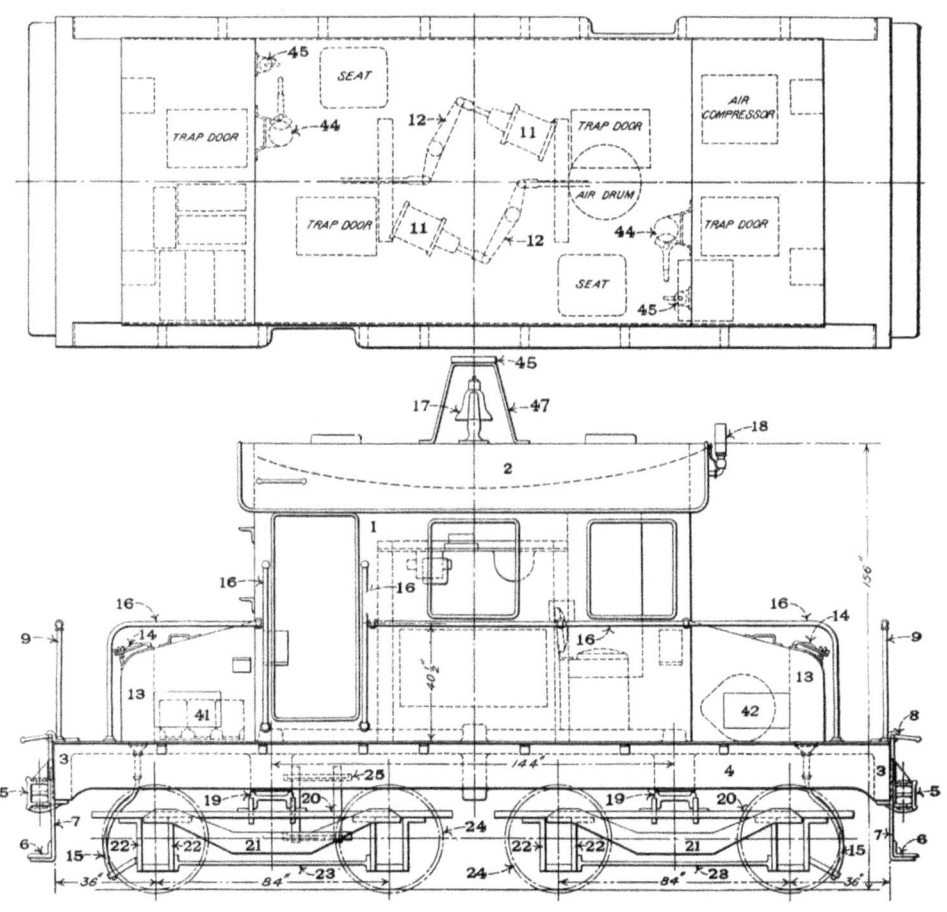

Figs. 4686-4687. Plan and Side Elevation of 560 H. P. Baldwin-Westinghouse Electric Locomotive for the Hoboken Shore Road.

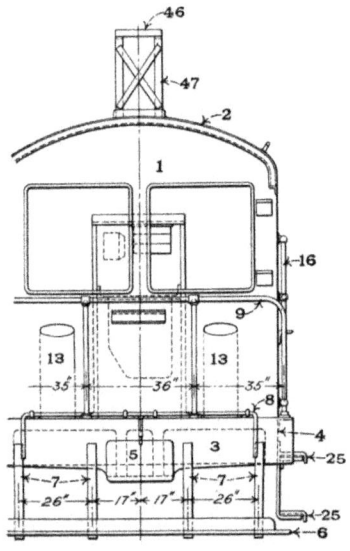

Fig. 4688. End Elevation of 560-H. P. Baldwin-Westinghouse Electric Locomotive for the Hoboken Shore Road.

Names of Parts of Figs. 4686-4691.

1 Cab
2 Cab Roof
3 Bumper
4 Side Frame
5 Coupler
6 Bumper Step
7 Bumper Step Hanger
8 Coupler Rod
9 Bumper Hand Rail
11 Brake Cylinder
12 Cylinder Lever
13 Sand Box
14 Sand Box Cover
15 Sand Pipe
16 Hand Rail
17 Bell
18 Air Whistle
19 Center Plate
20 Truck Frame
21 Equalizing Bar
22 Truck Pedestal
23 Pedestal Tie
24 Wheel
25 Truck Spring
26 Truck Spring Band
27 Pedestal Cap
28 Pedestal Cap Bolt
29 Truck Bolster
30 Motor
31 Brake Hanger
32 Brake Head and Shoe
33 Brake Hanger Carrier
34 Dead Lever
35 Brake Lever
36 Brake Rod
37 Dead Lever Guide
38 Lower Brake Rod
39 Brake Rod Adjusting Sleeve
40 Safety Chain Eye Bolt
41 Rheostat
42 Motor-Driven Air Compressor
44 Controller
45 Air Brake Valve
46 Trolley Base
47 Trolley Stand

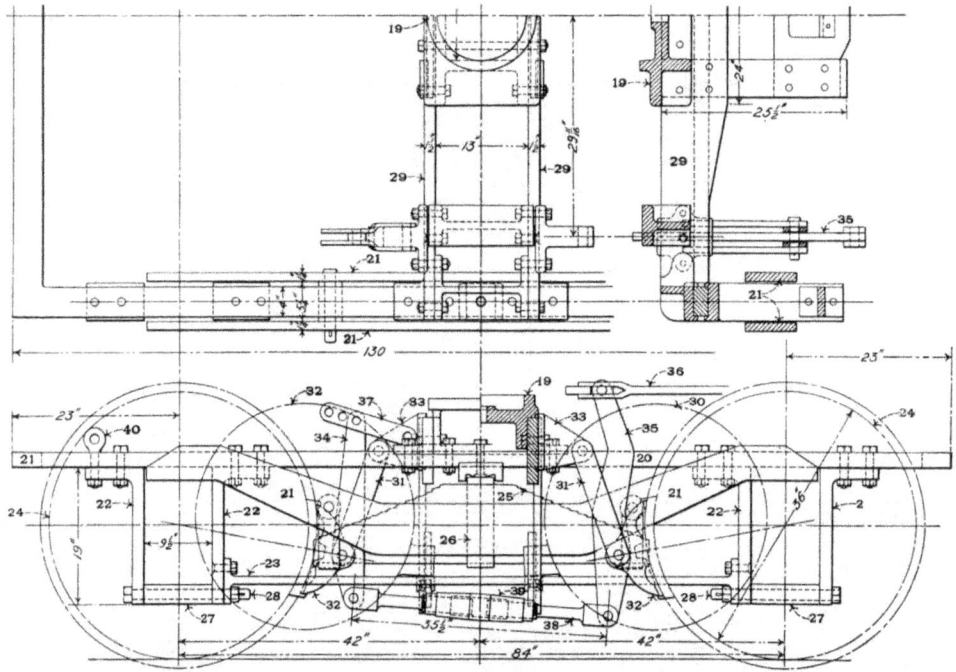

Figs. 4689-4691. Four-Wheel Motor Truck for 560-H. P. Baldwin-Westinghouse Electric Locomotive for the Hoboken Shore Road.

Figs. 4692-4710 RAILROAD STANDARDS, Pennsylvania Railroad.

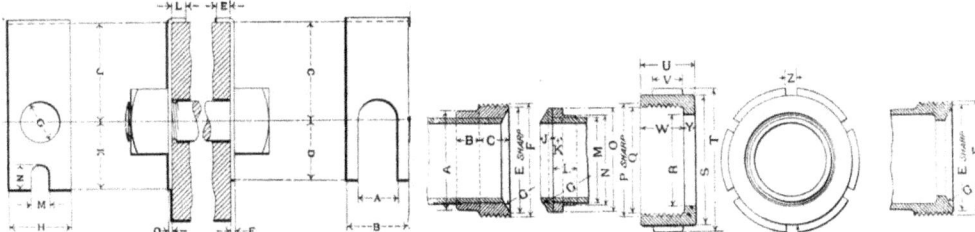

Figs. 4692-4694. Standard Nut Locks.

Figs. 4695-4699. Standard Unions for Copper Pipe.

Diam. of bolt. in.	Diameter for head lock.					
	A. in.	B. in.	C. in.	D. in.	E. in.	F. in.
1¾	2	3¼	2½	2⅝	½	.10
1½	1⅝	2⅞	3	2	½	.10
1¼	1¾	2	2½	1¾	½	.10
1⅛	1⅝	2	3	2¼	½	.10
1	1⅜	2	2	1¾	½	.10
⅞	1¼	1⅞	2½	1⅝	½	.10
1	1⅛	1¾	1¾	1⅝	½	.10
⅞	..	..	..	..	..	..
¾	..	..	..	..	..	..

Diam. of bolt. in.	Diameter for nut lock.						
	G. in.	H. in.	J. in.	K. in.	L. in.	M. in.	N. in.	O. in.
1¾	2	2⅞	2½	2¾	½	½	1⅝	.10
1½	1⅝	2⅞	3	2¼	½	½	1¼	.10
1¼	1⅜	2	2½	2	½	½	1	.10
1⅛	1⅝	2	3	2½	½	½	1	.10
1	1⅜	2	2	2	½	½	1	.10
⅞	1⅛	1¾	2½	1¾	½	½	1	.10
¾	1⅛	1⅜	1¾	1¾	½	½	⅝	.10
⅞	1	1½	1¼	1½	½	½	¾	.10
⅞	1	1½	1¾	1½	½	½	¾	.10

Size of copper pipe.	1 in.	1¼ in.	1½ in.	1¾ in.	2 in.	2¼ in.	2½ in.	2¾ in.
A	......	1.56250	1.81250	2.12500	2.37500	2.62500	2.87500	3.12500
B	......	.37500	.50000	.62500	.62500	.62500	.62500	.62500
C	......	.50000	.56250	.62500	.68750	.81250	.93750	.87500
E	1.29921	1.60629	1.94881	2.20078	2.49606	2.81102	3.05906	3.25590
F	1.42913	1.73622	2.10236	2.35228	2.64566	3.00000	3.24800	3.44488
G	......	1.25000	1.50000	1.81250	2.12500	2.37500	2.37500	2.96875
J	......	.31250	.31250	.31250	.31250	.34375	.37500	.34375
K	......	.18750	.18750	.18750	.25000	.18750	.25000	.21875
L	......	.43750	.46875	.50000	.56250	.50000	.68750	.75000
M	1.00000	1.25000	1.50000	1.75000	2.00000	2.25000	2.50000	2.75000
N	......	1.34670	1.62500	1.87500	2.12500	2.37500	2.68750	2.87500
O	......	1.56250	1.87500	2.12500	2.43750	2.75000	3.00000	3.25000
P	1.44881	1.75590	2.12598	2.37401	2.66929	3.02755	3.27500	3.47244
Q	1.31889	1.62598	1.97244	2.22244	2.51968	2.83862	3.08600	3.28345
R	1.12204	1.37795	1.75196	2.00787	2.18503	2.55906	2.75000	2.95275
S	1.71259	1.96850	2.48031	2.69684	3.14960	3.42519	3.75000	3.74015
T	1.96850	2.26378	2.87401	3.01181	3.56299	3.89763	4.12500	4.17322
U	.82677	.86614	1.06299	1.16141	1.45669	1.47637	1.62500	1.53543
V	.49212	.47244	.57086	.64960	.78740	.88582	.87500	.74803
W	.66929	.62992	.74803	.84645	1.14173	1.14173	1.31250	1.20078
Y	.15748	.23622	.31496	.31496	.31496	.33464	.31250	.33464
Z	.25000	.25000	.31250	.31250	.25000	.31250	.31250	.31250
t	12	12	10	10	10	8	8	8

Figs. 4700-4702. Dimensions of Standard Reamers.

D. in.	L. in.	A. in.	B. in.	C. in.	E. in.	F. in.	G. in.	S. in.	T. in.	Mark reamer. in.
½	8	½	¾	7-16	½	½	¾	½	½	½—No. 4
½	12	½	¾	7-16	½	½	¾	½	½	½—" 8
⅝	8	⅝	¾	9-16	½	½	¾	⅝	½	⅝—" 4
⅝	12	⅝	¾	9-16	½	½	¾	⅝	½	⅝—" 8
¾	8	¾	1 1-16	11-16	½	½	1	¾	½	¾—" 4
¾	12	¾	1 1-16	11-16	½	½	1	¾	½	¾—" 8
¾	16	¾	1 1-16	11-16	½	½	1	¾	½	¾—" 12
¾	20	¾	1 1-16	11-16	½	½	1	¾	½	¾—" 16
⅞	8	⅞	1¼	13-16	½	½	1⅛	⅞	½	⅞—" 4
⅞	12	⅞	1¼	13-16	½	½	1⅛	⅞	½	⅞—" 8
⅞	16	⅞	1¼	13-16	½	½	1⅛	⅞	½	⅞—" 12
⅞	20	⅞	1¼	13-16	½	½	1⅛	⅞	½	⅞—" 16
1	8	1	1¼	15-16	½	½	1¼	⅞	½	1—" 4
1	12	1	1¼	15-16	½	½	1¼	⅞	½	1—" 8
1	16	1	1¼	15-16	½	½	1¼	⅞	½	1—" 12
1	20	1	1¼	15-16	½	½	1¼	⅞	½	1—" 16
1⅛	8	1⅛	1½	1 1-16	½	½	1¼	1	½	1⅛—" 4
1⅛	12	1⅛	1½	1 1-16	½	½	1¼	1	½	1⅛—" 8
1⅛	16	1⅛	1½	1 1-16	½	½	1¼	1	½	1⅛—" 12
1⅛	20	1⅛	1½	1 1-16	½	½	1¼	1	½	1⅛—" 16
1¼	8	1¼	1½	1 3-16	½	½	1¼	1	½	1¼—" 4
1¼	12	1¼	1½	1 3-16	½	½	1¼	1	½	1¼—" 8
1¼	16	1¼	1½	1 3-16	½	½	1¼	1	½	1¼—" 12
1¼	20	1¼	1½	1 3-16	½	½	1¼	1	½	1¼—" 16
1⅜	8	1⅜	1½	1 5-16	½	½	1¼	1	½	1⅜—" 4
1⅜	12	1⅜	1½	1 5-16	½	½	1¼	1	½	1⅜—" 8
1⅜	16	1⅜	1½	1 5-16	½	½	1¼	1	½	1⅜—" 12
1⅜	20	1⅜	1½	1 5-16	½	½	1¼	1	½	1⅜—" 16
1½	8	1½	1½	1 7-16	½	½	1¼	1	½	1½—" 4
1½	12	1½	1½	1 7-16	½	½	1¼	1	½	1½—" 8
1½	16	1½	1½	1 7-16	½	½	1¼	1	½	1½—" 12
1½	20	1½	1¼	1 7-16	½	½	1¼	1	½	1½—" 16

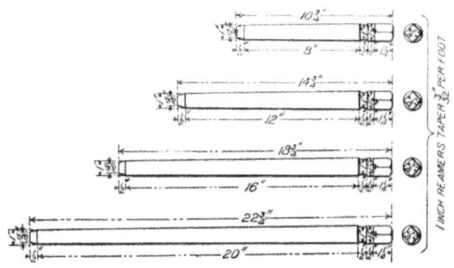

Figs. 4703-4710. Standard Taper Reamers.

To allow for grinding, each reamer is made 4 in. longer than longest bolt of its class. When a No. 12 reamer has been reduced 1/32 in. in diameter and goes in up to the top of flutes when reaming for longest bolt of its class, by cutting 4 in. from the small end, it can be used as a No. 8 reamer, and afterwards as a No. 4.

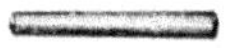

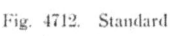

Fig. 4711. Standard Taper Pins. Taper ¼ in. in 12 in.

Number of pin.	Diam. at large end.	Minimum and maximum lengths.
0	.156	From ¾ in. to 1 in. inclusive
1	.172	" ¾ " " 1¼ " "
2	.193	" ¾ " " 1½ " "
3	.219	" ¾ " " 1¾ " "
4	.250	" ¾ " " 2 " "
5	.289	" ¾ " " 2¼ " "
6	.341	" ¾ " " 3¼ " "
7	.409	" 1 " " 3¾ " "
8	.492	" 1¼ " " 4½ " "
9	.591	" 1½ " " 5¼ " "
10	.706	" 1½ " " 6 " "

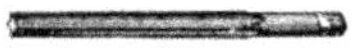

Fig. 4712. Standard Taper Reamer.

Size No.	Diam. at small end.	Length of flute. in.	Total length. in.
0	0.125	1 5-16	2
1	0.146	1 9-16	2⅜
2	0.162	1 13-16	2 11-16
3	0.183	2 1-16	3
4	0.208	2⅜	3 7-16
5	0.240	2⅝	4⅛
6	0.279	3⅝	5
7	0.331	4 7-16	6 1-16
8	0.398	5¼	7 1-16
9	0.482	6⅛	8⅛
10	0.581	7	9½

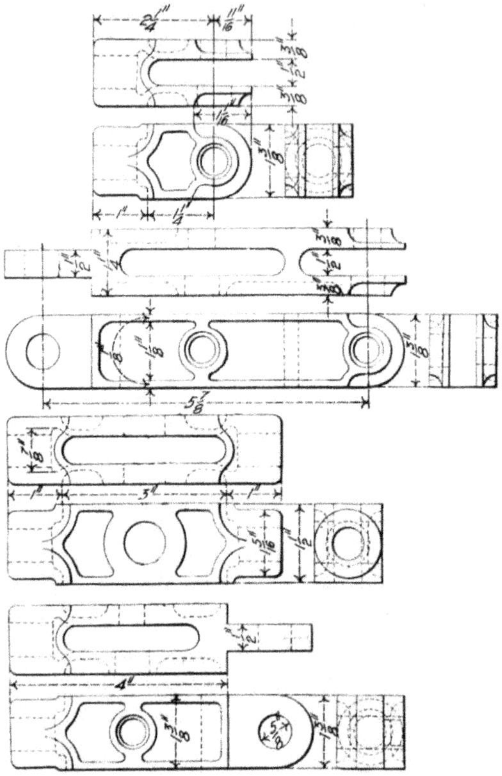

Figs. 4713-4720. Standard Malleable Iron Connections for ½-in. Pipes When Used as Operating Rods.

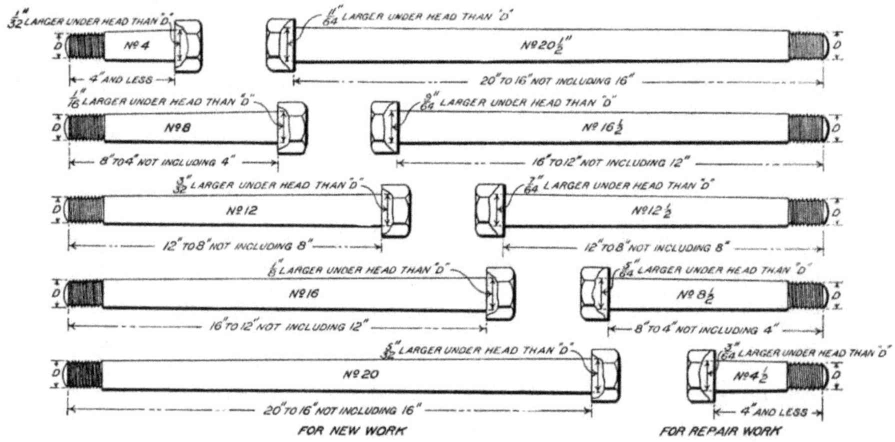

Figs. 4721-4730. Standard Taper Bolts.

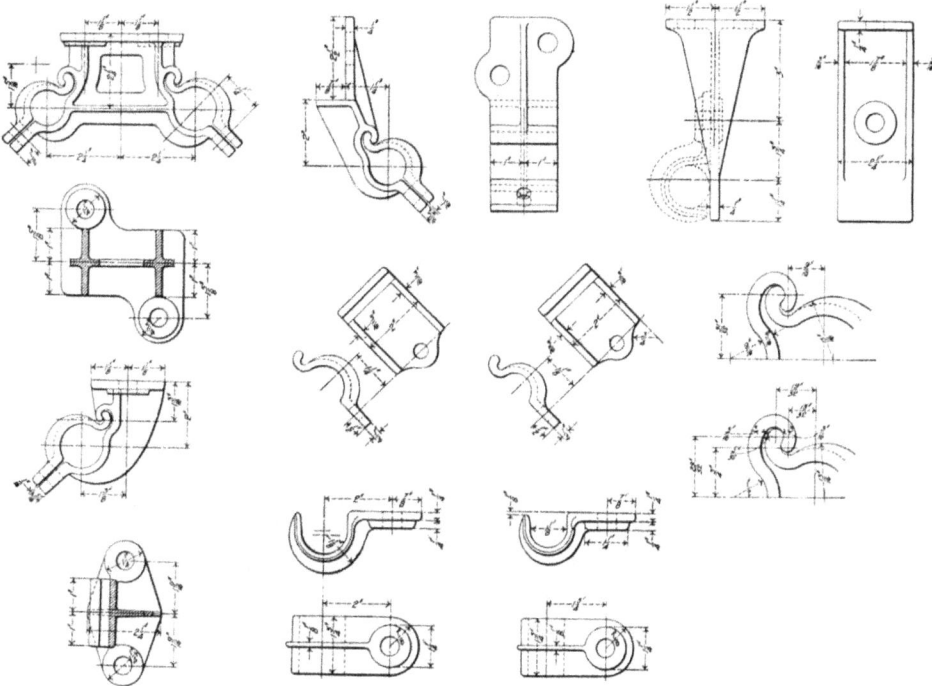

Figs. 4731-4748. Standard Clamps for Air Brake, Signal and Water Scoop Heater Pipes.

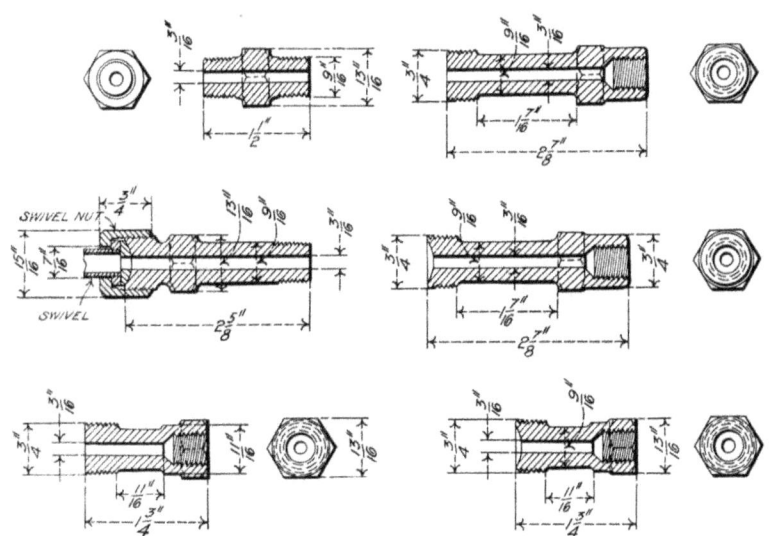

Figs. 4749-4759. Standard Connections for Steam and Air Gages.

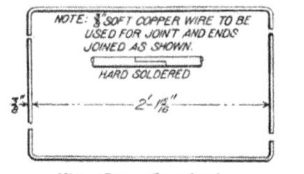

Fig. 4760. Standard Steam Chest Copper Joint.

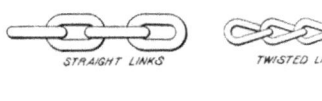
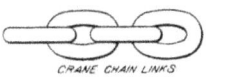

Figs. 4761-4764. Standard Chain Links.

RAILROAD STANDARDS, Pennsylvania Railroad.

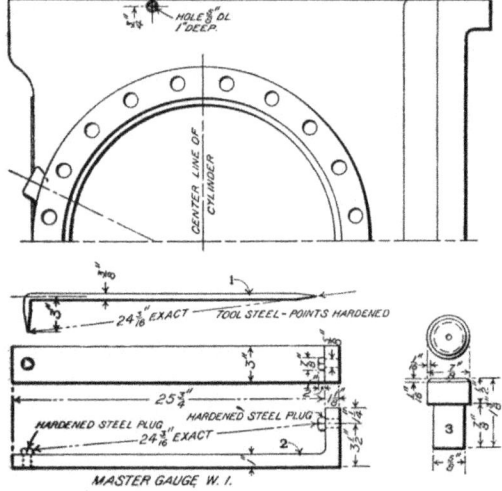

Figs. 4765-4770. Standard Datum Points, Master Gage and Tram for Valve Setting.

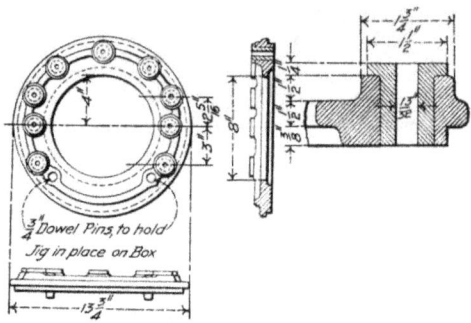

Figs. 4771-4774. Standard Jig for Boring Trailing Truck Boxes.

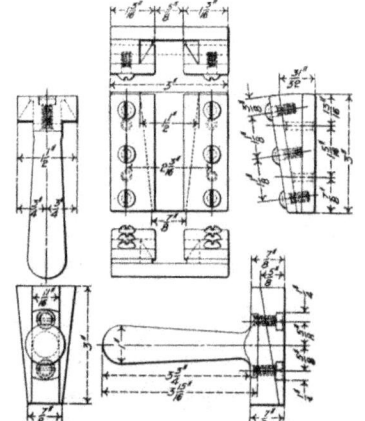

Figs. 4775-4781. Standard Gages for Fitting Lamp Brackets.

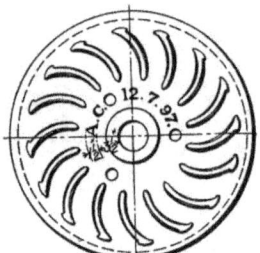

Fig. 4795. Standard Stenciling on Wheels, Showing Shop and Date Applied.

Fig. 4796. Standard Marking for Axles.

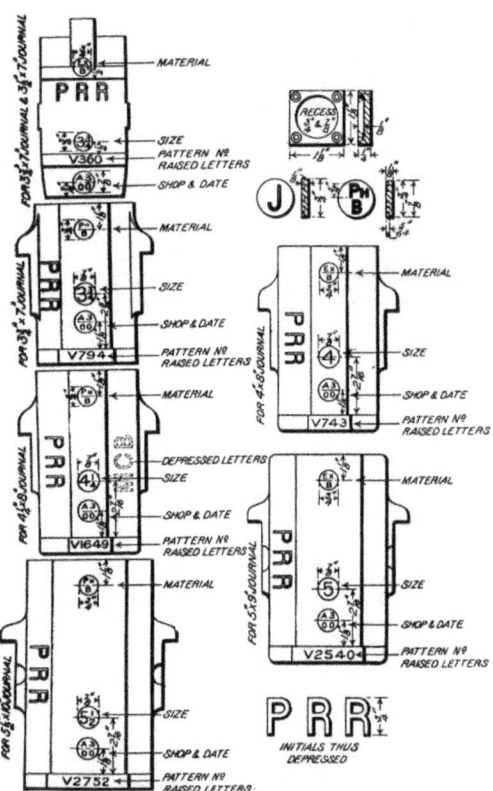

Figs. 4782-4794. Standard Markings for Journal Bearings.

(439)

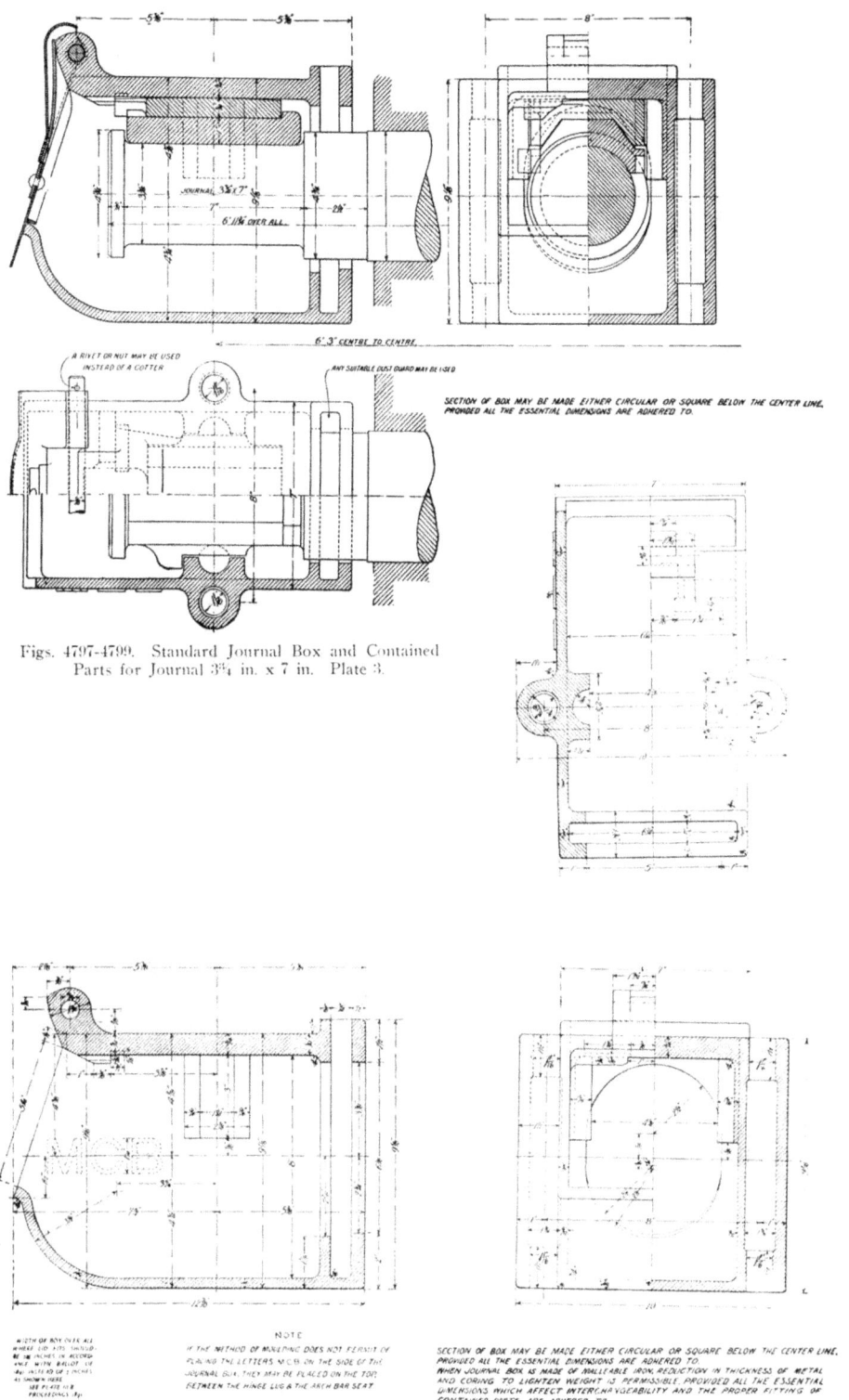

Figs. 4797-4799. Standard Journal Box and Contained Parts for Journal 3¾ in. x 7 in. Plate 3.

Figs. 4800-4802. Standard Journal Box for Journal 3¾ in. x 7 in. Plate 2.

MASTER MECHANICS' STANDARDS, Journal Boxes; Details. Figs. 4803-4819

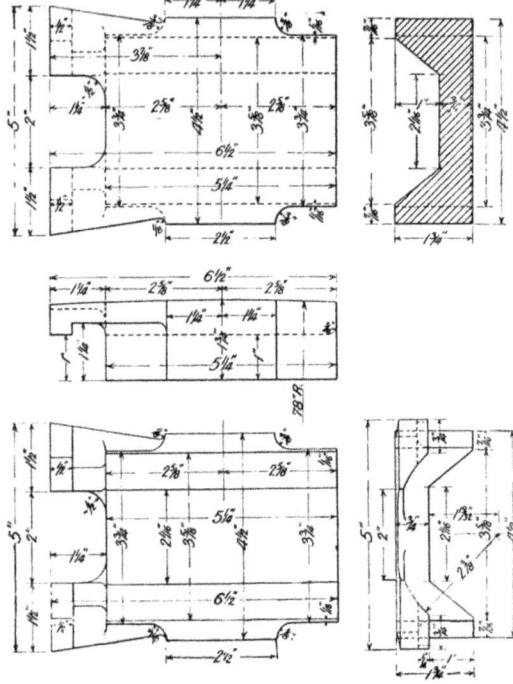

NOTE—*Skeleton wedge of malleable iron or steel may be used provided the essential dimensions are adhered to. The lid spring may be of any design and may be secured to the lid by any practicable method, provided that it works properly on the standard box and is of the designated section, 2 in. x 1/8 in. A rivet or nut may be used instead of a cotter in hinge pin if preferred.*

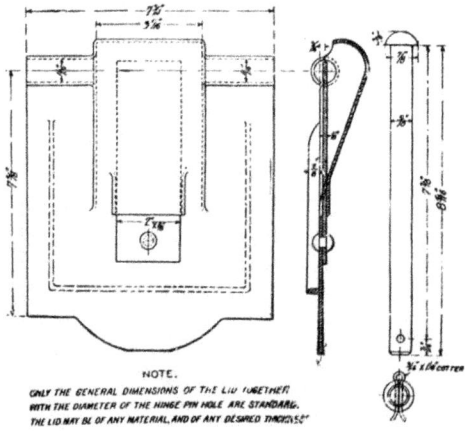

Figs. 4803-4807. Standard Wedge for Journal 3¾ in. x 7 in. Plate 4.

Figs. 4808-4811. Standard Journal Box Lid and Pin for Journal 3¾ in. x 7 in. Plate 4.

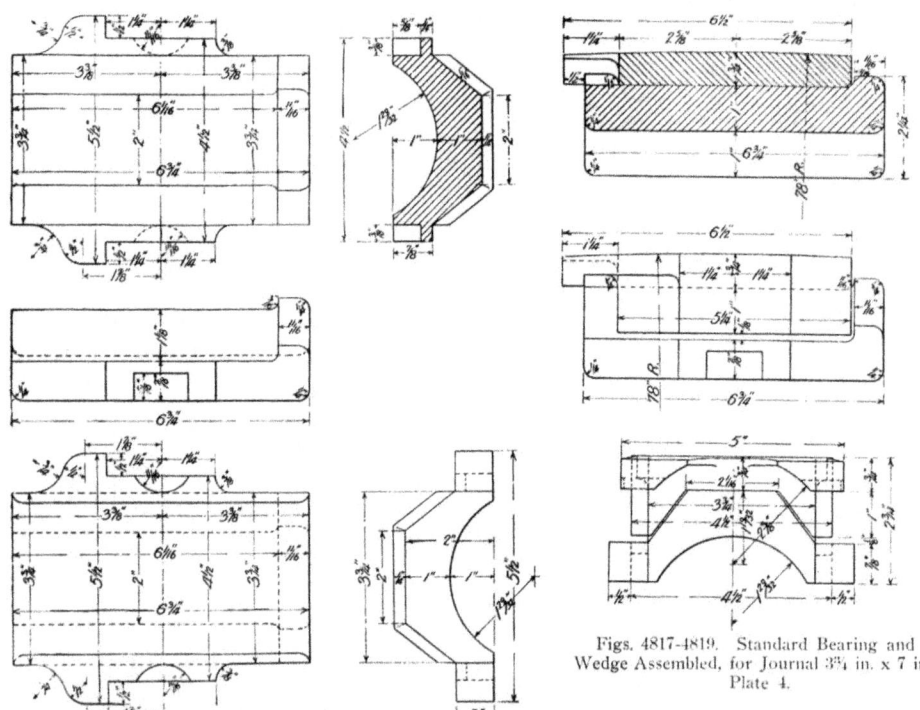

Figs. 4812-4816. Standard Bearing for Journal 3¾ in x 7 in. Plate 4.

Figs. 4817-4819. Standard Bearing and Wedge Assembled, for Journal 3¾ in. x 7 in. Plate 4.

Figs. 4820-4825 MASTER MECHANICS' STANDARDS, Journal Boxes.

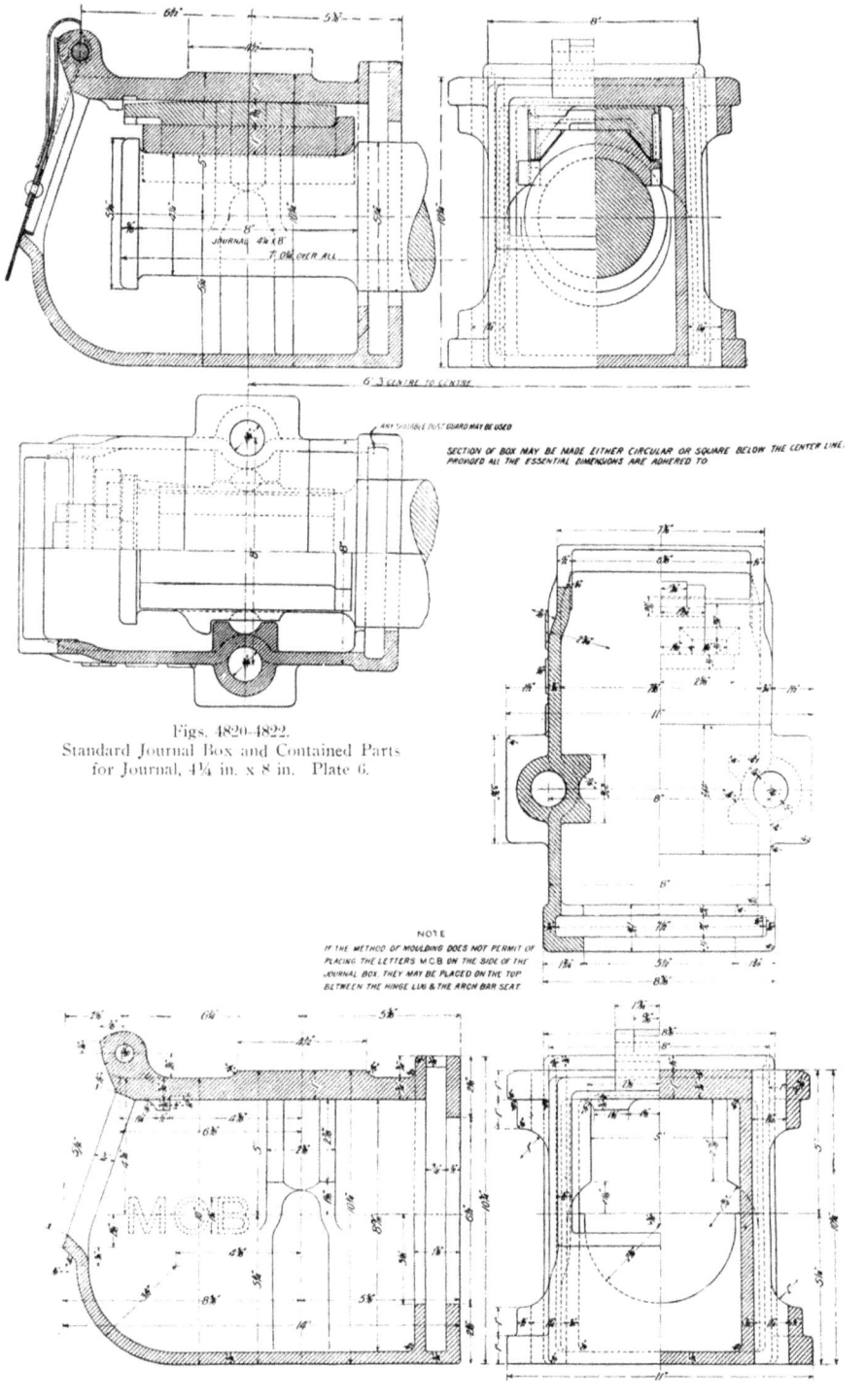

Figs. 4820-4822. Standard Journal Box and Contained Parts for Journal, 4¼ in. x 8 in. Plate 6.

Figs. 4823-4825. Standard Journal Box for Journal, 4¼ in. x 8 in. Plate 5.

MASTER MECHANICS' STANDARDS, Journal Boxes; Details. Figs. 4826-4842

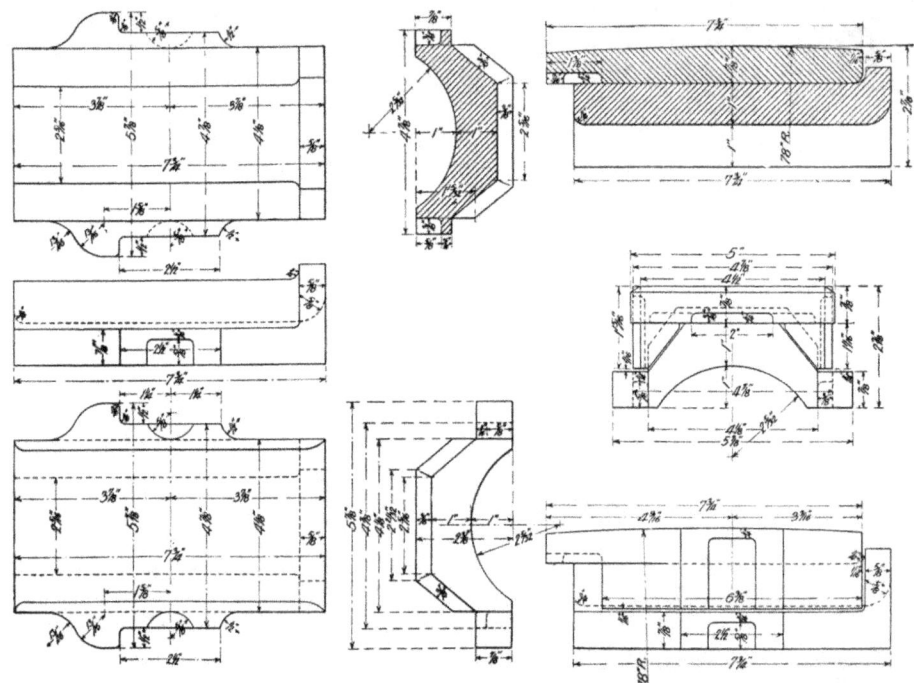

Figs. 4826-4830. Standard Bearing for Journal, 4¼ in. x 8 in. Plate 7.

Figs. 4831-4833. Standard Bearing and Wedge Assembled, for Journal, 4¼ in. x 8 in. Plate 7.

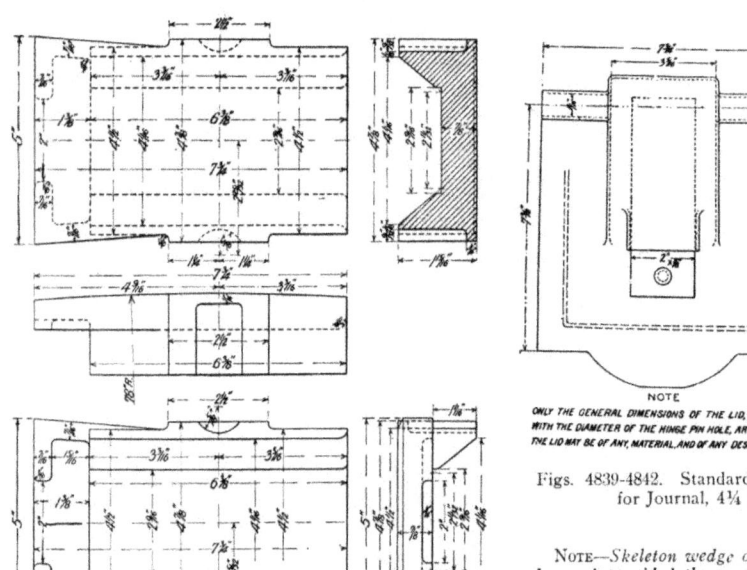

Figs. 4834-4838. Standard Wedge for Journal, 4¼ in. x 8 in. Plate 7.

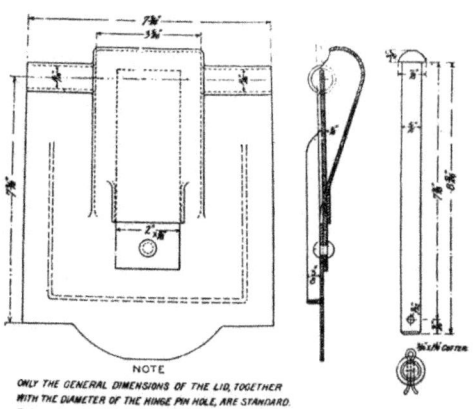

NOTE—ONLY THE GENERAL DIMENSIONS OF THE LID, TOGETHER WITH THE DIAMETER OF THE HINGE PIN HOLE, ARE STANDARD. THE LID MAY BE OF ANY MATERIAL, AND OF ANY DESIRED THICKNESS.

Figs. 4839-4842. Standard Journal Box Lid and Pin for Journal, 4¼ in. x 8 in. Plate 7.

NOTE—*Skeleton wedge of malleable iron or steel may be used provided the essential dimensions are adhered to. The lid spring may be of any design and may be secured to the lid by any practicable method, provided that it works properly on the standard box and is of the designated section, 2 in. x ⅛ in. A rivet or nut may be used instead of a cotter in hinge pin if preferred.*

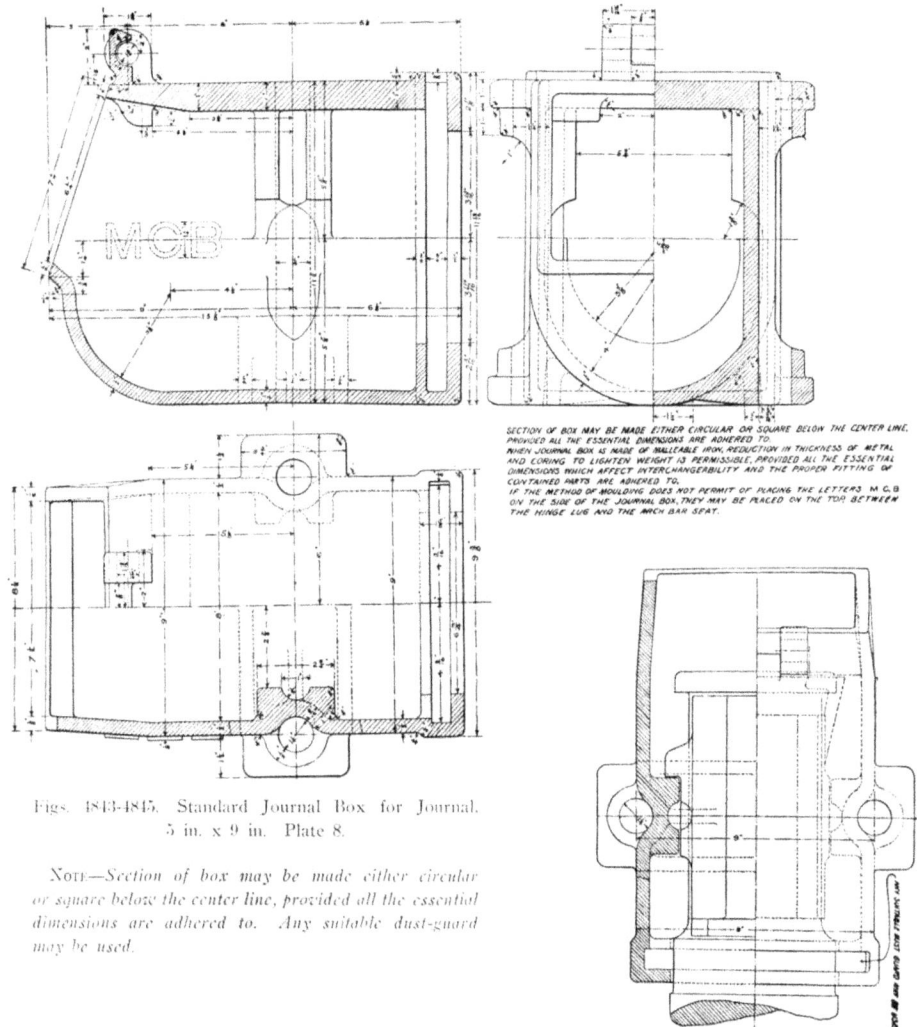

Figs. 4843-4845. Standard Journal Box for Journal, 5 in. x 9 in. Plate 8.

Note—Section of box may be made either circular or square below the center line, provided all the essential dimensions are adhered to. Any suitable dust-guard may be used.

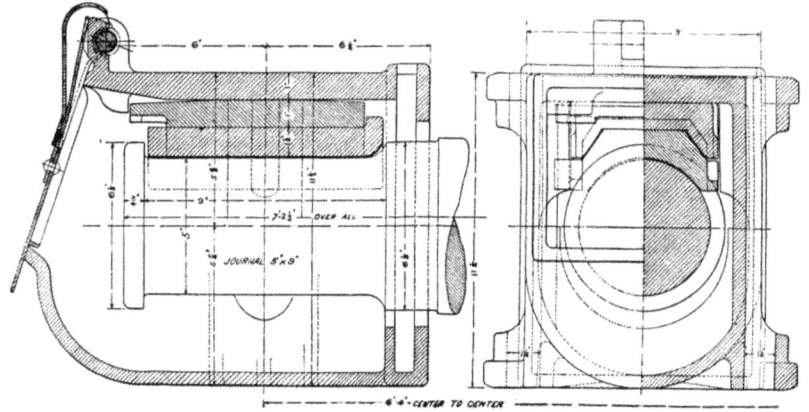

Figs. 4846-4848. Standard Journal Box and Contained Parts for Journal, 5 in. x 9 in. Plate 9.

MASTER MECHANICS' STANDARDS, Journal Boxes; Details.   Figs. 4849-4871

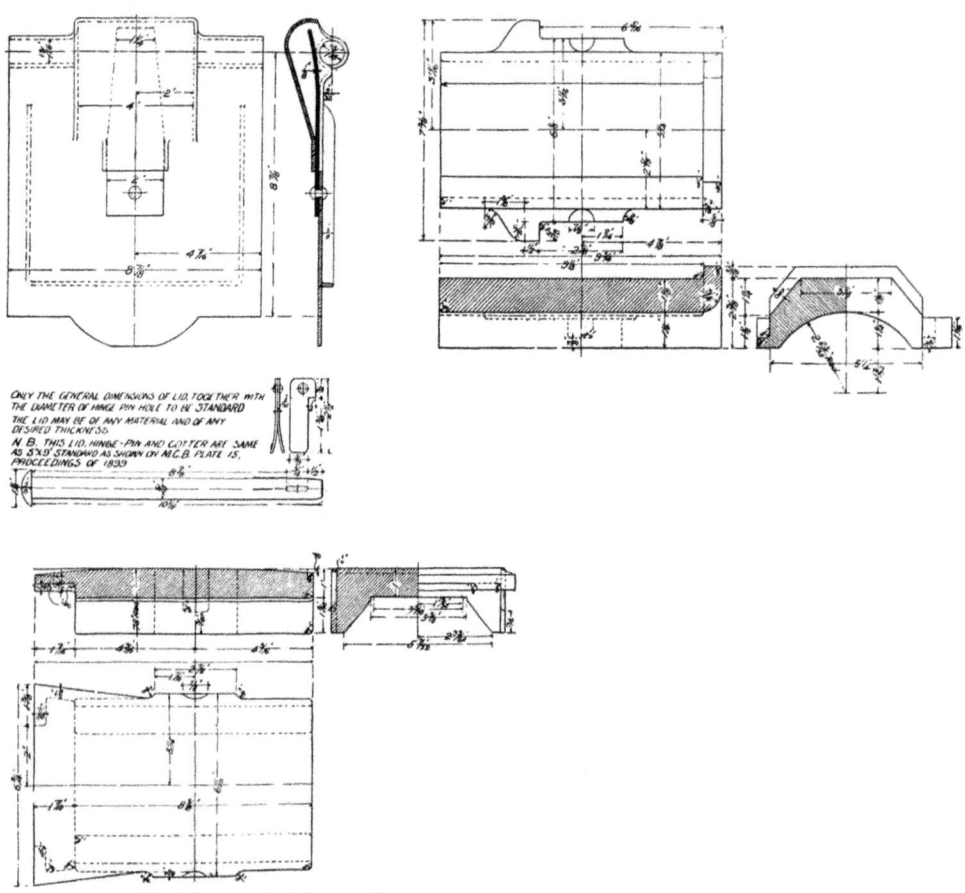

Figs. 4849-4859. Standard Journal Bearing, Wedge and Lid for Journal, 5½ in. x 10 in. Plate 13.

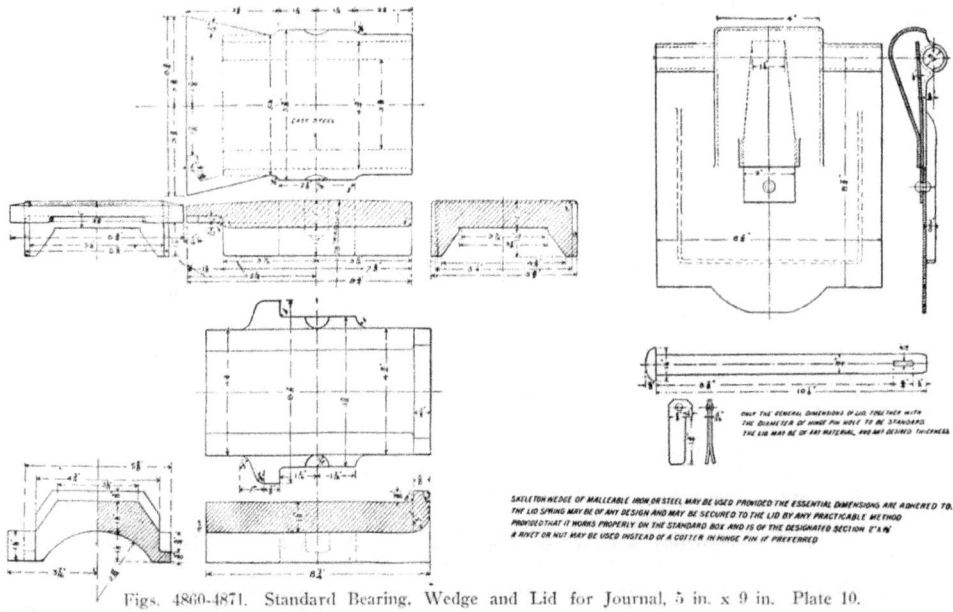

Figs. 4860-4871. Standard Bearing, Wedge and Lid for Journal, 5 in. x 9 in. Plate 10.

MASTER MECHANICS' STANDARDS, Journal Boxes.

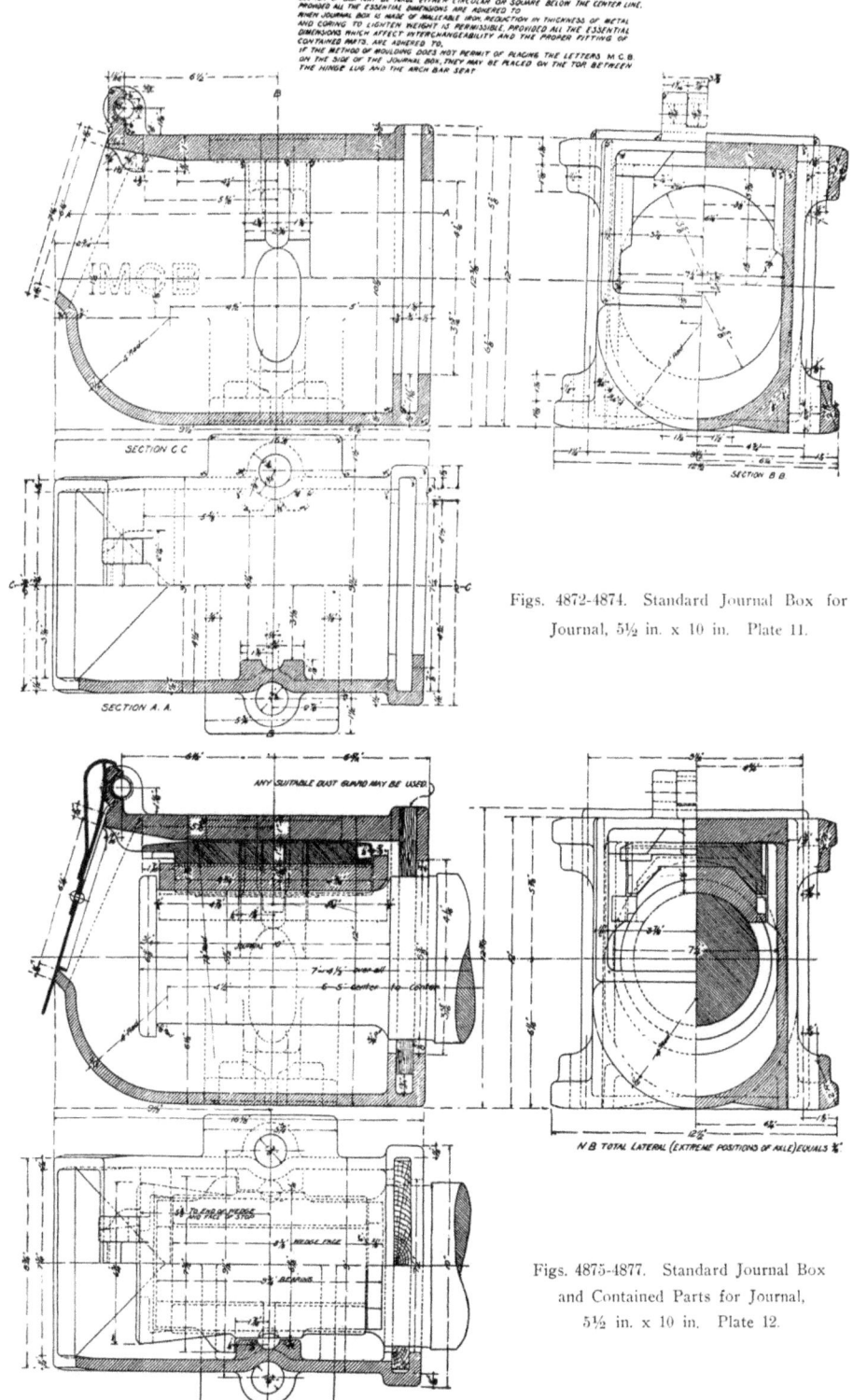

Figs. 4872-4874. Standard Journal Box for Journal, 5½ in. x 10 in. Plate 11.

Figs. 4875-4877. Standard Journal Box and Contained Parts for Journal, 5½ in. x 10 in. Plate 12.

MASTER MECHANICS' STANDARDS, Axles and Pedestal. Figs. 4878-4887

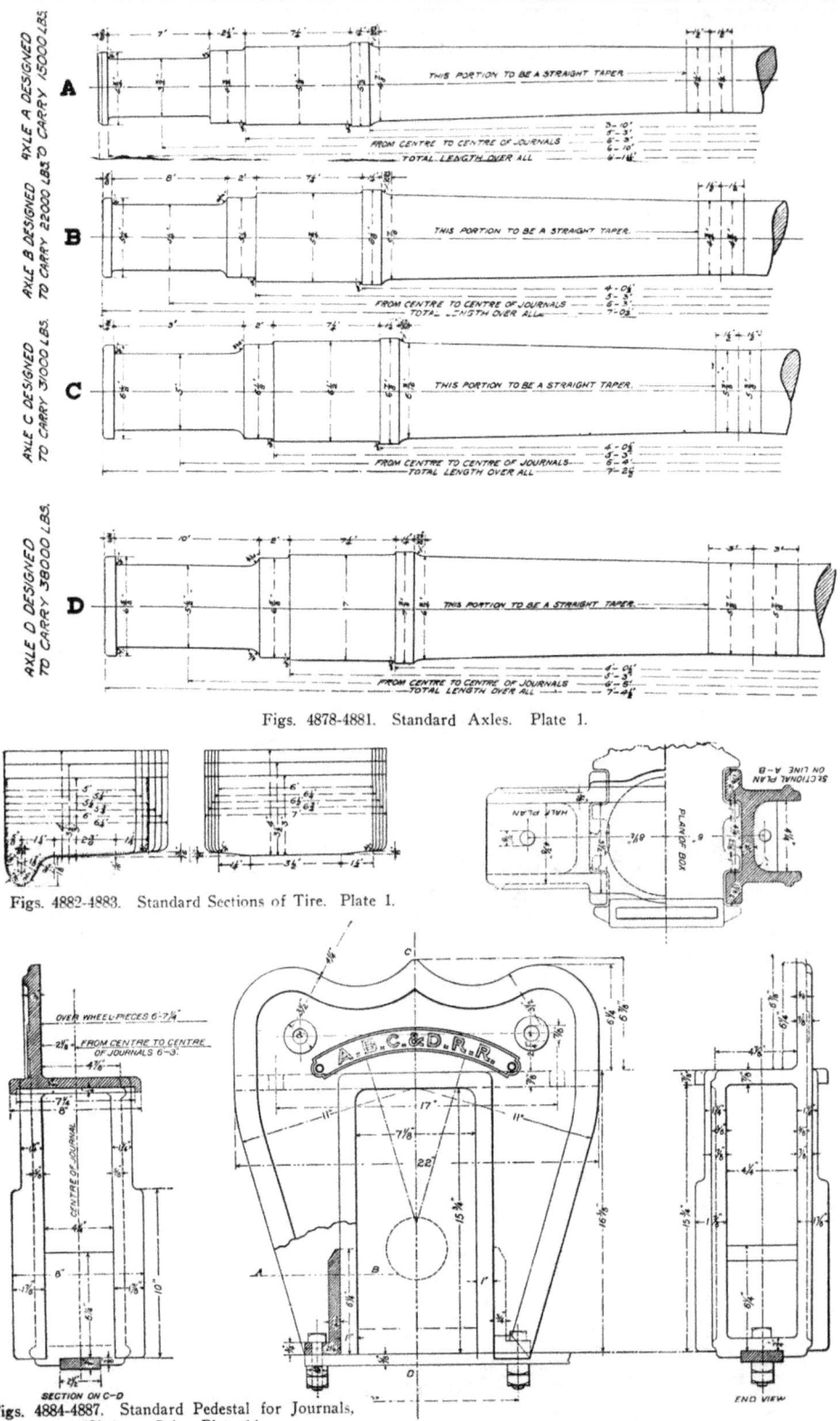

Figs. 4878-4881. Standard Axles. Plate 1.

Figs. 4882-4883. Standard Sections of Tire. Plate 1.

Figs. 4884-4887. Standard Pedestal for Journals, 3¾ in. x 7 in. Plate 14.

Figs. 4888-4892   MACHINE TOOLS, Bending Rolls and Bolt Threading Machines.

Fig. 4888. Heavy Plate Bending Rolls, Provided with Two Motors. One for Driving the Lower Rolls and the Other for Raising and Lowering the Top Rolls. Hilles & Jones Company.

Fig. 4889. National Double Head Bolt Cutter. National Machinery Co.

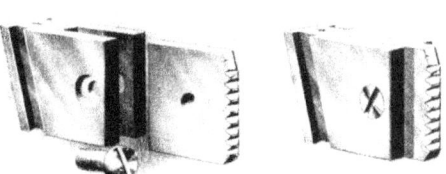

Figs. 4890-4891. National Interchangeable Case Dies. National Machinery Co.

Fig. 4892. 1½-Inch Double Stay Bolt Cutter. Acme Machinery Company.

MACHINE TOOLS, Bolt Threading and Horizontal Boring Machines. Figs. 4893-4895

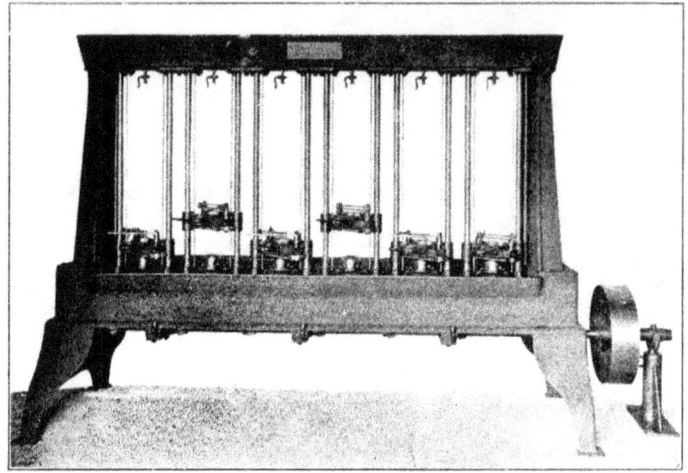

Fig. 4893. Stay Bolt Threading Machine. Edwin Harrington, Son & Co., Inc.

Fig. 4894. 1¼-Inch Double Bolt Cutter. Acme Machinery Company.

Fig. 4895. Horizontal Boring Machine. Betts Machine Co.

Fig. 4896. Horizontal Boring Machine. Binsse Machine Company.

Fig. 4897. Horizontal Boring Machine. Gisholt Machine Company.

Fig. 4898. Driving Box Boring Machine. Wm. Sellers & Co., Inc.

MACHINE TOOLS, Boring and Turning Mills.   Figs. 4899-4900

Fig. 4899. Tender Wheel Boring Machine. Niles-Bement-Pond Co.

Fig. 4900. Boring and Turning Mill. Niles-Bement-Pond Co.

Fig. 4901. Boring and Turning Mill. Gisholt Machine Co.

Fig. 4902. 84-Inch Tire Turning Mill. Betts Machine Co.

MACHINE TOOLS, Bushing Press, Cutting-Off and Centering Machine.   Figs. 4903-4905

Fig. 4903. 36-Inch Boring and Turning Mill Fitted with Turret Head. Bullard Machine Tool Co.

Fig. 4904. Portable Hydraulic Bushing Press. Watson-Stillman Co.

Fig. 4905. 12-Inch Double Cutting-Off and Centering Machine for Cutting Off and Centering Axles and Shafts of Any Diameter up to 12 Inches. Niles-Bement-Pond Co.

Figs. 4906-4908 MACHINE TOOLS, Cold Saws and Crank Pin Turning Machine.

Fig. 4906. Cold Saw Cutting-Off Machine, Fitted with Taylor-Newbold Cold Saw. Espen-Lucas Machine Works.

Fig. 4907. High Duty Metal Saw, Fitted with "Tindel" Saw Blade. High Duty Saw & Tool Co.

Fig. 4908. Portable Crank Pin Turning Machine. H. B. Underwood & Co.

MACHINE TOOLS, Crank Pin Press, Cylinder Boring Bar and Drills.   Figs. 4909-4915

Fig. 4909. Portable Hydraulic Crank Pin Press. Watson-Stillman Co.

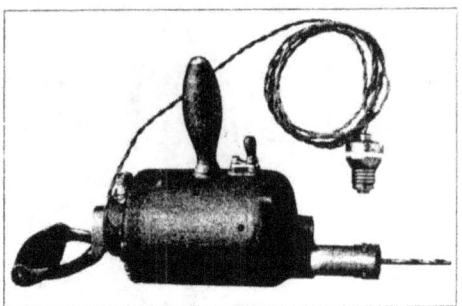

Fig. 4910. Motor-Driven Hand Drill. Hisey-Wolf Machine Co.

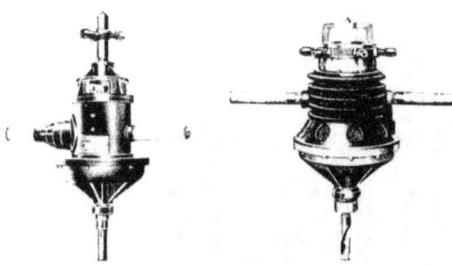

Figs. 4911-4912. Duntley Air-Cooled Electric Drills. Chicago Pneumatic Tool Co.

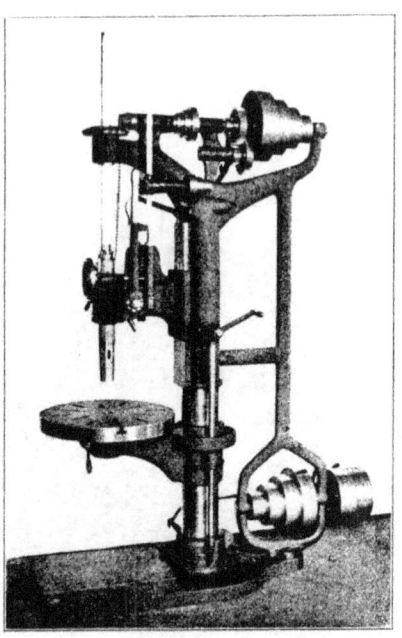

Fig. 4913. 36-Inch Upright Drill. Hoefer Mfg. Co.

Fig. 4914. Friction Drive Sensitive Drill. The Knecht Bros. Co.

Fig. 4915. Portable Locomotive Cylinder Boring Bar. H. B. Underwood & Co.

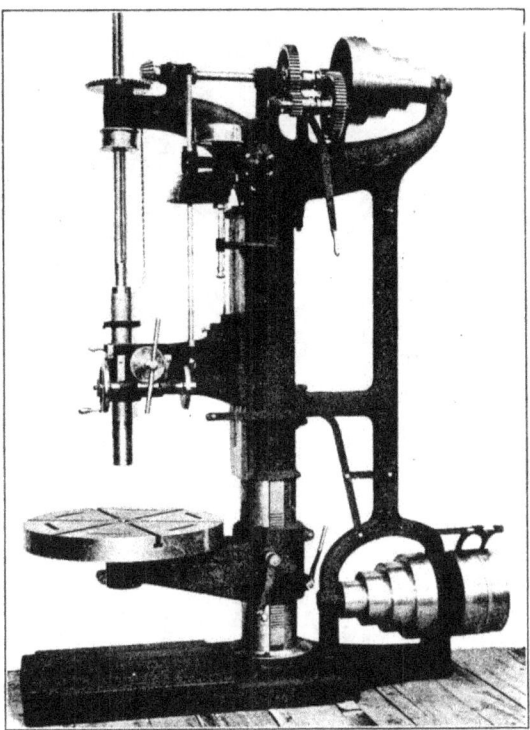

Fig. 4916. Upright Drill. Hamilton Machine Tool Co.

Fig. 4917. Special Combination Radial and Locomotive Frame Drilling Machine. American Tool Works Co.

Fig. 4918. Small Upright or Vertical Drill. H. G. Barr & Co.

Fig. 4919. Six-Spindle Multiple Drill. Niles-Bement-Pond Co.

Fig. 4920. Six-Spindle Mud Ring Drill. Bickford Drill & Tool Co.

Fig. 4921. Locomotive Frame Drill. Foote, Burt & Co.

Fig. 4922. Universal Radial Drilling Machine. Niles-Bement-Pond Co.

Fig. 4923. Plain Radial Drill, Fitted with Speed Box. American Tool Works Co.

MACHINE TOOLS, Drilling Machine and Flue Cleaning Machine. Figs. 4924-4925

Fig. 4924. Radial Drilling Machine. Fosdick Machine Tool Co.

Fig. 4925. Flue Cleaning Machine. Joseph T. Ryerson & Son.

Fig. 4926. McGrath Pneumatic Flue Welder. Draper Mfg. Co.

Fig. 4927. Stationary Forge. B. F. Sturtevant Co.

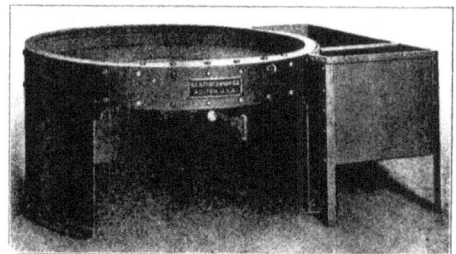

Fig. 4928. Stationary Forge. B. F. Sturtevant Co.

Fig. 4930. Stationary Smith Shop Forges. Buffalo Forge Co.

MACHINE TOOLS, Forges and Forging Machines. Figs. 4931-4934

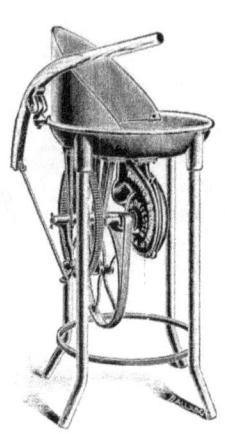

Fig. 4931. Portable Forge. Boynton & Plummer.

Fig. 4932. Portable Forge. Buffalo Forge Co.

Fig. 4933. Three-Inch Heading and Forging Machine. Acme Machinery Co.

Fig. 4934. Universal Forging Machine. Ajax Mfg. Co.

Fig. 4935. Flue Welding Furnace, Fitted with Oil Burners. Tate, Jones & Co., Inc.

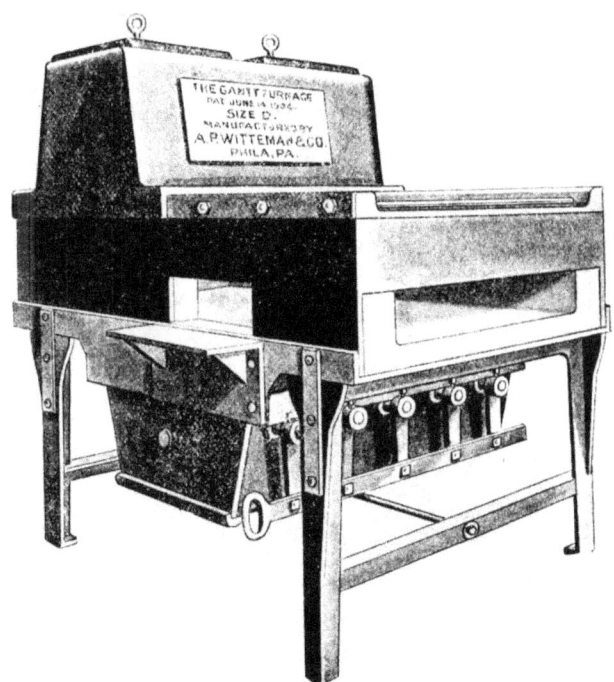

Fig. 4936. The Gantt Furnace. A. P. Witteman & Co.

MACHINE TOOLS, Grinding Machines.   Figs. 4937-4940

Fig. 4937. Motor-Driven Tool Grinder. Stow Mfg. Co.

Fig. 4938. Motor-Driven Universal Tool Grinder. Gisholt Machine Co.

Fig. 4939. Locomotive Guide Bar Grinding or Lapping Machine. Edwin Harrington, Son & Co., Inc.

Fig. 4940. Gap Grinding Machine. Norton Grinding Co.

MACHINE TOOLS, Grinding Machine and Power Hammers.

Fig. 4941. Tool Room Grinding Machine. Cincinnati Milling Machine Co.

Fig. 4942. Justice Power Hammer. Williams, White & Co.

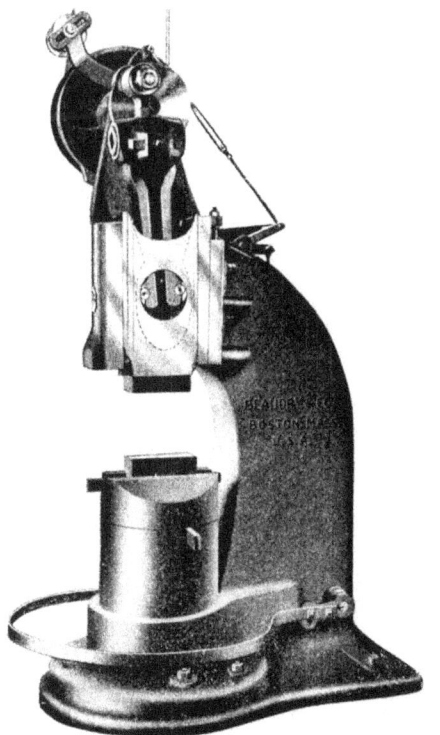

Fig. 4943. Champion Power Hammer. Beaudry & Co.

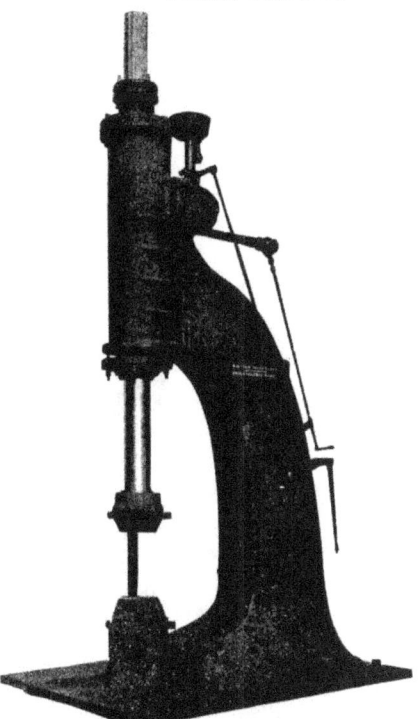

Fig. 4944. 2,000-lb. Single Frame Steam Hammer. William Sellers & Co., Inc.

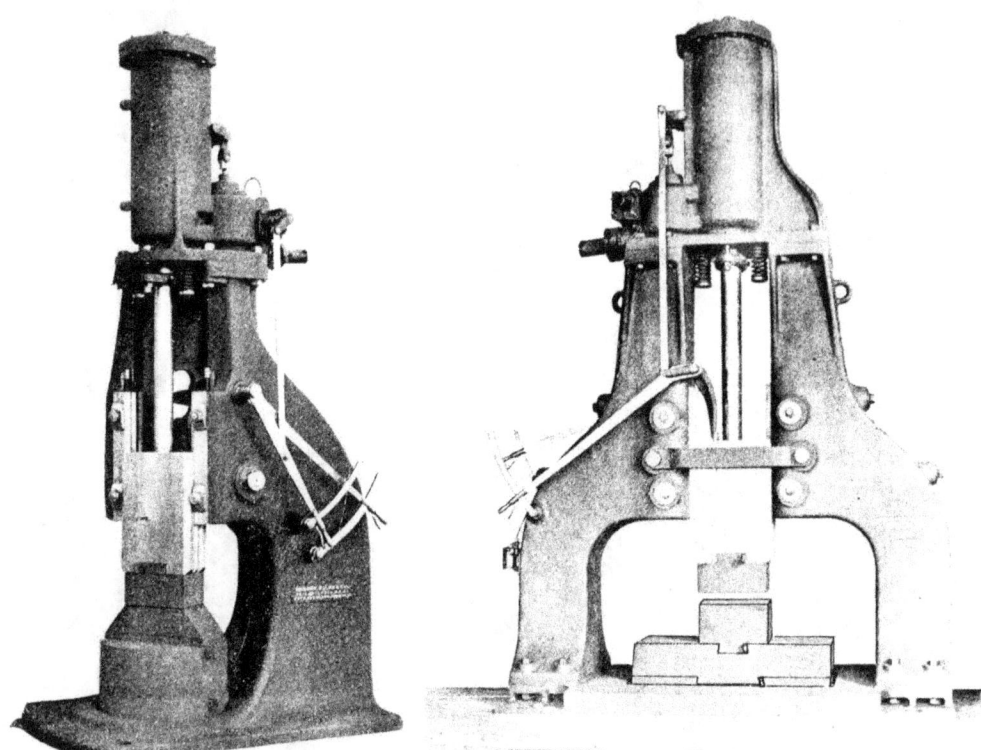

Fig. 4945. Single Frame Steam Hammer. Niles-Bement-Pond Co.

Fig. 4946. Double Frame Steam Hammer. Niles-Bement-Pond Co.

Fig. 4947. Heavy 90-Inch Driving Wheel Chucking Lathe. Niles-Bement-Pond Co.

Fig. 4948. Single Axle Lathe. Niles-Bement-Pond. Co.

Fig. 4949. Double End Axle Lathe. Lodge & Shipley Machine Tool Co.

Fig. 4950. Double Axle Lathe. Putnam Machine Co.

MACHINE TOOLS, Lathes.   Figs. 4951-4953

Fig. 4951. Double Axle Lathe. Niles-Bement-Pond Co.

Fig. 4952. 25-Inch Swing Roughing Lathe. Wm. Sellers & Co., Inc.

Fig. 4953. 22-Inch Swing Engine Lathe. Greaves, Klusman & Co.

Fig. 4954. 42-Inch Engine Lathe. Niles-Bement-Pond Co.

Fig. 4955. 42-Inch Swing, Triple Geared Engine Lathe. American Tool Works Co.

Fig. 4956. 30-Inch Swing, Patent Head Engine Lathe. Lodge & Shipley Machine Tool Co.

MACHINE TOOLS, Cylinder Boring Machines.

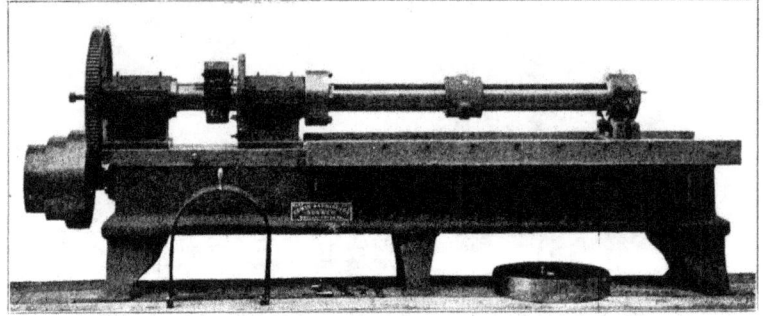

Fig. 4957. Cylinder Shell Boring Machine. Edwin Harrington, Son & Co., Inc.

Fig. 4958. Locomotive Cylinder Boring Machine. Niles-Bement-Pond Co.

Fig. 4959. Locomotive Cylinder Boring Machine. William Sellers & Co., Inc.

Fig. 4960. Locomotive Rod Boring Machine. Niles-Bement-Pond Co.

Fig. 4961. Locomotive Rod Boring Machine. Baker Bros.

MACHINE TOOLS, Milling Machine. Figs. 4962-4963

Fig. 4962. Locomotive Rod Boring Machine. Wm. Sellers & Co., Inc.

Fig. 4963. Duplex Milling Machine. Becker-Brainard Milling Machine Co.

Fig. 4964. Vertical Milling Machine. Niles-Bement-Pond Co.

Fig. 4965. Universal Milling Machine. Cincinnati Milling Machine Co.

Fig. 4966. Plain Milling Machine. Cincinnati Milling Machine Co.

Fig. 4967. Horizontal Milling Machine. Niles-Bement-Pond Co.

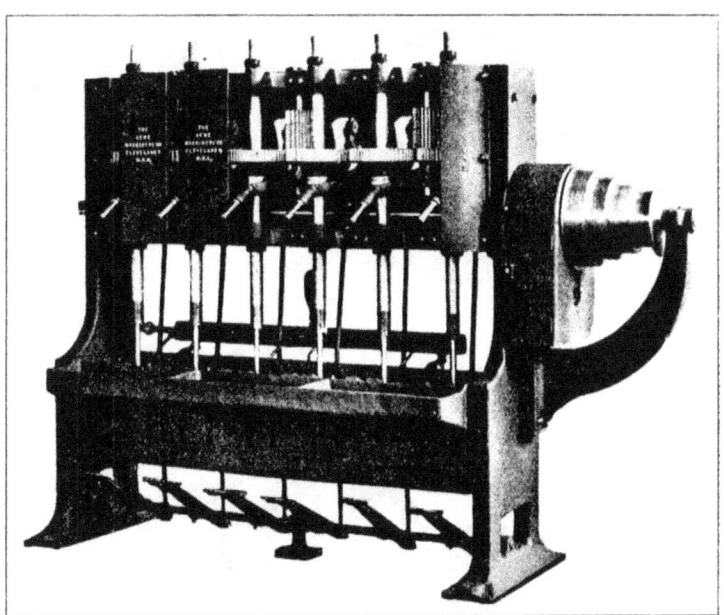

Fig. 4968. 1½-Inch Six-Spindle Nut Tapping Machine. Acme Machinery Co.

Fig. 4969. Pipe Bending Machine. Chicago Pneumatic Tool Co.

MACHINE TOOLS, Pipe Threading and Cutting-Off Machines. Figs. 4970-4972

Fig. 4970. The Standard Wieland Six-Inch Pipe Threading and Cutting Machine. Standard Engineering Co.

Fig. 4971. Six-Inch Standard Pipe Machine, Equipped with Sliding Die Head. Stoever Foundry & Mfg. Co.

Fig. 4972. Peerless Pipe Threading and Cutting Machine. Bignall & Keeler Mfg. Co.

Fig. 4973. Locomotive Connecting Rod Planer. Woodward & Powell Planer Co.

Fig. 4974. 48-Inch Planer. Betts Machine Co.

Fig. 4975. 48-Inch x 48-Inch x 10-Foot Planer. Cincinnati Planer Co.

Fig. 4976. 36-Inch x 36-Inch x 10-Foot Spiral-Geared Planer with Shifting Belts. William Sellers & Co., Inc.

Fig. 4977. Quick Return Planer. Chandler Planer Co.

Fig. 4978. "Little Giant" Piston Air Drill.

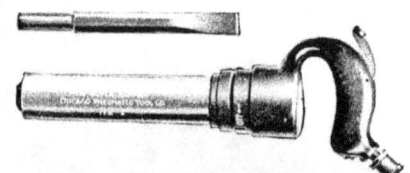

Fig. 4979. "Boyer" Riveting Hammer.   Fig. 4980. "Boyer" Chipping Hammer.

Chicago Pneumatic Tool Co.

Figs. 4981-4988   MACHINE TOOLS, Pneumatic Tools.

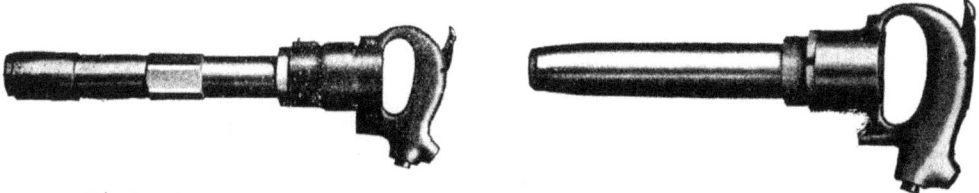

Fig. 4981. Pneumatic Riveting Hammer. Fig. 4982. Pneumatic Chipping Hammer.
Standard Railway Equipment Co.

Fig. 4983. Thor Pneumatic Long Stroke Riveting Hammer.
Independent Pneumatic Tool Co.

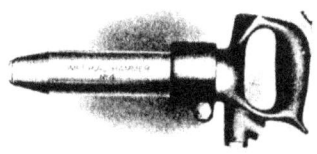

Fig. 4985. Imperial Chipping Hammer.
Ingersoll-Rand Co.

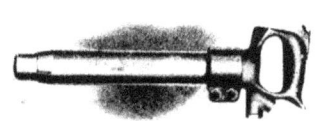

Fig. 4986. Imperial Long Stroke Riveting Hammer. Ingersoll-Rand Co.

Fig. 4984. Thor Piston Air Drill. Independent Pneumatic Tool Co.

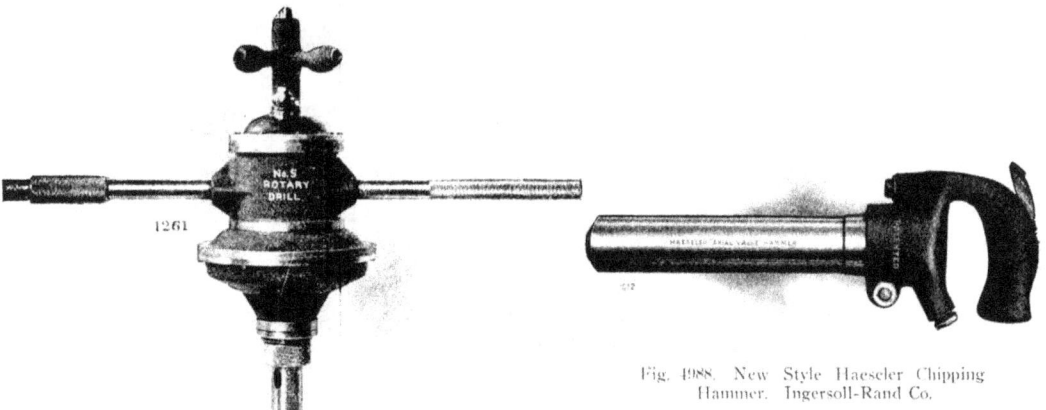

Fig. 4988. New Style Haeseler Chipping Hammer. Ingersoll-Rand Co.

Fig. 4987. Haeseler Rotary Drill. Ingersoll-Rand Co.

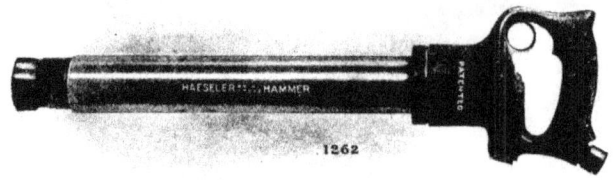

Fig. 4989. Haeseler Riveting Hammer. No. 9-H. Ingersoll-Rand Co.

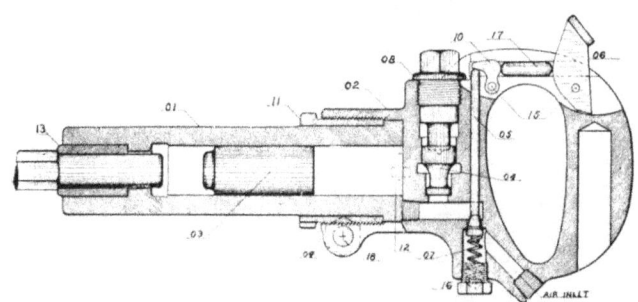

Fig. 4990. Green Chipping and Caulking Hammer, Class B, with Outside Trigger. Dayton Pneumatic Tool Co.

Fig. 4991. Deep Throat Punching Machine. Hilles & Jones Co.

Fig. 4992. Johns Patent Plate Shear Combined with Bar and Angle Cutter and Punch. Henry Pels & Co.

Figs. 4993-4994. Johns New Coping Machine. Henry Pels & Co.

Fig. 4995. Johns Patent Bar Cutter Combined with Shear. Henry Pels & Co.

MACHINE TOOLS, Punching and Shearing Machines. Figs. 4996-4997

Fig. 4996. Vertical Punch and Automatic Spacing Table.
Cleveland Punch & Shear Works.

Fig. 4997. Flush Front Shearing Machine.
Hilles & Jones Co.

Fig. 4998. 25-Inch Throat Double Punching and Shearing Machine.   Williams, White & Co.

Fig. 4999. Portable Pneumatic Punch.   Quincy, Manchester, Sargent Co.

Fig. 5000. Quartering Machine.   Niles-Bement-Pond Co.

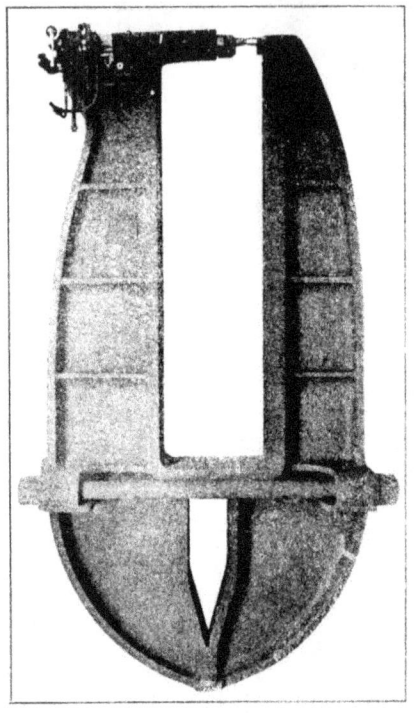

Fig. 5001. Hydraulic Riveting Machine. Chambersburg Engineering Co.

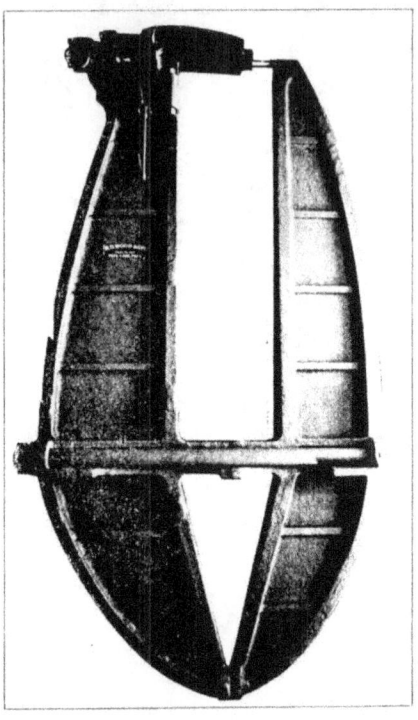

Fig. 5002. 50-Ton to 150-Ton Capacity, 17-Foot Hydraulic Riveting Machine. R. D. Wood & Co.

Fig. 5003. 25-Inch Back Geared Crank Shaper. John Steptoe Shaper Co.

Fig. 5004. Back Geared Crank Shaper.   Cincinnati Shaper Co.

Fig. 5005. 24-Inch Shaper.   Stockbridge Machine Co.

Fig. 5006. Double Traveling Head Shaper with Pull Cut Head.
Cincinnati Shaper Co.

Fig. 5007. Double Traveling Head Shaper.   Niles-Bement-Pond Co.

Fig. 5008. 16-Inch Traveling Head Slotter.   T. C. Dill Machine Co., Inc.

Fig. 5009. 18-Inch Slotting Machine. William Sellers & Co., Inc.

Fig. 5010. 15-Inch Slotting Machine. Betts Machine Co.

Fig. 5011. Double Head Locomotive Frame Crank Slotting Machine, Niles-Bement-Pond Co.

Fig. 5012. Straightening Rolls. Hilles & Jones Co.

Figs. 5013-5015 MACHINE TOOLS, Tire Expander and Turret Lathe.

Fig. 5013. Straightening Rolls. Niles-Bement-Pond Co.

Fig. 5014. Tire Expanding Device. Wells Light Mfg. Co.

Fig. 5015. Turret Lathe. Warner & Swasey Co.

MACHINE TOOLS, Turret Lathes.   Figs. 5016-5018

Fig. 5016. Big Bore Turret Lathe, Equipped with Bar Tools for Machining Crosshead Pins. Gisholt Machine Co.

Fig. 5017. Hartness Flat Turret Lathe. Jones & Lamson.

Fig. 5018. Pratt & Whitney Turret Lathe. Niles-Bement-Pond Co.

MACHINE TOOLS, Valve Seat Planer and Valve Setting Machine.

Fig. 5019. 20-Inch Full Universal Monitor or Turret Lathe. Dreses Machine Tool Co.

Fig. 5020. Portable Valve Seat Planing Machine. Quincy, Manchester, Sargent Co.

Fig. 5021. Farrington's Valve Setting Machine, Fitted with Mills Power Attachment. Sherburne & Co.

Fig. 5022. Hydraulic Driving Wheel Press. Watson-Stillman Co.

Fig. 5023. Hydraulic Driving Wheel Press. Niles-Bement-Pond Co.

MACHINE TOOLS, Motor Drive.

Power Required for Motor-Driven Machine Tools. Table of Actual Railroad Shop Installation Made by Crocker-Wheeler Co.

Machine Tool	Builder	Motor
18" by 8' Lathe	Flather & Co.	5 I, 5 HP CM
Two 20" by 8' Lathe	F. E. Reed Co.	5 I, 5 HP CM, each
25" by 6' Lathe	Putnam Machine Co.	7½ I, 7½ HP CM
42" by 8' Lathe	Niles-Bement-Pond Co.	15 I, 15 HP CM
24" by 12' Lathe	American Tool Works Co.	7½ I, 7½ HP CM
Axle Lathe	Niles-Bement-Pond Co.	25 I, 25 HP CM
72" Wheel Lathe	Niles-Bement-Pond Co.	25 I, 25 HP CM
Turret Lathes (two)	Jones & Lamson Machine Co.	5 I, 5 HP CM each
Turret Lathe	American Tool Works Co.	3 I, 3 HP CM
Turret Lathe	American Tool Works Co.	5 I, 5 HP CM
Turret Lathe	Warner & Swasey Co.	5 I, 5 HP CM
24" by 12' Lathe	American Tool Works Co.	7½ I, 7½ HP CM
30" by 15' Lathe	Putnam Machine Co.	10 I, 10 HP CM
Axle Lathe	Putnam Machine Co.	35 I, 35 HP CM
42" Car Wheel Lathe	Niles-Bement-Pond Co.	20 I, 20 HP CM
90" Wheel Lathe	Putnam Machine Co.	25 I, 25 HP CM
18" by 10' Lathe	Putnam Machine Co.	7½ I, 7½ HP CM
36" by 24' Lathe	Putnam Machine Co.	10 I, 10 H. P. CM
Hyd. Wheel Press, 200 Tons	Niles-Bement-Pond Co.	*7½ I, 7½ HP CM
42" Car Wheel Borer	Niles-Bement-Pond Co.	10 I, 10 HP CM
72" Boring Mill	Niles-Bement-Pond Co.	25 I, 25 HP CM
100" Hyd. Wheel Press	Putnam Machine Co.	*7½ I, 7½ HP CM
18" by 36" Horizontal Boring Machine	Betts Machine Co.	15 I, 15 HP CM
81" Quartering Machine	Niles-Bement-Pond Co.	(2) 5 I, 5 HP CM
51" Boring Mill	Baush Machine Tool Co.	15 I, 15 HP CM
Five 36" Drill Press		3 F, 4 HP CM, each
72" Radial Drill	Niles-Bement-Pond Co.	3 F, 4 HP CM
Heavy Two Spindle Drill	Niles-Bement-Pond Co.	(2) 7½ I, 9 HP CM
30" Drill Press	J. E. Snyder	5 I, 5 HP CM
30" by 30" by 8' Planer	New Haven Mfg. Co.	7½ I, 7½ HP CCM
60" by 60" by 20' Planer	Niles-Bement-Pond Co.	20 I, 20 HP CCM
30" by 30" by 8' Planer	Woodward & Powell Planer Co.	7½ I, 7½ HP CCM
42" by 42" by 12' Planer	Niles-Bement-Pond Co.	15 I, 15 HP CCM
42" by 42" by 12' Planer	Cincinnati Planer Co.	15 I, 15 HP CCM
12" Shaper	Hughes & Phillips	5 I, 5 HP CCM
24" Shaper	Gould & Eberhardt	7½ I, 7½ HP CCM
24" Traversing Head Shaper	Cincinnati Shaper Co.	7½ I, 7½ HP CCM
20" by 11' Lathes (2)	Putnam Machine Co.	7½ I, 7½ HP CM, each
34" Gisholt Turret Lathe	Gisholt Machine Co.	15 I, 15 HP CM
Slab Miller	Wm. Sellers & Co., Inc.	5 I, 5¼ HP CCM
12" Slotter	Betts Machine Co.	5 I, 6¼ HP CCM
19" Slotter	Putnam Machine Co.	10 I, 13 HP CCM
6" Pipe Cutter	D. Saunders' Sons	7½ I, 7½ HP CM
3" Pipe Cutter	D. Saunders' Sons	3 I, 3 HP CM
(3) 18" Emery Wheel Grinders	Bridgeport Emery Whl. Co.	3 D, 4 HP CM
Bending Rolls No. 2	Hilles & Jones Co.	7½ I, 7½ HP CCM
Bending Rolls No. 4	Hilles & Jones Co.	25 I, 25 HP CCM
Straightening Rolls No. 2	Hilles & Jones Co.	15 I, 15 HP CCM
Punch and Shear No. 3	Hilles & Jones Co.	10 I, 10 HP CCM
Punch No. 2 with Spacing Table	Hilles & Jones Co.	*10 I, 10 HP CCM
Punch 13/16" Hole, ⅜" Plate	Cleveland Punch & Shear Wks. Co.	*5 I, 5 HP CCM
Punch No. 5	Hilles & Jones Co.	*15 I, 15 HP CCM
Horizontal Punch	Hilles & Jones Co.	*10 I, 10 HP CCM
Shear No. 6	Hilles & Jones Co.	*15 I, 15 HP CCM
Angle Shear No. 1	Hilles & Jones Co.	*10 I, 10 HP CCM
60" Radial Drill	Dreses Mach. Tool Co.	5 I, 6¼ HP CM
Punch and Shears No. 4	Hilles & Jones Co.	15 I, 15 HP CCM

NOTE.

Standard motors used throughout.

"CM" indicates shunt motor. "CCM" indicates compound motor.

The letters "I" "F" and "D," indicate type of frame.

The number preceding the letter indicates the size of frame.

All motors marked with (*) are constant speed; all others are used as variable speed motors.

The ratings given are the standard ratings of the motors when operating under normal conditions, i.e., full field strength and 230 volts on the armature.

Fig. 5024. Eight-Wheel, Four-Coupled Tank Locomotive. London & South Western. Cylinders 18½ in. x 26 in.; Working Steam Pressure 175 lbs. per sq. in.; Total Heating Surface 1,191.68 sq. ft.; Diameter of Drivers 67 in.; Total Weight 122,500 lbs.

Fig. 5025. Eight-Wheel, Four-Coupled Tank Locomotive. North Eastern Railway. Cylinders 18 in. x 24 in.; Working Steam Pressure 160 lbs. per sq. in.; Total Heating Surface 1,097 sq. ft.; Weight on Drivers 67,440 lbs.; Total Weight 115,250 lbs.

Fig. 5026. Six-Coupled Goods Locomotive. North Eastern Railway. Cylinders 18½ in. x 26 in.; Total Heating Surface 1,658 sq. ft.; Diameter of Drivers 55½ in.; Weight on Drivers 106,740 lbs.; Total Weight 106,740 lbs.

Fig. 5027. Six-Coupled Goods Locomotive. Lancashire & Yorkshire. Cylinders 18 in. x 26 in.; Working Steam Pressure 160 lbs. per sq. in.; Total Heating Surface 1,216.41 sq. ft.; Diameter of Drivers 62 in.; Weight on Drivers 94,320 lbs.; Total Weight 94,320 lbs.

Fig. 5028. Six-Coupled Tank Shunting Locomotive. Great Eastern Railway. Cylinders 16½ in. x 22 in.; Total Heating Surface 988.17 sq. ft.; Diameter of Drivers 48 in.; Weight on Drivers 95,100 lbs.; Total Weight 95,100 lbs.

Fig. 5029. Six-Coupled Tank Shunting Locomotive. North Eastern Railway. Cylinders 16 in. x 22 in.; Total Heating Surface 731 sq. ft.; Diameter of Drivers 55½ in.; Weight on Drivers 82,160 lbs.; Total Weight 82,160 lbs.

BRITISH LOCOMOTIVES, General Views.   Figs. 5030-5032

Fig. 5030. Six-Coupled Goods Locomotive. Great Eastern Railway. Cylinders 19 in. x 26 in.; Total Heating Surface 1,706.58 sq. ft.; Diameter of Drivers 59 in.; Weight on Drivers 102,680 lbs.; Total Weight 102,680 lbs.

Fig. 5031. Six-Coupled Tank Shunting Locomotive. Great Northern Railway. Cylinders 18 in. x 26 in.; Working Steam Pressure 170 lbs. per sq. in.; Total Heating Surface 1,164.2 sq. ft.; Diameter of Drivers 56 in.; Weight on Drivers 115,910 lbs.; Total Weight 115,910 lbs.

Fig. 5032. Eight-Coupled Goods Locomotive. North Eastern Railway. Cylinders 20 in. x 26 in.; Total Heating Surface 1,675 sq. ft.; Diameter of Drivers 55¼ in.; Weight on Drivers 140,600 lbs.; Total Weight 140,600 lbs.

Fig. 5033. Eight-Coupled Goods Locomotive. Lancashire & Yorkshire. Cylinders 20 in. x 26 in.; Working Steam Pressure 180 lbs. per sq. in.; Total Heating Surface 2,038.64 sq. ft.; Diameter of Drivers 54 in.; Weight on Drivers 130,490 lbs.; Total Weight 130,490 lbs.

Fig. 5034. Eight-Coupled Goods Locomotive. Lancashire & Yorkshire. Cylinders 20 in. x 26 in.; Working Steam Pressure 180 lbs. per sq. in.; Total Heating Surface 1,900 sq. ft.; Diameter of Drivers 54 in.; Weight on Drivers 129,700 lbs.; Total Weight 129,700 lbs.

Fig. 5035. Eight-Coupled Goods Locomotive. Great Northern Railway. Cylinders 19¾ in. x 26 in.; Working Steam Pressure 175 lbs. per sq. in.; Total Heating Surface 1,438.84 sq. ft.; Diameter of Drivers 56 in.; Weight on Drivers 122,340 lbs.; Total Weight 122,340 lbs.

BRITISH LOCOMOTIVES, General Views.   Figs. 5036-5038

Fig. 5036. Ten-Wheel, Eight-Coupled Tank Locomotive. Great Northern Railway. Cylinders 20 in. x 26 in.; Working Steam Pressure 175 lbs. per sq. in.; Total Heating Surface 1,043.7 sq. ft.; Diameter of Drivers 56 in.; Weight on Drivers 129,920 lbs.; Total Weight 157,360 lbs.

Fig. 5037. Eight-Wheel, Four-Coupled Tank Locomotive with Radial Axle Boxes. Lancashire & Yorkshire. Cylinders 17½ in. x 26 in.; Working Steam Pressure 160 lbs. per sq. in.; Total Heating Surface 1,216.41 sq. ft.; Diameter of Drivers 68 in.; Weight on Drivers 78,960 lbs.; Total Weight 135,520 lbs.

Fig. 5038. Ten-Wheel, Six-Coupled Tank Locomotive with Radial Axle Boxes. Lancashire & Yorkshire. Cylinders 19 in. x 26 in.; Working Steam Pressure 180 lbs. per sq. in.; Total Heating Surface 2,038.64 sq. ft.; Diameter of Drivers 68 in.; Weight on Drivers 127,730 lbs.; Total Weight 184,600 lbs.

Fig. 5039. Ten-Wheel, Six-Coupled Tank Locomotive. Great Western Railway. Cylinders 18 in. x 30 in.; Working Steam Pressure 195 lbs. per sq. in.; Total Heating Surface 1,517.89 sq. ft.; Weight on Drivers 123,312 lbs.; Total Weight 169,120 lbs.

Fig. 5040. Ten-Wheel, Eight-Coupled Goods Locomotive. Great Western Railway. Cylinders 18 in. x 30 in.; Working Steam Pressure 200 lbs. per sq. in.; Total Heating Surface 2,142.63 sq. ft.; Weight on Drivers 137,990 lbs.; Total Weight 153,220 lbs.

Fig. 5041. Eight-Wheel, Single Driver Locomotive. Great Northern Railway. Cylinders 19 in. x 26 in.; Working Steam Pressure 175 lbs. per sq. in.; Total Heating Surface 1,296.6 sq. ft.; Diameter of Drivers 92 in.; Weight on Drivers 49,760 lbs.; Total Weight 108,890 lbs.

BRITISH LOCOMOTIVES, General Views. Figs. 5042-5044

Fig. 5042. Eight-Wheel, Single Driver Locomotive. Great Northern Railway. Cylinders 18 in. x 28 in.; Working Steam Pressure 160 lbs. per sq. in.; Total Heating Surface 1,045 sq. ft.; Diameter of Drivers 98 in.; Weight on Drivers 38,800 lbs.; Total Weight 101,400 lbs.

Fig. 5043. Eight-Wheel, Four-Coupled Locomotive. Great Northern Railway. Cylinders 17½ in. x 26 in.; Working Steam Pressure 170 lbs. per sq. in.; Total Heating Surface 1,249.8 sq. ft.; Diameter of Drivers 80 in.; Weight on Drivers 69,440 lbs.; Total Weight 106,400 lbs.

Fig. 5044. Eight-Wheel, Four-Coupled Locomotive. Great Eastern Railway. Cylinders 19 in. x 26 in.; Total Heating Surface 1,706.58 sq. ft.; Diameter of Drivers 84 in.; Weight on Drivers 77,040 lbs.; Total Weight 115,850 lbs.

Fig. 5045. Eight-Wheel, Four-Coupled Locomotive. Lancashire & Yorkshire. Working Steam Pressure 160 lbs. per sq. in.; Total Heating Surface 1,261.41 sq. ft.; Diameter of Drivers 87 in.; Weight on Drivers 69,440 lbs.; Total Weight 100,360 lbs.

Fig. 5046. Eight-Wheel, Four-Coupled Locomotive. North Eastern Railway. Cylinders 19 in. x 26 in.; Total Heating Surface 1,527 sq. ft.; Diameter of Drivers 82 in.; Weight on Drivers 79,960 lbs.; Total Weight 126,810 lbs.

Fig. 5047. Eight-Wheel, Four-Coupled Locomotive. London & South Western. Cylinders 19 in. x 26 in.; Working Steam Pressure 175 lbs. per sq. in.; Total Heating Surface 1,550 lbs.; Diameter of Drivers 79 in.

Fig. 5048. Eight-Wheel, Four-Coupled Locomotive. London & North Western. Cylinders 19 in. x 26 in.; Working Steam Pressure 175 lbs. per sq. in.; Total Heating Surface 2,009.7 sq. ft.; Diameter of Drivers 81 in.

Fig. 5049. Eight-Wheel, Four-Coupled, Four-Cylinder Compound Locomotive. Midland Railway. Cylinders 19 in. and 26 in. x 26 in.; Working Steam Pressure 195 lbs. per sq. in; Total Heating Surface 1,448 sq. ft.; Diameter of Drivers 84 in.; Weight on Drivers 86,800 lbs.; Total Weight 133,280 lbs.

Fig. 5050. Ten-Wheel, Four-Coupled Locomotive. Great Northern Railway. Cylinders 19 in. x 24 in.; Working Steam Pressure 175 lbs. per sq. in.; Total Heating Surface 2,500 sq. ft.; Diameter of Drivers 80 in.; Weight on Drivers 84,640 lbs.; Total Weight 146,720 lbs.

BRITISH LOCOMOTIVES, General Views.

Fig. 5051. Ten-Wheel, Four-Coupled Locomotive. North Eastern Railway. Cylinders 20 in. x 28 in.; Total Heating Surface 2,455.8 sq. ft.; Diameter of Drivers 82 in.; Weight on Drivers 87,530 lbs.; Total Weight 163,300 lbs.

Fig. 5052. Ten-Wheel, Four-Coupled, Four-Cylinder Compound Locomotive. Great Northern Railway. Cylinders 13 in. x 20 in. and 16 in. x 26 in.; Working Steam Pressure 200 lbs. per sq. in.; Total Heating Surface 2,500 sq. ft.; Diameter of Drivers 80 in.; Weight on Drivers 81,760 lbs.; Total Weight 154,600 lbs.

Fig. 5053. Ten-Wheel, Four-Coupled Locomotive. Great Western Railway. Cylinders 18 in. x 30 in.; Working Steam Pressure 225 lbs. per sq. in.; Total Heating Surface 2,142.9 sq. ft.; Weight on Drivers 79,750 lbs.; Total Weight 106,400 lbs.

BRITISH LOCOMOTIVES, General Views. Figs. 5054-5056

Fig. 5054. Ten-Wheel, Four-Coupled, De Glehn, Four-Cylinder Balanced Compound Locomotive. Great Western Railway. Cylinders 14 13-16 in. and 23⅝ in. x 25 3-16 in.; Working Steam Pressure 227 lbs. per sq. in.; Total Heating Surface 2,755.7 sq. ft.; Weight on Drivers 75,040 lbs.; Total Weight 159,940 lbs.

Fig. 5055. Ten-Wheel, Four-Coupled Locomotive. Great Central Railway. Cylinders 19½ in. x 26 in.; Working Steam Pressure 180 lbs. per sq. in.; Total Heating Surface 1,931 sq. ft.

Fig. 5056. Ten-Wheel, Four-Coupled Locomotive. Great Northern Railway. Cylinders 19 in. x 24 in.; Working Steam Pressure 175 lbs. per sq. in.; Total Heating Surface 1,442 sq. ft.; Diameter of Drivers 80 in.; Weight on Drivers 69,440 lbs.; Total Weight 129,920 lbs.

BRITISH LOCOMOTIVES, General Views.

Fig. 5057. Ten-Wheel, Four-Coupled Locomotive. Lancashire & Yorkshire. Cylinders 19 in. x 26 in.; Working Steam Pressure 180 lbs. per sq. in.; Total Heating Surface 2,052.6 sq. ft.; Diameter of Drivers 87 in.; Weight on Drivers 78,400 lbs.; Total Weight 131,600 lbs.

Fig. 5058. Ten-Wheel, Four-Coupled Tank Locomotive. Great Northern Railway. Cylinders 18 in. x 26 in.; Working Steam Pressure 170 lbs. per sq. in.; Total Heating Surface 1,123.8 sq. ft.; Diameter of Drivers 68 in.; Weight on Drivers 80,308 lbs.; Total Weight 138,770 lbs.

Fig. 5059. Ten-Wheel, Four-Coupled Tank Locomotive. Great Western Railway. Cylinders 18 in. x 30 in.; Working Steam Pressure 195 lbs. per sq. in.; Total Heating Surface 1,517.89 sq. ft.; Weight on Drivers, 64,960 lbs.; Total Weight 168,000 lbs.

Fig. 5060. Ten-Wheel, Six-Coupled Locomotive. Great Western Railway. Cylinders 18 in. x 30 in.; Working Steam Pressure 225 lbs. per sq. in.; Total Heating Surface 2,142.91 sq. ft.; Weight on Drivers 110,432 lbs.; Total Weight 157,240 lbs.

Fig. 5061. Ten-Wheel, Six-Coupled Locomotive. London & South Western. Cylinders 16 in. x 24 in.; Working Steam Pressure 175 lbs. per sq. in.; Total Heating Surface 2,727 sq. ft.; Diameter of Drivers 72 in.

Fig. 5062. Ten-Wheel, Six-Coupled Locomotive. Great Central Railway. Cylinders 19½ in. x 26 in.; Working Steam Pressure 180 lbs. per sq. in.; Total Heating Surface 1,917 sq. ft.

PRINCIPAL DIMENSIONS OF HEAVY BRITISH LOCOMOTIVES.

Gallons are imperial gallons and tons are 2,240 lbs.

Type.	Name of railroad.	When built.	Name of builder.	Simple or Compound.	Weight. On dvrs. lbs.	Weight. Total. lbs.	Diam. of cyls. in.	Stroke of piston. in.	Diam. of dvrs. in.	Type of boiler.	Working steam pressure. lbs.	Heating surface total. sq. ft.	Tubes. No.	Tubes. Outside diam. in.	Tubes. Length. ft. in.	Firebox. Length. in.	Firebox. Width. in.	Grate area. sq. ft.	Tank capacity water. gals.	Coal capacity. tons.
Six-wheel coupled goods, 0-6-0......	Midland.	1903	Midland.	Simple	98,144	98,144	18	26	63	Straight	175	1,427.9	258	1¾	11 2	75½	40¼	21.1	3,500	4
Eight-wheel coal...	Lanc. & York.	1899	Lanc. & Yorkshire.	Simple	120,400	120,400	20	26	54	Belpaire	180	1,914	225	2	15 0	86¼	38½	23	3,600	5
Ten-wheel tank, 2-6-2	Lancashire & Yorkshire.	1902	Lanc. & Yorkshire.	Simple	117,318	173,600	19	26	68	Belpaire	180	1,914	225	2	15 0	86¼	38½	23	2,000	3¾
	Midland.	1905	Midland.	Comp.	87,628	133,984	19—21	26	84	Belpaire	220	1,458.3	216	1⅞	12 7	99 7/16	40¼	28.4	3,500	7
	So. E. & Chat.	1905	So. E. & Chat. Ry.	Simple	78,176	117,040	19¼	26	78	Belpaire	175	1,532	266	1¾	11 5 11/16	75 11/16	40⅝	21.15	3,450	4
Eight-wheel, 4-4-0..	Great Eastern.	1904	Gt. Eastern Ry. Co.	Simple	77,168	115,808	19	26	84	Belpaire	180	1,706.58	287	1¾	12 1	75¾	40¼	21.6	3,450	5
	Cambrian Ry.	1904	R. Stephenson & Co.	Simple	66,416	101,304	18½	26	72	Belpaire	170	1,283	233	1¾	11 1⅝	71¾	41⅝	20.5	2,500	4
	Gt. N. of Scot.	1899	Neilson, Reid & Co.	Simple	71,456	100,576	18	26	73	Straight	165	1,207	220	1¾	11 0	63 11/16	41	18	3,000	5
	No. Brit. Ry.	1906	N. Br. Loco. Co., Ltd.	Simple	89,600	166,320	20	28	81	Belpaire	200	2,256.2	257	2	15 4¾	100⅝	41¼	28.5	4,240	7
	No. East. Ry.	1903	North Eastern Ry.	Simple	87,584	163,293	20	28	82	....	180	2,455.8	254	2	16 2⅝	99½	38½	27	4,125	5
	Gt. Northern.	1905	Vulcan Fdy. Co.	Comp.	82,880	159,040	14—23	26	80	Straight	200	2,514	*119	2¾	12 4	100 7/16	40	31	3,720	5
Atlantic, 4-4-2.....	Gt. Northern.	1905	Great Northern (Doncaster).	Simple or Comp.	81,760	154,560	13—16	20—26	80	Wide firebox	200	2,500	248	2¼	16 0	62[illegible]	71⅝	31	3,720	5
	Lon., Brighton & S. Coast.	1906	Kitson & Co., Airedale Fdy., Leeds.	Simple	84,590	150,080	18½	26	79½	....	200	2,459	246	2¼	16 0	71	81¼	30.9	3,500	..
	Lanc. & York.	1898	Lanc. & Yorkshire.	Simple	78,440	131,600	19	26	87	Belpaire	180	1,928	225	2	15 0	86¼	38½	23	2,290	5
	Lon. & S. W.	1905	Lon. & So. Western.	Simple 4-cyl.	117,600	165,760	16	24	72	Straight firebox. Fitted with 112 cross water tubes 2¾ in. in diam.	175	2,727	340	1¾	14 1½	107½	42	31.5	4,000	4
	Caledonian.	1906	Caledonian Ry.	Simple	122,100	161,968	20	26	78	Straight.	200	2,260	242	2	16 8	81	48	26	5,000	5
Ten-wheel, 4-6-0...	Glas. & S. W.	1903	N. Br. Loco. Co., Ltd.	Simple	111,664	150,304	20	26	78	Belpaire	180	1,852	209	2	15 9	88½	48	25	4,100	4
	The Highland Ry. Co.	1900	N. Br. Loco. Co., Ltd. (Glasgow Works).	Simple	98,224	131,824	19½	26	69	Straight	180	2,050	248	2	11 9⅛	89 9/16	42⅛	26.5	3,359	6½
	Lon. & No. W.	1905	Lon. & No. Western.	Simple	104,720	147,280	19	26	75	Straight	185	2,041	299	1⅞	13 0	89	48⅛	25	3,000	6

*Serve tubes.

BRITISH LOCOMOTIVES, Elevations.   Figs. 5063-5066

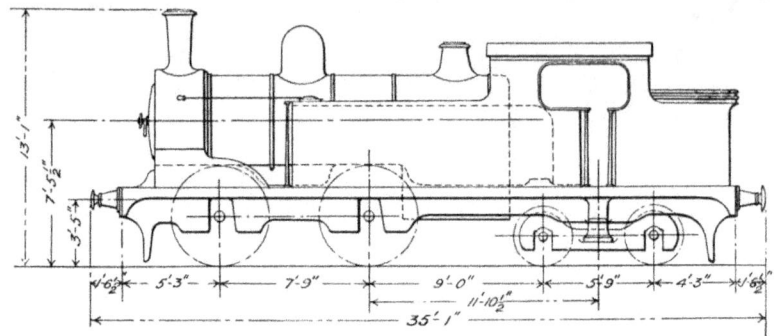

Fig. 5063. Side Elevation of Eight-Wheel, Four-Coupled Tank Locomotive. North Eastern Railway.

Cylinders .... 18 in. x 24 in. Total Heating Surface .... 1,097 sq. ft.
Working Steam Pressure ..... 160 lbs. per sq. in. Weight on Drivers .... 67,650 lbs.
                      Total Weight .... 125,250 lbs.

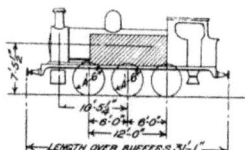

Fig. 5064. Six-Coupled Shunting Tank Locomotive. Lancashire & Yorkshire.

Cylinders .... 17 in. x 24 in.
Total Heating Surface .... 1,167.4 sq. ft.
Grate Area .... 17 sq. ft.
Diameter of Drivers .... 54 in.
Weight on Drivers .... 112,000 lbs.
Total Weight .... 112,000 lbs.

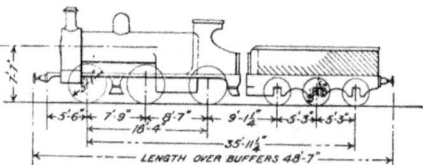

Fig. 5065. Six-Coupled Goods Locomotive. Lancashire & Yorkshire.

Cylinders .... 18 in. x 26 in.
Total Heating Surface .... 1,216.41 sq. ft.
Grate Area .... 18.75 sq. ft.
Diameter of Drivers .... 61 in.
Weight on Drivers .... 94,400 lbs.
Total Weight .... 94,400 lbs.

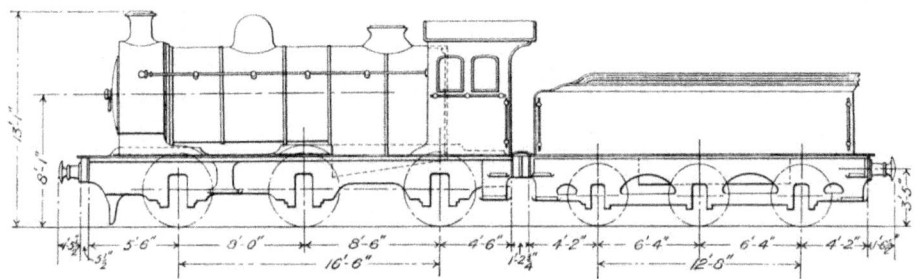

Fig. 5066. Six-Coupled Goods Locomotive. North Eastern Railway.

Cylinders .... 18½ in. x 26 in.   Diameter of Drivers .... 55½ in.
Total Heating Surface .... 1,658 sq. ft.   Weight on Drivers .... 106,740 lbs.
                      Total Weight .... 106,740 lbs.

BRITISH LOCOMOTIVES, Elevations.

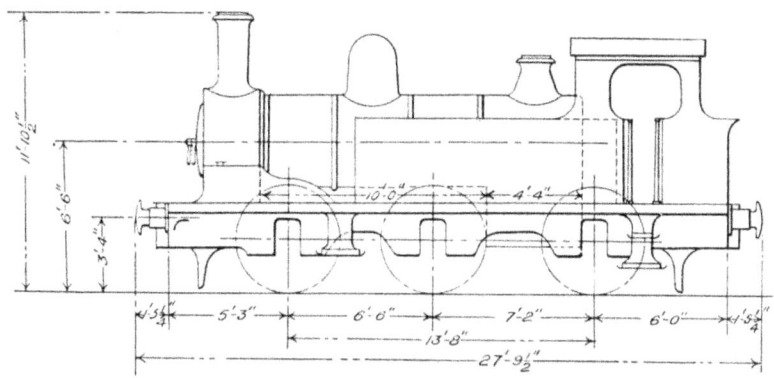

Fig. 5067. Six-Coupled Tank Locomotive. North Eastern Railway.

Cylinders .... 16 in. x 22 in.	Diameter of Drivers .... 55½ in.
Total Heating Surface .... 731 sq. ft.	Weight on Drivers .... 82,160 lbs.
Total Weight .... 82,160 lbs.	

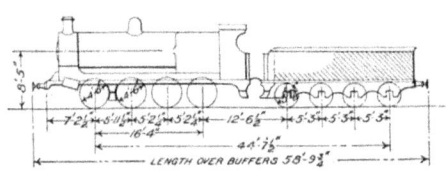

Fig. 5068. Eight-Coupled Goods Locomotive. Lancashire & Yorkshire.

Cylinders .... 20 in. x 26 in.
Total Heating Surface .... 2,038.64 sq. ft.
Grate Area .... 26.05 sq. ft.
Diameter of Drivers .... 54 in.
Weight on Drivers .... 130,490 lbs.
Total Weight .... 130,490 lbs.

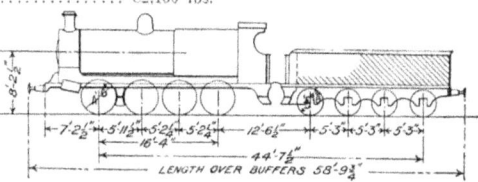

Fig. 5069. Eight-Coupled Goods Locomotive, with Corrugated Firebox. Lancashire & Yorkshire.

Cylinders .... 20 in. x 26 in.
Total Heating Surface .... 1,900 sq. ft.
Grate Area .... 26 sq. ft.
Diameter of Drivers .... 54 in.
Weight on Drivers .... 129,700 lbs.
Total Weight .... 129,700 lbs.

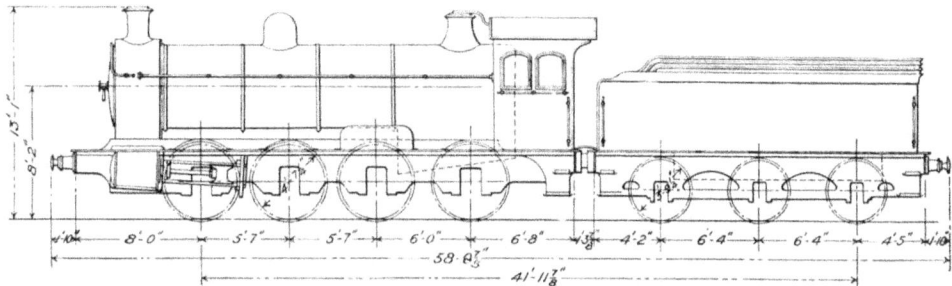

Fig. 5070. Eight-Coupled Goods Locomotive. North Eastern Railway.

Cylinders .... 20 in. x 26 in.	Diameter of Drivers .... 55¼ in.
Total Heating Surface .... 1,675 sq. ft.	Weight on Drivers .... 140,600 lbs.
Grate Area .... 21.5 sq. ft.	Total Weight .... 140,600 lbs.

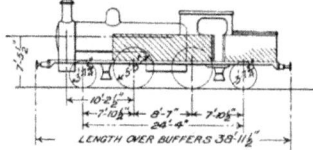

Fig. 5071. Eight-Wheel, Four-Coupled Tank Locomotive, with Radial Axle Boxes. Lancashire & Yorkshire.

Cylinders .... 17½ in. x 26 in.
Total Heating Surface .... 1,216.41 sq. ft.
Grate Area .... 18.75 sq. ft.
Diameter of Drivers .... 68 in.
Weight on Drivers .... 78,600 lbs.
Total Weight .... 135,520 lbs.

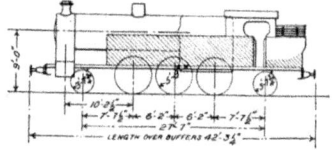

Fig. 5072. Ten-Wheel, Six-Coupled Tank Locomotive, with Radial Axle Boxes. Lancashire & Yorkshire.

Cylinders .... 19 in. x 26 in.
Total Heating Surface .... 2,038.64 sq. ft.
Grate Area .... 26.05 sq. ft.
Diameter of Drivers .... 68 in.
Weight on Drivers .... 127,730 lbs.
Total Weight .... 184,600 lbs.

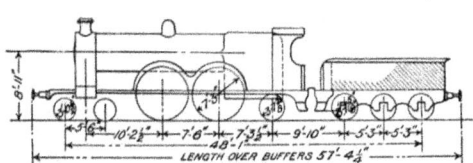

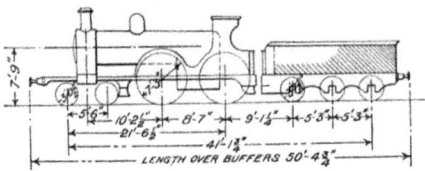

Fig. 5073. Ten-Wheel, Four-Coupled Locomotive. Lancashire & Yorkshire.

Cylinders	19 in. x 26 in.
Total Heating Surface	2,052.6 sq. ft.
Grate Area	26.05 sq. ft
Diameter of Drivers	87 in.
Weight on Drivers	54,900 lbs.
Total Weight	131,600 lbs.

Fig. 5074. Eight-Wheel, Four-Coupled Locomotive. Lancashire & Yorkshire.

Total Heating Surface	1,216.4 sq. ft.
Grate Area	18.75 sq. ft.
Diameter of Drivers	87 in.
Weight on Drivers	69,400 lbs.
Total Weight	100,360 lbs.

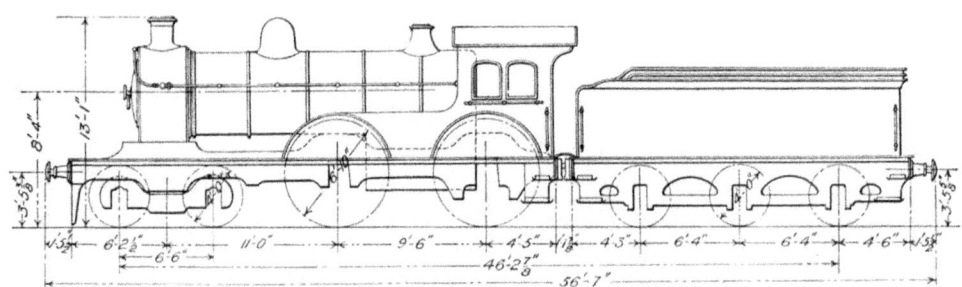

Fig. 5075. Eight-Wheel, Four-Coupled Locomotive. North Eastern Railway.

Cylinders	19 in. x 26 in.	Diameter of Drivers	82 in.
Total Heating Surface	1,527 sq. ft.	Weight on Drivers	79,960 lbs.
	Total Weight	125,910 lbs.	

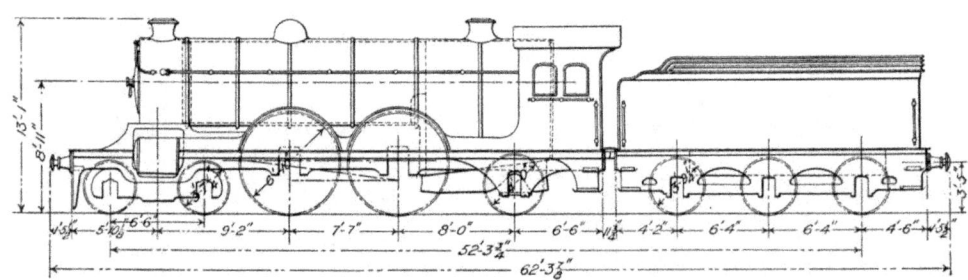

Fig. 5076. Ten-Wheel, Four-Coupled Locomotive. North Eastern Railway.

Cylinders	20 in. x 28 in.	Diameter of Drivers	82 in.
Total Heating Surface	2,455.8 sq. ft.	Weight on Drivers	87,530 lbs.
Grate Area	27 sq. ft.	Total Weight	163,300 lbs.

Figs. 5077-5078   BRITISH LOCOMOTIVES, Elevations.

Numbers Refer to List of Names of Parts on Opposite Page.

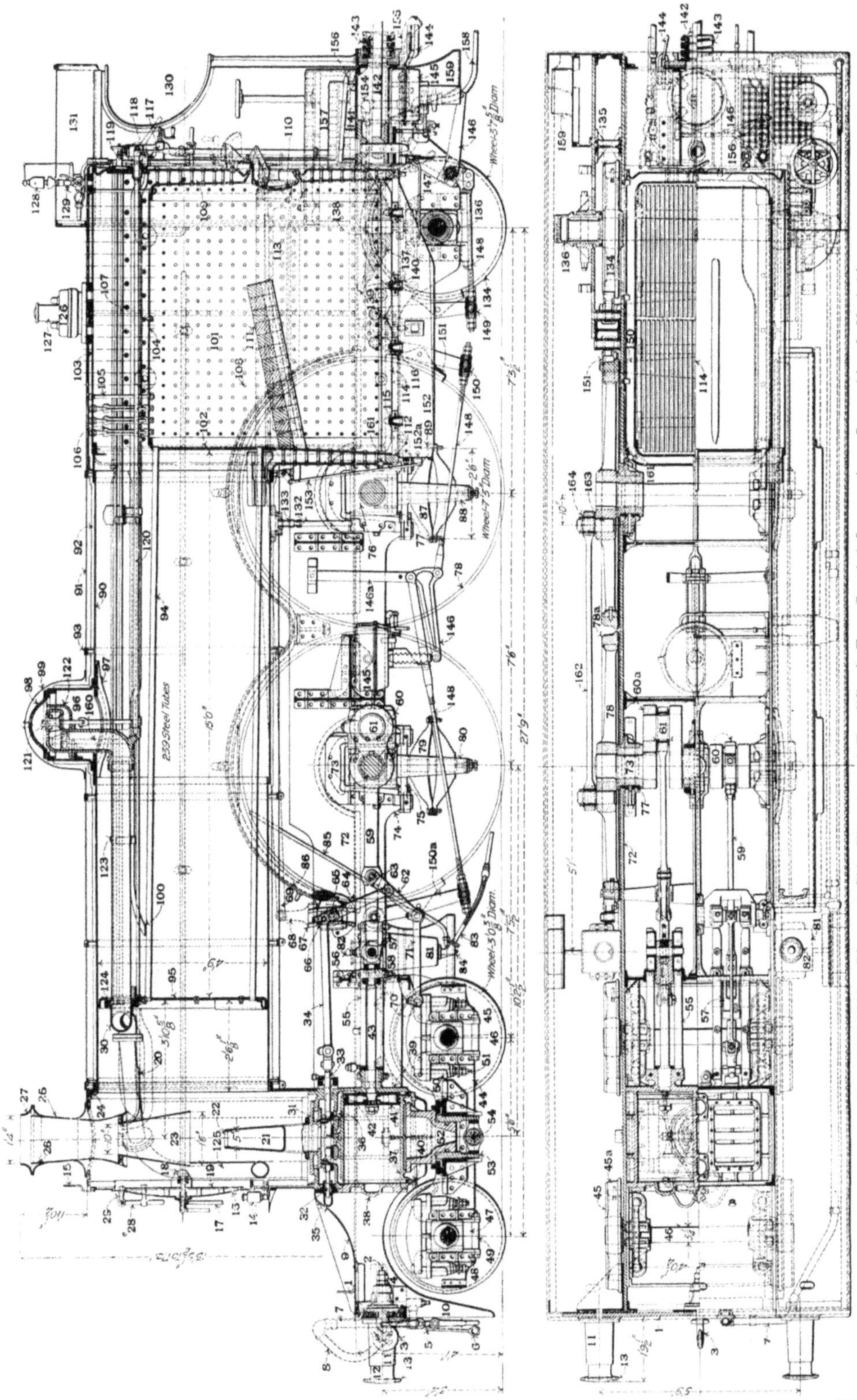

Figs. 5077-5078. Plan and Side Elevation of Ten-Wheel, Four-Coupled Locomotive. Lancashire & Yorkshire.

BRITISH LOCOMOTIVES, Boilers. Figs. 5079-5080

Names of Parts of Figs. 5077-5078.

#	Part	#	Part	#	Part
1	Buffer Beam	58	Crosshead Pin	114	Fire Bar
2	Drawbar	59	Connecting Rod	115	Fire Bar Bearer
3	Drawbar Hook	60	Connecting Rod Big End	116	Fire Bar Bearer Bracket
4	Drawbar Rubbers	60a	Crank	117	Regulator Lever
5	Screw Coupling	61	Crank Pin	118	Regulator Lever Quadrant
6	Screw Coupling Ball	62	Vibrating Link	119	Regulator Head
7	Vacuum Brake Pipe	63	Vibrating Link Pin	120	Regulator Rod
8	Vacuum Brake Hose	64	Combination Lever	121	Regulator Valve
9	Front End Plate	65	Link Block	122	Regulator Valve Case
10	Guard Iron	66	Valve Rod Pin	123	Steam Pipe to Cylinders
11	Buffer Guide	67	Link	124	Steam Pipe Joint
12	Buffer Rod	68	Link Lever	125	Smokebox Steam Pipe to Cylinders
13	Buffer Head	69	Reversing Rod	126	Safety Valve Casing
14	Lamp	70	Radius Rod Fulcrum	127	Safety Valve Column
15	Lamp Iron	71	Radius Rod	128	Whistle
16	Smokebox Door	72	Inside Frame Plate	129	Whistle Valve
17	Smokebox Door Handle	73	Driving Axle	130	Cab
18	Smokebox Door Fastening	74	Driving Horn	131	Cab Roof
19	Smokebox Door Baffle	75	Driving Horn Stay	132	Blow-off Pipe
20	Blower Pipe	76	Driving Axle Box	133	Blow-off Cock
21	Blast Pipe	77	Driving Axle Box Wedge	134	Trailing Wheel
22	Blast Pipe Nozzle	78	Driving Wheel	135	Trailing Wheel Tyre
23	Petticoat Pipe	78a	Driving Wheel Tyre	136	Trailing Wheel Axle Box
24	Smokebox Ring	79	Driving Wheel Spring	137	Trailing Wheel Spring
25	Chimney	80	Driving Wheel Spring Hanger	138	Trailing Wheel Spring Band
26	Chimney Lining	81	Sandbox	139	Trailing Wheel Spring Hanger
27	Chimney Cap	82	Sandbox Filling Lid	140	Trailing Wheel Spring Hanger Bracket
28	Hand Rail	83	Sand Pipe	141	Drag Plate Casting
29	Hand Rail Bracket	84	Sand Valve	142	Tender Coupling
30	Steam T-Piece	85	Air Pipe to Sand Valve	143	Tender Buffer Spring
31	Slide Valve	86	Wheel Splashers	144	Safety Chain
32	Slide Valve Tail Rod Gland	87	Coupled Wheel Spring	145	Vacuum Brake Cylinder
33	Slide Valve Rod	88	Coupled Wheel Spring Hanger	146	Vacuum Brake Lever
34	Slide Valve Intermediate Rod	89	Coupled Wheel Spring Bolts	146a	Vacuum Brake Lever Hanger
35	Front End Inspection Lid	90	Boiler Shell	147	Vacuum Brake Lever Shaft
36	Steam Port	91	Boiler Lagging Plate	148	Vacuum Brake Pull-on Rods
37	Cylinder	92	Boiler Clothing	149	Vacuum Brake Rod Adjusting Screw
38	Cylinder Front Cover	93	Boiler Clothing Band	150	Brake Beam
39	Cylinder Back End	94	Boiler Tubes	150a	Brake Beam Hanger
40	Cylinder Cocks	95	Boiler Tube Plate	151	Brake Block
41	Piston	96	Boiler Dome	152	Ashpan
42	Piston Rings	97	Boiler Dome Ring	152a	Ashpan Damper
43	Piston Rod	98	Boiler Dome Top	153	Ashpan Damper Rigging
44	Bogie Frame	99	Boiler Dome Cover	154	Feed Water Pipe
45	Bogie Wheel	100	Boiler Feed Water Pipe	155	Feed Water Hose
45a	Bogie Wheel Tyre	101	Firebox	156	Foot Board
46	Bogie Wheel Axle	102	Firebox Tube Sheet	157	Locker
47	Bogie Wheel Axle Box	103	Firebox Wrapper	158	Train Pipe
48	Bogie Horn Plate	104	Firebox Crown	159	Step
49	Bogie Horn Plate Stay	105	Firebox Crown Stay Bolts	160	Steam Pipe to Injector
50	Bogie Spring	106	Firebox Crown Sling Stays	161	Wash-out Plugs
51	Bogie Spring Hanger	107	Firebox Cross Stays	162	Side Rod
52	Bogie Pin	108	Firebox Side Stays	163	Side Rod Pin
53	Bogie Pin Casing	109	Firebox Water Space	164	Side Rod Bush
54	Bogie Spring Pin	110	Fire Door		
55	Slide Bar	111	Brick Arch		
56	Motion Plate	112	Foundation Ring		
57	Crosshead	113	Expansion Bracket		

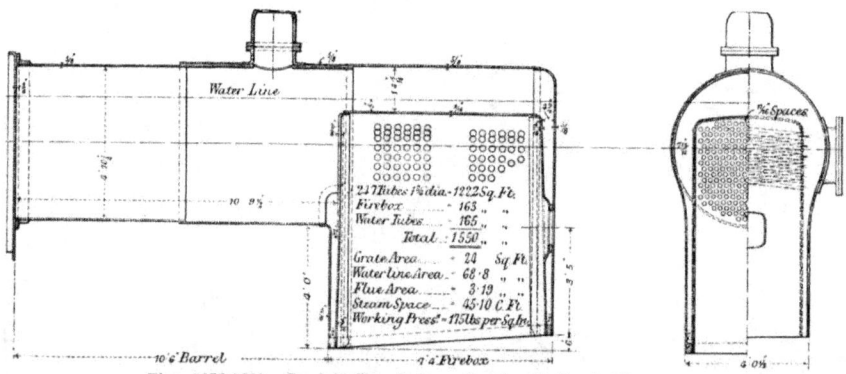

Figs. 5079-5080. Straight Top Boiler. London & South Western.

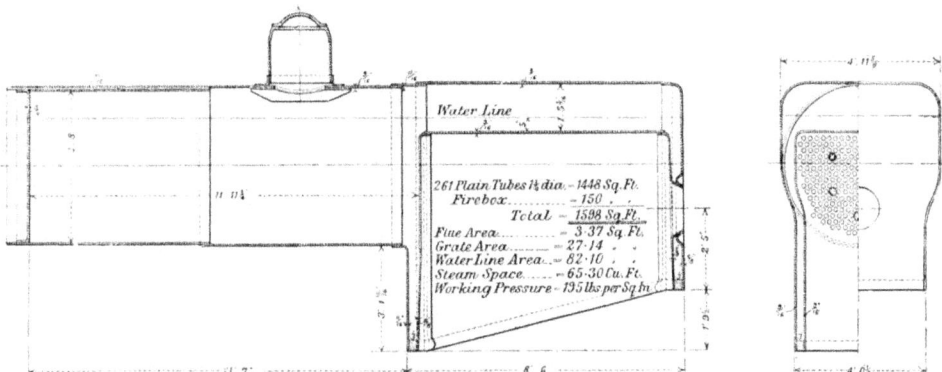

Figs. 5081-5082. Straight Top Boiler with Belpaire Firebox. Midland Railway.

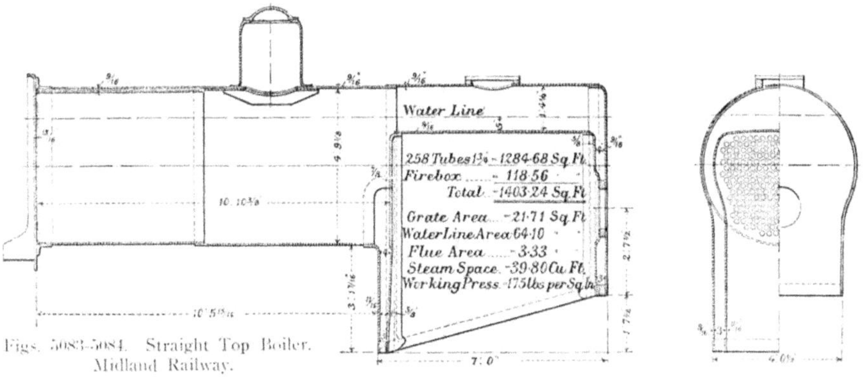

Figs. 5083-5084. Straight Top Boiler. Midland Railway.

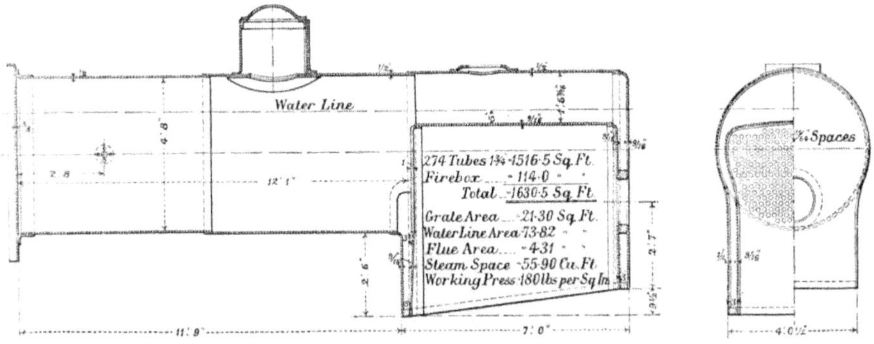

Figs. 5085-5086. Straight Top Boiler. Great Eastern Railway.

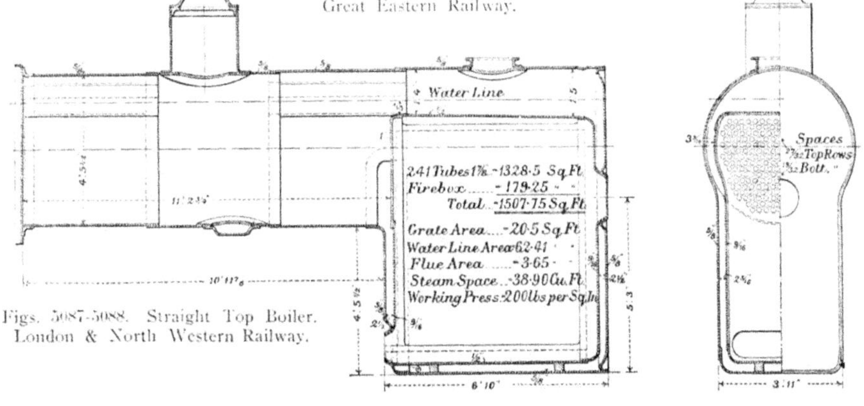

Figs. 5087-5088. Straight Top Boiler. London & North Western Railway.

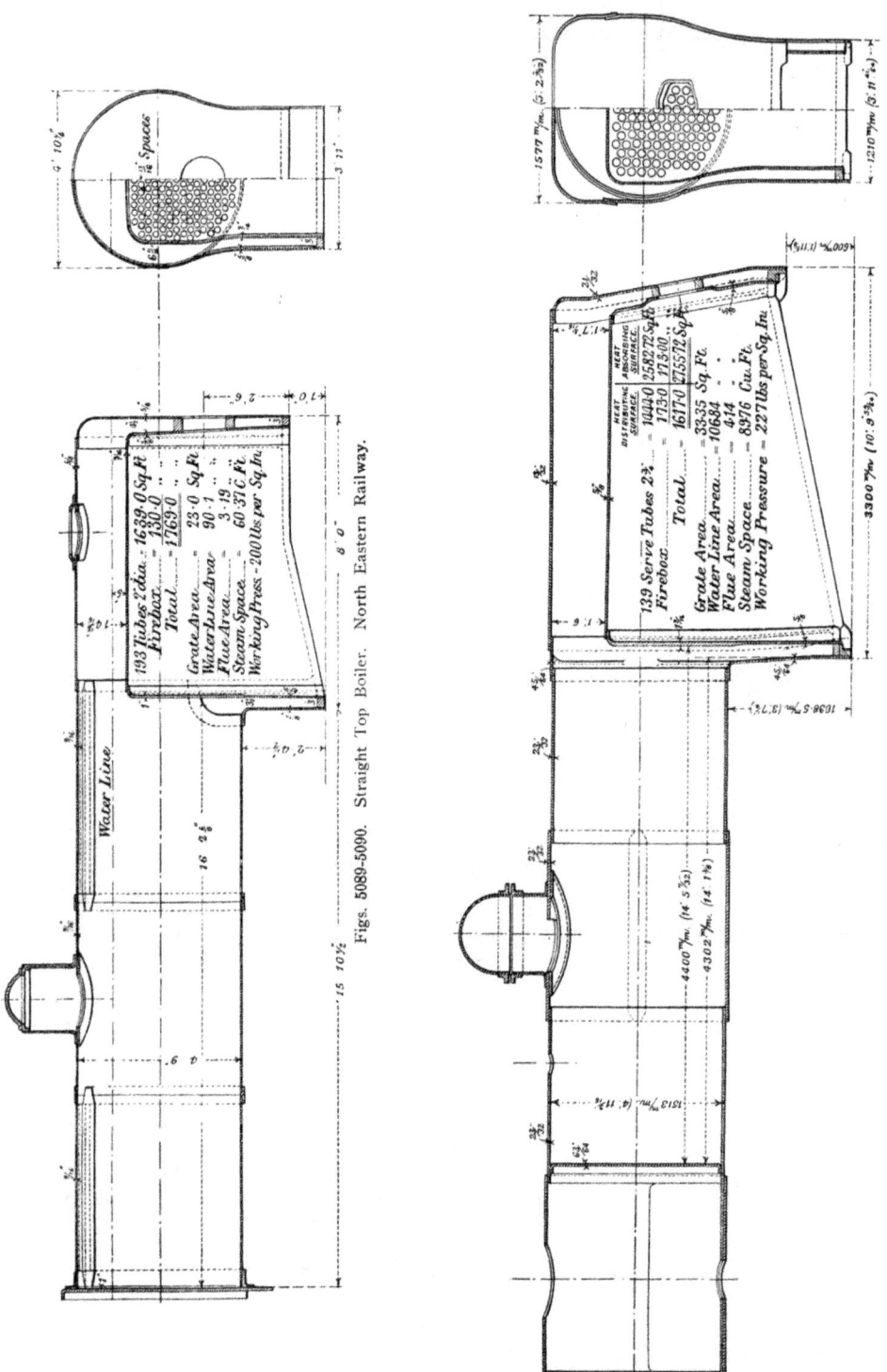

Figs. 5089-5090. Straight Top Boiler. North Eastern Railway.

Figs. 5091-5092. Straight Top Boiler. Great Western Railway.

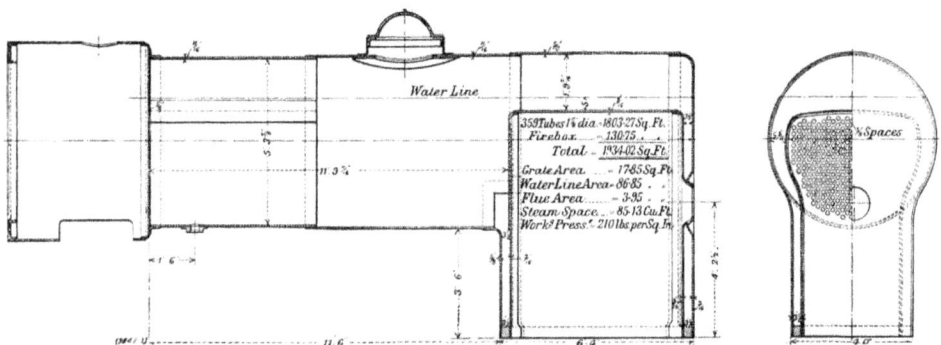

Figs. 5093-5094. Straight Top Boiler. Great Western Railway.

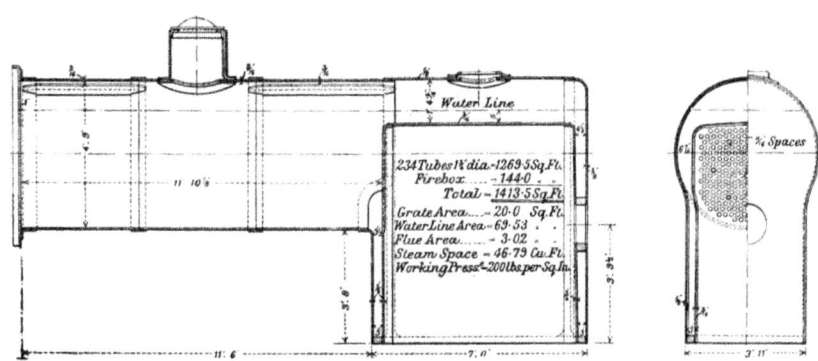

Figs. 5095-5096. Straight Top Boiler. North Eastern Railway.

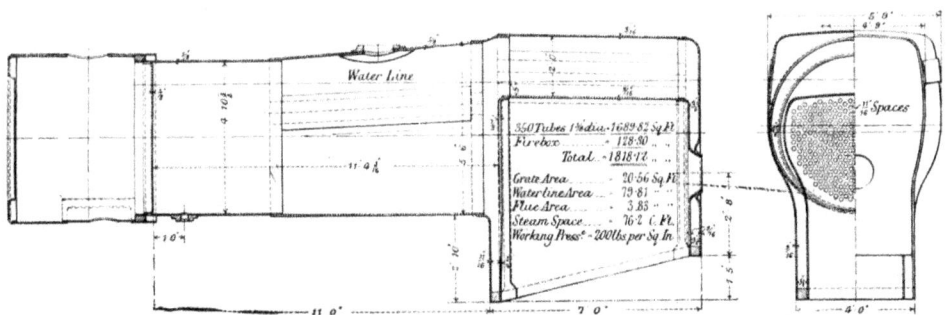

Figs. 5097-5098. Extended Wagon Top Boiler. Great Western Railway.

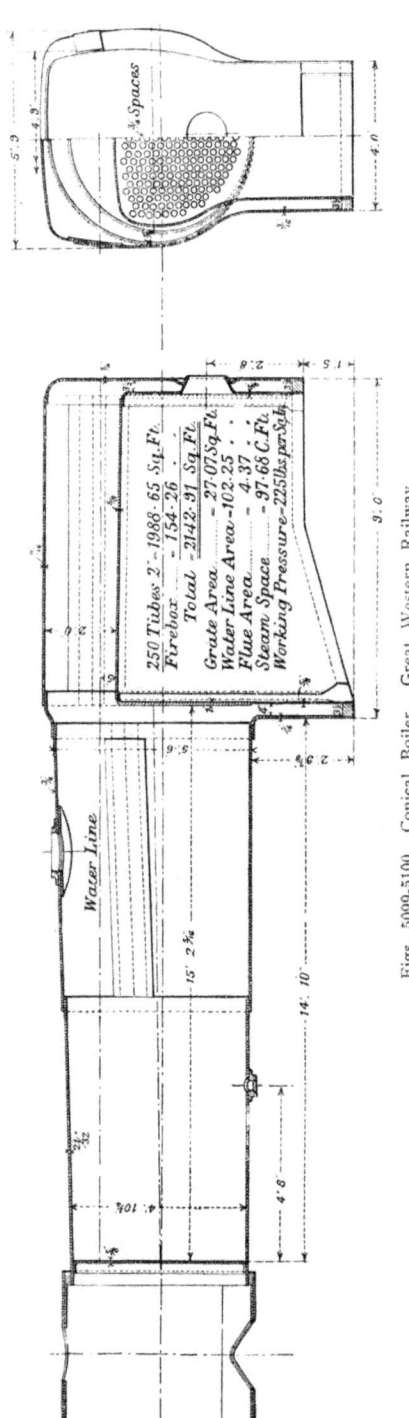

Figs. 5099-5100. Conical Boiler. Great Western Railway.

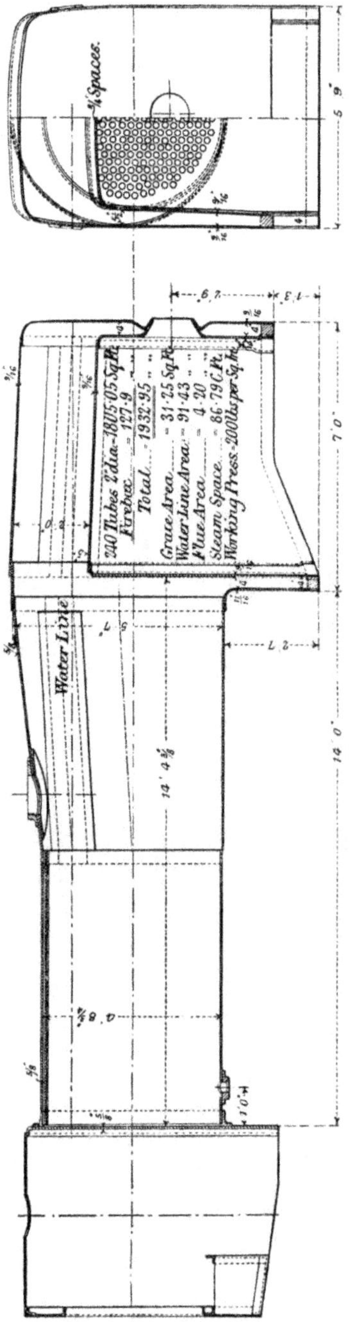

Figs. 5101-5102. Extended Wagon Top Boiler. Great Western Railway.

BRITISH LOCOMOTIVES, Boilers.

Figs. 5103-5110

Numbers Refer to List of Names of Parts on Opposite Page.

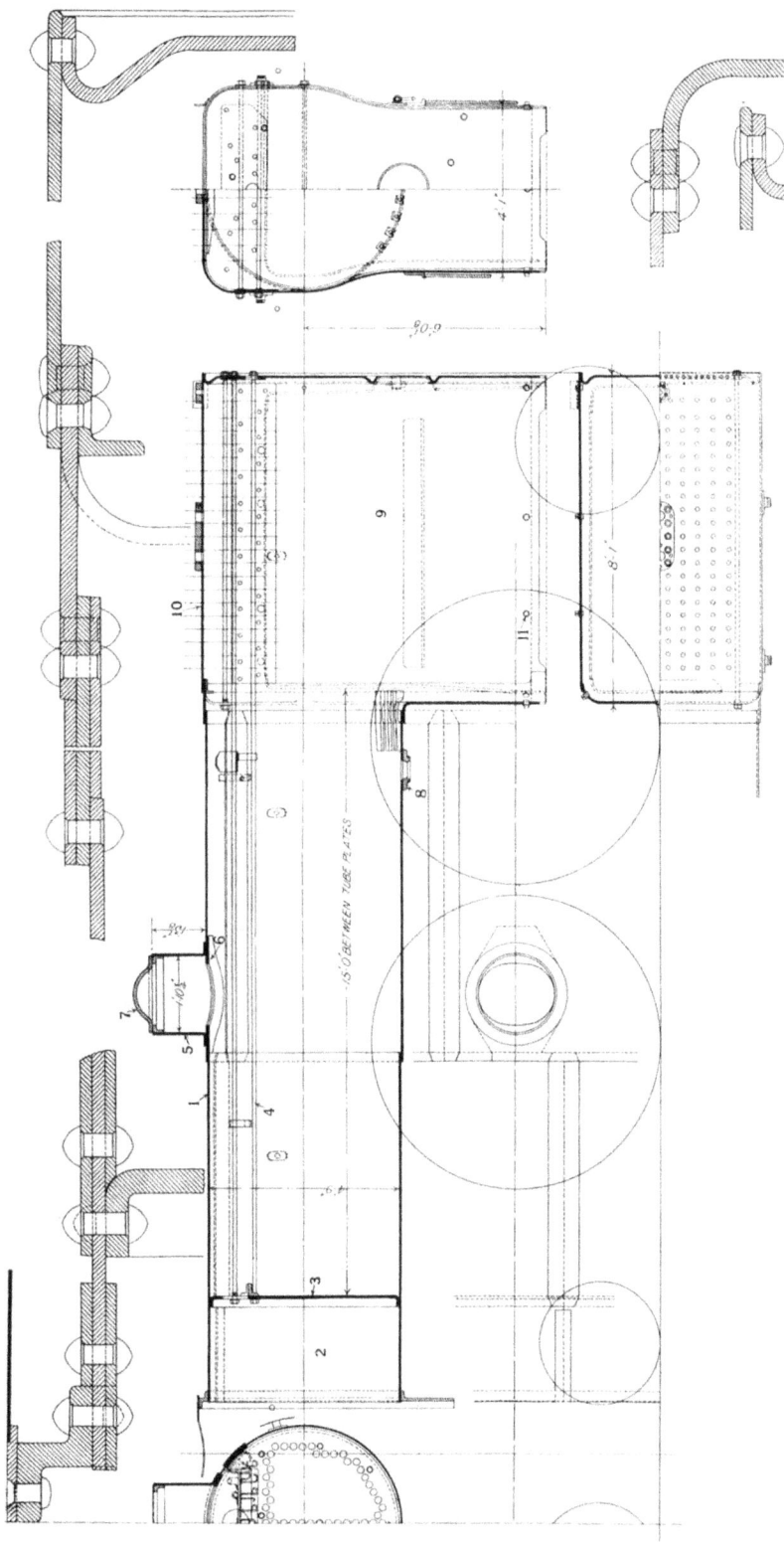

Figs. 5103-5110. Boiler for Ten-Wheel, Four-Coupled Locomotive. Lancashire & Yorkshire.

BRITISH LOCOMOTIVES, Boilers. Figs. 5111-5113

Numbers Refer to List of Names of Parts Below.

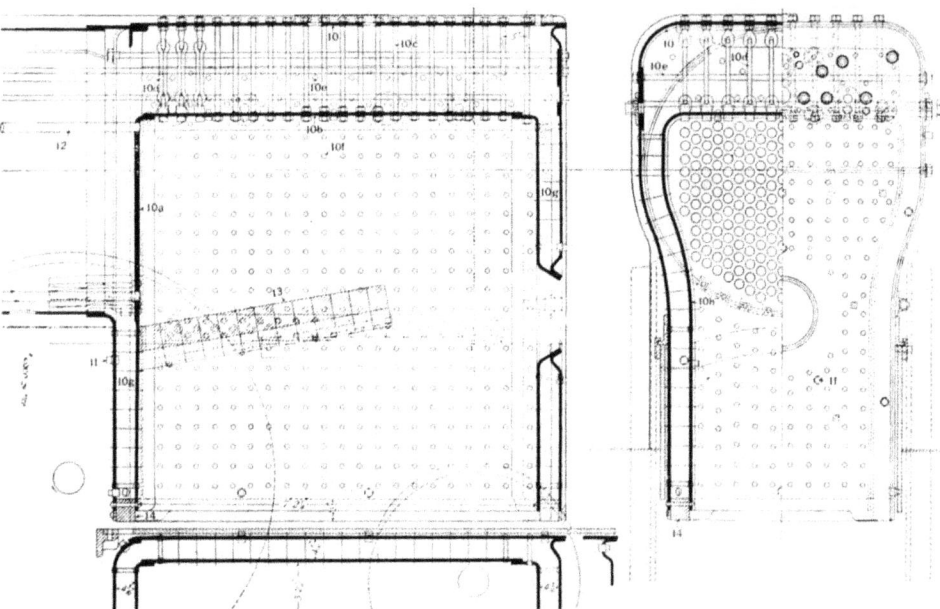

Figs. 5111-5112. Firebox of Boiler for Ten-Wheel, Four-Coupled Locomotive. Lancashire & Yorkshire.

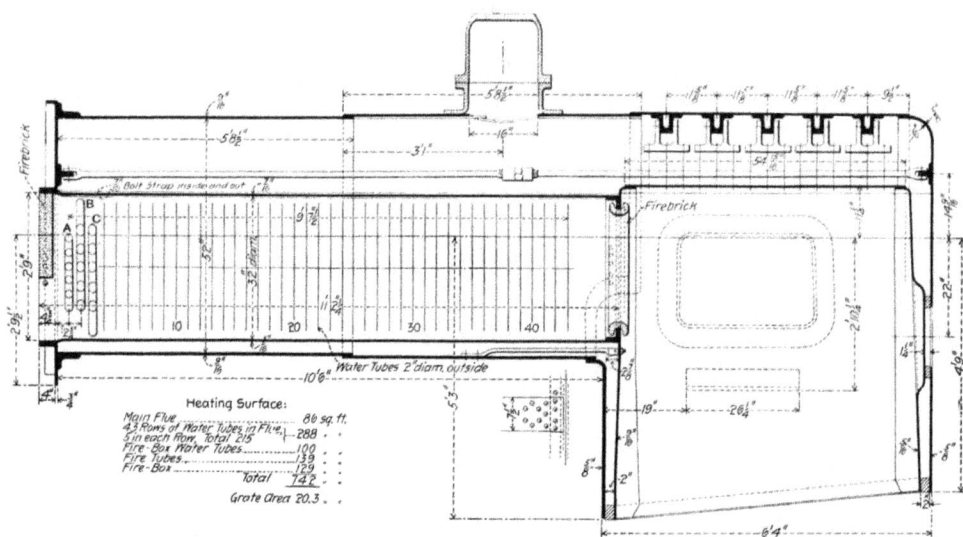

Fig. 5113. Water Tube Locomotive Boiler. London & South Western.

Names of Parts of Boilers, Figs. 5103-5117.

1 *Boiler Shell*	9 *Firebox*	10f *Firebox Side Stays*
2 *Smokebox*	10 *Firebox Wrapper Plate*	10g *Firebox Water Space*
3 *Smokebox Tube Plate*	10a *Firebox Tube Plate*	10h *Firebox Side Sheet*
4 *Tube Plate Stay*	10b *Firebox Crown*	11 *Wash-out Plugs*
5 *Dome*	10c *Firebox Crown Stay Bolt*	12 *Tube*
6 *Dome Ring*	10d *Firebox Crown Sling Stay*	13 *Brick Arch*
7 *Dome Cover*	10e *Firebox Cross Stays*	14 *Foundation Ring*
8 *Blow-off Hole Ring*		

(517)

Figs. 5114-5117 BRITISH LOCOMOTIVES, Boilers.

Numbers Refer to List of Names of Parts With Figs. 5111-5113.

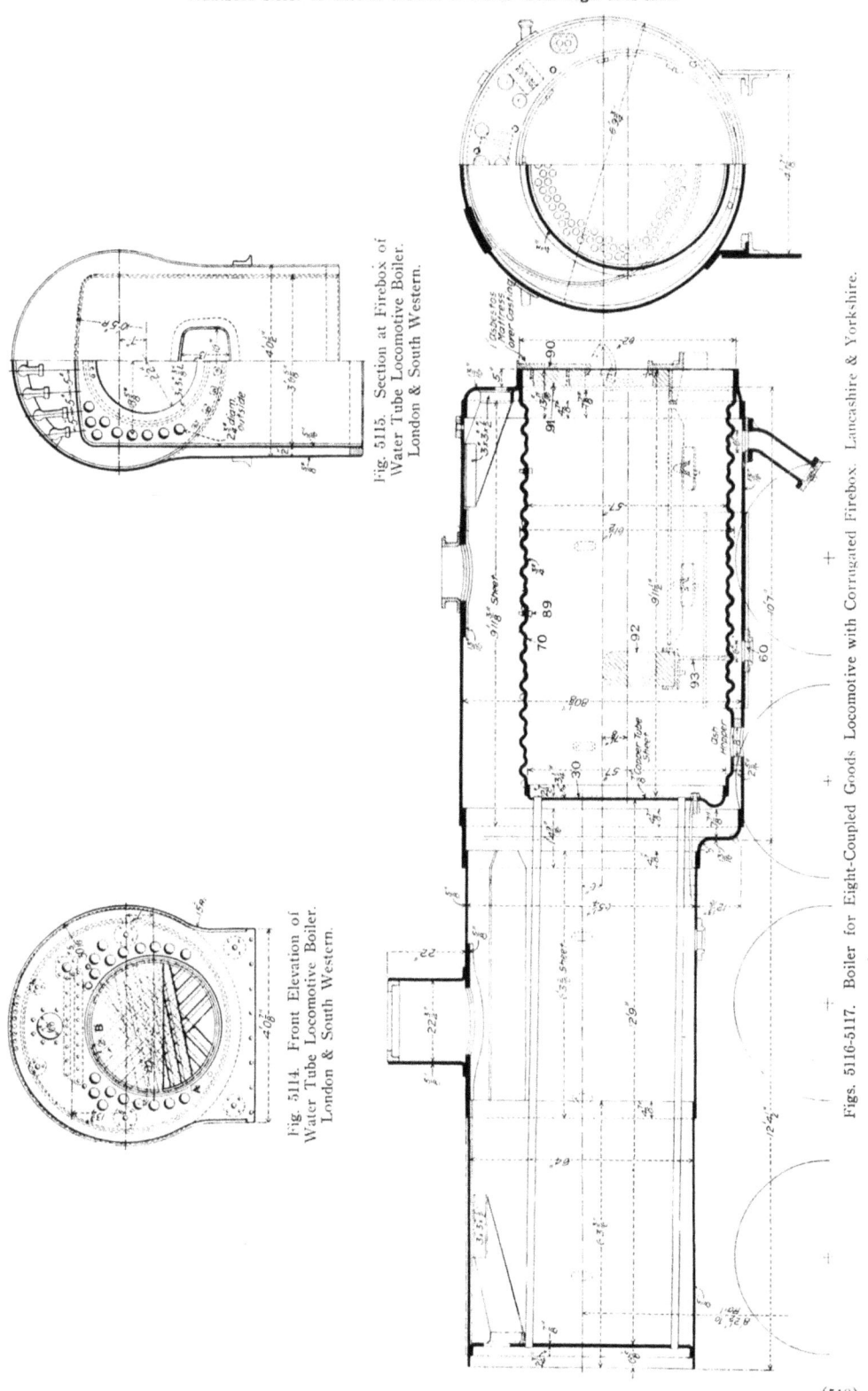

Fig. 5115. Section at Firebox of Water Tube Locomotive Boiler. London & South Western.

Fig. 5114. Front Elevation of Water Tube Locomotive Boiler. London & South Western.

Figs. 5116-5117. Boiler for Eight-Coupled Goods Locomotive with Corrugated Firebox. Lancashire & Yorkshire.

BRITISH LOCOMOTIVES, Cylinders and Valves. Figs. 5118-5125

Numbers Refer to List of Names of Parts Below.

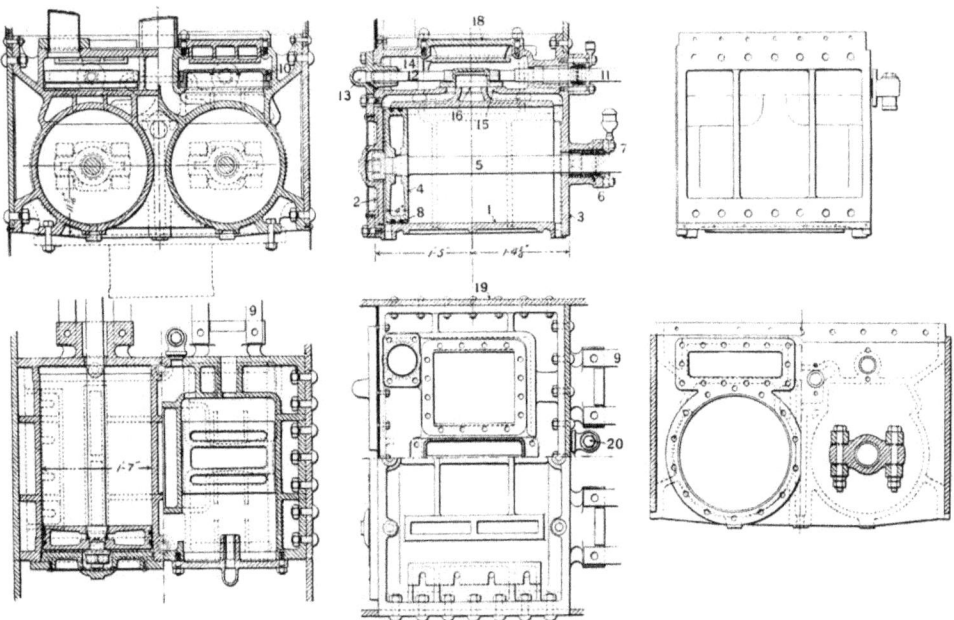

Figs. 5118-5123. Cylinders and Steam Chest for Ten-Wheel, Four-Coupled Locomotive. Lancashire & Yorkshire.

Names of Parts of Cylinders, Figs. 5118-5123.

1 Cylinder	8 Piston Rings	15 Steam Port
2 Cylinder Front Cover	9 Slide Bar	16 Exhaust Port
3 Cylinder Back End	10 Slide Valve	17 Steam Chest
4 Piston	11 Slide Valve Spindle	18 Steam Chest Cover
5 Piston Rod	12 Slide Valve Tail Rod	19 Engine Frame
6 Piston Rod Metallic Packing	13 Slide Valve Tail Rod Casing	20 Cylinder Relief Valve
7 Piston Rod Gland	14 Slide Valve Tail Rod Bush	

Figs. 5124-5125. Smith's Piston Valve. North Eastern Railway.

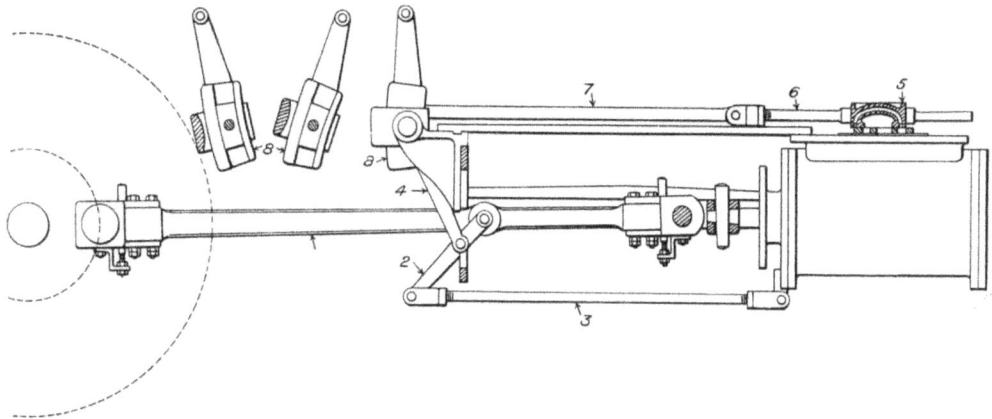

Fig. 5126. Joy Valve Gear.

Names of Parts of Joy Valve Gear, Fig. 5126.

1 *Connecting Rod*
2 *Vibrating Link*
3 *Radius Rod*
4 *Combination Lever*
5 *Valve*
6 *Valve Stem*
7 *Valve Rod*
8 *Link*
9 *Link Arm*

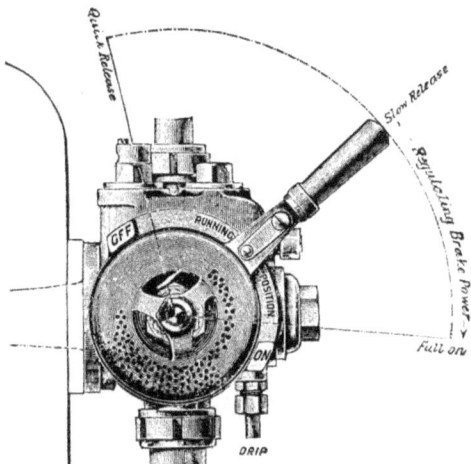

Fig. 5127. Locomotive Ejector.

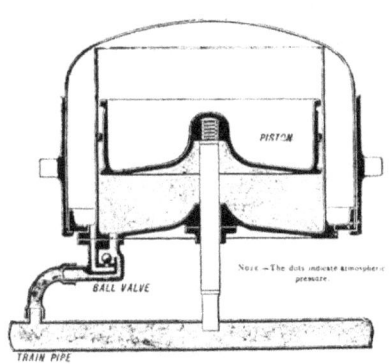

Fig. 5128. Brakes Applied. Fig. 5129. Brakes Off.

Vacuum Brake Cylinder and Ball Valve.
Vacuum Brake Co., Ltd.

(520)

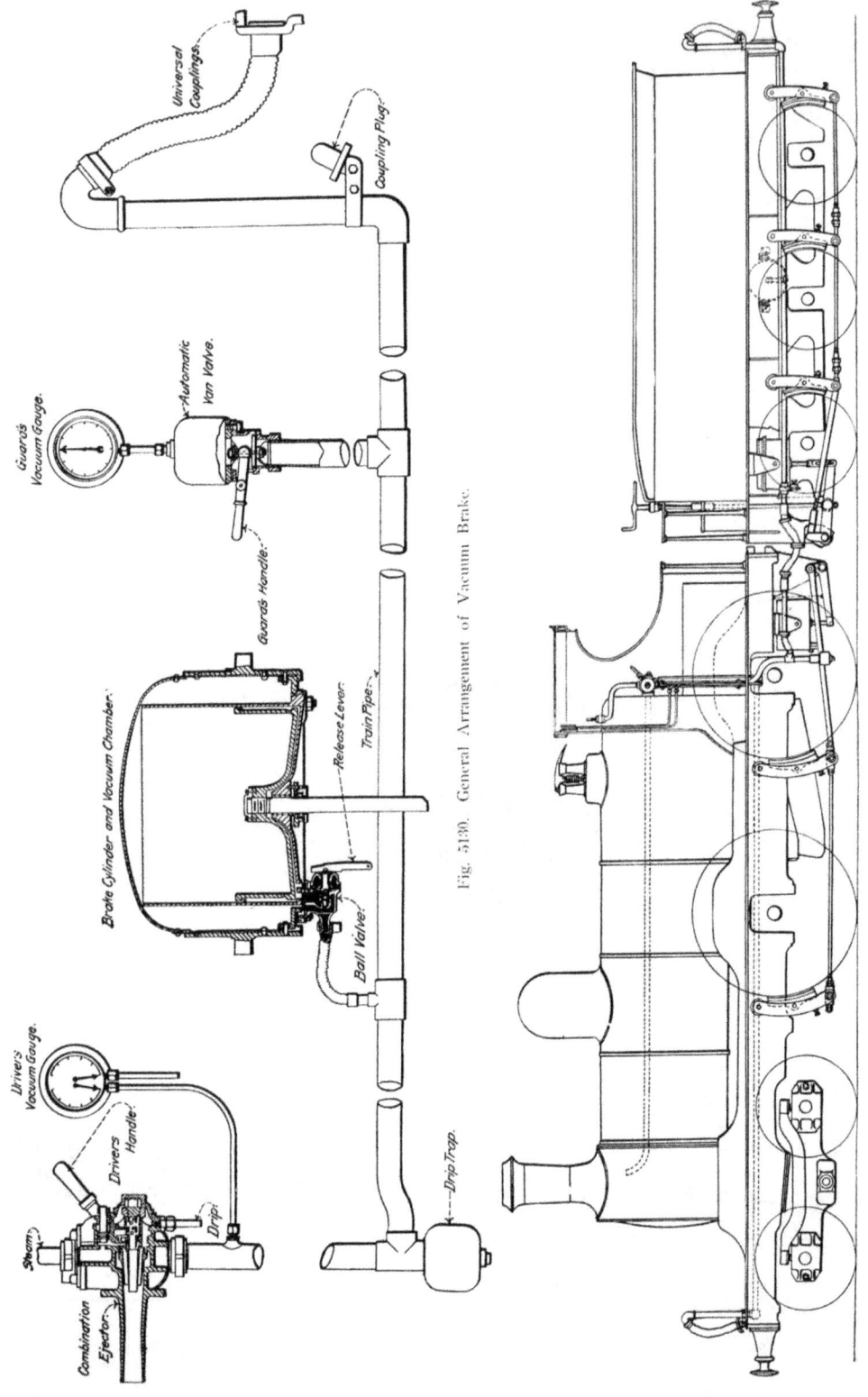

Fig. 5130. General Arrangement of Vacuum Brake.

Fig. 5131. Application of Vacuum Brake to Locomotive and Tender. Vacuum Brake Co., Ltd.

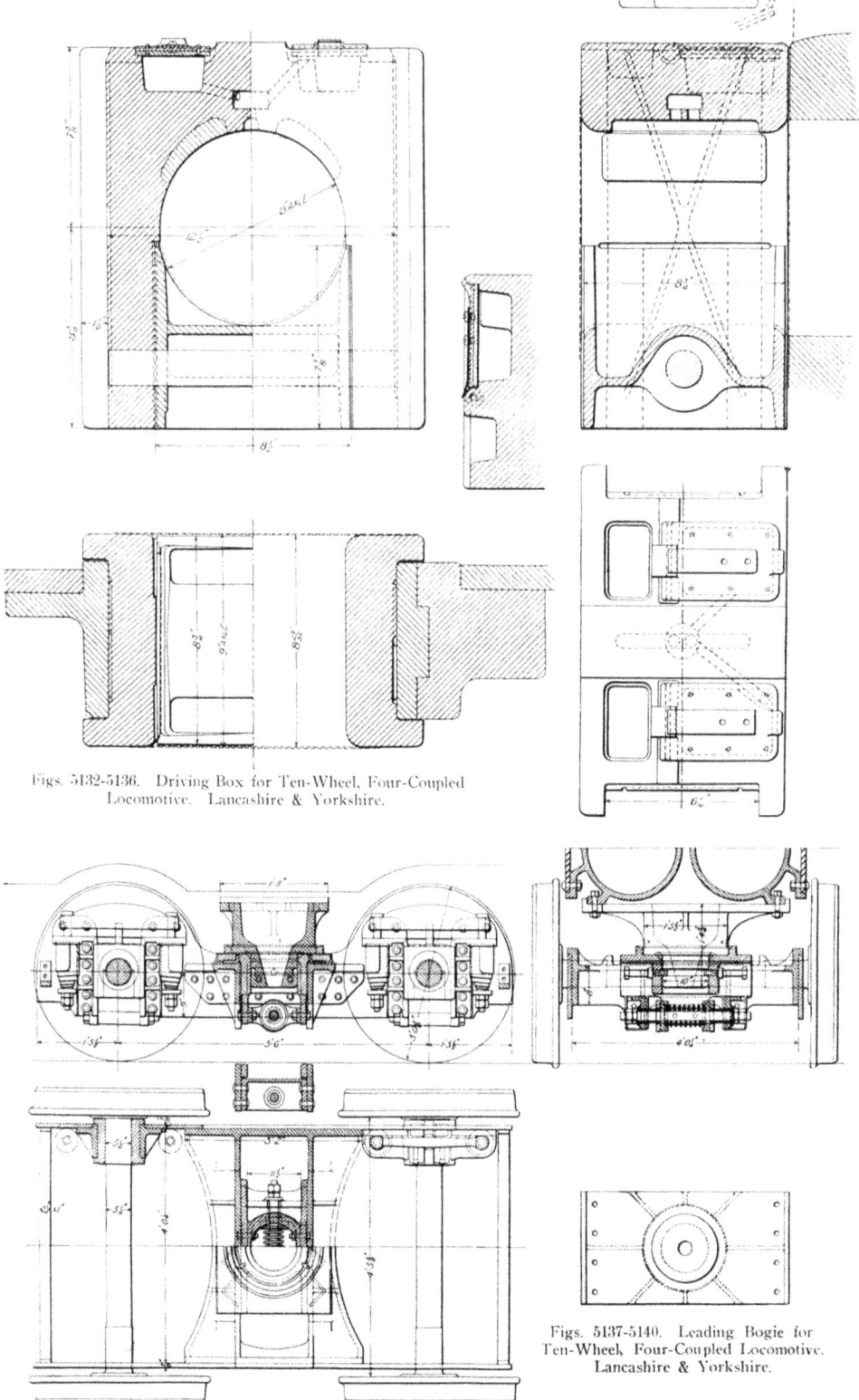

Figs. 5132-5136. Driving Box for Ten-Wheel, Four-Coupled Locomotive. Lancashire & Yorkshire.

Figs. 5137-5140. Leading Bogie for Ten-Wheel, Four-Coupled Locomotive. Lancashire & Yorkshire.

BRITISH LOCOMOTIVES, Water Scoops. Figs. 5141-5148

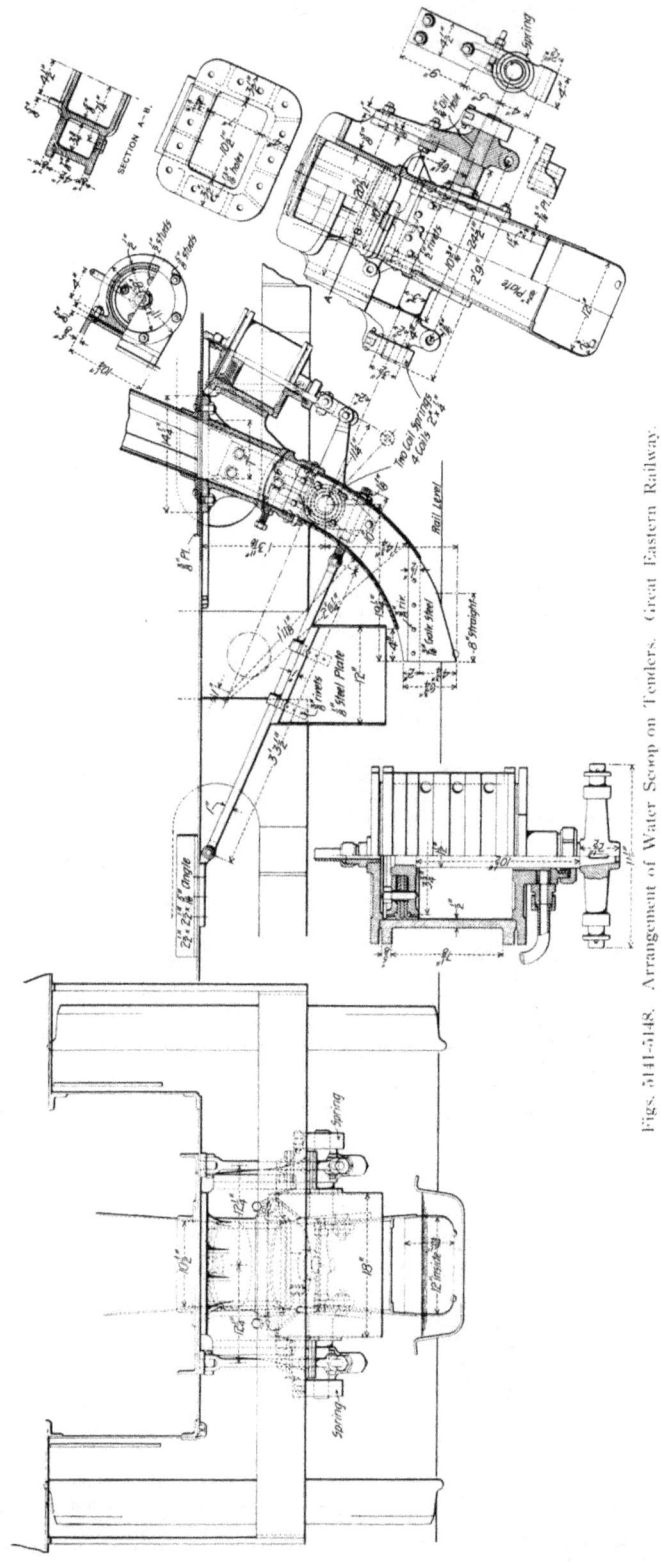

Figs. 5141-5148. Arrangement of Water Scoop on Tenders. Great Eastern Railway.

ADVERTISEMENTS.

SEE CLASSIFIED INDEX TO ADVERTISEMENTS FOLLOWING THE PREFACE.

American Balance Valve Co. 27	Nathan Mfg. Co. 24
American Brake Co. 4	National Machinery Co., The. 43
American Brake Shoe & Foundry Co. 22	National Malleable Castings Co., The 2
American Locomotive Co. 6, 7, 8, 9, 10	National Tube Co. 30
American Locomotive Sander Co. 28	Niles-Bement-Pond Co. 46
American Steam Gage & Valve Mfg. Co. 5	Norton Company 38
American Steel Foundries 39	Norton Grinding Co. 38
Ashcroft Mfg. Co., The 19	
Ashton Valve Co., The 23	Pels & Co., Henry 42
Ateliers Metallurgiques (L'd Co.) Les 14	Pratt & Letchworth Co. 18
	Pressed Steel Car Co. 2
Baldwin Locomotive Works 13	Prosser & Son, Thomas 25
Baltimore Railway Specialty Co. 21	
Betts Machine Co. 43	Quincy, Manchester, Sargent Co. 22
Buffalo Brake Beam Co. 42	
	Railway Steel-Spring Co. 29
Cincinnati Shaper Co., The 45	
Coes Wrench Co. 31	Safety Car Heating & Lighting Co., The .. 33
Columbia Nut & Bolt Co. 26	Sellers & Co., Wm. 40-41
Consolidated Car Heating Co. 35	Shaw Electric Crane Co., The 19
Consolidated Safety Valve Co., The 19	Shelby Steel Tube Co. 30
Crocker-Wheeler Co., The 19	Sherburne & Co. 26
	Standard Steel Works 32
Davis Pressed Steel Co. 18	Star Brass Mfg. Co. 25
Detroit Lubricator Co. 28	Steptoe Shaper Co., The John 45
Dudgeon, Richard 42	Stockbridge Machine Co. 45
	Symington Co., The T. H. 21
Flannery Bolt Co. 21	
Franklin Mfg. Co. 25	Underwood & Co., H. B. 44
	Union Steel Castings Co. 22
General Electric Co. 16, 17	United States Metallic Packing Co., The . 28
Gold Car Heating & Lighting Co. 34	
Gould Coupler Co. 20	Washburn Company, The 26
	Watson-Stillman Co. 43
Hancock Inspirator Co., The 19	Wells Light Mfg. Co., The 24
Hannoversche Maschinenbau-Actien-Gesellschaft ... 18	Westinghouse Air Brake Co., The 3
Hayden & Derby Mfg. Co., The 19	Westinghouse Electric & Mfg. Co. 37
	Witteman & Co., A. P. 44
Lima Locomotive & Machine Co., The 15	Woodward & Powell Planer Co. 45
Locomotive & Machine Co. of Montreal, Ltd 11	Worth Bros. Co. 12
Manning, Maxwell & Moore 19	
Mason Regulator Co., The 24	
McConway & Torley Co., The 36	

Tower and Climax Couplers

FOR

Freight, Passenger and Locomotive Service

See Pages 236, 237, 367.

NATIONAL BRAKE JAWS
NATIONAL BRAKE LEVERS
NATIONAL SAFETY CAR DOOR FASTENERS
NATIONAL JOURNAL BOXES
MALLEABLE IRON CASTINGS

The National Malleable Castings Co.

Works at

CLEVELAND   CHICAGO   INDIANAPOLIS   TOLEDO   SHARON

PRESSED STEEL CAR COMPANY

SAVING IN REPAIRS

LESS FLANGE WEAR OF WHEELS

PRESSED STEEL TRUCKS

of all types and capacities for freight cars and engine tenders.

FREIGHT, PASSENGER, BAGGAGE, POSTAL AND STREET CARS, COMPOSITE CARS.
STEEL UNDERFRAMES.   ENGINE TENDERS.
PRESSED STEEL SPECIALTIES.

OFFICES:

Pittsburgh   New York   Chicago   Atlanta   Mexico City   London   Sydney, N. S. W.

WESTINGHOUSE
NEW LOCOMOTIVE AND TENDER BRAKE EQUIPMENT
SCHEDULE "ET"

The Highest Development in the Art of Locomotive Braking

The Distributing Valve, the important feature of the "ET" Equipment.

RESULTS
MAXIMUM SIMPLICITY—MINIMUM MAINTENANCE

GREAT FLEXIBILITY because of—

    (a) Graduated application and graduated release.

    (b) Operation of locomotive brakes independently or in conjunction with train brakes, at will.

    (c) Ability to use either automatic or straight air as demanded by service conditions.

    (d) Combining the distinct advantages of the High Speed Brake, Double Pressure Control and the Combined Automatic and Straight Air Equipment.

ABSOLUTE RELIABILITY because braking power is—

    (a) Instantly available at all times.

    (b) Automatically and uniformly maintained in all brake cylinders irrespective of number, size, piston travel or cylinder leakage.

    (c) Unlimited, except by pump capacity, in successive applications immediately following release.

ONE STANDARD APPARATUS FOR ALL SIZES AND CLASSES OF LOCOMOTIVES. A PROFITABLE INVESTMENT.

THE WESTINGHOUSE AIR BRAKE COMPANY
WILMERDING, PA.

Offices in all the principal cities.

WESTINGHOUSE
American Automatic Slack Adjuster

Automatically regulates Piston Travel

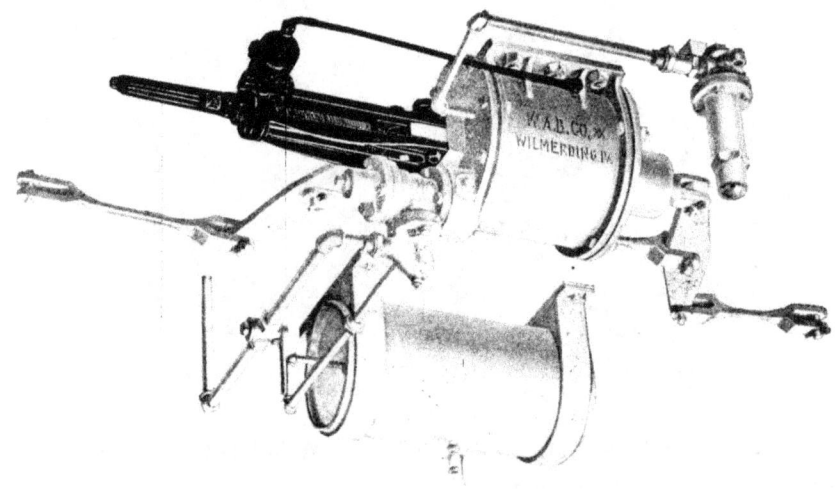

The American Automatic Slack Adjuster furnishes the only practical solution of the difficulties and dangers incident to the regulation of piston travel by hand. Its use secures

Automatically

Uniform Piston Travel
Maximum Brake Efficiency
Saving of Brake Shoes
Minimum Wear of ADJUSTER Parts:—
Device does not operate until adjustment is required.

For information address the

AMERICAN BRAKE COMPANY
1932 NORTH BROADWAY
ST. LOUIS, MO.

Manufacturers of
Driver and Engine Truck Brakes

The American Locomotive Muffled Pop Safety Valve

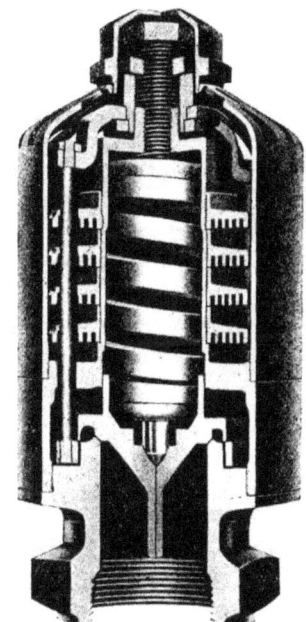

PATENTED

THE ENTIRE

Adjustment

is located directly beneath the cap at the extreme top of the valve

THE

Blow=Back

is adjusted by a slip ring connected with a swivel nut at top of the valve

The time required to adjust this valve is about one-fifth that required for other makes. No threads to stick; no parts to get out of order.

<u>POSITIVE</u>   <u>ACCURATE</u>   <u>EFFICIENT</u>

American Locomotive Steam Gauge

American Locomotive Steam Gauges are equally well constructed, insuring the maximum amount of accuracy and rigidity with the minimum amount of wear.

American Duplex Air-Brake Gauge

Manufactured exclusively by the

American Steam Gauge & Valve Mfg. Co.

New York
Atlanta

Boston, Mass.

Chicago
San Francisco

LOCOMOTIVES

STEAM   ELECTRIC   COMPRESSED AIR

Prairie Type Passenger Locomotive
Built at Brooks Works for Lake Shore & Michigan Southern Railway

Ten of the thirty-five 100 ton 2200 horse-power electric locomotives built for
the New York Terminal electrification of the New York Central
Lines by the General Electric Company and the
American Locomotive Company

Consolidation Freight Locomotive
Built at Richmond Works for Chesapeake & Ohio Railway

AMERICAN LOCOMOTIVE COMPANY
111 BROADWAY, NEW YORK, U. S. A.

LOCOMOTIVES

FOR ALL CLASSES OF SERVICE

Mogul Freight Locomotive
Built for Kiushiu Railway of Japan

Eight-Wheel Passenger Locomotive
Built for American-China Development Company

Consolidation Freight Locomotive
Built for Western Railways of Havana

AMERICAN LOCOMOTIVE COMPANY
111 Broadway, New York, U. S. A.
LONDON OFFICE: 26 Victoria Street, Westminster.

SMALL LOCOMOTIVES

Suitable for light logging, contractors, switching, or other service where runs are comparatively short and where short rigid wheel base or small driving wheels are important.

FORNEY TYPE LOCOMOTIVE

Suitable for contractors, rolling mills, industrial plants and general construction work.

Has entire weight available for adhesion, and is specially adapted for short heavy hauls.

FOUR-WHEEL SADDLE TANK

FOUR-WHEEL CONNECTED DOUBLE-ENDER

Suitable for light mixed and plantation service.

Designed for taking sharp curves easily, and makes a very satisfactory engine for all-round work.

SPARE PARTS ALWAYS ON HAND

AMERICAN LOCOMOTIVE COMPANY
111 BROADWAY, NEW YORK

ATLANTIC STEAM SHOVEL

COMMENDS ITSELF TO USERS FOR ITS

Simplicity of design,
    Large and efficient Boiler,
        Free steaming and low fuel consumption,
            Minimum breakdowns and repair costs.

GOLD DREDGES

BUILT FROM DESIGNS BY A. W. ROBINSON, M. AM. SOC. C. E.

AMERICAN LOCOMOTIVE COMPANY
111 BROADWAY, N. Y., U. S. A.

ROTARY SNOW PLOW

Used on many of the largest and most important roads in the U. S.
The only means of opening roads in deep snow.
Throws snow clear of tracks. Saves
Locomotives and men.

Front View of Rotary on
Denver, Northwestern and Pacific Railroad

AMERICAN LOCOMOTIVE COMPANY
111 Broadway, New York, U. S. A.

LOCOMOTIVES
STRUCTURAL STEEL   STEAM SHOVELS

Ten-Wheel Locomotive for Fast Passenger Service
Built for Grand Trunk Railway

Structural Steel for Bridges, Buildings, Roof Trusses, Viaducts, etc

Atlantic Steam Shovel—Size 50-17-3½
Built for Canadian Pacific Railway

LOCOMOTIVE & MACHINE COMPANY OF MONTREAL, LIMITED

IMPERIAL BANK BUILDING, MONTREAL, CANADA

LONDON OFFICE: 26 Victoria Street, Westminster

BALDWIN LOCOMOTIVE WORKS

Burnham, Williams & Co., Philadelphia, Pa.

Cable Address: "Baldwin," Philadelphia

LOCOMOTIVES
OF EVERY DESCRIPTION

Electric Locomotives Built in Conjunction with the Westinghouse Electric & Manufacturing Company

Pacific Type Locomotive, Built for the Great Northern Railway

Les Ateliers Métallurgiques (Ld. Co.)

Head Office: 1, Place de Louvain, Brussels (Belgium)
Works at Tubize, Nivelles and La Sambre.

PERMANENT WAY AND ROLLING STOCK FOR RAILWAYS AND TRAMWAYS.

Codes Used: Lieber's, A. B. C. (5th Ed.).

Télégraphic Address: Métal, Brussels.

SPECIAL PRODUCTIONS:
Locomotives, Passenger Cars. Open and Closed Goods Wagons, Tramcars, Bridges, Constructional Steel Work for Roofs, Wheels, Springs, Switches and Crossings, Spikes, Bolts and Nuts.

ASK FOR CATALOGUES AND PRICES.

THE EFFICIENCY OF RIGHT BEVEL GEARS IS 92%

ARE YOUR SIDE RODS DOING ANY BETTER?

This is the Service Obtained by the

SHAY GEARED LOCOMOTIVE

150-Ton Shay Locomotive built for C. & O. Ry.

For Heavy Freight and Combination Traffic on Branch Lines, Mountain Divisions or any sort of a railroad where Heavy Grades and Curves are found, the SHAY cannot be surpassed. Shows from *10 to 15 per cent. economy per ton-mile over* other types doing the above work. Better Investigate. Write for full particulars. Catalog No. 13 gives general information about 150-ton size, as well as other sizes. Built in weights 10 to 150 tons.

Mogul Locomotive

Our Direct Locomotives embody the most modern construction, and we are prepared to build Locomotives of this class of any design desired in sizes up to 20x26 cylinders. Catalog No. 14 gives information and illustrations Locomotives recently constructed. Give us a call.

THE LIMA LOCOMOTIVE AND MACHINE CO.
111 THIRD STREET, LIMA, OHIO, U. S. A.

General Electric Company

CURTIS STEAM TURBINE
GENERATING SET
For Train Lighting

Used By

Southern Railroad
Pennsylvania Railroad
Seaboard Air Line Railroad
Chicago & Northwestern Railroad
Chicago, Burlington & Quincy Railroad
Lake Shore & Michigan Southern Railroad
New York Central & Hudson River Railroad
Chicago, St. Paul, Minneapolis & Omaha R. R.

20 Kilowatt, 4,000 r. p. m., Curtis Turbine, Direct Connected to Direct Current 125-volt Generator.

Reliable in Service
Proper lubrication
Proper construction

Makes no Noise
Produces no vibration and
cannot annoy passengers

Locomotive Equipped with Curtis Turbine Train Lighting Set.

Requires Little Attention
Does away with expense
of a special attendant

Occupies Small Space
Can be located either in the
baggage car or on locomotive

The General Electric Company makes all fittings for electrically lighted trains—instruments, couplers, lamps, fans, etc.

824

New York Office:	Principal Office:	Sales Offices in all
44 Broad St.	**Schenectady, N. Y.**	large cities

General Electric Company

HIGH SPEED ELECTRIC LOCOMOTIVES

New York Central Type of Electric Locomotive. Direct Current—100 tons—2200 horse-power—80 m. p. h.
Built by General Electric Company and American Locomotive Company.

THE maintenance expense per mile for the 50,000-mile test run of the No. 6,000 locomotive, completed June 12, 1906, was $0.0126. This includes all maintenance expense on motors, brake shoes, tires, inspection and other miscellaneous items. The service given by this locomotive with a train averaging 200 to 400 tons was on a six-mile track. High-speed running under these conditions involved higher braking and accelerating duty than in regular operating service.

The 50,000-mile test run indicated that no material changes in design or construction were desirable for future locomotives of this type, which are to be identical with No. 6,000 in form.

Eight of the thirty-five 100-ton 2,200 horse-power electric locomotives built for the New York Terminal electrification of the New York Central Lines by the General Electric Company and the American Locomotive Company at Schenectady, N. Y.

| New York Office | PRINCIPAL OFFICE | Sales Offices in |
| 44 Broad Street | **Schenectady, N. Y.** | all large cities |

Davis Solid Truss BRAKE BEAMS

THE TRUSS IS FORMED IN ONE PIECE FROM A SOLID BAR

The only brake beam that fully meets the M. C. B. requirement, viz.: "not more than 1-16 in. deflection with a load of 15,000 lbs. at center."

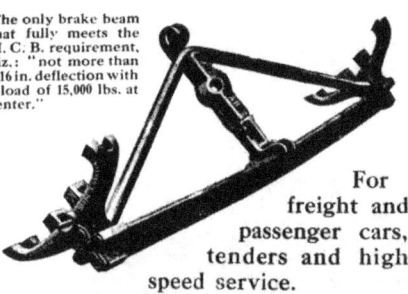

For freight and passenger cars, tenders and high speed service.

HIGH SPEED DEFLECTION, 1-16 IN. WITH A LOAD OF 30,000 LBS. AT CENTER

DAVIS PRESSED STEEL CO.

Wilmington, Delaware, U. S. A.

NATHAN H. DAVIS — President
THOS. C. DAVIS — Sec'y & Treas.

HANNOVERSCHE MASCHINENBAU= ACTIEN=GESELLSCHAFT

vormals Georg Egestorff

LINDEN vor HANNOVER

Telegraphic address: Maschinenfabrik Hannover-Linden

LOCOMOTIVES

for any width of gauge and for all purposes with Pielock-Superheater and Lentz's Valve Gear.

BOILERS, STEAM ENGINES, PUMPS.

For fitting locomotives with Pielock-Superheater and Lentz's Valve Gear Apply to

Société Anonyme de Perfectionnements Mécaniques

Paris, 43 Rue Taitbout,

Telegraphic Address: Soupape, Paris.

MALLEABLE IRON & STEEL CASTINGS.

LOCOMOTIVE & RAILROAD WORK

PRATT & LETCHWORTH COMPANY.

WORKS
BUFFALO, N.Y.
BRANTFORD, ONT.

COST OF LOCOMOTIVE OPERATION

By George R. Henderson

A complete analysis of the cost of operating a locomotive considered as a power plant, including chapters on fuel, water supply, lubrication, repairs, wages, etc. Cloth, 192 pages.

PRICE, $2.50

The Railroad Gazette
New York   Chicago   London

TO BUILD MODERN LOCOMOTIVES YOU MUST USE MODERN METHODS.

View of Modern Locomotive Shop, showing C-W Motor-Driven Tools. Note Absence of Belts.

Let us show you our work in this field. We are **EXPERTS** in Motor Drive

SEE RAILWAY BULLETIN No. 67%

CROCKER-WHEELER COMPANY
Manufacturers and Electrical Engineers
AMPERE, N. J.

MANNING, MAXWELL & MOORE
INCORPORATED

Machine Tools & Railway Supplies
OF EVERY DESCRIPTION

OWNING AND OPERATING

THE SHAW ELECTRIC CRANE CO.
The Shaw Electric Traveling Crane
The Shaw Wrecking Crane

THE ASHCROFT MANUFACTURING CO.
The Ashcroft Steam Gauge
The Tabor Steam Engine Indicator

THE CONSOLIDATED SAFETY VALVE CO.
The Consolidated Pop Safety Valve

THE HANCOCK INSPIRATOR CO.
The Hancock Inspirator
The Hancock Main Steam Valve
The Hancock Check Valve
The Hancock Globe Valve

THE HAYDEN & DERBY MANUFACTURING CO.
The Metropolitan Injector
The H—D. Ejector

GENERAL OFFICES
85-87-89 LIBERTY ST., NEW YORK

22-26 S. Canal St., Chicago.   721 Arch St., Philadelphia.   128 Oliver St., Boston.   Frisco Bldg., St. Louis.   Park Bldg. Pittsburg.   Williamson Bldg. Cleveland.   Kirk Bldg., Syracuse.   Woodward Bldg., Birmingham, Ala.
Tokio, Japan.

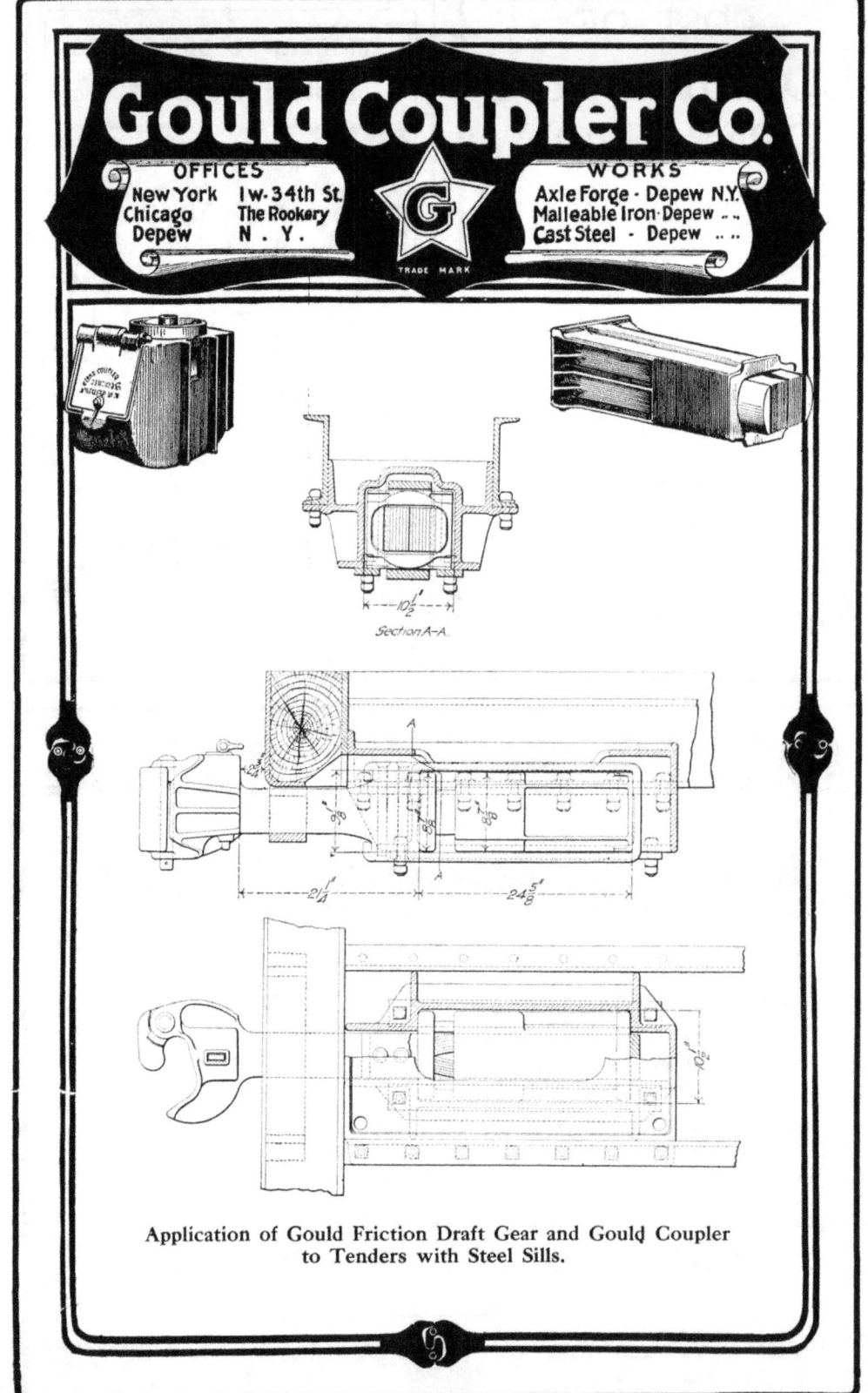

Application of Gould Friction Draft Gear and Gould Coupler to Tenders with Steel Sills.

THE SYMINGTON JOURNAL BOX

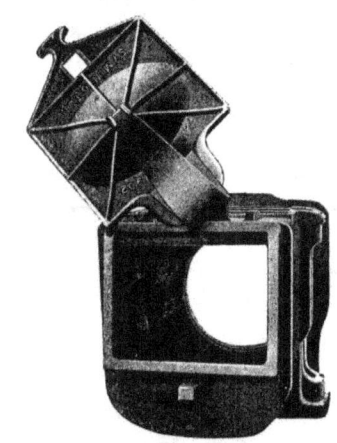

THE T. H. SYMINGTON CO.
BALTIMORE, MD.   CHICAGO, ILL.

BALTIMORE BALL=BEARING

CENTER AND SIDE BEARINGS

BALTIMORE RAILWAY SPECIALTY CO.
BALTIMORE, MARYLAND

THE T. H. SYMINGTON CO.
SELLING AGENTS

BALTIMORE, MD.   CHICAGO, ILL.

The Tate Flexible Staybolt

PATENTED
MAR.-1-1904
NO. 753329
FEB'Y.-20-1906
NO. 813120

Perfect in its Design
Strong and Serviceable
The IDEAL STAY
For Locomotive Fire Boxes

WE MAINTAIN that the fire box sheet when rigidly stayed—with the ordinary staybolt—buckles and bends in its effort to expand, throwing great stress on the bolt, which becomes fatigued, ruptures and breaks. The fire sheet soon deteriorates through the unnatural strains thrown upon it due to the old method of staying, collecting innumerable small surface cracks which expose the inner structure of the material to constant disintegration.

THE TATE FLEXIBLE STAYBOLT when properly applied, covering sufficient area to allow the fire box to expand in its natural course with less resistance, overcoming the transverse stress due to force of expansion—will not only eliminate the risk of cracking sheets, but will reduce staybolt breakages to an absolute minimum.

SERVICE RESULTS TESTIFY TO THE ARGUMENTS WE ADVANCE : : : : : : :

WRITE FOR LITERATURE

FLANNERY BOLT COMPANY
307-309 FRICK BUILDING
PITTSBURGH, PENN.
U. S. A.

B. E. D. STAFFORD, General Manager

QUINCY, MANCHESTER, SARGENT CO.

SUCCEEDING

Railway Appliances Co.—Q & C Company—Pedrick & Ayer Co.

OFFICES

Old Colony Bldg., Chicago   114 Liberty Street, New York

MANUFACTURERS OF RAILWAY MACHINERY AND SUPPLIES

Air Hoists	Portable Boring Bars	Portable Crank Pin Turners
Cranes	Gilman-Brown Emergency Knuckle	Q & C Priest Snow Flangers
Pneumatic Punches	Riveters, Pneumatic	Fewings Car and Engine Replacers
Metal Sawing Machines	Flue Cleaners	Portable Crank-Pin Turning Machine
Elastic Self-locking Nuts	Valve Seat Boring Bars	

SEND FOR CATALOG AND DETAILED INFORMATION

Union Steel Casting Co.

PITTSBURGH, PA.

Locomotive Castings

The Unflanged Steel Back Shoe for Engine Truck and Tenders.

HIGH SPEED BRAKES DEMAND STEEL BACK BRAKE SHOES

The Flanged Steel Back Shoe for Engine Truck and Tenders.

SAFETY   EFFICIENCY   ECONOMY

AMERICAN BRAKE SHOE AND FOUNDRY COMPANY

NEW YORK   MAHWAH, N. J.   CHICAGO

STEEL BACK BRAKE SHOES

The Combination Brake Head will accommodate American "T" and Westinghouse types of brake shoes. It is easier to operate, safer to use, and more economical than any other
BRAKE HEAD.

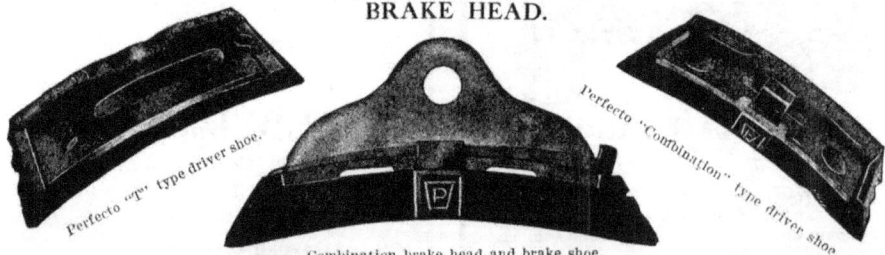

Combination brake head and brake shoe.

Ashton High Grade

Locomotive Mufflers, Open Pop Valves, Steam and Air Gages

The highest standard of excellence. Guaranteed to give satisfaction and greatest efficiency and durability.

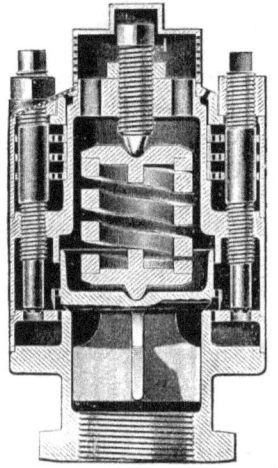

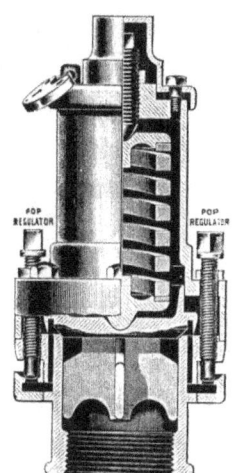

No. 30—Ashton Muffler

gives quiet relief without impairing efficiency. It has top outside adjustment of pop, and all working parts are made of best composition metal, with springs of Jessops steel.

No. 52—LOCOMOTIVE STEAM GAGE.

No. 28—Open Pop Valve

has downward discharge outlet, preventing cinders getting into the valve to clog it, also lock-up attachment, as well as other features as found in our standard muffler valves.

The Ashton Gages

embody the latest improvements in the art. They are accurately graduated, have non-corrosive movements and solid drawn seamless springs, carefully made and of best material.

No. 68—INSPECTOR'S TEST GAGE
with Air Brake Hose Coupling.

No. 62—DUPLEX AIR BRAKE GAGE.

THE ASHTON VALVE CO.,

271 Franklin Street, Boston, Mass.

Branches—New York, Chicago, San Francisco, London, Vienna.

(References, see pages 301, 302, 303, 312.)

The MASON

LOCOMOTIVE REDUCING VALVE

STANDARD OF THE WORLD

The
Mason Regulator Co.
Boston, Mass., U. S. A.

They Hold the Light in the Right Place

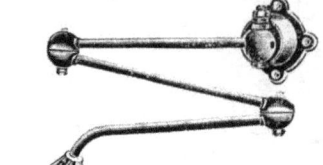

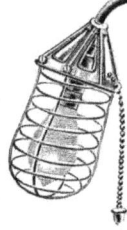

Wallwork's Universal Electric Lamp Brackets can be attached to any machine frame, work bench or desk. Simple, practical, durable and cheap. Write for illustrated folder showing full line.

THE WELLS LIGHT MFG. CO.
50 WASHINGTON STREET
NEW YORK CITY

Nathan Manufacturing Co.

92-94 Liberty Street, New York
Western Office: 485 Old Colony Building, Chicago, Ill.

INJECTORS AND LUBRICATORS

specially constructed for High Pressures grading from 25 to 300 lbs.

Makers of
Monitor, Simplex and Nathan Injectors

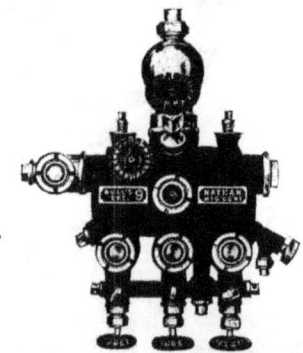

"NATHAN'S" SIGHT FEED LUBRICATORS
for Cylinder and Air Brakes

STEAM FIRE EXTINGUISHERS
for Switching and Yard Engines

Boiler Washers, Rod and Guide Oil Cups, etc.

SEND FOR CATALOGUE

Sole Agency of the Coale Muffler Safety Valves.

STAR BRASS MANUFACTURING CO.

Original and Exclusive Manufacturers of "Non-Corrosive" Steam and Air Gages. Extra heavy Muffled and Open Pop Safety Valves, Chime Whistles, Seibert Bulls Eye Lubricators, Automatic Water Gages, etc.

Globe, Angle, Check, Cross and Blow-off Valves.

Main Office and Works . . . . 108-114 East Dedham Street, BOSTON, MASS.
Branches: NEW YORK CITY   LONDON, ENGLAND

KRUPP STEEL TIRES

ON LOCOMOTIVE DRIVING WHEELS AND ON STEEL TIRED WHEELS GIVE THE BEST RESULTS FOR EVERY VARIETY OF SERVICE

THOMAS PROSSER & SON

15 Gold Street, New York   Old Colony Building, Chicago

American Locomotive Co., Pittsburgh Works.

ENGINE BEING LAGGED WITH OUR K. & M. 85% MAGNESIA SECTIONAL LAGGING

THE ONLY ECONOMICAL LAGGING MADE

FRANKLIN MFG. COMPANY

FRANKLIN, PA.

MILLS' PATENT ATTACHMENT FOR ROTATING LOCOMOTIVE DRIVING WHEELS with FARRINGTON'S MACHINE FOR SETTING VALVES AND ECCENTRICS

CAN BE EASILY APPLIED TO FARRINGTON'S VALVE SETTING MACHINES YOU MAY OWN AND HAVE IN USE

DESCRIPTIVE CIRCULAR SENT ON APPLICATION

These Machines are largely in use and giving excellent satisfaction

SHERBURNE & CO.
Proprietors

**53 OLIVER ST., BOSTON
MASSACHUSETTS, U. S. A.**

COLUMBIA LOCK NUTS

"The nut that will not shake off"

For use on **LOCOMOTIVES** and **MACHINERY** of all kinds

Our Special for Wrist, Knuckle and Cross Head Pins has proven a great success.

Inexpensive   Simple   Effective

Samples free for the asking

COLUMBIA NUT & BOLT CO.

"Original Columbia" Assembled—   Bridgeport, Conn.   New York: 25 Broad St.   —"Improved Columbia" Assembled

---

The Washburn Company
MINNEAPOLIS, MINNESOTA

Freight Engine and Passenger Couplers

Draft Rigging Simple and Friction Types

Railway and General Steel Castings

Trucks Bolsters and Side Frames

NOTICE.—We are turning out the above mentioned useful articles and shipping to all parts of America. If you can use any of them in your business WRITE TO US. If what we have does not suit you we will make something that does. If you are merely a collector of catalogues DON'T ANSWER THIS AD. Our time belongs to our patrons and not to the general public.

Balanced Main Valves

ANY TYPE OF VALVE. FOR ANY KIND OF SERVICE
AMERICAN SEMI-PLUG PISTON VALVE

Shipping Room: Shipping 60 a week to One R.R. which had 1,206 in Service June 1, 1906

WE HAVE MADE THESE VALVES FOR 750 LBS. PRESSURE AND CAN GUARANTEE THEM UP TO THAT
WE HAVE THEM IN SERVICE FROM 3 INCHES DIA TO 14 INCHES DIA., AND CAN MAKE THEM ANY SIZE

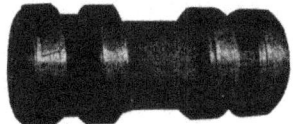
DOUBLE END VALVE

TRIPLE END VALVE

SINGLE END VALVE

SERVICE IS WHAT YOU WANT

We took a pair of these Valves out of a Locomotive after two years and nine months service. They are in PERFECT condition. We put a new set of valves in their place without boring the cages; valves still perfectly steam tight after 5 years' continuous service without reboring valve cages.

Over Ports Without Bridges

A pair of the above Valves have been doing this trick since July 1st, 1905, in a Switch Engine running night and day.

STILL IN PERFECT CONDITION
AND THE ENGINE CAN PUSH CARS

WE FURNISH VALVES ON APPROVAL YOU ARE THE JUDGE AND JURY

OUR JACK WILSON
DOUBLE ACTING SLIDE VALVES

Are made FOR pressure up to 250 pounds. They are balanced in all positions of stroke. They are made for internal or external admission. They are fitted to any old or new power.

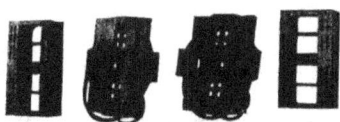
INTERNAL ADMISSION HALF VALVES

Main Office
SAN FRANCISCO, CAL.

Eastern Office and Works
JERSEY SHORE, PENNA.

AMERICAN LOCOMOTIVE SANDER CO.
PHILADELPHIA and CHICAGO

Pneumatic Track Sanders of Standard Design

METALLIC PACKINGS For Locomotive Piston Rods, Valve Stems and Air Pumps : : : : : :
Also THE GOLLMAR BELL RINGER

The U. S. Metallic Packing Co.
PHILADELPHIA and CHICAGO

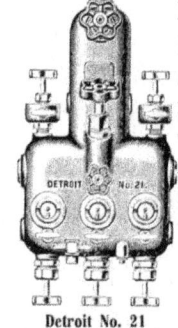

Detroit No. 21
Locomotive Lubricator

SAFETY, SIMPLICITY, ECONOMY.

In the Detroit No. 21 Locomotive Lubricator

All the essential and desirable features for a perfect locomotive lubricator are combined in the most compact and simple form. Descriptive pamphlet showing sectional views and fully explaining the various features will be sent on application.

DETROIT LUBRICATOR CO., Detroit, Mich.

Car Builders' Dictionary

THE 1906 edition was prepared under the direction of the Master Car Builders' Association, and is as accurate and comprehensive as skilled men could make it. The text gives correct descriptions of cars and all parts of cars. The 6,344 engravings show general views, scale drawings and dimensions of substantially all American cars their details and parts, and in addition the principal features of British car building practice are illustrated. It is probably the most expensive, as well as the most artistic technical book ever published. It is indispensable to makers, designers and users of cars or of any car furnishing or attachment, and it is of the highest interest and value to all, either old or young, who wish to know either thoroughly or superficially the modern practices in car building. Price $6.00.

THE RAILROAD GAZETTE
New York   London   Chicago

Railway Steel-Spring Co.

71 Broadway, New York

SPRINGS

LATROBE TIRES

STEEL TIRED WHEELS

BRANCHES

CHICAGO   LOUISVILLE   MEXICO CITY
ST. LOUIS   ST. PAUL   WASHINGTON

National Tube Company

Manufacturers of

KNOBBLED HAMMERED CHARCOAL
IRON LOCOMOTIVE TUBES

GENERAL OFFICES
FRICK BUILDING, PITTSBURG, PA.

LOCAL SALES OFFICES

NEW YORK,	Battery Park Building
PHILADELPHIA,	Pennsylvania Building
CHICAGO,	The Rookery
PITTSBURG,	Frick Building
SAN FRANCISCO,	16th and Folsom Streets

GENERAL AGENT FOR THE SOUTHWEST

National Tube Works Company
CHEMICAL BUILDING, ST. LOUIS, MO.

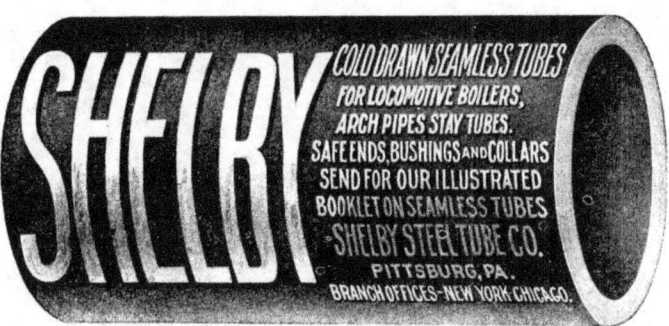

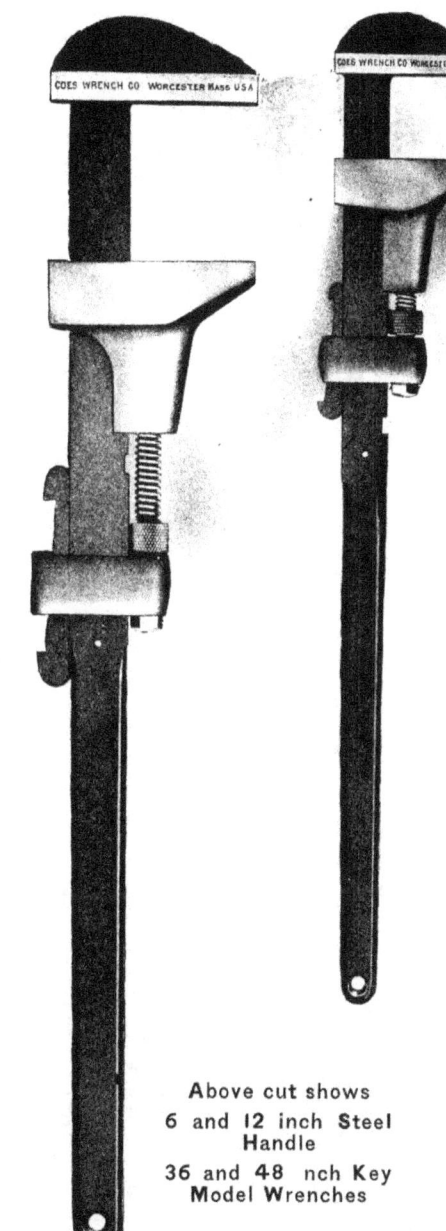

COES'
Genuine Screw
WRENCHES

Strongest
Best Finished
Longest Life
and
COES' Warrant

Sixty-six years of experience in Wrench Making

5 STYLES   48 SIZES
6 TO 48 INCH LONG

Catalogue and other literature on request

Above cut shows
6 and 12 inch Steel Handle
36 and 48 inch Key Model Wrenches

COES WRENCH COMPANY

WORCESTER, MASS.

N. Y. Agents { J. C. McCARTY & CO., 10 Warren Street
JOHN H. GRAHAM & CO., 113 Chambers Street

OR YOUR SUPPLY HOUSE

ELECTRIC MOTOR and TRAILER TRUCKS

For Railway and Suburban Service

STANDARD STEEL WORKS
Harrison Building, Philadelphia, Pa.

STEEL-TIRED WHEELS
SOLID FORGED ROLLED WHEELS
LOCOMOTIVE TIRES

Iron and Steel Forgings   Iron and Steel Castings

Railway Springs

The Safety Car Heating & Lighting Co.
160 Broadway, New York City

CHICAGO   PHILADELPHIA   ST. LOUIS   SAN FRANCISCO

Pintsch System Car and Buoy Lighting

Has been applied to 29,000 cars by 200 railroads in the United States, Canada and Mexico. In the World 148,000 cars, 6,600 locomotives, 1,900 buoys and beacons, 125 lightships and vessels are using this system and 375 gas works have been established. Gold medals for excellence at the World's Expositions at Moscow, Vienna, St. Petersburg, London, Berlin, Paris, Chicago, Atlanta and Buffalo.   Grand Prize St. Louis Exposition 1904.

NEW INVERTED MANTLE

LAMPS FOR PINTSCH GAS

Illumination increased over three times without additional gas consumption

A revolution in the lighting of railroad cars

SAFETY HEATING SYSTEMS

Practical service for the past 19 years has demonstrated the reliability, efficiency and adaptability of the Safety Systems of direct steam and hot water heating. Straightport Couplers and Automatic Steam Traps.
160 railroads using these devices on 19,000 cars.
Grand Prize St. Louis Exposition 1904

GOLD CAR HEATING AND LIGHTING COMPANY

Cable Address, "Gold," New York.
Long-Distance Telephone.

Whitehall Building, 17 Battery Place,
NEW YORK

LARGEST MANUFACTURERS IN THE WORLD OF CAR-HEATING APPARATUS.

Over 40,000 Cars and Locomotives already equipped—all giving Entire Satisfaction.
Competitive tests have invariably proven the Superiority of our devices.
Highest Award—A Gold Medal received at the Louisiana Purchase Exposition.

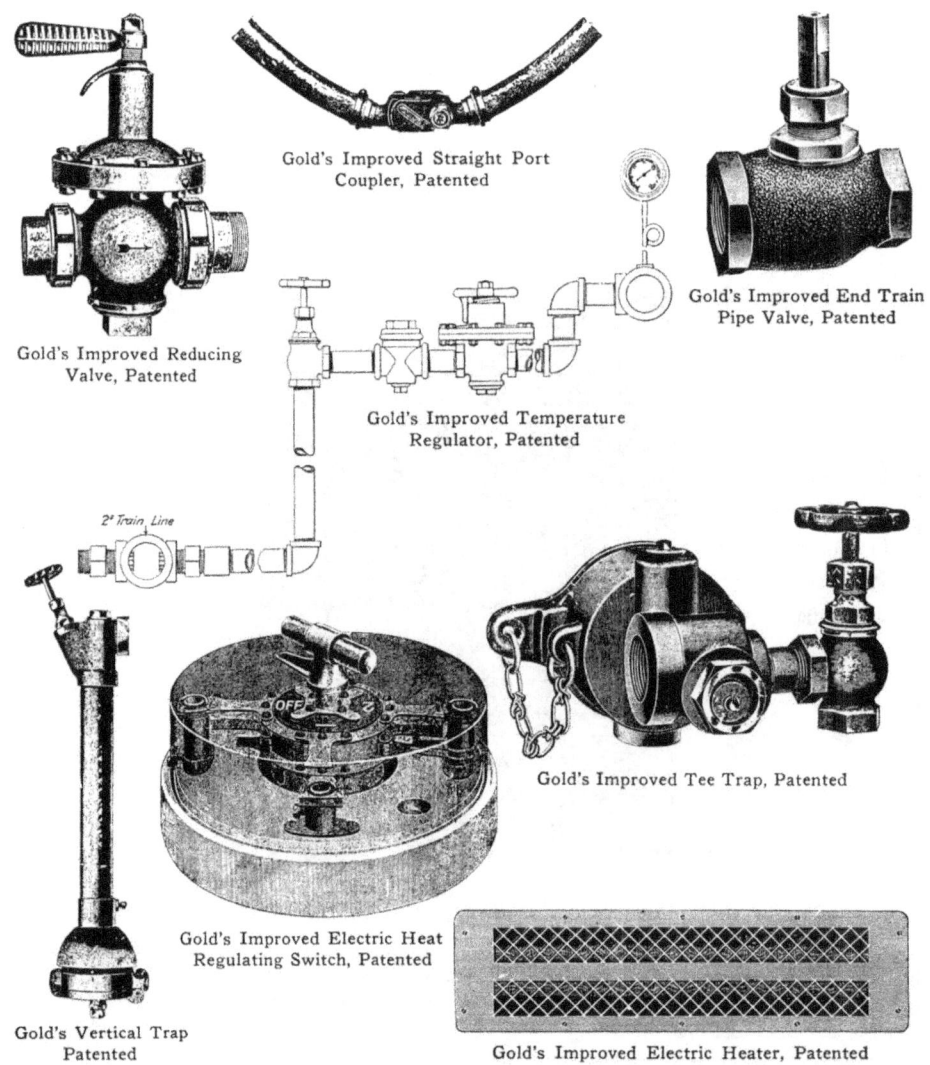

Gold's Improved Straight Port Coupler, Patented

Gold's Improved End Train Pipe Valve, Patented

Gold's Improved Reducing Valve, Patented

Gold's Improved Temperature Regulator, Patented

Gold's Improved Tee Trap, Patented

Gold's Vertical Trap Patented

Gold's Improved Electric Heat Regulating Switch, Patented

Gold's Improved Electric Heater, Patented

ELECTRIC, STEAM AND HOT WATER APPARATUS FOR RAILWAY CARS
EDISON STORAGE BATTERY FOR RAILWAY CAR LIGHTING

Catalogues and circulars cheerfully furnished

RELIABLE REGULATION *for* STEAM HEAT

CONSOLIDATED LOCOMOTIVE EQUIPMENT

Economically and efficiently supplies steam to the heating system. All parts of extra heavy pattern.

SPECIAL STEAM GAUGE No. 23.

SPECIAL PARTS LOCOMOTIVE EQUIPMENT

Reducing Valve, Throttle Valve, Steam Gauge, Automatic Relief Valve. All apparatus guaranteed.

AUTOMATIC LOCK COUPLER *for* LOCOMOTIVE *and* TENDER

Adapted for High-Pressure Work

COUPLER HEAD AND GASKET.

Prevent Steam Leaks

CONSOLIDATED CAR-HEATING COMPANY

ALBANY, N. Y.   COATICOOK, P. Q.

NEW YORK, 42 BROADWAY   CHICAGO, 1007 FISHER BLDG.

The Pitt Tender Coupler

A SIMPLE and efficient design of pivoted tender coupler, adapted for either the rear end of tenders or front end of locomotives. An adaptation of the latest development of the M. C. B. type of coupler for locomotive service, combining with the simplicity of the Janney coupler with the vertical locking pin all the up-to-date features required in an automatic coupler, complying fully with all the specifications and recommendations of the M. C. B. Association. The "Knuckle-Opener" of the Pitt coupler is positive in operation and opens the knuckle to its fullest range of movement from either a fully closed position or any partially open position *regardless of rust.*

MANUFACTURED ONLY BY

THE McCONWAY & TORLEY CO.
PITTSBURGH, PA.

Westinghouse
Single = Phase Electric Locomotives

We illustrate one of the thirty-five electric locomotives for the New York, New Haven and Hartford Railroad. These locomotives are designed to operate in passenger service, on both alternating and direct current systems, at speeds up to 70 miles per hour.

Westinghouse Electric & Mfg. Co.
PITTSBURG, PA.

Address Nearest District Office:

New York, Atlanta, Baltimore, Boston, Buffalo, Chicago, Cincinnati, Cleveland, Dallas, Denver, Detroit, Los Angeles, Minneapolis, New Orleans, Philadelphia, Pittsburg, St. Louis, Salt Lake City, San Francisco, Seattle, Syracuse.
Canada: Canadian Westinghouse Co., Ltd., Hamilton, Ontario.   Mexico: G. & O. Braniff and Co., City of Mexico.

ALUNDUM

IS THE

SHARPEST, HARDEST, MOST UNIFORM ABRASIVE IN USE

Norton Grinding Wheels

ARE MADE OF IT

Write for Particulars.

NORTON COMPANY
WORCESTER, MASS.

NIAGARA FALLS   CHICAGO

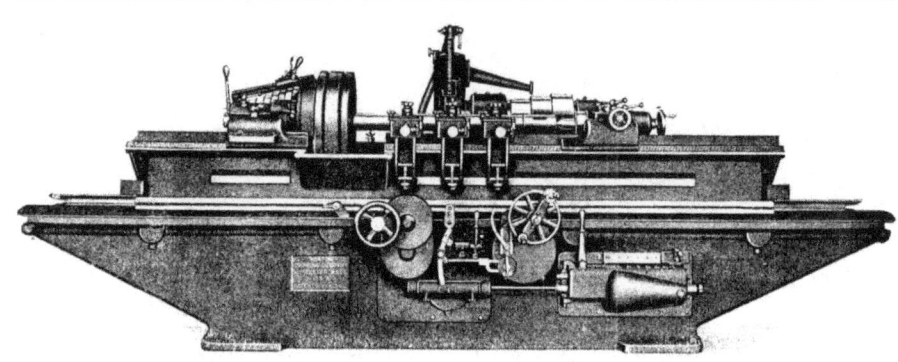

Norton Gap Grinding Machine

THIS is a machine made especially for Railroad work. It has been thoroughly tested by actual use and is in successful operation in shops of leading roads. It grinds piston rods with heads in place; no turning required in repairing old rods; no finish cut in lathe in case of new rods. It also grinds valve stems, crank pins, and axles. You can take two piston rods from an engine long in service, and grind them true, round, straight, smooth and ready for use in thirty minutes. Repairing by grinding increases the life of the rod and of the packing. Is there not a large saving by this method, as compared with your present methods?

The Norton Gap Grinder swings 30 inches in the gap, and takes work 8 feet long. It has self-contained devices for rapid work. It is of latest improved design, thorough in workmanship, and more powerful and rigid than any other machine built exclusively for this work.

NORTON GRINDING COMPANY   Worcester, Mass., U. S. A.

 # American Steel Foundries

SIMPLEX RAILWAY APPLIANCE CO.

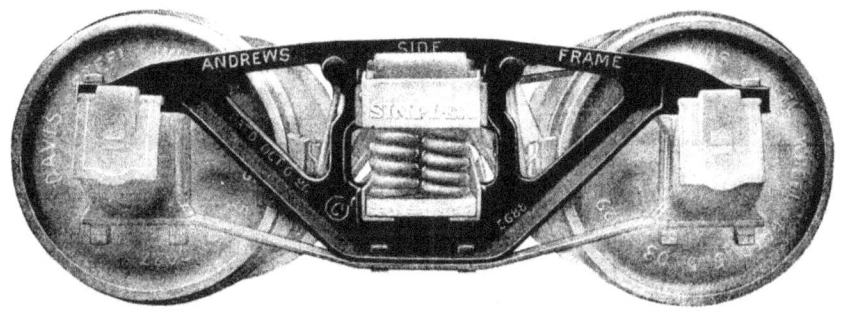

MANUFACTURERS OF

**Cast Steel Bolsters
R. E. Janney Couplers
Davis Steel Wheels
Truck Side Frames, and all kinds
of Miscellaneous Steel
Castings
Also, Susemihl Side Bearings;
Simplex Bolsters,
Brake Beams and Springs**

NEW YORK:	CHICAGO:	ST. LOUIS:
42 Broadway	1st National Bank Bldg.	Frisco Building

WM. SELLERS & CO.

INCORPORATED

PHILADELPHIA, U. S. A.

Locomotive Injectors and Valves

The Improved Self Acting Injector

Restarts automatically. Simple in Construction. Self Adjusting. Absolutely reliable under most severe conditions of service. No waste at low steam pressure. Parts interchangeable.

DUPLEX INJECTORS   **NON-LIFTING INJECTORS**

Combined Main Check and Stop Valves

Side or bottom inlet. Flanged or screw shank. Check valve and seat can be removed while the boiler is under steam.

FEED WATER STRAINERS   **BOILER WASHERS**

In addition to the Railways of the UNITED STATES, our Injectors are in use on Locomotives in ENGLAND, FRANCE, RUSSIA, BELGIUM, ITALY, SPAIN, JAPAN, CHINA, EGYPT, ENGLISH COLONIES, SOUTH AMERICA, MEXICO, &c., &c.

WM. SELLERS & CO.
INCORPORATED
PHILADELPHIA, U. S. A.

Modern Machine Tools

Pneumatic Clutch Planing Machine

Operated by single belt running only in one direction. Variable cutting speeds. Constant return speed. Crosshead extended back between uprights, and secured front and rear. Forced lubrication of ways.

Turntables

Car Wheel Borers	Traveling Cranes	Tool Grinders
Driving Box Borers		Drill Grinders
Cylinder Borers	Jib Cranes	Slotters
Rod Borers		Slabbing Machines
Wheel Lathes	Shafting, &c.	Steam Hammers
Axle Lathes		Transfer Tables

BUFFALO BRAKE BEAM COMPANY

30 Pine St. New York

Works Buffalo, N. Y.

SPECIAL SECTION BRAKE BEAM

FORGED FULCRUM

ROBT. W. HUNT & CO. TEST OF SPECIAL SECTION

Load	Deflection	Permanent Set
7500 lbs.	.039	.000
20000 "	.108	.000
35000 "	.207	.000

RICHARD DUDGEON

Inventor, Patentee and Original Manufacturer of

Hydraulic Jack, Hydraulic Punch, Roller Tube Expander.

Broome and Columbia Streets,   New York City

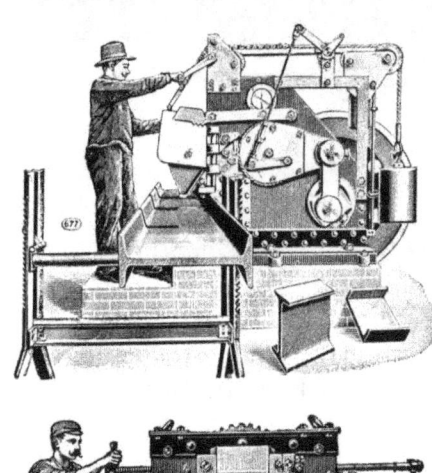

Cutting Punching Coping

of all structural steel done to advantage with unbreakable steel plate frame

MACHINES

Furnished to all leading Locomotive and Car Builders, Railroad Shops, etc., all over the world

ASK FOR CATALOGUE D

Henry Pels & Co. 68 Broad St. New York

THE MAN WITH A LOAD

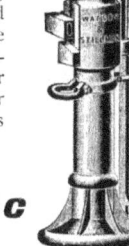

whether it be to push, pull or lift; in crowded places; or insecure foundations; outdoors, in mud, rain or cold, or wherever or whoever he is knows the value of

W. & S. HYDRAULIC JACKS

These jacks are made to stand the most severe service, are excellent in every detail and being made in over 200 regular varieties, there's rarely need of waiting for the jack you want. It's ready for you now. So's our catalog.

ALL KINDS OF HYDRAULIC TOOLS FOR RAILROAD SERVICE

WATSON-STILLMAN CO.
26 CORTLANDT ST., NEW YORK CITY
CHICAGO OFFICE, 453 ROOKERY
SELIG SONNETHAL & CO., LONDON

BETTS MACHINE CO.
WILMINGTON, DELAWARE, U. S. A.
MAKERS OF
HEAVY MACHINE TOOLS
For HIGH SPEED STEEL

VERTICAL BORING MILLS
HORIZONTAL BORING MACHINES
SLOTTING MACHINES
PLANING MACHINES
TIRE MILLS, Etc., Etc.

NATIONAL 1½-INCH SINGLE BOLT CUTTER.

The present National Line shows what competent engineers, experienced in this branch of tool building, can do when backed by abundant and progressive capital.

National Bolt Cutters
Single, Double, Triple—25 Styles and Sizes.

National Nut Tappers
Plain Geared and Semi-Automatic.

National Rivet and Track Bolt Headers
For Single Blow Work.

National Hammer Bolt Headers
For Square, Hex and Tee Head Bolts.

National Forging Machines
For Miscellaneous Requirements.

Portable Valve Seat Rotary Planing Machine

Portable Tools
FOR
Railway Repair Shops

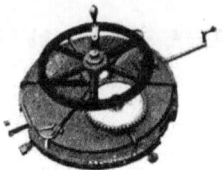
Locomotive Cylinder or Dome Facing Machine

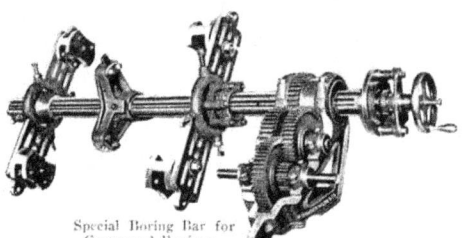
Special Boring Bar for Compound Engines.

Send for Catalogue. We solicit your orders.

Our guarantee is broad. Our prices moderate.

Planer Tool

H. B. Underwood & Co.
1025 Hamilton Street
PHILADELPHIA
U. S. A.

Portable Milling Machine

¶ The efficiency and economy of the "GANTT FURNACE" has been demonstrated by its installation by several of the leading drop forging concerns in the country.

First.—It imparts a through soaking heat.

Second.—It is non-oxidizing.

Third.—It is continuous.

MANUFACTURED BY

A. P. WITTEMAN & CO.

1223-1225 Spring St.
PHILADELPHIA

BOSTON OFFICE, 70 Kilby Street

EASTERN SELLING AGENTS FOR

Burgess High Speed Steel
Burgess Tool Steels
Cyclops Refined Steel
Cyclops Extra Refined Steel
Cyclops Double Extra Steel
Cyclops Triple Extra Steel

Stockbridge Two-Piece Crank Shapers

REMEMBER STOCKBRIDGE SHAPERS ARE DIFFERENT. THEY GIVE AN EVEN CUTTING SPEED AND A QUICK RETURN

TWICE ANY OTHER PLAIN CRANK SHAPER. "It's a Worker."

STOCKBRIDGE MACH. CO.
WORCESTER, MASS., U.S.A.

HEAVY DUTY SHAPERS

CRANK SHAPERS GEARED SHAPERS
TRAVERSE SHAPERS OPEN SIDE SHAPERS

THE CINCINNATI SHAPER CO.
CINCINNATI, OHIO

The Largest Exclusive Manufacturers of Shapers

Manning, Maxwell & Moore, Inc.

| New York, | Chicago, | Boston, | Philadelphia, | St. Louis, | Cleveland, |
| Milwaukee, | Syracuse, | Detroit, | Birmingham, Ala., | | Agents |

STEPTOE SHAPERS

THE length of stroke can be changed while the machine is in motion. The table support will permit the heaviest cuts with accuracy. The head can be swiveled by means of the lever at back of the head, saving time of opening fastening bolts and looking for wrenches. The feed is positive. No guesswork. No loss of time.

We would like to send our catalogue describing many more points for time saving. : : : : : :

The **JOHN STEPTOE SHAPER CO.,** Cincinnati, O.

See page 483

Woodward & Powell Planer Co.
WORCESTER, MASS., U. S. A.

WE MANUFACTURE

24" x 24" to 72" x 72" planers, any length. Widened planers. Railroad switch point planer. Railroad frog and crossing planer. Locomotive connecting rod planer. Duplex planer.

SEND FOR CATALOGUE

48" x 48" x 12' Planer.

LOCOMOTIVE SHOP MACHINERY  ELECTRIC CRANES AND HOISTS

42" Car Wheel Borer.

600-lb. Steam Hammer.

6' Radial Drill.

90" Driving Wheel Chucking Lathe.

No. 3 Double Axle Lathe.

Steel-tired Car-wheel Lathe.

Hydraulic Wheel Press.

Detailed descriptions with illustrations promptly furnished

NILES-BEMENT-POND CO.
TRINITY BUILDING, 111 BROADWAY, NEW YORK
BOSTON　　PHILADELPHIA　　PITTSBURGH　　CHICAGO　　ST. LOUIS　　LONDON

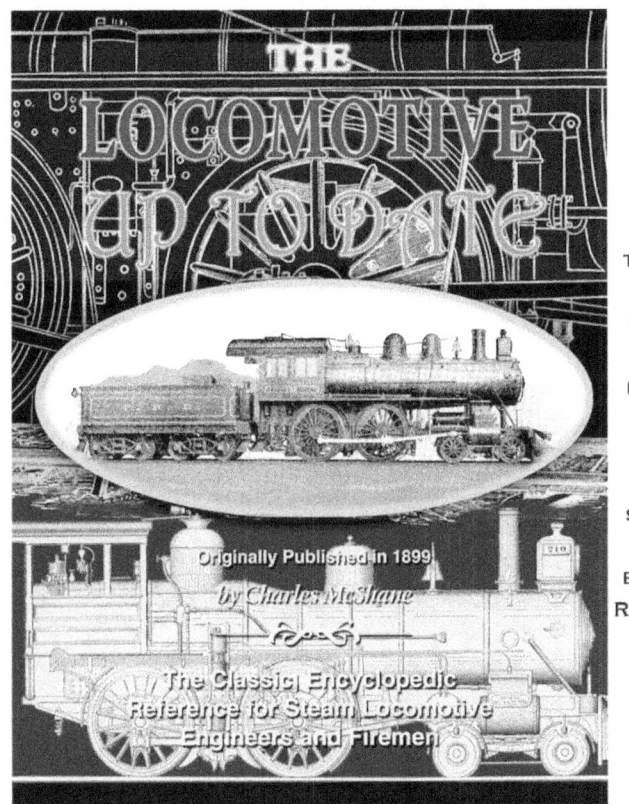

When it was originally published in 1899, **The Locomotive Up to Date** was hailed as "...the most definitive work ever published concerning the mechanism that has transformed the American nation: the steam locomotive." Filled with over 700 pages of text, diagrams and photos, this remains one of the most important railroading books ever written. From steam valves to sanders, trucks to side rods, it's a treasure trove of information, explaining in easy-to-understand language how the most sophisticated machines of the 19th Century were operated and maintained. This new edition is an exact duplicate of the original. Reformatted as an easy-to-read 8.5x11 volume, it's delightful for railroad enthusiasts of all ages.

Originally printed in 1898 and then periodically revised, **The Motorman...and His Duties** served as the definitive training text for a generation of streetcar operators. A must-have for the trolley or train enthusiast, it is also an important source of information for museum staff and docents. Lavishly illustrated with numerous photos and black and white line drawings, this affordable reprint contains all of the original text. Includes chapters on trolley car types and equipment, troubleshooting, brakes, controllers, electricity and principles, electric traction, multi-car control and has a convenient glossary in the back. If you've ever operated a trolley car, or just had an electric train set, this is a terrific book for your shelf!

ALSO NOW AVAILABLE FROM PeriscopeFilm.com!

©2010 Periscope Film LLC
All Rights Reserved
ISBN #978-1-935327-96-7   1-935327-96-8
www.PeriscopeFilm.com

www.ingramcontent.com/pod-product-compliance
Lightning Source LLC
Chambersburg PA
CBHW081752300426
44116CB00014B/2095